ELEVENTH EDITION

Sociology

David Popenoe

Rutgers, The State University of New Jersey

Prentice Hall, Upper Saddle River, New Jersey 07458

Library of Congress Cataloging-in-Publication Data

POPENOE, DAVID
  Sociology/David Popenoe. — 11th ed.
    p.   cm.
  Includes bibliographical references and index.
  ISBN   0-13-095745-3 (pbk.)
  1. Sociology.   I. Title.
HM585.P66   2000
301—dc21   99–40919
                                                 CIP

Editorial Director: **Charlyce Jones Owen**
Editor-in-Chief: **Nancy Roberts**
Managing Editor: **Sharon Chambliss**
AVP, Director of Production and Manufacturing: **Barbara Kittle**
Project Manager: **Joan Stone**
Manufacturing Manager: **Nick Sklitsis**
Prepress and Manufacturing Buyer: **Mary Ann Gloriande**
Creative Design Director: **Leslie Osher**
Art Director: **Anne Bonanno Nieglos**
Interior Design: **Anne Bonanno Nieglos and Joseph Rattan Design**
Cover Design: **Joseph Rattan Design, Dallas, Texas**
Cover and Chapter Opening Art: **© Robert Felker**
Photo Researcher: **Linda Sykes**
Image Specialist: **Beth Boyd**
Manager, Rights and Permissions: **Kay Dellosa**
Director, Image Resource Center: **Melinda Reo**
Line Art Coordinator: **Guy Ruggiero**
Electronic Art Creation: **Mirella Signoretto**
Marketing Manager: **Christopher DeJohn**

This book was set in 10/12 Minion by Lithokraft II
and was printed and bound by Webcrafters, Inc.
The cover was printed by Webcrafters, Inc.

© 2000, 1995, 1993, 1991, 1989, 1986, 1983,
1980, 1977, 1974, 1971 by Prentice-Hall, Inc.
Upper Saddle River, New Jersey 07458

Printed in the United States of America
10   9   8   7   6   5   4   3   2

ISBN 0-13-095745-3

Prentice-Hall International (UK) Limited, *London*
Prentice-Hall of Australia Pty. Limited, *Sydney*
Prentice-Hall Canada Inc., *Toronto*
Prentice-Hall Hispanoamericana, S.A., *Mexico*
Prentice-Hall of India Private Limited, *New Delhi*
Prentice-Hall of Japan, Inc., *Tokyo*
Pearson Education Asia Pte. Ltd., *Singapore*
Editora Prentice-Hall do Brasil, Ltda., *Rio de Janeiro*

Brief Contents

Contents

12 Age and Health in Society 263

13 Gender 291

Part Four: Social Institutions

14 The Family 311

Boxes

 ## Window on Sociology

 ## Global Society

 ## Applying Sociology

 ## Sociology of the Media

 ## Internet/Technology

Preface

riting any introductory college-level textbook is a challenge. The attempt to write a textbook designed to introduce the discipline of sociology is especially demanding. The broad scope of the discipline, the often conflicting sociological perspectives, the wide diversity of teaching approaches, and the varied backgrounds of the students all oblige the author to make a series of difficult decisions about content, purpose, and style.

The difficulty of this task, however, is far outweighed by the rewarding learning experiences that writing a book like this entails. The research that goes into the project gives the writer an opportunity to learn anew about sociological discoveries as well as theoretical explanations of the way society operates. Altogether, the experience stimulates the imagination. It encourages new ways of thinking about society and provides rich new insights. One of the primary goals of this book is to provide students with the same kind of intellectual reward. Hopefully, the sociological discoveries and theoretical explanations described in this introductory textbook will raise many questions for them and generate greater interest in the field of sociology.

In preparing the eleventh edition of this textbook, I have held uppermost in my mind the following general goal: to present basic sociology in a systematic yet scholarly way, while offering maximum social insight and emphasizing the applicability of sociological knowledge to everyday life. To achieve this goal I have tried to be comprehensive yet integrated, readable yet sociologically accurate, and up-to-date yet respectful of tradition. In dealing with the ideological debates that mark the field, I have sought to be fair and evenhanded, presenting all sides so that students can make their own judgments.

The extensive research that went into the eleventh edition of this book showed how society has changed in many unexpected ways. Today, more than ever, technology is playing a role in that change. The marvelous scientific discoveries that we are witnessing existed only in the imaginations of inventors and writers at the beginning of the twentieth century. Society now confronts many of the unintended consequences of these promising scientific discoveries. Therefore, it seemed particularly fitting to open the eleventh edition of this book with one of the most spectacular scientific achievements of the century—the cloning of Dolly, the lamb.

The possibility of human cloning has sparked many heated debates throughout the twentieth century—raising questions about its impact upon civilization and particularly the nature and function of the family. Could a scientific achievement like this fundamentally alter society? Aldous Huxley thought so. In his fictional account of *Brave New World,* he described how altering the family unit would create a rippling effect across all social institutions. Designer babies, created to serve a specific function in a multi-layered society, were supposedly the key to a utopian society. But, in fact, the ultimate message of Huxley's novel suggests that the complex nature of society is difficult to understand, let alone design. While the creators of this brave new world had created a smoothly operating society, that had come at an enormous cost—human freedom. This introductory book to sociology is designed to help students understand such messages.

A new feature of this edition—the Internet/Technology boxes—considers recent scientific advances that are changing society. The new Internet exercises found at the end of every chapter complement this new box and give students a chance to explore their interests along their own chosen paths. Another box new to the eleventh edition is the Sociology of the Media. The themes of this new feature are tailored to selected chapters and are designed to increase students' awareness about the way they consume media messages.

I have introduced many other changes in the eleventh edition designed to make the book more timely and relevant to the lives of students. Almost all chapters have been extensively revised, with the addition of substantial new material. An effort has been made throughout to improve readability, to clarify difficult concepts, and to use current and engaging examples that bring those concepts to life. I have tried to summarize the most salient of the new research into a form that will be easily accessible to the introductory student. Statistical data have been updated, charts and graphs have been revised, and there are numerous new illustrations. Most chapters contain detailed discussions of the United States, in addition to cross-cultural perspectives. Finally, the eleventh edition (like its four immediate predecessors) is offered in paperback, thus making it affordable to students.

PLAN OF THE ELEVENTH EDITION

The eleventh edition is divided into five parts. Part One, "Introduction," provides an overview of sociology, its history, and its methods. Chapter 1 introduces the discipline of sociology in general, including its basic assumptions, its history, its theoretical perspectives, and its uses. Chapter 2 provides a comprehensive discussion of the social research process, with clarifying applications and examples.

With the coverage of culture in Chapter 3, we begin Part Two, "Social Organization and the Individual." In Chapter 4, we take up what is commonly regarded as the central concern of sociological thought: society and social structure. This chapter provides an extended discussion contrasting the functionalist and conflict perspectives. In Chapter 5, moving from the macro level to the micro level, we discuss social interaction, including symbolic interactionism, dramaturgy, ethnomethodology, nonverbal communication, and social networks. Chapter 6, on socialization, includes material on theories of personal development and the life course. Chapter 7 presents a discussion of social groups, organizations, and organizational alternatives. Part Two concludes with a comprehensive discussion in Chapter 8 of sociological perspectives on deviance, crime, and social control.

Part Three is concerned with social inequality. Chapter 9 brings together the major theoretical materials on social class, social status, and social stratification. Chapter 10 covers social class and poverty in the United States, together with the array of new American social welfare programs that were created through the welfare reform legislation of 1996. Other bases of social inequality are ethnicity and race, the subject of Chapter 11, and age and health, the focus of Chapter 12. The concluding chapter in Part Three, Chapter 13, is concerned with inequalities of gender.

In Part Four, we turn to an overview of major social institutions. The family, perhaps the most basic social institution, is the subject of Chapter 14. Chapter 15, on education, and Chapter 16, on religion, have been updated. Chapter 17, which discusses power, politics, and government in world perspective, also contains a detailed discussion of the political and governmental system in the United States. Chapter 18, on the economy and work, treats not only worker alienation and satisfaction in the United States, but also variations in economic and work systems throughout the world.

Part Five, "Social Environments and Social Change," looks primarily at the major dimensions of social change in societies. Chapter 19, on population and ecology, looks at the twenty-first century. Chapter 20 deals with cities, urban development, and community change. Chapter 21, on collective behavior and social movements, takes into account both modern sociological thought and the important social movements that have taken place throughout the 1980s and 1990s. To conclude, Chapter 22 discusses social change and the future.

FEATURES

BOXED INSERTS. This text includes five different types of boxed materials.

Window on Sociology boxes amplify or deepen coverage of topics touched on in the main text. Some of these boxes summarize the main ideas of previously published articles and books.

Global Society boxes provide extended discussions of selected sociological aspects of societies around the world. Many of these focus on the notion of the global village, showing how other societies are increasingly affecting our daily lives.

Applying Sociology boxes are designed to give students a sense of the relevance of sociology and sociological research to everyday life. Many illustrate how research is conducted and how the results are used for practical purposes.

Internet/Technology boxes examine issues surrounding the Internet and the latest scientific discoveries. Many of these boxes illustrate the unexpected downside of seemingly revolutionary advances. Topics covered in these boxes range from First Amendment issues involving the Internet to modern discoveries that promise to lengthen the human life span.

Sociology of the Media boxes revolve around the themes of selected chapters and are designed to increase students' awareness about the way they consume media messages. These boxes tackle issues ranging from the impact of media polls to the effects produced by media portrayals of racial and ethnic groups.

READABILITY. A good textbook is one that students can and will read, and the readability of a book seems to depend primarily on three factors: internal organization, language, and interest level. To rank high in readability, textbook material must be well organized and clearly presented, one step at a time. Each chapter in this book is broken down into three or more major subject areas.

Clear and familiar language also makes a book readable. Students find it difficult to have to learn an entire vocabulary in order to understand new subject matter. This book, therefore, uses only the professional terminology that students must know in order to understand the fundamentals of sociology and to be prepared for more advanced courses. When important new terms are introduced, they are set in boldface type and clearly defined.

Relevance makes a book readable because it provides motivation to read. Sociological theories and concepts are illustrated in this book not only with the results of published studies and with discussion of major social problems and issues, but also with examples drawn from the students' own social environment—the daily behavior of friends, parents, classmates, and neighbors.

CHAPTER REVIEWS. Each chapter concludes with a set of questions to help students review the most important concepts. Many of these questions are designed to improve students' critical thinking skills.

KEY TERMS. Each new term is highlighted and clearly defined in the text when it first appears. Because a number of terms are important in chapters other than those in which they first appear, there is also a glossary at the end of the book.

GRAPHS, CHARTS, AND TABLES. Since sociology depends heavily on statistical data, it is important for the student to become familiar with the ways such data are commonly presented. This book includes many examples of graphs, charts, and tables. Each has been designed to ensure its accuracy, attractiveness, and comprehensibility.

ILLUSTRATIONS. Sociologists are among the first to point out that modern society is increasingly oriented toward visual images. All the photographs have been chosen to give visual impact and support to the text.

SUPPLEMENTS

Prentice Hall prides itself in offering the most comprehensive ancillary package available in the sociology market. Listed below are the key supplements that accompany *Sociology, Eleventh Edition*.

For the Instructor

Instructor's Resource Manual   For each chapter of the text, this manual provides a chapter summary, discussion questions, and additional resources available to enhance classroom presentations.

Test Item File   This carefully prepared manual includes over 1,500 test questions in multiple choice, true-false, and essay formats that are page-referenced to the text. **Prentice Hall Custom Text** is a test generator designed to allow the creation of personalized exams. It is available in DOS, Windows, and Macintosh formats.

Social Survey Software, Third Edition   *Student CHIP Social Survey Software* is an easy yet powerful program that allows users to investigate U.S. society and other nations of the world by calling on the best source of survey data available, the *General Social Survey*. Over 200 GSS items have been transformed into CHIP data sets linked to chapters in introductory sociology texts. An instructor's manual as well as an easy-to-understand student manual lead students through multivariate analysis of attitudes and behavior reported by sex, race, occupation, level of income and education, and a host of other variables. *Social Survey Software*, which investigators can now manipulate either by keyboard or by mouse, also has a new graphing feature. The *Student CHIP* microcomputer program was developed by James A. Davis (Harvard University) and is available in both IBM and Macintosh formats.

Film/Video Guide: Prentice Hall Introductory Sociology, Sixth Edition   This helpful guide describes well over 300 films and videos appropriate for classroom viewing for each of the chapters in the text. It also provides summaries, discussion questions, and rental sources for each film and video.

ABCNEWS **ABC News/Prentice Hall Video Library for Sociology**   Few will dispute that video is the most dynamic supplement you can use to enhance a class. However, the quality of the video material and how well it relates to your course still make all the difference. Prentice Hall and ABC News are now working together to bring you the best, most comprehensive video ancillaries available in the college market.

Through its wide variety of award-winning programs—*Nightline, ABC World News Tonight/American Agenda*, and *20/20*—ABC offers a resource for feature and documentary-style videos related to the chapters in the text. The programs have high production quality, present substantial content, and are hosted by well-versed, well-known anchors.

The authors and editors of Prentice Hall have carefully selected videos on topics that complement *Sociology, Eleventh Edition*.

ABC News/Prentice Hall Video Library, Sociology:

Volume I: Social Stratification

Volume II: Marriages and Families

Volume III: Race/Ethnic Relations

Volume IV: Criminology

Volume V: Social Problems

Volume VI: Introduction to Sociology I

Volume VII: Introduction to Sociology II

Volume VIII: Introduction to Sociology III

Volume IX: Social Problems II

Volume X: Marriages and Families II

Volume XI: Race and Ethnic Relations II (0-13-021134-6); (2113D-2)

Volume XII: Institutions (0-13-021133-8); (2113C-4)

Intructor's Guide for ABC News/Prentice Hall Video Library   For each ABC News video clip, this guide offers an abstract and suggested questions for discussion.

Prentice Hall Color Transparencies, Sociology Series V   Full-color illustrations, charts, and other visual materials from the text as well as outside sources have been selected to make up this useful in-class tool.

Instructor's Guide to Prentice Hall Color Transparencies, Sociology Series V   This guide offers suggestions for effectively using each transparency in the classroom.

For the Student

Study Guide   This carefully designed manual consists of chapter overviews and study questions keyed to the chapters of the text.

Critical Thinking Audio Study Cassette   This 60-minute tape will help students to think and read critically.

 **The New York Times Supplement, Themes of the Times, for Introductory Sociology**   *The New York Times* and Prentice Hall are sponsoring *Themes of the Times,* a program designed to enhance student access to current information relevant to the classroom. Through this program, the core subject matter provided in this text is supplemented by a collection of timely articles from one of the world's most distinguished newspapers, *The New York Times.* These articles demonstrate the vital, ongoing connection between what is learned in the classroom and what is happening in the world around us.

To enjoy the wealth of information of *The New York Times* daily, a reduced subscription rate is available. For information, call toll-free: 1-800-631-1222.

Prentice Hall and *The New York Times* are proud to cosponsor *Themes of the Times.* We hope it will make the reading of both textbooks and newspapers a more dynamic, involving process.

MEDIA SUPPLEMENTS

Sociology on the Internet 1999–2000   This guide introduces students to the origin and innovations behind the Internet and provides clear strategies for navigating the complexity of the Internet and World Wide Web. Exercises within and at the end of the chapters allow students to practice searching for the myriad of resources available to the student of sociology. This 96-page supplementary book is free to students when shrinkwrapped as a package with *Sociology, Eleventh Edition.*

Companion Website   In tandem with the text, students can now take full advantage of the World Wide Web to enrich their study of sociology through the Popenoe Website. This resource correlates the text with related material available on the Internet. Features of the Website include chapter objectives, study questions, as well as links to interesting material and information from other sites on the Web that can reinforce and enhance the content of each chapter. Address: http://www.prenhall.com/popenoe

ACKNOWLEDGMENTS

As in previous editions, the eleventh edition has benefited greatly from the energies and skills of a team of specialists who know and understand the interests and needs of beginning students of sociology. I want to extend my sincere thanks to all of the people who have made up this team. At Prentice Hall, the team consists of Nancy Roberts, editor-in-chief of social sciences; Sharon Chambliss, managing editor for sociology/anthropology; Joan Stone, project manager; Mary Louise Byrd, copy editor; Anne Bonanno Nieglos, design director; and Linda Sykes, photo researcher.

Thanks are due, most of all, to Professor Christine Von Der Haar of Indiana University, who systematically went through every chapter and made suggestions for rewriting, revising, and adding new material. Professor Von Der Haar is a highly skilled editor as well as a tremendously knowledgeable sociologist, and her outstanding contributions are deeply appreciated. She should be considered a major collaborator if not co-author of this edition.

I have had the great advantage of helpful suggestions from many users of the previous editions of this book. And, although I alone am responsible for the content of the text, portions of the manuscript of this and prior editions were reviewed in various stages of development by the following sociologists:

Patricia A. Adler, University of Colorado
Stan L. Albrecht, Brigham Young University
Majeed Alsikafi, University of Alabama
Robert S. Anwyl, Miami-Dade Community College
David Arnold, Sonoma State University
Jeanne Ballantine, Wright State University
Lawrence Beckhouse, College of William and Mary
Philip Berg, University of Wisconsin, La-Crosse
Judith Blau, State University of New York, Albany
R. Devon Boan, Gardner-Webb College
Lee Braude, State University of New York, Fredonia
Brent Burton, Iowa State University

Bruce A. Chadwick, Brigham Young University

Janet Chafetz, University of Houston

Karen Conner, Drake University

Harold Cox, Indiana State University

M. Richard Cramer, University of North Carolina, Chapel Hill

Dennis Crow, U.S. Department of Housing and Urban Development

Wayne Curry, Belmont College

Edward Z. Dager, University of Maryland, College Park

Jon Darling, University of Pittsburgh, Johnstown

Lynn Davidman, University of Pittsburgh

John DeLamater, University of Wisconsin, Madison

Norman K. Denzin, University of Illinois, Urbana

Stanley DeViney, University of Maryland Eastern Shore

Gordon DiRenzo, University of Delaware

Linda Donoian, Quinsigamond Community College

Rick Eckstein, Villanova University

Willie Edwards, Richland College

John F. Farley, Southern Illinois University, Edwardsville

Michael P. Farrell, State University of New York, Buffalo

Joe Feagin, University of Texas, Austin

Natalie Friedman, Columbia University

Larry H. Frye, St. Petersburg Junior College

Norval Glenn, University of Texas, Austin

Jeanne Gobalet, San Jose City College

Phillip B. Gonzales, University of New Mexico

Linda Grant, University of Georgia

Paul S. Gray, Boston College

Richard H. Hall, State University of New York, Albany

Michael J. Hart, Broward Community College

Frank Hearn, State University of New York, Cortland

Jerry Heiss, University of Connecticut

Charles C. Herrman, Jr., Western Maryland College

Bradley Hertel, Virginia Polytechnic Institute

Gretchen J. Hill, The Wichita State University

Michael Hughs, Virginia Polytechnic Institute

Janet G. Hunt, University of Maryland, College Park

Jon E. Iannitti, State University of New York College, Morrisville

Gary F. Jensen, University of Arizona

Narenda Nath Kalia, Buffalo State College

Dennis L. Kalob, Loyola University

Ali Kamali, Washburn University

Mark Kassop, Bergen Community College

Bruce Keith, West Virginia University

Michael Kimmel, SUNY-Stony Brook

Ross Klein, Memorial University, Newfoundland

Daniel Klenow, North Dakota State University

George A. Kourvetaris, Northern Illinois University

David F. Krause, Lake-Sumter Community College

Phillip Kunz, Brigham Young University

Betty Levine, Indiana University

Linda L. Lindsey, Maryville College, St. Louis

Alan E. Liska, State University of New York, Albany

Dale A. Lund, University of Utah

Gene M. Lutz, University of Northern Iowa

James Marshall, State University of New York School of Medicine, Buffalo

Susan E. Marshall, University of Texas

George T. Martin, Jr., Montclair State College

Ron Matson, The Wichita State University

M. Cathey Maze, Franklin University

Patrick McGuire, University of Toledo

Patrick H. McNamara, University of New Mexico

R. L. McNeely, University of Wisconsin, Milwaukee

Steven F. Messner, State University of New York, Albany

Dan Miller, University of Dayton

John S. Miller, University of Arkansas, Little Rock

Murray Milner, University of Virginia

Kent Mommsen, University of Utah

Robert Moore, St. Joseph's University

Neville N. Morgan, Kentucky State University

Carlo Morrissey, Quinsigamond Community College

Charles L. Mulford, Iowa State University

Dina B. Neal, Vernon Regional Jr. College

Elias T. Nigem, University of Toledo

Howard Nixon II, University of Vermont

Raphael J. Njoroge, Quinsigamond Community College

Anthony Orum, University of Illinois at Chicago

David Perry, State University of New York, Buffalo

Jeffrey Prager, University of California, Los Angeles

Jack Preiss, Duke University

David Preston, Eastfield College (Texas)

George Rent, Mississippi State University

Richard Robbins, University of Massachusetts, Boston

Dorothy M. Roe, Milwaukee Area Technical College

Elizabeth Rooney, San Francisco State University

Lawrence Rosen, Temple University

Jeffrey P. Rosenfeld, Nassau Community College

Saul Rosenthal, Creighton University

Robert Rothman, University of Delaware

Earl Rubington, Northeastern University

William A. Schwab, University of Arkansas

Harry Schwartzweller, Michigan State University

Raymond Scupin, Lindenwood College

Hans Sebald, Arizona State University

Denise Segura, University of California, Santa Barbara

Jan Smith, Ohio Wesleyan University

David A. Snow, University of Texas, Austin

Fred Snuffer, West Virginia State College

Louise Solomon, Pace University

James Steele, James Madison University

George F. Stine, Millersville University of Pennsylvania

Russell Stone, State University of New York, Buffalo

Victoria E. Sturtevant, Southern Oregon State College

Richard Sweeney, Modesto Community College

Kenrick S. Thompson, Northern Michigan University

Diana J. Torrez, University of North Texas

Peter Uhlenberg, University of North Carolina, Chapel Hill

Michael Useem, Boston University

Steven Vago, St. Louis University

Michael Vallante, Quinsigamond Community College

Christine Von Der Haar, Indiana University

Theodore Wagenaar, Miami University

Ruth Wallace, George Washington University

Kathryn Wark, Southern Illinois University

Russell Ward, State University of New York, Albany

Steve Warden, University of Arkansas

Susan L. Weeks, Sam Houston State University

Meredith Weiss-Belding, Quinsigamond Community College

Dennis Wenger, Texas A & M University

Douglas L. White, Henry Ford Community College

David M. Willems, Rutgers University

C. Ray Wingrove, University of Richmond

Michael Woodard, University of Missouri, Columbia

Wayne S. Wooden, California State Polytechnic University, Pomona

Bruce M. Zelkovitz, Washburn University

Irving Zola, Brandeis University

Finally, I want to give special thanks to my daughters, Becky and Julie, who have contributed many ideas and suggestions to this book, and also to express my deep gratitude for the continuing guidance and perseverance of my wife, Kate.

David Popenoe

avid Popenoe is Professor of Sociology and former social and behavioral sciences dean at Rutgers—the State University of New Jersey, in New Brunswick. Past chairperson and graduate director of the Rutgers sociology department, he is a leading scholar in the social organization and social change of modern societies, with a specialty in family and community studies.

Among his many publications are nine books, the most recent of which is *Life Without Father* (1996), a study of the importance of fatherhood and marriage for children and society. Other major books are *Disturbing the Nest: Family Change and Decline in Modern Societies* (1988), a comparative analysis of four affluent societies that focuses on the problematic effects of the welfare state on the institution of the family; *Private Pleasure, Public Plight* (1985), which examines the ways in which metropolitan living in three modern nations has become highly privatized, with a weakening of community ties; and *The Suburban Environment: Sweden and the United States* (1977), which compares the very different character of post-war housing and planning in the two nations and the effects of these environmental conditions on the lives of suburban residents.

Professor Popenoe has been a Fulbright Research Scholar to Sweden; has been awarded fellowships by the American Council of Learned Societies, the American Scandinavian Foundation, the Swedish Government, and the Rutgers University Research Council; and has served as a visiting faculty member or research scientist at the University of Stockholm, the Centre for Environmental Studies in London, the National Swedish Building Research Institute, New York University, and the University of Pennsylvania.

A native of Pasadena, California, Professor Popenoe graduated from Antioch College in Ohio and received his Ph.D. degree from the University of Pennsylvania. He began his professional career in the field of city planning and is a charter member of the American Institute of Certified Planners. Working on inner city problems and urban renewal, he held professional planning positions in Newark, New Jersey, and in Philadelphia. After joining the academic community, he served for several years as research director of the Urban Studies Center at Rutgers. In addition to the introductory course, he has taught courses in urban sociology, marriage and the family, the sociology of communities, city planning, environmental sociology, Scandinavian society, comparative social systems, social change, and social theory.

The father of two daughters, Professor Popenoe and his wife live in Princeton, New Jersey. He is currently co-director of The National Marriage Project at Rutgers, an academic initiative designed to provide research and analysis on the state of marriage in America and to educate the public on the social, economic, and cultural conditions affecting marital success and well-being.

CHAPTER 1

An Introduction to Sociology

With the arrival of Dolly, cloning a mammal is no longer science fiction. Would someone clone a human being? If so, for what purpose? And how would this affect society?

In February 1997, *Nature* magazine created a sensation when it published an article describing the method used to clone mammals from a single adult cell. This procedure was no longer just science fiction. Researchers had succeeded in cloning a lamb from an adult udder cell of a ewe. They named her Dolly.

With scientists claiming that human cloning was impossible just 20 years earlier, serious ethical debates about this issue never came about. Now speculation grew. With the impossible accomplished, was the unthinkable inevitable? Would someone clone a human being? If so, for what purpose? And how would this affect society?

Aldous Huxley was one of the first to address these questions in his futuristic novel, *Brave New World*, which was originally published in 1932. In this fictional account of a utopian society, he describes the "Bokanovsky Process," a scientific procedure similar to cloning that could produce up to 96 genetically identical human beings. When a young student in this story asks the Director of the Central London Hatchery and Conditioning Center about the advantage of this process, he receives a well-rehearsed lesson:

> "My good boy!" . . . "Can't you see? Can't you *see*?" . . . "Bokanovsky's Process is one of the major instruments of social stability!"
>
> *Major instruments of social stability.*
>
> Standard men and women; in uniform batches. The whole of a small factory staffed with the products of a single bokanovskied egg.
>
> "Ninety-six identical twins working ninety-six identical machines!" The voice was tremulous with enthusiasm. "You really know where you are. For the first time in history." He quoted the planetary motto. "Community, Identity, Stability." (Huxley, 1932, p. 4)

Indeed, peace and harmony did flourish in Huxley's "brave new world." In this utopian society, social problems did not exist. Everyone's needs were met, no one was sick, and happiness was at arms's length in the form of a tranquilizing drug called *soma*. The creators of this world knew that designing a "perfect" society required not only a vision of the goals sought but, as well, an understanding of the methods required to accomplish those goals. Cloning was a method needed to achieve social stability—a means to a perfect end.

Huxley was not, of course, portraying a perfect society. While social stability had been accomplished, it had come at a great cost. This was a place where neither freedom nor equality existed. Order was maintained by prefabricated social institutions that were centrally controlled by a handful of "directors."

In this technologically sophisticated society, neither mothers nor fathers existed; the words, themselves, were taboo. The family had been extinct for hundreds of years. In fact, a number of social institutions were either noticeably absent or had been radically altered in this world. For example, although the institution of education was still around, it was not designed to encourage critical thinking. On the contrary, education was simply a well-organized system for conditioning members of this society into a form of blind obedience and passive acceptance.

Religion, seemingly absent, had actually undergone a major transformation. Known as a "solidarity service," this weekly meeting was designed to create artificial bonds among members of 12-person groups. This was accomplished through their common enactment of meaningless rituals, in which they praised the only *god* they knew—Ford. In worshiping this symbolic figure, the participants were honoring what Ford actually represented—their own society. And it was this service that produced the social bonds that held their society together.

Huxley reveals the flaws in this society by showing it from the perspective of an outsider, the *Savage*, who was forced to live there as part of an experiment. Raised on a primitive reservation, where families formed the foundation of social life, he was never able to adjust to this "perfect" society. In contrast to the successfully conditioned members of this society, he questioned everything. He could neither understand nor accept promiscuous relationships that were devoid of love. Unable to accept the luxurious consumer civilization of this world, the Savage was never fully integrated into society. He never felt like he belonged. Tragically, in the end, he found his only escape in suicide.

Sociology is the systematic and objective study of human society and social interaction.

Novels like *Brave New World* help us understand how societies are structured and how the members of those societies attempt to accomplish certain social goals. They make it easy for us to see what values are important to these societies and how members of another society are shaped. It is far more difficult to recognize how our own society shapes us.

In the United States, institutionalized methods of cloning and conditioning do not shape our choices. Most of us see our future as a matter of personal choice. We feel that we are free to choose marriage or a single life, children or no children. The possibilities seem limitless. But, in fact, they are not. As Americans, we all share certain ideas about how people should think and act. People who do not behave as they are "supposed to" make us feel uncomfortable.

These social realities shape not only our ideas of who we want to be but also what we will eventually become. For example, most us will marry, and when we do, we will believe that we are making this decision freely. In reality, our choice, not only to marry but also about who we select as a life partner, is heavily influenced by the expectations of others around us.

Sociology is valuable because it can provide us with information about the social forces that mold our lives.

As you study society from a sociological point of view, you will begin to see that, alas, your own life is somewhat predictable. But you will also find that a knowledge of sociology can give you more freedom in forming and achieving your own personal goals.

WHAT IS SOCIOLOGY?

Sociology is the systematic and objective study of human society and social interaction. The discipline of sociology enables us to look beyond our limited view of the world to society as a whole—the values and ideas shared by its members, the groups and institutions that compose it, and the forces that change it.

There are many ways of studying society and social interaction. Perhaps the best way to introduce the discipline of sociology, then, is to look first at its *approach*—its special way of dealing with its subject matter.

The Sociological Approach

In its approach to the study of society and social interaction, sociology strives to be scientific. This means that sociologists do not rely on insight, unsubstantiated beliefs, or hearsay. Astute observers throughout history have commented on the relationship between people and their societies. The plays of Shakespeare, the essays of Voltaire, the novels of Dickens—all contain brilliant insights into human relationships and social systems. And folk proverbs such as "Love your neighbor, but don't pull down the hedge" and "The innkeeper loves the drunkard, but not for a son-in-law" contain much wisdom. But sociologists, however much they may want to believe such insights, cannot accept them as firm bases for understanding or explanation. They rely instead on scientific evidence obtained by the systematic study of human social life.

Whenever possible, sociologists use research techniques similar to those of the natural sciences, such as biology and physics. They often conduct research using the *scientific method*. Like other scientists, sociologists strive to reach conclusions and present findings that are *objective*—not biased by emotion or preferences. It is this commitment to the scientific method that makes sociology different from the nonscientific disciplines of the humanities, such as literature, religion, and philosophy. Sociology's ultimate aim is to develop a refined body of scientific knowledge that can explain and, in some cases, predict social events.

But it is not easy to be entirely unbiased when studying other human beings, and the use of the scientific method within sociology presents many problems. Human beings, unlike stones, stars, or molecules, have feelings, thoughts, and personal interests. The fact that sociologists, like their subject matter, are sensitive and moral beings places strict limits on what they can study and how they can study it. Sociologists cannot, for example, deprive children of love or human contact in order to test theories about human development. They cannot start a war to see how people respond or how much they can "tolerate." Nor can they dismantle existing social institutions to see how society would fare without them. (The issue of sociology as a science is discussed in Chapter 2.)

Because people are so different from the kinds of things studied by natural scientists, many sociologists modify the methods of the natural sciences. The discovery of sociological truth, these sociologists believe, also depends heavily on the personal understanding of the investigator.

Most sociologists have come to understand that the methods of the "hard," or natural, sciences alone are not enough to produce a full understanding of the human experience. Much sociological work reflects the perspectives of the humanities, especially philosophy. This interplay of approaches, a blend of science and the humanities, makes sociology the exciting and fascinating field that it is today.

Sociology: The Science of the Obvious?

It is sometimes charged by nonsociologists that sociology is a science of the obvious. Sociologists, it is said, spend a lot of money to "discover" what everyone already knows. This misconception exists because sociology deals with the familiar world of people and society. Indeed, everyone is, to some degree, an amateur sociologist, with a pet theory to explain what makes the world work and people tick. By contrast, the subject matter of the natural sciences is often outside the realm of common experience. Answers to problems in the natural sciences are most often cast in language and symbols that the average person can barely understand.

But because the subject matter of sociology is familiar, one must be extremely careful in working with sociological materials. Statements that sound like common sense, and the reasons given to support them, may not be—and often are not—true.

People with training in sociology approach problems in a different way from people without such training. The sociological perspective helps us to understand the many social forces influencing a problem, to grasp how the whole system in question operates and is held together. For example, to look at divorce from a sociological point of view requires that one realize that the problem is not just divorce but also involves the role of women, economic conditions, and the place of marriage and the family in society. Similarly, the problem of crime involves the law, societal value systems, and the conditions of life in large cities.

This way of seeing—looking at the whole context of a problem—often points out that life is not always what it seems. Sociology teaches us that things are more complex and different than they first appear, and that true understanding comes from looking below the surface for the underlying social reality. The process of looking below the surface of the "taken-for-granted" part of social experience has been dubbed *debunking* by sociologist Peter L. Berger (1963).

Being able to debunk taken-for-granted experiences and thinking can have major practical implications. A principal finding of social scientists in the last few decades, for example, is that much of the conventional wisdom about business organizations is not always correct. It had long been accepted that an organization that is tightly controlled from the top works best: "Take up the slack, cut out the fat, get everyone in step, streamline the goals, and the result is success, vitality, profits." Yet sociological research has found "that decentralized and loosely controlled organizations are often better at adapting, or that slack, foolishness, and some insubordination often provide new ideas and innovations" (*New York Times*,

WINDOW ON SOCIOLOGY

SOCIOLOGICAL INSIGHT

Is sociology just common sense? Do sociologists simply say what everyone already knows? According to Randall Collins (1992), this common perception might be created by sociologists' use of technical jargon that appears to do nothing more than put a new face on the familiar. But, in fact, Collins argues that "sociology does know some important principles of how the world operates."

To illustrate how sociological explanations "go beneath the surface of ordinary belief," consider the baffling behavior of one early American religious group known as the Shakers. Explaining why the public derisively referred to members of this group as Shaking Quakers, or simply Shakers, Mark Holloway (1966) described their religious practices as follows:

> At their religious meetings they shook and trembled, whirled like dervishes, danced, sang, and cried out in strange tongues derived from the spirit world." . . . (p. 56)
>
> In another service, an entranced person shouted to those who were dancing:
>
> Shake! Shake! Shake!! There's a great spirit on you—Shake him off! off! off!! (p. 76)

While colonial America tolerated different religious groups, the public did not necessarily regard groups like the Shakers as normal. In fact, some people thought the Shakers were "demented hooligans" who communicated with spirits and broke the Sabbath (Holloway, 1966).

Common sense reveals little about the Shakers' behavior. But sociology offers an explanation with keen insight. What is more, it can be applied to all religious groups, which share something in common with the Shakers—religious rituals. It is Durkheim's theory of religion.

To understand this theory, you must think in a different way. You must first discard the two most obvious positions that you can take about religion: (1) that you believe in it or (2) that you don't believe in it. Then you must adopt the position taken by sociology—that "the key to religion is not its beliefs but the social rituals that its members perform" (Collins, 1992, p. 32).

Common sense suggests that religious beliefs should precede religious rituals. So, for example, belief in a supernatural being would lead people to enact religious rituals as a form of worship. But Durkheim proposed just the opposite, Collins says, suggesting that "the correct performance of religious rituals is what gave rise to the belief in the sacred" (p. 34).

Durkheim's focus on religious rituals, along with the fact that he did not believe in supernatural beings, led him to speculate about a nonobvious function that religious rituals serve: the power to create binding attachments among members of a group. This profound idea, which shifts attention away from religious beliefs, identifies the mechanism upon which societies are built—the emotional reward of belonging to a group.

Although Durkheim did not believe in supernatural beings, he did believe that religion represented something real. Collins captured the essence of Durkheim's conclusion about religion, writing:

> There is one reality that does have all the characteristics that people attribute to the divine. It is not nature, nor is it metaphysical. It is society itself. For society is a force far greater than any individual. It brought us to life, and it can kill us. It has tremendous power over us. . . . This is the fundamental truth that religion expresses. *God is a symbol of society.* (p. 35)

Referring to this kind of insight as *non-obvious sociology*, Collins proceeded to explain further the reality of Heaven and Hell and their equivalents in various religions. With a focus on group membership, he said that adhering to the moral precepts of the group is required for members to be in good standing. The reward that is given in return is the security of belonging to the group. Symbolically, that represents Heaven.

In contrast, he said, exclusion from membership results from moral evil or a transgression against the group. It is a punishment that denies a member the feeling of belonging to society. "In the symbolism of Christian theology, Hell is the banishment of the sinner from God" (p. 38).

According to Collins, one of the primary advantages of belonging to a group is the emotional energy that members gain from participating in intense social gatherings. This enables them to do things that they could not or would not do alone. And, he argues, it is the reward of this emotional experience that explains the everlasting appeal of religion.

The rituals of religious groups today are often as puzzling to the public as the behavior of the early American Shakers. Whether these practices involve the chants of Eastern religions or the communion rituals of Christians, they all serve the same function. They constitute a mechanism that creates binding attachments among group members. While common sense fails to provide insight into this function, sociology offers an explanation rich with insight into how the world operates.

		Male		Female	
Age	Total[1]	White	Black	White	Black
All ages[2]	12.1	21.4	12.5	5.0	2.1
10–14 years old	1.7	2.4	2.3	1.0	—
15–19 years old	10.9	18.5	14.4	4.2	—
20–24 years old	15.8	27.4	25.9	4.4	3.9
25–34 years old	15.1	25.9	21.5	5.5	3.1
35–44 years old	15.1	25.5	16.2	7.1	3.0
45–54 years old	14.5	23.9	14.1	7.8	2.2
55–64 years old	14.6	25.7	9.7	6.8	2.6
65–74 years old	16.3	31.4	11.7	6.2	2.2
75–84 years old	22.3	52.1	16.3	6.1	—
85 years and over	22.8	73.6	—	5.4	—

TABLE 1.1   SUICIDE RATES PER 100,000 POPULATION, BY SEX, RACE, AND AGE GROUP, 1993

[1]Includes other races not shown separately.
[2]Includes other age groups not shown separately.

Source: U.S. Bureau of the Census, *Statistical Abstract of the United States*, 1994 (Washington, D.C.: U.S. Government Printing Office, 1994).

June 22, 1982, p. C2). Debunking, then, can reveal unexpected sociological insights.

Take, for example, the problem of suicide, which has become the second leading cause of death, after accidents, among young people in the United States. Which of the following statements about suicide and its causes would you say, on the basis of common sense, are true?

1. Because they are the dependent, even oppressed, sex, more women than men commit suicide.

2. More young people than old people commit suicide. When one is young, the stresses and uncertainties of life are greatest.

3. Because of years of inequality and discrimination, African-Americans have a higher suicide rate than whites.

4. More people commit suicide around the major holidays because it is during these times that people feel the loneliest and most depressed.

5. People are more likely to commit suicide after extensive media coverage of other suicides.

Sociological research has effectively debunked each of these statements. As Table 1.1 shows, the suicide rate is consistently higher among men than women (although women do attempt suicide more often than men do). The elderly commit suicide at a higher rate than the young, partly because of ill health. The suicide rate among African-Americans is relatively low compared to that among whites. Recent research has not supported the popular assumption that holidays are a risk factor in suicide (Phillips & Wills, 1987). Other studies have shown that people who are not already at risk of suicide are not more likely to take their own lives after exposure to extensive media coverage of suicides, although those individuals who are already at risk of suicide may be affected (Weiss, 1989).

Evidence of the sharp increase in suicide that occurs when societies become highly developed was first gathered systematically by one of the founders of sociology, Émile Durkheim (1858–1917). His book *Suicide* (1897/1950) was one of the pioneering scientific studies in sociology. The study of suicide, which has since become an important area of research, often turns up surprising findings like Durkheim's (Maris, 1981).

The Basic Sociological Assumption

Aside from the idea that our common-sense views can mislead us, there is something else of importance to be learned from sociological research into suicide: Suicide is not the arbitrary, patternless act of individuals who are simply "pushed to the brink." Variations in suicide rates suggest that suicide is closely connected to particular groups, areas, and times—almost as if each social category were "predisposed" to contribute a quota of suicides. No one can predict which individuals within each category will commit suicide, but the categories that will have the highest suicide rates can be predicted with confidence. For example, there has been a strong consistency over the years in the higher rates of suicide of whites over African-Americans, men over women, unmarried people over married people, and members of rich societies over members of poor societies.

What can we conclude from this social patterning of suicides? Of course, suicide is the result of a very personal decision, an individual judgment that life is no longer worth living. In this sense, suicide is a purely individual act. But this personal decision is reached more commonly by people in certain social circumstances. This fact suggests that suicide is not only an individual but also a social act—that is, an act heavily influenced by the person's social surroundings. The main conclusion to be drawn from the social patterning of suicide is that human behavior is molded in part by the social environments—families, organizations, communities, ethnic groups, societies, and historical eras—in which people find themselves. This conclusion is the basic assumption that sociologists make about all human behavior: *Human behavior is shaped by society and social circumstances.*

The Sociological "Why?"

The central question asked by every science is "*why*?" How did a certain situation come to be? Under which specific circumstances? Through which processes, and involving which mechanisms? In other words, how can the existence of a phenomenon be explained? These questions all contribute to answering the more general question "why?"

Durkheim was interested in knowing what sociology can tell us about why a person commits suicide. To fully understand his answer to this question is to comprehend sociology's role in the social sciences and the discipline's potential for the advancement of knowledge. Before discussing the sociological "why," let us review three nonsociological answers that might be given to the question of why a suicide is committed.

1. *Biological.* It may be that a biological or organic factor is involved—a biochemical imbalance, for instance, prompted a person to take his or her own life. Such an answer, of course, lies outside the social sciences and in the realm of the natural sciences. Sociologists do not deny the possibility of biological causation, but neither do they study it.

2. *Biographical.* The reason a particular individual committed suicide can be stated in terms of a sequence of events that led up to the act. The person was punished at school that day; this followed breaking up with a friend and a fight with a parent, events that were in turn precipitated by a recent divorce in the family, and so on. This is a helpful and valid approach to use in

Sociologists study suicide not as a function of biology, biography, or personality, but as a function of society. They would explain it in terms of the individual's social background and circumstances.

explaining why a *particular* suicide was committed; it is the one often used by journalists. It is not, however, often used by sociologists, who seek to generalize from the particular. The sequence of events involved in every case of suicide is unique and, therefore, does not lend itself to generalization.

3. *Psychological.* Probably the most common explanation for suicide is the psychological one, having to do with what was going on in the mind of the individual. The suicide victim may have left a suicide note, for example, that outlined his or her reasons for committing suicide—perhaps the person wanted to "get back" at a parent or could not cope with a deep feeling of guilt. In the psychological realm, one would also want to know what the personality dispositions of the individual were: Was this person suffering from mental illness, intense depression, a deep sense of shame? Such information could not be gleaned solely from the suicide note; an investigation of the person's prior mental state would be required.

Knowledge about a person's biology, biography, and personality could provide a plausible explanation of why a particular suicide took place; it is the kind of knowledge developed by biologists, private investigators, and psychologists. How, then, does the sociologist fit in? Sociologists study suicide not as a function of biology, biography, or personality, but as a function of society. The sociologist would explain an individual case of suicide in terms of the subject's social background and circumstances.

However, it is important to add that the discipline of sociology as a whole does not deal primarily with such questions as why a particular *individual* committed suicide (or committed a crime, failed to get married, flunked out of school, or became unemployed). The main focus of sociology is not on the individual act but rather on the social environment or circumstance in which the act takes place.

To the sociologist, suicide is seen less as an individual act than as what Durkheim termed a *social fact*. The sociologist does not want to know why a particular person committed suicide, but why certain social environments have higher or lower suicide rates than others. Answers are sought to such questions as: Why are suicide rates lower in rural areas (at least in Western nations) than in urban areas, or why do fewer Italians commit suicide than Austrians? What characteristics, for example, do rural areas and Italy have in common, and how might such common characteristics be related to suicide? The answers to these questions will not give a complete explanation of suicide, nor will they allow us to make predictions of suicide in individual cases. However, they will provide rich information not only about suicide but also about the fundamental nature of human social organization.

It is inaccurate to say that sociology focuses on society to the exclusion of the individual, however. While it is not the main goal of sociology to provide a full explanation for human behavior, sociologists realize that the abstraction called "society" is a human creation; it is a result of individuals interacting with one another. The principal interest of most sociologists is in the nature of the society thus created and its effects on individuals (as in the example of suicide). Yet many sociologists are also concerned with the process of social interaction itself. How is society created and re-created on a daily basis through people interacting? This division within sociology, between a focus on society and a focus on social interaction, is discussed later in this chapter.

Sociological Explanation

Using such abstract ideas as "society" or "human social organization," how would a sociologist explain or account for the social patterning of suicide? Why is the suicide rate much lower in rural Mississippi than it is in New York City and much lower in Italy than in Austria? To provide a full sociological answer to these questions would take us far afield at this point, but much insight can be gained into the nature of sociological thought from a brief discussion of the kinds of explanations generated by sociology.

What is it about groups, communities, and societies with low suicide rates that causes people in them to be less prone to taking their own lives? Durkheim argued that these social groupings are more cohesive, integrated, or tightly knit than others (Durkheim, 1897/1950; Pope, 1976). In these groupings, individuals tend to have a surer sense of meaning and purpose in life; they have a more specific social position; expectations of how they should behave are more clearly spelled out; and they feel more "plugged in" or socially attached to something beyond or higher than their individual selves. By the same token, these social groupings have greater control over their individual members and exert strong external constraints on individual behavior (Pescosolido & Georgianna, 1989).

These social characteristics are most prevalent the world over in stable, traditional, and deeply religious groups, communities, and societies. It is in these groupings that suicide rates are lowest. The individual tie to the group is so strong that, in a sense, the group acts to prevent a person from taking, or even considering taking, his or her own life. In fact, human life is thought of less in individual terms than in terms of group ties and purposes.

In contrast, suicide rates are highest in those groupings where the concept of individualism reigns supreme—where group ties are weak and group expectations are questioned, and where individuals, relatively free to pursue life as they see fit, can become socially isolated (Stack, 1990). In place of strong group purposes, the lives of socially isolated people are governed mainly by personal interests. The fact is that such personal interests, in the absence of strong group purposes, often appear to be insufficient in providing individuals with the will to live. One could almost say, therefore, that suicide is one of the costs people pay for having a great deal of personal freedom.

The sociologist does not make any moral judgment of this trade-off; it is not the mission of sociology to suggest that one society is better than another because it has a lower suicide rate or more personal freedom. That is a moral or political judgment to be made outside the realm of the social sciences. Yet sociology can provide much valuable factual information on which to base such judgments.

To add further complexity to our discussion, one special type of suicide must be mentioned because it is at striking variance with the most commonly accepted American beliefs concerning suicide—a type of suicide that is actually encouraged by strong groups. A familiar example is the Japanese kamikaze pilots in World War II,

TABLE 1.2   DURKHEIM'S FOUR TYPES OF SUICIDE

	Egotistic	*Altruistic*	*Fatalistic*	*Anomic*
DESCRIPTION	Individual does not feel connected to larger society	Individual places the group's welfare above his or her own life	Individual commits suicide because of feelings of powerlessness to regulate his or her life	Individual commits suicide when society lacks social order
EXAMPLES	Skid row residents	Aged Eskimos; Japanese kamikaze pilots	Prisoners	People who have lost everything in a stock market crash
PSYCHOLOGICAL INDICATIONS	Depression and melancholy	Sense of obligation; shame and guilt	Fear, resignation	Insecurity, disillusionment

Sources: Based on Émile Durkheim, *Suicide* (Glencoe, Ill.: Free Press, 1950; orig. pub. in 1897); and Mamoru Iga, *The Thorn in the Chrysanthemum: Suicide and Economic Success in Modern Japan* (Berkeley: University of California Press, 1986).

who were willing to give up their lives for the survival of the Japanese nation. Other examples are the traditional suicides of aged Eskimos, who felt they had become a burden to their families, and Hindu widows, who willingly threw themselves on their husbands' funeral pyres. In these cases it is a strong group identification, not a weak one, that is the cause of suicide.

This kind of suicide, in which an individual places the group's welfare above his or her own life, is called *altruistic suicide.* Altruistic suicide is, of course, viewed differently in moral terms than the suicide that is initiated by a person to serve his or her own needs or desires. (Altruistic suicide is just one of the four types of suicide identified by Durkheim. The other three major types of suicide—egoistic, anomic, and fatalistic—are summarized in Table 1.2.)

One final aspect of sociological explanation should be noted. If suicide is associated with the strength of group connections, what causes some groupings to be cohesive or strongly connected and others to lack cohesion and be loosely connected? Compared to rural areas, urban areas tend to be loosely integrated, and this in turn is associated with the higher suicide rates in urban areas. But why are people in urban areas more loosely connected than those in rural areas? Again, the answer could be framed in biological or psychological terms. It is not likely that urban people differ biologically from rural people, however, and any dissimilarities in urban and rural psychology are probably due not to innate differences but to differences in social settings.

Where, then, do the reasons for group differences lie? As with their explanations of individual suicidal behavior, sociologists tend to look for the causes of social phenomena such as levels of social integration in other social phenomena. It is largely through the interplay of social institutions, for instance, that communities and societies are shaped. The family is shaped by the economy, the economy is shaped by the government, the government is shaped by the laws, the laws are shaped by the morals, and so on. Each social setting is thus an intricate web of social forces interacting with one another.

We should, therefore, be careful about generalizing from culture to culture or even from group to group. While we can say that suicide rates are generally higher among the elderly in many cultures, we cannot say that suicide rates are always higher in either urban or rural regions. For example, in contrast to the United States, where the suicide rate is higher in urban areas, in Japan, suicide is more common in rural areas. Several factors help to explain this: In Japan, older people tend to live in rural areas, where they have lower incomes and are at the mercy of an inadequate welfare system (Iga, 1986). Exploring the web of social reality in other cultures, as well as in our own, is the task, and the challenge, of the discipline called sociology.

Sociology and the Other Social Sciences

Unlike a *natural science,* which is the systematized study of the physical world, a **social science** involves the application of scientific methods to the study of society and human behavior. Sociology is closely related to the natural sciences through the methods it uses. It is related to the other social sciences because its subject matter overlaps with theirs. The boundaries between sociology, economics, psychology, anthropology, and history are often unclear. For example, research into the problems of inner-city residents with incomes below the poverty level could easily be characterized as urban sociology, family economics, or urban political science. But boundaries do exist, and an accurate picture of sociology requires an understanding of each of the other social sciences.

Economics is the study of how goods and services are produced, distributed, and consumed. An important common ground between economics and sociology is the study of the social basis of economic behavior. Money does not move in and out of banks by itself or in response to impersonal forces. It is deposited by people who have made social decisions about accepting a job and saving for the education of their children or for the purchase of a condominium. It is withdrawn by people who want to start their own business instead of taking orders from a boss, or who want to buy a fur coat because a neighbor bought one last week, or who find themselves unemployed. Another link is the economic basis of much social behavior. Sociologists recognize that economic and material interests have a strong effect on the workings of society. (The sociology of economic life is addressed in Chapter 18.)

Political science focuses on government and the use of political power. Students of political science look at the ideas behind systems of government and at the operation of the political process. Sociologists, on the other hand, are more interested in political behavior—the reasons people join political movements or support political parties—and the relationships between political and other social institutions. (Political sociology is discussed in Chapter 17.) In recent years, political science and sociology have moved closer in methods, subject matter, and concepts, and it has become increasingly difficult to draw a firm line between them.

History looks backward in an effort to determine the causes, sequence, and meaning of past events. Historical analysis has shifted from presenting accounts about people and places to tracing broad social trends over time. In turn, sociologists have borrowed heavily from historical inquiry. They have drawn on history, for example, to compare the social effects of industrialization in the Western countries in the 1800s with trends in the developing countries of Africa and Asia today. Historical references are used often in this text to shed light on many present-day social events.

Psychology deals mainly with human mental processes. Psychologists study such operations of the mind as logic, reason, perception, dreams, and creativity, as well as neuroses, mental conflicts, and various emotional states. Psychology differs markedly from sociology because it focuses on individual experience rather than on social groups. But *social psychology*—the study of the ways in which personality and behavior are influenced by the individual's social setting—is closely related to sociology and draws on the knowledge and methods of both disciplines.

Anthropology is the study of human evolution and culture in all periods and in all parts of the world. *Physical anthropology* concentrates on human biological evolution and the physical differences among peoples of the world today. *Cultural anthropology* mainly studies the culture and development of premodern (sometimes called *preindustrial*) societies. By contrast, sociology principally focuses on modern civilizations. Sociologists have borrowed many anthropological concepts and approaches, however, and in a number of colleges and universities the two fields are combined into one department.

Anthropology is faced with a built-in limitation: There are few premodern societies left to study, and almost none of these has remained untouched by modern civilization. This is one reason why twentieth-century anthropologists have widened their field of study to include modern communities and societies. They have thus brought their field closer to sociology in subject matter. *Ethnographies*, anthropological reports that detail some aspect of a people's behavior or way of life, have helped sociologists to understand and compare societies from all over the world. (Chapter 3 explores the anthropological approach to the study of culture.)

THE HISTORY AND DEVELOPMENT OF SOCIOLOGY

Sociology began to take its present form only about a hundred years ago. The roots of the discipline, though, reach back to the eighteenth century. This period of European history is called the Enlightenment because its thinkers believed in reason and humanity's ability to perfect itself. The early assumptions of sociology derive from the ideas of these thinkers. One key assumption was that, just as scientists studying the natural world had been able to use reason to discover the laws of physics and the movements of the planets, so scientists studying the social world could use reason to discover the laws of human bahavior. Another assumption was that the laws of human behavior, once they were known, could be used to perfect society. But the Industrial Revolution of the nineteenth century set in motion a series of rapid and widespread social changes that challenged the optimistic ideas of the Enlightenment.

The Industrial Revolution began in England, where inventors perfected the spinning jenny and the power loom as methods of manufacturing large quantities of textiles quickly and cheaply. As the textile industry grew, along with iron smelting and other industries, large numbers of people crowded into the rapidly expanding towns and cities to take factory jobs. There they formed a new social class of industrial workers; their employers also became a powerful new social class. Other dramatic changes took place in the structure of families, the nature of politics, and the role of religion in people's lives. Workers' wages were often so low that husband, wife, and children all had to work to make ends meet. Some people worked as long as 19 hours a day, six or seven days a week. This did not mean that work was steady; layoffs were common. In addition to the long hours and lack of security, worker housing and sanitation were abysmal. Such conditions reduced the life expectancy of the new urban poor while increasing the crime rate. It was this terrible set of problems that the social thinkers of the early nineteenth century tried to understand and hoped to eliminate.

The Classic Figures

Although the Industrial Revolution began in England, the most famous early sociologists were French and German rather than English. One reason for this was the great intellectual curiosity that spread through continental Europe following the French Revolution, a curiosity that generated many new ways of thinking.

AUGUSTE COMTE

The person usually considered the founder of sociology is Auguste Comte (1798–1857), who had once been personal secretary to another early social thinker, Henri de Saint-Simon. Comte coined the term *sociology.* Previously, he had called the new discipline *positive philosophy,* both to stress its scientific nature and to distinguish it from traditional philosophy. The aim of sociology, as he saw it, was to find the "invariable natural laws" of society upon which a new order could be based. Comte did not have a purely scientific interest in analyzing society; rather, he wanted to establish a "spiritual elite"—led by himself—to run the new social order.

HERBERT SPENCER

Herbert Spencer (1820–1903), the son of a schoolteacher, is generally considered to be the most important English social thinker of his time. He put forth the idea that society is like an organism—a self-regulating system. Drawing an analogy to Charles Darwin's theory of biological evolution, Spencer suggested that societies, like

Many early sociologists sought to improve the social conditions of the poor. They were moved by deplorable working conditions and especially child labor, as exemplified by these young boys working a spinning machine.

animal species, evolved from simple to more complex forms. And just as Darwin had suggested, in his theory of natural selection, that animals better adapted to their surroundings were more likely to survive and reproduce, Spencer suggested that those societies better adapted to their surroundings were more likely to survive and develop than those that were poorly adapted.

Spencer was also an early advocate of what later came to be called *social Darwinism*—the view that the principle of survival of the fittest applies to societies and within societies. In other words, the traits of any society, including its inequalities, are the result of "natural" evolutionary principles, or laws. Unlike the reformist thinkers of his day, Spencer was against government intervention in social affairs because he felt that such intervention would interfere with these natural laws. Spencer's theories of social evolution have generally been discredited. His analogy between societies and organisms, however, is echoed in the *functionalist* school of modern sociology (discussed later in this chapter).

KARL MARX

Karl Marx (1818–1883) was born a German but lived much of his adult life in London, where he did most of his writing. Marx did not believe that society is an orderly system that regulates itself. Instead, he saw in society continuous conflict and change. Every society, he stated, contains the "seeds of its own destruction." In contrast to Spencer's view that societies are subject to "natural" laws,

Marx believed that societies are largely determined by economic forces. He saw human history as a series of inevitable conflicts between economic classes.

In the tradition of Comte, Marx felt that social scientists should try not only to understand society but also to change it. However, Marx's vision was much more radical; he believed that just as capitalism had replaced feudalism, so capitalism in turn would, through class struggle, be replaced by socialism. He devoted much of his life to bringing about this change. Marx's ideas and ideals have, in fact, inspired more social change than those of almost any other person in history, although not necessarily in the directions he foresaw.

Marx's view of social classes and the importance of economic factors in our lives is regarded as a major contribution to the social sciences. His views on class conflict are reflected in the *conflict* school of modern sociology (discussed later in this chapter). He also made important contributions to the sociological analysis of political and economic institutions (discussed in Chapters 17 and 18).

ÉMILE DURKHEIM

More than anyone, the French scholar Émile Durkheim (1858–1917) defined the subject matter of sociology and pointed out how it differed from philosophy, economics, psychology, and social reform. In *The Rules of Sociological Method* (1894/1950) and in *Suicide* (1897/1950), Durkheim argued that the main concern of sociology should be what he called *social facts*. These facts are external to people but exert control over them. Laws may be just words, for example, but people act as if laws were something tangible and real.

Social facts should be studied in their own right, Durkheim believed. He insisted that one has to explain social facts in terms of other social facts, not in terms of biological or psychological traits. Thus, in his view, to understand the meaning and development of a society's laws, one must look at the society's religion. To understand a society's organizations, one must look at its institutions, such as the government and economy, of which they are a part.

Like Comte and Spencer, Durkheim viewed society as a whole unto itself, greater than the sum of its parts. One of his central interests was how societies manage to hold together. Deeply distressed by the breakdown of the traditional values and social structures of preindustrial societies, Durkheim searched for the sources of social solidarity. Ultimately, he believed, societies are bound together by the shared beliefs and values of their members. Durkheim's emphasis on social solidarity is often criticized by Marxists and other radical sociologists, who are more interested in the sources of social conflict in societies. However, his analysis of the ability of religion to promote solidarity, presented in *The Elementary Forms of the Religious Life* (1915), continues to be regarded as a central contribution to the sociological analysis of religion (discussed in Chapter 16).

MAX WEBER

Max Weber (1864–1920) had perhaps the greatest influence on the development of modern sociology. He was particularly interested in the larger dimensions of society—its organizations and institutions—which he studied on a vast historical and worldwide scale. He is perhaps best known for his analyses of bureaucracy and capitalism, and he also did important work in social stratification, political sociology, and the sociology of religion. Much of Weber's thought contrasts strongly with that of Marx.

Weber was both a dedicated scholar and a man passionately involved with the problems of Germany in his time. As a scholar, he believed that social scientists can find objective solutions to problems only if they suspend their own value judgments in doing research and in drawing conclusions. This belief in *value-free* sociology was directly opposed to the tradition of Comte and Marx. Weber believed, however, that as citizens, sociologists should take an active role in public life. During World War I, he ran a military hospital and later helped to draft the constitution of the Weimar Republic.

Like Durkheim, Weber shaped the development of sociological research as well as sociological theory. Weber felt that sociology must also include the study of *social action*, the way people orient their behavior to one another. In his view, the study of interpersonal interaction should not rely only on objective and quantitative methods. It must also include what Weber called *Verstehen*, the "sympathetic understanding" of the mind of another.

The Development of American Sociology

Although its founders were Europeans, sociology became most strongly rooted in the United States. The intellectual climate in this country encouraged new ideas, and the social climate—one of great diversity and rapid social change—cried out for systematic analysis. Like many of the Europeans who preceded them, the early American sociologists were strongly interested in social reform.

From the beginning, American sociology and its practitioners (such as Lester Ward, Franklin Giddings, William I. Thomas, Robert Park, and William G. Summer) embarked on a crusade: to understand, evaluate, and solve the problems of the city (poverty, poor housing conditions, and intemperance, to name just a few). Although the early American sociologists tended to come from rural backgrounds, their strong religious and moral principles led them to promote urban reform (Hinkle & Hinkle, 1954; Reiss, 1968). The emphasis of the early American sociologists on solving the social problems of the urban poor differentiated them sharply from their European counterparts, who tended to be more ideological and less applied in their orientation.

THE CHICAGO SCHOOL

Sociology first became an established discipline in the Midwest. In 1892, the University of Chicago became the first university in the world to offer a doctorate in sociology. By 1905, graduate study in sociology had spread to the East, where Brown, Columbia, Dartmouth, and Yale introduced formal training in the field. By the 1920s, sociology had come to be widely recognized as an academic and practical discipline throughout the United States (Reiss, 1968).

The University of Chicago remained at the center of sociological research and instruction for many years. The researchers at the University of Chicago during this period came to be known collectively as the *Chicago School.* The Chicago School sociologists were interested in such typical American social problems as ghettos, immigration, race relations, and urbanization. They assembled a vast amount of useful statistical data and developed many important concepts that are still in use.

The leading figure at the University of Chicago was Robert Park (1864–1944), who began teaching there in 1914. Park was a unique combination of news reporter, social activist (he served for a while as publicity director and ghost writer for Booker T. Washington), researcher, and pure theorist. He co-wrote the first major introductory textbook in sociology (Park & Burgess, 1921). Many of his students later became influential sociologists at other American universities.

George Herbert Mead (1863–1931) was the major theorist of the *symbolic interactionist* branch of sociology that was born at the University of Chicago. (This approach is discussed in Chapter 5.) Mead stressed that humans respond to abstract meanings as well as to concrete experience. Unlike most theorists of the time, Mead claimed that the human mind and self-consciousness are largely social creations. Thus he helped to define that aspect of sociology that sees individual behavior as the product of society.

AMERICAN SOCIOLOGY AFTER WORLD WAR II

During the tumultuous years of the Great Depression, the federal government began to hire sociologists to do research and to advise such governmental agencies as the Works Progress Administration, the Department of Agriculture, and the Natural Resources Committee. With the advent of World War II, many sociologists were called to work in Washington. Sociologists used their skills to devise training programs for servicemen and to develop information campaigns for civilians, and they consulted with the War Department, the Office of Price Administration, and the Department of State. They also helped to develop the food rationing program that was instituted during World War II (Bulmer, 1984).

After the Depression and World War II, however, the Chicago School's optimistic zeal for social reform and for the collection of data dwindled. American sociologists became more interested in constructing theories of society. By the late 1940s, sociology had come so far and grown so fast that it was time to stand back and try to generalize the knowledge of society that had been collected. It was time again to construct, in the tradition of the founders of the discipline, abstract explanations for the workings of society. This shift was accompanied by an eastward shift in dominance, from Chicago to such universities as Harvard and Columbia.

The most important of all the American abstract theoreticians was Talcott Parsons (1902–1979), one of the founders of the sociology department at Harvard in the 1930s. Parsons combined the diverse approaches of several classical sociologists, mainly Weber and Durkheim, into a total system of thought that he called a *general theory of action* (Parsons, 1951; Parsons & Shils, 1951). In this general theory, he sought to develop a framework of concepts that could be used to analyze all types of social phenomena, from the major institutions of society to individual actions. He later applied the theory to a wide range of subjects, including religion, education, and race relations. Parsons had a strong influence on several generations of sociologists. Because of his fondness for abstraction, however, and his view of society as relatively static, he has also been heavily criticized.

Another influential American sociologist was Robert K. Merton (1910–1998). A student of Parsons, Merton worked within the Parsonian tradition, but he was especially interested in developing sociological theories of the "middle range." *Middle-range theories* take the middle road between narrow *specialized theories,* which focus on a single aspect of social life, and broad *general theories,* which are comprehensive attempts to explain how a wide range of social factors fit together. Merton's theories are not as abstract as the theories of Parsons and thus can be more easily tested empirically. One of Merton's lasting contributions is his theory of deviant behavior, discussed in Chapter 8.

In the early postwar period, many sociologists worked in the functionalist tradition, as did Parsons and

Merton. An exception was C. Wright Mills (1916–1962), a key figure in the development of what is now called the *conflict perspective.* (The functionalist and conflict perspectives are discussed in more detail later in this chapter.) Mills criticized both the Chicago School's "hard-core empiricists" and the Parsonian "grand theorists" for their lack of social concern. He once described himself as a "plain Marxist," but he was greatly influenced by Weber as well as Marx. Mills was passionately involved in the problems and politics of his time; he especially wanted to see wealth and power in America distributed more equally.

SOCIOLOGY TODAY

Today sociology is a well-established discipline in every advanced society and in many developing ones. It is still most strongly entrenched in the United States, where it is taught in every major university. (As of 1998, some 13,200 people were members of the discipline's professional organization, the American Sociological Association.) Sociology is also solidly developed in England, France, Germany, and other Western nations.

The role of sociology in Eastern Europe is less firmly established. The obstacles faced by sociology in what used to be the Soviet Union were also found in other communist countries. Research on Soviet society was restricted, and sociological findings inconsistent with the official image of existing social arrangements were silenced. In addition, Soviet sociologists lacked access to studies of their society produced by their Western counterparts (Nove, 1989). All of this changed with the far-reaching reforms initiated in the Soviet Union during the mid-1980s. No longer limited by party ideology and more familiar with the perspectives and techniques of Western sociology, Soviet sociologists saw their work influence decisions concerning women's employment, work conditions, health and child care, and schooling (Nove, 1989). In the Soviet Union and in neighboring countries like Hungary, sociology rose in prominence as the need for solutions to problems of social disorder—climbing rates of delinquency, crime, the breakup of the family, and suicide—became more urgent (Sanjian, 1991; Szalai, 1991).

Because the influence and appeal of sociology seem to grow during periods of social turmoil and disorder, we can expect the discipline to become even more important in the nations of Eastern Europe and in the former Soviet Union as these countries confront the tensions and dilemmas of rapid social change. For the same reason, sociology also may be reinvigorated in the United States.

As noted earlier, sociology originated amid the widespread confusion and chaos produced by the French and Industrial revolutions. The old social order had been destroyed, a new one had yet to emerge, and

sociology attracted support because of the new intellectual understandings it provided. In the United States, sociology took root during the first two decades of the twentieth century, also a period of massive social change generated by rapid and widespread urban and industrial development. Half a century later, in the late 1960s and early 1970s, sociology gained its greatest appeal in this nation as solutions were sought for the deep-seated social discord signaled by inner-city riots, the civil rights movement, and antiwar protests (Gouldner, 1970; Lemann, 1991). Today there is evidence that the United States may be on the verge of yet another era of domestic discord, based on an economic downturn, growing inequality in the distribution of income and wealth, and weakening bonds of national solidarity (Wolfe, 1991). The question being asked with increasing frequency is the one that gave rise to sociology in the first place: "What must we do to establish the basis of an orderly social life?" (Hearn, 1985).

SOCIOLOGICAL THEORY

Sociology is a well-established discipline, but that does not mean it is a discipline with a unified way of looking at the world. Sociologists do agree on many basic principles, but there is no single viewpoint that is dominant within modern sociology. Indeed, few academic disciplines, especially the newer ones like sociology, have a high degree of unity. Sociology is still in the process of defining itself—its subject matter, its methods, and the uses to which its findings can be put.

You should already have picked up some clues about the range of thought within sociology from the first parts of this chapter. In our discussion of the sociological approach, we pointed out that many sociologists want the discipline to be as scientific as possible, whereas others favor a more humanistic approach. And in our discussion of the sociological "why," we noted that most sociologists focus on society, but that some are concerned mainly with social interaction. Where sociologists stand on issues such as these is strongly related to their view of the discipline's role in society, the methods they use, and the questions they ask.

In the effort to understand how society works, different sociologists start with different assumptions about the basic character of human social life. Some see order and stability as more important than conflict and change; others take the opposite view. Some focus their attention principally on the larger institutional structures of society; others concentrate more on human interaction in small groups. Such choices define a sociologist's *theoretical perspective,* also sometimes called a *theoretical paradigm.* Theoretical perspectives help sociologists to select

.NET   INTERNET/TECHNOLOGY

THE GLOBAL VILLAGE

As we approach the twenty-first century, one technological innovation promises to revolutionize society. It is the Internet—a phenomenal scientific achievement that has captured the attention of a worldwide audience.

In simple terms, the Internet can be described as a network of computer networks. But science fiction writers, politicians, journalists, and even scientists, themselves, have depicted it more fantastically. It is cyberspace, a global village, the information superhighway, a supercommunity, and even an intergalactic network.

Of these images, Marshall McLuhan's term *global village,* which first appeared in 1964 in his book *Understanding Media,* probably captures the essence of the Internet better than any other. As a symbol of human relationships and laden with McLuhan's ideas about the effects of media, this term suggests the real power of the net—its potential to change society, to alter fundamentally the way we experience the world.

Expectations about the Internet's effects span an extreme range—all the way from its promise to remedy society's most challenging problems to actually exacerbating them or causing new ones. Regardless of the specific effects, this new media form is sure to conform to McLuhan's theoretical expectations. Writing on this subject in 1967, he said:

> Media are so pervasive in their personal, political, economic, esthetic, psychological, moral, ethical and social consequences that they leave no part of us untouched, unaffected unaltered. (p. 26)

Indeed, from the early sixteenth century, when the printing press introduced the age of information, the media have played a tremendous role in social change (Postman, 1993). The school, representative government, new forms of economic activity, new conceptions of knowledge and intelligence, and new forms of public discourse (newspapers, pamphlets, broadsides, and books)—all were social products of the printing press.

The telegraph, which eliminated distance as a constraint on communication, diminished both physical and social boundaries with far-reaching consequences for the United States. As Neil Postman noted: "The telegraph erased state lines, collapsed regions, and, by wrapping the continent in an information grid, created the possibility of a unified nation-state" (1993, p. 67).

Together telegraphy and photograpy introduced new ideas about information. It no longer required interconectedness or context, instancy gained favor over historical continuity, and fascination replaced complexity and coherence (Postman, 1993). It was not long before broadcasting signaled yet another stage in the information revolution.

Today computer technology marks the latest stage in the information age. While it is impossible to predict how computer technology will change the world, the Internet has the potential to spread democracy worldwide. This potential was tested during the attempted coup of the former Soviet Union in 1991. While Soviet newspapers, radio, and television were not free to report the truth, the Internet was. As Vadim Antonov, a founder of the Russian computer network,

claimed, it had put "communications in the hands of the people" (*Newsday,* August, 28, 1991, p. 4).

Indeed, it had. Electronic messages relayed back and forth between Soviet Internet users and sympathizers around the world helped to mobilize the resistance. On Wednesday, August 21, one anonymous activist wrote:

> To all people of good will! We want you to know that the democracy of the USSR is in great danger. . . . Right now the center of Moscow is surrounded by tanks and soldiers. . . . We need your moral support! . . . Down with the Communist tyranny! (*Newsday,* August 28, 1991)

As a worldwide audience responded, history would record that the Internet had played a major role in securing democracy. It had been a force in dramatic social change.

For most of us, the effect of the Internet will not be so sudden nor so discernible. It will gradually transform our daily lives and slowly alter American institutions. In fact, this process is already underway. Print and broadcast media, with perhaps the most to lose, are adapting to their latest competitor with Web sites advertising and supplementing their own form of communication. The economy is adjusting to new ways of working and spending. And the political system is being transformed by a cost-saving medium that allows two-way communication with citizens.

While the benefits of the Internet must be weighed against its abuses, it clearly promises to erase international boundaries and unify the world.

A unit of social structure is considered dysfunctional when it prevents society from meeting its needs. A school can be dysfunctional if it serves as a place where students learn undesirable behavior from their peers.

the questions that they ask about social life and the methods they use to seek answers to these questions. In other words, they shape the ways in which sociologists seek to explain society and social behavior. The three most common theoretical perspectives used by modern sociologists are functionalism, the conflict perspective, and interactionism.

The Functionalist Perspective

The **functionalist perspective** emphasizes the way in which each part of a society contributes to the whole so as to maintain social stability. According to this perspective, society is much like the human body or any other living organism. Like the parts of the body (such as the limbs, the heart, and the brain), the parts of society (such as families, businesses, and governments) work together in a systematic way that is usually good for the whole. Each part helps to maintain the state of balance that is needed for the system to operate smoothly. Functionalism, sometimes called *structural functionalism,* has its roots in the work of such early sociological theorists as Auguste Comte, Herbert Spencer, and Émile Durkheim.

More recently, Robert Merton pointed out that the functions of a unit of social structure may be either *manifest* (intended and recognized) or *latent* (unintended or unrecognized). For example, one manifest function of elementary school is to provide students with a solid background in such academic skills as reading and mathematics. A latent function of elementary school, however, is to teach children such important social skills as cooperation and organization. A unit of social structure is considered *dysfunctional* when it prevents society from

meeting its needs. A school can be dysfunctional if it serves as a place where students learn socially undesirable behavior from their peers.

An important perspective within cultural anthropology as well as within sociology, functionalism is especially suited to the study of stable, small-scale societies such as isolated communities on Pacific islands or small midwestern towns in the United States. It can help us understand how people in such communities live their lives in an orderly way with what appears to be a strong spirit of cooperation and a high degree of unity. In these kinds of settings, it is not difficult to assume that things will continue pretty much the way they always have—unless something from the outside upsets the balance. Indeed, the functionalist perspective normally interprets social change as something introduced from the outside that interrupts the system's smooth functioning.

Yet social life is not always tranquil. Much of the world is embroiled in wars, rebellions, and revolutions. Critics of functionalism believe that it fails to explain adequately such events. A second, and contrasting, theoretical perspective in sociology is the conflict perspective.

The Conflict Perspective

The **conflict perspective** emphasizes struggle over limited resources, power, and prestige as a permanent aspect of societies and a major source of social change. This perspective is based on the assumption that the parts of society, far from being smoothly functioning units of a whole, actually are in conflict with one another. This is not to say that society is never orderly—conflict theorists do not deny that there is much order in the world—but rather that order is only one possible outcome of the ongoing conflict among society's parts and that it is not necessarily the natural state of things.

Conflict theorists trace their roots back to Marx. They stress the dynamic, ever-changing nature of society. To them, society is always in a fragile balance. More often than not, social order (often quite temporary) stems from the domination of some parts of society over other parts rather than from the natural cooperation among those parts. Order is the product of force and constraint—domination—of the strong over the weak, the rich over the poor.

FUNCTIONALISM AND CONFLICT PERSPECTIVES COMPARED

We can illustrate these contrasting perspectives by discussing how sociologists using each of them would view the organization of a college campus. Note that although the two perspectives are quite different from each other, they are not necessarily incompatible. Each looks at a different aspect of social reality. Functionalists would see the campus as consisting of various "organic" parts: students, faculty, and administrators, as well as maintenance personnel, research assistants, cafeteria workers, and so on. All of the parts are interrelated, and all normally contribute to the smooth functioning of the campus. A disturbance in any one of the parts could temporarily upset this equilibrium. A student strike over the quality of the teaching or the food, or over larger political issues, could throw the campus into imbalance as surely as a blizzard. But since society is based on agreement and cooperation, such temporary imbalance would be swiftly righted to promote the good of the whole.

Conflict theorists would look through the surface calm of the campus to the self-interests of the different groups and the rivalries among them. For instance, the faculty might be fighting for a reduced classload. Sophomores might be upset at a new reduction of electives. Medical laboratory assistants might be forming a labor union to bring their salaries more in line with those they can get off-campus. And administrators might consider all the other groups ungrateful for their efforts to keep the school running in the face of government spending cuts. Conflict theorists would see the "order" of the campus as merely the fragile, momentary outcome of the competition among various groups. (Functionalism and conflict theory are discussed at more length in Chapter 4.)

Both of these theoretical perspectives have one thing in common: They are concerned primarily with the macro level of society, or large-scale social structures and how they relate to one another. Sometimes called *macrosociologists,* researchers using these perspectives typically focus on the major structural units of society, such as organizations, institutions, communities, and nations; on social processes, such as urbanization and social mobility; and on belief systems, such as capitalism and socialism.

These two theoretical perspectives also share a "structuralist" view of human society and behavior. The premises of the *structuralist view* are (1) that social structures should be treated and studied as social facts that are external to, and exert control over, individuals; and (2) that individual behavior is mainly the product of social structures and forces that are not of the person's own making. Stressing the coercive power of society over human thought and action, perspectives such as these minimize the importance of free will and individual autonomy.

The Interactionist Perspective

Another prominent perspective within sociology differs from those just discussed in that it is concerned mainly with the micro level of society—social interaction and the individual as a social being. This perspective, known as the *interactionist perspective,* focuses on how people interact in their everyday lives and how they make sense of this interaction. Persons favoring the interactionist perspective are sometimes called *microsociologists* because they study individuals and small groups rather than large-scale social structures. George Herbert Mead is generally considered the founder of the interactionist perspective. (Mead's theory of symbolic interaction is treated in Chapter 5.)

Perhaps because they observe human behavior at such close range, interactionists tend to see people as having more freedom of action—more freedom from the constraints of society—than do the macrosociologists of the functionalist and conflict schools. In other words, interactionists do not see society as a controlling force, at least not to the degree that the macrosociologists do. Interactionists stress that people are always in the process of creating and changing their social worlds. Moreover, they are as interested in what people think and feel as in how they act. Interactionists explore people's motives, their purposes and goals, and the ways they perceive the world.

We can illustrate the interactionist perspective by going back to our example of the college campus. Rather than viewing the campus in terms of either cooperation or conflict, interactionists would focus on such questions as how students look at campus life when they first arrive, what the college experience means to them, and how social interaction develops in the dorm. The interactionist is concerned not so much with the organization and operation of the college campus as with the nature of daily interaction on the campus and how this interaction is perceived by students, faculty, and administrators. Interactionists do not assume that a campus is a fixed organization to which its members must adapt their behavior. Rather, they see campus organization as something that evolves and changes through the interaction of the participants.

In addition to their focus on the individual, interactionists also typically differ from macrosociologists in the kinds of research methods they use. Because they are interested in what people think and feel, interactionists often use qualitative methods. These are methods designed to study people in natural situations. Macrosociologists, in contrast, are more likely to use quantitative methods, such as carefully controlled statistical studies. (Research methods are discussed at length in Chapter 2.)

The Three Perspectives: A Brief Assessment

The diversity of theoretical perspectives within sociology makes it clear that sociology is not a well-defined discipline with a unified view of the world. But this diversity should also point out the fact that neither is sociology a narrow, closed-minded academic pursuit. Indeed, such diversity is seen by many sociologists today as making their discipline a vital, vigorous, and intensely exciting enterprise, one that is always trying to plumb the depths of the human experience.

Also, it should be stressed that the differences revealed by these three perspectives typically do not stem from contradiction or antagonism but from complementarity. It is not a question of one perspective being right and the others being wrong; each complements the others by looking at a related aspect of the same social reality. Order and conflict are found in all social groupings; to study the one in the absence of the other is to be missing something real and important.

Similarly, the macro and micro levels of society are really two sides of the same coin (Collins, 1981). Macrosocial organization develops out of the interaction of people in microsocial situations; thus, the organization of the college campus is a product of the daily interaction of the participants. But it is equally true that every social situation is already organized by the people who have interacted in that situation in the past. Thus, students who arrive on campus find a preexisting social structure, one they experience as external to them and into which they must fit their lives.

Regardless of which perspective seems most appealing, pressing questions many readers are probably thinking at this point are: What's the use of all of this mental activity? How does sociology *apply*—to my society and, more importantly, to my own life? How can I use all of this information and insight about the human condition? We try to answer these questions in the remainder of this chapter.

SOCIOLOGY APPLIED

The main goal of sociology is to advance our understanding of the world we live in. This is a noble aim that in itself justifies the existence of sociology. But this is often not the goal of most interest to students taking courses in the subject. They wish to know how sociology can be used in "real life."

The question really subsumes two different issues. First, what is the practical importance of sociology for society as a whole? That is, how does society benefit from having sociologists in its midst? And second, why should you, the student, bother to study sociology? What's in it for you? Some answers to both types of questions are explored in the discussion that follows and also in special features throughout this book called "Applying Sociology."

Sociology and Society

Most sociologists work as teachers in colleges and universities. Their effect on society—through teaching—is indirect. As students learn the sociological perspective and the results of sociological studies, they become better educated and better able to solve the problems of their society. But what are the direct uses of sociology outside the university? This aspect of sociology, called *applied sociology,* has been growing rapidly (Monette, Sullivan, & De Jong, 1986; Olsen & Micklin, 1981). An increasing number of sociologists are working in the applied sector: in government agencies, nonprofit organizations, private research agencies, and such fields as communications, advertising, and technology (Huber, 1984).

We can begin to understand the difference between academic sociology and applied sociology by examining the distinction between basic and applied research. **Basic research** is concerned with knowledge for its own sake, without regard to the uses and applications of that knowledge. **Applied research** is designed to provide answers for the solution of immediate practical problems. It is addressed directly to the solution of real-world problems and is decision-oriented. Typically, applied research is requested by people who need information to help them make a specific decision or solve a certain problem, such as how to reduce street crime or the number of school dropouts.

A classic example of applied social research is a study of a Chicago neighborhood heavily populated by heroin addicts. This study, done by the Illinois Drug Abuse program and a team of sociologists from the University of Chicago, identified key factors involved in the process of drug addiction. A policy based on this information and carried out over a three-year test period resulted in a significant decrease in addiction (Hughes, 1977).

In practice, the distinction between basic and applied research is not always clear. Research designed to solve specific problems relies heavily on the results of basic research. And much research can be both basic and applied at the same time.

TYPES OF APPLIED RESEARCH

The five main types of applied research are evaluation research, the social experiment, policy-oriented social investigation, social prediction, and social monitoring and description.

EVALUATION RESEARCH. This common kind of applied research involves assessing the effects of a project or program that has already been undertaken. Evaluation research is used to answer such questions as Was the program a success? Did it accomplish what was intended?

A good example of evaluation research involves the famous television program *Sesame Street.* This program was designed by the Children's Television Workshop "to promote the intellectual and cultural growth of preschoolers, particularly disadvantaged preschoolers" (Cooney, 1968). Did it do so? Researchers found that children who viewed the show regularly—four times or more per week—did show some learning gains. But they also found that advantaged children watched the show more often than did disadvantaged children. As a result, the program seemed to be increasing the learning gap between advantaged and disadvantaged children. Thus, *Sesame Street,* although it may be helping some preschoolers, has not accomplished all that its designers had hoped (Cook et al., 1975).

A study of the impact of mandatory sentencing laws in Florida provides a more recent example of evaluation research (Bales & Dees, 1992). As part of the nationwide movement to "get tough" on crime, Florida established ten mandatory sentencing provisions; six of these were passed in 1988 and 1989 alone. The researchers wanted to know what effects these provisions were having. Their research suggested the following conclusions: (a) The new laws were indeed being used; the number of people sentenced under the mandatory minimum provisions for drug trafficking increased from 4 in 1979–1980 to 1,022 in 1989–1990; over the same time period the number of persons convicted under Florida's habitual felony offender statutes jumped from 21 to 1,084. (b) These laws contributed significantly to a fourfold increase in the state's prison population, from about 10,000 to over 40,000. (c) Because of prison overcrowding, officials were more frequently granting early release to those criminals who had not been sentenced under mandatory guidelines; as a result, the average percentage of sentences served in Florida dropped from 53 to 34 percent between 1987 and 1989. Furthermore, a considerable number of the prisoners who won early release had been convicted for serious violent crimes. The research thus suggests that mandatory sentencing laws may have unexpected consequences that could appreciably impair their ability to reduce the crime rate.

The tremendous surge in evaluation research since the 1960s has been one result of government-mandated assessments of many of its social programs (such as job training, education for the disadvantaged, and legal services for the poor). One prominent evaluation researcher has concluded, much to everyone's dismay, that few of these government programs have accomplished what they set out to do. However, the same researcher has suggested that her conclusions are probably influenced by the fact that, because of budgetary constraints, the evaluations had to be completed so hurriedly that it was impossible to identify accurately any of the programs' long-term effects (Weiss, 1987).

THE SOCIAL EXPERIMENT. Another type of applied social research—the social experiment—is conducted *before* a program begins. Despite this difference in timing, social experiments often use the same research methods as evaluation research. In one important social experiment, the U.S. Department of Housing and Urban Development (HUD) gave 25,000 low-income families direct payments to improve their housing rather than building subsidized housing for them. The purpose of the experiment, which lasted from 1973 to 1980, was to see if direct payments better served the housing needs of the poor.

Researchers found that the housing payments did indeed reach those families with the greatest need and did reduce the proportion of their income those families paid for rent. However, a stipulation of the program was that to receive these payments, families had to upgrade the quality of their housing to a rather high standard. It turned out that most families chose to make just a few repairs to their current residence or move to only slightly better quarters. In other words, instead of improving their housing very much, they chose to spend the greater part of their housing payments to improve their desperate financial situations. Because the experiment showed that a program of direct payments for housing would not greatly improve low-income housing, HUD shifted its focus to other approaches to the housing problem (Frieden, 1980).

POLICY-ORIENTED SOCIAL INVESTIGATION. A form of applied sociology that has gained importance in the last few decades is the large, policy-oriented social investigation. Such studies are usually financed either by the government or by private foundations. Their purpose is to provide public officials with information and tentative conclusions about major policy issues facing the nation.

One example is a major study conducted by a research team headed by sociologist James S. Coleman that compared levels of academic achievement in public, Catholic, and other private schools in the United States (Coleman, Hoffer, & Kilgore, 1982). The study had been requested by the National Center for Education Statistics as a means of evaluating proposed changes in educational policy. The goal of these changes, which included tuition tax credits or "educational vouchers" for private school attendance, was to reduce educational segregation. The study found that students in private schools had higher educational achievement and higher aspirations; this was ascribed to the more rigorous academic demands and more effective discipline of the private schools. However, private schools showed *less* racial segregation (but more economic segregation) than the public schools did.

APPLYING SOCIOLOGY

CRITICAL THINKING

Whether they are conservative or liberal, Americans love to express their opinions. And the airwaves give them plenty of opportunity to do so. Television and radio talk shows turn the passive broadcast medium into an interactive one with sensational controversial issues.

- Should physician-assisted suicide be legalized?
- Do we need stricter gun-control laws?
- Should schools be required to use a multicultural curriculum?

In forming opinions about these and many other issues, we must determine which experts are credible, which arguments are logical, and ultimately which conclusions to accept or reject. But despite—indeed, because of—so much available information, many of us may feel overwhelmed and confused. And few of us possess the expertise to adequately judge the news coverage on a particular subject.

To make matters worse, news organizations may contribute to our confusion. Consider, for example, the headlines that appeared in two national newspapers (Lee & Solomon, 1991). On May 6, 1989, *The New York Times* printed: "April Job Growth Eased Decisively, Stirring Concern." Two days later, a headline appearing in *USA Today* read: "Jobless Rate Increase Seen As Good News." Equally as puzzling were the headlines that appeared on April 13, 1989, in two different New York City newspapers. What were readers supposed to believe when *Newsday* printed the headline: "City School Dropout Rate Is Up," while *The New York Times*'s headline read: "Dropout Rate Unchanged, Despite More Spending"?

As these examples suggest, we cannot depend on the media to tell us what position to take on an issue. Even they

disagree. We must, therefore, develop the ability to recognize the strengths and weaknesses of an argument. We must learn to be critical thinkers.

Asking the Right Questions

In their guide to critical thinking, Browne and Keeley take a systematic approach to evaluating the information that bombards us on a daily basis (1991). Their first recommendation is to ask the right question. To help students get started, they compiled the following list of critical questions.

1. What are the issues and the conclusion?
2. What are the reasons?
3. What words or phrases are ambiguous?
4. What are the value conflicts and assumptions?
5. What are the descriptive assumptions?
6. What is the evidence?
7. Are the samples representative and the measurements valid?
8. Are there rival hypotheses?
9. Are there flaws in the statistical reasoning?
10. How relevant are the analogies?
11. Are there any errors in reasoning?
12. What significant information is omitted?
13. What conclusions are consistent with the strong reasons?
14. What are your own value preferences in this controversy?

Testing Your Critical Thinking Skills

To test your critical thinking skills, evaluate the following argument. If you do not know where to begin, use the questions that Browne and Keeley recommend.

The United States should not help sustain foreign regimes that flagrantly disregard basic rights.

China in particular, one of America's largest trading partners, violated the basic human rights of its citizens long before and since the massacre of pro-democracy demonstrators at Tiananmen Square. China imprisons, tortures, and kills citizens for their nonviolent expression of political and religious beliefs.

China often exports goods made by political prisoners in forced labor camps. The United States cannot encourage and sustain foreign oppression by purchasing products made with illegal labor. U.S. companies with strong ethical guidelines, such as Levi Strauss and Timberland, have already started pulling out of China. Why can't the U.S. government demonstrate the same backbone?

. . . Countries like China, . . . which ignore human rights pleas from other nations, will only respond to meaningful threats. With a widespread trade embargo, China . . . would lose [its] export markets. The resulting economic hardship and unemployment would force changes in the human rights policies of these countries.

. . . When the world's nations united to cut off trade with South Africa, it hastened democratic reforms, substantially improved human rights, and ultimately led to majority rule. . . .

. . . The United States cannot support and condone these violations by continuing to trade freely and offer most-favored-nation status to these countries. To allow our pursuit of money to replace our protection of human rights is to lose our soul. We spent trillions of dollars during the cold war to export our values. Let's not now sacrifice these cherished values for cheap labor and export markets. (Starer, 1995, p. 230)

The Issue and the Conclusion

So what do you think about this writer's position? Before you answer, make sure you have correctly identified both the issue and the conclusion. Perhaps you think they are perfectly clear. In fact, Browne and Keeley say that determining the basic question or issue in an argument is often easy. An obvious clue frequently appears in the title, or it may be explicitly stated at the beginning of an argument. A writer might, for example, open with a question: "Should capital punishment be outlawed?"

In our example, however, the writer has not made our job that easy. We must, therefore, infer what the issue is from the conclusion. One simple question will help us find this: "What is the writer trying to prove?" Indicator words can also point to the conclusion. These would include *therefore, thus, so suggests that, as a result,* and *proves that.*

A variation of one of these words appears in the last sentence of the third paragraph—*the resulting.* Using this clue, the conclusion seems obvious. It is fair to infer that the issue is whether or not the United States should cut off trade with countries that violate human rights.

The Reasons

Now that we have identified the conclusion, the next step is to evaluate the reasons given to justify it. Whether you agree or disagree with the writer's position, you should seek to understand why she has taken a particular position (Browne & Keeley, 1991). Her reasons may be strong or weak. But, as Browne and Keeley point out, to say "because I think so" is not a reason. It is merely a restatement of a conclusion. Look for beliefs, evidence, metaphors, and analogies. All of these qualify as reasons.

As with conclusions, certain words will typically precede a reason. These include *because, first—second—third, for example,* and *for one thing.* As you evaluate reasons, it should be helpful to remember that the "structure of reasoning is, 'This because of that'" (Browne & Keeley, 1991, p. 21).

The reasons given in this argument include the fact that China has a history of violating human rights, and the writer provides the Tiananmen Square demonstration as a vivid example to remind readers of this fact. To bolster her belief that curtailing trade is the solution to this problem, she also provides evidence to show how this strategy has worked in the past with South Africa.

Missing Information

Taken together, a writer's reasons and conclusions constitute the argument. While the writer in this example has provided some strong arguments, we must also consider what she has not said. Consider, for example, the reasons that a writer taking the opposite position might give. He might argue that curtailing trade with China would hurt the United States. And his evidence might consist of the fact that "U.S. exports of over $9 billion to China each year keep more than 165,000 Americans employed, especially in agriculture, aviation, and high technology" (Starer, 1995, p. 231). He might further reason that "because of trade, China's booming economy over the last decade has helped create a middle class with greater access to the Western media and information-disseminating machines like faxes, which spread new social and political views" (Starer, 1995, p. 231).

Another kind of missing information that we must consider involves the interests of the writer or speaker. Consider, for example, Henry Kissinger, who appeared as a foreign policy expert on ABC's program *Nightline* both before and after the Tiananmen Square massacre. Most Americans probably assumed that his experience as Secretary of State made him a credible source of information. Unfortunately, the program failed to mention that Kissinger was a paid consultant representing multinational corporations that dealt with China's leaders and that he headed up a company that "engaged in joint ventures with China's state bank" (Lee & Solomon, 1991).

Developing the Right Attitudes

In evaluating the position that the United States should take toward countries that violate human rights, did other kinds of questions pop into your head? If so, then you have probably developed the kinds of attitudes that characterize critical thinkers. If not, then consider the kinds of attitudes that might you want to develop. For starters, consider the following short list that Browne and Keeley compiled:

1. *Intellectual curiosity.* Look for causes and answers every chance you get.

2. *Open-mindedness to multiple realities.* Seek out and respect alternative viewpoints and perspectives.

3. *Flexibility.* Be willing to change your mind in the face of strong reasoning.

4. *Humility concerning your beliefs.* Recognize that certainty is almost always and illusion.

5. *Intellectual skepticism.* Require support for claims or opinions before adopting them.

The next time you find yourself debating the issues of the day, remember Browne and Keeley's recommendations. They will help you recognize how writers and speakers attempt to persuade an audience to adopt their position. And they will prepare you to defend your own.

As a result of past research on levels of academic achievement in public, Catholic, and private schools, some public schools are now making more rigorous demands on their students.

The researchers' report aroused a great deal of criticism, both for its methodology and for its conclusions. Some critics charged that it would be more effective to try to improve the learning environments of public schools than to channel more students into private schools (Finn, 1981). As a more general criticism, some scholars have charged that this type of policy research is sometimes done merely to support a government decision that has already been made (Massagli & McCullough, 1979).

SOCIAL PREDICTION. In the natural sciences, predicting events is a major goal of research. Because the social world is so complex, however, and the methods used to study it are relatively inexact, few social events can be predicted. It is not possible, for example, to know with any precision ahead of time whether wars, revolutions, economic depressions, or even minor civil disturbances will or will not take place.

Yet social science research can be used for prediction in more modest ways, with real practical effects. The most widely known example is the prediction of election outcomes. Only 50 years ago, predicting election results was mostly guesswork. Today, it is a refined art, and pollsters are able to predict the outcome of all but the very closest elections with great precision.

SOCIAL MONITORING AND DESCRIPTION. Not all applied social research produces definitive conclusions, much less predictions. Some merely accurately describe the way the world is. For example, Angus Campbell asked a nationwide sample of people over a number of years about their feelings, attitudes, and sense of well-being. He developed an understanding of which types of people in the American population have the highest sense of well-being and which have the lowest. The results in some cases were surprising. On the average, Campbell found married people to be more content than unmarried, separated, divorced, or widowed people. But having children did not increase the sense of well-being among Campbell's sample. A sense of community increased a person's satisfaction, and in general, this sense of community seemed to be more common in rural and small-town settings than in cities. But Campbell found only a small relationship between well-being and people's income level (Campbell, 1981).

When earlier and more recent studies of this sort are compared with each other, these snapshot descriptions can become *social indicators,* data that suggest how the pulse of the nation is changing over time. For example, recent government statistics show that the family unit has become less stable, as indicated by a 122 percent increase in the annual divorce rate from 1960 to 1990. Among other things, this means that more children live with only one parent (25 percent of all children in 1990, up from 9 percent in 1960) than before. And from 1960 to 1990 the average size of the American household dropped from 3.33 people to 2.63 people, clearly indicating a trend toward smaller families.

Although these data can be interpreted in many ways, such indicators do suggest where the nation is headed socially. Data developed by social monitoring over time are also used as a basis for forming or redirecting public policy.

OTHER APPLICATIONS OF SOCIOLOGY

So far we have emphasized the applications of sociology that involve the direct use of social research. Other applications include policy consulting, social criticism, and clinical sociology.

POLICY CONSULTING. The involvement of sociologists in the making of government policy is not limited to large-scale policy-oriented research. Government policy makers may turn to sociologists directly for the expert knowledge they can provide on social issues.

The most famous example of such use of social science expertise was in the U.S. Supreme Court's 1954 decision to ban segregated schooling. In the case of *Brown* v. *Board of Education,* the Court relied heavily on sociological and psychological evidence and testimony that attending segregated "separate but equal" schools was damaging to blacks (Horowitz & Katz, 1975). This was the first time that social science opinion and research had been given so much weight in an important case.

SOCIAL CRITICISM. Sociologists do not have to wait to be asked for their ideas on social policy. Many sociologists publish theoretical analyses of life in society that have strong policy implications. These analyses are often called *social criticism.*

An example is Daniel Bell's *The Cultural Contradictions of Capitalism* (1978), a book that was influential during the administration of President Jimmy Carter. Bell argued that American capitalism is being torn by two conflicting sets of values: a traditional set of values emphasizing independence, moderation, work, and thrift; and a modern set of values emphasizing instant personal gratification. The first set of values is needed to get people to produce goods and capital, the other to get them to buy those goods. Both are necessary for the U.S. economy, but they contradict each other. As people come increasingly to value instant gratification, they produce and save less, thus contributing to the nation's economic problems. (This thesis is discussed at greater length in Chapter 3.)

CLINICAL SOCIOLOGY. A growing number of sociologists, unhappy with the often detached and abstract nature of their discipline, are pioneering a new application known as *clinical sociology.* Like the psychologist who deals clinically with people's mental and emotional problems, and the doctor who deals with their physical problems, this new breed of sociologist is devising ways to help people directly with their social problems. Clinical sociology involves active intervention in social situations to change things for the better. And, as in other clinical practices, prior to the intervention the sociologist makes a professional diagnosis of the problem.

Clients range from individuals and families to large-scale organizations (Rossi & Whyte, 1981). Generally, clinical sociologists help clients to achieve their own stated goals rather than intervening to bring about institutional or social change. An example of clinical sociology is Kai Erikson's work (1977) on community life in Buffalo Creek, West Virginia, following a devastating flood in 1972 that ripped through the valley after a dam burst. Erikson assessed the personal and social impact of the flood on the 5,000 families that lived in the valley. Without the communal supports that had bonded the residents together, many of the people lost their morale, mental health, and respect for the law. Through his incisive analysis of the destruction of community life, Erikson succeeded in helping the victims win $13.5 million in damages from the coal company judged negligent in the disaster.

Why Study Sociology?

Up to this point we have been talking about sociology as it is applied by sociologists. But those of you who are not planning to become sociologists have a right to ask what use it is to you. There are, in fact, a great many ways in which sociology can be applied in our lives. A knowledge of sociological methods is of value for many careers. The study of sociology provides a special way of approaching problems—whether personal, job related, or political—that can help us to make everyday decisions.

CAREER PREPARATION

Among the useful skills that a sociologically trained person brings to any job are the abilities to observe a social situation and to be objective. Such a person has been taught to organize complex ideas, to use data in testing hunches and theories, and to reason clearly and logically. These are useful abilities for many jobs in which the word "sociology" is never spoken.

The technical skills of sociology are not the only important ones. Regardless of career choice, we need *social* skills—the skills required to get along with others. Because it improves your knowledge of the way people interact, the study of sociology can be of real help in this regard. In addition, *organizational* skills—skills required to survive and prosper within formal organizations—play a key role in many careers. Sociology can provide the knowledge on which such skills are based.

A pamphlet distributed by the American Sociological Association on the value of a sociology major as a preparation for careers in business suggests that students who major in sociology should focus on a particular subfield or subspecialty (for example, business organizations or social problems) as early as possible. Many sociology majors who develop an early interest in business organizations move toward careers in personnel, industrial relations, public relations, organizational planning, or international marketing. Those interested in social problems and social psychology often gravitate toward such "helping" professions as social work, counseling, or teaching.

MAKING EVERYDAY DECISIONS

Objective knowledge of the social world, sociological methods, and the sociological perspective can also help us to approach more rationally the decisions that we face in daily life. Using the findings of sociology, as well as the techniques that it employs, we are more likely to reach decisions that will enhance our personal well-being. Many of the special features in this book called "Applying Sociology" give examples of how sociology can help individuals in making everyday decisions.

UNDERSTANDING YOURSELF

C. Wright Mills stressed that the sociological perspective can serve as a major tool for interpreting and understanding our lives. He contended that we can understand our experiences and determine what we can expect to accomplish only by "locating ourselves" within our society and historical period. Mills referred to this process as the development of the **sociological imagination:**

> The sociological imagination enables us to grasp history and biography and the relations between the two within society. This is its task and its promise. . . . The first fruit of this imagination—and the first lesson of the social science that embodies it—is the idea that the individual can understand his own experience and gauge his own fate only by locating himself within his period, that he can know his own chances in life only by becoming aware of those of all individuals in his circumstances. (1977, p. 6)

Remember that Mills had a distinct mission in mind: to encourage the sociologist to become a social critic. For Mills, the "sociological imagination" was the ability to perceive when personal problems become public issues, to weave back and forth between the personal and the societal, to see the individual as both a unique person and as a part and product of a historical period.

The sociological perspective is a powerful tool in our individual search for identity and self-awareness. And such a perspective is essential if we are to have some control over our own destinies. It can be difficult to accept that our careers and our opportunities, even our feelings of happiness or frustration, are heavily shaped by forces external to us. But as Mills said, "In many ways it is a terrible lesson; in many ways a magnificent one" (1977).

CHAPTER REVIEW

1. The concept of cloning has received much attention over the course of the twentieth century. How would different disciplines treat cloning as a research topic?

2. What basic assumption do sociologists make about all human behavior? How does this assumption make sociology different from psychology? Does this assumption make sociology different from disciplines such as psychology, political science, or economics? Why or why not?

3. Compared with other disciplines, the field of sociology is relatively new. Why was the nineteenth century a particularly productive period in its history?

4. How was the field of sociology shaped by society and social circumstances?

5. Consider issues that politicians like to debate when they run for office, for example, educational reform or family values. How would the solutions that politicians propose be viewed from the perspectives of functionalism, conflict theory, and interactionism?

6. The Internet is bound to play a significant role in the way society changes over the course of the twenty-first century. Use your sociological imagination to predict how it will change our lives.

INTERNET EXERCISE

The Web destinations for Chapter 1 cover various aspects of academic and applied sociology. To start your explorations, go to the Prentice Hall Companion Web site: **http://www.prenhall.com/popenoe.** Next, choose **Chapter 1** (An Introduction to Sociology). Then select **web destinations** from the menu on the left side of the screen. There are a variety of sites to choose from. We suggest that you begin with the **SocioWeb.** This site contains a wide variety of resources on different aspects of sociology. When you arrive at the site, you may wish to click on **Giants of Sociology, Sociology in Action, Sociological Theory,** or **Learning Sociology.** If time permits, you may also wish to access the **Society for Applied Sociology.** Here, for example, you'll find information about getting a head start on a career as an applied sociologist and how the Internet may be utilized as a resource for job seekers in sociology. As you conduct your exploration, answer the following questions:

- Who are the "giants" of sociology?

- What are the major categories of sociological theory?

- What is the difference between "academic" and "applied" sociology?

- How do applied sociologists conduct their work?

- All in all, what aspect of sociology most interests you?

KEY TERMS

sociology	**conflict perspective**	**applied research**
social science	**interactionist perspective**	**sociological imagination**
functionalist perspective	**basic research**	

CHAPTER 2

The Process
of Sociological Research

few minutes spent watching television news programs or reading any major newspaper shows the extent to which reporters seem drawn to many of the same sorts of topics that also interest sociologists. The daily headlines are full of references to broken families, crime and drug abuse, unemployment, racial tension, and sexual harassment. Furthermore, the stories under the headlines frequently make explicit reference to research conducted by sociologists or by social science organizations and agencies.

The regularity with which this research is cited in the media is both a boon and a curse for professional sociologists. On the positive side, popular accounts of sociological research help increase people's familiarity with the discipline. Most members of the general public may not have a solid understanding of the character of sociology, but at least they know some of the sorts of things that sociologists study, and this general awareness doubtless contributes to some extent to the legitimacy accorded to the field. On the other hand, the themes that reporters choose to emphasize when they write about sociological research rarely seem to reflect issues that professional sociologists regard as of central importance. Furthermore, journalistic accounts all too often distort the research on which they are based.

These observations led two sociologists to conduct a program of research designed to find out how reporters decide what social science stories are likely to be of interest to their readers and how these stories are repackaged for the mass audience.

Carol Weiss and Eleanor Singer were concerned not only with the image of sociology presented to the general public but also with how media accounts affect policy makers in business and government (1987). Both had been actively involved in applied research, and they already knew from their previous work that policy makers ordinarily do not spend a great deal of time reading technical reports or social science journals. Instead, much like the rest of us, they rely heavily on mass media accounts of social science research. This suggests the possibility that national policy makers are making use of incomplete, biased, or even inaccurate reporting as the basis for decisions that affect millions of people. It further emphasizes the importance of carefully studying the process by which sociological research is modified when it is reported in newspapers and on television.

Weiss and Singer began by systematically searching the social science literature to see if any previous work had been done on this topic. They also engaged in some preliminary discussions with selected sociologists. Thus prepared, they developed a three-stage *research design* to investigate how social science research is filtered through the journalistic lens. First, Singer developed a detailed listing of all the social science stories that had appeared in the major media over a five-month period. (It turned out that there were more than 2,000 such stories!) Next, Weiss drew a sample of these accounts and conducted standardized telephone interviews both with the reporter who wrote each story in the sample and with the social scientist on whose research the story was based. Finally, Singer analyzed the content of each article to see how it had been modified by the reporters.

The researchers established that the reporters did not choose a topic because of its scientific importance but, rather, selected studies they believed would strike their audience as "important, interesting, and new." They found that, on the whole, the reporters were not trained in the social sciences and did not even attempt to judge the quality of the research about which they were writing or to place one study in the context of others, as any professional sociologist would certainly do. The social scientists whose work was reported in the stories were well aware of these realities and frequently complained that their research had been oversimplified, overdramatized, or fragmented in the effort to turn it into a news story.

Weiss and Singer also found that, contrary to their expectations, the reporters usually were alerted to what they regarded as interesting stories by the government and private agencies that sponsored the research rather than by the social scientists who actually did the work. This sometimes added another layer of distortion to the media reports.

THE PROCESS OF RESEARCH

Much of the sociologist's knowledge of the world is obtained through research like that just described. There is no mystery about research. It involves carefully framing a question, then finding the answer to that question in a systematic way. In the case described earlier, Weiss and Singer organized their study around three questions designed to explore the relationship between the social sciences and the media: (1) How well does the news reflect social science? (2) How do particular studies and people in the social sciences become a part of the news? (3) How accurately are these studies and people presented?

What is a researchable question? How does a social scientist design a research project to answer such questions? What methods do sociologists use to gather data? How do they produce explanations from the data? How do they state their findings and present them to other social scientists and to the general public? These issues are the focus of sociological **methodology,** the system of procedures that helps sociologists develop knowledge. Without methodology, sociology would be little more than idle guesswork.

Scientists, including social scientists, rely heavily on the **empirical method.** This method involves using the human senses, such as sight and hearing, to observe the world. The observations that result can then be checked for accuracy by other people using the same process. Thus, the empirical method is a very public and open path to knowledge. And because it relies on sense observations that can be reported and repeated, it lessens problems of individual human bias, emotion, and distorted reasoning.

The process of designing empirical studies and drawing conclusions from them must, of course, follow the rules of logic. But no scientific "truth" is ever accepted on the basis of logic or intuition alone. It is always subjected to empirical investigation. For example, logic and intuition may suggest that poverty is the main cause of revolutions, or that broken homes are the main cause of juvenile delinquency. We cannot know such things with any certainty until many careful observations of both revolutions and juvenile delinquency have been made over a long period of time.

Sociologists typically conduct two types of empirical studies. **Descriptive studies** are a first step in the pursuit of knowledge. They are designed to find out what is happening to whom, where, and when. They carefully collect data to describe some group, practice, or event. Crime statistics, public opinion surveys, television audience ratings, and reports on people's sexual habits are all examples of descriptive studies.

Although descriptive studies are a necessary first step, the long-run interest of sociologists is the kind of study that explains why things happen. **Explanatory studies** answer the questions "why" and "how." Why is the divorce rate rising? Why are people fleeing the cities to acquire a mortgage and a sliver of land in the suburbs? Why has there been such a striking increase in juvenile delinquency in recent decades? How do children become delinquent?

Sociological Explanation

Explaining social phenomena is what sociological theory is all about. Sociological theory is much more than speculation. Good theory is both the driving force behind and the final result of social research, and the practice of sociology consists largely of an interplay between theory and research. Each helps to guide and refine the other, as we will see in this section.

CONCEPTS AND VARIABLES

The building blocks of both research and theory are concepts and variables. A sociological **concept** is a generalization, a way of labeling similar things or processes.

Concepts can label tangible things, such as people or buildings, or intangible phenomena, such as peace or welfare or love.

Even before entering kindergarten, a child is exposed to many concepts. A four-year-old, for example, already understands the general concept of "car" (as distinct from particular cars) and knows that it includes Mom and Dad's new red Toyota, Uncle Bill's classic 1967 Mustang, and the neighbor's dune buggy. The concept directs a child's attention into certain channels. In this way, children learn to ignore the slight differences in color, size, and radiator design in particular automobiles—none of which is important to the general concept of "car."

In general use, concepts are often vague. The concept "family" can refer to just two parents and their children or to 193 second and third cousins. When someone uses a concept that can stand for many different things, we usually know what is meant by the context in which it is used. Suppose your mother tells you that she is going to buy a 25-pound turkey because the family is coming for Thanksgiving dinner. In this case, you know that she must mean the family that includes uncles and aunts, cousins, and grandparents.

In sociological inquiry, however, concepts like "the family" must be defined more precisely. Students reading a paper on communications systems within Chinese families should not have to guess at how the author is using the concept of "family." Therefore, like all specialists, sociologists have developed a set of concepts with agreed-upon definitions to describe the patterns and events they deal with frequently.

Many ordinary concepts, such as "car," refer to relatively constant or fixed things. Cars come in many sizes and shapes, but they are not thought of in differing degrees; that is, cars do not change or vary in their degree of "carness" along some dimension, such as time or space. Most concepts used by sociologists, however, refer to things that do vary in these ways. Concepts that refer to things that change across time or space, or from one person or group to another, are called **variables.** Age is a variable, for human beings can range in age from less than a second to over 100 years. Social class is another variable; people may belong to the upper, middle, working, or lower class. Other common sociological variables are income, level of education, and gender. Some of these variables, such as income and age, can be expressed in numbers. Others vary by category instead of by degree; gender, for example, is either male or female.

To do research, social scientists must translate general concepts into specific, measurable variables. This process is known as **operationalizing the variable.** For example, the general concept "quality of a college" can be measured by such **operational variables** as the percentage of the faculty holding doctorates, the size of the college library, and the ratio of applicants to admissions. "Social class," a very commonly used concept, has been operationalized by such variables as education, income, and occupation. It takes great skill and ingenuity to choose and define variables effectively.

HYPOTHESES AND EMPIRICAL GENERALIZATIONS

Sociological explanations most often take the form of statements about relationships between variables. A **hypothesis** is a tentative statement about the way in which two or more variables are related. For example, one could hypothesize that, in American society, the younger the age at marriage, the higher the divorce rate. This hypothesis suggests a relationship between two variables: age at marriage and frequency of divorce. Hypotheses are usually presented so that they can be rejected should the evidence warrant it. A hypothesis can never be confirmed in any absolute sense, however, because there is always the chance that further evidence will lead to its rejection.

Once research suggests that a hypothesis is reasonable, the hypothesis may become an **empirical generalization**—a statement, supported by empirical evidence (i.e., evidence based on observation), about the relationship between two or more variables. Let us again consider the hypothesis that divorce rates rise as marriage age falls. Can we refine this hypothesis? Surely there must be factors other than age at marriage that influence divorce rates. Under which conditions might the original relationship between the variables change? Suppose we measure how religious the families of the marital partners are. Reliable sociological research has shown that the divorce rate is lower for religious couples than for nonreligious couples. Is age at marriage still an important factor in divorce, and if so, could age at marriage be related to the couple's degree of religious involvement?

To answer these questions the research process would again be set in motion. Only after numerous studies had accounted for as many variables as possible—such as marriage age, extent of religious commitment, area of residence, and number of children—could a sociologist comfortably develop a sound empirical generalization.

THEORY

A **theory,** as opposed to a hypothesis, is a comprehensive explanation of observed relationships among variables. In constructing theories, sociologists try to look beyond valid empirical generalizations to seek explanations for them. Theories grow out of empirical generalizations. In turn, theories generate predictions about the way other

When someone uses a concept that can stand for many different things, we usually know what is meant by the context in which it is used. In sociological inquiry, however, concepts like "family" must be defined more precisely.

variables may relate to each other. These predictions can be tested against new empirical observations.

A study of self-esteem (feelings of self-worth) among urban schoolchildren conducted by Rosenberg and Simmons (1971) illustrates the give-and-take between theory and empirical generalization. These researchers wanted to know how children's personal images of themselves are shaped by their social experiences. Rosenberg and Simmons encountered some surprises when they looked at racially segregated schools and compared the self-esteem levels of African-American schoolchildren with the self-esteem levels of white schoolchildren. African-American pupils scored just as high as white pupils of comparable age and social background. These results were unexpected because prior research had found that many African-American children come from very disadvantaged social environments, and such environments are thought to cause feelings of low self-worth. What would account for this new finding?

Once the researchers had made sure there was no distortion caused by their research methods, they developed an explanation based on "social contexts." As social beings, humans continually compare themselves with others. Further studies showed that African-American children in all-black schools see themselves in a better light than do African-American pupils in integrated schools. According to Rosenberg and Simmons, in segregated African-American schools, where poverty and racial discrimination are facts of everyday life, no poor child feels uniquely disadvantaged; no one else seems to be in a better position. But in racially mixed schools, the differences between African-Americans and whites are obvious; compared with the privileged whites, the African-American children do feel disadvantaged.

This explanation seems plausible. The basics of a social theory that researchers can try to prove or disprove are present. The Rosenberg-Simmons theory of self-esteem states that the more consonant the social context—the more it resembles the child's own social position—the higher the child's self-esteem. But would this statement hold for college students as well as for younger schoolchildren? For successful students as well as for those who are doing poorly? In housing developments as well as in

According to the Rosenberg-Simmons theory of self-esteem, African-American children feel disadvantaged in racially mixed schools when compared with privileged white students. The researchers believe that the more consonant the social context (the more it resembles the child's own social position), the higher the child's self-esteem.

schools? The theory gives us a way of generating new issues to explore and new problems to solve. But there is always the chance that a competing theory may explain the facts better.

The Analysis of Variables

We have said that a hypothesis is a statement about the relationship between variables. Just what kind of relationships does sociological research explore? Sociologists, like other scientists, attempt to identify *cause* and *effect*. They might, for example, want to understand the causes of a rapid increase in juvenile crime. They would study suspected causes, such as dropping out of school, teenage unemployment, and drug and alcohol abuse. These likely causes, or explanatory variables, are called **independent variables.** The effect (the amount of juvenile crime) is the **dependent variable.** To put it another way, the dependent variable is the variable an investigator wants to explain, and the independent variables are the possible explanations.

In some studies, the dependent variables (effects) are known, so the research focus is on the independent variables (causes). Why do people buy one brand of coffee rather than another? Why do people move from one place to another? In other studies, the independent variables (causes) are known but the dependent variables (effects) are not. What are the effects or consequences of a political campaign? Of the surgeon general's warning against smoking? Of restrictive drug laws?

It is sometimes difficult to distinguish causes from effects. Does advertising "cause" people to buy? Some research has shown that people read car ads *after* they have bought a car. After making a decision, people tend to feel uneasy about the choices they rejected and thus seek reassurance that they made the best decision (Wicklund & Brehm, 1976). Thus, reading the ads is not a cause but an effect of buying (Wiggins, 1955).

Causes and effects can "change places," too. A son's criminal activities can lead a father to desert his family, just as a broken home can lead to juvenile crime. An independent variable at one point in time may become a dependent variable at another point in time. Why does it so often seem that minor bureaucratic officials are petty and rigid in their dealings with others? It has been proposed that not only do rigid individuals often select jobs as minor officials (personality being, in this case, the independent variable and job choice the dependent variable) but also that the red tape of the position reinforces the rigid tendencies of these officials (job choice influencing personality) (Merton, 1956a, 1956b). Another study has shown that high school seniors who enter the military adopt "military values" because their predispositions led them to join the military in the first place, not because of their training in the armed services (Bachman, Sigelman, & Diamond, 1987).

How do sociologists go about studying whether variables are linked in a cause-and-effect relationship? As a first step, researchers look for a statistical **correlation,** in which a change in one variable is associated in some way with a change in another variable. Suppose we wanted to determine the relationship between the murder rate and how much money a state spends on education. A statistical comparison of various states might find that when spending on education is low the murder rate is generally high. The exact degree of statistical association between the variables could be computed. Yet even if there were a correlation between the variables, we still could not say that lack of education causes murder. Perhaps both really stem from another variable, like poverty, for poverty might cause both low spending on education and a high rate of murder.

In short, simple correlation cannot prove that two variables are associated in a cause-and-effect relationship. Sometimes, in fact, two variables may be highly correlated even though there is no cause-and-effect relationship whatsoever. For example, there is a higher death rate in hospitals than in homes. Does this mean that hospitals cause deaths? It does not. The correlation is valid, but the conclusion is false. Correlations that are not based on causal connections are called **spurious correlations.**

Statistical Controls and Multivariate Analysis

When researchers discover that two variables are correlated, how do they try to find out if the correlation implies a causal relationship? They attempt to show that other factors are not the source of the correlation by applying *statistical controls.*

Two scholars were curious about the effects of the type of college people attended on their income later in life (Solomon & Wachtel, 1975). It is usually assumed that someone who graduates from a small, nonselective college will typically experience less economic success than a graduate of a leading university. The researchers did find a high statistical correlation between the institution attended and earnings in later life: People who attended higher-rated universities earned more. But was this really a result of the type of institution, or could it be that better students attended the better schools? The researchers applied statistical controls and determined that even when they compared only students of equal academic ability and drawn from the same socioeconomic backgrounds, the institution still made a difference: Those who attended higher-quality institutions earned more money. In other words, the quality of the institution had an *independent effect* on later earnings.

Simple cause-and-effect relationships are seldom found in society. Instead, a single social event is normally caused by a great many variables that affect it at the same time. Thus, much statistical research involves **multivariate analysis,** in which more than two variables are involved. The search for cause and effect focuses on finding the relative importance of several variables that together have an overall effect. Studies testing a number of variables can contribute further to our understanding of the high correlation between college attended and later earnings. Perhaps better-rated institutions attract better faculty, who are more likely to encourage students to go on to graduate and professional schools; or perhaps higher-paying organizations prefer graduates of more prestigious universities. Multivariate analysis allows us to untangle and analyze such complex relationships.

The Stages of Social Research

How does one conduct a research project? In this section, we outline six stages of research that together make up the *scientific method*—the set of procedures designed to ensure that research will lead to valid generalizations and theory. These stages are not followed exactly for all research projects in sociology or any other science. But they do provide a useful guide for sociologists and other scientists.

To explain the stages of the research process concretely, we show how each stage was conducted in an actual sociological research project. This project is a sociological classic: James S. Coleman's *The Adolescent Society* (1961). Although the study was conducted some years ago, its findings seem as important today as they were when first published.

Coleman had long been aware of a peculiar aspect of the social climate in American high schools. The value system promoted by teachers and parents seemed to run counter to the values held by the students. Teachers emphasized academic achievement, but students valued such things as athletic ability in boys and popularity in girls. Coleman wanted to find out which factors in the school and the community tend to promote one or another kind of high school social climate (or value system) and what the effects of the high school social climate might be on the students.

Stage 1: Develop a careful statement of the problem and formulate the hypotheses to be investigated. Before Coleman drew up a formal plan for research, he combed through previous studies to see how his research would extend existing knowledge. These studies provided a jumping-off point for his own work.

Next, Coleman formulated some specific hypotheses to be tested. This involved defining the research problem

WINDOW ON SOCIOLOGY

UNDERSTANDING CHARTS, TABLES, AND GRAPHS

1. Begin by reading the title, which should tell you precisely what you can expect to learn from the chart, table, or graph.

2. Check for other explanatory notes. Sometimes you will find a headnote explaining how the data were collected, the conditions under which they were gathered, or the reasons for the use of certain classifcations. Footnotes may explain the source of the data or indicate that, in some cases, they are incomplete or inaccurate.

3. For charts and tables, read the column headings across the top and the stubs down the left-hand side. For graphs, read the headings along the horizontal axis (on the bottom of the graph) and along the vertical axis (on the left-hand side). These tell you what data the chart, table, or graph contains.

4. Find out what units of measurement have been used. It is easy to become confused when figures are presented in thousands or millions. Rates are even more troublesome, because they can be expressed in a variety of ways—the number of times something happens per 100 or 1,000 or 1,000,000 people, for instance.

5. Estimate the range of variability in the data. Look for the highest figure, the lowest, and the average. You then have a basis for comparing individual entries.

6. *Comparing tables and graphs:* Tables and graphs can present the same information but in different ways. Both the table and the graph presented here show what proportion of households headed by people who have completed various levels of education (elementary school only, high school, and college) earn different levels of income. If we wanted to know exact percentages, the table would be a more effective way of obtaining this information. The graph, however, lets us visualize the relationships among the various sets of figures.

7. Draw conclusions about the significance of the chart, table, or graph. Does the data source seem reliable? How were the data obtained? Is there enough variation for the data to be meaningful? Could there be any bias in the way the data have been reported? Answers to questions like these will help you judge for yourself the significance of the chart, table, or graph.

TABLE 2.1   MONEY INCOME OF HOUSEHOLDS BY EDUCATION OF HOUSEHOLDER: PERCENT DISTRIBUTION, 1991

Education of Householder	*Household Income Level*						
	Under $5,000	*$5,000– 9,999*	*$10,000– 14,999*	*$15,000– 24,999*	*$25,000– 34,999*	*$35,000– 49,999*	*$50,000 and over*
Less than 9th grade	10.9	26.6	18.2	21.7	10.5	7.4	4.5
High school graduate	4.0	9.5	9.9	19.7	17.8	19.5	19.6
College graduate or graduate work	1.3	2.0	3.2	9.1	12.4	19.0	53.0

Source: U.S. Bureau of the Census, *Statistical Abstract of the United States, 1993* (Washington, D.C.: U.S. Government Printing Office, 1993).

very carefully and making statements about the ways in which the variables under study might affect one another. One hypothesis, for example, was that certain aspects of the social character of a community would be reflected in its high school's values. Thus, athletics would matter most in a small-town high school, and grades would be more important in a suburban high school. Another hypothesis was that in schools in which the adolescents were anti-academic, the best grades would be made by mediocre students because the most intelligent students would excel

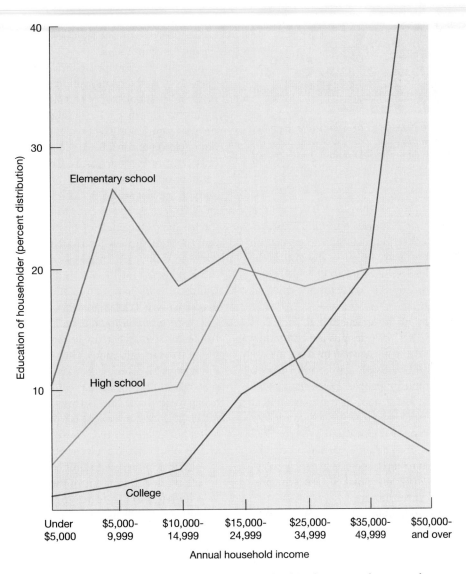

FIGURE 2.1 The higher a householder's education level is, the greater that person's likelihood of having a high income.

Source: U.S. Bureau of the Census, *Statistical Abstract of the United States, 1993* (Washington, D.C.: U.S. Government Printing Office, 1993).

in the nonacademic activities favored by students, not in those valued by teachers.

At this stage the researcher must develop *operational definitions*—that is, definitions of general concepts, such as student values—in terms of specific variables that can be measured. Coleman developed an operational definition of student values in terms of such measurable variables as prestige (What types of students have the highest prestige?) and student attitudes (How would a student most like to be remembered by his or her classmates?).

American high school students tend to value athletic ability and popularity more than the academic achievement that is valued by their teachers. Many social research projects deal with such conflicting values.

Stage 2: Develop a research design. A *research design* is a plan for the collection, analysis, and evaluation of the data that will allow us to confirm or disconfirm the original hypotheses. The design must specify which comparisons will be useful in building a case for one explanation rather than another.

As will be discussed at greater length in the next section, four basic types of research designs are commonly employed by sociologists: *Survey research* involves the use of questionnaires and interviews to gather information from relatively large groups of people. *Experiments* allow the particularly precise assessment of cause-and-effect relationships between variables and are usually conducted in social science laboratories under carefully controlled conditions. In contrast, *observation* is carried out in the natural settings in which research subjects live their everyday lives. Finally, *secondary analysis* makes use of data previously collected by other researchers.

Coleman chose to employ the survey research method—the single research design most frequently utilized in sociological studies. He collected his data with questionnaires given to students, their teachers, and their parents in 10 schools located near one another in northern Illinois. To vary the community character, he selected schools located in large urban centers, in suburbs, and in small rural communities.

Stage 3: Collect data in accordance with the research design. Coleman and his staff gave out questionnaires to a total of 8,900 students at the 10 high schools. The students answered questions about themselves and about life at their schools. Informal interviews with freshmen and seniors added vitality to the data collected from the questionnaires. A small sample of teachers and parents was also sent questionnaires.

Stage 4: Analyze the data in accordance with the hypotheses. In this stage the data are assembled, classified, and organized in a way that allows the researcher to test the hypotheses. In very small-scale studies, researchers can process the data themselves. This approach is impossible in large-scale quantitative studies like Coleman's because dozens of variables are examined at once (multivariate analysis). In such studies, researchers must process the data on computers.

When Coleman tested the hypothesis mentioned in Stage 1 about the relationship between community character and a school's social climate, he found that he had to reject this hypothesis. Definitions of success in school did *not* vary significantly by type of community. In no school did adolescents consider academic achievement the most important type of success. In fact, he found that the adolescent social climate in all the schools worked quite strongly against academic achievement. The values of the students seemed consistently to win out over the values of the teachers. One effect of this was that "in these adolescent societies, those who are seen as intellectuals, and who come to think of themselves in this way, are not really those of highest intelligence, but are only the ones who are willing to work hard at a relatively unrewarded [by students] activity" (Coleman, 1961, p. 265).

Stage 5: Interpret the findings and draw conclusions. In the end, researchers must make the leap from specific findings to generalizations. They must create a whole out of the various pieces of evidence. Coleman's general conclusions were: "Our society has within its midst a set of small teenage societies, which focus teenage interests and attitudes on things far removed from adult responsibilities," and "Our adolescents today are cut off, probably more than ever before, from the adult society" (1961, p. 9).

The accuracy and significance of scientific findings are often assessed in terms of their validity and reliability. **Validity** refers to the degree to which a study or research instrument actually measures what it is attempting to measure. For example, do "prestige" and "student attitudes"—the variables selected by Coleman to measure "student values"—really, in fact, measure such values? Might they not measure something else instead? **Reliability** refers to the degree to which a study or research instrument provides consistently accurate results. A reliable measure of student values would lead to the same results if the study were repeated by another researcher.

Consider as another example IQ tests, which seem reliable, but are they validly measuring innate human intelligence? The issue is open to question. Another example is a bathroom scale, which may consistently give a reading that is 5 pounds off. The reading is not valid, but it would still provide a reliable indication of weight change from day to day.

Stage 6: Publish your research findings. Publication is important for several reasons. First, it allows other sociologists to carefully examine and assess the quality of the research that you have done. When a social scientist has spent several years planning and carrying out a program of research as extensive as that reported in *The Adolescent Society,* it can be very easy to develop blind spots, which makes it difficult to detect errors in the operationalization of key variables, in the construction of the research design, in the collection and analysis of data, or in the development of theories to explain one's findings. By publishing detailed accounts of their research, scholars allow and even encourage members of the sociological community to point out problematic aspects of their work that they have themselves failed to detect.

Second, if a body of published research has been accepted as methodologically and theoretically sound by one's colleagues, it becomes available as a foundation for future research projects. Coleman stressed that his work should be considered as no more than a pilot study; further investigation was needed before firm, valid, and reliable conclusions could be drawn. Do the generalizations drawn from this research apply to other kinds of schools in other states or even in other nations? Are Coleman's findings as applicable to students in the 1990s as they appear to have been to those of the 1960s? These are examples of the sorts of questions that have been investigated by researchers inspired by Coleman's original research reports.

Finally, sociologists publish their work for a third, very different and highly personal reason: The quality and quantity of a sociologist's published research is the most important criterion on which his or her professional reputation is established. In sociology, as in all other contemporary academic disciplines, "publish or perish" is more than a slogan; it is a way of life!

RESEARCH METHODS

At the most general level, sociologists use two types of research methods: quantitative and qualitative. **Quantitative methods** are designed to study variables that can be measured in numbers—variables such as income, age, and educational level. Because quantitative measurement lies at the very heart of all sciences, most sociologists try to use these methods whenever possible. But many situations in human affairs cannot be measured with numbers, at least not very easily. Moreover, some sociologists feel that quantitative measurement can damage or distort the social reality they are studying.

Qualitative methods are designed to describe reality in accurate *verbal* terms, not in numbers and measurements (Denzin, 1978; Lofland, 1971; Schatzman & Strauss, 1973). Researchers using this approach to study social interaction, a common focus of qualitative methods, typically try to understand the social world from the point of view of the people they are studying, rather than from the perspective of an outside observer. Probably the most common technique of qualitative observation is *participant observation,* which we discuss in a later section.

In general, sociology uses a much wider range of methods than the natural sciences do. Much sociological research has both quantitative and qualitative aspects. It is common for an exploratory study of a topic to use qualitative methods; this initial study is then followed by quantitative studies of selected aspects of the same topic.

Survey Research

The most common quantitative research method used in sociology is the **survey,** a method of systematically questioning large numbers of people about their opinions, attitudes, or behavior to find out how they think, feel, and act.

Survey research is perhaps best explained through a discussion of the steps followed in a typical survey research process. Like all social research, survey research starts with a careful statement of the issues to be studied. The researcher must then identify the population to be examined, select a sample, design the research instrument, administer the instrument, and, finally, analyze the data.

IDENTIFYING THE POPULATION

Once the issues have been identified, the first step in survey research is to select the **population,** the total group of people to be studied. (The population is also sometimes called the *universe.*) The population might be all male citizens in Liberia, all working mothers in Milwaukee, or all members of the junior class at a community college. It always consists of the total number of people with the traits the researcher wants to examine. This first step is crucial. If the population is not specified carefully, the results of the survey can be virtually meaningless. If the aim of the survey is to predict the results of an election, for example, it is very important that, so far as possible, the population chosen consist only of people who will actually vote in that election.

SELECTING A SAMPLE

Because it usually costs too much or takes too much time to interview an entire population, the second step is to choose an appropriate sample. A **sample** is a limited number of cases selected to represent the entire population being studied.

SOCIOLOGY OF THE MEDIA

THE MEDIA AND PUBLIC OPINION POLLS

The issues addressed in media polls can create a lot of public debate. This is particularly true when it comes to political polls. But as the following newspaper headlines show (Babbie, 1995), the issue sparking a controversy is sometimes the poll itself.

- "Why Trust the Polls?"
- "Are Restraints Needed on Election Day Polls?"
- "Pollsters Bicker on Why Landslide Caught Them"
- "Polls' Divergence Puzzles Experts"
- "Networks Criticized on Polls"
- "First You Take a Poll—Not Always"
- "Dilemma of Voter Polls: Suspense or Knowledge"

Bad polls give critics all the evidence they need to argue that the public should not trust the polls. But the truth is that there are both good polls and bad ones. And the public must sort them out. But how can we tell the difference?

We can begin by recognizing the kinds of mistakes that contribute to distortions in public opinion. In order to detect these errors, we need to ask three questions:

1. Does the sample fairly represent the population surveyed?

2. Are the measurements valid? Do they measure what they claim to measure?

3. Does the interpretation of the results accurately reflect the poll's findings?

Does the Sample Fairly Represent the Population Surveyed?

The classic example of a flawed sample involved a poll conducted by the

Literary Digest in 1936. While this popular newsmagazine had been successful in predicting who would win the presidential elections in 1920, 1924, 1928, and 1932, its method failed in 1936. And that failure resulted from the way the magazine had selected its sample.

Over the years, names for these polls were drawn from two sources: telephone directories and automobile registration lists. Using the same procedure in 1936, the magazine sent 10 million ballots to respondents. And based on the more than 2 million responses that it received, the *Literary Digest* predicted that Alf Landon would beat President Franklin Roosevelt by a margin of 57 to 43 percent. But he did not. Roosevelt won by a landslide, with 61 percent of the vote.

As the source of respondents suggests, this sampling procedure failed to represent poor people, who were not able to afford either a telephone or a car. In the wake of the Depression, they were the ones who voted for Roosevelt and his New Deal recovery program.

Nonscientific polls like these have contributed to the public's mistrust of public opinion polls. This skepticism was reflected in a 1996 Gallup poll which showed that a majority

of Americans—68 percent—did not think that a sample of 1,500 or 2,000 people could accurately reflect the views of the nation's population.

This, of course, creates a curious paradox for public opinion critics. But it also reflects the public's misunderstanding of the scientific sampling methods that reputable pollsters use today. Using this method, which is based on mathematical probabilities, the chance of selecting each person in a target population is known. That allows pollsters to design a representative sample and to claim that it reflects the views of the population surveyed.

Today's preelection polls, which are based on probability sampling methods, allow pollsters to predict electoral outcomes on the basis of a relatively small number of respondents. In contrast to the *Literary Digest*'s sample, which contained millions of respondents, pollsters now predict election results on the basis of interviews with as few as 1,000 people (Babbie, 1995).

You can judge the accuracy of these polls yourself. Table 2.2 lists the results of several preelection media polls conducted the weekend before the 1996 presidential election.

As the results show, each of these polls reported slightly different results.

TABLE 2.2   PRE- AND POSTELECTION MEDIA POLLS

	Poll Findings		
	Clinton	*Dole*	*Perot*
PREELECTION POLL RESULTS			
CBS News/*New York Times*	50%	34%	8%
NBC News/*Wall Street Journal*	47%	37%	9%
CNN/Gallup/*USA Today*	50%	37%	7%
FOX News	49%	49%	9%
ACTUAL RESULTS (NOVEMBER 5, 1996)	49.2%	40.9%	8.5%

But none of them was "wrong." Pollsters call the range of results the *margin of error.* Along with a measure of uncertainty (a confidence level), pollsters report their results using a range of percentage points.

Consider the example of a pollster who expresses 95 percent confidence in the results of a national poll. A "3 percentage point margin of error" for this poll would mean that if every adult in the nation were interviewed with the same questions in the same way at about the same time as the first poll, that poll's answer would fall within plus or minus 3 percentage points of the complete count result 95 percent of the time.

The results of the 1996 preelection polls show that media polls did correctly predict the winner, and their percentages came very close to the final election results. The third-party candidacy of Ross Perot, which had caused pollsters problems in 1992, continued to create some problems in this election—as reflected in the percentages expected for Dole. But pollsters had learned from the 1992 experience and came much closer this time.

A number of questions will help you determine whether a poll fairly represents the views of the population surveyed. Most importantly, you should ask how the people were chosen. Scientific polls use a specific method for choosing respondents. Nonscientific polls do not, and, in fact, the respondents often choose themselves as participants. Nonscientific polls include 900-number dial-in polls, magazine mail-in polls, and instant polls found on the Internet. These kinds of polls are conducted primarily for entertainment purposes, and their results cannot be generalized to any other group.

Pay particular attention to how respondents are selected for political polls. While adults drawn from the American population appear to make up the appropriate sample, they do not. All Americans do not vote. Therefore, preelection polls and preprimary polls should be based on the sample that best represents Americans who go to the polls—registered voters, "likely voters," or previous primary voters (Babbie, 1995).

Are the Measurements Valid? Do They Measure What They Claim to Measure?

Question wording. According to Neil Postman, "The public's 'opinion' on almost any issue will be a function of the question asked" (1993). A number of examples illustrate his point. Take, for instance, the issue of abortion. The CBS/*New York Times* poll has used several different versions of questions for this issue. As the following comparison shows, the results vary significantly, depending on the wording of the question.

"Do you think there should be an amendment to the Constitution prohibiting abortions, or shouldn't there be such an amendment?"

For: 29%
Against: 67%

"Do you believe there should be an amendment to the Constitution protecting the life of the unborn child, or shouldn't there be such an amendment?"

For: 50%
Against: 39%

John Allen Paulos observed the same kind of effect for questions about political campaign finance funding (1995):

"Should laws be passed to eliminate all possibilities of special interests giving huge sums of money to candidates?"

Yes: 80%
No: 17%

"Should laws be passed to prohibit interest groups from contributing to campaigns, or do groups have a right to contribute to the candidate they support?"

Yes: 40%
No: 55%

Pollsters are well aware of these kinds of question-wording effects (Babbie, 1995; Schuman and Presser, 1981). In fact, experiments on the effects of question-wording date back to the early 1940s.

In recent years, Kenneth Rasinski has examined questions that asked the public to evaluate a variety of government spending policies (1989). His analysis showed that question-wording had a significant impact on the public's amount of support. Consider, for example, how the public responded to the issue of poverty, depending on how the problem was labeled:

"Are we spending too much, too little or about the right amount on welfare?"

Too Little: 23%

"Are we spending too much, too little or about the right amount of assistance to the poor?"

Too Little: 63%

As the comparison in Table 2.3 shows, these kinds of question-wording differences were observed for a number of other spending policies (Babbie, 1995).

These examples illustrate why it is important to examine the exact wording of poll questions. To determine whether the wording of a question could bias the results, consider your own reaction to it. And ask these questions:

- Is the question fair and unbiased?
- Are the possible choices balanced?

(continued on next page)

SOCIOLOGY OF THE MEDIA (continued)

TABLE 2.3   QUESTION-WORDING DIFFERENCES IN POLLS

More Support	Less Support
"Halting rising crime rate"	"Law enforcement"
"Dealing with drug addiction"	"Drug rehabilitation"
"Solving problems of big cities"	"Assistance to big cities"
"Improving conditions of blacks"	"Assistance to blacks"
"Protecting social security"	"Social security"

- Are the people you know knowledgeable enough to answer the question?

In some cases, pollsters overestimate what the public knows or understands about an issue. But the questions they design may allow respondents to answer anyway (Schiller, 1973; Schuman and Presser, 1981). And they will, because they don't want to look stupid.

Therefore, as you evaluate question-wording effects, you should also consider what sociologists call the *social desirability* of questions and answers (Babbie, 1995). Remember that when they answer questions, respondents

want to look good. If a question could embarrass respondents or make them look inhumane, or irresponsible, you should expect question-wording effects.

In addition to the bias produced by question-wording, other measurement problems can also affect whether polls reflect the real views of respondents. Consider, for example, the results of a 1988 CBS/*New York Times* poll conducted just prior to the primary election. This poll showed Jesse Jackson winning about 50 percent of all black voters. But on election day, the exit polls indicated that Jackson had captured 91 percent of all black votes. In analyzing these discrepant results, poll experts

believed that black voters had not revealed their true voting intentions to the CBS/*New York Times* interviewers—most of whom were white (Browne and Keeley, 1990).

When it comes to sensitive questions or issues, you should always compare the results of several different polls conducted by a number of organizations with a focus on the exact wording of questions.

Does the Interpretation of the Results Accurately Reflect the Poll's Findings?

The last source of bias that can distort public opinion requires us to distinguish poll findings from the interpretation of those findings (Dautrich and Dineen, 1996). In some cases, this kind of distortion is readily apparent. But in others, it is not.

Consider, for example, how one's personal values can interfere with objectivity. In an address to the American Association of Public Opinion Research (AAPOR) in 1968, Milton Rokeach expressed concern over the way that hidden value systems bias media polls (1968). Referring to a

---

Careful procedures have been established for selecting samples. The better the sampling procedure, the more closely the sample will represent the entire population and the more accurate the resulting generalizations or predictions will be. Consider the following example: In gathering data for her book *Women and Love: A Cultural Revolution in Progress* (1987), which concluded that a very high proportion of American women dislike their marriages, Shere Hite distributed 100,000 questionnaires. Most were distributed to women's organizations, and only 4,500 responses were obtained—a return rate of 4.5 percent.

Hite's sample could not be said to be representative of the population she was interested in studying—American women in the 1980s—in part because of the very low return rate and in part because members of women's organizations may well have different attitudes about marriage than those typical of American women in

general. The kind of error made when the sample selected does not represent the population as a whole is called *sampling error.*

Among the many procedures used in choosing a sample, the simplest is **random sampling.** In this method, the sample is chosen so that every member of the population has an equal chance of being picked for inclusion in the sample. One could select a random sample by pulling names from a hat. But such a procedure is not very practical in large-scale research. Instead, researchers frequently use random numbers, generated by computer or from a table, to decide which members of the population to include in the sample.

Other sampling procedures are more common in survey research. One is *systematic sampling,* in which a specific scheme is followed, such as choosing every tenth name in a telephone book or on an attendance list. Another is

Gallup poll that was reported in the *New York Times* on February 28, 1968, Rokeach claimed that the report reflected the high value that white society placed on freedom and the low value that it placed on equality.

Based on the public's response to the question: "What is the most important problem facing this community today?" the *New York Times* had written a story with the headline: "Poll Finds Crime Top Fear at Home." Rokeach argued that both the Gallup report and the *New York Times* had failed to "exercise their journalistic conscience" when they combined a handful of different responses to create what then became the most important problem: "crime and lawlessness."

Using a different value system, Rokeach argued, they could have combined other responses to make "racial problems" the most important problem. As it turned out, it ranked eighth in importance, which, he felt, would be viewed as less deserving of immediate attention.

Several things can help you detect biased interpretations of media polls. First, examine the exact wording of both questions and possible responses.

Second, compare the poll's results to those of different polls conducted by different organizations. And, third, consider the reason for the poll. In the case of media polls, that will most likely turn out to be the development of a good story.

The Value of Public Opinion Polls

Given all of the potential problems of public opinion polls, one might ask: Should the results of public opinion polls be reported? The answer is yes—for many reasons. First, media polls are conducted by reputable polling organizations that recognize the problems and take measures to avoid them. While the number of media polls are small, the public can compare the results of different polls and investigate discrepant results. In fact, these media groups compare the results of their polls to others and tend to act as watchdogs, themselves.

And, second, these polls serve a very important function in America. When George Gallup published his first report in client newspapers in 1935, he had great expectations for public opinion polls. He believed that they would not only provide citizens with information on the day's most important issues, but that they would also remove the greatest obstacle to an informed democracy—"the absence of a way to measure public opinion accurately and continuously" (Gallup, 1990).

The best piece of advice offered on the question of whether poll results ought to be reported was offered by Paul Lazarsfeld at the beginning of the polling age. He said:

> The results of well-conducted polls are scientific facts: these can be misinterpreted and misused. But the solution certainly is not the forbidding of polls—rather it would be to give thought to how polls are used and by whom. (Lazarsfeld, 1945, p. 404)

Source: Selections and "Question-Wording Differences in Polls" table from *Practice of Social Research*, 7th Edition by E. R. Babbie © 1995. Reprinted with permission of Wadsworth Publishing, a division of International Thomson Publishing. Fax 800-730-2215.

stratified random sampling, in which the population is first subdivided into groups, or strata—departments within a college, counties within a state, work groups within a factory—and a random sample is then drawn from each of the strata.

A small, representative sample can be far superior to a large, unrepresentative sample. In other words, it is not the size of a sample that is important but, rather, how well it reflects the traits of the population under study. For example, the Bureau of Labor Statistics monitors consumer prices by examining a "market basket" of goods and services in only 56 cities in the United States. This sample, however, has been carefully selected to represent American consumers as a whole, and the resultant Consumer Price Index has proved to be an accurate measure of the changing costs of food, housing, clothing, transportation, health, and recreation.

DESIGNING THE RESEARCH INSTRUMENT

Once the sample has been selected, the third step in survey research is to design *research instruments*—questionnaires, interviews, or tests. A single survey might combine several instruments. But whatever instrument is used, the questions themselves are of the utmost importance. Are they phrased so that they will be understood correctly and similarly by every respondent? For example, if a certain number of Americans say that they favor more environmental regulation, do they all have the same kinds of laws in mind? Probably not. To avoid confusion, the question must spell out what *exactly* is meant by environmental regulation.

Generally, the more specific a survey question is, the more probable that the same interpretation of that question will be made by respondents and the more easily comparable and accurate the answers will be. *Closed response questions,* which present respondents with a range of alternative answers (multiple-choice questions, for instance), are the most specific and are probably the most widely used in sociological research. *Open response questions,* which do not include response categories and which allow respondents to answer in their own words, are used less often.

In deciding which type or types of questions to include in the research instrument, the sociologist must consider the purpose of the survey, the chosen method of sampling, the size of the sample being surveyed, and the nature of the information being sought. For example, a survey of a random sample of 500 students at a local college campus to determine student levels of optimism about their personal future and the future of the nation as a whole may be best accomplished by a series of closed response questions in a multiple-choice format. This format would allow the researcher to control the respondents' interpretation of the questions and to build distinctions into the answer categories. On the other hand, a limited sample of neighborhood residents to determine the reaction to the introduction of a child with AIDS into the local school may lend itself to open response questions, which allow residents to use their own words in reporting their attitudes. This research design would permit the researcher to capture the respondents' modes of expression as well as to record their reactions (Converse & Presser, 1986).

One method of probing the answers to closed response questions is to follow up with open response questions. In the 1983 Detroit Area Study of attitudes toward welfare, for example, a significant majority of respondents agreed with the statement that "government is trying to do too many things that should be left to individuals and private businesses." However, when these respondents were asked the follow-up question, "What things do you feel should be left to individuals or private businesses," over 25 percent could not answer or give an example (Converse & Presser, 1986).

Survey research questions should also be designed to reveal the complexities of an issue. In one study in which respondents were asked if they favored banning private ownership of guns, a majority said "No." However, an equally large majority expressed support when asked if they favored a law requiring people to obtain a police permit before they could buy a gun (Wright, quoted in Converse & Presser, 1986). Such questions reveal the different sides of an issue, allow respondents to qualify their answers, and make it less likely that the researcher will use a potentially misleading single response to represent public opinion.

Furthermore, questions should be stated as neutrally as possible in order to minimize bias. In one survey in which people were simply asked if there should be a constitutional amendment "prohibiting abortions," the majority responded "No." However, when the question was rephrased to ask whether there should be an amendment "protecting the life of the unborn child" (language more supportive of the pro-life position), some 20 percent of the respondents changed their answer to "Yes" (Brower, 1988).

It is not hard for interviewers accidentally to introduce bias into a survey. For example, they may use expressions or make comments that encourage the respondent to answer in a certain way. It is important that interviewers be well suited to their task and that they be carefully trained in the techniques of interviewing.

Some attitude surveys and public opinion polls are conducted through personal interviews. These interviews range from highly structured to unstructured. A *structured interview* consists of a set of closed response questions with a checklist of answers. The questions and responses are always stated in the same way and in the same sequence, so the results are easily compiled and generalized.

In other types of research, when more information about attitudes or behavior is desired, the *unstructured,* or open-ended, *interview* has many advantages. With an unstructured interview, leads can be followed up and individual points pursued. As a result, the interviewer can better determine whether the person responding really understands the questions. The disadvantage of this type of interview is that the answers are harder to analyze and compare. Many interviews are *semistructured*—that is, they combine elements of structured and unstructured interviews.

ADMINISTERING THE RESEARCH INSTRUMENT

The fourth step in survey research is to administer the research instrument. To get the most accurate results, the entire sample must be surveyed, particularly if it is small. If some people refuse to answer or are otherwise not available, the sample is no longer as representative as planned, and the data will probably be less accurate. Often, when questionnaires are sent by mail, people fail to return them. Replies may come from only those who are interested in the issue under study. This generally biases the findings.

ANALYZING THE DATA

The final step in survey research is tabulation, analysis, and interpretation of the data. In all but the smallest surveys, this step normally involves the use of computers.

LIMITATIONS OF THE SURVEY METHOD

No technique is more useful than the survey in obtaining accurate information about large numbers of people. Surveys have their limitations, however. Respondents are generally accurate in reporting demographic information about themselves—that is, age, occupation, or education—though they do sometimes make errors. But their self-reported attitudes may be less truthful, or a gap may exist between their attitudes and their behavior. For example, people who are prejudiced against minorities may actively practice discrimination. But, knowing that others do not approve, they often will not admit to such discrimination. Or people may honestly say to an interviewer that they approve of something—for example, better schools. But on election day they may vote against improving the schools, perhaps because they consider it more important to keep taxes low.

Well-designed and well-executed research can help to bring out hidden attitudes such as these and reveal conflicting ideals. The sociologist must always be aware that attitudes expressed in interviews do not always reflect underlying values, and that behavior does not always follow stated attitudes.

Experiments

The experiment is the classic scientific technique for studying cause-and-effect relationships under carefully controlled conditions. Typically, an experiment is designed to test a hypothesis about the relationship between two variables. One of these, the *independent variable,* is introduced during the experiment to see what effect it has on the other, the *dependent variable.*

An ideal **controlled experiment** is designed to isolate the specific effect of the independent variable by controlling the effects of other variables that may influence the dependent variable. In the most basic form of a controlled experiment, the subjects are randomly divided into two groups that are identical in every way except that the independent variable is introduced into one group, called the **experimental group,** and not into the other, called the **control group.** The two groups are then compared to see if they differ in relation to the dependent variable. On the basis of this comparison, the hypothesis about the relationship of the two variables is confirmed or rejected.

For example, in one study the experimental group might be schoolchildren who learn to read by computer; the control group would be a similar group of pupils who use a standard reading text. Both groups would take a reading test at the beginning of the experiment, which might then run as long as the entire school year. At the end of the experimental period, both groups of students

A controlled experiment designed to measure how well children learn by computer would test two groups. The control group would continue to use standard textbooks; the experimental group would use computers only. At the end of the experiment, the progress of both groups of students would be compared.

would be retested to see whether the experimental group showed greater gains than the control group. If it did, the differences in the reading scores (the dependent variable) would be ascribed to the experimental curriculum (the independent variable). Of course, there could be other reasons why the computer group learned more, and the experiment might also include some measures of these. Perhaps the experimental group was more highly motivated by virtue of being selected for inclusion in the study, or perhaps the parents of the children in the experimental group were sufficiently intrigued by the new program to help their children more at home.

Not all experiments make use of traditional experimental and control groups. For example, researchers in a study of the effects of media violence selected two groups quite different from one another in social class and personality (as measured by a special personality questionnaire). One group was made up solely of volunteer undergraduates from affluent white families. The other group consisted of paid volunteers, in the same age group as the students, who lived in a racially mixed inner-city housing project. The independent variable in this experiment was exposure to a set of excerpts from 24 commercially produced films selected for their portrayal of violence: accidental death, assault, property destruction, murder, and rape. The dependent variable was the subjects' physiological response (as measured by skin conductance) to these violent scenes.

The study revealed that the inner-city subjects were more physically affected by portrayals of violence than the college students were. In particular, the college sample was much less affected by the depiction of rape than was the inner-city group. Why? The researchers believe the inner-city residents had stronger reactions to the violence depicted in these films because it mirrored their real-life experiences (Frost & Stauffer, 1987).

Many social science experiments take place in laboratories, where all conditions can be carefully regulated. For example, in one interesting laboratory experiment, two groups, each composed of 15 males and 15 females, listened to tape-recorded jokes. On the tape the experimental group heard, prerecorded laughter was included at the end of each joke. On the tape the control group heard, the laugh track was omitted. After each joke was presented, researchers measured "expressions of mirth," such as smiling and laughing. They found that there were more expressions of mirth in the experimental group than in the control group—that is, the laugh track tended to generate real laughter. Moreover, members of the experimental group could remember the jokes better than members of the control group when tested later (Chapman, 1973).

The use of such laboratory experiments is especially common in psychology. But in sociology, experiments typically move out of the laboratory and into the field—the school, the hospital, the street. Because it is often not possible or desirable to conduct a controlled experiment, sociologists take advantage of *natural experiments*—that is, real situations with experimental and control groups not set up by the researchers.

One excellent example of a natural experiment is provided by a study of aggressiveness among children over a two-year period in three Canadian towns (Jay, Kimball, & Zabrack, 1986). In one of these communities, which the researchers tagged "Multitel," residents could tune in to both the Canadian Broadcasting Network and three U.S. networks. In the second town, "Unitel," only shows from the Canadian Broadcasting Network could be received. Most crucially, residents of the third town, dubbed "Notel," could not view any television programming at all at the time the study began, but acquired TV reception one year later. The researchers

observed a much greater increase in the level of children's aggressiveness over the two years in Notel (the experimental group) than took place in either Unitel or Multitel (the control groups). This study strongly suggests that watching television stimulates aggressive behavior among children. Other natural experiments have investigated such topics as the academic success rate of students in large versus small colleges and childrearing in two-parent versus single-parent families.

LIMITATIONS OF THE EXPERIMENTAL METHOD

Laboratory experiments provide much better control over variables than do natural or field experiments. Nonetheless, the laboratory is an artificial setting, and this may distort findings. Although a natural experiment usually takes the manipulation of independent variables and the composition of experimental groups out of the investigator's hands, it may promote a better understanding of the dynamics of real-life social behavior.

Observation

To conduct *systematic observation,* sociologists look for promising research sites where it is possible to study social interaction as it occurs. The observer cannot really control any of the variables (except when observation is coupled with a controlled experiment). But it is possible to work out careful procedures for observing and recording behavior, so that any qualified researcher can repeat these procedures. Systematic observation may be conducted either in the laboratory or in the field.

LABORATORY OBSERVATION

Many research projects have involved the observation of small groups in a laboratory setting. For example, researchers have studied groups of young children by watching them through one-way windows. Or a small work group may be called in to discuss a specific problem. During the discussion, an unseen sociologist records how often certain kinds of behavior take place—giving and receiving opinions, agreeing and disagreeing, joking, criticizing, and so on (Bales, 1951). Although conducted in somewhat artificial surroundings, such research has produced much useful information.

FIELD OBSERVATION

Social scientists may also observe in homes, playgrounds, streets, or offices. Sometimes they watch formal groups—committees, therapy groups, or professional societies—in action. Sometimes they observe how a particular site is used—a sandbox, a street corner, or even a living room with a television set. For example, a psychiatrist and a social scientist observed elderly Bowery men and found that the popular conception of the skid row man as a total loner was inaccurate. Although these men did not see much of their families, they were involved in a considerable amount of interaction with other homeless men. These relationships could not be considered close personal friendships, but they were ever-changing, reciprocal encounters where one did favors for another and expected something in return very soon thereafter (Cohen & Sokolovsky, 1989).

In another field study, two British authors (Broadstreet & Segnit, 1975) observed TV watching in the homes of specially selected working-class families who were heavy viewers. They found that there was only a weak relationship between how long the TV set was on and how much people actually watched it. Family members often wandered in, flopped down briefly in front of the set, and then wandered off to eat or do chores. Sometimes the set kept running for hours, as if it were "just part of the wallpaper."

NONPARTICIPANT AND PARTICIPANT OBSERVATION

In **nonparticipant observation,** the researcher watches, but does not take part in, the activities or social situation under study. **Participant observation,** on the other hand, requires personal involvement. Researchers actually become members of the group they study in order to try to see the world through the eyes of that group's members. This technique, widely used in cultural anthropology, has undergone great refinement over the years. Sometimes a participant observer also uses questionnaires and interviews, although these instruments are employed more informally than in survey research.

In *overt participant observation,* the researcher participates in the social lives of the subjects, who are aware of his or her identity as a social scientist. In *covert participant observation,* the researcher attempts to become a member of the group being studied without revealing his or her identity or intentions. Covert participant observation raises serious ethical questions: Is it right to deceive people, and perhaps invade their privacy, in order to study them?

Most participant observation research takes the form of the **case study,** a detailed record of a single event, person, or social grouping. Case studies have played an important role in the development of the social sciences and have provided a major source of insights and hypotheses later applied to larger populations.

One classic case study is *Tally's Corner* by Elliot Liebow (1967). The unemployed African-American men

that Liebow studied knew he was an observer, but allowed him to share their lives on their "Corner" hangout in Washington, D.C. He talked, drank beer, and played pool with them, visited their rooming houses, and hung around the Carry-Out Shop (a take-out grocery). Liebow chose to focus his study on the men's personal relationships. He showed how, in the crumbling, ever-changing street world, human relationships are dark mirrors of the world outside. Friendships are quickly made and appear warm, yet friends frequently do not even know each other's last names. Loyalties are fierce, but fast-fading. The men like the idea of having children, but the fathers who are separated from their families are more tender with their children than are the men who live with their children. Liebow found that these men, who cannot find a place in the "legitimate" world, set up a shadow existence outside it.

Another famous example of participant observation research is the "hanging tongues" study done by William Thompson (1983). Thompson, a research sociologist, applied for a summer job at a meat-packing plant and was hired for the Slaughter Division, a site renowned for its overwhelming odor of live and dead cattle. At Thompson's station, beef tongues were processed and hung up to dry. Monotony, dehumanization, and the ever-present threat of physical injury were the everyday experiences of workers on this job. Hanging, branding, and bagging some 1,500 beef tongues per shift did not offer much in the way of rewards. The substantial salary seemed to be the job's only advantage.

In observing how his fellow workers coped with these dreary conditions, Thompson made some interesting discoveries. He found that they devised several ways to try to mentally escape from the monotony of their jobs. They daydreamed extensively about their families and their leisure pursuits. But most of all, the workers talked endlessly about the expensive things they had managed to buy: cars, vans, and motorcycles. These were the only things that made their work worthwhile.

LIMITATIONS OF OBSERVATION

There are special strengths and weaknesses of the participant observation technique. A major argument for participant observation is that, through firsthand immersion in a situation, the sociologist comes to understand intimately how the subjects see their world, how they interpret their daily experiences, and how they interact with one another. But participant observation also runs into some difficulties for this very reason. Perhaps the most important of these is the sociologist's struggle to remain objective despite becoming deeply immersed in a group's activities.

INTERNET/TECHNOLOGY

PUBLIC OPINION POLLS ON THE INTERNET

For over 60 years, pollsters have been asking Americans to express their opinions on just about everything—the president's job performance, the legality of burning the American flag, even the likelihood that UFOs are real.

The public's interest in these polls reflects the many functions they serve. In a democracy, they provide a measure of how closely decision makers actually represent the views of their constituents. Exit polls, which are conducted on election day, provide a way to measure voting irregularities. In all cases, knowing what others think gives us a way to evaluate our own opinions (Festinger, 1954). In the past, however, the results usually reached only a small audience. Even those who participated in the poll had no idea when the results would be published or broadcast. Today the Internet has solved that problem. Now every major polling organization makes the results of its polls available on the Internet.

As the latest technological advance in communications, the Internet provides pollsters with the best way to report poll findings. Besides the obvious advantage of increasing access to the results of public opinion polls, the Internet also eliminates the space and time constraints imposed by print and broadcast media. Poll findings no longer must be limited to a specified number of newspaper or magazine columns, or to 20 seconds of air time. The Internet allows pollsters to provide detailed information about the poll. The public can examine the exact wording of questions. They can see how different people (men and women, young and old, rich and poor) answered the questions. And they can search the archives to learn how American opinion has changed over time.

Finding the Polls

In most cases, finding the results of public opinion polls on the internet requires only a few steps. The Web sites for polls conducted by Gallup, Roper, Harris, and Yankelovich will take you directly to where you want to begin.

In addition to these polls, the media have also teamed up to conduct their own polls. These include the CBS/*New York Times* poll, the ABC/*Washington Post* poll, the NBC/*Wall Street Journal*, and the CNN/*Time* poll. As the product of a collaborative effort, the results of these polls may appear on the Web site of either organization.

In some cases, one member of the media team has set up a site designed for the sole purpose of reporting polling results. For example, CBS News has created a site for the CBS/*New York Times* polls, and the *Washington Post* has done the same thing for the ABC/*Washington Post* polls.

In all cases, you can conduct a search from the Web site of either team member to locate a poll. But keep this in mind: The name of the poll may vary, depending on the media Web site. So, for example, if you are searching for a poll from the *New York Times* Web site, search for *New York Times*/ CBS News polls.

A Word of Caution

Before you surf the Internet in search of public opinion data, remember that all polls do not fairly represent the views of the American public. Do not confuse scientific polls with those that are designed solely for entertainment purposes. In several cases, media organizations conduct both kinds of polls. For example, in addition to NBC/*Wall Street Journal* polls, NBC also reports the findings of its own poll of Internet users called "Live Vote." CNN has a similar Internet poll called "quickvote," and the *Washington Post* calls its Internet poll "poll taker." In each case, these polls represent only Internet users. And there is no guarantee that respondents have answered honestly or that they have answered the question only once.

To get a sense of how unrepresentative these polls can be, consider these differences. The results of an NBC "Live Vote" poll showed that 61 percent of Internet respondents believed that UFOs were actual visitors from outer space. But a Gallup poll, which NBC reported right next to these findings, showed that only 48 percent of the people they surveyed thought that UFOs were "something real." Remember, the sample for these Internet polls represents only people who log onto the Internet.

To separate scientific polls from those designed simply for entertainment purposes, look for information about how the poll was conducted. In many cases disclaimers regarding the scientific value of instant polls are provided. In other cases, you must be the judge.

Secondary Analysis

Sociologists need not always rush out to collect new data. Previous studies are important sources of information that can be refined, recombined, and reanalyzed to answer new questions. The reuse of previously collected data is called **secondary analysis.**

A great deal of data can be found in diaries, letters, autobiographies, and other personal documents, as well as in organizational records, historical archives, news articles, government records, and data banks of previous social science research. The single most important source of available data in the United States is the census. This periodic count (every 10 years, with special studies in between) of the population includes information about age, sex, race, marital status, income, household, and other variables. In addition, public records of vital statistics containing such information about each person as birth date, date of marriage, number of children, and date of death are available for research purposes.

The use of census data and vital statistics is subject to guarantees against invasion of privacy. Studies in Germany, however, have demonstrated that people can sometimes be identified from census data despite official claims of confidentiality (Gluckman, 1988).

CONTENT ANALYSIS

Content analysis is a research procedure often utilized in secondary analysis that involves examining a body of written documents or any other kind of communication (letters, for example, or comic strips, or the episodes of a television program) and applying a systematic coding scheme to it. For example, Linda Mooney and Sarah Brabant were interested in finding out how often and in what manner love is expressed in greeting cards. They selected a sample of birthday cards from greeting-card outlets at a city in Louisiana and set up a formal coding system for describing the format and content of each card. This coding scheme included *general features,* such as price, size, and total number of words; *cover features,* such as type of artwork; *tone* of the words, whether serious, funny, or neutral; *sentiments* expressed, such as love, joy, or appreciation; and the *status* of the sender and receiver, such as parent, sister, or sweetheart.

The study's most interesting finding was that the cards that mentioned love (and only about one-quarter of them did so) were generally geared toward relatives (especially female relatives), both as senders and recipients. Such cards were more expensive, more ornate, and more serious than other cards. According to the researchers, this lends support to the stereotype of the unemotional male (Mooney & Brabant, 1988).

Another example of content analysis is a study of the topics discussed by religious television programming (Abelman & Neuendorf, 1985). Three episodes of each of 27 prominent religious programs were classified as devoted to social, political, or religious topics, and the frequency and treatment of each of these topics were noted. This research found that the most common social topic discussed was death; the most common political topic was communism; and the most common religious topic was God.

Content analysis is a research procedure that involves examining a body of written documents or other kinds of communication and applying a systematic coding scheme to it.

Research Strategies

As well as making use of the four basic types of research designs already discussed—survey research, experiments, observation, and secondary analysis—sociologists may choose from one or more of several general research strategies. These include comparative analysis, replication, unobtrusive measures, and multiple research methods.

COMPARATIVE ANALYSIS

The availability of large bodies of data is often an important stimulus to comparative analysis. Although most sociological research includes some comparison, the term **comparative analysis** usually refers to research involving the comparison of several social systems—such as nations or major segments of nations—or of the same social system at more than one point in time (Warwick & Osherson, 1973).

Cross-national research is the comparative study of two or more nations. A good example of this kind of research comes from the work of a sociologist who set out to discover if nationality is related to "psychological modernity" (Inkeles, 1978). Among the traits that he defined as making up psychological modernity were openness to new experience, resistance to traditional authority, interest in the news and community affairs, ambition, and belief in the importance of science. He obtained samples of young men in six countries matched according to their education and occupation. Next, he measured the degree to which they showed the traits of psychological modernity. He found widespread national variation in the presence of these traits: Argentina and Israel led; Nigeria, Chile, and India followed; and Bangladesh trailed far behind.

Comparison of the same society at different points in time is, in effect, the study of social change. Sociologists study social change by means of longitudinal studies and cross-sectional studies. A *longitudinal study* follows the same people over a period of time. For example, one researcher examined the lives of men who were born between 1916 and 1925 and thus were teenagers during the Depression (Elder, 1974). He was particularly interested in how those difficult years affected their adult lives. Comparing men who were severely deprived during the Depression with those who were not, he found that the deprived men were much more child-centered as adults. They worked harder to provide for their children's comfort, security, and affluence—things they had missed in their own youth.

Because of the high cost of longitudinal studies, sociologists often choose to study social change through *cross-sectional studies,* which compare the responses of people of different ages, education, economic status, and ethnic background at a single point in time. One such study contrasted the way members of two different generations reacted to statements made about sex in advertising (Wise & Merenski, 1974). Parents were more likely than their college-age children to agree with the statement "Advertisers make too much use of sex appeal." We cannot assume that the college-age group will come to hold their parents' views when they age. But the study suggests that people's attitudes do change over time.

REPLICATION

Physical scientists commonly emphasize the necessity for **replication**—that is, the repetition of a study or experiment in order to check its accuracy. Replication is often easily accomplished in the physical sciences. Conditions are created in a laboratory, variables are introduced, and results are compared. But since relatively little sociological research is conducted in the laboratory, sociologists often need to develop new ways of replicating earlier studies. This task is frequently difficult and time-consuming.

Let us imagine that a careful analysis of the data from our hypothetical example leads us to conclude that delinquent behavior is more frequent among children from broken homes than among those from intact families. Before we began our research, we had developed hypotheses about the processes at work. Once we had actually collected the data for our study, we used certain statistical techniques to adjust for the factors that might influence our findings: length of time the child spent in a broken home, location of the home, socioeconomic status of the family, and previous incidents of delinquency, to name just a few. But would our findings hold up in a different sample?

We need to recognize the possibility that our study was based on an atypical sample of children and families. Therefore, we must *replicate* the study with a new sample to find out whether the results of a second study will support our original (seemingly proven) hypothesis about the connection between broken homes and delinquency. Replication allows us to find errors we may have made in the original study, as well as to gain a better understanding of the circumstances under which our previous findings will stand up—or be disproven.

Although some researchers replicate their own studies, it is more common for other teams of researchers to do the replication. This practice helps to screen out researcher bias and introduces a stronger element of objectivity into the study. All researchers have to accept the possibility that their findings will be modified by someone else in the light of new knowledge, new technology, or new methods of analyzing data. In fact, it is not uncommon for the results of a replication to contradict completely the results of the original study.

For example, research in the mid-1980s seemed to indicate that the greater the television coverage of news stories about suicide, the steeper the rise in suicides immediately thereafter (Phillips & Carstensen, 1988; Stack, 1987). But would real-life suicide rates also increase after *fictional* stories about suicide were aired on television? The answer to this question might help to test the validity of the conclusions of the original research. Study of teenagers in the New York City area found that suicide rates did indeed increase following televised fictional portrayals of suicide (Gould & Shaffer, 1986), thus supporting the original research.

But the original researchers were not satisfied with the New York sample, so they examined data on teenage suicide rates in California and Pennsylvania before and after fictional portrayals of suicide had been shown on television. Their doubts were confirmed; fictional accounts of suicide on television did not provoke a rise in suicides (Phillips & Paight, 1987).

What could be the reasons for this disparity in the findings between one location and another? Perhaps, the researchers speculated, the imitation of suicide is an urban phenomenon in general or is limited to the Northeast. To test these hypotheses, they reanalyzed their data, combining samples from New York City with those from California and Pennsylvania. None of the subsamples showed the same dramatic results as reported by the original studies. Thus, by successive and more refined replications, honing in on more and more specific possibilities, the researchers decided that it was premature to conclude that "fictional presentations of suicide may have a lethal effect."

UNOBTRUSIVE MEASURES

Some sociologists, not wanting to impose themselves on the subjects they are observing, stress the use of *unobtrusive measures,* such as the observance of physical traces of social behavior (Webb et al., 1966). Like detectives, sociologists have studied the wear and tear on the floors around museum exhibits (to identify visitor preferences), dog-eared library books (to study reading habits), and discarded liquor bottles (to study alcohol drinking in a "dry" town). These measures are seldom used alone. But they add to other sources of data and help ensure that the investigator has not somehow influenced the behavior under study.

MULTIPLE RESEARCH METHODS

Given the limitations of each of the four principal research methods, many sociologists choose to combine two or more of these procedures, a strategy sometimes called *triangulation.* By simultaneously using dissimilar approaches that entail different limitations, researchers gain increased confidence in the validity of their findings.

The use of multiple methods has been especially important in a type of research termed **community studies.** In this approach, a team of sociologists collects a broad range of information about a small or medium-sized town that will provide a holistic, in-depth understanding of the lifeways of the entire community. Participant observation techniques usually feature prominently in community studies, but they are augmented by both survey research and secondary analysis.

A classic example of a community study was an investigation of Muncie, Indiana, conducted by Robert and Helen Lynd (1929, 1937), who lived in this midwestern town for a number of years just before and during the Depression. The Lynds interviewed scores of Muncie citizens, methodically worked their way through newspaper files to find data about the past, and tried to enter fully into small-town life. They found that the citizens of Muncie put a premium on work, self-reliance, Christian faith, and national and civic pride.

A team of sociologists returned to Muncie to see how that community looked in the late 1970s. Had anything changed? The team found, surprisingly, that the same values were still very strong, despite such physical changes as shopping malls, fast-food restaurants, and discos. Most of the high school students agreed, for example, that the Bible "is a sufficient guide to all problems in modern life." But Muncie residents today are more tolerant of other views, probably because of the influence of television. Only a minority now consider Christianity "the one true religion" (Caplow, Bahr, Chadwick, Hill, & Williamson, 1982).

OBJECTIVITY AND ETHICS IN SOCIAL RESEARCH

The use of any research method gives rise to basic issues concerning objectivity, bias, and ethics in sociological research. We conclude with a discussion of these topics.

Objectivity and Bias

Surely, one of the biggest problems social scientists face is the issue of objectivity. Sociologists are frequently asked: "How can you, a creature of society like everyone else, with feelings, moral views, and prejudices, be detached and unemotional enough in your investigations so that your findings are truly objective? How do we know that you are reporting the facts as they are, rather than as you wish they were?" Although the subject matter of sociology would seem to leave it unusually open to the problem of objectivity, every scientific discipline faces this problem.

Sociologists address the problem of objectivity partly through the way their discipline is organized and partly through the way they conduct research. As in other academic disciplines, knowledge in sociology is derived from the work of many researchers. The specific points of view and biases of any particular sociologist are kept to a minimum by the checks and balances of research by other scholars on similar topics. Sociological findings are almost always reported publicly, with full statements of methods and sources. Others may look at the same evidence and try the same methods to see whether they come up with the same conclusions.

Controversial research tends to attract the greatest amount of scrutiny. For example, in the mid-1960s, James Coleman led a study of American educational institutions and their impact on student achievement

Some researchers find that their mere presence can distort the situation under study, as it has with this group being photographed.

(Coleman et al., 1966). The study had been commissioned by the U.S. Office of Education (now the Department of Education), which wanted to examine the common-sense idea that the quality of the facilities of American schools, which varies a great deal, largely explains the variations in the academic abilities of their students. Good students, in other words, were supposed to come from good schools.

Coleman found that there was indeed some variation in the quality of school facilities, but not nearly so much as had been thought. He found, as well, that these variations did seem to affect the performance of students, but not very much. In short, Coleman concluded, a connection that had been considered to be very strong turned out to be very weak.

These conclusions came as a surprise to most educators. They were also very controversial because they suggested that massive improvements in facilities (such as libraries and laboratories) might be relatively ineffective in improving students' academic performance. This was exactly the opposite of what the Office of Education had expected would be found. The Coleman Report was therefore subjected to intense examination, notably in a year-long professional seminar at Harvard University, where the report's assumptions, data, and conclusions were thoroughly examined. To this day, the methodology of this report remains the focus of sharp debate, and the findings are held by many to be inconclusive.

Another controversial social science study was the famous so-called Moynihan report on the African-American family, conducted by Daniel Patrick Moynihan (1965), now a U.S. senator from New York. Moynihan, then an aide to President Lyndon B. Johnson, focused on what he regarded as the excessively large number of African-American families headed by women. In effect, he argued that the increase in the number of such "matrifocal" units (i.e., family units headed by mothers) indicated that the structure of African-American families was disintegrating and that this was among the most important sources of African-American poverty.

Many sociologists and African-Americans rejected Moynihan's belief that families led by women are necessarily weak. In addition, many people regarded his report as a political document intended to justify the Johnson administration's Great Society programs, not as an objective study of the black family. For both reasons the study was examined and debated extensively.

A separate issue concerning bias in social research deals with the effects of the research process itself on the behavior of people being studied. Sociologists cannot afford to forget that theirs is a science of *human* behavior. People react to the research process—and sometimes in ways we do not expect. The mere presence of a researcher may distort the situation under study, a phenomenon often termed *reactivity.*

The classic case is the famous Hawthorne experiment, conducted in the late 1920s and early 1930s (Roethlisberger, 1949). The management of Western Electric's Hawthorne plant, located outside Chicago, wanted to find out if environmental factors, such as lighting, could affect workers' productivity and morale. A team of social scientists experimented with a small group of employees who were set apart from their co-workers. The environmental conditions of this group's work area were controlled, and the subjects themselves were closely observed. To the great surprise of the researchers, the productivity of these workers increased in response to *any* change in their environmental conditions—even when the changes (such as a sharp decrease in the level of light in the workplace) seemed unlikely to have such an effect.

It was concluded that the presence of the observers had caused the workers in the experimental group to feel that they were special. The employees came to know and trust one another, and they developed a strong belief in the importance of their job. The researchers believed that this, not the controlled changes in the work environment, accounted for the increased productivity. A reanalysis of the original data challenged the conclusions of the Hawthorne researchers on the grounds that the changes in human relations patterns, deemed so important by the researchers, were never measured in the original study. (Franke & Kaul, 1978). However, even if the original conclusions of the Hawthorne study must be revised, they nonetheless raise a problem that all social scientists must confront: the fact that research subjects who know they are being studied can change their behavior. Throughout the social sciences, this phenomenon has come to be called the **Hawthorne effect.**

Ethical Issues in Social Research

Because sociologists study human subjects, they must confront several important ethical problems. One of these problems involves the selection of subjects for research. The problem is most obvious in social experiments, such as sponsored jobs for ex-criminals, special training programs for unemployed teenagers, or enriched educational programs for minority children. How can sociologists ethically decide who will be in the experimental group—and receive special help—and who will be in the control group—and receive no special help at all? Does one choose those who will profit most from the program? Those who seem most needy?

A second problem concerns ending a subject's participation. Once people have been selected for special programs, is it ethical to force them to withdraw if they seem to be disrupting the research? Then there is the closely related question of freedom of choice. College students, for example, may ask whether they are really free to refuse to take part in an experiment when they depend on the instructor for grades.

A fourth ethical dilemma is posed by the conflict between the sociologist's desire to know and the subject's right to privacy. Sociologists are frequently involved in bringing behavior out of the "social closet." What gives them the right to inquire about a person's mistakes, conflicts, antisocial acts, or embarrassing experiences? Should people have the right to keep such matters secret?

A good example of this dilemma is provided by the work of Laud Humphreys (1970), who studied homosexual acts in public places. Humphreys posed as a lookout in a public rest room while other men performed homosexual sex acts. He was given the task of warning the participants if the police showed up. By recording their license-plate numbers, he was able to obtain the men's home addresses. About a year later, he went to their homes, posing as a researcher interested in an entirely different subject. He discovered that most of the men claimed to be strongly antihomosexual and seemed to be leading normal married lives. Although Humphreys's findings aroused great interest, many people criticized him for employing what they felt were unethical methods. They felt he should not have deceived the men whose private lives he was studying.

Professional associations of social scientists, as well as government sponsors of research, have taken an explicit position on the question of privacy in research. They agree that researchers must safeguard their subjects' rights to privacy. Subjects should be informed of the purposes of the research and the provisions set up for protecting their identities. Many research sponsors require that before a study begins, the subjects (or, if they are minors, their parents) give informed consent in writing.

Some official statements of research ethics recognize that social research is a two-way process. Potential subjects should know what the research is about; they should also find out what benefits they may gain from it.

All social science research must weigh benefits against costs. Does the increased knowledge that might result from the research outweigh the possible harm that may be done in the process of getting that knowledge? Such decisions are the responsibility not only of the social scientists conducting the research but of all of us, as members of a society that supports the social sciences (Rivlin & Timpane, 1975).

ETHICAL NEUTRALITY

One problem sociology shares with the natural sciences is the issue of ethical neutrality. In the sciences, *ethical neutrality* means that scientific truth should be pursued no matter whom it hurts, whom it helps, or what values it serves. The advent of nuclear weapons and other means of widespread destruction has called this position into question.

As private citizens, sociologists may express moral values, hold strong political opinions, and speak out on public issues. Many sociologists believe, however, that *in their work as social scientists* they must be guided mainly by scientific concerns, avoid political involvement, and be scholars rather than activists (Sibley, 1971). That is, they must remain ethically—or at least socially and politically—neutral. To do otherwise, they believe, would compromise sociology's position as an objective, scientific endeavor. This view, sometimes termed *value-free sociology,* was pioneered by Max Weber and remained largely unchallenged until the 1960s.

More recently, however, a large number of sociologists have come to see a potential social danger in ethical neutrality (Becker, 1967). They charge that "neutral" research, much of which is supported by "the Establishment," helps to maintain the existing social order. They feel that if sociology does not become involved in political and social issues, it, in effect, affirms the status quo (Gouldner, 1962). These critics argue that sociologists should become scholar-activists, even advocates for various ideological positions. They also believe that sociologists should use their research to bring about social change.

This debate is a continuing one, and many sociologists have rejected ethical neutrality in favor of greater social and political involvement.

CHAPTER REVIEW

1. Why is it important to understand the methodology that sociologists use in their research?

2. What kinds of problems does the empirical method seek to minimize?

3. Discuss the differences between descriptive and explanatory studies.

4. Which of the following terms are concepts: age, race, social class, male, female, poverty, religion, crime, racism, political party identification? Which are variables? Operationalize each variable.

5. Consider the relationships that might exist between the following variables: age, religion, crime, gender. Formulate a hypothesis using two of these variables. When would your hypothesis become an empirical generalization?

6. Propose a theory to explain the high divorce rate in the United States.

7. One researcher hypothesizes that crime rates are lower for religious people. Another researcher hypothesizes that older people are more religious. Identify the independent and dependent variables in each of these hypotheses. How would a researcher determine whether there is a relationship between these variables?

8. What does it mean when a researcher discovers that a correlation between variables is spurious?

9. Why would a researcher use multivariate analysis?

10. Discuss the difference between validity and reliability. Give an example of each.

11. What kind of methodology is used to measure public opinion?

12. Does survey research involve quantitative or qualitative methods?

13. Why do sociologists survey a sample instead of the population?

14. Why must survey researchers use random sampling?

15. When would a researcher use a controlled experiment?

16. How do an experimental group and a control group differ?

17. Identify the most common form of participant observation research.

18. Suppose your professor requires a research paper that involves secondary data analysis. Where could you find the data for the project?

19. If you were asked to conduct a content analysis of the evening news, how would you proceed?

20. For what purposes would a sociologist conduct comparative analyses?

INTERNET EXERCISE

The Web destinations for Chapter 2 relate to the process of sociological research. To begin your explorations, go to the Prentice Hall Companion Web site **http://www.prenhall.com/popenoe.** Next, choose **Chapter 2** (The Process of Sociological Research). Then, select **web destinations** from the menu on the left side of the screen. You will find a variety of sites to choose from. We suggest that you begin with **A Sociological Tour Through Cyberspace.** This site offers a wide variety of resources and other links that are relevant to research in sociology. When you arrive at the opening page, a number of other sites "to stimulate the sociological imagination" are listed. Click on **Methods and Statistics.** You may wish to explore **StatSoft: An Electronic Textbook, Statistical Resources on the Web,** or **Sociological Methodology.** After you have explored these and other links, and keeping the text's discussion in perspective, answer the following questions:

- How do sociologists analyze different variables?
- What are the stages of social research?
- What are the major research methods employed by sociologists?
- Why is it important to be objective in conducting sociological research?

KEY TERMS

methodology	dependent variables	control group
empirical method	spurious correlations	nonparticipant
descriptive studies	multivariate analysis	observation
explanatory studies	validity	participant observation
concepts	reliability	case study
variables	quantitative methods	secondary analysis
operationalizing the	qualitative methods	content analysis
variable	survey	comparative analyses
operational variables	population	replication
hypothesis	sample	community studies
empirical generalization	random sampling	Hawthorne effect
theory	controlled experiment	
`independent variables	experimental group	

CHAPTER 3

Culture

oday, in America, as in many Western countries, Asian-born newcomers earn a high percentage of awards and academic honors in mathematics and science, from grade school through graduate school. And topflight American research laboratories from Silicon Valley in California to Woods Hole in Massachusetts employ a high proportion of Asian-born scientists and engineers.

Why? Are Asians smarter than other people? Do they possess some fundamental secret to success that Westerners have somehow lost? Do Asians simply try harder?

Although the popular press at some point has responded "yes" to all of these questions, we, as students of sociology, need to debunk these relatively superficial explanations. A recent study tracked the academic success in the United States of over 500 school-age children of Southeast Asian "boat people" (Caplan, Choy, & Whitmore, 1992). The refugee children arrived knowing little English, after having suffered harrowing experiences during their flight from Vietnam and Laos and having lost out on much schooltime. In spite of these obstacles, they soon were doing exceptionally well in mathematics and science in American schools. For example, in national tests, 27 percent of Asian-born students achieved scores placing them in the top tenth of all mathematics students. When it came to grades in math and science, A's and B's were the norm, C's were rare (17 percent), and only 4 percent of these students had grade-point averages below a C.

One sociological explanation of the Asian students' success in math and science can be found in the values they held. The researchers found a high correlation between the students' achievement-oriented values and their academic success. Values vary from one society to another. What is taken for granted in one place or time may not be in another. Values are an important part of what is called *culture,* and the concept of culture is one of the most important ideas in the social sciences. It is to an examination of this concept that we now turn.

WHAT IS CULTURE?

What is the difference between a group of college students and a group of chimpanzees? You might find this a strange question, but the answer is not as straightforward as you may think. Probably the most important quality that sets humans apart from chimps and gorillas—our close "relatives" in the natural world—is culture. In everyday speech, culture is often used to mean refinement or sophistication in the arts. It might be used, for example, to distinguish between people who like classical music—the "cultured"—and those who prefer pop music—the

"uncultured." Clearly, however, this definition of culture will not help us tell chimpanzees from humans, for we all know people who have no special interest in the arts and yet are quite different from chimps.

Sociologists and anthropologists commonly define **culture** as the shared products of a human group or society. These shared products include not only values, language, and knowledge but also material objects. The people of any group or society share **nonmaterial culture**—abstract and intangible human creations such as definitions of right and wrong, some medium of communication, and knowledge about the environment and about ways of doing things. They also share **material culture**—a body of physical objects that reflect nonmaterial cultural meanings. Elements of material culture include tools, money, clothing, and works of art.

Although culture is shared, it must also be learned by each new generation through the process of social interaction. Thus, culture is passed on from generation to generation and accumulates over time.

In the most general sense, then, culture is the whole way of life of a people that is transmitted from one generation to the next. Although the concept of "culture" is often used interchangeably with "society," the two should not be confused. Strictly speaking, *society* refers to interacting people who share a culture, whereas *culture* is the product of that interaction. In reality, human society and culture cannot exist independently of each other (although dead societies leave behind cultural remains that are discovered by archeologists). Culture is created through people interacting, but human interaction takes its form through the sharing of culture.

Although humans are the only animals whose social groups are defined by culture, we are not the only social animals. Chimpanzees live together in stable groups and show a sense of community. They often react to outsiders with hostility, for instance, and cooperate in searching for fruit and stalking game. Ants live in self-sufficient societies marked by an extremely complex division of labor. Each ant has a part to play: Smaller ants work inside the nest, medium-sized ants operate outside, and ants with large heads act as soldiers.

As patterned as some animal and insect societies are, however, the behavior of neither ants nor chimpanzees is shaped by shared values, knowledge, or other distinctive features of culture. In place of culture, animals rely on strong **instincts**—fixed, biologically inherited, complex behavior patterns. Animal behavior is thus programmed genetically, and the social organization of any single species is alike from one place and time to the next. Depending only on their instincts, all beavers the world over build dams and raise their young in a very similar manner; all birds of a single species build the same kind of nests. These animals do not have to be taught to do these things.

By contrast, human societies vary greatly because they are patterned not only by human genetics but also by their cultures. (Human societies are the subject of Chapter 4.) Unlike chimpanzees and ants, humans are not born knowing how to act. We must learn culture after birth, and our behavior is profoundly affected by the culture into which we are born.

Returning to the difference between college students and chimpanzees, it is not quite accurate to say that chimps are ruled by biology and college students by culture. Human beings have no strong instincts of any kind, but we do share with chimps and other higher animals biological *drives,* inborn impulses to satisfy such needs as food, water, and sleep. Much of human culture is, in fact, organized around such drives.

In turn, chimpanzees possess some traits that could be labeled as cultural. These close relatives of humans use primitive tools and pass on the skills of making and using them to their young. Chimps have been known to use sticks as clubs for fighting, to split open tough nuts with rocks, and to use straws to fish termites from their nests. It is possible that chimps have all the basic skills needed for language, except the ability to actually speak words (Premack, 1985). A number of researchers have successfully taught chimps to recognize and use American Sign Language, a hand language used by the deaf in North America (Sanders, 1985). Some observers even assert that the chimps' use of these symbols constitutes language (Gardner & Gardner, 1975). Others dispute this, however,

Researchers have successfully taught chimps to recognize and use American Sign Language. Some observers assert that the chimps' use of these symbols constitutes language; others dispute this, saying that chimps are not capable of forming real sentences.

saying that chimps rarely string together more than two words and are not capable of forming real sentences (Terrance, 1979).

In any case, if chimps live in groups with a degree of structure, possess some symbolic abilities and a body of learned behavior, and use tools, can it therefore be said that they have culture? Most observers would agree that chimps do have the basics of culture, or at least something like culture, but that what they have is far less complex than human culture. To understand this difference, we need only compare the subtlety and variety of meanings that we can express through language with the limited meanings that chimps can get across by combining two or three symbols. In addition, our material culture and the social rules that guide our behavior and organize our societies are infinitely more complex than those of the chimps. Compare, for example, some of the advanced "tools" of the average American student—computers, calculators, VCRs—with the termite straws of our closest relative in the animal kingdom.

The Evolution of Culture

The earliest signs of human culture date from about 3 million years ago. Because values and meanings (nonmaterial aspects of culture) do not fossilize, fragments of the material culture of the earliest societies are all that have survived. The earliest tools were simply pebbles from which flakes were chipped to form a cutting edge.

Perhaps the most important cultural adaptation in the early history of humanity was the shift to big-game hunting. There is some evidence that the immediate ancestors of the earliest humans, the australopithecines, foraged for plant material and meat from already-dead animals. The bones of large animals found around early human sites, however, suggest that the first true humans had begun to hunt big game and bring it back to a home base. Radically new social patterns, including food sharing, division of labor by sex, cooperation, and the making of tools, probably evolved along with this change to hunting. Hunting may also have facilitated the development of language.

This shift to a hunting way of life occurred roughly 1 to 3 million years ago. During this period, the family as we know it today—based on a bond between one male and one or more females—probably first took form. Prehuman primates had mated only when the females were in estrus (heat), thus forcing the males to compete on the basis of strength for a chance to reproduce. Through evolution, human females—unlike any other female members of the animal kingdom—became sexually receptive more or less at all times. Many anthropologists think that the change to a more permanent male-female bond is related to the development of big-game hunting. Once the males hunted game while the females gathered plants, it became an advantage to mate with fewer partners and to choose partners on the basis of hunting and gathering skills.

Observation of modern hunter-gatherers such as the San of the Kalahari and the Aborigines of Australia has given us some idea of what early human social organization might have been like. The first humans probably lived in bands consisting of about 25 related men, their wives, and their children. Leadership roles were probably informal and shifting. Informal rules of conduct guided most activities. The men probably hunted big game, and the women trapped small animals, gathered plants, and nursed children.

Before the development of culture, humans could adapt to changes in the environment only through biological evolution, a process that can take hundreds of generations. Darwin's theories of evolution and natural selection, introduced in *On the Origin of Species* (1859), hold that those who are best adapted to their environment will be most likely to survive and reproduce. (Herbert Spencer later called this process the "survival of the fittest.") The development of culture meant that, for the first time, humans could alter the environment to their advantage. They could also change their behavior to adjust to changing environmental conditions.

Knowledge of useful behavior—how to make a shelter or where to find a certain kind of food—could be passed on from one generation to the next. As game of one kind died out, strategies for hunting other animals were developed. As temperatures fell, clothing was invented. Other species became extinct because they could not adjust to such changes so well.

The development of culture, in turn, influenced the evolution of the human body itself. For example, early humans who had relatively large brains and flexible hands were able to create more sophisticated tools and thus accomplish more specialized tasks. The individuals with these abilities were more likely to survive and therefore to reproduce. Over time, larger brains and nimble thumbs and fingers became increasingly common in human populations. Thus, just as changes in the environment promoted developments in culture, the evolution of culture led to progressive changes in the biological character of humans (Campbell, 1985).

During the past million years, the pace of cultural change has increased in a series of dramatic steps (Lenski & Lenski, 1987). By about 40,000 years ago, humans wore clothes, constructed shelters, and occupied most of the world. The climates in which they could survive ranged from tropical to subarctic. They buried their dead, cooked with fire, and participated in what may have been religious rituals.

Observation of modern hunter-gatherers such as the San of the Kalahari has given us some idea of what early human social organization might have been like.

Sometime around 10,000 B.C., humans began to produce their own food; the practice of domesticating animals and cultivating crops became widespread during the centuries that followed. Agriculture ushered in perhaps the most profound changes in all of human history. Humans no longer had to move from place to place, following big game. Crops and domesticated animals allowed the establishment of large, settled communities. As agricultural output increased, economies became more specialized: Some people made goods or governed or traded, while food was supplied to them by others. Some of the early settlements grew into towns and later urban areas. By about 5,000 years ago, *states*—independent political units consisting of several communities sharing a central government—had been formed in the Near East and in Greece (Stavrianos, 1983). The state soon became the dominant political form in the world.

By the late 1700s, another tremendous change comparable in importance to the development of agriculture—the Industrial Revolution—was under way in England. Machine technology has totally altered economic, political, and social structures. It has made possible communication and transportation on a worldwide basis and has enabled us to produce a vast array of tools, labor-saving devices, medicines, luxuries, and forms of entertainment. It has also enabled us to produce weapons that can destroy the human race. Culture has made humanity the most successful species on earth.

MAJOR COMPONENTS OF CULTURE

Symbols

The existence of culture depends on people's ability to create and use symbols. A **symbol** is anything that a group of people have agreed upon as a way of meaningfully representing something other than itself. All words and numbers are symbols; so are a clenched fist, the American flag, and the cross. Human beings, unlike their primate ancestors, can transmit extremely complex information to others—everything from "I love you" to technical data about the physical universe—and they can learn a great deal from the experience of others. The key to these critical human abilities is the use of symbols. Through symbols, we can make sense of reality and transmit and store complex information. In short, we can both create and learn from our culture. (Gusfield & Michalowicz, 1984).

Symbols are extremely important in helping us comprehend abstract concepts like "God," "justice," and "patriotism." Because such concepts are hard to understand, we often compare them to things we already understand. Thus, the ideals and sentiments underlying our system of laws are frequently represented by a blindfolded woman holding the scales of justice. Such symbols serve the important function of helping us comprehend complex ideas by linking them to ideas or concepts that are simpler. In this way they help us make sense of reality and communicate with greater ease.

Symbols sometimes resemble the ideas they represent. For example, birds may stand for "freedom" because, to earth-bound humans, they seem to be able to go where they please. However, our use of such symbols may affect the way we perceive what they represent. When symbols are not understood as things separate from what they stand for, a great deal of intellectual and social confusion can arise. A symbol not only stands for something else, but it also conveys a certain attitude toward what it represents (Goffman, 1976). Some symbols are so charged with certain meanings that they predefine the things they represent in socially significant ways.

The symbolic "goodness" of white and the "badness" of black, for example, seem to have an influence on the way white and black people see themselves and each other. In one study, a picture-story technique was used to measure racial bias in preschool children (Williams & Stabler, 1973). The children were first shown pairs of pictures—one of a dark-skinned person, the other of a light-skinned individual. The researchers then told a story about a person. The children were asked to say which person—the dark-skinned one or the light-skinned one—the story was about. The children tended to associate the light-skinned figures with the positive stories and the dark-skinned figures with the negative stories. In effect, the negative meanings associated with the color black seem to attach themselves to black people, who are predefined to some extent as a result. This is just one example of the way in which the symbols of a culture can shape that culture, often in ways that are unexpected and undesired.

LANGUAGE. **Language,** defined simply as human speech in both its spoken and written forms, is our most important set of symbols. Through it, the ideas, values, and norms of our culture find their most complete expression. Although we use many other media—painting, music, sculpture, and dance are examples—to express culture, only language is flexible and precise enough to convey all the complex subtleties that humans can understand.

In fact, without language, much of human thought would not be possible (Crystal, 1988). Through language, children learn how their society understands the world, the past, and the future. They learn what is expected of them largely through the language of their parents, teachers, and friends. Language, therefore, is essential to social organization. It allows us to build and transmit culture more fully than any other system of symbols.

Although language is an integral part of our lives, no one knows how it began. One theory holds that language started with the imitation of sounds of nature—for example, "splash" and "roar." Another is that language arose out of spontaneous sounds prompted by pain or other strong emotions. Still another theory asserts that language developed to accompany repeated muscular acts—for example, "heave" and "haul."

A more likely explanation, however, is that early humanlike creatures began to blend calls from their primitive signal systems to create new meanings (Hockett & Ascher, 1964). Calls such as barks and squeals presumably made up a set of signals with fixed meanings. The evolution of these call systems into language would have made hunting and other cooperative activities much more effective. Groups possessing advanced language skills would be more likely to survive than those whose language skills were less developed.

Research by the noted linguist Noam Chomsky strongly suggests that human beings may have evolved a biological structure within the forebrain that facilitates the learning of language (1975). This "language acquisition device" is a general blueprint or program establishing the basic logic whereby all human languages are constructed. Chomsky calls this program a *universal grammar.* It does not, of course, include specific words or the grammatical principles of any particular language.

These features are distinctly different for every culture, but they are learned in congruence with the underlying logic of the universal grammar.

Evidence for the existence of an inherent language acquisition device comes from the fact that children in all cultures learn language at about the same age. Further, they master the same aspects of their particular language at similar rates and make similar errors—presumably reflecting principles of the universal grammar—before they master the grammatical peculiarities of their own language.

The languages of the modern world are very diverse. Certain sounds in the language of one culture are not found in others. For example, French people often have difficulty pronouncing "thin" (the French language does not have the initial *th* sound) and instead pronounce it like "sin." The sounds used in American English are not identical with the sounds used in British English. Languages also differ in the way they combine sounds to make up words, as well as in the way they combine words to make up sentences. In English, for example, word order is very important to the meaning of a sentence. In other languages, such as German, each word has an ending that indicates its meaning in relation to the others in the sentence, so word order is less important.

The vocabulary of a language also reflects the culture and environment of its speakers. Samoans, for example, who depend on fish for food, have a wealth of words to convey precise information about fishing and boating. Likewise, Arabs who live on the edge of the Sahara have many words for sand.

Some linguists and social scientists have argued that the differences among languages do not just reflect the needs and environments of their speakers but that they actually shape the way their speakers view the world. This view, developed by Edward Sapir and Benjamin Lee Whorf, is called the *Sapir-Whorf hypothesis.*

Sapir and Whorf argue that language and thought are so intimately related that the speakers of one language may actually think about the world differently than do the speakers of another. Whorf points out, for example, that English has three tenses that divide time into past, present, and future, but that the language of the Hopi Indians does not have these tenses (although it does have ways of expressing the sequential relationship of events in time). Whorf argues that, as a result, speakers of English think of time in a more objective way than do speakers of Hopi. For speakers of English, time is something that can be measured; for speakers of Hopi, it is not. Whorf suggests that this difference may explain such things as the interest of English-speaking people in record keeping, calendars, and history (Harris, 1988; Whorf, 1941).

Although symbols are found in every culture, most specific symbols are associated with a particular culture. The Chinese yin-yang symbol represents the two complementary forces of Earth and Heaven that comprise all aspects of life. The symbol of the Statue of Liberty is uniquely American.

In its "strong form," the Sapir-Whorf hypothesis asserts that "the real world is to a large extent unconsciously built up on the language habits of the group. . . . We see and hear and otherwise experience very largely as we do because the language habits of our community predispose certain choices of interpretation" (Whorf,

1941). That is, language mandates certain ways of thinking about reality because other ways simply cannot be expressed.

Abstract words can be influential in shaping the character of a culture. They are much more numerous in the modern languages of the West, especially English, than in the languages of preindustrial cultures or in those of classical antiquity. Nonetheless, the strong form of the Sapir-Whorf hypothesis probably exaggerates the importance of language in shaping human thought. In their later writings, Sapir and Whorf suggested a weaker form of the original hypothesis. According to this weaker form, language *predisposes* people to see reality in certain ways, but its effect is not nearly so constraining as the strong hypothesis suggests.

Language varies not only from culture to culture but also from group to group within a society whose members speak the same language. Regional and ethnic differences in language are well known, such as those in the United States between southerners and northerners or between people with Italian and Jewish backgrounds. Similarly, the United States and Great Britain share the same basic language but have many linguistic variations. Some groups have even created a *restricted language* of their own—a severely reduced linguistic system used only for a special activity. One such restricted language is that of American truck drivers using citizens band (CB) radios. The CB language is filled with colorful words and phrases that are generally unintelligible to outsiders. Examples of "CBese" are *bears* (police), *eyeballs* (headlights), *five-finger discount* (stolen goods), *motion lotion* (fuel), and *super cola* (beer) (Crystal, 1988).

Finally, language can reflect cultural values. A study of English as spoken in Australia suggested that certain of its linguistic practices reflect the value placed by Australians on informality, good humor, and antisentimentality. Thus, the Australian tendency to shorten words and add an "ie" or a "y" to the end (for example, *prezzie* for present and *matey* for mate) can be seen as a way of expressing jocularity and easy friendship or familiarity without sentimentality (Wierzbicka, 1986).

Values

A **value** is an idea shared by the people in a society about what is good and bad, right and wrong, desirable and undesirable. Values are general, abstract ideas that shape the ideals and goals of a society. They are usually emotionally charged and provide the basis of justification for a person's behavior (Kluckhohn, 1961; Williams, 1970).

The Asian-born refugee children mentioned at the beginning of this chapter were found to hold values that helped them to excel in math and science. One value of traditional Indochinese culture, and still transmitted from parent to child in the United States, is the central importance of the family. For example, homework is considered a shared family obligation, with older children helping younger siblings and parents freeing children from household chores to allow them ample time to study. Typically, after dinner the table is cleared, and the family does homework at the table. The average time spent by Indochinese high school students on homework was three hours and ten minutes a night, compared to about one and a half hours for American students. Naturally, such an investment brings noticeable results.

Studies of other immigrant groups have found similar values at work. Indeed, middle-class Americans traditionally emphasize educational achievement and hard work, just as Asians do, but Americans tend to feel that it is more the individual who does the achieving rather than the family (Caplan, Choy, & Whitmore, 1992).

The main values of a culture are passed on through its symbol systems. Values may be portrayed in folklore, mythology, art, entertainment, and any number of other media. Consider, for example, the English Arthurian legend, with its colorful cast of characters: King Arthur, Queen Guinevere, Sir Lancelot, Merlin, and dragons and other fabulous beasts. To this day, reading these stories allows us to admire the fatherly care bestowed by Arthur on his subjects. We approve of Lancelot's bravery and loyalty, and we are fascinated by Merlin's mysterious power and cleverness. These traits and others embody the values of medieval culture.

Like symbols, values do not exist in isolation. Rather, they relate to one another to form a unified pattern. In medieval society, the ideal of a fatherly king was consistent with the loyalty demanded of all the king's subjects, who were encouraged to view themselves as members of a "family" rather than as individuals. Our contemporary stress on individualism would have been quite inconsistent with medieval English society's values. Likewise, the value we place on profit-oriented economic life would have been quite foreign to medieval people united by "familial" bonds.

The values of a culture typically come in pairs, so that for every positive value there is a negative value. For every admired quality there is a quality that is disapproved of. For example, people in the Middle Ages admired bravery but were repelled by cowardice. Sometimes, as in the case of Lancelot, the same character embodies both positive and negative qualities. Lancelot is both a "knave" (because he carries on an extramarital affair with King Arthur's wife, Guinevere) and a "hero" (because he rescues Guinevere from being executed for infidelity).

SOCIOLOGY OF THE MEDIA

SYMBOLS IN ADVERTISING

In 1877, a small oatmeal-processing company in Ravenna, Ohio, decided to illustrate its packages with the Quaker Oats man. Today he is a cultural icon. Over the years, illustrators have updated his image by replacing his sober expression with a smile. But they have never tampered with the key to this successful trademark—its link to American culture. The Quaker Oats man reflects our history and the values on which this country was built.

Companies have used symbols like the Quaker Oats man to advertise their products since the middle of the nineteenth century (Morgan, 1987). In 1851, Procter & Gamble marked its packages with a moon and stars. Trademarks like Arm and Hammer, Bull Durham, White Owl, and the Underwood devil were introduced in the 1860s. In the following two decades a number of other symbols appeared, including the Quaker Oats man, the Smith Brothers, the Baker's chocolate waitress, the Coca-Cola signature, the Anheuser Busch eagle, and John Deere's leaping deer.

By the turn of the century, advertising symbols reflected ingrained racist attitudes. Racial stereotypes and caricatures, which Americans accepted as a common form of humor, depicted blacks in menial jobs—cheerful cooks, polite porters, dancing minstrels, and servants (Sivulka, 1998). Native Americans were shown as savage warriors selling Red Cloud Tobacco, Calumet baking powder, and Hiawatha corn. And Asian-Americans wearing long braids and Asian clothes were portrayed swallowing rats to sell products for extermination.

These kinds of images, which reinforced and shaped negative stereotypes, became familiar household personalities. In an 1897 ad for Cream of Wheat, Chef Rastus admired his own image with a caption that read: "Ah reckon as how he's de bes' known man in de worl.'" While the most offensive racial caricatures have now vanished from circulation, some, such as Aunt Jemima as a black "mammy," persisted for years. Eventually Quaker Oats changed Aunt Jemima's appearance by slimming her down, discarding her handkerchief, and giving her pearl earrings.

Like Aunt Jemima, a number of trademark personalities that were created in the early part of the twentieth century became as famous as national heroes—Buster Brown (1906), the Campbell's kids (1910), Mr. Peanut (1918), the Morton Salt girl (1921), and Cracker Jack (1924). As American as apple pie, cultural symbols like these possess the power to steal our hearts and bond one generation to the next. In contrast to symbols like the racist caricatures mentioned above, these kinds of symbols adapt to transformations in other dimensions of culture and achieve their own kind of immortality.

The "retro-marketing" of the 1990s, which revived slogans, jingles, and trade characters from earlier decades, illustrates how advertisers use transformed cultural symbols to appeal to American consumers. Consider, for example, how ads for Coppertone suntan lotion adapted to changing attitudes and values. The first ad for Coppertone suntan lotion in 1944 depicted an Indian chief with the slogan "Don't Be a Paleface" (Sivulka, 1998). Although the company kept the same slogan in 1953, a scantily clad Little Miss Coppertone replaced the Indian chief. Adapting to the health-conscious 1990s, Little Miss Coppertone changed again, donning a hat and T-shirt to pitch a suntan lotion that offers protection from the sun's ultraviolet rays. Advertisers recognized that ads with familiar personalities like Little Miss Coppertone appealed to baby boomers because they conjured up pleasant childhood memories (Sivulka, 1998).

The relationship between advertising and culture is complex. At the height of its power in the 1920s, advertising exerted considerable influence on American culture—shaping the attitudes and values of the public (Fox, 1983). Since then, it has increasingly acted as a mirror, reflecting American culture more than shaping it. And that suggests that other dimensions of American culture have actually influenced advertising.

Regardless of the direction of influence, advertising symbols are an important dimension of American culture. Whether it is the Quaker Oats man, the Nike "swoosh," the Golden Arches, or the enduring Levi's jeans patch, these symbols mark the physical objects of our culture with a distinct American identity.

How do values relate to behavior? There are two conflicting points of view on this issue (Spates, 1983). One theory holds that values mold behavior. Basic values, according to this theory, are absorbed early in a person's life. Once they are fixed, they serve as a guide in choosing behavior and in forming attitudes. According to Talcott Parsons:

There is reason to believe that, among the learned elements of personality in certain respects the stablest and most enduring are the major value-orientation patterns and there is much evidence that these are "laid down" in childhood and are not on a large scale subject to drastic alteration during adult life. (1951, p. 208)

This theory also holds that specific patterns of behavior evolve in a society because they are the logical outcome of its values. In the United States, for example, those in business set prices on the basis of what they think they can get people to pay, without the interference of government. This practice reflects the basic value of personal economic freedom. Such a value logically leads to the idea that government regulation of private exchange is wrong.

The opposing theory gives much greater attention to the independent importance of behavior in creating values (Blake & Davis, 1964). As originally stated by the pioneering American sociologist William G. Sumner (1906/1960), this theory suggests that social habits develop naturally within societies over a period of time. To justify these habits, and perhaps also to hide the fact that they may be irrational, people in the society invent abstract explanations for them. In other words, values are a kind of afterthought—explanations by which the already ingrained habits of a society are shown to be desirable.

This theory can be applied to our example of the free-market way of setting prices. Seen in this light, the American pricing system began in the context of a migration to a rich and unclaimed country in which government was very weak. In practice, the best way for an individual to become successful was to charge as high a price as the market would bear. This became a habit in doing business, and the habit was later justified, both morally and socially, by inventing the value of economic freedom.

Both points of view seem valid, and it is not easy to choose between them. As in many controversies concerning theory, some truth exists on both sides. There is indeed a set of basic values that underlies every known society. (The principal values of American society are discussed later in this chapter.) On the other hand, values do not develop overnight. They are formed, reinforced, and changed through day-to-day behavior. In this sense, it is reasonable to assert that values are preceded by behavior and that, over time, behavior shapes values as much as values shape behavior (Rokeach, 1973, 1979). In other words, the relationship between values and behavior is reciprocal.

Norms

Sociologists refer to expectations of how people are supposed to act, think, or feel in specific situations as **norms.** Norms can be either formal or informal. *Formal norms* have been written down or codified, often in the form of *laws* (see below), and carry specific punishments for violators. *Informal norms* are not written down but are widely understood by the members of a society. The most important norms are generally those shared by large segments of society. For instance, most people in American society obey the norms that prohibit murder, robbery, and strolling through one's neighborhood in the nude.

Other norms apply only to particular groups or categories of people. We think of musicians as highly unconventional people, unconcerned with rules. The fact is that, for musicians, as for all of us, there are distinct norms governing behavior. Paradoxically, one of these norms is the importance of being "different" and flouting conventional social norms. Many musicians like to tell stories of the unconventional things they have done, as in the following example:

> We played the dance and after the job was over we packed up to get back in this old bus and make it back to Detroit. A little way out of town the car just refused to go. There was plenty of gas; it just wouldn't run. These guys all climbed out and stood around griping. All of a sudden, somebody said, "Let's set it on fire!" So someone got some gas out of the tank and sprinkled it around, touching a match to it and whoosh, it just went up in smoke. What an experience! The car burning up and all these guys standing around hollering and clapping their hands. It was really something. (Becker, 1963, p. 87)

Most norms, however, are concerned with the behaviors expected of people occupying specific social positions and playing specific roles, such as mother, man, employee, or date. A physician's role in treating a patient, for example, consists of a set of norms. Doctors are expected to appear calm, stable, sympathetic, and responsible at all times. Many norms associated with doctors' roles do not apply to any other position. Yet others in the health professions may imitate the way doctors behave in an attempt to be identified with them and to win some of the respect or other rewards that doctors receive. (Social position and social role are discussed in Chapter 4.)

The noun *norm* and the related adjective *normative* should not be confused with the concept *normal.* "Normal" behavior is behavior that is statistically most common. It is not normal to be left-handed or to have red hair, but both traits are normatively acceptable—that is, regarded as right and proper.

Although values and norms are closely related, the two should not be confused. *Norms* are specific, concrete, and situation-bound. They are usually expressed as behavioral guidelines: One should or should not act in a particular fashion. *Values* are general, and often serve as a standard by which norms may be judged (Williams, 1970). Our society, for example, values financial success. Certain norms govern the way we may seek to legitimately achieve that value—getting an education, starting a business and trying to make a profit, or obtaining a job and seeking promotions.

FOLKWAYS. Norms vary greatly in their social importance. Many can be broken without serious consequence. For example, although men are currently expected to wear their hair relatively short, some still wear their hair very long or even in a ponytail. There are norms against such behavior, but they have little strength and may, within broad limits, be easily broken. Norms like these are called *folkways,* or social customs (Sumner, 1906/1960). Rules specifying expected table manners or other rules of etiquette provide another example.

MORES. Some norms are almost considered sacred, and violating them is likely to result in serious consequences. When a person violates the norm against murder, his or her action will not be excused or overlooked on the grounds that it happened only once. The murderer will be punished. Strongly held norms that are considered essential and are strictly enforced (like the norm prohibiting murder) are called *mores* (pronounced MOR-aiz).

Mores can be either prescriptive or proscriptive. *Prescriptive mores* state what a person *must do,* such as care for infants and children who are unable to care for themselves. *Proscriptive mores* state what a person *must not do,* such as break into other people's homes. A particularly strong proscriptive more is a *taboo.* One proscriptive more that is a cultural universal is the incest taboo—a powerful moral prohibition against sexual relations between certain categories of relatives.

LAWS. **Laws** are formal norms, usually mores, that have been enacted by the state to regulate human conduct. It is possible for an action to be illegal (against the law) but at the same time acceptable when judged by certain informal social norms. For example, many people in the United States under the age of 21 drink alcohol. Although this behavior is technically illegal, the informal norms of society sometimes allow the law to be overlooked. Most police officers would not arrest a man who gives his 14-year-old son a sip of beer, and underage drinking has often been overlooked on college campuses as long as it goes on "behind closed doors."

Sanctions

If a society is to operate, it must have some way to enforce its norms. People must be made to *conform,* or behave in socially acceptable ways, even when it is hard or unpleasant for them to do so. Violation of the norms of a society is called *deviance.* Conformity is encouraged through the pressure of **sanctions,** a process known as *social control* (Gibbs, 1966, 1981). (Deviant behavior and social control are the subjects of Chapter 8.) Sanctions can be either positive or negative. A *positive sanction* is a reward for behaving as expected and desired. A *negative sanction* is a punishment for violating significant norms.

Body piercing can be considered a folkway. There are norms against such behavior, but they have little strength and may, within broad limits, be easily broken.

Sanctions range from *formal* (those applied by a person or group in a position of authority) to *informal* (those applied by one's friends or peers). An example of a formal negative sanction is the three-year jail sentence given to a man who was caught robbing a grocery store. Examples of formal positive sanctions are a promotion given to an employee who has faithfully served the company's interests, and a cash reward paid to a young girl who tells the FBI the license number of the car she saw leaving the scene of a bank robbery.

Formal sanctions are often a last resort, used only after informal sanctions have failed. Informal sanctions appear constantly in the course of daily life. For example, a West Point cadet who has broken the honor code is likely to be rejected by his or her peers. A spectator at the opera dressed in jeans and a ripped T-shirt may receive informal negative sanctions in the form of icy stares from other opera patrons. Some studies have suggested that informal sanctions can be more effective than formal sanctions (Hollinger & Clark, 1982).

Sociological research has pointed to the many highly imaginative informal sanctions that occur within groups (Blau & Scott, 1962). Some examples of common negative sanctions were observed by a team studying a

Artifacts found when archeologists dig up the remains of ancient cities help to reconstruct some of the nonmaterial values and norms of the culture.

group of factory workers. These workers kept a greater than normal physical distance from, and walked a longer route to avoid passing the desk of, a worker being sanctioned. They did not laugh at that person's jokes, failed to express sympathy over the worker's problems, and violated his or her normal rights of privacy. To express approval of someone's behavior—a positive informal sanction—the members of the working group might say the person's name frequently, often addressing him or her by name before making any remark. They might pat the person on the back, or they might adopt a suggestion he or she made about work procedures.

Extensive sanctions are usually not needed in everyday social behavior, however, precisely because most norms are accepted by members of society in the course of their upbringing. In fact, the crucial test of how well norms are functioning is the degree to which people follow them of their own free will.

Finally, it is important to add that it is not desirable that an individual or group obey the norms too consistently. Culture and society must be able to adapt to changing conditions. Allowing some deviation from current norms may help keep a society flexible (Merton, 1968).

Material Culture

The physical objects that are typically found within a society—machines, tools, books, clothing, and so on—are called *material culture*. For many thousands of years, human beings have been using the elements of their natural surroundings to increase their chances for survival and to enrich their lives. They have turned soil, trees, rocks, metals, animals, and other natural resources into shelter, tools, clothes, and forms of communication.

The nature of the material culture produced by a given society is a function of, among other things, the society's level of technology, the resources available to it, and the needs of its people. Modern societies have access to minerals, enormous labor pools, and highly advanced technology. When we apply these material and nonmaterial resources to the problem of transportation, for example, we produce cars, trucks, trains, airplanes, and other kinds of vehicles. Because pre-twentieth-century Plains Indians had a much more limited set of resources, a less elaborate technology, and more modest needs, they solved the problem of transportation more simply. They carried their possessions on their backs or used a travois—a horse-drawn vehicle made up of two trailing poles supporting a platform or net.

When archeologists dig up the remains of an ancient city, it is the material culture that they find: a broken pot, a necklace carefully stored in a little wooden box, the foundations of a house. From these *artifacts*—articles made or used by humans—they are able to reconstruct some of the nonmaterial values and norms of the culture.

The meanings of artifacts may vary from culture to culture, and may even have contrary meanings in different societies. An object that we might interpret as a baby's rattle may be used by various Indian tribes in religious ceremonies. A bowl used for eating in one culture might serve the purpose of collecting alms in another. A colored piece of cloth we honor and revere as our national flag might be viewed by another culture as nothing but material for clothing.

People create material culture and people can change it. But we can also think of developing material culture as a part of social life to which elements of nonmaterial culture—norms, values, language, traditions, and the like—must adapt. For example, the invention of the automobile, which was condemned by early twentieth-century social critics as a "bedroom on wheels," and the later introduction of the birth control pill have profoundly altered many aspects of American sexual norms and values. Similarly, advances in modern medical technology have forced us to rethink many important ethical issues surrounding the question of when death actually occurs.

ANALYZING CULTURE

Although most social scientists normally study some aspects of culture, their work is usually not called *cultural analysis* unless they try to describe and understand a culture as a whole. Analyzing a whole culture involves identifying its major values and norms, seeing how they are reflected in social behavior, and studying the way in which they shape and are shaped by the material culture.

Describing and analyzing premodern cultures have been the main tasks of cultural anthropologists. The analysis of modern cultures is the primary concern of sociologists. Although anthropology and sociology come from different traditions and draw on the work of different scholars, today they are quite similar in interest and approach. Many cultural anthropologists are studying modern as well as premodern cultures, and sociologists are indebted to anthropology for many concepts and techniques useful in cultural analysis.

Perspectives on Cultural Analysis

When looking at the belief system, rituals, institutions, or other aspects of a culture, the sociologist or anthropologist usually starts by asking a fundamental question: "Why does this aspect of culture exist?" Social scientists examine this question from a variety of perspectives. In this section, we look at three of the most important perspectives: the functionalist, the conflict, and the ecological.

THE FUNCTIONALIST PERSPECTIVE

From the functionalist perspective (introduced in Chapter 1), a particular aspect of culture is seen as existing because it serves an important social function. One of the most widely used perspectives on cultural analysis, functionalism was the main approach of leading British anthropologists before it became popular in American sociology after World War II. To answer the question of why an aspect of culture exists, the functionalist asks a further question: "What functions does it serve?" The perspective stresses the contributions, both positive and negative, that a unit of culture makes to the society as a whole.

An excellent example of the use of the functionalist perspective is the explanation by the classic British anthropologist A. R. Radcliffe-Brown (1952) of childbirth practices among the Andaman Islanders, who live off the coast of India. The following cultural facts were to be explained: When an Andaman Island woman is expecting a child, the baby is named while it is still in the womb. From that time until the baby is born, nobody is allowed to call the parents-to-be by their personal names. Instead, they must be referred to in terms of their relationship to the child. Also, during this period both parents must not eat certain foods that are normally part of their diet.

The islanders believe that these practices magically ensure the safe delivery of the child. But Radcliffe-Brown determined that they also serve important latent social functions of which the islanders were generally not aware. According to Radcliffe-Brown, the practice of calling parents by names that show their relationship to the child may strengthen their sense of being parents and improve the chances that they will properly fulfill their parental roles. Similarly, not eating certain foods may dispose them toward attitudes of self-sacrifice in their new parental roles. Thus, cultural practices that appear to have little practical utility actually serve an important social need.

One of the most widely discussed and controversial functional analyses of American culture was developed by Herbert Gans (1971), who identified the positive functions of American poverty. Compared to other wealthy, industrial societies, America has a much higher percentage of poor people, yet provides fewer government programs to combat poverty. This lack of government effort is commonly explained by the fact that Americans see their nation as "the land of opportunity" and therefore tend to feel that poverty is the fault of those who are poor. Anyone can get ahead, it is said, who wants to get ahead. Yet Gans suggested that a latent reason why so little is done about poverty in America is that the poor serve important social functions. Most importantly, without the poor, society's "dirty work"—menial jobs, requiring no special training or education—would not get done. Thus, despite the high value placed on equality, American society has a stake in keeping part of the population poor.

THE CONFLICT PERSPECTIVE

From the conflict perspective (introduced in Chapter 1), a particular aspect of culture is seen as existing because it protects or promotes the interests of one group over another. A basic assumption of this perspective is that there are, or may be, conflicting cultural traits in a society, each of which promotes the interests of different interest groups or social classes. Using this perspective, sociologists try to find out which groups support which ideas, values, and beliefs, and for what reasons.

Central to the conflict perspective is the concept of **ideology**—a set of cultural beliefs that legitimates or justifies the interests of a class, group, or other sector of society in its struggle with other groups for prestige and dominance. Marxian cultural analysts argue that ideologies primarily serve the purpose of defending (or challenging) the power of economically defined social classes. Thus, the widespread acceptance in America of the view that anyone who works hard can expect to achieve economic success would be interpreted in Marxian thought as an ideology that serves to deflect calls for fundamental economic reform and therefore helps to defend the power and privileges of the economic elite.

Counterideologies may arise that support the interests of subordinate groups. In America, these counterideologies range from the moderate challenge to the status quo provided by the reformist left wing of the Democratic party to radical ideologies such as those supported in the early twentieth century by pro-communist labor unions like the International Workers of the World. These movements flatly denied the right of the capitalist elite to rule and demanded dramatic changes in the fundamental institutions of American society.

Other conflict ideologies focus less explicitly on economics. For example, in recent years, American cultural conservatives have rallied around a set of ideological beliefs that are sometimes referred to as "traditional American family values" while their opponents adhere to a different ideology that emphasizes the right of each individual to choose the way he or she will live. The conflict approach identifies similar contesting ideologies in a variety of other important struggles, including those between industrialists and environmentalists, advocates and foes of gay rights, and African-American integrationists and separatists, among many others.

A historical example of the conflict approach to cultural analysis is provided by Guy Swanson's study *Religion and Regime* (1967). Swanson set out to show that during the sixteenth century various princes of Europe embraced either Catholicism or Protestantism, depending on which religion best served as an ideology to support their political authority. The princes were fighting a series of religious wars that could be understood as struggles for power between minor princes and central kings. According to Catholicism, the pope and, to a lesser extent, the kings who were governed by the Church were representatives of God on earth. The strong central kings, Swanson reasoned, would naturally prefer this belief and therefore choose Catholicism, which would function as a cultural buttress to their political power. By contrast, Protestantism emphasized a more private, individual experience of God and tended to undermine the authority of the central kings. The lesser princes, Swanson believed, would naturally prefer this doctrine.

Swanson found that both the kings and the princes did indeed espouse religious ideologies that promoted and protected their interests. The kings adhered to Catholicism because this religion affirmed the power of a central authority, whereas the princes preferred Protestantism because it advocated exactly the opposite: an emphasis on individualism and much less reliance on a centralized source of authority.

THE ECOLOGICAL PERSPECTIVE

A third perspective on the analysis of culture draws on *ecology,* the study of the relationship between organisms and their environments. Cultural ecology asserts that culture traits are shaped by the resources and limitations of the surrounding environment and by changes in that environment.

The anthropologist Julian Steward (1955), who laid much of the foundation for the ecological approach, compared the cultures of different societies with the same level of subsistence technology. Each of the societies used bows, spears, and deadfalls in order to hunt animals. Steward theorized that the culture of the societies would vary with the kind of animals they hunted. He hypothesized that if the main game animals were found in large migrating herds, as are bison and caribou, the societies that hunt these animals would tend to be fairly large and organized into multifamily groups. This is because these societies would have to develop large-scale cooperative hunting practices. If, on the other hand, the game was found in small, scattered herds that did not migrate, the societies would tend to be small and organized into single-family groups. Steward cited three societies that hunt small game but in radically different environments as evidence to support his hypothesis. The San, who live in the desert; the Negritos, who live in a rain forest; and the Fuegians, who live on a cold, rainy coastal plain—all exhibit the culture expected of small-game hunters.

Although it is easy to see how the economic activities of a society are affected by environmental conditions, it is even more revealing to see how cultural elements in other areas—religion, law, science, art—are strongly influenced by environmental factors. In a controversial study, the anthropologist Marvin Harris (1989) explained the Aztec practice of ritual human sacrifice and cannibalism in terms of the nutritional needs of the population. Harris believes that no custom can survive if it does not help adapt a population to its environment. Because the Aztecs did not raise large animals, they lacked an adequate source of protein in their diet. The cannibalistic ritual arose and persisted because it filled this nutritional requirement.

Although the ecological approach is useful for explaining some culture traits, it cannot explain all of them. It would be difficult, for example, to account for the variations in governments found in the modern world solely in terms of their environments. Democratic Costa Rica exists in essentially the same ecological region of the world as do its neighbors Honduras and Nicaragua, which have tended toward dictatorial rule over much of their history.

The Diversity and Unity of Culture

CULTURAL DIVERSITY

Each culture is different because it is adapted to meet a specific set of conditions, both physical and social. Cultural ecologists have made us aware of the principal factors that help shape a culture—climate, geography, population, plant and animal life. A society of people who live in the South Seas is not going to obtain food by hunting seals and polar bears. The physical environment requires them to eat the fruit that grows there and to learn how to fish in lagoons or the open sea. This type of environment is associated with settled communities. Magic or religious rites intended to ensure the safety of the fishermen are also likely to develop. And living in a warm and fertile climate may mean that it takes less time to meet the basic needs of survival—food and shelter—so more attention can be devoted to developing art and ritual.

But physical conditions, important as they are, often have less influence on a culture than do social factors, particularly in complex societies. Social factors include the society's level of technology, its language, its prevailing beliefs, and the extent of its contact with other cultures. Social factors such as these determine how each particular South Seas society is governed, whether the incantations over the departing fishing fleet are uttered by a priest or a magician, and whether the society's art is more likely to depict love or aggression.

CULTURAL UNIVERSALS

It is easy to place too much stress on cultural differences, however. Comparative research in anthropology has shown that all cultures share many basic social structures and cultural meanings, commonly referred to as **cultural universals.** One anthropologist has listed some 60 cultural universals, including cooking, feasting, folklore, funeral rites, music, and laws (Murdock, 1956).

All human beings are basically alike biologically, which may explain many of the known cultural universals. We all must eat and find shelter. We all must take care of young and helpless children, deal with the problem of aging and ill parents, and face death.

Other cultural universals stem from the basic requirements of human social life. In order to function, every society must replace people when they die, leave, or become ill or infirm. It must teach new members to play useful roles. It must produce and distribute goods and services, preserve order, and maintain a sense of purpose. No society, if it is to survive, is exempt from these requirements.

Cultural universals are also related to what is possible in, or limited by, the natural environment. Nearly every culture has used fire for heat and light. Nearly every society has created a form of bread. No group uses a square wheel, because it does not work.

Marriage and the family are two important cultural universals. Every society is characterized by a division of labor by sex, and every society must raise its children. A human society that has no marriage and no family system has not yet been found. However, as with other universals, the *specific form* of marriage and the family may vary significantly from one society to another.

Ethnocentrism and Cultural Relativity

The first descriptions of other cultures by travelers and missionaries were often highly biased. The people who wrote the reports tended to judge the cultures they were observing by the standards of their own. They often labeled customs that were incompatible with their values and beliefs as uncivilized or barbaric, but praised and accepted those that conformed to their values. This tendency to evaluate other cultures in terms of one's own, and to automatically evaluate one's own culture as superior, is called **ethnocentrism.**

Today anthropologists and sociologists who study other cultures try very hard to avoid ethnocentrism. Because everyone has both consciously and unconsciously accepted a particular set of norms and values, it is not possible to be totally unbiased when analyzing another culture. But the first principle of cultural analysis is that every culture should be judged as much as possible on its own terms. This principle, known as **cultural relativity,** holds that one cannot truly understand or evaluate cultural traits except in terms of the larger cultural and social system of which they are a part.

The painful conflict between objective judgment of another culture and emotional commitment to one's own is apparent even in the life of so careful a scientist as Franz Boas, one of the first American anthropologists. To a reader of his books, essays, and even his collected field observations, Boas sounds extremely detached and objective. But his personal diaries and the letters he wrote to his family reveal the struggle between his ideal of objective observation and his personal values. Telling of his work with the Indian tribes of the Canadian Northwest, particularly the Eskimos and the Bella Coolas, he wrote:

> Then I went to the Bella Coolas, who told me another idiotic story. . . . The fact that I obtain these stories is interesting, but the stories themselves are more horrible than some of the Eskimo stories. (Diary entry, October 3, 1886)
>
> In the meantime, screaming dirty children run about; sometimes a meal is eaten. Dogs and children force their way between the people; fires smoke so that one can hardly see. . . . In short, the whole thing is a test of patience. (November 8, 1886) (Yampolsky, 1958)

Ethnocentrism can serve a positive function in societies. If people believe that the norms and values of their culture are right and good, they will be more likely

TABLE 3.1	COMMON ITEMS AND THEIR ORIGINS
Item	*Country of Origin*
Cigars	Brazil
Coffee	Abyssinia
Forks	Medieval Italy
Glass	Ancient Egypt
Pajamas	East India
Rubber	Ancient Mexico
Silk	China
Soap	Ancient Gual
Towels	Turkey
Trains	England
Umbrellas	India
Waffles	Scandinavia

Source: Ralph Linton, "The One Hundred Percent American," *The American Mercury,* 40 (1937): 427–429.

to conform to them. This, in turn, promotes social order and stability. But extreme ethnocentrism can lead to social isolation by preventing cultural exchanges that promote growth and development. And ethnocentrism can be politically misused. Hitler used an extreme form of ethnocentrism—the glorification of German culture—as a means of increasing his popularity.

In today's world, too much ethnocentrism is undesirable because nations have become so dependent on one another. The world's economic development and even its survival depend in part on our ability to appreciate the cultures of others. Table 3.1 lists just a few of the many items common in American life that have their origins in foreign countries. On the other hand, *xenocentrism*—the belief that other cultures are better than one's own—should also be avoided. Xenocentrism is sometimes referred to as "reverse ethnocentrism."

Subcultures

Not every society is characterized by a single culture that is equally shared and accepted by all members of that society. What is called a society's culture is often only a common strand found among the diverse cultural elements of which it is composed.

When a group of people within a society has a style of living that includes features of the main culture and also certain distinctive cultural elements not found in other groups, the group culture is called a **subculture.** A subculture may develop around occupations, such as those in the

medical or military field. It may reflect a racial or ethnic difference, as does the subculture of African-Americans. A subculture may be based on regionalism, as in the case of southerners, or on national origins, as with Mexican-Americans or Italian-Americans. Members of these ethnic subcultures have partly adapted to mainstream American culture as a consequence of their residence in the United States but have also maintained some distinctly non-American norms, values, and language patterns.

Every complex modern society contains many subcultures. Individual members of a society often function in more than one subculture, and they may pass through different subcultures over the course of life. Among the most visible of these temporary subcultures are a variety of adolescent groupings closely associated with specific types of popular music that have thrived and then faded away after a few years. Most of the specifics of these subcultures vary from era to era, but all of them are fueled by adolescent rebellion against parents, teachers, and other authority figures. In the 1950s, the most widely publicized of these subcultures was one organized around early rock 'n' roll, black leather jackets, and "ducktail" and "beehive" hairstyles. In the 1960s, folk and protest music generated an important subculture; in the 1970s, disco did the same; in the 1980s, the punk rock subculture was popular; and on the contemporary scene, we can see the alternative rock and hip hop (or rap) subcultures.

A subculture that directly challenges the values, beliefs, ideals, institutions, or other central aspects of the dominant culture is known as a **counterculture.** Countercultures are often found among the young. The hippie counterculture of the late 1960s, for example, strongly rejected established lifestyles and directly opposed popular beliefs about the desirability of work, patriotism, and material possessions (Gitlin, 1987). Other examples of countercultures include the Ku Klux Klan, the Amish, and the Branch Davidian movement led by David Koresh that was destroyed in a 1993 raid on its Waco, Texas, headquarters.

Cultural Integration

Many of the elements of modern American culture seem to be consistent with one another. Our belief in science, the value placed on material progress, the emphasis on efficiency, the material products of modern technology—all these seem to form a consistent whole. When cultural traits are logically consistent with one another, we say that a culture displays a high level of **cultural integration.**

Cultural integration can be seen in relatively limited parts of a culture as well as in a culture as a whole. For example, in Christianity the confession of sins, the absolution of sins through the communion service, and the emphasis given to Jesus' teaching about turning the other cheek are all logically consistent expressions of the central Christian value of forgiveness.

However, cultural elements may also sometimes contradict one another. That is, they may be logically inconsistent. For example, the norms of a society may not be fully consistent with its values. As a result, people may not always practice what they preach. This can happen, for instance, when they find that in order to succeed, they must deviate from such values as honesty, openness, and fair play. It also occurs when a society goes to war yet argues that it is doing so in order to secure peace and other life-sustaining values. Sometimes sociologists refer to such a clash between what people believe and what they actually do as a contrast between *ideal culture* and *real culture*.

Instances of cultural contradiction may also arise when elements of one culture conflict with elements of another into which they are introduced. When this happens, the members of the receiving society often feel ambivalent about the changing norms and values. For example, many Asian immigrants to America have great difficulty in adjusting to what they see as the excessive sexual permissiveness of American society. Similarly, many Asian families, which are traditionally very close-knit, experience culture shock when they are exposed to the high rates of separation and divorce in the United States.

Finally, cultural components may be neither integrated nor contradictory, but simply neutral in relation to one another. For instance, a clothing designer might create a new fashion at the same time as an inventor develops a new kind of computer. One has little or no relationship to the other. Human societies are so complex that many beliefs, practices, and innovations can coexist without much interrelationship.

Cultural Change

Although the last chapter in this book is devoted solely to cultural and social change, our discussion of cultural analysis here would not be complete without a brief introduction to the topic. Cultural change is both necessary and inevitable. The natural and social environments constantly change, and so must the relationship of any human society to them. Cultural change can be set in motion by developments within a culture or by the influence of foreign cultures. Within a culture, change can result from a wide variety of tensions, conflicts, and new developments. A common source of cultural change from within is *innovation*, the development of a new culture trait—a new idea, norm, or artifact. Sometimes an entirely new culture trait is created, for example, atomic energy. At other times an existing trait is adapted to a new

The Amish are an example of a subculture contained within a complex modern society. Much of their lives are lived within the confines of their own culture, yet they still must cope with a broader modern society.

situation, such as the use of laser technology in surgery. Cultural change can also be brought about by *cultural diffusion*, the process by which traits or patterns are transmitted from one group or society to another.

Cultures can come into contact with one another for many reasons, including trade, travel, and warfare. In the modern world, most cultures are especially closely connected with one another through the mass media and trade. Over the last 200 years, expanded communication and transportation have made far more contact possible than ever before. Not all of this contact has been gradual—or friendly. In some cases, military, political, and commercial interests have prompted members of one society to conquer, dominate, and exploit other groups. In these cases, cultural contact often does violence to the beliefs and customs of the less powerful society.

AMERICAN VALUES

Because the United States is the society most often analyzed and discussed in this book, it is helpful to give an overview of one main aspect of American culture: the shared values and beliefs that give coherence and meaning to American life. Such an overview also provides a chance to look more closely at the culture of one particular society.

The values that are found in American culture are so familiar to us that it is hard to notice them. They blend into the background of our lives, as does water in the lives of fish. They are basic assumptions we take for granted. Yet, from the time we are born to the moment of our death, our culture shapes us. If the culture were different, we would not be the same people that we are.

A hurricane relief effort is an example of moral concern and humanitarianism. Americans are often generous when people are in distress through no fault of their own.

The American people are diverse in ethnicity, occupation, and religion. The United States, therefore, has one of the world's most varied cultures. Coal miners and corporate executives, African-Americans and Chinese-Americans, Bostonians of Irish Catholic descent and Creoles from New Orleans—all are part of American society and add to its culture. Despite this variety, however, certain value patterns can be clearly identified.

Traditional American Values

In his study *American Society: A Sociological Interpretation,* Robin M. Williams, Jr. (1970), identified a set of American values that provides the basis for the discussion in this section. But many other social scientists have isolated a similar set of shared American values. These observations have been confirmed by foreign visitors, who recognize the same "typically American" traits, and by opinion polls taken among American citizens, whose responses show that they still believe in what Gunnar Myrdal (1962) referred to as the "American Creed." Williams listed the following traditional American values:

PERSONAL ACHIEVEMENT. One of the most prized of all American values is personal achievement. Ideally, Americans honor and reward those who produce, accomplish, and achieve, especially when this is done through hard work. A person's worth is often equated with his or her achievements in business, the arts, or some other important area of American life. But the stress on achievement, especially as measured by economic status, conflicts with the idea that one should be respected simply for who one is.

WORK. American society was founded on hard work. The settlers who pioneered in the wilderness had to work hard not only to achieve a better life but also just to survive. Moreover, the country's abundant natural resources provided a strong incentive to make the most of what was available. And as the settlers saw that the labor of a farmer, trapper, or miner brought wealth not only to that individual but also to the community at large, they came to value work as a means of achieving a better life. The open, fluid social structure of the new country promised "room at the top" for those willing to work hard. Work for its own sake continues to be a dominant value in American culture.

MORAL CONCERN AND HUMANITARIANISM. As part of their devout religious faith, America's first settlers showed deep concern for the welfare of others less fortunate than themselves. Americans do not always put these ideals into practice, however. Sometimes these values contradict certain other equally strong values. For example, the American ideal of personal achievement makes it hard for many Americans to accept welfare programs. To them, it is wrong for part of society to support those who do not work. But when people are in distress clearly through no fault of their own (victims of a drought, for example), Americans are often generous. The struggle to resolve contradictions between key values such as personal achievement and moral concern is often difficult and can easily lead to confusion and instability at the individual level.

EFFICIENCY AND PRACTICALITY. Americans tend to judge things on the basis of practicality: Does it work? Will it pay off? This emphasis stems partly from the American frontier tradition. The dangers of the frontier left American pioneers with contempt for tools, weapons, or even people that were not efficient or practical.

As a practical people, Americans like to solve whatever problems are at hand as quickly as possible. Americans value technology and have a strong desire to control the physical world. They are less willing to pursue long-term, visionary goals.

PROGRESS AND MATERIAL ADVANCEMENT. As a nation based largely on hope, America has always found the idea of progress attractive. One source of this value was the stress placed on work, which led to the belief that toil would help to bring about a better world. Early Americans strove to increase their levels of material prosperity and comfort. This effort caused the idea of progress to be linked with technological change: If it was new, it was bound to be better. As the ideas of progress and material advancement became intertwined, they both came to symbolize "the good life." It is no wonder, then, that American corporations adopt such slogans as "progress is our most important product," and advertisers constantly try to entice us to buy their products because they are "new" and "improved."

EQUALITY. The early colonists, drawn mostly from the middle and lower classes, tended to reject rigid class distinctions. Many of the social inequalities of the Old World dissolved in America. The country's vast natural resources, which provided plenty for all, further strengthened the concept of equality.

Like most major American values, equality comes into conflict with other values and is not always followed in the practices of society. Again, we see the contrast between ideal and real culture. One argument used to justify the obvious lack of equality in American life is that conforming to this value requires only that everyone be guaranteed an equal *opportunity* to achieve success, although even by this modified standard, America falls short of living up to this value. Nevertheless, many members of the upper and middle classes explain their privileged position in society as fair reward for their greater personal achievement, which is also an American value.

FREEDOM. Of the many values in American culture, none is more highly regarded than freedom. To Americans, the word *freedom* means both a lack of restraints on their behavior and the specific, positive forms of freedom. These include freedom of the press, freedom to gather peacefully, freedom to maintain a multiparty government, and freedom of private enterprise.

Although Americans accept some limits on their freedom, most distrust any central government that becomes too powerful or tells a person how to live. This distrust is justified by the belief that people should run their own lives.

This American skepticism regarding government control leads to an ongoing conflict in our culture between the two values of freedom and equality (Lipset, 1963). Without government control, some people will inevitably become both wealthy and extremely powerful. However, great extremes of wealth tend to go hand in hand with the oppression of the poor and disadvantaged, which violates our strong acceptance of the value of equality or at least of equal opportunity. In an effort to resolve this contradiction, Americans have emphasized the importance of mass public education and the policy that the rich should pay a greater portion of their income in taxes than the poor.

NATIONALISM AND PATRIOTISM. Most Americans believe that their way of life is the best and that it should be adopted in other lands. Even today, citizens who offer constructive criticism of American society are sometimes thought to be unpatriotic.

TABLE 3.2	MEANS OF PERSONAL VALUE RANKINGS FOR AMERICAN AND ENGLISH ADULTS	

Personal Values	United States	England
1. Good health	7.86	8.25
2. Happy marriage	6.38	7.37
3. Meaningful life	6.29	5.43
4. Sense of peace	5.85	5.28
5. Close friends	4.76	5.64
6. Control of life	4.71	4.06
7. Respect from others	4.43	4.48
8. Having children	4.01	4.40
9. Good in work	3.76	3.69
10. Moral purpose	2.33	2.67
11. Sense of teamwork	2.15	2.38
12. Earning a lot of money	1.60	1.61

Note: Rankings are scored ranging from 0 (least important) to 10 (most important).

Source: H. Wesley Perkins and James L. Spates, "Mirror Images? Three Analyses of Values in England and the United States," *International Journal of Comparative Sociology,* 27 (1986): 31–50.

It is interesting to note that recent sociological studies have found a strong similarity in personal values between citizens of the United States and residents of England. As Table 3.2 shows, both American and English urban adults ranked "good health" and "happy marriage" as the most important of 12 personal values and "moral purpose," "sense of teamwork" and "earning a lot of money" as the least important. However, the strength with which specific values are held differs between the two countries. Marriage and friends mean more to the English; a "meaningful life" has more significance for Americans. It has been suggested that these differences reflect an underlying dissimilarity between the two cultures: a stronger collective orientation in England and a more individualistic outlook in the United States (Perkins & Spates, 1986).

Other Analyses of American Values

Although Robin Williams, Jr., noted that certain American values conflict with one another, he did not stress such conflict as a major factor in American culture. Neither did he discuss at length how these values are related to each other. But conflict and the relationships between values have been the focus of analyses developed by other sociologists in recent decades. In addition, some scholars suggest that major American values may be in a process of dramatic change.

.NET INTERNET/TECHNOLOGY

CYBERPORN AND AMERICAN VALUES

When the founding fathers of this nation amended the Bill of Rights to the Constitution in 1791, they created a legal document that guaranteed the widest protection of individual freedom ever written (Alderman & Kennedy, 1991). Nowhere is this more evident than in the First Amendment, which reads:

> Congress shall make no law respecting an establishment of religion, or prohibiting the free exercise thereof; or abridging the freedom of speech, or of the press; or the right of the people peaceably to assemble, and to petition the Government for a redress of grievances.

Society has changed dramatically since the authors of this document considered how future generations would interpret its meaning. As the wording of this amendment indicates, for example, they had considered the only existing form of mass media at the time—the print media (Croteau & Hoynes, 1997). But they were fully aware that governments had a clear interest in controlling the free flow of communication. They had witnessed European governments persecute authors, printers, and publishers. Taxes on newsprint, laws that required licenses to publish, and the vigorous prosecution of libel suits—all served to restrain the press.

In seeking to prevent this kind of control, the United States adopted the "hands-off" policy that is embodied in the First Amendment (Croteau & Hoynes, 1997). This worked particularly well for print media, but the later emergence of broadcast media presented some problems and led to the creation of a new set of rules. Now the Internet, which promises to dominate the media in the next century, presents its own unique set of challenges for the First Amendment.

Praised as the most democratic form of media yet to exist, the Internet's danger lies in its abuse—as a vehicle for the distribution of pornography. *Cyberporn,* as it is known, grabbed national attention in July 1995 when it appeared as the cover story of *Time* magazine. According to the article, cyberporn is not only popular, it is pervasive and strikingly perverse. Indeed, in an 18-month study carried out by a team at Carnegie Mellon University, researchers examined 917,410 sexually explicit pictures, descriptions, short stories, and film clips. Particularly troubling were the kinds of hard-core sex pictures that are not widely available—pedophilia (nude photos of children), hebephilia (youths), and various forms of paraphilia, including images of bondage, sadomasochism, urination, defecation, and sex acts involving animals.

As the *Time* story pointed out, "This is the flip side of Vice President Al Gore's vision of an information superhighway linking every school and library in the land." It not only raises parental concerns about children being exposed to the seamiest side of sexuality, but it also instills the fear that child molesters are lurking in electronic chat rooms.

In response to these kinds of concerns, President Clinton signed the Communication Decency Act into law on February 8, 1996. As a subsection to the 1996 Telecommunication Act, the CDA outlawed the display of "indecent" material on the Internet and online services without a screening mechanism to keep minors out. Violators were subject to prison terms of two years and a $250,000 fine.

PARSONS' VIEWPOINT

Talcott Parsons (1964, 1967), whose theories of society greatly emphasize the significance of cultural values, felt that the dominant value pattern in American society could be termed *instrumental activism.* By *activism,* Parsons meant that Americans favor mastery of the environment, rather than the more passive lifestyle of, say, Buddhists. By *instrumental,* he was pointing to the fact that American society is not directed toward specific high-level or "ultimate" goals or values so much as it is committed to very general "improvement" or "progress." The main values that it endorses—efficiency, economic development, science, and the pursuit of knowledge—are simply *instruments* for achieving individual and collective human happiness.

Parsons emphasized that American culture has been strongly influenced by the moral and spiritual tradition of Puritanism. Puritans held the view that all people are instruments of the Divine Will and as such must be committed to working actively for a better world. Their concern was to build a Kingdom of God in this world, rather than waiting for "the next one." And the Puritans believed that individuals are capable of, and fully responsible for, guiding their own actions in a way that expresses this basic religious commitment. Instrumental activism, therefore, implies that the good society is one in which each person is actively working for the common good of all.

A coalition of some 50 plaintiffs, ranging from the American Civil Liberties Union to the American Library Association, launched a challenge to this act, arguing that the law violated the First Amendment. In fact, while the CDA was supposed to make the Net safe for children, the legislation was so vague and broad that uploading *Ulysses* to the World Wide Web could be construed as a felony (Quittner, 1998).

While the First Amendment has successfully protected the media from many government attempts to regulate the content of media, *obscenity* is not protected speech. But what is *obscene*? That question had plagued the U.S. Supreme Court in the past and was particularly destined to create problems for cyberporn.

In *Miller* v. *California* (1973), the Court created three guidelines for establishing whether material was obscene:

1. whether the average person, applying contemporary community standards, would find that it appeals directly to prurient (obscene) interest

2. whether the material depicts or describes, in a patently offensive way, sexual conduct specifically defined by the applicable state law

3. whether the material, taken as a whole, lacks serious literary, artistic, political, or scientific value

According to this three-pronged test, a book, movie, song, television or radio program, magazine article, or any other form of media is legally obscene if it fits all three criteria. Broadcast media are, moreover, subject to even stricter standards than print media when it comes to nudity, language, and sex. Rooted in the idea that airwaves are a scarce public resource, broadcasters are subject to tighter control because they operate under licenses granted by the federal government. So one of the issues that the Supreme Court needed to consider was whether the Internet was more like print or broadcast media. Another problem that this three-pronged test created was its reference to contemporary community standards. Determining how to apply this guideline has been difficult for cases involving other types of media, and it will be particularly challenging for a medium that has essentially erased all community boundaries.

In June 1997, the U.S. Supreme Court decided that the Internet was indeed more like print media, and the justices unanimously ruled that the CDA was unconstitutional. Writing on their decision, the judges described the Internet as "a profoundly democratic channel for communication that should be nurtured, not stifled" (Quittner, 1998). And they claimed that it deserved as much constitutional protection as print media, if not more.

Despite the Court's decision, cyberporn is destined to remain an issue for years to come. Internet providers themselves have begun to discuss self-policing guidelines. While parents might initially welcome this form of self-censorship, critics fear that this is even more dangerous than government regulation because self-censorship does not enjoy the protection of the First Amendment.

CRITICAL PERSPECTIVES

A pointed critique of the conflicts in current American culture was provided by Daniel Bell in his book *The Cultural Contradictions of Capitalism* (1978). Bell suggested that capitalism, the American economic system, has emphasized two conflicting sets of cultural values at different points in its development. In its early stages, capitalism stressed independence, work, achievement, thrift, and moderation. These values led to increased worker productivity and encouraged owners to build up their assets by plowing profits back into their businesses. However, as early capitalism grew into large-scale corporate capitalism and more money was needed to keep businesses running, huge sums had to be spent on advertising to encourage consumers to spend more on consumer goods and services. Such exhortation promoted a different set of values, including personal pleasure, expressiveness, and spontaneity.

Bombarded by constant urging to spend money, have a "good time," travel, drink beer, and continuously enjoy life, Americans found themselves in conflict with older values of hard work, frugality, and moderation. People still had to follow the old values to secure the means to enjoy the new values. Yet these two sets of values contradict each other in so many ways that it is hard to reconcile them. Moreover, Bell felt that the apparent long-run trend toward what he referred to as *hedonism*—the belief that personal pleasure is the highest good—threatened to undermine the American capitalist system. People's desires for instant gratification threatened to reduce their drive to save, to work, and to produce. If Bell is right, American culture has come a very long way from the beliefs and practices of the Puritans.

Bell is not the only contemporary sociologist to argue that fundamental American values are undergoing a major change toward hedonism. In his best-selling book *The Culture of Narcissism* (1979), the social historian Christopher Lasch argued that the value of competitive individualism that long had ruled American life was giving way to "purely personal preoccupation" or the search for self-fulfillment. Even definitions of success were changing, he noted—from self-improvement through hard work and delayed pleasure to "self-preservation, with the desire for immediate rewards and satisfaction."

As a result of this growing self-absorption, self-improvement has become increasingly popular in such forms as health foods and the emphasis on personal fitness and learning to "relate." Lasch saw this change in values as a symptom of a personality disorder, which he called *narcissism,* or extreme self-centeredness. The rise of the narcissistic personality was, in turn, directly linked to broader changes in society, in particular the rise of large-scale bureaucracies in which most people today work. The sheer scale of bureaucracies in modern societies caused people to doubt whether their old values and behavior patterns could still function adequately in such a radically changed social environment. At the same time, narcissistic people found that their ability to manipulate others could lead them to great success in the corporate world.

More recently, a widely discussed critique of American values was developed by a team of sociologists led by Robert Bellah. In a book entitled *Habits of the Heart* (1986), Bellah and his colleagues agree with Bell and Lasch that self-fulfillment has become a predominant value of our time. Bellah and his colleagues see self-fulfillment as a modern extension of individualism, a value that has long been central to American life. The main problem with this contemporary form of individualism, in their view, is that people are becoming less committed to the collective goals of society and are retreating into their private lives. Earlier in American history, they argue, the self-orientation that is inherent in individualism was held in check by strong ties to family, church, and local community. With these institutions now weakening, however, people more and more are putting aside public concerns (such as assisting the poor) that are necessary for the survival of a free, democratic society.

Building on the analysis of American culture in *Habits of the Heart,* Bellah and his colleagues focused on social, economic, and political institutions in *The Good Society* (1991). Stressing that strong institutions are absolutely essential because they help to counteract people's selfish impulses and promote the common good, the authors detail the consequences of the institutional weakening that can be seen all around us. Families, businesses, and the nation as a whole are mired in debt; poverty, homelessness, and pollution continue to grow; America's children are in trouble; and natural resources are not being renewed. Only through taking greater responsibility for our institutions, they argue, can we truly take responsibility for ourselves.

WHAT THE OPINION POLLS SHOW

The increasing hedonism that Bell observed in American culture is certainly related to the narcissistic personality that Lasch saw emerging, and both are associated with the new individualism discerned by the Bellah group. Yet these analyses remain speculative, based on personal observation and insight, or in the case of the Bellah group on interviews with only a few hundred Americans. The tentative nature of the data on which these views are based gives rise to an interesting question: To what extent are they supported by changes in American attitudes and values as reflected in public opinion polls?

Measuring changes of opinion in the period from the mid-1960s to the late 1970s, the pollster Daniel Yankelovich (1981) found evidence for what he said was a "cultural revolution" in American values. He saw this revolution as a swing from the self-denial of our Puritan forebears to an ethic of self-fulfillment. Part of the evidence he cited is the fact that during the period under study, the number of Americans who said that they believed "hard work always pays off" fell from 58 percent to 42 percent, or well below a majority, and that 80 percent of Americans had become committed in some degree to the search for self-fulfillment. Yet he remained optimistic, suggesting that the tide may have turned and that "Americans are growing less self-absorbed and better prepared to take [a] step toward an ethic of commitment" (p. 259).

Whether or not Americans are willing to take "a step toward commitment," public opinion polls suggest that they are becoming increasingly cynical and disillusioned with public institutions (see Table 3.3). For example, during the last decade Americans' confidence in Congress plummeted to an all-time low (Gallup, 1999). In March of 1991, 30 percent of Americans said they had a great deal or a lot of confidence in Congress. By October of that same year, however, this rating had dropped to 18 percent—the lowest confidence rating of any institution in the history of the Gallup poll.

Although confidence ratings of institutions fluctuate over time and often reflect short-lived economic recessions or scandals, many U.S. institutions have received low

TABLE **3.3**   CONFIDENCE IN MAJOR U.S. INSTITUTIONS, 1973–1998
(PERCENT SAYING "GREAT DEAL" OR "QUITE A LOT")

	1973	1983	1988	1993	1998
Military	n/a	53	58	68	64
Church/organized religion	66	62	59	53	59
Police	n/a	n/a	n/a	52	58
Presidency	n/a	n/a	n/a	43	53
Supreme Court	44	42	56	44	50
Public schools	58	39	49	39	37
Newspapers	39	38	36	31	33
Banks	n/a	51	49	37	40
Television news	n/a	n/a	n/a	46	34
Organized labor	30	26	26	26	26
Big business	26	28	25	22	30
Congress	42	28	35	18	28

Source: The Gallup Poll, 1999.

or declining marks over the past 25 years. For example, American confidence in public schools fell from a rating of 58 percent in 1973 to 37 percent in 1998. And banks have never regained the confidence they enjoyed before the savings and loan and banking scandals of the 1980s. Dropping from a rating of 60 percent in 1979 to a low of 30 percent in 1991, they gradually inched up to 40 percent in 1998. Even institutions that have historically received high marks have suffered declines over the last 25 years. Organized religion, which ranked second in 1998, remained well below the historic high levels that it reached before the televangelism scandals of the 1980s.

The U.S. military, which has outranked other institutions for over ten years, reached a confidence rating of 85 percent immediately after Operation Desert Storm in 1991. Its consistently high marks stand in stark contrast to those given to the presidency. Since 1888, when Gallup first asked Americans to rate their confidence in this institution, its ratings have been as high as 72 percent and as low as 38 percent. To the surprise of some, the confidence rating of the presidency was relatively high in June of 1998 despite the Monica Lewinsky scandal.

A NEW CULTURAL SHIFT?

In a recent article prepared for the Brookings Institution, Daniel Yankelovich (1994) proposed new grounds for optimism that we may be on the verge of a new cultural shift—if not back to "traditional values," then at least away from the radical individualism of the last few decades. This trend has also been trumpeted by the mass media, which increasingly report that Americans are becoming more "family oriented" and less enamored of "materialism."

If indeed such a change is taking place, there are several possible ways of explaining it. At a relatively superficial level, it may be connected with the gradual aging of the baby boom generation, that enormous segment of the population born between the end of World War II and the early 1960s and whose members have dramatically influenced American cultural patterns simply because of their great numbers. The individualism and hedonism of the past several decades may have been promoted by the fact that the baby boomers were adolescents, college students, or young unmarried adults, still relatively unrestrained by the realities of job and family. In the 1990s, most members of this generation had settled down to raise children and devote themselves to their careers, pursuits that surely encouraged them to shift to a more collective set of values.

Yankelovich himself suggests an equally believable explanation rooted more in economics than in generational change. As he sees it, the driving force of cultural change is affluence, and the process of change takes place in three stages. In stage 1, which in America occurred during the highly prosperous 1950s, affluence is new and people do not expect it to last. They tend,

GLOBAL SOCIETY

CONDUCTING BUSINESS ABROAD

Have you ever thought of an international career in business? If so, consider this. Conducting business in foreign countries may end in failure, even disaster, when cultural differences are ignored. For example, when the Thom McAn Company tried to sell its shoes in Bangladesh, more than 50 people were hurt when a riot erupted (Morrison, Conaway, & Borden, 1994). It turns out that the Thom McAn signature printed inside the shoe resembles the Arabic script for "Allah." Muslims thought that Thom McAn was desecrating God by walking on his name. This was particularly insulting in Bangladesh where the foot is considered unclean.

To avoid problems like this and to improve your own chance of success in foreign markets, you should learn how cultural differences influence the expectations of foreign clients. The kinds of questions you should ask include:

- How are appointments handled? Will clients be on time or will they keep you waiting?

- How should you dress?

- Is a handshake the appropriate greeting? Do men and women shake hands?

- What will give you the advantage in negotiations?

- How should you behave at social gatherings?

- What kinds of gestures are offensive or obscene?

- What kinds of gifts are appropriate?

The answers to these questions vary widely from country to country. To illustrate, let's consider them in several different countries.

Appointments

The predominant attitude toward punctuality in the United States can be summed up in three short words: "Time is money." This attitude is shared by Italians, who conduct business, especially in northern Italy, with "American-style pressure and efficiency" (Morrison, Conaway, & Borden, 1994). Punctuality is similarly valued in both China and Japan, where you are expected to arrive on time for everything, including social gatherings. Being late or canceling a meeting is a serious affront in China. In contrast, do not be surprised if clients in countries like Israel and Saudi Arabia keep you waiting or fail to show up entirely. Punctuality is not valued in many Middle Eastern countries. In fact, it is standard practice to keep clients waiting.

Dress

Although the finest clothes cannot guarantee a successful business deal, dressing inappropriately can cost you dearly. In general, conservative suits are appropriate for business meetings. But never assume anything. Even your leather briefcase can unwittingly blow

a deal for you. Wearing or carrying anything made of leather will offend Hindu clients who revere cows and do not use leather products.

But insulting a client will be the least of your worries in other places. No one can save you if you dress improperly in countries like Saudi Arabia, where Muslim religious beliefs dictate a strict dress code. Women, who are particularly subject to these standards, must dress very modestly with high necklines and long sleeves. And they should wear long skirts, perhaps even ankle-length. If their skirts are too short, the *matawain* (religious police) will use camel whips on their legs (Morrison, Conaway, & Borden, 1994).

Greetings

Graduating business students in the United States are commonly advised to greet businesspeople with a firm handshake. According to conventional wisdom, this signifies warmth and strength. And graduates are strongly cautioned against a weak handshake. While shaking hands is a common Western greeting, do not always expect a firm grip. A German handshake will be firm but brief. But French handshakes are not as firm as those in the United States, and Japanese handshakes often feel weak. Contrary to popular notions in the United States, handshakes do not reveal anything about a person's character.

While handshakes are common in China, wait for a client to extend a hand. The client may choose a more traditional greeting—a nod or bow. If

---

therefore, to hold strongly to such values as family solidarity, hard work, and self-sacrifice. At stage 2, from the late 1960s through the 1980s, people become used to affluence and anticipate that it will continue indefinitely. At this stage, people can afford to favor, as Yankelovich puts it, "personal choice" over "social

bonds." "They and their nation can now spend freely without worrying about tomorrow . . . they believe they can indulge themselves and make up for lost time" (p. 18). In stage 3, however, a fear of losing affluence sets in. If prosperity ends, people reason, they will lose many opportunities for personal choice and will again have to you visit a factory, you may be greeted with applause. You should applaud back.

Finally, be aware that handshakes are not always acceptable. In India, for example, religious beliefs prohibit Muslim men and women from touching one another. Therefore, it is wise to know how to perform the traditional Indian greeting known as the *namaste*. Holding your palms together (as if you are praying) below the chin, nod slightly and say *namaste*.

Negotiating

Negotiating styles vary widely across cultures. Some of them are very confrontational; others require extraordinary politeness. For example, temper tantrums, threats, and walkouts are typical of Russian negotiations (Morrison, Conaway, & Borden, 1994). In fact, if you have not walked out at least twice during this process, Russians will think you are too easy. And do not be offended by Israelis; they love to argue. You do not have to agree with them. On the other hand, it is not a bad idea to incorporate the words "I'm sorry" into your vocabulary before you begin to negotiate with the Japanese. It is not necessary to be ingratiating, just polite.

If you think that jokes will lighten up a situation, think twice. The Japanese are very serious when it comes to business. Italians do not appreciate off-color jokes. And never make fun of the Royal Family in front of the English.

Ultimately, the key to success is patience. And it is the virtue that all

U.S. businesspeople need to learn when dealing with foreign clients.

Gestures

Along with language, we also use gestures to communicate our feelings, reactions, and intentions. These, far more than the spoken word, can offend and unwittingly create serious misunderstandings. Take, for example, the sign for "O.K." in the United States—a circle created by the index finger and thumb. If you use this gesture in Japan, you might cause some confusion, but you probably won't offend anyone, because it is a sign for money. However, in many countries, including Spain, Brazil, and Guatemala it is a rude, if not obscene, gesture. In Colombia, it is the sign used for a homosexual, when it is placed over the nose. U.S. businesspeople should also refrain from using the "thumbs up" gesture, which is considered rude in Australia and throughout the Middle East.

Social Gatherings

Because business entertaining usually involves eating and drinking, the pitfalls are everywhere. Here is a short list of do's and don'ts for a few countries. Remember, alcohol and pork are illegal in Saudi Arabia. And eating must be done with your right hand only. Always use your utensils in Germany; few things are eaten with the hands. And be careful with your chopsticks in China. Never drop them or place them parallel on top of your bowl. Both are signs of bad luck. It is also

rude to stick chopsticks straight up in your rice bowl. In Greece, many dishes are ordered and then shared by everyone at the table. But if you are in India, you must never offer someone else food from your plate. Once it is put on your plate, it is considered "polluted." Even touching a communal dish with your hands may cause other guests to avoid it.

Gifts

Finally, exercise good judgment when giving a gift. Gifts made from leather products should never be given to Hindu clients in India, and alcohol is illegal in Muslim countries. Also, be careful with flowers. Frangipani blossoms are associated with funerals in India, as are chrysanthemums in Italy and all types of white flowers in Japan and China.

The color of gifts or wrapping paper may also be associated with funerals. In China, where color has particular significance, you should avoid white, black, or blue, which are associated with funerals. Preferred colors include red (a lucky color), or pink or yellow (happy, prosperous colors).

rely more on others. In a shift away from individualism, therefore, they modify their values and lifestyles to reemphasize social bonds.

Owing to our growing economic problems, the United States has clearly entered stage 3. Yankelovich writes: "Americans in all walks of life are now adjusting

their expectations downward and adapting to what they now see as a more difficult, less open, less fair, more demanding, and more stressful economic environment" (p. 19). Just how far this cultural shift will go, however, and whether it will result in a renewal of American institutions, remain to be seen.

CHAPTER REVIEW

1. Give examples of both material and nonmaterial culture in the United States. Which of these can you trace to the nineteenth century? Which of these first appeared in the twentieth century? What does a comparison of nineteenth and twentieth century American culture teach you?

2. Identify five symbols that you take for granted everyday. Would someone outside the United States recognize these symbols?

3. What does American slang of the late twentieth century tell you about our culture?

4. Identify five common American folkways. How important are these in your everyday life?

5. Discuss the role that media play in perpetuating American ideology.

6. Find an example of ethnocentrism in a newspaper. Where are you likely to find an example of cultural relativity.

7. Describe a subculture from your own community. Include specific examples of its symbols, values, and language.

8. What basic American values are common in professional sports?

9. What direction is the dominant value pattern taking in America? How will this change the world in which you live?

INTERNET EXERCISE

The Web destinations for Chapter 3 are related to different aspects of culture. To begin your explorations, go to the Prentice Hall Companion Web site **http://www. prenhall.com/popenoe.** Then choose **Chapter 3** (Culture). Next, select **web destinations** from the menu on the left side of the screen. There are many different sites to investigate. We suggest you begin with **The Web of Culture.**

In Chapter 3, the *Global Society* installment deals with the cultural implications of conducting business abroad. **The Web of Culture** is billed as the "premier Web source for global business competency . . . providing customized research for [your] business needs." Fundamentally, this Web site is a direct result of globalization: In order to be successful, today's businessperson must be "culturally competent"—that is, be thoroughly familiar with and informed about the customs and traditions of other cultures and societies.

An example is found in the world of automobile sales. The Chevrolet division of General Motors introduced its "Nova" line of cars in Mexico. Sales proved to be dismal and no one could understand why until someone recognized that *no va* means "it doesn't go" in Spanish. Compare this with the circumstances surrounding the Thom McAn shoe company marketing its products in Bangladesh, as described in the *Global Society* insert. These situations make it clear how crucial it is to understand the cultural implications of business decisions. After you have explored the Web of Culture site, answer the following questions:

- How might a thorough knowledge of cultures other than one's own give a person the advantage in business negotiations?

- How might your dress, the way you greet people, your punctuality, or whether you are confrontational affect your business dealings with members of different world cultures?

KEY TERMS

culture	norms	ethnocentrism
nonmaterial culture	folkways	cultural relativity
material culture	mores	subculture
instincts	laws	counterculture
symbol	sanctions	cultural integration
language	ideology	
value	cultural universals	

CHAPTER 4

Society and Social Structure

n William Golding's famous novel *Lord of the Flies,* a plane carrying a group of English schoolboys aged 6 to 16 is shot down during World War II. The plane crashes on a deserted island, leaving the children with no leaders or organization. It is not long, however, before the boys begin to develop some familiar social characteristics.

Soon after the crash, Ralph, a large, handsome older boy, says, "Seems to me we ought to have a chief to decide things." Jack, a rival for the position of leader, declares right away, "I ought to be chief . . . because I'm chapter chorister and head boy." Everyone agrees that there should be a vote. Ralph is elected, but he appoints Jack to a leadership role. "Jack's in charge of the choir. Who do you want them to be?" Ralph asks. "Hunters," Jack replies. "They are to kill pigs for food." Another group, the "littluns," those aged about six, is also formed. They "led quite a distinct life. . . . They seldom bothered with the biguns and their passionately emotional and corporate life was their own."

When the fire is allowed to go out, there is a call for more order. Ralph says, "We've got to have more rules." Jack agrees, "We've got to have rules and obey them. After all, we're not savages. We're English. . . ." He declares, "I'll split up the choir—my hunters, that is, into groups, and we'll be responsible for keeping the fire going." Soon, when the boys begin to imagine monsters, fear, paranoia, and panic enter their world. When Ralph insists, "The rules are the only thing we've got!" Jack shouts back, "Ballocks to the rules! We're strong—we hunt!" They divide into warring groups. Fortunately, they are rescued by adults before they kill one another off entirely.

Golding's novel imaginatively envisions the formation of a small-scale society. We see the emergence of a division of labor and of social structure—the pattern of rules and groupings that shape the way people relate to one another. Finally we see the social structure break down into anarchy and warfare.

In this chapter, we provide an introduction to the nature of society and the social world. We discuss the concept of social structure and explain the differences between *statuses* and *roles.* We also discuss the main units of social structure within societies, the types of societies, and the functionalist and conflict perspectives regarding the nature of societies.

SOCIAL STRUCTURE

Most sociologists agree that society has an existence of its own, apart from the people who compose it. As societies develop, statuses and roles, groups and organizations, institutions and communities emerge. These concepts are best thought of as part of the society as a whole rather than as belonging to particular people. Individuals view these things as external to themselves and sometimes as coercive in the sense that they compel us to modify our behavior in various ways.

These emergent concepts are collectively referred to in sociology as *social structure.* The term *structure* refers to the ways that the parts of a whole are related to one another. **Social structure,** then, refers to the ways in which the components of a group or society relate to each other.

We tend to take much of everyday social life for granted, but when we apply the sociological imagination to our daily routines we can easily see the extent to which social structure influences human behavior. Our schools or employers determine how we must time our daily arrivals and departures, our waking and sleeping. Our parents and the demands of the job market help to shape our goals of good grades or academic achievement. And schools and employers define a great deal of the behavior necessary to meet these goals.

Social structure often remains largely stable from one year to the next, despite constant minor modifications and pressures for change. In a high school, for example, the student body is composed of different people each fall; some students have graduated, and a new class has entered. Every day sees a slightly different group within the walls of the school: A new student transfers from another school; someone drops out to take a job; someone else stays home sick. Each week new policies are handed down from the superintendent's office. Each year some changes are made in the curriculum. But no one would deny that there is a fairly stable whole called, for example, George Washington High School, with structural traits that remain essentially the same over a long period of time. One could confidently say, "This is an educational institution and not a grocery store," or "The relationship between the students, teachers, and principal remains about the same from year to year." In other words, although people, policies, and programs are always changing, the general social nature of the school itself remains fixed.

This relatively fixed quality of a school is its social structure. Students and teachers know, in general, how they are supposed to interact with other members of the group. That is, they know what the duties of students, teachers, administrators, and other personnel are. This year's school is much the same as last year's school because the group members are organized in approximately the same way.

Despite this stability, not all schools are smoothly functioning places where everyone follows the rules. The rules themselves may be unclear. And even when they are clear, occasional departures from the rules are built-in

Although the student body of a high school changes from year to year, the social structure of the school remains the same.

and expected parts of every organization. This is not necessarily a sign that the social structure of a school is weak. In fact, some variation in behavior, and even a certain amount of conflict, can be as highly patterned and predictable as is behavior that conforms to the rules. High school students may, for example, be allowed to be absent from class in certain cases. And they may sometimes hand in homework late, if their excuse is clever enough or if the teacher is in a good mood.

The school example can also be used to demonstrate the importance of social structure in our lives. Imagine what it would be like if students, teachers, and administrators came to school each morning with no orderly or patterned way of relating to each other. To proceed with the business of education, they would have to go through a long, tedious process of trial and error to find out which teachers could teach which subjects, which students wanted to take those subjects, and how each subject should be taught. Then, if a student were sick or a teacher decided to quit and new people joined the group, the whole process would have to start all over again. Clearly, very little would be learned—except the need for social structure!

Social structure allows us to perform most of the activities of everyday life with a reasonable degree of efficiency. It spares us the hundreds of little choices that would otherwise have to be made before every act, and it gives groups and societies stability and continuity.

Yet, like most things in life, social structure has both positive and negative sides. It makes efficient human activity possible, but it can also restrict personal freedom.

People in small, isolated towns may feel these restrictions particularly strongly. Even more restrictive is the coercive social climate that characterizes totalitarian societies or police states such as North Korea. But all of us, no matter where we live, experience the coercive power of social structure at one time or another. Our parents, our bosses, the police—all sometimes act in ways that we feel are restrictive. If these restrictions are severe enough, they can lead to pressure for change in the social structure. Attempts at change can vary from requests for minor modifications in the rules to violent social revolutions.

THE UNITS OF SOCIAL STRUCTURE

Clubs, families, churches, schools, governments—these common groupings are important units of social structure, and they are central elements of the subject matter of sociology. But when sociologists analyze structure, they cannot use everyday language. They must chart a very careful "conceptual map" of social structure, with a set of clearly defined terms. Because society is so complex, this is far from easy. In fact, social scientists have never been able to agree fully on a common set of concepts and terms for describing social structure.

In this section, we use a simplified conceptual map based on ideas from the work of many sociologists. The units of social structure are presented in a sequence, beginning with those closest to the individual. The discussion concludes with society and the world system of societies—the most abstract units and the ones farthest removed from the individual. Many of the units of social structure briefly introduced here are the subjects of entire chapters later in this book.

Status

Central to the analysis of social structure are the concepts of status and role. A **status** is a socially defined position in a group or society. Being female, black, a lawyer, or a father are examples of statuses. The list of possible statuses seems endless, but the most familiar ones concern sex, marriage, age, education, ethnic background, religion, and occupation.

There are two major types of status. A status that is obtained over the course of one's life as a result of individual effort, or lack of effort, is called an **achieved status.** Most occupational positions in modern society, from corporate executive and doctor to shoeshiner and trash collector, are achieved statuses. Other examples include an individual's level of educational attainment (college graduate or grade-school dropout), religious affiliation, or social class position. Some family statuses, including parent and spouse, are also achieved. At least in principle, achieved statuses can be changed if an individual desires to do so.

A social position to which an individual is assigned and that usually cannot be changed is termed an **ascribed status.** Examples include race and ethnicity, age, gender, and certain family statuses, including oldest son or granddaughter. The usual basis of ascribed statuses is parentage. Children inherit the social position of their father or mother. But ascribed statuses could also be based on the place, time, or circumstances of a person's birth. As an example of the influence of such factors, consider the birth of quadruplets. This event brings the children fame, a certain prestige, and gifts of money simply because they were born as a set of four.

Most important statuses are *ranked* in terms of respectability, power, or prestige in comparison with other related statuses. Thus, for example, some occupations carry far more prestige, and rewards, than others. (Table 9.3, on page 198, lists the relative prestige ranking of a number of important occupational statuses in contemporary American society.) Similarly, statuses within the military are ranked from generals at the top to privates at the bottom, and high school classes are ranked from lowly freshmen to godlike seniors. Indeed, this is the meaning of "status" when it is used in everyday conversation, as when we say that someone who drives a BMW has "a lot of status." Sociologists, however, regard the issue of ranking as secondary in importance and use the term *status* in many cases to refer to positions in society that are not necessarily differentially ranked in comparison with other positions.

Clearly, each person occupies more than one status, and the possible combinations of statuses can reveal a great deal about the structure of a society. In the United States, for example, there are more male lawyers than female lawyers and a higher percentage of young, unemployed blacks than young, unemployed whites. Having one status may make it easier to acquire others. For example, the president of a bank may be asked to serve as United Way chairperson, museum trustee, and corporation board member because his or her occupational status is highly ranked.

Because most individuals occupy many different statuses, some high and some low, a problem can arise concerning what one's overall social position is—especially in the eyes of others. Everett Hughes (1945) pointed out that one way societies resolve this problem is by agreeing that certain statuses are more important than others. Hughes calls a crucial status that determines a person's general social position a **master status.** For most adults in our society, occupation is normally one's master status. But an ascribed status—a handicap, exceptional beauty, or great inherited wealth—can also be a master status. Consider, for example, the case of a person who has great wealth but a "lowly" occupation. When a young woman from the Kennedy family becomes a social worker, she still carries the high master status of a rich person. Among the European aristocracy, family background is a master status. A poor prince receives the prestige due a prince, not a pauper.

Role

A **role** is defined as the behavior expected of someone with a given status in a group or society. According to Ralph Linton (1936), one *occupies* a status but *plays* a role. For each highly structured social interaction, society provides a "script," complete with the roles assigned to the various members. To learn a role is to understand the behavior that is expected or required of a particular status—in other words, to know which *norms* apply to persons occupying that status. In *My Fair Lady*, Eliza Doolittle could not play the role of a duchess until Henry Higgins had coached her on the behaviors expected of a duchess. All of us must learn to play the roles connected with our statuses.

A status may carry with it many related roles. English teachers are expected to teach Shakespeare to their students. But they may also have to meet with anxious parents, advise the drama club, order books for the library, give reports at teachers' meetings, and attend workshops. None of these role demands is directly connected to the teacher-student relationship, but they are all expected of any individual occupying the status of English teacher. The whole set of roles associated with a single status is called a **role set** (Merton, 1968).

If a status is new, some of the roles that go with it may still have to be worked out. In American society, the statuses of single parent and businesswoman are relatively new. The roles connected with each of these statuses are slowly being defined through the actions of those people now occupying the statuses. In time, the norms that prove most successful and acceptable will become standard. Thus, newcomers to each status will better understand what is expected of them from the outset.

Moreover, roles are always being redefined (Turner, 1990). For many years, widows were expected to keep themselves apart from others after the death of their husband. Now they are more likely to resume many of their former activities as soon as they can. Some retired workers now have the chance to pocket their gold watches and begin second careers. These changes are taking place in part because people live longer today. There are simply more elderly people in our society than in earlier generations, and as the elderly grow in numbers, they assert themselves as a group in pushing for social change.

GLOBAL SOCIETY

CROSS-CULTURAL DIFFERENCES OF GENDER AND LANGUAGE

A famous doctor had a brother who died.

The man who died didn't have a brother.

So how were the famous doctor and the man who died related? (Brandreth, 1985)

This riddle is a favorite among young American schoolgirls who quickly realize that the missing information in this puzzle is a linguistic marker signifying that *this* doctor is a woman.

The significance of this missing information may not, however, occur to them. In American society, one's occupation is normally a crucial status—one that determines a person's general social position. When a woman enters a predominantly male occupation, attention is drawn to this unusual "invasion" of male territory through the use of a linguistic marker—"lady doctor." This is done intentionally to protect the status of the men in this occupation. Without the marker, society might erroneously conclude that most doctors are women, which would diminish the respect, power, and prestige of the male members of this profession (Bonvillain, 1998).

The use of language to signify status differences occurs in many societies. For example, in German, feminizing suffixes transform some masculine

nouns to designate that a female occupies this position, as *der Lehrer* "the teacher," *die Lehrerin* "the woman teacher" (Bonvillain, 1998). In Spanish, feminizing suffixes alter the meaning of the masculine nouns in another way. Instead of referring to a female member of a profession, it refers to one's wife. For example, "el medico" refers to a male doctor but "la medica" refers to his wife. Linguistic markers like these represent men as the usual or generic persons in an occupation and women as unusual or derivatives.

In Japan, status differences between men and women are particularly pronounced, extending even into the privacy of family life. Thus, for example, a husband will typically address his wife in a familiar form—by her first name or by one of two second-person pronouns: *omae* or *kimi*. Superiors generally use *omae* to address persons of lower status, while the pronoun, *kimi,* is used with subordinates or intimates but not superiors (Lee, 1976). In contrast, women will attach the honorific suffix *san* when they use their husband's first name. Spouses may also address one another as father (*otoosan*) or mother (*okaasan*). In this case, the higher status of men is reflected in the asymmetric frequency with which this is done. On a more impersonal level, Japanese wives may refer to their husbands as either *uit no hito* "person of my house" or as *shujin* "master."

In some societies, language reflects the respect given to women. For

example, in contrast to European languages, which reflect the subordinate status of women, the Mohawk language reveals the value and worth accorded to women. In traditional Mohawk culture, women performed important economic roles, supplying their families with corn, beans, and squash. In Mohawk mythology these crops were symbolized as females and are referred to as "Our Life Supporters."

In this matrilineal kinship system, women were also valued for their reproductive roles. And the prestige attached to this role was reflected in the semantics of feminine pronouns. Thus, most people addressed older women, relatives, and/or women who had gained their respect with the pronoun {ye-}. The pronoun {ka-} was used more frequently to convey a neutral or even negative attitude toward the woman. While the pragmatic meanings of these pronouns have changed, {ye-} is still used today to show respect toward women, and it continues to reflect the valued symbolization of women in Mohawk culture (Bonvillain, 1998).

As the most important set of symbols in society, language expresses the ideas, values, and norms of a culture. The examples given here illustrate how deeply other dimensions of culture become embedded in language. And they show how language reflects the inequalities in a society.

Rather than being banished to the wings, they want active roles to play. (These topics are discussed in more detail in Chapter 12.)

There is sometimes a difference between the norms that apply to a particular role and the way people actually play that role. In other words, **role expectation,** society's definition of the way a role ought to be played, does not always match **role performance,** the way a person actually plays a role. The gap between expectation and performance

can have many causes. People may not fully understand their roles. Or they may refuse to perform according to expectations for personal reasons. For example, a study of emergency medical technicians found that paramedics sometimes get so caught up in the spirit of "doing anything to save lives" that they extend their roles beyond the prescribed expectations (Palmer & Gonsoulin, 1990). Paramedics will occasionally make their own decisions about medications or they will choose a specific hospital for a particularly imperiled patient, no matter what the formal rules are. Another reason for the gap is that the expectations may be unclear, especially when the roles are new. But even if people do not play their roles exactly as expected, they are still said to be playing those roles.

The terms *status* and *role* are powerful tools for analyzing social structure. Suppose we want to study the structure of the high school discussed in the opening pages of this chapter. We could first identify all the statuses found in that school: student, teacher, secretary, nurse, principal, cafeteria worker, and so on. Next we could find out how someone occupying each of these statuses is expected to relate to each of the others. The organized web of statuses and roles that we would thereby uncover is the social structure of the school.

ROLE CONFLICT AND ROLE STRAIN

In the course of any one day's social interaction, a person plays many different roles. If opposing demands are made on an individual by two or more roles linked with two or more entirely separate social statuses, the situation is called **role conflict.** For example, many women want to have both a career and children. The demands of the roles connected to the statuses of businesswoman and mother often conflict, and women must work out compromises. They may leave their careers for several years when their children are young, rely on day-care centers, or share the parenting role with their husbands. Role conflict typically leads to a feeling of being pulled in many different directions.

Another example is the dilemma presented by the fact that the role expectations associated with the status of Little League coach may well conflict with the role expectations associated with the status of father for coaches whose children are also members of the team that they coach.

Sometimes opposing demands are built into a single role. The personal stress caused by such a situation is called **role strain** (Goode, 1960). Take the case of military officers. To be successful, officers must have the affection and trust of their subordinates, for they may have to ask them to risk their lives. But at the same time, officers are authority figures who must be obeyed instantly and without question. The first part of the role calls for behavior that seems kind, personal, and sympathetic. The second part of the role calls for behavior that appears stern and uncompromising. Similarly, a doctor must show compassion toward a cancer patient and at the same time be objective. And priests are supposed to protect a confessor's privacy even if he or she has committed a crime. In each of these cases, playing the role can lead to personal strain and anxiety.

Roles are always being redefined. As the elderly population grows in number, its members assert themselves as a group in pushing for social change. The elderly want to play active roles, such as returning to the work force.

ROLES AND SELF-IDENTITY

How do people deal with role expectations that clash with their values or self-image? They may try to resolve the problem by changing the role, so that their usual behavior will meet its demands. They may try to leave the role. Or they may distance themselves from the demands of the role, establishing what Erving Goffman (1986) calls *role distance,* and merely go through the motions of performing the role. Acting in this way is like wearing a sign that says, "I'm only doing this because I have to. I don't really believe in it." If none of these ways of handling the conflict is possible, a more drastic solution is to try to compartmentalize oneself by saying, "I am this kind of person here but that kind of person there." This course of action can, however, lead to psychological problems.

The roles we play can strongly affect our self-identity. We can all think of cases in which taking on a new role changed a person. For example, a medical student who becomes a doctor usually displays such traits as a reassuring bedside manner and a commanding attitude. These traits emerge not as some magic bonus attached to the medical degree, but because playing the role of doctor requires their development. In fact, doctors must show these qualities in order to do their job well.

Occasionally, people may modify their values and self-images so dramatically in order to make them fit with their major life roles that they seem to lose themselves in their role behavior, a pattern that Ralph Turner (1978) calls *person-role merger.* This is particularly likely when an

This group of commuters would be regarded as an aggregate. They engage in little if any true social interaction, share no sense of unit or common identity, and have no common goals or expectations.

individual is playing roles that, as Turner puts it, are "difficult to put aside." We all know police officers, elementary school teachers, and college professors who seem incapable of separating their personal identities from their occupational role demands even when they are away from the job. Similarly, some people seem to have merged with their gender or age roles to the point where they always act like wives or senior citizens, for example, whether or not these roles are particularly germane to the interactional situations in which they find themselves.

Social Groups and Organizations

Roles and statuses typically are components of social groups and organizations. The term *social group* is used by sociologists and nonsociologists alike to refer to many kinds of human associations. In strict sociological usage, a **group** consists of two or more people who have a common identity and some feeling of unity, who interact, and who share certain goals and expectations. All groups, of course, have a social structure. But they can be as loosely organized as shoppers waiting in line or as tightly structured as an army platoon in which each member has specific tasks.

Any group can also be called a **social system.** To say that groups are social systems—a term favored by functionalists—is to stress that they share certain basic structural properties with all kinds of systems. Automobile engines, plants, the human body, and the solar system are all systems because each is a set of interrelated parts. Each part contributes to the whole, and the whole is greater than the sum of its parts. When one element of a system changes, all of the other elements change in response.

As we have defined it, *group* is a very broad and general term. We need to look at the ways in which particular groups vary. For example, groups differ greatly in size and in the length of time they last. The Roman Catholic Church has lasted for centuries; an encounter group might last only one weekend. In the discussion that follows, we consider groups in terms of three less obvious qualities that are especially important to sociologists: groups' level of structure, their degree of intimacy, and their connection with social inequality and human diversity.

THE LEVEL OF STRUCTURE IN GROUPS

Certain human collectivities are not groups in the sociological sense because they have no social structure at all. An example is people who merely share a particular social trait: liberals or conservatives, females or males, high school or college graduates. Sociologists call such a collectivity a **social category.** The members of social categories do not necessarily interact, know one another, share a social structure, or have anything in common other than the trait that they share.

Although a social category is unstructured, being classified together may awaken in its members a feeling of shared interests or goals that leads to the formation of a real social group. For example, feminist groups have been started by women whose joint classification as "female" led to the sharing of common experiences and viewpoints.

Another type of collectivity that sociologists do not regard as a true group is an **aggregate,** a number of people who find themselves face-to-face in a particular setting but do not interact and lack more than a minimal social structure. Examples include people riding a bus or patients sitting in a dentist's waiting room. It is true that certain basic understandings are shared among members of an aggregate. For example, there is a widely accepted way to distribute seats on a bus—first-come, first-served in most cases—but the handicapped, the elderly, and pregnant women may receive special consideration. However, people in aggregates engage in little if any true social interaction, share no sense of unity or common identity, and have no common goals or expectations.

Note that, as with a social category, if the members of an aggregate are given a reason to interact, social structure may well develop and a true group may emerge. If one of the passengers on an elevator suffers a heart attack, this aggregate will more likely than not be transformed into a group as the different riders cooperate to help their stricken fellow.

In addition to aggregates, there are many loosely structured groupings that are more spontaneous and temporary than are the collective entities that sociologists usually call social groups. Examples are the crowds that gather at fires, protest rallies on college campuses, and riots in inner-city ghettos. The actions of people in such groupings are called *collective behavior* (the subject of Chapter 21).

Every modern society has thousands of small and often loosely organized groups that are more stable than those involved in collective behavior. Examples are families, groups of friends, discussion groups, and committees. Some sociologists use "group" to refer only to such small and fairly stable *face-to-face* groupings. (These small social groups are discussed in Chapter 7.)

Larger and more structured groups are called *organizations,* groups that have been purposely formed to achieve particular goals (Etzioni & Lehman, 1980). Examples of organizations include business firms, colleges and universities, and branches of the government. Within organizations, there is normally an elaborate division of labor and power, as well as a precise definition of the role and status of each member. Thus, behavior is much more highly patterned in an organization than in other kinds of groups. (Organizations are also discussed in Chapter 7.)

The Degree of Intimacy in Groups

Another common way of classifying groups is according to their degree of intimacy. *Primary groups* are small and unspecialized. Their members communicate openly and intimately. The most familiar primary group is the family. Other examples are playmates, teenage gangs, and small clusters of longtime co-workers.

Secondary groups, by contrast, are larger, more specialized groups in which the members interact in a limited, impersonal way. The most familiar secondary group is an organization. Primary groups may exist within an organization (lunch partners within a firm, teenage cliques within a school). But an organization requires patterns of behavior in which people must set aside personal styles or preferences in order to attain the aims of the group. (Primary and secondary groups are discussed in more detail in Chapter 7.)

Inequality and Diversity in Groups

In every known human society, people and social positions tend to be ranked in terms of such things as wealth, power, and prestige. Sociologists call this ranking *social stratification.* (It is the subject of Chapter 9.) Social ranking can create very strong social groups. For example, *caste groups,* as in India, are among the most rigid, highly structured social groups ever to exist. Some sociologists analyze race relations in the United States as a form of caste. Caste membership is passed from parents to children and is fixed for life.

In Europe during the Middle Ages, social rank was based on membership in groups called *social estates.* The three main social estates were the nobility, the clergy, and the peasantry. Social estates have sometimes been referred to as "diluted castes," because membership in them was not quite as fixed as it is in a caste system. As the medieval estate system declined and towns and cities flourished, the social estates were replaced by *social classes.* These classes were a kind of diluted version of the social estates. Social classes—such as the working class, middle class, and upper class—were organized around the ownership of industrial production.

Another familiar social grouping is the ethnic group. An *ethnic group* consists of people who share a common social and cultural background and a feeling of identity with each other. The term *ethnic group* usually refers to people who hold a minority status in a society that is dominated by a group with a different culture. *Minority groups* are those groups in a society whose members possess particular biological or social traits that cause them to become the object of prejudice or discrimination. (Ethnic and racial minority groups are discussed in Chapter 11.)

Macro Social Groupings

We can actually see crowds, or families, or work groups in action, but some important units of social structure are not so easily seen. The concepts used to analyze these *macro social groupings* are among the most abstract in sociology.

Social Institutions

One such concept is the social institution. A **social institution** is a relatively stable cluster of social structures that is intended to meet the basic needs of societies. One basic need, for example, is the replacement of a society's members. This is done by the institution known as the *family* (see Chapter 14). This institution consists of such specific social structures as family groups and family roles and statuses (See Figure 4.1). Sexual behavior takes place between husband and wife, and in most societies, the

INSTITUTION	NEEDS	VALUES	NORMS	STATUSES/ ROLES	GROUPS
Family	Survival	Security Cooperation Loyalty	Practice monogamy.	Mother Uncle	Immediate family Extended family
Religion	Community	Cooperation	Do not lie, cheat, or steal, The "golden rule."	Rabbi Priest Minister	Parish Synagogue
Political system	Governing/ maintaining order	Freedom Democracy	Vote.	Governor Secretary of State	Political parties
Economy	Exchange of goods and services	Hard work Competition	Make a profit.	CEO Secretary	American Marketing Association
Media	Communication	Education Freedom Entertainment	Inform the public.	Editor Producer	CBS New York Times

FIGURE 4.1   Basic Components of the Social Structure

offspring are cared for by this pair. Husband and wife are expected to teach their children to behave in acceptable ways.

Other institutions meet other basic needs. The institution of *education* passes advanced culture on to the young so that they can act as full members of society. The institution of *religion* reinforces people's commitment to the shared values that hold them together as a society. Societies produce and allocate goods and services by means of the *economic* institution. And they distribute power by means of the *political* institution. (These four institutions are examined through the functionalist and conflict perspectives in Chapters 15 through 18.) Still other institutions, such as sports, provide recreation and leisure activities while teaching or reinforcing the values of the larger society.

COMMUNITIES, SOCIETIES, AND THE WORLD SYSTEM

The terms *community* and *society* are often confused with one another. Sometimes they are used interchangeably simply to refer to any cluster of people who live together and share a common culture. But sociologists generally distinguish between the two on the basis of size, degree of independence, and degree of self-sufficiency.

When the cluster of people is focused on individual homes and places of work, and based on daily patterns of interaction (such as those involved with work, shopping, and school), the grouping is usually called a **community.** Examples of communities are villages, towns, cities, suburbs, and metropolitan areas. (Communities are discussed more fully in Chapter 20.)

In many past societies, such as the Greek city-states, community and society were one and the same, as they are in many preliterate societies today. In such settings, there was no larger social unit beyond the local population cluster. Today, however, advances in communication and transportation have vastly increased the range of human activity. The local community is often a fairly small and by no means independent or self-sufficient part of a larger cluster of people known as a society.

Like all groups, a society is a collection of people who share a common identity, a feeling of unity, and collective goals. But it is much more than this. A **society** is a comprehensive, territorially based social grouping that includes all the social institutions required to meet basic human needs. Such comprehensiveness is not found in a family, an organization, or a local community.

Societies can be structured in many ways, as is discussed in the next section. But all types of societies display the following traits (Olsen, 1968):

1. Nearly all the social relationships of a society's members occur within the boundaries of the society. Those that do not are generally subject to strict formal control. Relationships with foreign countries, for example, are carefully regulated. A citizen needs a visa or passport to travel abroad.

2. A society establishes the social procedures and mechanisms by which resources—economic and otherwise—are obtained and distributed in order to satisfy people's needs.

3. The final authority to make decisions and resolve conflicts rests within a society.

4. A society is usually the highest level of organization to which its members are loyal and which they are prepared to defend. Most Americans who are willing to serve in an army would not be willing to serve in any army but that of their own society.

5. All of a society's members share a common and unique culture and usually a common language. In American society, we share such cultural symbols as the Fourth of July, Hollywood, and McDonald's, and we share such cultural values as individualism and "getting ahead."

Because of the growing interdependence among societies, sociologists have recently identified what is now called the **world system** (Wallerstein, 1974). This is the system of economic, political, and cultural relationships that links all the societies in the world. We cannot fully understand any society without knowing about its relationships with other societies and the history of those relationships. Like any other social system, the world system has a structure. There is, for example, a division of labor and a hierarchy of power among societies. Some societies supply natural resources; others manufacture finished products. Some are weak and dependent; others have great economic and military power.

The units of social structure, then, range from status and role to the world system. These units are the main concern of most sociological thought and analysis. Although it may sometimes sound as if social structure is static, it is not. The units of societies, such as families, schools, and communities, are always in the process of change. The last chapter of this book is devoted to the most abstract and general subject in sociology, the process of social change in societies as a whole.

TYPES OF SOCIETIES

All human beings share a common set of basic needs—eating, sleeping, reproducing, producing, learning, and keeping order. But an amazing variety of social forms can answer these needs. This variety is clearly evident when we look at the many types of societies that have existed throughout world history.

Sociologists have not agreed on a single way to classify societal types. It is not that they have not tried; in fact, many of the classic sociologists made such a classification the basis of their theories. These theories were often combined with ideas about how societies change from one type to another. And historians and philosophers were inventing classification schemes before sociology was even recognized as a discipline.

Strong value judgments about the societies being classified often flawed the schemes of the classical sociologists. An example is the theory suggested by the anthropologist Lewis Henry Morgan (1877). He divided all societies into three groups: savage, barbarian, and civilized. Essentially, "civilized" meant having the traits of modern Western societies; non-Western societies were automatically regarded as either savage or barbarian!

Similarly, Auguste Comte (1877) suggested that all societies evolve from lower to higher stages. The theological stage lasted from the dawn of civilization to about 1300 A.D. and was marked by a distinctly and pervasively religious outlook. The metaphysical stage lasted from 1300 to 1800 and was characterized by a more rational approach to life. And the positivistic, or scientific, stage, extending from 1800 on, is committed to scientific knowledge.

Such broad classification schemes are no longer in favor among sociologists, although in its day Comte's theory was an important scholarly advance. In this section, we look at a classification scheme commonly used today. It is based on how the members of a society make a living—their *mode of subsistence.*

Mode of Subsistence

The most basic human activity is to provide for such vital needs as food, clothing, and shelter. These are called *subsistence needs* because they allow us to stay alive. Many classification schemes have been based on the way societies are organized to meet these needs.

One of the best classification schemes is that developed by Gerhard Lenski (Lenski, Lenski, & Nolan, 1991). In Lenski's scheme, the oldest and simplest type is the *hunting and gathering society.* Such a society is characterized by a small, sparse population, a nomadic way of life, and primitive technology. The family is very important, and there is little specialization; that is, each member of the society can adequately perform most of the important social and economic roles in that society. The social structure in these societies is thus very simple, consisting of a few statuses based on sex, age, and kinship. The common experiences of these small societies result in shared values and essentially equal statuses. The absence of personal possessions—the result of a nomadic lifestyle—plays an important role in creating equality among members of this society. It also explains why warfare is extremely uncommon. There is nothing to fight over. Decisions in these societies are made by group discussion. Political institutions do not exist.

The social structure of a hunting and gathering society is reflected in its religion, which does not include beliefs about a powerful god or gods who play an active role in human affairs. Instead, members of these societies

The Masai tribe is a pastoral society. Pastoralism produces a reliable food supply that can be increased over time through animal husbandry.

tend to believe in spirits that must be acknowledged, but not necessarily worshiped.

The vast majority of societies throughout human history have relied on a hunting and gathering strategy. Some examples of this type of society still exist in the twentieth century, such as the San of the Kalahari Desert of Africa and some groups in New Guinea. These societies are rapidly being destroyed, however, as more technologically advanced peoples encroach on their lands.

As societies came to rely more and more on plants such as wheat, rice, and other grains, the *horticultural society* was born. The first horticulturalists probably appeared near fertile river valleys in the Middle East about 9,000 years ago. The members of these societies cultivated cereal grains and ate wild plants and animals as dietary supplements. These societies were the first to establish permanent communities, some of which were as large as 1,000 people. Owing to their more settled way of life, the members of these communities made many tools and household objects, such as pots and dishes. Eventually, horticulture became so efficient that not everyone had to produce food. Specialized statuses and roles, such as shaman, trader, or craftperson appeared. As certain people took charge of distributing food to non-farming members of the society, inequalities in wealth and power began to arise. And so, too, did political institutions, which took the form of hereditary chieftainships. The surplus of goods in this kind of society also made warfare more common.

Ancestor worship was practiced most frequently in horticultural societies and reflected this society's concept of the kinship group, which included both living and dead members. Religious rituals were performed to appease the spirits of dead ancestors who were thought to live among them.

Some societies rely on capturing, taming, and breeding animals as the most important source of their food supply. *Pastoral societies* came into existence at about the same time as horticultural societies. Whereas the members of horticultural societies tended to remain stationary, moving only when the soil became exhausted, pastoral societies were mostly nomadic, wandering from place to place in search of fields in which to graze their herds. Pastoralism produced a reliable food supply that could be increased over time through animal husbandry. As the surplus food supply exceeded the needs of this society, pastoralists developed trading relationships, exchanging livestock for clothing and other types of food. These kinds of cooperative relationships were advantageous, but disputes over grazing rights also led to war.

Pastoral societies also developed religious beliefs and practices that reflected their everyday lives. Their gods and goddesses took an interest in humans and, like good shepherds, looked after their needs. This kind of relationship is still reflected in the beliefs of the three major world religions, which originated in pastoral societies—Judaism, Christianity, and Islam. Many pastoral societies still exist in Africa and the Middle East.

By 3000 B.C., *agrarian societies* had developed. The plow helped to control weeds and keep the soil fertile. This permitted predictable crop surpluses and ended the need for regular moves to new fields. In turn, these factors led to important social changes, including the further stratification of people into unequal social groups (some worked the land; others collected the surplus), the establishment of bureaucracies to control the expanding economy, and the rise of the first cities. A money economy developed, and important advances in technology were made, such as the invention of gunpowder, clocks, windmills, and, most important, the process of smelting iron.

Political institutions evolved into more complex systems. Hereditary monarchies wielded absolute power over their subjects, elaborate courts and government bureaucracies developed, and a separate institution—the military—evolved for the defense and expansion of the empire. Religion also emerged as a separate institution with specialized roles for officials. And, as in earlier societies, religious beliefs and practices reflected the power and inequalities of this society.

In the eighteenth and nineteenth centuries, the Industrial Revolution began another period of major social change that led to *industrial society*. The primary economic enterprise of industrial society was the production of manufactured goods. Many forms of work were now done by machine, and cities became much more densely populated. In this kind of society, the family lost many of its functions and, therefore, became less important. It no longer served as the basic unit of economic production. Responsibility for educating children shifted to a separate institution. And religion began to lose its influence. In its place a new institution arose—science. As these shifts occurred, the state began to assume increasing responsibilities for education, welfare, and economic activity.

Finally, some social scientists today speak of *postindustrial society* (Bell, 1973). In this type of society, the office has come to replace the factory, the computer has taken over from the machine, and the metropolitan area has supplanted the town or the city. In contrast to industrial society, the main economic enterprise of postindustrial society is the provision of services in such diverse areas as health, education, transportation, and communication, as well as business and government. Most of the economically advanced societies in the world today, including the United States and the nations of Western Europe, fit this description.

THEORETICAL PERSPECTIVES ON SOCIETIES

At this point, it is instructive to reintroduce two of the three major sociological perspectives, *structural functionalism* and *conflict theory*, which were briefly outlined in Chapter 1. Both of these are macro-level perspectives that are principally concerned with the dynamics of large-scale social systems and whole societies. Here we explore these two perspectives in greater detail and see how they can be used to analyze the operation of societies. A third major sociological perspective, *symbolic interactionism*, which focuses on micro-level human social behavior, is not generally used to analyze large systems or entire societies; we discuss it at length in Chapter 5.

The Functionalist Perspective

The basic tenets of functionalism were developed in the nineteenth century—in many ways, a century that was dominated by the science of biology. Knowledge of the human body, of microscopic forms of life, and of plants and animals kept increasing. In one of the greatest achievements of the century, Charles Darwin drew on this vast body of new knowledge to explain evolution in terms of natural selection. Biology had never before enjoyed such high prestige. Excited by these steps forward, early social thinkers naturally began to apply some of the concepts of biology to society.

Auguste Comte and Herbert Spencer proposed the most basic principle of functionalism: *A society is similar in many ways to a living organism.* There are three main elements of this idea. First, a society, like a living thing, has structure. An animal is made up of cells, tissues, and organs; a society is likewise made up of groups, classes, and institutions. Second, like an organism, a society is a system whose needs must be satisfied if it is to survive. Societies must, for example, be able to get food and resources from their surroundings and distribute them to their members. Third, like the parts of a biological organism, the parts of a social system work together in an orderly way to maintain the well-being of the whole.

Following the lead of the Italian sociologist Vilfredo Pareto, Spencer and his followers maintained that the natural tendency of systems is toward equilibrium or stability, and that each part of a society has a function that adds to this stability. Thus, a society is viewed from the functionalist perspective as a complex system made up of parts that function to fulfill the needs of the whole so as to maintain stability.

Later scholars took the basic idea of functionalism—that society is similar to a living organism—and refined and added to it. Émile Durkheim (1893) is often thought of as the founder of modern functionalism. He saw a society as a special kind of organism, one ruled by a consensus regarding moral values. He distinguished between societies based on mechanical solidarity and those based on organic solidarity. Societies based on mechanical solidarity are held together because their members perform very similar economic roles and therefore share the same values. Societies based on organic solidarity are held together because their members perform very specialized economic roles and are therefore highly dependent on one another. Functionalism was also the major perspective of the British founders of cultural anthropology.

In the United States, Talcott Parsons was the leading figure in developing functionalism into a general yet systematic theory of sociological analysis. A society, he said, will remain functional—that is, maintain its order and stability—if it can meet four basic needs (Parsons, 1951; Parsons & Smelser, 1956). These four needs, sometimes called *functional requisites,* are the achievement of goals, adjustment to the environment, integration of the various parts of a society into a whole, and control of deviance. Parsons (1951) placed special emphasis on the need to integrate the parts of a society, which he felt required that people accept and follow their society's *shared values*. These shared values, he said, served as a kind of "glue" holding a society together. If too many people reject these values, social stability will break down.

Robert Merton (1968) refined Parsons' functionalist perspective and made it more useful for guiding empirical research. He began by focusing on the function

INTERNET/TECHNOLOGY

THE INTERNET IN POSTINDUSTRIAL SOCIETY

In 1973, Daniel Bell described his expectations for the future of society in his book, *The Coming of Post-Industrial Society*. In contrast to the manufacturing base of industrial society, postindustrial society would rely on knowledge and information as it evolved from an economy that produced goods to one that would provide services.

The Internet, the technology that would make this possible, was in its infancy when Bell's book was published. While many Americans today regard the Internet as technology's latest toy, it is actually the product of the Cold War. The tensions between communist and noncommunist nations fed constant fears of a nuclear war. As a result, the United States wanted to develop a communications network that could survive such an attack. Ideas for such a system began to develop in the mid-1960s. And in 1969, the U.S. Defense Department commissioned the Advanced Research project Agency to create ARPANET—a huge military computer network.

The system they created allowed data to move freely around this military network so that if any of its computers became damaged, the data could be moved via alternate routes. When the American military split away from ARPANET in the early 1980s, the system became known as the Internet. Shortly thereafter, both academic institutions and other government agencies (particularly the National Science Foundation) joined the Internet and connected their own computer networks to the system.

Today over 30 million households are connected to the Internet (*Newsweek,* January 27, 1997). (See Figure 4.2.) That number is expected to jump to over 60 million worldwide by the year 2000, convincing many businesspeople that the Internet will become the "powerful engine of economic growth" (*Time,* Spring 1995). Recent transformations in the American workplace indicate that this is already happening.

Consider, for example, the *virtual workplace.* This term, which sounds more like science fiction than reality, refers to any worksite located outside the traditional office setting where work is done (Bredin, 1996). This is typically a high-tech home office that connects workers to other members of this virtual organization or to their clients.

Many Fortune 500 companies are decentralizing their operations in this way and re-creating themselves around their information networks. The Internet, along with fax machines, toll-free telephone lines, and overnight mail services, makes all this possible. Virtual workplaces turn out to be bargains for corporations that want to cut the high cost of office space, especially in pricey urban areas. For example, Citibank has relocated its credit operations to South Dakota (*Time,* Spring 1995). Dell Computer, which employees 25 corporate sales executives working out of their homes in the suburbs of Manhattan and Seattle, operates a retail store with no location. And Journal Graphics, the vendor of transcripts for television programs, lists Grant Street, Denver, as its address but actually operates out of its employees' homes.

While some sociologists have questioned Bell's predictions about postindustrial society, these examples illustrate many of the changes that he foresaw. It is clear, for example, that we are entering the information age and that we have the technology necessary to support an economy based on its exchange. As the transmission of credit information becomes more secure, businesses will increasingly use the Internet to market financial and travel services (*Newsweek,* January 27, 1997). And they have already recognized that the Web is particularly well-suited for business-to-business marketing.

Changes in the American workplace also illustrate how businesses are decentralizing their operations and abandoning bureaucratic organizational styles in favor of more flexible forms. The Internet has created a superhighway that allows workers to telecommute. But, as Bell predicted, this may have some drawbacks. While the Internet will increase relationships among people, these are likely to be temporary and unstable.

The Internet clearly provides the kind of technology necessary for

---

of a given unit of social structure. Earlier theorists often explained the presence of a part by saying that it contributed to the maintenance of the whole. It was difficult, however, for them to see any social unit as harmful to the whole. If a unit of social structure existed, they thought, it must be functional. But Merton pointed out that not all parts of a social system need be functional. A unit of structure is **dysfunctional** when it prevents society, or one of its parts, from meeting its needs.

Religion is functional when it binds together the members of a society; an army is functional when it protects a society from harm; a political machine is functional when it helps to integrate immigrant groups into a society by providing them with needed information

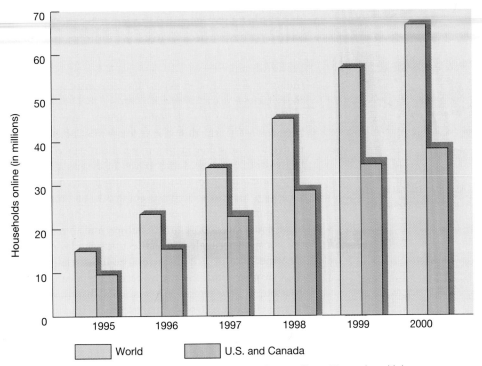

Use of the Web (1996, in percent*)	
Browsing	77%
Entertainment	64
Education	53
Work	51
Business research	41
Academic research	36
Shopping	19

World   U.S. and Canada

*Based on the responses of 10,332 Americans, allowed to mark multiple answers.

FIGURE 4.2 It's a Wide, Wired World

Source: Newsweek, January 27, 1997, © 1997 Newsweek, Inc. All rights reserved. Reprinted by permission.

postindustrial society. But will the kind of economy it promises be good for society? Social analysts take two opposite positions on this question. Some, like Bell, are optimistic and believe that technology will free people from alienating labor. The Internet will spare Americans from many stressful parts of work—long commutes, rigid bureaucracies, and the watchful eye of the boss. But others see an increasingly stratified society that has no place for poorly educated, unskilled workers. While the Internet is regarded as the most democratic of media—where people are judged not by their race, gender, or social class—it is out of reach for millions of those people who lack access to a computer and a high-speed telecommunications link. For these Americans, the Internet does not promise such a rosy portrait of postindustrial society.

about government and social services. But religion that promotes political strife, as in Northern Ireland, is dysfunctional (Darby, Dodge, & Hepburn, 1990). So is an army that drains resources away from other pressing social needs, such as health or education, or a political machine that relies on graft and creates corruption in public life.

It is also important to point out that the functions of a unit of social structure may not be limited to its "official," or intended, functions. Besides its recognized, or **manifest, functions,** a unit of social structure also has unrecognized, unintended **latent functions.**

One manifest function of colleges and universities, for instance, is to educate people and prepare them for

Draining resources away from pressing social needs by creating an atom bomb, as occurred in both Pakistan and India in 1998, could be viewed as a dysfunctional act of government.

specialized roles in society. A latent function of colleges and universities may be to keep part of the population out of the job market and so prevent strains in the economy.

Functionalism has been criticized on many grounds, but mainly because its view of society is inherently conservative. Since it stresses shared values and regards society as composed of parts that function together for the benefit of the whole, functionalism seems to leave little room for people who do not share society's values or who try to change them. Critics charge that functionalism largely ignores dissent and social conflict. By focusing so heavily on order, stability, and consensus, functionalism may even distort the true nature of societies. Unlike the parts of an organism, argue the critics, the parts of society do not always function together for the benefit of the whole. Some societal parts are in conflict; some parts benefit at the expense of others.

The most forceful criticism of the functionalist perspective comes from a group called *conflict theorists*. They agree that the functional perspective may be valuable in studying stable societies. But a look at the world today suggests that societies are changing at a rapid rate, and that conflict is not the exception but the rule.

The Conflict Perspective

The *conflict perspective* is not nearly so unified a viewpoint as is functionalism. It consists of a varied body of theories that has been given the conflict label only in recent years. The one belief shared by all conflict theorists is that societies are always in a state of struggle over scarce resources. One of the most important of these scarce resources is power. Therefore, conflict theorists argue, a society is best viewed as an arena in which there is a constant struggle for power.

A major assumption of many conflict theorists is that, rather than being held together by the "glue" of shared values, societies, social institutions, and social order are maintained principally through force. The more powerful members of a society are able, partly through the use of force, to compel the less powerful members of the society at least to appear to accept their values. One of the main concerns of conflict theorists, therefore, has been to identify the dominant groups in a society and to understand how they maintain their dominance—and, in fact, how they achieved their power in the first place.

Sometimes conflict theory simply means Marxist sociology. Marxist sociologists emphasize the importance of economic forces in societies rather than the shared cultural values stressed by functionalists. And they focus on the constant struggle between economic classes. Marx identified two principal classes: the industrial working class, or *proletariat,* and the owners of the means of production, or *bourgeoisie.* He predicted that the conflict between these two classes would eventually lead to the revolutionary overthrow of capitalist societies, with a classless society as the final outcome (Marx & Engels, 1848).

The fact that Marx's prediction has not come to pass does not mean that conflict theory is invalid or even that the class struggle has ended in capitalist societies. Neo-Marxist conflict theorists continue to agree with Marx in emphasizing that most societies are torn by conflict and struggle between economic classes. In general, neo-Marxists argue that social progress will occur only when the power of capitalists—the dominant class—is diminished (Braverman, 1975).

The term *conflict theorist* typically includes many non-Marxist sociologists as well. Perhaps the best-known living non-Marxist conflict theorist is the German sociologist Ralf Dahrendorf, former head of the London School of Economics. Dahrendorf attacks the central premise of functionalism—that society is basically orderly. He regards that premise as utopian (1958) and directs attention to society's "ugly face"—conflict. In contrast to Marx, Dahrendorf sees conflict more as a struggle for power than as a fight between classes over economic resources. But, like Marx, he views society as always tending toward instability and change. Indeed, he maintains that social change, not social order, should be the main focus in the analysis of society (1959).

The founder of the conflict perspective in the United States was C. Wright Mills. Mills felt that he was working in a Marxist tradition, but there is also much in his thought that comes from Max Weber. In addition, Mills's work reflects midwestern populism, a political ideology of the late nineteenth century that viewed "the people" as pitted against corrupt "big interests" in American life. In his best-known book, *The Power Elite* (1956), Mills tried to discover who really rules in America. He concluded that this nation is dominated by leaders drawn from three increasingly interrelated spheres: the top management of the big corporations, key officials in the executive branch of the government, and the top ranks of the military. Moreover, corporate executives often join the government, and retired generals are frequently elected to the boards of large corporations. Thus, Mills believed, a small and very centralized group makes most of the major decisions in our society about war and peace, money and taxes, civil rights and responsibilities.

The ideas developed by Mills are central to much of modern conflict theory (Domhoff, 1978, 1983, 1990). Despite visible signs of success, conflict theorists note, the people who make up the power elite are often less aware of their power than they are of other people's resistance to it. To deal with this resistance and to keep public resentment within bounds, those in power try to blur the line between themselves and the masses. Nonetheless, the masses are aware of their powerlessness, and they resent it. This tension between the strong and the weak becomes the breeding ground for social conflict. The people who benefit the most from the existing social order will seek to preserve it. Those who are deprived, work to change it. The conflict resulting from the opposition of these groups can lead to significant social change.

Most sociologists today, no matter what their personal preference, accept both perspectives—functionalist and conflict—as valuable, recognizing that each explores a different aspect of society. Functionalism examines how people work together in everyday life. It provides some useful answers to the question: Why are people who have their own special needs and interests often cooperative with one another? Conflict theory, on the other hand, focuses on the strains and tensions in life, on the lack of equality in societies, and on breakdowns in the social order. Just as functionalism may sometimes err in seeing more cooperation and order than actually exist, conflict theories may err in believing social conflict to be the major form of social interaction. But both perspectives point out aspects of our social existence that are basic and universal.

CHAPTER REVIEW

1. Where do you fit in the social structure? What is your master status?

2. Explain the fundamental difference between a status and a role.

3. What is the key difference between role conflict and role strain?

4. Do the members of your sociology class constitute a group or an aggregate? Why?

5. Is the media a social institution? Why or why not?

6. How would you describe the community in which you live? What are its boundaries? Compare your answer with that of a classmate from a different place.

7. Describe the role that the Internet plays in the world system.

8. Explain why war is more likely in some societies than in others.

9. Describe one dysfunctional part of the American social structure.

10. Some politicians have argued that the media constitute a cultural elite. What do they mean, and what would Karl Marx say about that claim?

INTERNET EXERCISE

The Web destinations for Chapter 4 cover various aspects of society and social structure. To begin your on-line exploration, go to the Prentice Hall Companion Web site **http://www.prenhall.com/popenoe**. Next, choose **Chapter 4** (Society and Social Structure). Then, select **web destinations** from the menu on the left side of the screen. There are a variety of sites to choose from. We suggest you begin with

Intentional Communities. This site contains fascinating materials relating to communal and associational societies. As described in this site, *intentional community* is an inclusive term for ecovillages, cohousing, residential land trusts, communes, student co-ops, and urban housing cooperatives. You may want to visit one of the many Web sites managed by *actual* communal organizations, like the **Eastwind Community, The Farm,** or the **Bruderhof Communities.** After you have conducted your explorations, answer the following questions:

- What are the major differences between the lifestyle in intentional communities compared with the average American family today?

- What would you find appealing or disturbing about social life in intentional communities? Why?

KEY TERMS

social structure	role performance	community
status	role conflict	society
achieved status	role strain	world system
ascribed status	group	dysfunctional
master status	social system	manifest functions
role	social category	latent functions
role set	aggregate	
role expectation	social institution	

CHAPTER 5

Social Interaction and Social Networks

s he picked at his breakfast, Joe kept asking himself, "How will it go today?" In an hour he would have an interview with the dean of admissions at a prestigious local business school. He felt that his future was on the line. Mentally rehearsing for the interview, Joe played both his part and the admissions officer's.

He got in his car and drove to the campus. He was nervous, but to an outsider he was the image of the rising young executive: well groomed, wearing polished shoes, dressed in a conservative jacket and tie, and sporting a new briefcase.

At the interview, Joe tried to put his best foot forward, despite the butterflies in his stomach. He wanted to show the dean that he was bright, articulate, and, above all, businesslike. He asked what he hoped were discerning questions about elective specialties and intern programs. He was very careful to speak properly, yet naturally.

After the interview was over, Joe was relieved and elated. He felt that he had done well and that he had impressed the interviewer with his polish and eloquence. He had certainly tried hard enough. He hoped he had presented the image that the dean expected. Then he went home and changed into jeans and his favorite flannel shirt.

What had Joe done? The main point is that he had crafted his actions and appearance in order to present himself in a certain way. His attire, speech, posture, and expression can all be understood as carefully designed to meet his audience's expectations. He tried to project an image that emphasized the features of his personality that he felt were important for success in the interview.

Depending on the particular situation, we all emphasize different elements of ourselves at different times. We do this according to rules constructed and shared by the members of our society. The interactions between Joe and the dean were patterned by what each expected of the other. The dean expected to meet someone alert, polite, highly motivated, carefully dressed in business clothes, and well prepared with remarks and questions suitable for an admissions interview. Joe expected to meet someone authoritative, knowledgeable about the school, and adept at asking probing questions.

In this chapter, we discuss how sociologists analyze daily interaction among people. We also look at the main forms of social interaction in societies, including the social networks in which our lives are embedded.

WHAT IS SOCIAL INTERACTION?

Almost all human behavior is oriented toward other people, for we are constantly aware of the effects that our actions and reactions have on others. In our everyday face-to-face encounters with people, we are often conscious of the way we think they expect us to behave and the way we expect them to think, feel, and act toward us. We continually alter our behavior to suit both where we are and the people we are with. We act differently when eating in the high school cafeteria or college lunchroom than we do when we are eating in a fancy restaurant or at home. Our behavior in class is different from our behavior outside of class. People who work together in an office interact differently at work than they do when socializing together after work. And when we do not know what the "right" behavior is—if we run into the boss at a bar, for example—we often feel uncomfortable.

Even when we are not consciously thinking about others, our actions may be patterned by expectations we learned in the past that have become ingrained. Routine, seemingly private actions, such as strolling down the street, looking around a room, or even sleeping in our own beds, are heavily shaped by what other people expect about how such actions should be performed. For example, the looks that strangers give to one another when they pass on the street generally follow a common pattern. In a process that has been called *civil inattention,* strangers typically look at one another long enough to acknowledge each other's presence, but not so long as to suggest any special curiosity. Civil inattention usually takes the form of "eyeing the other up to eight feet . . . and then casting the eyes down as the other passes—a kind of dimming of the lights" (Goffman, 1963/1980).

This type of awareness of what others expect of us occurs even when we are not with other people. We may be alone and thinking of someone else, or imagining someone else thinking about us. We may be trying to assess the quality of a friendship or the importance of a recent **social encounter.** Or we may be wondering how we can impress our professors or supervisors. In short, we are almost always involved in **social interaction,** the process in which people act toward, or respond to, others in a mutual and reciprocal way. In one form or another, social interaction makes up a major part of human existence.

Interaction and Meaning

Humans are not unique in engaging in social interaction. However, nonhuman organisms respond to one another with a much more fixed set of behaviors. Imagine, for instance, two dogs circling each other, just about to fight. In a sense, the two animals "converse" with each other by snarling, baring their teeth, and barking. An action by one dog brings forth an instinctive response in the other.

But this kind of "conversation" is fundamentally different from the interaction between, say, a husband and wife deciding how to spend a summer weekend. Human interaction is meaningful: The husband and wife are consciously aware of the motives or intentions behind what each says. Each is aided in making sense of the other's behavior by their years of experience together, not to mention their common language and culture. By contrast, animals interact by responding to a series of stimuli. They probably do not consciously think about the meaning of their own behavior or that of the animal with which they are interacting.

Max Weber was one of the first sociologists to stress the importance of studying interaction and meaning. In fact, he argued that the main goal of sociology is to explain what he called "social action." In order to do this, Weber felt, sociologists must put themselves in the position of the people they are studying and then try to interpret their thoughts and motives. He called this approach *Verstehen*, or "sympathetic understanding."

However, Weber never put these ideas into practice. Most of the work he did was at the level of macrosociology. It was, instead, an American—George Herbert Mead—who was among the first to make a systematic study of meaning in human interaction. His approach came to be called *symbolic interactionism*.

SYMBOLIC INTERACTIONISM

George Herbert Mead

Mead was a teacher at the University of Chicago from 1894 to 1931 (see Chapter 1). His studies were focused on what he saw as the basic unit of human behavior, which he called the "act." According to Mead, an act is the total reaction of a person in a situation. It includes not only people's actual behavior but also their focusing of attention on specific objects or people in the environment, along with their feelings and thoughts about those objects or people (Strauss, 1956).

Humans do not simply react to the behavior of others without thinking, as animals do. They think very carefully about what they are responding to. They plan their responses and even rehearse them in their minds before acting.

Humans, Mead said, are also different from animals in that we have a *self*. Mead's use of this term emphasizes the fact that we "act" toward ourselves as we might toward another person. We compliment ourselves, debate with ourselves, take pride in ourselves, or take ourselves to task. In all of these "actions," we are addressing our self, an inner "person" to whom we "speak" as if we were talking to another individual. The process of "talking" to ourselves, according to Mead, is the most important single feature of human consciousness.

Furthermore, Mead stressed that human interaction is heavily influenced by cultural meanings and that

People are almost always involved in social interaction— the process in which people act toward, or respond to, others in a mutual and reciprocal way. Social interaction makes up a major part of human existence.

most cultural meanings are symbolic (see Chapter 3). A colored piece of cloth on a flagpole symbolizes a nation. A smile may mean that another person is pleased.

It was Mead's main insight, then, that in their everyday existence, humans are constantly learning socially constructed and shared symbolic meanings and "conversing" with themselves about these meanings. Human interaction, according to Mead, is a process of acting on the basis of meaningful symbols (Blumer, 1962).

Principles of Symbolic Interactionism

In Chapter 1 we briefly introduced three major sociological perspectives: structural functionalism, conflict theory, and symbolic interactionalism. Because the first two of these general perspectives focus on large-scale, or macrosociological, phenomena, we devoted considerable attention in Chapter 4 to exploring each of them. We now turn to a detailed discussion of **symbolic interactionism,** a sociological approach that emphasizes the importance of symbols and meaning at the microsociological level. The essence of symbolic interactionism has been best summarized by Herbert Blumer, a student of Mead who spent much of his career refining and extending his teacher's ideas.

Blumer (1986) summarized the interactionist viewpoint in three basic principles. First, we act toward things according to the meanings we give them. Second, the meaning we give to things results from social interaction. Third, in any situation, we go through an internal process of interpretation—we "talk to ourselves"—in order to give the situation meaning and decide how to act.

Imagine, for example, a customer in a restaurant paying the bill at the cashier's desk. The customer gives the check to the cashier and reaches into her pocketbook. The cashier prepares to accept the money and give change. They are both acting toward the check according to the meaning they have given it, a meaning they share (the first principle). They know the meaning of the check because they learned it through many previous similar interactions (the second principle).

Now suppose the customer finds that she does not have enough money to cover the check. She acts embarrassed and says she will go to the bank next door to get some money and come right back. The cashier has to interpret this new situation, give it a meaning, and decide how to act (the third principle). He asks himself whether he should trust the customer or call the manager. Does she look honest? Is she a regular customer? Has the cashier encountered a similar situation? What happened then? All of these factors help to determine the cashier's interpretation; and understanding this process of interpretation is, according to Blumer, an important goal of an interactionist analysis (Wallace & Wolf, 1986).

According to symbolic interactionism, when we act, we must adapt our behavior so that it fits with what other people in the social situation are doing or thinking. To do this, we must first interpret the symbolic meaning of other people's acts. A young salesperson who blithely describes the latest round of office practical jokes during lunch with the boss and a potential client has not correctly interpreted the situation. If the salesperson fails, moreover, to understand the meaning of a sharp glance from the boss, he or she may well be excluded from future interactions with this group.

How do people gain an understanding of the meanings that other people attribute to symbols? Mead argued that this crucial understanding develops out of a process he called **role taking.** Individuals imagine themselves in the position of the person or group with which they are interacting. By paying close attention to the way these people use words or other symbols, we are able to intuit the meanings they intend their words and behaviors to convey. Thus, the young salesperson, by mentally taking the boss's role, learns that the boss wants the client to think that the firm is staffed with serious, competent people. As a result, the salesperson comes to share the boss's interpretation of the situation. By taking the role of the boss, the salesperson learns the meaning of the boss's behavior and modifies his actions accordingly.

Many social situations demand a kind of creative give-and-take. Each person must constantly interpret the actions of others and adjust his or her responses to them. For example, a woman giving a serious speech may shift her tone of voice slightly to show that she is going to tell a joke. People in the audience perceive this change and adjust their attention to the speaker so that they laugh at the right moment. In the same manner, the speaker listens to herself and may change her words according to how she believes they are affecting her listeners. If the audience does not appear to respond to her humor, the speaker may adopt a more obvious joke-telling manner. In this way the "scripts" of much social interaction are created on the spot rather than written once and repeated again and again.

Shared Definitions

In performing most of our everyday activities, we assume that, in general, others apply the same meanings as we do not only to words and other specific symbols but also to routine social situations. Many of these shared meanings, or "definitions of the situation," are acquired unconsciously. Neither the customer nor the salesperson, for example, is likely to stop and think deliberately about the social interaction they are involved in as they flip through the new blazers on the coat rack. Each understands his or her own role and also that of the other person. Imagine how difficult and uncertain life would be if people did not know how to interact when buying a toothbrush, answering a teacher's question, or typing a letter for an employer. Shared definitions of such routine situations enable people to see the world as a stable place that can be more or less taken for granted (Schutz, 1962).

This kind of agreement on definitions is the key to human interaction. Because the members of a society interpret and define most of the same situations in the same way, they can act together in an organized manner.

One of the founders of American sociology, W. I. Thomas, pointed out the great importance of *shared definitions* when he wrote: "If men define situations as real, they are real in their consequences" (Thomas & Thomas, 1928, p. 572)—an observation that is sometimes called *the Thomas theorem.* Our shared definitions guide human activity even when these definitions are objectively inaccurate. If people believe that witches really exist or that AIDS can be spread by sneezing, then they are likely to burn the people whom they believe to be witches at the stake and to shun AIDS victims who have the flu, despite the fact that such behaviors are based on faulty premises (which makes little difference to the "witches" or AIDS sufferers who are victimized).

There are some social situations in which definitions are not clear, in which case people develop the definitions they need through social interaction. From the information others provide about themselves, mostly through their patterns of behavior, an individual learns what to expect and what is expected. For example, two people at a dinner party given by a new business colleague must define the situation: What is the purpose of the party? Why were they invited? How should they act toward each of the other people there? Each guest may find that the other has a definition different from his or her own. One person may be using the gathering to conclude a business deal, and another may see it as a chance to flirt with someone else's spouse. On the other hand, the host and hostess may consider it primarily an occasion to show off their newly decorated living room.

Another instance in which people's definitions of a situation may vary occurs when a familiar custom is in flux. In the 1970s, for example, the custom of men automatically holding doors open for women was widely challenged. This ritual was felt by some to be a symbol of male control and female passivity. When one sociologist asked her students to observe and record who opened doors for whom and how they felt about it, she found that these encounters had become increasingly complex, problematic, and nonroutine. In other words, a new set of definitions about how men and women should act toward each other had created a situation in which a familiar custom was also being redefined. Many sociologists believe that such changes in customary behavior often lay the groundwork for significant future shifts in society's values on substantial issues (Walum, 1974).

CRITIQUE

Critics of symbolic interactionism argue that the approach's single-minded focus on the way individuals interact fails to account for how people's behavior is often shaped by larger forces that are beyond their control. In other words, it ignores many of the effects of social structure on our lives. The approach seems to deny the constraints that history, society, and the economy impose on us, and it gives a false impression of unlimited personal freedom.

In reply to these criticisms, Blumer and other symbolic interactionists point out that, whatever the impact of these larger social forces, we always experience them as people interacting with one another. We cannot truly understand society, they emphasize, without first understanding the way people interact within it (Adler & Adler, 1980).

OTHER APPROACHES TO SOCIAL INTERACTION

Sociologists have developed a number of perspectives that elaborate and extend the central insights of symbolic interactionism (Adler, Adler, & Fontana, 1987). Among the best known of these perspectives are dramaturgy and ethnomethodology.

Dramaturgy

When we talk to a person we do not know well, we immediately start asking ourselves questions about that individual. What does he or she do for a living? Where does the person live? What does he or she hope to gain from the conversation? All these questions help us to define the situation. We can also draw inferences based on the way the other person dresses, what has happened in the past in similar situations, and so on. However, the person we are getting to know is likely to be fully aware of the mental process we are going through and, as a result, he or she will actively attempt to influence the sorts of interpretations that we are making.

Erving Goffman thoroughly studied the process by which people attempt to shape the impressions others have of them. Goffman's approach to the study of social interaction, which views people as though they were actors in a theater, is called the **dramaturgical perspective.** According to Goffman, as people play their roles, their performances are judged by an audience that is constantly alert for slips that might reveal something about the actors' true characters (Goffman, 1959, 1963, 1971).

A central feature of human interaction, according to Goffman, is **impression management** or the **presentation of self**—the attempt to display ourselves to others so they will see us as we wish to be seen. For example, many people create impressions that make them seem sociable. A guest at a party might show great interest in the stock market for the benefit of a group of people introduced as stockbrokers. Similarly, salespeople tend to cultivate impressions that jibe with what they are selling. Thus, a person trying to sell vitamins might spend time under a sunlamp in order to look healthier. Similarly, aspiring rock stars may dress and act in ways that are sure to get them noticed.

In situations in which a first impression is critical, people often carefully plan their performances so that their actions are consistent with the impressions they wish to create. For example, a teacher preparing for the first day of school made the following remarks about the relationship he wanted to establish with his students:

> You can't ever let them get the upper hand on you or you're through. So I start out tough. The first day I get a new class in, I let them know who's boss. . . . You've got to start off tough, then you can ease up as you go along. If you start out easy-going, when you try to get tough, they'll just look at you and laugh. (Becker, 1952)

There are many possible goals of impression management. The actor may want to defraud, insult, confuse,

INTERNET/TECHNOLOGY

SOCIAL INTERACTION ON THE INTERNET

Cyberspace, the new frontier: Whether you recognize it as a familiar place or consider it foreign territory may well depend on the language you speak. For example, how many of the following words can you define? *Cyberporn, lurking, flaming, spamming,* and *newbie.* If you are having problems, then consider yourself a newbie—a newcomer to cyberspace.

If you did not know what newbie meant, then you probably were not offended by the condescending implications of the term. But forget my bad manners, you may need an introduction to manners yourself—that is, *netiquette,* the behavior expected of Internet users.

When we engage in everyday activities, we take most words for granted. We tend to acquire shared definitions unconsciously. We also tend to take the way we interact with others for granted. We question neither the meanings of our conversations nor our manners. That is, until we step outside our own culture. In this unfamiliar world, it is easy to unwittingly insult others. It can be as simple as looking directly into someone else's eyes, addressing the person improperly, or talking about taboo subjects.

The Internet is a foreign culture to newbies. And they must learn the "standards of conduct" that longtime inhabitants have established. If they violate the norms of this culture, they might receive a mild warning. But repeated or serious offenses are not tolerated. The norms of this culture

structure the social interaction within all of the Internet's networks (discussion groups, data bases, e-mail). And violators may be threatened with a loss of access to a group or even expelled (Croteau & Hoynes, 1997).

If you want to enter this new territory and do not want to be *flamed*—"toasted with nasty messages from all over" (Tapscott, 1998)— here are a few rules to follow:

1. DO NOT SHOUT. Typing words in all caps is called shouting. Do not do it. It is rude.

2. Read the *FAQs* (frequently asked questions). FAQs refers to a list of the most commonly asked questions for a particular Internet site. Proper netiquette requires that you read them before you post any questions.

3. *Lurk* before you speak. Lurking is a form of eavesdropping on the Internet, but it is expected and even advised. It refers to reading newsgroup messages that are posted by other people without responding to them. It gives you a chance to hear an ongoing conversation before you presume to know and understand a conversation.

4. *Spamming* is not allowed. Internet spam should not be confused with your favorite canned meat. It refers instead to newsgroup junk mail. Spamming— posting the same message to multiple newsgroups to

advertise a product or service— will not only irritate others, it will violate a deeply held conviction, that the Internet should be an ad-free medium.

If you violate these rules or insult other Internet users, they will probably express their anger by flaming you. And we all understand the emotion underlying a nasty message. But the Internet does not automatically supply us with many of the nonverbal cues that we rely on to read other people's reactions—a smile, a wink, or a frown. These are so necessary to the process of communication, however, that Internet users have developed their own way of attaching these meanings to their messages. The Internet has body language!

If you just aren't sure what someone meant by an e-mail message, check for some emotional cues (nonverbal information) or, as they are more commonly called, *smilies.* These consist of a few characters to create a face with an expression. Turn the book to the right to see these faces:

:-)	a person smiling
:-D	a person laughing
8-	a person with glasses
=:-)	a punk rocker
:-o	shocked or amazed

If you feel like you have just been *WNOHGB* (where no one has gone before), then take *JAM* (just a minute) to review this box. Before you know it you will be incorporating these kinds of abbreviations into your everyday language and saying things like *ttfn* (ta-ta for now) and *CUL8r* (see you later).

---

mislead, or get rid of others. Whatever the goal, as Goffman points out, it is always to the advantage of the actor to control the conduct of others. This is done by presenting an image that will bring about the desired behavior.

Goffman calls actions intended for strangers or casual friends *frontstage* behavior. Only people on more intimate terms are allowed to see what is going on *backstage*—that is, to know the actor's real feelings. Imagine, for instance, a customer complaining to a department store clerk about a defective garment. The clerk makes an apology, saying with a smile that every now and then a bad item slips past the inspectors. After the customer leaves with a new garment, the clerk turns to a co-worker and expresses what was "backstage": "Some people have nothing better to do with their time than complain!"

Frontstage and *backstage* may also refer to the actual physical place where a particular performance is given. In a typical middle-class suburban home, the living room is likely to serve as a frontstage area, carefully and tastefully decorated to reflect as positively as possible on the people who perform there, whereas the unplanned disarray of the den or family room testifies to its backstage character. In a high school, the teachers' lounge is a backstage area; the classroom, frontstage.

Sometimes two or more people work together as a *team* to create a desired impression. Two clerks might team up to express approval of a customer's choice of suit, when they really only want to hurry things along so they can close for the day.

On occasion, when presenting an impression, the actor, almost without knowing it, "gives off" a clue that makes the audience aware that it has been watching a performance. A speaker's voice may quaver. A person being interviewed may exaggerate being at ease, thereby betraying nervousness. Or a smile may break through the surface anger of a parent attempting to discipline a child. Disruption of a performance can also occur if someone in the "audience" mentions a fact or asks a question that weakens the image the actor is trying to present.

According to the dramaturgical approach, *embarrassment* occurs when an actor realizes that his or her performance has failed to make the desired impression on the audience. A professor who is supposed to be an authority on economics but is unaware of an important government document on the subject is likely to be embarrassed if his or her ignorance is exposed in class. A renowned soprano will probably be embarrassed if she fails to hit the E above high C for which she is so famous. Because of embarrassment, the performer may engage in *face work*—behavior intended to avoid losing face. The economist may express scorn for government documents in general, saying that they are biased and unreliable; the opera star may say that she inhaled a speck of dust just as she was about to hit her glass-shattering note.

Goffman pointed out, however, that embarrassment by a performer is usually accompanied by embarrassment by the audience. To avoid such embarrassment, members of an audience often ignore or overlook flaws in a performance and thereby help the performer to save face. Goffman used the term *studied nonobservance* to describe such a process. The class may downplay the importance of the government's economic report to help

Many parents experience frontstage and backstage behavior on a daily basis. In this picture the parents are exhibiting backstage behavior, in their home life with their children, and have just completed a day at work filled with frontstage behavior.

the economist save face; reviews of the opera may avoid any reference to the diva's failure to hit the high note. Studied nonobservance is a form of *tact*—a broader, more general term for the variety of ways an audience helps a performer to save face.

CRITIQUE. The dramaturgical approach has been criticized for presenting an overly static view of the self (Denzin & Keller, 1981). According to some sociologists, our self-image is actually slightly different in every interaction. As Charles Horton Cooley's notion of the looking-glass self suggests, we see ourselves reflected in the way that specific others react to us, and because each person sees us somewhat differently, we actually are, to some extent, different when in the presence of various other people (1902). Thus, we are a somewhat different person when interacting with our father, with our teacher, with our best friend, or with a bus driver. But Goffman seems to envision a stable, unchanging self, concerned in all interactions only with presenting the best possible impression.

Other critics have argued that Goffman goes overboard in portraying people as cynical and amoral. We do not always manipulate social situations; sometimes we try to present ourselves honestly and authentically (Douglas et al., 1980). Still other critics say that Goffman's cynicism may be appropriate as a description of the behavior of some contemporary Americans, but that it is much less applicable to other Americans or to people in different societies.

In his later work, Goffman indirectly responded to these criticisms by broadening his single focus on impression management, which he readily admitted is only one aspect of social reality.

Ethnomethodology

Harold Garfinkel (1967) coined the term **ethnomethodology** when studying jury deliberations. Garfinkel wondered how jurors could work together and reach decisions without having previously known each other and without understanding the technical rules of law. He decided that there must be a set of rules—*ethnomethods*—that we all implicitly understand and that we can call on in order to know how to behave in novel situations, such as on a jury. These ethnomethods, in other words, are a sort of shorthand that allow people to communicate and interact effectively, even when they do not know each other.

Ethnomethodologists share with Goffman and the dramaturgical approach an interest in the techniques that people use to create impressions in social situations, but they ask a different question about these techniques. They ask: How do such techniques or rules help form a common sense of reality, a feeling among people that their understandings are shared? Whereas mainstream symbolic interactionists see the rules by which we interact as an outcome of the process of interaction, ethnomethodologists are not interested in the origins of these rules. Rather, they are interested in the way people draw on the rules so that they know how to interact in a given situation (DeNora,1986; Wallace & Wolf, 1986; Whalen & Zimmerman, 1987).

The folk rules that govern social interaction involve a great many implicit understandings and expectations, or background assumptions, that people have about one another. These background assumptions are generally so taken for granted that they are rarely noticed. Yet when they are disrupted or challenged, their influence on social behavior becomes evident. A man who wears jeans and a T-shirt to a formal wedding has not followed the generally understood rule of "dressing for the occasion." Some guests may merely be puzzled at his failure to obey the rule; others may shun his company altogether.

Ethnomethodologists point out that even casual meetings are governed by shared assumptions. To show just how true this is, Garfinkel (1967) devised what he called *breaching experiments*. In these experiments, people act as though they do not understand the basic, unspoken assumptions behind a conversation. The following is an

exchange that occurred between the subject (*S*) and the experimenter (*E*):

(*S*):   Hi, Ray. How is your girlfriend feeling?
(*E*):   What do you mean, "How is she feeling?" Do you mean physical or mental?
(*S*):   I mean how is she feeling? What's the matter with you? (He looked peeved.)
(*E*):   Nothing. Just explain a little clearer what do you mean?
(*S*):   Skip it. How are your Med School applications coming?
(*E*):   What do you mean, "How are they?"
(*S*):   You know what I mean.
(*E*):   I really don't.
(*S*):   What's the matter with you? Are you sick? (p. 42)

Not only did these two people have trouble communicating, but the person who made the assumptions was upset by the other person's refusal to share them.

In another breaching experiment, students were asked to interact with their families for a period of up to one hour as though they were not familiar with the family's shared assumptions. None of the assumptions on which the family usually based its interaction was to be taken for granted. Strict formality was observed; for example, Dad and Mom were addressed as "Sir" and "Madam." The result was a breakdown in communication, with the family members becoming annoyed and upset. In attempting to restore the normal situation, the student could easily identify the family's shared assumptions.

CRITIQUE. Many mainstream sociologists, especially macrosociologists, are not familiar with ethnomethodology, and many distrust it. These critics argue that it is far removed from such major issues in sociology as the nature of institutions and the use of power in society. Moreover, it seems excessively vague and abstract. Yet the discovery of the rules of the social game, which ethnomethodology holds as its central goal, is clearly of universal interest.

Some sociologists are trying to link these micro-level rules with the macro-level rules governing communities and nations (Alexander et al., 1987; Collins, 1981). Such a link would provide an exciting and powerful new means of viewing social life.

Conversation Analysis

Harvey Sachs, a student of Erving Goffman and a colleague of Howard Garfinkel, led in the early development of **conversation analysis** (1992). Like them, he believed that everyday behavior revealed a great deal about human interaction. Sachs studied a variety of conversations—

from the trivial exchanges between friends to emergency calls for help. He found a number of characteristics common to all conversations: turn-taking, transitions between speakers, and interruptions.

Early research in conversation analysis focused on the way that speakers organize their verbal interaction into a coherent sequence. Turn-taking determines the order of speakers—who may speak and who may not. This process involves signals that indicate that a message has been understood and that another speaker can now proceed. Consider, for example, when someone asks a question such as "How is your mother doing?" The other person is expected to respond with a logical response: "She's fine, thank you." This response indicates that the question was understood and that the conversation may now continue. A failure to respond or hesitation indicates confusion and signals the need for further clarification. In this case, perhaps the mother has died.

While early conversation analysis focused on the way people organized verbal interaction into coherent sequences, subsequent studies have focused on other aspects of conversation (Boden, 1994; Campbell et al., 1992; Heritage & Greatbatch, 1991; Hopper, 1991; Maynard & Clayman, 1991; Schegloff, 1991; Whalen, 1990; Zimmerman, 1992). For example, Harvey Molotoch and Deirdre Boden analyzed videotapes of the Watergate hearings to study how power struggles played themselves out over the course of the investigation (1985). In her studies of the way men and women communicate, Deborah Tannen also examined how power displays itself in conversation (1990). According to Tannen, conversations between men and women reveal fundamental differences in the way they view the world. Thus, she argues that, for men, "conversations are negotiations in which people try to achieve and maintain the upper hand," whereas for women, they are "negotiations for closeness in which people try to seek and give confirmation and support" (1990, pp. 24–25). That, she argues, explains why men and women often fail to understand one another.

NONVERBAL COMMUNICATION

As we interact with other people, we respond not only to what they say but also to what they do. Suppose, for example, that a professor says he or she is greatly interested in your thoughts on a subject. As you are speaking, however, you notice the telltale signs of a suppressed yawn. This nonverbal part of the professor's behavior is bound to affect your actions from that point on.

An astonishing amount of nonverbal communication takes place in the course of everyday human interaction. According to one estimate (Birdwhistell, 1970), most people speak for a total of only about 10 to 11 minutes daily. In an average two-person conversation, words carry less than 35 percent of the social meaning of the situation. The nonverbal content makes up the remaining 65 percent.

Communication that is conducted in symbols other than language is called **nonverbal communication.** Physical appearance, dress, personal possessions—all may be types of nonverbal communication. Two of the most important forms are body language, which includes gestures and facial expressions, and personal space.

Body Language

Facial expressions are probably the richest source of nonverbal information because they reveal emotions so directly. In talking toothers, we continually watch their faces for reactions to what we say. We also try to keep close control over the expressions on our own faces. Yet interpreting facial expressions is often difficult because they can be hard to read.

There is some evidence that expressions of certain emotions, such as fear, happiness, surprise, and anger, are universal. When researchers showed photographs of these expressions to people from both modern cultures and isolated traditional cultures, they were correctly identified by all (Ekman & Friesen, 1971). It is widely accepted that such facial expressions reflect innate biological programming—that is, nature rather than nurture. It is for this reason that they do not have to be learned and that they convey the same meaning in virtually all cultures.

In contrast, *gestures*—movements of the body or limbs to express an idea, emotion, or attitude—vary widely from culture to culture. In the United States, for example, nodding the head up and down means "yes," and shaking the head from side to side means "no." But the Semang of the Malay Peninsula thrust their head forward to indicate "yes," and the Malayan Negritos say "no" by looking downward. To Ethiopians, the hand flick gesture (placing one wrist on top of the other and moving the hands back and forth simultaneously in opposite directions) is used to symbolize a declaration of love to a woman; in Israel, the same gesture has taken on a military meaning and now signifies "imprisoned" or injured hands. The hand purse gesture (made by sticking out the hand, palm up, and bringing the five fingers together in a point) is interpreted by Ethiopians as begging for food, but by Israelis as a signal to "slow down and be patient" (Schneller, 1985).

Posture, the way people position the body or limbs, is also a form of body language. Unlike facial expressions and gestures, which are under fairly conscious control, people often do not think about their postures. Thus, through posture they often "give off" information that they did not intend to divulge.

Facial expressions are probably the richest source of nonverbal communication. The meaning of certain expressions, such as these signifying happiness, fear, surprise, and anger, is universally understood.

Personal Space

People can deliberately employ *personal space*—the immediate area surrounding them—to convey certain meanings. However, this is more often done unconsciously. One aspect of personal space, the *personal distance* between people conversing, is especially meaningful. Personal distance is usually measured by physical distance. The anthropologist Edward T. Hall (1966), who has studied this subject extensively, uses the following examples to show how physical distance can indicate people's feelings about one another:

> People who are very angry or emphatic about the point they are making will move in close, they "turn up the volume," as it were, by shouting. Similarly—as any woman knows—one of the first signs that a man is beginning to feel amorous is his move closer to her. If the woman does not feel similarly disposed, she signals this by moving back. (p. 144)

Hall has developed a theory suggesting that there are four basic zones of personal distance, each characterized by its own types of activities and relationships. The particular distance at which people choose to interact reflects and sometimes shapes their relationships. It is important to note that this theory may apply only to the people Hall studied—healthy, middle—class adults in the northeastern United States.

At *intimate distance,* from actual contact to 18 inches from one another, the presence of the other person is overwhelming. At this distance, one can smell the other person's breath and feel, hear, and see in detail the other's body. This is the distance for lovemaking, comforting, and protecting. This distance is not considered proper in public by many adults, though children may frequently be observed at this distance in public places of all kinds.

Personal distance, 18 inches to 4 feet, is the range within which close friends and lovers normally interact. *Social distance,* 4 feet to 12 feet, is the zone in which impersonal business is carried on. People at a casual social gathering also stand at this distance, except where space is limited. Beyond 12 feet is the zone of *public distance.* Public figures address others at this distance.

Hall argues that similar kinds of personal space exist in other cultures, although the specific distances vary from one society to the next. Continental Europeans normally speak to one another at a distance that in America is reserved for more personal relationships. One American whom Hall (1966) interviewed said, "These people get so close, you're cross-eyed. It really makes me nervous. They put their face so close it feels like they're *inside you*" (p. 145).

Cultural definitions of personal space also extend to the way in which rooms, doors, and offices are regarded. Germans feel that the door preserves the integrity of the room and provides a needed boundary between people. In German offices, doors tend to be solid and are kept closed. In America, however, a closed door may imply an antisocial air or even a hint of conspiracy (Hall, 1966; Schwartz, 1967). And while both Americans and Germans tend to assign top-ranking business executives to corner offices, the French consider the most prestigious office to be the center one. In France, both offices and towns are often laid out as radiating stars, with the most important people, places, and institutions at the center (Hall, 1988).

There is also evidence that the amount of personal space used varies with gender. One researcher has noted that men tend to need more personal space than women (Epstein, 1986). Perhaps as a consequence, they are more negatively affected than women when in a crowded room (Freedman, 1975).

FORMS OF SOCIAL INTERACTION

Building on the pioneering work of George Simmel, a late nineteenth-century German sociologist, a number of major forms of social interaction have been identified and analyzed. Those forms most prominent in human social life are exchange, cooperation, conflict, competition, and coercion. Although we discuss each of these separately, they are commonly combined in various ways.

Exchange

A relationship in which a person or group acts in a certain way toward another in order to receive a reward or return is an **exchange relationship.** Many relationships are of this type; a good example would be that between employer and employee. If the employee behaves the way the employer wishes, he or she will be rewarded with a salary.

Rewards do not have to be tangible. Many social exchange relationships offer emotional rewards, as when people tailor their behavior toward another in order to receive gratitude. People expect gratitude more often than is realized (Blau, 1964, 1987). Making change for a stranger who wants to buy a candy bar from a machine, helping an elderly person across the street, sending a small gift to a co-worker who is ill—underlying all these actions is the desire to have the other person feel grateful for what you have done.

The exchange relationship is also important in intimate interactions. One person's love for another is not based solely on an expected return. Nonetheless, that

GLOBAL SOCIETY

THE GYPSIES

Have you ever hailed a gypsy cab to take you to a rough part of town where licensed taxicabs do not like to travel? Have you ever been "gypped"? Do you refer to an independent trucker as a gypsy? These slang terms refer to Gypsies—a mysterious group that is commonly associated with an itinerant lifestyle whose members have acquired the reputation for swindling naive members of society. In fact, while most Americans have probably incorporated these slang terms into their vocabulary, few have ever met a Gypsy. If you have, she was probably a fortune-teller. They seem to be everywhere and yet nowhere at all.

Are these just negative stereotypes? It is actually hard to say. Even researchers admit that their "cultural patterns are difficult to grasp" (Kephart & Zellner, 1994). But their lifestyle, and the social network which supports it, are fascinating. While the public might view Gypsies as crooks, devoid of any form of social control, Gypsies do indeed live by rules, which form an effective system of social control. In order to understand how their system operates, we must first understand who the Gypsies are.

The word *Gypsy* is derived from "Egyptian," but today we know that this group originated in India. In fact, the language of Gypsies, Romany, has its roots in Sanskrit. According to Kephart and Zellner, Gypsies

> have been variously described as being descended from the criminal and Wandering Tribes, as being deported prisoners of war, and as being "a loose federation of nomadic tribes, possibly outside the Indian Caste system." (1994, p. 97)

Scholars believe that Gypsies left India at different times, starting perhaps during the first few centuries A.D. Some appear to have settled around Persia and Syria by the fifth century. By the 1300s, Gypsies had settled in southeastern Europe (Greece, Hungary, Romania, Serbia), and by the 1400s, they lived in western Europe (France, Germany, Italy, Holland, Switzerland, and Spain). Today Gypsies live in almost every European country, North Africa, the Near East, South America, the United States, and Canada.

Gypsies, who refer to themselves as *Rom*, live in an alien culture. And they draw sharp lines between themselves and outsiders, whom they call *gadje* (non-Gypsies). These boundaries are maintained in a number of ways, including deception, avoidance, misrepresentation, and lying. As many researchers have discovered, studying the Rom is "like trying to penetrate a secret society" (Kephart & Zellner, 1994, p. 101).

The Gypsy community is strongly rooted in an interlocking system of extended families. The *familiyi* (extended families) form part of a larger kinship group called the *vista*. These, in turn, are linked to one of four tribes, or *natsiyi*: Lowara, Machwaya,

expectation is a part of the relationship. If a person never receives any affection or gratitude for the love offered, his or her feelings of love will probably diminish.

In these examples, we see at work a basic principle of much social exchange: *reciprocity*. According to reciprocity, every transfer from one person to another involves the expectation of a return. The return may be immediate or delayed, but the expectation that one will eventually receive an equitable reward governs the entire relationship. Reciprocity assumes a basic equality between those who take part, and it helps to maintain that equality by creating continuing mutual obligations.

Exchange relationships are the focus of what is called *exchange theory.* Based on assumptions quite different from those of symbolic interactionism, microsociological exchange theory is best represented by the work of George Homans. Homans's theory applies to sociology the principles of behavioral psychology, or *behaviorism,* a branch of psychology that is concerned only with behavior that can be observed and measured.

Drawing on the work of his Harvard colleague, the behavioral psychologist B. F. Skinner, Homans (1974) argues that self-interest is the universal motive behind people's actions toward one another. People, like the animals in Skinner's psychology experiments, do things for rewards. And if behavior is positively reinforced or rewarded, it is more likely to be repeated in the future.

This perspective assumes that individuals think in terms of *net rewards*—that is, rewards minus costs. Even when considerable psychological pain results from a relationship, for example, people will not break off the relationship so long as the rewards from it continue to be greater than the costs. Moreover, they may continue in relationships that are not rewarding because they are not aware of, or have no chance to engage in, relationships that offer more rewards, or fewer costs, or both.

Thus, according to exchange theorists, much of human social life can be reduced to a kind of arithmetic of rewards and costs. This logic has been applied to marriages, friendships, and even the simple act of doing good

Kalderacha, and Churara. While Gypsy customs may vary from one *familia* to the next, one instrument of social control has a powerful binding force. It is called *marime*, which means defilement or pollution.

Gypsies believe that the upper parts of the body are pure and clean, and the lower parts, especially the genital and anal areas, are *marime*. In order to avoid pollution, the upper part of the body must never come into contact with the lower part. Ronald Lee, a Gypsy, described the kind of hygienic rituals that are designed to prevent pollution:

> You can't wash clothes, dishes, and babies in the same pan, and every Gypsy has his own eating utensils, towels, and soap. Other dishes and utensils are set aside for guests, and still others for pregnant women. Certain towels are for the face, and others for the nether regions—and there are different colored soaps in the skin, each with an allotted function. (cited in Kephart & Zellner, 1994, p. 103)

Gypsies view the *gadje* as *marime* because they do things that contaminate the upper part of their body. For example, non-Gypsies may forget to wash their hands in public bathrooms, they may eat with a fork that has fallen to the floor, they may wash face towels with underwear, or they may put their feet on a tabletop (Kephart & Zellner, 1994).

Marime restricts the interaction between *Rom* and *gadje* and effectively prevents the assimilation of *Rom* into the larger society. An older Gypsy woman described the important function of *marime* to an interviewer who asked her if she thought *marime* was beginning to weaken in Gypsy society. She replied: "Maybe. I hope not. Some of the young kids don't know it but it's what holds us together" (Kephart & Zellner, 1994, p. 107).

In Gypsy society, informal social control is far more effective than formal social control. No written rules exist. Instead, traditions, customs, rituals, rules of behavior, and moral codes hold the society together. Together these constitute what Gypsies call *romania*. Individuals who violate the unwritten rules embodied in *romania* will not be arrested, nor must they fear jail. But they will be subjected to gossip, ridicule, and wisecracks; and in this tight-knit, closed society this type of informal social control is highly effective. If the offense is serious enough, an individual may be declared *marime* and ostracized from the group. In Gypsy society, where people are never really alone, this is the ultimate punishment. If the *marime* is considered permanent, a Gypsy may even prefer to end his life by committing suicide.

Source: Based on William M. Kephart and William W. Zellner, *Extraordinary Groups,* 5th ed. (New York: St. Martin's Press, 1994).

for someone. Stable patterns of interaction between people are formed and maintained because the individuals find the interaction rewarding.

One important application of exchange theory has been in the study of the relationships of couples (Levinger, 1979). Most couples do not consciously analyze their relationship in terms of costs and rewards, debits and credits. But, in fact, they are engaged in many kinds of exchange. The items exchanged may include such tangible things as domestic work and financial support, as well as such intangibles as emotional support and physical pleasure. According to Levinger, the stability of a relationship depends on how satisfying these exchanges are to both members. In a stable, enduring relationship, the exchanges are taken for granted. When a relationship turns sour, the members begin to pay close attention to what they do for each other. If they feel that the give and take is inequitable, they may try to restore balance. But, ultimately, if they feel that costs outweigh benefits, the relationship is likely to end.

Criticisms of exchange theory and behaviorism have, in general, been impassioned within sociology, especially from symbolic interactionists. Exchange theory is regarded by symbolic interactionists as conceptually narrow because it tends to dismiss those very elements of social life they feel are centrally important: meanings, values, motives, intentions, and the self (Denzin, 1986a). Symbolic interactionists ask, for example, "How do you know what is rewarding and what is costly unless you understand preexisting values and meanings?" Nevertheless, the importance of exchange relationships in societies is hard to deny. And exchange theories are currently becoming more prominent within sociology.

Cooperation

Cooperation is interaction in which people or groups act together in order to achieve common interests or goals that might be difficult or impossible to attain alone. As emphasized by the functionalist perspective, all social life

Habitat for Humanity is an example of directed cooperation. People cooperate together under the aegis of a large organization.

is, in a broad sense, based on cooperation; society could not exist without it. People band together in groups and societies in order to meet environmental crises such as floods, famine, and disease. They work together to supply individual needs efficiently and to obtain mutual protection against threats from other groups.

Four main types of cooperation have been identified (Nisbet, 1970). The oldest and most universal is *spontaneous cooperation*, or mutual aid. It arises directly out of the needs and possibilities of a situation, as when two people cooperate on a homework assignment so that they can both get better grades, or when witnesses to an accident work together to help the injured.

Sometimes cooperation that began spontaneously becomes fixed in a society's customs. The cooperation thus institutionalized is called *traditional cooperation*. On the frontier of early America, for example, settlers had a tradition of gathering to help one another put up barns and bring in the harvest.

Modern societies rely less on traditional cooperation than on *directed cooperation*—that is, cooperation mandated and coordinated by a third party in a position of authority. The third party may be an employer who tells two co-workers to pool their efforts to accomplish a certain task. Or the third party may be a swimming instructor who tells students to pair up when they go into the water.

Modern societies also depend on *contractual cooperation*, in which individuals or groups formally agree to cooperate in certain ways, with the duties of each clearly spelled out. A group of young parents is involved in contractual cooperation, for example, when its members take turns caring for one another's children so that each can have time to do other things.

Conflict

Conflict, the opposite of cooperation, is the struggle for a prized object or value (Nisbet, 1970); the defeat of an opponent is thought to be essential to achieving the desired goal. As stressed by the conflict perspective in sociology, conflicts arise because benefits and rewards are limited. Individuals must compete in pursuing scarce resources. Each person tries to subdue the others as much as is necessary to achieve his or her own desires.

Georg Simmel (1955) outlined four major types of conflict: wars between groups, conflict within groups, litigation (conflict that is handled legally and is often settled in the courts), and the clash of impersonal ideals. Conflicts over ideals, rather than over concrete possessions, have often been the most merciless and destructive. Today, for example, differences in religious ideals underlie many of the world's most serious conflicts, such as those in the Middle East and in Northern Ireland.

Because conflict has so often produced misery, people tend to view it negatively. However, some contemporary sociologists, following the lead of Simmel, have pointed out that it has some positive aspects (Coser, 1956). Conflict can serve as a force that bonds the people on opposing sides firmly into groups. Conflict may also lead to needed social change—by forcing groups to talk to one another and face their problems, for example. These sociologists point out that even if society could somehow succeed in doing away with conflict, such a step might not be desirable. A conflict-free society would be lifeless and dull.

Competition

Competition is a kind of cooperative conflict governed by rules that make the goal being sought more important than the defeat of one's opponents. As in conflict, one party will attain the goal and another will be defeated, but defeating the competitor is not the main aim. Unlike those who take part in cooperative interaction, competitors go about achieving their goals separately and in rivalry with one another.

To keep competition from turning into conflict, the parties must agree ahead of time on the "rules of the game," and they must cooperate in sticking to these rules. This applies to competition in the marketplace, among students in a classroom, and between football teams. Competition is especially common in Western societies. It is central, for example, to the American system of individualistic capitalism.

Coercion

Coercion occurs when one person or group forces its will on another. To a substantial extent, all forms of coercion rest on the ultimate threat of the use of physical force or violence. But coercion is usually much more subtle than this. Love for a parent, respect for one's national flag, faith in God, and fear of loneliness can all be used as weapons of coercion.

Like conflict, coercion is usually viewed as a negative kind of social interaction. But coercion also has positive social functions. Although parents and educators use many strategies in raising children, the threat of punishment often underlies the teaching of social rules: The misbehaving boy is sent to his room; the girl who rode her tricycle onto the highway receives a spanking.

SOCIAL NETWORKS

Another approach to the study of social interaction focuses on the social networks to which people belong. A **social network** consists of an intricate web of ties among individuals. Networks have certain similarities with groups: Their members interact on occasion, often share a loose sense of identity and unity, and may have some common goals and expectations. However, the relationships among the members of networks are generally much more limited and diffuse than those that bind the members of groups, even secondary groups.

We all form networks naturally throughout our lives. As we move toward adulthood, we become members of networks of relatives, neighbors, schoolmates, and our parents' friends and colleagues. Though we join such networks effortlessly and usually with little thought, the resources they provide in our later lives can have profound effects on our socioeconomic status as adults. With respect to career mobility, for example, network analysis confirms what many have long suspected: In spite of the lip service paid to the idea of equal opportunity, what often counts in reality is not "what you know but whom you know."

Social networks perform several important functions. For one, many decisions and preferences are influenced by networks of friends, family, and co-workers. Networks are also a primary source of information and advice, whether for an immigrant searching for a place to live, a student seeking a summer job, or a parent looking for a good day-care center. Networks can also provide individuals with companionship.

The term *networking* has become a key word in the professional world. It usually signifies interacting for the purpose of meeting the "right" people. For example, a worker in a large company might try to network with members of the corporate management, say, at a company party or at the golf course, hoping that they will like him and help further his career.

Network Characteristics

Networks vary tremendously in their character and qualities (Höllinger & Haller, 1990). One group whose networks have been carefully studied are the British-Canadian East Yorkers of the greater Toronto area (Wellman, 1979). East Yorkers were asked detailed questions about such topics as whom they felt closest to, where these people lived, whether their intimates were kin, friends, or co-workers, and how they kept in touch. The researchers also determined whether the intimates named were connected with each other through social networks. Even though many of these people lived in other parts of metropolitan Toronto and beyond, the East Yorkers reported that weekly contacts in person or by phone were common.

Most of these networks were found to be "loosely knit"—that is, the majority of respondents belonged to multiple networks that were not strongly connected to each other rather than to single, tightly bonded groups. Living within such loosely knit networks does not, however, mean experiencing a sense of isolation. Only 2 percent of respondents reported having no one outside the home to whom they felt close, and 61 percent reported at least five intimate ties.

As this case points out, one major way in which social networks vary is their *density;* they range from being loosely knit to being tightly knit, or dense. Density

APPLYING SOCIOLOGY

NETWORKING ON THE INTERNET

Getting a good job is never easy. Employment agencies can cost a fortune, with no guarantee that you will find the job you want. And reading the Sunday classifieds quickly turns into exasperation for most people. Frustrations like these are common, and research explains why. Employment agencies locate about 9 percent of jobs for professional and technical people. And ads account for the placement of about 10 percent (Camden & Schwartz, 1995). But do not despair. Successful methods for finding jobs do exist. According to Mark Granovetter, a Harvard sociologist, 75 percent of all successful job searches result from "informal contacts" or, as it is more commonly called, "networking" (Camden & Schwartz, 1995).

This method of searching for jobs is based on the idea that your own social network—the web of ties available to you through personal contact—is your most valuable resource when looking for a job. Most people know at least 30 adults (Camden & Schwartz, 1995). If each of them gives you access to 3 more people, you have built a starting network of about 90 people who can help you gain access to the person who is hiring for the job you want.

Using this method, you might have to talk to 250 people before you land the job you want (Camden & Schwartz, 1995). Professional career counselors estimate that it can take 10 to 15 contacts to generate one formal interview, and 5 to 10 formal interviews to get a job offer. And you might consider five offers before you get the job you want.

Networking is a full-time job, in and of itself. Telephone calls can turn into telephone tag, and written correspondence can take weeks or even months. But today the Internet—the network of computer networks—can make the best method for getting a job even better. In fact, many recruiting departments are using the Internet today to screen job applicants.

Consider these advantages. First, the Internet can significantly increase the base of your initial list of contacts. Bulletin boards and listservs can put you into contact with people far beyond the leads developed through your own personal contacts. Second, the Internet provides valuable information about the labor market. For example, if you are looking for information about growing industries, salary projections, or market statistics check out the Web site for labor statistics (http://www.stats.bls.gov).

The Internet also gives you immediate access to information about companies that interest you. You can quickly find articles about the company online. Or pay a "virtual visit" to the company that interests you. Many companies provide a great deal of valuable information at their own Web sites.

Once you have completed your initial research, pursuing and contacting leads is your next step. Carrie Straub recommends a number of strategies (1998). For example, search the lists]ervs for leads. You might even post a question on a listserv about the career or industry that interests you. Or use a bulletin board to make connections. Finally, check out the Web sites for professional and trade associations.

As you pursue leads, keep an intermediate goal in mind—an informational interview. While busy schedules may prevent representatives of companies from meeting with you personally, the Internet is the perfect way to make that initial contact. Later, an informational interview can be conducted over the Internet. Contacting potential employers in this way has an added advantage. It will impress them with your Internet skills, an increasingly marketable skill for today's job market.

In fact, many recruiters may expect you to send an online résumé to them. In this case, you need to design it so that a computer will recognize your experience and talents (Graber, 1998; Straub, 1998). The use of keywords will increase the chances of your résumé being read by the person who is doing the actual hiring. The company's own job description is the best place to find keywords. Read it carefully and tailor your résumé to fit that description.

A number of Web sites will be helpful as you begin to network on the Internet. Check out the following:

America's Job Bank (http://www.ajb.dni.us/html/seekers.html)
CareerMosaic (http://www.careermosaic.com)
Internet Business Network (http://www.interbiz.com)
Internet Job Locator (http://www.joblocator.com/jobs/)
National Business Employment Weekly (http://www.nbew.com/)
Job Hunt: Meta List (http://www.job-hunt.com)
JobTrak (http://www.jobtrak.com)
Kaplan (http:kaplan.com)
The Monster Board (http://www.monster.com/home.html)
Online Career Center (http://www.occ.com)
The Riley Guide (http://www.dbm.com/jobguide)

refers to the degree of connectedness of the individuals in the network. If most of your friends know each other in addition to knowing you, your friendship network is tightly knit, or dense. If they generally do not know each other, your friendship network is loosely knit. There is much evidence that urban dwellers usually have looser knit social networks than do rural dwellers.

Another characteristic of networks is the degree to which they are multistranded. *Multistrandedness* refers to the number of ways in which two people are involved with each other. Relationships can vary from the simple and one-dimensional, such as those between a salesperson and his or her clients, to the multistranded, such as those between people who are involved in family life (Choldin, 1984). One study of northern California residents has revealed that young people, employed people, and people with high levels of education are particularly likely to have multistranded relationships (Fischer, 1982). Furthermore—and contrary to earlier theories suggesting that contacts among urban dwellers would be more numerous but also more superficial than those among rural dwellers—the northern California study revealed that people with larger networks have more multistranded ties. When we gain access to more people, the study concluded, we "may actually enjoy richer social lives" (p. 143).

Social ties have also been analyzed in terms of weakness and strength. A *strong tie* is one in which the amount of time invested, the level of emotional intensity, the degree of intimacy, and the extent of reciprocal services provided are all relatively substantial. To whom do we turn for help during a personal crisis? Probably to one of the small number of people with whom we have *strong ties*. In all likelihood, these people will be family members, close friends, or neighbors of the same sex. We tend to differentiate among our intimate ties, expecting sympathetic listening and understanding from some people, and small services from others. And we fully expect to reciprocate when these people need our help (Wellman & Wortley, 1990).

A *weak tie* is one in which these investments of self are less substantial or lacking altogether (Granovetter, 1973). Most people have many more weak ties than strong ties, but the importance of the weak ties should not be underestimated. A study of people who had changed jobs showed that, for most of those interviewed, a social contact had provided information about the new job, and "in many cases, the contact was someone only marginally included in the current network of contacts" (Granovetter, 1973, pp. 1371–1372). Weak ties are also important in fostering a sense of solidarity among people in numerous technical and professional specialties and in

allowing information and ideas to flow at meetings and conventions.

The Small-World Project

One interesting attempt to measure the interconnectedness of networks across the United States was the small-world project, named after the idea of this being "a small world after all" (Travers & Milgram, 1969). The researchers wanted to see how long it would take to get a document delivered from a person in Omaha, Nebraska, to a person in Sharon, Massachusetts, *using only personal contacts.* Documents were mailed to a random sample of Omaha residents containing the name of the target person in Sharon, instructions about how to proceed, and postcards to keep the researchers informed about the progress of the efforts. Participants were told that if they didn't know the target (a stockbroker) personally, they should pass the document along to someone more likely to know him.

The result? The median number of intermediaries required to connect volunteers with the target individual was just over five. Considering the large size of the nation, it is surprising that roughly five intermediaries can connect any two people. These results have important implications for our view of cities in particular. They show that even large and seemingly amorphous population centers are actually full of networks. Later research has even suggested that a chain of even two or three friends of friends may often be enough to link any two people in the *world* (Kochen, 1989).

The Importance of Network Analysis

Traditionally, sociological research has focused on the characteristics of individuals and groups. Network analysis has begun to make an important contribution to sociology because it concentrates on the personal connections among individuals. This more dynamic perspective provides fresh insights into the inner workings of social systems. Like each of the other perspectives discussed in this chapter, network analysis emphasizes that the individual has an active role in the social process, rather than passively adapting to larger social forces Fischer, 1982; Fischer et al., 1977).

According to symbolic interactionists, the members of a society can act together in an organized manner because they can define situations in the same way. But although definitions are widely shared within a society, they may differ sharply from one society to another; greetings, for example, can be expressed by an enthusiastic hug or a formal bow.

CHAPTER REVIEW

1. In what way does human interaction differ from the interaction of other animals?

2. Consider an inner conversation you had with yourself. What did you learn from this conversation?

3. How can role taking decrease misunderstandings between people?

4. How would Erving Goffman explain embarrassment? Why is it important to allow others to save face?

5. List five rules that you take for granted in everyday social interaction.

6. What kind of social interaction would characterize a healthy marriage?

7. How do politicians use social networks?

INTERNET EXERCISE

The Web destinations for Chapter 5 deal with various aspects of social interaction. To start your explorations, go to the Prentice Hall Companion Web site **http://www.prenhall.com/popenoe.** Next, choose **Chapter 5** (Social Interaction and Social Networks). Then, select **web destinations** from the menu on the left side of the screen. You will find a number of interesting sites to choose from. We suggest that you begin with **Business Netiquette International.** This site parallels the discussion in the *Internet/Technology* box in Chapter 5 entitled "Social Interaction on the Internet." The manager of the Business Netiquette International site is also the author of the Business Start Page, devoted to concerns of those who are trying to begin a new business venture. The site contains discussion of such topics as spamming, junk e-mail, international considerations, first names and titles, capitalization, and signatures. After you have explored the Business Netiquette International site, answer the following questions:

- Why do you think it is important to learn about using socially accepted procedures in communications on the Internet/World Wide Web?

- What are some of the consequences of failing to heed the rules of "Netiquette"?

KEY TERMS

social interaction
symbolic interactionism
role taking
dramaturgical
    perspective
impression management

presentation of self
ethnomethodology
conversation analysis
nonverbal
    communication
exchange relationship

cooperation
conflict
competition
coercion
social network

CHAPTER 6

Socialization

uppose you had spent your infancy and childhood locked in a room with no meaningful human contact. Would you be able to speak a language? Would you have a personality? Or feel human emotions?

Some answers to these questions were provided by the discovery of three separate cases of children who had been raised in extreme isolation: Anna, Isabelle, and Genie (Davis, 1940, 1947; Gromkin et al., 1974). Anna was kept hidden in a room by her mother, who was ashamed of the fact that her child had been born out of wedlock. When she was found, at 6½ years of age, Anna could not walk, talk, feed herself, or keep herself clean. She showed almost no emotion and was indifferent to humans. After she was discovered, Anna was first placed in a home for retarded children and then sent to a foster home. Her social skills gradually improved, and by the time of her death, at age 11, she had started learning to speak.

Isabelle, also born out of wedlock, was kept hidden by her deaf-mute mother. Although Isabelle had not mastered spoken language, she and her mother communicated with each other through gestures. Like Anna, she was discovered when she was 6½ years old. When she was first found, her behavior toward other people was described as "almost that of a wild animal." However, unlike Anna, Isabelle was provided with an intensive training program by the people who had taken over her care. Within only a few years, Isabelle had attained a developmental level that was normal for children her age.

Genie, who was discovered when she was about 13 years old, had been locked in a small room since she was about 18 months old. During much of her childhood, her father had her tied to a potty chair, where she stayed for many days and nights. When she was not imprisoned in the chair, she was kept in a crib in a windowless room. Her blind mother was allowed to feed her, but her father would not permit noise of any kind in the house. Her father and older brother did not even speak to her; rather, they barked at her like dogs.

By the time she was found, Genie was an emaciated, emotionally disturbed adolescent who could neither stand nor speak. Because doctors could find no evidence of biological defects, psychologists concluded that the social isolation in which she had spent her life had deprived her of the ability to speak. In the hospital to which she was later taken, Genie seemed to understand words but could not produce any herself until she had been there for a year. And although she made progress in many areas—such as learning to use the toilet—she never mastered the art of speaking in sentences (Pines, 1981).

These cases of children raised in isolation are rare, of course, but they point out that people are born emotionally and socially, as well as biologically, helpless. To survive and develop as complete human beings, people must have regular interaction with others. They must learn from others how to think and behave. This process of interaction and learning is called **socialization.** Formally defined, socialization is the process of social interaction through which people acquire personality and learn the ways of a society or group.

No matter where a child is born—whether in Los Angeles, Bombay, or the Trobriand Islands—the process of socialization is similar in broad outline, even though the cultural content may be very different. Through interaction with other people, infants are transformed from helpless human animals into social beings. As people pass through childhood, they are taught socially expected patterns of behavior, language, skills, and how to perform a variety of social roles. Even in adulthood the process of socialization continues, with new roles and skills still to be learned. Thus, socialization continues throughout the life course—the sequence of developmental stages in one's life, including birth, childhood, adolescence, adulthood, old age, and death.

Socialization is essential not only for the survival and development of the individual but also for the survival and effective operation of society. In fact, without socialization there can be no society (Elkin & Handel, 1978). A society will survive only as long as its members act together to support and maintain it, and therefore every society seeks to shape the behavior of its members toward this end. From society's point of view, the socialization process is working effectively when people feel that they want to do what they are expected to do, and when what they are expected to do is in the best interests of society.

HUMAN BIOLOGY AND SOCIALIZATION

The process of socialization is intimately connected with human biology. Human beings remain in "infancy"—that is, they are totally dependent on others—for about 6 years, and they do not leave the "juvenile phase" for another 14 years. Thus, they depend on their parents for 15 to 25 percent of their total life span. Compared with other animals, even other primates, this is a very long time. Yet it is this extended period of dependency that provides the time needed for learning cultural meanings and social skills, while creating lifelong social and emotional ties to others and to society as a whole.

Socialization would not be necessary if human beings had strong *instincts,* or fixed, biologically inherited behavior patterns. As noted in Chapter 3, however, such instincts are absent in human beings, and culture takes their place. Human beings must learn cultural patterns in order to survive and develop. This is the purpose of the process of socialization.

In lower animals, where instincts rather than culture guide social life, the young can function independently at a very early age. Animal young treat the first moving object they see after birth as "mother"—a process called *imprinting*—but a baby duckling will follow its instincts to search out water and swim even if the first moving object it sees is a hen. Lacking instincts, an unprotected human infant would have less chance of survival than most newborn animals, but at the same time, animals' dependence on instincts limits them to a rigid set of behaviors.

Although few scientists have argued that there are true human instincts, many have held that the social behavior of human beings is heavily influenced by inherited biological traits. This view was especially popular in the nineteenth century. Today, most social scientists stress the importance of cultural influences on social behavior, yet the issue of biology versus culture, or "nature versus nurture," remains unsettled.

Even the human body is affected by culture and the environment. Social class is one environmental factor that has been extensively studied. Sociological research has shown that children with fathers from higher-income groups tend to be taller than children with fathers from lower-income groups (Reynolds, 1976). One reason: High-income families can afford better nutrition. To take another example, the onset of puberty in girls is part of a developmental process begun by genes. But the average age of onset has been declining at the rate of four months per decade during most of this century. This has been attributed to such environmental factors as improved diet, personal health care, and medical treatment.

Sociobiology

Few scientists would argue that human behavior is determined entirely either by genetics or by the environment. Most agree that it is shaped by both. They disagree, however, on the extent of the genetic influence. The debate on this issue has focused on the work of a group of theorists called *sociobiologists* and led by the Harvard biologist Edward O. Wilson (1975, 1978).

Pointing out that humans differ from apes in only 1 percent of their genetic material, sociobiologists see much human, as well as animal, social behavior as the outcome of organic rather than cultural evolution (Gribben & Gribben, 1988). They assert that the genetic makeup of human beings contains a vast amount of "information" that programs the way we behave socially, just as it shapes our physical features. The specific genetic

information that is found in present-day human beings is the product of natural selection.

Darwin's theory of *natural selection* holds that those individuals who are best adapted to their environments will be most likely to survive and reproduce. This is the familiar theory of "survival of the fittest." We most often think of fitness in terms of physical traits—being taller, stronger, faster. But the concept of fitness, say sociobiologists, also applies to social traits such as the ability to love and to get along well with others. Whether the traits are physical or social, the better adapted are more likely to survive and thus pass their genes on to the next generation. Over many generations, the favored genes will spread throughout the population, and eventually the whole species will have the traits associated with those genes.

In biological terms, fitness and survival can have three meanings: *personal* fitness and survival (living a long life), *reproductive* fitness and survival (having numerous and healthy offspring), and *genetic* fitness and survival (the continued existence of all those with the same pool of genes, which includes all one's close relatives, not just one's own immediate offspring). Sociobiologists focus especially on this third meaning to explain some important aspects of human social behavior.

Take, for example, *altruistic behavior*—actions that reflect a concern for the welfare of others. This is a form of social behavior often thought of as entirely cultural, the exact opposite of the "law of the jungle." It is believed by many to be religious in origin or to stem from some other high-level value system. But sociobiologists point out that much altruistic behavior principally benefits family members and other close relatives and is, therefore, strongly biological. If a woman sacrifices her life (the ultimate altruism) to save her brother's children from a fire, for example, she is actually being "selfish" in genetic terms (Dawkins, 1976). She is enhancing the survival of the genes of her close kin. In a similar way, couples who stay married "for the sake of the children" may also be promoting the survival of their own genes through their children, insofar as a more secure environment is created for their children's upbringing (Barash, 1977). Sociobiologists can also explain other common human behaviors and aspects of social organization, such as aggression, homosexuality, social inequality, and gender-role differences, in biological terms.

Most sociobiologists argue that genes only set general limits to social behavior, and readily admit that society and culture strongly influence human interaction. Nonetheless, most social scientists feel that sociobiologists explain too much social behavior by biological causes. Critics of sociobiology note, for example, that in many societies kinship is as much socially defined as it is

Through interaction with their parents, babies learn to see themselves as distinct individuals, to build relationships, and to develop both moral concepts and language.

biologically determined. An extended patriarchal family (see Chapter 14) can include people who have hardly any genetic relationship to one another. When people behave in an altruistic manner to benefit such a family, they are obviously doing so for social, not biological, reasons (Sahlins, 1978).

In response to the claim of some sociobiologists that humans are innately aggressive, critics argue that aggression is no more biologically determined than is peaceable behavior: We are capable of both. Cultural rules, not biology, determine whether we behave aggressively or peacefully. As one noted anthropologist has pointed out, human beings, whom sociobiologists sometimes portray as grateful to find an outlet for their aggression (as in war), are in fact often terrified by the prospect of combat (Sahlins, 1978).

A fundamental criticism of sociobiology is that its claims about human behavior are not strongly supported by the evidence (Kitcher, 1987). No one has yet isolated a gene responsible for any particular aspect of social behavior (Lewontin, Rose, & Kamin, 1984). And because controlled breeding experiments of humans would be unethical, sociobiologists must rely on indirect evidence for the genetic determination of behavior (Gould, 1971). A basic contention of sociobiologists in this regard is that certain social behaviors are found in all societies and are therefore genetically, rather than culturally, determined. Critics argue, however, that these researchers pay too little attention to the larger historical, economic, and political

dimensions and focus instead on only those details that support their case.

The issues raised by sociobiology have not been resolved. But even the firmest advocates of a cultural explanation of human behavior realize that each of us is a biological organism. And all social scientists recognize that, in the early years in particular, the satisfaction of biological needs is an important part of the socialization process. It is to the early socialization of children that we now turn.

THE SOCIALIZATION OF INFANTS

Socialization begins the moment parents first hold their babies. This human contact is the first step in a long process through which babies learn to see themselves as distinct individuals, to build social relationships, to develop moral concepts, to learn language, and much more. During the first few months of their children's lives, parents try to satisfy the most basic biological needs of their children. But the very actions that are required to meet these biological needs respond to the infants' emotional needs as well.

When babies are nursed or held against their parent's body while being bottle-fed, they receive three necessities of life: warmth, food, and human contact. Although less tangible than warmth and food, human contact is no less important for development and even survival.

The psychologist Harry F. Harlow's experiments with rhesus monkeys showed that contact—both bodily contact—and interaction with others—is a basic biological need of monkeys. If this need for contact is not met early in a monkey's life, serious physical and emotional problems result. The need for physical contact is so great that when monkeys were placed in a cage with two substitute "mothers"—one made of wire and the other covered by soft cloth—the monkeys spent most of their time clinging to the soft-cloth mother. Even if they received food only from the wire mother, they preferred the soft-cloth mother. When the cloth mother was removed, the monkeys developed severe behavior problems. The cloth mother provided some of the comfort of a real mother. However, many of these "cloth-mothered" monkeys, although at first seemingly normal, later proved completely unable to parent, and many of the females could not reproduce at all (Harlow, 1959).

Although generalizing from animal research and applying it to human behavior is considered to be inherently risky, most experts believe that babies, like infant monkeys, have a basic biological as well as emotional need for contact and interaction. The pioneering work of René Spitz (1945) provided some of the first evidence that such a need exists. Spitz compared children who were cared for by their mothers, and who were free to move around, with babies in an institution for abandoned children. The latter were given only minimal care by nurses and could not leave their cribs. By the end of the first year, the deprived children had developed more slowly and caught more diseases—and many were deeply depressed.

Further evidence of the positive effects of human contact—both physical and social—on infants has come from research on children in various institutions. In one recent study, premature infants were massaged three times a day for 15 minutes (Goleman, 1988). These infants gained weight 47 percent faster than others who were left alone in their incubators. In another study, nurses were asked to spend an extra 20 minutes a day with some infants. The infants given extra human contact showed increased attention to external objects; they learned to grasp an object 45 days earlier, on average, than did the babies without the extra human contact.

Emotional Development

By about 3 months of age, infants can recognize specific human faces, such as those of their parents. In order to

In a famous series of experiments, psychologist Harry F. Harlow showed that infant rhesus monkeys have a biological need for physical contact. This baby monkey clings to a cloth-covered "mother," going to its wire "mother" only to feed from the milk bottle it holds.

TABLE 6.1	EMOTIONAL DEVELOPMENT: A SEQUENTIAL PROCESS
Average Age at Which Emotion Is Present	*Emotion*
Birth	Pleasure
	Surprise
	Disgust
	Distress
6–8 weeks	Joy
3–4 months	Anger
8–9 months	Sadness
	Fear
12–18 months	Tender affection
18 months	Shame
2 years	Pride
3–4 years	Guilt
5–6 years	Social emotions:
	insecurity
	humility
	confidence
	envy
Adolescence	Romantic passion
	Philosophical brooding

Research has shown that human emotions develop in a specific order. Knowing this can help parents gain realistic expectations about their children's behavior.

Source: Daniel Goleman, "Order Found in Development of Emotions," *The New York Times*, June 19, 1984, p. C1. Copyright © 1984 by The New York Times Company. Reprinted by permission.

develop into emotionally healthy adults, at this stage babies must begin to send and receive strong emotional messages. At first, these messages are sent nonverbally—for example, by body and facial movements. In an observational study, researchers found that infants were able to distinguish between smiles and fearful looks from their mothers and responded appropriately; they did not, however, respond to the varied facial expressions of strangers (Zarbatany & Lamb, 1985).

Research conducted in recent years has suggested that human emotions develop in a fixed sequence (Goleman, 1984) (see Table 6.1). Newborns seem to experience only four emotions: pleasure, surprise, disgust, and distress. The capacity for joy makes its appearance after 6 to 8 weeks, anger after 3 to 4 months, and sadness and fear after 8 to 9 months.

At 12 to 18 months, children are sufficiently aware of the outside world to feel affection for their mothers or for anyone who plays the maternal role. Shame, pride, and guilt enter the child's behavioral "repertoire" at 18 months, 2 years, and 3 to 4 years from birth, respectively.

Not until children reach 5 or 6 years of age do they begin to display what can be thought of as truly social emotions, such as insecurity, humility, confidence, and envy. Still more complex emotions, such as romantic passion and philosophical brooding about the meaning of life and the nature of evil, do not arise until adolescence.

Although the researchers investigating this developmental sequence think it has essentially biological origins, they have also found that life experiences can upset the "timetable." Thus, for example, abused children display fear at about 3 months of age, not the 8 to 9 months that would be usual (Gaensbauer & Hiatt, 1984).

THEORIES OF PERSONAL DEVELOPMENT

During the interaction between infants and their parents, infants are not only developing biologically and emotionally, but they are also becoming persons in the social sense of the term. They are forming personalities.

What is personality? In day-to-day conversation, "personality" often refers to social skills. This is what we mean when we say that someone has a "great personality," or that we are trying to build a "better personality." For sociologists and other social scientists, however, **personality** refers to the particular pattern of thoughts, feelings, and self-concepts that make up the distinctive qualities of a particular individual. Personality has been divided into three main components: a *cognitive* component (thoughts, intelligence level, perception, and memory), a *behavioral* component (talents, skills, and competence levels), and an *emotional* component (feelings and sentiments).

People tend to regard their personalities as unique. Sociologists and social psychologists, however, see personality as more the product of surrounding social and cultural forces (Parsons, 1964; Wallace, 1970). Even such seemingly individual traits as competitiveness and quickness to anger are socially and culturally patterned. They are more common in some cultures and in some parts of a given culture than in others.

One aspect of personality that has been of special interest to sociologists is called the **self.** Self refers to a person's awareness of, and feelings about, his or her personal and social identities—who one is and how one differs from others. The development of the self—self-identity—depends heavily on the process of socialization.

At birth, infants do not fully understand that there is a difference between themselves and their parents. They have not yet formed any sense of self. In the months following birth, they gradually come to see themselves as one person and their parents as others. They may gain a

vague sense of their parents as protectors and themselves as dependents. Gradually, interactions become more complex. Babies learn that they are small and that their parents are large; that they are pupils, their parents teachers; that they are sons or daughters, their parents mothers and fathers.

As we have seen, children reared in social isolation—those who are *unsocialized*—are severely handicapped both emotionally and socially (Davis, 1940, 1947). They are deprived of the opportunity to see themselves reflected in the eyes of others—to develop an understanding, through social interaction, of their own identities. Indeed, we depend on social interaction throughout our lives to develop and maintain our sense of self. Through the responses we receive from others, we constantly alter our self-image.

How do our personality and sense of self develop as we grow from childhood to adulthood? This basic question has been the subject of much theory and research within sociology and social psychology. However, no single answer has been able to satisfy all scholars. In the following sections, we review some important theories in this field, many of which view personality and self-development as a series of stages through which each person must pass. See Figure 6.1 for a comparison of three of the theories discussed in this section.

Charles Cooley: The Looking-Glass Self

Charles Horton Cooley (1864–1929) was one of the first sociologists to develop a theory of the development of the self. According to Cooley (1902), the self emerges as a social product through a series of three steps. First, we perceive the way our behavior appears to others. Second, we perceive other people's judgments about our behavior. Third, we evaluate our behavior based on our interpretations of the responses of others. In short, people come to understand themselves by imagining how other people feel about how they act and look. For example, if we think that people who are important to us approve of something we do, we will probably approve of it, too. Because people's sense of self can thus be said to reflect what they think others think of them, Cooley called this self the **looking-glass self.**

Cooley believed that the self develops most fully in primary groups (see Chapter 7). The family, Cooley felt, was the most important such group. In it, children form a sense of self through their "sympathetic" relationships with their parents. By paying attention to the gestures and words of their parents, children come to know what parents expect from them, how parents judge their actions, and their parents' opinions of them. Armed with this

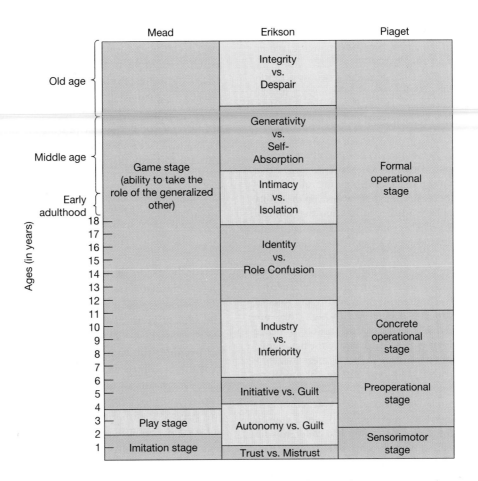

FIGURE 6.1 A Comparison of the Theories of Mead, Erikson, and Piaget.
Cooley's theory of the development of self is not included because Cooley
did not see this process as occurring in distinct stages.

knowledge, children try to become the sort of self that
their parents expect them to be.

George Herbert Mead: Role Taking

George Herbert Mead (1863–1931), the most important
figure in the development of symbolic interactionism
(discussed in Chapter 5), regarded himself primarily as a
philosopher. His work became accessible to sociologists
mainly through the publication of his teachings by students at the University of Chicago after his death (e.g.,
Mead, 1934).

According to Mead, in the early months of life children do not realize that they are separate from others.
As they develop language and learn to understand symbols, they begin to develop self-concepts. When they can

envision themselves in their own minds as objects distinct
from everything else, their self has been formed. They can
"talk" with themselves and "react" to themselves. They
become objects to themselves.

Mead divided the self into two parts: the "I" and the
"me." The "I" consists of the spontaneous, unique, and
"natural" traits of each person, such as the unrestrained
impulses and drives found in every normal infant and
child. The "me" is the social part of the self—the internalized demands of society and the person's awareness of
those demands. The "I" develops first. Because the infant
must first learn what society expects, the "me" takes much
longer to emerge. Mead suggested that the development
of the self involves a continuing "conversation" between
the "me" and the "I" in which the "I" constantly reacts to
the changing "me."

In Mead's view, the "me" takes form during socialization in three distinct stages: imitation, play, and game.

1. The *imitation* stage takes up the first two years of life. During this phase, children merely engage in what Mead called a "conversation of gestures" with their parents, mimicking their physical movements. At this point, no true "me" has developed.

2. In the second, *play* stage, which begins at the age of 2 and lasts several years, children start to engage in **role taking:** They imagine themselves in the role or position of another person and thereby develop the ability to see themselves and the world from the point of view of the other. This practice results initially from the discovery that there is a gap between their minds and intentions and those of their parents. Most often this realization is engendered by frustration caused by a parent's failure to meet one or more of their needs.

   Initially, children begin by taking the roles of **significant others**—people with whom they are closely involved and who have the greatest influence on their development of self. Generally, the first significant others are parents or parent figures; later, siblings, family friends, and some outsiders are added to the child's repertoire. During this stage, as children play at taking the roles of others, they practice the attitudes and actions that the significant others expect. Children might first play at being "bad children" who steal cookies, then pretend to be their scolding "parents," and finally play at being the "police officers" who come to settle the matter. It is at this stage that children first begin to see themselves as social objects: "*I* do this," "*Maria* want candy." Although the "me" begins to develop during this stage, children do not yet understand the significance of role taking; they merely play at the social roles of life.

3. The *game* stage unfolds in the years immediately after age 4. During this stage, children begin to relate to many people and groups beyond their families and to view their families as groups of which they are a part. Children become concerned about the roles they play in nonfamily groups, including society as a whole. They develop conceptions of the demands and expectations of people in general, or of what Mead termed the **generalized other.** In a game like baseball, for example, children must take into account the likely behavior of many people playing many different roles at the same time. They must decide in advance what the actions of all the other players might be and respond to these actions. They need to understand the whole situation. In so doing, they *take the role of the generalized other.* When they can do this, they have internalized "society," and the formation of the "me" is complete.

The theories of Mead and Cooley remain highly influential in modern sociology, but both men based their work on an image of a much simpler social reality than we are faced with today. Cooley paid insufficient attention, for example, to the way in which the self is influenced by those rapidly emerging social forces that lie outside the primary group, such as the mass media. And Mead's concept of the generalized other takes little account of today's social pluralism. In contemporary America, with its many subgroups and subcultures, it is difficult to think of the "larger society" as presenting a single, uniform set of demands and expectations.

Sigmund Freud: The Unconscious

Sigmund Freud (1856–1939), the Vienna-born founder of psychoanalysis, is one of the key figures in the study of human behavior. No discussion of socialization is complete without reference to his work. Unlike Cooley and Mead, who stressed the harmony between the individual and society, Freud saw a basic conflict between the two. He even went so far as to say that the more civilized we become, the more unhappy we must be (Freud, 1930/1962). This is because civilized life requires that we repress many of our underlying biological desires. Where Cooley and Mead interpreted the self as a social product and stressed the importance of language and other symbol systems, Freud emphasized the biological bases and emotional forces involved in socialization. Finally, Freud argued that much of our psychological life takes place in an unconscious realm, to which our conscious and "rational" minds do not have easy access. Indeed, Freud's "discovery" of the unconscious is regarded as one of the great achievements of the twentieth century.

Freud conceived of the human personality as being divided into three parts: the id, the ego, and the superego. The *superego* roughly corresponds to Mead's "me"—internalized, socially learned "shoulds" and "oughts." It is the censor, conscience, and social monitor of the personality. The *id* contains unconscious memories and biological and psychological drives, especially sexual drives. Freud's emphasis on the id was a hallmark of his theory. The *ego* acts as a mediator—mostly within the unconscious—between the demands of the superego and those of the id. According to Freud, these three parts of the personality must be in harmony throughout life if a person is to be mentally healthy.

A simple example may help to clarify the functions of the id, the ego, and the superego. Imagine that you are driving behind someone who is traveling very slowly. You are rushing to make an 8 o'clock appointment, but you will never get there at a rate of 15 miles per hour. You blow the horn and flash your bright lights, but the driver in front of you refuses to go any faster. At this point, your id may make you want to slam down the accelerator in order to teach the driver of the other car a lesson. The ego might be considering the probable consequences of this action: ruined cars, higher insurance premiums, and perhaps lost lives. The superego, or conscience, would question the morality or "rightness" of your action: Do I have the right to smash my car into that car in front of me? Doesn't the other driver have the right to go slowly? The final result: You will probably mumble, or perhaps scream in frustration, but you are unlikely to ram the car in front of you.

Critics attack Freud on many grounds. For one thing, they charge that his entire theory is rooted in the strict, middle-class Viennese society in which he grew up, a culture that is hardly universal. Cross-cultural studies have, in fact, challenged the universality of some of the psychosexual conflicts that Freud described. Some of the harshest criticism of his work has come from feminist psychologists and sociologists who feel that his theory is deeply permeated with sexist and even outright misogynistic assumptions. For example, orthodox Freudians argue that when little girls notice that they lack penises, they assume that they have been "mutilated" and much of their future development is shaped by the resultant "penis envy." They also tend to assume that a psychologically normal female is submissive and even masochistic, rather than being assertive and self-confident.

Another common criticism is that Freud's theory is too rigid in claiming that a child's personality is all but fixed for life during the early years of socialization. There is considerable evidence that people are capable of some degree of personality change throughout their lives. Also, Freud implies that people would not be as disturbed and unhappy if sexual expression were more open. Since Freud's day, sexual mores in the West have become more relaxed, but there does not seem to be any less unhappiness. This suggests that many factors in addition to sexual conflict are at the root of personal problems (Mussen, Conger, & Kagan, 1974). Finally, some of Freud's theories are criticized harshly because they lack adequate supporting empirical evidence.

Many sociologists today feel that Freud put too much stress on the biological factors that mold personality and not enough on the social factors. But Freud did place great importance on the child's social experiences within the family. Besides his theory of the unconscious, Freud's most lasting and widely accepted contribution is probably his analysis of the impact of childhood events on later life.

Erik Erikson: Identity Crises

Erik Erikson (1902–1994) was heavily influenced by Freud. However, because he modified Freud's theories, he is commonly referred to as a "neo-Freudian." Freud emphasized the drives of the id; Erikson's main concern was the more "rational" world of the ego. Erikson saw self-development as proceeding through eight *psychosocial* stages that involve the way we respond to the changing demands made on us as we go through life. Freud focused on childhood; Erikson's stages continue into old age. Thus, Erikson believed that the personality is molded throughout life, not just in childhood.

According to Erikson (1963), each stage of development is defined by an "identity crisis." A stable self-identity results from the positive resolution of these identity crises, which are widely thought to encapsulate many of the basic concerns of life in modern societies. A summary of Erikson's eight identity crises follows (based on Elkind, 1970):

1. *Trust versus mistrust* (infancy): The infant whose needs are adequately met develops trust, a sense that the world is a safe place. But if care is not consistent or adequate, or if the infant feels rejected, a basic mistrust is fostered that will be carried through to later stages of development. The problem of trust versus mistrust (like all later problems) is not fully resolved during the first year of life. Trust can change into mistrust, and vice versa, as one moves through life.

2. *Autonomy versus doubt* (early childhood): Autonomy (sense of independence) emerges during the second stage, as a result of the child's developing motor and mental skills. If parents recognize their young children's need to do what they are capable of doing—at their own pace—children develop a sense that they are able to control their muscles, their impulses, themselves, and their surroundings. On the other hand, children sometimes feel doubt, or even shame—for example, if they are toilet-trained but lose control on a visitor's lap. When parents are impatient and do for children what the children could do for themselves, they reinforce this sense of doubt. Children who leave this stage feeling more shame and doubt than autonomy will have trouble achieving autonomy in adolescence and adulthood.

3. *Initiative versus guilt* (preschool years): By the time they enter this stage, children can control their bodies. They now begin new motor activities, as well as language and fantasy activities. Whether a child leaves this stage with a sense of initiative or a sense of guilt depends on how the parents respond to the child's self-initiated activities. If children are made to feel that their actions are bad, their questions a nuisance, and their play silly, they may develop a strong and lasting sense of guilt.

4. *Industry versus inferiority* (school age): This stage encompasses the elementary school years. During this period, children want to know how things are made, how they work, and what they do. When adults

encourage children in their efforts to make, do, or build practical things, allow them to finish their projects, and praise them for the results, the children's sense of industry is enhanced. But parents who see their children's efforts at making and doing things as "mischief" or as "making a mess," or teachers who demand that children conform to strict adult-oriented rules, encourage a sense of inferiority.

5. *Identity versus role confusion* (adolescence): When children move into adolescence, their bodies change. Adolescents develop new ways of looking at and thinking about the world. Childhood roles such as daughter, son, friend, and student are joined by new ones: boyfriend, girlfriend, athlete, scholar, and many more. These new roles must somehow be smoothly combined with the old to promote a strong self-identity. Young people who have mastered the earlier stages and reach adolescence with a strong sense of trust, autonomy, initiative, and industry have a better chance of gaining a strong sense of self-identity and avoiding feelings of role confusion than those who have not.

6. *Intimacy versus isolation* (young adulthood): This stage includes courtship and early family life. When Erikson spoke of intimacy, he meant the ability to share with and care about another person without fear of losing one's sense of self-identity. If a person cannot be intimate, he or she will live with a sense of isolation. The ability to be intimate depends greatly on the strength of one's self-identity.

7. *Generativity versus self-absorption* (middle age): In middle age, after surveying what one has accomplished, a person becomes more concerned with others beyond his or her family, with future generations, and with the nature of the society in which those generations will live. Erikson called this concern "generativity." People who do not develop generativity fall into a state of self-absorption in which their personal needs and comforts become their main concerns.

8. *Integrity versus despair* (old age): In this final stage, the individual's major life activities are nearing completion, and there is more time for thought. A sense of integrity arises from a person's satisfaction with his or her life. At the other extreme is the person who sees the past as a series of missed opportunities and wrong directions and therefore falls into despair.

Erikson's model of development has been criticized as being biased toward the experiences of the middle class. It is true that Erikson, for the most part, based his model on studies of middle-class people. He also studied personal development at a very general level (as did the other theorists), taking no account of differences in social class, ethnic group, or available opportunities. Another criticism of Erikson's model is that it is difficult to study

empirically. How, for example, can we measure a person's success in getting through a given stage? Finally, Erikson's model implies development toward some abstract ideal, but what is that ideal? Happiness? Conformity to middle-class values? Mental health? Erikson did not provide the answer.

Jean Piaget: Cognitive Development

The theories we have discussed so far concern personality development as a whole. The final theory we shall take up, that developed by the Swiss scholar Jean Piaget (1896–1980), is more limited in focus. It concerns cognitive development, or the way we learn to think.

Many people feel that Piaget was the world's leading expert on how children learn to think and reason. He tried to answer such questions as: What do children know at birth? What tools can they use to get new knowledge? What kinds of knowledge are acquired at specific ages? Piaget's major contribution to our knowledge of the socialization process has been to describe how children think at various stages of their development.

Piaget asserted that at each stage of development, from infancy through adolescence, a certain type of mental operation marks all of the child's activities and gives a structure to the child's knowledge. He believed that although some children may go through the stages faster than others, all children must go through all the stages in the same sequence. Piaget thus felt that a statement like "Any child can be taught anything at any time" is not only false but actually absurd.

Learning is an *active process,* according to Piaget. In order to learn, children must take knowledge into themselves and process it. Piaget believed that the development of children's mental processes proceeds through the following stages (after Elkind, 1968):

1. *The sensorimotor stage:* For the first one and a half to two years of life, children learn about the world exclusively through their senses. Children reach out, touch, sit, walk, and explore. Their actions are haphazard at first, but show more and more purpose as the months pass. In this first stage, children learn to construct and reconstruct objects in their minds. For example, if a newborn baby looks at an object that is then removed from its field of vision, the baby's eyes will not follow it. For the baby, "out of sight" is literally "out of existence." When the object is not in sight, it simply does not exist. Toward the end of the sensorimotor period, however, the child can retain a mental image of the object.

2. *The preoperational stage:* During this stage, which lasts from about ages 2 to 7, children learn to use and

understand symbols, to speak, and to make their first attempts to draw objects. Preoperational children focus on one aspect of a situation at a time and ignore the rest. They may incorrectly insist that a tall, thin glass holds more water than a short, wide glass, even when they see the contents of the first glass poured into the second. This is because children at this stage do not have an understanding of such abstract concepts as width, depth, density, quantity, and causality. Children in the preoperational stage are highly *egocentric*—that is, they see the world almost entirely from their own perspective, and thus are unable to take the roles of others and see the world from other points of view.

3. *The concrete operational stage:* Between the ages of 7 and 11, children learn to conceive of a concrete object or of a category in more than one way, and they can form notions about the ways things relate to one another. For example, children at this stage know that an object can be a ball, a toy, and a round thing all at the same time, and they can connect events in terms of cause and effect. They also develop the ability to imagine themselves in the position of another person.

4. *The formal operational stage:* During this final stage, which runs from about age 12 to age 15, young adults develop the capacity for highly abstract thought. They can consider alternatives to reality, construct ideals, and reason realistically about the future. This ability also enables adolescents to think logically about statements that are contrary to fact.

Although Piaget's work has inspired a major school of thought among developmental psychologists and has influenced many other theorists and researchers, it is not without its critics. One major criticism is that his work is not systematic or scientific. It is difficult to repeat his procedures and reach the same conclusions he did.

But modern technology may provide some further insight into Piaget's original ideas. Using positron-emission tomography (PET), scientists can see how a baby's brain develops. They have already measured the brain activity of infants from the moment of birth and have discovered that the primitive structures of the brain that control respiration, reflexes, and heartbeat are already wired at birth. The neural circuits in higher regions of the cortex, however, are undeveloped. And most of the connections that an infant's neurons will make will be determined by early experiences (*Newsweek*, 1997).

While scientists have just begun to understand how experiences after birth hard-wire the brain, they do know that these experiences exert a dramatic and precise impact (*Newsweek*, 1997). Different parts of the brain are wired at different ages. Creating these connections is natural and does not require parents to engage a child in

According to Piaget, children between the ages of 7 and 11 enter the concrete operational state and develop the ability to perform abstract mental operations such as arithmetic. They also develop the ability to imagine themselves in the position of another person.

structured activities like using flash cards. Nor are expensive toys required. Pots and pans, blocks, beads, peekaboo, and talking to babies—the kinds of stimulation that commonly occur in most households—will provide the proper kind of stimulation for brain development. When children are isolated or deprived of sensory experiences, however, their brains do not get hard-wired—and that can produce irreversible damage.

Lawrence Kohlberg: Moral Development

Piaget also studied how children make decisions about what is right and wrong. His observations led him to propose that moral reasoning develops in two stages. When children are between the ages of 4 and 7, the first stage, they believe that rules are objective and absolute. And they do not consider a person's motivation for behaving in a certain way. Thus, they would say that breaking a window is wrong, even if someone did it to save a child who was caught in a burning building. During the second stage, from about the age of 7, children start to view rules as more subjective and relative. They now weigh the intentions behind people's actions when they decide whether an act is right or wrong. This tendency is related to the child's new ability to see situations from the perspective of others.

Lawrence Kohlberg built upon Piaget's theory to develop a more sophisticated model of moral development (1963). Using stories that contained moral dilemmas, he asked subjects how the problem should be resolved. Consider, for example, the following story that Kohlberg used:

GLOBAL SOCIETY

THE SOCIALIZATION OF RUSSIAN CHILDREN

On his trip to Russia in September 1998, President Clinton spoke to university students about the crisis facing their country. The footage that appeared that evening on television stations across America focused on students' questions and comments. It was clear that American journalists shared something in common with Russian parents—they both believed that these students were the future of Russia.

So, too, are the youngest students who were also shown on the evening news as they headed off for their first day of school—little boys neatly dressed in gray uniforms and little girls in brown dresses with crisp white pinafores and white hair bows. In one hand they clasped the hand of a parent, in the other, fresh flowers for their teachers. This scene had been described by past visitors to the Soviet Union and remains remarkably unchanged (Pearson, 1990; Shipler, 1989; Smith, 1976). Tearful Russian mothers and fathers, who have a reputation for overprotecting their children, had a hard time letting go of their children.

Karl Marx and Frederich Engels, who had described the family as an oppressive institution, would be astounded. Under communism, the family, like the state, was supposed to wither away. And its major functions, including child rearing, would be transferred to society at large (Shipler, 1989).

When Lenin came to power in 1917, plans to eliminate the traditional family took the form of specific programs that would reduce the importance of the

traditional family, including communal children's houses and dining halls (Shipler, 1989). By the late 1920s, educators were discussing ways to implement these ideas. Anatoly Lunacharsky, the commissar of education, wrote:

> Our problem now is to do away with the household and to free women from the care of children. It would be idiotic to separate children from their parents by force. But when, in our communal houses, we have well-organized quarters for children, connected by a heated gallery with the adults' quarters, parents will, of their own free will, send their children to these quarters, where they will be supervised by trained pedagogical and medical personnel. There is no doubt that the terms "my parents," "our children," will gradually fall out of usage, being replaced by such conceptions as "old people," "adults," "children," and "infants." (Shipler, 1989, p. 89)

While efforts to eliminate the family in the Soviet Union failed, the state did succeed in gaining a great deal of control over the training of children. Hedrick Smith, who spent three years (1971–1974) as the Moscow bureau chief for the *New York Times*, described how children were indoctrinated (1976). By the age of 2 or 3, they were singing patriotic songs about Lenin that portrayed him as "the most perfect human who ever lived"—a combined George Washington, Santa Claus, and Christ figure" (1976). Their reading materials were similarly filled with communist ideology. Thus, for example, while beginning readers in the United States introduced children to "Dick and Jane," Soviet readers

began with a lesson about socialism: "The first country of socialism in the world became the first country of children's happiness in the world" (Smith, 1976).

The primary goal of political indoctrination was to produce a collectivist mentality—a person who would not think of himself apart from society. Individuality in Soviet children was, therefore, discouraged. And the biggest mistake a child could make in kindergarten was to be different. Smith and a number of other Western visitors saw evidence of the strong pressure to conform in children's art, which they claimed all looked alike (Shipler, 1989; Smith, 1976).

Children were taught not only to conform but, as well, to inform on those who did not. This form of institutionalized tattling, which was common in many Soviet classrooms, involved one child, known as the *zvenovoi*, who would report on children who had broken the rules.

The political indoctrination of children, which stressed collective responsibility, self-discipline, and conformity, continued throughout the school years in the classroom and in children's organizations such as the Octobrists, Young Pioneers, and Komosomol. While these groups have been compared to American youth groups like the Boy Scouts and Girl Scouts, they actually served to further indoctrinate young people with political ideology.

The story of one Pioneer illustrates the degree to which these youth groups controlled young people. Pavel Morozov, a 14-year-old boy, was immortalized by the Communist party as a Pioneer hero and martyr for practicing his civic duty. During the harsh period of farm collectivization in 1932, Morozov turned in his own father for hiding grain from the state. Private farmers who opposed collectivization responded by murdering the boy.

The tragic story of Pavel Morozov illustrates the extent to which the state was able to undermine the family unit. But it provides no insight into the deep love that Russian parents have for their children. While Russian teachers have earned a reputation for strict discipline, Russian parents are known for overprotecting and spoiling their children. A number of Western visitors personally witnessed parents pampering their children—working extra jobs to buy them beautiful clothes or provide them with extra portions of food, (Shipler, 1989; Smith, 1976). Children were also spared household chores and were not expected to work outside the home.

Whereas American parents may encourage teenagers to make money for themselves through part-time jobs, Soviet teenagers had no incentive to work. Viewed from the perspective of collective responsibility, any money they made belonged to their family. Earning money for themselves was not viewed as a form of self-reliance, as it is in the United States, but as a sign of selfishness.

But this was destined to change before the turn of the twentieth century. By the 1980s, Soviet teenagers were starting to show signs of rebellion. They openly embraced Western attitudes, music, and fashion. They were particularly fond of American jeans, which symbolized the hippie, the protester, and the rock star (Shipler, 1989). In response, the Soviet press criticized this generation for its lack of values, its materialism, and its lack of respect for elders.

Under the leadership of Gorbachev, some of the political rhetoric changed, and the state did admit that it was not the perfect guardian of Soviet children (Pearson, 1990). Nevertheless, "it reserved the right to define the moral code of communism" and continued its efforts to instill the lessons of Lenin (Pearson, 1990).

In 1989, Landon Pearson, an expert in childhood development and the wife of a former Canadian ambassador to Russia, returned to Russia to see how children had changed since she and her husband left six years earlier. When she asked a group of teenagers to think about the year 2000 and to predict the future for themselves and Russia, students were slow to respond. The director explained that children must now think for themselves—and that just took more time. None of the students wanted to go into politics. One wanted to be a teacher, another a doctor. And one saw himself working in industry. But when Pearson asked him if he were interested in business, he wasn't sure what she meant.

That, too, is bound to change in the near future. Today a new hero is influencing young minds. He is Misha the Bear—a character in a book called *Economics for Little Ones: How Misha Became a Businessman* (Reeves, 1996). Designed for a 7-year-old audience, this book opens as Misha is waking up from his winter hibernation. He promptly decides to open a shop to sell honey and berries. Phil Reeves, a reporter for *The Independent*, sums up the story:

Helped by other animals in the forest, including a magpie who handles his advertising, he institutes a harsh regime of under-cutting his

How does Russian education differ from education in the United States? Have the changes in Russian government made the educational system better? How do you feel about government's involvement in the rearing and education of children?

competitors—notably the rival capitalist, Winnie the Pooh. He opens a furniture factory, before finally becoming so rich that he can afford to take a post as the forest's finance minister. (1996, p. 15)

The chapters in this book illustrate just how far Russia is moving toward capitalism. One chapter is called "How Misha Converted His Capital into Money," another "Why Misha's Factory Made a Profit." And they suggest how the socialization of Russian children is changing as well.

In Europe, a woman was near death from cancer. One drug might save her, a form of radium that a druggist in the same town had recently discovered. The druggist was charging $2,000—ten times what the drug cost him to make. The sick woman's husband, Heinz, went to everyone he knew to borrow the money, but he could only get together about half of what it cost. He told the druggist that his wife was dying and asked him to sell it cheaper or let him pay later. But the druggists said, "No." The husband got desperate and broke into the man's store to steal the drug for his wife. (Kohlberg, 1963, pp. 18–19)

Based on the responses that his subjects gave to stories like this, Kohlberg proposed that people proceed through three main levels of moral development, which are further subdivided into six separate stages. In the first level (preconventional), people judge right from wrong on the basis of expected rewards and punishments. At stage 1 (punishment and obedience orientation), people who are asked to decide whether Heinz was right or wrong might say that he was wrong because he would be caught and put in jail. Or they might say he was right because the chances of getting sent to jail are slim. In the second stage (naive hedonistic), people might reason that stealing the drug is alright because the man needs his wife. In both stages, the moral reasoning is based on one's needs and desires and does not take the perspective of others into account.

In the second main level (conventional), laws are the guidelines for deciding what is right or wrong. At stage 3 ("good boy" morality), people are concerned with pleasing others and being perceived as good. Thus, someone at this stage might say that Heinz was wrong because his family would be ashamed of him. At stage 4 (law and authority), maintaining the social order is most important. So stealing the drug could be viewed as wrong because Heinz broke the law.

The third main level (postconventional) is based on an application of abstract moral principles that are often rooted in concerns for justice and the good of all. At this level, one's own conscience acts as the guide for deciding right from wrong. At stage 5 (morality of contract, of individual rights, and of democratically accepted law), a person might say that Heinz was wrong because the laws are created in a democratic fashion to protect the rights of everyone, including other sick patients who might need this drug. At the sixth stage (morality of individual principles of conscience), someone might say that Heinz's action is right because his conscience told him that it would be wrong to let his wife die.

Over the years, Kohlberg's theory of moral development has attracted a great deal of attention. Research has shown that children do progress through the stages in the order that he predicted (Colby et al., 1983; Walker, 1989). But critics claim that his model is biased. Few people ever rise to the sixth stage in Kohlberg's model. But Americans from the middle class are more likely to score high in this scheme than those from the lower class (Dannefer, 1984). Women tend to score lower than do men (Gilligan, 1993); and so do non-Westerners (Miller & Bersoff, 1992; Snarey, 1985).

Overall, these differences suggest that the values of different groups have a bearing on the level to which people rise in Kohlberg's scheme of moral development. For example, Carol Gilligan argues that women place more value on compassion than on abstract rules, which would explain their lower scores on Kohlberg's scale (1963). Likewise, the emphasis placed on friendships and social responsibility that characterizes some non-Western cultures would also explain lower scores on his scale.

APPROACHES TO CHILD REARING

The personalities and social development of children are strongly affected by the child-rearing approach used by their parents. Especially in complex societies such as the United States, child rearing differs greatly among parents and from group to group.

Child-rearing approaches can be described as varying from *authoritarian* to *permissive.* Authoritarian parents demand that their children obey without question. They emphasize such values as order and stability, and are likely to use physical punishments. Permissive parents, on the other hand, are more open and flexible with their children, more likely to reason with them and to compromise on rules. In addition, they are likely to reinforce rules with emotional appeals or with threats of disapproval, and they are much less likely to use physical punishment.

In a review of research done in the 1940s and 1950s, the psychologist Urie Bronfenbrenner (1958) concluded that middle-class parents are likely to be more permissive and working-class parents more authoritarian in their child-rearing approaches. Such social class differences in child rearing may be explained in part by the roles the parents assume at work. The traits stressed by middle-class parents—flexibility, initiative, self-control, and personal achievement—are needed for middle-class jobs. Similarly, the stress placed by working-class parents on discipline and conformity reflects their on-the-job experience. Factory or construction work requires more obedience and conformity than independence and initiative (Hyman, 1953; Kohn, 1963).

It is probably true, however, that class differences in child rearing are diminishing over time. One researcher, for example, found only a weak correlation between social class level and the use of physical punishment in the 1970s (Erlanger, 1974). In addition, other studies have suggested that most of today's parents, not just those from the middle class, stress individual initiative and personal responsibility much more than parents did in the early part of the twentieth century. This shift is associated with a diminishing respect for social institutions and the continuing growth of individualism (Alwin, 1988).

One long-range study concluded that the parents who are most effective at raising independent, socially responsible children are neither authoritarian nor permissive, but rather *authoritative* (Baumrind, 1980). Authoritarian parents think children have few rights yet many adult duties, and permissive parents regard children as having few duties yet many adult rights. Authoritative parents, in contrast, try to strike a balance reflecting the child's particular stage of development. These parents expect their relationship with their children to be complementary. That is, they feel that the responsibilities that they have toward their children and that their children have toward them should balance each other and change as the children mature.

AGENTS OF SOCIALIZATION

A wide variety of persons, groups, and institutions is involved in the process of socialization. The most important and influential of these groups are called **agents of socialization.** The main agents of socialization are the family, schools and day-care centers, peer groups, and the mass media.

The Family

Since the beginning of human history, the most important agent of socialization has always been the family (discussed in detail in Chapter 14). The continuing importance of the family stems from its position on the front line of socialization during the critical early years in a person's life. Socialization begins at home, where children learn who they are, what they can and should expect from their society, and what their society expects from them.

The family is ideally suited in many ways to the task of socialization. Because it is usually a small primary group in which the members have extensive face-to-face contact, children's actions can be closely monitored. Mistakes and inappropriate behavior can be detected and corrected early.

Yet, even during a child's first few years, alternative agents of socialization are challenging the family's leading role in the socialization process. With both parents working outside the home in more than half of all families, and with many families headed by just one parent,

children may now spend more time watching television than they spend with their parents. Furthermore, the lives of children are increasingly centered around schools, day-care centers, and peer groups. All of these agents of socialization outside the family have become highly influential in the last few decades.

Schools and Day-Care Centers

The first major agent outside the family involved in socializing children has historically been the school. Through formal schooling, children are taught both the skills and attitudes they need in society and the heritage of their culture. In such a complex and technologically advanced society as the United States, formal education is an important and lengthy undertaking, lasting as long as 20 years in some cases. In simpler societies that need to pass less specialized knowledge on to their members, formal schooling occupies a much briefer period in a child's life. (Education is discussed in more detail in Chapter 15.)

The social roles children learn at school are oriented more toward the wider society than are those that they learn at home. The teacher tells them what is expected of them as students, as members of their community, and as citizens of their nation. In addition, for the first time the child is evaluated in a systematic way in comparison with others. The teacher may comment informally on the behavior of students, praising and criticizing them. And in most schools, report cards periodically evaluate not only the students' academic progress but their social progress as well. This is reflected by such criteria as "obeys rules and regulations," "shows self-control," "gets along with others," and "follows directions." This nonacademic dimension of education has been called the "hidden curriculum" (Snyder, 1971).

Socialization at school emphasizes conformity to impersonal rules and authority, an adjustment basic to successful functioning in modern societies. At home, children learn to obey their parents and recognize them as authority figures. But the nature of the relationship between parent and child is personal and emotional. Love and a recognition of dependency make children obey their parents. At school, however, children learn to obey "the rules," not just an individual.

Day-care centers are a popular mode of child care today, largely because many mothers want or need to work outside the home (Kahn & Kamerman, 1987; MacKinnon & King, 1988). The quality of a day-care center's staff and program, as well as the attitudes that parents and children have toward them, determines the center's effectiveness. Day-care centers are still controversial in the United States, but they have been widely

Children attending day-care centers become exposed, at an early age, to an important agent of socialization—the peer group. The interaction children experience in these groups can have important effects on their development.

regarded as successful for years in many European countries (Kamerman, 1991; Kamerman & Kahn, 1981).

Peer Groups

When children attend day-care centers or, at the latest, when they start school, they become more heavily exposed to another important agent of socialization, the **peer group.** This term refers to a group of people who have roughly equal social status and are usually of similar ages. Members of a peer group do not have to be friends. For example, the children in a given second-grade class are a peer group, although they may not all be emotionally close to one another.

In childhood, peer groups are formed largely by accident. Later in life, more choice is involved. At 7 years of age, one's peer groups are generally the members of one's class at school (or subgroups of that class) and other children of the same age who live in one's neighborhood. Adults select their peer group more on the basis of common interests and activities and similar incomes, occupations, or social positions. Age limits are more flexible in adulthood, so that people between the ages of 30 and 45, for example, might readily qualify as members of a 37-year-old's peer group.

A relatively new idea about early childhood development, called the *interpretive approach* to socialization, suggests that children do not merely absorb information from the adult world but actively produce their own unique peer cultures (Corsaro, 1992; Corsaro & Eder, 1990; Corsaro & Rizzo 1988; Ochs 1988; Schieffelin 1990; Wentworth, 1980). During preschool and early elementary school years, children are concerned with two things:

participating in activities with their peers and taking control of their own lives (Corsaro, 1997; Corsaro & Eder, 1990). As it turns out, efforts to achieve these goals are compatible. When children first enter school, they quickly develop a strong group identity (Corsaro, 1985). This is strengthened in two ways (Corsaro, 1997; Corsaro & Rizzo, 1988): through sharing, which gives children an opportunity to do things together; and through their attempts to control their lives, which is also something they want to share with classmates. Children attempt to control their lives by challenging authority. Mocking teachers is a common method used to do this, and it often involves the participation of many children.

Social participation and the development of friendships are central interests of children at this age. But conflict also exists, along with an increasing separation between boys and girls. This is so obvious by elementary school that Barrie Thorne claims "it is meaningful to speak of separate girls' and boys' worlds" (1986). At the same time, she argues that past research has focused on the differences between boys and girls and ignored the similarities (1995). And she shows how boys and girls engage in activities that are designed to take them into the other's world.

The interaction that children experience in peer groups produces a positive effect on the development of children (Berndt & Radel, 1989). Research shows that by adolescence, peer groups acquire a particularly strong influence on teenagers, as they help them find their place in a society of equals (Eder, 1991; Eder, Evans, & Parker, 1995). In the family, by contrast, the status of young people is always subordinate. Also, adolescent peer groups are very important in helping young people reduce their dependency on adults.

Adolescent peer groups can become a historical force. In any society, members of the same generation tend to undergo common experiences and respond to them in common ways; in this sense they are a kind of peer group writ large. The generation of adolescents and young adults of the 1960s and 1970s, the sum of all the peer groups born from 1945 to 1963, has been particularly important in American social and cultural history. This group, born in the economically prosperous years immediately following World War II, is substantially larger than any other American generation, before or since. For this reason, they are frequently called the "baby boom" or "boomers."

Members of the baby boom grew up during the early years of television, a fact that profoundly shaped their awareness and set them apart from their parents' generation. During the 1960s and 1970s, this media-nurtured sense of difference led to much discussion of what was termed a "generation gap" between the boomers and their elders. Another factor that contributed to this generation's sense of its own uniqueness and importance was the development of a commercialized youth culture whose rapid growth reflected both the baby boom's size and its connection to the electronic media (Gitlin, 1987).

In their adolescence and early adulthood, many baby boomers, especially those born to middle-class families, strongly but temporarily embraced a variety of sharply countercultural patterns that seemed not only different but were actually opposed to the values accepted at the time by the adult world. The common defining experiences of this counterculture included the civil rights movement, the assassinations of John and Robert Kennedy and Martin Luther King, opposition to the Vietnam War, the hippie movement, and the Watergate scandal. Many baby boomers passionately believed that radical politics, recreational drug use, sexual freedom, long hair, and rock music would soon usher in a genuinely new era in history—what one enthusiast called "Consciousness III" (Reich, 1970). Most of these immoderate hopes were dashed, although many of the boomers continue to retain a very strong sense of their own generational distinctiveness.

By the mid-1980s, the peer groups of middle-class college men and women were widely perceived as being more interested in conforming and making money than in working for social change, a logical development in an age of diminishing economic opportunity (Astin et al., 1984). Yet the impact of the baby boom on American culture remained strong, continuing to influence heavily everything from television programming to key political and social issues.

Some journalists and other observers have suggested that there may yet be another generation developing among America's adolescent and college-age peer groups. This new generational consciousness, termed "Generation X" or "the thirteenth generation," is being shaped by the continuing cultural domination of the baby boom and the difficult economic times of the 1990s. More materialistic than the boomers but less so than the generation of the Reagan era, they see a real need for social reform but worry that the escalation of the national debt may make it impossible to implement needed changes. Their numbers will swell in the closing years of the twentieth century as the children of the baby boom generation enter college; their defining consciousness will continue to evolve in the years ahead.

The Mass Media

In modern societies, the *mass media*—those means of communication that reach and influence large numbers of people, especially newspapers, magazines, television,

and radio—have come to play an extremely important role in socialization. Before the mass media appeared, few people could read, and information traveled slowly, by word of mouth. Today it zips around the world in a matter of seconds. With the flick of a dial, people can listen to music or watch news, comedy, or drama. In fact, about two-thirds of Americans now identify television as their main source of news (Robinson & Levy, 1987).

Of special concern to many people in recent years, including social scientists, are the effects of television viewing on children. In 1994, 98 percent of American homes had a television, with an average of 2.2 sets (U.S. Bureau of the Census, 1995). The average American household has the TV turned on for 7 hours per day, although this does not mean that people usually pay close attention to all of this programming (Kubey & Csikszentmihalyi, 1990). According to one estimate, by the time the average American high school student reaches graduation, he or she will have spent 20,000 hours watching television. This figure exceeds the total amount of time spent in the classroom (Barwise & Ehrenberg, 1988).

Given this extensive exposure, the content of television programming has received a great deal of attention (Croteau & Hoynes, 1997; Ehrenhaus, 1989; Ryan & Wentworth, 1999). Television gives children a great deal of information about both real and imaginary worlds and about human behavior. But children are not adults and can easily misinterpret what they see and hear. For example, people, unlike cartoon characters, cannot be hit over the head or pushed over a cliff and come back smiling.

In some respects, children's programs reinforce the values taught by other socializing agents. A peer group may watch a certain program, discuss it, act it out, and thus reinforce the group's unity and values. But ideas learned from television may also conflict with those taught at home and in school (Comstock & Strasburger, 1990). For instance, children may learn from their parents and teachers that in order to get ahead they should work hard and get a good education. In contrast, television may teach them that one should enjoy life to the fullest while still young.

Social scientists have long known that children model their behavior after that of the people around them. Researchers, therefore, have tried to discover whether children imitate the people they see on television and, specifically, whether or not violent television programs engender violent behavior in children. This is a complex matter because it may be that children who are already inclined to aggressiveness prefer to watch violent television shows.

A major review of television and social behavior, sponsored by the National Institute of Mental Health

SOCIOLOGY OF THE MEDIA

TELEVISION IMAGES OF MOM AND DAD

Television images of the American family have changed dramatically since the 1950s. Nowhere is this more evident than in one of the most popular programs of the 1990s, *The Simpsons*. Consider, for example, one episode in which Sherry Bobbins is hired as a nanny to spell Marge, whose hair is falling out from stress. By the end of the show, Bobbins is binging on alcohol—in worse shape than Marge ever was. Crying uncontrollably, she laments her failure to help the Simpsons. But they reassure her, saying that they are happy with things the way they are. Then they break into the following song:

Homer: Around the house I never
        lift a finger.
        As a husband and a father
        I'm subpar.
        I'd rather drink a beer,
        Than win father of the
        year.
        I'm happy with things the
        way they are.
Marge: The house is still a mess.
        And I'm going bald from
        stress.
        But we're happy just the
        way we are.
Lisa: I'm getting used to never
        getting noticed.
Bart: I'm stuck here 'til I can
        steal a car.

Family: But we're happy just the
         way we are.

The Simpsons are a far cry from television families of the 1950s—the Cleavers (*Leave It to Beaver*), the Nelsons (*Ozzie and Harriet*), and the Andersons (*Father Knows Best*). The fathers in these families were well respected by their families and communities. They were ideal dads—intelligent, good providers, loving, and wise. Their authority was unquestioned, and they set an example that was difficult, if not impossible, to follow. Cast as the partner in a traditional marriage, mothers were also unrealistically ideal. They never worked outside the home. They were happy homemakers who catered to their families' needs and deferred to the good judgment of their husbands. Their homes looked like models for *House Beautiful*, and so did they.

The most serious problem facing these families usually involved the mischievous antics of a son who was either trying to prove himself or accomplish something on his own (Miller, 1986). Once it was discovered, the misdeed was dealt with in a calm father-to-son talk. Rationality reigned. Problems never escalated into emotional arguments or power struggles. Mom and Dad never fought. And that was because everyone accepted the chain of command: Dad was the boss. But these ideal families did not represent the typical family of the 1950s.

By the 1970s, television images of mothers and fathers began to change dramatically. The program that revolutionized these images was Norman Lear's *All in the Family*, which revolved around contemporary social and political issues. Archie Bunker, the pugnacious patriarch of the family, commanded no respect and was ridiculed for his oversimplistic, bigoted views. Always stumbling from a malapropism, Archie was an easy target for his son-in-law, Mike (Meathead). In contrast to the previous generation of fathers and sons, Archie and Mike were constantly at each other's throat. Emotional rather than rational, the two of them created far more problems than they solved.

Ironically, Archie dubbed Edith the "dingbat." He dreaded her stories, which went on and on with no apparent underlying logic. And he often ended the story for himself by pretending to hold a gun to his head and then firing. While Archie often made Edith look smart, her adoration of him seemed irrational. Taking his abuse in stride, she constantly aimed to please him. Cheerfully catering to his every whim and fancy, she would characteristically jump from her chair and run to the kitchen to fetch a beer for him.

While the Bunkers did fight, and their world was filled with real problems, neither were they the typical American family. What, then, explains the dramatic change in the television images of mothers and fathers? Mark

(1982), examined some 900 studies of the effects of television violence and concluded:

> The consensus among most of the research community is that violence on television does lead to aggressive behavior by children and teenagers who watch the programs. . . . In magnitude, television violence is as strongly correlated with aggressive behavior as any other behavioral variable that has been measured.

Another study has suggested that these findings are also applicable to adults. It is not as though adults run out and commit crimes when they see violent acts portrayed on television, but they are more likely to harbor aggressive thoughts and to exchange hostile words and criticisms with family members after they have watched a violent show (Linz & Donnerstein, 1989). It should be noted that none of the present studies takes into account the newer modes of home entertainment—cable

Crispin Miller suggests that television characters changed to meet the demands of a consumer society (1986). The new portrayals of parents were designed to please the television viewers who watched the commercials—women and children.

In fact, the demise of Dad's status and power, began long before Archie. It took hold in the mid-1960s. According to Miller:

> The sixties generally revealed that Dad's prerogatives were threatened—not by a rise in real authority among women, but by the rising influence of TV and its corporate advertisers. (p. 201)

Because mothers ran the household and bought the products needed to do so, they appeared more powerful than previous mothers. Samantha, the mother in *Bewitched*, illustrates this idea particularly well. While she ultimately did obey her husband (Darrin), she actually had more power because she was a witch. And the program revolved around the predicaments produced when she exercised that power.

The reversal of roles in domestic relationships became the recipe for successful sitcoms. Fathers stayed home with the kids and cleaned house (*Who's the Boss?*), and mothers either landed glamorous jobs (*Growing Pains*) or returned to school for advanced degrees (*Home Improvement*). Mothers got smarter; fathers became the butt

Television images of the American family have changed dramatically in the last century from the wholesome, well-rounded family on the show Happy Days *to the somewhat dysfunctional family portrayed on the television show* The Simpsons.

of jokes. And role reversals were not limited to spouses. Fathers reversed roles with their adolescent sons. Dads became kids and were commonly portrayed as nothing more than nincompoops who, stripped of all dignity, deserved no respect.

While some nostalgic programs like *Happy Days* did take us back to the 1950s, the dads (like Tom Bosley) lacked the authority of Ward Cleaver. Other programs like *The Cosby's* did portray dads as both cool and successful, but audiences did not regard families like these as real.

It is easy to see that television sitcoms do not portray realistic images of moms and dads. But to believe that these programs are simply a form of entertainment is naive. You can bet your bottom dollar, as do advertisers, that the effects are very real. And once you have viewed *The Simpsons,* that is indeed a sobering thought.

television and VCRs—and their effects on viewers (Stipp & Milavsky, 1988).

Increased awareness of the potentially damaging effects of televised violence has led to periodic efforts by concerned citizens and advocacy groups to pressure the networks to reduce the level of violence in their programming. One campaign was mounted in 1993 in response to publicity concerning ABC's controversial show *N.Y.P.D. Blue,* and it resulted in the airing of advisories concerning violent content at the beginning of a number of programs. It remains to be seen, however, whether broadcast executives will continue such practices once public attention is diverted elsewhere.

By the age of 20, the average American has watched about 1 million commercials (Postman, 1981). During 1 hour of prime-time television in 1996, there were over 15 minutes of commercials. Daytime programming averaged over 20 minutes per hour (Katz 1997). Most commercials teach that problems can be easily and quickly solved if a certain product is purchased. One study concluded that children who watch unusually large amounts of television are prone to believe that medicine works magically and without fail (Chira, 1983).

Moreover, television often reduces people and institutions to simple stereotypes, and it may reinforce these stereotypes in the minds of its younger viewers. By the mid-1980s, for example, television was being criticized for what appeared to be the return of the "woman as victim" theme. And at different times, the ratio of white male characters to white female characters has been as high as four to one (Basow, 1992; Gerbner et al., 1980).

Media scholars have devoted substantial attention in recent years to the issue of whether television has had even deeper and more subtle effects on life in modern societies. The Canadian scholar Marshall McLuhan pioneered this line of inquiry, arguing that television has fundamentally redefined the meaning of literacy and is gradually uniting the entire world into a kind of "global village" (1964). More recent analyses have been less optimistic. Neil Postman argues that the electronic media degrade and trivialize public life by implicitly teaching viewers that every aspect of culture must be entertaining (1985).

In a particularly incisive discussion, Joshua Meyrowitz developed a dramaturgical analysis suggesting that television blurs the distinction between frontstage and backstage areas of social life (1985). When children are able to watch parents on TV discussing how to rear their offspring, parental authority is weakened and the dividing line between childhood and adulthood, very clear in the era of the print media, becomes increasingly blurred. Similarly, when the media relentlessly search out and publicize the failings of virtually all of our political leaders, whether major (e.g., Richard Nixon's Watergate tapes) or minor (e.g., Bill Clinton's involvement with Monica Lewinsky), public confidence in leaders is shaken. Indeed, Meyrowitz wonders whether, in the modern era, it is possible for anyone to continue to believe in heroes, a trend with potentially major ramifications for our political culture.

The effects of television are certainly not all negative, however. Television programs, including commercials, provide much useful information. Children can gain a broad knowledge of people, places, and events and learn about the roles of doctors and lawyers, police officers and fire fighters, from television. A television program may bring a geography lesson to life or spark an interest in science (see Chapter 15 for more about the uses of television in education). And television commercials do help introduce children to the role of consumer and to the knowledge that theirs is a consumer-oriented society.

In sum: Television is a powerful socializing agent that has some harmful effects, especially on children, but also has great potential for making a positive contribution to society.

SOCIALIZATION THROUGH THE LIFE COURSE

We have thus far concentrated our discussion on the socialization that takes place in childhood. But socialization does not end at a particular age; it continues throughout life. As we mature, we take on new statuses and roles. Many of us will be married, for example, and perhaps later divorced or widowed; we will be parents, employees or employers, and senior citizens. Even in old age, near the end of the life course, people must adjust to new situations and create new self-images. In a complex society such as ours, life presents an ever-changing array of new parts to play.

Adolescence and Youth

Adolescence is a sensitive time. Because their bodies and minds are changing dramatically, and because they must develop the ability to fill new social statuses and play new roles, adolescents have much to learn and to which to adapt (Clarke-Stewart & Friedman, 1987).

The relation of adults to adolescents varies from one society to another. In the United States and other modern societies, adolescents tend to be regarded essentially as children, whereas in premodern societies they are typically experienced workers and are thus treated as adults. Indeed, in premodern societies, adolescence as a separate and prolonged stage of the life course does not really exist (Stone & Church, 1975).

In modern industrial societies, most adolescents are likely to be less under the influence of their immediate families and more subject to the influence of peers and school than they were when they were younger. For those who cannot integrate the new with the old, adolescence can be a time of great confusion and turmoil (Adelson, 1980; Hogan & Astone, 1986).

To a greater extent than children, adolescents can adopt the viewpoints of others and carefully examine their own personalities. Their worldviews, however, are still highly subjective-that is, based on their own immediate experiences and feelings. They frequently become overly concerned that others are judging their behavior. And they tend to fluctuate between egotism (constant, excessive reference to oneself in speaking or writing) on the one hand and low self-esteem on the other.

Adolescence is the time when people develop the ability to think abstractly. It is also the time when most people develop a sense of humor. Apparently, as the power to understand increases, so does the ability to appreciate humor.

Much adolescent socialization takes the form of **anticipatory socialization,** a process of social learning that is directed toward playing future roles. While anticipatory socialization spans the entire life cycle, it is especially visible in adolescence as teenagers "rehearse" their future adult roles of spouses (by dating), parents (by baby-sitting), and employees (by holding part-time jobs).

Many observers claim that in recent decades the ties between adolescents and their parents have weakened, especially in middle-class families, creating the so-called generation gap mentioned earlier. Most adolescents are still financially dependent on their families at a time when they are growing more independent in other ways. This can produce a powerful and troublesome conflict of feelings.

Three important and widely discussed areas of conflict are clothing, hairstyles, and curfews. Another common complaint of teenagers is that parents sometimes try to impose their goals on their children without bothering to find out what the teenagers themselves would like. Despite such conflicts, several British and American studies have shown that most teenagers and their parents have positive relationships with one another (Coleman & Hendry, 1990).

In recent years, scholars have begun to note a period of limbo between adolescence and adulthood—between biological maturity and full entry into the adult world. During this period, young people are old enough to vote, marry, and have children but often are still dependent on their parents or families for economic support. Because of the importance of a college education in the job market, many young people remain in the preadult stage until their mid-20s. This period of life has come to be called *youth* (Keniston, 1970). Recent census figures suggest that, partly in response to the difficult economic climate of the 1990s, an increasing number of young adults are still living at home. In fact, roughly 30 percent of all unmarried people between the ages of 25 and 29 had failed to establish a residence apart from that of their parents in 1991. If this trend continues, it seems likely to delay even further entry into true adult status for millions of young Americans.

Adulthood

By the time adulthood is reached, what is sometimes called **primary socialization**—the basic preparation for the various roles of adult life that takes place during the early years—has been completed. People who have reached adulthood normally have developed images of

Adolescence can be a time of powerful and troublesome conflict. Some ways young people test their independence is in their clothing and hairstyles.

the self, both real and ideal; some commitment to the norms and values of the society; a certain degree of self-control; and a willingness to subordinate some personal desires to society's rules. But adults' personalities have not become totally fixed. Indeed, there is a growing body of evidence that personalities continue to grow and change throughout adulthood (Brim & Kagan, 1980; Levinson et al., 1978). In addition, many new social roles (such as husband, wife, father, and mother) must be learned in adulthood. For these reasons, socialization continues throughout life.

Adult socialization differs from childhood socialization in several major respects (Brim, 1968). Adults are more motivated than children and are able to choose roles of their own free will. They may, if they want, change religions or marital status or jobs, or they may return to school. Children generally do not have the freedom to make these kinds of choices.

Adult socialization also involves the redefinition or re-creation of a current role when the content of the role changes. Rather than "role taking," the adult becomes involved in "role making." A good example of a change in role content is the new definition of the role of wife. In the past, wives were expected to care for their homes and families, to help their husbands find peace and contentment, and to undertake few, if any, duties outside the home. This role definition is now under heavy criticism, and a major restructuring of the wife's role is well underway.

Around the age of 40 many men find themselves doubting the value of their achievements and fearing that they have not managed to accomplish what they set out to do. Sometimes this "midlife transition" ushers in a period of reevaluation and change (Parker, 1985; see also Coche & Coche, 1986). One study found that men who experienced midlife transition seemed especially preoccupied with their work: the kind they had chosen, the self-identity they derived from it, and whether they had made the right career choices in early adulthood (Filene, 1987). Some people cannot manage such reevaluations; they enter a period that has been labeled the "midlife crisis." This crisis can be characterized by acute depression or unhappiness, but those who weather the storm often find late adulthood to be one of the most satisfying times of their life.

Later Life

Scholars such as Erik Erikson believe that some of the most difficult changes in attitudes and behavior occur in the last years of life. During this period, one usually must reconcile oneself to lower prestige, decreased physical ability and the prospect of death, and to one's failures in life (Erikson, 1982).

Old age is sometimes viewed in modern societies as a time of helplessness, uselessness, and dependence. It may also be a time when one's self-identity weakens. The self identity of most American men and women depends on their job roles and how independent and self-supporting they can be. Retirement puts an abrupt end to job self-identity and is painful for many people. Women who have based their self-identities on the roles of wife and mother sometimes feel lost or useless if they become widowed or divorced, or when their children leave home. (The process and problems of aging are discussed in Chapter 12.)

Death and Dying

Geoffrey Gorer has argued convincingly that modern Americans regard death with such distaste that it constitutes a kind of nonsexual pornography (Gorer, 1965). We deny death, lie to the dying about their condition, and remove all traces of death from our everyday lives. We put the dying in hospitals not only to ease their suffering but also to remove them from our sight. We discourage mourning and try to remove the aftereffects of a death from our lives as quickly as possible (Ariès, 1981). As a result, socialization for death has commonly been limited or nonexistent.

The Experience of Dying

Although some people seem to face death with composure, this calmness usually comes at the end of a long emotional struggle. Facing death is never easy, not even for those who seem courageous about it. Elisabeth Kübler-Ross (1969), a physician who spent years studying how the terminally ill react to the prospect of death, suggested that most people go through five stages leading toward acceptance of death. The first is denial and isolation, the second anger, the third bargaining (in which the dying person makes an "agreement" to die willingly if God or fate will allow him or her to live a little longer), the fourth depression, and the fifth acceptance. Most people do not experience these stages in strict sequence; they accept death only in "flashes," sometimes shifting between moments of hope and moments of despair.

Kübler-Ross's attempt to outline the process of dying was originally meant to help doctors and nurses understand what their patients were going through. At times, however, the "stages of dying" have been interpreted too literally. Doctors and nurses have tried to lead patients mechanically from one stage to the next; some patients have felt anxiety over not being at the "right" stage.

Charles Corr argues that Kubler-Ross's model is useful for developing theoretical perspectives on coping with death (1993). And he recommends a task-based model for dealing with death that includes both a greater understanding and an empowerment of dying patients. This model, therefore, encourages them to make cricial decisions about their deaths and allows the participation of others who are coping with death and all aspects of dying.

Mourning, Grief, and Bereavement

We go through the process of *mourning* when faced with *bereavement*—the loss of a loved one. If there has been a protracted illness, mourning usually begins before the actual death and involves the dying person as well as the survivors. The news that someone is going to die can produce a bout of *anticipatory grief* almost as intense as news of death itself. To work through their grief over a loved one's present condition, many people try to "fix" a mental image of how the dying person looked when healthy. One of the reasons why unexpected bereavement may be especially difficult for survivors is that sudden death allows no chance for anticipatory grief (Lundin, 1984). It remains unclear, however, whether the anticipation of death always helps the survivors adjust to the loss (Lund, 1989).

When death actually occurs, the response to it may take place in several phases. Four successive phases of emotions that typically accompany loss have been identified: first, shock, a kind of numbed refusal to acknowledge that anything has happened; second, protest, often accompanied by anticipating the dead person's reappearance; third, despair, frequently in the form of severe depression; and finally, adaptation, in which the survivor attempts to build a new life (Weis, 1988). These phases may not, however, occur in orderly sequence (Lund, Caserta, & Dimond, 1986).

Although grief is universal, everyone grieves differently. Bereaved people may mourn by weeping and then suddenly lash out in anger at the dead person for having "abandoned" them. Or a survivor may relive arguments that took place 20 years earlier, brooding over failures to communicate with the dead person or to live up to that person's expectations. Such feelings of guilt and anger are part of the process of separation, which finally leads the bereaved individual to acknowledge that the dead person cannot be brought back to life (Lund, 1989).

RESOCIALIZATION

As socialization proceeds throughout the life course, most of what we become is built on an unchanging foundation of the values that we learned and the self-identity that we established during primary socialization. However, in some cases, adolescents and adults undergo a process called **resocialization** in which old values and behavior patterns are unlearned and new values and behaviors are adopted. An extreme example of this process is the "brainwashing" sometimes forced on prisoners of war (Schein, 1961).

Resocialization often takes place in what Erving Goffman called **total institutions:** places where people are confined 24 hours a day under the complete control of an administrative staff for the purpose of fundamentally changing their personalities, values, and self-identities (Goffman, 1961). Basic training in the military is a familiar and relatively moderate example of a total institution. The goal of basic training is to modify recruits' civilian self-image in order to rebuild a military self-image.

Although grief is universal, everyone mourns differently. Some suffer in silence and isolation, while others are publicly consumed by despair.

This change is accomplished in two distinct stages. First, once the recruits have been removed from their civilian environment and confined on a military base, they undergo a process of *stripping* or *mortification* in which their commitment to their old selves is systematically eroded. They are required to give up the clothes they wore in their old lives and given uniform hairstyles. Personal names are used as little as possible; instead, they are addressed as "soldier" or "sailor" or by rank. They are allowed little if any contact with former friends and relatives and are subjected to long hours of physical labor and considerable sleep deprivation. As a result of these strippings, their old identities start to weaken and they become increasingly dependent on the total institution, much as young children are dependent on their parents.

In the second phase, a new, military self is reconstructed. The recruits are indoctrinated with the behaviors that will now be expected of them through exposure to positive role models who reinforce such things as saluting officers, being concerned with presenting a neat and orderly appearance, and following orders without question. A few weeks ago, the recruit was a civilian; now he or she is a soldier, a sailor, or a marine.

Research suggests that military training successfully weakens such civilian values as self-determination (acting on the basis of one's own decisions), which is replaced by values such as obedience to authority that will be essential if the recruit is to perform adequately in his or her new role (Stouffer et al., 1949).

Another example of resocialization within a total institution is the process of conversion to the types of unconventional religions that many people call "cults." However, research suggests that most members of cults eventually return to their previous self-images and values. One report estimated that only 5 percent of a cult's original recruits remained in that group for more than five years (Petranek, 1988). Another study found that the majority of members who voluntarily left another group had belonged to it for less than one year (Galanter, 1982). Such research suggests that resocialization is usually only effective if the convert's new self-image is continually reinforced by those with whom he or she comes into regular contact, a condition that is more likely in the case of the socially approved new identity of soldier or sailor than in the generally devalued role of cult member.

Goffman's theory of total institutions provides an important insight into why prisons and, to a lesser extent, mental hospitals often fail to effectively resocialize their inmates. To some extent, this failure may be attributed to the fact that prisoners and some mental patients, unlike military recruits and (contrary to popular opinion) most cult joiners, are undergoing resocialization involuntarily, but the example of successfully brainwashed prisoners of war suggests that resocialization can be effective up to a point even without the consent of the subject. The great failing of prisons and other unsuccessful total institutions is that they strip and mortify effectively but then provide few positive role models and little reinforcement for the new values and self-identities they are supposedly promoting.

Not all forms of resocialization are as dramatic as those discussed here, and not all resocialization takes place in total institutions. Resocialization into prestigious career fields such as medicine and the law can serve as a good example. This process can be particularly difficult and stressful. One doctor reflected back on her experience in medical school and noted that, like most first-year students, she believed at first that it would be her job to cure patients. It took her a while to learn that this was an oversimplification: Some patients simply cannot be helped because the medical profession lacks the knowledge to do so. Medical students are gradually resocialized so that their idealism becomes tempered by the harsh realities of medical practice (Klass, 1988).

SOCIALIZATION AND PERSONAL FREEDOM

Our discussion of how people learn to accept the patterns of thought, feeling, and behavior expected in their society may seem to imply that people are merely passive conformists. People often seem overwhelmed by the demands of schools, business organizations, and other social forces. However, people are far more than puppets, manipulated by society through socialization. Society is a human invention, though not an individual one, and people are as much a part of society as society is a part of them (Wrong, 1961). People create social rules through their interactions.

The relationship between the individual and society has occupied the great minds throughout history. Although the philosophical assumptions of social scientists vary, most tend to see people as active beings who can and do create and change culture and social structure even though they often act in expected ways.

Although the process of socialization may seem to restrict individual creativity and personal freedom, it is important to note that socialization also makes positive contributions to the creative process. Creative people must have great self-confidence to enter upon new and sometimes risky projects, as well as to endure the loneliness and isolation that often accompany such work. This confidence ultimately derives from the socialization provided by one's parents and one's peers.

Furthermore, all forms of socialization, even those that occur early in infancy, require the cooperation of the individual. Except in a few situations—such as in some total institutions—an unwilling subject cannot be socialized. Each of us has the ability to reject some of the dictates of society. Socialization is not an automatic process. When people feel that an action is unlikely to be rewarding, they may reject expectations that they learn or carry out the action.

As people grow older, their power to control their lives usually increases. We all know of individuals who have made dramatic changes in their adult lives that run counter to major social patterns. The man who gives up a highly paid business career to become a minister and the housewife who starts a new career in middle age are examples. So is the college dean who gives up a position at a prestigious university to teach at a small, southern black college. All are people who have rejected the scripts of society to seek roles they believe will be more personally satisfying. Less dramatic examples occur daily as people adapt their roles to meet their changing needs.

In summary, no matter how complex a society may seem or how much conformity it may demand, it is still a human creation that can be changed. Sometimes society is changed by the actions of an exceptional individual: a Napoleon or an Alexander the Great. More often, change comes through steady pressure from nameless individuals. One act of nonconformity may be a deviation. But when the act is repeated over and over, it can become a social revolution.

INTERNET/TECHNOLOGY

THE NET GENERATION

First there were bookworms. Then came couch potatoes. Now there are *chipheads*. While it is difficult to assess the exact impact of media on human beings, the transformations that these terms describe suggests that the effect produced is related to a particular type of media.

Despite the negative connotation of "bookworm," Americans generally view books positively; and campaigns to remove or ban certain books from schools and libraries have failed. But television has not fared so well. It has earned a bad reputation for being a lazy, poorly educated, and at times violent baby-sitter. What is more, television is a medium that denies children a voice (Tapscott, 1998). They are not permitted to question or disagree. They are the passive consumers of a one-way medium.

Now, even before researchers fully understand how television has affected one generation of children, the Internet is producing another. Referring to them as the *net generation*, Don Tapscott identifies them as the generation of children who will be between the ages of 2 and 21 in 1999.

Internet critics express concern about these young people, arguing that they will be nothing more than the next crop of couch potatoes. But Tapscott vigorously disagrees. According to him, the Internet is fundamentally different from television. Children are not just passive observers on the Internet but active participants. And that, he claims, translates into children who are tolerant, curious, assertive, and self-reliant.

In contrast to television, he argues that the Internet provides children with an interactive world that stimulates curiosity and the pursuit of adventure. Children can travel to faraway places and meet all kinds of people. They have access to the world's knowledge. And, because the Internet does not reveal whether you are rich

D. Tapscott believes that the interactive world of the Internet, unlike television, helps to stimulate curiosity and adventure, which translates into children who are tolerant, curious, assertive, and self-reliant.

or poor, male or female, or black or white, children will judge others only on the basis of their ideas.

Tapscott also argues that the Internet encourages critical thinking. In contrast to television, which involves no work at all on the part of viewers, the Internet requires users to think and to figure out how to get from place to place, how to download information, and how to respond to other Internet users. As a form of social interaction, the net encourages children to question, challenge, and disagree.

In contrast to many adults, children feel comfortable on the Internet. They are not afraid to surf the net—to explore unfamiliar places. As a result, they naturally develop problem-solving skills. For example, in contrast to their parents, kids can quickly figure out how to find and download a game that interests them.

Unfortunately, growing up on the net can also mean growing up too fast. Critics warn that the Internet is not always a safe place for children. It provides easy access not only to the

world's knowledge but, as well, to parts of the world for which they are unprepared—hate groups, pornography, even pedophiles. The Internet, too, can be a bad baby-sitter.

Overall, though, the Internet is most likely to benefit children. And the real problem with it actually lies in the fact that all children do not have access to it. Those who do will benefit in the ways that Tapscott described. They will develop critical thinking skills and the ability to access information at the stroke of a key. These are the skills that a postindustrial society demands, and they are the ones it will reward. Children who do not have access to the Internet will not be prepared for the twenty-first century. In a society with dwindling manufacturing jobs, they will fall even farther behind than their parents. For them the Internet does not promise a future full of opportunities. And, unfortunately, this means that the net generation will not include all children who will be between the ages of 2 and 21 in 1999.

CHAPTER REVIEW

1. Explain the difference between personality and self.

2. Could the concept of the looking-glass self be used to explain self-esteem? Why or why not?

3. Compare the concepts of Mead's theory of the development of the self to those that Freud used to describe the personality.

4. How would you describe the child-rearing practices of parents today?

5. The mass media, especially television, create images of a society's agents of socialization. Describe the images on television today. Do they accurately reflect the process of childhood socialization in America? Why or why not?

6. What is the purpose of the military's basic training program?

7. Is socialization just a form of brainwashing? Why or why not?

8. Describe the five stages that terminally ill patients usually go through. How can an understanding of this process help families cope with the death of a loved one?

INTERNET EXERCISE

The Web destinations for Chapter 6 are related to various aspects of socialization. To begin your explorations, go to the Prentice Hall Companion web site **http://www.prenhall.com/popenoe.** Next, select **Chapter 6** (Socialization). Then, choose **web destinations** from the menu on the left side of the screen. There are a variety of interesting sites to investigate. We suggest that you begin with **Homeschoolzone.** This site provides a wealth of information of the homeschooling movement in American society. Homeschooling poses a controversial alternative to public education. After you have explored the Homeschoolzone, answer the following questions:

- Schools are an acknowledged "agency of socialization" in American society, along with family, peers, and the media. Are homeschooled youngsters "missing out" in terms of their overall socialization? Why or why not?

- Do you think children should choose whether they are homeschooled or attend regular school, or should their parents make this decision for them?

KEY TERMS

socialization	significant others	primary socialization
personality	generalized other	resocialization
self	agent of socialization	total institutions
looking-glass self	peer group	
role taking	anticipatory socialization	

CHAPTER 7

Groups
and Organizations

aniel Defoe's Robinson Crusoe is one of the most intriguing figures in literary history. Generations of readers have been fascinated—and horrified—by imagining themselves stranded, totally alone, on a desert island. How do you think you would react if you found yourself a modern-day Crusoe, cut off for a long time from all human contact?

On the one hand, it might be nice to live without being told what to do by other people. You could sleep as late as you liked, dress as you pleased, sing out of tune at the top of your lungs, belch and scratch yourself without ever having to worry that others would disapprove. Such freedom might be heavenly—for a while.

But for how long? For most of us, the answer is: not very long at all. Even the most antisocial person would soon start missing human company. If we lived alone, with whom would we celebrate our successes, and who would console us when we were depressed? For how long would we be content hearing no voice other than our own, and exposed to no ideas other than those rattling around in our own minds?

In reality, people who have been forced to endure prolonged periods of isolation frequently experience profound disorientation and may even be driven mad by lack of human companionship. It is not surprising that the most severe punishment possible in traditional prison systems was solitary confinement. Similarly, the strongest negative sanction available to many communal religious groups is "shunning," or forced separation from the group. Just as Robinson Crusoe was overjoyed when he eventually encountered another person on his island purgatory, anyone who has ever endured even relatively brief periods of forced isolation knows that contact with other people is as basic a human need as are food, water, and shelter.

Chapter 6 extensively documented people's need for human contact in order to be properly socialized. We also depend on others for most of our basic physical needs and for our psychological health as well. We work, play, study, and worship with others; in fact, so much of human life takes place in groups that people who prefer to keep to themselves are commonly labeled as "loners" and stigmatized as deviant. It is a fundamental sociological assumption that humans are innately social animals, and it is in groups of all sizes and types that human life is lived.

Because social groups serve such important purposes and play such a major part in our lives, they are a basic topic of study in sociology. We begin this chapter with a discussion of the nature and structure of **small groups,** or groups that are small enough to allow their members to relate to one another on an individual basis.

After a consideration of the ways small groups work, we turn to the larger social groupings known as *organizations* and conclude with a consideration of some alternatives to traditional organizational structures.

THE NATURE OF SOCIAL GROUPS

The study of small groups was a central focus of American sociology during the 1930s, 1940s, and 1950s. Our discussion of social groups draws heavily on the classic research done in this period, although more recent work will be cited when appropriate. We begin by addressing a basic sociological question: What, precisely, is a social group?

What Is a Social Group?

As pointed out in Chapter 4, the members of a group, unlike the members of mere collections of people or social categories, display distinct patterns in the ways they relate to one another. In other words, they develop a social structure and expect certain things from fellow members. Groups also develop cultures with distinct meanings and norms. They have a character all their own and are different from the personalities, beliefs, and values of the individual people who belong to them. By sharing the group's meanings and norms, the people in a group develop a sense of identity as group members. Those in the group are clearly distinguished from outsiders. A **social group** can thus be defined as two or more people who have a common identity and some feeling of unity and who share certain goals and expectations about each other's behavior.

Although the term *social group* can be applied to units as large as whole societies, it also has a more specific meaning. The term is often used by both sociologists and nonsociologists to mean a small face-to-face grouping whose members all know one another. For example, if we were to look around a park on a warm Sunday afternoon, we might see many clusters of people. One cluster might be gathered around a hot-dog stand, waiting to buy food. A pack of five or six teenage boys, all dressed in jeans and T-shirts, might come barreling down a path on their bicycles, scattering joggers, strollers, and children. Off to our left, some adults and children might be enjoying a picnic at a park table. Which of these sets of people are social groups?

The people waiting to buy hot dogs are not a social group, because they do not have a distinct social structure or shared culture. They do not know one another and they have little in common except a desire to get what they are waiting for as quickly as possible. They are together in one place only because they all want hot dogs.

Sociologists sometimes refer to such collections of people as *aggregates*. (Of course, if all the people in the hot-dog line were family members or friends, they would make up a social group—but not because of their common goal of buying hot dogs.)

Our park scene does include two likely social groups, however. The boys on bicycles probably are a social group: They share specific patterns of behavior and a set of values and role expectations. One boy might be a clown, another the leader, and a third his "right-hand man." Their clothes, their style of speech, their code of behavior, and their sense of group unity distinguish them from mere aggregates of people. And the cluster of people at the picnic table is also probably a social group—perhaps a family or close friends on a Sunday outing.

A well-known example of a small group is Alcoholics Anonymous (Denzin, 1986b). Alcoholics Anonymous (AA) groups, ranging from 5 to 30 or more people, meet at least once a week and are headed by a chairperson. Ritual is an important part of group meetings; prayers and readings from AA texts are recited, and a special status is conferred on those offering the recitations. The members are united by a pledge that reaffirms the group goal of sobriety. They also share their identity as alcoholics—discussions are opened with "My name is _____, and I am an alcoholic." Communication is the central activity of the meetings. AA members share past experiences and vow to keep coming back to meetings in the future, thus giving the group continuity.

Primary and Secondary Groups

As briefly discussed in Chapter 4, sociologists have long distinguished between two general types of groups: primary and secondary. Throughout history, a basic unit of human society—perhaps the most important kind of social group—has been the **primary group,** a relatively small, multipurpose group in which interaction is intimate and there is a strong sense of group identity. The most important primary group is the family. Other primary groups include youthful peer groups, such as children's play groups and teenage gangs; some neighborhood friendship circles and adult social clubs; and informal groups within complex organizations, such as cliques of factory workers and groups of student friends.

The meaning of the term *primary* as applied to groups has expanded somewhat since it was first used by Charles Horton Cooley (1909). Cooley used "primary" principally to mean first. He called the family and children's play groups primary groups because they are the first agents of socialization that we encounter. Referring to them as the "nursery of human nature," Cooley believed that they were centrally important in shaping the

A social group can be defined as two or more people who have a common identity and some feeling of unity and who share certain goals and expectations about each other's behavior. Can you identify anyone in this photograph as being in a social group? Are there aggregates?

human personality. Since Cooley's day, the term has commonly been broadened to apply to all groups in which relationships are like family ties. Fraternities and sororities, some sports teams, and even small political groups whose members share a sense of identity can be analyzed as primary groups.

PRIMARY RELATIONSHIPS

Perhaps the best way to understand the nature of these groups is to look at the type of relationship that binds their members—the primary relationship. This type of relationship is not only found in all primary groups, but it is also present in almost every kind of organization and in almost all social settings. A **primary relationship** is a personal, emotional, and not easily transferable relationship that includes a variety of roles and interests of each individual. It is characterized by free and extensive communication and the interaction of whole personalities. These traits are explained more fully as follows:

1. *The people in the relationship play a variety of roles in it and bring many personal interests to it.* For example, a professor and an undergraduate student typically

Office workers are a common secondary group. As defined, a secondary group is a specialized group designed to achieve specific goals; its members are linked mainly by secondary relationships that lack emotional intensity and involve only limited aspects of one's personality.

relate only in terms of these specific roles; they do not have a primary relationship. If, however, the student were to begin graduate school and to work closely with this same professor, the two might develop a primary relationship—becoming friends and meeting after work for social reasons. They might even become rivals.

2. *Because the primary relationship includes a wide variety of roles and interests, it involves the whole personality.* For example, members of a primary group of office workers are likely to come to know one another outside the office as well. By meeting socially after work and by chatting casually during office hours, they learn how the others handle their finances, spend their leisure time, and relate to their children. Because they can observe one another in many roles and situations, they may ultimately come to value one another as much for the nonwork roles as for the work roles they share.

3. *Primary relationships are characterized by free and extensive communication.* People in a primary relationship usually feel that they can and should communicate intimately. We neither expect nor wish our butcher to tell us why he feels depressed on a given morning. But we would expect our spouse to do so. By communicating openly and by observing each other's behavior, the people in a primary relationship reveal their inner selves and thus become more intimate.

4. *Because primary relationships involve many aspects of the personality, they are laden with emotions, though they need not be strongly affectionate.* Some members of a primary group may even detest some of the others. Members who dislike one another maintain their primary relationship because their membership

in the group gives them something besides affection—perhaps respect or support.

5. *Because primary relationships involve a special response to the unique traits of another person, they cannot be easily transferred from one person to another.* If you feel that your druggist is rude and careless, you can find another druggist. But in the case, let's say, of a boyfriend or girlfriend, close feelings cannot be shifted to someone else so quickly or easily.

We can see from this discussion that primary relationships, and therefore primary groups, provide people with the chance to develop their personalities. These relationships help us to expand our self-image as complex, multifaceted individuals. Moreover, the primary group is a main source of identity and security during conflicts with other people and groups. Because the primary group accepts the whole person, it gives one the feeling of having "someone on my side"—a necessary kind of emotional support.

Just how important primary groups and primary relationships are is apparent when we consider the case of a child who loses a parent through death or divorce, an adult who loses a spouse, or an elderly person whose friends have all died. In each of these cases, the individual suffers a major personal loss from broken primary ties.

Yet primary groups can also affect people negatively. By suppressing individuality and sometimes personal achievement, some primary groups can limit a person's social development. We all know cases of people who have had to "break free" of their families in order to develop as separate individuals.

SECONDARY GROUPS AND RELATIONSHIPS

Although the terms *secondary group* and *secondary relationship* were not used by Cooley, they are used widely by sociologists today. A **secondary group** is a specialized group designed to achieve specific goals; its members are linked mainly by secondary relationships. In contrast to a primary relationship, a **secondary relationship** is specialized, lacks emotional intensity, and involves only limited aspects of one's personality.

Secondary relationships are increasingly prevalent in modern societies. Office workers, colleagues in university departments, and officials in government bureaus are all most commonly members of secondary groups. These people often communicate indirectly, through memos, the phone, or e-mail. This impersonality reflects the purpose of secondary groups: to achieve practical goals, not to provide emotional support or to be vehicles for self-expression. The most familiar secondary group is the formal organization, discussed later in this chapter.

TABLE 7.1   CHARACTERISTICS OF PRIMARY AND SECONDARY RELATIONSHIPS

Primary Relationship	*Secondary Relationship*
1. Includes a variety of roles and interests of each of the participants. General and diffuse in character.	1. Usually includes only one role and interest of each participant. Specialized in character.
2. Involves the total personality of each participant.	2. Involves only those aspects of the personalities of the participants that are specifically relevant to the situation.
3. Involves communication that is free and extensive.	3. Limits communication to the specific subject of the relationship.
4. Personal and emotion-laden.	4. Relatively impersonal and unemotional.
5. Not easily transferable to another person.	5. Transferable to others; that is, the participants are interchangeable.

Note: Primary relationships are usually important sources of emotional expression and gratification. Secondary relationships are more efficient for transacting business and are especially characteristic of modern urban-industrial society.

Table 7.1 summarizes the differences between primary and secondary groups.

Why Do We Form Groups?

Sociologists believe that there are two basic and quite different reasons why people form social groups, connected to two separate types of needs shared by all members of society and closely related to the distinction between primary and secondary groups.

Some groups meet *instrumental needs*—that is, they help members do jobs that they could not easily accomplish alone. Many instrumental groups are absolutely necessary; for example, a single player could not possibly win a football game. Other instrumental groups are less essential. People can lose weight without such groups as Weight Watchers, and students can certainly pass tests without the informal study groups they form at exam time, but such groups often accomplish a goal much more effectively than one person can.

Other groups form chiefly to meet *expressive needs*—that is, they help to fulfill their members' emotional desires, usually for support and self-expression. Most groups of friends serve this purpose; so do fraternities and sororities, though in a more structured way.

In practice, many social groups—perhaps most of them—serve both ends. Instrumental groups, for instance, often meet expressive needs as well. Members of sports teams can develop close ties that are the basis for friendships off the playing field. Musicians can develop friendships as a result of their close contact, over extended periods, in rehearsals and performances.

GROUP STRUCTURE

If people spend enough time together, they almost always develop a social structure. Juries, work crews, and even people trapped in an elevator may at first be mere collections of strangers, but after they have been together a while, they form an integrated system of norms, statuses, and roles. Why do human groups have this tendency? The importance of social structure was discussed in Chapter 4. Here we sharpen that discussion by focusing on small groups.

According to Robert Bales (1951), a pioneering small group researcher, social structure arises from each person's need for a stable social environment. When two or more people meet for the first time, there is a degree of tension. Each individual tries to reduce this tension by establishing relatively stable patterns of group interaction. Once such patterns have been established, the members come to know what behavior to expect from one another, and in turn they can shape their own behavior within the group. Thus, social structure solves a basic problem every group member faces: How should I behave in the presence of others?

The different talents and personal qualities of the group members can also contribute to the developing social structure. Some people find it easier to lead; others, to follow. Some may have special insight into a group's values and so take on the role of trendsetter. Gradually, group roles evolve. In a peer group of high school students, for example, the most sociable member may hold the parties, while the most intellectual might have the greatest influence on the opinions of the other group members.

APPLYING SOCIOLOGY

COOPERATIVE LEARNING

How do you learn best? That is a question that educators ask year after year as they attempt to reform our school systems. Today three different approaches are practiced in the United States: (1) the individualistic approach, (2) the competitive approach, and (3) the cooperative approach. Teachers can use each of these methods effectively (Johnson & Johnson, 1987). The key lies in matching the appropriate method to the learning goal they wish to accomplish. For example, individualistic learning is well suited to the acquisition of skills and knowledge, such as memorizing spelling words or scientific concepts like the chemical elements in the periodic table (Putnam, 1997). Working independently, but with assistance and feedback from the teacher, students can move at their own pace.

Competitive learning is also well suited for practicing skills and for recalling information. It does not, however, accommodate individual rates of achievement. In fact, student interaction is designed to reward those who perform better than others. Spelling bees, sporting events, and music competitions are designed to help students improve their skills by identifying their own strengths and weaknesses (Putnam, 1997).

Cooperative learning is suited for all kinds of learning and involves long periods of interaction among students. Contributing to the group in the form of helping and sharing are the key characteristics to this approach to learning.

Over the last 60 years, education in the United States has stressed only competitive and individualistic learning (Johnson & Johnson, 1987). Competitive learning, which gained the support of the business community in the 1930s, became so popular that by the 1960s it was considered the "traditional" approach to educating students. During the 1960s, the individualistic approach gained favor in written curricula and teacher-training programs (Johnson & Johnson, 1987).

Studies have shown that teachers use these two styles 85 to 95 percent of the time (Johnson & Johnson, 1987). Used properly, these approaches can achieve positive results, but educators must also recognize their weaknesses. For example, while competitive learning can motivate students to try harder, it also draws attention to the fact that all students do not move at the same pace. Labeling students as winners and losers accentuates this fact and contributes to feelings of low self-esteem in those who perform poorly. Students who learn in this way tend to follow one of two paths. Either

they work very hard in an effort to do better than other students, or they give up without even trying, convinced that they never had a chance to win (Johnson & Johnson, 1987).

The individualistic approach, on the other hand, offers no opportunity for student interaction, which is necessary for developing communication and leadership skills. As a result, students are unprepared for the adult world, where they will be required to interact cooperatively with others in the workplace, in their communities, and at home.

The third approach that teachers can take—cooperative learning—is used less often than either individualistic or competitive methods, despite the research that shows its many advantages. Students who are taught using this method show higher levels of achievement and higher level reasoning abilities. They value the subjects they study, have higher self-esteem, and develop strong interpersonal skills (Hill & Hill, 1990; Johnson & Johnson 1987; Putnam, 1997).

Elements of Cooperative Learning

Learning in groups can take many forms—games and simulations, role playing, discussion groups, and study groups (Reynolds, 1994). However, cooperative group learning is distinguished by five basic elements

Group Size

How does the size of a group affect the behavior of its members? Many classic sociologists, especially Georg Simmel (Wolff, 1950), were interested in this topic.

The smallest possible group, a **dyad,** is a group made up of just two members. The dyadic bond is potentially uniquely strong; such a group can develop a sense of unity and intimacy not found in larger groups. But, because the dyad depends on a single relationship, the members must always take each other into account. And

in a dyad there is no opportunity to let others carry on the interaction. If one member drops out, the group is effectively extinguished.

According to Simmel, the **triad,** a group of three members, is in some ways the least stable of all small groups. In any group of three people, one individual can always become an outsider, or an "intruder" (Caplow, 1969). On the other hand, sometimes the third person can act as a mediator.

As a group gets larger, it grows more complex and formal. With each additional member there is a geometric

(Johnson, Johnson, & Holubec, 1993; Putnam, 1997):

1. Positive interdependence
2. Individual accountability
3. Cooperative skills
4. Face-to-face interaction
5. Group reflection and goal setting

Positive interdependence. Working together to accomplish a goal is the distinguishing characteristic of cooperative learning (Putnam, 1997). The group's success depends on each member's willingness to take responsibility not only for her or his own work but for the achievement of all members as well. All group members must play a role in planning, decision making, and negotiating.

Individual accountability. Cooperative learning requires the full participation of all group members. If individual members fail to do their jobs, the group is impaired. Even if other members make up the unfinished job, the failure of one member disqualifies this as a truly cooperative learning group. Each member of the group is held accountable by other members.

Cooperative skills. Young children begin to develop cooperative skills by staying with a group and taking turns. As they mature, children should learn how to listen actively and to contribute their own ideas to the group. In doing so, they acquire the interpersonal skills that they will need as an adult.

Face-to-face interaction. Interacting with group members can take many forms and is not necessarily an indication that cooperative learning is taking place. For example, sharing answers to a homework assignment is not the kind of face-to-face interaction that characterizes a cooperative learning group. Real cooperative tasks involve planning, discussions, and negotiations. In some cases, individualistic learning is a component of cooperative learning—for example, researching arguments for a debate (Putnam, 1997). But, as this example illustrates, it is only one component and ultimately requires the group's attention.

Group reflection and goal setting. The final component of cooperative learning involves an evaluation of how well the group functions. Members identify strengths and weaknesses of the group effort and prepare solutions for the problems they encountered.

While learning occurs in many ways, it is primarily a social act (Putnam, 1997). Cooperative learning is, therefore, one of the most effective approaches teachers can take. In fact, as Table 7.2 shows, the three most effective ways that people learn are key components of cooperative group learning (Putnam, 1997). They learn what they SAY, what they SAY and APPLY in life, and what they TEACH others.

TABLE 7.2	**WHAT PEOPLE LEARN**

10% of what they READ
20% of what they READ and HEAR
30% of what they SEE
50% of what they SEE and HEAR
70% of what they SAY
90% of what they SAY and APPLY in life
95% of what they TEACH others

Source: Adapted from M.D. Alcorn, J.S. Kinder, & J.R. Schunert, *Better Teaching in Secondary Schools* (Chicago: Holt, Rinehart and Winston, 1970); cited in JoAnne Putnam, *Cooperative Learning In Diverse Classrooms,* (Upper Saddle River, NJ: Prentice Hall, 1997).

increase in the number of possible social relationships within the group. For example, in a three-person group consisting of A, B, and C, only three friendship pairs are possible: AD, AC, and BC. As soon as one more person (D) is added to the group, the number of possible pairings increases to six: AB, AC, AD, BC, BD, and CD. If another person (E) enters the group, ten two-person alliances could be formed: AB, AC, AD, AE, BC, BD, BE, CD, CE, DE. Thus, the number of possible pairings in the group increases from three to ten when the group size increases by only two.

Large groups can be either more or less productive than smaller ones, depending on the group's task (Nixon, 1979). A group whose task results are limited by the weakest or least efficient member of the group will usually be less efficient at problem solving than one or two creative individuals will be. But a task that relies on a concerted group effort in which each person's input is valuable (as in obtaining signatures for a political petition) will usually be more easily accomplished by a large group of volunteers—provided they do not get in one another's way (Wood, Polek, & Aiken, 1985).

For a dyad—a group of two people—to endure, both members must pay attention to and respond to each other. The triad or three-person group may be less stable, since coalitions can form and two members may sometimes exlude the third.

The "proper" size for a group is thus strongly dependent on its purpose, and many groups function best when they are relatively small. For such special-purpose groups as counseling groups or day camps for emotionally disturbed children, a group size of less than 10 people seems to be optimal. Groups between 12 and 30 members are recommended in educational settings (Skidmore, Hon, Thackeray, & Farley, 1988).

Group Norms

As already mentioned, one trait that makes a social group distinct from a mere aggregation of people is a set of shared norms. Group norms prescribe how members should behave and what it means to be deviant.

Among the best early accounts of group norms and their origins is William Foote Whyte's classic study *Street Corner Society*. In the late 1930s and early 1940s, Whyte immersed himself in the activities of a street gang in "Cornerville," a neighborhood in "Eastern City"—actually the North End of Boston, the city's Italian district. Most "respectable" Bostonians knew little about the area, believing "that bathrooms are rare [in Cornerville], that children overrun the narrow and neglected streets, that the juvenile delinquency rate is high, that crime is prevalent among adults, and that a large proportion of the population was on . . . relief . . . during the Depression." Thus, to the rest of the city, Cornerville was nothing more than "a formidable mass of confusion, a social chaos" (Whyte, 1943/1981).

Whyte's subjects were young men in their 20s and early 30s who hung out together almost every night. These "corner boys" shared a set of norms that were at least as strict as the norms of Beacon Hill, an elite Boston neighborhood. Their sense of hierarchy, for example, was highly developed. At the top of the ranking stood the gang's leader, "Doc." Immediately below him were three assistants, and below them nine or so followers. Relations among these three levels were governed by the firm belief that the leaders should take precedence over the followers.

Traditions governed almost all of the group's actions. Just about every night the members would meet at the same bar. And whenever they did so, they would try to sit in the same position at the same table. "The right to these positions is recognized by other Cornerville groups. When strangers are found at the accustomed places, the necessity of finding other chairs is a matter of some annoyance."

The members of the group were also bound by elaborate rules of mutual aid. "The code of the corner boy requires him to help his friends when he can and to refrain from doing anything to harm them." These obligations varied from member to member. A gang leader had to be a free spender; he was expected to shower gifts and benefits on his followers. It would be beneath the dignity of such a man to accept favors in return, especially from the lower-ranking gang members. For the members of low rank, however, helping the chief was a route to enhanced status.

Far from being socially disorganized, then, Whyte's street corner society was characterized by elaborate group norms that regulated the behavior of all of the members. Its norms were just as meaningful as the norms of any other society: They told the corner boys exactly how to behave in most situations, even though that behavior might seem peculiar to other Bostonians.

Group Roles

As Whyte's *Street Corner Society* shows, many group norms take the form of role expectations. Group roles can arise spontaneously. For example, if we suddenly found ourselves in an emergency, such as an auto accident, each of us would probably automatically assume a different role. One person might act as a doctor's helper, another as a crowd controller, and another as a messenger. This is an example, of how incidents, such as accidents, can transform an aggregation of people into a group.

Many attempts have been made to identify the roles that commonly arise in small groups. In the most famous of these efforts, Robert Bales and his colleagues studied various small task-oriented groups and found that in every one the same basic roles arose. Each role contributed in a different way to the group's task or activity. Some people took the role of talkers and kept the conversation going. Others provided the group with ideas. Still others served to keep the conversation on track. Finally, the best-liked people played the role of harmonizer. They helped resolve tensions and promote unity (Parsons & Bales, 1955).

Another famous study of group roles was conducted by Philip Zimbardo. Zimbardo and his colleagues wanted to study abuses of power by prison guards, such as withholding of privileges, beatings, and throwing prisoners into solitary confinement. Zimbardo wondered if brutal, callous people are drawn to jobs as prison guards, or if there is something within the social environment of a prison that engenders violent behavior.

To find the answer to this question, Zimbardo (1972) simulated a prison in a basement at Stanford University and advertised for young men to participate in the experiment. More than 70 people applied for the job, which paid $15 a day. Zimbardo used psychological and physical tests to select 24 seemingly stable, normal middle-class students from the United States and Canada to take part in the experiment. The students were then randomly assigned one of two roles: prisoner or guard. The students chosen to be "prisoners" were actually arrested by the local police and brought to the basement jail, where they were put into three-man cells and told that they would be held for two weeks.

At the end of six days, the mock prison was closed down because the researchers were so concerned about the behaviors their experiment had brought about (Zimbardo, 1971). The students chosen to be "guards" actually took on the role of stereotypical prison guards, treating the "prisoners" like animals and delighting in dehumanizing them. Meanwhile, the "prisoners" quickly adopted the prisoner role, thinking only of their survival and escape.

Critics have pointed out that the Zimbardo research may not be fully applicable to actual prisons. In real life, inmates generally are able to develop their own informal social structure, which helps them resist some of the pressures to which they are exposed. Furthermore, in actual prisons, guards know that they will be interacting with prisoners for months and years, not just for a week

Interactions between prisoners and correctional officers are commonly harsh and confrontational. Zimbardo's study suggests that this is more a result of the expectations associated with the roles of guards and prisoners than of the personalities of the people playing these roles.

or two, and most of them come to understand that they need to establish reasonably positive relations with the prisoners because an extremely hostile work environment will only make their jobs more difficult and riskier. However, despite such cautions, the results of the Zimbardo experiment have been widely interpreted as suggesting that the causes of prison violence lie less in the particular personalities of the guards and the prisoners and more in the social structure of the prison itself. In this research, both sets of students—"guards" and "prisoners"—played their group roles in a way that strongly supports the notion that structural demands may easily overwhelm personal preferences.

LEADERSHIP

Every group includes positions that enable certain people to wield power over others. Bales (1951) determined that there are two main types of leaders in small groups. *Instrumental leaders,* also called task leaders, attempt to guide the group toward its goals. *Expressive leaders,* also called *socioemotional leaders,* seek to create group unity and to maintain harmony. Both forms of leadership are needed for a group to be successful.

The two types of leadership roles are usually played by different people. According to Parsons and Bales (1955), this division of leadership can be seen clearly in the traditional American nuclear family: The husband-breadwinner provides instrumental leadership;

the wife-homemaker provides expressive leadership by supplying the family with warmth, comfort, and emotional security. (For other views on gender roles in the family, see Chapter 13.)

Besides promoting different ends, leadership can take a variety of *styles*. The social psychologists Kurt Lewin, Ronald Lippit, and Ralph White did the classic work on small group leadership styles in the 1930s. They exposed groups of 11-year-old boys to three leadership styles-authoritarian, democratic, and laissez faire—and observed the effects on behavior (Lippit & White, 1952).

These leadership styles differed in several key respects. In the authoritarian setting, the leader was the only person who determined group policy and assigned tasks. In the democratic setting, policy was determined and tasks were allocated through group discussion, which the leader assisted. In the laissez-faire setting, the boys had complete freedom, with minimal involvement by the leader. In addition, the way the leaders praised and criticized the boys differed in each setting. The authoritarian leaders were personal in their criticism; the democratic leaders tried to be objective and fair; and the laissez-faire leaders commented infrequently on the boys' actions and did not try to regulate the group.

How did the boys react to these leadership styles? There was vastly more hostility and much more aggression in the authoritarian group than in the democratic group. Also, under authoritarian leadership, group members engaged in more scapegoating—that is, finding others to blame—than in the other settings. The democratic leaders were liked better than the authoritarian leaders by 19 of 20 boys, and 7 of 10 preferred the laissez-faire to the authoritarian leaders. And though there was no substantial difference in group productivity, observers judged the products of the democratic groups to be superior to those of the others (Shaw, 1976).

There are some important limitations to the studies of Lewin, Lippit, and White (Nixon, 1979). For one, their research focused on leadership imposed from outside rather than on leadership that arose informally from within (Golembiewski, 1962). Another limitation is the study's obvious preference for the democratic style. Later researchers have tried to correct this bias by using terms such as *directive* and *participatory* instead of the emotionally charged words *authoritarian* and *democratic*.

Later researchers have also been more receptive to the idea that a democratic style may be less beneficial than an authoritarian style in some situations. For example, in classroom settings where members need to acquire basic skills, a strong directive approach often works best until students reach a certain level (McKeachie, 1954). Furthermore, there are some settings, such as the army and some factories, where leaders are expected to be

authoritarian, and in such places productivity may decline and members become dissatisfied when democratic leadership is introduced (Hare, 1976). Similarly, in Third World nations lacking a democratic political tradition, authoritarian leadership may be preferred in a variety of small group settings. In short, the effects of leadership styles depend on the nature of the leadership and where and when it is exercised.

It is important to stress that leadership is not a fixed quality. Although there are individual characteristics, such as persuasiveness, innovativeness, and decision-making ability, that are critical for successful leadership, there is no distinct set of traits that all leaders possess (Hall, 1999). A leader in one group will not automatically become a leader in another. Leadership depends on each particular group's values, needs, and goals.

HOW GROUPS WORK

Decision Making

How do groups make decisions? In an influential study of *task-oriented groups*—groups whose purpose is to solve a problem—Robert Bales and Fred Strodtbeck (1951) discovered that decision making occurs in four distinct phases. In the orientation phase, group members are introduced to the problem and analyze the facts. In the evaluation phase, the members assess the problem and respond to the views of others. In the third phase, the group comes to a decision. During the struggle to reach consensus, factions may develop and emotions build. When a decision is finally reached, the fourth phase begins. During this phase, the group seeks to restore its initial harmony. Members may joke or kid one another, for example, to ease tensions and rebuild group unity.

Conformity

What determines the choices a group will make? What leads a group to make a certain decision? To answer these questions we must explore the nature of group **conformity**—action in accordance with customs, rules, or prevailing opinions. Several experiments have shown just how powerful the pressure to conform within a group can be.

In order to measure a group's impact on its members, Muzafer Sherif (1936) asked subjects in an experiment to look at a fixed point of light while sitting alone in a darkened room. In such a setting, a point of light will appear to move slightly, although it really remains fixed. Subjects were then asked to report how far they thought the light had moved. After several rounds, each subject's estimates became relatively fixed—two inches for one subject, three for another, and so on. Then the subjects were put into small groups, and the experiment was repeated. Each subject was again asked to estimate how far the light had moved, but this time each subject was allowed to hear the estimates of other group members. Sherif found that people's individual estimates began to converge around an emerging group norm. Finally, each subject was again tested separately. The subjects conformed to the group norm instead of returning to their original estimates.

Sherif's findings strongly supported the idea that members of a small group tend to reduce the ambiguity of a situation by settling on a common view of reality. The group members internalize the common view and continue to hold it even after leaving the group.

The Sherif experiment studied a situation that was inherently vague in the sense that the light appeared to have moved when it really had not. In a later study, Solomon Asch (1955) showed that even in a task that was not so ambiguous, there was a remarkable tendency for subjects to suppress the evidence of their own eyes and conform to group expectations. Asch asked groups of eight males, seven of whom were following a script written by Asch and one of whom was an unwitting subject, to take a series of "perceptual" tests. Asch held two large cards before the group. On one card was a single line. On the other card were three lines of different lengths, one of which was exactly the same length as the line on the first card. In the presence of all the others, each member of the group, including the naive subject, was asked to announce which of the three lines on the second card was the same length as the single line on the first card. Asch set up the experiment so that the naive subject always answered last, after each of the seven confederates had already announced his judgment.

Eighteen tests were given to each group; in every case, the empirically correct answer was obvious. Asch's seven confederates gave unanimous but incorrect answers in 12 of the tests in order to create a clear conflict for the naive subject between the evidence of his own senses and his desire to conform to what appeared to be the group consensus. Asch found that only one-fourth of his subjects never yielded to the group, whereas more than one-third of the 50 subjects went along more than half the time. The remaining subjects occasionally conformed but mostly stuck by their guns, although this posture was often accompanied by what appeared to be substantial emotional stress on the part of the naive subjects.

What distinguished the yielders from the nonyielders? Interviews with the subjects revealed that those who never yielded either placed great trust in their own judgment, cared little about the opinions of the group, or were doubtful about going against the group but wanted to perform competently anyway. Of those who yielded, most

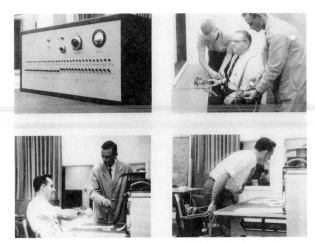

Milgram's experiment is a classic demonstration of how far people will go in following the dictates of authority. Copyright 1965 by Stanley Milgram. From the film Obedience, *distributed by Penn State Media Sales.*

perceived the lines correctly but concluded under group pressure that their perceptions were wrong. A few knew that their observations were correct but were overpowered by a need to conform.

The experiments conducted by Sherif and by Asch provide us with examples of *informational conformity*. The subjects in these studies did not perceive any explicit pressures from group members to conform to their opinions or judgments, but they decided to accept the group point of view simply because they felt that the members of the group must have had good reasons for their expressed choices. In contrast, *normative conformity* involves real or imagined social pressures from others. For example, many students may drink alcohol or engage in other similar behaviors because they believe that their friends may reject them if they do not go along (Insko et al., 1985).

Obedience—the "acceptance of real or imagined leadership expectations" (Crosbie, 1975)—is a third kind of conformity. In the early 1960s, the Yale psychologist Stanley Milgram launched a famous, or perhaps notorious, investigation of obedience to authority. Milgram placed ads calling for "assistants" to help him in an experiment. When people responded to the ads, Milgram explained that he was attempting to test instructional methods. Each "assistant" was taken into a room where a "learner," who sat strapped to a chair, was taking an oral test. Any time the "learner" provided a wrong answer, Milgram told the "assistant" to give him an "electric shock."

Of course, the whole thing was a setup. The "assistant" was the true subject of the experiment. The "learner" was really an actor who howled with pretended pain when the "assistant" gave him an imaginary electric shock. The point of the deception was to find out whether and to what extent people would follow Milgram's orders, even when the consequence was inflicting pain on others.

The results of the experiment were daunting. No less than 65 percent of the "assistants" did everything Milgram asked, even though the actors shrieked with pain and in some cases pretended to faint (Milgram, 1963). Many of the subjects said that they followed orders because they respected the authority of the scientists who were conducting the experiment.

Although Milgram's experiment gave rise to a serious debate about the place of ethics in the social sciences, it remains a classic demonstration of how far people will go in following the dictates of "authority."

THE RISKY SHIFT

Pressure to conform clearly affects the kinds of decisions groups make. In a series of experiments, several scholars (Stoner, 1961; Wallach, Kogan, & Bem, 1962) found that groups often make riskier decisions than people working alone. In a typical experiment, subjects were asked to decide whether a person should risk leaving a secure but unrewarding job to work for a new firm that would pay more and would offer a share of the profits but that might go under. The subjects were first asked to decide alone and then to reach a second decision in a group. The group decision was consistently riskier that the individual one, a phenomenon called *the risky shift*.

One explanation for the risky shift is that people in groups feel less personally responsible for a collective decision that they do when deciding alone. The group "frees" them to make riskier decisions. Another explanation relates to the Sherif experiments discussed earlier—the risky shift results from pressure to conform. (S. Wilson, 1978). Group discussions let people see how their views compare with those of others, and they then modify their views to reach a common decision. But why is the group decision often riskier than individual decisions? It may be because the people with the most extreme initial views in the group are likely to change them the least during the group discussion. As a result, to arrive at a common decision, the other group members must move toward the extreme position. It is important to note, however, that not all group decisions involve a risky shift. In some cases, group decisions are more cautious than individual decisions might be (Nordhøy, 1962).

GROUPTHINK

In his study of foreign policy fiascos, Irving Janis (1972, 1983) provides an excellent example of another type of group conformity pressure. Janis describes a process he calls *groupthink*—a way of thinking that is common in very cohesive groups when the desire for unanimity overrides the need to think critically. Janis sees groupthink as responsible for President John F. Kennedy's 1961 decision to send a brigade of Cuban exiles to invade the Bay of Pigs in Cuba. Some of government's most talented and experienced people were involved in this decision. Yet all of them failed to see that the plan, which had been drawn up by an ambitious group of CIA officers with little military experience, grossly underestimated Castro's popularity and military power. As it turned out, Castro's army surrounded and captured the brigade within a day of the invasion.

How could such a plan have been approved? According to Janis, Kennedy's advisory group developed several illusions that interfered with critical thinking. (Illusions are typical of groupthink.) One of these illusions was the notion that the advisory group was immune to failure. This caused the group to ignore odds of 140 to 1 against military success. Another illusion was the belief that almost everyone at the decision-making meetings was in agreement, which led some individuals to suppress their criticism. Also, many group members later wrote of suppressing their doubts out of fear of being labeled cowards.

Another characteristic of groupthink is the emergence of "mindguards," or members of the group who stamp out potential dissension and protect the comfortable consensus. In the Bay of Pigs fiasco, Attorney General Robert Kennedy took on this role. Finally, President Kennedy himself allowed inexpert CIA officers to dominate the meetings in a way that stifled dissenting opinion. Thus, by seeking consensus instead of critical debate, President Kennedy and his advisers created an atmosphere that led them to ignore the obvious risks of the operation.

The 1977 gymnasium controversy at Kent State University provides a second example of groupthink. Kent State's trustees decided to build an addition to the school's gymnasium at the very site of the tragic shootings of May 4, 1970, where the Ohio National Guard and Kent State students confronted one another in an antiwar demonstration that resulted in the death of four students. Despite pleas from the student body, faculty, and government officials, the trustees refused to alter their position. They felt locked into their decision after thousands of dollars and years of planning had been lavished on the project. The construction took place as planned.

Social scientists analyzing the controversy have suggested that the trustees' decision to complete the construction was a result of groupthink. The trustees were a homogeneous group of people from northeastern Ohio. Middle-aged professionals and executives, they were very concerned with retaining one another's approval. And because the media gave extensive publicity to the situation, the trustees wanted to insulate themselves from public scrutiny or criticism. They sought to accomplish this by presenting a united front and refusing to modify their plans (Hensley & Griffin, 1986).

Group Boundaries: Ingroups and Outgroups

It should be clear from our discussion that the groups to which we belong have powerful social effects. But groups to which we do not belong also may influence us. One of the earliest principles of group interaction was formulated by William Graham Sumner (1906/1960), who coined the terms *ingroup* and *outgroup* to describe the feelings of group members toward their own and other groups. Group members normally have special feelings for their **ingroups**—the groups to which they belong. They regard other groups, or **outgroups**—the groups to which they do not belong—with suspicion and as less worthy than their own. The virtues that each of us tends to find in our ingroups may reflect our need for a positive self-image (Tajfel & Turner, 1979). Group membership can be essential in developing such a self-image (Rosenberg, 1990).

Definitions of group membership depend on the existence of clear group boundaries. Without boundaries, we could not distinguish group members from nonmembers. Boundaries often take the form of a special language, which helps group members to feel a sense of unity and of separateness from those not belonging to the group (Denzin, 1984). Some group boundaries are formal and reinforced by symbols and codes. The clothing of priests, for example, identifies the group to which they belong. Professional groups, such as lawyers, use advanced degrees and membership in professional associations as symbols of group boundaries.

In what are generally referred to as the "Robbers' Cove" studies, conducted in the late 1940s and early 1950s, Muzafer Sherif and Carolyn Sherif (1953) showed how conflict affects the relationship between ingroups and outgroups. The subjects of this research were 11-year-old boys who thought they were going to an ordinary summer camp and never knew they were involved in an experiment. In the first few days of the "camp," the researchers let the boys form their own spontaneous friendship groups. Then they arbitrarily split the camp in two, breaking up the groups that had formed. The two new groups quickly developed their own distinct social structures, with leaders and followers, and adopted symbols of group boundaries, such as names and special colors.

When the researchers pitted the new groups against each other in athletic contests, the boundaries between them grew sharper. Friendships between boys from different groups broke down. When the two groups were forced to be together, they would fight and call each other names.

This Youth Ministry chorus is an example of a positive reference group. Sociologists believe the values and norms of positive reference groups can be the base from which we view the rest of the world.

Restoring harmony proved to be very difficult; only when the researchers created a series of "emergencies" in which the two groups had to work together toward common goals did the sense of hostility begin to recede.

Like the obedience-to-authority research conducted by Stanley Milgram, this sort of study, which manipulates subjects and forces them to endure unpleasant or even horrifying experiences, would not be done today. After all, should children be made to fight with their friends so that academics can publish articles? The common practice today is to require that subjects be told in advance as much as possible about the experiments in which they are participating and about their possible consequences. But the old kind of research—with its sometimes disturbing indifference to the feelings of its subjects—did reveal a great deal about the way social groups shape our behavior.

Reference Groups

To conclude our discussion of groups, it is important to note that some groups, called "reference groups," have more influence than others on our sense of who we are and on the way we interact with the world. A **reference group** is a group that is especially important in shaping a person's beliefs, attitudes, and values. A reference group need not be a small group of the type we have been discussing in this chapter. Nor is it always a group to which a person already belongs; it may be a group that someone wants to join. Premed students, for example, may regard students in medical school as their reference group. In other words, they model their actions after a group that has already achieved a goal they, too, want to achieve. Reference groups may be either positive—as in the example of students in medical school—or they may be negative. High school students wishing to avoid alcohol and drugs may regard the delinquent subculture at their school as a negative reference group, a model of exactly how they do not care to be seen.

Sociologists view reference groups as essential to life in modern societies. Because each of us is required to play many different roles, reference groups act as a psychological anchor against the changing demands and expectations of other groups. The values and norms of our positive reference groups are the base from which we view the rest of the world (Sherif & Sherif, 1953).

THE NATURE OF ORGANIZATIONS

As with so many other aspects of our society, we tend to take organizations for granted. You may belong to a church or synagogue, a union, or a fraternity. You probably do your banking at a branch of a large bank, shop at a branch of a supermarket chain, and attend classes at a university or college. Yet how often have you considered the nature and structure of the organizations with which you have daily contact?

Even those people who live their lives within organizations rarely consciously consider how these social units affect them, or how organizational structures such as bureaucracy and leadership develop. The complex system of bureaucratic management that we now take for granted did not simply spring to life by itself. How do organizations arise? Why do people create them? How are they managed? What influence do they have over our work, our private lives, and the ways we relate to each other? These questions are among the many we consider in this section.

Organizational Goals and Traits

Within human societies, people have long formed groups to achieve special purposes. These special-purpose groups are called organizations. An **organization** is a social group that has been deliberately constructed to achieve specific goals (Etzioni & Lehman, 1980; see also Hall, 1999). Clubs, schools, churches and synagogues, hospitals, prisons, corporations, and government agencies are all examples of organizations. Modern urban-industrial societies are characterized by an abundance of large-scale, complex organizations that extend into all areas of life. This is due mainly to the high value placed on rationality and efficiency in modern times, for it is in the achievement of these ends that organizations excel.

Organizations come in a variety of types, ranging in scope from a Cub Scout pack with six members to the federal government with its millions of workers. Our first task is to describe the basic nature of organizations in all of their many forms. Although all groups strive to accomplish goals, these aims are often very general or unstated; sometimes each person in a group has a separate goal. In an organization, however, the goals are specific, clearly stated, and usually well understood by the members.

Besides having clearly stated and specific goals, organizations typically display the following basic traits (Etzioni & Lehman, 1980):

1. A division of labor and authority designed to make the group a highly efficient agent for achieving its goals.

2. Some concentration of power in the hands of leaders or executives, who use that power to control the activities of the members of the organization and direct them toward the organization's goals.

3. Membership that is not firmly fixed, which allows the organization to endure or persist beyond the lifetime or tenure of any particular individual. Members who die, resign, retire, or are fired are routinely replaced.

Many groups do not have all of these features. A family is not usually considered an organization because its members cannot be routinely replaced and because it does not have specific goals. An ethnic category, such as Italian-Americans, is not an organization. But a group like the Sons of Italy, made up of persons of Italian descent who join together to improve the public image of Italian-Americans, definitely is. A group of friends—even when they have a highly patterned set of relationships—is not usually an organization because it lacks clearly defined goals.

Organizational Structure

Organizations are commonly analyzed in terms of two aspects of their social structure: the formal aspect and the informal aspect.

FORMAL STRUCTURE

The **formal structure** of an organization is the stated set of rules, regulations, and procedures that guides the activities of that organization's members. The formal structure includes charts, constitutions, bylaws, chains of command, and timetables for meeting goals. Usually the rules and procedures are written down, but this is not always the case. A small group, such as a club, may be formally organized in that there are officers, a goal, and a method of conducting meetings that is agreed upon, but it may not maintain any written records. Because the club is small and simple, the members can retain the organizational structure in their heads.

The intended (manifest) function of the formal structure is to meet organizational goals efficiently. Each member is assigned some share of the group's task. At the same time, each member must be clear about his or her relationship to the members assigned to carry out other parts of the task. Thus, the amount of power each member has over the others and the expected patterns of communication and coordination among members are carefully spelled out. Each member knows where, when, by whom, and by what method decisions will be made, and where he or she stands in the organizational hierarchy.

Some formal means of discipline must also be provided—explicit sanctions, both positive and negative, that members can employ to attempt to ensure that those in the group obey the rules. Positive sanctions, which in the business world can include promotions, raises, titles, plush offices, and fringe benefits such as expense accounts, cars, and invitations to social events, are used to motivate or reward people who carry out their assigned tasks. Negative sanctions, such as being demoted, fired, or passed over for promotion, are imposed on members who do not follow the rules. It is common for a large, complex organization to set up some formal means of measuring the performance of its members—a salary review, for example, or a yearly evaluation by a superior.

An organization in which the formal structure is dominant is termed a **formal organization.** Most organizations, including churches and synagogues, corporations, schools, and governments, are of this type (Clegg & Dunkerley, 1980).

INFORMAL STRUCTURE

An organization's formal structure is always supplemented by an **informal structure,** which consists of the personal relationships that form as the members interact. Although they are unplanned, informal relationships are necessary to an organization's efficient functioning. The formal rules and procedures do not cover all the problems that an organization encounters and, in some cases, may be less efficient than the informal rules that emerge. For example, when air traffic controllers were negotiating for higher wages, they employed the strategy of obeying all the formal rules and *only* those rules. They ignored the many timesaving informal rules they normally used. A serious work slowdown was created, and the controllers showed that "going by the book" alone was not an efficient way to get things done.

Informal structure helps an organization adapt to changing circumstances that might otherwise reduce its efficiency and make it harder to achieve its goals. A foreign correspondent for the *Washington Post* described one element of the informal structure that arose within the vast system of the former Soviet Union (Kaiser, 1976). Factories had to meet formal economic production quotas set by the central state planning commission. In order for this to happen, raw materials and parts had to be assembled so that the finished products could be supplied on time. Unfortunately, this did not always happen, and the resulting breakdown nurtured an illegal, informal structure, a part of which was the *tolkach:*

> A good factory usually has a good *tolkach* or "pusher." A successful *tolkach* appears to have many of the personal qualities of a good door-to-door salesman, plus a large capacity for vodka and friendly relations with the chefs and managers of the best restaurants in his area. He devotes these assets to the cultivation of officials in various supply organizations. If a *tolkach* tells his factory director he needs some money for a banquet, a gift or even a payoff, the director is likely to pay up. In return, the *tolkach* finds the materials the factory needs to meet its targets. (Kaiser, 1976, p. 354)

The *tolkach* thus helped to reduce bottlenecks in the Soviet economy for which there were no solutions within the formal structure.

Informal structure often helps an organization achieve higher levels of efficiency. A sociologist studying a Chicago machine company discovered an informal structure, which he described as the "game of making out," that was central to the shop-floor activities of the firm's operators (Burawoy, 1984). Workers earned incentive pay for producing more than 100 percent of the formally defined quota. The operators' *informal quota* was 140 percent, based on their assumption that regularly turning in anything more than that would result in an increase in the formal standard. Operators usually produced more than 140 percent but turned in only 140 percent, using the remainder as a "kitty" to be drawn on in times when difficult or time-consuming tasks prevented them from producing at the informally accepted level.

> Indeed, operators would "bust their ass" for entire shifts, when they had a gravy job, so as to build up a kitty for the following day(s). Experienced operators on the more sophisticated machines could easily build up a kitty of a week's work. There was always some discrepancy, therefore, between what was registered in the books as completed and what was actually completed on the shop floor. . . . Both the 140 percent ceiling and the practice of banking [keeping a kitty] were recognized and accepted by everyone on the shop

floor, even if they didn't meet with the approval of higher management. (Burawoy, 1984, p. 232).

Despite its inconsistency with the formal rules, norms, and procedures, the "game of making out" ultimately promoted the company's interests. It made the shop floor a less tedious, more satisfying place for the operators. It transformed management-worker conflict into intragroup competition among the operators. Finally, it enhanced the company's profit margin (Burawoy, 1984). In short, this informal structure enabled the company to achieve its goals more efficiently.

In some circumstances, however, informal structure can have negative effects. For example, the informal social controls that a "whistle-blower"—a person who reports or informs on wrongdoing—encounters are likely to prevent many workers from reporting illegal or dangerous activities in the workplace. Such informal controls include hostility and retaliation from co-workers and supervisors alike (Near & Miceli, 1989).

Organizational Culture

The study of organizational culture became popular in the 1980s, when American corporations realized that they were losing ground to the Japanese. Despite its image of prosperity, the American economy lagged far behind those of other nations, making it the second lowest of nine leading economies. Disappointed with the cost and quality of American goods, consumers began to purchase Japanese cars, televisions, and computers. Mass layoffs hit a number of industries—automobile, steel, textiles, and high-tech Silicon Valley—and the standard of living dropped (Smith, 1995).

Searching for answers to the economic problems of American companies, management theorists began to focus on the cultures of successful Japanese companies (Morgan, 1997; Smith, 1995). Many of these studies suggested that American corporations should adopt elements of Japanese culture to regain their position in the global economy. But other management experts focused on the corporate cultures of successful American companies (Deal & Kennedy, 1982; Peters & Waterman, 1982). They suggested that the key to success lay in strong cultures—ones with well-cultivated identities, clearly defined values, and heroes who personified both.

The lesson common to both approaches was the idea that corporate culture plays a critical role in the success of an organization. According to Linda Smircich (1985), the term *culture* refers to an attribute or quality that is internal to a group. It is "a fairly stable set of taken-for-granted assumptions, shared beliefs, meanings, and values that form a kind of back drop for action" (p. 58).

Every organization can be identified by its culture (Handy, 1995; Scott, 1998). For example, stability and predictability characterize the cultures of life insurance companies, the civil service, and state industries (Handy, 1995). This kind of culture, which assumes that tomorrow will be like yesterday, differs dramatically from the kinds found in advertising agencies or consulting firms, which thrive on change and the uncertainty which that brings. As this suggests, all cultures consist of the same basic elements, but they vary by their attributes (Handy, 1995; Scott, 1998).

According to Terrence Deal and Allan Kennedy (1982), the basic elements of culture include values, heroes, rites and rituals, and the cultural network. Values constitute the essence of a company's philosophy. By providing the guidelines by which a company operates, they give employees a common direction and meaningful purpose for their daily lives. Companies with strong cultures succeed in creating an identity that is rooted firmly in its values. As the following examples show, slogans often capture the essence of a company's values:

The heartbeat of America. (Chevrolet)

We make it simple. (Honda)

You asked for it, you got it (Toyota)

The ultimate driving machine. (BMW)

Symbols can achieve the same result as slogans. Consider, for example, the Levi Strauss patch, which depicts two horses trying unsuccessfully to pull a pair of Levi's in opposite directions. For over a century, this image has symbolized the values upon which the company was founded: durability and quality.

Heroes are the people who personify an organization's values (Deal & Kennedy, 1982). People like Henry Ford (Ford), Thomas Edison (GE), John D. Rockefeller (Standard Oil), Estée Lauder (Estée Lauder), and Bill Gates (Microsoft) show employees what they must do to succeed. Heroes like these often become national celebrities and become part of the folklore of American industry (*Time*, 1998).

Rites and rituals are also important elements of organizational culture. They bring order to the daily routines of organizational behavior by showing employees what is expected of them. For example, a ritual enacted every Monday night for Tupperware distributorships involves a process called "Count Up," in which salespeople march up on stage in the reverse order of their previous week's sales (Morgan, 1997). Amid a great deal of hoopla, their peers applause and celebrate their achievement by joining in "All Rise." More extraordinary rituals—ceremonies—include the celebration of heroes, myths, and sacred symbols. They, too, are designed to reward those who follow the rules and embrace the organization's values.

The last element of corporate culture is the cultural network. A variety of characters make up this hidden hierarchy, which bears no resemblance to the formal organizational chart. They include storytellers, spies, and whisperers whose unofficial job is to get the real story and communicate it to everyone else off the record (Deal & Kennedy, 1982). For example, while the official explanation for the resignation of an executive might be that he wanted to pursue other interests, a spy might reveal the real truth—that he refused to travel as extensively as his boss expected.

When the basic elements of corporate culture reinforce one another, they create a strong culture. This, according to some organizational theorists, gives them a competitive edge in the marketplace (Deal & Kennedy, 1982; Peters & Waterman, 1982). A number of researchers have continued to explore just how these kinds of cultures are created and maintained (Cameron & Quinn, 1996; Scott, 1998; Schneider, 1990).

Research on corporate cultures clearly helps us understand why some corporations succeed while others fail. Unfortunately, organizations often find it difficult to incorporate the lessons that these studies reveal. The reason lies in the stability of organizational cultures. While members may come and go, organizations remain highly resistant to change (Hall, 1999; Harrison & Carroll, 1991; Smith, 1993).

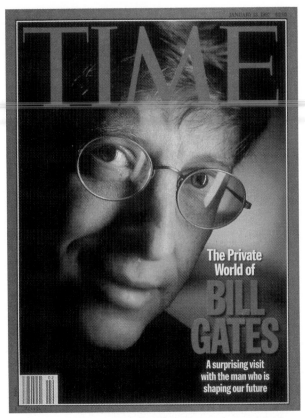

Bill Gates's success and celebrity status have guaranteed him a place in the folklore of American industry, along with other past industry giants such as Rockefeller, Ford, and Edison.

Bureaucracies

Most organizations in the modern world are examples of a special type of formal structure that sociologists call *bureaucracy*. Indeed, the trend toward bureaucracy has been so marked over the course of history that large, bureaucratic organizations have come to dominate our economic and political institutions, and many people today use the terms *bureaucracy* and *formal organization* as synonyms.

People often associate bureaucracy only with red tape, waste, delay, long forms, and even longer lines. And the image evoked by the word *bureaucrats* is one of narrow-minded people so tied up by red tape that they have lost sight of their original function. Sociologists, however, define **bureaucracy** as a hierarchical authority structure that operates on the basis of explicit rules and procedures.

The classic analysis of bureaucracy was developed by Max Weber in the early twentieth century. Weber saw the major social trend in the modern world as **rationalization**—a process by which older, traditional methods of social organization are gradually replaced by numerous explicit, abstract, and formal rules and procedures. The rationalization process can be seen everywhere in our society, from educational institutions, where courses with enrollments of 500 students have all but eliminated student-teacher contact in some universities, to the workplace, where huge multinational corporations with thousands of employees have replaced simple "mom and pop" stores.

George Ritzer developed a penetrating analysis of the rationalization process, which he calls, only partly tongue-in-cheek, "McDonaldization," as it applies to postindustrial society (1993). Ritzer argues that the model of organization that typifies McDonald's restaurants is relentlessly expanding into almost every aspect of modern life. "McDonaldization" encompasses four basic themes: (1) a tremendous emphasis on efficiency, (2) quantifiability (the *Big* Mac) coupled with speed (*fast* food), (3) predictability (all McDonald's serve exactly the same menu), and (4) the substitution of nonhuman for human technology (McDonald's is highly mechanized and its workers are allowed virtually no discretion in their

GLOBAL SOCIETY

ORGANIZATIONAL CULTURES: LEARNING FROM THE COMPETITION

By the middle of the twentieth century, the American automobile industry seemed indomitable—sales were booming, the public loved their cars, and auto executives exuded the confidence of champions. That all seemed to change overnight. By the 1980s, sales figures for American automakers were plummeting. General Motors, the giant of giants, suffered its first financial loss in 60 years—and it was huge—$760 million (Smith, 1995). Reeling from the oil crisis that had hit the United States in the mid-1970s, Americans wanted small, affordable, fuel-efficient cars (Morgan 1997; Smith, 1995). American automakers could not deliver, but the Japanese could—and did.

While the oil crisis had contributed to the decline of the American automobile industry, leaders of American companies failed to recognize an even more important factor in the success of the Japanese: They had revolutionized the manufacturing process. And the well-disguised key to this revolution lay deeply rooted in its national culture. According to Hedrick Smith (1995), the cultures of European and American automakers had also contributed to their past success. And he argues that the lessons that automakers learned from the shifting giants in the global marketplace came from a collision of three cultures—German, American, and Japanese.

In seeking to understand how organizational culture affects the organization's ultimate success or failure, let us consider Smith's insightful analysis of three automobile giants: Mercedes-Benz, General Motors, and Toyota.

Mercedes-Benz (Germany)

When Karl Benz and Gottlieb Daimler decided to produce the Mercedes-Benz,

they reportedly claimed: "We will produce the best or nothing" (Smith, 1995). The mind-set of Mercedes-Benz—"Quality at Any Cost"—reflects this philosophy. It also suggests how Germany's unique history and culture influenced the development of its automobile industry. Born in Europe, the car was originally designed for the aristocracy, who expected luxury and demanded quality. Cost was no obstacle for this class. So production was on a relatively small scale, and the engineering and craftsmanship were superb (Smith, 1995).

Taking pride in one's work is a German trait and can be traced back to the guild system of the Middle Ages. A master craftsman, called a *meister,* demanded perfection and held his apprentices to high standards. As a product of their culture, producing quality goods thus came naturally to German workers. And to guarantee the best, every Mercedes-Benz that rolled off the assembly line was subjected to a thorough final inspection. According to Smith, "Teams of blue-coated meisters and experienced assemblers worked every slightest defect, no matter how long it took" (1995, p. 40).

Mercedes-Benz became so successful in the luxury car market that by the mid-1980s hundreds of thousands of Europeans and Americans were willing to pay whatever it cost for the quality of this car. That, however, changed when the Japanese entered the upscale market in the 1990s.

General Motors (United States)

General Motors took a completely different attitude toward automobiles. Based on Ford's revolutionary idea about manufacturing cars for the average American, GM's mind-set was "Mass Marketing" (Smith, 1995). In order to cut costs, GM produced cars in high volume. In contrast to German *meisters* and their emphasis

on craftsmanship, relatively unskilled workers assembled cars in a repetitive fashion. One plant alone would produce 250,000 copies of one model. But cutting costs meant that less attention was paid to quality and variety. Models that appeared different on the outside—Buicks, Oldsmobiles, Chevrolets, and Pontiacs—were actually the same underneath.

This mass marketing approach had been the hallmark of GM's success for years. And when Roger Smith took charge in 1981, he did not intend to change it. Instead, he planned to invest heavily in technology—computers and robots—and reduce GM's dependence on workers. But by 1986, Smith's strategy was not producing the expected results. Despite its huge investment in technology, GM was still less efficient than its competitors. According to one study conducted by MIT in 1986, GM workers took more than 40 hours to assemble a car, whereas Toyota workers took only 18 (Smith, 1995). A number of other problems compounded GM's troubles: GM's competitors took less time to design and produce new models, defects in GM's cars resulted in massive callbacks, and GM was losing its loyal customers.

Toyota (Japan)

Japan's entrance into the automobile industry was late compared to that of Germany and of the United States. Developing in the aftermath of World War II, Japan's economic success in the automobile industry has been remarkable, especially given its lack of natural resources (Morgan, 1997; Smith, 1995). But scarcity had posed challenges for Japan throughout its history. And, ironically, it shaped a culture that ultimately played a central role in Japan's success. Smith attributes Toyota's phenomenal success to a mind-set that he describes as "Flexible and Lean." While Toyota's success may have seemed to occur overnight, these particular values have shaped Japanese culture for centuries.

According to Murray Sayle, an expert on Japan, modern organizations like Toyota are shaped by two strong influences from the past: Japan's reliance on rice fields for survival, and the spirit of service of the samurai (Morgan, 1997). Sayle argues that the cooperative nature of work—a hallmark of Japan's success—can be traced back to its dependence on the difficult process of growing rice. Survival, which depended on this crop, required backbreaking teamwork and a deep sense of communal responsibility. As a result, people respected and depended on one another.

The samurai spirit of service explains two other features that are associated with Japan's success—style of management and the way that organizations relate to one another. The samurai looked after the rice farmers, who, in turn, provided them with rice. The role that the samurai played in the Japanese military is paralleled by the role that managerial elites play in Japanese society today (Morgan, 1997). Thus, the most important features of their management style include service to one another, the protection of employees, and accepting one's place in the organization. This style also characterizes the relationships that Japanese organizations develop with one another. The organizational culture of Toyota clearly embodies these qualities.

The reason that these particular values contributed to Toyota's success starts with an understanding of the mentality of Japanese consumers. While they value quality the way Germans do, they do not subscribe to the aristocratic idea of "quality at any cost" (Smith, 1995). As their past suggests, scarcity developed an attitude of "waste not want not." But keeping prices down posed a challenge. Toyota recognized that it could carve out a niche for itself by responding to customers' desires for small innovations. However, this required a manufacturing process that could react to change quickly, one that was designed for low-volume runs. It also required skilled workers who were trained to do multiple tasks and change equipment quickly. As such, this model challenged the American idea that cost-saving required mass production. And, yet, the Japanese devised a way to make a low-volume system work.

As management theorists would later understand, this system did not depend on sophisticated technology but on the workers. The key to Toyota's success, it turns out, was deeply rooted in its organizational culture, which understood scarcity and valued quality, flexibility, and people. And this meant that customers got what they wanted, at the price they could afford, without sacrificing quality.

The scarcity that had shaped Japanese culture for centuries now contributed to its phenomenal success. For example, in contrast to GM, which produced and stored car parts for future use, Toyota relied on a decentralized system of outside suppliers that manufactured and delivered parts just before they were needed. While this system required the cooperation of dependable outside suppliers, it saved money by eliminating waste.

This system gave Toyota the kind of flexibility it needed to succeed in the global marketplace. And the result was impressive. In comparing a Toyota plant to the standardized production at a GM plant, Hedrick Smith wrote:

In one day at one plant Toyota rolled out ninety-one different types of engines on thirty-eight different models of cars. For that day's production, the order had come in from customers on a computerized system in the previous two weeks. That's how close to market Toyota was. (1995, p. 51)

Ultimately Toyota's success depended on its workers. And the company recognized that. The degree to which Toyota valued its workers was reflected in the power that they were given—any worker could stop the assembly line at any time. In contrast to workers at GM, they played a key role in troubleshooting, and that paid off in terms of quality. The Japanese realized that stopping the assembly line to fix problems cut costs. It was far more expensive to allow defective cars to move along the line, because that only increased costs at the end. Ironically, the Japanese had learned this particular lesson from an American management expert, W. Edwards Deming (Morgan, 1997).

Lessons Learned

Learning from the Japanese, Mercedes-Benz abandoned its rework area at the end of the assembly line and adopted the philosophy that doing it right the first time reduces waste and inefficiency. The company also incorporated more flexibility into its production process and gave more responsibility to workers. General Motors suffered huge financial losses before it finally decided to change. Under new leadership, it, too, adopted elements of the Toyota mind-set by applying concepts of flexibility and simplicity along with leaner management and efforts to improve relations with labor.

Smith's analysis of Mercedes-Benz, General Motors, and Toyota shows how organizational cultures influence both the nature of work and the quality of a product. And it shows why management must never dismiss the human component—both workers and customers—in the manufacturing process.

behavior). These principles are being extended, according to Ritzer, to everything from education and religion to sex and the production of tomatoes. Incidentally, Ritzer, like Weber before him (1922), sees this process of bureaucratic rationalization as an ominous trend that is difficult, if not impossible, to resist.

Weber utilized a method in studying bureaucracy that he called **ideal type** analysis. An ideal type model of a phenomenon such as bureaucracy is a description of the most essential or characteristic qualities of it. An ideal type does not strive to incorporate only those qualities of what it is describing that are most commonly found in the real world, but, rather, it stresses those traits that the theorist regards as most reflective of the heart, core, or essence of the phenomenon, sometimes to the point of exaggeration. Thus, an ideal type description of a German shepherd would include only those qualities that most clearly define the breed, even though few if any actual German shepherds display all or even most of those traits. Furthermore, an ideal type is not "ideal" in the sense of "good"—one can construct an ideal type description of a child molester or a concentration camp as easily as one can build one of a saint or of a hospice.

Thus, it is unlikely that any organization fully displays every one of the following ideal type traits of bureaucracy. Yet this description has proven extremely useful in organizational analysis:

1. *Division of the total staff into smaller units, called offices or bureaus.* The responsibility of each bureau is carefully described, and the jobs of the officials who work in it are carefully planned in advance.

2. *Clear-cut lines of authority and responsibility.* Employees are located in a hierarchy, with each official responsible to a superior on the next level. This structure permits coordination of activities into one comprehensive goal-seeking effort.

3. *Employment of personnel solely on the basis of their technical or professional qualifications.* In a bureaucracy, it is common to hire only people for each job who have specific qualifications-certain educational credentials, so many years of experience, and so on. People are hired on the basis of how closely their personal qualifications meet the job requirements.

4. *Elaborate rules and regulations governing the way officials are expected to perform their jobs.* The authority of employees to issue orders and commands is strictly limited by rules that cannot be changed to suit individual abilities or inclinations.

5. *The establishment of a bureaucratic career, with specific lines of promotion or advancement and rewards in the form of tenure and seniority for lengthy and meritorious service.*

BUREAUCRATIC STRUCTURE: PROS AND CONS

While the main purpose of bureaucratic structure is to promote organizational efficiency, bureaucracy has several additional positive features. By establishing the principle that a bureaucratic position is theoretically independent of an individual and his or her unique personality, it is possible to minimize many potential problems such as personal, job-interfering antagonisms. This also tends to reduce the degree to which individual ethnic, racial, or gender bias can interfere with the efficient functioning of an organization: It is no coincidence that women and minorities have historically achieved more success in rigidly bureaucratic local, state, and federal government positions than they have in any other sector of the economy.

Bureaucratic structure also promotes continuity. Since the individual performing a job is likely to change from time to time, employee loyalty is directed to the total organization rather than to an individual. The periodic review of each official's work also contributes to organizational efficiency and continuity.

However, bureaucracy also has many shortcomings. The very procedures intended to promote efficiency may create problems. Bureaucracies have a tendency to become rigid; their highly formal structures can stifle innovation and creativity. Furthermore, bureaucracies tend to result in *oligarchy*—rule by the few. There is always the danger of economic, political, or social power becoming too highly concentrated in the hands of those people who hold the highest positions in the most important organizations. Finally, bureaucracies can produce an overcautious attitude, a strong desire not to disturb the status quo, in their employees.

The same impersonality that makes the organization efficient also creates potential problems in human terms. Bureaucracies engaged in public service, for example, have a tendency to treat the people they are supposed to be serving in the same impersonal manner in which they treat their employees—a manner that often interferes with the accomplishment of their service goal. And this impersonality is difficult for employees to deal with in their own jobs, too. Workers like to believe that they are personally valuable. Indeed, the human consequences of impersonality have become a significant issue in modern societies.

The ongoing theoretical debate over the social impact of large-scale bureaucratic organization tends to be divided into two camps. Functionalists, who generally accept the mainstream, Weberian position, argue that the routinization, centralized hierarchical structure, impersonal formal rules and regulations, and top-down administration that characterize bureaucracies are generally important to organizational efficiency. Conflict theorists claim that these features of organization are valued less for their contribution to efficiency than for their capacity to strengthen managerial control over both the work process and the workers involved in that process (Hearn, 1988).

ORGANIZATIONAL PROCESSES AND CHANGE

Institutionalization

When an organization is successful in recruiting members, secures their loyalty, is efficient in achieving its goals, and is generally accepted by the larger community, it usually settles into an orderly pattern of operation with a relatively stable structure and set of goals and values. In short, it becomes *institutionalized.* Some organizations, such as the Catholic Church, endure for centuries or even millennia; most fold fairly quickly. Those that survive the longest are usually those that are able to perpetuate themselves by effectively recruiting and training new members (Hannan & Freeman, 1989).

When it is first formed, an organization is relatively free to experiment. Its goals are fluid, it can choose among many different ways to pursue these goals, and the relationships among its members tend to be informal and adaptable. But as an organization grows, its structure typically becomes dominated by institutionalized forms.

First, a set way of carrying out the group's activities, sometimes referred to as *standard operating procedure* (SOP), becomes established. SOP eventually limits the freedom of the organization to choose among alternative actions. Second, as procedures become more fixed, the relationships among the members become more formal. As a result, the behavior of the organization becomes more stable and predictable. But as informal relationships become less important, it becomes harder to create new paths of communication and new structures. Third, the goals of the organization become increasingly inflexible.

Although institutionalization may produce excessive rigidity, it also yields many benefits. As relationships become more orderly and predictable, increased coordination develops among members and organizational continuity is improved. As knowledge and experience grow, there is less need to resort to inefficient trial and error to discover the best methods of functioning.

GOAL DISPLACEMENT

Another negative effect of institutionalization is **goal displacement,** a process that occurs when the members of an organization become more concerned with perpetuating the organization itself and their positions in it than with meeting the actual goals of the organization. Goal displacement takes many forms. For instance, the members of an organization can become so concerned with preserving their own positions that they subvert the organization to this end. To give an example, most unions are characterized by a formally democratic structure—the leaders are elected by the rank and file. But, once in office, union leaders may try subtly to discourage democratic processes to protect their elected jobs. Allowing the organization to remain highly democratic might mean a loss of office and status for the leaders (Lipset, Trow, & Coleman, 1956).

Goal displacement also occurs when the rules of an organization become ends in themselves. Rules are initially established to help an organization meet its goals efficiently. They can, however, take on a "sacred" character and interfere with the organization's ability to deal with new or unusual situations. Employees may come to view their role as to conform to the rules, whether or not such conformity actually promotes the organization's goals. This is the kind of behavior that people have in mind when they complain about "bureaucrats" and "red tape" (Merton, 1968; Sills, 1970). Robert Merton coined the term *bureaucratic ritualism* to describe such a bureaucratic preoccupation with rules and regulations as ends in themselves rather than as means to achieve organizational goals.

A third form of goal displacement involves the development of informal structures among employees that lead them to protect their own interests rather than the needs of the organization (Sills, 1970). Workers in a factory, for example, sometimes informally agree on how many units they should produce in a day, then resist management attempts to increase productivity.

Goal displacement has been the subject of many humorous attacks on the nature of organizations. According to Parkinson's law (Parkinson, 1964), for example, "work expands so as to fill the time available for its completion" (see also Porter, 1980). Similarly, the Peter principle describes a common problem in bureaucracies involving promotions. Employees who do well in their current jobs are generally advanced up the hierarchy; for example, good teachers become assistant principals, and good nurses are promoted into administrative positions. Promotions continue until the worker eventually is placed in a position in which he or she does not do particularly good work. At this point, the organization will be hesitant to fire or demote the employee for fear of demoralizing others who are climbing the bureaucratic ladder, so there is a tendency for "deadwood" to accumulate toward the top. Or, as Laurence Peter puts it, "in a hierarchy, every employee tends to rise to his level of incompetence" (Peter, 1985; Peter & Hull, 1969).

Organizational Change

As the process of institutionalization demonstrates, every organization has within it the seeds of change. Extensive organizational change can result from such internal events as a shift of power relationships among the components of the organization, the breakdown of leadership, or the protest of workers. Yet much organizational change is induced by factors that are external to the organization, factors located in what is called the *organizational environment.* Indeed, the relative importance of internal versus external change is currently a major topic of debate among organizational theorists (Hall, 1999). In some cases, organizations are able to control their environment (McNeil, 1978; Perrow, 1979); in others, the organizations themselves are largely under environmental control (Pfeffer & Salancik, 1978).

Most organizations compete with other organizations for the attention of the publics they serve. Competing organizations can have great influence over one another. When one organization is less successful than another—for example, if one business earns smaller profits—basic changes may be necessary in the less successful organization to improve its position. The American auto industry, which was required to make many painful changes when Japanese auto imports began to capture a large share of the U.S. market, is a case in point. General Motors found that it needed to revise many of its most basic operating assumptions in order to hold its own in an extremely competitive market. And Ford began to use some of the management techniques pioneered by its Japanese partner, Mazda, in some of its American factories (*New York Times,* February 27, 1990).

It is possible for just one new individual to alter the course of an organization, especially if the new member is in a position of leadership. The owners of professional athletic teams bank on this fact when they fire the coach after too many poor seasons and hire a new one. Typically, the new coach shifts players to new positions, attempts to improve morale, and alters team strategies. All these changes are designed to transform a losing organization into a winning one.

Other external sources of change include the development of new technology, the opening up of new markets or sources of supply, and changing interests, attitudes, and values in the population as a whole. If the people an organization serves change their needs or demands, the organization must also change to take these new needs and demands into account. However one looks at it, an organization, especially one that is large and complex, is an entity whose future is always in doubt.

ORGANIZATIONAL ALTERNATIVES

Amitai Etzioni (1975) noted that there are three basic methods by which the people within an organization can be made to do what is expected of them: They may be forced, paid, or convinced to obey. From this basic observation, Etzioni derived three ideal type models of organizations: coercive, utilitarian, and normative.

A *coercive* organization relies primarily on physical force, whether actual or potential, to secure the obedience of those who are under its control. Because this type of organization must devote a large percentage of its resources to social control, it is relatively inefficient in its pursuit of goals other than obedience, so it is generally employed only when no other means of securing order and obedience is feasible—in particular, when the organizational members are present involuntarily. Examples of coercive organizations include prisons, concentration camps, and some public schools.

A *utilitarian* organization relies principally on monetary incentives to secure compliance; most businesses are of this type. Utilitarian organizations need to devote far fewer resources to social control, but on the other hand, the loyalty of their members is always limited by the calculative nature of their involvement with the organization.

The greatest commitment with the lowest expenditure of organizational resources can be obtained if the members participate primarily because they personally accept the goals of the organization as their own. They feel a sense of involvement in the organization; if it succeeds, they feel that in a real sense *they* have succeeded. Such groups are termed *normative* organizations or, more commonly, **voluntary associations**—organizations by which individuals freely pursue some common interest. Voluntary associations are commonly less bureaucratic than most other large organizations (Sills, 1968). Familiar examples include the Boy Scouts and Girl Scouts, PTAs, the League of Women Voters, some professional associations, amateur sports teams, many churches, political interest groups, and service organizations like Rotary International.

Voluntary Associations in American Society

Social observers have long noted that the United States is unusually rich in voluntary associations; indeed, the propensity of Americans to join such organizations is one of the fundamental themes in Alexis de Toqueville's classic analysis *Democracy in America,* which was based on nine months of observation conducted in 1831 and 1832.

Modern sociologists continue to be very interested in the social functions of voluntary associations (Tomeh,

1974). One such function is to provide members with a vehicle for pursuing social goals they could not achieve as individuals. This function is especially evident in the realm of politics. A large, well-organized voluntary association can have substantial influence on the government. In recent years, for example, the Right to Life movement has successfully mobilized voters to support antiabortion political candidates.

Another important function of voluntary associations is to bridge the gap between large bureaucratic organizations—governments, schools, corporations—and individuals. Voluntary associations like the League of Women Voters help involve individuals in the political process. Parent-Teacher Associations smooth the relationship between parents of schoolchildren and the formal bureaucracy of the school system. And most formal organizations, like churches and synagogues, hospitals, and even the armed forces, create voluntary associations in an effort to reach out to the individuals from whom they draw support (Litwak & Meyer, 1966).

Although voluntary associations provide many beneficial functions to society, they have been criticized as well. A criticism from the political left is that many such groups may reduce the pressure on government to carry out its rightful responsibilities, in areas such as health, welfare, and recreation. Similarly, some feminists have suggested that voluntary associations, in effect, exploit women, who, they argue, should demand payment for their many "voluntary" activities rather than serving as unpaid volunteers (Hartmann, 1976). In addition, it has often been noted that the people who could most benefit from the opportunities provided by voluntary associations (i.e., those who are on the fringes of society) are the least likely to join them.

Flexible Organizations

Many large organizations are highly bureaucratic—the armed forces, government agencies, and some businesses, to name just a few. But rigid bureaucratic structure is becoming less common in the industrial sector, where bureaucracies had dominated for nearly half a century. Why? The highly varied, continually fluctuating, and unpredictable markets of the 1990s are very different from the stable settings in which rigid bureaucracies work best. Instead, more flexible organizations seem to have the edge in today's industrial environment.

A *flexible organization* encourages new product design and continuous product differentiation rather than the product standardization promoted by bureaucratic organizations. Also, flexible organization encourages more democratic, less adversarial labor-management relations by favoring a broader diffusion of responsibility.

Onsite day-care centers have become a part of many flexible organizations. Studies have shown that these organizations are showing a decrease in employee absenteeism and therefore an increase in productivity because of the convenience of onsite day-care.

To be "flexible" means to promote close collaboration between managers, workers, customers, and suppliers–all of whom are involved in generating and implementing new ideas.

The production process is often more costly in flexible organizations than in standardized (bureaucratic) ones. But because new computer technologies permit highly efficient production, even in short production runs, it is possible for industries to adapt quickly and economically to demands for new products (Hearn, 1988). As a result, a flexible organization's ability to shift product designs can produce a greater payoff in the long run than a bureaucratic organization's ability to cut costs by standardizing its work systems and products.

Two widely introduced components of flexible organization are flexible hours and job sharing. With *flexible hours* (also called *flex-time*), an employee is able to set his or her work hours (for example, from 11 A.M. to 7 P.M. rather than from 9 A.M. to 5 P.M.). In *job sharing,* two or more employees share one job. Flexible hours have been effective in keeping qualified men and women in their chosen industries, and job sharing has allowed part-time workers to maintain their careers while pursuing other options or raising families. At the same time, companies have benefited from a more qualified and motivated work force. Such programs would be completely unacceptable in traditional bureaucratic settings in which rules are enforced with little attention to individual needs.

Japanese Organizations

In 1997 Japan's economy began to collapse, causing experts to fear that Japan's reckless use of the world's capital in the 1980s could cause a worldwide banking collapse (Hirsch, 1997). It is still too soon to predict the long-term effects of this financial crisis, and it is hard to say how it will affect Japanese organizations—if it affects them at all. In fact, many features unique to Japanese organizations make them particularly stable, and one of these is the emphasis placed on long-term (as opposed to short-term) profit-maximizing planning. Concern for the long-term survival of the organization explains why Japanese managers have been less likely than their American counterparts to become involved in risky financial deals involving mergers or acquisitions (Christopher, 1983).

Another feature contributing to the stability of Japanese organizations is the relationship between workers and employees. In the West, the relationship between worker and employer is based on a negotiated contract (written or implied) between an individual and the organization; this relationship frequently involves conflict. In contrast, Japanese organizations are renowned for their sense of commitment to the well-being of their workers. For larger companies, this means supplying employees with subsidized housing, social programs, health benefits, retirement plans, and vacation resorts. In turn, workers frequently involve the company in what many Americans would consider private matters: marriage arrangements, education of children, and the like.

Japanese organizations also rely on *generalist managers,* as opposed to specialists. Unlike American managers, who tend to become experts in one field, Japanese managers typically spend their careers moving through the various parts of one organization. As a result, Japanese managers gain an overall knowledge of the operations of an entire company rather than mastery of one specific area (such as manufacturing processes or marketing) within that company. This increases their value to the organization.

Japanese organizations also encourage consensus decision making. This often involves a "bottom-up" approach, in which a proposal slowly makes its way up the organizational hierarchy, with modifications made and approval given at each higher level, until it reaches the top. This system differs greatly from the typical Western approach, in which decisions are made at the top and the details of implementation are left to the lower echelons. In theory, employees at lower levels of the Japanese organization are more committed to the decision that is eventually made because they have been involved in the decision-making process from the very beginning.

Most American workers have an "up or out" attitude toward their jobs—that is, they expect regular raises and promotions as a reward for their work. If they do not get what they think they deserve, they start looking for another job. This is not the case in Japanese organizations, in which the usual pattern is slow, highly structured promotion. Related to the promotion system is the fact that employees (except for top executives) are usually paid according to seniority, rather than on the basis of individual performance or merit (Christopher, 1983). This system reflects the group-oriented (as opposed to individualistic) emphasis of Japanese culture.

All of these factors contribute to the establishment of stable Japanese organizations, which foster the commitment of workers. But despite these observations, some researchers have argued that Western students of Japanese organizations tend to present an overly rosy picture (Azumi, 1977; Morgan, 1997). Like workers in the West, Japanese workers report varying degrees of satisfaction, depending on the company for which they work and the character of the work they do; assembly-line workers, for instance, report less satisfaction than executives. Overall, while they may work harder, Japanese workers report less satisfaction than workers in the United States and Western Europe.

In addition, many of the benefits traditionally enjoyed by Japanese workers seem to be eroding. The permanent employment system, long an important aspect of the Japanese business world, has begun to fall by the wayside. Furthermore, Japanese management theory is not always Japanese management practice. One researcher reviewing the administration of Japanese hospitals found that planning decisions were made by top officials, and that "the technical-level staff do not appear to play any more of a role in decision making in Japan than in America" (Goldsmith, 1984, p. 127).

While the financial crisis in the late 1990s suggests that some organizational researchers did paint an overly optimistic picture of Japanese organizations, their studies still offer some valuable lessons. One of the most important ones is that concern for workers' welfare, attention to workers' individual needs, and utilization of workers' views improve competitiveness, the quality of output, and productivity (Lincoln & Kalleberg, 1990).

INTERNET/TECHNOLOGY

ORGANIZATIONS IN THE AGE OF COMPUTERS

The sole purpose of many organizations is to collect information. Consider, for example, the functions of the Census Bureau, the IRS, the CIA, and the FBI. These organizations know Americans better than anyone else. Or, at least, we thought so. Today you cannot be sure.

Gathering information on people has never been easier. And computers are the reason. Starting with a name, commercial data-base services can create a personal profile within minutes, revealing all kinds of facts: date of birth, social security number, driver's license, current and past addresses, telephone number, and a history of personal finances such as liens, civil judgments, property tax filings, and bankruptcies (Bernstein, 1997). If you thought that personal information like this was private, then you failed to consider one of the unforeseen consequences of the modern computer age. Your life is literally an open book.

In the past, collecting this kind of personal information took private investigators weeks, and it did not come cheap. The computer age has revolutionized this business, giving private investigators—and others—the information they need at the push of a button. Some of this information comes from governments that sell digitalized public records. For instance, the state of Illinois makes $10 million a year from sales of this kind of information. And Rhode Island makes $9.7 million by selling motor vehicle records.

Companies that buy these kinds of records then use software programs to compile related pieces of information. In less than three minutes, subscribers to these services can type in someone's name and retrieve all kinds of personal information. The cost—as little as $1.50—is then billed to the subscriber's account.

Private investigators are not the only ones using these kinds of services. Other common subscribers include bill collectors, insurance agents, journalists, and Fortune 500 companies. Access to these services is as close as the Web. And with Web sites like Dig Dirt and SpyForU, they are easy to find (Bernstein, 1997).

While this might suggest that individuals are the only victims of the unforeseen consequences of the computer age, they are not. Organizations are vulnerable, too. In their eagerness to increase the productivity of their employees, organizations provided workers with desktop computers. Connecting these computers to the Internet seemed like the next logical step. Ironically, instead of increasing productivity, access to the Internet actually led to a decrease. Rather than spending time at the water cooler, employees now spend time surfing the Net—estimated to be as much as five to ten hours a week (Harmon, 1997).

In some cases, surfing the Internet at work has created problems serious enough to warrant the firing of employees (Dedman, 1998). For example, in the course of teaching other employees how to surf the Internet, a young man employed by a small advertising agency in Traverse City, Michigan, mentioned his own Web page. He was fired after several co-workers expressed their concern about a fictional story they found at his site that described a violent incident involving murder. In another case, a young woman who called herself SexyChyck quit her job at a small publishing company when her boss ordered her to remove her place of employment from her personal Web page (Dedman, 1998). Her Web site, which showed her posing in leopard print underwear, carried ads for hardcore pornographic sites.

While some Americans are expressing serious concerns about the invasion of privacy that the Internet makes possible, this ironically illustrates how others use it to expose many private aspects of themselves. Now, in contrast to the past, companies must be concerned about how the personal lives of their employees can affect their businesses.

Strangely enough, companies that create Web pages to advertise their products and services may, like SexyChyck, be exposing more than they should. According to competitive intelligence experts, Web pages that contain organization charts, executive biographies, customer lists, and news-release archives provide valuable information that can be analyzed to reveal corporate strategies (Sreenivasan, 1998). Consumers as well as competitors are using the Web to make important decisions.

While we assume that technology means progress and that our lives will improve because of it, we often neglect to consider the unforeseen consequences of it (Postman, 1993). Blinded by our enthusiasm about how the Internet can provide us with the information we want, we may fail to consider how it may invade our own privacy.

ORGANIZATIONS AND MODERN SOCIETY: A HUMANISTIC PERSPECTIVE

The rise of large-scale organizations has been accompanied by social losses as well as gains. One of the big gains is *social efficiency*—the organization of people and resources in ways that seem best for "getting the job done." No modern society has been able to resist the pull of social efficiency; and no advanced society, at least so far, has been willing to forgo efficiency in the interest of a more "personalized" society or more individual freedom.

Yet around the world today we can see some signs of change. In America, in particular, there is strong evidence that people are growing restive under increasing levels of organizational complexity. The antigovernment attitude that has spread through most of the society in recent years does not necessarily represent resistance to government, per se, or even to particular policies. Rather, it is a negative reaction to big government, to out-of-touch bureaucrats, and to the dominance of bureaucratic structures in our lives. Although not as widely publicized, similar oppositional attitudes have developed toward big business, big universities, and even the big bureaucracy of religious organizations (Perrow, 1984).

Will these attitudes succeed in counteracting a social trend that until a few years ago was believed to be unstoppable? At this time, no one can tell. It may be that the limits of organization have been reached, that the losses from a more organized society have begun to outweigh the gains. Yet, at the same time, we can all think of many areas of society in which enhanced organized efficiency would seem to be desirable. We tend to support improved efficiency wherever it benefits us directly, whether in welfare programs, old age and retirement benefits, veterans' benefits, or the preservation of the environment. When such programs are not administered effectively, our own shoes pinch.

The main task ahead, if advanced societies are to preserve democracy, is to maintain popular control over large organizations. One term that is often used in this connection is *accountability*. The natural tendency of an organization, like that of a person, is to operate in its own best interest. Just as people are held strictly accountable in a bureaucratic organization, so must organizations be held accountable in a democratic society. Because of the seriousness of this task, the years ahead may see a rapid increase in such activities as public representation on the boards of large corporations and class action suits. Such activities are directed toward making large organizations, in government or the private sector, more socially responsible.

CHAPTER REVIEW

1. Some college courses have enrollments that exceed 300 students. Are large classes like these social groups or simple aggregates?

2. Explain why secondary groups are common in modern society.

3. Explain why both instrumental and expressive leaders are needed to build a winning sports team.

4. What kinds of groups are college fraternities and sororities? Use examples of the way members of fraternities and sororities behave to explain the following concepts: dyad, triad, primary group, secondary group, ingroups, and outgroups.

5. Identify the likely reference groups for each of the following: a pre-med student, a pre-law student, a teacher, a skinhead, a General Motors employee.

6. How do you think the Internet might change the structure of business organizations?

7. In what ways would you expect the organizational culture of a bank to differ from that of a cosmetics company?

8. Describe both the formal and informal structures of your college.

9. What kinds of organizations do not fit the characteristics of a bureaucracy?

10. How do we use Weber's concept of the ideal type every day?

11. Does the March of Dimes illustrate the concept of goal displacement? Why or why not?

12. Consider the differences among coercive, utilitarian, and normative organizations. Which is most likely to foster high levels of membership commitment? Why?

INTERNET EXERCISE

The Web destinations for Chapter 7 are related to various aspects of groups and organizations. To begin your explorations, go to the Prentice Hall Companion Web site **http://www.prenhall.com/popenoe.** Then choose **Chapter 7** (Groups and Organizations). Next, select **web destinations** from the menu on the left side of the screen. You will find a number of interesting sites to choose from. We suggest you begin with **The Cooperative Learning Center at the University of Minnesota.** This site offers a wealth of information about cooperative learning. In the *Applying Sociology* box in this chapter, cooperative learning is discussed as an alternative to the more familiar "competitive learning," which was the more traditional approach to educating students by the 1960s. After you have explored the Cooperative Learning Center site, answer the following questions:

- How is cooperative learning distinguished from other types of learning?
- Which style of learning do you tend to favor? Why?

KEY TERMS

small group	triad	formal organization
social group	conformity	informal structure
primary group	ingroups	bureaucracy
primary relationship	outgroups	rationalization
secondary group	reference group	ideal type
secondary relationship	organization	goal displacement
dyad	formal structure	voluntary association

CHAPTER 8

Deviance, Crime, and Social Control

It is fairly safe to assume that most people in any particular society believe that they have a good understanding of what sorts of behavior are properly regarded as deviant. Deviants are bad people; people who break the laws; people who act or think in ways that most of our friends and family regard as fundamentally wrong. We may be vaguely aware that people in other societies sometimes define crime and deviance differently than we do, or that acts (like women wearing slacks) that were once looked down on by Americans are now widely regarded as acceptable, but such knowledge is unlikely to challenge seriously our own basic sense of what is and is not proper and moral.

It is a critical, if unsettling, insight of the sociological imagination that in reality what is defined as deviant is almost entirely relative. While a few acts—murder is the best example—are indeed universally regarded as wrong (although what sort of killing is considered to be murder varies greatly from society to society), there is enormous variation concerning what types of behavior are condemned. Different acts will be regarded as more or less deviant depending on when, where, and by whom they are committed.

Consider, for example, the seemingly simple issue of which teenagers are to be defined as juvenile delinquents. This seems to be a pretty straightforward matter of identifying those adolescents who have violated the criminal law. But research by William J. Chambliss (1973) shows that the reality of the situation is considerably more complex. Chambliss studied two different groups of high school students, one of which he called the "Saints" and the other the "Roughnecks." The Saints were constantly truant from school, and on weekends they engaged in a steady round of drinking, theft, and vandalism. They shouted obscenities at women from their cars and they ran red lights at high speeds. They also vandalized construction sites and abandoned houses.

Were these boys delinquent? Most of us would probably think so, but most of the members of the community in which they lived did not. As the sons of respected citizens, they were regarded in general as responsible students, good boys who played an occasional prank. The community treated them as future leaders and expected them to do well. The police mostly left them alone.

Meanwhile, the "Roughnecks"—a group of boys from the lower class—engaged in many of the same delinquent acts as the Saints did but were regarded by the community as troublemakers. Each Roughneck was arrested at least once during the time Chambliss observed the gang, which the police harassed from time to time. Moreover, because they had only occasional access to cars, the Roughnecks' stealing, drinking, and vandalism usually took place in their own community, where they were highly visible. The Saints, in contrast, were careful to misbehave in distant neighborhoods where they were not known. Thus, the extent of their delinquency was largely hidden from the residents of their own community.

As this study suggests, there is a fine line between sowing wild oats and being a juvenile delinquent. In this case, the two groups differed not so much in how they misbehaved but in the public perception of these acts. The lower-class Roughnecks, labeled as delinquents, were thus encouraged to think of themselves as outlaws; most of them continued their deviant behavior into adulthood. Most of the middle-class Saints, however, went on to college and successful careers.

The nature of juvenile delinquency, as well as that of other forms of deviance, is much more complex than most people realize. In this chapter, we explore some of this complexity. We begin by discussing the general nature of deviance and exploring its relationship with the concept of *social control*—social mechanisms that are intended to make people conform to important social norms. Next we describe the major biological, psychological, and sociological explanations that have been proposed for deviant behavior. We conclude with a discussion of the criminal justice system and of *crime,* those deviant acts that are punishable by law.

THE NATURE OF DEVIANCE

Behavior that violates the significant social norms of a group or society is called **social deviance.** However, this simple definition leaves many questions unanswered—for example, which norms are considered to be significant. In some communities, so-called blue laws that ban certain commercial activities on Sunday are still on the books, yet are widely ignored; merchants who open their stores on Sunday are not considered deviant. Another such question is: What are the circumstances surrounding the violation of the norm? Does it matter who breaks the social norms, why they are broken, or when they are broken? The norms require that we stop at a red light. But is running a red light a deviant act when a driver is rushing a sick person to the hospital?

As suggested at the beginning of this chapter, definitions of deviance vary from one year to the next and from one place to another. For example, a 1984 federal law gave states until 1987 to make 21 the legal drinking age; otherwise, they would lose part of their federal highway funds. Although all 50 states ultimately complied, individual state laws differ regarding the maximum legal level of alcohol a person can have in the bloodstream while driving. Defining deviance is a major issue not only for sociologists but also for societies in general.

Would you consider the people in this photograph to be exhibiting deviant behavior? Why or why not? As defined, deviant behavior is not necessarily bad or unacceptable behavior; the term deviance *can imply nonconformity.*

Defining Deviance

Initially, it should be emphasized that social deviance is a very different concept from *statistical deviance,* which simply refers to what sorts of behavior occur more or less frequently. Collecting matchbook covers is not a very popular hobby and is therefore statistically deviant, but it is not a violation of a social norm and sociologists would not regard it as social deviance. On the other hand, certain behaviors that are widespread in society, like running the occasional stop sign or cheating on one's income tax return, are at least mildly socially deviant despite the fact that they are statistically common.

One approach to defining deviance is based on an analogy with medicine (Merton, 1968; Parsons, 1967). Conformity, the opposite of deviance, can be considered healthy or functional, because it stabilizes the social system. Deviance, then, would be called pathological or dysfunctional, because it disrupts social stability. But this definition is flawed. It is hard enough to know objectively what a healthy society is, much less what promotes such health. In addition, sociologists have observed that some forms of deviance can actually improve social functioning. (The positive functions of deviance are discussed later in this chapter.)

What is or is not considered deviant behavior depends on various social circumstances. For example, prostitutes may solicit openly on the street one day without being bothered by the police. But if they do it the day after newspapers feature a story on corruption in the police department, an arrest is much more likely.

As the case study of the Saints and the Roughnecks suggests, people who are relatively socially powerless—especially minorities and the poor—may be much more easily stigmatized as social deviants than the rich and powerful. Thus, to continue with the example of prostitution, streetwalkers, who are disproportionately women of color and whose customers are generally men of modest means, are far more likely to be arrested than are call girls, who serve a much more elite clientele.

Definitions of deviance also change over time. Not long ago, divorce brought shame to the families of both partners and marked their children as the products of a "broken home." Divorce was generally assumed to signify a lack of morality. Today, when nearly half of all first marriages in America end in divorce, many people are beginning to think that marriages lasting until "death do us part" are unusual.

Definitions of deviance vary from place to place and from culture to culture. What is considered normal behavior in some parts of New York City might subject you to arrest in Dubuque, Iowa. Behavior encouraged in so-called open marriages in the United States—specifically, sexual relations outside the marriage—might cause the participants to be stoned to death in some Islamic societies.

Finally, there is a sense in which behavior, to be considered deviant, must be observed, defined, and labeled as deviant. For instance, a youth caught stealing a watch by a salesperson who simply demands that the item be returned will not be labeled deviant if the salesperson tells no one about the incident. If, however, the salesperson presses charges and the youth goes to reform school, the act becomes known to many people. As a result, the youth becomes publicly identified as a deviant. Howard Becker (1963) has suggested that deviance be defined not as a quality associated with a certain act but as the outcome of social interaction between the person who commits the act and those who label the act deviant. (We discuss the significance of this viewpoint, which is known as *labeling,* later in this chapter.)

MISCONCEPTIONS OF DEVIANCE

Very often the words *deviance* and *deviant* conjure up only pictures of individual degenerates, perverts, and madmen. It is important, therefore, to keep the following five points in mind as you study deviance:

1. *Deviant behavior is not necessarily bad or unacceptable behavior.* The term *deviance* can imply "nonconformity," which, in turn, can be translated into the creative genius of novelists, artists, composers, and the like (Sagarin, 1975).

Sometimes behavior is formally deviant, but because the norms that are broken are not widely accepted, the violations are not regarded as particularly immoral. For example, the Volstead Act, which banned the sale of alcoholic beverages in the United States during Prohibition, was opposed by a broad segment of the population. Accordingly, bootleggers, operators of speakeasies, and other violators of this act were commonly accepted by many, although not all, of their fellow citizens.

In certain cases within bureaucratic organizations, deviance from the formal rules may actually be necessary in order to cut through the red tape and accomplish the organization's central goals. A classic study describes how violating a bureaucratic rule in an aircraft factory helped workers to do their jobs (Bensman & Gerver, 1963). An informal network of peers and supervisors encouraged workers to use a particular tool that made their work much easier but weakened the construction of the planes. The use or even the possession of the tool was grounds for immediate dismissal, yet all the mechanics used it with the tacit approval of both their peers and their supervisors. Although this behavior was officially deviant, it was, in practice, socially approved.

Robert Merton's distinction between aberrant and nonconforming behavior is yet another example of a circumstance in which deviance may be viewed positively (1976). Aberrant deviants are people who basically accept the validity of a social rule but break it for personal gain. Most criminal activities fit into this classification. Virtually everyone disapproves of aberrant deviance, even the deviant actor in most cases. However, nonconforming deviance is a different issue. Nonconforming deviants believe that a rule is so bad that it is morally necessary to challenge it by deliberately and publicly violating it. Unlike aberrant deviants, who hope to hide their behavior, nonconforming deviants attract attention to their actions. Their goal is not personal gain but to cause the rule to be changed. This type of deviance is an act of conscience based on a social ideal, and nonconforming deviants are often regarded as heroes by their supporters and, if they are successful in their efforts, ultimately by the entire society. Examples include the students who sat in at segregated lunch counters in the South in the early phases of the civil rights movement, civil disobedience as practiced by protestors opposed to nuclear power, and the public announcement of his or her homosexuality by a soldier hoping to change the military's antigay policies. Thus, nonconformity in Merton's terms, like the eccentricities of creative artists, the violation of widely unpopular laws, or rule-violating practices designed to cut through bureaucratic red tape, is deviant behavior that is not necessarily bad or devalued.

2. *Deviant behavior is not always voluntary.* For example, people who are physically handicapped are sometimes treated as deviant. According to one researcher, people with physical disabilities violate basic norms of social identity by not being "whole" (Sagarin, 1975). However, because society does recognize that such disabilities are involuntary, this type of deviance is usually viewed with relative tolerance. Steps may be taken to restrain these people, such as putting them in institutions, but they still are not held fully accountable for their behavior. Those who can conform but fail to do so, on the other hand, usually must accept full responsibility for their actions. Thus, murderers who are judged to have been of "sound mind" when they committed their crimes face long prison terms, whereas those who are found to have been insane are treated more leniently.

   The line between inability to conform and failure to conform is often hard to draw. Some theorists believe that almost any antisocial act is the result of an inability to behave differently at a given time and place. But such a broad definition makes the concept of personal responsibility, which is basic to our system of justice, meaningless.

3. *Deviant behavior does not necessarily mean criminal behavior.* While most criminal behavior is deviant, not all deviant behavior is criminal. In general, an action can be (1) both criminal and deviant, such as committing murder; (2) criminal but not significantly deviant, such as gambling; or (3) deviant but not criminal. For example, whistle-blowing (reporting or informing on wrongdoing or illegal activities, especially in business or government) is widely considered deviant behavior, but it certainly is not criminal. Whistle-blowing can have many positive effects on a society (Gummer, 1985–86). Obese people, people with tattoos, and members of religious cults are all considered deviant, but their deviance is a departure from the norms of society, not criminal behavior.

4. *Deviant behavior, although disapproved, is a cultural universal.* Émile Durkheim noted that deviance is "an integral part of all healthy societies" (1958, p. 67). No known society has failed to include a substantial amount of behavior that its members defined as deviant; even the Puritan colonies of early New England, highly conformist by modern-day standards, found many of the actions of their members blameworthy (Erikson, 1966).

5. *Deviance may be committed by groups or organizations as well as by individuals.* Some kinds of crime and deviance, such as embezzlement (Cressey, 1953), are the result of one person acting alone. Others, such as the crimes committed by the Saints and the Roughnecks, are the behavior of groups. Some of the most serious acts of deviance have been committed by corporations or government agencies. A corporation

Would you define the behavior of President Clinton and Monica Lewinsky as social deviance? As defined in the text, social deviance is the violation of important social norms. Such violation normally results in efforts by society to punish the offenders and to attempt to reduce or eliminate further misbehavior.

is deviant, for example, when it illegally dumps toxic wastes; the FBI was deviant when it violated its charter by obsessively attempting to smear Martin Luther King, Jr.'s, reputation during the 1960s.

Social Control and Deviance

Social deviance, as already defined, is the violation of important social norms. Such violation normally results in efforts by the society to punish the offenders and to attempt to reduce or eliminate further misbehavior. Efforts intended to discourage deviance and encourage conformity are termed **social control.** There are two main types of social control: internal and external. *Internal social controls* consist of those processes that cause people to be self-motivated to act in a conforming manner. *External social controls* consist of pressures on people to conform through the use of various formal and informal social sanctions.

INTERNAL CONTROL OF DEVIANCE

Internalization is the acceptance of the norms of a group or society as part of one's identity. (It is one aspect of the socialization process discussed in Chapter 6.) Once a social norm has been internalized successfully, a person generally continues to obey it even when no one is watching. All of us, of course, sometimes deviate from what our group or society expects of us; internalization is never perfect (Sykes & Matza, 1957).

The conformity to norms that results from internalization is quite different from the conformity caused by fear of getting caught. The latter is a response to external controls applied by society. The successful internalization of social norms causes people to refrain, for example, from stealing someone else's money, not because they are afraid of being arrested and sent to jail, but because they believe stealing is wrong. Their conscience acts as an internal mechanism of social control.

Internalization is the most effective means of socially controlling deviant behavior. Although everyone feels some deviant impulses, the internalization of social norms tends to keep these impulses in check. People may lie to their parents, teachers, or friends; they may steal a CD, book, or scarf from a store; they may cheat an employer by taking a day off from work. But in most cases, internalized social norms lead to remorse and guilt and a lessening of one's sense of self-respect. As a result, the deviant behavior is likely to be abandoned.

EXTERNAL CONTROLS OF DEVIANCE

External controls over deviant behavior involve the use of social sanctions (see Chapter 3). Some sanctions are applied *informally*—that is, through the actions of people with whom we interact on a daily basis. Other sanctions are applied *formally*—that is, by agents charged with that particular task by society.

INFORMAL MECHANISMS OF SOCIAL CONTROL. Applying social sanctions informally is one of the main functions of the primary group. Negative sanctions can range from a gesture of disapproval to complete social rejection by the group or even physical punishment. Peer response is a very important informal mechanism of social control; even when people are motivated to break the rules, as one sociologist put it, "they usually squelch those impulses so that they will maintain the respect of friends and relatives" (Tittle, 1980, p. 321). Although this may put the case too strongly, the importance of informal sanctions in our daily lives cannot be denied.

Outside of primary groups, informal social control is commonly applied in the workplace and by people who happen to be nearby when an offense is committed. One employee may reproach another for goofing off; a teacher may informally tell parents about a student seen using drugs; and the elderly woman down the block may scold the neighborhood children for ganging up on one little boy.

Informal sanctions can be very effective, but their effects are often limited. One reason is because such sanctions are often vague. The individual does not really know what punishment, if any, will be forthcoming if a deviant act is observed or detected. Another is that personal feelings, relative social statuses, and feelings of group solidarity can negate the desire or ability to apply sanctions. A student who sees a friend cheating on a final exam might condemn the friend's action but not report the cheater for fear of ruining their friendship. In fact, those who do report cheaters may be labeled "squealers" and become social outcasts themselves.

Feelings of solidarity within a close-knit group of friends can affect social control in two conflicting ways. Deviance is a threat to solidarity, so the group wishes to limit it. But that same sense of solidarity restrains group members from applying strong sanctions to a deviant fellow member. It has been suggested that the members of a close-knit group will tend to protect the deviant *except* under three conditions: (1) when the deviance can easily be observed by outsiders; (2) when the deviant can readily be identified with the group; and (3) when the group is liable to be severely punished because of the deviant's behavior (Cohen, 1966).

FORMAL MECHANISMS OF SOCIAL CONTROL. Because of the limitations of informal social control mechanisms, societies have created organizations and special statuses that specialize in social control. Such statuses include police officers, judges, prison guards, and lawyers. Legislators, social workers, teachers, members of the clergy, psychiatrists, and doctors also practice social control as part of their duties. In modern societies, the network of such formal positions has become increasingly important, and social control has thus, in general, become much more impersonal.

At times, however, formal means of social control can be quite informal and even personal. One sociologist studied how prison guards relate to prisoners (Cloward, 1960). He reported that the guards often bargain with the inmates. By "forgetting" to enforce some rules, guards motivate prisoners to cooperate in observing other rules.

The informal ways that police carry out their formal social control duties have been examined in detail. Police officers do not always exercise their power of arrest even though they know that a crime has been committed (Sykes, 1978). They may wish to use the lawbreaker as a source of information. Or, for any number of other reasons, they may let criminals off with a warning or simply overlook deviant acts. In fact, very little police work is initiated by the police themselves; most of it is in response to citizen complaints. If the complainant shows a desire for leniency, the police are not likely to make an arrest (Black, 1971).

Other agents of formal social control also exercise a great deal of personal discretion. In order to ensure a conviction, prosecutors frequently engage in plea bargaining—that is, they allow someone to plead guilty to a lesser charge. Or prosecutors may drop the charges against an offender if they do not have enough personnel to go ahead with the case or if they feel that the evidence is insufficient to convict.

It is hard to think of any situation in which agents of formal social control do not have some discretionary power. Without this power, justice would be excessively rigid. Furthermore, if all adulterers, all husbands speeding pregnant wives to hospitals, all marijuana smokers, stop-sign passers, litterers, and public nuisances were suddenly arrested and brought to trial, our criminal justice system would be even more swamped than it already is.

Social Functions and Dysfunctions of Deviance

So far we have looked at deviance mainly in terms of the individual. Another important aspect of deviance is the ways in which it influences society as a whole. What are the effects on society when citizens do not pay their parking tickets or when they beat up and rob others? What are the effects on society of corporate bribery or political corruption? Most people probably think first of the *dysfunctions* of deviance—the effects that are negative or disruptive—but sociologists have also identified several latent positive functions of deviance. (The following discussion is drawn from Cohen [1966].)

SOCIAL FUNCTIONS OF DEVIANCE

Although deviance is seldom thought to be desirable, sociologists believe that it sometimes actually helps a social system to function and change in desired directions. The following are some of the positive social functions of deviance:

1. *Deviance can help to clarify and define social norms.* Many social norms remain rather vague until they are broken. The group's reaction to the violation then further clarifies the norm. Students sharing a kitchen, for example, might establish a rule stating that the sink, stove, and refrigerator are to be kept clean. But since "clean" is an imprecise term, the students do not know exactly what is expected of them. If one student leaves stains on the stove and no one notices, while another leaves dirty dishes all over the kitchen and everybody complains, the users of the kitchen will then better understand the norm of cleanliness.

2. *Deviance can increase group solidarity.* According to George Herbert Mead (1964), "the attitude of hostility toward the lawbreaker has the unique advantage of uniting all members of the community in the emotional solidarity of aggression." Group members find that they share a common attitude toward the deviant, and in many cases, they must take some common action to control or suppress the deviance.

Sometimes the group unites on behalf of a deviant member, and this, too, increases group solidarity. The group may want to protect one of its members from the consequences of his or her deviance or help the deviant learn to conform. Because members feel that it is worth the trouble and effort to keep the group intact, both these actions promote group solidarity.

3. *Deviance can bring about needed change in a social system.* Social change through deviance is the goal of nonconforming deviants, as discussed earlier. Sometimes, as a result of the deviant actions of some members, the rest of the group realizes that a rule is not a good one or that it contradicts other, more important rules. The rule is then changed. For example, in the civil disobedience campaign begun by Dr. Martin Luther King, Jr., the breaking of laws mandating segregation called the nation's attention to their unfairness. The civil rights movement ultimately caused these laws to be changed. At other times, if initially disapproved behavior becomes widespread, it may become generally accepted even though there was no deliberate campaign to cause social change. Examples include the gradual acceptance of women smoking in public or of earrings being worn by young men.

4. *Deviance makes conformity seem more desirable.* This occurs only when the deviant is unsuccessful and is punished. When everyone conforms, conformity is not considered a special virtue. But when a deviant is punished, all those who did not deviate are rewarded by not being punished and by the feeling of having done "the right thing." The conformist's desire to obey the rule is strengthened.

SOCIAL DYSFUNCTIONS OF DEVIANCE

Because society can absorb a large amount of deviance without serious effects, it is rare for one act of deviance or the deviance of one person to affect the functioning of society. But long-term or widespread deviance can be socially dysfunctional in several ways.

For one thing, if deviance is widespread, it may weaken people's motivation to conform. If you are taking an examination and you know that many of your fellow students are cheating, you may start to wonder why you bothered to stay up late studying. If all of your friends cheat on their taxes, why should you be honest? If deviance and conformity are equally rewarded, why conform?

Deviance can be harmful also because it makes life unpredictable and dangerous. All complex social interaction is based on the assumption that people will usually stick to their defined roles. If people, especially those occupying important statuses, do not live up to important role expectations, social life becomes problematic and risky. We feel safe on the highways because almost everyone obeys the rule that drivers should keep to the right. People bouncing on a trampoline expect their spotters to remain alert and catch them if they fall. Soldiers in battle constantly stake their lives on the willingness of their fellows to live up to their obligations. Deviance in such situations can weaken the fabric of trust that makes social life possible.

In any discussion of the social dysfunctions of deviance, it helps to distinguish between deviance and social disorganization, two concepts that are sometimes used as if they had the same meaning. **Social disorganization** refers to a breakdown of social institutions. A highly organized social system can stand a great deal of deviance without becoming seriously disorganized. Only when deviance is practiced by large numbers of people over long periods of time, only when it seriously undermines belief in the values of basic social institutions or when it produces conflict that cannot be contained, does it lead to social disorganization. At the same time, social disorganization can be caused not only by excessive deviance but also by wars, population changes, technological innovations, and calamities such as floods, fire, and famine.

THEORETICAL PERSPECTIVES ON DEVIANCE

Now that we have defined deviance and explored some of its effects on society, we can look at its causes. *Why* do some people break the rules of a group or society? Many theoretical perspectives have been developed to help explain deviant behavior. Note that, since deviance ranges from the persistent failure to greet a neighbor to a lifelong career of crime, no single theory can shed light on all its forms. Most perspectives reflect the special view of the discipline that developed them. For example, psychologists stress psychological factors in deviance, whereas sociologists emphasize social factors. In addition, it is important to remember that these theories deal more with the *general* causes of deviance than with the causes of a specific act. They try to explain why deviance occurs, not why a particular person has committed a specific deviant act. Although social scientists can state with some assurance which social situations are likely to generate a relatively large amount of deviance, they can rarely predict which people in those situations will actually commit deviant acts.

The search for scientific explanations of deviant behavior has been carried out on three main levels. Some scholars believe that certain *biological traits* are chiefly responsible for deviance. Psychologists, along with much of the public at large and, probably, most individuals working within the criminal justice system, attribute deviance mainly to *psychological* problems. But even though biological and psychological factors undoubtedly play important roles in the causation of deviance, sociologists feel that the *social environment*—the social context in which deviance is generated, sustained, and sometimes transformed—also makes a major contribution.

Biological Perspectives on Deviance

Many researchers have wondered whether biological factors might help explain deviance, especially criminal deviance. The nineteenth-century Italian researcher Cesare Lombroso (1918) suggested that criminals were biologically less evolved than law-abiding citizens. The American physical anthropologist Ernest Hooten (1939) concluded that criminals typically had multiple genetic and physical defects. And the American psychologist William Sheldon (Sheldon et al., 1949) argued that body type could be linked to criminality; an unusually high percentage of the criminals he studied had what he termed a *mesomorphic* body build—muscular and with heavy bones.

Because of the poor quality of the research, the conclusions of these early studies are widely regarded as incorrect. The search for biological factors, however, continues. In the late 1960s, two scientists reported that many men who had committed violent crimes were found to have an extra male chromosome, giving them an XYY configuration (Amir & Berman, 1970). But there is no solid evidence that this condition causes violent behavior, and most violent criminals do not have this abnormality (Sarbin & Miller, 1970). At a 1980s convention of medical specialists, several researchers stated their belief that up to 90 percent of excessively violent individuals have brain defects (*New York Times,* September 17, 1985). Recent research has also suggested but not proven a relationship between violent crime and diet (especially excessive use of sugar). It is also likely that aggressiveness and perhaps criminality are influenced by the level of the male sex hormone testosterone in the body.

One of the best ways to study the role of biological factors in deviance is to compare the occurrence and types of crimes committed by identical twins, since such twins are genetically identical. The results of such studies, however, have been contradictory. One careful study of twins in Norway concluded that inherited traits are not a significant cause of crime (Dalgard & Kringlen, 1976). Yet other research has suggested the reverse, especially for major crimes. One study found that inherited criminal behavior is more likely to involve theft than violence (Gabrielli, Hutchings, & Mednick, 1984).

Despite the paucity of research findings firmly linking deviance with biological factors, there is an increasing tendency in modern society to interpret deviant behavior as the result of illness, whether physical or mental—a trend called the *medicalization of deviance.* As a result, such deviant behaviors as drug addiction, hyperactivity, and drunkenness are now more commonly regarded as medical problems than as moral failings (Conrad & Schneider, 1980).

This process of reinterpretation seems to fit today's rapidly changing culture better than the traditional view that such lapses represent sins (Light, 1989). What was once the sin of drunkenness, for example, has been medicalized into the disease of alcoholism; what was once a moral failing is now regarded as an illness that requires professional treatment. Although medicine has been able to help many deviants cope with their problems, medicalization is not always a helpful approach. For example, the homeless often display symptoms such as dizziness and disorientation, which leads to their being labeled "mentally ill"; however, it is likely that such symptoms result not from illness but from the lack of adequate diet and housing to which the homeless are subject. Thus, the medicalization perspective may encourage us to look for individual pathology rather than the underlying social causes of major social problems (Snow, 1988).

Psychological Perspectives on Deviance

Both psychologists and sociologists have suggested that certain types of personalities are often correlated with deviant behavior. One of the most important researchers holding this point of view is the British psychologist Hans Eysenck (1977), whose theory blends biological and psychological perspectives. According to Eysenck, no one is *born* deviant, but some people may be genetically more *prone* to deviance than others. One personality type that is especially likely to become deviant is the *extrovert*—a person who is sociable but also impulsive and who has a strong need for variety and excitement. (*Introverts,* the opposite personality type, are quiet and controlled.) Extroverts, says Eysenck, are likely to overstep the bounds of acceptable behavior because they have a biological need for thrills and risks. Whether or not they actually become deviant depends principally on how they have been socialized.

Another important psychological perspective emphasizes that violence and thus often deviance are *socially learned.* The social psychologist Albert Bandura (1973) argued that people learn aggressive behavior by observation and imitation, even if they do not actually engage in it. For instance, children watch violence on television and imitate it in play. In this way they learn how to

Psychologists argue that much deviant behavior is socially learned through observation and imitation. This child, for example, may be imitating violent behavior he observed on television or at the movies.

be violent (how to shoot a gun, for example), even if they do not actually display the behavior they have learned. If they later find that behaving violently brings them a reward and does not lead to punishment, they are likely to resort to violence.

A third popular psychological explanation of violence suggests that aggression is often produced by frustration. When a need is not fulfilled, people may become frustrated. As explained by the *frustration-aggression* hypothesis, the amount of frustration is based on the strength of the needs, impulses, or wishes that are obstructed (Berkowitz, 1962). The degree of aggression, in turn, is related to how frustrated a person becomes. Frustration may result from a lack of money, love, or any of a number of things. In fact, the theory can be stated broadly enough so that it will cover just about any situation.

Sociological Perspectives on Deviance

Where psychological explanations stress individual traits that can motivate people to act in deviant ways, sociological perspectives focus on the social environment. These two approaches have been called *kinds-of-people* theories and *kinds-of-situations* theories, respectively (Cohen, 1966). Kinds-of-people theories try to show that deviants are different from other people, either biologically or

psychologically. Kinds-of-situations theories attempt to figure out what kinds of situations would make an otherwise ordinary person violate norms. In pursuing the situational approach, sociologists focus on three broad questions: Why are some social environments more likely to produce deviance than others? Why are acts that are deviant in some social situations highly valued in others? Why do deviants break some rules and not others?

STRUCTURAL STRAIN THEORY

An early and very influential sociological theory of deviance was advanced by Robert Merton in 1938. Building on Durkheim's classic concept of **anomie**—a social condition in which norms and values are conflicting, weak, or absent—Merton suggested that deviance is likely to result when there is a strain or conflict between a society's culture and its social structure.

More specifically, all cultures put forth certain goals (such as financial success) as universally desirable and also specify certain means (working hard, going to school) as the legitimate or socially approved ways of seeking to obtain those goals. However, in circumstances of rapid social change or widespread social inequality, certain groups of people are likely to have little or no opportunity to achieve their culture's success goals using the approved means. The social structure restricts their chances of success. As a result, people in such groups will experience anomie in that they may lose their interest in the goals, in achieving them through the legitimate means, or both. Thus, Merton's **structural strain theory** seeks to explain widespread deviance within certain sectors of society—those experiencing blocked opportunities—as a result of cultural pressure to achieve goals without corresponding access to legitimate ways of achieving them.

Merton suggests that there are five ways that members of these blocked groups—principally minorities and the poor—may respond to their anomic dilemma:

1. The most common response is *conformity*: to keep working to achieve desired goals using the culturally approved means, even though the chances of success are relatively remote. Fortunately, this is the most common response to anomie.

The four other possible responses are all, to a greater or lesser extent, deviant:

2. *Innovation* consists of accepting the goal—seeking to become wealthy—but rejecting the approved means and substituting new, illegitimate ones, as when a person sells drugs in order to buy a new car.

3. *Ritualism* is a relatively uncommon pattern in which the blocked individual accepts the means but rejects the goal, as when one goes to school to obtain a degree that almost certainly will not lead to a job.

4. *Retreatism* consists of rejecting both the goal and the means, as in the case of a hermit who goes off to live by himself in the woods.

5. *Rebellion* involves rejecting the approved goals and means of one's culture and substituting new ones, usually in concert with others. For example, a group of college students may drop out of school and abandon hopes of conventional success, instead forming a radical environmental action group that works for new goals using unconventional means.

Merton's theory has been criticized on several grounds. For one thing, certain deviant acts, such as rape, simply are not explained by the scheme (Gibbons & Jones, 1975). Furthermore, the theory explains only the deviance of people who are members of groups whose opportunity to succeed is limited; it says nothing about deviance among society's privileged. Finally, it does not help us predict which response a particular individual will choose when experiencing anomie.

CULTURAL TRANSMISSION THEORY

By itself, anomie does not invariably lead to deviance. Many ghetto children, for example, whose chances for education and financial success are often stifled at every turn, do not become drug addicts, thieves, or revolutionaries. As psychological learning theorists note, in order to become deviant, people must have an opportunity to *learn* deviance. People who learn ideas that favor deviant actions are more likely than others to act in deviant ways.

The idea that deviance, like conformity, is learned from one's social environment is supported by research by Clifford Shaw and Henry McKay that was conducted in certain Chicago neighborhoods characterized by consistently high crime rates. Shaw and McKay (1929) noted that a high crime rate persisted in those neighborhoods for over 20 years, even though the ethnic composition of the neighborhoods changed several times during the two decades. The researchers concluded that the recent arrivals learned deviant behavior from people already living in the area, mainly in children's play groups and teenage gangs.

More recently, Richard Cloward and Lloyd Ohlin (1964) pointed out that, although social institutions attempt to teach conformity to social norms, they do not always do so consistently. Parents, teachers, religious leaders, and other socializing agents sometimes transmit attitudes supporting deviance rather than conformity. In

telling her daughter always to obey the laws, for example, a mother teaches conformity. Yet, if that mother receives a parking ticket while she and her daughter are shopping and says, "Oh, I'll just throw the ticket away; they will never know the difference anyhow," she teaches the girl that certain kinds of deviance are acceptable.

Ironically, sociologists have noted that many places intended to correct deviance actually teach deviant behavior. In prisons, new inmates are exposed to the attitudes of hardened criminals. Older prisoners often teach younger inmates more effective methods of committing crime. In mental institutions, deviant behavior tends to be reinforced by the subculture of the institution.

No one is ever exposed exclusively to deviance. Members of delinquent gangs who are taught by older gang members how to steal a car are also taught by others that car theft is morally and legally wrong. Many members of religious cults grew up in conventional households. Why, then, are some people attracted to deviant patterns and others lean toward conformity?

Edwin Sutherland (1947) developed what may well be the most systematic attempt to answer this question. Sutherland's theory of differential association argues that everybody is exposed to both conforming and deviant behaviors. These influences compete in the mind of the individual, and the stronger wins out. If socialization to deviance is stronger than socialization to conformity, the person will become deviant. Sutherland identified several factors that work to tip the balance toward deviance: The more intense the relationship with the person teaching deviant behavior, the greater the number, frequency, and duration of contacts, and the younger the age of contact, the more likely it is that an individual will become deviant.

CONTROL THEORIES

The structural strain and cultural transmission perspectives share the assumption that conformity is the normal state of affairs and that it is deviance from the norms that requires explanation. Social control theory takes a different position. Departing from traditional sociological explanations of crime, it is based on the assumption that human beings are self-interested and antisocial (Barkan, 1997; Livingston, 1996). Instead of asking why people commit crimes, this theory focuses on why they do not. And it suggests that crime results because society fails to instill effective controls within people before they reach adulthood.

Control theory also dismisses another idea common to other sociological theories of crime—that different groups within society subscribe to different definitions of law and morality. It argues that the law and moral codes

Some criminologists believe that as an enduring trait, the lack of self-control explains why deviant children become deviant adults. Do you agree? Are these children destined to be deviant adults because they lack the self-control needed not to paint the wall with graffiti?

are clear and that people have a clear sense of right and wrong for most crimes. People are, thus, fully aware of breaking the law.

Finally, control theory rejects environmental causes of criminal behavior—social class, economic status, and culture. The basis for this departure from other sociological theories lies not only in theory but in empirical research as well. In fact, control theory gained support when findings from self-report studies of criminal behavior failed to show significant differences in criminal behavior between the lower class and the middle class and between whites and blacks (Livingston, 1996).

Control theories come in many varieties. One type builds on psychology by arguing that some people are less able to contain their inner impulses than others. According to Walter Reckless's (1967) *containment theory,* criminals are generally people who lack a positive self-concept and as a result are unable to resist deviant temptations. Similarly, Howard Becker (1963) suggests that "normal" people control their deviant impulses by thinking about what will happen if they carry them out. They do not want to risk soiling their self-images. Others have trouble restraining these impulses because they lack commitment to themselves or a strong sense of identity. Still others cannot see the link between their failure to restrain their deviant impulses and the effects of becoming deviant. And some people may simply view themselves as worthless and feel that what happens to them does not matter.

Today many criminologists regard Travis Hirschi's **social control theory** as the most influential theory of criminal and delinquent behavior (Akers, 1994; Barkan, 1997; Livingston, 1996; Lynch et al., 1993). Since it was first presented in his book *Causes of Delinquency* in 1969, this theory has been tested in over 71 investigations (Kempf, 1993). Consistent with other control theories, the most interesting question about criminal behavior for Hirschi was not why people commit crimes, but why they do not. According to him, it is the bond that human beings form with society and its moral code that prevents them from breaking the law.

He suggests that four social bonds control deviant impulses in most of us, but are typically weak in criminals. They include *attachment* to conformist others, especially parents and peers; *commitment,* by which he means investment of time and effort working toward conventional goals (such as attending college) whose attainment would be threatened by deviant behavior; *involvement* in conventional activities, which reduces the time available for deviance; and *belief,* the acceptance of conventional moral attitudes.

Twenty years after the publication of *Causes of Delinquency,* Hirschi collaborated with Michael Gottfredson to produce a revised version of control theory known as **self-control theory** (Livingston, 1996). Rejecting biological, psychological, and even sociological explanations of crime, including Hirshi's idea about the social bond, they claimed that people commit crimes for a simple reason—because they lack self-control, the ability to control impulses and defer gratification.

As an enduring trait, the lack of self-control explains why deviant children become deviant adults (Livingston, 1996). It also accounts for many forms of deviance—drinking and drugs, domestic violence, job instability, accidents, and premature deaths. And it eliminates the need to tailor special theories for different crimes. Robbery, rape, and white-collar crimes can all be explained by one variable—the lack of self-control.

According to Gottfredson and Hirschi, ineffective childrearing seems to be the major cause of low self-control (Gottfredson & Hirschi, 1990). Parents who do not recognize and correct inappropriate behavior fail to instill self-control in their children.

CONFLICT THEORY AND DEVIANCE

Earlier in this chapter, we introduced several ways in which, according to the functionalist perspective, deviance promotes the stability of a social system. Merton's structural strain theory also draws on functionalism; it assumes, for example, that all members of a society share values relating to the desirability of certain success goals.

In contrast, conflict theorists deny that all members of a society share the same goals and values. Instead, they argue that the values of the relatively powerful groups in society are often quite different from those of the powerless. Because the rules and laws of a society are largely shaped by the preferences of the powerful, the greater frequency of deviance among the powerless simply reflects the fact that the rules do not reflect their particular way of looking at reality. From this perspective, if poor people, minorities, and women made the laws, then wealthy white males would be more likely than anyone else to be judged criminal!

Two general schools of conflict theory may be identified: *culture conflict theory* and *Marxian conflict theory.* The first tradition emphasizes the fact that complex societies contain a number of distinct subcultures, each with its own set of norms and values. These subcultures may be centered around ethnicity, gender, lifestyle, geographic location, or many other factors. What is seen as deviant by one group may well be accepted behavior by another. However, the more powerful subcultures are able to effectively define many of the values of the less powerful subcultures as deviant.

Culture conflict theorists, thus, frequently ask why the norms of some groups rather than others are made into laws, and why these laws are enforced more rigorously against the members of some groups than they are against the members of others. For example, why is smoking marijuana, a relatively harmless drug, considered deviant, whereas drinking Scotch, which is much more clearly linked to the cause of various diseases, perfectly acceptable? Culture conflict theorists would point to the greater social power of Scotch drinkers as opposed to that of pot smokers.

Regarding the differential enforcement of laws, two researchers using the culture conflict approach observed public reactions to staged incidents of shoplifting in public places (Steffensmeier & Terry, 1973). The found that whether or not a witness reported an incident of shoplifting often depended on the appearance of the shoplifter. Public willingness to report the offense increased when the shoplifter was perceived to be a hippie—a member of a devalued and relatively powerless group.

One culture conflict theorist has even tried to define precisely the conditions that turn cultural differences into overt legal conflicts (Turk, 1969). He argued that the outcomes of such conflicts depend on the power, organization, and sophistication of the groups involved. For example, a highly organized group with little power and little sophistication—a street gang, for example—is especially likely to come into conflict with the law. A highly sophisticated member of a powerful segment of society acting alone or with a few others—a building contractor who bribes a city inspector, for example—is much less likely to run afoul of the law.

Marxian conflict theories focus more narrowly on the differential power of social classes rather than on that of a variety of different subcultures. This perspective argues that class conflict, not cultural differences in general, is the best explanation of much deviance. The most serious crimes in a capitalist society are those like embezzlement, which are committed by the poor against the rich; in contrast, the crimes of the rich, such as tax fraud or the savings and loan scandal, are regarded and treated by the law as relatively minor, especially in proportion to the amount of harm that they cause. The purpose of most of the criminal law in our society, according to the Marxian perspective, is to maintain the status quo and in particular to defend the interests of the rich and powerful at the expense of the poor and powerless. Marxian conflict theorists view the legal system as working with education, the mass media, and religion to focus public attention on lower-class deviance, especially street crimes like mugging and petty theft. As a result, our attention is diverted from the far more costly crimes of the rich and from the basic underlying cause of deviance: the great inequalities of American life (Greenberg, 1986).

Despite their differences, both Marxian and non-Marxian conflict theorists reject two commonly held notions about our legal system. Laws are not, they say, designed to protect all members of a society equally, and laws do not necessarily reflect the moral thinking of the entire society.

LABELING THEORY

The sociological theories we have just examined help us to understand some of the causes of deviant behavior, but they cannot explain all aspects of it. Some people spend time with deviants and even perform deviant acts, but are not publicly identified as deviants. Furthermore, in some cases, committing deviant acts leads to a career of deviance; in others, it does not. To explain these facts, a group of sociologists known as *labeling theorists,* drawing on symbolic interactionism, has focused on the *process* of deviance rather than the *causes* of deviance. Labeling theorists strongly emphasize the fact that deviance is relative. An act and the person who commits it become deviant only when labeled as such by others.

One of the first sociologists to develop the labeling perspective was Edwin Lemert (1951, 1967). Lemert distinguished between *primary deviance,* occasional involvement with acts that violate social norms with no lasting effect on the individual's psychological makeup or performance of social roles, and *secondary deviance,* involvement in norm violations that are labeled as deviant by others and accepted by the deviant as such. In secondary deviance, deviants must reorganize their behavior and self-concepts around the deviant role. They may dress in certain ways or use a special kind of slang known only to other deviants. The more clearly the deviants define themselves as deviant, the more likely they are to be treated as deviants by others. After a period of time, even people who do not know their reputation may be able to recognize them as deviants because of the image they present.

Labeling theorists have isolated three major steps in the process of becoming a career deviant. First is the *observation* of the act of deviance by the authorities or by people who are close to the person committing the act. Second is the *labeling* of the individual as deviant. Third is the person's *joining a deviant group* or subculture that provides social support for the deviant behavior. Once all three of these steps have been taken, the chances are that the person will not give up his or her deviant ways and return to conformity. The individual will have embarked on a **deviant career**—the adoption of a deviant identity and lifestyle within a supporting deviant subculture. This concept can be useful in understanding the stages of deviant behavior—not only the steps that lead up to it, but also the degree to which a person becomes committed to deviance and the identity that goes with it.

OBSERVING THE DEVIANCE. An act of social rule breaking known only to the deviant may have no social consequences for that person, even though it is performed frequently. Studies show that this kind of behavior is extremely common. In one nationwide survey, interviews were conducted with a sample of 847 boys and girls; 88 percent of the youths admitted having committed at least one delinquent act in the previous three years. Yet only 20 percent had had any contact with the police, and only 16 youths had been sent to juvenile court (Williams & Gold, 1972). It is safe to conclude that most delinquent acts are not detected, at least by the authorities.

For a deviant act to have social consequences, significant people must observe it. The number of people who know about the act need not be large; more important is *who* knows about the act. If a store employee steals money from the cash register and is seen by only one person—a customer who says nothing to anyone—that employee will probably suffer no social consequences. But if the one observer is the employee's boss, the results can be very different.

LABELING THE DEVIANT. Being publicly labeled a deviant is probably the most significant step in the deviant's career. The deviant is *typed*—placed in a social category that creates a negative impression. Labeling may give the deviant a public reputation of being a "nut,"

"junky," "faggot," "bum," or whatever name seems to fit the situation. When the act of deviance violates the law, the person may be called a criminal as well.

A label may be applied formally, as in court or at a sanity hearing, in which case a ritual called a *degradation ceremony* will often be conducted in order to officially transform the individual's public identity from normal to deviant. Labels may also be applied informally, by friends or family. An example would be the process by which a child acquires the reputation of being bad or a troublemaker. Labels can also be self-applied. Many gays voluntarily come "out of the closet" and publicly announce their sexual orientation in order to avoid the negative effects of pretending to be what they are not (Schur, 1971).

Labeling people as deviants can have long-lasting effects (Link & Cullen, 1990). Those so labeled are no longer treated simply as students, plumbers, parents, or church members, but as persons who are somehow outside of normal society. The social effects can be the same even if the individual never actually committed the deviant acts implied by the label.

Howard Becker (1963) has pointed out that a deviant identity tends to be a *master status,* one that dominates all others and thereby defines a person's social position:

> One will be identified as a deviant, before other identifications are made. The question is raised: "What kind of person would break such an important rule?" And the answer is given: "One who is different from the rest of us, who cannot or will not act as a moral human being and therefore might break other important rules." The deviant identification becomes the controlling one. (pp. 33–34)

People labeled as deviant are often rejected and isolated by society. This rejection may be physical—as when the deviant is sent to a jail, mental hospital, or some other corrective institution—or it may be social. For example, friends and families may withdraw some of their former trust and affection, or employers may fire labeled deviants. In many cases, the deviant acquires a **stigma**—a label that identifies the deviant as socially unacceptable. Social rejection and isolation tend to push labeled individuals further into a life of deviance. In work, with friends, and in their outlook on life, people stigmatized as deviant slowly begin to organize their entire lives around the deviant role.

JOINING THE DEVIANT GROUP. For many deviants, the final step in a deviant career is to join and identify with a group of other deviants. The group serves two important functions for the person. The first is practical:

When one moves into a deviant group . . . he learns how to carry on his deviant activity with a minimum of trouble. All the problems he faces in evading enforcement of the rule he is breaking have been faced before by others. Solutions have been worked out. Thus, the young thief meets older thieves who, more experienced than he is, explain to him how to get rid of stolen merchandise without running the risk of being caught. (Becker, 1963, p. 39)

The second function of the group is to provide its members with emotional and social support. Within the group, people understand and sympathize with one another. The group also rationalizes its deviant behavior. Group members may assert, for example, that the normal world is full of hypocritical deviants, but that the group members are at least honest about their behavior. These explanations are substitutes for the harsher assessments made by the outside society, and they partially relieve group members of their burdens of guilt and self-hatred.

Joining a deviant group makes it more likely that one will continue a deviant lifestyle. The pressure to return to conventionality diminishes, and the deviant self-image is reinforced. As one girl explained, she realized she was a drug addict when she noticed that she no longer had any friends who were not addicts (Becker, 1963). There is irony in the fact that some conformity pressures exist in all groups, whether that group is socially acceptable or deviant. An individual who rejects the rules of society and joins a deviant group may find himself or herself under substantial pressure to conform to the deviant lifestyle.

Sometimes, especially in illegal occupations, there is a strict hierarchy among those who have embarked on deviant careers. For example, one researcher conducted interviews with 28 male prostitutes in Chicago and found that there were three main levels of male prostitution: street hustling (in which the prostitute plies his trade in parks or bus stations), bar hustling, and escort prostitution arranged through agencies. Most of the prostitutes moved from street hustling to bar hustling, and some eventually rose to escort prostitution. There was a clear hierarchy in the way these positions were ranked. The main determinants of this hierarchy were income, privacy, and security from arrest. For instance, street hustlers earned about $10 to $15 per encounter; bar hustlers, about $50 to $75; and escorts, the highest ranked, about $100 plus tips.

The researcher found that there were certain prerequisites for ascending each step of the ladder. Street hustlers simply had to look reasonably presentable. Bar hustlers had to be at least 21 years old, attractive, and at ease with people. Escorts actually had to fill out job applications

Joining a deviant group like this female street gang makes it more likely that one will continue a deviant lifestyle. The pressure to return to conventionality diminishes, and the deviant self-image is reinforced.

about their personal backgrounds, education, and experience (Luckenbill, 1986)!

The labeling perspective has not gone unchallenged. To imply that the labeling of people as deviant is what makes them so is often an exaggeration. Many criminals pursue their careers principally because crime provides substantial monetary rewards or for other reasons not related to the fact that society labels their activities deviant. And even though labeling may be part of becoming a deviant, it cannot explain the initial deviant act. The labeling perspective is not a substitute for theories that attempt to explain the causes of deviance in a society, but it clearly does offer important insights into this puzzling social reality.

CRIME AND THE CRIMINAL JUSTICE SYSTEM

Types of Crime

Crime can be defined as behavior that is prohibited by a governmental authority and that can be punished through the application of formal sanctions. Experts have traditionally divided such behavior into several main categories, including crime against persons, crime against property, and victimless or moral crime. In recent years organized crime and white-collar and corporate crime have also received substantial attention.

The most widely feared crimes are probably murder, rape, and aggravated assault. All are classified by public authorities as "violent crimes" committed against persons. Even though violent crimes receive the most

TABLE 8.1	CRIMINAL OFFENSES IN THE UNITED STATES KNOW TO THE POLICE, 1997	
All Crime	*Number*	*Percent*
Murder	18,209	0.14
Forcible rape	96,122	0.73
Robbery	497,950	3.78
Aggravated assault	1,022,492	7.76
Burglary	2,461,120	18.68
Larceny-theft	7,725,470	58.64
Motor vehicle theft	1,353,707	10.27
Total	13,175,070	100.00*

*Rounded.

Source: U.S. Department of Justice, 1998.

attention, they actually make up only a small proportion of the total number of crimes recorded by official agencies. (Refer to Table 8.1 for data on major offenses known to the police.) Larceny, burglary, robbery, car theft, and arson fall into the category of "crimes against property." This category also includes white-collar crime (discussed later in this chapter).

On an international scale, according to official statistics, approximately 20 percent of all crimes are crimes against the person; 72 percent are crimes against property; and about 8 percent are drug offenses. Developed countries report much more crime than developing countries, by a margin of more than 2 to 1. The types of crimes committed also differ. In developing countries, the number of crimes against the person is about equal to the number of crimes against property, but in developed countries (such as the United States) there are many more crimes against property (Mueller, 1983).

ORGANIZED CRIME

There is a great demand for, and hence a great profit to be made from, illegal gambling and the provision of drugs and sexual services. The fact that these services and products are banned by the law allows the people who sell them to charge a high price, even though the cost of providing them is often relatively low. These realities are central to any explanation of why organized crime has thrived in the United States, although its activities extend beyond these traditional realms to such diverse areas as labor racketeering, loan sharking, and money laundering.

Until recently, the popular image of organized crime was strongly associated with Italian-Americans. Beginning in the 1930s, Americans became fascinated by the criminal syndicate commonly known as the Mafia. Books, movies, newspapers, magazine articles—anything purporting to shed light on this group—have always sold well. In the early 1980s, according to the Federal Bureau of Investigation, 24 traditional organized crime families were still operating in the United States, loosely grouped together in an organization called La Cosa Nostra (Italian for "our thing" or "our work"). Specific crimes that police intelligence reports have linked to such families include illegal gambling, hijacking, loan sharking, labor racketeering, and cocaine and heroin trafficking.

Of increasing concern to law enforcement officials today, however, are newer organized gangs of diverse ethnic backgrounds, including the Colombian drug cartels. These new groups, typically heavily engaged in the drug trade, are considered to be both more violent and less well organized than the Mafia.

Members of organized crime should not be confused with professional criminals. A *professional criminal* is a person who makes a career out of a particular crime, such as burglary, safecracking, or armed robbery. Unlike organized crime syndicates, which can include hundreds of members, professional criminals tend to work either alone or very closely with one partner or a few accomplices. In most cases, professional criminals have developed sophisticated techniques (often learned from other professional criminals in prison or on the streets) that allow them to ply their trade with a great deal of precision and considerable immunity from apprehension. Professional criminals who are especially good enjoy a great deal of prestige in the criminal underground.

WHITE-COLLAR AND CORPORATE CRIME

When we think of crime, most of us visualize muggings, burglaries, rapes, or perhaps the rackets of organized crime. Published crime statistics and newspaper reports tend to support such a view. *White-collar crimes*—those committed by business executives, corporations, politicians, and professionals—are also common, but we think about them much less frequently. White-collar crime is not as familiar to most of us, in part because the people involved are usually powerful and sophisticated and therefore can often avoid detection. If apprehended, they are usually processed through the civil courts rather than the criminal courts and so do not show up in crime statistics (Clinard, 1979; Sutherland, 1940).

Most white-collar crimes are committed for money. Such crimes include price-fixing, fraudulent advertising, and bribery—what Al Capone called "the legitimate rackets" (Sutherland, 1940). These crimes can be committed by people acting for their own personal gain or by corporate officers working together to benefit their company.

Some forms of white-collar crime may be committed for reasons other than personal monetary gain. For example, current liability laws require that people engaged in insider trading must profit personally from the misuse of confidential information in order to be prosecuted, but studies have shown that insider trading is often undertaken primarily for the purpose of advancing the firm and its clients rather than its individual employees (Garten, 1987). Other researchers have noted that the "race to be first" in scientific research sometimes leads to the falsification or manipulation of data (Merton, 1984; Zuckerman, 1988).

The "indirect robbery" committed by white-collar criminals is not as personally threatening to the public as are street crimes. A mugging at gunpoint certainly seems more threatening than a big corporation evading millions of dollars in taxes. But white-collar crime involves much greater losses than do other types of crime. Estimates of the amount of money involved run into the hundreds of billions of dollars. The total cost of the 1980s savings and loan scandal alone may exceed $500 billion.

VICTIMLESS CRIMES

One of the most important types of crime in America today is variously categorized as moral crime, public order crime, or victimless crime. *Victimless crimes* result from using the criminal law to attempt to prohibit the exchange between consenting adults of strongly desired goods and services. These exchanges are said to be victimless in that the parties involved in the transaction do not see themselves as being harmed. Prostitution, pornography, and the sale and use of illicit drugs are examples. American history reveals a long and generally unsuccessful tradition of attempting to enforce victimless crime laws, highlighted by Prohibition and by the contemporary "war on drugs" (Musto, 1987).

Currently, a heated debate is underway between advocates of retaining our drug laws and their opponents, who believe that criminalization has failed and encourage adoption of a policy of decriminalization combined with an intensified emphasis on education and therapy. This is similar to the way in which alcohol and tobacco are currently controlled. Supporters of keeping drugs illegal argue that decriminalization would lead to massive increases in drug abuse, in part because it would send the wrong message to young people who are considering using drugs.

Advocates of decriminalization respond that drug prohibition has been no more successful than alcohol

Victimless crimes result from using criminal law to attempt to prohibit the exchange between consenting adults of strongly desired goods and services. Prostitution is an example of victimless crime.

prohibition was. People who wish to use illegal substances have no difficulty obtaining them, and their illegal status may even encourage some people to experiment with them—the "forbidden fruit" effect. Furthermore, the drug laws clog our courts and prisons with users and sellers, making it more difficult to prosecute predatory street criminals (Nadelman, 1992).

Despite such arguments, victimless crime laws remain in effect in most states, partly as a result of the efforts of "moral entrepreneurs"—persons or groups who proclaim certain behaviors to be unacceptable and attempt to have them classified as criminal.

For instance, a group called Women Against Pornography has been instrumental in launching a campaign against what it perceives as the exploitation of women in the mass media, in advertising, and even in medical textbooks. But, in fact, contemporary American attitudes toward pornography are ambivalent. As one scholar has noted, pornography is considered deviant, yet is widely tolerated or overlooked except when children are involved. Most Americans believe that those who purchase pornography have the right to do so (Press et al., 1985). The antipornography movement has failed to turn pornography into a crime, simply because many Americans are not fully convinced that pornography is a moral evil (Goode, 1990).

Crime Statistics

Every year when the Federal Bureau of Investigation publishes its annual *Uniform Crime Reports*, it singles out eight specific crimes for special attention (see Figure 8.2).

GLOBAL SOCIETY

INTERNATIONAL COMPARISONS OF CRIME

In 1994, Michael Fay, an American teenager, was convicted of spray-painting cars in Singapore. His punishment for this crime—a severe whipping with a bamboo rod—caused an international protest from opponents of corporal punishment (Schmalleger, 1997). It also led Americans to question how crimes vary from one society to another. Unfortunately, this is not an easy question to answer. For one thing, the way that crimes are defined varies from one country to another. For example, sodomy, seduction of a child, incest, prostitution, and "lewdness" are classified as separate crimes in the United States. But in Greece they are all classified as one crime—rape (Schmalleger, 1997).

Another problem with international comparisons involves the way that crimes are reported. No international standard exists. Therefore, agencies that collect information from different countries have no way of determining the accuracy of the data they receive. Today international crime data are gathered by four main groups: Interpol (the International Police Organization), the United Nations, the World Health Organization (WHO), and the Comparative Crime Data File

(CCDF). In some cases the results of these groups are consistent, but in others they are not (Bennett & Lynch, 1990). And, unfortunately, data are not gathered on a regular basis.

These problems make most international comparisons of crime impossible. Murder is one exception. While it might be difficult to identify the murderer, a dead body is certain proof that this crime has been committed. And because murder is a serious crime—one that is universally condemned—it is almost certain that it will be reported. As it turns out, the United States has by far the highest murder rate when compared to other industrialized nations (see Figure 8.1). The International Police Organization (Interpol) claims that the murder rate is 3 times higher in the United States than in Canada and 5 times higher than that in Europe. Data gathered by the World Health Organization indicate that the difference is even greater. According to WHO, the rate is 5 times higher in the United States than in Canada and 7.5 times higher than in Europe.

Explaining American Violence

Many reasons have been offered to explain the high murder rate in the United States. Cultural theories focus on the relationship between tolerant

attitudes toward aggression and violence and violent crimes (Livingston, 1996). One explanation that has received a great deal of attention over the years suggests that television programs provide children with an abundant source of violent images. According to one estimate, the average American child will view 8,000 murders on television before completing elementary school (Clark, 1993). While the results of research on media violence are mixed, one examination of over 200 existing studies concluded that there is "a positive and significant correlation between television violence and aggressive behavior" (Paik & Comstock, 1994). According to Brandon Centerwall, an epidemiologist, there would be 10,000 fewer murderers in the United States if television had not been invented (1993).

Of course, tolerant attitudes toward violence are not new. The United States has a long history of violence. According to the historian Richard Maxwell Brown, the United States "was conceived and born in violence" (1990, p. 5). Good causes justified it, and interpersonal disputes required it (Barkan, 1997). Colonists engaged in "savage guerrilla warfare" in their fight for independence. And pioneers resorted to it as they moved westward into uncivilized territory.

These eight, which are collectively referred to as *index crimes,* include four violent crimes—homicide, forcible rape, aggravated assault, and robbery—and four crimes against property—larceny-theft, burglary, auto theft, and arson.

FBI data suggest that index crime is committed mostly by people under the age of 25, although the extent to which this is true varies from crime to crime. For example, in 1997 people in this age group were responsible for 55.5 percent of all murders, 64.8 percent of all robberies, and 43.6 percent of all rapes. Persons aged 25 and over, however, were most frequently involved in such

nonindex crimes as fraud, gambling, drunkenness, and offenses against the family (U.S. Department of Justice, 1998).

These FBI figures also prove that crime is generally a male activity, although some offenses, such as prostitution, have traditionally been defined so that they are almost the exclusive domain of women. But women are involved in more criminal activities than they used to be. In 1997, 25.5 percent of all persons arrested for index offenses were women, compared to 12 percent in 1967. The crimes for which women are most often arrested are nonviolent, however. In 1997, women accounted for

In order to preserve law and order, law-abiding citizens became involved in vigilante behavior, producing a "wild west" mentality of violence. The history of violence in America also includes the particularly brutal treatment of three groups—Native Americans, African-Americans, and industrial workers (Barkan, 1997). According to historians, the massacres of tens of thousands of Native Americans, the brutality of slavery, and a violent history of labor disputes all contributed to the development of tolerant attitudes toward violence in America.

Another explanation for the higher murder rate in the United States focuses on the social structure and suggests that economic inequality produces higher rates of violent crimes (Barkan, 1997; Livingston, 1996). In fact, a number of studies have found that nations with greater inequality also have higher murder rates (Avison & Loring, 1986; Braithwaite & Braithwaite, 1980; Krahn et al., 1986; Messner, 1982).

Finally, some criminologists argue that the greater availability of handguns in the United States explains its high murder rate (Barkan, 1997; Livingston, 1996). According to the findings of one study, 29 percent of U.S. respondents owned a gun

compared to less than 10 percent of respondents in most European nations (Van Dijk et al., 1991). While this suggests that violence in the United States is more likely to result in death, cultural theorists argue that the explanation still lies in an underlying attitude

toward deadly violence. According to Jay Livingston, "Even if every murder by gun were removed from the statistics, the U.S. murder rate would still be double that of most European countries" (1996, p. 150).

FIGURE 8.1 The United States has far higher rates of rape and murder than other industrialized nations.

Source: United Nations Human Development Programme, *Human Development Report, 1997*, p. 213. © 1997 by United Nations Development Programme. Used by permission of Oxford University Press, Inc.

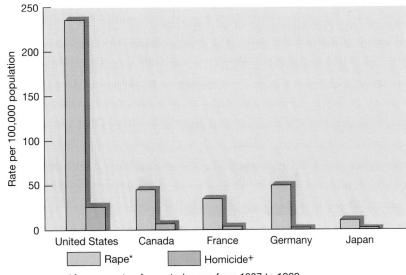

*Average rate of reported rapes from 1987 to 1989.
+Average rate of homicides committed by males from 1985 to 1990.

16.2 percent of violent crime arrests, compared to 28.8 percent of property crime arrests (U.S. Department of Justice, 1998).

The *Uniform Crime Reports* also shows that the crime rate for blacks is higher than it is for whites, although the figure varies from one type of crime to another. Blacks make up about 12.7 percent of the U.S. population; in 1997, they constituted 30.4 percent of all arrests. A number of reasons have been put forth to account for the higher crime rate among blacks. These include (1) differential law enforcement—blacks are often arrested for offenses that either would be ignored or

dealt with informally if committed by whites; (2) the social experiences of blacks, which may predispose more of them to criminal involvement; and (3) distortions of official data—white-collar crime, most often committed by whites, goes largely unreported, but the types of crime most frequently committed by blacks are carefully recorded (Gibbons, 1977; Goode, 1990).

Finally, crime rates show considerable variation by community size and by region of the country. Large cities display higher crime rates than do small cities, and urban areas have more crime than rural areas. The Northeast has the lowest rates of homicide, forcible rape, aggravated

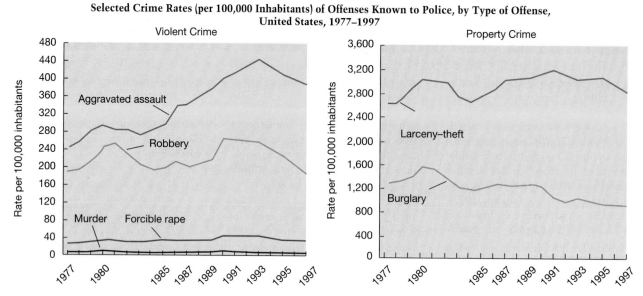

FIGURE 8.2 Although crime levels decreased after 1981, the late 1980s saw a rise in the number of violent crimes. After leveling off, violent crime began to decrease in the 1990s.

Source: U.S. Bureau of the Census, *Statistical Abstract of the United States, 1997* (Washington, D.C.: U.S. Government Printing Office, 1997); U.S. Department of Justice, Federal Bureau of Investigation, *Uniform Crime Reports for the United States, 1997* (Washington, D.C.: U.S. Government Printing Office).

assault, burglary, and larceny-theft. The Midwest has the lowest rate for robbery. The South, on the other hand, has the highest rates for homicide, forcible rape, aggravated assault, burglary, and larceny-theft (see Figure 8.3).

The overall rate for Crime Index offenses in 1997 was estimated at 4,923 Crime Index offenses for each 100,000 in the United States population—the lowest since 1974. Nationally, this rate is down 10 percent from the 1993 rate and 13 percent from the 1988 level.

"REAL" VERSUS REPORTED CRIME

We must look at official crime statistics with a critical eye, however. Crimes officially known to the police make up only a small fraction of all crimes committed. And although the FBI collects data from all over the country, the police agencies that contribute these data vary tremendously in the accuracy of their methods of data collection. In fact, sometimes data are purposely recorded in a way that presents the police in a good light.

Ironically, it appears that the sharp decline in crime rates in recent years has actually put pressure on some police departments to falsify crime reports. In 1998, police departments in New York City, Atlanta, Philadelphia, and Boca Raton, Florida were charged with

altering crime statistics (*New York Times,* August 3, 1998). By systematically downgrading property crimes like burglaries to vandalism, trespassing, or missing property, a Boca Raton police captain reduced the city's felony rate by almost 11 percent in 1997. And, he did so with the knowledge of the police chief. Philadelphia had to withdraw its crime statistics from the FBI's system for 1996, 1997, and the first half of 1998 because police there had altered crime statistics in a similar way.

While police departments can tamper with the information they provide to the FBI, they have no control over another major source of data about crime—the National Crime Victimization Survey (NCVS), which is collected by the Bureau of Justice through a cooperative arrangement with the Census Bureau. The first NCVS was conducted in 1972 in an attempt to determine the "true rate of crime" in urban America. The U.S. Census Bureau was asked to conduct a victimization survey in 13 large cities: Twenty-two thousand randomly selected residents and 2,000 businesspeople were asked if they had been victims of crime. This survey reported two or three times more crime than was shown for the same period by the official reports of the FBI. In one large city, the survey revealed five times more offenses than were officially reported. In some cases, cities have rates of victimization close to the ones reported in the Uniform Crime Report. New York City, which has had a reputation for being a high-crime city, turned out to have one of the lowest rates of self-reported victimization (Schmalleger, 1997).

The results of the first National Crime Victimization Surveys changed the way that criminologists thought about crime. They realized that people may fail to report crimes for many reasons. Studies show that they do not expect the police to be able to do anything, or that too much time and effort are required, especially for minor crimes. Some people fear the criminal may take revenge on them. Some—rape victims, for example—fear insensitivity and harassment by the police. Also people are less likely to report crimes committed by friends and relatives than crimes committed by strangers. The poor report crimes less often than do middle-class victims. And commuters, tourists, and others passing through an area often fail to report crime because they do not have time to follow through with investigations. As a rule, the more serious a crime—if it involves a weapon, for example, or personal injury—the more likely the victim is to report it (Booth, Johnson, & Choldin, 1997; Skogan, 1979).

Today, National Crime Victimization Surveys are conducted twice a year with a national sample of 42,000 households. Despite the attempts of a few police departments to portray their own crime statistics in a better light, the 1997 figures from the NCVS confirm the information contained in the Uniform Crime Report, which indicates that crimes rates in the United States have continued to drop in recent years. According to the NCVS figures, violent crime fell nearly 7 percent to its lowest rate in at least 24 years, and property crime dropped to its lowest level since the government conducted the first NCVS (*Star Tribune*, December 28, 1998).

Public perceptions of crime are not necessarily linked to official statistics like these. For example, even though actual crime rates have continued to drop in recent years, many people believe that there is more crime in the United States today than in the past. Thus, the findings of a recent Gallup Poll showed that 56 percent of Americans thought that there was more crime in the United States in 1998 than there was five years earlier. Only 35 percent thought there was less crime.

Surprisingly, this same poll showed that the public's fear of crime has dropped. When asked about five

FIGURE 8.3 Homicide data reveal that killers and their victims are usually intimates, and that both male and female murderers are more likely to kill males than females.

Source: Federal Bureau of Investigation, *Uniform Crime Reports, 1998* (Washington, D.C.: U.S. Government Printing Office).

Composite Portrait of Homicide Rates in the United States

	Most Frequent	Least Frequent
Geographical region	South	Northeast
Size of community	Large cities	Very small communities
Weapon used	Firearms	Poison
Murderer	Family member or friend of victim	Stranger to victim
Murderer's race	Same as victim	Different from victim
Socioeconomic status of murderer	Low	High
Sex of murderer and victim	Male murderer, male victim	Female murderer, female victim

different types of crime (murder, mugging, burglary, rape, and being attacked in a car), fewer people expressed high levels of worry in 1998 than in 1993. The responses to other questions asked in this poll suggest that Americans' fear of crime has dropped for a number of reasons. Some people feel less threatened by crime because of changes they made in their own lives to protect themselves. Others indicate that they have more confidence in the police's ability to protect the public. And some cite a lower crime rate.

THE ISSUE OF GENDER

If one were to pick a single factor that is more often associated with the commission of crime than any other, that factor would probably be gender. In all cultures, women commit far fewer crimes (and are less deviant in general) than men. And, as noted earlier, the crimes that women do commit are principally nonviolent property crimes; the motivation for these crimes is largely personal economic gain (Simon & Landis, 1991).

The reasons for this relationship between crime and gender have been the subject of much research and discussion. One possible explanation is that women are by nature physically weaker and less aggressive than men (Gove, 1985; Leonard, 1982). Some social scientists put more emphasis, however, on the different positions of males and females in the social structure. One such explanation focuses on the gender roles into which males and females are socialized. Women act on deviant impulses less often because of the conservative nature of their gender roles (Jensen & Raymond, 1976), it is argued, whereas men exhibit more deviance because male gender roles are commonly characterized by aggressiveness and machismo (Thornton & James, 1979). Many social scientists have noted that males and females have very different opportunities to commit crime; also, most cultures place a much greater stigma on female criminals than on male criminals (Heidensohn, 1987). To date, however, the evidence to support these various theories is limited, and the issue of the role of gender in crime and deviance remains an active and exciting topic of sociological research.

Historical Trends in Crime Rates

When the FBI implemented the Uniform Crime Report Program in 1930, it received crime information from law enforcement agencies in 400 cities in 43 states. Today over 17,000 city, county, and state law enforcement agencies provide crime information to the FBI. Since 1930, the trends in crime rates have shown two major shifts. The first occurred during the early 1940s when a large number

of young men entered the military to serve in World War II. In the absence of the most crime-prone group in the population, crime rates feel (Schmalleger, 1997).

The second major shift involved a dramatic increase in crime rates beginning in the 1960s. One factor that sociologists link to this shift is the effect of the high birth rate following World War II (Steffensmeier & Streifel, 1991; Schmalleger, 1997). As we noted in the last section, criminal behavior is heavily concentrated in the younger age groups. Between 1960 and 1975, the population aged 14 to 25 increased by 63 percent, more than six times the increase in all other age groups combined. Charles Silberman (1978) estimated that this increase in the number of young people in the population alone should have brought about an increase in crime amounting to 40 to 50 percent, all other factors being equal. But the actual increase in serious crime during that period was closer to 200 percent.

Sociologists do not agree on what accounts for the difference between the expected 50 percent increase and the actual 200 percent increase in crime in the 1960s. Some have emphasized the fact that addictive drugs became more widely available in this decade. Others cite the heightened sense of deprivation encouraged among the poor by TV portrayals of the "good life." Still others point to increased violence on television and the growth of a variety of deviant subcultures. Finally, a case can be made that there were simply too many young people all at one time for the nation to be able to socialize them properly.

One factor that experts associate with high rates of violent crimes is the widespread popularity of drugs. In earlier decades, law enforcement officials estimated that only about 20 percent of people arrested for serious crimes were using drugs. However, research conducted in major cities during the summer of 1992 found much higher percentages of persons arrested for major crimes testing positive for the recent use of illicit drugs, with figures ranging from highs of 80 percent in Philadelphia and 77 percent in New York City and San Diego to lows of 48 percent in San Antonio and Omaha (U.S. National Institute of Justice, 1992).

Most of the violent crime associated with drugs takes the form of shootings associated with conflicts among drug distributors over turf; these crimes are a direct result of the high profits that can be generated by drug sales rather than from the chemical effects of drugs, per se. However, some drugs, especially PCP, do break down inhibitions and can lead directly to violence. Furthermore, the use of highly addictive drugs like crack cocaine frequently impels addicts to engage in crimes of violence such as robbery in order to obtain funds to support their habits.

SOCIOLOGY OF THE MEDIA

CELEBRATED CRIME CASES

On Tuesday, June 20, 1893, a jury declared Lizzie Borden not guilty of murdering her father and stepmother. Despite the verdict, this case would go down in history as one of this country's most celebrated. Lizzie Borden became a cultural legend, immortalized by schoolchildren in the rhyming cadence:

> Lizzie Borden took an axe
> And gave her mother forty
> whacks;
> When she saw what she had done
> She gave her father forty-one.

(Spiering, 1984, p. 202)

Cases like this are atypical. They are what Samuel Walker calls "celebrated cases"—the ones that make the news (1994). In reality, it might be more accurate to say that the news makes them. Consider, for example, the *New York Times* account of the Borden murders that appeared on Friday, August 5, 1892:

> Andrew J. Borden and wife, two of the eldest, wealthiest and most highly respected persons in the city, were brutally murdered with an axe at 11 o'clock this morning in their home on Second Street within a few minutes walk of the City Hall. The Borden family consisted of the father, mother, two daughters and a servant. The elder daughter has been in Fairhaven for some days. The rest of the family have been ill for three or four days and Dr. Bowen, the attending physician, thought they had been poisoned.
>
> Miss Lizzie Borden, the youngest daughter, was in the barn when she heard a cry of distress coming apparently from the house and she ran in. Going directly to a sitting room leading from the main hallway in the house she saw the father

lying back on the sofa, lifeless and covered with blood.

> She ran out again shrieking and her cries attracted the servant and a neighbor. They made a hasty search for the mother and found her upstairs in a spare room lying dead, face downward, on the floor. The women ran downstairs terrified and summoned Dr. Bowen who lives opposite. He found both of the victims dead. Then the daughter and servant fainted.
>
> The city is thoroughly excited over the murders and about a dozen different theories have been advanced by the police who have as yet not the slightest clue to the murderer. The stomachs of both victims were removed and placed in alcohol. They will be sent to Boston tomorrow for analysis to determine whether milk poisoning was attempted. The police are suspicious of John V. Morse, brother-in-law of Mr. Borden by his first marriage.

(Cited in Spiering, 1984, pp. 43–44)

This story was designed to capture national curiosity (Spiering, 1984). In fact, neither Lizzie Borden nor the servant fainted. But that fabrication created the kind of melodrama that would appeal to readers. And it contributed to the mystery surrounding the identity of the murderer.

In the 100 years that have passed since the Borden murders, many celebrity cases have made the news. In recent years these have included the cases of Bernard Goetz, Claus von Bulow, Jeffrey Dahmer, the Menendez brothers, and O.J. Simpson. Each of these cases received immense publicity—the key characteristic of celebrity cases (Walker, 1994). The media dubbed the O.J. Simpson case the trial of the century and turned it into a national soap opera. Americans tuned

in daily to catch the latest twist in the double murder mystery. One sociologist described the unprecedented media coverage as follows:

> Even before the trial began, the Simpson case received daily attention from the national media. Near its finish, media watchers declared that the Simpson trial had received more coverage than any other single event in the history of television—with networks and cable channels broadcasting thousands of hours of courtroom testimony, talkshow interviews with key personnel, and expert testimony. (Schmalleger, 1997, p. 17)

Cases like that of O.J. Simpson illustrate the adversarial system of criminal justice—a model that involves fierce fights between the prosecutor and defense attorney. Success ultimately depends on the legal skills and the power of oratory, which explains why the celebrities in these cases are not defended by public defenders or court-appointed attorneys but by high profile celebrity defense attorneys, like Simpson's "dream team."

This kind of drama fascinates the public and drives media coverage. Unfortunately, what the public receives is a distorted perception of the criminal justice system. Unlike celebrity cases, typical cases do not involve the full criminal process (Walker, 1994). These cases are not hotly contested and do not entail controversies about the admissibility of evidence, the credibility of witnesses, or the competence of the prosecutor, judge, and defense attorney. In fact, the typical case does not involve a jury trial, but rather a negotiated settlement. And without the benefit of a "dream team," most of these defendants plead guilty (Barkan, 1997).

Crime Control: The Criminal Justice System

In the United States, the criminal justice system is an interlocking network of three distinct institutions: the police, the courts, and the correctional system.

THE POLICE

Crime control is the police function most in the public eye. Yet, until the twentieth century, the major function of the police was to maintain order rather than to enforce the law. The maintenance of order—for example, police intervention in domestic squabbles—rarely leads to arrests (Carey, 1978). And even today, enforcing the criminal law probably occupies no more than 20 percent of police officers' time. The main activity of most local police forces is traffic control.

The police are always under great public pressure to "perform," a pressure that has promoted the development of a distinct police subculture. One element of this subculture frequently noted by sociologists is a high level of suspiciousness—a belief that people cannot be trusted and are dangerous (Manning, 1974; Skolnik, 1966; Westley, 1970; Wilson, 1968). Stemming from the danger that the police continually face as a part of their job, this belief sometimes colors their general attitudes, isolating them from the average citizen and confining them to their own special world.

While in training at a police academy, new recruits undergo formal socialization processes. Among other things, they must learn the formal rules that govern the use of force, a right given exclusively to them by society. Yet society does little to help them make the often difficult decisions regarding when the use of force is warranted and just how much to use. They must internalize the distinctions between *legal force*, that which is sufficient to take a suspect into custody; *normal force*, that which is required under specific circumstances (though not always lawful or highly regarded); and *excessive force*, that which is brutal and unnecessary. In practice, much of the socialization of police officers is completed on the street—an informal learning process or "second training" that is as important as that in the academy (Hunt, 1985).

THE COURTS

The second part of the criminal justice system is the courts. In theory, the courts serve to determine the guilt or innocence of individuals accused of crimes and to decide on the punishment for those convicted. A prosecuting attorney represents the state; a defense attorney represents the defendant; and a judge mediates the process. A defendant who can afford to do so hires his or her own defense attorney; otherwise the court appoints one. If the defendant pleads guilty, there is no trial; the judge simply decides on the sentence. If the defendant pleads innocent, there may be a jury trial.

The popular image of the courts as a place where the state and the defense present cases against and for the defendant is far from accurate, however. The court system is actually a complex bureaucracy, and most cases are settled through a process of negotiation. In order to handle the increasing number of cases, the courts have resorted more and more to *plea bargaining*. This is a process in which judges and prosecutors negotiate with defendants to get them to plead guilty to lesser crimes than the ones with which they are charged, thus avoiding jury trials, saving money, and taking some of the strain off an already overcrowded system. In many courts, more than 90 percent of all felony indictments are decided by plea bargaining.

The prevalence of plea bargaining probably contributes to growing public dissatisfaction with the criminal justice system. Dissatisfaction is also expressed with the courts' sentencing of criminals once they are convicted. Increasingly, people feel that sentences need to be tougher. One study of persons arrested on felony charges in 11 states found that 62 percent were convicted but that only 36 percent ended up serving time in jail. One-third of those convicted of violent crimes were sentenced to serve more than a year in prison (*New York Times*, January 19, 1988).

The court system is not always adequately prepared to handle new legal issues that arise as a result of technological innovation or cultural change. For example, 46 states enacted computer crime statutes between 1981 and 1985. Despite this concentrated legislative activity, a national survey of county prosecutors in states with computer laws found very low levels of prosecutorial activity. Why? There were no precedents for this new category of crime in the court cases. Consequently, it was difficult to know how to apply such traditional legal concepts as theft and fraud to computer abuse (Pfuhl, 1987).

The court system has also been taken to task in recent years for its treatment of women. Is the courts' traditional conception of what a "reasonable man" would do in a given set of circumstances fully applicable to what a "reasonable woman" would do? Aren't some current courtroom procedures biased against women? For example, some have argued that the requirement of giving testimony in public in front of a relatively large group of people may put some women at a disadvantage, because "domestic isolation will have given them fewer chances for public performances than men" (Carlen & Worrall, 1987, p. 13).

It is clear, however, that the women's movement has had some impact on the treatment of women in the courts. In response to the feminist demand for equal treatment, there has been some movement away from the relative lenience with which courts have traditionally handled women—especially middle-class white women—who are accused of crimes. The "chivalry hypothesis" appears to be losing its validity. Furthermore, rape is punished more severely than it was previously (Heilbrun & Heilbrun, 1986), and a variety of steps have been taken in many jurisdictions to make it easier and less traumatic for women to prosecute men who rape them.

THE CORRECTIONAL SYSTEM

The correctional system was established to apply sanctions and other measures to criminals convicted by the courts. At the heart of the correctional system in the United States are the prisons. This nation has the highest rate of imprisonment in the world; the number of imprisoned Americans increased from 196,000 in 1970 to 789,000 in 1991 (U.S. Bureau of Justice Statistics). The great majority of convicted criminals are either on probation or parole, however. *Probation* is a period of time during which offenders, instead of serving a prison term, are more or less closely supervised while continuing to live in the community. *Parole* is the conditional release of offenders from prison, usually for good behavior, before their full sentence is served.

A correctional system may, in theory, be designed to accomplish one or more of four basic purposes: *retribution,* seeking revenge for a crime on behalf of both the victim and society as a whole; *incapacitation,* restricting the freedom of the offender so that he or she will be less able to commit further crimes; *rehabilitation,* seeking to reform the offender so that he or she will return to law-abiding ways; and *deterrence,* attempting to reduce criminal activity by instilling a fear of punishment.

Although humanitarians would like to see additional emphasis placed on rehabilitation, many experts doubt that this goal is achievable in the prison setting. One review of rehabilitation programs in prisons concluded that no type of rehabilitation has been very successful because it is impossible to produce changes in unwilling individuals under the conditions of constraint or indifference prevalent in prisons (Wilson, 1985).

Even changing the conditions of prisons may not help. When prisons are changed to make them more humane, research suggests that no more rehabilitation takes place in them than in traditional penal institutions (Kasselbaum, Ward, & Wilner, 1971). If rehabilitation is to have a chance to become successful, it seems reasonable to suppose that correctional institutions should be

The United States has the highest rate of imprisonment in the world. What are your thoughts on rehabilitation programs in the prison system? Do you think the idea of deterrence works? Would social reform lead to a reduction in crime?

better integrated into the community. As one researcher has noted, punishment must be coupled with fundamental changes in the prisoner's social environment in order to have any positive effect (Saney, 1986).

Deterrence has been the most widely debated purpose of the correctional system in recent years; it has also been the subject of much research. Deterrence is based on the (not entirely realistic) idea that people are rational beings and calculate the risks versus the benefits of committing a particular crime. If deterrence is working, the crime rate should be low when the risk of punishment is high.

Punishment can vary according to *certainty* (likelihood of imprisonment), *severity* (length of sentence), and *swiftness*. Each of these dimensions may play a role in deterrence. Some evidence suggests that crime can be reduced by making the punishment more severe and especially more certain (Gibbs, 1975; Zimring & Hawkins, 1973). Other research (Minor & Harry, 1982; Saltzman et al., 1982) has disputed these findings, however, and it is fair to say that at the present time no firm conclusions about deterrence can be drawn.

The lack of clarity surrounding the effectiveness of both rehabilitation and deterrence lends support to the far-reaching programs of crime prevention long espoused by most sociologists. Though complex, expensive, and politically difficult to enact, broad programs of social reform leading to the reduction of crime-associated factors such as poverty, discrimination, unemployment, broken homes, and inadequate housing may in the long run be the only solution to the problem of crime.

CHAPTER REVIEW

1. The U.S. House of Representatives considered many aspects of President Clinton's behavior before it voted to impeach him. Do you consider what he did social deviance? Why or why not?

2. Give examples of the positive functions that social deviance can serve.

3. Is underage drinking on college campuses a form of social deviance? Why or why not?

4. What kinds of social control could a university use to reduce underage drinking at events that take place on its campus?

5. What kinds of norms have you internalized and consider important enough to teach your own children?

6. Draw the distinction between the social dysfunctions of deviance and social disorganization.

7. Explain why the concept of anomie is central to Merton's structural strain theory.

8. Describe each of the steps involved in the development of a deviant career.

9. Discuss the problems associated with gathering reliable data on crime.

10. Should victimless crimes be decriminalized? Why or why not?

11. Describe the criminal justice system. Do you think your perception of this system fits the actual experience of celebrity defendants like O.J. Simpson? Why or why not? What about the average defendant?

12. Critique each of the following theories: structural strain theory, cultural transmission theory, control theory, culture conflict theory, and Marxian conflict theory.

INTERNET EXERCISE

The Web destinations for Chapter 8 relate to various aspects of deviance, crime, and social control. To begin your search, go to the Prentice Hall companion Web site **http://www.prenhall.com/popenoe.** Then select **Chapter 8** (Deviance, Crime, and Social Control). Next, choose **web destinations** from the menu on the left side of the screen. There are a number of very interesting sites to choose from. We suggest you begin with the **Vera Institute of Justice.** The main screen lists a wide variety of sites that are relevant to criminal justice issues. You may wish to expand your explorations according to your personal interests. You might start by clicking on **Bureau of Justice Statistics.** After you access that site, click on **Key Facts at a Glance.** After you have done this, answer the following questions:

- Based upon the statistics presented by the Bureau of Justice, how would you characterize the crime problem in the United States?

- What do you think explains the high rate of crime in American society?

KEY TERMS

social deviance	**social disorganization**	**deviant career**
social control	**anomie**	**stigma**
internalization	**structural strain theory**	**crime**

CHAPTER 9

Social Stratification

On the morning of April 15, 1912, what was at the time the world's largest passenger ship sank in the icy North Atlantic on its very first voyage. It took this great ship about three hours to go down. Unfortunately, there were not nearly enough lifeboats to save all the passengers. Afterwards, much was made of the fact that, despite the great loss of life, the passengers aboard the *Titanic* had taken care to observe the social norm of saving "women and children first." Perhaps this claim was necessary so that the British public and government could find some solace in the face of this disaster. Women and children were more likely to survive the *Titanic's* sinking; 69 percent of female and child passengers lived, but only 17 percent of male passengers did so.

However, in this case, as in many events that sociologists examine, things were not exactly as they seemed to be. A sociological analysis shows that the first-class section of the ship was populated largely by the wealthy; second class was composed largely of middle-class professionals and businesspersons; and third class (and lower) was occupied largely by poor, working-class immigrants coming to the United States. When the survivorship rates aboard the *Titanic* are compared according to sex and social class, we see that only 26 percent of third-class passengers survived, compared to 44 percent of second-class passengers and 60 percent of first-class passengers. Male passengers in first class survived at a slightly higher rate than did children in third class. Perhaps it would be more accurate to say that the social norm that applied in the case of the *Titanic* was "first- and second-class women and children first."

The story of the sinking of the *Titanic* is just one illustration of the importance of social class. Desirable things in life are distributed unequally in all societies. In this chapter, we discuss the unequal distribution of desirables, what accounts for this pattern of distribution, and how this inequality both reflects and affects a society's social structure. In the following chapter, we will focus more narrowly on wealth and poverty in the United States.

THE DISTRIBUTION OF DESIRABLES

From birth, people in all known societies face inequality—a lack of equal access to the desirable things offered by their society. What is considered desirable varies from culture to culture, and may include material objects (cattle, gold, fresh food, tickets to the World Series) or nonmaterial valuables (prestige, respect, fame). No matter what the desired object, though, one thing is certain: It is scarce, meaning that the demand for it exceeds the supply. Not everyone can own large amounts of gold or be famous. Some people have greater access to the good things in life than others do.

Who are the privileged few in a society? Among animals, it is fairly clear that the rewards go to the physically strong. There is a pecking order among chickens, a ranked organization of hunting packs among wolves and lions, and a dominance hierarchy among many primates, especially certain species of monkeys. In each of these cases, the leaders use their strength to get the other members of the group to cooperate and obey.

Human inequality, in contrast, is based on much more than sheer physical power. In the simplest human societies, personal qualities alone may explain most of the social inequality. The leader of a band of hunter-gatherers, for instance, usually wins that role through bravery, age, and personal strength. But in more complex human societies, personal traits combine with social factors—such as race or the wealth of one's parents—to determine privilege.

Inequality in complex societies is somewhat like the ranking of apartments in an urban high rise, in which the desirable goods include sunlight, distance from street noise, and a scenic view. The best apartments are located in the upper stories, where there is a lot of light, not much noise and pollution, and a good view. Further down, the air is not as clean, the apartments get less direct sunlight, and the view disappears. The rents also drop, bringing these apartments within reach of less affluent people. Each floor can be thought of as a separate layer, or *stratum,* of privilege. By the time we get to the basement, where the building's maintenance workers have their quarters, we have reached the opposite of the top-floor penthouse with its outdoor gardens and pool, unlimited light, and 360-degree view.

The residents of such a building, like the members of societies, are arranged in a system of **social stratification**—an enduring pattern based on the ranking of groups or categories of people into social positions according to their access to desirables. In an influential analysis that is still the basis for many sociological studies of inequality, Max Weber (1919/1946) identified three key dimensions of social stratification. Using terminology modified somewhat from that employed by Weber, we usually call these dimensions *wealth and income* (economic status), *power* (political status), and *prestige* (social status).

These dimensions are sometimes called the "rewards" of society, but the term *rewards* is misleading because it implies that those who receive them have done something to deserve them. Yet children born to royalty, for instance, are given wealth and prestige at birth and power as soon as they are old enough to exercise it. Often, then, social desirables are given to people who happen to be in a good social position, not only to those who achieve them on the basis of personal merit.

Income and Wealth

Wealth consists of all the economic assets of a person or group—not only money but also material objects, land, natural resources, and productive labor services. Some of the objects defined as wealth may have value because of the hours of skilled labor that go into making them, some because of their beauty, and some because they will bring future economic rewards. Diamonds have value, for instance, because they are both scarce and beautiful. A letter signed by George Washington has value because it is rare and has historic, patriotic, and sentimental appeal. Land is valued because it can be used to produce other economic assets in the form of crops or minerals.

Closely related to wealth is **income**—the economic gain derived from the use of human or material resources. The concepts of wealth and income should not be confused. *Wealth* refers to the total of all the possessions owned by a person or group. *Income* typically refers to the amount of money that a person or group receives on a regular basis. When we say that a man is "worth three million dollars," we are giving an estimate of his wealth— the sum total of all his liquid and nonliquid assets: his house, his car, his investments, his bank accounts, and the money in his wallet. When we say that the same man earns $350,000 annually, we are describing his income.

Income is typically expressed as a flow of money per unit of time. But not all income is in the form of money. When family members do their own home repairs and housework, for example, these actions do not produce money. But they do increase the real value of the household. They produce "nonmoney income": If the members of the family did not do these tasks themselves, they would have to pay someone else to do them.

Although almost all of us would like to possess wealth and income, some people always have more than others. Among nations, too, there is an unequal distribution of economic reward. In Turkey, the per capita *gross national product*—a country's total economic output divided by the number of people living in the country— was $3,130 in 1997. In the United States in the same year, it was $28,740, more than 9 times higher. In Bangladesh, one of the poorest countries in the world, the per capita gross national product is only $270 (World Bank, 1998). A nation's wealth is based largely on its natural resources, the strength of its economy, and the kinds of power (military, for example) it can use to obtain resources from other nations.

The pattern of the unequal distribution of income in the United States is based on place of residence, race,

Social desirables are not only given to those who achieve them on the basis of personal merit, they are also given to people who happen to be in a good social position. Athena Roussel-Onassis, heir to the Onassis fortune, will be one of the wealthiest people in the world simply because she was born an heiress.

education, gender, occupation, and other variables. For example, in 1997, the median household income for Connecticut residents was $43,985—a substantially higher amount than the median income of families in Arkansas, which was only $26,162. Looking at the ethnic and racial pattern of income distribution, we see that the median U.S. family income was $38,972 for a white family, $26,628 for a Hispanic family, and $25,050 for an Afican-American family (U.S. Bureau of the Census, 1998). These income differences are even more significant than they may seem at first because the average family size of nonwhites is larger than that of whites. Thus, the lower incomes of nonwhite families must be stretched to meet the needs of more people.

The degree of inequality in the distribution of income in the United States is underscored by other important data. The wealthiest 20 percent of American families receive 49.4 percent of the total national income, whereas the poorest 20 percent receive only 3.6 percent (U.S. Bureau of the Census, 1998). Table 9.1 shows the percentage of total income received by the bottom and top fifths of the populations in 10 countries.

The distribution of wealth in the United States is considerably more unequal than that of income. In 1990, when the top 1 percent of income earners received about 13 percent of all income, the top 1 percent of wealth holders held 31 percent of all net wealth. Indeed, a study conducted by the Federal Reserve Board found that the net

TABLE 9.1   PERCENTAGE OF PRIVATE INCOME RECEIVED BY BOTTOM FIFTH AND TOP FIFTH OF POPULATION, 1995

	Algeria	Brazil	China	Colombia	El Salvador	Indonesia	Mongolia	Nepal	Paraguay	United States (1994 data)
Bottom Fifth	7.0%	2.5%	5.5%	3.1%	3.7%	9.2%	7.3%	7.6%	2.3%	4.8%
Top Fifth	42.6%	64.2%	47.5%	61.5%	54.4%	39.3%	40.9%	44.8%	62.4%	45.2%

Source: From *World Development Indicators,* 1998 (www.worldbank.org/data/pdfs/tab2_8.pdf)

worth of the top 1 percent of the population exceeds that of the bottom 90 percent (Gilbert & Kahl, 1992)!

In the U.S. economy, the poorest people are often those who are the least productive economically. They may be too old or too young to work; they may not be educated enough to get high-paying jobs; they may be discriminated against in finding or advancing in jobs; or they may have to stay home to take care of children. No matter what the reason is, the result is the same: The amount of a family's income is closely tied to how much that family produces, as measured in the economic marketplace.

The pattern of income and wealth distribution in the United States may seem natural, but it is by no means universal. Because the American economy has expanded for most of its history, we often assume that wealth is something a person earns. In a more static economy, however, where the amount of wealth is relatively fixed, wealth is more likely to be something that one inherits rather than something one gains through personal achievement.

In socialist societies, at least ideally, wealth is based on need rather than on what one produces. In other words, "To each according to his needs, from each according to his abilities." A very large family in a socialist country, for example, might receive special payments to help with its additional expenses. People who do not produce through no fault of their own—such as the old and the sick—also receive state support. Even in these societies, however, "productive" people have access to rewards not available to others. In both the People's Republic of China and Cuba, for example, the distribution of income is far from equal (Azicri, 1988; Tsui, 1991).

Power

Sociologists use the term **power** to refer to the capacity of people or groups to control or influence the actions of others, whether those others wish to cooperate or not. Sociologists study power not only in order to determine

who exercises it but also to see why it is exercised and who benefits from its use.

Of the three main types of desirables—wealth and income, power, and prestige—power is the hardest to measure. Most studies of power are nothing more than educated guesses. Many forms of power are so well hidden that they are fully understood only by the power holders themselves. Because it is so hard to measure, and because it is so closely connected to questions of *ideology* (the set of cultural beliefs that is linked to, and helps to maintain, various political, social, and class interests), the subject of power—who holds it and how it is used—is much debated in sociology. Some social scientists maintain that power in America is concentrated in the hands of a few people who share a common background and who tend to act together (Domhoff, 1978, 1983, 1998; Dye, 1995). For example, C. Wright Mills (1956) suggested that America is run by a "power elite" and calculated its total number at no more than 300 people. Other sociologists disagree strongly, arguing that power in America is divided among many groups and people (Riesman, 1961; Rose, 1967).

Sociologists do agree that real power does not always lie where we think it does. The mayors of some cities, for example, are sometimes mere figureheads and the actual decisions are made by a handful of business leaders who stay behind the scenes. And some decisions are made at lower levels where the work is carried out. Such is often the case with the police officer on the beat or the teacher in the classroom. (The distribution of power in America is discussed further in Chapter 17.)

Clearly, power may exist without wealth: Not all the rich are powerful, and not all the powerful are rich. But the two dimensions are closely related. Wealth can sometimes buy power. In national politics, for instance, candidates for office are often wealthy. The Kennedy brothers, the three Rockefeller governors, and the Roosevelts are only a few examples of men of wealth who have become powerful in politics. Moreover, power is often useful in acquiring wealth. How many lawmakers or generals retire in poverty?

Prestige

The third dimension of social stratification is **prestige**—the favorable evaluation and social recognition that a person receives from others. Prestige comes in many forms: public acceptance and fame, respect and admiration, honor and esteem. Prestige can be gained in many ways. People who are unusually kind, generous, brave, creative, or intelligent are often rewarded with prestige. Money can buy prestige, and power can compel it, or at least its outward appearance. For example, when John D. Rockefeller, Sr., made his first millions in oil, he was publicly despised. Over time, however, he used his great wealth to gain prestige, not only for himself but also for his heirs, by funding museums, parks, foundations, and charities.

Sometimes the process works in reverse. A person may win prestige first and then translate it into wealth. The novelist and journalist Norman Mailer won prestige as a novelist with his first major work, *The Naked and the Dead*. Since its publication, Mailer has turned out a number of best-selling books.

Most often, however, prestige comes from holding a well-regarded occupational position. In American society, for example, prestige is routinely accorded those who are employed in medicine, science, and law. High prestige can also be attained through success in fields much in the public eye, such as television broadcasting, sports, and the film industry.

SOCIAL STATUS AND STATUS RANKING

In general sociological usage, a social status is a socially defined position in a group or society. This usage of social status was discussed in Chapter 4. In relation to stratification, however, the term *social status* has a more specialized meaning: a ranked position in a social hierarchy or stratification system. This usage of social status is commonly referred to by sociologists as **socioeconomic status,** or **SES.** SES is a measure of social status that takes into account a person's educational attainment, income level, and occupational prestige. People who share the same socioeconomic status have access to about the same amount of society's desirables.

Recognizing Social Status

Because so much of life is based on social ranking, pinpointing another person's social status is often important. But recognizing status can be difficult in modern urban

The social status of American athletes is recognized globally. The products they endorse or put their names on have become status symbols for many people in and outside the United States.

settings. We often do not personally know many of the people we meet, yet we must make quick judgments about them. Two conditions must exist if we are to recognize an individual's status correctly: We both must all be aware of the system used to rank status in our society and there must be some generally understood symbols that let us assess the status level of an unknown person.

In everyday life, one can often accurately determine a person's social status by observing how that individual interacts with others and how other people behave toward him or her. Is the person shown a great deal of respect and treated with formality, or is he or she treated informally? What do people say about and to the person? How does he or she react?

We can also look for what sociologists call status symbols. A **status symbol** can be anything—an obviously cheap or expensive object, a style of dress, a manner of speech—that communicates to others that an individual displaying it occupies a particular level of status.

People on low status levels, of course, do not deliberately display symbols of their low ranking. But people on higher status levels do try to advertise their status and to protect that status from being undervalued. Indeed, the farther up the status ladder people are, the more status symbols they are likely to deliberately display.

Think, for instance, about male attire. The symbolic meanings of a blue work shirt and a dress shirt, tie, and jacket are obvious: The man wearing the blue work shirt probably does some kind of physical labor. And the man wearing the tie and jacket probably does "intellectual" work, giving him higher prestige and a larger salary. Many people can also recognize more subtle differences between varieties of suits. A cheap, mass-produced polyester suit differs visibly from an expensive wool suit from

SOCIOLOGY OF THE MEDIA

MEDIA PORTRAYALS OF SOCIAL CLASS

Where do we get our ideas about how the social world is structured? Most of us would say the media—newspapers, magazines, broadcast news, and even programs that entertain us, like soap operas and situation comedies. In fact, images of social class permeate media content (Croteau & Hoynes, 1997). But how close do they come to reality?

A number of studies suggest that the media portray a distorted view of social class in America. Television programs, films, and especially advertisements profile the comfortable lifestyles of middle-class and upper-class Americans. Noticeably absent are images of the lives of the working-class and poor.

How many entertainment programs can you identify that feature working-class or poor Americans? You might have thought of some of those listed in Table 9.2, but there are not many more. In an examination of 262 situation comedies that aired between 1946 and 1990, Richard Butsch found that only 11 percent included blue-collar,

clerical, or service workers (1992). And over 70 percent of the programs portrayed middle-class families. When Butsch examined situation comedies in 1992, approximately 15 percent of the work force in the United States were professionals. And yet 44.5 percent of television families were headed up by a professional (Croteau & Hoynes, 1997). For every nine doctors there was one nurse; for every three professors, one schoolteacher; and the ratio of lawyers to accountants was 9 to 1. The lifestyles of these high-income families exceeded the wildest dreams of the average American family. Incredibly, more than one in five of them employed a servant. As these percentages suggest, such programs do not accurately reflect the distribution of social classes in America.

Even the evening news, which is supposed to be objective, fails to present an accurate picture of our social world. Instead, it features people in positions of power (Croteau & Hoynes, 1997; Gans, 1980). Nothing much has changed in this respect since Herbert Gans studied the people who regularly appeared in the news during

the 1960s and 1970s. His analysis of news stories showed that five kinds of well-known people took up between 70 and 85 percent of all domestic news. They included incumbent presidents, presidential candidates, leading federal officials, state and local officials, and well-known alleged and actual violators of the laws and mores.

Today, politicians and professionals dominate public affair programs such as *Nightline* and the *MacNeil-Lehrer News Hour* (Croteau & Hoynes, 1997). Working-class people do not appear, nor do representatives of organizations that might speak on their behalf. According to David Croteau and William Hoynes, "We might argue that, for many journalists, the very working definition of news is what those in power say and do" (1997, p. 158).

Over the years, a few news stories have focused on consumer concerns. But journalists tend to avoid these kinds of reports because they can jeopardize relationships with advertisers. Take, for example, what happened to the *San Jose Mercury News* in 1995 when it ran a story that suggested what

an exclusive men's store. Within the upper status levels, however, even more subtle distinctions exist that outsiders may not perceive. These distinctions—between a suit from a good men's store, for example, and one that is custom-made—are often crucially important to members of high-status groups.

Many other items are used as symbols of status. A house, a neighborhood, a rug, a choice of words, a breed of dog, a car, a painting on the wall—all these things are potential signs of social position to those who know how to read them. And we are all skilled at reading at least the symbols of our own status level, though we may do this without thinking consciously about it.

When people demonstrate their socioeconomic status by blatantly displaying status symbols, they are engaging in **conspicuous consumption** (Veblen, 1899/1967). Examples are ownership of expensive and

economically unproductive items, such as well-tended lawns and fur coats. People who have recently acquired great wealth sometimes try to demonstrate their new status through conspicuous consumption. These newly wealthy people, referred to as "nouveau riche," buy expensive things—such as polo ponies and yachts—which symbolize the lifestyle of the very wealthy.

Yet status symbols can also mislead. A status symbol may be used fraudulently by people who do not in fact possess the status reflected by the symbol. To present the impression of higher economic status, families may buy furniture for their living rooms or cars that they can barely afford. Executives in large companies sometime spend money and behave in ways that are more appropriate for the status level above them. In this way, they hope to convince their bosses that they should be promoted. If they get the promotion, they expect that the consumers should consider when buying a new car. Fearing that stories like this would jeopardize their car sales, 47 local auto dealers canceled 52 pages of advertising in the paper's weekly "drive" section (Croteau & Hoynes, 1997)—a $1 million loss for the paper. While the Federal Trade Commission eventually ruled that the auto dealers' action was illegal, this case illustrates how powerful groups influence—directly and indirectly—what appears in the news.

According to Daniel Rossides, even though the mass media tend to homogenize what the upper and lower classes experience, the media industry still promotes the worldview of the upper classes (1997). It is actually in the media's interest to do so. With a heavy reliance on advertisers for revenue, the media must appeal to readers and viewers with enough money to buy the products that they advertise (Croteau & Hoynes, 1997). Thus, for example, while 80 percent of Americans do not own stock, newspapers devote pages to stock market reports in their business sections. Evening news programs also make these

reports a major feature of their 22-minute broadcasts.

In an effort to reach wealthier customers, the *Los Angeles Times* actually increased the price of the paper from 35 cents to 50 cents in inner-city neighborhoods, while it reduced the price to 25 cents in wealthier ones (Cole, 1995). Reflecting a similar strategy, ABC created a profile of the audience it sought to capture (Croteau & Hoynes, 1997). The network entitled it: "Some People Are More Valuable Than Others" (Wilson & Gutierrez, 1995, p. 23).

TABLE 9.2	TELEVISION PROGRAMS FEATURING WORKING-CLASS OR POOR AMERICANS	
Program	*Occupation of Main Character*	
The Honeymooners	Ralph	Bus driver
The Flintstones	Fred	Crane operator
All in the Family	Archie	Dock worker
Sanford and Son	Fred	Garbage collector
Roseanne	Roseanne	Factory worker
Family Matters	Carl	Police officer
Married with Children	Al	Shoe salesman
Simpsons	Homer	Nuclear power plant technician
Grace under Fire	Grace	Factory worker

higher salary that goes along with the new job will cover their costs.

C. Wright Mills (1956) once suggested that "status panic" was prevalent in the American middle class, partly because of the spread to the working class of such status symbols as cars and nice clothes. The middle classes, he argued, devote much attention to their choices of where to live and in their pursuit of leisure in order to achieve more exclusive status symbols.

Because most status symbols can be displayed by those outside the appropriate status ranking, the most useful symbols are those that are hardest to fake. Thus, symbols of high status are often costly, and they change frequently. The lower classes, for example, cannot possibly afford to keep up with the changing high fashions in clothing. And many status symbols have a faddish aspect—one year high-status people have Yorkshire

terriers, and the next they have Shar-Peis. Such symbols are especially useful because it takes time for outsiders to notice the changes.

The Ranking of Social Statuses

Many of the examples of status given so far pertain to occupation, primarily because in modern societies one's occupation is the most important social position a person holds (Blau & Duncan, 1967). Both income and prestige levels are typically heavily influenced by occupation. The connection is not, however, always as close as it might seem at first. Table 9.3 shows a ranking of occupations by prestige. We can see from the table that jobs that pay the most tend to be highest in prestige and those that pay the least are generally the lowest. But this is not always the case. A justice of the U.S. Supreme Court, one of the

TABLE 9.3   DISTRIBUTION OF PRESTIGE RATINGS

Occupation	Rating	Occupation	Rating
Physician	86	Secretary	46
Lawyer	75	Insurance sales	45
Postsecondary teacher	74	Public transportation attendant	42
Dentist	72	Data-entry keyer	41
High government official	70	Auto mechanic	40
Clergy	69	Receptionist	39
Civil engineer	69	Brick/stone mason	36
Registered nurse	66	Hairdresser	36
Accountant and auditor	65	Sales counter clerk	34
Air traffic controller	65	Bulldozer operator	34
Elementary school teacher	64	Bus driver	32
Airline pilot	61	Billing clerk	31
Police/detective	60	Truck driver	30
Dietician	56	Cashier	29
Firefighter	53	Taxi driver/chauffer	28
Social worker	52	Waiter/waitress	28
Dental hygenist	52	Garbage collector	28
Manager, administrator	51	Bartender	25
Electrician	51	Farm worker	23
Computer operator	50	Household servant/cleaner	23
Funeral director	49	Janitor and cleaner	22
Machinist	47	Garage, service station occupations	21
Mail carrier	47		

Note: This table shows the way the American public ranks various occupations. Research has shown these prestige rankings to be relatively constant over time.

Source: James A. Davis and Tom W. Smith, General Social Survey Cumulative File, 1972–1994, *Cumulative Codebook* (Chicago: National Opinion Research Center, 1994), Appendix F.

highest ranked positions, makes more than $100,000 a year. But a director of a large company or a successful doctor or lawyer who works in a big city like New York or Los Angeles earns even more. The high prestige of the justice is due to the power this position holds and to the years of education and experience required to attain it. The position is also highly selective: There are only nine U.S. Supreme Court justices.

The prestige ranking of various occupations has remained remarkably stable over time. One study found that very little change had occurred in the rankings since 1925 (Hodge, Siefel, & Rossi, 1964; see also Guppy & Goyder, 1984). Another study comparing the prestige rankings of occupations in 1947 and 1963 showed an almost perfect (.99) correlation. There was, however, a slight increase in the prestige of jobs in the sciences and a mild drop for "culturally oriented" occupations, such as teaching.

The prestige ranking of occupations is also similar in different communities and regions within the United States and among nations. A study of six communities of different sizes in two different regions found that prestige rankings, along with other aspects of the stratification system, were similar from place to place. This seems to reflect a national pattern (Curtis & Jackson, 1977). Another study comparing status rankings in 60 countries, including the United States, also found a high (.83) degree of correlation (Treiman, 1977). An even higher correlation was established by previous studies that focused only on modern, industrial societies (Inkeles & Rossi, 1956).

Still, important differences exist between the United States and other cultures. In the former Soviet Union, for example, working-class occupations were generally accorded higher prestige (and income) than they are in the United States. In fact, the Soviet population consistently placed routine white-collar jobs near the bottom of the prestige ladder, above unskilled manual workers but below skilled manual workers (Lane, 1987). This preference in favor of skilled manual occupations continues to be widely held in modern-day Russia. However, it is increasingly challenged as recently unleashed market forces reduce the importance of old and obsolete industries and encourage the development of new enterprises and a middle class (Horn, 1991).

But occupation and income are not the only important factors that determine an individual's social status ranking. In the United States, many people base status ranking in part on skin color (Hughes & Hertel, 1990). In fact, cross-cultural studies have suggested that lighter skin colors are preferred not just in the United States but also throughout the world. In Japan, for example, matrimonial ads in newspapers frequently mention light skin as a desirable quality in a prospective spouse. This is why Japanese women looking for husbands frequently use facial powder, parasols, and face hoods to make themselves appear paler (Frost, 1986). Religion is also ranked (in the United States, Protestants have higher status than Catholics and Jews; among Protestants, Episcopalians rank highest), as is education (those who have earned graduate degrees are at the top; those who never went to school are at the bottom).

In most cultures, men have traditionally been ranked higher than women. Also, people who are married generally have a higher status than those who are either single or divorced. Finally, there still exists a ranking based on ethnicity: Descendants of the original Anglo-Saxon settlers rank at the top, and those of foreign-born non-European heritage rank toward the bottom.

Status Inconsistency

Although each individual occupies many ranked social statuses, people generally show a marked degree of **status consistency.** That is, people who rank high in one area also usually rank high in other status hierarchies. For example, an individual with high occupational rank usually also has a high income. Furthermore, a high ranking in education, ethnicity, and color often helps a person to achieve high occupational rank. The various status levels may not be exactly equal, but people in any given quartile of one status hierarchy will generally be in the same quartile of the other major status hierarchies. Research has shown that people whose general social position is toward the middle levels of the hierarchy tend to have somewhat lower status consistency than do those at the upper and lower levels (Gilbert & Kahl, 1992).

It is not uncommon, however, especially in the United States, for people to display **status inconsistency.**

Would you consider former Chief of Staff, General Colin Powell's achievement both professionally and personally an example of status inconsistency? Were all opportunities available to him? Did he have to work harder to achieve this status because of his racial background?

That is, an individual may rank high in one status area and low in another. Status inconsistency results, for example, when education and personal skill help a person rise above ethnic background or residence to achieve a high-status job. An African-American physician is an example of status inconsistency. Another is Justice Sandra Day O'Connor of the U.S. Supreme Court. Occupationally, her status is very high, even though her sex is generally ranked lower.

Some status inconsistency is built into work that has high prestige but low income, such as the ministry. Although they have high occupational prestige, the clergy typically make less money than, for example, lower-ranked accountants and airline pilots (see Table 9.2 for prestige ratings). The average minister cannot afford to live in the style that is associated with high occupational status.

People with inconsistent statuses generally attempt to claim the highest one as their "overall" status. For example, royalty from foreign countries often expect to be treated as royalty, even by those who are not their subjects. But others may be inclined to treat them simply as "foreigners" or noncitizens.

HISTORICAL SYSTEMS OF STRATIFICATION

Stratification systems vary in different historical eras and economic structures. Sociologists consider the most significant types of stratification to be slavery, caste, estate, and class systems. Each type is characterized by a different kind of economic relationship between major social groups.

Slavery

Freedom or liberty is a highly valued nonmaterial desirable. **Slavery** is an extreme system of stratified inequality in which freedom is denied to one group of people in society. Many societies, including the antebellum South, found it expedient to forcibly import slaves from other societies.

The essential feature of slavery is an economic relationship: Some people own other people. Because they are owned, slaves provide an inexpensive form of labor for their owners. In addition, slaves are themselves commodities that can be sold in the marketplace for a profit (Collins, 1990).

Slavery is most compatible with an economy in which production methods are relatively primitive and require large amounts of human labor. The antebellum South is a good example. It was characterized by an agricultural economy centered around plantations, or very large farms. The major crop was cotton, which required a great deal of human labor to plant, cultivate, harvest, process, and transport.

All stratification systems are justified by an ideology that defends the interests of the higher-ranked individuals and that, more or less successfully, convinces members of the lower-ranked category that their inequality is just and proper. Without such an ideology, it would be difficult or impossible to secure compliance and maintain order among the losers in the struggle for wealth and income, power, and prestige. In the case of American slavery, African-Americans were very different from those who enslaved them, especially with respect to culture and physical appearance. This facilitated the spread of an ideology that defined those who were enslaved as biologically and culturally inferior, perhaps even subhuman.

Slavery was the most visible feature of stratification in the United States for the first 200 years of its history. It is important to note, however, that this system of stratification required a great deal of repressive social control. Slaves often resisted their condition by revolting or running away. This demonstrates that the ideology that justified slavery, while broadly accepted by the slaveholders, was frequently rejected by the slaves themselves. Although slavery was abolished more than 125 years ago, its effects linger in the form of racism and discrimination against African-American people in the United States today.

Caste

A caste system is a system of stratified inequality in which status is determined at birth and in which people generally cannot change their social position. In a caste system, it is usually very difficult to marry someone from another rank.

The best-known caste system in history was found in traditional India, where there were only four principal castes (*varnas*), but over a thousand subcategories (*jati*). Each *jati* was characterized by its own traditional occupation, place of residence, and rules for dealing with members of other castes. Indians learned early in childhood to recognize the status symbols that identified the members of the various castes. The highest castes were those of priests (Brahmans) and warriors (*kshatriyas*). Many people, however, were not members of any caste. These people, called "untouchables," were considered the lowliest in society, and other caste members were forbidden to come into certain kinds of contact with them.

The caste system in India was justified by an ideology based on the Hindu religion. A principal tenet of Hinduism is the belief in *reincarnation.* After death, souls are reborn into another life on earth. Being born as an untouchable was considered to be the result of not having performed well in one's previous life. The Hindu religion encouraged the untouchables to accept their low social position dutifully (Tumin, 1985).

There have been major changes in India's caste system since the nation achieved independence from Britain after World War II. For example, the Indian constitution bans discrimination against untouchables. However, the Indian caste system is about 4,000 years old, and it has been slow to change.

Some scholars have viewed the situation of African-Americans in the United States as having many caste-like features. One anthropological expert on India found the details of "caste in India and race relations in America . . . [to be] remarkably similar in view of the differences in cultural content" (Berreman, 1960, p. 80).

Estate

The **estate system** of stratification is associated with a type of social and economic system called *feudalism.* Agrarian Europe in the Middle Ages was characterized by such a system.

The ideology supporting the European estates granted special privileges to members of the first estate—the priests—and to those of the second estate—the nobles—in contrast to the rights allowed the commoners, including the peasantry, who were classified as the third estate. This ideology was sanctioned by both the Catholic Church and by the laws of the state.

Dominance in the feudal system was maintained by the landowning nobles. On the feudal manor, peasant and lord were bound together in a relationship of *vassalage:* Peasants, or serfs, provided labor and military service in return for protection and material support from the noble.

With the development of extensive trading in late feudalism, a new social group appeared: merchants. The merchants, the first group in the feudal system whose wealth did not depend on inherited ownership of land, were instrumental in the decline of feudalism and the rise of capitalism (this major socioeconomic change is discussed in Chapter 18). In effect, the merchants were the first capitalists. As an industrial economic system developed, social class became the dominant form of social stratification.

SOCIAL CLASS

The most common type of stratification in the modern world is the **class system,** a relatively open form of stratification based mainly on economic status. The class system is characterized by boundaries between groups that are less rigidly defined than those in slavery, caste, and estate systems. In a class system, there is considerably more mobility between groups, and achievement (as opposed to ascription) plays a larger role in ranking individuals. Even though a class system allows a relatively high degree of social mobility, however, it also includes strong elements of both stability and hierarchy. Thus, a class system still includes extensive inequality among groups of people.

The ideology that supports modern class systems is wholly secular. In essence, the greater privilege of the elite is justified by the argument that, because a substantial amount of social mobility up or down the class ladder is possible, those who succeed do so largely on the basis of their own merit. This means not only that individual determination and hard work are believed to pay off in the end with wealth and high status (Fallows, 1988; Rossides, 1990) but, more crucially, that the poor are seen as primarily responsible for their poverty. If they had applied themselves more diligently, they would not be poor. Thus, the class system is defended as eminently fair, and both the upper and the lower classes have no one to thank, or to blame, for their fate but themselves.

Sociologists disagree about the nature of social class systems. The major debate revolves around the theories of Karl Marx and Max Weber. For Marx, class is defined by access to the means of production—that is, the sources of wealth. The upper classes (the *bourgeoisie*) own and control the means of production and exploit the labor of the lower classes (the *proletariat*). Marx saw the bourgeoisie and the proletariat as inevitably destined to conflict. This **class conflict**—or struggle between competing classes—takes the form of events such as strikes and revolutions (Marx's views of class are more fully discussed in Chapters 17 and 18).

Weber, in contrast, viewed class systems as having two important dimensions of stratification in addition to

Would this family agree that social mobility up or down the class ladder is possible? As American sociologists point out, class division and inequality still play a major role in this nation's life.

economics: power and prestige. According to Marx, power and prestige are ultimately derived from wealth. To Weber, they are relatively independent of economics. Also, according to Weber, the relationship between classes in capitalism is not necessarily conflictful. It can even involve mutual dependence and cooperation.

The term *social class* is somewhat ambiguous because it stands for a very complex social reality. In American sociology, the concept of social class has often been defined broadly enough to include many different economic groupings, as well as groupings based on power and prestige. To the average American, however, "social class" means about the same thing as "social standing" and does not refer to specific groupings (Coleman & Rainwater, 1978).

Class Divisions

A society is said to have extensive **class divisions**—perceived and real differences between its classes—when the levels of reward given to members of various classes are very different; when the members of these classes are fully aware of these differences; and when there are only limited opportunities to move from one class to another.

In the United States, the boundaries between the classes are relatively indistinct, awareness of class is low, and movement from one class group to another is fairly common. Class divisions do exist in the United States, however. One of the outstanding contributions of American sociologists in the first half of the twentieth century was to point out the major role that class divisions and inequality still play in this nation's life (Page, 1969).

Class divisions are found in cultures throughout the world—not just in advanced, industrialized, or

APPLYING SOCIOLOGY

THE MIDDLE-CLASS MENTALITÉ

Sociologists include social class as a variable in all kinds of research. But social class is a difficult concept to define, and sociologists take many different approaches in measuring it. Some researchers take the objective approach and use a set of variables, such as income and wealth, education, and occupation, to determine social class. Unfortunately, even though this approach is particularly useful for quantitative research, it does not necessarily fit the classification that people assign to themselves.

According to Alan Wolfe, most Americans take the subjective approach to defining social class, which means that you are middle class if you say so (1998). And, in fact, public opinion polls show that most Americans do just that. From 1972 to 1994, the General Social Survey showed that no more than 10 percent of Americans classified themselves as either lower class or upper class. And a 1992 CBS/ New York Times poll showed 75 percent

of the American people responding positively to the question: "When presidential candidates talk about the middle class, do you think they mean people like you?"

Results like these led Wolfe to say that "nothing captures better the love affair between America and middle-class status than the propensity of Americans to define themselves as middle class whether or not they are" (1998, p. 1). Despite this discrepancy, sociologists will continue to assign people to social classes on the basis of objective criteria such as income, wealth, education, and occupation. But public opinion polls suggest that we are not measuring one of the most important dimensions of social class—one that offers insight into the way Americans understand their society and their place in it. And many people, including politicians, would argue that this subjective dimension is the most important. But what is it?

According to Wolfe, it is something that the French call a "mentalité—a cluster of attitudes, beliefs, practices, and lifestyles that defines what it

means to live in a way not too poor to be considered dependent on others and not too rich to be so luxuriously ostentatious that one loses touch with common sense" (p. 3). In the past, politicians had a clear sense of this mentalité, for historically the middle class was unified in its disdain for the way that both the poor and rich led their lives. Today, however, some people do not believe that this definition captures how the middle class understands itself. Critics from both ends of the political spectrum have argued that the middle class is radically split. Viewed as a "culture war," this perception suggests that middle-class anger is the result of either lost jobs and income (liberals), declining morals and fears for physical safety (conservatives), or both (populists). Wolfe argued that if this perception of the middle-class were true, then the democratic stability that has held the country together since the Civil War would be at stake. In fact, he seriously doubted that this perception was correct, and he set out to test the hypothesis that "middle-class Americans no

Western nations like the United States. For example, Korea, a country whose class structure was poorly defined before World War II, now has four clearly defined classes: a wealthy and powerful capitalist class; a white-collar and small-business class; a working class; and a marginal group at the very bottom of the social ladder (Rossides, 1990).

DETERMINING CLASS DIVISIONS AND PLACEMENT

What determines the major class divisions? Who is a member of which social class? Most sociologists today treat these issues as important areas of empirical study. But because class is a very complex concept, there are no easy answers. Universally accepted criteria do not exist for determining who belongs to a social class, as they do for deciding who belongs to a stamp club or football team.

Sociologists have developed three approaches—the objective, the reputational, and the subjective—to assign individuals to particular social classes.

THE OBJECTIVE APPROACH. In this approach, people are assigned by researchers to a social class on the basis of such objective criteria as their amount of income and wealth, type of work, and level of education. Sociologists thus arbitrarily establish class boundaries by defining the "cutoff points" for membership in each social class. Examples of social classes formed in this manner are Marx's "capitalists" and "workers" and the modern distinction between the middle (or white-collar) and working (or blue-collar) classes.

Clearly, the use of this method to determine social class placement is not without difficulties. Critics contend that the cutoff points between classes are sometimes illogical. A person whose annual income is $24,999 will longer share a common moral worldview but are bitterly divided into traditionalist and modernists wings" (p. 21).

In seeking to find the truth, Wolfe designed a study called the Middle Class Morality Project. Keenly aware of the strengths and weaknesses of both quantitative and qualitative research, he tried to combine ethnographic and survey methods. But he soon recognized that gaining insight into the what middle-class status meant to Americans required him to lean toward the ethnographic approach. And he accepted the fact that he could not claim that his survey was representative of America as a whole.

Wolfe gave a great deal of thought to how he would select subjects for this study. In seeking to interview middle-class Americans who varied in terms of economic, racial, cultural, ethnic, and job-related characteristics, he chose eight suburbs from four different regions in the United States: Brookline, Massachusetts; Medford, Massachusetts; Southeast DeKalb County, Georgia; Cobb County Georgia; Broken Arrow,

Oklahoma; and Sand Springs, Oklahoma. While Wolfe did find differences in the attitudes and beliefs of Americans drawn from these distinct parts of the country, one of the most important findings involved the way that researchers have measured the attitudes and beliefs of Americans. According to Wolfe:

> Over and over again, the Middle Class Morality Project found ways in which polls do not get opinion in this country quite right and, on a few occasions, get it downright wrong. (p. 277)

In contrast to the results of these polls, Wolfe found little support for the idea that middle-class Americans are bitterly divided into traditionalist and modern camps and are fully engaged in a culture war. In fact, Wolfe found middle-class Americans to be moderate in their outlook on the world, hesitant to pass judgment on others, and reluctant to impose their own values on others. While they do not accept homosexuality as normal and are opposed to bilingualism,

middle-class Americans do accept many things, including the changes in the family, legal immigration, multicultural education, and the separation of church and state.

Wolfe also argued that terms such as *traditional* and *modern* fail to express how middle-class Americans think about issues. In fact, he said that those who would be labeled traditional have accepted the social changes of the 1960s. They send their children to integrated schools and do not blame one group for divorce, drug use, teenage pregnancy, and working women. And modern Americans—those who rejected the middle-class morality and lifestyle of their parents in the 1960s—now live in the suburbs, fear crime, raise children, and deal with their aging parents. Overall, the results of the Middle Class Morality Project led Wolfe to one main conclusion: America is not experiencing a culture war. We are one nation, after all.

be placed by the objective method in a lower class than one whose annual income is $25,000, for example, if an annual income of $25,000 is the cutoff point for membership in the higher class. Furthermore, critics are concerned because the members of these "objective" classes are often unaware of their class membership.

On the positive side, however, the objective method is particularly helpful in allowing sociologists to perform quantitative research. Also, while the lifestyle of a person with an annual income of $24,999 is admittedly no different from that of a person with an annual income of $25,000, both of these individuals probably live quite differently than does a person with an annual income of $100,000.

THE REPUTATIONAL APPROACH. In this method, community members are asked to identify the number and nature of classes in their town or area. These people

are also asked to name the class to which community members belong—that is, to place people in classes according to their "reputation." Sociologists who use this approach feel that only insiders can understand the social class structure of a given community.

Critics claim that the reputational approach puts too much stress on prestige and not enough on more objective economic and political factors. Moreover, this approach works best in small communities where everyone knows everyone else. It is not as effective in large communities or for comparing one community with another.

THE SUBJECTIVE APPROACH. Investigators using this approach ask people to place themselves within a social class. The approach thus captures the subjective aspect of social class—how people themselves see the class system and their own positions in it. One problem with using the subjective approach is that some cultures tend to deemphasize the importance of class differences. In the United States, for example, the sociologically important distinction between the middle and working classes is often blurred because the media and politicians routinely characterize everyone who is not rich or destitute as "middle class."

Furthermore, many working-class Americans see themselves as having middle- rather than working-class status, partly as a result of the rise in their economic standard of living since World War II. They can now afford the goods and, to some extent, the lifestyles that were once the mark of the white-collar middle class (Wright & Martin, 1987).

Class Consciousness and False Consciousness

The shared awareness that members of a social class have concerning their common situation and interests is called **class consciousness.** Compared with citizens of other advanced countries, Americans have very little class consciousness. This low level of awareness is especially characteristic, as previously noted, of the American working class.

Marxist sociologists are likely to see this low level of class consciousness in America as an example of **false consciousness**—any situation in which a person's subjective understanding of reality is inconsistent with the objective facts of that situation. False consciousness is clearly promoted by acceptance of the core ideology of equal opportunity that underlies the American class system and also by repeated pronouncements by politicians and other public figures identified with the American upper class that class is not an important feature of American social life. Thus, most Americans do not see their nation's social system as reflecting inequities in the distribution of goods that disproportionately benefit a small elite class.

Low class consciousness in American society is also a result of racial, religious, ethnic, and regional differences that often cut across, and even submerge, class differences. There is so much diversity in American life that social class is only one way that Americans divide themselves. Instead of thinking about class, Americans tend to focus on inequities in age, sex, education, race, and religion.

The highest degree of class consciousness in American life is probably held by members of this country's upper class, especially those who have been wealthy for generations. This group is sharply aware of being in a unique situation and of sharing a distinct background and common interests (Coleman & Rainwater, 1978).

SOCIAL MOBILITY

Social mobility refers to a change on the part of an individual or a group of people from one status or social class to another. In common usage, "social mobility" means upward movement or social improvement. But for sociologists, *upward mobility* is only one of several kinds of social mobility. People may also move to a lower status (*downward mobility*). Either upward or downward movement in an individual's status is called *vertical mobility.*

Open and Closed Societies

Stratification systems differ in the ease with which people within them can move from one social status to another. A completely *open* society has never existed. But if it did, people could achieve whatever status their natural talents, abilities, and desires allowed them to attain. An open society would not be a society of equals; unequal social positions would still exist, but these positions would be filled solely on the basis of merit. Therefore, such a system could be described as a perfect *meritocracy.*

In a completely *closed* society everyone would be assigned a status at birth or at a certain age. That status could never be changed. No society has ever been completely closed, although some have been fairly close to this extreme.

The chief distinction between relatively open and relatively closed societies concerns the mix of statuses each contains. Open societies are characterized by greater reliance on *achieved* status than are closed societies; closed societies rely more on *ascribed* status. (Achieved and ascribed statuses were discussed in Chapter 4.) Many studies have shown that industrial, technologically advanced societies such as the United States tend to be relatively open (Hazelrigg & Garnier, 1976). In contrast, preindustrial societies with economies based on agriculture tend to be relatively closed (Eisenstadt, 1971).

India before the time of Gandhi is an example of a relatively closed society. During this era, the rules of the caste system were enforced by law. Yet even in this society, some social mobility was allowed. People could sometimes marry into higher castes or acquire education and better jobs by obtaining the patronage of higher caste members. Such individuals, or at least their children, were later able to move into those higher castes. Sometimes entire groups were mobile, in which case the hierarchical ranking system of the entire society changed.

The Conditions of Social Mobility

Sociologists commonly analyze two types of social mobility: intergenerational and intragenerational. The first type, *intergenerational social mobility,* compares the social position of parents with that attained by their children or grandchildren. In contrast, *intragenerational social mobility* refers to an individual's change in social position within his or her lifetime, as when someone starts out in a lower social class and rises to affluence. Both types can, however, entail either upward or downward mobility.

UPWARD MOBILITY

One pioneering study uncovered two conditions that seemed especially likely to foster upward mobility within a particular society: advanced industrial development and a large educational enrollment (Fox & Miller, 1965). As societies become more industrialized, the low-salaried, low-status jobs that require few skills are slowly eliminated. These are the jobs most easily performed by machines. At the same time, more jobs are added at the middle and upper levels. The upward mobility that results from such changes in the social or economic system—rather than from individual personal achievement—is called **structural mobility.**

The higher-level jobs will not be filled, however, unless the children of lower-status parents are given the needed knowledge and training. Advanced societies have tried to meet this need with a system of public secondary and higher education. One study concluded that in America "the best readily observable predictor of a young man's eventual status or earnings is the amount of schooling he has had" (Jencks et al., 1979). It is not known, however, whether this is principally because of the knowledge and skills schooling provides or because schooling serves as a kind of filtering system that allocates people to jobs.

Mass communication, urbanization, and geographic mobility are other factors related to high levels of upward mobility (Treiman, 1970). In addition, there is a relationship between upward mobility and a society's form of government. Autocratic governments tend to have a negative effect on upward mobility and income equality, but political democracy tends to have a positive effect (Tyree, Semyonov, & Hodge, 1979).

Several social conditions can discourage upward mobility. Traditional societies provide few upper-level social positions and therefore few chances for people to move up. In fairly closed societies, such as traditional India, movement from one status to another may be forbidden by tradition or law. Furthermore, industrialization alone does not always ensure upward mobility, because the number of people employed in high-status jobs may remain fairly constant. In India and Egypt, for instance, the professions have expanded very little as these countries have become industrialized, and as a result, many college graduates have had great difficulty finding jobs (Matras, 1984).

In the United States, much individual upward mobility results from what Ralph Turner (1960) calls a contest among equals; in contrast, in England, it is more common for members of the elite to identify promising recruits in the middle classes and to deliberately recruit them for membership in the higher ranks, a process Turner terms sponsored mobility.

DOWNWARD MOBILITY

Common sense might suggest that the conditions leading to individual downward mobility are simply the opposites of those leading to upward mobility. To some extent, this is true. Not getting an education, marrying very young, and raising a large family are all related to downward mobility. Being born into a very large family also can lead to downward mobility, if the family cannot provide schooling and other advantages for all the children.

Other conditions leading to downward mobility can be less straightforward. Although living in a city is usually considered to be associated with upward mobility (Lipset & Bendix, 1964), some research has shown that urban living can also promote downward mobility (Fox & Miller, 1965). For instance, downward mobility is typically the lot of newly arrived immigrants to a city (Margolis, 1990). In short, city life promotes mobility of all kinds. Small-town and rural life, however, are definitely associated with lower rates of mobility.

Downward mobility has received surprisingly little attention from sociologists, in part because so many opportunities for upward structural mobility have existed throughout American history that downward mobility may not have seemed like a very important topic. However, recent changes in the American economy, to be discussed in the next chapter, suggest that we may be on the brink of a new era in which downward mobility may become more common than it ever was before, a trend that could have a variety of negative consequences for both individuals and the society as a whole.

The Social Mobility of Women

Until recently, most studies of social mobility have focused exclusively on men, typically comparing sons with their fathers. Studies of the mobility of women, which have turned up some important findings, have become increasingly common as more and more women have entered the labor market. These studies also have had to consider some interesting methodological questions. Should a daughter's job be compared with that of her father or her mother, or both? Doesn't a woman achieve mobility through marriage as well as through the job market?

One study showed that a woman's occupational mobility is affected by the occupational status of both of her parents (Rosenfeld, 1978). Whether or not the mother works outside the home and the occupational position

WINDOW ON SOCIOLOGY

THE RICH AND THE SUPERRICH

How many rich people do you know? How much money does someone have to make in order to be rich? Many Americans would put the figure at an annual income of $1 million. With that as a guideline, that would mean that almost 70,000 Americans are rich—at least according to the 1994 figures of the Internal Revenue Service (Hacker, 1998). But who are they? Well, you might not know any of them personally, but you can guess who some are. Many professional athletes would make the cut. According to Andrew Hacker, 246 football players, 241 baseball players, and 159 hockey players made at least $1 million in 1995. The National Basketball Association does not like to report the salaries of individual players, but it is fair to say that nearly half of them also make at least $1 million, as the average salary for players was $1.6 million.

Hollywood stars also make six-figure incomes. In 1996, *Entertainment Weekly* reported that 133 stars made at least $1 million per year. These superstars included 96 men and 37 women. Jim Carrey, John Travolta, Mel Gibson, Tom Hanks, and Arnold Swartzenegger command about $20 million per picture. Demi Moore and Julia Roberts make about $12 million, and Sandra Bullock and Michelle Pfeiffer each make about $10 million per picture.

When Americans think about celebrities like these, they might assume that they are the richest people in the United States. But, in fact, their wealth does not even come close to those at the top. Oprah Winfrey, arguably the most powerful woman in the media, is only worth $125 million (*Forbes*, 1998). Steven Spielberg has amassed only $175 million. And even Jerry Seinfeld, with $225 million, falls short of what it takes to make the *Forbes* list of the richest Americans.

The superrich are in a league by themselves. In 1998, making the list required a personal fortune of $500 million. But the stakes are bound to surpass $1 billion in the near future. Nearly half of the *Forbes* list of the 400 wealthiest Americans are already billionaires. With a fortune estimated at $58 billion, Bill Gates topped the list for the fifth straight year. The fortunes of the top nine individuals on the list amounted to over $10 billion each. Five of these people inherited their wealth from Sam Walton, the founder of Wal-Mart. If he were alive today, he would be giving Bill Gates a run for his money with a net worth of $55 billion.

When *Forbes* compiled its first list of the richest Americans in 1918, it was limited to 30 names and required one to have $50 million (Hacker, 1998). With a fortune estimated at about $1.2 billion (the equivalent of $12.8 billion in 1997), John D. Rockefellar topped a list of industrial giants—H. C. Frick (steel), Andrew Carnegie (steel), George F. Baker (banking), William Rockefeller (oil), Edward Harkness (oil), J. Ogden Armour (meatpacking), Henry Ford (autos), and William K. Vanderbilt (railroads).

Unlike the billionaires of today, it took years to amass these fortunes. Wealth was based on assets such as steel mills, railroad tracks, or manufacturing plants (Hacker, 1998). No one became rich overnight. Once you had enough capital to start a business, you then had to build a plant and then make sure the process operated properly (Sloan, 1997). What is more, while the market could increase the value of an enterprise, the price of goods could not vary too much from their actual cost or what customers were willing to pay. The shift from manufacturing to high technology in the last 20 years has fundamentally changed the way that Americans get rich (see Table 9.4). Today, fortunes are made on soaring stock valuations. And this is particularly true in companies that deal with computer technology.

As the primary source of wealth shifts from the tangible to the intangible—from manufactured goods to ideas—we will continue to see fortunes made overnight. But this new economy is not bound to benefit all Americans (Sloan, 1997); in fact, many will be left behind. However, if you think they will resent the new rich, think again. Even though it is hard to justify the $25 million salaries

she holds are important factors that must be considered in studies of female mobility. Increasingly, of course, these will have to be considered in studies of male mobility as well. According to one such study, there seems to be a positive correlation between working mothers and the job status of their sons, but not that of their daughters (Sewell, Hauser, & Wolf, 1980).

Another researcher found that women may achieve greater social mobility through marriage than men do through their jobs (Chase, 1975). This study determined of superstar athletes like Michael Jordan or the $20 million that movie stars make for one picture, Americans willingly contribute to their fortunes (Hacker, 1998). So, too, are they contributing to the fortunes of superrich people like Bill Gates.

TABLE 9.4   PAST AND PRESENT FORTUNES

Name	Source	Billions
1918		
John D. Rockefeller	Oil	$12.8
H. C. Frick	Steel	2.4
Andrew Carnegie	Steel	2.1
George F. Baker	Banking	1.6
William Rockefeller	Oil	1.6
Edward Harkness	Oil	1.3
J. Ogden Armour	Meatpacking	1.3
Henry Ford	Autos	1.1
William K. Vanderbilt	Railroads	1.1
Edward H. R. Green	Inheritance	1.1
1998		
William Gates III	Computers	$58.0
Walton Family	Wal-Mart	55.0
Warren Buffet	Investment	29.0
Paul Allen	Computers	22.0
Cox Family	Media	14.2
Michael Dell	Computers	13.0
Steven Anthony Ballmer	Computers	12.0
John Kluge	Media	9.8
Gordon Moore	Computers	7.0
Sumner Redstone	Media	6.4

Note: 1918 figures adjusted for inflation.

Source: 1918 figures from *Newsweek,* August 4, 1997, p. 50. Copyright © 1997 Newsweek, Inc. All rights reserved. Reprinted by permission. 1998 figures from *Forbes,* October 12, 1998; http://www.forbes.com. Reprinted by permission of *Forbes* Magazine. © Forbes Inc. 1999.

that in his first job a man tends to "inherit" the occupational status of his father. A woman, however, often marries a man with an occupational status quite different from that of her father and becomes associated more with her husband's status. Marriage may not always involve upward mobility; one study concluded that mobility through marriage is as often downward as it is upward (Glenn, Ross, & Tully, 1974).

In general, research has suggested that the process of gaining an education and getting a job has become

Is Hillary Clinton's social mobility and occupational status associated more with her role as the President's wife or with her own accomplishments as a successful lawyer and politician?

very similar for both working men and working women (Treiman & Terrell, 1975). The qualifications needed for a job are the same for both sexes, and the route to a higher-status job is typically through education. Women, however, are still heavily concentrated in "pink-collar" clerical and service-oriented jobs, which tend to be low in pay and prestige (Bernard, 1981).

THEORIES OF STRATIFICATION

Why does social stratification occur? Why do social positions differ so greatly in wealth, power, and prestige? These questions have long been the focus of theoretical probing, as well as empirical research, by sociologists. Two basic contrasting answers have emerged. The functionalist theorists hold that some degree of social inequality is necessary in order for society to function properly. The conflict theorists hold that such inequality is neither functional nor just, but rather is the result of the exploitation of those at the bottom by those at the top. Both functionalists and conflict theorists typically focus on occupation as the most important measure of social position.

Functionalist Theories

The functionalist point of view is best expressed in a classic analysis developed by Kingsley Davis and Wilbert Moore (1945). Their basic argument is that social inequality is not only inevitable but, in fact, is required for the proper functioning of society.

They start with the observation that some jobs are more important than others in any society. In particular, it is crucial that certain occupational positions be filled by the best qualified individuals in order to ensure that they are performed properly. Examples that come readily to mind are doctors, top leaders in the political, military, and corporate spheres, engineers, and lawyers. If the people who hold these jobs are less than competent, the social consequences may be catastrophic.

This is not to argue that many other positions, such as truck drivers, garbage collectors, or cooks, are not important, only that the social harm done if the people in these occupations are incompetent is relatively less serious. If garbage collectors are not very good at their jobs, we may end up hip-deep in orange peels and coffee grinds; if we allow stupid and clumsy people to become brain surgeons, the results will be far more problematic.

Note that most of the critical occupations singled out by Davis and Moore require a great deal of education or training. Most people seeking such positions spend many years preparing themselves in order to qualify for them. Furthermore, most of these occupations place great demands of time, energy, and self-sacrifice on their incumbents. Successful doctors, engineers, and political leaders rarely work 40-hour weeks!

The question then arises how the most able people can be convinced to make the sacrifices necessary in order to take on these challenging occupations. Davis and Moore respond that this is ensured by providing substantially more incentives—wealth, power, and prestige—to those able to fill society's most critical occupational roles. Thus, they argue, we *all* benefit from the disproportionate rewards given to certain workers because we thereby guarantee that tasks that *must* be performed skillfully will be accomplished by the best and brightest among us.

This perspective, while reasonable up to a point, has been subjected to heavy criticism (Tumin, 1953; Wrong, 1959). For one thing, it is fairly clear that certain occupations are very richly rewarded that, although they may require skills possessed by very few people, do not contribute to any important social ends. Obvious examples include professional athletes and rock singers. Along the same lines, such occupations as schoolteachers, day-care workers, police officers, and social workers, which certainly ought to be staffed by highly able people, in fact command very low wages. As a result, they do not always attract the most capable workers, a reality that has caused great social damage.

Another problem with the Davis-Moore thesis is that ascribed or inherited advantages may interfere with the logic of differential resource allocation. For example, the untalented offspring of a capable and richly rewarded business executive may be able to draw on his or her father's resources in order to secure a high-level position, whereas the far more capable child of a working-class parent goes unrewarded. The differential advantages that accrue to males over females and whites over nonwhites may similarly interfere with ensuring that the most capable people fill the most crucial slots.

Finally, some critics accept the basic logic of the functional argument but are distressed by the extent of the disparity of rewards that are available in contemporary societies. It is all well and good, they admit, to pay doctors more than unskilled laborers, but is any social benefit likely to come from allowing some people to become billionaires while millions of others live in such extreme poverty that they are unable to develop their innate skills and abilities, talents that, if nurtured, might well allow them to contribute to the good of the society in elite occupational positions?

Research on the functionalist view has yielded mixed results. One scholar found that the functionalist view was supported in the allocation of rewards to players of different positions on baseball teams (Abrahamson, 1979). Yet other researchers did not find support for the functionalist view in their analysis of the allocation of rewards to business executives (Broom & Cushing, 1977).

Conflict Theories

Do people in high positions acquire large amounts of wealth, prestige, and power because those positions are valuable to society? Or do they acquire wealth, prestige, and power because they have gained a monopoly over scarce resources and act in their own interest to prevent those resources from being more widely dispersed? Conflict theorists tend to hold the latter viewpoint. What determines who gets what? In a word, *power* (Dahrendorf, 1959; Mills, 1956).

To conflict theorists, inequality is not a necessary part of the operation of societies. It is the result of more powerful groups' exploitation of the less powerful. The powerful determine which people will fill which jobs and who will get what rewards. Conflict theorists deny that extreme inequality in occupational rewards is necessary either for motivating people to work or for effective social functioning.

Most contemporary conflict theories build on the classic views of Karl Marx. According to Marx, capitalism is marked by conflict between two classes. As introduced earlier in this chapter, the dominant class is the bourgeoisie, who own and control the means of production. The subordinate class is the proletariat, who must sell their labor to the bourgeoisie in order to live. The

distribution of desirables in capitalist societies is principally an outcome of class-based power imbalances (Rossides, 1990).

Marx believed that the ruling class is able to maintain its power primarily because social institutions reflect its interests. Religion, education, and the political order all generally serve to preserve the status quo rather than encourage change and a reduction of inequality. Marx also believed that the oppressed proletariat are frequently subject to false consciousness, failing to understand that the social order is not just and that they cannot achieve their fair share of society's rewards so long as the bourgeoisie remain in control. Acceptance of the ideology of equal opportunity that underlies class inequality in a capitalist society leads to an inability of the workers to organize to pursue effectively their true class interests. Marx was hopeful that eventually the proletariat would be able to cast off such false consciousness, achieve true class consciousness, and rise in violent revolution against the class that oppressed them. Developments in the previously Marxist societies of Eastern Europe and in the former Soviet Union have shown Marx to have been a poor political prophet, but they have not necessarily undermined the value of the conflict view of stratification that he pioneered.

Modern conflict theorists have modified Marx's views in order to make them better reflect the economic, political, and social realities of the late twentieth century. These theorists have abandoned much of Marx's rigid political posturing while retaining his fundamental insight that stratification systems disproportionately benefit the wealthy and powerful and that ideologies generated by the elites can blind the middle and lower classes to the extent that the cards are stacked against them. Modern conflict theorists also modify Marx by considering stratification systems based on factors other than economic class (such as gender, race, and age) and sometimes acknowledge that a certain amount of inequality in society may be inevitable in view of the fact that people do differ greatly in their talents and skills. However, all conflict theorists would agree that structured social inequality is best understood as the outcome of unequal struggle between the powerful and the powerless, and all would agree that modern societies are characterized by far more inequality than is defensible except by people who are attempting to justify their own immodestly large share of society's desirables.

Lenski's Theory

Gerhard Lenski (1966, 1984) has persuasively argued that both the functionalist and the conflict perspectives have some empirical validity and that the two perspectives

Having access to high-quality education, such as that of Oxford or Cambridge, Britain's elite youth establish themselves as the next generation of leaders in business and government.

should be combined to produce a more accurate analysis of stratification. Moreover, he suggests, a broad historical view of stratification is essential because the character of stratification has changed over time.

In small, premodern societies, Lenski points out, goods and service go to members largely on the basis of need. Power has almost nothing to do with social reward. As a society becomes more modern, however, power does become increasingly important in shaping the stratification system. Given the choice between someone else's interests or their own, Lenski suggests, most people naturally will choose their own. Thus, when societies first begin to produce more goods than are required for day-to-day survival, the strong are able to arrange for themselves to get a greater share.

But is the power of the strong always based on their economic position? Unlike Marx, Lenski holds that power has other sources as well. One such base is strong political leadership. Lenski agrees with Marx, however, that dominant economic classes can and often do influence the distribution of desirables to their own advantage.

In contrast to many conflict theorists, Lenski believes that some inequality may actually promote the functioning of society. And he does not hold out much hope for a classless society. In making these points he aligns himself with central themes of functionalist thought.

STRATIFICATION AND MOBILITY IN OTHER SOCIETIES

In this section, we examine stratification and social mobility in three nations: Great Britain, Brazil, and the former Soviet Union. The systems of stratification in these countries are contrasted with the system in the United States (which is explored more fully in Chapter 10). Britain is a nation much like the United States, but with a more rigid class system. Brazilian stratification displays a pattern more typical of a developing society. The stratification pattern of the Soviet Union reflected a socialist economic system.

Great Britain: Class Society and Welfare State

For many years following World War II, Great Britain was governed by the Labour party. Principally representing the interests of the working class, this party transformed the nation into a welfare state, with extensive social services such as state-financed health care and education. Even so, Great Britain, which has always had a pronounced class structure, remains a country characterized by substantial social inequalities. The upper class, with roots in a centuries-old aristocracy, still controls most of the nation's wealth. Although the prosperous years of the 1950s and 1960s raised the incomes of all Britons, the distribution of wealth and income among social classes did not change significantly (Goldthorpe, 1987; Westergaard & Resler, 1976).

This pattern of income inequality, however, is not very different from that of many other advanced societies, including the United States. More distinctive is the way Britons themselves view their social class structure. In contrast with Americans, who see their society as composed of many vague and overlapping classes, Britons view theirs as having only a few, very distinct classes. In addition, whereas most Americans define class membership in terms of income and occupation, Britons are more likely to define class membership in terms of authority and the control of wealth (Bell & Robinson, 1980). The British social world has traditionally been divided into "us" and "them," and boundaries have been maintained by well-recognized differences in speech, education, and lifestyle.

The upper class in Britain has maintained its position of wealth and power through inheritance and shared educational background. Many people in positions of influence are educated at exclusive private schools (called public schools in Britain). The expense of these schools limits access to them mainly to the children of the wealthy. Half the college-bound students from these schools go to either Oxford or Cambridge, the most highly respected universities in Britain. Only 10 percent of the college-bound students from state-run schools go to Oxford or Cambridge. This background of exclusive and high-quality education strengthens a sense of shared values among the members of the upper class and helps them establish lifelong contacts that make it easy to enter positions of power and leadership (Noble, 1981).

This pattern is gradually changing, however. Although the large family fortunes of modern Britain are still based mainly on inherited assets (1 percent of the population controls about one-quarter of the country's wealth), the country's high rates of taxation may gradually reduce these fortunes. And even though most of the members of a list of Britain's 200 richest men and women inherited their money, 86 members of the list made their fortunes themselves (Knight, 1989). Indeed, some observers believe that the emphasis placed by the Conservative government of recent years on encouraging the growth of private business has led to a weakening of class boundaries and a mixing of the classes unheard of in Britain before the late twentieth century.

Upward social mobility in Britain did increase significantly in the postwar years. In 1951, for example, 73.6 percent of employed British men had manual jobs, and 26.4 percent held nonmanual jobs. By 1966, these percentages had nearly reversed themselves: 34.2 held manual jobs, and 65.8 had nonmanual jobs (Noble, 1981). This change is probably due at least as much to structural mobility resulting from the expansion of the British economy as it is to welfare state measures. This expansion came to an end in the 1970s, and the mobility rate of British society was then said to be at a virtual standstill (Goldthorpe 1987).

In the 1980s, under the administration of Prime Minister Margaret Thatcher, the British economy entered a period of very strong growth (Ryder & Silver, 1985). The effects of the Thatcher years on social stratification are still to be determined, but some critics believe that the policies of her administration—which dismantled some of the welfare state and stressed the importance of a free market—increased class differences in income, health, and living conditions (Hudson & Williams, 1989). By the late 1990s, under the administration of Tony Blair, the British economy remained quite strong.

Brazil: Tradition and Expansion

Brazil is a large and important nation of the Third World. A key feature of the Third World is its poverty. Brazil's per capita gross national product is only about 18 percent of that of the United States and 25 percent of that of Great Britain. Before World War II, the son of a poor man in Brazil was almost certain to remain poor, and the son of a

Although Brazil's class structure has changed since World War II, social inequalities have not diminished much. Most of Brazil's poor still live in extreme poverty.

rich man was almost sure to remain rich. Thus, class membership was virtually always inherited, and there was little chance for upward mobility.

Pre–World War II Brazilian society was composed of two major social classes: a small upper class of landowners, professionals, and government officials and a very large lower class of manual (mostly farm) workers and artisans. The power of the upper class depended largely on their ownership of large agricultural estates. Members of this class controlled both rural and urban society and ran the national government. Lower-class Brazilians were poor and uneducated and had a wretched standard of living.

The relationship between the two classes was one of client to *patrao* (patron). In this paternalistic relationship, the lower-class workers were dependent on upper-class patrons, who might be employers, landlords, or creditors. The workers offered loyalty to their *patrao* in return for protection and material support (Norris, 1984).

Since World War II, the economy of Brazil has grown rapidly, and it has shifted from an agrarian to an industrial base. Brazil's agricultural sector is still important—it grows more coffee than any other country in the world—but today the country's economy is increasingly centered around such industries as steel, automobiles, textiles, ships, appliances, and petrochemicals (*World Almanac*, 1994). This industrial expansion has led to important changes in the nation's social structure—the rapid growth of a middle class, the emergence of an urban working class, the growth of a rural working class not bound by the client—*patrao* relationship, and the emergence of a new urban elite (Raine, 1974; Saunders, 1971; Wagley, 1971).

Brazil's changing class structure does not mean that social inequalities have diminished very much, however (Roniger, 1987). In 1997, the poorest 40 percent of the Brazilian people earned only 8.2 percent of the national income, whereas the richest 10 percent earned 47.9 percent (World Bank, 1998). Most of the rural and urban poor still live in extreme poverty, some in a state of semistarvation.

Inequality in a Classless Society: The Soviet Union

The 1917 Russian Revolution, which led to the creation of the Soviet Union, was guided in part by a Marxist commitment to the abolition of the bases of class inequality, in particular the private ownership of property. The Soviet government, controlled by the Communist party, portrayed itself as a dictatorship of the working class. This meant that other classes would be denied power and prestige and would ultimately disappear, making the Soviet Union a single-class—or classless—society. Seventy-five years after its birth, the Soviet Union was dead, mortally wounded by an array of powerful forces, some of which resulted from the presence in this supposedly classless society of a system of structured inequality that arose despite official efforts to prevent such a development.

In the Soviet system, government officials, intellectuals, and many artists, athletes, and performers had much greater access to valued goods and services than did ordinary Soviet citizens. Even a casual observer of life in the Soviet Union could see this, and proponents of the Soviet model did not argue this point (Daniloff, 1983; Theen, 1984). What they did dispute is whether these inequalities represented class divisions.

The official Soviet position concerning this sort of inequality was basically functionalist: People who fill difficult jobs that require years of training must be rewarded more than others. Rewards included such things as access to special stores, chauffeur-driven cars, and the right to live in Moscow or other preferred areas (*New York Times,* February 10, 1979). Defenders of the Soviet system argued that these inequalities were very different from true class divisions. One reason they gave was that the schooling needed to obtain high-status positions was open to all Soviet citizens on a merit basis. Another was that since wealth was not owned privately, inequality did not benefit the personal interests of owners but rather served to promote the efficient functioning of the state, which worked for the common good (Yanowitch & Fisher, 1973).

In reality, there were four main strata, or social divisions, within the Soviet Union: the political elite (very few of whom were women), the intelligentsia (including lower government officials and professional workers), urban manual workers, and rural workers (Lane, 1984; Lane, 1987). Members of the political elite staffed the bureaucracy that ran the country. They received the usual rewards of the upper class. They did not own property, but had unequal access to the use and enjoyment of state property. They also earned higher incomes than members of the other social strata.

The major cleavage in the Soviet Union (as in all Communist societies) was between the ruling Communist party, including the political elite and the intelligentsia, and the mass of nonparty citizens. The party elite sought to prevent the formation of classes, an act they justified in terms of the ideal of classlessness. However, this behavior was also based on fear that "classes, like any other independent social collectivity or organization, might attempt to challenge the Party's authority" (Parkin, 1971, p. 139) and its ability to maintain the system of inequality on which the privileged positions of its members rested.

Within the nonparty segment of the population, there was a marked distinction between the wealth and prestige of nonmanual and manual workers. And among manual workers, there was a further division between rural workers and urban workers. Many manual workers had moved to urban areas because of the jobs created there by industry; urban manual workers were better off than rural manual workers, and were well aware of this (Connor, 1979).

There was also a division between workers according to gender. Soviet women had one of the highest full-time paid employment rates in the world. Until the economic collapse that took place in the final two years of the Soviet Union's existence, nine out of ten Soviet women aged 20 to 49 were employed. Women filled the majority of posts in education, culture, and entertainment, and were frequently employed in what might be considered traditionally "male" occupations, such as mine engineering and commercial fishing. But despite their seemingly liberated status, women were still generally responsible for home care and childrearing. And, partly because they had so little time left to pursue the additional education that would have helped them to secure better jobs, women were concentrated in economic sectors characterized by lower status and pay (Lapidus, 1982). For instance, even though women made up 90 percent of workers in the medical professions, men usually became the heads of hospitals or chief physicians.

Despite the existence of widespread inequalities in the Soviet Union, manual workers had more prestige and income relative to white-collar occupations than manual workers do in the United States. For example, Gerhard Lenski (1984) found that U.S. executives received 20 to 200 times the minimum wage and 12 to 125 times the average income, but that Soviet executives received only 15 to 25 times the minimum wage and 5 to 10 times the average income. Lenski (1984, p. 313) concluded that "income inequality is much less pronounced in the Soviet Union than in the United States." Also, there was less inheritance of elite positions in the Soviet Union than there is in the United States, although top officials were known to resort to bribery to get their children into the schools that virtually ensured advancement (Daniloff, 1983; Nove, 1982).

In short, the evidence suggests that the Soviet system did overcome class stratification to some extent, and while the country's major resources were distributed unequally, this was true to a lesser degree than in market economies like that of the United States. The key point is that in the Soviet Union, as in all command economies, the distribution of resources was determined by a central political authority—in this case, the Communist party. Possessing a monopoly on power, the party was able to reduce many economic inequalities. This same power, however, also allowed it to engage in many human rights violations, to suppress political dissidence with violence, and to control tightly vast areas of Soviet citizens' social and personal life (Parkin, 1971, p. 184). In the early 1980s disenchantment produced by these arrangements,

combined with the economic failures resulting from the party's bureaucratically rigid central plan, sparked a widespread challenge to the Soviet system.

The reforms made from 1985 to 1991 under Mikhail Gorbachev's policy of *perestroika* (economic restructuring) legalized certain kinds of markets and private ownership. One example of the type of private enterprise permitted was the family farm, on which farmers were able to lease land and equipment from collectives in order to grow what they wished (Schlapentokh, 1988). Individual entrepreneurship in manufacturing was also allowed on a limited basis (*Congressional Quarterly*, 1986).

But Gorbachev's reforms proved too little, too late. On Christmas Day 1991, he resigned under pressure, three months after the Communist party had been stripped of its power and outlawed, and four days after the leaders of 11 Soviet republics announced their withdrawal from the Soviet Union. Most of these new independent countries immediately began the arduous process of constructing the complex bases of a market economy. Far-reaching changes in the social structures of these countries are currently under way. As markets and private ownership come to fill the vacuum left by the demise of massive bureaucratic state agencies, we may expect to see the expansion of both the middle class and class inequalities in this part of the world (Dahl, 1990).

Given the continued flux and uncertainty that mark these historic developments, it is difficult to know to what extent the stratification systems that emerge in the countries of the former Soviet Union will resemble those found in Western market societies. Some argue that an egalitarian, democratic socialism or a Scandinavian type of social democracy will emerge in some of these countries (Landy, 1991), while others predict the development of a right wing, nationalistic form of totalitarianism (*Time*, January 13, 1992). One thing we can be reasonably certain about, however, is that the fundamental source of social inequality in these countries for three-quarters of a century—the Communist party's virtually unchallenged concentration of power—has been completely destroyed.

CHAPTER REVIEW

1. How does wealth differ from income?

2. Does wealth buy power in the United States? If so, give an example.

3. Why is prestige commonly associated with a person's occupation?

4. Consider the occupations listed in Table 9.2. Identify the status symbols that are commonly associated with people who hold these kinds of jobs.

5. Is socioeconomic status a good measure of social class in the United States? Why or why not?

6. A number of well-known Americans are likely to exhibit status inconsistency. Who are they?

7. Describe the four major historical types of social stratification systems. Why do you think systems of inequality like these can last so long?

8. Does class conflict exist in the United States today? If so, give an example.

9. What is the best way to determine class divisions? Why?

10. Why is class consciousness relatively low in the United States? What members of American society are most likely to experience false consciousness?

11. Why did the transformation from an agricultural society to a postindustrial one increase social mobility in the United States?

12. How will the shift from an industrial society to a postindustrial one affect structural mobility?

13. Several theories attempt to explain why occupations vary so much in prestige, wealth, and power. Which theory do you favor? Why?

INTERNET EXERCISE

The Web destinations for Chapter 9 deal with the topic of social stratification. To begin your tour, go to the Prentice Hall companion Web site **http://www. prenhall.com/popenoe.** Next, choose **Chapter 9** (Social Stratification). Then select **web destinations** from the left side of the screen. There are many interesting sites to choose from. We suggest you begin with **Social Stratification.** This site contains a wide variety of links to relevant sites on various aspects of social stratification. Click on **Stratification and Society,** then click on **Some Principles of Stratification.** After you have read the contents of the essay presented, answer the following questions:

- What are the basic principles of stratification from a sociology perspective?

- Where do you place yourself in the stratification hierarchy?

KEY TERMS

social stratification	conspicuous consumption	class conflict
wealth	status consistency	class divisions
income	status inconsistency	class consciousness
power	slavery	false consciousness
prestige	caste system	social mobility
socioeconomic status (SES)	estate system	structural mobility
status symbol	class system	

CHAPTER 10

Social Class and Poverty in the United States

It's a warm Saturday afternoon in June and four American men in their mid-30s are enjoying leisure-time activities.

James arranged earlier in the week for his private pilot to fly him to his estate, located a few miles outside Aspen, Colorado. If it were winter, he would doubtless be skiing, but instead he and his wife, Helen, are lounging in their pool and sipping Champagne while a sizable staff of servants prepares for the evening's activities that will center around a catered dinner party for several dozen guests, most of whom are highly successful businesspeople and lawyers.

Charles is jogging through the streets of his pleasant suburban town; his wife, Ann, is shopping at a mall for a new outfit she will wear that evening to dinner at a gourmet restaurant downtown. Afterward, they will drop in for a few hours at a cocktail party given by one of Ann's fellow college professors.

At about the same time, Pete is playing in a hotly contested softball game on a public field a few miles from his modest home in an older suburb; his wife, Doreen, is working at her second job as a supermarket checker this afternoon. Later they will have a pizza delivered to their home and spend the evening with relatives watching television.

Eddie is playing basketball with some of his friends on a court that was built by the city on a vacant lot near his inner-city apartment. He pauses from time to time to take a sip from a bottle of inexpensive beer. Later on he may shoot some pool, visit the home of his ex-wife, Barbara, to spend a little time with their two children, or just hang out on the street corner.

Most Americans don't like to think very much about social class; in fact, we often hear politicians denouncing anyone who draws attention to class divisions in this society as being somehow "un-American." Our reluctance to discuss class openly probably results from Americans' widespread acceptance of the ideology that suggests that people's economic success is almost entirely a reflection of their own effort and ability. Thus, to acknowledge that someone is anything less than middle class amounts, in many people's minds, to accusing them of being incompetent or lazy. Talking about class simply isn't polite.

But sociologists don't have the luxury of being polite; they must describe society as it is. Furthermore, sociological research strongly suggests that the American ideology puts too much blame on the shoulders of individuals for their class placement. Ability and effort *do* matter, but so does one's parents' class position; and upward mobility, especially for those born into poverty, is much more difficult than most people imagine. In any event, as the different leisure-time activities of James, Charles, Pete, and Eddie suggest, there are indeed classes in America, and our class position has a great deal of impact on the way that we live our lives.

Of course, class differences go far beyond an individual's choice of leisure activities. Other, more important differences include access to health care and educational and career opportunities. In this chapter, we examine the range of living standards in the United States, as represented by social classes and the connections between social class position and the quality of life, with special attention devoted to the subject of poverty. Finally, we include a brief overview of the range of programs called "social welfare."

SOCIAL CLASSES IN THE UNITED STATES

In small and medium-sized communities across America, the importance of social class is quite evident. Most people tend to choose friends, spouses, employees, and associates from within their own social class. Furthermore, powerful barriers to relationships outside one's own class may exist. Factory workers know mainly factory workers and others who do similar work; they normally have little contact with members of other classes, especially those far from their own level. Corporation presidents may lead even more sheltered lives because their power and wealth shield them from contact with people outside their own class.

In large urban areas, it is sometimes more difficult to identify class groupings that are as clearly defined as those in a small town. It is harder still to identify social classes that span the whole society. However, because jobs are ranked in similar ways nationally, and because income and wealth can be judged objectively, most sociologists speak of society-wide social classes in America.

How many classes are there in the United States? Some sociologists recognize only three: the upper class, the middle class, and the lower class. Lloyd Warner (1949), the author of a classic study on American social stratification, divided each of the three main classes into an upper and lower level, yielding a total of six classes. Warner's system is still often used by sociologists, although variations are common. Many sociologists, for example, identify only five classes, omitting the distinction between the lower-upper and upper-upper classes. We use this somewhat arbitrary five-class division in the discussion of American social classes that follows. A summary of attributes of each of the five classes is found in Figure 10.1 on page 218.

The Lower Class

The lower class consists of the people who are the most deprived of wealth, power, and prestige in American society. It currently includes roughly 20 percent of the adults without political and economic power. Through unions and other forms of collective action, such working-class occupational groups as sanitation workers and bus drivers have been able to secure fairly high wages. In fact, they often make more money than do people with higher educational qualifications, such as clerical workers and teachers.

Members of the working class do not interact with their co-workers off the job as much as do middle-class people, and at home they tend not to talk about their jobs very frequently (Komarovsky, 1964; Rubin, 1976). In their spare time, members of the working class may watch ball games, go camping, and work on their cars. These activities, however, are, to some extent, shared by all Americans.

Lower-class people appear in some ways to be stuck at their level because of the lack of resources available to them with which to escape.

Working-class people, despite their relatively low incomes and lack of job security, are not without political and economic power. Through unions, working-class occupational groups are able to fight for increased wages and job security.

in the United States and is disproportionately made up of members of racial and ethnic minority groups. Children are also overrepresented in the lower class. The defining traits of members of the lower class are a low level of education and a lack of marketable skills. Unemployment is high, and economic insecurity is chronic.

In view of these conditions, it is little wonder that lower-class people tend to be pessimistic, cynical, resigned, and distrustful (Rosenberg, 1956). Although they may want to be in the mainstream of society, lower-class people join fewer groups and vote less than do the members of any other class. Lower-class people appear in some ways to be stuck at their level, for they have few resources with which to escape.

The Working Class

Consisting of people who are steadily employed in manual labor, the working class is the largest of the main social classes, with about 40 to 45 percent of the labor force in its ranks. Members of this class typically feel that work is not a "central life interest" (Dubin & Goldman, 1972). The condition of the working class has improved steadily, especially since the Great Depression of the 1930s. Its members, however, are not free of financial worries, job layoffs, or unrewarding work. The recent massive layoffs in many blue-collar industries underscore the persistent job insecurity of the members of this class.

Despite their relatively low incomes and lack of job security, members of the working class are not totally

CLASS (AND PERCENTAGE OF TOTAL POPULATION)	GENERAL						
	INCOME	PROPERTY	OCCUPATION	EDUCATION	PERSONAL AND FAMILY LIFE	EDUCATION OF CHILDREN	
Upper class (1–3%)	Very high income, most of it from wealth	Great wealth, old wealth, control over investment	Managers, professionals, high civil and military officials	Liberal arts education at elite schools	Stable family life	College education by right for both sexes	
Upper middle class (10–15%)	High income	Accumulation of property through savings	Lowest unemployment	Graduate training	Autonomous personality		
Lower middle class (30–35%)	Modest income	Few assets	Small business people and farmers, lower professionals, semiprofessionals, sales and clerical workers	Some college	Better physical and mental health and health care	Educational system biased in their favor	
		Some savings		High school	Longer life expectancy	Greater chance of college than working class children	
Working class (40–45%)	Low income	Few to no assets	Skilled labor	Some high school	Unstable family life	Tendency toward vocational programs	
			Unskilled labor	Grade school	One-parent homes		
		No savings	Highest unemployment	Illiteracy, especially functional illiteracy	Conformist personality		
Lower class (20–25%)	Poverty income (destitution)		Surplus labor		Poorer physical and mental health	Little interest in education, high dropout rates	
					Lower life expectancy		

FIGURE 10.1   The five social classes in America differ widely in wealth, prestige, and power.

Source: From Daniel W. Rossides, *Social Stratification: The American Class System in Comparative Perspective,* © 1990, pp. 406–408. Reprinted by permission of Prentice-Hall, Inc., Upper Saddle River, NJ.

The Lower Middle Class

This "white-collar" class makes up about 30 to 35 percent of the work force. It includes people who run small businesses as well as those who work in large organizations within the government, business, and industry. Members of this class do work that is intellectual rather than manual. Typical jobs include clerk, insurance agent, schoolteacher, and salesperson. The lower middle class is higher in prestige than the working class. But because its members tend not be unionized, this class in some ways may have less collective power than the working class.

Members of the lower middle class sometimes show a special concern for prestige and status and tend to be *status seekers* (Mills, 1951). That is, they invest a substantial percentage of their disposable income in goods and services that can be used as status symbols. These include cars, homes, and leisure activities.

Traditionally, the members of this class have relatively strongly adhered to the "Protestant ethic" (a term coined by Max Weber)—a set of moral and ethical principles emphasizing the importance of hard work, honesty, sexual modesty, and responsibility (Rothman, 1978). (This ethic is not, of course, limited to Protestants.)

The Upper Middle Class

The upper middle class is the most recent class to emerge in modern societies (Bensman & Vidich, 1971). It appeared mainly because of the need for expert knowledge in a technological society. Members of this class constitute about 10 to 15 percent of the labor force and fall into the upper one-fifth of the nation's income

PRESTIGE				POWER	
OCCUPATIONAL PRESTIGE	SUBJECTIVE DEVELOPMENT	CONSUMPTION	PARTICIPATION IN GROUP LIFE	PARTICIPATION IN POLITICAL PROCESSES	POLITICAL ATTITUDES
High occupational prestige	Consistent attitudes	Tasteful consumption	High participation in groups segregated by breeding, religion, ethnicity, race, and function	High participation in voting and other forms of political participation, including monopoly on high governmental positions	Belief in efficacy of political action
	Integrated self-perception	Affluence and comfort			Support for civil rights and liberal foreign policy
		Modest standard of living			Negative attitude toward governmental intervention in economy and toward welfare programs
Low occupational prestige	Inconsistent attitudes	Consumption of mass "material" and "symbolic" culture	Low participation in group life		Tendency to discount value of political action
	Unrealistic self-perception	Austere consumption		Tendency not to vote or participate in politics	Except for minorities, opposition to civil rights
Stigma of worthlessness on the labor market	Greater prevalence of mental illness	Physical suffering	Social isolation		Support for more nationalist foreign policy and governmental programs that provide economic help and security
		Acute economic anxiety			

distribution. They enjoy substantial power and prestige, as well as income. Much of their power derives from their membership in strong professional groups, such as the American Medical Association. These groups have been very effective in promoting their own interests.

Compared to members of the other classes, members of the upper middle class are more likely to find work a central life interest, and much of their social life revolves around work (Dubin & Goldman, 1972).

Members of the upper middle class come from relatively diverse social backgrounds, at least in comparison to members of the upper class, and they hold a variety of jobs, ranging from self-employment as dentists, lawyers, and physicians to positions as salaried corporate executives. This class reads more magazines, books, and newspapers—and watches less television—than do members of the lower social classes (Rossides, 1990).

The Upper Class

The upper class is the most powerful and wealthiest group in America. Constituting only about 1 to 3 percent of the U.S. population, members of the upper class hold many of the top-level positions in big business, entertainment, industry, government, and the military (Rossides, 1990). Despite the great wealth and power of this class, however, its members enjoy a less than perfect reputation in the eyes of many people. This is partly because of their ability to distance themselves from the day-to-day problems of less fortunate Americans.

The lifestyle of the upper class is typically conservative, often elegant, and distinguished by education in private schools and membership in exclusive clubs. Many members of the upper class try to preserve their family name, for example, through foundations and charities. As

SOCIOLOGY OF THE MEDIA

POVERTY: INVISIBLE NEWS

On November 30, 1998, the *St. Louis Post-Dispatch* ran a story entitled "In the Midst of Plenty, the Disadvantaged Struggle to Get by." In contrast to most newspaper articles on poverty, the reporter, Dave Dorr, put faces on an invisible part of American society. Referring to them as neighbors who need our help, he identified 10 of the 100 neediest cases in the city. They included:

Case 21

Mr. A. fought to gain custody of his two sons after he learned they were abused by their mother. Both boys, ages 10 and 11, have asthma. The oldest boy often is hospitalized with asthma attacks.

Mr. A. is without adequate health insurance. He's accepted temporary jobs, but when he works, his medical benefits are taken away and this scares him because of the severity of his oldest son's asthma.

He's in need of clothing and shoes for his sons, but what would really brighten the holidays for this family would be a substantial job for Mr. A. that would allow him to put himself back on his feet.

Case 23

Ms. G., 28, is divorced. She's taken on the responsibility of raising her nephew, 5, after he was abandoned by his mother. Ms. G.'s caseworker calls this act of kindness "admirable," particularly in light of the fact that Ms. G. is out of work.

Living room furniture is a priority, as well as winter clothing for Ms. G. and her nephew.

Case 26

Ms. J., 27, lost many of her possessions in a fire at her home. A neighbor awoke and saw flames. After calling the fire department, the neighbor kicked in the door to Ms. J.'s home to alert her and her three children.

She is unemployed and unable to offer her children the promise of a good Christmas dinner and some gifts. What the family needs more are blankets, sheets, and kitchen items.

Case 27

After Ms. H., 34, was let go from her job, she moved with her two children, ages 5 and 2, into her mother's basement because she couldn't afford rent.

Her caseworker said Ms. H.'s 5-year-old son told her, "My mom stays hungry," because she gives her children most of the food. A donation of $200 would allow her to buy food and get Christmas gifts for her children.

While most Americans know situations like these, the media rarely cover poverty or the plight of the poor. Unlike the White House, Wall street, or City Hall, they are not regular newsbeats. Poverty is a seasonal

---

noted in the last chapter, members of the upper class show more class consciousness than do people from other social classes. They are well aware of their privileged position in society.

The members of the upper class tend to define their class as a category that one is born into. The "new rich" (*nouveau riche*) may gain nominal acceptance, but their status is never quite the same as that of those whose names have been in the social register for generations.

While upper-class men are often professionals or financiers, upper-class women tend to gravitate toward volunteer work in their communities. These women do not push carts down hospital corridors or answer school telephones, but they do conduct fund-raising campaigns for museums, symphonies, children's welfare boards, and other similar cultural and social causes (Ostrander, 1984).

SOCIAL MOBILITY IN THE UNITED STATES

How open is American society compared to those of other highly industrialized or advanced nations? How easily can a person move from one social class into a higher, or lower, class? The United States has been called the "land of opportunity," meaning the opportunity for upward mobility. Yet a classic objective study in the 1950s found that the rates of social mobility in the United States were roughly the same as those in other advanced societies (Lipset & Bendix, 1959). In each of the nations studied, about a third of the children of manual (blue-collar) workers had moved into nonmanual (white-collar) jobs. Switzerland showed the greatest upward mobility and West Germany the lowest, with the United States in the middle of the pack.

feature—popular at Thanksgiving and Christmas (Lee & Solomon, 1991).

In fact, David Croteau and William Hoynes argue that "the only regular features on working-class and poor people are likely to come from the reporter on the crime beat" (1997, p. 158). And that has not changed since Herbert Gans studied the media in the 1960s and 1970s (1980). In describing who usually appeared in the news, Gans did not neglect to identify those who did not. He wrote:

> Stories about the poor or about poverty are also rare; in 1967, less than 1 percent of the television news, and from 1967 to 1971 a similar percent of the newsmagazine columns, were devoted to stories centering on the poor or poverty and most of these were about the federal War on Poverty or anti-hunger policies. Subsequently, the poor have dropped out of the news, except as law violators. (1980, p. 26)

Today, coverage of poverty usually involves official government reports that are periodically issued by the Census Bureau. While these reports always contain data showing the wide income gap between the rich and the poor, news stories bury facts about class divisions (Lee & Solomon, 1991). Journalists hesitate to draw attention to these differences, and "class conflict," which is bound to stir up Marxist notions, is a media no-no.

In the future, it seems unlikely that media coverage of the poor will increase. It is simply not in the media's interest; and reporters who think otherwise put their careers on the line. Consider, for example, the case of Sydney Schanberg, a well-respected journalist whose career at the *New York Times* included positions as foreign correspondent, city desk editor, and columnist. He made the mistake of investigating a real-estate deal in New York City called Westway. While developers took out ads in magazines and newspapers touting the project as

good for the city, their motives were less than altruistic (Lee & Solomon, 1991). In fact, developing that part of New York City would displace many poor and minority households. It is no surprise that Schanberg's column was canceled after he criticized the project. This kind of column was just not in the interest of the newspaper, which relied on the huge ad revenues from landowners and developers who were involved in this project.

As the current trend toward increasing concentration of media ownership by huge multinational corporations continues, it seems unlikely that media coverage of the poor will change. While reporters might remember them on Thanksgiving or Christmas, they are likely to remain invisible the rest of the year.

The study concluded that the mobility rates in advanced societies are similar because these nations share a common pattern of economic development. In each nation, the main reason for upward mobility was structural: The number of white-collar jobs increased in relation to blue-collar jobs, thus reducing the proportion of blue-collar workers and increasing the proportion of white-collar workers (see also Goldthorpe, 1987).

A later cross-national study gave further support to these findings (Fox & Miller, 1965). It concluded that, overall, the United States is quite similar to other advanced nations in the opportunity for movement from manual to nonmanual occupations. One exception was noted, however. In the United States there was substantially more mobility of people from working-class origins into the professional elite—from very low statuses to very high statuses.

Have the chances for upward mobility in the United States improved in recent years? During the late 1960s and early 1970s, a slight trend toward increased upward mobility was found (Blau & Duncan, 1967; Featherman & Hauser, 1978). But more recently the trend toward upward mobility has slowed or even reversed (Blumberg, 1981; Levy & Michel, 1991).

In recent years there has been an extensive sociological debate over what some critics consider the "disappearing" American middle class (Blackburn & Bloom, 1985; Newman, 1988; Pampel, Land, & Felson, 1977). Median family income, adjusted for inflation, grew rapidly after the end of World War II until about 1973, but since then it has remained roughly stable, despite the fact that the costs of such necessities as housing and medical care have increased at a pace much faster than that of

Relocation by American manufacturers to other countries may have created an increase in downward mobility for middle- and working-class people in the United States.

inflation. The result has been a pronounced economic pinch on all of the classes other than the rich.

Long accustomed to the assumption that each generation would be able to maintain a higher standard of living than its parents, children of the middle and working classes are today facing the bleak reality that they may have to be fortunate as well as hardworking in order to do even as well as their parents did. Millions of middle-class families fear that they may drop to working-class status, while marginal members of the working class are confronting the real possibility of poverty. Such formerly attainable goals as a second car, an annual vacation, a college education for the children, and even homeownership seem to be slipping away.

It is important to stress that the reasons for this ominous increase in downward mobility have little to do with the capabilities or job performance of individual workers but, rather, are principally the result of changes in the structure of the American and world economies. One such factor is *deindustrialization*—a decline in some parts of the American manufacturing sector because management has found it more profitable to produce cars, enter data, program computers, and manufacture microelectronics in foreign countries, where wage rates are much lower than in the United States. Another factor is the high number of corporate mergers and acquisitions that took place in the 1980s. Both factors reduced the number of middle management positions available (Bluestone & Harrison, 1982; Harrison & Bluestone, 1988). The

dramatic downsizing in middle management positions by many corporations in the early 1990s continued this trend. Promotion to these kinds of positions has traditionally been a key to upward social mobility.

Another aspect of the middle class's decreased mobility, it has been argued, is the lower promotion potential of the baby boomers who entered the labor market in the 1970s and 1980s. Because of the size of this generation, there are simply too many candidates to be promoted far beyond entry levels. Therefore, many baby boomers will not experience the upward mobility they had been raised to expect.

CLASS DIFFERENCES IN LIFE CHANCES

Social class position (socioeconomic status) has a tremendous impact on us. Our family and work lives, our leisure pursuits, and our political attitudes are all influenced by our social class position. Perhaps the most important effect of social class is on our **life chances**— the likelihood of attaining important goals in life. In this section we review the relationship of class position to overall life chances.

Social Class, Health, and Longevity

Health is a basic determinant of life chances, and there is a very strong relationship between people's socioeconomic status and the quality of their health and the length of their lives. One of the key measures of health in a society is the infant mortality rate. Because African-Americans in our society generally have lower socioeconomic status than whites, a comparison of the infant mortality rates for these two groups can help us understand the magnitude of the effects of class on health. (It is important to note that although blacks are disproportionately represented in lower-status groups, most lower-status people are white, and most blacks are not members of the lower class.) In 1996, the infant mortality rate for blacks was 14.2 per 1,000 live births, compared to 7.2 per 1,000 for whites (U.S. Bureau of the Census, 1998).

Another indication that people from the lower social classes have worse life chances than the rest of us is provided by longevity statistics. In 1996, whites could expect to live an average of 76.8 years, but African-Americans could expect to live only 70.3 years. The life expectancy of black men was only 66.1 years (U.S. Bureau of the Census, 1998).

One reason for these dramatic differences in life expectancy is that both chronic and infectious diseases occur more frequently among the lower classes. The lower classes are additionally disadvantaged by inadequate knowledge concerning how to maintain good health. Not only do they find it difficult to come up with money for nourishing meals, but they also lack information about how to choose a balanced diet. Because diet and health are closely related, it is not surprising that malnutrition and high blood pressure are much more common among the poor than in the rest of the population (Geiger, 1971; Syme & Berkman, 1986). Mental illness is also more prevalent among the poor (Kessler & Clery, 1980).

Not only do low-income people fall ill more often, but they also receive lower quality medical care than do those who have higher incomes. Physicians are scarce in impoverished areas. The poor are thus often forced to use public medical facilities, which tend to be large and over-crowded and to have less qualified staffs than do private medical facilities. To make matters worse, many hospital facilities available to the poor in major urban centers were closed during the 1970s and 1980s because of fiscal problems (Farley, 1995).

A lack of trust in professionals and the low percentage of minority doctors also tend to keep poor minority group members from seeking medical help (Cockerham, 1998). Moreover, the poor commonly lack adequate health insurance. In 1997, 59 percent of families with incomes of less than $20,000 were uninsured (Bagby, 1998).

It is important to note that many authorities feel the most serious problems of lack of access to health care are found not among the very poor, who are eligible for Medicaid, but among the working poor and lower working class, who do not qualify for Medicaid benefits. Individuals in these categories frequently work in jobs that do not provide health insurance coverage, and they cannot afford to purchase private insurance.

To make matters worse, lower- and working-class people are more likely to be subject to a variety of work and home hazards. Some industrial diseases, such as black lung and cancer caused by asbestos, are found chiefly among manual workers who have no choice but to work in unhealthful industries. The victims of on-the-job accidents are almost all from the lower classes. Furthermore, low-status Americans have more household accidents. Carbon monoxide poisoning (often caused by space heaters needed to keep below-standard houses warm in the winter) and lead poisoning (from fires and flaking paint) occur much more often in lower-class homes. Lower-income people are also more likely to live in areas seriously affected by environmental pollution and the dumping of toxic wastes. Thus, at work and at home, lower- and working-class people are considerably more likely than are middle- and upper-class people to have their lives shortened by exposure to poisons.

There is a very strong relationship between people's socioeconomic status and the quality of their health and length of their lives. Low-income people, forced to use public medical facilities, receive lower quality health care and typically suffer from poorer health and lower life expectancy.

Finally, persons of the lower classes are the most likely to die from "unnatural causes." The number of deaths per 100,000 persons resulting from accidents and violence in 1990 was 142 for black males, 81.2 for white males, 38.6 for black females, and 32.1 for white females. But the largest difference between blacks and whites was in homicide rates. In 1995, the rate was 56.3 per 100,000 among black males, compared to only 7.8 per 100,000 among white males (U.S. Bureau of the Census, 1998).

Social Class and the Law

Extensive research strongly suggests that one's social class position affects how he or she is treated by the law (Albonetti, 1991). In principle, all Americans have the right to equal treatment. Yet this is sometimes not the case. Lower-class criminals are more likely to be caught than wealthy criminals and, once apprehended, are less likely to be able to afford highly skilled legal representation (Blumberg, 1970). When they appear in court, their life history—which often includes quitting school, unemployment, divorce, and an apparent lack of responsibility when judged by middle-class standards—may work against them. As a result, lower-income criminals are likely to receive heavier penalties than higher-income criminals for the same crime. And because they often cannot afford bail, lower-income criminals often have to wait for trial in jail cells rather than in the comforts of their own home. (See Chapter 8 for more on the ways in which social class and crime are related.)

APPLYING SOCIOLOGY

AMERICAN PERCEPTIONS OF THE RICH AND POOR

Do you think it is possible nowadays for someone in the United States to start out poor and become rich by working hard? According to a 1996 poll conducted by CBS and the *New York Times,* 78 percent of Americans thought so. In fact, some of America's wealthiest people are self-made billionaires, including Bill Gates (Microsoft), Philip Knight (NIKE), and Ross Perot (EDS).

The idea that anyone can start out poor and achieve unimaginable wealth was made popular by Horatio Alger (1832–1899), who incorporated this theme into more than 100 books that he wrote during the last half of the nineteenth century. His first book, *Ragged Dick* (1868), told the story of a poor shoeshine boy who rose to wealth through his own hard work. In the books that followed, Alger repeated the recipe for success over and over again: Through honest, hard work, and cheerful perseverance, a

poor boy would reap his just reward. These stories were extremely popular with the American public and were particularly well-suited for a time when opportunities for advancement in America seemed unlimited and men were building huge personal fortunes. More than 100 years after the publication of Alger's books, the "Alger hero" lives on in the American language and in the imaginations of the American public.

But times have changed. Society is far more complex and so, too, are ideas about poor people. In some cases it seems that Alger's formula for success has been turned upside down to blame the poor for their misfortune. Consider, for example, some of the common stereotypes about poor people who rely on welfare. According to Daniel Rossides:

Many Americans believe that the welfare rolls are filled with deadbeats and cheats, able-bodied individuals who don't want to work. They believe that welfare makes

people dependent and that people don't want to get out of poverty. Many believe that welfare spending is the reason for their high taxes. (1997, p. 143)

Ideas like these gave welfare reform the support it needed, but they are not necessarily based on the facts. For example, most people on welfare are actually children (who cannot work), mothers, and the elderly. Most poor people would work if it were available. And able-bodied men are not eligible for welfare benefits no matter how poor they are. Finally, the amount of money spent on welfare is small and barely provides enough to get by.

This would suggest that Americans are insensitive to the problems of the poor. But, in fact, that may not be the case. When Americans are asked about "poor people" instead of "welfare recipients," many do seem to understand the causes of their misfortune. Consider, for example, the results of a 1999 Gallup poll that asked Americans why some people are rich and others

Social Class and Education

The opportunity to obtain an education is another life chance that is strongly affected by social class position. Education is critical in order to have a chance to enjoy many of the benefits of American society; the average yearly earnings of college graduates, for instance, are nearly 50 percent higher than those of people with less education. One classic study of some 9,000 students determined that those from high socioeconomic level families had almost 2.5 times the chance of continuing with their education past high school than did those from low socioeconomic level families (Sewell, 1971). Another study concluded that educational attainments are strongly dependent on social class level, even for people with similar IQs (Bowles & Gintis, 1976). The relationship between class level and educational attainment is partly explained

by the fact that children from families in the higher classes are more strongly encouraged to seek and to value higher education (Kerckhoff, 1986), but simple inability to afford the cost of higher education is also an important factor in the equation. (See also Chapter 15.)

Social Class and Social Participation

One pioneering study indicated that people of the lower class, compared to those of higher classes, have less chance for, and receive fewer benefits from, social participation (Axelrod, 1956). They have fewer friends, know fewer of their neighbors and co-workers, join fewer groups—in short, they have fewer social contacts of any kind. A later study of residents in North Carolina came to a similar conclusion (Houghland, Kim, & Christenson, 1979).

poor. Over half of them (53 percent) attributed the success of rich people to strong effort. In contrast, less than half (43 percent) said that a lack of effort explained poverty. And about the same number (41 percent) attributed the plight of the poor to factors beyond their control.

While Americans still believe that hard work is the most important factor in getting ahead, they also recognize that many other factors contribute to success (see Table 10.1). Today, 92 percent of Americans believe that getting the right education or training is important, 87 percent cite parents and family, 69 percent say that you must be willing to take risks, and 68 percent believe that knowing the right people is important. Six in 10 Americans think that ability or talent explains why some people succeed, and half believe that good looks make a difference. Less than half of Americans think that good luck (43 percent), inheritance (42 percent), gender (33 percent), or race/ethnicity (30 percent) are important factors.

And only 24 percent think that dishonesty helps people get ahead.

While most Americans do not blame the poor for their misfortune, the ranking of these reasons does not suggest that they blame an unfair system. Indeed, as this list indicates, they give the lowest rankings to the five factors that would lead to this conclusion—race/ethnicity, gender, inherited wealth, luck, and dishonesty.

TABLE 10.1	**PERCEPTIONS OF WHY SOME PEOPLE GET AHEAD AND SUCCEED IN LIFE**	
Hard work and initiative		92%
Getting the right education/training		92
Parents and family		87
Willingness to take risks		69
Connections/knowing right people		68
Ability or talent one is born with		60
Physical appearance/good looks		50
Good luck/in right place at right time		43
Money inherited from family		42
Gender		33
Member of particular race/ethnic group		30
Dishonesty and willingness to take whatever one can get		24

Source: The Gallup Poll News Service, July 6, 1998; http://www.gallup.com

POVERTY

Poverty is a condition of scarcity or deprivation of material resources characterized by a lack of adequate consumption of the necessities of life. For those who experience it, poverty is highly personal—a feeling of emptiness in one's gut and of seeing hunger in the eyes of one's children. The widespread problems of poverty in America today make it a social condition that demands extensive sociological analysis.

Definitions of Poverty

The definition of poverty is a controversial issue because it is influenced by political and moral values, as well as by economics. Definitions of poverty can be relative or absolute.

Relative definitions place a certain proportion of the members of any society in the poverty category. An individual is relatively poor if he or she has substantially less than is considered to be normal in a given society. Some sociologists, for example, consider the poverty income level to be one-half the national median income, and they place in relative poverty anyone who falls at or below this income level.

Absolute definitions of poverty set an income level below which a person or family cannot sustain a minimal standard of living. Using an absolute definition of poverty, it is theoretically possible to have no poverty in a given society.

Although there is no entirely satisfactory way to define poverty, a quantitative definition is necessary in order to administer social welfare programs. The government and other agencies must have some numerical

poverty level—a specific income that is used to identify who will officially be regarded as poor—in order to determine who is eligible for certain social welfare benefits. The federal government has established a method of calculating the poverty level that reflects an absolute definition of poverty and is based on the amount of income believed necessary to purchase enough food for a subsistence diet. State and local governments and private agencies also frequently rely on this definition. The poverty level is recalculated each year to take into account changes caused by inflation and varies according to family size. In 1998, the poverty level was $16,655 for a family of four.

First developed in the 1960s, the federal government's poverty level is based on a minimum food budget calculated by the U.S. Department of Agriculture. This budget is just enough to purchase the nutritional minimum necessary to sustain human life. This basic food budget is then multiplied by 3 to determine the poverty level; in other words, expenses for food are assumed to represent one-third of the poor family's total budget. This can be illustrated by the following breakdown of expenses for a poverty-level family of four (based on 1998 Census Bureau data):

Total income	$16,655.00	
Food	5,551.67 =	$3.80 a day per person
Shelter	5,551.67 =	$462.64 a month
Other necessities	5,551.67 =	$115.66 a month per person for clothing, transportation, medicine, utilities, etc.

It is important to note that this poverty level refers only to cash income and does not take into account non-cash (in-kind) benefits that many poor people receive, such as food stamps. The exclusion of these benefits may be compensated for, however, by the fact that the poverty-level food budget is extremely low. Some social scientists, in fact, have charged that the government's poverty level is set much too low. One researcher concluded that "a much-improved measure that included in-kind benefits, taxes paid, and underreporting of income, while adjusting the multiplication factor and raising the food budget, would probably show anywhere from 5 to 20 million additional poor" (Rodgers, 1982, p. 25).

Incidence of Poverty

The incidence of poverty varies over time. Poverty is affected not only by the condition of the economy but also by government policies. Table 10.2 shows the changes in the poverty population in the United States from 1959 to 1997 as measured by the U.S. government.

TABLE 10.2   POVERTY IN THE UNITED STATES, 1959–1997

Year	Poverty Level	Number of Poor Persons (millions)	Poor Persons as Percentage of Total Population (poverty rate)
1959	$ 2,973	39.5	22.4
1965	3,223	33.2	17.3
1973	4,540	23.0	11.1
1979	7,412	25.3	11.6
1987	11,611	32.5	13.5
1991	13,924	35.7	14.2
1997	16,400	35.6	13.3

Source: U.S. Bureau of the Census, *Statistical Abstract of the United States, 1998* (Washington, D.C.: U.S. Government Printing Office, 1998).

What economic conditions and government policies account for the changes in the poverty rate over the last quarter-century? Although the subject of sharp debate, the decline in poverty between 1959 and 1965 is usually attributed principally to the healthy state of the economy. The continued decline between 1965 and 1973 seems to have been the result of continued prosperity, together, more likely than not, with the effects of the multi-billion-dollar War on Poverty of the 1960s. Throughout the 1970s, there was little change in the size of the poverty population. But in the early 1980s, the poverty rate began to rise again, and this is usually explained by two major factors: the state of the economy and controversial government cuts in social welfare programs.

The overall poverty rate in 1997 was 13.3 percent, the lowest level since before the last recession in 1989 (*New York Times*, 1998). While poverty levels remain the lowest for non-Hispanic whites (8.6 percent in 1997), other selected groups have also benefited from three consecutive years of growth in income. Declining from 32.7 percent in 1991 to 26.5 percent in 1997, the poverty rate for African-Americans is at its lowest point since the federal government began collecting poverty data for African-Americans in 1959. The poverty rate also declined for other groups during this period: Hispanic-Americans (from 28.7 to 27.1 percent), children (from 21.1 to 19.9 percent), and the elderly (from 12.4 to 10.5 percent) (see Figure 10.2).

The Poor and Employment

Although many poor people are unable to work, a majority of them do work, at least part time. The main reason that these wage earners remain below the poverty line lies in the fact that they are chronically *underemployed*—that is, they work at jobs that pay very low wages. The 1998 minimum wage was $5.15 an hour. This rate would have produced an annual, full-time income (at 40 hours of work per week with no days off) of only $10,712, which is well below the 1998 poverty level of $16,655 for a family of four.

The largest group of nonworking poor people are people who stay at home keeping house and taking care of young children. These are mainly female householders who have no husband present. The next largest group of poor people who do not work are those who are ill or disabled. Very few nonworking poor people are able-bodied adults without young dependent children.

The Causes of Poverty

BLAMING THE VICTIM

As previously mentioned, there is a long-standing belief in America that the poor are to blame for their own misfortune. According to this view—which social scientists often describe as an example of "blaming the victim"—we have equal opportunities to advance ourselves through hard work. If someone is poor, his or her poverty must be due to some personal failing. This ideology is at the heart of the resentment many people feel toward welfare programs. Recipients are thought to depend on welfare because they are too lazy to work or because their immoral behavior has resulted in large and often broken families. Supporting the poor through welfare is thus seen as a waste of the taxpayers' money and as encouraging people to continue in their misguided ways, including widespread welfare cheating (Kluegel, 1987).

Social scientists generally reject this view (Felson, 1991). Poverty is not the fault of the poor, they argue, but is overwhelmingly the result of conditions over which the victims have little control (Ryan, 1976). According to one perspective, there is a *culture of poverty* that prevents the poor from acquiring the qualities they need to advance in middle-class society. According to another, there are *structural* barriers built into our economic system that make it almost impossible for the poor to break out of their circumstances.

THE CULTURE OF POVERTY

The idea that there is a distinctive **culture of poverty**—a set of norms and values common to poor people—was developed by the anthropologist Oscar Lewis in a series of

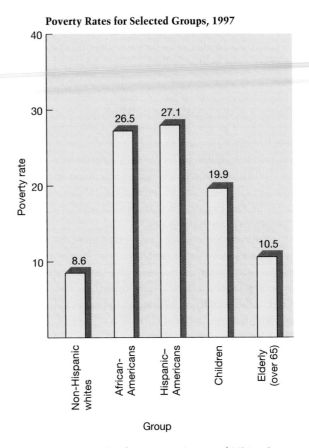

Poverty Rates for Selected Groups, 1997

FIGURE 10.2 Both African-Americans and Hispanic-Americans have higher overall poverty rates than non-Hispanic white Americans do.

Source: U.S. Bureau of the Census, *Statistical Abstract of the United States, 1998* (Washington, D.C.: U.S. Government Printing Office, 1998).

studies of slum dwellers in Mexico and Puerto Rico (1959, 1961, 1964, 1966). Lewis argued that the culture of poverty is characteristic of many urban poor the world over. When a group of people suffers economic deprivation for several generations, a culture develops as an adaptive response to the deprivation—that is, it enables the poor to cope with their extreme circumstances. The characteristic traits of the culture of poverty include a sense of resignation, unwillingness to plan for the future, inability to defer the gratification of impulses, and suspicion of authority. These values are adaptive in an environment in which there is no hope that conditions will improve.

Unfortunately, however, the culture of poverty, like any cultural tradition, is self-perpetuating. According to Lewis:

> Once [the culture of poverty] comes into existence it tends to perpetuate itself from generation to generation because of its effect on children. By the time slum children are age six or seven, they have usually absorbed the

basic values and attitudes of their subculture and are not psychologically geared to take full advantage of changing conditions or increased opportunities which may occur in their lifetime. (1966, p. xiv)

The culture of poverty concept had substantial influence on the social programs that were developed during the War on Poverty of the 1960s (discussed below). Many of these programs were designed to alter the personal qualities, including the cultural values, of the poor, in the hope that this would enable them to participate more effectively in the job market. Job training, job counseling and placement, and compensatory education are examples of such programs.

Critics of the culture of poverty perspective argue that it is just a more sophisticated way of blaming the victims of poverty for their own condition. In their view, it is not cultural values but social injustice that causes poverty. Additionally, critics argue that Lewis does not effectively demonstrate that there is a culture of poverty distinct from the culture of the rest of society. It can be argued, for example, that the inability to defer the gratification of impulses is no more characteristic of the poor than of the middle class. The only difference is that the members of the middle class can confidently expect a future when they will be able to satisfy those impulses. The poor do not have the luxury of that certainty (Harris, 1988; Valentine, 1968, 1971).

STRUCTURAL EXPLANATIONS

In the late 1960s and early 1970s, many sociologists became dissatisfied with explanations of poverty that focused on the personal and cultural qualities of the poor. They began to look instead for **structural explanations of poverty,** explanations that attribute poverty to persistent inequalities in society, such as the distribution of power, wealth, and other resources that, in effect, force some people to remain in poverty.

Many structural factors reduce the access of the poor to jobs. For example, the rapid outflow of manufacturing jobs from the central cities (where many of the poor live) to the suburbs (where few poor people can afford to live) has left behind primarily jobs that are either low-paying or that require a high level of training and skills (Wilson, 1987, 1996). Thus, as mentioned earlier, even when the urban poor can find jobs, their wages are often so low that work only marginally reduces their poverty. The ability of many minorities to get any but the most low-skill, monotonous, and low-paying jobs may also be hindered by *institutional racism,* persistent discrimination built into our social and economic institutions. (This topic is discussed in Chapter 11.)

Poor people also suffer various kinds of exploitation by powerful economic interests. For example, it is in the interest of business to pay the lowest wages possible, to keep costs down. And in its efforts to reduce inflation, the government sometimes uses methods that drive up the unemployment rate, especially among unskilled workers.

The undeniable importance of structural factors does not mean that we do not need also to take account of personal and cultural factors. Some research, in fact, suggests that the two are intertwined in complex ways to perpetuate welfare dependency. For example, "welfare mothers" have difficulty getting jobs for both personal and structural reasons. Often, they cannot leave their young children to go to work, and they may be ill because of the conditions in which they live and their lack of access to adequate medical care. These are structural factors. But welfare mothers also may lack the education and the work experience that would allow them to find work steady enough to achieve financial independence. Although there are structural reasons for their lack of education and experience, these are also personal and cultural factors that could be changed through educational and job training programs.

SOCIAL WELFARE

Social welfare is a system of programs, benefits, and services that seeks to enable people in need to attain a minimum level of social and personal functioning. Broadly speaking, social welfare includes four major components: income maintenance programs and health, education, and welfare services. Here, the discussion of social welfare is confined to income maintenance and welfare services; health and education are the topics of Chapters 12 and 15.

A Brief History of Social Welfare

WELFARE IN THE COLONIES

Americans have been greatly influenced by the values of the early Puritan settlers, who regarded poverty as a sign of moral weakness. The colonists viewed paupers, beggars, vagrants, and all other classes of the needy (except for the elderly, most of whom were longtime members of the community) as objects of contempt. Support for the needy was a local responsibility exercised by the parish or town government. Relief was provided for the poor either in kind—food, clothes, fuel—or in the form of a fee paid to families who agreed to support paupers in their homes. Often, the town and the families keeping boarders supplied barely enough aid to keep the poor and infirm alive.

In addition, their keepers sometimes beat and punished the needy, especially those from out of town.

NINETEENTH-CENTURY REFORMS

The nineteenth century was an era in which the *poorhouse,* which came into being after reformers criticized the mistreatment of the poor under the colonial system, attempted to shelter virtually everyone in need. Poorhouses were typically rundown buildings bought cheaply by towns or counties and often supervised by minimally qualified political appointees (Friedlander & Apte, 1980).

In the early nineteenth century, the poorhouse policy tended to treat the needy as a single category, offering the same services to all. Elderly and sick people were thrown together with tramps, the blind, the deaf, the mentally and physically handicapped, and the insane. Able-bodied residents sat idle all day. Walls, furnishings, and "sanitary" facilities were filthy (Katz, 1986).

By midcentury, private charitable organizations began to establish specialized institutions for children, invalids, and the elderly to remove them from the wretched conditions of the poorhouse. Meanwhile, because caring for certain other types of the needy had become too costly for towns and counties, state governments set up insane asylums and jails.

THE GREAT DEPRESSION: ENTRY OF THE FEDERAL GOVERNMENT

The general economic collapse of the Great Depression changed popular beliefs about who should get welfare and which organizations should give it. A general consensus remained, however, regarding how much welfare funding should be given: as little as possible.

Up to one-third of the American work force was unemployed in the years following the stock market crash of October 1929. Until that time, many people believed that economic misfortune could only befall those who were morally defective in some way. But the sheer scale of unemployment during the Depression suggested that the American economic system, not the individual, must have been at fault (Piven & Cloward, 1982). Because local and state governments and charities, long the source of relief, were nearly bankrupt, masses of citizens accepted the necessity for federal action.

When Franklin Delano Roosevelt became president, he responded with a series of programs, collectively called the New Deal, which culminated in the Social Security Act of 1935. This act became the cornerstone of the welfare system for over 60 years; it set up a nationalized pension

The Great Depression of the 1930s was a time of great poverty in the United States. Here unemployed men wait in line for free coffee and doughnuts.

plan for the elderly known as Social Security (see Chapter 12) and provided relief to unemployed workers in the form of unemployment insurance. It also mandated Aid to Families with Dependent Children (AFDC) and assistance to the aged, the blind, and the disabled.

One consequence of the New Deal was that for the first time in U.S. history the federal government took responsibility for those who could not care for themselves: the elderly, the disabled, and the poor. By providing unemployment compensation, the government also accepted an obligation to cushion the effects of the boom-and-bust cycles that had become a part of America's industrial capitalist economy.

The Depression and the New Deal also marked the beginning of a shift in public attitudes toward welfare. Some people began to accept the view that receiving help from a public agency is not a sign of moral weakness (Wilensky & Lebeaux, 1965). It is important not to exaggerate this shift in attitudes, however. Public acceptance of welfare programs varies according to the program. Old age benefits, for example, are extremely popular, but programs designed to benefit poor families remain controversial. And the belief that the able-bodied poor should work and take care of themselves remains strong.

THE GREAT SOCIETY AND THE WAR ON POVERTY

During the 1960s, President Lyndon Johnson initiated a series of measures to extend welfare benefits. Taken together, these programs became known as the Great Society and the War on Poverty.

WINDOW ON SOCIOLOGY

FACES OF POVERTY

What does the face of poverty look like? Is it a black woman living in a rat-infested apartment in an inner city? Perhaps you see a white woman in Appalachia whose wrinked face leads you to assume that she is the grand-mother—not the mother—of the children who surround her. Or perhaps you see the face of a homeless person, sleeping under bridges, in subways, or on a door stoop. Most of us do not know the poor. These invisible Americans live in separate neighborhoods, their children attend different schools, and we do not work together.

In her book *Portraits of Women and Children on Welfare,* Jill Berrick gives us insight into the problems of the poor by profiling the lives of five typical welfare mothers. The only one that you might recognize is Cora. Her own self-description seems to fit that of a stereotypical "welfare queen":

I already feel like I'm old. You know, I think me bein' at home all this time sort of like got me on the lazy side—sort of ruined me. What slowed me down was, you know, I was gettin' high and then I didn't go nowhere. I'd just lay around and get high. Get up in the morning, do the same thing, over and over again. So the routine just layin' around the house all the time just broke my spirit, and next thing I'm getting fat and I'm forty-one years old. 'Cause I started doin' that when I was about twenty-nine. I been doin' it ever since then. Next thing I know I'm forty years old. I can't get in the spirit like I used to. There goes fifteen, twenty years of my life doin' nothing. (Berrick, 1995, p. 113)

Cora spent her entire adult life—from the age of 17—on welfare. And, as her story suggests, she fits the image of a welfare queen. But she is only one of the faces that Berrick reveals, and she is by no means typical of the kind of women who receive public assistance.

Far more typical is Ana, a woman who slipped from the working class into poverty because of circumstances beyond her control. In contrast to Cora, Ana was a hard worker. After marrying at 17, she earned her high school diploma at summer school and later attended a community college. With the support of her mother, she was able to continue working after the birth of two children. In fact, she

What does the face of poverty look like? Most of us do not know the poor. These invisible Americans live in separate neighborhoods, their children attend different schools, and they work in different places—if they have jobs.

became the family's sole provider when her husband's drug problem led him to leave the family for weeks at a time. Eventually, Ana was making $31,000 a year as a civil servant in the Department of Motor Vehicles. And after 15 years, she had saved several thousand dollars.

While she considered buying a house, she decided to invest the money in her own business—a bar. But she did not give up her job at the

---

This new legislation came largely in response to demands made by the civil rights movement. At first, urban blacks in the North called on city governments to provide more jobs and to be more responsive to their needs. When their calls went largely unanswered, they began to demand housing and jobs from the federal government. To meet these needs, the administration extended previous benefits and created new ones. The new benefits took several forms, including general cash grants, subsidies earmarked for specific purposes, and training programs for the employable poor. Congress greatly increased Social Security benefits to the elderly and expanded the AFDC program.

The 1996 Welfare Reform Act

In 1997, the welfare system that dated back to the New Deal era was officially dismantled in compliance with the 1996 Welfare Reform Act (see Figure 10.3, page 232). By shifting responsibility for the needy and unemployed to individual states, this landmark welfare-reform legislation effectively ended welfare as an entitlement program. Under the new system, the federal government will provide block grants to the states, which they will then use to design their own welfare programs.

One block grant, known as Temporary Assistance for Needy Families, phases out Aid to Families with

DMV. Instead, she hired a new boyfriend to manage the bar during the day and she, herself, worked evenings. But Ana's hope of achieving the American dream soon turned into a nightmare. Her business began to fail, and with debts mounting, she learned that she was pregnant. But she still had her steady income from her position at the DMV and was paying off her creditors.

Unfortunately, her luck just kept getting worse. Her real ordeal began at work when she fell from the top stair of a truck, splitting a vertebra and damaging three disks in her neck. After 3 weeks of rest, Ana returned to work with doctor's orders of "light duty." But her boss soon pressured her to resume her old work. Shortly thereafter she found herself unable to get out of bed. And her doctors took her off work. Ana assumed that she would receive workers compensation and began to withdraw money from her small savings account.

Incredibly, misfortune hit again. She and her baby were badly burned while she was cooking. After a couple of days in the hospital, Ana and the baby were able to go home. But at this point, she had no income. She held a garage sale and sold everything but her most precious and basic possessions. When her family could no longer help her, Ana turned to welfare.

Her attitude toward welfare was different from Cora's. She said:

[The people at welfare] were very helpful. They tried to work with me, and that was surprising. But I didn't want to go in there [to the welfare office]. First of all, I really thought I would be belittled. I expected them to look at me and say, "There's a dork, good-bye. You don't belong here." I just kept saying to myself, "I don't belong here." And I felt a little bad. You really do. You feel real depressed. I thought people were staring at me. And the people. . . . It was like they were very loud. I had this feeling that they didn't really want to get out of it. It's almost like they were always going to be there, you know? No matter what day of the week you'd go in there, you'd find them in there.

[The worker] asked me a lot of questions, but that was good. I don't believe they police people well enough. They were very thorough with me. I think they're very thorough before you get through the door, but once you are in, the door locks. They were thorough, and they were quick about it.

(Berrick 1995, pp. 29–30).

Ana eventually received her workers compensation check. And she was able to return to work after about 6 months. Although the details of her circumstances are unique, the reason she needed welfare is typical. American men and women rely on income maintenance programs like unemployment insurance, workers compensation, food stamps, local food banks, and welfare benefits to help them get through temporary financial crises. Unfortunately, when Americans think of people who need help, Ana is not the first face they see. Instead, it is Cora's—an unrealistic representative of America's poorest.

Source: Jill Berrick. Faces of Poverty: Portraits of Women and Children on Welfare (New York: Oxford University Press, 1995).

Dependent Children (AFDC). Under the provisions of the new law, states must put half of all AFDC recipients to work by the year 2000, and families are eligible to receive benefits for only a limited number of months. The Child Protection Block Grant replaces 23 federal child-protection programs, including programs that provided foster care, adoption assistance, and child abuse services. Another nine federal child-care programs have been replaced by the Child Care and Development Block Grant, which is designed to provide child-care services to low-income families. And the Family Nutrition Block Grant replaces a number of federal nutrition programs, including WIC (Women, Infants, and children), the Child and Adult Care Food Program, the Summer Food Program, and the Homeless Children Nutrition Program. While states must decide how to use the funds from this block grant, they will be required to provide food to low-income pregnant women, infants, and young children at risk for poor nutrition. Finally, the School-Based Nutrition Block Grant is replacing lunch and breakfast programs, summer food programs, and special milk programs of the school systems.

The 1996 Welfare Reform Act also scaled back other programs. A cap was put on funds allocated to the food stamp program so that as the number of households receiving food stamps increases, each one will receive

OLD SYSTEM	NEW SYSTEM	FUNDING
Programs	Block grants	Federal government will provide
AFDC (Aid to Families with Dependent Children)	Cash welfare block grant	$15.4 billion in temporary assistance for each year from 1997 to 2000
23 Federal child-protection programs	Child protection block grant	$4.4 billion in 1997, $5.6 billion in 2000
9 Federal child-care programs	Child care and development block grant	$2.1 billion annually between 1997 and 2000
WIC, Child and adult care food programs, summer food program, homeless children nutrition program	School-based nutrition block grant	$4.6 billion in 1997, $5.3 billion by 2000

FIGURE 10.3   Public Assistance before and after the 1996 Welfare Reform Act

Source: Based on Meredith Bagby, *Annual Report of the United States of America* (New York: McGraw-Hill, 1997).

proportionately less benefits. Other restrictions under the new law also prevent legal and illegal immigrants from receiving Supplemental Security Income (SSI), cash welfare, social service block grants, Medicaid, and food stamps. The eligibility requirements for SSI and the cash benefit program are also stricter for the blind, disabled, and elderly. And neither drug addiction nor alcoholism is considered a disability under the new system. Finally, single mothers on welfare who do not identify the fathers of their children can lose at least 20 percent of their benefits. And unwed teen mothers must live at home and stay in school in order to receive benefits.

The changes required by the 1996 Welfare Reform Act are expected to save the federal government $55 billion over a period of 6 years. While it is still too early to judge this new system, critics are concerned about the effects that it will have on the poor and especially children (Piven, 1996). The first year, however, looked promising. The new requirements to work, along with a healthy economy, reduced the number of welfare recipients (Bagby, 1998). And feedback from individual states suggest that the reforms have not produced significant negative effects. Data from states that have taken the lead in forcing people off welfare rolls, like Iowa and Wisconsin, show little evidence so far of homelessness and destitution.

While the welfare-reform legislation of 1996 required major reforms in public assistance programs, it did not affect the social insurance programs that were also created under the Social Security Act of 1935. In contrast to public assistance, which is paid for from general tax revenues, social insurance programs are based on contributions by workers and employees, and benefits are related to these contributions. The two most important social insurance programs are Social Security and Unemployment Insurance.

SOCIAL SECURITY. Old Age, Survivors, and Disability Insurance, popularly known as *Social Security,* was signed into law by Franklin Delano Roosevelt in 1935. This program, which was designed to guarantee income to the elderly after retirement, has become one of the most expensive social programs in the world (Bagby, 1998). Taking in more than 22 cents for every dollar of tax revenue, the Social Security Administration estimated that it spent $370.8 billion in 1997.

When this program began, its future seemed secure with the ratio of workers to recipients at 15 to 1. But with Americans living longer than ever, that ratio has started to decline. By the year 2000, the number of Americans receiving Social Security benefits is expected to grow to nearly 47 million people and to reach nearly 90 million by the middle of the twenty-first century. By the time baby boomers reach retirement age, the ratio of workers to Social Security recipients will be 2 to 1, which has led economists to predict that the program will go bankrupt by the year 2029 (Bagby, 1997).

A number of plans have been proposed to reform this system, including investing Social Security money in mutual and index funds. While this could yield higher funds, critics fear that investing in the stock market is far too risky for retirement savings. Other proposals have suggested a reduction in benefits, an older age for retirement, increased payroll taxes on higher incomes, increased penalties for early retirement, and lower cost of living adjustments (Bagby, 1997).

UNEMPLOYMENT INSURANCE. Unemployment Insurance (UI) is intended to protect the incomes of workers who are laid off. This program is financed by a tax on employers (and, in some states, on employees as well) and proceeds from the tax are distributed to state-run programs that are subject to federal guidelines. Eligibility rules require a minimum period of employment and a minimum level of earnings before benefits are paid. Partly because the poor are the workers who are least able to meet these requirements, they are the least likely to be covered.

The UI program was originally intended to help adult male workers through occasional periods of layoff until improved economic conditions would allow them to return to their jobs (Ford Foundation, 1989). But in today's rapidly changing economy, many laid-off workers do not have jobs to return to. Therefore, many of these workers need retraining for new kinds of jobs.

CHAPTER REVIEW

1. How do the life chances differ for members of the five major social classes in the United States?

2. Why is poverty defined in both relative and absolute terms?

3. Describe how a family under the poverty line survives.

4. How has poverty in the United States fluctuated over the course of the last century? What have been the main causes of poverty?

5. Give an example of "blaming the victim."

6. Explain the differences between culture of poverty and structural explanations of poverty.

7. Describe the changes brought about by the 1996 Welfare Bill.

8. Consider the various proposals for reforming the Social Security program. Which do you favor? Why?

INTERNET EXERCISE

The Web destinations for Chapter 10 cover varous aspects of social class and poverty in American society. To begin your explorations, go to the Prentice Hall companion Web site **http://www.prenhall.com/popenoe.** Then select **Chapter 10** (Social Class and Poverty in the United States) from the menu on the left side of the screen. There are numerous sites to choose from. We suggest you begin with **Welfare.** From the opening screen, you will find a wide variety of links to issues regarding welfare reform. In this chapter, you read about the 1996 Welfare Reform Act. Click on **Welfare Reform—A Complete Description of the New Law.** After you have familiarized yourself with the 1996 Welfare Reform Act, answer the following questions:

- Do you agree that the U.S. welfare system is in need of reform?
- What other suggestions do you have for improving America's approach to welfare issues?

KEY TERMS

life chances	culture of poverty	social welfare
poverty	structural explanation	
poverty level	of poverty	

CHAPTER 11

Ethnic and Racial Minorities

ost visitors to the United States are immediately struck by the remarkable ethnic and racial diversity of its population. New York City alone has Chinatown, Little Italy, Harlem, and Spanish Harlem; large numbers of Greeks, Colombians, Jews, and Koreans; and smaller populations of dozens of other groups. The nation's ethnic and racial diversity has enriched its cultural life greatly. Jazz, salsa, rap, and reggae, as well as cuisine from every part of the world, are only a few of the contributions made to our society by ethnic and racial groups.

Ironically, although at one level the United States has traditionally welcomed diversity, it also has a history of discrimination against the people responsible for that diversity. Inequality in the United States results, in part, because people in positions of power limit the opportunities of others on the basis of ascribed characteristics. Ethnicity and race are both ascribed traits. Thus, many members of ethnic and racial groups in this country are singled out for prejudice or discrimination because they have particular biological or social characteristics. Sociologists characterize such groups as minorities.

In this chapter, we define the terms *ethnic, racial,* and *minority groups* and discuss the nature of prejudice and discrimination. We then describe the major patterns of acceptance and rejection of minorities, and conclude with a discussion of the various ways in which minority members may respond to their status.

ETHNIC AND RACIAL GROUPS

The earliest societies were probably so homogeneous that, like some premodern societies today, they may have had no familiarity with minority groups with cultural or physical traits different from those of the majority. But the written records of the first civilizations do speak of minorities and address the questions of how they should be treated (Castive & Kushner, 1981).

Minority groups are usually the products of *migration,* which is often brought about by environmental, economic, or political conditions such as famine, unemployment, and war. These conditions cause people who may or may not be part of the cultural majority of a society to leave that society and search for a better place to live. Although migration is sometimes voluntary, it is often forced. History is filled with examples of involuntary migrations. The residents of the ancient cities of Akkad and Babylon were forced to move to the Persian Gulf when their fertile lands around the Euphrates River turned to desert. Millions of Africans were captured and brought to America as slaves. More recently, large numbers of Afghans fled to Pakistan to escape persecution by Soviet invaders.

A **minority group** is any group in a society that consists of people who are identified by some biological, social, or cultural trait and who are singled out as objects of prejudice and discrimination. The difference between a "minority" and a "majority" group is not a matter of numbers but, rather, concerns how much social power is held by each group. In South Africa, for example, blacks have historically been treated as a minority group, even though they greatly outnumber whites. It has been suggested that the terms *dominant* and *subordinate* are more descriptive than *majority* and *minority,* for they make it clear that the crucial difference between the groups is one of power. A subordinate population is one whose interests are not fully represented in the political, economic, and social institutions of its society (Banton, 1988). In this chapter, we will use the terms *minority* and *dominant groups.*

For a group to be viewed and treated as a minority, its members must share common characteristics that can be distinguished by both the minority group members and the dominant society. Examples of factors that can result in "us versus them" thinking are language, style of dress, skin color, hair texture and style, and religion. These traits can be divided into two general categories: (1) those that are culturally determined, such as hairstyle, dress, and language, and (2) those that are biologically caused, such as skin color and hair texture.

Groups with distinctive social and cultural characteristics are called *ethnic groups.* Groups with distinctive physical characteristics are called *racial groups.* But ethnicity, race, culture, and biology are often closely connected. Furthermore, the significance of the various cultural and biological differences among various groups in a society is always determined by the dominant group. Not all peoples who are culturally distinct are singled out and treated as ethnic groups. Similarly, race is primarily a cultural concept, not a biological one. Only certain physical differences between groups are regarded by the dominant group as socially significant enough to constitute a basis for racial identification.

Ethnic Groups

The definition of the term *ethnic group* varies widely. Some sociologists use the term to mean all people from a certain geographic region, such as the Irish, the Italians, and the French. Others use the term to mean a group of people who speak the same language or have the same religion. Many contemporary sociologists, however, define an **ethnic group** as any group that is socially distinguished from other groups, has developed a distinct subculture, and has "a shared feeling of peoplehood" (Gordon, 1964).

The bond that makes Jews an ethnic group is not race, religion, or culture—it is their shared feeling of peoplehood, of Jewishness. Here a group of Holocaust survivors gather outside the Capitol in Washington, D.C.

An important factor in the determination of ethnicity by people outside the group is the recognition of social differences between members of the ethnic group and those outside it. Italian-Americans are called an ethnic group, for example, because certain traits shared by the Italians who immigrated to the United States set them apart from the larger American society and from other ethnic groups. Among these traits are speaking Italian, being Roman Catholics, and cooking certain traditional foods. But in Europe, the general term "Italian" is not used to refer to a single group. It is too broad to have much social significance. Europeans are aware of northern Italians, southern Italians, and Sicilians, and view each as having specific characteristics. And within Italy, even these categories are too broad to be meaningful. There, groups are identified on the basis of regional dialect, local customs, and physical traits, such as hair and eye color.

In most groups with strong ethnic identities, social and cultural differences are recognized not only by outsiders but also by group members. Group members see themselves as different from outsiders, who are "not of our people." The social and cultural bonds that hold such groups together may be religious or linguistic. But more generally, it is a strong identification with a particular population, a special feeling that sets one's group apart from all others. Within a strong ethnic group, a social system develops that is substantially separate from that of the larger society and has its own distinct processes of socialization.

Many ethnic groups are racially and culturally diverse. An example is the Jewish people, who are considered an ethnic group both by others and by themselves. But what exactly do Jews have in common? It is not race.

Their racial origins (called *Semitic*) are the same as those of the Arabs. The Egyptian Jew and the Egyptian Arab look alike. And European Jews have intermarried with gentiles (non-Jews) for so long that Semitic features often do not distinguish them from other Europeans. Nor is religion the common bond among Jews. The practices and beliefs of Jews vary greatly, and some people who identify themselves as Jews no longer practice or believe in any form of the Jewish religion. Nor do Jews share a common culture. A Russian, Polish, or German Jew has an entirely different culture from a Syrian or Moroccan Jew.

The bond that makes the Jews an ethnic group, despite their varied social characteristics, is their shared feeling of peoplehood, of Jewishness. Jews regard themselves as descendants of the biblical group of exiles who received the Ten Commandments. They remember their ancestors as a group that has been discriminated against, persecuted, and pursued by powerful enemies all over the world for more than 2,000 years.

Racial Groups

Like ethnicity, the concept of race is extremely difficult to define. Historically, trying to identify and classify the human races has been the job of physical anthropologists and biologists, who have categorized skin colors, measured heads, and classified strands of hair. For years, human beings were loosely divided into three groups on the basis of their physical characteristics: Caucasoid, Mongoloid, and Negroid.

As Western scientists made contact with and studied more of the peoples of the world, however, it was found that some peoples did not fit easily into these general categories. Polynesians and Australian Aborigines, for example, do not fit any of the three basic types. This problem gave rise to more and more new categories, and gradually the idea that a small number of basic racial stocks could be identified was largely abandoned.

All the attempts to establish a fixed number of racial groupings were based on the assumption that races could be defined in terms of certain physical traits shared by all members of the group. As knowledge of human variation increased, the choice of traits traditionally used as the bases for racial classification seemed increasingly arbitrary. The Caucasoid stock, for instance, was distinguished from the Negroid stock mainly on the basis of hair texture and facial features. But some Caucasoid Asiatic Indians are as dark-skinned as most Negroid peoples, and some Negroids, such as the Kalahari Bushmen, are light-skinned. Because there is no scientific reason to use hair and facial features over skin color as criteria for racial grouping, the selection of traits seems arbitrary (Coon, 1982; Jolly & Plog, 1979).

Today most anthropologists and sociologists view race as a cultural concept rather than a biological one. Racial categories are considered to reflect social and cultural factors more than physical variations. In fact, most American institutions that seek to categorize a person by race—for example, for Affirmative Action purposes—have abandoned the traditional three categories and replaced them with eight to ten classifications, including Native American, African-American, Asian-American, Hispanic, and white American (Banton, 1988).

Although, as we have seen, race has little validity as a biological concept, it remains an important way to distinguish certain social categories into which people place one another. That is how the term is used in this text: A **race** is a group of people who are *believed* to share certain physical traits and to be genetically distinct. In other words, race is a *social fact* much more than it is a biological fact.

The fact that ethnic and racial groups frequently overlap often causes confusion. African-Americans and Asian-Americans are relatively distinct racial groups in the United States, and for the most part, they are also ethnic groups. Yet some people belong to these groups racially but not ethnically. An example is a Japanese-American whose family has lived in the United States for two or three generations and who has little or no familiarity with Japanese culture and traditions. Furthermore, some people—for instance, those whose skin is very light because of intermarriage—may be ethnically African-Americans or Asian-Americans but may not fit into these groups racially. Finally, an ethnic group may include more than one race. In India, for example, there has been so much intermingling of the races that racial divisions are often difficult to establish. In cases like these, language, rather than race, is frequently used to clarify the distinctions between people.

Levels of racial consciousness vary sharply from society to society. In the United States, for instance, physical appearance is commonly used as a basis for social classification. But this is generally less the case in Latin America, where social identification depends as much on socioeconomic status as it does on appearance (Boucher, Landis, & Clark, 1987; J. Stone, 1985).

RACE, INTELLIGENCE, AND CHARACTER

A major question about race that has caused much debate is whether physical differences among the basic racial stocks, as they have been traditionally defined, are accompanied by significant mental and behavioral differences in qualities such as intelligence or emotional makeup. Scientific research has yet to offer a firm answer to this question. Because the so-called races are so heterogeneous

Today most anthropologists and sociologists view race as a cultural concept rather than a biological one. Racial categories are considered to reflect social and cultural factors more than physical variations.

in their genetic makeup, it is impossible to study pure racial types. And such studies are made even more complex by the difficulty of separating culturally learned behavior from biologically inherited traits, as well as by the problem of measuring emotional and intellectual characteristics accurately and without bias.

The first modern tests that promised an objective measure of intelligence were developed in 1905 by Alfred Binet and Théophile Simon of France. Using these and later tests, social scientists have made numerous comparisons of abilities between the races. The results of early tests showed a wide variation among various racial and ethnic groups in what was thought to be intelligence. Particularly controversial were the tests that consistently yielded lower scores for African-American children and for children of the lower classes (Schiff & Lewontin, 1986).

In recent years, scientists have been reexamining this evidence and have concluded that it is misleading (Gould, 1981; Irvine & Berry, 1988; Miller-Jones, 1989; Schiff & Lewontin, 1986). For example, in 1912, Henry Goddard, a pioneer in intelligence testing in the United States, gave "intelligence" tests to new immigrants at Ellis Island. He found that 83 percent of the Jews, 90 percent of the Hungarians, 79 percent of the Italians, and 87 percent of the Russians were "feeble-minded" (Kamin, 1974, p. 16). What Goddard's tests measured was not intelligence, however but, rather, the ability to perform a very narrow range of intellectual tasks, some of which were more familiar to Americans than to immigrants from other societies. Furthermore, the fact that most of the immigrants were illiterate in English—and some in their native languages as well—clearly influenced their scores. When some of these immigrants were tested again after having lived in the United States for a number of years, their test scores increased (Schiff & Lewontin, 1986).

Although reasonably accurate in predicting academic success, all the tests used today to measure intelligence reflect the social, cultural, and academic standards of the educated middle class. Scoring well on an intelligence test requires mastery of the English language as it is spoken by white middle-class Americans. Even sections that are supposedly nonverbal, such as the matching of shapes or colors, still require certain language skills in order to fully understand the instructions. Moreover, some of the "right" answers to the questions are much more obvious to members of the middle-class groups who construct and administer the tests.

Today most social scientists believe that there are probably no significant innate or inherited differences in intelligence among the racial groups. An exception is Arthur Jensen (1969, 1973a, 1973b), an educational psychologist whose ideas have caused much debate in the scientific community. Pointing to the fact that, on the average, blacks score slightly below whites on the most commonly used IQ tests, Jensen argues that environmental explanations of this difference are inadequate. He suggests that since there are differences in physical characteristics among racial groups, it is likely that their inherited mental characteristics also vary. These genetic differences, he contends, are the primary source of variations in the average IQs of blacks and whites.

Jensen's position has been attacked on many grounds (Taylor, 1975, 1980; Wilson, 1986). One of the main points raised is that neither white nor black Americans are distinct races in any genetically meaningful sense. It is estimated that 80 percent of all African-Americans have some white ancestry, and that nearly a quarter of Americans classified as white have some African ancestry.

A review of the research on ethnic-racial IQ differences suggests the following conclusions (Loehlin, Lindzey, & Spuhler, 1975):

1. Differences in the average IQ scores of members of various ethnic and racial groups in American society probably reflect three factors: biases in the tests themselves, differences in environmental conditions among the groups, and genetic differences among the groups.

2. On the basis of the current evidence, a wide range of positions can be supported concerning the relative importance of each of these three factors.

3. Regardless of the position taken on the significance of these factors, it seems clear that differences among individuals *within* ethnic and racial groups greatly exceed the average differences among these groups.

It is even more difficult to draw conclusions about racial variations in emotional makeup. Many stereotyped generalizations about racial personality and "character" are based on casual observation. Although there may be some differences in the emotional makeup of various racial groups, these differences are probably learned culturally and are not biologically based.

Minority Groups in America

Every large American city includes neighborhoods that are inhabited principally by members of different ethnic or racial groups. Most large cities contain a Little Italy, a predominantly Jewish section, and perhaps a Chinatown. Newspapers and magazines are published in many languages, and the ingredients for many kinds of ethnic dishes are sold in specialty grocery stores. The Irish celebrate St. Patrick's Day; the Italians, Columbus Day. In Lorain, Ohio, people dance the Hungarian *czardas;* in Gallup, New Mexico, the Zuñi Rain Dance; and in Delano County, California, the Mexican Hat Dance. The United States is a nation with literally hundreds of well-established ethnic minorities. Here we discuss five of the most visible ethnic minority groups: African-Americans, Hispanic-Americans, Asian-Americans, Native Americans, and white ethnics.

AFRICAN-AMERICANS

Slavery sharply differentiates the history of African-Americans from that of all other minority groups in the United States. In the course of their forced entry into the United States (beginning in the early 1600s) and their long years as slaves, the native cultures and traditional family relationships of African-Americans were radically disrupted, and individuals were legally denied identities. Although the Thirteenth Amendment to the U.S. Constitution freed all slaves in 1865, laws passed after the Civil War restricted the rights of African-Americans. Not until 1954 were such laws declared unconstitutional.

There are about 34 million African-Americans in the United States today, 12.7 percent of the country's population. The percentage of African-Americans has decreased since the country's early days. In 1776, African-Americans made up slightly more than 20 percent of the total population of the 13 colonies. Since that time, immigration to the United States has been almost exclusively nonblack.

SOCIOLOGY OF THE MEDIA

IMAGES OF RACE IN THE MEDIA

Images of nonwhite racial groups have reflected America's racism for over 200 years. In the late 1770s, while newspapers printed the Declaration of Independence declaring that "all men are created equal," advertisements for slave auctions portrayed slaves as inanimate objects—to be sold as property. Advertisements would continue to create and perpetuate symbols and messages of racial inequality for years to come. African-Americans would be portrayed in menial occupations as cheerful cooks, polite porters, dancing minstrels, and servants. While trademark characters like Chef Rastus (Cream of Wheat) and Aunt Jemima (pancake mix) became American icons, their identities were firmly fixed in subservient roles, reinforcing stereotypical racist ideas.

Characters like "Sambo," who appeared in novels and plays at the end of the eighteenth century, also contributed to the development of stereotypical ideas about African-Americans (Croteau & Hoynes, 1997). White actors in blackface and gaudy dress played the role of Sambo, a comical figure with pretentious manners whose speech was filled with malapropisms. Dancing around the stage singing nonsense songs, this character was the object of ridicule and became the precursor of racist stereotypes that would appear in mass media. During the nineteenth century, writers continued to develop racist stereotypes. In *The Spy,* James Fenimore Cooper cast African-Americans in the roles of loyal, content house slaves who feared ghosts and believed in superstitions.

Even Harriet Beecher Stowe's antislavery novel, *Uncle Tom's Cabin,* perpetuated racist stereotypes. In this case, blacks were depicted as gentle victims with childlike innocence (Croteau & Hoynes, 1997).

With the end of slavery, new racist images began to appear. Writers now created images of angry, free black men. In 1915, with the release of D. W. Griffith's film *Birth of a Nation,* racist images filled the big screen. Other early films depicting white supremacy and promoting racism were: *The Wooing and Wedding of a Coon* (1905) and *The Nigger* (1915). Films like *The Greaser's Revenge* (1914) created stereotypical images of Mexicans as bandits, rapists, and murders. *The Yellow Menace* depicted Asians as a threat to American values. And *The Aryan* (1916) promoted white supremacy over American Indians (Wilson & Gutierrez, 1995).

The content of media products continued to reveal the deeply ingrained racist attitudes of Americans well into the twentieth century. But after World War II, when the attitudes of white Americans began to change toward black Americans, the demeaning images of nonwhite racial groups began to vanish. By the end of the 1960s, the civil rights movement had confronted America with the discrepancy between the sacred words of the U.S. Constitution and the racist images and words of the media.

In response to the protests of social activists, racist stereotypes began to vanish. The Frito Bandito character disappeared after Mexican-Americans protested this stereotyped image of a "gun-toting Pancho Villa look-alike" who held up people in supermarkets and on picnics in search of his favorite

snack (Sivulka, 1998). Jell-O dropped an award-winning 1959 commercial that featured a Chinese baby who could not eat his Jell-O with chopsticks, saying: "But, ah! Mother brings great Western invention—the spoon! Spoon invented to eat Jell-O, Chinese Baby velly happy!" (Sivulka, 1998, p. 320). And other characters, like "Injun Orange" and "Chinese Cherry," which appeared in Funny Face fruit juice ads were renamed—"Choo-Choo Cherry" and "Jolly Olly Orange." Movies like *Little Big Man* (1970), *Dances with Wolves* (1990), and *Geronimo* (1993) restored Indian dignity and expressed American guilt about the subjugation of Native Americans (Croteau & Hoynes, 1997).

While blatant racist images have disappeared, some critics argue that these changes only mask a more subtle form of racism (Croteau & Hoynes, 1997; Entman, 1992; Rossides, 1997). They claim that while entertainment programs like *The Cosby Show* (1980s) have depicted the African-American family in a positive light, other more "realistic" shows depict black males as absent and irresponsible. Critics also worry that biased news coverage of African-Americans, which focuses on the problems of poor African-Americans (drugs, crime, and violence), can lead the audience to reason that since some blacks succeed, ample opportunities exist for all blacks.

It is difficult to predict how the media will present race in the future. But subtle forms of racism will probably continue to exist until greater numbers of nonwhite racial groups own, publish, and produce media products.

Hispanic-Americans celebrate their culture with picturesque murals that are found in many U.S. cities. Hispanic-Americans are the fifth largest national block of Spanish-speaking people in the world.

Before the Civil War, most African-Americans lived as slaves in the South. After emancipation, they gradually began to migrate to the urban North. About the time of World War I, this migration increased to massive proportions. Between 1915 and 1918, an estimated 250,000 to 350,000 African-Americans left the South for northern industrial cities (Cruse, 1987).

After World War II, African-American migration to the North became even more rapid, constituting one of the largest internal migrations in this country's history. At the end of the war, more than 80 percent of all African-Americans still lived in the South. Today, only 53 percent do so. The move northward seems to have come to an end, however, partly because of recent increases in job availability in the Sun Belt (see Chapter 19) and perhaps also because "it became apparent that the North was not the racial paradise that many southern blacks once believed" (Farley, 1988, p. 199).

The image of the African-American citizen as a farmer and rural resident has given way to a new reality—the urban African-American. In 1998, 54.7 percent of blacks in America lived inside central cities, as opposed to 22 percent of whites. Blacks also have higher percentages of single-parent households (64 percent versus 26 percent for whites) and out-of-wedlock births (69.9 percent versus 25.3 percent for whites) (U.S. Bureau of the Census, 1998). The median family income of blacks is considerably lower than that of whites, too: $23,482 for blacks versus $37,161 for whites in 1996 (U.S. Bureau of the Census, 1998).

We discuss African-Americans in more detail later in this chapter.

HISPANIC-AMERICANS

People of Hispanic origin represent a rapidly growing segment of the American population. Members of this group share a language (Spanish); typically, a religion (Roman Catholicism); and a historical experience of Spanish colonialism. But otherwise they are quite diverse (Portes & Truelove, 1987). The life of a middle-class Cuban refugee, for instance, is very different from that of a Mexican industrial laborer or a Puerto Rican garment worker in Spanish Harlem. This is one of the reasons that some Hispanic-Americans object to being labeled "Hispanic." Hispanic-Americans are a widely disparate people—varying in background, nationality, attitudes, and values—and the term *Hispanic-American* tends to lump them into a category that negates their diversity (Gann & Duignan, 1986). It is usually preferable, therefore, to refer to Americans of Hispanic heritage by their nation of origin—for example, as Mexican-Americans, Cuban-Americans, and Puerto Ricans.

Collectively, the Hispanic-American population, most of which comes from Mexico and Central and South America, constitutes about 29.3 million people, or 11 percent of the total population (U.S. Bureau of the Census, 1998). As of October 1996, the estimated population of undocumented immigrants was 5 million (U.S. Immigration and Naturalization Service, 1997). Most of these illegal aliens were Hispanic, which makes Hispanic-Americans the fifth largest national bloc of Spanish-speaking people in the world. Some demographers predict that by the year 2000 the number of Hispanics in America will increase to 30 million (U.S. Bureau of the Census, 1998).

Currently almost three-fourths of the Hispanic population in the United States reside in five states—California, Texas, New York, Florida, and Illinois (U.S. Bureau of the Census, 1998). But the Hispanic presence can be seen and felt all over the country—from big cities, where murals by Hispanic artists decorate buildings and Mexican restaurants have become widely popular, to such unexpected places as the Pennsylvania Dutch country, where there is a sizable settlement of Hispanics. The two largest Hispanic groups in this country are Mexican-Americans and Puerto Ricans.

MEXICAN-AMERICANS. The history of persons of Mexican ancestry in the United States dates back to the acquisition of what is now the American Southwest (much of which was originally part of Mexico). As the border states grew, the demand for cheap labor, as well as enduring poverty in Mexico, stimulated the immigration of Mexicans from across the border (Langley, 1988). In recent decades, much of the immigration from Mexico has been illegal, creating a large group of "invisible" and insecure people in Mexican-American communities. As of October 1996, the estimated number of illegal Mexican immigrants in the United States was 2.7 million (U.S. Immigration and Naturalization Service, 1997).

There are currently about 18.8 million persons of Mexican ancestry living legally in the United States, a large majority of whom reside in the southwestern states of Texas, Arizona, Colorado, New Mexico and California. Mexicans and Mexican-Americans have been a major component of the migrant agricultural labor force since the 1940s. But as agriculture becomes increasingly mechanized and the demand for farm labor decreases, more Mexican immigrants are moving to cities like Albuquerque, Los Angeles, Phoenix, Denver, and Chicago (Langley, 1988).

Although there have been few formal laws segregating Mexican-Americans, this minority group still finds it hard to buy homes in certain neighborhoods in the Southwest. Some realtors, for example, have secretly created home buyers' qualifying systems—based on income, credit rating, "ethnic affinity," and social standing—that effectively prevent Mexican-Americans from purchasing homes in affluent areas (Feagin & Feagin, 1999).

Job opportunities can also be restricted. Most Mexican-Americans not engaged in agricultural work are employed as unskilled or semiskilled laborers in factories and packing plants, or in service jobs as maids, waitresses, and delivery personnel. In 1991, the Mexican-American unemployment rate was 10.4 percent (compared to 6.0 percent for whites).

The language barrier has slowed efforts to improve the socioeconomic standing of this group. Some Mexican-American children start school unable to speak English. This contributed to a high school dropout rate in the past. Recent trends show some improvement in the educational status of Mexican-Americans, however. Younger people are getting more education than their parents did, and many are now enrolled in colleges and universities. In 1998, 48.6 percent of Mexican-Americans had completed high school (U.S. Bureau of the Census, 1998). Indeed, a sizable percentage of Mexican-Americans have been highly successful, and they make up a growing Mexican-American middle class. By the mid-1980s, for the first time in American history, farm workers did not constitute the most significant proportion of the Mexican-American labor force (Gann & Duignan, 1986). In 1997, 12.1 percent of all Mexican-American workers were employed in managerial and professional positions, and 22 percent were working in technical, sales, and administrative jobs (U.S. Bureau of the Census, 1998).

PUERTO RICANS. The movement of Puerto Ricans to the United States mainland began in 1898, after the American annexation of the island of Puerto Rico following the Spanish-American War. After World War II, migration increased steadily, until it peaked in the early 1950s. Factors that spurred this movement include rapid population increases in Puerto Rico, lack of economic opportunities on the island, the absence of legal or political restrictions on migration, and the availability of inexpensive transportation to the mainland (Gann & Duignan, 1986).

The approximately 3.2 million Puerto Ricans on the United States mainland today make up a large and visible ethnic minority. Most live in New York City and its environs, but other large Puerto Rican communities can be found in and around such cities as Chicago, Cleveland, and Philadelphia (U.S. Bureau of the Census, 1998).

Puerto Ricans experience many of the same difficulties as African-Americans and Mexican-Americans. Their educational, occupational, and income statuses tend to be low. Of Puerto Ricans over the age of 25, only 12.1 percent are college graduates (U.S. Bureau of the Census, 1998).

Because they are U.S. citizens, Puerto Ricans' political concerns frequently differ from those of other Hispanic groups. None of them, for example, are illegal aliens. An issue of great concern to most Puerto Ricans, however, is the official status of the island. Puerto Rico became a commonwealth in 1952. As such, it has a local government much like that of a state but without representation in Congress. A few Puerto Ricans favor independence, many favor statehood, and a small majority prefers the current status or some variation of it.

OTHER HISPANIC-AMERICAN GROUPS. The third largest group of Hispanic-Americans are Cuban-Americans, who number around 1.3 million (U.S. Bureau of the Census, 1998). Most came to the United States to escape the regime of Fidel Castro, who became premier of Cuba in 1959, and many settled in southern Florida. Unlike most Mexicans and Puerto Ricans, who left poverty to come to the United States, those who fled Cuba tended to be drawn from the educated middle class. As a group, therefore, their socioeconomic status is somewhat higher than that of other Hispanic-Americans. About 25 percent of Cuban-Americans are employed in managerial and professional positions (U.S. Bureau of the Census, 1998).

A large proportion of the sizable increase in the Cuban-American population in the 1980s followed Fidel Castro's decision in 1980 to allow Cuban immigration to the United States. Many of the more recent immigrants are poorer and less educated than those who arrived a generation earlier. This has caused friction between the newer immigrants and the more established Cuban-Americans living in Miami (Fallows, 1983; see also Portes & Rumbaut, 1990).

U.S. Immigration from Selected Asian Countries, 1960–1995

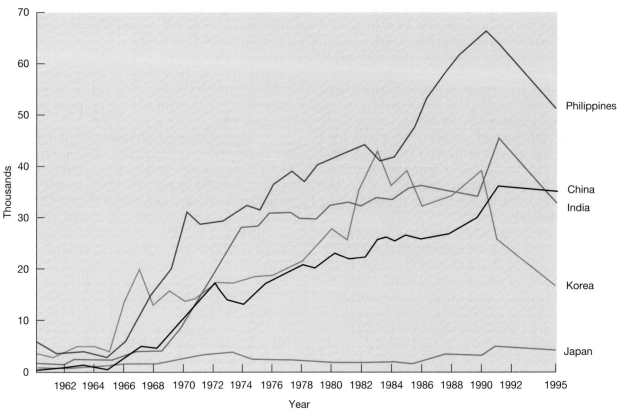

FIGURE 11.1 The Asian country sending the most immigrants to the United States is the Philippines.

Sources: James T. Fawcett and Benjamin V. Carino, *Pacific Bridges: The New Immigration from Asia and the Pacific Islands* (New York: Center for Migration Studies), 1987; *World Almanac and Book of Facts, 1992* (New York: Scripps Howard); U.S. Bureau of the Census, *Statistical Abstract of the United States, 1993* (Washington, D.C.: U.S. Government Printing Office, 1993), U.S. Bureau of the Census, *Statistical Abstract of the United States, 1998* (Washington, D.C.: U.S. Government Printing Office, 1998).

Another 4.3 million Hispanics come from other Central and South American and Caribbean countries, including the Dominican Republic, El Salvador, Colombia, Guatemala, Honduras, Peru, Ecuador, Brazil, and Argentina. They make up sizable communities in certain areas of the country (U.S. Bureau of the Census, 1998).

ASIAN-AMERICANS

Asian immigrants to the United States have encountered dramatic differences between themselves and the American people—differences in race, religion, culture, and social organization (Fawcett & Carino, 1987). Like many other immigrant groups, they have experienced racism, segregation, prejudice, and discrimination. Most

Asian immigrants have entered the United States at the West Coast, and they have tended to remain in the western states; far more Asian immigrants live in California and Hawaii than in any other state.

In 1960, none of the 10 countries sending the most immigrants to the United States were Asian. By 1985, however, six of the ten largest streams of immigrants into the United States were Asian. The four Asian countries sending the most immigrants to America today are the Philippines, Korea, India, and China (see Figure 11.1). Here we briefly discuss two of the first Asian groups to arrive, the Chinese and the Japanese, and three groups of more recent arrivals: the Vietnamese, Koreans, and Filipinos.

CHINESE-AMERICANS. People of Chinese ancestry are now the largest group of Asian-Americans, having surpassed the Japanese in numbers during recent decades. The Chinese-American population now stands at 1.65 million (U.S. Bureau of the Census, 1993).

The Chinese immigration, which started in the 1840s, was the first significant movement of Asians to the United States. When it began in earnest during the Gold Rush of 1849, it consisted almost exclusively of male laborers. Thousands of Chinese men were brought to the United States as indentured workers to build the railroads and work the mines and the farms of California (King & Locke, 1980). At first, the Chinese were welcomed to their new homeland and appreciated for their willingness to do these difficult jobs. As more Chinese arrived, however, and as they began to compete with whites for jobs, they encountered widespread hostility that eventually coalesced into an anti-Chinese movement. As a result of this movement, they were persecuted, beaten, and subjected to laws that restricted their political and economic rights and educational opportunities. The climax of the anti-Chinese movement came in 1882, with the passage of the Chinese Exclusion Act that prohibited Chinese immigration altogether. This law was not repealed until 1943.

In spite of the hostile treatment they received, the number of Chinese in California continued to grow rapidly before the ban on immigration—from approximately 25,000 in 1852 to more than 50,000 ten years later. Through the 1870s, over 10 percent of California's population was Chinese.

As a result of discriminatory laws and racial antagonism, many of the immigrants were forced to abandon more desirable work and find jobs in noncompetitive situations such as domestic service, laundries, and small shops. The Chinese came to dominate the laundry business and to work in substantial numbers in the shoe and cigar industries (Daniels & Kitano, 1970; King & Locke, 1980). As recently as 1920, more than half of the employed Chinese in the United States worked in the laundry business or in restaurants (Sowell, 1981).

Partly because of the hostility they faced and partly because their own cultural values remained strong, the Chinese generally lived in separate communities isolated from the majority population. As they spread across the United States, they created "Chinatowns"—distinct ethnic enclaves within urban settings. Although many Chinese-Americans today still live in Chinatowns, many others have moved into integrated urban and suburban neighborhoods (Daniels, 1988).

The Chinese-American population more than doubled after legislation in the 1960s opened the door to Asian immigrants. From 1960 to 1985, more than 553,000 Chinese arrived in the United States (Feagin & Feagin, 1999). Chinese-Americans have become one of the best-educated minority groups. Their educational

Despite the move of many Chinese-Americans to urban and suburban neighborhoods, Chinatowns still flourish in many large cities.

achievements are reflected in their occupations, which are heavily concentrated in white-collar jobs (Feagin & Feagin, 1999). The 1990 census showed that the proportion of Chinese-Americans holding managerial and professional jobs exceeded that of European-Americans.

JAPANESE-AMERICANS. The more than 848,000 persons of Japanese ancestry in the United States make up the third largest group of Asian-Americans (Filipinos are the second largest) (U.S. Bureau of the Census, 1993). Their history in this country is somewhat similar to that of the Chinese. They were brought to the United States to work as laborers and quickly became the targets of racial discrimination.

The main wave of Japanese immigration followed the influx of the Chinese and began around 1870. Most of the Japanese settled on the West Coast, taking jobs as agricultural and service workers and in small businesses. Some set themselves up as shopkeepers. Like the Chinese, they lived together in their own communities, segregated from the American mainstream (Kitano, 1985).

The industriousness and economic success of the Japanese made them the target of laws that barred them from many professions and occupations that required licensing. Also, laws were passed (in 1913 and 1920) that prevented the original immigrants from owning land. In spite of such restrictions, Japanese agricultural businesses flourished.

During World War II, more than 110,000 Japanese were forced to leave their homes and were placed in "relocation camps"; most were American citizens. This is regarded by many as one of the most racist acts ever committed by the U.S. government.

What is often regarded as one of the most racist acts ever committed by the U.S. government was directed against Japanese-Americans. In March 1942, subsequent to the Japanese attack on Pearl Harbor, the government interned (imprisoned) all individuals of Japanese descent living on the West Coast. More than 110,000 people were forced to leave their homes and were placed in "relocation camps." Most were American citizens with few remaining ties to Japan—ordinary people who posed no threat to the country's war effort. They were forced to live in closely guarded, specially built camps until early 1945, when the U.S. Supreme Court ordered the internment ended.

Today Japanese-Americans continue to be concentrated on the West Coast, although many live in other parts of the country. Like the Chinese, many of the Japanese have achieved high socioeconomic status. They are now one of the highest-income and best-educated groups in America, and a large number are engaged in professional occupations (Feagin & Feagin, 1999).

VIETNAMESE-AMERICANS. There are more than 615,000 persons of Vietnamese ancestry living in the United States, many of them refugees who fled their country during or shortly after the Vietnam War (U.S. Bureau of the Census, 1993). Upon their arrival in the United States, the refugees lived in special camps until sponsors could be found who would assist them in finding jobs and housing and in settling into their new lives (Leba, Leba, & Leba, 1985).

When compared to other refugee groups, such as those who fled Nazism in the 1930s and 1940s and the

Hungarian refugees of 1956, the Vietnamese are faring poorly in terms of employment. Most work at jobs far below the levels of professional status they had reached in their native land, and some live below the poverty level (although not as commonly as refugees from the neighboring war-torn countries of Cambodia and Laos [Fischman, 1986]). Many reasons have been suggested for the socioeconomic difficulties of Vietnamese immigrants, including the lack of an established ethnic community to aid them, cultural and language barriers, and the weakened state of the U.S. economy at the time of their arrival (Freeman, 1989; Stein, 1979).

KOREAN-AMERICANS. There are over 799,000 Korean-Americans in the United States today (U.S. Bureau of the Census, 1993). Like other Asian immigrants, the first Koreans to come to the United States found that discrimination and the language barrier prevented them from obtaining employment compatible with their educational backgrounds and abilities. As a result, many of the early Korean immigrants—including some with high levels of education—were forced to take jobs as farm laborers, kitchen helpers, and janitors. By the 1940s, however, a few Korean-Americans had begun to establish small family-owned and -operated businesses. This tradition expanded and continues to this day, especially in major cities like New York and Los Angeles, where Korean-Americans are often either middlemen, serving the poorer segments of their own communities, or entrepreneurs, catering to more heterogeneous groups (Portes & Rumbaut, 1989).

The wave of Korean immigrants that arrived in the United States in the mid-1960s and 1970s included many professionals (mathematicians, scientists, doctors) and entrepreneurs. By 1990, Korean Americans were most likely to be employed in service occupations.

FILIPINO-AMERICANS. Filipino men first began to leave their homeland in the 1920s, when they were recruited as farm workers for sugar plantations in Hawaii and on the West Coast. Most of these men worked 12-hour days for meager wages. Despite these conditions, a steady flow of Filipinos arrived in the United States until 1934, when restrictive immigration legislation was passed. The second wave of Filipino immigration to the United States began after World War II and has continued in recent decades (Daniels, 1988). According to the 1990 census, there were over 1.4 million Filipino-Americans in the United States, making them the second largest group in the Asian-Pacific category (Feagin & Feagin, 1999).

Like many other Asian-American groups, Filipino-Americans have been relatively successful educationally and economically. The Filipino-American median family income is one of the highest of any Asian-American group (Feagin & Feagin, 1999). While Filipino-Americans are concentrated in white-collar jobs, they are more likely to be employed in technical, sales, and administrative support jobs than in managerial and professional positions.

NATIVE AMERICANS

The history of Native Americans has been one of conquest and depopulation. The original population of the area that was to become the United States has been roughly estimated at between 1 million and 10 million. By 1850, that number had been reduced to 250,000 as a direct and indirect result of contact with whites. Since then, better living conditions and a high birth rate have led to a current population of about 2.3 million (U.S. Bureau of the Census, 1998).

Native Americans are probably the poorest, most marginal, and most neglected group in the United States today. They have had the lowest median family income of any racial or ethnic group for decades (Feagin & Feagin, 1999). The 1990 census showed that more than 26 percent of all Native American families and 47 percent of those on reservations fell below the official poverty level. The unemployment rate for Native Americans averages about three times that of the white population. The dire economic conditions of this group are reflected in its suicide rate, which has remained above the national average (Thorton, 1987). The mortality rates for other causes of death also indicate the extent to which this group has been neglected. Death rates from alcoholism and tuberculosis are more than five times those of the total population (Feagin & Feagin, 1999).

As legal wards of the federal government, Native Americans have found themselves in a unique situation among minority groups (Boucher, Landis, & Clark, 1987). It was not until 1924 that Indians were even granted the right of citizenship in the United States, their native land. In the past, the federal government tended to treat all tribes alike, without regard for their vast differences in heritage and lifestyles, and it showed much insensitivity to tribal cultures. During the nineteenth century, for example, the government tried to convert Indians into small farmers. By allocating land to individuals, the government damaged Native American tribal organization, which was based on the principle of communal ownership.

The education of Native Americans has been a continuing problem. The present system, which divides responsibility among local public, private, and federal schools, is associated with a high dropout rate and low achievement and self-confidence levels among Native American children. New efforts are now being made to establish tribally controlled schools that can serve as centers of community life and emphasize Indian values and traditions in their curricula.

Native Americans are probably the poorest, most marginal, and most neglected group in the United States today. Death rates from alcoholism and tuberculosis are more than five times those of the total population.

The militant demonstrations and protests by Native Americans that occurred in various parts of the country throughout the 1970s and 1980s indicated a deep dissatisfaction with their lack of access to the material rewards available in the wider society and an unwillingness to accept the judgments and laws of the dominant culture. Two groups in particular, the National Indian Youth Council and the American Indian Movement, have opposed the policies of the Bureau of Indian Affairs (BIA), the U.S. government agency responsible for the welfare of Native Americans. These groups argue that the BIA has a long history of neglecting, discriminating against, and lying to Native Americans. In response, the federal government reduced appropriations to the BIA in the 1980s and is now encouraging tribal self-government (Trimble, 1987).

WHITE ETHNICS

More than half of all Americans may be described as *white ethnics*. This label is used to characterize European immigrants who came from countries other than the United Kingdom.

Most of the white ethnics who entered the United States prior to the late nineteenth century were from the nations of northern and western Europe, especially Ireland, Germany, France, and the Scandinavian countries, and were relatively culturally similar to the English-descended Anglos. Nevertheless, the members of these groups encountered considerable prejudice and discrimination when they arrived in America, especially the Irish, who entered in great numbers during and after the potato famine of 1845–1849. However, successive generations have lost so much of their ethnic identity through Americanization and intermarriage that it is debatable if they still constitute minority groups.

The minority status of the second great wave of white ethnics is much more evident. Most of these immigrants came to the United States in the late 1800s and in the first decades of the twentieth century, and most were from eastern and southern European nations, especially Italy, Russia, Poland, Greece, Hungary, and Czechoslovakia. The majority settled in the large industrial cities of the Northeast and the upper Midwest, where they took jobs as factory workers and laborers.

This second wave of white ethnics also met substantial hostility. Not only were their cultures quite different from that of "old stock" Americans but most were Catholic or Jewish, unlike the Protestant Anglos. Religious bigotry was a continual theme voiced by supporters of nativistic political groups in this era, culminating in the passage in 1924 of the National Origins Act. Under this legislation, a quota was established that limited how many immigrants would be accepted each year from different nations; these quotas had the effect of radically reducing migration from eastern and southern Europe while encouraging continued immigration from the Protestant nations of northern Europe. This act remained in force until 1965.

Over the course of the twentieth century, most southern and eastern European white ethnics have followed the general pattern of the Irish and Germans who preceded them, gradually blending in with the larger culture, abandoning the ethnic neighborhoods in which they first settled, and moving up the class ladder. About half of all white ethnics now attend college, and they constitute a large and growing segment of the middle class. Overt discrimination against white ethnics is relatively uncommon, although lingering prejudice is evident in negative stereotypes about dumb Poles and criminally oriented Italians.

Many of the members of these groups retain a considerable sense of ethnic consciousness, in part because they are still generally no more than four generations removed from their European roots and in part because they have made deliberate efforts to keep their heritage alive. These efforts parallel, and may have been inspired by, the example of the black pride movement that began in the late 1960s. They may also result from a realization by the grandchildren and the great-grandchildren of immigrants that if they do not learn more about their family backgrounds now, they may permanently lose the opportunity to do so. As a consequence, Italians, Poles, Czechs, Greeks, Croatians, and many others are showing a strong interest in the traditional foods, costumes, music, and literature of their native lands (Alba 1985).

PREJUDICE AND DISCRIMINATION AGAINST MINORITIES

Prejudice and discrimination occur in many situations. An individual who proclaims, "My school is the best in the city and all the rest are no good," shows prejudice. An employer who hires a job applicant solely because the applicant graduated from the same college as the employer engages in discrimination against other job applicants. But such actions, though they may lead to misunderstandings and disappointments, are relatively random and affect only a few people. In this section, we discuss the more serious issue of prejudice and discrimination against minority groups in a society.

Prejudice

The Latin root of the word *prejudice* means "judging before"; thus, a prejudice is, literally a *prejudgment*. Prejudice includes two components: a belief and an associated attitude. The belief component of a prejudice is termed a **stereotype,** a simplified or unsubstantiated generalization applied to an entire category of people, objects, or situations. The attitudinal component consists of an evaluative judgment about the object of prejudice. **Prejudice,** thus, may be formally defined as the judgment of people, objects, or situations in a stereotypical way. A prejudice can be positive, such as the view that African-Americans are outstanding athletes, or it may be negative, such as the opinion that people on welfare are lazy. Although negative prejudice is obviously especially harmful, it is important to note that even positive prejudiced thinking distorts reality and forces individuals into preestablished categories.

A certain amount of prejudice is inevitable, and even useful, in some situations. For example, if you were alone on a street, about to be attacked by someone with a knife, and you saw two men nearby who might help you, one muscular and tall, the other skinny and short, which one would you ask for help? The tall, muscular man, of course. In reality, that man might be afraid of knives, nauseated by the sight of blood, and not inclined to get involved in someone else's troubles. The short, skinny man, on the other hand, might be very brave and have a black belt in karate. But the circumstances call for a prejudgment that cannot be based on anything more than the relative size of the two men.

In a less dramatic way, similar examples of prejudice occur almost daily. A business executive hiring a secretary, a college student requesting a certain type of roommate, or a family choosing a suburb in which to live—all engage in some prejudgment in that they base their actions on preformed generalizations.

Prejudice becomes a problem when someone's preformed judgment remains unchanged even after the facts show it to be untrue. To return to our example, suppose you recognized the skinny man as someone who had recently won the world championship in karate. In that case, your decision about which man to choose to assist you would be influenced by that knowledge. You would think: "Big, muscular men are often better fighters than short, skinny men, but this man has proved to be a good fighter, so I'll be safer if I choose him." In other words, you would discard your prejudice because it did not help you to make the right decision in this situation. Some people, however, are unable to do this. They have believed for so many years that a skinny man cannot be a good fighter, and are so thoroughly convinced of it, that they simply cannot accept (and may even refuse to consider) any evidence to the contrary.

The social problem of prejudice, then, is not so much prejudgment—which in many cases is necessary for social interaction—as it is the failure to discard a prejudgment in the light of additional evidence.

Substantial evidence indicates that some people may be more psychologically prone to prejudiced thinking than others. Research conducted shortly after World War II by T. W. Adorno and his associates (1950) suggested that a large percentage of Americans displayed what the researchers called the *authoritarian personality*. Authoritarians view the world as rigidly divided between the strong and the weak, the good and the bad, superiors and inferiors. They thrive on hierarchy and are uncomfortable with ambiguity. They tend to view their own group in idealized terms and to look down on all outsiders. The authoritarian personality is ingrained in early childhood, in part as a result of harsh and inflexible parental discipline, and it is commonly passed down through the generations.

However, authoritarianism is only part of the story in explaining the origins of prejudice. While personality factors may make an individual more or less susceptible to prejudiced thinking, sociologists emphasize that prejudice is always learned. No one is born with prejudice. We learn it from our parents, at school or church, from our friends, and from the books we read and the television programs we watch. Prejudice may be built into a culture. Protestant children growing up in Northern Ireland, for instance, commonly learn prejudice against Catholics from nearly all their social experience. In such an environment, much of what is learned reinforces *ethnocentrism*, the tendency to see one's own culture as superior

Sociologists emphasize that prejudice is learned. We learn it from our parents, at school or church, from our friends, from the books we read, and from the television we watch.

and to judge other cultures by the standards of one's own. As we noted in Chapter 6, people's thoughts, attitudes, and feelings are heavily influenced by social pressure to accept prevailing beliefs—including stereotypes.

What leads a social group to formulate prejudicial views of other groups? Situational changes in a society are a major factor in this process. In particular, prejudice tends to arise when an established group feels economically threatened by another group. For example, when new groups of immigrants arrived in the United States in the early part of the twentieth century, they came into competition with longer-established immigrants for jobs. As a result, the earlier immigrants often developed prejudice and hostility toward the new groups. Conversely, prejudice can decrease when people feel less threatened than they once did.

Several studies have shown that certain groups of people are more likely to be prejudiced against minority groups than others. Because working-class whites frequently compete with blacks for jobs, they are usually more prejudiced against blacks than are whites of higher social standing. For similar reasons, prejudice against Jews is particularly common among upper class non-Jews (Williams, 1964). Some sociologists have noted that low-status groups in general tend to be more prejudiced than high-status groups (Simpson & Yinger, 1972). This tendency may be due in part to the indirect boost in status that prejudice gives those who rank lower on the social ladder. If another group is forced still lower than themselves, their status is raised.

Discrimination

Prejudice and discrimination are often regarded as an inseparable pair. Although they do frequently occur together, it is important to understand that they are two separate concepts. Prejudice is an *attitude* based on a belief, whereas discrimination is an *action* or *behavior*. More precisely, **discrimination** means the unfair or unequal treatment of people because of the groups or categories of which they are members.

Prejudice and discrimination do not always occur together. It is possible to be prejudiced but not to express that prejudice through discrimination. For example, some people may believe that Asians are inferior. But because these people are also committed to democratic ideals, they will not try to stop Asians from living in their neighborhoods, joining their churches, and competing freely for jobs. Conversely, discrimination is possible without prejudice. Company officials may be aware that Ms. Smith has the ability to perform the duties of a vice president, yet still refuse to promote her to that position because they are afraid their clients will not be willing to deal with a female executive. This excuse—"I don't have anything against Ms. Smith personally, but it would ruin my business if I promoted her"—is used to justify discriminatory actions that do not reflect personal prejudice.

Typically, though, prejudice and discrimination reinforce one another. Many forms of discrimination result from prejudicial attitudes, and continuing discrimination can create prejudice. If, through discriminatory practices, members of a group are kept from obtaining adequate educations, others may come to view that group as intellectually inferior. It may eventually be forgotten that the group's educational deficiency is the result of discrimination.

Many kinds of discrimination have been legal and even required by law at one time or another in the United States. Take, for example, voting restrictions. In most of the original 13 colonies, only white males over the age of 21 who owned property had the right to vote. This restriction discriminated against the poor, the nonwhite (including Native Americans), the young, and women. During the early nineteenth century, voting discrimination against poor white males was outlawed. In 1870, discrimination against black males in voting was legally abolished, though many more subtle discriminatory practices remained. In 1920, women were given

the right to vote. Finally, formal electoral discrimination ended in 1924, when Native Americans received the franchise.

Informal patterns of discrimination, some of them very subtle, are still common in everyday life in the United States. Consider, for example, the bigoted employer who turns down every black job applicant, claiming that all are unqualified. Or the admissions officer of a college who personally sets a quota for Jews and refuses to accept more than that number. Or the real estate agent who will not show homes in certain neighborhoods to Hispanics with the explanation, "You really wouldn't enjoy living in that part of town."

Discrimination, of course, is not a uniquely American phenomenon, but is found worldwide. In many countries, the suppression of minorities is legally sanctioned, particularly when minorities are political or religious dissidents.

Changing Patterns of Prejudice and Discrimination

In the last few decades many laws have been passed in the United States that outlaw discriminatory behavior. Laws, however, do not automatically change attitudes and feelings, and therefore it has not been easy to enforce them. It is difficult to prove that potential renters were turned down by the owner of an apartment building because they were black, or that a job applicant was not hired because he or she was Italian. Even when the evidence is clear, long and costly court cases are often necessary to enforce antidiscrimination laws.

Can increased contact between opposing groups lessen prejudice? In a pioneering study, social psychologist Gordon Allport (1958) concluded that, under certain conditions, contact does have this effect. Prejudicial attitudes tend to diminish if people from dominant and minority groups are working toward common goals, if they need to cooperate and depend on each other in order to reach those goals, if they have an equal status while they are together, and if their contact is sanctioned by widely accepted laws or customs. Furthermore, many studies of whites and blacks in newly desegregated situations have shown that their attitudes toward each other improve markedly following integration (Lipset, 1987; Pettigrew, 1971).

Yet increased contact is not a universal solution. Sometimes it can even make matters worse. One study, for example, compared the attitudes of high school students in Oak Ridge, Tennessee, before school integration and then a year after desegregation and found that antiminority attitudes had actually strengthened (Campbell, 1971). A review of 25 years of research concluded that we really do not know whether integration and increased contact between people of different races reduce prejudice (Ford, 1986).

As members of minority groups gradually achieve higher economic, social, and political status, however, their improved position typically helps to modify the attitudes of other groups. For example, increasing numbers of African-Americans are getting high school and college educations, thus improving their chances of finding better jobs at higher salaries. The improved economic circumstances of African-Americans may help to weaken some of the stereotypes that still prevail in our society (Pettigrew et al., 1982).

PATTERNS OF MINORITY RELATIONS

The treatment of minority groups may vary greatly within any particular society. This can be clearly seen in the United States, where French, German, and Swedish immigrants have not faced the same enduring discriminatory treatment as have African-Americans, Mexican-Americans, Puerto Ricans, and Native Americans. In this section, we examine the different ways in which dominant groups may treat minorities. In the next section, we look at the various ways in which minority groups may respond to their status.

It is useful to discuss minority relations in terms of two broad categories representing opposite positions: acceptance and rejection. Patterns of *acceptance* attempt to bring minority groups to full and equal status in the dominant society. Patterns of *rejection* prevent or minimize the acceptance of minorities.

Patterns of Acceptance

If a society values equality and freedom, it is likely to respond to the presence of minority groups with at least some level of acceptance. It will try to open its doors to the newcomers so that they can gain full and equal social participation.

ASSIMILATION

Many Americans regard **assimilation**—the absorption of an incoming group into the dominant society—as the ideal pattern of minority group relations.

There are two basic types of assimilation: cultural and structural. *Cultural* assimilation occurs when an immigrant group gives up much of its traditional culture, including not only language and clothing styles but also in many cases important political, social, and religious values, and adopts those of the society into which it has moved. Cultural assimilation can be extremely

wrenching, but it is often largely completed by the third or fourth generation. In contrast, *structural* assimilation, in which members of the minority group are fully accepted into the schools, businesses, neighborhoods, and families of the dominant group, may be a much more lengthy process.

Americans have long believed that assimilation proceeds according to what is called the *melting pot model*. In this interpretation, all of America's ethnic subcultures—English, Irish, black, Italian, Japanese, Mexican, and the many others—are believed to have blended to form an entirely new culture. Sociologists recognize the appeal of this image, but they suspect that the reality is somewhat different. The *Anglo-conformity model* recognizes that, while many different ethnic groups have contributed to the melting pot, some groups have had to abandon most of their own cultures and others, particularly those from the British Isles, have had to change relatively little. Advocates of this perspective point out that America's political, legal, and social structures and its culture, including its language, are essentially lightly modified versions of patterns brought to this country by white Anglo-Saxon Protestants.

The Anglo-conformity model helps to explain why assimilation tends to take place much more easily and quickly if the minority group is similar both culturally and physically to the dominant group. Thus, light-skinned, English-speaking Protestant groups (Scots and Canadians, for example) assimilate easily into American society; non-Christian, dark-skinned peoples who do not speak English assimilate only with great difficulty. Ease of assimilation is also closely related to the status ranking of ethnic groups. The highest status ethnic groups (as viewed by members of the dominant group, of course) meet the least resistance.

Although assimilation may be a generally positive way for minority groups to adapt to a society, it is not entirely beneficial. Strong ethnic subcultures can constitute a natural resource for a society, providing alternative ways of thought and behavior that promote new ideas and social insights. Moreover, many members of minority groups resist full assimilation. Feeling that their own cultures are valuable, they are reluctant to disappear into the melting pot.

Conflict can arise when an ethnic group resists pressures for assimilation and seeks to retain a strong ethnic identity. In Sri Lanka, for example, the Sinhalese and the Tamils—two ethnic groups with different religions and languages—are struggling to coexist in harmony (Arasaratnam, 1987). In India, a country characterized by many different ethnic groups, languages, and religions, conflicts among Sikhs, Hindus, and Muslims are endemic.

.NET   INTERNET/TECHNOLOGY

RACISM AND THE WEB

In 1997, 8,049 hate crimes were reported to the FBI by various law enforcement agencies. Over half of these incidents were racially motivated. The others involved hate directed toward members of various religions or ethnic groups, homosexuals, or persons with disabilities.

In recent years, the number of hate groups has grown in the United States. According to a report issued by the Southern Poverty Law Center in Montgomery, Alabama, 474 hate groups and group chapters were involved in racist behavior in 1997 (Intelligence Report, 1998). Many of these are survivalist groups that are actively seeking to bring about their own vision of a future America (Schmalleger, 1997). Law enforcement agencies are particularly concerned about these kinds of groups because they are reportedly well organized, well financed, and extremely well armed. These groups have been called "the radical right," "neo-Nazis," "skinheads," "white supremacists," and "racial hate groups." They include the White Patriot Party; the Order, Aryan Nations, Posse Comitatus; the Covenant, the Sword, and the Arm of the Lord; the Ku Klux Klan; and the Christian Conservative Church.

Recent increases in hate groups like these have been surprising, since experts believe that tough economic times—not prosperous ones—contribute to their growth (see Figure 11.2). But it now appears that the Internet may be playing a role in their expansion. The first neo-Nazi Web site was created in 1995, by a member of the Ku Klux Klan. In 1998, 81 hate groups had created and were maintaining 163 sites on the Internet (Intelligence Report, 1998). Some

groups, like the Ku Klux Klan, claim to be respectable Christian organizations. The Christian Conservative Church even cites biblical verses to validate the legitimacy of their claim that members of the white race are God's chosen people. Based on the growing number of churches that are joining the Christian Identity movement, which bases its belief in white supremacy and anti-semitism on the Bible, it appears that this approach is working.

Other groups do not rely on religious beliefs for legitimacy. Instead, they promote hatred and justify violence on the basis of personal rights. These groups design messages that appeal to negative emotions—fear, hatred, hostility, insecurity, and inadequacy. Take, for example, the Web site of White Aryan Resistance, which opens with an illustration of interracial violence. The cartoon shows a young white man apparently defending himself from a young black man who has approached him with a gun. As the black man falls backward from the knock-out punch of the white man, the message reads: ". . . Believe it or not, White Man . . . In the long run, it costs far less . . . to take *a stand now!* Get busy. . . . Defend your way of life . . . or lose it."

These kinds of emotional appeals, which are rooted in the feeling that one's way of life is being threatened, are designed to recruit young people into an organization that will fight for their rights. The Web sites of other hate groups link their messages of hate and white supremacy to popular elements of youth culture (T-shirts, music, and videos), seeking to make young recruits feel like they belong. Thus, for example, the Web site for White Pride resembles the kind of high-tech, razzle-dazzle video games popular with adolescent boys. Access to the

inner chambers of the site is limited; it requires clicking on a door labeled "whites only." This kind of exclusive membership creates the feeling that one is special and reinforces the idea of white pride. Once recruits identify with the group, they can purchase T-shirts (available through this site) to promote their support of the organization. Pages of this Web site are also filled with racist jokes, complete with violent depictions of interracial violence and messages that seek to justify the dehumanizing violence directed toward nonwhites.

A number of European countries have laws that make it a crime to put sites like these on-line (Olson, 1997). In France, it is illegal to put Nazi sites, or any other material that incites racial hatred, on-line. In 1997, under the sponsorship of the United Nations Human Rights Center, an international group met to discuss how to apply the legal prohibition against hate speech of European countries to the Internet. While 148 countries signed a pact to enact measures to eliminate sites that promote racial discrimination, many problems still exist. For one thing, shutting down a site in one country usually means that it will just resurface in another one where it may actually be protected under the law. In fact, even though the United States signed the international pact to eliminate these kinds of sites, it said it would not pass laws that violate the First Amendment, which guarantees the right to free speech.

Some service providers have already taken steps to eliminate these kinds of sites from the Internet. While choice of providers allows parents to monitor the kinds of messages that reach their children, it cannot prevent these groups from finding other ways to recruit them.

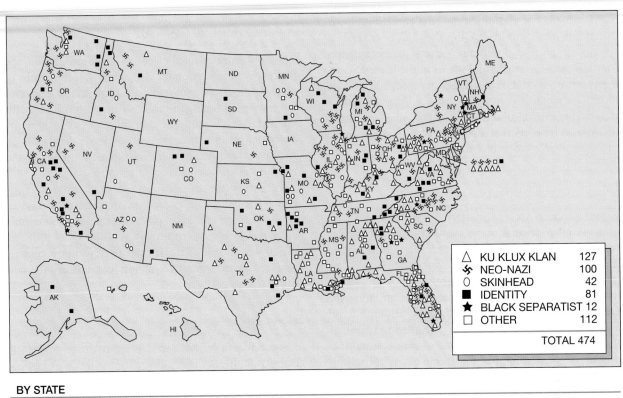

△	KU KLUX KLAN	127
ϟ	NEO-NAZI	100
O	SKINHEAD	42
■	IDENTITY	81
★	BLACK SEPARATIST	12
□	OTHER	112
	TOTAL	474

BY STATE

ALABAMA	18	IDAHO	8	MISSOURI	15	PENNSYLVANIA	21
ALASKA	2	ILLINOIS	26	MONTANA	4	SOUTH CAROLINA	8
ARIZONA	7	INDIANA	10	NEBRASKA	3	SOUTH DAKOTA	1
ARKANSAS	8	KANSAS	4	NEVADA	3	TENNESSEE	10
CALIFORNIA	35	KENTUCKY	12	NEW JERSEY	5	TEXAS	18
COLORADO	5	LOUISIANA	21	NEW MEXICO	1	UTAH	2
CONNECTICUT	1	MARYLAND	10	NEW YORK	9	VERMONT	1
DELAWARE	1	MASSACHUSETTS	8	NORTH CAROLINA	21	VIRGINIA	13
FLORIDA	48	MICHIGAN	14	OHIO	19	WASHINGTON	10
GEORGIA	16	MINNESOTA	8	OKLAHOMA	8	WEST VIRGINIA	5
HAWAII	1	MISSISSIPPI	13	OREGON	11	WISCONSIN	10

FIGURE 11.2 Active Hate Groups in the United States in 1997.

Source: Intelligence Report (Winter 1999).

AMALGAMATION

Whereas assimilation means the social and cultural merging of ethnic and racial groups, **amalgamation** refers to the biological merging of an ethnic or a racial group with the dominant population. Some amalgamation always occurs when two groups live together, but only rarely is amalgamation the dominant pattern of acceptance. Marriage between blacks and whites in the United States, for example, has not been widely approved, and the two races have remained physically distinct. True amalgamation can be seen in Hawaii and Polynesia, where people of many races have intermarried so frequently that a single racial and ethnic group has resulted.

CULTURAL PLURALISM

Cultural pluralism is a pattern in which minorities achieve full participation in the dominant society yet retain many of their cultural and social differences. Although cultural pluralism is sometimes described as the dominant pattern of acceptance in the United States, it has not been completely successful. Many minority groups have not yet achieved full participation. But, by and large, immigrant groups are permitted to maintain their religious affiliations and some of their cultural traditions. Greek immigrants, for example, are free to join the Greek Orthodox church; they are not required to become Protestants. They can continue to eat lamb *shashlik* instead of cheeseburgers. They must, however, learn English, dress in American clothes at work, and conform to many other American social customs if they are to function successfully in American society.

A good example of a functioning society based on cultural pluralism is Switzerland. German, French, and often Italian are spoken everywhere in Switzerland. So long as a person speaks any one of these three languages, he or she can participate fully as a citizen. The Swiss are free to choose between the Protestant and Catholic churches, which have equal status. The French-speaking Catholics and the German-speaking Protestants live in relative harmony; neither group dominates the other. But this situation is not without limitations. If the Swiss gave the same treatment to a dozen other ethnic groups, their society might well become hopelessly divided.

Patterns of Rejection

In the rejection patterns examined below, discrimination and prejudice are highly organized and focused. These patterns often reflect a deliberate policy agreed upon by a society. Throughout history, full or partial rejection of incoming groups has been the most common pattern of majority–minority group relations. The dominant group, which already holds social power, is reluctant to share it. Immigrants are feared as potentially disruptive, and it is felt to be socially necessary to reject them.

ANNIHILATION AND GENOCIDE

The most extreme form of rejection is **annihilation,** the process by which a dominant group causes the deaths of large numbers of minority group members. Societies have resorted to such brutality throughout history. In ancient Assyria and nineteenth-century Turkey, for example, annihilation was a routine practice. Both nations established a policy of butchering many of the residents of conquered cities or countries.

Sometimes annihilation takes the form of **genocide**—the deliberate and systematic destruction of an entire ethnic or racial group. The most infamous example of genocide in modern history is Hitler's "solution" to the presence of Jews in Europe. The Nazi government rounded up an estimated 6 million Jews and sent them to gas chambers.

EXPULSION

A second form of rejection that has occurred frequently throughout history is **expulsion,** or the forcing of a people out of an area or a society. Expulsion can be nearly as costly as annihilation in terms of lost lives. If a minority group is reluctant to leave its home, force will be used. And because the dominant group often shows little concern for the suffering of the minority, the trip to a "new home" may become an ordeal. In the 1830s, when U.S. Army troops forced the Cherokees to move from their native lands in Georgia to a reservation in Oklahoma, over 4,000 of the 10,000 who made the trip died along the way. The Cherokees called this journey the "Trail of Tears" (Starkey, 1946). And because their culture was not suited to the living conditions in Oklahoma, thousands more Cherokees died after they settled on the reservation.

Often no attempt is made to resettle those being expelled. A familiar biblical example is that of the Jews, who were turned out more than once into the uninhabitable desert. A modern example is the expulsion of ethnic Chinese by Vietnam. The Chinese were forced to emigrate by sea, and as many as half are estimated to have died.

PARTITION

Partition is the reorganization of a nation in order to make political boundaries correspond more closely to ethnic or racial boundaries. The groups involved sometimes agree on partition, as when India was divided after the end of British colonial rule in response to antagonism between the dominant Hindus and the large Muslim minority. The Hindus were given control of most of India. The Muslims were given the western part of the country (West Pakistan), together with a smaller piece of land in the eastern corner (East Pakistan, now the independent nation of Bangladesh), where they could live peacefully in their own nation. On the other hand, sometimes partition is imposed without the consent of those involved. Palestine, for example, was divided by the British into separate areas for Arabs and Jews in 1947.

Historical evidence suggests that partition is not a permanent solution to the problems of conflicting ethnic groups. It frequently generates hostilities that last for years. Although it may have been the best solution at the time, the partition of India has not ended widespread discrimination against the minority group remaining within each country (Shaw, Nordie, & Shapiro, 1987). And hostility between the two nations has continued, and even escalated, over the years. More than 40 years after the partitioning of Palestine, the Arabs and the Israelis remain in a constant state of conflict. Relationships between Catholics and Protestants in Ireland, which was partitioned along religious lines in 1921, are also marked by extreme bitterness and hostility.

SEGREGATION

Segregation is the separation of residential areas, institutions, or other facilities on the basis of the ethnic or racial characteristics of the people using them. It is a kind of internal partitioning, but the boundaries it erects are social and legal rather than political. Members of the segregated minority group may be forced to live in one particular part of town. They may be legally forbidden to leave except to go to work. And they may not be permitted to attend the same churches or schools as members of the dominant group, to participate in the government, or to form any kind of intimate relationships outside their own group.

For more than a century after the Civil War, segregation was the dominant pattern of relations between blacks and whites in the United States. When the nation was founded, the situation was different. Africans were originally brought to colonial America as slaves to meet demands for labor, particularly in the agricultural South. At that time, slaves—but not all blacks—experienced high levels of discrimination. There were several ways in which slaves could be freed, and once free, they enjoyed all the rights and privileges of any other citizen. In the eighteenth and early nineteenth centuries, however, when the growing southern plantations became increasingly dependent on the cheap and stable labor of the slaves,

For more than a century after the Civil War, segregation was the dominant pattern of relations between blacks and whites in the United States. Although segregationist laws and policies have been abolished, de facto segregation still exists.

laws were passed that discriminated against all blacks, both slaves and free citizens. As a result, African-Americans were gradually forced into a segregated and servile status.

After the Civil War, a less restrictive pattern of segregation developed in the South. Under some circumstances, close relationships between blacks and whites became possible, and certain social activities were shared. It was assumed, however, that public facilities should be equal but separate. The Civil Rights Act of 1875 sanctioned "separate but equal" accommodations in public facilities; in 1883, a U.S. Supreme Court decision applied the same principle to the schools. Especially in the South, however, schools and facilities were not, in fact, equal; white facilities were far superior to those provided for blacks.

In recent decades, this pattern of segregation has broken down. The 1954 *Brown* v. *Board of Education* decision and the Civil Rights Act of 1964 overturned the "separate but equal" principle and forbade discrimination in public facilities. African-Americans now have the right to attend the same schools, go to the same movie theaters, and ride in the same sections of buses as white people do. But some whites still oppose integrated housing and social clubs and interracial dating and marriage.

In the North, most of the social segregation of African-Americans has been the result of customary as opposed to legally required segregation of neighborhoods (Darden, 1989). Several studies have shown that the residential segregation of African-Americans in the North is no less extreme than that in the South, although there is some evidence that such segregation is declining in the newer metropolitan areas of the Sun Belt (James,

McCummings, & Tynan, 1984; Massey and Denton, 1995). The segregation of African-Americans has endured in part because of the obvious and immutable difference in skin color. The physical distinctness of African-Americans has slowed their full acceptance into a white-dominated society.

The most radical form of segregation is *apartheid,* the term used to describe a system that was mandated by law until very recently in South Africa. The policy of apartheid—a Dutch word that means "separateness"—was first adopted in 1947 by the Afrikaner-dominated National Party. The rationale for apartheid was that the races were so different in heritage and ability that they should each develop separately. What resulted was a system in which South African blacks and whites lived almost completely apart. Blacks were allowed in white areas only to work, and this work was usually menial. Through apartheid, the much smaller white population was able to keep the blacks relatively powerless.

After decades of tremendous internal and international pressure to change this system, the South African government finally took steps toward creating a more equitable system. Apartheid officially came to an end on February 1, 1991, when South African president F. W. de Klerk announced the repeal of all remaining apartheid laws. It remains to be seen, however, whether the racial, class, and ethnic tensions that have endured for decades can be alleviated simply by changing the laws (Schlemmer, 1991; Van den Berghe, 1990).

Structured Inequality in the United States

Most forms of racial discrimination are now illegal, and public opinion polls suggest that racial prejudice has diminished. But American society is still far from realizing true equality. In fact, living conditions for some minorities may actually be getting worse. Many scholars, therefore, have urged researchers studying ethnic and racial relations to devote more attention to racism and to the *social structures* that oppress minorities (Feagin & Feagin, 1999; Jencks, 1985).

Racism

The term *racism* is one of the most difficult to define in the entire field of sociology. Minority advocates and political liberals tend to view racism as any attitude or action on the part of a dominant group that is harmful to members of a minority group. Note that this approach does not require that racism be intentional, but only that it have harmful consequences. Note, also, that, by this definition, minorities cannot be racist.

Political conservatives are more likely to favor a very different definition of the concept. They regard as racist any attitude or action that treats people differently on the basis of race. Under such a definition, both a Ku Klux Klan rally and preferential hiring under a court-ordered affirmative action plan would be considered racist.

Most sociologists attempt to avoid this ideological mine field by focusing more on attitudes than on actions. Thus, **racism** is frequently defined as an ideology which holds that one race is innately superior or inferior to another.

Institutional Racism

Some scholars, especially those who are comfortable with the "liberal" definition of racism, believe that the most important type of racism in American society is *institutional racism,* a term coined by Stokely Carmichael and Charles V. Hamilton in their book *Black Power* (1967). **Institutional racism** consists of policies that appear to be race-neutral or colorblind and that are usually not the result of intentional efforts to discriminate but nevertheless have the effect of limiting the opportunities of members of minority groups. This type of discrimination is found in almost all institutional spheres of American life despite decades of legal efforts to ensure equal treatment of minorities.

An often-cited example of institutional racism concerns the minimum height requirement for fire fighters in New York City. This requirement was established years before Puerto Ricans began to migrate to New York in large numbers, and there is no reason to believe that it was deliberately enacted in order to keep Puerto Ricans (who tend to be short) from being hired as fire fighters. Still, the actual result of the requirement, regardless of the original intent, has been to limit the opportunities of Puerto Ricans.

Let us look at how institutional racism works in several important spheres of public life.

ECONOMIC INSTITUTIONS. Under the American market system, large numbers of people can be unemployed at any given time, especially during economic recessions. Under normal circumstances, white-collar workers and professionals are relatively well protected from economic cycles; unionized blue-collar laborers are also protected by relatively good wages, unemployment insurance, and other benefits. But a disproportionate number of people from minority groups work in jobs that are seasonal or subject to regular layoffs. They have no security, earn low pay, and receive few benefits.

Many observers have noted, therefore, that there exists in our society a "dual labor market." The economy includes a primary market in which pay and job stability are good, and a secondary market characterized by low pay and little stability. But why, if racial discrimination is illegal, is it disproportionately members of minority groups who are employed in the secondary market? One reason is that as a result of past overt and legal discrimination, minority group members were often prevented from gaining the skills, experience, and seniority that they need to participate in the primary labor market. Thus, the dual labor market, by its very structure, and without any overt prejudice or illegal discrimination, works to the great disadvantage of minority groups.

Tables 11.1 and 11.2 record recent inequalities between whites and other groups in the United States. Whites have had consistently lower rates of unemployment and higher incomes than members of other groups.

EDUCATIONAL INSTITUTIONS. Because education is the chief means of gaining access to the primary labor market, it is one of the main avenues of upward mobility. In a society dedicated to equal opportunity, a value shared by most citizens of the United States, we would expect educational opportunities to be equal. But until fairly recently, African-Americans were barred from access to quality education by overt and often legal discrimination. Prior to the 1960s, for example, some colleges and universities used quota systems that limited the number of African-American students who would be admitted. And studies of segregated schools have repeatedly demonstrated that, to this day, many schools with primarily African-American student bodies are significantly inferior to schools in which the students are mostly white (Willie, 1984).

Youths who receive a poor education at understaffed and underequipped segregated schools are less likely to be able to meet the high academic standards that

TABLE 11.2 PROPORTION OF WHITES, BLACKS, AND PEOPLE OF SPANISH ORIGIN BELOW POVERTY LEVEL IN THE UNITED STATES*

Year	Whites	Blacks	People of Spanish Origin†
1959	18.1	55.1	‡
1970	9.9	33.5	‡
1975	9.7	31.3	26.9
1980	10.2	32.5	25.7
1987	11.0	31.1	27.3
1989	10.0	30.7	26.2
1992	11.3	32.7	28.1
1998	8.6	26.5	27.1

*In percentages.
†People of Spanish origin can be of any race.
‡Not available.

Sources: U.S. Bureau of the Census, *Money Income and Poverty Status of Families and Persons in the United States, 1983* (Washington, D.C.: U.S. Government Printing Office, 1983); U.S. Bureau of the Census, *Current Population Reports, 1987* (Washington, D.C.: U.S. Government Printing Office 1987); U.S. Bureau of the Census, *Statistical Abstract of the United States, 1993* (Washington, D.C.: U.S. Government Printing Office, 1993), U.S. Bureau of the Census, *March 1998 Current Population Survey* (http:www.census.gov)).

TABLE 11.1 UNEMPLOYMENT RATES BY RACE AND ETHNICITY, 1980–1999

Year	White	Hispanic	Black
1980	6.3	10.1	14.3
1988	5.3	8.2	11.7
1990	4.8	8.2	11.4
1995	4.9	9.3	10.4
1999	4.3	7.4	7.9

Sources: U.S. Bureau of Labor Statistics, "Employment and Earnings, 1990" (Washington, D.C.: U.S. Government Printing Office, 1991); U.S. Bureau of Labor Statistics, "Labor Force Statistics from Current Population Survey," 1999. (http:stats.bls.gov)

colleges and employers require. Although the purpose of these standards is not to discriminate against a particular group, they have that effect because of past educational inequalities. Another example of institutional discrimination in education is the high cost of college, a serious impediment to higher learning for poor minority students (Farley, 1995). Between 1989 and 1990 alone, college tuition costs increased an average of 6 to 7 percent, while state and federal financial aid did not rise proportionally.

CRIMINAL JUSTICE SYSTEM. Minority group members are arrested and convicted for many types of crime more often than their numbers should warrant. Every study of crime using official data shows that African-Americans are heavily overrepresented among persons arrested, convicted, and imprisoned. Blacks are four times more likely than whites to be arrested for violent crimes and three times more likely to be arrested for crimes against property (Wilson & Herrnstein, 1985).

One reason for these statistics is that minorities are more likely to be arrested and convicted than are members of the dominant group who have committed the same crimes. Careful research has shown that nonwhites are stopped by the police for questioning more often than whites, that black offenders are more likely to be arrested than white offenders for the same types of acts, and that police officers display more authoritarian and belittling behavior toward black suspects (van Oudenhoven & Willemsen, 1989). Also, the kinds of crimes characteristically committed by lower-class minority group members are more likely to result in arrest and conviction than are the kinds of crimes more typically committed by members of the middle class. Thus, the criminal justice system seems to operate in a way that leads to unequal justice for minorities.

Institutional discrimination also occurs in politics, housing, the mass media, and many other spheres of American life. This discrimination often does not encompass any deliberate actions intended to harm minorities, but the effects can be just as harmful as those of intentional discrimination.

AFFIRMATIVE ACTION

The principal mechanism that American society has developed to respond to institutional racism, especially in education and the economy, is **affirmative action**—policies that grant preference to minority group members in order to make up for the effects of prior discrimination. Such policies may vary from simply taking pains to be sure that opportunities are well publicized in the minority community to actually reserving a certain number of jobs or college admissions slots for minority applicants.

Affirmative action has been legally required in a variety of situations since the late 1960s. In recent years, courts have become less willing to endorse so-called "hard quotas," but the basic principle of minority preference seems firmly established as constitutionally allowable. Affirmative action is, however, intensely controversial. Advocates argue that there is no other way by which we can make up for the harmful effects of prior deliberate discrimination. In order to make the playing field truly level, a certain amount of handicapping is necessary. Furthermore, they note, research strongly suggests that businesses and educational institutions that have been required to conform to affirmative action guidelines have desegregated far more rapidly and completely than have those that have not been so ordered.

Opponents of affirmative action programs also have some strong arguments. Many people decry affirmative action as "reverse discrimination" and ask why whites today should suffer in order to make right the consequences of the sins of their ancestors. Furthermore, affirmative action may be seen as insulting to minorities. An African-American who is hired under an affirmative action plan may always have to fight the suspicion that he or she would not have been good enough to get the job

without special help. Finally, opponents note that affirmative action is so unpopular among whites that its continuation will only inflame already sensitive race relations in this country.

Perhaps a middle position can be found by noting that affirmative action was never intended to be a permanent policy but, rather, one designed only to provide minorities with enough assistance to overcome the lingering effects of prior deliberate oppression. As a result of almost three decades of affirmative action, the black middle class has expanded dramatically. It may be that the need for special help to this group is no longer as great as it once was. On the other hand, most members of the minority underclass, whose problems dwarf those of the black working and middle classes, are not likely to be able to take much advantage of the educational and occupational advantages provided by affirmative action.

INTERNAL COLONIALISM

What are the origins of institutional racism? And why has it endured despite laws intended to eliminate discrimination against minorities? One group of theorists argues that the answers to these questions can be found in the early history of the United States. Institutional racism, they say, is the result of a pattern of economic exploitation called *internal colonialism* (Blauner, 1969).

Internal colonialism is similar to, and grew out of, the colonialism that European nations imposed on much of the world beginning in the fifteenth century. When the Europeans colonized a region, they established themselves as the dominant group and the native population as the subordinate group. They used the usually unwilling native people as a cheap source of labor. In the process, they often destroyed, or tried to destroy, indigenous cultures and values. Even though most of the former European colonies are now independent, many are still dominated economically by a European minority and still depend on European nations for economic survival. They remain *internally* colonized. India, for example, was a British colony until 1947. Since that time, its progress toward modernization has been slower than that of many other developing countries. Some believe that this is partly due to India's continuing economic dependence on Britain.

The native population in North America was small, and it was nearly eradicated early in the process of colonization. As a result, the European settlers were obliged to import a source of cheap labor: African slaves. As was the case with the native peoples of former European colonies elsewhere, American blacks were kept in an economically subordinate position even after slavery was abolished. Even today, they are disproportionately likely to work in menial jobs for low wages. According to proponents of the internal colonialism view, African-Americans have remained, in effect, a colonized people and have been kept in a subordinate status that is reflected in the persistence of institutional racism.

Critics of the internal colonialism view argue that African-Americans were not the only group to come here originally as a source of cheap labor. The waves of European immigrants—Irish, Italian, and Jewish—who emigrated in the nineteenth and early twentieth centuries were all initially exploited as low-paid laborers and faced discrimination. Yet these groups have since achieved substantial upward mobility.

Responding to this criticism, advocates of the internal colonialism view note some crucial differences between African-Americans and other ethnic groups: The Africans were brought here entirely against their will, and most of their native culture was destroyed. European ethnic groups came here voluntarily in search of economic opportunity. They were able to keep their cultural heritage at least partially intact, and, unlike African-Americans, they were not legally prevented from taking advantage of the educational and economic resources of the country (Feagin & Feagin, 1999; Kitano, 1985).

THE DECLINING SIGNIFICANCE OF RACE?

The importance of race in inequality has become the focus of sharp scholarly controversy in recent years. In one highly influential work, sociologist William J. Wilson (1978) put forth the view that "class has become more important than race in determining black life chances in the modern industrial period" (p. 150). Wilson believes that since World War II, the increased availability of white-collar employment, the passage of civil rights legislation, and the expansion of the African-American middle class have made racial oppression decreasingly important in the lives of many African-Americans. Wilson goes on to note that, at the same time, the great inequality faced by poor, lower-class African-Americans is mainly class-based and less the result of racial discrimination than in the past.

In a more recent book, Wilson (1987) argues that the worsening situation of this urban "underclass" is largely the result of economic forces, especially the flight of many jobs from the central cities. As the cities move from industrial to postindustrial economies (see Chapter 22), skilled and unskilled blue-collar jobs—in which a high number of minorities are employed—are diminishing rapidly. As a result, many minorities have been unable to obtain new positions because many of the jobs available today require high levels of education or technical skills. Wilson also suggests that the situation has been exacerbated by the flight of the African-American middle class to the suburbs, leaving the remaining ghetto population with few middle-class role models.

Wilson's theories are very controversial. Critics note that at the same time that the African-American middle class was supposedly rising, the unemployment rate among African-Americans increased 100 percent, as opposed to only 25 percent among whites. Citing these statistics, Wilson's detractors argue that only a very small percentage of African-Americans moved upward into the middle class—a percentage so small, they believe, that Wilson's work distorts the social experience of African-Americans and overstates the amount of progress that has been made in the last few decades (Pinkney, 1984).

If this is the case, then the significance of race may not be declining at all. In fact, some critics see a growing white backlash—a strong adverse reaction on the part of whites resulting in increased discrimination—that may actually increase the significance of race in the coming years (Feagin & Feagin, 1999).

SOCIAL AND PSYCHOLOGICAL RESPONSES OF MINORITY GROUP MEMBERS

Because a minority group is, by definition, relatively powerless, the actions of the dominant society normally determine the main patterns of intergroup relations. All human relationships are mutual, however, and the actions of the dominant society will always in some way be influenced by the responses of the minority group. The responses of minority group members have ranged from passive acceptance to active hostility and aggression.

Passive Acceptance

One course open to minority group members is simply to accept their situation. They can adjust to their subordinate position and make the best of it. The classic example of passive acceptance is Uncle Tom, the black servant in Harriet Beecher Stowe's novel *Uncle Tom's Cabin* (1852). Resigned to his status, Tom tries to act in a way that will make his life as comfortable as possible. He does as he is told, never causes trouble, and is faithful to his master's interests. Because of this passive behavior, he is treated well by his master and even achieves some of his personal goals.

In the sense that it maintains intergroup harmony, passive acceptance may seem the easiest answer for a minority group member. But those who use it often pay for outer peace with inner anxiety. To appear to accept personal inferiority while privately believing otherwise is very stressful because it requires the concealment of one's true feelings. Accepting the role of an inferior and at the same time maintaining self-respect can be difficult, if not

APPLYING SOCIOLOGY

RESPONDING TO RACIAL DISCRIMINATION

What is the best way to respond to racial discrimination? If you think that you will never face this problem, think again. A number of cases in recent years have shown that discrimination is still a problem in corporate America. And while you might not be the victim of discrimination, you might be required to testify in court about it. Recent cases have shown that racial discrimination can start at the top and that company policies may be intentionally designed to discriminate against members of minority groups. This kind of discrimination is not imagined. And executives at the head of America's largest corporations have been required to testify about it.

Consider an incident that involved Ray Danner, the CEO of Shoney's, Inc., the second largest family restaurant chain in the United States. During a surprise inspection of a store run by Ron Murphy, the only black manager out of dozens in the Nashville area, Danner picked up a flounder and put it into an Igloo cooler. He was unhappy that the fish was underweight—one and one-half ounces instead of two. He then returned to the corporate headquarters of Shoney's. An official of the company by the name of Jerry Garner later testified about what happened the next day:

On Monday morning after this weekend inspection, approximately

twelve or thirteen of the highest level supervisors in that area, including a group vice president, gathered for a meeting in the Central Office in Nashville. These Monday morning conferences were regular occurrences.

"At the meeting, Danner put the Igloo cooler on the conference table, reached into it and picked out the fish he had brought back from Ron Murphy's restaurant, which was thawed out by that time, and threw it against the wall where it stuck."

Garner, who was one of those present, said Danner then addressed the conferees.

"That," Danner is purported to have said, "is a prime example of black management in our company." (Watkins, 1997, p. 2)

Danner's racist attitudes shaped discriminatory policies. According to one longtime vice president, everyone knew Danner's laws: "Blacks were not qualified to run a store. Blacks were not qualified to run a kitchen of a store. Blacks should not be employed in any position where they would be seen by customers" (Watkins, 1997; p. 5).

On April 9, 1989, a lawsuit charging racial discrimination was filed against Danner and his company. During the trial that followed, white managers of Shoney's restaurants testified that their superiors ordered them to blacken the "O" in the word

"Shoney's" on the applications of minorities. It was on that basis that blacks were screened out and passed over for jobs.

The company eventually settled out of court for $132.5 million. The company forced Danner, who was the 266th richest person at the time, to pay half of this. One of the surprising aspects of this case turned out to be who initiated it. They were two white managers, who were fired because they refused to comply with the company's orders to reduce the number of black employees and to demote a black assistant store manager (Hammond, 1997).

This story did not receive much attention from the media. One reason was that the settlement was announced on November 3, 1992, when journalists were absorbed with covering Bill Clinton's presidential victory over George Bush. But since then, a number of other cases involving racial discrimination at some of America's corporate giants have received national news coverage. In the largest settlement to date, Texaco agreed to pay $140 million and to adopt new policies to promote equality and eliminate discrimination (*New York Times*, 1997). Other settlements have included Boeing, $15 million; United Parcel Service of America, $12.1 million; Pennzoil, $6.25 million; and Denny's, $54.4 million for two class-action suits.

Members of subordinate groups respond to discrimination in a variety

impossible. Total acceptance can lead to self-hatred and a variety of other pathological responses.

Furthermore, passive acceptance tends to support a social pattern of prejudice and discrimination. Because the minority member appears satisfied, members of the dominant society see no reason to change. Passive acceptance can also become a **self-fulfilling prophecy**—a

belief or prediction that comes true as a result of the behavior it produces. In other words, if the members of a minority group respond with passive acceptance because they believe their situation is hopeless, it is unlikely that their situation will ever change; the minority group cannot improve its position because its members believe improvement is not possible. The belief is self-fulfilling.

of ways—from deference or withdrawal, to verbal confrontation and physical confrontation, to legal action (Feagin & Feagin, 1999). During the civil rights movement in the 1950s and 1960s, victims of racial discrimination joined forces to fight back in organized ways. Today, some cases require legal action. But research shows that legal action is not always necessary (Feagin & Sikes, 1994). Individual victims who contest discrimination can turn a one-way action into a two-way negotiation. Consider, for example, the case of a black woman manager in a U.S. corporation who confronted her boss about an evaluation of her job performance. She described the meeting as follows:

We had a five scale rating, starting with outstanding, then very good, then good, then fair, and then less than satisfactory. I had gone into my evaluation interview anticipating that he would give me a "VG" (very good), feeling that I deserved an "outstanding" and prepared to fight for my outstanding rating. Knowing, you know, my past experience with him, and more his way toward females. But even beyond female, I happened to be the only black in my position within my branch. So the racial issue would also come into play. And he and I had some very frank discussions about race specifically. About females, but more about race when he and I talked. So I certainly knew

that he had a lot of prejudices in terms of blacks. And [he] had some very strong feelings based on his upbringing about the abilities of blacks. He said to me on numerous occasions that he considered me to be an exception, that I certainly was not what he felt the abilities of an average black person [were]. While I was of course appalled and made it perfectly clear to him. . . . But, when I went into the evaluation interview, he gave me glowing comments that cited numerous achievements and accomplishments for me during the year, and then concluded it with, "So I've given you a G." You know, which of course, just floored me. . . . [I] maintained my emotions and basically just said, as unemotionally as I possibly could, that I found that unacceptable, I thought it was inconsistent with his remarks in terms of my performance, and I would not accept it. I think I kind of shocked him, because he sort of said, "Well I don't know what that means," you know, when I said I wouldn't accept it. I said, I'm not signing the evaluation. And at that point, here again knowing that the best way to deal with most issues is with facts and specifics, I had already come in prepared. . . . I had my list of objectives for the year where I was able to show him that I had achieved every objective and I exceeded all of them. I also had . . . my sales performance: the dollar amount, the

products . . . both in total dollar sales and also a product mix. I sold every product in the line that we offered to our customers. I had exceeded all of my sales objectives. You know, as far as I was concerned, it was outstanding performance. . . . So he basically said, "Well, we don't have to agree to agree," and that was the end of the session. I got up and left. Fifteen minutes later he called me back in and said, "I've thought about what you said, and you're right, you do have an O." So it's interesting how in fifteen minutes I went from a G to an O. But the interesting point is had I not fought it, had I just accepted it, I would have gotten a G rating for that year, which has many implications. (cited in Feagin & Feagin, 1999; pp. 25–26).

In this case, the victim did not accept the negative evaluation and successfully challenged it. Today middle-class African-Americans have the resources to contest this kind of discrimination. And they are doing so successfully. Research shows that victim's first response is important (Feagin & Sikes, 1994). While it may only be the first step in fighting discrimination, it can be an individual's most effective strategy.

Source: Excerpt from *Racial and Ethnic Relations*, 6/e by Feagin/Feagin, © 1999, reprinted by permission of Prentice-Hall, Inc., Upper Saddle River, NJ.

Individual Aggression and Acts of Violence

Another common response of minority group members is aggression. This response can take the form of physical violence against the dominant group, such as the Apache raids on white settlements in the late nineteenth century or the riots in American central cities in the late 1960s.

Because those who are caught in such acts of violence are often severely punished or even killed, this response is generally used only as a last resort.

Usually minority individuals seek safer ways to express their aggression, such as through verbal and written channels. Minority group members may shout threats or spray-paint them on walls. They may write books expressing their anger. By making the attitudes and actions of the dominant group appear ridiculous, jokes can also reflect aggression.

Another outlet for aggression is by sabotaging, deliberately or not, work done for the dominant group. Slaves in the South sometimes had "accidents" that ruined crops or killed livestock. A cook may burn the family's dinner on a special occasion or break a valuable dish. Minority factory workers may bungle their jobs, causing a slowdown in the assembly line.

Some sociologists have suggested that many crimes committed by minority persons may be interpreted as aggressive responses to their condition of oppression. Minority individuals who rob higher status people at gunpoint may be doing more than just trying to improve their economic condition. They may also be using crime as an aggressive protest against society (see Gibbons, 1977; Pettigrew & Martin, 1987).

Collective Protest

Protest movements, which have occurred throughout history, have dealt with many different issues. Movements among minorities to gain civil rights are a fairly recent phenomenon, yet they have quickly become perhaps the most common form of minority response in America.

Many scholars see the civil rights movement as rooted in the experience of World War II. The great demand for labor to support the war effort brought large numbers of African-American and other minority workers into skilled and semiskilled jobs that had never before been open to them. Less directly involved, but also important psychologically, was the end of the European colonial empires that followed World War II.

Political gains that have resulted in part from civil rights protests have put minorities into policy-making positions in many parts of the country. African-Americans have been elected mayors of about 300 cities, including Los Angeles, Detroit, Chicago, Atlanta, Philadelphia, New York, and Washington, D.C. A number are now representatives in Congress, and many hold key federal and state government positions. However, even though minorities have been accepted to some extent into the power structure, they still have a long way to go before they achieve full acceptance.

Self-Segregation

The process by which a minority group voluntarily tries to keep itself apart from the dominant society is called **self-segregation.** Unable to find satisfactory ways to relate to the dominant group, minority group members try to limit their contacts with outsiders through this process.

The black nationalist tradition in the United States is an outstanding example of this pattern of response. Beginning with the mass movement headed by Marcus Garvey in the 1920s and continuing today through the modern Nation of Islam, black nationalists have consistently taken a stand against integration, arguing that African-Americans will never be treated fairly by whites. Instead of trying to assimilate, nationalists advocate that blacks establish and support their own separate educational, economic, and religious institutions.

The most extreme form of self-segregation is **separatism,** in which the minority group aspires to set up a totally independent society of its own. Separatism may be carried out through migration or by partition. One of the few successful attempts at separatism occurred in 1947 when Palestine was partitioned and the Jewish state of Israel was born. The African nation of Liberia is another example of separatism. Under the sponsorship of the American government, which did no more than arrange for their emigration, a group of freed slaves colonized Liberia in 1822. The first 100 years of the colony were difficult. In addition to a lack of capital and technology needed to develop their nation's economy, the colonists also had trouble with the tropical climate and unfriendly indigenous people. Only in recent years has Liberia made progress toward achieving a satisfactory standard of living, but it shares the political instability common to other African nations. Today the descendants of the original colonialists have lost much of the power they once held.

Voluntary Assimilation

Another response of minority group members to the dominant society is voluntary assimilation. Individuals who choose this response try to learn the dominant group's language, style of dress, patterns of behavior, and other cultural characteristics so well that it is difficult to tell that they are actually minority group members.

For many European ethnic groups, assimilation has meant dropping old customs, simplifying foreign-sounding names, and moving to the suburbs. An illustration of this pattern can be seen in a suburban Cleveland community of second- and third-generation Poles and Czechs. All the houses, built on streets named for U.S. presidents, are in the American colonial style, with brass eagles over the door. On some mailboxes the last syllable of the owner's name has been neatly painted out: Joseph Rudenski has become Joe Ruden, and Robert Marcowiak is now Bob Marco.

The decision to assimilate can be painful because it involves turning away from an ethnic heritage that may still carry emotional meaning and social connection.

Sometimes those who choose this path are bitterly criticized by their parents, siblings, and other relatives for giving up the family name, history, language, and cultural traditions. The daughter of strict Orthodox Jewish parents who marries a non-Jew may be cut off from her family. They may even hold a symbolic funeral service and pronounce her dead.

THE FUTURE OF ETHNIC AND RACE RELATIONS

As we have seen, ethnic and racial tensions are a major source of internal and international conflict. Dominant and minority groups have been a social fact throughout history, and these boundaries do not appear to be breaking down very rapidly (Marrett & Leggon, 1985). What can be done to reduce tensions in the future?

The key to improved dominant–minority relations may lie in changing the way people *think* rather than in passing legislation regarding the way people *act.* Because ethnocentrism appears to be at the base of most prejudice and discrimination, societies can counter the strength of ethnocentric feelings by teaching *altrocentrism,* the ability to see events as they appear to others. Being able to put oneself in the shoes of a minority group member will surely go a long way toward decreasing cross-cultural misunderstandings (Stagner, 1987).

Some sociologists believe that the international economy and culture that have begun to emerge in the last few decades will eventually result in improved ethnic and racial relations. The increasing environmental and economic interdependence of all parts of the world, these scholars believe, will bring about a new commitment to interracial and interethnic equality, along with a pragmatic recognition that one country's welfare depends to a large extent on the well-being of other nations. With these changes, the world could see an increasing amalgamation of racial and ethnic groups, together with a declining significance of race and ethnicity as sources of tension (Stack, 1986).

CHAPTER REVIEW

1. Does the term *Hispanic* refer to race or ethnicity? Why?

2. What problems could the Census Bureau encounter as it attempts to classify the population on the basis of race and ethnicity?

3. Why do people stereotype members of different racial and ethnic groups?

4. Give examples of both positive and negative prejudice.

5. Can employers practice discrimination and get around the law in the United States today? If so, how do they do it?

6. Describe the processes that occur when a society responds to the presence of minority groups with some level of acceptance.

7. Describe the ways used by the dominant group in a society to reject members of a minority group.

8. Is cultural pluralism desirable? Why or why not?

9. Give an example of institutional racism.

10. Describe the process by which a minority group voluntarily tries to keep itself apart from the dominant society.

INTERNET EXERCISE

The Web destinations for Chapter 11 deal with topics that are relevant to ethnic and racial minorities. To begin your explorations, go to the Prentice Hall Web site **http://www.prenhall.com/popenoe.** Then, select **Chapter 11** (Ethnic and Racial Minorities). Now, choose **web destinations** from the menu on the left side of the screen. There are a number of interesting sites to access. We suggest you begin with **One America,** which is among the presidential initiatives sponsored by the White House. Click on "What You Can Do." There you will find a list of suggestions for Americans in terms of their attitudes toward ethnic and racial minority groups. If you would like to find out more about the *One America* program, you may click on different descriptors within the site After you have explored the *One America* site, answer the following questions:

- Do you agree with the *One America* initiative? Why or why not?
- How would the nation benefit from being able to actually accomplish the *One America* initiative?

KEY TERMS

minority group	amalgamation	racism
ethnic group	cultural pluralism	institutional racism
race	annihilation	affirmative action
prejudice	genocide	self-fulfilling prophecy
stereotype	expulsion	self-segregation
discrimination	partition	separatism
assimilation	segregation	

CHAPTER 12

Age and Health in Society

o one in American society, it seems, wants to grow old. Virtually everyone tries in one way or another to ward off old age. Advertisers spend billions of dollars every year trying to convince us that their products—certain cars, particular styles of clothing, and different types of yogurt, to name just a few—will make us feel young.

When your hair turns gray, chances are you will at least consider dyeing it. At the first sign of a bulge, you may begin feverishly exercising and dieting in the hope of regaining your "youthful" slenderness. As you move through middle age into the "autumn" of life, you may also consider liposuction, a face-lift, or a hairpiece.

The fear of growing old and the hope that the aging process can somehow be held at bay contribute to America's having by far the world's largest health-care system. Age and health are related, of course. A large part of a person's lifetime health-care expenses are incurred in the last few months of life (Kovar, 1986; Kovar, Hendershot, & Mathis, 1989; Riley, 1987). And with a growing elderly population, the nation's health-care bill is bound to rise.

In this chapter, we explore these and many other aspects of the relations between age, health, and society. As we shall see, age and health are not only biological facts of human life but also very important social phenomena. Age, for example, has a very different social meaning when applied to different groups of people. Ballplayers are said to be "over the hill" at about age 35. Gymnasts' careers end at about age 22. Politicians, however, are considered young if they run for office in their 30s and even 40s, and Ronald Reagan has demonstrated that being well into one's 70s is not an irrevocable handicap for becoming president.

AGE AND SOCIETY

The study of age and aging is one of the newest fields of sociological inquiry. Nevertheless, it has quickly gained importance; for despite the heavy accent on youth in American culture, our society is aging very rapidly. In fact, the median age of the American population (35.3 in 1998) is one of the highest in the world.

Caused primarily by changes in the ratio of deaths to births, the "aging of America" is part of a shift toward older populations that has gradually occurred throughout the developed world. As this trend continues, it will have increasingly profound social consequences.

The Demographic Shift

Before the Industrial Revolution, infectious disease killed an enormous number of children. One study showed that between 1770 and 1789, half the infants baptized in London were dead before the age of five (Edmonds, 1835/1976). But with advances in medical knowledge and improvements in living conditions in the nineteenth and early twentieth centuries, the infant death rate declined sharply. As a result, populations began to expand dramatically, often without any increase in the birth rate. Partly because so many children were surviving, the average age of these populations dropped (McKeon, 1976). Today, as medical and sanitary conditions improve in the developing countries, such as those of Africa and Asia, their infant mortality rate is declining and their populations are also becoming younger.

In the developed countries today, however, another trend has reversed this shift toward younger populations: Women in these nations are choosing to give birth to fewer children. Because children make up an ever smaller part of the population, the average age of these societies is now growing older each year.

This trend is clearly evident in the United States. Since the late 1960s, the American *fertility rate*—the average number of children each woman bears—has sharply declined. The children born in the postwar baby boom are now between 35 and 54 years of age, swelling the middle range of the age distribution. When this generation reaches 65, it will contribute to a "seniors boom."

This trend toward an older society has already brought strong pressure for added attention to the needs of the elderly. In the future, the needs of senior citizens will loom even larger than they do today. To meet these needs, a major reordering of our current social priorities and values may be necessary.

Historical Development of the Stages of Life

The concept of age may seem to be obvious and unchanging. But, in fact, social attitudes toward age and aging have changed greatly over the centuries. In Western societies, two notable trends seem to have had contradictory effects. One trend decreases the social importance of age; the other has the opposite effect (Neugarten & Hagestad, 1976). These two trends help to explain some of society's inconsistent attitudes toward aging and the elderly.

The first trend is that social perceptions of what is "appropriate" behavior for various age groups now permit much more personal freedom than they did in the past. For example, people are marrying later, having children later, switching careers in their 50s, and returning to school in their 60s. It is not unusual to see mothers and daughters both wearing blue jeans, listening to rock music, and even dancing the same dances. Young men and women have been elected to offices previously held only by their elders. Colleges, where the old once taught the young, are now frequently staffed by relatively young men and women and attended by students who, not infrequently, are retired people wishing to resume or complete their educations.

The second trend is equally significant, though less obvious. More than ever before, people are being sorted and segregated according to age. Though we once tended to view ourselves as either old or young, we are now faced with more and more age-based categories, including adolescence, young adulthood, and late middle age. Government and institutional programs sift and divide people into age groups, with special policies for each group. In many companies, retirement is expected at 65, if not before, and this age has become an arbitrary marker of the beginning of old age.

Indeed, it may come as a surprise that even such concepts as childhood and adolescence are very new in historical terms. Childhood was not treated as a separate life stage until the seventeenth and eighteenth centuries. Adolescence was "invented" only 100 years ago. Middle age is an even more recent "discovery."

Colleges, where the old once taught the young, are now staffed by relatively young men and women and attended by students who are not infrequently retired people wishing to resume or complete their education.

CHILDHOOD

In medieval Europe, children past infancy were not clearly distinguished from adults. Almost as soon as they could walk and talk, they entered adult society, becoming helpers in the fields or apprentices in workshops (Ariès, 1962). Children even dressed like adults, for clothes were determined more by social class than age. Not until the seventeenth century—as we can see from the paintings of that period—did children begin to dress in a manner different from that of adults. It was during this same period that childhood was first identified as a distinct stage of life.

The most critical element in the "invention" of childhood was probably the idea of formal education, especially the requirement that all children attend school. This trend reinforced the then-new view that children were not to be seen as part of the work force but as creatures who needed to be carefully molded into adults. Childhood became a time when people were to be protected, cared for, and taught. Furthermore, during the nineteenth and early twentieth centuries, access to certain kinds of sensitive knowledge that sets adults apart from children was available only to those who had mastered reading in school. Finally, the physical isolation of children in the schools promoted the development of a distinct youth subculture that further served to separate childhood from adulthood.

Some scholars believe that this trend may now be reversing. Since the advent of the electronic media in the latter half of the current century, adult secrets are revealed to any child old enough to understand what is displayed on a TV screen. This has resulted not only in a loss of innocence among many contemporary children but also, some argue, in a more general weakening of the distinction between children and adults (Postman, 1982).

ADOLESCENCE AND YOUTH

The period between childhood and adulthood was not perceived as a separate stage of life until the late nineteenth century. G. Stanley Hall, a pioneer in child psychology, first described this stage in *Adolescence* (1904). Hall regarded adolescence as a kind of "second birth" marked by a rise of "moral idealism, chivalry and religious enthusiasm." In the twentieth century, laws mandating compulsory school attendance until age 16 advanced the concept of adolescence even further (Eisenstadt, 1956). For the first time, young people were required to remain in school so long that sexual maturity and adult economic responsibility did not occur simultaneously.

In modern society, the postponement of adulthood has been extended yet further. Indeed, so much time now elapses between biological maturity and full entry into the adult world that yet another stage of life, called "youth," has come into being, especially among the middle and upper classes (Keniston, 1970). During this period, young people are old enough to serve in the military, marry, and have children, but they often still depend on their families for economic support. Today only a little more than half of all Americans between the ages of 16 and 19 are full-time members of the labor force; almost all of the rest are in a life stage that has been called "studentry" (U.S. Bureau of Labor, 1999). Because of the increasing demand for highly educated and skilled workers, many young people remain in a preadult state well into their 20s and beyond.

MIDDLE AGE

For years, middle age was regarded as a time of personal turmoil—a time particularly distressing for men, who were expected to experience a *mid-life crisis* (Levinson et al., 1978). The theory suggested that at this point in life, men might believe that that they no longer had a chance for a promotion. In the factory, a manual worker might finally admit to himself that he would never become a farmer or an independent businessman. Even men who have fulfilled their career dreams were expected to ask themselves painful questions: What have I given up for success? Was it worth it?

Although many middle-aged men were expected to be depressed or despondent as a consequence of such bitter reflections, experts did not believe women would experience the same problems. Having only recently entered the labor force in large numbers, middle-aged women did not seem to face life crises. If anything, the expectation was that women had gained psychological strength and self-confidence through participating in the world of work, even though juggling the twin demands of work and family life has often proved to be taxing (Sheehy, 1976).

As it turns out, new research suggests that the mid-life crisis was just a myth (*Los Angeles Times,* 1999). And, in fact, middle age may be the most fulfilling time of life. A 10-year study, which included mail surveys of over 7,800 adults between the ages of 25 and 74 and interviews with over 3,000 people, showed that many middle-aged people were happy. They described their relationships in positive terms, as stable and happy, and they felt secure in their jobs. And over 70 percent considered themselves in excellent health. Finally, there was no evidence that middle-aged men wanted to abandon their families for a red sports car and a younger woman. In this study, 90 percent of those surveyed indicated that they had never experienced the proverbial mid-life crisis.

OLD AGE

Old age as a distinct stage of life is also a relatively recent social creation (Elder, 1975). Usually thought to begin at retirement, old age is often marked by a loss of status. Just as youth is seen as the most desirable time of life, so old age is often seen as the least.

For centuries, however, aging was associated with an increase rather than a loss of status, as it still is in many non-Western cultures. For example, among the Kipsigis

people of rural Kenya, the older the person, the higher his or her social ranking (Krymkowski & Middleton, 1987). Why, then, have the elderly lost status in the developed societies? One scholar has observed that the main shift in attitude apparently took place between 1770 and 1880 (Fischer, 1978). In this era of rapid social and political change, the idea that high status and power belonged by right to elderly leaders was displaced by the ideal of social equality. Because it challenges the entrenched authority of elderly leaders, equality tends to favor the young over the old. Accompanying this change in cultural values were the broad economic transformations brought about by industrialization and the movement of people to cities, which also tended to reduce the status of the elderly (Cowgill, 1986).

Property ownership previously gave the old much of their power over the young. But in modern industrial societies, ownership and control are not always linked, and the young have opportunities for advancement—through education and business—that do not depend on the good graces of powerful older people. Older people used to be more highly valued for their knowledge and skills than they are today. But because of the rapid rate of technological change, many skills held by the old become outdated quickly. Furthermore, the ascendancy of the nuclear family has frequently relegated elderly parents to a relatively peripheral role in the lives of their adult children (and their offspring), again reducing their status. Nevertheless, older people are still often considered to be sources of good advice and are consulted from time to time on a wide variety of matters.

Age and Social Structure

Sociologists have developed an important perspective for analyzing the significance of age in society, using the concepts of status and role. As defined in Chapter 4, a *status* is a socially defined position in a group or society, and a *role* is the behavior expected of someone occupying a given status.

AGE STATUSES AND ROLES

Just as society assigns statuses and roles to people according to their class, race, and sex, it also assigns them on the basis of age (Riley, Foner, & Waring, 1988; Riley, Johnson, & Foner, 1972). For example, adolescents typically hold statuses and play roles such as student, friend, and family member. Certain "rites of passage," such as graduating, getting a first job, marrying, and having a child, mark transitions from adolescent to adult statuses.

A status based on a person's age is called an **age status.** Associated with each age status are **age roles,** or expectations about the behavior of people occupying particular age statuses. Like other roles, age roles are expressed in social norms, or standards, which define what people at a given age should think and do. These are called **age norms.** For example, laws governing the behavior of "minors" reflect social judgments about the age at which one may leave school, as well as the age at which one is responsible enough to engage in sexual behavior.

Age norms are not unalterable; they can, and do, change over time. Two surveys, one from the late 1950s and the other from the late 1970s, illustrate dramatic differences in some age norms over this 20-year span (Rosenfeld & Stark, 1987). When asked at which age most men should have settled on a career, 74 percent of the men in the earlier survey responded 24 to 26; only 24 percent of those in the more recent survey gave that response. An even greater change has occurred in norms concerning the "best" age for a woman to marry: Ninety percent of the women in the 1950s survey chose 19 to 24, compared to only 36 percent of those responding in the 1970s survey.

It should be noted that age norms are ideas not only about age conformity but also about age deviance. **Age deviance** is behavior that violates the age norms of a group or society. A man who remains a bachelor until the age of 45 is considered age deviant; so is a woman of 45 who marries a man 10 years her junior. Yet, if a man of 45 marries a woman of 35, he is conforming to the age norm.

Age Statuses in Social Institutions

Like other statuses, age statuses are a basis for social ranking in major social institutions. Let us look further at age statuses and roles in some of the principal areas of life.

AGE STATUSES AND THE FAMILY. In the family, the unfolding sequence of age statuses and their accompanying roles is more clearly defined and predictable than it is in most areas of society. A daughter or son moves from childhood to adolescence to adulthood. Age status changes are usually marked by clear-cut biological or social events: graduation, marriage, the birth of the first child, the birth of the first grandchild, and the death of a spouse, for example. At each point, people take on new statuses, and their social ranking typically changes in relation to that of other family members (Neugarten & Moore, 1968). When students graduate from college, for example, they gain prestige, as may women when they marry. The voluntarily childless couple may lose prestige, as may a couple going through a divorce.

AGE STATUSES AND EDUCATION. Traditional educational milestones that indicate a change in age statuses include entering high school, graduating from high school, and graduating from college. Because adulthood is popularly linked to the completion of schooling, educational milestones play an important part in defining one's "social age," or one's age status apart from chronological age. A blue-collar worker—for example, an electrician licensed to practice at age 20—passes the age status mark of adulthood earlier than a law student, who remains in school until the age of 24 or 25. The electrician is "socially older" at a younger age.

AGE STATUSES AND WORK. Work roles are closely linked to age statuses, especially in advanced industrial societies. Aside from marriage and the completion of school, the most important sign that one has reached the socially recognized age status of "adult" is entry into the labor market. Earning a living implies social maturity. Similarly, retirement—the exit from the labor market—signals another critical change in age status. It implies the fulfillment of adult duties and leads to the lower-ranked status of "senior citizen."

AGE STATUSES IN LAW AND POLITICS. The age at which one is able to vote is another important milestone of adulthood, and is linked to the belief that the judgment needed to participate in the community as an adult takes some time to acquire. Great controversy arose when men of 18 became old enough to be drafted but still were considered too young to vote. Legal age limits on driving, the consumption of alcohol, the signing of contracts, and criminal prosecution also reflect the strong tie between age and responsibility.

Political participation and leadership are also tied to age. The more responsible the political position, the older the person who fills it generally must be. The minimum ages at which people can assume the positions of congressional representative, senator, and president are fixed by the U.S. Constitution.

Age Status Inconsistency

As we have seen, social definitions of age can vary from one area of life to the next. One result of this variation is the 18-year-old who is a "minor" and an "adult" at the same time. In some states, for example, the driving age is 16; the voting age, 18; and the drinking age, 21. Inconsistency among the social expectations associated with the various age statuses a person holds is called **age status inconsistency.** Age status inconsistency can also be experienced by the precocious youth who acquires a social rank normally held only by older people. An extreme case was Wolfgang Amadeus Mozart (1756–1791), who performed his own piano works at age six for the Empress of Austria. A more common example would be a woman in her 60s who begins a new career in business in an entry-level position usually filled by people in their mid-20s.

GLOBAL SOCIETY

THE AGING CRISIS

As the twentieth century comes to an end, so too, it appears, will our preoccupation with youth. The simple reason is because the elderly will soon outnumber the young. The entire world is beginning to undergo this demographic transition toward old age, but the effects of this trend will hit developed countries first (see Figure 12.1). Consider these statistics. In 1950, 27.3 percent of the population in developed countries was under the age of 14; only 11.7 percent was over the age of 60. In the year 2000, people in developed countries over the age of 60 will for the first time in history outnumber those under the age of 14. And by 2050, experts predict that the number of people in developed countries over the age of 60 will rise to 32.5 percent, whereas the percentage of those under the age of 14 will increase to only 15.3 percent (*U.S. News & World Report*, 1999).

This trend concerns experts, who believe that global aging will become the most important issue in the twenty-first century. According to Peter Peterson (1999), the huge imbalance between the young and the old will bring economic and social costs that could bankrupt even the wealthiest countries if they do not prepare themselves for this future.

Within the next thirty years, the official projections suggest that governments in most developed countries will have to spend at least an extra 9 to 16 percent of GDP annually simply to meet their old-age benefit promises. To pay these costs through increased taxation would raise the total tax burden by an unthinkable extra 25 to 40 percent of every worker's taxable wages—in countries where total payroll tax rates often already exceed 40 percent. Or, if we resort to deficit spending, we would have to consume all the savings and more of the entire developed world. (p. 18)

A number of factors are contributing to global aging. For one thing, people are living longer. In the last 50 years, the human life span has grown more globally than it did in the previous 5,000 years (Peterson, 1999). Between 1972 and 1999, it jumped from 49.5 years to more than 63 years. At the same time, women are having fewer babies. In 1972 worldwide, the typical woman had 5.6 children over her lifetime. Today, the number is just 2.7. In developed countries the fertility rate is even lower—1.6, which is 25 percent below the rate needed to replace the population.

As this suggests, the ratio of retirees to workers has already started to decline. In the developed world today that ratio stands at about 3 to 1. If nothing changes, it is expected to fall even more—to 1.5 to 1 by 2030. At that point the burden on working people will be huge. In the United States, the payroll taxes needed to cover retirees are projected to rise from the current level of 15.8 percent to 31.9 percent in 2030. The situation is even more grave in Italy, where the payroll taxes are expected to jump from a current 37.6 percent today to a whopping 71.5 percent.

The global aging crisis raises a number of questions. First, although longevity has always been viewed as a positive sign of a nation's health, we must consider what will happen as medical progress also means increasingly scarce resources. Peterson asks: Should money be spent on the latest high-tech treatment to prolong life, or should it be used to educate the young? The answer to this question inevitably leads to other, more troubling questions: Who should live? Who should die? And who should decide?

Peterson proposes a number of strategies to deal with the aging crisis, including increasing the age of retirement, raising more children, stressing filial obligation, and requiring people to save for their old age. While his strategies might work, all of them will be difficult to implement. Regardless, it seems inevitable that we will experience some major social and cultural changes in the twenty-first century in response to global aging.

Ageism

As we have noted, the people of industrialized societies tend to disparage the elderly and honor the young, the strong, and the beautiful. Television, books, and films have traditionally presented us with distasteful portraits of old people, who are often depicted as unimportant, unhappy, or undignified (Ryan & Wentworth, 1999; Signorielli, 1983). Although old people tend to watch more television than younger people do, one survey of 1,700 Canadian TV commercials showed that fewer than 2 percent of the featured characters were elderly (Moore & Cadeau, 1985).

This ignoring of older people is a reflection of **ageism,** the ideology that holds that the elderly are biologically or socially inferior, and the discrimination that results from acceptance of this belief. The old, according to this view, are isolated, dependent, emotionally unstable,

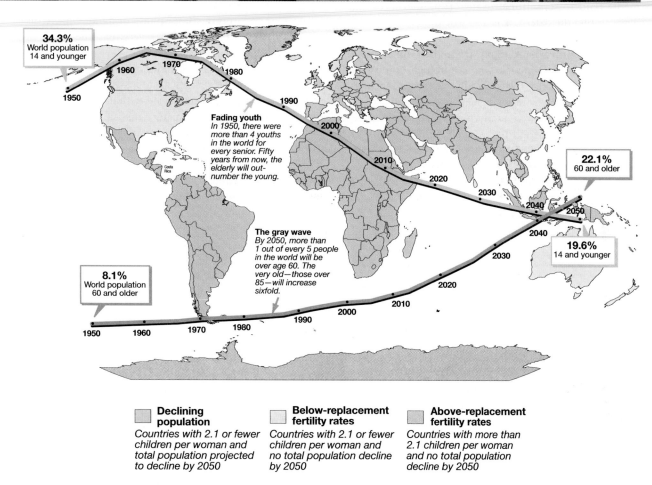

34.3%
World population 14 and younger

1950 1960 1970 1980 1990

Fading youth
In 1950, there were more than 4 youths in the world for every senior. Fifty years from now, the elderly will out-number the young.

2000 2010 2020 2030 2040 2050

22.1%
60 and older

The gray wave
By 2050, more than 1 out of every 5 people in the world will be over age 60. The very old—those over 85—will increase sixfold.

2040 2030 2020 2010

19.6%
14 and younger

8.1%
World population 60 and older

1950 1960 1970 1980 1990 2000

■ **Declining population**	■ **Below-replacement fertility rates**	■ **Above-replacement fertility rates**
Countries with 2.1 or fewer children per woman and total population projected to decline by 2050	*Countries with 2.1 or fewer children per woman and no total population decline by 2050*	*Countries with more than 2.1 children per woman and no total population decline by 2050*

FIGURE 12.1 How countries around the world are aging. Developed countries like the United States will have fewer young people to support the elderly than less developed countries like Saudi Arabia.

Source: Copyright March 1, 1999, *U.S. News & World Report.* Visit us at our Web site at www.usnews.com for additional information.

and feeble. Some older people do, of course, reflect these qualities, but so do many younger people. Research indicates that ageist stereotypes of old people are mostly false (Cockerham, 1991; Cox, 1988).

Fortunately, older people perceive themselves more favorably than the rest of the population does. One Harris poll showed that most older Americans think they are open-minded, adaptable, bright, alert, and capable of achieving their goals. Although about 35 percent of those under the age of 65 felt that the elderly tend to do little or nothing, only 15 percent of those over 65 agreed. In general, the poll showed, the old do not feel that the aging process has greatly altered their lot in life.

Older people are, however, exposed to certain special problems because of their age. Contrary to popular opinion, they are less likely than people of any other age to be victimized by crime (except for personal larceny with contact—mainly purse-snatching—and fraud). But they nevertheless express an extremely high-level *fear* of crime (Alston, 1986; Cox, 1996; Schmalleger, 1997). This anomaly may be explained in part by the fact that the media tend to sensationalize the crime that does take place among the elderly. It is also true that, if victimized, elderly people sometimes lack the physical and financial ability to bounce back easily from their misfortune. Finally, those elderly people who live in high-crime areas do indeed experience relatively high victimization rates, as well as suffering from such great concerns about crime that they sometimes virtually place themselves under "house arrest," fearing to leave their homes (Barrow & Smith, 1979; Cox, 1996). In addition, a number of elderly people—it is impossible to say how many—are neglected or abused by their own children (Cox, 1996; Krauskopf & Burnett, 1983; O'Toole & Webster, 1988). Medical quacks, too, prey on the fears of the aged.

GROWING OLD

What exactly happens when people grow old? It is useful to distinguish biological changes from social developments, although the two are often closely related.

Biological Changes

Physical and mental changes are an inevitable part of aging. These changes result in the physical appearance that we associate with old age (for example, wrinkles, hair loss, and stooped posture), and they certainly have some bearing on the social behavior and status of the elderly, partly because we attach social expectations to biological changes (White, 1988). In this section, we consider the biological aspects of the aging process.

Our understanding of what happens to the body with age has increased greatly over the past few decades, but it is still far from complete. Many of the ailments commonly associated with age are often lumped under the catchall term *senility*. The symptoms include decreased appetite, loss of muscle tone, and reduced sexual vigor. These complaints are by no means limited to old people, though; most can strike at any age. And they certainly do not afflict all old people.

Some conditions, however, are a definite part of the aging process and sooner or later affect all people who survive into old age. For example, visual acuity lessens with age. Hearing, too, declines continually after the age of 20. Taste and smell decline as well, and reflexes slow. Despite individual variations, the aging process eventually affects everyone's sensory and mental functioning, sexual behavior, health, and physical appearance to some degree (Cockerham, 1998; Cottrell, 1974).

SENSORY AND MENTAL FUNCTIONING

Sensory impairments often reduce the older person's capacity to function fully in society. These impairments represent an "intermediate" phase of aging—more disruptive than wrinkles, yet less severe than the graver illnesses that may come later.

By age 65, over 50 percent of all men and 30 percent of all women experience hearing losses that make social interaction difficult. Studies show that hearing impairment seems to create a greater sense of frustration and social isolation than does loss of keen eyesight. For instance, paranoia—the belief that others are talking about you or plotting against you—often accompanies hearing loss (Hendricks & Hendricks, 1986). With diminished hearing, you are more likely to imagine that you are the focus of other people's actions and words.

Psychomotor response, the amount of time that elapses between receipt of a sensory impulse and a physical response, also lengthens with age. One laboratory test found that older pilots, though more accurate in their judgments, took longer to respond to physical stimuli than did their younger colleagues (Botwinick, 1967; Hendricks & Hendricks, 1986).

Many other aspects of mental functioning are impaired as a result of the aging process. Older people can and do learn new things, but, with some exceptions, it generally takes them longer than it takes younger people. Similarly, the amount of time needed to retrieve facts from one's memory, especially recently learned facts, increases with age. Long-term memories of past events, however, do not seem to be as strongly affected by the aging process.

Men and women may not be affected equally by the decline of mental functioning. Research has shown that women typically retain significantly better mental functioning than men do. This may stem in part from the fact that men tend to get sick and die at a younger age than women do. Also, well-educated, intellectually active people tend not to exhibit the same rate of decline in mental functioning as do their contemporaries who have less opportunity or inclination to exercise their mental faculties (Hendricks & Hendricks, 1986).

Alzheimer's disease is a common mental disorder frequently associated with the elderly. For victims of Alzheimer's, "names, dates, places—the interior scrapbook of an entire life—fade into mists of nonrecognition. The simplest tasks—tying a shoelace, cutting meat with a knife, telling time—become insurmountable" (*Newsweek,* December 3, 1984). In the end, usually within eight years, the victims cannot walk or control themselves in any way; they lie curled in bed, awaiting death. Alzheimer's is a remarkably widespread ailment, affecting an estimated

4 million people in the United States. While researchers have identified a number of possible causes for Alzheimer's disease, studies have not yet confirmed any one of these (Cox, 1996).

SEXUAL FUNCTIONING

Certain physical changes affect the sexual functioning of older people. Masters and Johnson reported that erection is slower and ejaculation less forceful in older men than in younger men. Also, in older men, a longer period is required between erections. Older women have less vaginal lubrication than younger women (Ludeman, 1981; Masters & Johnson, 1966, 1970). However, these deficits do not mean that sex cannot still be practiced and enjoyed.

Indeed, many studies (e.g., Turner & Adams, 1988) have shown that older people do not lose interest in sexual activity. Among the Abkhasians, for example, it is apparently not unusual for men to retain their potency long past the age of 70; furthermore, 13.6 percent of the women continue menstruating after the age of 55 (Benet, 1976). Marriages are celebrated by people in their 90s, and one man was reported to be planning a marriage at the age of 108, though he insisted that he was really only 95.

Some people wrongly believe that older people do—and perhaps should—lack the ability and desire to function sexually. In one study, university students and nursing-home staff members rated stories depicting sexually active older couples as less believable (and also less moral) than stories concerning sexually active younger couples (La Torre & Kear, 1977; Ludeman, 1981). Such attitudes toward sexuality among older people can have important negative effects.

PHYSICAL HEALTH

Most of the illnesses of younger people are the result of an *acute condition:* There is a definite beginning of the illness, a crisis point, and a finite recovery period. The cause of the illness usually lies outside the body, most often in infectious microorganisms. Later in life, however, there is an increased tendency toward illness that results from *chronic conditions.* That is, the illness develops slowly, without a marked crisis point, and lingers. Unlike many acute conditions, chronic conditions cannot always be explained by a single external cause and cannot be cured.

The most common causes of illness and death among the elderly are diseases of the heart and circulatory system, including *strokes,* which occur when a blood clot blocks the supply of oxygen to the brain (National Center for Health Statistics, 1997). Although cancer is by

Many people mistakenly believe that the elderly have no sexual desires or needs. This is just one of the manifestations of ageism.

no means restricted to the elderly, certain kinds, such as cancer of the stomach, the intestinal tract, the prostate, and the kidneys, are more common among the old than the young. One of the most debilitating age-related diseases is *arthritis.* Although rarely a cause of death, arthritis can severely hamper the well-being of those who suffer from it (Hendricks & Hendricks, 1986).

While debilitating chronic diseases are more common among the old than among the young, it is important to keep in mind that many old people are healthy, active, and independent. Their activity levels may be reduced and some physical deterioration is inevitable, but the popular image of old people as continually weak and ill is far from true. In fact, a national study of the "oldest old" (those over age 80) found that one-third of the group was still physically able (Harris et al., 1989).

Perspectives on Social Gerontology

Gerontology is the multidisciplinary study of aging and the special problems of the elderly. The study of the social aspects of aging is called *social gerontology.* A new but rapidly growing field, social gerontology, has already inspired a number of important theories. Gerontology is to be distinguished from *geriatrics,* the study of medical aspects of aging and the medical practice that specializes in the treatment of elderly patients.

One of the principal interests of social gerontologists is the process of transition to old age. They have developed several interesting perspectives on the attitudes and behavior of older people as they adjust to their new social roles: disengagement theory, activity theory, continuity theory, and the aged as a subculture.

DISENGAGEMENT THEORY

Disengagement theory is one of the earliest explanations of the social situation of the elderly. Although widely challenged, it remains important because of the attention it has generated and the theories that have been put forth to counter it.

Disengagement theory was first formulated in 1961 (Cumming & Henry). Its central thesis is that as we grow older, we draw inward, becoming progressively less involved in the social activities in which we have participated throughout adult life. Disengagement theory argues that such a transition is a natural and universal response as the elderly grow increasingly aware of death and of the diminished resources of time and energy that are available to them. Disengagement theory also posits that society as a whole has an equally natural need to withdraw from extensive interaction with the elderly.

Disengagement theory has been controversial almost from the time it was proposed. How inevitable is the disengagement process? How universal? Although it is clear that some older people do indeed disengage themselves from social life, it is by no means clear that all old people do—or should. The original formulation of the theory did not take into account individual differences in temperament, social and economic status, or health.

One of the originators of the theory later altered it to account for the fact that personalities continue to develop throughout life, even in the face of death, and that people can turn inward without completely disengaging from society (Henry, 1965). Individuals who usually deal with stress by withdrawing probably do disengage as death approaches. But people who have responded actively to life may not be disposed to withdraw (Hendricks & Hendricks, 1986).

ACTIVITY THEORY

The *activity theory* of aging contradicts some of the central tenets of disengagement theory. Activity theory holds that if older people reduce their levels of physical and social activity, it is because of the way society is structured. Especially in modern societies, people lose some of their social roles—as active members of society, as providers, as nurturers—as they grow old. The more roles they lose, the less satisfaction they experience from life. If activity levels remain high—even if changed from the peak levels typical during earlier stages of life—life satisfaction will remain high. Social gerontologists who accept activity theory therefore believe that the more older people are allowed to participate in society, the better off they will be.

The loss of roles that may accompany aging has been termed *role exit* (Blau, 1981). The most dramatic examples of role exit are the loss of a spouse and retirement. Stressing that the maintenance of familiar roles is essential to the well-being of the elderly, some proponents of activity theory assert that adaptation to role loss poses one of the greatest problems for the aged.

Other activity theorists take a more optimistic view of role loss. One scholar has noted that most people do not depend entirely on one role (Atchley, 1988). Thus, provided that older people have enough money and supportive friends, they can adapt fairly easily by diverting energy from a lost role to a role that was previously less important. For example, a man who worked on the railroad may construct miniature railroads for his grandchildren or for a local school or orphanage. A woman who was a homemaker may find new satisfaction in the student role she abandoned 40 or 50 years earlier.

Activity theory cannot fully account for all of the adaptations that old people must make. Declining physical and mental capacities are a reality of the aging process. Although some elderly people regret the drop in activity that aging forces on them, many accept it as inevitable and adapt to their new circumstances with no loss of self-esteem (Havighurst, Neugarten, & Tobin, 1968).

Furthermore, activity theory is clearly grounded in a particular set of values. In American society, activity is valued over passivity, strength over weakness. Because of our respect for the high activity level associated with youth, people are persuaded throughout their lives that to "do nothing" is to be useless. This belief has the inevitable effect on older people of making them feel that unless they remain active, they will lose the respect of society.

CONTINUITY THEORY

The *continuity theory* of aging, one of the most popular in social gerontology today, stresses that individuals continue to develop throughout the life course. It therefore considers "old age" to be merely the latter part of a person's life, not a separate "stage" of existence. This perspective seems to be more in accordance with the way most people view life: not as occurring in distinct stages but, rather, as undergoing a slow, gradual process of development. According to continuity theorists, stage theories that treat old age as a time of life always marked by disengagement or decreased levels of activity present an artificial, overly simplistic, and fragmented view of human existence.

Unlike disengagement theory, which emphasizes primarily the physical and social activities of the elderly, continuity theory also takes into account individual differences in personality and values. As people age, they do not necessarily or "naturally" withdraw from work and other activities. Rather, they choose to continue satisfying life patterns and to discontinue unsatisfying ones. For old men and women, this process may entail leaving a harsh climate for one that is milder, leaving a job to do volunteer work, or selling their home in order to travel extensively. These decisions are not so much consequences of being old but, rather, choices made by people who are financially and socially secure and able to do what they want to do with their lives.

THE AGED AS A SUBCULTURE

Yet another perspective put forth to account for the attitudes and behavior of older people suggests that the *aged make up a distinct subculture.* With the growth of retirement communities, the presence of inner-city pockets of the elderly, and the abandonment of rural areas by the young, older people find themselves increasingly segregated from other age groups. Social policies concerning retirement and pensions tend to isolate old people still further from the rest of society. Those who favor this perspective argue that these factors have encouraged the development of a support network among the elderly that constitutes a distinct subculture with its own values and beliefs.

According to the subculture perspective, participation in peer-group activities and a sense of subcultural bonds help the elderly to make a smooth transition into old age (Hendricks & Hendricks, 1986; Rose, 1965). Some activities that might have this effect include widow-to-widow programs, in which the elderly give one another social support; the Retired Senior Volunteer Corps, through which the elderly help society at large; and the Foster Grandparents Program, in which the elderly help the young.

Has the seeming affinity of the elderly for people their own age and the growing awareness of their special position in society actually led to a distinct subculture? The answer is not clear. In their search for identity, and in the growth of organizations and social movements dedicated to promoting their rights and privileges, older people seem to have much in common with the members of other subcultures, such as racial and ethnic minority groups. But most older people may still be too integrated into the dominant culture to be accurately analyzed as a separate subculture.

The continuity theory of aging stresses that individuals continue to develop throughout the life course. Volunteer work among the elderly enables them to remain social and active members in the community.

SOCIAL CONDITIONS OF THE ELDERLY IN THE UNITED STATES

In the United States, 34.3 million people (12.7 percent of the population) are older than 65, and about 4.1 million are over 85. The elderly are scattered around the country, of course, but some places have higher concentrations of elderly people than others. California, Florida, and New York have the largest numbers of elderly—in 1997, 3.5, 2.7, and 2.4 million, respectively. About half of this country's older people reside in just nine states—California, Florida, New York, Texas, Pennsylvania, Illinois, Michigan, Ohio, and New Jersey (Administration on Aging, 1998). In this section, we examine the social conditions of the elderly in the United States.

Retirement

We tend to associate aging with retirement from work. But the concept of retirement is relatively new. In the past, people remained economically productive members of society for as long as they were physically able. In 1900, for example, more than 65 percent of men over age 65 were still in the work force (Foner & Schwab, 1981). By 1992, this figure had dropped to about 16 percent for men and 8 percent for women. In many developing countries, retirement is still a rarity.

It was not until 1935, when the Social Security Act was passed, that the concept of retirement was officially recognized in the United States. The act, which established a national pension plan, was originally designed to help reduce the ranks of the involuntarily unemployed during the Depression. Because in theory the act enabled older people to achieve financial security while making more jobs available to younger workers, unions supported it. After the Social Security Act was passed, however, many employers began to set an age for mandatory retirement. The "normal" retirement age became 65, the age at which full Social Security benefits could be received.

Many factors have combined to encourage or force older people to retire and to make it economically feasible for them to do so. One hundred years ago, about 50 percent of the people in this country worked on farms, compared with less than 2 percent today; there were also more self-employed people. Now most people work in large organizations. Farmers and other self-employed people can decide on their own when to stop working. In large organizations, however, such decisions are constrained by impersonal rules.

But if in the past older people had more freedom to continue working than they do now, they probably lacked the financial resources to stop working, even if they wanted to. Although many workers today face mandatory retirement, some retirees can count on some financial support from company pension plans, as well as from government programs.

Nonetheless, the great majority of today's retirees are obliged to live on reduced incomes. In 1997, 10.5 percent of people over age 65 had incomes below the poverty level as defined by the federal government (U.S. Bureau of the Census, 1998). For the average retired person, income from Social Security and pensions amounts to about half their preretirement income (Cox, 1996).

It was once thought that adjustment to retirement was very difficult and that, in general, retired people were dissatisfied. Recent evidence suggests that this is not so. In general, people's feelings and interests after retirement are a continuation of those from their preretirement days (Johnson & Williamson, 1987). Most retired people report that they are satisfied with their lives and, if they had to make the choice again, would retire at the same time or even earlier (Parnes, 1983). Those who are dissatisfied feel unhappy not because they are no longer working but because they are sick or do not have sufficient incomes.

TRENDS IN RETIREMENT

The average age of retirement from work has dropped over the past 25 years. In 1950, 85 percent of men between 55 and 64 were still in the work force. By 1995,

the number had fallen to 63.6 percent (Organization for Economic Cooperation and Development, 1998). One investigator learned from interviewing retirees that about half had retired voluntarily before turning 65 (Parnes, 1981).

A favorable economic climate and a series of government policy decisions have promoted this trend toward earlier retirement. In 1961, the government allowed people to choose to collect partial Social Security at 62 instead of waiting for full payments at 65. Medicare was established in 1966, reducing much of the burden of medical expenses paid by the elderly. In the early 1970s, Congress pegged Social Security benefits to the cost of living, so that people's buying power would not be undermined by inflation. As a result, people found that they could afford to retire at an earlier age, and many chose to do so (Deviney & O'Rand, 1988; Weinstein, 1980).

But several economic and demographic developments now threaten this trend. As we have pointed out, the proportion of the elderly in our population is growing. The Social Security system, however, is supported directly by payments made by today's working people. If current retirement patterns continue, the ratio of working people to retired people will shrink precipitously. In 1937, 12 workers contributed the benefits for each retired person. In 1980, three workers contributed the benefits for each retired person (Weinstein, 1980). It is estimated that by the year 2030, only 2.5 workers will have to bear this same burden (Petersen, 1999).

In time, these developments may seriously strain the Social Security system, and no solution that is likely to please everyone is in sight. To maintain both the current level of benefits and the pattern of early retirement puts an unfair burden on working people. Reducing benefits would relieve the pressure on the system, but it would also strain the resources of the retired. The government is currently planning on gradually increasing the age at which people will be able to collect full Social Security benefits. This will have the effect of encouraging the elderly to continue working. However, if they do so, this plan will also reduce the number of jobs and the opportunities for promotion available to younger people.

Housing

One of the most important housing needs of the elderly is to reside near essential services. As people find it increasingly difficult to get around, the distance from home to laundries, medical facilities, and community centers becomes a major concern. Access to services for the elderly has been a particularly serious problem in the United States, where communities tend to be spread out and public transportation is minimal.

Some effort has been made to design housing specifically for older people. Since the Housing Act of 1959, the federal government has spent billions of dollars on homes for the elderly—usually low-rent, high-rise public projects. Even so, only 3 percent of the elderly live in such housing.

A growing number of affluent older people are moving to retirement communities. Often set apart from other communities, they are common in the Sun Belt but can be found in all areas of the country. *Congregate housing,* another form of housing for older people, has also attracted much attention. It is intended for people who have disabilities that make it difficult for them to take care of themselves but who are otherwise in good health and do not need to be in nursing homes or hospitals. Residents retain their own living units but eat in a common dining room and have access to other shared services, such as medical care and housekeeping. Congregate housing is costly and is generally available only to higher-income groups (Ackelsberg et al., 1988; Williams, 1985).

All these special forms of housing have been criticized for isolating older people in "old-age ghettos" away from younger people. A number of studies have shown, however, that most old people who voluntarily choose to live in age-segregated communities are happy to be among their peers and away from the noise and annoyance of the young (Cox, 1996; Lawton, 1977).

Health and Personal Care

FAMILY CARE

The burden of caring for older people has often fallen on the family, especially when the elderly are ill, incapacitated, or financially dependent. This is true not only in the less developed nations, where public health care is minimal, but also in the United States (Khullar, 1988).

Many older people seem to prefer family care. If their husbands or wives are dead, they are inclined to turn first to their children for assistance and then to other close relatives. Yet families often find it difficult to care for aged parents or relatives. They may have children of their own and live in cramped quarters; the stress of feeding and housing another dependent can lead to tension, financial hardship, and even emotional problems. Under such circumstances, the physical or emotional abuse of the elderly relative becomes a distinct possibility. Thus, the economic and psychological cost to a family that takes on the burden of caring for an aging member can outweigh the benefits to that person and can, therefore, make institutional care preferable.

Despite these strains, many families are still willing to provide care for an aging relative. They will delay

Congregate housing, like this facility in Florida, is very costly and is generally available only to higher income groups.

putting a relative in an institution for as long as possible. Today many of the services provided by home health care are covered by Medicare because the costs are generally no greater and may be lower than institutional care (Lassey, Lassey, & Jinks, 1997).

Shifting social patterns may soon alter this picture, however. With fewer children born, there will be fewer adults available to care for a growing number of aging relatives. The proliferation of new family forms, the increase in single-parent households, the changing roles of women, the rise of the two-career family, and continued high residential mobility will also reduce the ability of family members to care for elderly relatives.

CARE OUTSIDE THE FAMILY

While only about 1 percent of Americans in the 65- to 74-age range are confined to institutions, the figure rises to 17.7 percent for those 85 and over (National Center for Health Statistics, 1998; U.S. Bureau of the Census, 1998). Most families seem to postpone institutionalization of any kind for as long as possible, often longer than they should (Hendricks & Hendricks, 1986). Most people who are sent to institutions are without families or the resources necessary to maintain independence. Thus, the institutionalized aged are mainly poor, without families, and alone. But this group also includes people whose medical and mental conditions are so severe that proper home care is not feasible.

Since the introduction of Medicare, the national medical assistance program for elderly people, older people have made increasing use of short-stay hospitals (Shanas & Maddox, 1976). There has also been a marked

Despite economic and psychological strains, many families are still willing to provide care for an aging relative.

expansion in the use of long-stay facilities, especially nursing homes. The elderly are also commonly institutionalized in mental hospitals. Under the best conditions, each kind of institution can offer excellent health care. Yet in other circumstances, they can be expensive, dismal, and neglectful way stations on the road to death.

Nursing Homes

Only 5 percent of the population over 65 (a total of about 1.4 million people) lived in nursing homes in 1995 (National Center for Health Statistics, 1998). Yet it is estimated that 25 percent of the elderly will spend some time in a nursing home before they die (Cox, 1996). What are the characteristics of nursing-home residents? Why do some people end up in them while others do not? Family status is an important factor. Those who are single, separated, divorced, or widowed are more likely to become nursing-home residents. Older people without children, or those with only one surviving child, are also more likely than others to be in nursing homes.

Nursing homes vary widely in the quality of the care they offer. Almost 80 percent of them are commercial enterprises (Hendricks & Hendricks, 1986). Those that cater to the affluent differ dramatically from those serving the poor in the type of facilities available, treatments used, and staff attitudes. In nursing homes for the poor, employees tend to have limited education and training. Such facilities are often merely rundown private homes converted to public use, frequently in undesirable locations.

One reason for these poor conditions is the staggering cost of running a nursing home. Nursing-home care is one of the largest and fastest-growing areas of national health-care costs. Between 1980 and 1995, spending on nursing-home care increased from $20 billion to $75.2 billion (U.S. Bureau of the Census, *Statistical Abstract of the United States, 1993, 1998*). The factors involved in this enormous rise include the increasing life expectancy of the elderly and the growth in such nursing-home expenses as fuel and salaries (U.S. Bureau of Labor Statistics, 1984).

Although the financial cost of nursing-home care is very high (about $3,135 per month), there is another, less well documented cost—the psychological one. Regardless of the quality of the facility, a move to a nursing home is often a very stressful experience. Unfortunately, the very nature of a nursing home lends itself to experiences of dislocation. The elderly may be pressured—and sometimes "tranquilized"—into dependent behavior. As in prisons and mental hospitals, managing the patients may take precedence over treating them. And it has been said that whether they are ill or not, nursing-home residents are expected by the staff, fellow patients, and family members to *act* ill while in the home (Cox, 1988). Thus, the nursing-home setting seldom lends itself to building up or even utilizing the considerable personal resources of its residents. Rather, it can lead to the destruction of any individuality and independence that the elderly still possess.

THE ELDERLY IN OTHER SOCIETIES

We tend to forget that contemporary American attitudes toward the elderly and their place in society are by no means universal. Although many *problems* of the elderly—housing, health care, and the financial burden of dependency and chronic illness—are almost universal, American *solutions,* such as nursing homes, Social Security, retirement pensions, and the like, are not. Let us look at the situations of the elderly in a few other societies.

China: Veneration of the Elderly

The Confucian tradition encourages the veneration of the elderly. Historically, age and power went together, and parents had absolute authority over their children. But the social turmoil and political changes that began in China about a century ago have gradually undermined the power of the elderly. Since the Communists came into control in 1949, the Chinese government has acted to equalize the status of the young in relation to the old. In addition, the authorities have, from time to time, deliberately encouraged youthful political ferment—the Cultural Revolution of the 1960s is the most dramatic example—to discredit traditional values. Much veneration of the elderly has survived these upheavals, however, and it remains particularly strong in the countryside (Treas, 1979; Yin & Lai, 1983).

The Chinese social security system is not funded by worker contributions but by state-owned enterprises, and benefits—about 70 percent of preretirement earnings—are generous by American standards. Although older employees who are no longer needed are "encouraged" to retire, there is no mandatory age when they must do so. The current social security system mainly helps those who live in cities and work in factories, however; it does not cover elderly people in the villages and countryside—about 85 percent of the population—who are still cared for almost entirely by their families (Brown, 1990).

Retired people in China seem to suffer little loss of prestige. They are often entrusted with useful and valued work, such as housekeeping and child care. And they also continue to play important roles in the local committees that control much of Chinese community life.

Israeli Kibbutzim: Integration of the Elderly

The Israeli kibbutz is a form of voluntary collective enterprise—usually, but not always, a farm. It typically is a small settlement of about 500 people. Kibbutzim (the plural of kibbutz) were first established early in the twentieth century, and they played an important role in the creation of the state of Israel.

Kibbutzim provide total social and economic security for their members. All members are expected to work according to their abilities and are supported according to their needs. On the kibbutzim, property is owned collectively and production decisions are made by members.

One study concluded that the kibbutz integrates the elderly in a way that minimizes many of the problems of aging found in American society (Wershow, 1969). The elderly living on a kibbutz never have to worry about housing or economic support. They can continue to do productive work as long as they are able (Am-Ad, 1988). They are not isolated from the others, and they interact with people of all ages. Compared to the Chinese elderly, however, the elderly of the kibbutzim suffer more loss of status when they surrender leadership and valued productive roles to younger members.

The Ik: Rejection of the Elderly

In the society of the Ik, a tribal people in Uganda, the elderly have neither status nor any regular means of support. The Ik view the elderly as useless parasites who ought to be dead (Turnbull, 1972).

This was not always so. About a generation ago, the Ik were turned out of their traditional lands, which were made into a game preserve, and forced to live in a hilly and barren area nearby. This catastrophe made the Ik

Regardless of the quality of the facility, a move to a nursing home is often very stressful on the family and the patient. Unfortunately, the very nature of a nursing home lends itself to experiences of dislocation.

vastly poorer than they had been, and everything in their society had to adjust to that reality. The adjustment involved the almost complete erosion of social solidarity.

It is unusual for Iks to help one another in any way, especially when they do not anticipate receiving a favor in return. Because most of the elderly lack physical strength—the one personal virtue this society regards as important—they receive little aid and must scavenge for food on their own. So, far from helping the elderly, the younger members of the tribe insult, abuse, and even murder them with impunity.

HEALTH AND HEALTH CARE IN THE UNITED STATES

In the United States and other developed nations, older population groups have by far the highest rates of mortality. This fact might seem to be too obvious to deserve mention. But in preindustrial societies—including many still in existence—it is the very young who have the highest death rates. Also, the elderly in our society die of "old people's" ailments: chronic, noninfectious diseases, notably stroke, heart disease, and cancer (National Center for Health Statistics, 1998). These are the leading causes of death within the population as a whole. However, in the preindustrial world, infectious diseases and starvation are the primary killers, chiefly of the very young. In short, health and illness are *social facts,* in addition to being biological facts. They are influenced by the societies in which they occur.

In the following sections, we look at health and illness as social phenomena. To begin, we examine the health and health-care situation in the United States today.

APPLYING SOCIOLOGY

GENETIC DISCRIMINATION IN HEALTH INSURANCE

During the 1990s, concerns about health care rose to the top of the public's list of America's most important problems. In fact, a 1991 Gallup poll showed that more than 9 in 10 Americans thought that we faced a national health-care crisis. The rising cost of health care was identified as the single most important problem. And 85 percent of Americans said that the health-care system in the United States needed reform (Gallup Monthly Poll, August 1991).

But by the end of the decade not much had changed. President Clinton's proposals were defeated, and no one came up with a different plan. And many Americans still lacked health insurance—in 1997, an estimated 43.4 million people, or 16.1 percent of the population (U.S. Bureau of the Census, 1998). Over one-third of Hispanic-Americans lacked coverage, compared to 12.0 percent of non-white Hispanics. And

21.5 percent of blacks and 20.7 percent of Asian or Pacific Islanders lacked health insurance.

While Americans have expressed concern about those who have do not have health insurance, they might not expect to become a member of this unfortunate group. But, in fact, they could. As we learn more and more about the causes of serious diseases, the basis for unequal access to health insurance might change. Ironically, medical discoveries that promise to save many lives could be used to deny certain people health insurance or to increase health insurance rates. The ability to identify the genetic causes of serious diseases—breast cancer, diabetes, Down's syndrome—also means that insurers will have a way to identify patients who are at the greatest risk. And that may serve as the basis to screen out candidates and keep costs down (Hollowell, 1999).

Many Americans favor higher insurance rates for people who engage in behaviors that put them at risk for serious diseases. For example, a 1999

Gallup poll showed that 55 percent of Americans believe that people who smoke should pay higher insurance rates than nonsmokers; 42 percent did not. But the overwhelming majority of Americans do not believe that genetic profiles should determine who pays higher rates. Thus, 88 percent of them do not believe that a person whose genetic profile shows potential problems should pay higher health insurance rates than someone whose profile does not. More than 9 in 10 Americans do not believe that insurance companies should have access to one's genetic record or DNA without permission. And 95 percent do not believe that employers should be able to obtain access to employees' genetic records for DNA without permission.

While insurers claim that genetic discrimination will not happen, many states are passing laws to make sure it does not (Hollowell, 1999). According to the Council for Responsible Genetics, over 30 states have passed laws protecting people from genetic discrimination when applying for

The Social Distribution of Health

Measured by life expectancies, the American people have never been healthier than they are today. In 1900, life expectancy at birth among the general population was 47.3 years; by 1996, this figure was 76.1 years. Certain segments of the population have experienced an even more dramatic improvement. Among black females, life expectancy at birth rose from a mere 33.5 years at the turn of the century to 74.2 years in 1996 (U.S. Bureau of the Census, *Statistical Abstract of the United States, 1998*). This extension of the life span is largely, but not entirely, due to advances in medicine.

But even though the figures for life expectancy show that the health of Americans has been improving, it is still not as good as that of people in many other industrialized nations. In 1997, some 19 nations—including Japan, Sweden, Israel, Canada, Greece, and Australia—enjoyed longer life expectancies than the United States.

And in 1997, at least 17 countries had a lower infant mortality rate, an important measure of a nation's overall level of health (Brunner, 1998).

SOCIAL EPIDEMIOLOGY

In every society, health and illness are not distributed in either an equal or a random way. Some groups of people are more likely than others to get sick, and many diseases are more common among some groups than among others. Lung cancer, for example, is especially common among cigarette smokers. Black lung disease is endemic among coal miners. And poor people generally have more health problems than do affluent people.

The study of the social distribution of disease and the relationship of this distribution to social and environmental characteristics is called **social epidemiology.** Drawing heavily on sociological methods, social epidemiologists try to discover what the victims of a particular jobs or insurance. And over 70 genetic discrimination bills are pending in 24 states. Although the Health Insurance Portability and Accountability Act of 1996 makes it illegal to deny insurance based on preexisting genetic factors, in some states it is legal to raise premiums when insurance is renewed. And while it may be against the law to order genetic tests, information that already exists in one's medical record can be considered.

Operating on the assumption that healthy members of the population will pay for sick ones, insurance companies must spread their risk over a large population in order to make money. They are, therefore, legally allowed to raise premiums for people who have certain medical conditions when they want to renew a policy. Thus, while genetic testing could potentially save lives, it will also help insurance companies screen out the riskiest clients.

While all people do not want to know whether they are genetically predisposed to serious diseases they might suffer from later in life, many do. In fact, 64 percent of Americans polled by Gallup in 1999 indicated that they would like to know. And 64 percent said that they would like to know if the genetic profiles of their children indicate that they could suffer from a serious disease (see Table 12.1). As it stands, experts recommend that people be covered by health insurance before they get tested.

TABLE 12.1	WHAT CAN GO WRONG: SOME OF THE GENETIC DISORDERS THAT CAN BE DETECTED BEFORE BIRTH
Disorder	*Incidence*
Cystic fibrosis	1 out of 2,500 white births
Down's syndrome	1 out of 800–1,000 births
Duchenne muscular dystrophy	1 out of 3,300 male births
Fragile X syndrome	1 out of 1,500 male births
	1 out of 2,500 female births
Hemophilia A	1 out of 8,500 male births
Huntington's disease	4–7 out of 100,000 births
Polycystic kidney disease	1 out of 3,000 births
Sickle-cell anemia	1 out of 400–600 black births
Tay-Sachs disease	1 out of 3,600 Ashkenazi Jewish births

Source: Based on *Time*, January 11, 1999, and The Gallup Polls.

disease have in common in order to identify the factors that cause the disease (Cockerham, 1998). This kind of knowledge is a very important aspect of disease prevention.

What factors are involved in the possibility that a person will contract a disease? Some are genetic—that is, people inherit susceptibility or resistance to certain diseases in the same way they inherit eye and hair color. But other important factors are social. Income level, occupation, place of residence, lifestyle—all these and more affect proneness to disease (Graham & Reeder, 1979). By identifying the relationship between such factors and various diseases, social epidemiologists provide information that is invaluable in the formulation of public health programs.

One of the main assumptions of social epidemiology is that contracting a disease is merely the last in a complex series of events bringing the victim into contact with a disease-producing agent. Probably the first researcher to demonstrate such a causal chain was Sir Percival Pott, in a study published in 1755. Pott was interested in the fact that one particular occupational group in England, chimney sweeps, had a much higher incidence of scrotal cancer than did other occupational groups, and he uncovered a series of social factors that contributed to this disease. People needed heat in the winter. To provide heat they used space heaters. These heaters burned fuel that produced a lot of soot, so chimneys needed frequent cleaning. This created a need for chimney sweeps, who were thus in frequent contact with soot, which contributes to scrotal cancer (Graham & Reeder, 1979).

In what has been dubbed "popular epidemiology," the members of a community—rather than its health officials—seek out the social and environmental causes of the diseases that affect their lives. Families in Woburn, Massachusetts, for example, alerted the scientific community to the link between industrial carcinogens dumped into the town's supply of drinking water and the high rate of leukemia among the community's children (Brown, 1987). Citizen activists have also been responsible for bringing other environmental hazards—such as Agent Orange, pesticides, and asbestos—out of the shadows and into the public eye.

THE UNEQUAL DISTRIBUTION OF HEALTH AND ILLNESS

One of the most important social epidemiological findings is that health and illness are unequally distributed on the bases of age, sex, race, ethnicity, and socioeconomic status.

AGE. As previously noted, ill health that leads to death is found disproportionately among the elderly in the United States. People who survive infancy are likely to live to old age. The death rate reaches a minimum (3 per 1,000 persons) between ages 5 and 12 and then rises slowly until about age 50, when it starts to increase more rapidly as the body's ability to resist disease weakens.

SEX. In the United States, and in most societies throughout the world, women tend to live longer than men (Hoover & Siegel, 1986). The death rate among women is lower than that among men at all ages. In 1996, for example, American women lived an average of 6.0 years longer than men did. The higher mortality among men is rooted in both biological and social factors. A number of disorders, including circulatory problems and severe bacterial infections, are more common among male than female infants. In general, males who survive infancy are beset by social forces that include greater work stress and higher rates of cigarette smoking and alcohol abuse than are found among females.

Females report illness and use health services more often than males do, however, even when maternity care is excluded. Some evidence suggests that this is because women are more willing than men to acknowledge signs of illness and to seek help for it (Cockerham, 1998).

RACE, ETHNICITY, AND SOCIOECONOMIC STATUS. With the exception of Asians, members of non-white minorities in the United States tend to die at a younger age and have more health problems than whites. Blacks, for example, have the poorest health overall of any major racial group. In fact, the most dramatic change in the health of the American population in the last decade has been a sharp decline in the health of blacks (Cockerham, 1998). The most disadvantaged person in the nation in terms of health is the black male, whose life expectancy dropped from 65.2 years in 1987 to 64.9 years in 1988—although it had climbed back to 66.1 by 1996. White males, in contrast, enjoyed a life expectancy in 1996 of 73.8 years, while black females showed a life expectancy of 74.2 years and white females 79.6 years. The exact causes of the worsening health of blacks have not been conclusively identified, but strong evidence suggests that they are at greater risk because of smoking, high blood pressure, high cholesterol levels, alcohol intake, excess weight, and diabetes—health problems often associated with low incomes and stressful life circumstances (Otten et al., 1990).

Asian-Americans represent the opposite extreme. They have achieved a higher socioeconomic status than any other minority group in the nation—by some measures, it even exceeds that of whites—and, on the average, they enjoy extremely good health. Mortality rates among both infants and adults are lower than those for any other racial or ethnic group.

As these facts suggest, if income and related environmental differences among racial and ethnic groups were eliminated, many health problems would diminish as well. The poor are more susceptible to disease in part because their living conditions tend to be substandard. Poor people live disproportionately in crowded housing, in unsanitary conditions, and in violent neighborhoods—among subcultures in which alcoholism and drug abuse are common. Poor nutrition and the mental and physical stresses that accompany poverty often weaken their resistance to disease or worsen already existing health problems. The poor are more likely not only to become ill but also to lack access to quality medical care. Their illnesses, therefore, tend to be more disabling than the illnesses of higher-income people (Dutton, 1989).

The Health-Care System

The **health-care system** consists of all the people and formal organizations that deliver, finance, and regulate health care. The health-care system in the United States, with its hundreds of thousands of doctors, nurses, orderlies, and technicians and its thousands of doctors' offices, hospitals, medical schools, and nursing homes, is a fairly recent creation. It is useful, therefore, to review its historical development and the forces that produced it.

A BRIEF HISTORY OF HEALTH CARE

During much of the nineteenth century, the practice of medicine was largely unrestricted. A variety of healers, including formally trained physicians, herbal doctors, and homeopaths (who believe that treating symptoms constitutes treating the disease), were legally allowed to compete freely for the consumer's money. Many members of the public distrusted trained physicians because their relatively crude techniques, based on sketchy scientific information, were unpleasant and often lethal. Favorite remedies included bleeding, strong laxatives, and chemicals that induced vomiting.

By the early twentieth century, the science of medicine had advanced markedly, however. Better-trained physicians had eliminated much of the nonscientific competition and had established control over the process of treatment (Starr, 1982). The enhanced ability of physicians to cure their patients gave them an advantage over other healers and improved their standing in the public eye. Physicians came to be regarded as the symbol of healing by all social classes in America (Freidson, 1979).

One key to physicians' success was *professionalization*. A profession is a high-status occupation, usually oriented toward providing a service, that is characterized by prolonged training in a body of specialized knowledge including both theory and practice (Goode, 1960). Professions are inevitably concerned with setting up criteria for membership and standards of performance, training new members, and excluding those who do not meet their standards. Professional organizations generally succeed in defending the economic privileges and social prestige of their members.

In 1847, physicians established a professional organization, the American Medical Association (AMA). By the 1920s, the AMA had become the foremost influence on medical care in the United States. What gave the AMA much of its authority was its role in reforming medical education. Before 1900, anyone who could afford medical school could become a doctor, and the quality of education at all but a few schools was very poor. In 1910, Albert Flexner wrote a report that severely criticized the quality of most medical education in the United States and recommended stringent reforms. The AMA assumed responsibility for the certification of medical schools and thus came to have almost complete control over medical education.

The professionalization of medicine had two important consequences—marked improvement in medical education and medical care and greatly enhanced prestige and power for physicians in general and the AMA in particular. The AMA exercised discipline over its members by excluding those whom it deemed unfit to practice medicine. Membership in the AMA came to be essential for the success of practices that depended on referrals and other professional contacts.

THE RISE OF HOSPITALS. The development of hospitals is closely connected to the evolution of medical technology. Until the end of the nineteenth century, hospitals were generally little more than places where the very poor went to die. The death rate at these hospitals was high because of filthy conditions, widespread infection, and harsh medical techniques. The demand for hospital care was so small that in 1873 there were only 178 hospitals in the United States (Cockerham, 1998).

Advances in medicine greatly increased the chances that people who entered hospitals would emerge with improved health. Because private physicians did not have the means to acquire and house the new medical technology, hospitals became the centers of technology and research. In addition, medical schools, under pressure from the AMA, began to base more of their teaching in hospitals. Gradually, the hospital became a key facility for medical research and education as well as a source of patient care (Rosenberg, 1987). In 1996, the number of hospitals in the United States was 6,201 (Health, 1998).

SHIFTS IN THE FINANCING OF HEALTH CARE. Earlier in this century, patients either paid for the services of doctors and hospitals out of their own pockets or became the objects of charity. Government involvement in the provision, regulation, and financing of health care was minimal.

With the rise of health insurance during the Depression, payment for medical services by third parties became prevalent. At the same time, doctors organized insurance plans that covered doctor bills (Blue Shield) and private hospitalization (Blue Cross). These plans were bought by the middle class and by employers, but the poor and elderly remained largely unprotected.

In 1965, Congress passed the Medicare and Medicaid amendments to the Social Security Act. Medicare provides hospital and supplemental medical insurance for people over 65, regardless of income. (Some disabled persons under 65 also qualify for Medicare.) Medicaid channels federal subsidies to state-operated programs that pay certain hospital and doctors' costs for the poor. With Medicare and Medicaid, the government became deeply involved—for the first time—in the financing, administration, and regulation of medical care, though mostly for the old and the poor.

The role of government in other health matters was also expanding. Early in the twentieth century, most state governments took responsibility for controlling contagious diseases, and they enforced sanitary standards in public areas and industry. The states did not provide direct patient care except in certain areas that physicians ignored, such as the treatment of chronic mental illnesses. By the mid-1960s, the federal government had become the largest source of funding for medical research, a major influence on the private provision of health care through the Medicare and Medicaid programs, and a large-scale provider of health care in its own right, through some 170 Veterans Administration hospitals. Nonetheless, U.S. health care is still delivered largely by private physicians who remain relatively free of government control.

The majority of the American public today (about 83 percent) are covered by some form of private or government medical insurance. Only 1 percent of those over 65 are not covered (U.S. Bureau of the Census, *Current Population Reports,* 1998). For those without health insurance—some 16.1 percent of the population, or about 43.4 million people—the costs of medical care can be devastating (see Figure 12.2). The large number of people without health insurance is a major social problem.

THE ORGANIZATION OF HEALTH CARE

Health care in the United States is delivered by a large number of autonomous organizations and individuals. There is no central agency that coordinates, controls, and plans the various elements of the health-care system. As a result, American medicine is often marked by considerable conflict among the many groups involved. One way to understand the American health-care system is to identify the major secondary and primary providers of health care.

Persons and organizations that perform health care directly are termed *primary providers*. This includes physicians, nurses and paramedicals, and hospitals. *Secondary providers* invent and sell the technology and train the personnel used in the direct provision of health care. The key groups in this category are medical schools, nursing schools, and other institutions that train health-care workers, as well as drug manufacturers and medical-equipment suppliers.

PHYSICIANS. Physicians are the most familiar primary-care providers. About 80 percent of all patient services are provided in physicians' offices. In 1996, there were approximately 737,764 active physicians, a majority of whom work out of their own offices. The rest were interns, residents, or full-time staff members of hospitals or clinics.

The number of women entering the field of medicine has increased over the last 20 years. During the 1980–81 academic year, only 27 percent of the total student enrollment in allopathic schools of medicine were women. During the 1995–96 academic yeaar that number had grown to 42 percent (Health, 1998).

Early in the twentieth century, most doctors were general practitioners (GPs) rather than specialists. GPs treat "the whole patient"; they are familiar with all of their patients' medical problems, coordinate their care, and refer them to specialists if necessary. Today, however, most doctors are specialists. There are more than 50 medical specialties; and patients may see any number of doctors, depending on the nature of their complaint. Often no single doctor is familiar with all their problems.

Several explanations for the trend toward specialization have been suggested. The major reason is that medical knowledge has grown so complex that one person cannot possibly keep up with the information necessary to provide a high level of care. But also contributing

to the trend is the fact that specialists have more prestige and make more money than general practitioners do (Cockerham, 1998). As a result, even general practice has been turned into a specialty: family practice.

Physicians occupy a privileged position in American society. They enjoy a higher occupational prestige and have greater earnings than members of almost any other profession. Located at the top of the hierarchy of health care, they exert an unusual amount of control over the conditions of their work.

PARAMEDICALS. Paramedicals are medical support personnel, including nurses, pharmacists, and laboratory technicians, who generally work under the supervision of a physician. Paramedicals care for patients or do work closely related to patient care but have much lower prestige than physicians do. This situation has frustrated persistent efforts to fully professionalize the paramedical occupations. Moreover, a disproportionate number of paramedical personnel come from minority and lower-middle-class or working-class backgrounds (Freidson, 1970; Cockerham, 1998).

Nurses have had more success at professionalization than most other paramedical groups. About 75 percent of nurses work in nursing homes or hospitals, where they have often succeeded in relegating unpleasant tasks, such as bedside care, to lower-prestige workers. In recent years, nurses have broadened their activities, in many cases entering aspects of health care previously restricted to physicians. Nurses have acquired roles as administrators and also as nurse practitioners, trained to give physical exams, order laboratory tests, give referrals, and perform other routine tasks usually done by physicians (Fox, 1989; Cockerham, 1998).

HOSPITALS. The most important location of institutional health care today is the hospital, which carries out such functions as the treating of patients, doing medical research, training medical personnel, and offering preventive medicine for the general public. Although most health services are provided in doctors' offices, hospitals absorb the largest share of health expenditures—some 35 percent of the total, compared with only 20 percent spent on physicians (U.S. Health Care Financing Administration, 1997). Hospital charges have consistently been among the most rapidly rising items on the consumer price index.

There are three main types of short-stay hospitals in the United States. Government-owned hospitals (31 percent of the total) tend to be less well staffed and equipped than other hospitals. They are often located in urban poverty areas and are the hospitals on which the poor depend. Voluntary nonprofit hospitals (50 percent of the total) tend to be located in suburban areas and deliver high-quality care to the middle and upper classes.

Percent of all persons (and poor persons) never covered by
health insurance during the year, by selected characteristics

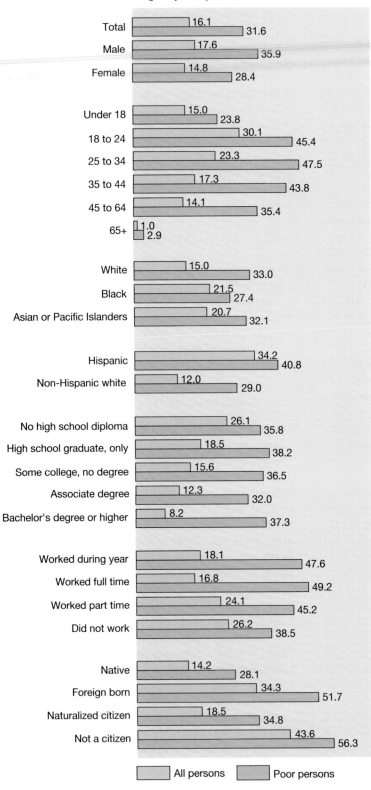

FIGURE 12.2   Americans Lacking Health
Insurance, 1997

Note: Persons of Hispanic origin may be of any
race. The percent is derived by dividing the number
of uninsured people in a particular category by the
total number of people in that category.

Source: U.S. Census Bureau, March 1998 Current
Population Survey.

Similarly, private for-profit hospitals (18 percent of the total) offer quality care to the relatively well-to-do near their homes and tend to be smaller than the other types of hospitals.

Several recent trends are expected to greatly affect America's hospitals. Inpatient admissions to many hospitals have been declining of late, a situation that is expected to continue. Another current trend is a decrease in the average duration of hospital stays; many patients are released days earlier than they would have been in the past. These two trends have already forced the closing of some underutilized hospitals. A major factor in the declining utilization of hospitals is the rise of out-of-hospital sources of primary care (Blendon, 1985).

OTHER SOURCES OF PRIMARY CARE. A variety of organizations other than hospitals provide health care. These include nursing homes, hospices, ambulatory-care centers, emergency-care centers, rehabilitation institutes, diagnostic centers, surgical centers, health maintenance organizations, and neighborhood health centers.

The *health maintenance organization (HMO),* a prepaid group practice in which members pay a monthly sum for comprehensive health-care services, is one of the most rapidly growing types of providers. Participating physicians are paid annual salaries or fixed amounts per patient. This arrangement gives doctors an incentive to keep patients healthy through the practice of preventive medicine. HMO physicians tend to prescribe fewer unnecessary treatments, which would reduce the organization's profits. In 1997, enrollment in HMOs had reached 67 million, double the enrollment in 1991 (Health, 1998).

Neighborhood health centers are federally funded clinics designed to provide medical care to people living in poor areas. Although they have made medical care more accessible to the poor, their staffs tend to be less well trained than the staffs of other organizations.

In addition to relying on health-care organizations, about 4 million Americans now receive some form of personal health care at home. New technologies have made home health care feasible for patients requiring chemotherapy, kidney dialysis, intravenous antibiotics, or special painkillers or nutrients. Such patients are typically under the care of for-profit home health businesses or nonprofit agencies that charge between 30 and 70 percent less than the average cost of a hospital stay.

A COMPARISON WITH OTHER NATIONS. The health-care systems in most other industrial nations differ from that in the United States (Lassey, Lassey, & Jinks, 1997). The United States and South Africa are the only industrialized nations that do not have some form of national health insurance. Sweden and Great Britain, for example, have systems in which the government runs its own national health service. In these countries, health care is financed by taxes and is provided virtually free to all citizens. Almost all physicians work for the government.

The health-care systems in communist countries, including Cuba and the People's Republic of China, are also highly centralized and provide essentially "free" and comprehensive medical care. They are often criticized for being impersonal and regimented (Ucko, 1986). Other countries, such as Germany and Japan, have more decentralized national health programs, with compulsory insurance and health services that vary according to one's occupation and place of employment. Such services are typically financed by employers' and employees' contributions rather than by the government itself, which serves mainly as an administrator (Cockerham, 1998).

ISSUES IN HEALTH CARE

Developments in medical technology, soaring costs, and cuts in public health-care spending have intensified the pressure for change in America's health-care system. And modern medicine and new diseases have raised a host of unforeseen social and moral issues. In this section, we explore some of the major health-care issues currently under debate.

The Medicalization of Life

Not so long ago, the foods that people ate, the kind of exercise they got, the way they raised their children, and the quality of their sex lives were seen by most people as personal issues. Today, to varying degrees, all these spheres of life, and many others as well, have come under medical jurisdiction. That is, medical scientists have researched diet, exercise, child rearing, and sex, and have given physicians a store of knowledge on which to draw in recommending certain courses of action over others and in treating "problems" in these areas. This expansion of medical jurisdiction to include problems that once were not regarded as medical has been termed the *medicalization of life* (Illich, 1976).

Medicalization has been especially rapid with regard to certain behaviors that expose an individual to negative social sanctions, a process termed the *medicalization of deviance* (see Chapter 8). Alcoholics and the mentally ill were once almost universally regarded as evil; now they are more commonly labeled "sick." Child abuse, drug abuse, and a number of related types of criminal behavior have also been at least partially redefined as illnesses. Once a person acquires a label as sick, the medical profession receives a mandate to treat the condition. The physician is, in effect, transformed into an agent of social control charged with "curing" the deviant (Zola, 1972).

Even if medicine is unable to consistently effect a cure, its monopoly over problems that are defined as medical ensures that deviance that has been redefined as illness will fall under the authority of doctors.

When such deviant behavior as alcoholism is no longer labeled immoral and punished as such but is rather regarded as a disease subject to medical treatment, the change may be humane. But defining deviant behavior as illness does not erase all negative moral judgment. It merely shifts the moral judgment into the medical realm. Although such terms as "health," "disease," and "syndrome" seem to be morally neutral, the use of such medical terminology often has far-reaching implications. For example, in recent years, feminist critics have objected to the medicalization of premenstrual syndrome (PMS). This medicalization, they argue, seems to imply that women are "risks" because they are physically and emotionally handicapped for a certain amount of time each month (Conrad & Kern, 1990). Such thinking can provide a rationale for job and other forms of discrimination.

In addition, from the patient's viewpoint, medicalization converts a personal problem into a social problem. When doctors take charge of behavior disorders, patients become vulnerable to medical methods of social control, including the use of drugs. Nonconforming behavior can be quelled with a pill or injection (Conrad & Schneider, 1980).

Preserving Life Through Medical Technology

During the twentieth century, medical science has succeeded in conquering most infectious diseases, once the leading killers just about everywhere, by discovering and manufacturing relatively inexpensive drugs and vaccines. It has been pointed out, however, that "the cheap elimination of one disease simply makes way for other more expensive ones" (Morison, 1979, p. 282). People are surviving the easily cured illnesses, so the resources of medicine have been freed to focus on diseases that are more difficult to cure. As a result, medicine has developed technologies that can extend the life of critically ill people, although sometimes at enormous cost.

Treating patients who are greatly deformed, terminally ill, or experiencing so much pain that survival becomes a goal they themselves question raises several ethical problems. For example, neonatal intensive-care units have been developed to provide critically ill and premature babies with nonstop care. Sophisticated technologies and a highly specialized staff have raised the cost of treating a relatively small number of infants to at least $1.5 billion a year. Given the limited supply of medical and financial resources, the question naturally arises: Should they be allocated to treating illness among a few babies rather than to some other medical or societal purpose, such as preventive health or better nutrition, which would benefit much larger numbers of people?

Attempts to develop rules for allocating lifesaving medical technology must address basic questions of social equity. In the United States today, physicians and manufacturers of medical equipment exert major influence on decisions about what technologies will be developed. Should this much power rest in these people's hands? Whose medical problems should be given the greatest emphasis? Those who suffer most? The oldest? The youngest? To some extent, the marketplace determines who can afford medical technology and, therefore, who will benefit from it. And to some degree the various private and public medical insurance plans equalize access to expensive medical care. But who should have the highest priority for using high-cost lifesaving equipment? Only those who can afford it, or all who need it? Those who are socially useful, or those who have suffered previous wrongs from society? Such questions are extremely difficult to answer.

The Crisis of Rising Medical Costs

The American health-care system is the most expensive in the world. During 1996, the nation spent a staggering $1,035.1 billion on health care—over 13.6 percent of the gross domestic product (GDP). This figure has grown in recent decades. In 1960, only 6 percent of GDP was devoted to health care. No other nation spends a higher percentage of its GDP or as much per capita on health care (Health, 1998; Lassey, Lassey, & Jinks, 1998) (see Figure 12.3).

Why is health care so expensive in the United States? A key factor is the system's built-in bias toward expensive care in institutions such as hospitals and nursing homes. Both Medicare and Medicaid pay more liberally for such care than for less expensive home services. In some cases, even though medical authorities agree that the patient would be better off at home, Medicare or Medicaid policies make costly institutional care the only option.

The system of third-party payment, in which public programs or private insurance companies reimburse doctors and hospitals for services rendered, also helps keep costs high. Doctors suggest, and consumers accept, expensive treatment partly because insurance spreads the cost, even though taxes or premiums must eventually rise to match expenses. Although insurance companies frequently pressure hospitals and doctors to cut costs, it is often easier for insurers to raise premiums than to risk retaliation by doctors and hospitals in the form of boycotts or repeal of discounts to favored companies.

.NET   INTERNET/TECHNOLOGY

THE FOUNTAIN OF YOUTH

People have searched for the fountain of youth for centuries. In 1513, the Spanish explorer Ponce de León set out to find a miraculous spring that the Indians claimed would rejuvenate those who drank from it. The only thing he discovered, however, was Florida. Today, despite many claims to the contrary, no one has learned how to reverse the aging process. But the possibility no longer seems so remote.

In 1991, scientists made the first major breakthrough in understanding how human beings age. They discovered that the tips of chromosomes in tissue cells shorten when cells replicate—a process that continues over and over again through about 50 replications. At that point, which is called the Hayflick limit, the cells stop dividing entirely (*Time,* January 11, 1999).

For years, scientists tried to reactivate an enzyme called telomerase to lengthen the tips of chromosomes. Finally, in 1998, a team of researchers at the Geron Corporation succeeded.

By activating the telomerase, they lengthened the life span of two types of human tissue cells well beyond the Hayflick limit. Skin cells treated in this way had replicated 40 more times after untreated ones stopped dividing.

During this procedure, a vital component of telomerase, which is used in egg and sperm cells to maintain a youthful length, is inserted into tissue cells. All human cells have a gene that makes this component, but in almost all normal cells it is turned off. Cancer cells, which are the exception, have turned the gene on, causing cells to grow indefinitely (Wade, 1998).

While this procedure was done in test tubes, the inventors of this new technology believe that it will be used to treat many diseases of aging (Wade, 1998). Using cells from a patient's own body, scientists can restore the telomerase and replace older cells. The most promising uses for this new technology include the treatment of wrinkled skin, certain types of eye degeneration, and hardening of the arteries. Researchers also hope that this technique can be used to grow new skin cells for patients suffering from serious burns. And they

believe that they will learn how to switch off telomerase in cancer cells. The biggest hope, however, is to reverse the entire aging process and to extend the human life span.

While skeptics were not convinced that this new technology could be used to rejuvenate all kinds of human cells, another major breakthrough by the Geron Corporation indicates that this can be accomplished. In November 1998, researchers at Geron reconstituted the telomerase of embryonic stem cells, which have the ability to turn into any type of cell. That conceivably makes it possible to rejuvenate parts of any organ with a simple injection (*Time,* January 11, 1999).

Despite these phenomenal achievements, scientists must hurdle at least one more obstacle before they can claim to have discovered the fountain of youth. So far, all of this research has been conducted in a test tube. Now they must show that it will work in the human body. If it does, society will face a completely new set of problems, including questions about how the extended life span of human beings will affect life as we know it.

Another factor explaining soaring national health-care expenditures is the greatly increased cost of services and resources used in providing medical care, especially labor costs. In addition, the advent of new technologies—ranging from specialized laboratory tests to advanced medical equipment—has not come cheaply. The soaring cost of medical malpractice insurance is frequently cited by physicians in explaining the rise of medical costs. At a deeper level, the fact that most of the American health-care system—HMOs are an exception—operates on the basis of a fee-for-service philosophy, which allows providers to charge separately for everything that is done for a patient rather than establishing a flat fee for treating a particular condition, also encourages costs to spiral upward. Finally, high medical costs are due in part to the privileged position of certain suppliers. Physicians as

a group command high pay, and drug companies have consistently been able to earn high profits compared to other industries. Perhaps consumers are the only party with a strong interest in reducing the costs of the health-care system. Thus far, however, they have not organized effectively enough to reduce prices.

In an effort to contain health-care costs for Medicare patients, the government has recently begun to establish *diagnosis-related groups (DRGs)*. Under this system, hospitals are reimbursed according to predetermined rates for some 460 categories of medical diagnoses. If the actual cost of the patient's care is lower than the rate paid by the DRG, the hospital makes a profit. If the cost is higher, however, the hospital runs the risk of loss or even bankruptcy.

Not surprisingly, DRGs have excited a great deal of controversy. Strong opposition comes from the AMA,

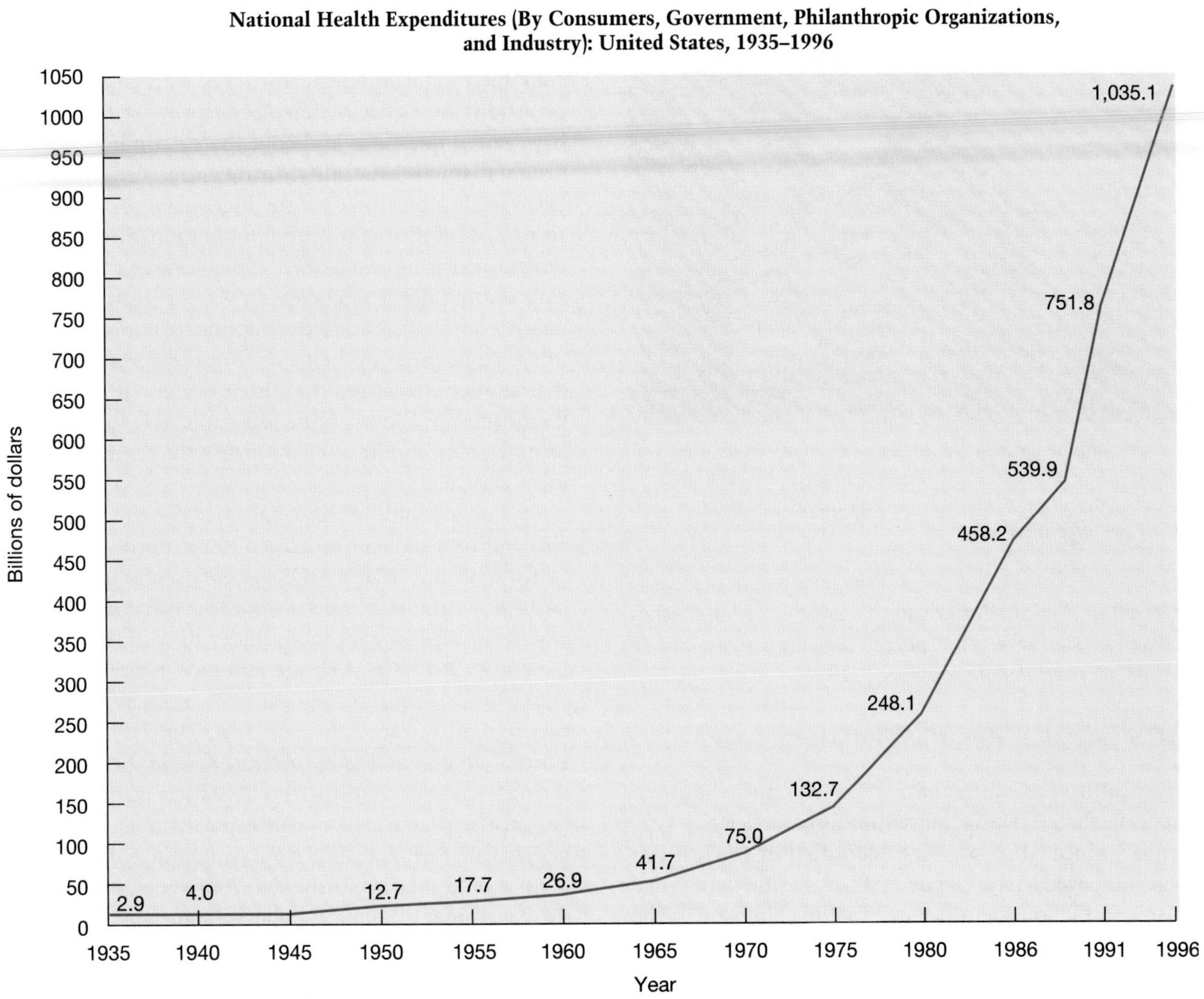

National Health Expenditures (By Consumers, Government, Philanthropic Organizations, and Industry): United States, 1935–1996

FIGURE 12.3 Since 1950, the amount of money spent annually on health care in the United States has grown enormously, at an exponential rate.

Sources: U.S. Department of Health and Human Services, Public Health Service, *Health: United States 1990*, p. 184, and Table 103 (Washington, D.C.: Government Printing Office, 1984, 1991), p. 177, Table 66; U.S. Health Financing Administration, *Health Care Financing Notes*, September 1986; U.S. Bureau of the Census, *Statistical Abstract of the United States, 1993* (Washington, D.C.: U.S. Government Printing Office, 1993); U.S. Department of Health and Human Services, *Health: United States 1998* (Washington, D.C.: Government Printing Office).

which fears that physicians are rapidly losing professional status and control within the health-care system (McKinley & Stoeckle, 1988). Others worry that the patient will get "lost" in the DRG process. For example, DRG classifications make no distinction between severe and mild forms of the same illness. Will hospitals turn away the more troublesome (and, therefore, more costly) cases? Or, conversely, will hospitals admit more patients (but for short-term stays) simply because they have the financial incentives to do so (Davis, 1986)?

The high cost of medical care has literally driven some Americans out of the medical marketplace. Principally, these are the 16.1 percent of the population without health insurance. They are the near-poor rather than the true poor (who are covered by Medicaid). Typically, the near-poor have low-income jobs that do not provide health insurance benefits. Thus, they make too much money to qualify for Medicaid but not enough to purchase private health insurance. Hispanic-Americans make up the highest portion of the uninsured (34.2 percent),

Clean needle programs are available in many inner-city communities. Do you think that these programs will help stop the spread of AIDS? Or do you think that they encourage illegal activity?

followed by African-Americans (21.5 percent) and Asian or Pacific Islanders (20.7 percent) (U.S. Bureau of the Census, *Current Population Survey,* 1998).

AIDS: Social, Economic, and Moral Issues

Few health-care issues have received more national attention than AIDS (acquired immune deficiency syndrome). Since AIDS was first identified in 1981, it has been compared to the Plague, or Black Death, that struck Europe in the fourteenth century, killing almost half the population in just four years (Platt, 1987). AIDS develops much more slowly and has a far lower infection rate than the Plague did.

By the end of 1997, 641,086 Americans reported that they had contracted AIDS (Centers for Disease Control, 1998). At least 60 percent of them have now died. During the early years of the epidemic, increases in AIDS cases ranged from between 65 percent and 95 percent each year. The epidemic has now slowed significantly due to the introduction of combination therapies for HIV. The estimated AIDS incidence dropped for the first time in 1996, with a decline of 6 percent from the previous year. The number of deaths attributed to AIDS also fell for the first time in 1996—by 25 percent.

But as new treatments prolong the lives of people with AIDS, the prevalence of AIDS continues to increase. Today experts estimate that between 650,000 and 900,000 Americans are living with HIV. At least 40,000 new infections occur each year. AIDS strategists agree that because we do not have a cure for the disease or a vaccine against it, the public, especially young people, must be educated about how the AIDS virus is transmitted. They then must be persuaded to modify their behavior accordingly.

The central purpose of AIDS education is to help change public habits so that the epidemic may be contained and irrational fears may be quelled. Other ways of modifying behavior have been proposed; they, too, have raised questions and engendered conflicts between pragmatism and morality. Intravenous drug users, for example, belong to one of the high-risk groups that can spread AIDS throughout the population. So far, education alone has not impressed addicts enough for them to stop sharing needles. Therefore, should clean needles be handed out to drug addicts? Proponents have argued that this type of program helps to stop the spread of AIDS; detractors have argued that the program encourages an illegal activity. Clean-needle programs have been tried in several places despite opposition, but the results are as yet inconclusive.

Public health officials, and society as a whole, must also confront the enormous economic burdens imposed by the epidemic. Many AIDS patients cannot afford care, partly because it is so expensive and partly because the disease seriously impedes their ability to work (*Newsweek,* December 2, 1996). Medicare and local government revenues must, therefore, assume costs not covered by the patient or by private insurance (Ergas, 1987). This leads to various ethical and legal problems. Should society pay for the medical costs of those who have been warned of their dangerous practices, yet continue them anyway? Can people who contract AIDS from contaminated blood sue? If so, should they sue insurance companies, hospitals, or the government? Similarly, who is financially responsible for children who have, innocently, contracted AIDS?

The AIDS epidemic has also raised a number of ethical issues concerning private rights versus the public good. For example, should testing for the AIDS virus be mandatory? Some civil libertarians say no, but what if a patient who is suspected of having AIDS needs surgery and refuses to be tested? In such situations, what are the rights of the medical staff? Does the army (or any other organization, for that matter) have the right to test personnel for AIDS, or is this an invasion of privacy? Also, should confidentiality be preserved at any cost? Or should an AIDS victim's family be informed, as well as others who are at risk or may already be infected? Can a state quarantine AIDS sufferers, or would this violate their individual rights?

Public opinion polls show that Americans have a wide range of opinions about questions like these and that they have changed over the last 10 years. In fact, Americans are less concerned about AIDS today than they were at the end of the 1980s. In 1987, a Gallup poll showed that 68 percent of Americans believed that AIDS was the most urgent health problem facing the country. By 1997, only 29 percent did so (Moore, 1997). The public's concern about contracting the disease had also diminshed. In 1987, 42 percent of Americans expressed some concern over getting AIDS. Only 30 percent said so in 1997.

But some attitudes about AIDS have not changed much over the last decade. About half of all Americans believe the government is not doing enough about the problem of AIDS; about the same percentage who said so in 1987. At the end of the 1990s, just under half of the public felt that people should be made to carry a card indicating they have AIDS. Ten years earlier, 54 percent thought they should. And Americans still hold people who contract AIDS somewhat responsible. In 1997, 4 in 10 Americans said that it is someone's own fault if he or she gets AIDS; 5 in 10 said so in 1987. Finally, in 1997, 31 percent of Americans said that AIDS is a punishment for the decline in moral standards; 43 percent said that in 1987.

The most dramatic changes in Americans' attitudes toward AIDS since the late 1980s involve the ways that people try to avoid the disease. In 1987, 43 percent of Americans said that they would not associate with people they suspected had AIDS; 42 percent said they would avoid elective surgery that would require a blood transfusion, and 28 percent said they would avoid using rest rooms in public facilities. By 1997, the number of Americans taking these particular steps to avoid AIDS had dropped. The percentage responding to each of the above items was, respectively, 15 percent, 33 percent, and 12 percent. Finally, by the end of the decade only 7 percent of Americans thought people with AIDS should be isolated from the rest of society. In 1987, 21 percent favored the idea.

Today AIDS no longer ranks among the top ten leading causes of death in the United States, but it is not clear whether this crisis is over. While scientists have made progress in the AIDS battle, many of the moral, ethical, and legal questions raised by this epidemic remain. And they may be with us long after we find a cure for AIDS.

CHAPTER REVIEW

1. What kinds of social and cultural changes would you expect to accompany an aging American population?

2. Identify and discuss the kinds of attitudes Americans express about different stages of life.

3. Describe the kinds of statuses, roles, and norms that characterize different stages of life. Give examples of age deviance and age status inconsistencies for different age groups.

4. How do the media perpetuate ageism?

5. Compare and contrast the theories developed by social gerontologists to explain the process of transition to old age.

6. Do you expect mandatory retirement policies to change in the twenty-first century? If so, why, and how will they change?

7. How will the housing needs of the elderly change over the next 30 years?

8. What can social epidemology tell us about cross-cultural differences in health care?

9. Describe how the health-care system in the United States has changed since the nineteenth century.

10. What kinds of ethical issues surround advances in medical technology?

INTERNET EXERCISE

The Web destinations for Chapter 12 cover various aspects of age and health in society. To begin your explorations, go to the Prentice Hall Companion Web site: **http://www.prenhall.com/popenoe.** Next, choose **Chapter 12** (Age and Health in Society). Then select **web destinations** from the menu on the left side of the screen. There are a number of interesting sites to choose from. We suggest that you begin with a comparison of two sites: **the HMO Page** and **the Humana Organization.** The **HMO page** is managed by *Physicians Who Care, Inc.,* a nonprofit organization supporting the private practice of medicine. Clearly, the contents of this site involve some very critical views of health maintenance organizations in particular and managed care in general; their motto: "You never expected justice from a *company,* did you?" In contrast, the **Humana Organization** is one of the best-known managed-care consortiums, with many subsidiaries nationwide. After you have explored these two sites, answer the following questions:

- What are the central issues surrounding managed health care?

- What are your reactions to the criticisms leveled at managed care in the **HMO Page** Web site? Do you agree or disagree with this critique? What are your views on managed care in general?

KEY TERMS

age status	**age status inconsistency**	**health-care system**
age roles	**ageism**	**paramedicals**
age norms	**gerontology**	
age deviance	**social epidemiology**	

Gender

n the fall of 1993, new students at Antioch College in Yellow Springs, Ohio, underwent the familiar process of learning their way around campus, moving into dorms, and signing up for classes. However, they were also provided with a less traditional socialization experience: an introduction to the college's Sexual Offense Policy.

Concerned about sexual violence in general and the problem of date rape in particular, Antioch had prepared a code that was intended to empower women, who traditionally have been the primary victims of sexual aggression and harassment, by specifying exactly how students are expected to behave when dating.

The code stressed that all sexual contact must be entirely consensual. Implicit assent is not adequate; there must be open and explicit discussion before any sexual activity whatsoever takes place. Similarly, before a sexual encounter moves to a higher level of intimacy—from kissing to physical caresses, for example, or from fondling to actual intercourse—there must again be explicit consent by both parties. The responsibility for securing assent is assumed to rest with the individual who chooses to escalate the intimacy of the encounter.

Antioch's new policy received nationwide attention, probably in large part because it struck many outside observers as bizarre. At the same time, however, it is obvious that the code, while admittedly difficult if not impossible to implement, represents a serious response to a very real problem in contemporary American life.

If asked to analyze why policies like this one have been developed in the 1990s, a sociologist might well cite the classic work of Émile Durkheim, who observed that in societies where there was a high level of agreement regarding values and norms, there were rarely many formal rules precisely because everyone understood what was expected of him or her. There was no need to write everything down. In contrast, societies lacking strong moral consensus were characterized by an extensive body of formal law (Durkheim, 1969). Applied to Antioch's dating policy, Durkheim's insight suggests what most of us probably already know: Relations between men and women are undergoing very rapid change, and many people in modern society are experiencing tremendous confusion about how to behave toward members of the opposite sex.

Historically, male and female behavior has usually been explained by inborn biological factors. Women, who were seen as innately maternal and social, were believed to be naturally suited to managing the household and looking after the children. Men, who were assumed to be bold and competitive, rational, and not easily swayed by the emotions, were said to be naturally suited to managing government, war, and commerce. If men tended to dominate women, even to the point of sometimes using force to obtain what they wanted, that was assumed to be a result of man's genetic character.

But if the behavior of men and women was mostly determined by biology, then it is unlikely that it could change as dramatically as it has over the past few decades. This observation leads most social scientists to believe that socialization is a major cause of gender-role differences. They see traditional gender distinctions as being heavily influenced by social conditioning and by the social circumstances in which men and women find themselves. And, as a consequence, they believe that it is possible for us consciously to change these roles in order to promote greater equality between the sexes. Most efforts to change gender roles are less extreme than the Antioch College dating policy, but it is obvious to even a casual observer that contemporary American gender roles are undergoing dramatic changes.

In this chapter, we begin with an assessment of the significance of the biological and psychological differences that do exist between the sexes. We then review the history of gender roles and gender-role socialization and examine how patterns of gender inequality are deeply woven into American society. Finally, we briefly consider some current efforts to change traditional gender-role patterns.

CHAPTER 13

DIFFERENCES BETWEEN THE SEXES: BIOLOGICAL AND PSYCHOLOGICAL

To what extent can the different ways in which men and women behave be explained by biological and psychological factors? This is an important issue to which scholars have recently begun to pay close attention. In this section, we look at some of the results of research on sex and gender differences from the disciplines of biology, psychology, and anthropology.

Biological Differences

The effects of biological factors on the behavior of men and women are complex and not yet fully understood. Although we know that males and females are genetically, hormonally, and anatomically different, we still know surprisingly little about the extent to which these differences influence behavior.

Research has shown that the behavior of primates is clearly differentiated by sex, even when the animals are isolated from cultural influences. Rhesus monkeys raised by surrogate "mothers" made of barbed wire and soft cloth, for example, acquired the primary social characteristics of their sexes by the time they were two months old (see Chapter 6). The males were more aggressive and the females more passive (Harlow, 1962, 1965).

Yet there are widespread variations in sex roles among different species. Male rhesus monkeys are generally uninterested fathers, but male owl monkeys are deeply involved in infant care. Male baboons outrank females in the dominance hierarchy, but among several species of macaques mother-infant pairs are dominant. Thus, although the behavior of female primates differs from that of male primates, the character of the differences is not always predictable (Abbott, Kitovitch-Winer, & Worell, 1986). And because there is so much variation in sex-related behavior among primates, one must be very careful in extending any of these findings to humans.

In order to understand the relationship between biology and behavior, it is useful to distinguish between the biological differences that appear prenatally and those that take effect after birth, with maturation. This distinction is reflected in the following discussion of two basic biological elements: chromosomes and hormones.

CHROMOSOMES

When a baby is born, we can tell its sex immediately by looking at its genitals. But in other physical respects, the two sexes resemble each other closely. Without the familiar "pink and blue" code to identify a diapered infant as male or female, mistakes of identification can easily occur.

Long before birth, the biological distinction between males and females is determined genetically. Each cell of the human embryo carries 23 pairs of **chromosomes,** the threadlike structures in the nucleus that hold *genes,* which carry the programming for all inherited traits. The members of each chromosome pair are alike—except in the case of the pair that determines the sex of the child. About half the sperm cells produced by the male have an X chromosome and half contain a Y chromosome. The female egg cell always contains an X. The union of two X chromosomes results in a girl; an X and a Y produce a boy.

Regardless of whether it is an XX or an XY, the embryo shows no signs of sexual differentiation until about six weeks after conception. At this time, the Y chromosome of a male embryo, together with an X, programs the development of testes. The two X chromosomes of the female program the same mass of cells to become ovaries (King, 1996).

HORMONES

Shortly after their formation, the sexual organs begin to produce **hormones,** chemical substances that promote or restrain biological processes vital to growth and body functioning. There are three primary sex hormones: *testosterone,* the so-called male hormone; *progesterone,*

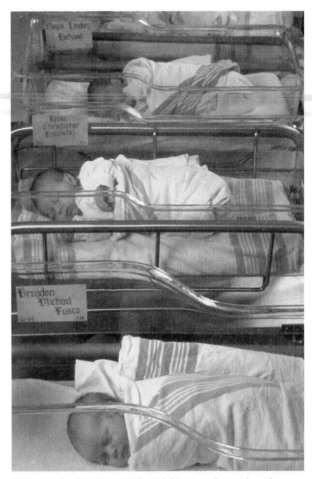

Without the familiar "pink and blue" code to identify a diapered infant, mistakes of identification can easily occur.

the pregnancy hormone; and *estrogen,* the so-called female hormone. All three hormones are produced by the sex organs of both males and females. What stimulates fetal tissue to grow into either male or female internal and external sexual organs is the particular mix of hormones. The male testes produce testosterone in very large amounts, but the female ovaries produce much less testosterone than estrogen and progesterone.

During puberty, the ovaries begin to produce increased amounts of estrogen, and the testes manufacture more testosterone. The result is the development of secondary sex characteristics, such as breasts, pubic hair, and deepened voices, as well as the capacity to reproduce. This hormonal activity brings about the rapid physiological changes that take place during adolescence; most researchers believe that it also causes psychological and behavioral changes. The shift from childish to adult behavior during adolescence is due at least in part to hormonal changes.

Some researchers believe that new mothers quickly gain the sense that they can interact with a baby on a nonverbal level, whereas fathers prefer to interact with older children, who respond to verbal communication and need less physical care.

Later in life, when women reach menopause, the amount of estrogen produced by the ovaries drops considerably. Similarly, there is some decrease in the production of testosterone in older men.

To what extent do hormones influence behavior? Some evidence suggests that they do play a role in affecting certain forms of behavior that vary by sex. Boys seem to expend more energy than girls do, especially in outdoor activities and sports; boys are more territorial in play than girls and engage more frequently in competitive rivalry for positions of dominance. By contrast, girls are more likely to rehearse the roles of parenthood (Money, 1977). It is important to note, however, that *both* sexes engage in these forms of behavior; it is just that some forms are more prevalent in one sex than in the other.

Sex researcher John Money believes that the different mix of hormones in males and females merely *predisposes* them to certain behaviors—that is, makes them more or less sensitive to environmental triggers (Money, 1988). These predispositions, he argues, can be overridden to some extent by socialization.

CHILDBIRTH AND THE MATERNAL INSTINCT

The capacity to bear and nurse children is clearly an area in which the sexes differ biologically; in fact, it represents the most clear-cut expression of *sexual dimorphism,* or the existence of two different forms of a species. Men's inability to bear or nurse children has been considered by some, such as Margaret Mead (1949/1975), as the best explanation for many exclusionary customs among males in primitive societies. Mead saw such customs as attempts by men to compensate themselves for their limited role in the central mystery of life—the creation of a new human being.

It is still an open question whether this biological capacity to bear children goes along with some kind of maternal instinct (Lindsey, 1997). Some research indicates that women are better than men at responding to the needs of newborns until the infants are around 18 months old—that is, until they begin to speak. According to these findings, new mothers quickly gain the sense that they can interact with a baby on a largely nonverbal level. New fathers, even second-time fathers, feel no such "interpersonal competence" in dealing with newborns and prefer to interact with older children, who respond to verbal communication and need less physical care (Rossi, 1984).

Other research, however, has suggested that nurturing behavior is dependent on social expectations regarding how a person should behave. In Fiji, where sex typing is low, both parents enjoy caring for infant babies (Basow, 1984). The same appears to be true in Bali (Coltrane, 1988).

In summary, current evidence suggests that there are some significant biological differences between men and women, but that genetic programming and hormonal

TABLE 13.1   SELECTED SEX DIFFERENCES

Strongly Supported by Evidence	*Ambiguous or Questionable*
Boys tend to be more aggressive than girls—both physically and verbally—in cultures in which appreciable aggressive behavior has been observed.	Some studies have found that males tend to be more active than females in social play, but others contradict this finding. More detailed research is needed to establish lifelong differences.
From adolescence through adulthood, males tend to have greater visual-spatial ability than females. Visual-spatial ability involves the visual perception of objects in space and how they are related to one another.	Some studies find males to be more competitive than females, but other studies do not.
Beginning at about age 12, males' mathematical skills tend to increase faster than females' skills.	Males make more efforts to dominate each other than do females. But dominance in relations between the sexes is a complex issue, and the longer the relationship lasts, the more equal the influence becomes.
From about age 11 through 18, females' verbal abilities tend to become superior to males' and may remain superior throughout life.	Most evidence suggests that females are not more passive than males. Both sexes are equally willing to explore new environments and to be involved in social situations. Although boys are more aggressive, girls are no more often the passive victims of aggression than are boys.

Source: Eleanor Emmons Maccoby and Carol Nagy Jacklin, *The Psychology of Sex Differences* (Palo Alto, Calif.: Stanford University Press, 1974).

effects are in no way complete explanations of gender-role differences. It is crucially important that we also consider the impact of psychological and social factors.

Psychological Differences

The subject of the psychological differences between the sexes is controversial. By "psychological differences," social scientists mean differences in behavior, mental ability, and personality. To what extent are such psychological differences inherent rather than the result of socialization?

One way to approach this issue is to make use of cross-cultural data. If certain differences appear in most cultures, they may be inherent rather than learned. However, because the socialization process begins at birth, we cannot be sure what causes the differences. The best we can say is that the more universal the differences and the earlier they appear, the more likely they are to be inborn.

Cross-cultural studies have suggested that girls generally touch and seek assistance more than boys, and that girls are more nurturant and supportive than boys. Boys, on the other hand, seek attention, assert dominance, and engage in aggressive behavior more often than girls. Of these behaviors, those that appear earliest and are thus most likely to be biologically based are aggressive behavior in boys and touching behavior in girls. Nurturant behavior in girls and the assertion of dominance in boys appear later, and therefore are more likely to be affected by socialization (Barry, Bacon, & Child, 1957; Stockard & Johnson, 1980; Whiting & Edwards, 1973; Whiting & Whiting, 1975; Williams, 1987).

In one of the most thorough attempts to identify the psychological differences between the sexes, psychologists Eleanor Maccoby and Carol Jacklin (1974) reviewed and interpreted data from more than 1,600 studies. Their aim was to provide a clear and unbiased summary of the current knowledge and to look beyond the stereotypes about men and women. The conclusions of their study are summarized in Table 13.1. Maccoby and Jacklin found little evidence to support many stereotypes, such as those concerning competitiveness in males and passivity in females. They did find strong evidence, however, for a tendency toward aggressiveness in boys and for some differences in mental abilities between the sexes. In a later study, however, Maccoby and Jacklin softened their conclusions about aggressiveness in boys by linking it to certain situations and not to others (1980).

Maccoby and Jacklin's work has not gone unchallenged. One scholar has argued that most of the studies they reviewed uncovered many more sex differences than they acknowledged (Block, 1976). For example, many surveys have found that males are less social than females (Maccoby, 1966; Terman & Tyler, 1954; Tyler, 1965). Obviously, more research needs to be done before we can reach scientifically valid conclusions about the extent of psychological differences between the sexes (Stockard & Johnson, 1980).

GENDER ROLES

The sense of identity each of us has includes knowing what it is like to be male or female. But if asked, how would we describe masculinity or femininity? We would probably begin by distinguishing between the sexes. We might mention the obvious differences in genitalia (the primary sex characteristics) or the variations in secondary sex characteristics, such as muscular structure and body hair. Yet, as we have already seen, the experience of being male or female includes much more than biological traits. It is important to differentiate between **sex**— the biological traits that distinguish the male and female members of a species—and **gender**—the social and psychological traits associated with masculinity and femininity. As a biological trait, sex is constant for virtually all members of a population. Gender, however, is in large part socially and culturally determined, and so is subject to extensive variation. There are only two sexes. But there are many concepts of gender, which reflects social ideas about masculinity and femininity that have changed dramatically through history.

A society operationalizes its concepts of gender through the social roles it assigns to each sex. As discussed in Chapter 4, a social role is the behavior expected of someone occupying a specific position in a group or society. A **gender role** is a social role associated with being male or female.

It is not easy for us to recognize our own cultural assumptions about gender roles. We often take it for granted that our ideas of what is masculine and what is feminine follow directly from the biological differences between men and women. But much research has suggested that gender roles are not necessarily determined by sex. Anthropologist Margaret Mead came to this

conclusion as early as 1935, when her research showed that gender roles in several primitive tribes were vastly different from those in most modern societies. Among the Tchambuli of New Guinea, for example, gender roles seemed to be "reversed." Women were the principal economic providers, and men stayed home and raised the children. The Tchambuli regarded women as properly dominant and assertive, and men as emotional and creative (Mead, 1935/1963).

Nonetheless, in most societies, men and women have traditionally played—and typically continue to play—gender roles that would be familiar to most Americans. Often these roles are very apparent, as when a woman at a party acts delicate, helpless, or seductive—all passive roles—even though she may have spent the day as an executive negotiating a complex business deal. Likewise, a man may be aware that he has a gentle nature but may feel compelled to act "tough" or "macho" in order to fulfill what he believes are society's expectations for him.

Traditional gender-role expectations shape many of our daily activities. In general, men in our society are expected to work hard to support their families and to be competitive, aggressive, and successful. Women are to some extent still expected to play the traditional "feminine" roles associated with being mothers, wives, teachers, or secretaries—all roles that stress nurturance—but not those associated with being football referees or construction workers. (It is important to note, though, that this is not equally true of women in all racial and socioeconomic groups. Most African-American and working-class women have historically worked outside the home.)

Because gender roles are defined by culture, they vary over time, from one culture to the next, and even between a society's different racial groups and socioeconomic classes. Yet no matter what gender roles we play, we normally maintain a single **gender identity**—our conception of ourselves as either male or female. Gender identity is even unrelated to *sexual orientation* (the manner in which people experience sexual arousal and sexual pleasure). Homosexual men, nurturant heterosexual husbands who enjoy child rearing, and men who hold traditional views regarding the appropriate relations between the sexes all have a male gender identity, even though they do not all play the same gender roles or have the same sexual preference. Thus, being male or female includes having a personal sense of gender, as well as filling culturally defined roles.

A Brief Social History of Gender Roles

Each of us receives a lengthy training in the gender-role behavior that is considered appropriate by our culture, community, and historical period. A glance at some

GLOBAL SOCIETY

CROSS-CULTURAL VARIATIONS IN GENDER

Gender is a key trait used for the organization of social relationships in every known culture (Andersen, 1997). While gender-role expectations vary cross-culturally, most societies recognize only two genders—male and female. And in most Western cultures, male and female constitute two exclusive and opposite categories. But some cultures recognize more than two categories for gender and, in some cases, they do overlap.

The term *berdache* was used to describe a third gender that was prevalent in many North American Indian tribes (Bonvillain, 1998; King, 1996). The origin of the term can be traced to the medieval French word meaning "male homosexual." But that does not adequately capture the Native American concept of this third gender. A better translation would be "halfman-halfwoman" or "manwoman." And the preference today is to refer to this gender as a "two-spirit."

Callender and Kochems describe a "two-spirit" as "a person, usually male, who was anatomically normal but assumed the dress, occupations, and behavior of the other sex to effect a

change in gender status" (1987, p. 443). "Two-spirits" married other men who were not "two-spirits." But Native Americans did not consider this a homosexual relationship—as judged by contemporary Western standards. Both partners were regarded as ordinary men. And only the "two-spirit" was seen as a third gender.

One indication that a boy would become a two-spirit was his unusual interest in the work of women during his childhood. Later, during adolescence, his change in gender status to a "two-spirit" was generally confirmed by a supernatural vision. This new status brought respect and honor to the individual, not humiliation or shame. In fact, "two-spirits" were highly valued for their ability to go back and forth between genders and were sought as mediators for conflicts between men and women (Roscoe, 1992). This ability, along with their tendency to excel in traditional female subsistence and caretaking tasks, was highly respected and valued in Native American societies.

The hijras of India offer another example of cross-cultural variations in the concept of gender roles (Andersen, 1997). Similar to the "two-spirits," the hijras are considered a third gender. Born as males, hijras choose to change

their gender status to one that is neither male nor female. The rite of passage that marks the transition to the hijra status involves a cultural ritual in adolescence during which a boy's penis and testicles are cut off. Although this renders them impotent, hijras are thought to possess the combined power of man and woman.

The hijras, who belong to a religious community of men, represent the Hindu belief that all individuals possess both male and female principles. And their sexual ambiguity, which is a trait of Hindu gods, is valued. Hijras play an important role at Indian weddings—where they bless the newlyweds' fertility—and at events to celebrate the birth of a male child.

Although biological males typically constitute the members of a third gender, biological females have also assumed this status (Andersen, 1997; Lorber, 1994; Nanda, 1990). Described as "manly hearted women," these "female men" have existed in some African and Native American societies. Unlike the "two-spirits" or hijras, they neither dress nor act like the opposite sex. They merely need to have enough money to buy wives.

aspects of the history of gender roles can help us to understand some of the forces that are shaping these roles today (Tannahill, 1980).

Gender-role definitions in Western society have been said to reflect a tension between two opposing forces—the similarities between the sexes and the differences between them (Bloch, 1978). Two periods have been identified during which gender roles among the English and American middle classes underwent especially significant changes. The first period was during the Protestant Reformation and the rise of preindustrial capitalism and cottage industry in the sixteenth and seventeenth centuries, and entailed an increase in the

similarity between male and female gender roles. As capitalism replaced feudalism, the home and family increasingly became the center of religious, educational, and commercial activity. This focus on the home strengthened the importance of women. There were thought to be relatively few innate differences between the sexes, yet women remained generally subordinate to their husbands.

This pattern of higher social involvement for women, although combined with their continued subordination, was especially visible in economic life. Women frequently engaged in productive work but always under the direction of their husbands. A woman married to a potter, for example, might work as hard as he did at the craft and even take over the business after his death, but she would never attain a social status equal to his. Women were denied formal apprenticeships and membership in craft guilds.

A second major change in gender roles occurred in the eighteenth and nineteenth centuries. Now the differences in character between the sexes began to be stressed. Men were believed to be "rational" and women "emotional." Men were dominant in the more competitive economic and political worlds, while women held sway in sacred, moral, and emotional spheres, particularly in the family.

Underlying these changes were economic forces during this period that resulted in the decline of production in the home and the transformation of domestic work into an activity without commercial value. Women increasingly withdrew from the paid labor force once they started families, and motherhood became the ideal feminine role. As economic forces led more and more men to work away from home, women became almost completely responsible for child rearing.

Although these nineteenth-century Victorian gender-role conceptions have continued to influence twentieth-century norms, some earlier notions stressing the similarity of the sexes have recently regained considerable influence. Neither model has eclipsed the other, and both continue to affect gender-role distinctions today.

Gender-Role Socialization

Gender-role expectations are taught and reinforced through socialization from the moment of birth onward. Two distinct mechanisms are primarily responsible for gender-role socialization: differential treatment and identification with role models.

During infancy, the dominant mechanism of gender-role socialization is *differential treatment*. Indeed, the first question that parents usually ask after the birth of a child is: "Is it a boy or a girl?" As friends and relatives repeat the question, a chain of related issues arises: Will he grow up to be a dentist, a farmer, an engineer? Will he be smart enough to succeed? Will she be strong enough to take care of herself? Will she be pretty? Immediately, social conventions and expectations start to affect the newborn child.

Gender-role socialization begins as soon as parents learn the sex of their child. Even when male and female infants look and behave very much alike, adults frequently respond to them in terms of stereotyped images. For example, an infant's crying tends to be attributed to anger if the child is a boy and to fear if it is a girl. Fathers tend to handle boys more roughly than they would

handle girls (Fausto-Sterling, 1986; Jacklin, DiPietro, & Maccoby, 1984; Siegal, 1987). Parents also describe their newborn infants in stereotyped ways. One study showed that parents tend to describe daughters, more often than sons, as little, beautiful, cute, and resembling their mothers, even when, in terms of actual physical appearance, this was not true (Rubin, Provenzano, & Luria, 1974).

How important is early gender-role socialization? One of the most compelling arguments in this regard revolves around a case study of two twin boys. When the two seven-month-old boys were being circumcised by electrocautery (a surgical technique using a heated needle), one of the boys accidentally had his penis burned off. After several months, the distraught parents decided that surgery was the best solution to the dilemma, and the boy was transformed into a girl and raised as such. By the time the twins were five years old, each was acting out his or her traditional gender role. Each preferred gender-typed clothing, toys, and activities; the girl was neat and tidy, while the boy was messy (Money & Ehrhardt, 1972). Some researchers in the 1970s regarded this case as unassailable evidence of the influence of nurture over nature (see Chapter 6).

However, the results of a follow-up study seem to suggest that biology plays just as important a part in gender-role formation as does socialization. By the time the "girl" reached age 13, she was experiencing severe psychological problems concerning her role as a female. She had a very masculine walk, hoped to be a mechanic, and felt that boys had better lives than girls. It was not entirely clear whether she knew about her operation or remembered that she had been born a male, but she did seem to be an unhappy person (Diamond, 1982). On the basis of the later developments in this important case, it is reasonable to conclude that neither nature nor nurture is the main determinant of gender behavior. Rather, the behavior associated with sex differences seems to be the product of both forces acting simultaneously at crucial periods in an individual's development (Money, 1986).

In any event, differential treatment continues as children grow. For example, parents tend to use physical punishment on boys more often than on girls, and boys especially are strongly discouraged from playing with the "wrong" toys, such as dolls (Best, 1983). Whether the gender-role expectations reflected in these and related socialization experiences are reinforced in the course of a child's development depends on family attitudes and the nature of other influences in the outside world. But the first imprint has been made. As the child grows, he or she quickly learns what people mean by "masculine" and "feminine."

Over time *identification with role models* becomes an increasingly important form of socialization. The most powerful role models are the child's parents, but in modern societies, people portrayed by the mass media, especially television, are also very important. The images children see on television can have a strong impact on their understandings about themselves.

At school, children may receive differential treatment from their teachers. Even though school policy usually dictates that boys and girls be treated equally, policy and reality often differ. Depending on the teachers' personal values and prejudices, subtle or not so subtle information about the nature of gender roles is passed on to students. Studies have shown, for example, that teachers (as well as parents) tend to praise boys more often than girls for similar achievements; this holds true whether the teachers themselves are male or female (Lipman-Blumen, 1984). Boys are also criticized more frequently than girls, but this can turn out to have positive effects, because boys then learn how to handle criticism (Sadker & Sadker, 1988, 1994).

The attitudes and expectations teachers have concerning male and female students have been called a "hidden curriculum" that usually reinforces traditional gender-role stereotypes. Because many teachers expect boys to be more active and difficult to control than girls, much classroom time is typically spent catering to boys' interests and trying to subdue them (Sadker & Sadker, 1994; Sadker, Sadker, & Klein, 1986). When girls do better than boys academically—which they usually do, at least until high school—teachers may regard them as merely conscientious and diligent, in conformity to the female stereotype. In contrast, boys who achieve may be thought to have "real" creativity and to be more interesting than girls. Thus, if a girl does what is expected of her, she is not given the same recognition as a boy. These practices are likely to have an impact on a child's academic self-image (Entwisle et al., 1987).

A child's identification with the role models in the school setting is affected by the sex ratio among teachers and school officials. In 1996, 74.4 percent of all public school teachers were women (U.S. Department of Education, 1997). But even though women are responsible for the day-to-day education of children, the final decision-making authority almost always rests with a man. At all levels, the majority of principals in public schools are men. Public high schools have the highest percentage—86 percent (U.S. Department of Education, 1999).

Because female teachers hold less power in schools and colleges than men do, the attitude that women are less professionally competent than men is communicated to students, which in turn may affect—consciously or unconsciously—the expectations that female students have for themselves (Fennema, 1976; see also Basow & Silberg, 1987; Dobbins, Cardy, & Truxillo, 1986).

These children have already absorbed many of their culture's traditional norms regarding the behavior expected of men and women. The divisions of labor within the home and career choices in later life are often subtly guided by awareness of these norms.

Adult Gender Roles

Although gender roles in American society today are in the process of change, especially among the educated middle classes in metropolitan areas, the following description of adult gender roles nevertheless still holds true for much of our society. As girls move through high school and college, their image of themselves as lacking the ability to do rigorous intellectual work—a view usually acquired during puberty—can, and sometimes does, become a self-fulfilling prophecy. Even women who are talented at and enjoy academic work may lack confidence in their abilities. They may see men constantly being rewarded for intellectual achievement, while women often are not so rewarded. Some women are also made to feel that when they reach levels of achievement the same as, or higher than, those of men, they are overstepping "natural" boundaries.

These attitudes persist and may even intensify in college. One study found that women speak much less often than men do in coed college classes and also experience sharper drops in self-confidence (American Association of University Women, 1992). Other studies have found that college women were disproportionately likely to experience a loss of motivation for careers in science (Holland & Eisenhart, 1990; Masters, 1994).

Just as our culture has traditionally equated femininity with intellectual inferiority, it has identified masculinity with unemotional or unexpressive behavior. The media often present tough "cowboy" images that encourage men to see themselves as strong and silent or as sexual conquerors. As a result of these socially constructed images, men who are gentle, emotional, and sexually responsible may not be viewed as fully masculine (see Brittan, 1989). Men who try to overcome these stereotypes may find themselves judged as "nice but weak" and "unlikely to amount to much." Thus, men who are not afraid to cry, who give their home life high priority, who reject sexual adventurism, or who support their spouse's careers at the expense of their own may be viewed with suspicion. Women displaying the same attitudes and engaging in the same behavior are considered "normal."

As men and women proceed through the life course, they continue to encounter different gender-role expectations. Society often considers a woman of 40 to be "middle-aged," but a man of the same age is "in his prime." Women may sometimes dye their hair at the first sign of "going gray," but men may regard a "touch of gray" as a sign of being "distinguished." These attitudes are constantly reinforced by the mass media, which urge women to remain youthful. Though men, too, are expected to show youthful vigor, they are urged mainly to achieve maturity and success, which often come with age. The prospect of growing old may make some women over 40 lie about their age, even though they may be vigorous, attractive, and accomplished.

Divorced or widowed men can marry considerably younger women without experiencing much social disapproval. Women, though, are generally limited to choosing partners of their own age or older, although it is now becoming somewhat more acceptable for women to have relationships with younger men. Divorced men may often select female companions from among a large number of young, single women, but social pressures tend to force a divorced woman to choose from a limited number of divorced men and older widowers.

Remarriage is mainly a male prerogative among the elderly: Eight times as many older men remarry as do women. This is the case largely because it is much easier for men to find new spouses, but it is also a matter of income and education. The more financial resources and educational background an elderly woman has, the less likely she is to remarry; the opposite is true for elderly men (Benokraitis, 1999).

Another difficult situation awaits older women who must reenter the workplace. Many older divorced or widowed women lack experience in the business world and must contend with employers' preferences for hiring "girls" rather than mature women. A woman of 45 or 50 can be made to feel that her "useful years" are over, but a man of this age knows he still has 15 to 20 productive years left.

GENDER AND INEQUALITY

Just as societies are characterized by inequalities based on race and ethnic background, they also display inequalities based on gender. Gender is a major source of social inequality. Not only are men and women assigned different roles, but these roles are judged and regarded unequally. Put differently, men and women have unequal access to social rewards.

Social inequality based on gender can be seen in a society's language and mass media. In virtually all societies, these reflect the basic assumption of **male dominance**—the social situation in which more power and prestige are given to men than to women. Male dominance does not mean that all men intentionally oppress women, or that individual women cannot overcome their situations and match men's achievements. But male dominance is built into cultures, and it unconsciously shapes the perceptions and daily interactions of the members of those cultures.

Because language is an essential part of culture, it is not surprising that the forms and usage of English—and many other languages—reflect male dominance. In languages that have separate male and female pronouns, the male form is usually more basic—only the male form can be used to refer to a group of men and women together. English is no exception: The pronoun "he" has traditionally been used to denote a single person, whether male or female. And the word "man" has been used to refer to *all* people—as, for example, in "mankind" and "all men are created equal." In recent years, many professional organizations have attempted to delete sexist language from their reports and publications, but it is not always easy to implement nonsexist language policies. One study found that although 24 out of 32 professional social work journals tried to eliminate sexist language, only 10 succeeded in doing so consistently (Else & Sanford, 1987).

Although the situation has been changing gradually, male dominance is also reflected in the mass media—in television and radio programming and commercials, in magazines, in popular music, and even in textbooks. Women have consistently been underrepresented on television. Until the early 1980s, only 30 to 45 percent of all television characters were women (Bretl & Cantor, 1988; Dambrot, Reep, & Bell, 1988; Stockard & Johnson, 1980; Tuchman, 1979). Children's shows, too, featured twice as many men as women. Also, men and women characters typically have played roles that reflect male dominance. A compilation of studies examining role portrayal and stereotyping on television found that women are usually depicted on television as young, holding traditional roles, and working at low-level occupations (Signorielli, 1985, 1989).

Recently, however, the networks' reluctance to portray women in strong roles on prime time has yielded to an even stronger imperative: the need to attract as viewers—and consumers—the growing number of American women now in the work force. Prime-time TV now offers more programs with strong, competent, dynamic women as leading characters. Donna Reed has been replaced by Ally McBeal, Scully (*The X-Files*), and Carol Hathaway (*ER*).

The content of the print media has also tended to reflect traditional gender stereotypes. For example, until fairly recently, the fiction printed in women's magazines, such as *McCall's, Redbook,* and *Ladies' Home Journal,* usually portrayed women in traditional roles with men as the centers of their lives. But these stories have begun to strike a less rosy, more realistic tone in which employed women are featured as working a "double day"—eight hours at the office, then several hours at home on household chores (Henry, 1984). Magazine advertisements also now more accurately reflect the diversity of women's social and occupational roles than they used to (Sivulka, 1998; Sullivan & O'Connor, 1988).

Of course, gender inequality is not limited to language and the mass media. In the rest of this section, we discuss sociological theories of gender stratification and the ideology of sexism and then we consider the relationship between gender and some major social institutions: marriage, work, and politics.

Sociological Theories of Gender Stratification

Sociologists studying gender inequality have speculated about its origins and, in particular, about the virtual universality of male dominance in human societies. Here we discuss the two main theoretical approaches used by sociologists—the functionalist and conflict perspectives—to explain male dominance and gender inequality.

FUNCTIONALIST PERSPECTIVE

Functionalist theory analyzes society as a system of interlocking statuses and roles. These statuses and roles are based on shared values, beliefs, and expectations and are arranged into social institutions. Functionalists hold that society has a basic tendency toward equilibrium and that the roles and statuses are normally in harmony and complement one another. Thus functionalists tend to view traditional gender-role differences as contributing to efficient societal operation.

According to the functionalist view, modern male and female gender roles derive from and reflect the sex-based division of labor that developed in the earliest societies. Women's childbearing capacities shaped their work roles; most of their time was spent near home, nursing and caring for children. Through much of human history most infants did not survive to adulthood, and it was necessary for each woman to give birth to and care for between six and ten children in order to be sure that their society's population did not decline. This, combined with the fact that few people in traditional societies lived much more than 35 or 40 years, severely limited women's work options. On the other hand, because men were not constrained by the need to stay close to home and also because of their superior physical strength, in the earliest societies they hunted and helped to defend the group against predators and enemies. Their strength and ability to withhold food enabled men to become the dominant sex. Gradually, this dominance was institutionalized in the values, norms, and roles of societies around the world.

The traditional sex-based division of labor may well have been the most efficient, or functional, arrangement in premodern societies. But is it still functional in the modern world? In a classic analysis of the family, Talcott Parsons and Robert Bales (1955) concluded that the traditional, clear-cut division of labor between men and women was indeed still a very effective social arrangement. Their analysis was based on the application to the family of principles derived from the study of the dynamics of small groups.

In an earlier work, Bales (1953) had found that two types of leaders are necessary if a small group is to function effectively (see Chapter 7). *Instrumental leaders* direct the group toward achieving its goals. *Expressive leaders,* in contrast, resolve group conflict and promote harmony and social cohesion.

Parsons and Bales together (1955) observed that most families are organized along instrumental-expressive lines, and that this organization may be as necessary for their effective functioning as it is for any other small group. Through his work outside the home, the man provides for the economic needs of his family and thereby assumes the instrumental role. Because of her biological ties to childbirth and nursing, the woman stays home and does the domestic work, providing for the family's emotional needs. The woman thus plays the expressive role.

The structure of gender roles in the traditional American nuclear family corresponds very closely to Parsons and Bales' view. But Parsons and Bales also claimed that this gender-role structure was universal in character and that it was essential to the successful functioning of the nuclear family. They believed that the structure had evolved because the instrumental role was the most natural for men, and the expressive role the most natural for women. Disregarding the fact that more and more women were entering the labor market, Parsons and Bales argued that a woman's primary role within the family was as an "expressive" housewife.

More recent functional analysts continue to emphasize the importance to society of an intact family consisting of a married couple and their children. They maintain that the playing of traditional gender roles by mothers makes it possible for children to form stable bonds and to benefit from strong and enduring role models. Without intensive mother-child contact during the first years of life, children can grow up relatively disoriented, isolated, and anxious, and can fail to develop a strong sense of self. Such children may come to value material things over human relationships (Berger & Berger, 1983; see also Gerson, 1984).

CONFLICT AND FEMINIST PERSPECTIVES: POWER AND DOMINANCE

Although most conflict theorists agree with functionalists regarding the origins of traditional gender roles, they argue strongly that these roles are outmoded in modern society. The conflict perspective stresses that culture is shaped by economic and technological forces. Throughout history, economic and technological change has brought about shifts in gender-role arrangements. For example, it has been argued that women originally adopted their domestic roles partly because of the lack of modern medicines and effective methods of birth control and also because the technology did not yet exist to replace the need for the male's physical strength (Lengermann, Marconi, & Wallace, 1978). But over time, these situations changed.

During the Industrial Revolution, when the home ceased to be a center of production, women's roles initially grew narrower, eventually shrinking to only those of homemaker, mother, and wife. But industrial economies are characterized by periodic needs for extra labor, and so women were gradually allowed to enter the market economy (Banner, 1984). The first of these women were recruited from the lower classes; middle-class married women were still expected to stay home (Wertheimer, 1984). As the economic, social, and technological constraints against women's full participation in the labor force were gradually removed, however, the possibility arose for a significant change in women's roles.

Conflict theorists also stress that male dominance is a major feature of our society. As the dominant group, men can and do limit women's access to the social, economic, and political power that men enjoy, thus sparing themselves from female competition (Reskin, 1988). Only a basic structural change in society can alter this pattern (Jacobs, 1989).

Some of the conflict theorists who analyze gender roles are Marxist feminists, who see gender inequality as an outgrowth of broader stratification systems (Lengermann & Wallace, 1985). These scholars suggest that when early agrarian societies first evolved, men laid claim both to communal economic resources and to women as their personal property. As this stratification system became entrenched, gender inequality came to be permanent as well. According to this perspective, only the destruction of the system of private ownership of economic resources will reverse this situation (Chafetz, 1988; Wallace, 1989).

Sexism

As we have noted previously, social inequality is commonly justified by an *ideology,* a set of beliefs that supports a particular social point of view. The ideology that supports gender inequality and justifies male dominance is called **sexism.** Like racism (see Chapter 11) and ageism (see Chapter 12), sexism justifies the dominance of one group—in this case, men—over another, usually on the basis of what are held to be biological facts. Sexism is based on the widespread perception, regardless of evidence to the contrary, that innate differences between men and women make them necessarily unequal. These perceptions often evolve from *gender stereotypes,* oversimplified and inaccurate beliefs about the characteristics of men and women.

Social inequality can be maintained only if the ideology that supports it is accepted to some degree by the subordinate, as well as the dominant, group. Many women in our society have long accepted their traditional roles as "natural"—principally because they have had few other options and have been socialized within this narrow framework. Although this is becoming less common, some women still believe that they suffer from a kind of "natural inferiority."

It is very difficult for an individual woman to challenge sexism. Like minorities, older people, and the poor, women may find that their survival depends on at least appearing to accept the prevailing ideology—in this case, sexist ideology. Furthermore, sexist attitudes and assumptions are often built into major social institutions.

Gender and Marriage

The vast majority of Americans today—about 85 percent—are expected to marry sometime during their lives. Thus, despite controversy surrounding the institution, it is evident that marriage is still by far the preferred lifestyle in the United States.

Some studies have suggested that men, despite their supposedly weaker commitment to marriage, typically gain more from it than women do (Bernard, 1982; Lindsey, 1997). This is especially true for traditional marriages in which the woman is a full-time homemaker. Why might this be true? One reason is that wives traditionally have tended to their husbands' physical and psychological needs, enabling the men to function more effectively outside the home. Women may gain relative economic security from marriage but in return are obliged to take care of their own physical and psychological needs as well as those of their husbands and children.

Many married women who do work outside the home are caught in a double bind. Working wives find themselves doing two jobs at once, often with little or no physical or psychological support from their husbands (Benokraitis, 1999; Crouter & Perry-Jenkins, 1986). A tired husband returning from work may expect to be fed and to play with his children. A tired woman coming home from work, however, must get ready for the "second shift" in which she will be expected to feed her husband and children, to check on the children's homework, and to listen to her husband's account of his day (Hochschild,

As more women enter the job market, husbands have gradually begun to share home responsibilities.

1989). And a recent study suggests that many of today's college students still do not anticipate being in relationships in which working men and women share household responsibilities (Spade & Reese, 1991).

Nevertheless, the situation has begun to change in recent years. As more and more women have entered the job market, husbands have gradually begun to share home responsibilities with their wives (Benokraitis, 1999; Lewin, 1998; Pleck, 1985; Pleck, Lamb, & Levine, 1986). A study conducted by the Families and Work Institute showed that in 1977 men spent 30 percent as much time on workday chores as women; in 1998, that figure rose to 75 percent (*New York Times,* April 15, 1998, A18). The study also showed that today's fathers are spending more time with their children, compared to fathers' time with their children 20 years ago.

However, when a clash of priorities arises, a woman is still likely to subordinate her interests to those of her husband and family. It is also still likely that a working wife will feel disproportionately responsible for any problems her children might have. And although some women may feel guilty for not staying home to take care of their children on a full-time basis, men are still likely to assume that it is normal and natural for them not to be present.

Gender and Work

Men and women commonly receive significantly different economic rewards for their work. To understand how and why this situation developed, it is useful to look briefly at the past.

TABLE 13.2   EARNINGS BY OCCUPATION AND SEX, 1997

Occupation	Median Weekly Earnings	
	Men	Women
Managerial and professional specialty	875	632
Executive, administrative, and managerial	868	605
Professional specialty	883	662
Technical, sales, and administrative support	598	403
Technicians and related support	667	498
Sales occupations	603	352
Administrative support, including clerical	514	403
Service occupations	372	282
Private household	*	213
Protective service	575	451
Service, except private household and protective	317	280
Precision production, craft, and repair	569	382
Mechanics and repairers	581	489
Construction trades	538	445
Other precision production, craft, and repair	588	362
Operators, fabricators, and laborers	436	313
Machine operators, assemblers, and inspectors	449	313
Transportation and materials moving occupations	505	373
Handlers, equipment cleaners, helpers, laborers	343	299
Farming, forestry, and fishing	302	257

*Note: Data not shown where base is less than 50,000.

Source: 1998 Statistical Abstract of the United States.

As noted earlier, the Victorian view of women as qualitatively different from men arose in part because of the Industrial Revolution: As men's work moved away from the home, women's work became more centered and lost its commercial value. Though women's work was considered "useful," men's work contributed to the market economy and so had a clear monetary and exchange value. Since power and prestige in a market system are gained mainly through earning money, those with the most earning power receive the highest status. Consequently, men's work came to be evaluated as much more important than women's work.

But in this century, and especially in the last few decades, the situation has begun to change. Partly because of increased economic pressure on the family, but also because they have obtained more education, women now make up a substantial portion of the labor market. In 1950, women over the age of 16 constituted 29.6 percent of the civilian labor force; in 1997, they constituted 59.8 percent (U.S. Bureau of the Census, *Statistical Abstract of the United States, 1998*). In spite of their increased participation in the work force, however, women have lagged behind men in both salary and status.

The "pay gap" between the average wages earned by men and women has gradually narrowed over the past couple of decades. In 1960, women as a group earned 61 percent of what men earned; today, women earn about 65 percent as much as men do (see Table 13.2). A sizable gap still remains, however, partly because of the concentration of women in low-status, poorly paying jobs. In 1997, 98 percent of preschool and kindergarten teachers were women; so were 99 percent of secretaries; 94 percent of registered nurses, 95 percent of housekeepers, and 97 percent of receptionists (U.S. Bureau of the Census, *Statistical Abstract of the United States, 1998*). Even within the same occupation, the average earnings of women workers are typically lower than those of men. This holds true even for occupations in which men and women have equal education and training.

Women have made advances in admission to professional schools, however. Since the early 1970s, the enrollment of women in pharmacy schools has doubled; that in medical schools has tripled; and that in dental schools has risen by 2,500 percent.

Yet even in the occupations most open to women, men usually hold many of the more prestigious and higher-paying positions. In retail sales, for example, more men than women are paid by commission and sell expensive goods; women tend to be paid low hourly wages to sell clothing and small items. Similarly, even though there are far more waitresses than waiters, virtually no women work in this capacity at the most exclusive, expensive restaurants. Also, teachers in high schools and colleges tend to be men, while elementary school teachers tend to be women. Men are more likely to teach the sciences, while women tend to teach literature and language classes.

When women enter high-paying, traditionally male-dominated fields such as medicine and law, they tend to be overrepresented in the less prestigious areas of these fields (Bellas, 1993; Fox, 1995; Kaufman, 1995). Women physicians are overrepresented in the low-ranking specialties of anesthesiology, obstetrics, gynecology, and pediatrics. Similarly, women lawyers tend to be steered into family law or into trust and estate work (Pollock & Ramirez, 1995). The former is a field that men do not typically choose and as a result has become known as a "woman's field." The latter is a specialty that requires extensive research and relatively little client contact (Epstein, 1988). This often hinders the advancement of women in law firms because making contact with clients is usually essential to the promotion process.

Furthermore, women who have landed jobs in traditionally male-dominated fields are usually concentrated in the lower echelons of those fields. As women entered pharmacy, for example, they were generally employed by hospitals, while male pharmacists continued to work in retail stores (where the pay is higher). Similarly, although bus driving is now an "integrated profession," many women work as part-time drivers for schools, while men hold most of the best-paying jobs as city bus drivers (England & McCreary, 1987).

Some social scientists have pointed out that men tend to work in the *primary* occupations—those that pay high wages and offer good working conditions, real opportunities for advancement, and substantial job security. Women—and also minority workers—are more likely to fill the *secondary* sector, which includes jobs with low wages, limited opportunities, and little security (Blau

& Jusenius, 1976; Rossides, 1997). It has been noted that women rarely displace men in high-paying, highly desirable jobs because many women's jobs lead only to other traditional women's jobs (DiPrete & Soule, 1988). Only when jobs stop being desirable to men are they opened to women (Tavris & Wade, 1984). For example, when the job of bank teller was an entry-level position that often led to a future in banking, it was held almost exclusively by men. Today it is often a dead-end job, held mainly by women and minority workers. There may, however, be some cause for optimism, as over 20 states have now enacted laws to eliminate sex-based wage discrimination (Burns & Nelson, 1989).

What are the typical experiences of women who do manage to succeed professionally? Research shows that these women possess qualities that are beneficial to modern corporations (Helgesen, 1990). In contrast to the typical leadership style adopted by men—one that reflects the corporate hierarchy—female managers describe a "weblike" structure of leadership. According to Sally Helgesen, this model rests on "skills and attitudes that have value in the workplace" (1990, p. 37). And it is particularly well suited to today's organizations whose success relies on qualities such as innovation and creativity.

Differences in the management styles of men and women are culturally conditioned (Helgesen, 1990; Lindsey, 1997; Rosener, 1990). Women managers are more likely to encourage participation, share power and information, and develop relationships with employees at all levels of the organization.

EXPLAINING GENDER INEQUALITY IN THE WORKPLACE

Why do women continue to be at a disadvantage in the workplace? Several explanations have been proposed: the human capital model, the considered choice model, and the discrimination model.

The *human capital model* suggests that sex stratification in the workplace is a result of the unequal resources that men and women bring to the labor market. In other words, women earn less than men do because they have less "human capital" to offer. For example, women tend to have less experience and higher turnover rates than men do, and so are valued less by employers (Blau & Jusenius, 1976). This theory has received mixed empirical support. Even when there is no difference between men and women in experience and training, women still earn less than men do. In addition, women's earnings tend not to increase as much as men's do, as a result of either increased education or extensive experience (Lipman-Blumen, 1984).

The second explanation is the *considered choice model*. This theory argues that women are disadvantaged in the workplace because of decisions they have made (or have been forced to make). Because of women's dual roles—family and work—they tend to choose jobs that will enable them to be both homemakers and employees. Typically, these are poorly paid part-time jobs that lead nowhere (Fuchs, 1988; Hochschild & Machung, 1989).

The *discrimination model* holds that women are routed into segregated jobs, given differential pay and job titles for the same work, and handicapped by unequal chances for promotion (Baron & Bielby, 1986; Bielby & Baron, 1986; Jacobs, 1989). The causes of such discrimination range from stereotypical ideas regarding gender roles to outright sexism. One scholar has argued that men in the workplace simply are not willing to allow their jobs to be threatened by women, and estimates that only a minuscule proportion of men (less than 10 percent) really support equality for women in the world of work (Astrachan, 1986).

CROSS-CULTURAL PERSPECTIVES

As a great deal of sociological research has demonstrated, gender inequality in the workplace is not an exclusively American phenomenon. According to a report issued by the United Nations,

> If women's unpaid work in the household were given economic value, it would add an estimated one-third ($4 trillion) to the world's annual economic product. When wage discrimination is added, the figure rises to $11 trillion. (cited in Lindsey, 1997, p. 127)

Comparative studies of the world's industrial societies point to two recurrent themes: (1) Women are noticeably underrepresented in administrative and managerial positions in government, business, and banking (the jobs that pay the most); and (2) despite the fact that many women work full time, most of these women still assume primary responsibility for raising children and taking care of the home (Coltrane, 1988; Roos, 1985).

In the state-run economy of the former Soviet Union, women were treated very much like women are treated in the U.S. market economy. Although the proportion of women in the Soviet labor force was the highest of all industrialized societies, inequalities of position and pay, for example, were widespread. Soviet women made up only 35 percent of all engineers, but they constituted 71 percent of the technicians in engineering production and design—jobs with much lower prestige and pay (Roos, 1985). Soviet women were channeled into low-paying, menial clerical and service jobs and were underrepresented in managerial positions (Peers, 1985). At the same time, Soviet working women bore the primary burden of domestic responsibilities (Allott, 1985; Gray, 1990). Today, Russian women are more highly represented in professions such as law, medicine, and engineering compared to Western women. But they also constitute a greater proportion of those in low-paying and menial jobs (Lindsey, 1997; Shapiro, 1992).

It is difficult to anticipate the consequences of the introduction of market principles to the Commonwealth of Independent States that replaced the Soviet Union at the start of 1992. The transition from a state-run to a market economy in Hungary has improved the labor market position of women. One study found that 32 percent of the owners, managers, and employees of small new Hungarian enterprises were women (Szalai, 1991). In contrast, a similar transition within the German Democratic Republic (East Germany) after its 1990 unification with the Federal Republic of Germany (West Germany) has worsened the situation of women: They have disproportionately borne the costs of unemployment and have encountered greater difficulties than men in finding new jobs (Rosenberg, 1991). Conditions in the newly independent countries that once formed the Soviet Union more closely resemble those found in East Germany than those prevailing in Hungary—not an encouraging sign for women in these countries who desire more equitable labor market opportunities (Sanjian, 1991).

In India, too, women continue to experience social inequality on all fronts, particularly in education and employment. Most Indian women are illiterate and are employed as agricultural laborers or day workers (D'Souza & Natarjan, 1986; Duley, 1986). But gender inequalities are perhaps the most blatant in Latin American countries, where women inhabit an altogether different world from men. In these countries, most women's jobs are poorly paid, nonunion, and dead-end. Production of goods in the home is common, but this does not make it any easier on the women. Many Latin American women work as many as 15 hours per day, in addition to taking care of the home and children (Nash, 1986).

On a final note, it is interesting to point out that industrial societies generally do not separate the men's world from the women's world to the extent found in many developing societies. Amazonian Mundurucu men, for example, do not even sleep in their wives' houses (Blain & Barkow, 1988). The Bedouins of northern Arabia rigidly divide women's work from men's, and the sexes eat and drink separately (Coltrane, 1988).

Gender and Politics

Just as women and men do not have equal status in the workplace, neither are they equally involved in the political life of our society. Studies have shown that American women and men have similar political opinions, and that a larger percentage of women than men vote (58.3 percent compared to 56.4 percent). Women are also as likely as men to be active campaign workers. But overwhelmingly, it is men, not women, who hold political office.

Although many women candidates have been elected to office, most of these offices have been at the local, rather than national, level. Until the 1970s, only three women had been elected governor, and all three had succeeded their husbands.

There were only 47 women in the U.S. House of Representatives and 10 women in the Senate in 1997. Women who serve in Congress usually do not have the same power as men, for they often lack the seniority to be appointed to major committees or other powerful posts. One reason for this is the fact that male candidates are able to start their political careers earlier than women, who generally must wait until their children are grown so that they will not be branded as "neglectful mothers" when they run for office (Lynn, 1984).

Until 1981, when Sandra Day O'Connor was appointed, no woman had served on the U.S. Supreme Court. In 1993, a second woman, Ruth Bader Ginsburg, joined the Court. But perhaps the most significant gain made by women in politics is reflected in the number who have been appointed to the president's cabinet. In 1999, these women included Madeleine K. Albright (Secretary of State), Janet Reno (Attorney General), Alexis M. Herman (Secretary of Labor), and Donna E. Shalala (Secretary of Health and Human Services).

Despite these recent gains, we must still ask: Why does such a discrepancy exist between the number of women who vote and the number of women who are elected to govern? Three theories have been advanced to account for the discrepancy. The first explanation holds that women, by nature, are essentially uninterested in politics. The second theory suggests that the structure of women's personal lives does not allow them to participate easily in politics. Because they spend so much time fulfilling their roles as wives, homemakers, mothers, and economic providers, they have little time for political participation. The third theory argues that women are socialized into a more politically passive role than men are (Nock & Kingston, 1989).

The first theory is clearly sexist, and both the first and the second theories do not take into account important findings to the contrary. Most research has supported the third theory. For example, one scholar has pointed out that boys and girls appear to have similar interests in politics (Sapiro, 1983, 1988). Yet, because of the gender roles they later learn, boys are more likely than girls to pursue professional political careers.

The Feminist Movement

In the early 1960s, Betty Friedan published a book called *The Feminine Mystique.* And thus, according to the conventional wisdom, the *feminist movement*—a movement designed to raise the status of women—was born. But, as important as Friedan's book was, feminism actually began much earlier. Mary Wollstonecraft, an English author, wrote "A Vindication of the Rights of Woman" in 1792. In 1848, Elizabeth Cady Stanton organized the first women's rights convention in America at Seneca Falls, New York. After the Civil War, Stanton continued her work with the help of Susan B. Anthony. Together, the two women founded the National Woman Suffrage Association, which saw enfranchisement for women as the first step to equality. In 1923, Alice Paul drew up the first equal rights amendment to the U.S. Constitution.

The 1960s did mark a turning point for feminism. Two years before the publication of *The Feminine Mystique,* President John Kennedy set up the Commission on the Status of Women. The commission's report left no doubt that women's status was considerably lower than that of men. Partly in response to the commission's report, Friedan wrote *The Feminine Mystique* (1963) to explore "the problem that had no name." According to Friedan, the central problem for women was the never-ending difficulty of being defined by one's relationship to men rather than having an identity of one's own.

Three years later, in 1966, in part as a result of ongoing networking among women who had participated in President Kennedy's commission, the National Organization for Women (NOW) was born, with Friedan as its first president. NOW's primarily white, middle-class membership was committed to the goal of bringing about fundamental changes in the position of women in society.

By the early 1970s, the feminist movement had evolved in two directions. NOW and other relatively moderate groups continued to work to change political and economic institutions in order to allow women greater equality of opportunity. Other feminists, mostly young and with a history of active participation in the civil rights and anti–Vietnam War movements, took a more radical path. This second stream of feminism focused heavily on raising the consciousness of individual women, arguing against NOW's "top-down" approach to social change. Many of the more radical feminists charged that NOW's traditional bureaucratic structure inhibited the freedom of its members to liberate themselves fully from male-dominated society. However, both varieties of feminists agreed on many specific policy goals, including increased participation by women in the political process.

SOCIOLOGY OF THE MEDIA

THE INTERVIEW OF THE CENTURY

The media touted it as the interview of the century. She had remained silent for over a year since news leaked about this sordid, political sex scandal. Now she was prepared to tell all. More than 70 million people tuned in to hear Monica Lewinsky describe her affair with President Clinton, making it the most highly rated news program ever. After the interview, presidential historian Michael Beschloss remarked during an interview on ABC's *Good Morning America* program that Lewinsky had changed history, saying that she caused Clinton nearly to lose his office, and that if the American public had known about this affair, Bob Dole could very well have won the 1996 election.

Barbara Walters' interview with Lewinsky probably did not add much to what the public already knew about a scandal that resulted in the only impeachment of an elected president in American history. But the interview did reveal something interesting about what Lewinsky understood as acceptable and unacceptable behavior between members of the opposite sex. In response to one question, Lewinsky said she understood the rules of being involved with a married man. But at no point did she indicate that she understood the rules about not being involved with a married man, the rules about becoming involved with superiors at work, or the rules about telling the truth.

But confusion over the rules of relationships between members of the opposite sex is not new. For years the news has been full of stories that demonstrate this fact. Just prior to the media's obsession with the Clinton-Lewinsky affair, the story of another woman had made national news. Her name was Kelly Flinn. In 1997, she left the Air Force—and a career to which she had devoted her entire life—after the military charged her with adultery, lying, and disobeying an order (*Newsweek*, November 24, 1997, p. 54). Flinn, a graduate of the Air Force Academy, had served four years of active duty as a lieutenant in the Air Force. Her claim to fame was the fact that she was the first female pilot to fly B-52s.

Flinn's version of her own story sounds all too familiar. In an excerpt from her book, *Proud to Be,* she asked: "Why did I fall so completely for a man whose own mother says he's a pathological liar? Who knows?" (*Newsweek,* November 24, 1997). The story picked up by the media suggested that the military was persecuting Flinn for adultery and that a double standard existed when it came to men and women in the U.S. military. But, in fact, Flinn knew the rules. The military instructs all personnel about the kinds of relationships considered improper for members of different military ranks. And the military saw this case quite differently. According to General Ron Fogelman, it involved lying (*Newsweek*, November 24, 1997, p. 60). And the true story was about Kelly Flinn's refusal to take responsibility for her actions and the military's need to trust people whose

---

During the 1970s, feminist activities became international in scope. The United Nations declared 1975 "International Women's Year" and 1975–1985 "The United Nations Decade for Women." Three major women's conferences were convened: one in Mexico City in 1975, a second in Copenhagen in 1980, and a third in Nairobi in 1985. These conferences were not without their difficulties. Some of the participants disagreed among themselves, and conservative groups tried to disrupt the meetings. But by the time of the Nairobi conference, it seemed that the women involved had developed a strong sense of unity and had made some progress toward understanding the problems of women on a worldwide scale (Lindsey, 1997).

A decade later Beijing, China, hosted the largest United Nations conference on women's issues in history. With attendance estimated to exceed 50,000, it was evident that debates over women's issues could no longer be ignored. The message of this conference was clear: Nations would be held accountable for ending gender inequality (Lindsey, 1997).

One of the central elements of the American feminist movement has been its support of the Equal Rights Amendment (ERA). This proposed legislation sought to end all forms of discrimination against women; it would have been the twenty-seventh amendment to the Constitution. But, although it was passed by Congress in 1972, the ERA failed to win the support of the three-fourths of state legislatures necessary for ratification. The amendment has been reintroduced into Congress annually in recent years, but Congress has not passed it again.

By the early 1980s, some feminist leaders were suggesting that it was time to shift gears, to help women jobs involve decisions that risk human life. But just as this story was beginning to gather steam, it faded away. The media became absorbed in another sex scandal—one that went all the way to the top—to the commander in chief—President Clinton.

The media thrive on scandals like these. But despite the immense coverage devoted to them, you have to wonder if we ever learn anything? The ever-increasing number of high-profile media stories about scandalous sexual affairs and sexual harassment suggests that we do not. Cases like that of Paula Jones leave us confused. Taking a settlement does not constitute a clear-cut victory. And we are left without a clear understanding of what constitutes sexual harassment. What is more, media stories increasingly seem to suggest that women end up being the victims, one way or another.

It is somewhat surprising, therefore, that media coverage of cases like these actually produces some positive effects. Consider, for example, the case of Anita Hill versus Clarence Thomas. President Bush nominated Judge Clarence Thomas, a Yale Law School graduate, to replace U.S. Supreme Court Justice Thurgood Marshall. While Thomas's nomination was controversial, it looked like he would be confirmed for the position. Then Anita Hill came forward with accusations of sexual harassment.

This scandal monopolized the attention of the American public. According to a CBS/*New York Times* poll, over 80 percent of those surveyed watched all or some of the three days and nights of the televised hearings (Paletz, 1999). As it turned out, Thomas was narrowly confirmed for the position by a vote of 52 to 48, suggesting that the main effect of the massive media coverage was only to reinforce the original voting intentions of senators.

But David Paletz argues that while this sexual harassment battle was lost, the media played a role in a larger victory. Anita Hill became a symbol of sexual harassment who drew attention to this issue and made it a legitimate concern. Following the Judiciary Committee hearings, the number of sexual harassment complains filed with the Equal Employment Opportunity Commission rose dramatically. Laws were passed that made it easier for women to sue their employers for discrimination, and the law allowed victims compensation as high as $300,000 for damages. Paletz also argues that media coverage of the Senate Judiciary Committee's Clarence Thomas–Anita Hill hearings prompted women to run for Congress, which reached a record number in 1992. Finally, he also attributes the rise in campaign contributions to feminist organizations to the media's coverage of this national issue.

It is hard to say what effect the media's coverage of the Clinton-Lewinsky scandal has had. But *Time* magazine claims that it taught America many important lessons, including the importance of telling the truth (February 22, 1999, pp. 32–37).

combine a career with the satisfactions of home and family life. In her book *The Second Stage* (1981), Friedan noted that many women who had found rewards in the workplace were worried that they had not left themselves enough time and freedom also to be good mothers. Some felt that they were caught in the same career traps that had ensnared men. They had broken down barriers, but had they created prisons for themselves at the same time? Friedan suggested—and many agreed—that it was time for men and women to work together to restructure social institutions so that work and family activities could be better coordinated for both sexes.

The feminist movement lost some steam during the Reagan years. But by the end of the 1980s, it revived as women's groups began to coalesce around the "pro-choice" position in the nationwide abortion debate (see Chapter 21).

What has the feminist movement accomplished? Although equality of the sexes is still far from being achieved, women have made many important advances over the past few decades (Gornick, 1990). In the United States and Canada, for example, women have been starting their own businesses twice as often as men. Many Christian churches, once opposed to women preachers, have become more liberal. There are now 21,000 female ministers in U.S. churches. In a number of countries, women have held the position of prime minister, and in 1989, the Japanese Liberal party appointed its first female chief cabinet officer (Naisbitt & Aburdene, 1990). Prospects for pay equity also seem to be improving. In 1989, women earned only about 65 percent of what men did. By 1997 full-time working women were making 75 percent of men's median pay (*New York Times,* February 9, 1989; *New York Times,* September 5, 1997, p. A20).

CHAPTER REVIEW

1. How do biological sex differences influence the roles that men and women assume?

2. What do cross-cultural studies show about the differences between boys and girls?

3. Explain the differences between each of the following concepts: gender role, gender identity, and sexual orientation.

4. What effect did the Industrial Revolution have on gender roles?

5. Describe the mechanisms by which gender-role expectations are acquired.

6. Give examples of how gender is reflected in language and mass media.

7. Explain how functionalists use the distinction between instrumental and expressive leadership styles to explain gender roles in the family.

8. How will changes in the economy and technology affect gender inequality in the twenty-first century?

9. How is sexism expressed in American society today?

10. Why do women gain less from marriage than men do? Will this ever change?

11. Why have women traditionally held low-paying, low-status jobs, and have found it difficult to advance even if they are in prestigious professions?

12. Identify and discuss the barriers women face when they run for political office.

13. How would you describe the feminist movement today?

INTERNET EXERCISE

The Web destinations for Chapter 13 cover various aspects of gender and gender inequality. To begin your explorations, go to the Prentice Hall Companion Web site: **http://www.prenhall.com/popenoe.** Then select **Chapter 13** (Gender). Next, choose **web destinations** from the menu on the left side of the screen. There are a number of very interesting sites you may wish to investigate. We suggest that you begin with the **Introduction to Sexual Harassment Site.** This site provides legal definitions, background information on a number of actual cases of sexual harassment, relevant theory and analysis, and a host of links to other Web sites related to this topic. After you have explored the Introduction to Sexual Harassment site, answer the following questions:

- What is the currently accepted definition of sexual harassment?
- What behaviors may constitute sexual harassment?
- What are people's legal rights and appropriate procedures if they feel they have been sexually harassed?

KEY TERMS

chromosomes	gender	male dominance
hormones	gender role	sexism
sex	gender identity	

CHAPTER 14

The Family

f you are thinking about running for political office, one of the tried-and-true ways of convincing people to vote for you is to express your concern about the "collapse" of the American family and to stress that you will work to restore "family values." But if you should find yourself trying to promote your candidacy in front of a group of sociologists, you had better be prepared to answer some sharp questions concerning exactly what you mean by "family."

A few generations ago, this was a fairly easy question to answer. It was generally assumed that a family consisted of a man and a woman, married to each other, and several children. It was further assumed that the husband made most of the decisions in the family and that, unless the family was from the lower classes, he was the sole breadwinner and his wife stayed home and looked after the children.

No other social institution has changed as rapidly in recent decades as the family. For example, female-headed, single-parent families increased from 11 percent to 24 percent of all families with children between 1970 and 1996. In 1960, about 31 percent of all married women held paying jobs; by 1997, over 61 percent did so (U.S. Bureau of the Census, 1998). A bewildering variety of family forms confronts the modern observer: cohabiting couples with and without children; couples in which the wife works and the husband stays home; gay couples seeking to adopt children. And the number of people who choose to live alone increases each year.

This increased diversity has led many observers, especially those who are strongly supportive of the traditional model, to fear that the family institution is in steep decline. Some of the evidence that we will review in this chapter, such as the very high American divorce rate, lends support to this view. Other evidence, such as the high remarriage rate, does not. In any event, in order to address crucial questions concerning the future of the family, we need to understand the social forces that are transforming the modern family. Will the family continue in the future to be—if it still is—the primary unit of child socialization? Of sexual gratification? Of human intimacy in general? What will the family look like in the next century? The answers to these and related questions are explored in this chapter. The other major *social institutions* (relatively stable clusters of social structures that are organized to meet the basic needs of a society)—education, religion, politics, and economics—are the subjects of the following four chapters.

THE FAMILY IN SOCIETY

The family has been present in one form or another during every historical period and in every known society. All other social institutions, including religion, government,

and education, were formed and developed within early family systems. Only late in the process of cultural evolution did these institutions become distinct sectors of society.

The Functionalist Perspective

In many small, preliterate societies, the family is largely self-sufficient and thus provides for most of its members' physical and emotional needs. The entire family cooperates to make tools, build shelters, and hunt, gather, or grow food. Parents and other older relatives teach children the skills they will need as adults, as well as help them to develop a sense of right and wrong. Religious practices are woven into the pattern of daily family life. The head of the family decides who does what and settles disputes.

In modern, complex societies, the family is more specialized and provides fewer functions than in preliterate societies. Schools and teachers are largely responsible for formal education, churches and clergy for religion, government and police for social control. But functionalists stress that the remaining family functions—socialization, affection and companionship, sexual regulation, and economic cooperation—are very important for the well-being (and smooth functioning) of society. Let us look at these four functions in some detail.

SOCIALIZATION

Socialization begins at home. There, children learn who they are, what they can and should expect in life, and how to behave toward other people. In many ways, the family is ideally suited to the task of socialization. It is a small group in which the members enjoy a great deal of face-to-face contact. The children's progress can be closely watched, and adjustments in their behavior can be made as necessary. Furthermore, parents are usually highly motivated to socialize their offspring. Viewing their children as biological and social extensions of themselves, parents have a strong emotional stake in childrearing.

But not all families are effective or efficient agents of socialization. Parents are rarely explicitly trained for the task. Essentially, most parents reproduce what they are able to remember from their own upbringing, adding (not always well-informed) ideas acquired from others. This is one of the reasons why today socialization has increasingly become the responsibility of the schools, the "helping" professions (such as psychology and social work), and other agents of society. Indeed, the socializing role of agents outside the family has become so important in modern industrialized societies that these agents have sometimes been accused of contributing to the weakening of the family (Berger & Berger, 1983; Lasch, 1977).

Alternatives to the family, however, have not proved very successful. Societies trying to effect dramatic change have occasionally experimented with new methods of socialization that at first seemed to be more effective than the socialization provided by the traditional family structure. In the early years of the Communist regime in the former Soviet Union, for example, government officials tried to reduce greatly the role of the family for political reasons (the family was seen as a bulwark of capitalism) and to introduce new patterns of collective childrearing. The attempt was a failure (Perevendentev, 1983). Indeed, for many decades the Soviet Union was characterized by a relatively strong family system compared with those of other industrially advanced countries (Imbrogno & Imbrogno, 1986; Lapidus, 1982). However, by the late 1980s, amid the massive changes brought by *glasnost* and *perestroika,* the Soviet Union's divorce rate rose to become the highest in Europe. Soviet sociologists identified this marital and familial instability as the primary cause of the increase in juvenile delinquency that occurred at the time (Sanjian, 1991).

The most extensively researched alternative-family experiments have taken place in Israel, where children in *kibbutzim* (collective settlements) live in houses separate from those of their parents. In these houses, small groups of children of about the same age live with specially trained adults who are members of the *kibbutz.* Several studies show that this approach to socialization has been successful in teaching the values and attitudes of the Israeli society (Bettelheim, 1969; Bowes, 1989; Spiro, 1958).

But the kibbutzim are unique. They are small, strongly integrated communities whose members share both common values and the constant fear of terrorist attacks. And although the children sleep away from their parents, they go to their parents' homes every day, in the mid-to-late afternoon, and have dinner together in the communal dining hall before they return to the children's houses in the evening. Moreover, evidence suggests that the family is gaining strength in the kibbutzim; a growing number of kibbutz children now live with their parents, and many mothers want to take on a stronger parental role (Palgi et al., 1983; Tiger & Shepher, 1975).

AFFECTION AND COMPANIONSHIP

A second major function of the family today is to provide love and affection for its members. Affection is as important to children as is learning, and it remains important throughout life. The evidence is clear that a lack of intimate caregiving can harm the physical, intellectual, and emotional growth as well as the social development of a child (see Chapter 6).

Although they may not die from lack of love, adults also need affection and companionship. In the past, many people spent their entire lives in the communities in which they were born and raised. After marrying and having children of their own, they continued to live with, or near, their parents and siblings. By remaining in familiar communities with relatives nearby, families had abundant opportunities for friendly contact and emotional support.

Most sociologists agree that in modern societies there are fewer opportunities for friendship and support from relatives outside the immediate family. Parents and children often live apart from other relatives and visit them only occasionally. Also, most families move when a parent accepts a job in another location or when they purchase a home in a different neighborhood. These trends force immediate family members to depend heavily on one another for affection as well as companionship (Melville, 1988; Parsons, 1955).

Because the family is one of the few sources of affection and companionship in modern societies, a high percentage of people continue to marry, even though it is now more socially acceptable for single men and women to have active sex lives outside of marriage. At the same time, because affection and companionship have become so important, families are more likely to break up if a spouse's emotional needs are not being met within the family circle—even if all other family functions are being satisfactorily performed. In this sense, the provision of affection and companionship has become the central function of the modern family. This is particularly true for men; a nonworking wife who is economically dependent on her husband is less likely to seek to dissolve a marriage because it fails to meet her emotional needs (Bernard, 1982; Blumstein & Schwartz, 1983).

SEXUAL REGULATION

As far as we know, no society has ever advocated total promiscuity. But norms governing sexual behavior do vary widely from society to society and from one period of history to the next (Howard, 1986; L. Stone, 1985). For example, Denmark and Bangladesh represent two extremes regarding attitudes toward young people's sexuality. The Danes approve of adolescent sexual activity for both sexes. Concerned about the transmission of AIDS, Danish schools began in the late 1980s to distribute free condoms to adolescents as young as age 14 (Kjoller, Hansen, & Segest, 1989). In Bangladesh, on the other hand, adolescent sexual activity among unmarried females is forbidden. If a young woman is not a virgin, she is labeled an outcast and considered unworthy of marriage. This is the case even if she has been raped.

Although a wide variety of sexual norms can be found throughout the world, no society leaves sexual matters entirely to the discretion of the individual. An important reason for this social concern about sexual behavior is the possibility of pregnancy. Because children need extensive care, it is in society's best interest that, once a baby is born, its biological or designated parents be held clearly responsible for providing food, shelter, and affection. Institutionalized norms of sexual behavior have as their primary, underlying goal the provision of proper child care and a smooth transition from one generation to the next. As a result, most societies strongly promote *legitimate birth* (birth to a mother and father who are married to each other) over *illegitimate birth* (birth to a mother who is not married to the child's father).

Social pressures for legitimacy also serve to ensure that each child receives appropriate *social placement*. This means that there is little or no ambiguity concerning the child's inherited or ascribed social statuses. A legitimate birth confers on the child a definite religious, ethnic, and class identification, as well as a defined position as a member of the families of each of its parents. The social statuses of children who are born illegitimately are generally less clear, which can result in substantial ambiguity concerning how the child ought to be treated.

Sexual norms in the United States have traditionally been quite strict, a legacy first of Puritanism and then of the morality of the Victorian Age. These norms were tied to religious beliefs and many are still enforced by law; for example, some states prohibit sexual relations outside of marriage, and some limit the sex acts of married couples to genital intercourse. Laws prohibiting sodomy ("unnatural" sex acts) are still on the books in 24 states (*West's Federal Practice Digest*, 1987).

But attitudes about sex and, to a lesser extent, actual sexual behavior are changing in modern societies (Blumstein & Schwartz, 1983; W. C. Wilson, 1975; Zelnik, Kantner, & Ford, 1981). In the past, men were permitted greater sexual freedom than women, but in recent decades, this double standard has been at least partially undermined. One team of researchers has suggested that the decline of the double standard represents the most significant change in sexual attitudes that has ever taken place in America (Klassen, Williams, & Levitt, 1989). Tolerance for sexual activity outside of marriage has fluctuated over the last 20 years. In 1982, one survey showed that 49 percent of Americans disapproved of premarital sex and 92 percent disapproved of extramarital sex; by 1988, those numbers had dropped to 38 percent and 67 percent, respectively (*General Social Survey*, 1988). But in 1998, American attitudes toward adultery had taken a conservative turn. According to a Gallup poll,

four out of five of those interviewed said that extramarital sex is always wrong (Gallup Poll, 1998).

The effect that these changes will have on the family remains to be seen. If all rules against extramarital sex were removed, people might no longer feel the need to marry or remain with their mates if they did marry. Serious problems could occur in the socialization of children and concerning the family's role as a stable source of affection and companionship. But this prospect is unlikely. The most recent trend, partly a result of the AIDS crisis, has been away from the casual or promiscuous sex sometimes associated with the sexual revolution of the 1960s and 1970s.

ECONOMIC COOPERATION

The family is often defined, in part, as a group of people who form an economic unit and cooperate in economic pursuits. In rural and peasant societies, the family was, and still is, a major unit of production. Families in these societies commonly engage in agricultural production or in cottage industries, such as pottery, weaving, or metalsmithing.

In modern societies, most productive work takes place outside the home, yet the family remains an important unit of economic activity. The main economic activity of the family, however, has changed from production to consumption. The family as a unit makes most major consumer purchases, such as houses, cars, and television sets.

In economic terms, women and men typically have different relationships with the family. Nonworking wives depend on their husbands as their primary source of financial support. Working wives, who generally earn less than their husbands do, are also more economically dependent on their husbands than their husbands are on them. This situation is changing, however, with the massive entry of married women into the labor force and with the rise of single-parent families.

Conflict Perspectives

Our discussion so far has emphasized the functionalist viewpoint, stressing the ways that the family functions in the interests of society as a whole. Conflict theorists view the family in a different light. They stress that the sexes are competing with each other in various ways and that the family benefits some members much more than others. And the history of the family, they point out, is also the history of the domination of women by men.

Feminist conflict theorists note that many laws, norms, and governmental policies support male dominance (Rothman, 1989). Male dominance has become so embedded in American culture, they argue, that most people see the woman's traditionally subordinate role in the family as not only acceptable but also natural. This subordinate role is clearly expressed in the traditional marriage ceremony. Although an increasingly large number of couples are opting for a more egalitarian ceremony, traditionally brides were asked to say that they would "honor and obey" their husbands. Clergy pronounced the couple "man and wife" (rather than "husband and wife"). Women moved from the status of "Miss" to "Mrs." and relinquished their last names. Feminists see these ceremonial traditions as the symbolic beginnings of an unequal marriage relationship.

Although there is little solid information on the origins of the human family, some evidence suggests that there has always been a division of work roles within the family based on sex. Throughout early human history, it is thought, women were less mobile than men because of pregnancy and the nursing of infants. Women generally stayed home with the children and gathered food from nearby areas. Men, on the other hand, went on distant hunts for food and were often the primary economic providers. They also engaged in warlike activities (Gough, 1975; Harris, 1988).

This division of work roles within the family may have been the original basis for gender inequality, and to a large extent both the division and the inequality still exist today. Conflict theorists thus see the family as the primary arena in which gender inequality is played out. This inequality is reflected in the different social roles that mothers and fathers (and daughters and sons) play and in the distribution of power within the family; in most cases, the father still rules.

Some feminist analyses of the balance of power within the family suggest that male domination emerged in early human societies only after the advent of agriculture. While people were still hunters and gatherers—a period that includes most of human history—a more equitable working relationship between the sexes may have prevailed. As the primary food gatherers, women, not men, were the principal economic providers. Also, the tribe, not the family, was the basic economic unit, and the role of males in reproduction was imperfectly understood (Campbell, 1988). Male domination resulted, according to this view, not from the male role as provider, but only after agriculture (and warfare) were established (Blumberg, 1978; Eisler, 1987; Harris, 1977; Lipman-Blumen, 1984).

Marxian theorists have been especially concerned with the relationship between the modern family and capitalism. The male-dominated family, they assert, has greatly assisted the rise of capitalism by providing society with important forms of labor—reproduction and care of children, food preparation, and daily health care (all traditionally the responsibilities of women)—for which wages are not paid (Zaretsky, 1978). This free labor enables men to maintain their position of power and perpetuates the subordinate position of women. It is in the best interest of capitalists to try to maintain the existing gender inequality within the family (Zaretsky, 1976). Unless the capitalist system is changed, many Marxian theorists argue, gender inequality cannot be overcome (Firestone, 1971).

FAMILY STRUCTURE

Although families around the world perform many of the same functions and display many of the same inequalities, family structure differs significantly from society to society and even from group to group. Because family structure is such an important aspect of premodern societies, it has always been a special focus of the discipline of social anthropology. Widespread variations in family structure are also found in modern societies, however.

Kinship and Family

Sociologists and anthropologists make an important distinction between the family and the kinship network, although both are commonly called "families" in the English language. **Kinship** refers to a social network of people who are related by common ancestry or origin, by marriage, or by adoption. Kin can include parents; brothers and sisters; aunts and uncles; grandparents; great-aunts and great-uncles; first, second, and third cousins; and so on. The exact membership of a kinship network is determined by particular cultural norms. In some societies, kin includes more distant relatives than in others.

Kin do not always live together and function as a group. They do, however, recognize certain rights, responsibilities, and obligations to one another. In American society, kin may come together for Thanksgiving or Christmas, for marriages and funerals, or perhaps only once in a lifetime for a family reunion.

Because families take so many diverse forms, defining the family has always been a difficult task. A **family** is a relatively small domestic group of kin (or people in a kinlike relationship) who function as a cooperative unit. In the United States, the family is usually a small group consisting of parents and their children. In many societies, though, the family includes relatives from three or more generations. For example, a group of brothers and their wives, their sons and their unmarried daughters, and their sons' wives and children may live together or near one another, cooperating to raise food, maintain the home, and care for children and the elderly. If the individuals

INTERNET/TECHNOLOGY

.NET

BRAVE NEW WORLD

On November 20, 1997, Bobbi McCaughey gave birth to seven healthy babies, making headlines around the world. The media had waited for months for this historical moment. The McCaugheys called the multiple births a miracle, but medical ethicists questioned whether science had gone too far—whether multiple births like these constituted an abuse of modern high-tech medicine.

While it allows many couples to have the families they so desperately desire, critics have questioned the ethics of playing god. Some fertility specialists, who recognize the risks to mother and child, follow self-imposed guidelines in their procedures. But others do not. And the McCaughey success troubled many fertility experts who believed that couples desirous of children would minimize the complications involved in multiple births. In fact because they are more likely to be born premature, multiple-birth babies are at risk for a wide range of health problems. And the estimated cost for each baby is astronomical—as high as $250,000 for each one before it even leaves the hospital.

The McCaugheys were aware that Bobbi McCaughey could have multiple babies. She had taken the drug Metrodin to stimulate egg production. Doctors generally use a vaginal ultra-sound to determine how many eggs have been produced. And, if a woman has produced too many, doctors usually advise the couple to abstain from sex. It is not clear what happened in this particular case. The only clue came from Bobbi's physician, who responded to reporters' questions with one of her own: "Should we as a society dictate to individuals the size of their families or their choices of reproductive care?" (*Newsweek*, December 1, 1997).

Before anyone even attempted to answer this one, another woman by the name of Nkem Chukwu made the news with the announcement that she was carrying eight babies—another record. Like McCaughey, she too had used high-tech fertility techniques to become pregnant. Unfortunately, she and her husband were not as lucky as the McCaugheys—one of their babies did not survive.

Most parents will not face the prospect of multiple births, but soon enough they will have some options when it comes to planning their families. They are more likely to consider a question like this: What traits would you like your child to possess?

While that might seem farfetched, scientists expect to have that ability within a few decades (*Time*, January 11, 1999). And, in fact, pollsters have already asked Americans what they think. According to a *Time*/CNN poll conducted in December 1998, 60 percent of Americans would use genetic engineering to rule out a fatal disease. One-third of them would use it to ensure greater intelligence. And about 1 in 10 would use it to determine the sex of a baby or to influence the baby's height or weight.

This might stir up images straight out of Aldous Huxley's 1932 novel, *Brave New World*. But there is one big difference. In Huxley's utopian society, the government controlled the process of eugenics. In the United States, individual parents would. And that could

---

function as a single unit, sociologists consider them a family. If, however, they simply live next door to one another and do not pool their resources, they are considered separate families but still members of a single kin group.

During their lifetimes, most people are members of two different types of family groups. The family into which they are born and in which the major part of their socialization takes place is called the **family of orientation;** the family that people create when they marry and have children is called the **family of procreation.** Societies differ in the cultural emphasis they place on these two groups. Among the Pueblo Indians, for example, the family of orientation is accorded a special significance, whereas the family of procreation is a more casual arrangement. When a Pueblo Indian couple marry, the woman stays in her mother's household, and her husband moves in. If the couple do not get along and divorce, the husband moves back to his mother's household with little fuss. And even while the couple are married, they separate at times of celebration and for harvests; the wife remains with her family of orientation and the husband returns temporarily to his. For both, the family of orientation remains the most important family.

Americans recognize both the family of orientation and the family of procreation as "family," but our primary allegiance is typically to the family of procreation. Rarely do modern American families split at holidays, for example, with the husband and wife each returning to his or her own family of orientation.

spell disaster. Ironically, the only thing to prevent that would be government control (Wright, 1999), but public opinion today suggests that that will not happen. The results of the *Time*/CNN poll also showed that when it comes to whether the government should regulate the use of genetic testing to pick the traits of unborn children, Americans disagree. In fact, they are almost equally divided: 46 percent said yes; 49 percent said no.

How would society change with genetic engineering? Will the differences that make up who we are become a thing of the past? What are your thoughts on genetic engineering?

Nuclear and Extended Families

Although the culturally ideal American family is the **nuclear family**—a two-generation family group that consists of a couple and their children, usually living apart from other relatives—variations on this pattern are common. Death and divorce leave many families with only one parent. An elderly grandparent may join the household. Economic problems may force a married child to bring his or her spouse and children to live with the family of orientation. A daughter still living at home may have a child. When a family is a group that consists of three or more generations, it is called an **extended family.** Because the nuclear family typically places its primary emphasis on the husband-wife relationship, it can be called a *conjugal family*. When a family (usually an extended family) places primary emphasis on the "blood ties" with various relatives, it can be called a *consanguine family*.

The "intact" nuclear family is most typical of the American middle and upper classes; the single-parent family, although found throughout the class spectrum, is more common among the lower classes. Single-parent families are generally the result of divorce and separation, out-of-wedlock birth, and male unemployment. The extended family is also more common among the lower classes, mainly because of economic conditions.

Most middle-class nuclear families can afford to hire someone to babysit for their children, to help them move to a new house, or to care for the sick. They are able

The nuclear family is made up of a husband, wife, and their children; the extended family is a group consisting of three or more generations.

to borrow money from the bank when they need it for emergencies and can also afford to buy a new car. Thus there are few economic reasons for a middle-class family to be extended.

The purchase of many of these products and services is a luxury that poorer families often cannot afford. Such families generally must rely on family members and relatives to provide the goods and services they cannot afford to buy. A sister will babysit. A grandmother will come to care for a sick mother or father. A brother will lend $50 to his sister until the next payday. A cousin will take the children to a dentist, if necessary. And all the able-bodied members of the family will lend a hand on moving day. Without this network of mutual assistance, families with low incomes would not be able to provide for their needs or handle many types of emergencies. The more family members who are available, the more likely one is to get assistance (Harris, 1989; Stack, 1974). Thus, large, extended families and kin groups with strong ties can be a real advantage—indeed, a necessity—to the poor.

THE GLOBAL FAMILY TREND

Family structure around the world has been gradually changing in the direction of the nuclear form. Called the *global family trend,* this transition is thought to have begun in England (Goode, 1963). In preindustrial rural England—a time when the extended family was still prevalent in much of Europe—families of three or more generations were already a distinct minority (Goody, 1983; Laslett, 1977; Laslett & Wall, 1972).

Today, the trend toward the nuclear family seems to be closely associated with urbanization, industrialization, and the worldwide modernization of societies (Harris, 1983; Kerr et al., 1964; Moore, 1979). As industry replaces agriculture as the main form of work, younger family members typically leave the farms and rural villages and move to the cities where jobs are located, often weakening ties with those left behind. Once in the cities, families continue to move for employment and other reasons (such as better housing conditions, retirement, and a more comfortable climate) (Mintz & Kellogg, 1988; Thernstrom, 1973). The agricultural family is likely to be extended and tied to a piece of land, while the industrial family is nuclear and much more mobile.

The decline of the extended family is thus promoted by the changing nature of work. In rural societies, as among the poor in industrial societies, the extended family offers an economic advantage. Each member of the family does some productive work. Children, the elderly, and the handicapped do not do the same work as able-bodied adults, but each can contribute to the economic welfare of the family unit. In industrial societies, however, the young, the elderly and the physically handicapped are more economically expendable and are employed only under certain conditions (for example, during a labor shortage). They therefore produce little for the family unit, yet they consume at about the same rate as do producers. The extended family can therefore constitute a burden rather than an advantage in industrial societies.

The transition from the extended to the nuclear family has brought with it much greater freedom and personal mobility for the individual. In the extended family, individual needs are generally subordinated to the demands of the larger group. Privacy, for example, is difficult to find.

But there are drawbacks to the nuclear family, too. Although individuals are freed from a broad range of responsibilities and obligations, other family members are, conversely, no longer as obligated to or responsible for them. Because the family is now a smaller unit, emotional and economic support may be more limited. Each family member has fewer people available to turn to for gratification, affection, companionship, or assistance. The result may be the increased social isolation of individuals (Popenoe, 1988; Zaretsky, 1976).

Authority in the Family

Throughout Western history, family authority has always been patriarchal. A **patriarchal family** is a family structure in which most of the authority is held by the oldest male. The *patriarch* may be a grandfather or an uncle in an extended family, or the father in a nuclear family. The patriarch has the final word in family decisions—where the family will live, how its goods will be used, whom the children may marry. Within patriarchal families, women generally have their own realms of authority, usually concerning the home and the children, but even in these areas final authority rests with the dominant male. The day-to day operation of the kitchen, for example, may be the responsibility of the woman, but a major purchase, such as a new oven, will require the approval of the patriarch.

Conversely, a **matriarchal family** would be a family structure in which most of the authority is in the hands of the oldest female. Some social scientists have claimed that at a very early stage of human history, matriarchy was the predominant family form. This claim was commonly made in the nineteenth century (Bachofen, 1861/1967; Engels, 1884/1977). Most modern scholars disagree, however (Bamberger, 1974; Harris, 1989; Webster, 1975; Westermarck, 1894/1901). There is no solid evidence to suggest that women ever held the level of familial and, therefore, societal authority that men do now.

In patriarchal societies, women may rule individual families by default. A family in which a woman is the central and most important member is called a **matrifocal family.** Such a pattern occurs when men are absent because of war or distant employment, or, more commonly in modern societies, when there are high rates of divorce and illegitimacy. Many of these families may be matrifocal only in a formal sense, however, as live-in boyfriends and even absent or former husbands may in reality wield considerable power.

Although most American families still tend to be patriarchal, a new pattern is emerging in modern societies: the **egalitarian family** (Malmaud, 1984; Young & Willmott, 1974). This is a family in which the husband and wife are roughly equal in authority and privilege. Like many family trends, the rise of the egalitarian family is related to industrialization. In modern societies, men are often away from home for 8 to 12 hours of every workday, which necessarily reduces their authority. Because wives are also increasingly members of the labor force too, they are less economically dependent on their

husbands, which enhances their power within the family. Because of such changes, more and more husbands and wives are sharing family authority.

Yet even in relatively egalitarian families, many important decisions are commonly still made by the husband. The husband's occupation, for example, typically determines where and how the family will live. Only rarely does a family move because the wife has been transferred or offered a better job in another city, although a number of dual-career couples today have become "commuter couples." These women and men pursue careers in different cities and spend weekends together in one of their two residences (Taylor & Lounsbury, 1988).

Marital Residence

Another important family pattern with regard to which societies differ concerns marital residence—where a couple settle after marriage. In some societies, **patrilocal residence** is the custom. A married couple live in the household or community of the husband's parents. In these cultures, a son brings his bride to live in or near his parents' house, and a daughter moves to her new husband's household. In societies that practice **matrilocal residence,** the opposite occurs. A married couple live in the household or community of the wife's parents. Daughters stay in their parents' household, and sons go to live with their wives and her parents. The Pueblo and Navajo Indians of the American Southwest, for example, practice patrilocal residence, while the traditional customs of the northeastern Iroquois and Huron tribes are matrilocal.

Although some American families follow matrilocal or patrilocal patterns, particularly first- and second-generation immigrants, most newlyweds set up separate homes. The pattern in which a married couple live apart from either spouse's parents or other relatives is called **neolocal residence.** This gives the couple enhanced privacy, mobility, and individual identity, but it also tends to isolate families from their kinship networks.

Descent and Inheritance

The way in which kinship and lineage are traced over generations is referred to as *descent*. Descent may be traced, and property inherited, in three ways. In **patrilineal descent,** the father's side of the family, but not the mother's, is defined as kin. In a patrilineal system, males inherit property through the male side of the family; females generally are not permitted to inherit. In **matrilineal descent,** the mother's side of the family, but not the father's, is defined as kin; descent is traced on the female side of the family, with property typically passed from mother to daughter. In **bilateral descent**—the system

In some societies, parents or village elders arrange mate selection. This is done to ensure the family's economic and social standing.

typical of most industrial societies, including the United States—children's kinship is tied to both sides of the family, and both male and female children are entitled to inherit.

MARRIAGE, DIVORCE, AND WIDOWHOOD

In extended family systems, the selection of a son's or daughter's marriage partner is very important to the entire family. A lazy spouse or a spouse who wants to lure a son or daughter away from the extended family is a serious threat to family stability. Also, because marriages play an important role in establishing the entire family's economic and social standing, mate selection is a way of making connections between kinship groups. In such societies, mate selection is typically considered too important to be left to the individuals involved and is arranged by parents or village elders. Sometimes the arranged choice of a spouse violates the children's wishes.

Young people in modern societies may find the practice of arranged marriages hard to understand, much less to accept. It should be realized, however, that marriage in these extended families is more a matter of economics than of love. Also, an "imperfect" spouse does not

matter as much in a large extended family as it does in an isolated, nuclear family. Marriage is but one of many close, personal relationships in an extended family.

In modern Western societies, romantic love and individual choice, rather than economics and parental arrangement, have become the principles on which marriage is based (Davis, 1985; Goode, 1959). Because the main function of marriage in these societies is to provide companionship and intimacy—perhaps the most intimate relationship people ever know—strong emphasis is placed on personal choice. Alliances between families are relatively unimportant, and married couples usually live apart from their kin. The choice of a marriage partner, therefore, may not directly affect anyone but the couple and the children they may have.

Choosing a Marriage Partner

All societies place some restrictions on the choice of sexual and marriage partners. The **incest taboo**—a powerful moral prohibition against sexual relations between certain categories of relatives—is an almost universal restriction. Incest taboos typically apply to the members of the nuclear family, but sometimes to more distant relatives as well. In the United States, sexual relations and marriage between parents and children and between brothers and sisters are strictly forbidden. A few states also outlaw marriages between first cousins. Some societies have prohibited marriage between relatives as distant as sixth cousins.

Very few officially allowed exceptions to the rule that prohibits sexual relations between brothers and sisters are known to have existed historically. Two exceptions occurred in the royal families of ancient Egypt and Hawaii, where brothers and sisters married each other because they were the only members of society of high enough rank for each other. These exceptions applied only to the royal family, however; incest was strictly prohibited for everyone else. Another exception is found in modern Sweden, where brother-sister incest has been decriminalized (Harris, 1989).

Many theories have tried to account for the near universality of the incest taboo (Murdock, 1949). Biological theories, which typically focus on the mental and physical degeneration that may result from inbreeding, are questionable for two reasons. First, inbreeding does not necessarily produce degeneration; and second, the negative effects of inbreeding generally occur too slowly to be noticed over the course of a few generations. Many social scientists, therefore, believe that the incest taboo is culturally determined (Harris, 1989). One common explanation is that the incest taboo helps to prevent conflict within the kinship group. Without the taboo, rivalries could seriously disrupt family stability. A daughter might compete with her mother for her father's affections, for example, or brothers might become hostile toward one another as each pursues a sister.

In addition to incest taboos, some cultures have norms that prescribe **endogamy,** marriage within one's own group. In American society, endogamy is still the norm among some ethnic groups. Orthodox Jews, for example, traditionally mourn children who have married non-Jews as though they were dead. Many American Greeks also encourage endogamy; they feel that marriage to non-Greeks weakens their culture, because Greek-Americans who marry outside the group are less likely to pass the Greek language and traditions on to their children (Schultz, 1981).

Other cultures encourage **exogamy,** the social norm that prescribes marriage outside one's own group. This is often the norm in small societies in which almost everyone is, at least distantly, related by blood or marriage. In such societies, marriage partners must come from another village. This practice helps to strengthen ties between neighboring groups, as each spouse has kin living in another community. Building on these kinship ties, the alliance between the villages can lead to strengthened economic relations through the exchange of goods and services (Lévi-Strauss, 1969). The norm of exogamy can also be seen in the traditional Christian rule prohibiting marriage between persons closer than third cousins.

In the United States, only a few patterns of marital choice are prohibited. Prospective partners may not already be married; they must be of legal age; they may not be close relatives; they must be of different sexes; and they may not be members of a religious community that requires a vow of celibacy. However, all other marriages are legally permitted. Officially, whites can marry blacks, Jews can marry Protestants, and socialites can marry janitors. But in practice, most Americans choose to marry people of roughly the same class, racial, ethnic, and religious background as themselves. This pattern of marriage between individuals having similar social characteristics is called **homogamy.**

Homogamy is based in part on the subtle discouragement of exogamy by many American subcultures. It often has been difficult, for example, for a Catholic to marry a non-Catholic in a church ceremony unless both partners promise to raise their children in the Catholic faith. Parental pressure and perhaps the threat of disinheritance have prevented many a debutante from marrying someone of lower social status. And widespread social disapproval of interracial marriages among all races lessens the chances of such marriages.

Homogamy serves two important functions. First, and probably most important, it increases the chances that the children of a union will be exposed to reasonably consistent socialization experiences. When strongly non-homogamous people marry, it is likely that they will disagree about many aspects of how they should raise their offspring, with negative consequences in many cases for the next generation. Marital homogamy is also an important way in which disputes over issues other than child socialization can be minimized. Because people who are very much like each other socially tend to share common values, homogamous marriage increases the chances of a relatively happy marriage and decreases the odds of divorce.

In traditional societies, homogamy was usually assured by the practice of arranged marriages. In modern life, it is typically a reflection of the fact that most people prefer to associate mainly with "their own kind." And even if they do not share such a preference, their chances of meeting and mixing with members of their own group are much greater than their chances of associating with "outsiders."

Americans tend to marry others of the same religious faith and from the same racial group. While the rate of interracial marriages has been increasing, only 2.4 percent of the nearly 55 million married couples in the United States in 1998 were interracial. Of the black/white couples, two thirds consisted of a black husband and a white wife (U.S. Bureau of the Census, *Current Population Reports,* January 7, 1999).

Although interclass marriages are more common in the United States than either interfaith or interracial unions, there is, nonetheless, a strong tendency for people to marry within their own class (Benokraitis, 1999; Clayton, 1975; Simon, 1987). People also usually marry within their own age group. The median age difference between spouses in the United States is only about two years, with most husbands being older than their wives (U.S. Bureau of the Census, *Statistical Abstract of the United States, 1998*).

Although people tend to marry others much like themselves, another tendency—called the marriage gradient—operates as well. The **marriage gradient** is the tendency of men to marry women who are younger than they are, have less education, and work at less prestigious occupations.

Courtship and Romantic Love

Most Americans believe in "love" as the most important basis for marriage (Cancian, 1987; Walster & Walster, 1978). We talk about it, sing about it, and write novels, plays, and poems about it. The kind of love that is typically considered essential as a basis for marriage is a mixture of sexual attraction, feelings of excitement and even ecstasy, and idealization of the loved one. The entire complex of norms surrounding marriage is tied to this ideal of romantic love. Many people even believe that the loss of this kind of love is cause for divorce.

Romantic love has not always been considered important in marriage, however. In traditional societies, as we have seen, an individual may not choose his or her own marriage partner at all, much less choose the partner because of love. Individuals who live in these societies are expected to put the needs and desires of their families or tribes above their own. If a marriage partner is a good choice for the family, she or he is considered a good choice for the individual as well.

In Western industrial societies, though, there is a strong belief in the rights of the individual. We try to choose our marriage partners principally on the basis of personal fulfillment (although economic necessity remains an important factor for many couples).

What effect does this cultural value have on the institution of marriage? It is likely that romantic love alone is not the ideal basis on which to establish a lasting marriage. Many people meet, fall madly in love, and marry in one great sweep of emotion. They expect the excitement of new love to survive years of domestic and economic routine. They feel cheated when their spouse's romantic feelings diminish. The idea that the excitement should last forever puts a strain on both partners. Disappointment may lead to bitterness within the marriage, to adultery, and perhaps to divorce.

Mutual support and social similarity, rather than romance, appear to be of central importance for lasting marital love. One scholar has aptly described a good marriage as "that relationship between one person and another which is most conducive to the optimal development of both" (Foote, 1953, p. 247). In order to satisfy each other emotionally, the marriage partners must recognize each other's needs and desires, share experiences, and value each other as individuals. This kind of love is highly related both to the personal maturity of each partner and to the similarity, or at least the compatibility, of their basic values and beliefs. As one scholar put it, "romantic" love must grow into "rational" love—a love characterized by realistic acceptance of the other, communication, and giving and receiving (Zastrow, 1986).

There are strong indications that such compatibility may be the most important social factor in marital stability (Zimmerman & Cervantes, 1960). Many studies have shown that in marriage opposites do *not* attract—for very long. A study of 331 military couples, for example, found that the couples least satisfied with their marriages were those in which the husband's attitudes toward sex roles were traditional and the wife's, modern (Bowen & Orthner, 1983). Another study concluded that people with similar dispositions usually achieve greater happiness and marital stability. Similarities in need for intimacy, inclinations toward extroversion, preferred leisure activities, and interpersonal and argumentative styles contribute strongly to the compatibility of married couples (Buss, 1984). The most satisfying relationships seem to be based on unions between men and women with roughly equal combinations of beauty, charisma, influence, intelligence, wealth, and other resources.

Marriage

Marriage is sociologically defined as a socially approved mating arrangement, usually involving sexual activity and economic cooperation, between a man and a woman. The marriage system of the United States is based on **monogamy**—that is, marriage between one man and one woman. Marriage involving more than one man or woman at the same time is called **polygamy.** The most common type of polygamous marriage is called **polygyny,** in which one man has more than one wife at the same time. The opposite situation, in which one woman has more than one husband, is called **polyandry.**

Polygyny is widespread around the world. George Murdock's classic study (1949) of 238 societies (most of which were premodern) found that 193 were characterized by polygyny, 43 by monogamy, and 2 by polyandry. Polygyny is still prevalent in parts of Africa and Asia and in tribal societies in the Middle East, where Muslim males are permitted to have four wives at one time. The wives and all the children usually live together under one roof, sharing domestic responsibilities. Typically based on economic necessity, polygyny helps to increase the number of births in a society or to make up for the shortage of men that may result from war.

The great majority of Americans marry and spend most of their lives in a family group. Indeed, a higher percentage of people in the United States marry than in any other modern society. In 1990, 92 percent of all women over the age of 40 were or had been married, and husbands and wives living together headed approximately 75 percent of all American families with children under the age of 18 (U.S. Bureau of the Census, *Statistical Abstract of the United States, 1998*).

But the current trend is toward marrying later in life. The median age of first marriage for women is now 25.0, the highest since the government began keeping that statistic in 1890. For men, the median age at first marriage is 26.7 (U.S. Bureau of the Census, *Current Population Survey,* January 7, 1999). And a growing number of people are choosing not to marry at all. Between 1970 and 1997, the number of single-person households more than doubled, increasing from 10.9 million to 25.4 million. Single-person households now account for about one-quarter of all households. The largest increase occurred among single women, who constitute 58 percent of all persons living alone. In 1990, 31.0 percent of all women aged 25 to 29 had never been married (U.S. Bureau of the Census, *Statistical Abstract of the United States, 1998*). The factors explaining these trends include women's new opportunities to get an education and to have a career.

One fear common to young people who choose either not to marry or to postpone marriage is that their marriage might be unhappy. Just how happy is the average marriage in the United States? Accurate data about the emotional quality of married life are not easy to obtain, and there is probably a tendency for people to report their marriages are happier than they really are. Nonetheless, some evidence suggests that there is a wide gap between the ideal marriage and reality, especially in the working class.

In a pioneering study of 58 working-class marriages, Mirra Komarovsky (1964) found that the couples expected relatively little from each other. Husbands and wives tended to lead separate lives. The husband usually spent time with his buddies, the wife with female relatives and friends. In general, these people did not seem to think closeness and companionship were especially important. About one-third of the couples in the sample described their marriages as happy, one-third as unhappy. As long as the family stayed together and remained financially stable, the spouses were more or less content. Most considered marriage to be a necessary and useful relationship.

Another well-known study of family life in the working class was conducted by Lillian Breslow Rubin. In her book *Worlds of Pain* (1976), Rubin reached conclusions very similar to those of Komarovsky: Marriage within the working class usually came at an early age, after a very short courtship. In these marriages, little attention was paid to such qualities as sharing, communication, or intimacy. The most important marriage goals were being able to provide a reasonably good living and "being good to the children." However, a more recent study of families in one midwestern American town over a 58-year period (from 1920 to 1978) presents a different picture. The attitudes of the working-class families in this town did not differ significantly from those of the business-class families. Couples from both classes expressed satisfaction with their relationships and indicated that open communication and mutual support were the primary qualities that contributed to their happiness (Bahr et al., 1982).

Studies that include a representative cross section of the U.S. population have found a relatively high level of marital happiness (National Opinion Research Center,

In the United States, a higher percentage of people marry than in any other modern society.

1992, 1994; Glenn & Weaver, 1988). One survey of married couples reported that 60 percent rated their marriages as very happy, 36 percent as pretty happy, and only 3 percent as not too happy (*General Social Survey,* National Opinion Research Center, 1994). Another study showed that over half of all married couples would marry the same person again, if they could do it over again (Patterson & Kim, 1991). Research also suggests that, for most Americans, overall happiness depends more on having a good marriage than on any other variable, including job satisfaction and family relations (Glenn & Weaver, 1981).

Divorce and Remarriage

Divorce was relatively uncommon during the nineteenth century. But after the turn of the century, the divorce rate began to rise and grew steadily for most of the twentieth century. In 1970, for every 1,000 married people living with their spouses, there were 47 divorced people. This figure rose to 100 in 1980 and to 138 in 1989—almost triple the 1970 rate (U.S. Bureau of the Census, 1990b). By 1990, there were 1,182,000 divorces per year. In recent years, the divorce rate has declined slightly. In 1997, the total number of divorces granted was 1,163,000, the lowest number in 20 years.

Many family relations specialists are alarmed by increases in the number of divorces involving families with dependent children. In 1956, 361,000 children were involved in divorces. By 1988, the number had almost tripled to 1,091,000 children (National Center for Health Statistics, 1989). It has been estimated that 41 percent of all children will experience the disruption of their parents' marriage by age 15 (National Center for Health Statistics, 1989).

Research into the impact of divorce on children indicates that some of its negative effects can be quite enduring. The factors related to these consequences include the absence of a parent, lower family income, failure in school, a child's age and gender, and the reactions of outsiders (Benokraitis, 1999). One study concluded that, compared with children from intact families, children from divorced families perceive their relationships with their parents as less positive—that is, more distant, less affectionate, and less communicative (Fine, Moreland, & Schwebel, 1984). Other research suggests that in the long run divorce tends to be more emotionally destabilizing to older children than to very young ones, who have few memories of life before the breakup and, unlike older children, feel no responsibility for it. Older children are also more likely to carry fears of abandonment into their subsequent relationships than younger children (Camara, 1986; Wallerstein & Kelly, 1981).

Regardless of their age at the time of a divorce, research shows that divorce does often hurt children (Biblarz & Rafferty, 1993; Walther, 1991). Children from divorced families are more likely than children from intact families to have problems at school, to isolate themselves from others, and to become addicted to drugs or alcohol. They are also more likely to suffer from eating disorders, to shoplift, and to become promiscuous.

At the time of the divorce, children experience a range of feelings, most commonly fear, abandonment, rejection, sadness, worry, loneliness, conflicting loyalties, anger, and guilt. However, a child's long-term adjustment to divorce cannot be predicted by his or her early responses to it. Some psychological effects may remain dormant and show up only at later stages of development or even in adulthood. In one study that interviewed children of divorce 10 to 15 years after the divorce had taken place, 50 percent of the respondents reported that their parents' divorce occupied a central emotional position in their lives (Wallerstein & Blakeslee, 1989).

The quality of family relationships following divorce has a strong influence on the way children adjust to the breakup of the marriage. Children have a better chance of adjusting if their parents maintain positive communication, show respect for one another, and demonstrate a low level of conflict (Bohannan, 1985). However, the quality of the mother-child bond appears to be the most critical factor in determining how children feel about themselves and how well they function in various areas of their lives in the years following the divorce of their parents (Wallerstein & Blakeslee, 1989).

Although divorce is generally regarded negatively, it can be a positive event for children in certain situations, especially for those children whose parents have abused them or fought violently (Demo & Acock, 1988). In fact, some research indicates that the children who suffer the most after a divorce are those whose parents had not behaved violently or bitterly at home (Bohannan, 1985).

The situation of a divorced parent with children is often more difficult in the United States than it is in other modern societies. Most West European nations support families with a wide range of social and welfare services, including family allowances (money given to all families with dependent children), preferential access to public housing, child-care programs for the children of working mothers, and free childhood health care (Kamerman & Kahn, 1981; Morgan, 1986). These services help to ease the strains of family breakup.

In contrast, the family in the United States is commonly looked on as part of the private sphere and thus not an entirely suitable focus of governmental action (Steiner, 1981). When family services are provided in the United States, it is usually only after the family has already broken up.

The children of divorced couples in the United States must often rely heavily on child-support payments from their father. But almost 50 percent of all fathers fail to support their children (Hewlett, 1990). Whether or not such payments are required typically depends on the mother's social status. In 1991, 56 percent of the 9.9 million women living with children under 21 whose fathers were not present in the household had legal agreements to receive child-support payments from the fathers (U.S. Bureau of the Census, *Statistical Abstract of the United States, 1998*). While 68 percent of white mothers had child-support agreements, only 41 percent of Hispanic mothers and 35 percent of black mothers had such agreements. Also, more college-educated women were awarded child-support payments than women with only a high school education. Moreover, being granted child-support payments in court did not necessarily mean that payments were actually made. Of the women who had been granted child support in 1989, only 75 percent actually received any money from the fathers of their children (U.S. Bureau of the Census, 1993).

REMARRIAGE

A majority of divorced people remarry. Indeed, more than 4 in 10 of all marriages today involve a remarriage for one or both spouses (Benokraitis, 1999). Divorced men and women usually remarry within three to four years after their divorce. And approximately 8 in 10 remarriages involve children acquired in previous marriages (Kantrowitz & Wingert, 1990). Certain personal characteristics influence the probability of remarriage: young, white, affluent men and poor women are more likely to remarry (Benokraitis, 1999). The odds of success in second marriages are not as high as in first marriages, however. Overall, 60 percent of remarriages have failed in recent years; when children are involved, the failure rate increases to 75 percent (DiCanio, 1989).

One explanation for the high divorce rate in second marriages is that remarried couples may monitor their relationships more closely than do people in first marriages. Because they are more sensitive to the warning signs, they are more likely to bail out before the predictable—and bitter—end (Frank Furstenberg, Jr., reported in Cox, 1983). The fact that they have already been through one divorce makes another one much easier to contemplate. Furthermore, a carryover of feelings and problems from the first marriage can interfere in the development of a successful new relationship (DiCanio, 1989). The problems associated with stepparenting are also contributing factors (Cherlin, 1983).

The common pattern of marriage, divorce (or widowhood), and remarriage, which may repeat several times in a person's life, has led some sociologists to characterize the American marriage system as "serial monogamy" or "sequential polygamy." That is, many Americans have several spouses in their lifetimes, but they have only one at a time. One prominent scholar noted that "probably more persons practice plural marriage in our society . . . than in societies that are avowedly polygamous"(Bernard, 1956).

ANALYZING THE DIVORCE RATE

The statistics on marriage, divorce, and remarriage may imply that many Americans have a negative opinion of married life. But the opposite seems closer to the truth. Although individual Americans may give up on particular marriages, as a group Americans remain strongly committed to the institution itself. Our very high marriage and remarriage rates testify to this.

Some of the primary social characteristics of divorcing persons have been identified. Divorce rates tend to be high for those who marry in their teens, have only a short acquaintanceship before marriage, do not attend religious services, and live in urban rather than rural areas (Kitson, Babri, & Roach, 1985). Other researchers have found that disapproval of the marriage by friends and family is an important indicator of instability ahead, since this disapproval represents not only a prediction by people who know the couple but also a vote of nonconfidence from those who could have helped bind the couple together (Goode, 1982). Early studies found that divorce rates were higher in the lower and working classes than in the middle and upper classes. This pattern was generally explained by reference to economic pressures. But in recent years divorce rates have increased more steeply in the higher classes than in the lower classes, and the differences in divorce rates between the classes have all but disappeared.

Some researchers have concluded that the employment situations of the husband and wife have a marked effect on whether a marriage will last. Couples are more likely to divorce if the husband has trouble finding or keeping a job and also if the wife has the ability to earn her own living. The wife's work situation is of particular importance. It appears that women who are able to support themselves rather than depend on their husbands' incomes do not have to stay in unhappy marriages, and they therefore divorce at a higher rate (Blumstein & Schwartz, 1983; Rix, 1989; Ross & Sawhill, 1975).

It is more difficult to determine why a particular marriage has failed. The reasons for divorce often include personality conflicts, economic hardship, conflicts over childrearing, religious differences, trouble with in-laws, and sexual incompatibility.

On a broader level, the high divorce rate in the United States is related to a variety of the characteristics of our society (Cherlin, 1983). Some of these characteristics, such as the relative isolation of the nuclear family, were discussed earlier. Others include the high rate of residential mobility (the movement from one home to another); the ongoing redefinition of family and gender roles; and the great ethnic diversity of American society, which means that people with different backgrounds and conflicting values are more likely to meet and to marry.

Over the years, divorce laws in the United States have become more liberal; that is, divorces have become easier to obtain because the legal grounds for divorce have been expanded. In many cases, it is no longer necessary to prove blame. In 1970, California became the first state to accept the concept of "no-fault divorce." This principle, which eliminates the need for costly and painful court battles when an amicable settlement can be reached voluntarily, has now been adopted by many other states. Such changes in the law may have contributed to the rising divorce rate, but they are also a reflection of changing attitudes about divorce.

Widowhood

There are approximately 13.7 million widowed men and women in the United States. Women make up the sizable majority of widowed persons, because they tend to live longer than men and also because they usually marry men a few years older than themselves (U.S. Bureau of the Census, *Statistical Abstract of the United States, 1998*). Widowed women do not remarry as often as widowed men, so many widowed women remain unmarried for the rest of their lives.

In the United States, many older women whose husbands die find themselves in a difficult position. Although some move in with married sons or daughters, others lead exceedingly lonely lives, cut off from family and married friends who tend to prefer to socialize with other couples. Unlike widowers, widows tend to experience serious economic problems as well. Because many widows depended on their husbands for financial support, they are often inadequately prepared to enter the labor market. With the rising cost of living, the widows' main means of support—pensions, Social Security, and life insurance policies—often prove inadequate. Better educated widows have an easier time reconstructing their lives after their loss, financially and socially, than do those with little education (Lopata, 1986, 1987).

THE CHANGING AMERICAN FAMILY

Where is the American family headed? Demographic trends, increasing numbers of single-parent families and stepfamilies, changes in the family's relation to work, family violence and child abuse, and alternatives to marriage and the nuclear family are all having an impact on the American family today.

Single parents face an array of economic, social, and emotional problems. One challenge is having to perform the functions of both parents.

Demographic Trends

Many changes in the family stem from underlying demographic trends that are found in all modern societies. The average life expectancy for a person born in 1920 was 55 years. Today, however, the average man can expect to live to be 73, the average women, 79 (U.S. Bureau of the Census, *Statistical Abstract of the United States, 1998*). In addition, childbearing and childrearing are no longer the lifelong jobs that they were when parents typically had their first children early in life, raised large families, and died young. An increasing number of women born since World War II have been postponing the birth of their first child until they are well into their 20s, and many have been having only one or, at most, two children (Rix, 1989; Wilkie, 1981). In fact, an increasing number of couples are electing not to have any children at all.

These trends have greatly lengthened the number of years at the beginning and end of the family life cycle in which a woman has no childrearing functions. Even allowing for increases in the age at which the first child is usually born, most women with only two children will have reached the so-called empty-nest stage while in their 40s. This significant reduction in the amount of a married woman's life that is devoted to childrearing is strongly associated with the move of women into the labor force.

Single-Parent Families and Stepfamilies

The prevalence of divorce and remarriage has led to a significant increase in the number of single-parent and stepfamilies in the last few decades. Single parents today head more than one-fourth of all families in the United States. The majority of these single-parent families—84 percent—are headed by women. And it has been estimated that half of all American children born today (45 percent of all white children and 86 percent of all black children) will spend at least part of their childhood in a family headed by a mother who is divorced, separated, unwed, or widowed (Garfinkel & McLanahan, 1986).

Single-parent families struggle with a wide array of economic, social, and emotional problems. These families often experience economic instability, periodic loss of income, relocation, changes in family roles and responsibilities, and emotional stress. One study showed that single parents frequently reported problems with child discipline, guilt, insecurity, ex-spouses, lowered standards of living, and depression (Garfinkel & McLanahan, 1986). Single parents of either sex also struggle with the problems and challenges of performing the functions of two parents.

Since most divorced people remarry, however, there is an increasing number of *stepfamilies,* or *blended families.* These are families in which children are present from previous marriages, and sometimes from the current marriage as well, with the adults being parents to some of the children and stepparents to others (Bohannan, 1985; DiCanio, 1989). In 1991 (the most recent data available), nearly 10 percent of children lived in stepfamilies (Benokraitis, 1999). About half of all children born in America after 1970 can expect to live in stepfamilies at some time in their lives, the majority of whom will be the children of divorced parents. Stepfamilies often become quite complex. Unfortunately, few guidelines exist for successfully creating blended families, and hostility, jealousy, insecurity, and competition frequently result from the tensions between stepchildren and adults struggling to form new family units. The roles of the "real" parents and the stepparents are often confusing to the adults and resented by the children.

In general, members of blended families usually report that it takes anywhere from three to six years to form a solid identity as a new family. Children's adjustment to the new family, it has been noted, is enhanced when they are given opportunities to express their feelings and to participate in making decisions.

Another major problem that divorced parents commonly face concerns the issue of child custody. One increasingly popular solution to this problem is the *joint custody* arrangement, in which the two parents share authority over the children (Atkins, 1986). In this arrangement, the children may move back and forth between the homes of the parents weekly, monthly, or perhaps semiannually. Parents must be on reasonably friendly terms for joint custody to work well, and they must make extra efforts to instill a sense of security in the children.

Work and the Family

The movement of married women into the labor force has been called one of the most significant social revolutions of the twentieth century (Shreve, 1984; Smith, 1979). Women now constitute over 45 percent of the paid American work force. Among mothers with children under the age of six, 64.8 percent are now in the labor force, a dramatic increase from 36.7 percent in 1975 (U.S. Bureau of Labor Statistics, 1998).

The entry of married women into the paid labor force has altered the traditional gender-role division in many families. This change has taken place largely in families of the higher classes, where the increase in female labor force participation has been greatest and where women tend to be more career-oriented than are women of the working and lower classes. In working and lower-class families, gender roles have been more resistant to change.

One unforeseen consequence of changing gender roles is that approximately 2.1 million children between 5 and 13 years old have no adult supervision after school (Select Committee on Children, Youth, and Families, 1989). Called "latchkey children," these youngsters tend to have higher than average in-home accident rates and are also more subject to problems at school. In some cases, local libraries have become alternatives to expensive day care, hiring sitters, or leaving children alone at home. Libraries report increases over the last few decades in the numbers of children who wait there after school to be picked up by a parent (DeCandido, 1988).

American society has changed in some ways in order to adapt to the increases in the participation of mothers in the labor force. A growing (but still very small) number of husbands and wives, especially in the middle class, are sharing household chores and responsibility for child care. And, although most children of working mothers are still cared for informally by friends or relatives, there has been an increase in the availability of institutional day care. There were over 98,000 licensed child-care centers in the United States in 1997 (U.S. Bureau of the Census, 1998). Many of these, however, are private facilities, operated by businesses and industries for their employees. As yet, there are relatively few public day-care centers, and very little public funding for day care is available in the United States. In fact, one survey found the lack of affordable, available day care to be the third leading problem in urban areas today (U.S. Conference of Mayors, 1988).

This situation is in stark contrast to the child-care systems found in many of the world's nations. More than 100 countries have national child-care policies, and many European nations operate extensive day-care programs. In Denmark, for example, 44 percent of children younger than three and 69 percent of children three to five years of age are enrolled in public day-care facilities.

Efforts to improve the child-care system in the United States have met with mixed success. At the state level, California, Minnesota, Massachusetts, New York, and Connecticut have been leaders in providing funds for day-care facilities, but many states have no programs at all. The city of San Francisco recently initiated an innovative approach: All developers of commercial office space are now required either to provide an on-site child-care center or to contribute to the city's child-care program.

At the national level, there is little chance for the passage of legislation establishing a federal system of day-care services. However, the Family and Medical Leave Act, which was signed into law by President Bill Clinton in

February 1993, does represent a significant effort to respond to the special problems of families with working mothers. The act requires companies with 50 or more employees to allow up to 12 weeks of unpaid leave so that an employee, male or female, can care for a newborn or newly adopted infant (or for themselves or a family member who is seriously ill). While on leave, employees are entitled to continued health-care coverage and they are guaranteed their old job or a comparable new one when they return to work. But this act will benefit only about 40 percent of the American work force; employees of small firms, part-time workers, people who have been at a company less than one year, and the highest paid 10 percent of a company's work force are exempt from coverage (Scanlan, 1993).

A decline in maternal care for children, without compensation from either fathers or public services, could have lasting implications for American children. Many concerned people, therefore, are seeking ways to get fathers more involved in childrearing. They are also trying to provide more flexible working schedules for the parents of young children, as well as to expand community services for child care and development (Hunt & Hunt, 1982; Galinsky, 1986).

DUAL-EARNER FAMILIES

Many married women still work only part time or repeatedly enter and leave the labor market. But there is a growing number of families, called **dual-earner families,** in which both partners work continuously and full time over an extended period of time. These families are frequently committed to sharing household tasks and putting equal emphasis on the jobs of both spouses,

There are several advantages to dual-earner families. Besides a larger income, dual-earners can provide a positive and egalitarian role model for their children.

though the career timetables of the wives may differ from those of the husbands (Fava & Genovese, 1983; Hertz, 1986).

Dual-earner families offer several advantages. They can provide wider employment horizons for women and more positive and egalitarian role models for children. They can accommodate the desire "to break out of stereotypic roles so that family members may strive for personal accomplishment" (Rapoport & Rapoport, 1978). And, of course, dual-earner families enjoy larger incomes.

These advantages, however, are frequently accompanied by hectic, high-pressure lifestyles, particularly for mothers (Johnson & Johnson, 1980). Although traditional gender-role expectations have shifted slightly, research shows that working women continue to assume the major responsibility for household chores, child care, and social arrangements (Bielby & Bielby, 1989). American mothers who work full time spend, on the average, 40 hours a week on their jobs and 36 hours on their homes and children (Crouter & Perry-Jenkins, 1986). Two-career couples, therefore, need to develop a variety of strategies for the special problems that arise when no "wife-mother" is present to tackle child care, social events, and home chores or to buffer the other demands of ordinary life (Hochschild, 1989; Nadelson & Nadelson, 1980).

As an alternative to juggling employment and family, some women have taken to "sequencing" their roles (Cardozo, 1986). The typical sequence is as follows: First, the woman builds her career for a number of years. Then she takes a few years off to stay at home as a full-time mother, following which time she may return to work part time. Finally, she reincorporates her career into her family and home life. This pattern allows a woman to "have it all," but also requires that she take the risk of sacrificing occupational gains when she leaves the work force to raise her children. The success of sequencing also relies to some extent on the willingness of employers to offer opportunities to women who have been away from the work force for some time.

Family Violence

It is not known for sure whether American families are more abusive today than they were in earlier times, or whether violence in the home is merely attracting more attention now. What is clear, however, is that the problem of family violence is widespread, and that both the severity of reported cases and the number of fatalities are increasing (see Figure 14.1) (Benokraitis, 1999). According to a 1994 Gallup poll, one in seven Americans reported being a victim of child abuse (Moore, 1994). This national survey also showed that 13 percent of the

	TYPE OF VIOLENCE	ESTIMATED INCIDENTS YEARLY	VICTIMS	ABUSERS
VIOLENCE AGAINST CHILDREN	Physical abuse and neglect	Over 3.1 million cases reported. As many as 9 million possible; 46 per 1,000 children.	52% of victims are female; 47% are male. 26% were 3 years or younger. Over 50% were less than 8; 26% between 8 and 12, and 21% teenagers.	Teen mothers are more abusive than older mothers. 70% of men who abuse their wives also abuse their children.
	Sexual abuse (Fondling to sexual intercourse)	Rate estimated at 0.7–1.4 per 1,000 children.	346,000 cases in 1995. Girls are abused 3 times more frequently than boys.	Over 25% are birth parents; 25% are nonbirth parents (stepparents); 50% are relatives or acquaintances.
	Incest	Unknown, but not a rare phenomenon.	One survey shows that 15% of adults said they had been sexually abused as children	Most cases involve fathers and daughters or stepfathers and stepdaughters.
	Fatalities	2,000 in 1995.	Mean age 2.8.	Mothers are most likely murderer for children under 2 years old. 25–33% of child murderers are single mother's boyfriends.
VIOLENCE AGAINST ADULTS	Wife battering (kicking, beating, biting, threatening, using weapons)	2–4 million.	Women of all social classes and educational levels.	Men from all social classes, though more likely to be low-income. A high percent are unemployed. 33% repeat violence in 6 months. 1 in 8 husbands commit "milder" forms of abuse each year–pushing, grabbing, shoving.
	Marital rape	Most common form of rape; estimate is 1.2 million.	Women of all social classes and educational levels. Most often victims of nonsexual abuse also. Often socially isolated, typically economically dependent.	Men of all classes and educational levels.
	Husband abuse (hitting, pushing, throwing things, hitting with object: rarely, but occasionally, threatening with weapons)	Commonly not reported. Estimates vary; one study shows 49,000.	In many cases, man, too, is abusive; the two form a violent couple.	In many incidents, act in self-defense.
	Abuse of the elderly	500,000 to 2 million. Estimated that 5% of the elderly are abused.	Mostly women, 75 or older: many are physically or mentally impaired.	Primarily caretakers of the elderly. Most commonly women. A smaller percentage are sons and grandchildren.

FIGURE 14.1 Family violence profile

Source: Garbarino, 1989; Kelley et al., 1997; Kurz, 1993; McCormick, 1994; Moore, 1994; Patterson & Kim, 1991; U.S. Advisory Board on Child Abuse and Neglect, 1995; U.S. Department of Health and Human Services, 1996; Violence Against Women, 1994; Wiese & Daro, 1995; Zawitz, 1994.

respondents had been punched, kicked, or choked by a parent or adult guardian. And 5 percent reported even more severe physical abuse. In 1995, more than 3 million cases of child abuse were reported to child protection agencies. It is estimated that as many as 9 million American children are abused annually (Kelley et al., 1997; Wiese & Daro, 1995).

Battered children are not necessarily infants or toddlers. In 1995, about one-fourth of the victims were 3 years old or younger, more than half were younger than

8 years old, one-fourth were between 8 and 12 years of age, and one-fifth were teenagers (U.S. Department of Health and Human Services, 1996, 1997). While the rate of sexual abuse is higher for girls than for boys, boys are at higher risk of serious injury than are girls.

Child abuse is not the only form of family violence. Siblings beat each other; indeed, this is the most common form of violence in the family. Some husbands batter their wives, and some wives abuse their husbands (Straus, Gelles, & Steinmetz, 1980; *Gallup Monthly Poll*, October 24, 1997).

The abuse of parents and elderly family members by children is another form of family violence that has received increased attention (Costa, 1984). Abuse of the elderly takes many forms: physical battering, psychological abuse, negligence, financial exploitation, and even sexual abuse (Crouter & Perry-Jenkins, 1986). One in ten parents report that they have been hit by their children, and 3 percent of all parents report being the victims of a severe form of violence by their children at least once. This translates into 900,000 victims of parent abuse each year (Gelles & Straus, 1988).

The sexual abuse of children, a taboo subject until recently, is now being widely reported. At least 22 percent of all children in America are estimated to be victims of sexual abuse (Crewdson, 1988; Van Hasselt et al., 1988). Although most instances occur in the child's own home or in the home of a neighbor, several cases of widespread sexual abuse at day-care centers have also come to light. By far the most common situation is the father who sexually abuses his daughters, especially his stepdaughters. A recent study of sexually abusive fathers showed them typically to be socially isolated and insecure people with weak impulse control, poor judgment, and great insensitivity to the consequences of their actions (Karen Kirkland & Chris Bauer, reported in Levenson, 1984; see also Crewdson, 1988).

Family violence is not evenly distributed throughout society—some groups are more likely to engage in certain forms of violence than others are (Straus, Gelles, & Steinmetz, 1980). Wife abuse is highest among black families, while African-American sibling violence is relatively rare. Younger parents are more violent than older parents.

Family violence is related to income. In general, the poorer the family, the more likely it is that it will be violent. This relationship is weaker with respect to sibling violence and stronger with regard to child abuse. Income level makes the most difference in the occurrence rates of spouse abuse, which is five times more likely to occur in very poor families than in very rich ones (Straus, Gelles, & Steinmetz, 1980). However, income level makes relatively little difference in sexual abuse, which is more likely than other forms of abuse to occur in middle and higher-income homes. The information concerning correlations between income and child abuse will remain incomplete, however, until doctors and other professionals, particularly those in private hospitals, report incidences of child abuse among the middle and upper classes more readily.

Serious attempts to understand the causes of family violence have been made only recently. It has been observed that abused children do commonly grow up to abuse their own children, but this circular pattern does not tell us why family violence occurs in the first place. The stresses that go along with economic hardship undoubtedly play an important role in family violence, although it should be emphasized that millions of jobless people living on public assistance never harm their children. Substance abuse and neurological factors also play a part (Van Hesselt et al., 1988). The norms of American childrearing may also indirectly promote child abuse, in that the physical punishment of children is expected and even encouraged. When carried too far, such punishment becomes child abuse. The relative isolation of the nuclear family, which permits abuse to be kept fairly private, also may encourage family violence (Cazenave & Straus, 1979; Gelles, 1978).

Since the early 1960s, there has been a growing public awareness of family violence, and some measures are being taken to lessen both its occurrence and its effects. Women's groups have set up shelters both for battered women and for battered children. In 1977, there were only four shelters for battered women; by 1987, there were more than 1,000. Child-abuse hotlines, through which cases of violence against children may be reported anonymously, are now operating in most major cities. Agencies are providing nurseries and counseling for parents who want to stop abusing their children. And ads about this problem are regularly displayed in public places. The National Commission for the Prevention of Child Abuse believes that the posters, hotlines, and public awareness campaigns have been responsible for the dramatic increases in child-abuse reporting. In 1986, there were 33 reports per 1,000 children; by 1995, reports had climbed to 46 per 1,000 children—an increase of 49 percent (Benokraitis, 1999). The future of public funding for many of these programs is uncertain, however.

On a final note, it should be pointed out that family violence is not solely an American phenomenon. One report has indicated that wife beating, reported in 85 percent of the 90 societies studied, is the most common form of family violence in the world. Physical abuse or punishment of children was reported in 75 percent of these countries, while husband beating was reported in 7 percent. Analysis of these statistics has led scholars to speculate that culturally sanctioned male dominance is the underlying cause of wife beating and that children are most likely to be severely abused in societies where people believe in malevolent supernatural spirits (Van Hasslet, Morrison & Bellack, 1988).

Alternatives to Marriage and the Nuclear Family

Remaining single has always been an alternative to marriage, and it is an increasingly popular option in the United States today. There are many reasons for voluntarily remaining single, especially since sexual relationships outside of marriage are no longer widely condemned. Some men and women feel that they cannot manage both a career and a marriage, and they opt for a career. Others remain single because they feel a strong responsibility to their parents, or because they do not intend to have children and see no other reason for marriage. And some people do not marry because they are homosexual. Although there have been some efforts to allow gay couples to marry, such unions are still not recognized by law—although seven U.S. cities, including Los Angeles and Seattle, now have "domestic partnership" laws that ensure a variety of spousal rights (including insurance benefits, bereavement leaves, and tax credits) for registered cohabiting homosexual couples (*Newsweek,* May 12, 1990).

Heterosexual cohabitation is becoming increasingly popular as an alternative to marriage or to remaining single. The number of unmarried couples living together rose nearly sevenfold between 1970 and 1996, from 523,000 to 3,958,000 (U.S. Bureau of Labor, *Statistical Abstract of the United States, 1997*). According to a nationwide Gallup poll in 1996, about half of respondents between the ages of 18 and 29 reported that they had lived with their spouse before marriage (Newport, 1996).

As one might expect, studies have shown that unmarried couples living together generally do not hold traditional social values (Blumstein & Schwartz, 1983; Markowski, Croake, & Keller, 1978; Peterman, Riddley, & Anderson, 1974). Cohabitation is often a prelude to marriage, however. In a survey of some 300 men and women, about half saw living together as a test of compatibility, a step toward marriage (Simenauer & Carroll, 1982).

Does living together before marriage decrease the chances of having a good marriage? There is some evidence that it does. A study using Swedish data found that women who cohabit premaritally have almost 80 percent higher marital dissolution rates than those who do not (Bennett, Blanc, & Bloom, 1988). The primary reason for this finding may be that cohabitors are less likely to subscribe to the traditional conventions of marriage in the first place. But people who live together before marriage also report lower levels of happiness in their marriages (Newport, 1996).

A few young adults have tried *group marriage,* in which three or more individuals live as a family unit and share sexual and personal intimacies. Although they provide some advantages similar to those of the extended family, in addition to sexual variety, few group marriages have been successful—mainly because of the strong tendency for interpersonal conflicts (such as jealousies) to arise (Constantine & Constantine, 1973).

The Future of the Family

As documented throughout this chapter, the institution of the family has changed dramatically over the last 30 years. Fewer persons are marrying. Those who do choose to marry are doing so later in life and are having few children. More marriages end in divorce, and the number of single-parent families has grown substantially. As more and more people live alone or with someone to whom they are not married, the percentage of "nonfamily" households in the population has risen sharply. There were almost 23 million people living alone in 1990, more than a 20 percent increase over the number of one-person households in 1980 (U.S. Bureau of the Census, 1990a). And because families are less stable and have shorter life spans than ever before, people today typically live within family units for a smaller percentage of their lives. Taken together, these trends have caused some people to suggest that the institution of the family is at death's door.

Although sociologists believe that the family is still very much alive, a growing body of evidence suggests that its role in most people's lives is declining (Popenoe, 1988). The family's importance as a unit of procreation has diminished as the birth rate has dropped to below replacement levels and more couples have chosen to remain childless—a decision that has become increasingly socially acceptable (Rix, 1989). And the family—once the primary agent of childhood socialization—today is just one of several such agents. Some scholars have even argued that television and other forms of mass media, in addition to schools and the state, are already more significant influences on children than are families (Meyrowitz, 1985).

Care of the elderly, another traditional responsibility of the family, is also declining in importance. More elderly people are living alone today than every before, and many are moving into newly developed, age-segregated retirement communities. Still others are cared for in nursing homes or in day-care centers for the elderly.

In light of such developments, it is not surprising that individual family members have generally become more autonomous and less bound by the family group. The family has also yielded some of its power and authority to other institutions, especially to the state and its agencies. As a result, many people have become some-what less willing to invest time, money, and energy in family life (Goode, 1984).

These changes should not be seen as completely negative. Many of them result from improvements in the status of women and promote a new psychological climate within marriages that can be emotionally rewarding for both partners. Still, many people are concerned about the negative effects of recent family changes on specific groups, especially children. Some family changes have been linked to increased child poverty, rising rates of juvenile delinquency, and increased depression among teenagers. Because children represent the future of society, any negative consequences for them are especially significant.

There is no assurance that recent family trends will continue unchanged in the future. The majority of young people today still view a lasting, monogamous relationship that includes children as a major life goal. And family values remain extraordinarily strong, especially in the United States. The search for alternatives to the nuclear family may continue, but so will the realization that the family is still a driving force that shapes people's personalities, values, and opportunities.

CHAPTER REVIEW

1. Identify the most important functions that the family serves. Discuss social problems that suggest that the family does not always function in the interest of society.

2. What do you think about the conflict perspective of the family? Is it in the best interest of modern capitalists to maintain gender inequality in the family? Why or why not?

3. How have changes in societies over time affected the structure of the family? Describe the family structure you expect to see in the United States in your lifetime.

4. Consider the concepts used to describe different family structures such as patriarchal family, matrilocal residence, and bilateral descent. What do they tell you about relationships within and between families?

5. Why is the incest taboo virtually universal?

6. Explain the advantages and disadvantages of both endogamy and exogamy.

7. Why do arranged marriages tend to be more stable than ones based on romantic love?

8. What would you change about the way most Americans view marriage today?

9. How will changes in the way Americans work in the twenty-first century affect the family?

10. What kinds of changes in American society might reduce the high divorce rate?

11. Consider the research on family violence in the United States. Will this social problem get better or worse during your lifetime? Why?

INTERNET EXERCISE

The Web destinations for Chapter 14 cover various aspects of the family. To begin your explorations, go to the Prentice Hall Companion Web site **http://www. prenhall.com/popenoe.** Then select **Chapter 14** (The Family). Next, choose **web destinations** from the menu on the left side of the screen. There are a number of different sites that will be of interest. We suggest you begin with **The Fertility Network** and **Strohecker's Pharmacy.** Both of these sites deal with issues surrounding infertility problems and fertility drugs. You will find fascinating information about actual fertility drugs that are available, counseling services, and a variety of facts concerning how these products are administered. After you have explored these sites, answer the following questions:

- In conjunction with the *Internet/Technology* box in this chapter, what are the key social issues surrounding infertility and fertility drugs?

- Fertility drugs are obviously "big business." What are the implications of this fact for family relationships today?

- In your personal assessment, what are the "pros" and "cons" of fertility drugs?

KEY TERMS

kinship
family of orientation
family of procreation
nuclear family
extended family
patriarchal family
matriarchal family
matrifocal family
egalitarian family

patrilocal residence
matrilocal residence
neolocal residence
patrilineal descent
matrilineal descent
bilateral descent
incest taboo
endogamy
exogamy

homogamy
marriage gradient
marriage
monogamy
polygamy
polygyny
polyandry
dual-earner families

CHAPTER 15

Education

Does it ever seem as if you have spent your entire life going to school? Particularly if you entered college right after you finished high school, you may be so used to organizing your life around the rhythms of the academic calendar that it will feel strange after you graduate to realize that September is not really the beginning of the year nor is May the end of it. Comprehensive education is crucial in the modern world, required of virtually everyone who hopes to obtain a decent job or to maintain the standard of living deemed normal by our society.

Extensive formal education is a fairly recent development. Prior to industrialization, education was reserved for a small, elite group of people. The vast majority remained unschooled and illiterate. However, the changing nature of the modern job market has greatly increased the importance of formal education, to the point where over 82 percent of all Americans graduate from high school and over 23 percent hold college degrees (U.S. Bureau of the Census, *Statistical Abstract of the United States, 1998*). In fact, as you probably already realize, if you want to have a good chance for success in a wide range of specialized fields, you will need to continue on after you receive your bachelor's degree for substantial postgraduate work. And making ourselves more employable is only one of many reasons why we attend school. As the functionalists note, schools also pass on the major values of our culture, help us to learn how to get along with other people, provide us with our first experience with bureaucratic organizations, and keep us occupied so that our parents can work rather than look after us at home.

But education plays an even more important role than this listing would suggest. Americans tend to believe that schools can also serve as an effective means of remediating a wide range of thorny social problems. Perhaps the most obvious example concerns the struggle to improve opportunities for minorities, an effort that has shaped much of American public life for the past four decades. While minority opportunities have expanded in virtually all sectors of society, special attention has been devoted to ensuring that the schools promote this goal through such controversial programs as busing, magnet schools, multicultural curricula, and affirmative action admission plans.

In addition, we have tried to use the schools to address such problems as substance abuse (through informational programs like D.A.R.E. and organizations like Students Against Drunk Driving), teenage pregnancy (through sex education courses and the distribution of condoms in high schools), inadequate parenting skills (through special classes designed to improve such skills), and even anomie (through values clarification programs). And the schools remain the primary means by which we attempt, by establishing special scholarships and similar assistance, to ensure that the children of poor families have an equal—or at least a decent—chance to compete for economic success along with the rest of society.

Needless to say, American schools perform some of these tasks much more effectively than others. In this chapter we discuss these and related issues, beginning with a comparison between the functionalist and the conflict perspectives on education. We next examine some of the characteristic ways in which education is organized in the United States and other postindustrial nations, and we consider a variety of important trends and issues in modern education. The chapter concludes with some observations concerning the impact of education on earnings and on people's values and attitudes.

SOCIOLOGICAL PERSPECTIVES ON EDUCATION

Learning is the lifelong process of social and personal experiences that alters an individual's knowledge, attitudes, and behavior. No society leaves such experiences to chance. **Education** is the formal institution that directs many of these learning experiences within a particular society.

Educational activities range from a parent teaching a child to ride a bike to a professor lecturing on physics to 800 students. Modern societies have established complex formal educational organizations employing specialized professionals. Vast sums of money are devoted to educational activities, and no one is exempt from formal education. Indeed, in many respects, the institution of education has become one of the great controlling forces in modern societies.

Like the family, education readily lends itself to functional analysis. We begin our discussion of education from this perspective.

The Functionalist Perspective

In organization and content, formal education around the world takes an enormous variety of forms. Summerhill (a world-famous "permissive" school), in England, for example, is loosely structured. The children roam about freely and attend only the classes that interest them. In contrast, students in the rigidly organized French *lycée* (more or less a high school) are sometimes required to memorize long passages from classic French plays and to devote several hours a day to written exercises. In the People's Republic of China, education has often been combined with organized exercise, factory work, and the "socially useful labor" of cleaning schools.

SOCIOLOGY OF THE MEDIA

EDUCATIONAL TELEVISION

Television is one of America's most effective educational tools. In fact, researchers have known for over 40 years that children pick ideas up from television with ease and quickly incorporate what they have learned into their behaviors (Bandura, 1973). Ironically, that is precisely why television concerns so many parents and educators. In 1961, Wilbur Schramm, Jack Lyle, and Edwin Parker captured the essence of a problem that remains with us today:

> The question of what a child learns from television has been second in the public mind only to the question of what a child learns from school. Whereas there has been worry lest the child not learn *enough* in school, there is a corresponding fear that he might learn *too much* and the wrong kind of thing from television. (1961; p. 75)

Over the years, the Federal Communications Commission has tried to influence the content of children's television in various ways. The FCC's concerns have included the quality of children's shows, depictions of violence, the effects of advertising on children, and the amount of children's programming (Kunkel, 1998; Ryan &

Wentworth, 1999). After repeated attempts to enact legislation to improve the quality and quantity of children's programs, it appeared that some progress had been made. The Children's Television Act of 1990 stipulated that in order to hold a broadcast license, stations would have to air three hours of educational programming for children per week. As it turned out, this law made little difference in what children saw on television. In a loose interpretation of the term "educational," broadcasters included such programs as *The Flintstones, The Jetsons, Mighty Morphin Power Rangers, Yogi Bear,* and *America's Funniest Home Videos.* In 1996, the FCC addressed this abuse by clearly defining educational programming.

The prolonged battles over educational television suggest that producing educational programs that appeal to children is a difficult, if not impossible, task. But, in fact, the success of several educational programs shows that it is not—and that it is certainly no more difficult than producing shows like *The Flintstones* or *America's Funniest Home Videos.* Consider, for example, ABC's *SchoolHouse Rock.* Schoolchildren would have a tough time distinguishing these cartoons from those whose primary purpose is

entertainment. Created to resemble a typical cartoon character, Schoolhouse Rocky takes children to places like the Conjunction Junction Diner, where they can sing along to tunes such as "Conjunction junction. What's your function? Hooking up words and phrases and clauses," or "Lolly, lolly, lolly, get your adverbs here." Multiplication Rock teaches children basic mathematics, and America Rock teaches children about American history and government. While children may not notice, *SchoolHouse Rock* is very different from most Saturday morning cartoons—it does not attempt to sell children toys.

The epitome of "good" educational television has always been *Sesame Street* (Hendershot, 1998). In contrast to its predecessors, which focused on creative play (*Romper Room*) or emotional development (*Mister Rogers' Neighborhood*), *Sesame Street* stressed cognitive development in children. Joan Cooney, the originator of *Sesame Street,* met the challenge of competing with television designed to entertain children by capitalizing on an idea that was totally foreign to the concept of educational television. In contrast to the low-budget, locally produced educational programs of the time, which commonly relied on a teacher explaining concepts in front of a blackboard,

In spite of these differences, the schools of all three nations serve very similar social purposes, or functions. Five main social functions of education have been identified: (1) socialization, (2) social control, (3) selection and allocation, (4) assimilation of newcomers, and (5) social innovation and change.

Not every educational organization promotes all these functions; some schools specialize. Such specialization is related to an organization's position in the educational hierarchy. At one extreme are nursery schools, whose purpose is mainly socialization; at the other end

are research-oriented postdoctoral institutes, which emphasize innovation and change.

SOCIALIZATION

The most familiar socialization function of education is the transmission of knowledge and technical skills. In the narrowest sense, this can mean vocational training. For example, among the Mbuti of Africa, fathers teach their sons how to make a straight arrow shaft, how to attach an arrowhead securely to the shaft, and how to shoot the

Cooney created a program that had the quality of network television. Reflecting her keen understanding of the program's target audience, she said: "Children are conditioned to expect pow! wham! fast-action thrillers from television [as well as] . . . highly visual, slickly and expensively produced material" (Hendershot, 1998, p. 144). Few would realize that Cooney's model for *Sesame Street* was a popular 1960s program, Rowan and Martin's *Laugh-In,* which entertained audiences with quick, humorous vignettes.

When it first aired, the budget for *Sesame Street* was the largest ever allocated for educational television—$8,191,100. While that, no doubt, contributed to its success, another program showed that even low-cost educational television programs could succeed. And that cartoons could be educational. Created by Bill Cosby, the show was *Fat Albert and the Cosby Kids,* a cartoon that featured characters straight out of Cosby's own childhood—poor, black, inner-city kids. Cosby introduced and closed each cartoon episode with the lesson that it illustrated, such as do not steal, do not lie, or do not play hooky. Some programs even touched on serious social problems such as drugs. One episode, entitled "Talk, Don't Fight,"

Do you think government should be able to regulate television programming? Are educational television shows truly educating children or just entertaining them? Were you influenced by what you watched on television as a child?

depicted the violent consequences of gang warfare—the murder of one of Fat Albert's friends, who is shot when he tries to save his brother from getting involved in gang violence. Praised for its prosocial messages, *Fat Albert and the Cosby Kids* gained respect as an educational cartoon, at least in part because it employed a panel of sociologists, psychologists, and educators to review the content of its scripts (Hendershot, 1998).

Programs like *Sesame Street* and *Fat Albert and the Cosby Kids* show that creating quality educational television programs for children is an attainable goal. These kinds of productions can ease parents' fears that children will learn too much and the wrong kind of thing from television. And the success of these programs shows that a market exists for this kind of educational television. We must, therefore, wonder why so few good educational programs exist today.

finished arrow at a moving target. Vocational high schools in the United States teach students how to repair car engines or to run a drill press. The Mbuti boy learns to be a hunter; the American learns how to be a mechanic. Both are taught technical skills that help them survive and function in their societies.

In modern industrial societies, which depend on many highly educated specialists, it is important that each new generation learn a large body of knowledge and skills, most of which are not specifically job-related. Because this knowledge is so extensive, formal education

in these societies takes many years. And because the content of this knowledge changes constantly, it is difficult for parents to pass it on to their children. Thus, specialized personnel such as an eighth-grade science teacher and specialized educational organizations such as a school of engineering are needed to transmit knowledge.

The transmission of knowledge is like the tip of an iceberg. It is the part of education with which everyone is familiar. Most of the activities in a school—reading textbooks, giving reports, taking exams, receiving report cards—are concerned with the transmission of knowledge.

"Doing well" in school usually means learning what is presented in class. But, as we have already noted, students learn much more than this in school. They also learn the values and norms of their culture, a process that sometimes is called the *hidden curriculum* (Broudy, 1987; Lickona, 1988).

Schools are expected to teach children such values as democracy, the rule of law, and even the desirability of monogamous marriage (Waller, 1932/1961). Normative socialization (that is, the teaching of norms and values) is also implicit in much that a child reads and is allowed to do.

For example, when students in college English classes read Herman Melville's *Moby Dick* and study the subculture of nineteenth-century seafaring New Englanders, they also learn about American attitudes toward good and evil as they read about Captain Ahab's bitter pursuit of the white whale. The teacher may discuss some of these attitudes with the class; others will be left for the students to infer. Either way, the result will be an increased familiarity with important American values. Similarly, when Chinese students leave their classrooms in the middle of the day to do several hours of factory work, they gain insights into the importance their society attaches to industrial production (Ann-Ping, 1988).

SOCIAL CONTROL

The socialization function of education goes far beyond merely teaching values and norms. Schools are also expected to persuade their students that it is necessary to behave according to these principles (Goslin, 1965). Indeed, students are graded not only on how well they learn but also on how well they cooperate, how orderly they are, and even on personal grooming. This, too, is part of the hidden curriculum. In the early years of schooling, these are sometimes the only criteria on which they are graded. If children do not behave according to certain norms (for example, those requiring cooperation and cleanliness) by the time they enter second or third grade, they will probably have a difficult time in school, no matter how well they perform in academic subjects. Thus, through the process of socialization, schools are directly engaged in social control. They attempt to instill loyalty, obedience to authority, and even submissiveness in the students (Raskin, 1972; Rothstein, 1987; Willis, 1981).

One way schools promote social control is by teaching children to idealize their nation's leaders. People in power are sometimes presented in ways that make it hard to question their authority. Conflict theorists see this aspect of education as an important reason why capitalist societies developed systems of mass education in the first place (Bowles & Gintis, 1976).

Is this an appropriate function for education? Certainly the citizens of any nation need to have a reasonable commitment to its core political institutions if they are to be properly integrated into society. On the other hand, blind loyalty to specific leaders can interfere with the periodic need for political change and with efforts to root out corruption and inefficiency.

The social control function of education extends well beyond socialization. Schools also serve as "custodial" institutions for the nation's young, keeping children off the streets for many hours of the day, many days of the year. In addition, after-school activities often extend this custodial time period late into the day.

Schools also try to channel young people toward socially approved activities. When children show interest in disapproved areas or are identified as having "behavior problems," the schools may keep close watch over them for years—for example, by alerting their teachers in each successive grade.

SELECTION AND ALLOCATION

The main burden for selecting and allocating people to enter particular occupational positions rests with the schools. This is an especially important function in modern society with its thousands of highly specialized occupational roles. If there are too few qualified people, the work will not get done; if there are too many, unemployment rates will rise and people's skills will be wasted.

In China, with its centralized system of economic planning, much of this is done by the state. In some cases, students are directly recruited by the government to study particular areas for which more workers are needed. Their tuition is paid for by the state with the understanding that they will work after graduation in the fields that have been chosen for them (Hawkins, 1988). Not all of the Chinese system involves schools, however. For example, within a community, the government pays certain "specialized households" to disseminate scientific and technical knowledge concerning such topics as techniques of modern farming.

In the United States, the mechanisms of selection and allocation are less formalized. For example, trade schools and colleges select course offerings largely on the basis of supply and demand. Should the demand for a particular specialty ebb, courses in that subject will be reduced or eliminated. New courses in high-demand fields are always being added. The dramatic expansion in the past two decades of computer-related educational programs is an excellent example of this pattern.

However, knowing that a certain number of computer programmers will be needed by 2000, and providing the programs for training them, does not solve the problem of selecting the particular people to fill these jobs. Although each individual ultimately decides whether to prepare for and accept a particular job, a major function of education is to select and channel people into jobs and careers and to help students develop useful and appropriate work skills (Lersch, 1988).

Both high schools and colleges employ personnel specifically trained in career guidance. Colleges maintain placement bureaus where students can get information about careers and job openings. Colleges also open their doors to recruiters from government and industry.

ASSIMILATION

In culturally diverse societies such as the United States, another major purpose of education is to assist in the process of **assimilation**—the absorption of newcomers into the dominant society. Teaching the English language and U.S. history and traditions is one way this function is promoted. A more subtle way by which this is accomplished is through the teaching of patriotism. Patriotism is instilled through such means as the ritual of pledging allegiance to the flag, displaying pictures of the president, and playing "The Star-spangled Banner" before assemblies or sports events.

Education is one of the primary vehicles by which many immigrants have become full participants in American life. Today the assimilation function in schools is also geared toward including the poor and disadvantaged in the mainstream of American society, whether or not they are recent immigrants.

Some argue that the goal of assimilation in American education has been overemphasized and that we now need to protect cultural diversity (McCormick, 1984). These critics claim that membership in a cultural minority should not be regarded as a "problem" and that America should be much more forceful in its attempts to maintain its subcultures. The strong interest in ethnic studies in many colleges and universities reflects this position, as do attempts to promote bilingual education in many primary and secondary schools.

INNOVATION AND CHANGE

It might seem from our discussion of the first four functions of education that one of the principal effects of this institution is to maintain the status quo. This is indeed the case; education is more often than not a conservative social force. However, some aspects of education do promote social change. One of the most important ways education contributes to change is by producing and spreading new knowledge, values, and beliefs.

The most familiar example of the production of knowledge is the research done by university professors. In addition to teaching, professors are expected to conduct research that will contribute knowledge to their fields of interest. This research is often supported by the government or by grants from private foundations.

Some research is *basic* in the sense that it is designed not to respond to specific practical needs but, rather, to uncover fundamental, underlying aspects of reality. An example from sociology might be efforts to understand the general dynamics of small group behavior. Other research is *applied* in that it is intended to solve specific real-world problems. Thus, sociologists may conduct studies designed to identify the most effective ways to teach schoolchildren to avoid experimenting with illegal drugs. Once research is completed, whether basic or applied, the knowledge gained is disseminated outside the academic institution, usually through articles and books.

Some critics of higher education believe that American universities are too involved with research. They feel that this emphasis keeps the university from adequately performing its other functions. Professors are sometimes hired solely for their research abilities, for example, and introductory courses are not infrequently taught by unskilled or overworked graduate students. This has been a problem in every large university in the United States.

The university's emphasis on research can be defended, however, on several grounds. In a highly industrialized, knowedge-oriented society, innovative research is essential. And even though most students are not personally involved in research activities, they benefit indirectly from the increased intellectual stimulation that research contributes to their university. Also, from a practical standpoint, research projects attract funds to the university and these funds allow the institution to hire more and better instructors and to expand its course offerings and teaching facilities. The largest donations by corporations and foundations are normally given to universities that have the most impressive research programs. For better or worse, the economy of a modern American university depends heavily on its research capacity.

Besides new knowledge, educational organizations also produce and disseminate new values and beliefs that can be potent generators of social change. Science, for example, is a belief system that was spread throughout society largely by the medium of the school system.

Another way education can promote social change is by encouraging a critical climate, one in which it is seen as acceptable to criticize or even rebel against the system. Such a climate exists at many colleges and universities. For example, a classic study at Bennington College

Are there preconceived notions on the success of these groups of students? Conflict theorists believe that "low-track" students often come to feel that they are unlikely to succeed at anything that requires extensive education.

(Newcomb, 1943) found that as students moved toward graduation, they increasingly tended to adopt the liberal social and political attitudes of their teachers.

On the other hand, during the late 1970s and 1980s, the general climate of student opinion on most college campuses became decidedly more conservative, more inclined to accept society as it is. One long-term study of men at Williams College found that after the mid-1970s, students there became markedly less concerned about social and political issues and more conservative in morality and religion (Hastings & Hoge, 1986). Another study noted that attitudes among college freshmen changed noticeably between 1970 and 1987. The number of students classifying themselves as "liberal" dropped from 34 percent in 1970 to 22 percent in 1987, while the number classifying themselves as "middle of the road" rose from 45 percent to 56 percent (U.S. Bureau of the Census, 1989). There are some tentative indications that

the pendulum is now beginning to swing back in a more liberal direction, but there seems little likelihood of an imminent return to the widespread popularity of left-wing perspectives that characterized many campuses during the 1960s and early 1970s.

The Conflict Perspective

We have thus far examined education and the educational system from the functionalist point of view. But the functionalist perspective tends to minimize the role that education can play in social conflict. For a discussion of the "other" side of education, we must turn to conflict theory, which suggests that education is one of the primary means by which those in power maintain their positions.

Rather than identifying the formal and informal purposes of education in society, conflict theorists see education principally as a tool used by the ruling classes to perpetuate social inequality, both by controlling access to schooling (Ballantine, 1997) and by training docile, disciplined workers (Rothstein, 1987). Two important ways by which these goals are promoted are tracking and credentialism.

TRACKING

As the functionalists note, one of the principal purposes of the schools is the selection and allocation of students into various specialized occupational roles. One of the major means by which this is accomplished is through the system of **tracking**—dividing students into different groups or classes on the basis of academic ability. This process of selection actually starts as soon as a child enters school. As early as first grade, the schools begin a regular routine of formal testing and grading. Those who do well on the tests are often given enriched programs that proceed at a faster pace and cover more material than regular classes do. Perhaps they will be assigned additional independent projects—books to read or reports to prepare. Students who test poorly may be placed in "slow learner" classes. These students generally cover less difficult material and receive special attention from their teachers. The stated purpose of tracking programs is to allow each student to learn at his or her own pace and thereby avoid boredom on the part of the fast learners and frustration among the lower-track students.

Tracking is particularly common at the middle and high school levels, where it often takes the form of college-bound and vocational tracks. Although these programs are well intentioned, conflict theorists point out that low-track students often come to feel that they are unlikely to succeed at anything that requires extensive education or specific knowledge. Their career aspirations diminish, and when they are old enough, they frequently drop out of school.

The real problem with tracking, according to conflict theorists, is that there is a good deal of evidence suggesting that the lower tracks tend to be disproportionately populated by minority students and by students from lower-class backgrounds (Lee & Ekstrom, 1987; Oakes, 1986; Passow, 1988; Sorensen, 1989; Vanfossen, Jones, & Spade, 1987). As a result, tracking systems tend to perpetuate existing patterns of inequality rather than helping disadvantaged students to achieve upward mobility. Poorer students placed in lower tracks are unlikely to receive encouragement and high-quality education, and frequently cannot afford to go on to college. These students, therefore, are unable to compete for the better-paying, more prestigious jobs—which are often filled by people who have degrees from expensive universities. In this manner, the cycle of poverty and inequality is reinforced through the educational system.

CREDENTIALISM

Functionalists see **credentialism**—the requirement that an applicant possess advanced degrees in order to be considered for certain jobs—as a way of making sure that the most capable people are hired to fill important positions. Conflict theorists, in contrast, contend that the more degrees granted, the less bearing they have on people's ability to do a job. An Ontario, Canada, study found that although teachers' average level of credentials has increased, the credential "inflation" affecting all jobs has actually diminished teachers' status (Filson, 1988). And although studies have shown that the average income for those with advanced degrees is higher than for those with basic degrees, this difference may be relatively insubstantial.

Credentialism has also been criticized as perpetuating certain myths about education—for example, that an advanced degree necessarily indicates greater intelligence rather than just a higher level of educational attainment. Other critics take issue with what seems to be a contemporary overreliance on credentials, saying that capable or even exceptional people are barred from jobs simply because they lack the necessary degrees. Finally, the time and expense involved in getting an advanced degree are seen by many conflict theorists as almost guaranteeing that high-paying professions traditionally demanding years of schooling—such as law and medicine—are unfairly limited to an elite composed of those people who can afford such schooling.

Conflict theorists thus see American education as, in essence, a vast and frequently unfair filtering system. At each level, lower-class and minority students are disproportionately likely to drop out, whereas middle-class and white students are encouraged to continue (Apple, 1993; Giroux, 1994; Hotchkiss & Eberst, 1987; Jencks & Riesman, 1977; Lee & Bryk, 1988; Parsons, 1959).

Conflict theorists identify several additional weaknesses of the American system of education, including the following:

1. Schools and colleges place a very high premium on such skills as a good memory and superior test-taking ability. Yet, in many high-status occupations, these traits may not be as useful as, for example, creativity or leadership ability.

2. Tests that claim to measure intelligence and ability do not always do so. Besides low intelligence, there are many reasons (such as low levels of motivation and distraction resulting from stress) why a child may perform poorly on a standard IQ test. A child's real intellectual capacities may not be truly reflected by such tests.

3. Sometimes the educational system holds back those who are naturally late achievers. Because they have already been placed in low tracks and guided into lower-status jobs, it may be extremely difficult for these people to attain high career goals.

The American educational system is not unique in containing inequities. Conflict theorists note, for example, that places in Great Britain's "public" schools (similar to private schools in the United States), which emphasize high academic standards and confer much prestige on their graduates, are filled mostly by students from the upper classes. Attendance at these schools is an important first step toward being accepted at a prestigious university. Since members of the lower classes cannot afford such schools and the networking possibilities they provide, lower-class access to highly ranked universities—and thus to high-paying jobs—is limited. Indeed, much research supports the idea that social class is a factor in education throughout the world (da Silva, 1988).

EDUCATIONAL ORGANIZATION

In this section, we examine selected aspects of the structure of contemporary American education. First we briefly discuss some consequences of the movement toward universal education. Then the basic logic of the organization of education is reviewed, followed by consideration of some issues concerning governmental support and parental choice. The section concludes with an examination of the roles of teachers and students and with some comments on the means by which student performance is evaluated.

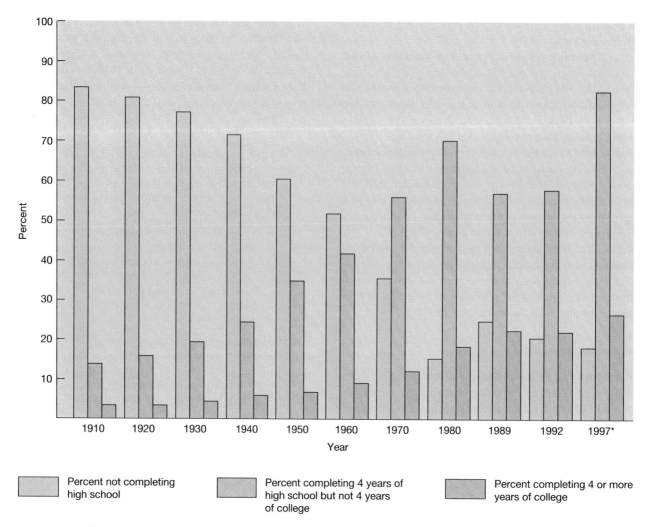

FIGURE 15.1 Level of school completed by persons 25 years and over, 1910–1997.

Source: Thomas D. Snyder, *Digest of Educational Statistics, 1987* (Washington, D.C.: National Center for Education Statistics, 1987); U.S. Bureau of the Census, *Statistical Abstract of the United States* (Washington, D.C.: U.S. Government Printing Office, 1993, 1998).

Universal Education

Education is no longer the privilege of the few. More and more Americans have been completing more and more years of formal schooling. For the academic year 1959–1960, the total enrollment in all American educational institutions was 45.2 million. By 1996, that figure had climbed to 70.3 million, more than a 55 percent increase. In part, this increase stems from growth in the size of the school-age population. But the higher number also reflects increased educational participation.

The growing proportion of the U.S. population completing high school is perhaps the clearest indication of the trend toward universal education. In 1900, only about 7 percent of young people finished high school. Today, the majority of people—about 82.1 percent—graduate from high school. In 1990, the median number of school years completed by people 25 and older was 12.7 (U.S. Bureau of the Census, *Statistical Abstract of the United States, 1993*). (See Figure 15.1.)

Although not everyone who goes to college earns a degree, the number of college graduates also has increased dramatically in this century. In 1900, 30,000 people received bachelor's degrees; by 1940, the figure was 362,000; in 1990, it reached 1,050,000; and in 1995, 1,160,134. The number of advanced degrees has increased as well. In 1995, 397,629 master's degrees and 44,446 doctoral degrees were conferred.

To achieve nearly universal education, schools have had to relax academic standards somewhat, especially at the secondary and college levels. This lowering of standards, along with reorienting the curriculum toward subjects believed to be useful to a greater number of students, began in the 1920s, when school enrollments first started to increase rapidly.

Over the past several decades, continuing lowering of academic standards has caused widespread concern.

Worried by the early Soviet space achievements in the 1950s, many Americans feared that our system of mass education was leading to reduced quality. Subsequently, nationwide attempts were made to upgrade public education, primarily through increased government financial support (see Figure 15.2). Declining scores on standardized tests of verbal and mathematical ability have provoked additional concern in recent years.

The dilemma of providing both universal education and academic excellence remains unresolved. A practical solution lies in balancing special programs for the academically gifted with those for the academically handicapped. But the balance point is not easily determined, and students who fall between these two extremes are always in danger of being overlooked.

FIGURE 15.2 The amount of money spent on education tends to be more in higher-income countries.

Source: Organization for Economic Cooperation and Development, *Education at a Glance,* 1996; and unpublished data.

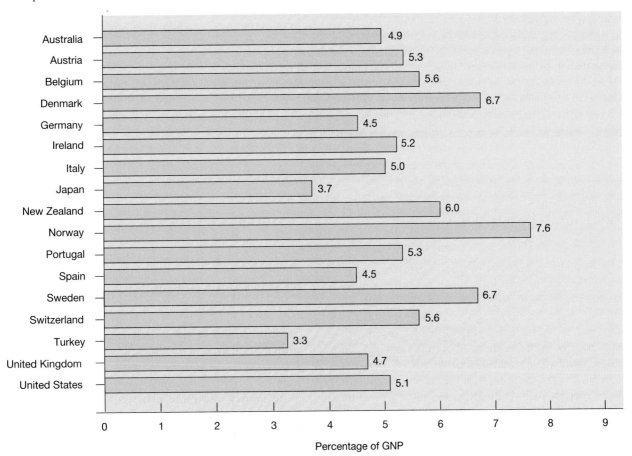

GLOBAL SOCIETY

CROSS-CULTURAL VARIATIONS IN EDUCATION

Today many American schools are struggling to prepare their students for the future. Getting students to achieve even the most basic educational requirements is a tough challenge for many schools. With neither the financial resources nor answers for the problems facing their students, some schools have fallen hopelessly behind others. And the situation is not likely to improve in the near future. As we enter the twenty-first century, they will face even stiffer competition. They will be compared not only to other American schools but to schools worldwide.

In fact, the results of the Third International Mathematics and Science Study showed that when they were tested in advanced subjects such as physics and mathematics, even the best American students performed worse than students from other countries (Bronner, 1998). Students in the Netherlands, Sweden, Denmark, Switzerland, Iceland, and Norway

scored above the international average in math; students in the United States had scores close to the international average. The scores for advanced math were even worse for American students. Not only were they lower than the international average, but students from less well-off countries like Cyprus, Lithuania, and Russia received scores that were above the international average. American students also received scores that were lower than the international average on the physics exam. Students in Norway, Sweden, Russia, and Denmark scored above the international average.

These results trouble American educators and political leaders, who recognize that maintaining a competitive edge in the global economy of the twenty-first century will depend on the math and science skills of this country's population. However, assessing the differences between educational systems that produce math and science stars and those that do not is not easy. Consider, for example, how much money different countries spend on education. Overall, the amount of

money allocated per student for education is more in higher income countries than in lower ones. Broken down as expenditures per student by level of school, the United States ranks near the top of industrialized nations. In 1993, it spent $5,492 per student in the primary level, $6,541 per student in the secondary level, and $14,607 per student in higher education. Only Switzerland spent more per student across all of these levels—$5,835, $7,024, and $15,731, respectively. As this suggests, money does not explain everything.

But what about the sizes of classes, homework, social life, or the amount of time spent watching television? Even these do not explain much (Bronner, 1998). Experts claim that students worldwide spend several hours a day watching television. And data on the leisure activities of eighth-grade students support that conclusion.

Some research suggests that the explanation for the differing performances of students on international tests of math and science lies in deeply

Educational Organization in the United States

The formal organization of public primary and secondary schools in America includes two main groups: a teaching staff directly responsible for the education of the students and an administrative staff—the principal and administrative assistants—responsible for coordinating the activities of the teachers. Above the principal is the superintendent, an administrative official who must coordinate the activities of all the schools in a district. The superintendent is hired by, and must answer to, a school board or board of education. The board members are usually elected by the voters of each district. In some cases, board members are appointed by an elected city official, such as the mayor (Ballantine, 1997).

At the level of teacher and principal, private schools display the same general organization as public schools. But the next higher link in the chain of responsibility is the organization that sponsors the school—a church, if the school is parochial, or a board of trustees, if the school is an independent private institution.

The organization of American colleges and universities differs in significant respects from that of primary and secondary educational systems (Parsons & Platt, 1973). In higher education, there is a more definite hierarchy in the organization of teachers, with more money and more privileges going to those at the top. The result is more competition for positions than is typical among primary and high school teaching staffs. Also, the faculty in a university has greater autonomy from the administration. The administration—

ingrained cultural values that influence attitudes toward education and ultimately student achievement. For example, Japanese society places a great deal of pressure on its students to achieve. By the time they reach junior high school, students are competing fiercely to get into the best high schools. Unlike American students, their lifetime opportunities depend on which high school they attend. These young students know that and so do their parents, who spend several thousand dollars a year sending their children to private cram schools called *jukus* to prepare them for the high school entrance exams that will determine their future (Smith, 1995).

If, in fact, this explains the consistently superior performance of Japanese students, then that does not really offer much hope to American educators. This suggests that the achievements of Japanese students are due more to the *jukus* and the family than to Japan's public school system (Walters, 1993). Changing a national culture requires far more than making specific changes in an educational

system. And it seems unlikely that most Americans would want to adopt these Japanese strategies for improving education.

But before educators and political leaders make any changes in the American educational system, they would be wise to find the explanation for the most puzzling aspect of international comparisons of academic performance: Even though American students perform poorly on international tests of math and science, the United States continues to dominate a global economy that is based increasingly on information and technology (Bronner, 1998).

Some experts suggest that American students catch up in college. And, in fact, the number of students who receive bachelor's degrees in the United States is impressive. The ratio of bachelor's degrees conferred per hundred 22- to 23-year-olds was 32 in the United States in 1994. By comparison, that ratio was only 1 in Italy and 2 in Portugal. However, education experts also pay particular attention to the percentage of graduates in math and

science fields. And, in 1994, the countries with over 30 percent of graduates in these fields included Germany, Finland, Belgium, Switzerland, Japan, and Austria. In contrast, the United States reported under 20 percent of graduates in these fields.

Cross-cultural variations in educational systems provide some insight into why students in certain countries perform better on international tests than students in other countries. But no one believes that the explanations for performance differences are clear or simple. And no one yet understands why the United States continues to dominate the global market despite the poor performance of its students on international tests of math and science. Until we do, it is unlikely that American educators will adopt the methods used by other countries to build math and science skills.

---

president, treasurer, deans, registrar—concentrates on such concerns as raising and allocating funds, admitting and disciplining students, and building new dormitories and classrooms. Unlike school principals, college presidents rarely supervise the teaching staff directly. Decisions about curriculum, division of teaching responsibilities, and hiring of new teachers are generally left to the faculty members.

The ultimate responsibility for decisions about the operation and policies of a college or university is often less clearly defined than it is at lower levels of education. Because they use public funds, state-supported colleges and universities must account to their state legislatures and governors. But in a private college, the president is responsible to a policy-setting board of trustees, an organizational pattern similar to that found in business

corporations. In a corporation, however, the board is eventually accountable to the stockholders, who have the power to remove unsatisfactory officials by a majority vote. The trustees of a private college often have no clear responsibility to any outside group except, perhaps, to the alumni or to others who donate to the school.

Models of Educational Organization

The structure of most educational organizations in modern societies has become relatively bureaucratic (see Chapter 7). Activities are divided by function: Teachers instruct, while administrators oversee. Personnel are hired or promoted on the basis of their technical and professional abilities. Clear-cut lines of authority run from school boards or boards of governors down to custodians. And the schools operate according to fixed rules, which must be strictly followed (Bidwell, 1965).

This bureaucratic structure is a source of much controversy. Some see educational organizations as efficient and rational, rewarding the people who contribute the most. In fact, some observers even believe that further efforts to bureaucratize education are necessary so that schools can be run as "tight ships" (Parelius & Parelius, 1987). Others view educational bureaucracies as awkward and inefficient. They think that these organizations are not sufficiently responsive to social change or adaptable to local needs, and that bureaucracies stifle creativity and are drowning in senseless, never-ending paperwork (Rothstein, 1987).

Teachers frequently complain that the bureaucracy of the public school system prevents them from doing enough real teaching. All too often, they charge, paperwork requirements change teaching time into administrative time. Teaching hours are too often taken up with filling out seating plans, attendance sheets, and absence and detention reports, and, in higher education, with committee work. Moreover, administrators and clerks are often able in practice to dictate what is to be taught and how it is to be taught (Ballantine, 1997; Goslin, 1965; Rogers, 1969).

The idea that educational organizations are overly bureaucratic can be pushed too far, however. It is clear that the organization of education substantially differs from that of government, business, and industry. Some scholars see educational organization as a "loosely coupled system" in which (Weick, 1976) the various parts (for example, departments) enjoy considerable autonomy and are only loosely interconnected (Goodlad, 1987; Tyler, 1985). Another model envisions schools as organized along the lines of a baseball team in which team effort would be as important as individual performance and in which "managers" (superintendents, principals, and so on) would be free to make the best possible use of the talents of the "players" (teachers and aides) (Timar, 1989).

Government Support and Parental Choice

Both public and private schools are supported by the government, but in different ways. The majority of the resources of public schools comes from local governments, which finance such items as teachers' salaries, buildings, and equipment. Partly to balance out regional inequities, state and federal governments have become increasingly involved in public education. Funds from these two levels of government are used to serve hot lunches at school, to improve the teaching of math and science, to buy school supplies for low-income students, and to construct new school buildings. In addition, over the years the federal government has established and funded special programs to combat the social problems of low-income, disadvantaged, and minority students. An example is Project Head Start, designed to strengthen the basic academic skills of preschoolers.

Although principally supported by tuition fees and private donations, private schools also receive some government funds for such purposes as bus transportation and feeding disadvantaged students. Government funding of nonpublic schools has been a controversial issue for many years. One reason is that most nonpublic schools are church-related, and government support of them may violate the principle of separation of church and state. The prevailing opinion is that although it may be acceptable for the government to provide parochial schools with fringe benefits and even textbooks, government should not contribute directly to religious programs.

Since nearly all public primary and secondary schools in the United States receive some state and federal support, they have also had to accept increasing levels of government supervision and control. Government agencies set standards for teacher competence. These agencies also insist on certain policies—desegregation, for example—as a condition for financial support. And because sometimes only certain subjects receive government subsidies, state and federal governments thus indirectly influence what courses are offered.

The public schools are sometimes used by higher levels of government as an arena in which important social programs are implemented. Integrating black and white Americans is one such program. Another is providing compensatory education for disadvantaged children. Also, public health agencies use schools for widespread vaccination and immunization against contagious diseases.

As a small but potentially significant supplement to government funding of schools, some of America's corporations are now contributing financially to public education. They are also lobbying for increases in government funding, all in an effort to create a work force that is not only literate but also capable of innovative thinking.

COMMUNITY CONTROL OF PUBLIC SCHOOLS

In most modern societies, major decisions regarding education are generally made by centralized governmental agencies. In contrast, the American model emphasizes the tradition of **community control,** meaning that residents of local communities are able to influence directly the actions of the public schools in which their children are educated. This pattern of control is highly controversial.

In general, the American public favors more community control and less input from Washington or from state capitals (Gallup & Clark, 1987). Residents in some communities complain that local public schools do not respond to their opinions about what and how their children should be taught (Andrews, 1987; Green & Raywid, 1987). Many ethnic and racial minorities, for example, would like to see more programs directed to their special needs. They want to be consulted about what courses will be offered, which teachers will be hired, and what disciplinary measures the schools will use. Because so many people consider a successful education to be the key to upward mobility for low-status groups, such issues arouse much emotion.

However, most teachers and school administrators oppose expanded community control, claiming that professional and technical knowledge is needed to make important decisions about educational methods and policies. They say it is essential to keep "politics" out of the schools. Municipal officials are also frequently opposed to expanding the influence of community members over education. They believe that centralized administration of schools is necessary for efficiency, and they fear that local control will increase educational costs, thus placing a severe strain on their budgets.

The conflict between parents and school officials and the municipal government has sometimes become bitter, especially in large cities. At times, it has been expressed as a racial issue between blacks and whites, worsening a problem that remains unresolved in American education (Andrews, 1987).

The Roles of Teacher and Student

THE TEACHER

It is surprising how complex the role of teacher can be. To the school board, a teacher is an employee; to the principal, a subordinate; to other teachers, a colleague. To students, a teacher must not only be a disciplinarian, judge, confidant, purveyor of morality, and parent substitute but also a knowledgeable person who is able to communicate effectively.

The public image of the teacher has varied dramatically over time. At various points in American history, the teacher has been seen as a strict schoolmaster with rod in hand, a puritanical schoolmarm without a sense of

Community control allows for a more active role for parents and community on school-related issues such as the controversy over school vouchers in Miami.

humor, an absentminded professor, a revered scholar, and a sympathetic adviser of youth. In a classic sociological statement on teaching, Willard Waller (1932/1961) analyzed the teacher as a taskmaster and the teacher-pupil relationship as a form of institutionalized dominance and subordination.

Whatever image may dominate at any particular time, American ideas about teachers have often been unrealistic. Parents wish teachers to participate in the life of the community but not to share its faults (Havighurst & Neugarten, 1978). They also expect teachers to hold strong values, yet remain neutral and objective on controversial public issues.

Today, moreover, teachers must cope with the increasingly widespread suspicion they are poorly trained and educated. In recent years, high school seniors planning to major in education earned an average combined (math and verbal) score of 812 (out of a possible maximum score of 1,600) on the Scholastic Achievement Test. This score was lower than the average score earned by the senior class as a whole, which was 893. Meanwhile, schools of education have been widely derided. Some educators, themselves, believe that their training did not prepare them well for teaching (Harris & Associates, 1991). And many teachers return to college for advanced degrees (National Center for Education Statistics, 1995).

There are, of course, a multitude of intelligent and well-prepared teachers. But the public image of the teacher has plummeted, and with it the number of students who hope to enter the teaching profession. In 1970, 20 percent of first-year college students wanted to teach. That percentage dropped steadily over the next 20 years and has only increased recently. In the face of teacher shortages, school districts are using a number of strategies to attract good teachers (Ballantine, 1997). But it will be difficult to recruit the kind of candidates who entered the field of teaching in the past. Top-ranking women students, who once accounted for much of the best academic talent entering the profession, have been deserting it for law, medicine, and engineering (Williams, 1984).

THE STUDENT

What are the main characteristics of the role of student in a typical school? Some scholars see independence and achievement as central traits (Dreeban, 1968; Parsons, 1959). Others look at the issue less idealistically. According to one anthropologist, the key to being a good student is simply "giving the teacher what she wants" (Henry, 1955). The author of an influential article entitled "Kindergarten as Academic Boot Camp" suggests that the most important dimension of the student role is "quiet obedience" (Gracey, 1970). This trait is first learned in kindergarten, much as raw recruits learn to be good soldiers in boot camp. Still other scholars point out, along similar lines, that the most prominent trait may be patience (Boocock, 1980).

However we may describe the student role, from the school's standpoint it is important that students fit into the bureaucracy. This means that students must learn such norms as punctuality, respect for the teacher, and academic honesty.

STUDENT SUBCULTURES. Partly in response to the bureaucratic setting of the school and partly because they share many common experiences and problems, students generally develop their own subculture. Indeed, there are usually many student subcultures within any particular school. The precise form these subcultures take is related to the character of the school and of the community it serves, as well as to the students' perceptions of their roles.

A classic and still relevant study by James Coleman (1961) suggests that many student subcultures systematically reject adult academic values and have more influence over their members than teachers do. Most boys, Coleman found, value success in sports more than good grades; and girls may try to attract boys by pretending to be less intelligent and studious than they really are.

Another famous research project revealed how a student subculture—this one in a medical school—

developed. At this school, the students were treated, to a large extent, as a single group. Every student went to the same courses, handed in the same assignments, and took the same exams. And, it seems, everyone suffered from an overwhelming workload. Because these students all shared the same pressures, they tended to interact a great deal. After much discussion, they decided to take collective action—to turn in only those reports and other assignments they felt were reasonable. This group action was ultimately accepted by their teachers. Thus, through developing a strong and active student subculture, these students were actually able to modify their educational program (Hughes, Becker, & Geer, 1962).

But the environment at this school was not typical. In less highly structured schools, student subcultures may not be so active or purposeful. And in most schools there is a diversity of subcultures. Three adolescent subcultures seem to have been present in almost every high school across America during the last few decades; they have been called the academic subculture, the fun subculture, and the delinquent subculture (Cohen, 1979).

The *academic subculture* is made up of students who work hard at their studies, generally earn the highest grades, and are college oriented. As the intellectual leaders of their schools, they are heavily involved in student government, edit the student newspaper and literary magazine, and take part in the debating team, as well as in other similar student organizations.

The *fun subculture* is made up of socially active students who are involved in athletics, dating, parties, and student organizations. They are the most popular students in school—mainly because they are involved in athletics and student government—and usually achieve moderately good grades.

The *delinquent subculture* is made up of students who reject many of their school's academic and social values. Over the years, they have been called "greasers," "hippies," "stoners," "punks," and "dirtbags" (the labels tend to change every few years). These delinquent groups share a rebellious attitude directed against authority, structure, conformity, and the "middle-class" values that, as they see it, overemphasize the importance of schooling. They are strongly opposed to rules, except for those established by their own group. It is not unusual to find members of this subculture strictly enforcing standards of behavior—loyalty to friends, for instance—and maintaining dress codes that mark them as members of a distinct group of "outsiders."

As in the larger society, hierarchies often form among student subcultures. The more power each group has or is perceived to have, the higher its place in the hierarchy. The relationships between these subcultures

Trenchcoat Mafia, Columbine High School, Littleton, Colorado. *There are a number of different subcultures that develop within a school. Most fit one of three categories: academic, fun, or delinquent. Do you feel that the schools should monitor these subcultures more closely?*

may echo the relationships between elements of society outside of school, in which boundaries are often drawn according to race, gender, sexual orientation, and religious and political beliefs. But the way students view these within-school divisions does not necessarily reflect what they have learned outside of school (from their parents, for example). One study found that students were much more tolerant about race than their parents were (Grant & Sleeter, 1988). Another study, in an Australian all-boys high school, focused on the relationships between four subcultures, three reflecting the particular sport the members excelled in and one group, the "three friends," stigmatized as "poofs." The researcher found that the students who held the most tolerant views of the fourth group belonged to the most ethnically mixed of the other three subcultures, thus suggesting that personal experience of diversity inclines people toward greater tolerance of individual and group differences (Walker, 1988).

Evaluation of Students

From kindergarten to graduate school, students are constantly being evaluated. Details of this process vary from grade to grade, but the intention is always the same: to measure, to classify, and often to label. In kindergarten, children are observed as they play. The teacher's perceptions of each child's abilities are recorded in a permanent file. Guidance counselors and teachers write evaluations. As the child moves through the grades, other methods of evaluation are used. Students' files go with them from grade to grade, and usually from school to school.

In addition to his or her formal, written record, a student often acquires an informal reputation passed on through the remarks teachers make to one another. Students may be labeled "leaders," "bossy," "eager," or "sloppy," and these labels may follow them through the rest of their academic careers.

Two underlying aspects of this evaluation process are vitally important to students. The first involves how much teachers' evaluations of students reflect cultural stereotypes. As members of the society around them, teachers are just as likely to be affected by stereotypes as is anyone else. What effect does this have on students? Suppose a teacher evaluates a similar action when it is performed by two different children—one white, one black. Say, for example, that the children are speaking out of turn. Will the teacher judge the white child to be "eager" and the black child "undisciplined"? Will a boy who gives direction to a classmate be seen as "a leader," but a girl who does the same be seen as "bossy"? These examples only hint at the way evaluations can reflect cultural stereotypes.

The second important aspect of student evaluations is the issue of how much they actually affect the way students perform. In one widely reported study, a standard IQ test was given to all the children from the first through the sixth grades. The teachers were told that this was a special test, one that would predict intellectual "blooming." A random selection of students, not based on the results of the test, was then made and the teachers were told to expect that the selected students would be the "bloomers," or achievers. The IQ tests were repeated a few months later and once again the following year. The test results showed that those children who were expected to bloom actually did so (Rosenthal & Jacobson, 1968).

This study caused a stir in both the academic and nonacademic worlds. Later, unsuccessful attempts to replicate the findings raised questions as to whether the results were valid. But other studies have produced similar findings. Teachers' stereotypes of students in the primary grades may be especially important, as they often form an important part of the basis on which students are later assigned to high or low tracks, an assignment that not infrequently becomes a self-fulfilling prophecy. Thus, the way that individual students are treated in the classroom can affect how they perceive themselves and how they perform on tests. Such perceptions have been shown to be closely related to the probability of a student's dropping out of school (Natriello, Pallas, & Alexander, 1989).

GRADING

The use of number or letter grades to assess student performance has long been criticized as rigid and unfair. Many substitutes for the conventional grading system have been suggested, but none has gained a wide following. Among the options are pass/fail grading, contract grading, and no grading. The pass/fail system is in limited use at many colleges. In contract grading, the student and teacher agree on what kind and how much work will merit a certain grade. In systems that dispense with grades entirely, the teacher typically writes lengthy evaluations of each student.

All of these alternatives to the usual grading system assess student performance in ways that have some meaning to the students and teachers involved. The problem is how to convey this meaning to outsiders—to colleges for high school students, for example, and to graduate schools for college students. This, in turn, is related to the bureaucratic character of the educational institution. As bureaucracies, colleges and graduate schools experience difficulty dealing with unusual cases—in this case, evaluating applications from students lacking standardized assessments of their academic performance. This is a major reason why alternative grading systems have failed to gain widespread acceptance.

STANDARDIZED TESTS

Scandals involving stolen test information have focused public attention more closely on the validity of reported scores on national tests and on the ability of these tests to assess accurately students' abilities. These concerns relit the fires of a debate that first arose in the early part of the last decade.

In 1980, Ralph Nader and Allan Nairn published *The Reign of ETS*, a critical study of the Educational Testing Service. ETS produces the Scholastic Achievement Test (SAT), on which many students' college hopes rise or fall. The controversy that followed the report's publication inspired another study that concluded that the SAT is simply not necessary. The researchers contended that, although the SAT may predict college success fairly accurately, it does not necessarily *improve* prediction when it supplements information already available from the high school about the student's coursework and grades (Crouse & Trusheim, 1988).

But although the ETS tests have been criticized for testing only a narrow range of abilities (on the SAT, verbal and mathematical skills) and for being easily coached, the researchers generally did not suggest abandoning all standardized testing. They cited as a model the College Board's Advanced Placement Program, which is characterized by a much closer match between what is tested and what is taught, thus yielding more accurate test scores. And, since the Advanced Placement Test questions are based on high school courses jointly planned by colleges and high schools, the scores more accurately predict the academic success of students in college (Crouse & Trusheim, 1988).

WINDOW ON SOCIOLOGY

THE END OF EDUCATION

When it comes to issues, education is a perennial American problem. Year after year, Americans give low grades to teachers and public schools, and they have compiled a long list of complaints. According to a 1997 Gallup poll, only 40 percent of Americans expressed a high level of confidence in public schools—a drop of 10 percentage points since 1987 and nearly 20 points since 1973 (Moore & Saad, 1998). In 1996, the problems most frequently cited by the public included lack of discipline, lack of financial support, violence, the use of drugs, and overcrowding (U.S. Department of Education, 1997, "The Annual Gallup Poll of the Public's Attitudes Toward the Public Schools"). Teachers saw the problems from another perspective. In 1993–1994, their list of the most serious problems included students being unprepared to learn, lack of parental involvement, student apathy, poverty, and student disrespect for teachers (U.S. Department of Education, 1997, "Schools and Staffing Survey").

In response to these concerns, educators typically propose solutions that address the means of attaining an education (Postman, 1995). Some people suggest that we should privatize schools. Some believe that national standards of assessment are needed. Some consider how we ought to teach reading, and yet others ask how we should use computers. According to Neil Postman, all of these possible solutions have one thing in common: They fail to address the *purpose* of school. And that is what is wrong with them.

In his book, *The End of Education,* Postman argues that schools today lack the kind of shared narratives that inspire students to learn (1995). Some of the past great American narratives include the great story of democracy. Described from the perspective of foreign eyes, Alexis de Tocqueville called it "the principle of civic participation"; Gunnar Myrdal referred to it as "the American Creed." From his own perspective, Postman sees Thomas Jefferson as the Moses of the democracy-god. And because Jefferson helped to write this narrative, Postman says that he knew the purpose of schools—"to ensure that citizens would know when and how to protect their liberty" (p. 13). Another narrative that has inspired American students is known as the Protestant work ethic. This story has motivated thousands of Americans with the idea that hard work, self-discipline, and deferred gratification will be taken as a sign of God's favor.

These kinds of narratives inspire people; and schools can use them to help students understand the purpose of education. They also arouse curiosity, motivate students, and help them focus their attention. But most importantly they give students common "gods," which, Postman argues, are more important than common goals. And that is because public education does not serve a public; it creates one. What kind does it create? Postman wonders himself:

A conglomerate of self-indulgent consumers? Angry, soulless, directionless masses? Indifferent, confused citizens? Or a public imbued with confidence, a sense of purpose, a respect for learning, and tolerance? (p. 18)

As the national schools and staffing survey cited earlier suggests, teachers' perceptions of students as unprepared to learn, apathetic, and disrespectful suggest that students sense no purpose in education. Postman would describe them as alienated and would argue that they experience education as a meaningless endeavor. Educators and political leaders who focus on the details of managing schools to solve educational problems are, therefore, looking in the wrong direction. National exams, teacher accountability, class size, and computers cannot solve America's educational problems. Only those who recognize the importance of helping students understand the purpose of education are on the right track.

The title of Postman's book, *The End of Education,* can be taken as a pessimistic expectation about the future of education. But, in fact, he intentionally chose a title that would allow a different interpretation, one that sees an optimistic future. This view is based on the notion that "end" can mean the achievement of a worthy goal—one that inspires students, arouses their curiosity, and focuses their attention. Embodied in narratives relevant to the twenty-first century with modern "gods," Postman hopes that students will think of the end of education in terms of the spiritual and intellectual dimensions of learning. Therein lies the real solution to America's educational problem.

TRENDS AND ISSUES IN AMERICAN EDUCATION

As one of the most powerful and important institutions in American society, education has been subject to a variety of criticisms and is presently undergoing a number of changes designed to remedy the failings identified by its critics. In this section, we begin by introducing some of the primary weaknesses of American education and then consider some of the responses to these problems,

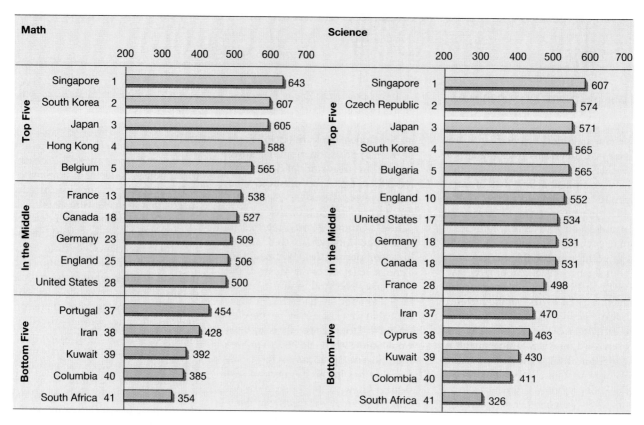

FIGURE 15.3   Ranking math and science skills: a study of student achievement in math and science ranked 41 countries. Scoring was on a scale of 200 to 800 points.

Source: International Mathematics and Science Study, 1996, courtesy of William Schmidt.

including the increased use of computers and television in the classroom, the back to basics movement, and voucher plans. Next we review some of the characteristics of private schools, which may suggest some ways in which public schools might improve their performance. We conclude with a look at some special concerns related to the education of minorities and to the ability of the schools to promote enhanced opportunity for their graduates.

Critiques of American Education

In recent years, the principal concerns of the American public about schools have remained fairly constant: lack of discipline and proper financial support, violence in school, the use of drugs, the difficulty of obtaining qualified new teachers, weak curricula and low academic standards, and overcrowding (U.S. Department of Education, 1997, "The Annual Gallup Poll of the Public's Attitudes Toward the Public Schools").

Such concerns gave rise in the early 1980s to a number of national investigations of public schooling. Among the most important reports stemming from these investigations were *A Nation at Risk* (1983); *Action for Excellence* (1983), from the Task Force on Education for Economic Growth; and *A Nation Prepared: Teachers for the 21st Century* (1986), by the Task Force on Teaching as a Profession. A common theme of all these reports is the relation between technical and scientific education, on the one hand, and the national economy on the other. The reports argue that the advanced economies of the future will depend heavily on high-level skills that can be provided only by education. Furthermore, they add, America's students are seriously deficient in such skills, particularly as compared with students in Japan, America's main economic competitor.

The reports point as well to the relatively low quality of the students who now enter the teaching profession, and they suggest ways of attracting better teachers in the future. Paying educators more money might seem to be the obvious solution, but in an era of reduced government funding, the reports tend to stress other answers. Two proposals much in favor are minimum competency tests for teachers and merit pay for those with special teaching abilities (as opposed to an overall rise in teacher salaries). Merit pay is controversial; objections include the concern that monetary awards for merit may have the effect of depressing the overall salary level of teachers (Ornstein, 1988). Another proposal is "extended preparation," requiring five years of schooling for prospective teachers rather than four (Hawley, 1989). Critics of this proposal argue that the costs of such a program would be prohibitive for many aspiring teachers and would divert public funds from other, more productive programs.

Another report, "An Impoverished Generation," by the Carnegie Foundation for the Advancement of Teaching (1987), calls for efforts at improvement to be concentrated in inner-city schools. The report argues that problems in these schools are of a different kind than those found in suburban districts. Poverty, malnutrition, racism, drugs, and deteriorated facilities, the report says, make efforts to raise academic standards in inner-city schools ineffective without additional help (*Washington Post,* March 19, 1988). Polls suggest that a majority of Americans would be willing to pay more taxes toward reaching this goal (Elam & Gallup, 1989).

Innovations in Teaching

During the 1960s and 1970s, there were high hopes for many educational innovations. Not all of these innovations met with success, although some laid the groundwork for developments of the last few years.

Educators once had great expectations for *teaching machines* and *closed-circuit television* as classroom aids. Teaching machines promised to make instruction more individualized by providing students with immediate feedback; closed-circuit television could reach a large student audience and provide a more diverse education. But these devices are costly to purchase and maintain, and teachers have tended to use them only with reluctance, perhaps fearing that the educational process might become depersonalized. In addition, there has not been enough training in the use of these devices, nor has much research been done on how to utilize them effectively in the classroom.

Another innovation was *team teaching,* in which several teachers were assigned to one classroom. This was meant to provide students with teachers who have a greater variety of skills and therefore more command of individual subjects. But because the technique required

so much planning and analysis and because teachers were used to exercising exclusive authority in the classroom, team teaching has not been very successful.

The *open classroom* is an informal environment in which students are taught individually or in small groups. Although it has been sucessful in some European countries, it has never become very popular in the United States. The greater freedom granted to each student in an open classroom is made possible only by a great deal of planning.

Performance contracting involves the hiring of private organizations to teach students such subjects as reading and math. Typically, these organizations have relied on various kinds of teaching machines. This approach has improved students' test scores only minimally, and many experiments of this kind have been discontinued.

Although none of these innovations has been notably successful, others have fared better and have become a part of American education. One example is the wide use of *paraprofessionals* in schools—men and women who do not have the full professional training required of teachers. The use of paraprofessionals helps to ease the workload of teachers, and it also can provide disadvantaged mothers with jobs and the chance to later become full professionals.

COMPUTERS IN EDUCATION

Another important, fairly recent innovation in education is the use of *personal computers* as learning tools. These desk-sized and fairly inexpensive devices have become almost universal in our schools. In 1995, the typical public school owned 72 computers. And two thirds of schools had Internet access by 1996 (U.S. Department of Education, 1997).

Schools use computers both to instruct students in the use of computers themselves—for computer education, in other words—and to teach about other subjects. Computer education is the less controversial of the two uses, for it is impossible to learn how to run a computer without having access to one. Even here there is debate, however. Most schools stress programming skills—how to write the programs that tell the computer what to do; other schools prefer to teach their students to make use of the many ready-to-use programs that are available commercially.

Whatever their advantages and drawbacks as an educational medium, computers have become an established part of school curricula. Fear that their students may be left behind in this age of computers has encouraged secondary school systems to give the computer a prominent place in education. This attitude is supported by a majority of Americans, who feel that computer training should be basic to a high school education, both for college-bound and noncollege-bound students (Gallup & Clark, 1987).

For over 10 years, there has been substantial controversy over the use of computers in the classroom. Some experts have argued that there are few classrooms where children are learning anything on computers that they could not learn without them (*New York Times,* August 6, 1989). The Center for Social Organization of Schools at Johns Hopkins University has suggested that not enough use is being made of computers to enhance instruction (*New York Times,* August 9, 1989). Others, pointing to the apparent effectiveness of computers in some classrooms, have noted that the greatest benefit from using computers in schools may be due not to the computers themselves but, rather, to the individualized instruction and attention from teachers received by students learning to use a computer (Walker, 1987). And, more recently, critics have questioned the educational value of the Internet when so many American students cannot even solve basic math problems (*New York Times,* October 25, 1997).

TELEVISION IN EDUCATION

Television rivals and may even surpass computers as a teaching tool. Although television has been long cast as a villain responsible for decreasing IQ levels and attention spans, recent research has suggested that it can be an effective educational asset when properly harnessed. It is now regarded as an excellent way to introduce students to other societies, to encourage new ideas, and to increase

motivational levels in the classroom (Fontana, 1988). By providing vicarious role models and social interactions that may be missing from their own lives, television is particularly valuable in teaching adolescents (Luker & Johnston, 1988).

From programs (such as *Sesame Street*) directed at very young children, to those that allow older students to earn high school credit, to those that promote reading and math skills, TV's potential as a medium of education has barely been scratched. International teleconferencing is seen by some sociologists as the wave of the future. In the future, classrooms may participate in global electronic universities that allow access to programming from all over the world (Pelton, 1988).

BACK TO BASICS AND HIGHER STANDARDS

According to many current critics, the American educational system must set higher standards and return to an emphasis on the traditional areas of reading, writing, and arithmetic. In order to accomplish these goals, the critics propose that schools spend less time on "frills," such as art and music appreciation, race relations, drivers' training, and physical education. Conservatives believe that the schools have become overburdened by trying to deal with the "whole child"; this is one major reason, they argue, for the schools' failure to teach the fundamentals adequately.

Moreover, these critics believe that a misguided concern with students' social adjustment has permitted many youngsters who have not mastered basic academic skills to pass on repeatedly to the next grade. Mastery of traditional subject areas, they feel, is more important than "self-discovery."

A Nation at Risk, the influential 1983 report of the National Commission on Excellence in Education, recommended tougher standards and increased competition among students and schools. Some modest changes along these lines have already been made. Most states have recently raised the requirements for graduation from high school, and many now require students to pass minimum competency tests in order to graduate.

THE VOUCHER SYSTEM

The *voucher system* is a much-discussed innovation in government support of education. Under this plan, parents would be given a "voucher" with which they could select the school of their choice, public or private. Public schools would be financed on the basis of the number of vouchers taken in, rather than being supported directly by taxes. Advocated mainly, but not solely, by conservatives, this system is designed to increase competition

Source: © 1970 by Janice and Stanley Berenstein. *Source:* Gerald Lesser, *Children and Television: Lessons from Sesame Street* (New York: Random House, 1974).

among schools and thus to raise educational standards. The federal government has supported voucher systems in several areas on a trial basis.

Many education experts have criticized such voucher programs. Some suggest that vouchers would make schools more segregated. Others fear that public schools might turn into dumping grounds for those students who could not gain admission elsewhere. Public response to the voucher system has been mixed. A 1995 Gallup poll showed that 69 percent of the American public favored allowing students and their parents to choose which public schools in the community the students attend, regardless of where they live. But only 33 percent said that they favored allowing students and parents to choose a private school to attend at public expense (U.S. Department of Education, 1997, "The Annual Gallup Poll of the Public's Attitudes Toward the Public Schools").

Private Education

Over 44 million American children currently attend public elementary and secondary schools. Under 6 million attend private schools (U.S. Department of Education 1997). Catholic schools account for most of the total private school enrollment, but their share of students has declined. In 1967, 87 percent of all students in private schools attended Catholic schools; by 1994, this figure had dropped to just under 51 percent (U.S. Department of Education, 1997). Fundamentalist Protestant schools have been growing rapidly in recent years.

Does the increase in private school enrollments tell us anything about the quality of a private versus a public education? According to sociologist James Coleman (1987), students are flocking to private schools for good reason: They receive a better education there. Under a contract from the National Center for Education Statistics, a federal agency, Coleman studied nearly 59,000 students in 1,015 public and private high schools throughout the country. In his widely discussed report, *Public and Private Schools,* Coleman concluded that even when differences in family backgrounds are taken into account, the average private school does a better job of educating students than does the average public school.

Coleman attributes the greater effectiveness of the private schools to several factors. He notes that private schools maintain better discipline than public schools; sophomores in public schools, for example, are twice as likely to get into fights, disobey their teachers, or vandalize their schools. Also, private schools offer greater academic challenges; the nation's 1.3 million private high school students outperform their public school counterparts in basic reading, writing, and arithmetic, as well as in science, civics, and vocabulary. Coleman found that the low student/teacher ratios of most private schools contribute to these positive results and that minority and white students benefit equally from private education. Although there is a smaller proportion of blacks in private schools than in public schools, there is less racial segregation in the private setting, a fact that may partly account for the academic success of minority, low-income private school students.

In a reexamination of his data, Coleman found that Catholic schools have an especially low dropout rate, even when compared to other private schools. He attributes this to the supportive community that surrounds most Catholic schools (*New York Times,* March 30, 1988).

Not surprisingly, Coleman's report inspired angry reactions from some public school officials, who denounced it as poorly researched, biased, and inaccurate. The critics focused especially on the comparability (or lack thereof) between public and private school populations, pointing out that 70 percent of private school students take academic programs with entering college as their goal, but that only about 33 percent of public school students pursue similar academic programs. Thus, students in private school are virtually certain to outperform their public school counterparts.

There were many other criticisms of Coleman's study. Some questioned the validity of the achievement tests Coleman used to measure performance, as well as his claim that private schools are less racially segregated than public schools. They also attacked the way he controlled for socioeconomic status (Page, 1981). Another researcher argued that, by controlling for variables that Coleman had ignored—sex, physical handicaps, region of residence, and hopes for college attendance—he could show that pupils in Catholic private schools "do no better—or worse—than [those in] public schools" (Noell, 1982).

Apart from the issue of academic quality, private schools are sometimes criticized in America on egalitarian grounds. Because of their high tuition, a sizable portion of young Americans cannot attend private schools. In particular, the academically elite schools, especially boarding schools, are viewed by some scholars as perpetuating the dominance of the American upper class (Cookson & Persell, 1985). One way to increase access to private schools would be to adopt the sort of voucher plan discussed in the previous section, which could cover part or even all of a student's tuition. However, many observers believe that the use of government vouchers to pay for tuition in parochial schools may be a violation of constitutional requirements mandating the separation of church and state.

One of the many difficulties facing teachers today is having to know how to communicate with and motivate a diverse student body.

Education and Minorities

Few issues in education today are more important than those that arise with regard to minority students. In this section, we consider two such issues: the special educational needs of minorities, especially those raised in poverty-level families, and the efforts that have been made to end racial segregation in the schools.

TEACHING MINORITY STUDENTS

Because they frequently enter school lacking language, values, and skills that most middle-class children have already acquired at home, lower-class minority students pose a particularly serious challenge to educators. It is generally assumed that the children who are most at risk of dropping out of school are those raised in poverty, those raised by a single parent, and those who understand little English—characteristics that often occur in the same individual.

Most educators agree that language is frequently a major problem among minority students. It is not uncommon, for example, for children from Puerto Rico, Mexico, and such Asian countries as Vietnam to start first grade without knowing more than a few words of English, the language in which all their classes are taught. Children of various ethnic backgrounds may have accents and use words that teachers cannot understand. The resulting frustrations can cause children, even at an early age, to view school as a place where they cannot possibly hope to succeed. As a result, they sometimes give up trying or even attending.

How should we educate children whose native language is not English? In 1974, the U.S. Supreme Court required all schools to provide special assistance to such children, but it did not specify what kind of assistance should be made available. The federal government's Office of Civil Rights chose to interpret this decision as a call for what became known as transitional *bilingual education:* giving students instruction in their native languages until they could attend classes taught in English. Proponents argued that students taught in this way would be able to go on learning other subjects while they mastered English, and that they would progress more quickly in both areas than they would if they were forced to attend classes conducted in English before they fully understood it. It has also been suggested that bilingual education could help foreign-language students retain contact with their cultures of origin (see Yu & Atkinson, 1988).

The results of bilingual education programs are not at all clear. Some studies seem to indicate that they have worked; others show that they have had no effect at all; and still others report that they actually have had a negative impact (Baker & de Kanter, 1983; Levine, 1996). Moreover, not everyone believes that students from abroad should be encouraged to maintain their original language and culture. One advocacy group, known as "U.S. English," has been fighting to have English declared the official language of the United States. So far, more than one-third of the states have passed legislation to that effect.

Another program connected with teaching minority-group children is deciding what type of educational material is appropriate. Until recently, typical grade-school reading books dealt with the lives of white, middle-class, small-town American families. To African-American children on Chicago's South Side or Mexican-Americans in southern California, such families seemed utterly alien. Responding to pressure from ethnic groups, educators and publishers have begun to develop more relevant educational materials. Many elementary readers now portray African-Americans and Asian-Americans as frequently and as positively as they do whites, include pictures of urban as well as suburban settings, and attempt to depict childhood in a more realistic way.

The realities of economic deprivation, however, continue to work against some minority children from the lower classes. Fatherless children with mothers who work nights cannot bring their parents to special events such as parents' night and the school play. This can embarrass or distress such children. Teachers often cannot confer with parents from these families about problems their children are having at school, nor can such parents easily assist their children with homework.

Also, the teachers, typically white and middle class, may not know how to motivate minority-group children to do their best in school. Mexican-American or Native American students, for example, may be unwilling to respond directly to a teacher's negative comments. The teacher may misread such an attitude as a display of defiance. Or a Puerto Rican child, accustomed to a highly nurturant and emotionally expressive home atmosphere, can be hurt and disappointed by the reserve of a teacher who may be sincerely trying to reach out to the child—but in a way the child cannot understand.

Minority-group students may also be harmed by displays of prejudice and discrimination from their classmates or, more seriously, from their teachers. A few teachers consciously discriminate—denying minority children extra help or the chance to participate, ignoring their raised hands, or grading them more strictly. More commonly, the discrimination may be unconscious and more subtle. For example, a prejudiced teacher may assume that African-American children who do poorly in math are performing as well as can be expected, but that white children who do poorly are underachievers. The white children, as a result, get extra instruction. Thus, because white students are expected to do better, they tend to learn more math than do black children who are equally capable.

Students from minority groups do not always fare poorly in American schools, however. One study showed that Sikh youths performed better than white students in both Great Britain and California (Givson & Bhachu, 1988). At the high school level, Asian-American students, as a group, often outscore other minorities and white students on standardized tests (So, 1986). Asian-American high school students also tend to take more courses in mathematics, the natural sciences, and foreign languages than do other students and are overrepresented in college-preparatory curricula and in programs for the gifted and talented (Ornstein, 1985). At the college freshman level, most minorities are better represented in two-year institutions than in four-year institutions, public or private. Asians are the only minority group with a higher enrollment in four-year colleges than in two-year colleges (American College Testing Program, 1986).

RACIAL INTEGRATION

American schools enrolling exclusively or primarily African-American children are, on average, of lower quality than those serving white children. Classes are larger, facilities are frequently outmoded or worn out, and library collections are smaller. Such conditions discourage many of the best-qualified teachers from working in these schools. Segregation, then, usually means inferior education (Coleman et al., 1966).

Many public school systems in the United States historically followed policies of **de jure segregation,** or segregation based on local law. In a 1954 Supreme Court decision, *Brown* v. *Board of Education, de jure* segregation was declared unconstitutional.

But it would be a mistake to believe that segregated schools no longer exist. An even more complex problem is created by **de facto segregation,** which results from residential patterns. Because of their typically lower incomes and also as a result of continuing discrimination, African-Americans and other minority groups often have a limited choice of housing. Thus, they commonly live clustered together in ghettos. Since most public schools in the United States serve the residents of a particular neighborhood, the schools in these districts typically enroll few white children. Segregation, therefore, continues to exist in de facto form-mainly in the primary schools (Kirby et al., 1973). Because they draw their students from more than one neighborhood, secondary schools and community colleges are usually less segregated.

De facto school segregation is a serious national problem. Since residential patterns cannot be easily changed, the only way to reduce this segregation is to partially or completely abandon the neighborhood character of schools. Some communities have reorganized their school systems to do just this. A town large enough to have three neighborhood primary schools, for example, can use one school for grades one and two, another for grades three and four, and the third for grades five and six. This plan allows all children of the same age group to attend the same school.

However, this solution, and others like it, necessarily involve transporting some children to schools outside their own neighborhoods. Popularly known as *busing,* this strategy has prompted strong opposition, especially in white neighborhoods with strong local identities (Buell, 1980). Parents sometimes object to busing on grounds other than opposition to integration: the tiring ride across town, the risk of their children becoming lost or confused about which bus to take, and decreased contact between parents and teachers (Armor, 1989). But the evidence suggests that white opposition to busing is at least as much a reflection of racial and political attitudes as it is caused by concerns over neighborhood identity and the problems of the bus ride itself (Sears, Hensler, & Speer, 1979; Weatherford, 1980).

Some research (Coleman, Kelly, & Moore, 1975) has cast serious doubt on the effectiveness of forced busing in the long run. In the early 1970s, for example, the city of Boston was ordered to desegregate its educational system by busing pupils across school districts. Although whites in Boston at first opposed busing, sometimes violently, by the mid-1980s opposition to it was dead. At the same time, however, the number and proportion of white students in Boston's public schools fell sharply, presumably because white families chose to move out of the city, a trend known as "white flight." The schools thus ultimately became more segregated than ever. Today, Boston as well as many other cities has dropped busing as an educational strategy.

ALTERNATIVES TO BUSING: CHOICE PLANS. Some alternative approaches to desegregation have been formulated that do not involve busing. These so-called choice plans include two main components. The first is a program called *majority to minority transfer,* or open enrollment, in which free transportation is offered to a student who transfers from a school in which his or her race is the majority to one in which his or her race is in the minority (Armor, 1989). The other, more visible, component is the *magnet school.* Usually located in inner cities, magnets are schools with special academic programs intended to make them more attractive to the kind of middle-class white student who would otherwise attend a private school or move to the suburbs.

The first magnet schools were established in the early 1970s. By the 1980s, they had become an important tool for achieving school integration: Dallas, Houston, Los Angeles, Milwaukee, and San Diego were required by court orders to found them; Chicago, Cincinnati, Indianapolis, and Seattle set them up in hopes of sidetracking legal trouble; a few cities, including Cambridge, Massachusetts, even established them without the threat of a court order. By 1992, 5,000 magnet schools existed nationwide (Ballantine, 1997).

Despite the proliferation of magnet schools across the country, they are not without their problems. One criticism is that magnet schools deliberately skim off the brightest students and teachers, thereby reducing the quality of the other schools in the district. A study analyzing admissions policies found that magnet schools consistently tended to admit students with high test scores, solid mastery of English, and no learning problems, as opposed to students from low-income families, who read below grade level, had attendance and learning problems and whose native language was not English (Moore & Davenport, 1989). Moreover, magnets often cost more money to set up and run than ordinary schools do. Also, legal and financial restrictions make it impossible to transfer across district boundaries, as is usually necessary if minority students are to be placed in predominantly white suburban schools (Armor, 1989). Nonetheless, studies show that magnet schools can offer more choices to students, aid in the desegregation of schools, and improve education (Blank & Archibald, 1992).

The prospect for choice programs is far from gloomy. Several large districts across the United States have successfully maintained a diverse racial mix through these strategies. In San Diego, 7,000 minority students use the majority to minority transfer plan, and nearly 30,000 white and minority students attend magnet schools. In Savannah, Georgia, a magnet program that replaced busing attracted nearly 1,000 white students back to public schools from private institutions (Armor, 1989; Rist, 1989; Rossell & Glenn, 1988).

Education and Equality

Schools in America are often blamed for promoting inequality in all areas of life. If only schools had equal resources, facilities, and teachers, it is argued, America would be well on the way to ending inequality. Several major national studies in the last few decades, however, have cast serious doubt on this premise.

The first was the famous Coleman Report (Coleman et al., 1966). James Coleman set out to study to what extent the unequal status of blacks and whites could be explained by the differential quality of the education each group received. Coleman found that "schools bring little influence to bear on a child's achievement that is independent of . . . background and general social context." By background and general social context, Coleman particularly meant the economic status of the child's family, cultural life in the home, neighborhood conditions, and peer relationships.

The home environment, which is greatly affected by the family's economic status, helps mold cognitive skills that are valuable in school. Students from "culturally rich" homes—for example, those with many books—tend to be more academically oriented than students from "culturally deprived" homes. Also, the family's attitudes toward education help to determine how far a student will go in school. Middle-class high school graduates tend to enter college even if they do not particularly enjoy school, whereas students from working- or lower-class families more commonly drop out of school if they dislike it.

Coleman's findings were by and large supported by those of another major study, *Inequality,* conducted by Christopher Jencks (Jencks et al., 1972). Jencks concluded that "the evidence suggests that equalizing education opportunity would do very little to make adults more equal." The reason for this, he states, is "that the character of a school's output depends largely on a single input, namely the characteristics of the entering children."

These researchers would argue that Americans hold unrealistic expectations for their schools. If Americans

FIELD	BATCHELOR'S DEGREE	MASTER'S DEGREE	DOCTORAL DEGREE
Humanities	$25,078	—	—
Social Sciences	$25,103	—	—
Accounting	$30,154	$33,636	—
Computer Science	$37,215	$44,331	$63,058

FIGURE 15.4 Annual salary offers according to degree, 1997.

Source: U.S. Bureau of the Census, *Statistical Abstract of the United States, 1998* (Washington, D.C.: U.S. Government Printing Office, 1998.)

want more equality, Jencks suggests, the best way—although it may not be politically feasible—is simply to redistribute income through the process of taxation.

Not all research supports this view of schools, however. One example is a 16-year study of the effects of high-quality preschool education on the subsequent careers of poor African-American children with low IQs in Ypsilanti, Michigan (Berrueta-Clement et al., 1984). This group of children, who started preschool at the age of three, needed less remedial help in their elementary and high school years and included fewer dropouts and lawbreakers than a similar control group of students who did not attend the special preschool program. Moreover, twice as many went on to higher education or full-time work as did children in the control group. However, the program, widely heralded when it was first reported, still did not bring the children up to the academic level of middle-class students.

Education and Earnings

Everyone has heard of the people who barely finished grade school yet became millionaires, and of Ph.D.s reduced to driving taxis or working in convenience stores. However, these exceptional cases obscure the general pattern: People who have more years of schooling typically earn higher incomes. Figure 15.4 documents the salaries that are offered to college graduates in different fields and to persons holding advanced degrees.

The following excerpt summarizes the findings of a variety of studies that have investigated the question of whether a college education for men is worth the cost (Jencks et al., 1979):

All these studies show that men with a lot of education work in higher-status occupations and earn more money than men with less education. Of course, not all of this difference has to do with the number of years spent in a classroom. Those who stay in school are often the kind of people who already have qualities and skills that employers value, no matter how many years of schooling they complete. And they are likely to come from affluent families, giving them an economic advantage no matter how successful they are academically.

Yet even among men from the same type of homes, with identical test scores and similar initial occupations, college graduates end up obtaining substantially higher-status jobs than high school graduates. In addition, research has shown that earning a bachelor's degree has a strong effect on income. Men who complete high school probably earn some [51] percent more than men from similar backgrounds who drop out of high school. In contrast, men who complete college may earn as much as [76] percent more than those from similar backgrounds who do not graduate.

What about the advantages of going to a "good" college? One study shows that for men with similar backgrounds, the differences in the reputation of college have little effect on occupational status—that is, on the prestige of the jobs the men eventually get. College selectivity is important, however, in regard to earnings. The study shows that men who graduate from "selective" colleges earn 28 percent more than men who graduate from "nonselective" ones.

CHAPTER REVIEW

1. What is the difference between learning and education?

2. Identify and discuss the functions that education serves.

3. How do tracking and credentialism perpetuate inequalities in education?

4. How can educators resolve the conflict between the need to maintain academic excellence and the desire to provide equal educational opportunites for everyone?

5. Why do most teachers and administrators oppose community control of education?

6. Describe the culture of a typical American school. Include an analysis of conflicting roles, norms, and values.

7. Discuss the different proposals for improving the quality of education in America. Identify the strengths and weaknesses of the arguments on different sides of these proposals.

8. Do private schools provide a better education than public schools? Why have private schools been criticized?

9. Does segregation in American schools today result in an inferior education for minority students? If so, what solution would you propose for this problem?

10. How does a student's education affect his or her entire life?

INTERNET EXERCISE

The Web destinations for Chapter 15 are relevant to various issues surrounding education. To begin your explorations, go to the Prentice Hall Companion Web site **http://www.prenhall.com/popenoe**. Next, choose **Chapter 15** (Education). Then, select **web destinations** from the menu on the left side of the screen. There are several sites to choose from. We suggest you begin with the **National Center for Education Statistics (NCES).** This site contains some very interesting facts and statistics about education in the United States. For example, the *National Assessment of Education Progress (NAEP) 1998 Reading Report Card for the Nation and the States* is presented, including the results of the NAEP Reading assessment for the nation and for participating states or jurisdictions. After you have explored the National Center for Education Statistics, answer the following questions:

- Based upon the contents of the NAEP web site, do ou believe that America is still "a nation at risk" in terms of education?

- Do you think it is a good idea for all public schools and classrooms to be connected to the Information Superhighway (Internet)? Why or why not?

KEY TERMS

learning	tracking	de jure segregation
education	credentialism	de facto segregation
assimilation	community control	

CHAPTER 16

Religion

hen institutional aspects of society function properly, they respond to important social needs. When they are not operating as they should, they can cause a great deal of harm, as when a school fails to educate its pupils or when a sector of the economy is unable to sustain or create badly needed jobs. But no malfunctioning part of society can create such utter chaos as a religion gone bad.

You could ask the followers of Jim Jones's People's Temple about this—if they were still alive. Jones was an itinerant minister from Indiana who moved his flock to California in the mid-1960s and, fearing political persecution, migrated again to the South American nation of Guyana in 1977. Isolated and increasingly paranoid, Jones compelled his followers to labor long hours erecting buildings for their settlement, called Jonestown. After work, the believers were subjected to increasingly incoherent daily sermons lasting four to six hours and aired on loudspeakers throughout the compound for the benefit of anyone too ill to attend in person.

Convinced that his enemies were preparing to destroy the cult, Jones established the ritual of White Night, in which his followers willingly drank what they were told might, or might not, be poison. In 1978, Congressman Leo Ryan was assassinated by Jones's followers after he had visited Jonestown in order to investigate complaints that some People's Temple members were being held against their will. Realizing that this incident could not be ignored by the outside world, Jones ordered one last White Night, this time for real. Nine hundred and twelve men, women, and children drank cyanide-laced Flavor-Aid and died, leaving a stunned world to contemplate the extremes to which a religion could impel its believers (Bainbridge & Stark, 1979; Johnson, 1979; Mills, 1979; Naipaul, 1980).

Fifteen years later, after memories of the Guyana mass suicide had begun to recede, history repeated itself, this time in the unlikely location of Waco, Texas. The group was called the Branch Davidians, an offshoot of an offshoot of the Seventh-day Adventists, and the leader was a 33-year-old former rock musician and self-proclaimed prophet who was born Vernon Howell but had assumed the name of David Koresh.

Like members of the People's Temple, the Branch Davidians had retreated from the world into an isolated, communal lifestyle. Both groups featured practices that outside observers found bizarre: Koresh, a ninth-grade dropout, married a number of the female believers, some as young as 12, and fathered many of the children who lived in the Branch Davidian compound. Obsessively worried about the activities of his enemies, Koresh, like Jones, prepared for an attack, in this case by accumulating a sizable armory of firearms.

On February 28, 1993, agents of the Federal Bureau of Alcohol, Tobacco, and Firearms attempted to raid the compound, but failed to secure their objective. Four agents and six cult members died. A 51-day standoff ensued that ended on April 19 with an assault by FBI and BAT forces to which Koresh's group responded by setting fires that destroyed their compound and killed 86 Davidians including at least 17 children under the age of 14 and Koresh himself (Beck, 1993; Kantrowitz, 1993a, 1993b).

Within five years, the mass suicide of yet another religious group, Heaven's Gate, would make headlines. In all, 39 corpses—21 women and 18 men—were found inside a 9,200-square-foot mansion located in Rancho Santa Fe, California. The discovery was eerie. Each body was draped with a diamond-shaped purple shroud, and all wore a new pair of black Nike running shoes. The coroner eventually discovered that at least a half dozen of the men had been surgically castrated, including the cult's leader, Marshall Herff Applewhite. The autopsies showed that Applewhite's followers had died from overdoses of phenobarbital, but many apparently died from suffocation caused by the plastic bags that the men and women had placed over their heads after ingesting drugs and alcohol (*Newsweek,* April 7, 1997).

Their deaths were technically suicides. But Applewhite, who was regarded as a masterful manipulator, played a critical role in persuading his followers to end their own lives. Videotapes, written documents, and Internet postings indicated that Heaven's Gate members had prepared themselves for a Higher Kingdom. Absorbing themselves in the fantasy worlds of *Star Trek* and *The X-Files,* they became convinced that a spacecraft was on its way to take them to "Their World." The sign was the comet Hale-Bopp, which grew bright in the dark evening sky. Applewhite had promised them that their deaths would free them and that they would ascend to a higher place.

Sociologists who specialize in the study of religion are often called upon to help explain tragedies such as those that occurred in Jonestown and in Waco; and some of the content of this chapter may help you to understand how believers can become so absorbed in their religion that they are willing literally to die for their faith. However, the sociology of religion devotes most of its attention to the more conventional varieties of religious expression in American society.

Research suggests that Americans are more religious as a group than are the citizens of most other industrial or postindustrial societies. Recent statistics show that 96 percent of all Americans believe in God (Shorto, 1997). Not only is formal church membership in the United States common, but the long-term historical trend is strongly upward. In 1861, only 37 percent of Americans belonged to a church or synagogue compared with more than 68 percent of all Americans in 1997.

If these figures are accurate, why do so many people believe that the United States is a secular society where religion is gradually losing importance? Perhaps part of the explanation lies in the definition of what it means to be religious. Can all people who claim membership in a formal religious organization be considered "religious"? Or is religion a more intensely personal experience that cannot be measured by attendance in a religious organization? These are some of the questions explored in this chapter, which examines theoretical perspectives concerning the way religion relates to society, the organization of religion, religion in American life, and the process of secularization.

RELIGION AND SOCIETY

Both sociologists and theologians agree that the term *religion* can be applied to many kinds of behavior. One dictionary defines religion as "the service and adoration of God or a god as expressed in forms of worship, in obedience to divine commands . . . and in the pursuit of a way of life regarded as incumbent on true believers." But this definition is too narrow to cover the many forms of religious behavior and experience. Because it is so diverse, religion is not easy to define, and all sociologists do not agree on a definition. A good working sociological definition identifies **religion** as "a system of beliefs and practices by which a group of people interprets and responds to what they feel is sacred and, usually, supernatural as well" (Johnstone, 1988, p. 13).

No matter how the term is defined, most observers agree that religion involves a focus on the *supernatural* (Hammond, 1985; Stark & Bainbridge, 1979, 1985). Because of this emphasis, religion almost always involves *faith,* a belief that is not or cannot be supported, or disproved, by scientific proof or evidence.

Varieties of Religion

Theism, belief in a god or gods, is the type of religion most familiar in Western society. There are three major religious groups of particular historic importance to the West: Christianity, Islam, and Judaism. Each is a form of **monotheism,** or the belief in only one god. All three types include formal religious organizations, sacred rituals, sacred writings, and a form of ministry or priesthood.

Christianity includes the Roman Catholic Church, the numerous Protestant denominations, and the Eastern Orthodox Church and, with over 1.9 billion faithful, is the world's largest religion. The next largest religion is

TABLE 16.1	ESTIMATED WORLD RELIGIOUS MEMBERSHIP, 1997	
	Membership	
Religion	*Thousands*	*Percent*
Christians	1,929,987	33.0
Roman Catholics	1,040,354	17.8
Protestants	360,913	6.1
Orthodox	223,204	3.8
Anglicans	54,785	1.0
Other Christians	287,857	4.9
Muslims	1,147,494	19.6
Nonreligious	760,280	13.0
Hindus	746,797	12.8
Buddhists	353,141	6.0
Atheists	146,615	2.5
Chinese folk religionists	363,334	6.2
New religionists	98,699	1.7
Ethnic religionists	231,694	4.0
Sikhs	22,518	0.4
Jews	14,890	0.3
Spiritists	11,467	0.2
Confucians	6,112	0.1
Baha'is	7,666	0.1
Jains	4,016	0.1
Shintoists	2,672	0.1
Other religionists	1,357	0.0
Total Population	**5,848,739**	**100.0**

Note: Totals not exact due to rounding.

Source: Adapted with permission from the Encyclopaedia Britannica *1998 Britannica Book of the Year;* © 1998. Encyclopaedia Britannica, Inc.

Islam. It numbers over 1.1 billion adherents and is the fastest growing of the major religions *(World Almanac and Book of Facts, 1999).* Judaism is one of the smallest of the world's major religions, with about 18 million followers. (For the estimated membership of the world's religions, see Table 16.1.)

The Hindu religion, practiced mainly in India, is an example of **polytheism,** or the belief in more than one god. Hinduism is a loose collection of hundreds of localized systems of belief and ritual and it claims over 746 million adherents. In India, each village and caste has its own particular god, who is honored on feast days. A certain place—either a temple or a sacred well, tree, or field—is reserved especially for worship. The gods of other villages or castes may also be worshiped if those deities are believed to be especially powerful or to secure success in an important aspect of life, such as the harvesting of crops or childbirth.

The other major religions of the world—Buddhism, Confucianism, Shintoism, and Taoism—are less familiar to Westerners. These religions of **transcendental idealism** do not worship a god but center instead on a set of ethical, moral, or philosophical principles. (Many Buddhists do, in practice, revere Buddha as a god, but this is not a formal teaching of their religion.)

Buddhism, Confucianism, and Taoism are all dedicated to achieving a kind of moral or spiritual enlightenment. The means to this achievement—the "way" of Buddha, the laws of Confucius—are the central focus of these religions. Shintoism, practiced largely in Japan, is a system of rituals and rules of conduct that glorify one's ancestors. It makes duty toward one's parents (a part of many religions, including Christianity) the center of religious feeling and devotion. Confucianism has no priesthood, but the other Eastern religions include a special group with the responsibility of carrying out religious duties and preserving religious values. All have rituals and sacred scriptures.

All of these religions have long histories. (Hinduism, probably the oldest religion, began over 6,000 years ago.) Over many centuries, they have evolved into complex systems of belief and behavior. Yet they are "modern" in the sense that they have adapted to meet conditions of twentieth-century life throughout much of the world.

In comparison, the religions of preliterate societies often face difficult challenges when they must change to respond to modern conditions. A common form of religion among preliterate peoples is **totemism,** the veneration of an animal (or, in rare cases, a plant) as both a god and an ancestor. This sacred object, the **totem,** is almost always something important to the community, such as a food source or a dangerous predator. During religious rites, people learn and perform special dances that mimic the behavior of the totem, and they wear special costumes and other totemic symbols. They may also consume the totemic animal in communal ritual banquets or enter into some form of communion with the totem. Some sociologists have suggested that totemism was the first religious principle and that other forms of religious organizations evolved from it (Durkheim, 1915).

Other forms of religion practiced in preindustrial societies include **simple supernaturalism,** a type of religion that does not recognize specific gods or spirits but that does believe in supernatural forces that influence people's lives; and **animism,** a type of religion that recognizes active ("animate") spirits operating in the world. Some forms of simple supernaturalism in the Western world include such superstitions as lucky four-leaf clovers

and unlucky Friday the 13th. Animistic religions, which often see spirits behind such natural forces as the wind, the snow, and the rain, frequently center around magic rituals developed to influence these forces. The rain dance is one of the most common forms of animistic ritual.

Totemism is still practiced by Australian Aborigines and among some New Guinea tribes. It was common among Native Americans, including the tribes of the northwest coast of the United States, who carved elaborate and decorative wooden "totem poles." Simple supernaturalism is still practiced on the islands of the South Pacific, and animism remains common among some African tribes.

Religion and the Human Condition

Like the family, religion is one of the universal human institutions and thus must "speak" to some basic aspects of the human condition. Here are some of the most important ways in which it may be useful in the lives of believers:

1. *Religion provides support and consolation that help to overcome fear of the unknown and anxiety about the future.* Because life is inherently unpredictable, people often feel anxious and fearful. Religion helps us to face life's uncertainties. By holding out the promise of an afterlife, most religions also offer specific reassurance and hope regarding death, the final unknown.

2. *Religion gives meaning and purpose to human existence.* For millennia, people have sought to answer the question "Why am I here?" Religion helps to provide an answer by explaining humanity's role in the larger, sacred or supernatural scheme of things. Part of the search for the meaning of life is also a search for absolute moral significance and standards, and these can also come from religion. Religion can thus serve as a yardstick for judging actions, goals, ideals, and ideas, even society itself.

3. *Religion allows people to transcend everyday reality.* Most people seem to desire some kind of relationship with the "other," the realm outside the mundane limits of daily life. Religion helps to fulfill this desire through its beliefs in the sacred "otherness" or "beyondness." These beliefs foster and encourage the feeling of stepping outside or above oneself.

4. *Religion helps people to develop a sense of identity.* Religion helps us answer the question "Who am I?" by providing membership in a special kind of organization. Religious organizations provide a stronger bond of identity than most others because they encourage people to share "ultimate" values and beliefs.

5. *Religion helps people during transitional stages in life.* All religions take note of the major events of the human life cycle: birth, puberty, marriage, and death.

Around these events grows a system of rituals, which anthropologists refer to as **rites of passage.** These periods of transition are times of special strain on people and their family and friends. Religious rites of passage—weddings, baptisms, funerals—help to ease this strain. Sometimes they provide consolation, as in the case of rituals surrounding death and dying. At other times they give instruction in coping with new roles. Rites of passage concerning puberty and marriage (such as bar mitzvahs and weddings) serve this purpose.

Religion is not the only institution that can help people cope with the problems of human existence. A strong occupational commitment can do the same. Ties to a family, a neighborhood, a work organization, or a nation can build a sense of identity. Social and political movements can give people a feeling of self-transcendence, too. But no other institution, except the family, is as effective as religion in helping people to deal with problems about the meaning and value of life, and none is as successful in creating a strong sense of allegiance and participation.

Other than the family, there is no institution as effective as religion in helping people deal with problems about the meaning and value of life. The people of this Oklahoma community meet together to pray for themselves and their nieghbors after devastating tornadoes destroyed their homes.

The Functionalist Perspective: Religion and Social Stability

Most sociologists are less interested in the ways that religion responds to the needs of particular individuals than they are in the functions that religion provides to society as a whole. The functionalist perspective emphasizes the important role of religion in promoting social stability. There are at least four ways in which religion tends to encourage the status quo:

1. *Religion binds the members of society together through sacred rituals.* Émile Durkheim (1915) observed that the faithful commonly sense a tremendous and mysterious power underlying the beliefs and rituals of their religion. A theologian would probably explain the origin of this power in supernatural terms: It is the power of God that awes the worshiper. But sociologists, compelled to offer only empirical explanations for social phenomena, cannot make use of theological conceptions. Durkheim suggested, based on his analysis of the sacred totems of the Arunta, a tribe of Australian Aborigines, that the empirical source of the awesome power that believers feel when participating in religious activities was actually the coercive power of society over its members. Durkheim's insight, one of the most important in the sociology of religion, was that in celebrating the power of the sacred and the supernatural, we are in fact constructing a kind of analogy that permits us to express our subconscious awareness of the tremendous power of society over the individual.

Durkheim noted further that we sense this power most keenly when we are in the presence of others who believe as we do and especially when we are engaged in religious rituals that explicitly celebrate our commitment to other members of our society. Thus, the ritual dances of the Arunta in honor of their totems, the symbolic expression of the unity of the tribe, led to an abandonment of self-interest and to a heightened sense of the tribesmen's unity with their fellows. The totem became the visible symbol of the society's ability to accept or reject, shape and mold, the individual.

2. *Religion strengthens society's basic norms and values.* Social norms are the foundations of all social organization. By giving norms and values enhanced moral meaning, by making some of them sacred, religion consoles people for the sacrifices they must make when their personal wishes conflict with social requirements, as in times of war.

Respect for parents is a social norm taught at home and at school. This norm is made sacred for both Christians and Jews by the biblical commandment "Honor thy father and thy mother." Similarly, the norm prohibiting sexual relationships outside marriage is given strong moral backing by the biblical commandment "Thou shalt not commit adultery."

Another way of expressing this function is to note that religion helps to control deviant behavior. Secular society encourages conformity by means of rewards and punishments administered by human beings. Religion adds another dimension: the supernatural. Those who

SOCIOLOGY OF THE MEDIA

PRIME-TIME RELIGION

In the wanton world of Hollywood's evening entertainment line-up, who could imagine that a show about God could succeed? The very notion of prime-time religion sounds absurd. Who does not know that prime-time slots are reserved for Sodom and Gomorrah, not Bethlehem? Apparently that would be Martha Williamson, the executive producer of *Touched by an Angel.* Even though the pilot for the program did not show much promise, Williamson still had faith in it (*People,* February 22, 1999). During its first season, it barely survived. But, perhaps, that was no surprise since it was pitted against the immensely popular *Roseanne.* Williamson was able to convince network executives to renew *Touched by an Angel* by showing them an episode about a Little League coach dying from cancer. And once it was moved to a different time slot, its ratings began to soar. By the first week of 1999, it was even beating out *60 Minutes* for top ratings, with an audience of 16.3 million viewers.

The success of *Touched by an Angel* led television executives to produce other shows with religious themes. By the fall of 1997, four prime-time programs featured the clergy (Goodstein, 1997). They included *Good News, Seventh Heaven, Soul Man,* and *Nothing Sacred.* Each of these programs contained the elements commonly associated with the form rituals take in the United States—the Bible, singing choirs, and messages of love and forgiveness. Each show also involved some kind of conflict and ended with a moral. Critics, though, claimed that they lacked spirituality. In commenting on this weakness, Laurie Goodstein said, "Television has missed an opportunity to take audiences further than it has before into the realm of mysterious, transcendent religiosity" (1997, p. 37).

But, in fact, these programs were not designed to do that. In contrast to *Touched by an Angel,* which features angels as the main characters, each of these programs depicted religious people as human beings who are vulnerable to worldly temptations. While this has a certain appeal, programs like *Soul Man* and *Seventh Heaven,* which emphasize the paternal role of ministers, end up being less about spirituality and more about family values. And programs like *Nothing Sacred,* which showed a Catholic priest departing from the church's teachings, risk cancellation. In fact, complaints from the Catholic League for Religious and Civil Rights caused a number of advertisers to pull their commercials from this program (Ryan & Wentworth, 1999).

The unique success of *Touched by an Angel* reflects the degree to which its message resonates with viewers. The show's ability to inspire and lift people out of the depths of despair is reflected in the letters written by fans. One woman wrote:

I am a recovering alcoholic with a painful background. I am now 10 years sober, but the drinking wasn't really the hard part. It's the guilt, low self-esteem and forgiveness that I have trouble with. I tried to commit suicide twice in the past, because I felt like I couldn't make it in this life. On Sunday night, when your show comes on, it feels like God is in that room talking to me. Those Special Angels give me hope that someday I can find out the true meaning of happiness. It was a hard step but I recently started counsel[ing] with my church. I pray God will keep your show going for years. (*People,* February 22, 1999, p. 86)

Another young viewer wrote:

My favorite show was the one with the police officer. He was shot and he became addicted to his pain-killers. He always carried with him the bullet that shot him. Then he became addicted to drugs. The message in that show was that God loves you, and that not all the drugs in the world can replace His love. I am 14 years old. Every week your show talks about how much God loves us all, even for all our faults. When you don't know what to do, you pray to God and ask him for an answer. And when the time is right you will receive that answer. God has perfect timing. (I learned that from *Touched by an Angel).* (*People,* February 22, 1999, p. 86)

As this particular letter suggests, *Touched by an Angel* has been successful in conveying the message that "God loves you," a line repeated over and over again by Monica, the naive angel who takes the role of a caseworker. With the help and guidance of her own heavenly angel, Tess, and Andrew, the Angel of Death, Monica enters the lives of troubled mortals—unwed mothers, suicidal teens, the terminally ill, drug addicts, and others who have fallen into despair. These angels do not provide ready-made solutions for earthly problems. Nor do they preach. But they do address the questions that revolve around the ultimate meaning of life:

1. Why are we here?

2. What is the purpose of life?

3. Why do we suffer?

4. Is there any justice?

5. What happens after we die?

No one knows the answers to these questions, and the producers of *Touched by an Angel* do not pretend to either. They wisely leave it up to the viewers to seek the answers for themselves.

obey religious laws and conform to social norms are promised rewards that are beyond the ability of humans to bestow: divine assistance in times of crisis, protection against enemies, eternal life. Those who deviate from commandments and norms are threatened with supernatural punishments, such as constant bad fortune or everlasting torture.

Furthermore, religion adds a kind of supernatural "detective" power to the social control process. Deviance is subject to negative social sanctions only when a person commits a deviant act that is both seen and reported (see Chapter 8). By extending control to cases of unseen and unreported deviance, religion minimizes the need for anyone to play the role of observer. God, or whatever supernatural power the faithful believe in, can always see the wrong and will punish the wrong-doer. Some religions go so far as to condemn mere thoughts of deviance; planning to kill someone or imagining a person's misfortune will evoke religious punishment even though the intended victim is never harmed. Thus, religion can be a major influence on an individual's conscience.

Religion also provides ways for deviants to atone for their sins and be accepted back into society—rituals of purification, for instance. In many modern religions, atonement often requires some mild form of penance, such as more regular church attendance, limited fasting, or the denial of some pleasure or comfort. Because most deviants know exactly how to go about making atonement and because it is clearly understood when they are to be received back into society, the system of atonement is effective. Social stress is reduced and social control is maintained.

3. *Religion may legitimate governmental authority.* Social stability is usually strengthened if the people of a society fully accept the legitimacy of the political authorities, because such acceptance increases their willingness to obey governmental laws and regulations. Early political systems commonly made this function very explicit. The pharaohs of ancient Egypt, for example, were simultaneously regarded as kings and as gods. Anyone who defied their authority risked both secular and supernatural sanctions. The absolute monarchs of European history were not regarded as divine, but it was widely believed that they ruled with God's blessing and that disobedience to the king amounted to a violation of God's will. Although the Church of England was officially disestablished as a state religion in 1869, British kings and queens are still installed in office by the Archbishop of Canterbury, the leader of the church. Some contemporary nations, such as Iran, remain *theocracies,* societies in which church and state are at least partially merged.

Even the United States, a highly secular nation, retains some aspects of this function of religion. Public funds are used to pay the salaries of chaplains in the U.S. House of Representatives and Senate, persons taking oaths of office customarily do so with their hand resting on the Bible, and our coins and paper money carry the motto "In God We Trust."

4. *Religion helps reconcile people to the hardships and inequities of their society.* Certain kinds of religious belief are commonly held more strongly among the poor and the oppressed. (These beliefs may include a particularly stringent moral code and a strong emphasis on salvation and the hereafter.) The poor often need a special reason to conform to the dictates of a social order that has placed them at the bottom. Because they are not being well compensated in the usual ways for participating in society, they need additional rewards for social conformity.

Religion can provide those needed reasons and rewards. Every religion offers its followers the chance to achieve a high moral status, which can help make up for their low social status. Some religions stress the equality of all believers. Others regard their adherents as a special elite.

Religion also approaches the problem of inequality by trying to influence the behavior of the higher classes. Religions often call for charity, mercy, kindness, sharing with the less fortunate, and renouncing pride and vanity. Though it may do nothing to remedy the actual condition of the poor and powerless, such advocacy may help to ease the dissatisfactions of the socially oppressed or disadvantaged.

DYSFUNCTIONS OF RELIGION

Although the ability of religion to promote social stability and to underlie the status quo is generally regarded positively, there are certain circumstances in which religion's conservative nature may create problems for some or all of the groups within a society. There are two principal ways in which religion may, in this sense, prove dysfunctional.

1. *Religion may prevent needed change.* This dysfunction was clearly identified by Karl Marx when he wrote that religion was "the opiate of the masses." Marx thought of religion as the active ally of the established capitalist social order (Marx & Engels, 1848/1969). He contended that, just as an opiate dulls people to the pain of physical injury, religion lulls people, and especially the downtrodden poor, into accepting the inequities of their society. Thus, Marx felt that religion reduced people's willingness to demand needed social change.

Similarly, religion can retard change in the realm of ideas. When a powerful religious establishment lends its weight to prevailing norms or other elements of culture, this tends to make those cultural traits sacred and accordingly more resistant to change. One prime example is the

WINDOW ON SOCIOLOGY

INTERFAITH MARRIAGES

Should people of different religions marry? Historically, couples have been strongly discouraged from doing so. In fact, Americans are more likely to date and marry someone with the same religion. And this has been true for many years. Forty years ago couples were even likelier to marry within their own religion (Crohn, 1995). Back then only 6 percent of Jews, 12 percent of Catholics, and 17 percent of Baptists married outside their own faith. While recent figures on mixed marriages show no increase for Baptists, 21 percent of Catholics and 32 percent of Jews are married to someone of a different faith today. The percentages of interfaith marriages vary widely for other groups. Hindus are the least likely to intermarry—only 5 percent do so. Lutherans (25 percent), Mormons (30 percent), Episcopalians (31 percent), and Muslims (40 percent) fall in the midrange. Nearly six out of every ten Buddhists intermarry, putting them at the upper end of the range.

Altogether the number of interfaith marriages today involve about 33 million Americans. While most Americans do marry someone with the same faith, studies indicate that the trend toward interfaith marriages will continue. In their study of sexual relationships in dating and marriage, Ed Laumann and his colleagues (1994) found that only 56 percent of long-term relationships involved couples with similar religious backgrounds.

Even though religion appears to be losing its influence in the selection of a mate, couples should recognize that they may face more problems than those who marry within their faith. In fact, research shows that mixed marriages have higher divorce rates and slightly lower levels of marital satisfaction than do homogamous ones (Glenn 1982; Heaton & Pratt, 1990; Price-Bonham & Balswick, 1980; Schwartz & Scott, 1997). The factors operating against interfaith marriages include the lack of support from one's family, church, and society. Cultural hostility can also contribute to the destabilization of these unions.

In his book, *Mixed Matches,* Joel Crohn discusses the kinds of problems that can result from marriage between people who come from different cultural backgrounds. He describes a typical example as follows:

A Jewish-American woman married to an Italian-American man: She feels her husband is too strict with their children, while he sees her as tolerating behavior his parents would never have put up with. And even though she had almost broken off their engagement because he wasn't Jewish, when he converted to Judaism five years later, she was upset that he had become "too carried away with religion." She describes herself as a "cultural Jew" and is uncomfortable with him taking their children to synagogue regularly. (1995; p. 4)

Today, young people are not likely to consider religion in their choice of dating partners (Asmussen & Shehan, 1992). But religious beliefs do shape who we are. And they ultimately constitute highly resistant ways of thinking and feeling (Schwartz & Scott, 1997). They can, therefore, create serious problems when couples in interfaith marriages plan to have children (Crohn, 1995). Then they must decide which religion their children should follow and which holidays to celebrate. Couples must figure out how to carry on cultural traditions and how to deal with the reactions of friends and family. One of the most difficult challenges facing parents, however, is how to instill a sense of identity in their children.

According to Crohn, interfaith marriages can be successful, but this depends upon couples' willingness to meet the challenges. And he suggests that they undertake five tasks. These include

- Facing the issues
- Clarifying the different cultural codes of your spouse
- Sorting out confusion about individual identities
- Becoming aware of the social context
- Finding your own path and helping your children find theirs.

Religious differences do not have to separate people who love one another. But couples must be prepared to deal with the problems that different religious backgrounds can create.

---

opposition of the medieval Catholic Church to Galileo's discovery that the earth orbits the sun rather than the sun circling the earth. Having committed itself to the latter notion, the church forced Galileo to repudiate his discovery, thus significantly retarding the development of the science of astronomy. The rejection of Darwin's theory of evolution and the continued acceptance of creationism by many fundamentalist Protestant churches in the United States today is another example of this dysfunction of religion.

2. *Religion may make political conflicts more difficult to resolve.* Most political struggles are ultimately about access to valued resources, such as land or jobs. However, when the two sides in such a dispute identify each other by religious labels, it frequently becomes more difficult to resolve the conflict. It seems to be easier to compromise with one's opponents when the other party is identified in secular terms than when they are seen as religiously, and thus in a sense morally, different from oneself. This is a primary explanation for the protracted conflict in Northern Ireland between rival communities identified as Protestants and Catholics (Beach, 1977). It also is a factor in the struggles between Hindus and Muslims on the Indian subcontinent and in the long-standing conflict between the Arabs and the Israelis in the Middle East.

RELIGION AND THE FAMILY

The role of religion in promoting social stability is especially evident within the institution of the family. Religion probably began as a family activity. And the family is often still deeply embedded in religious meaning.

The impact of religion on the family begins with the concept of marriage. By enforcing the norm of chastity and condemning sexual activity outside a lawful union, many religions promote the sanctity of marriage. In addition, religion influences a person's choice of a marriage partner. Although most of America's major religions have relaxed their prohibitions against interfaith marriages, they generally continue to encourage believers to marry within the faith.

Studies have shown that religious affiliation is associated with marital stability and a low divorce rate (Albrecht, Bahr, & Goodman, 1983; Heaton & Pratt, 1990; Gallup Organization, 1988d; Kitson, Babri, & Roach, 1985). Several theories have been proposed to account for this. It may be that participation in a religion encourages people to conform to social expectations; religion may thus make them cling more tightly to the social ideal of marriage. Another viewpoint holds that religious couples are likely to share the same norms and ethical beliefs. Also, by overtly discouraging or even prohibiting divorce, religious groups may help to keep the marriages of their members intact.

By influencing the socialization of children, religion has a further effect on the family. Religions socialize children explicitly—through parochial schools and educational programs—and indirectly—through the promotion of certain social norms of parenting and childrearing.

It is significant that the divinities of most religions are themselves thought to be members of a family network. The deities of some religions are husband and wife, like Hinduism's Siva and Kali. In other cases, the deities

The divinities of most religions are members of a family network. Hinduism's Siva and Kali, depicted here, are husband and wife.

are brother and sister, like Artemis and Apollo in ancient Greek religion. The Egyptian deities Osiris and Isis were both husband and wife and brother and sister. Parent–child relationships are also common among divinities, as in the father–son relationship between God and Jesus in Christianity. The worship of a mother figure, thought by some researchers to be the oldest form of religion, is strongly reflected in prehistoric religious art. The cult of the mother is still alive and well today in the worship of many Hindu goddesses and in the veneration of Mary, the mother of Jesus. The most common type of deity today, however, is the father figure, who both loves and chastises his children, the believers.

The Conflict Perspective: Religion and Social Change

The promotion of social stability is probably the most important role that religion has played in society. Certainly it is the role most frequently analyzed by sociologists. But religion does not always support the status quo. As conflict theorists writing in the tradition of Max

Weber emphasize, religion can also be a divisive force, a rallying point for the disaffected as they attack other institutions and seek social change. A religious group can bring together discontented citizens, give them a community of interest, and provide the power of organized numbers. It can also supply them with a sacred ideology justifying the need for social change. In short, it can be a ready-made base for altering the social order. Throughout history, religious fervor and ideals have caused or fueled many national revolutions and international conflicts. Two important examples are the Protestant Reformation of the sixteenth century and modern Islamic militance.

THE PROTESTANT REFORMATION AND THE RISE OF CAPITALISM

During the sixteenth century, the nature of European society was dramatically altered. A major factor associated with this change was the emergence of a new institutional form of Christianity—Protestantism. Two aspects of the Protestant movement, which affected every sphere of European life, were especially important in generating social change. One was the ability of the movement to unify diverse elements of society; the other was the support the Protestant ethic gave to the development of capitalism.

In 1500, Europe still operated under the feudal system. The economy was agricultural and the barter system was in common use. There was a very small middle class and almost no social or physical mobility. Only a small percentage of the population lived in cities. The lives of almost all Europeans were minutely regulated by ties of dependence to social superiors and ties of obligation to social inferiors.

With its own internal structure closely paralleling the feudal organization of the secular world, the Roman Catholic Church strongly supported the social and political systems of the time. Papal edicts and threats of excommunication against rebels helped more than one king defend his throne against rebellion and uprising.

By 1600, much had changed. A trade and manufacturing economy was steadily growing. Cities were expanding and began to play a more important role in national affairs. As more and more opportunities arose for making a profit without the large capital investment necessary for agriculture, the size of the middle class greatly increased. Aided by new religious developments, the feudal system began to disintegrate.

The Protestant Reformation began in the sixteenth century as a doctrinal dispute among a group of Catholic clergymen in a remote part of Germany. Soon, however, Protestantism attracted many people who were unhappy with the existing social system, drawing adherents from all walks of life. Social dissidents from the city and the country, from the lower and the upper classes, and from the capitalistic and the feudal segments of the economy were united by their Protestant religious beliefs. Protestantism gave them a single, emotionally charged cause around which they could rally. The bonding power of religion brought these people together into a major force for restructuring society.

Protestantism was an especially effective agent of change in the economic sphere—in the shift to capitalism. In his landmark study *The Protestant Ethic and the Spirit of Capitalism* (1930), Max Weber pointed out the close connection between the values of the Protestant religion and those needed for success in a capitalist economy. The Protestant belief in the virtue of hard work, and the doctrine that worldly prosperity is a mark of God's favor, dovetailed perfectly with the capitalist values of thrift, initiative, competition, and acquisitiveness.

Weber's views on the role of Protestantism in the growth of capitalism have not gone unchallenged. Some critics have argued that the growth of capitalism encouraged the emergence of Protestantism, not vice versa. Proponents of this position argue that the great economic power of the new capitalists allowed them to influence the development of the church in ways that supported their economic activities.

No doubt many forces were at work in the momentous economic and social changes of the sixteenth century. *The Protestant Ethic* presents a convincing argument that the beliefs of Protestantism promoted the emergence of capitalism. But it also seems to be true—as Weber himself believed—that the growth of capitalism supported the growth of Protestantism. A new religious system and a new economic system emerged in tandem, each supporting the other and encouraging the other's growth.

MILITANT ISLAM AND THE IRANIAN REVOLUTION

The fall of the Iranian monarchy in 1979, followed by the establishment of a new government and a dramatically transformed society, is a more recent example of religion acting as a revolutionary social force. In this case, Shi'ism, a branch of Islam and the national religion of Iran, became the vehicle for revolution. Shi'ism provided opponents of the Shah (Iran's established monarch) with a communications network, institutional structures, ideas, and personnel that allowed the revolution to spread and grow strong. An important leader of the Shi'ite clergy, the Ayatollah Khomeini, became the leader of the revolution. The fusion of the revolutionary movement with religion enabled the Ayatollah to succeed in accomplishing what others had attempted and failed—

the overthrow of the Shah (Benard & Khalilzad, 1979; Dilip, 1985; Khalilzad & Benard, 1984).

Clearly, the Iranian revolution could not have had its far-reaching effects if the Iranian people did not continue to be fiercely dedicated to the religious ideals that helped bring it about. For Muslims, Islam is more than a religion. It is a prescription for a complete way of life. Muslims believe that their God, Allah, has directed them to live simply. This simplicity involves emulating the life of the prophet Mohammad and living in a state of equity, avoiding both extreme poverty and extreme wealth. Western materialistic values, sexual permissiveness, and military power are seen as threats to the integrity and traditions of the Islamic religion. The Iranian revolution thus represented more than a tension between the old and the new; it also signified a deeper conflict between the sacred and the secular that endures today.

The primary aims of the Iranian Islamic government have been to construct a society based on justice according to the laws of Islam and to combat oppression, eradicate corruption, and prevent the intervention of foreigners in the affairs of Muslims. The government has succeeded to some extent in these policies, but some of its actions have been widely perceived by outsiders as extreme. Before his death in 1989, the Ayatollah ordered the assassination of Salman Rushdie, whose novel *The Satanic Verses* was perceived as heretical and insulting to the Islamic faith. The death edict sent shock waves through the world. Many leaders rallied in support of Rushdie, vehemently arguing that the Ayatollah had no right to order the death of a writer with whom he disagreed.

The close ties between religion and politics in Iran illustrate an important point: that the two social institutions tend to become tightly intertwined when a country is fighting for its freedom or identity. Will the Iranian revolution succeed in its goals? How significant will the Islamic religion be in shaping the political and social systems of other countries in the world? The answers remain to be seen, but it is clear that radical Islam has positioned itself as a strong force to be reckoned with in the modern world.

THE ORGANIZATION OF RELIGION

So far, we have discussed the variety of religions and the general ways in which religion affects individuals and societies. But religion must also be understood as an institution in itself. Knowledge of the central elements of religion and the main types of religious organization can help us to understand better the nature of religion as a social institution—an institution that many consider the most important element in their lives.

Elements of Religion

Most religions contain four common elements: sacred objects or places, rituals, a system of beliefs, and an organization of believers.

THE SACRED

According to Durkheim, the **profane** consists of all the elements of everyday life that are considered part of the ordinary physical (natural) world. The **sacred,** on the other hand, is anything set apart from everyday life that is capable of evoking deep respect and awe. This sense of awe in the presence of the sacred is the underlying and most basic religious impulse, whether one regards the ultimate source of awe as the supernatural or transcendent itself or whether one agrees with Durkheim's theory that it is the subconscious recognition of the power of society over the individual that is the best explanation for the awe experienced by the believer. In any event, when confronted by the sacred, people generally feel in touch with the eternal source of life and believe that they are experiencing a special power that cannot be understood by reason alone. Because the sacred is so supremely desirable, it arouses feelings of great attraction. Because of its power, the sacred also can provoke feelings of dread.

The experience of the sacred is frequently linked with material objects, such as an altar, a statue, or a cross. Almost anything can be considered sacred: certain locations, such as a grove of trees, a spring, or a cave; particular times, such as sunrise or Easter; or animals or plants, such as cows, rattlesnakes, or trees. Sometimes, the sacred is connected with unusual events, such as erupting volcanoes or overflowing rivers. People with rare abilities and the dates of unusual occurrences may also be regarded as sacred.

The olive tree, for example, is considered sacred by Muslims. To Christians, the bread and wine of the communion ritual represent the body and blood of Christ. In India, Hindus believe that bathing in the Ganges River can purify both the body and the spirit. Jews from around the world make pilgrimages to Israel, the "Holy Land," in order to pray at the sacred Wailing Wall in Jerusalem.

RITUAL

A religious **ritual** is an established pattern of behavior closely associated with the experience of the sacred. It is typically performed to express or revive powerful experiences of the sacred or to ask the sacred power for some favor. By holding certain ceremonies along the banks of the Nile, for example, the ancient Egyptians felt that they could bring on, or symbolically participate in, the annual

Ritual is an established pattern of behavior associated with the experience of the sacred. In the Hindu religion, worshippers purify themselves through ritual bathing in the Ganges River. In the Christian ritual of baptism, new members are admitted to the faith by symbolic washing.

flooding that brought needed water and silt to the fields. Ritual is also a way of protecting the sacred from contamination by the profane. A sacred chalice or cup is not

routinely used for drinking water. It may be used only in special ceremonies, when it is filled with special wine and passed from one person to another.

Ritual is a means of organizing the believers of a religion; it brings them together in a group. The repetition of a ritual, psychologists believe, helps to restore people's feelings of integration, identity, and security. By worshiping the crocodile in formal ceremonies, for example, certain African tribes felt that they were protecting themselves from attack by these frightening beasts.

Ritual itself can become sacred through its connection with the sacred. The objects used in ritual—the herbs or potions consumed, the clothes worn by the participants, the place where the ritual is conducted—can all come to be revered. For this reason, a house of worship, the location of religious ritual, is generally considered to be sacred.

A SYSTEM OF BELIEFS

The system of religious beliefs is the element of religion that has undergone more development than any other. In traditional religions, the main function of the belief system was to relate sacred objects to religious rituals and to define and protect the sacred. In the Old Testament, for example, God is portrayed as a superhuman figure who nevertheless can be understood in human terms. The abstract concept of God is transformed into a symbol that people can identify with and relate to.

Belief systems also explain the meaning and purpose of ritual. Muslims, for instance, learn that they must wash before evening prayers because physical cleanliness is a sign of moral cleanliness, and one must always appear morally clean before God. In light of this knowledge, the ritual of washing becomes a meaningful event.

Most modern systems of religious belief go far beyond merely supporting the other elements of religion. They often include moral propositions (such as the equality of all people) that are considered important truths. Although not necessarily considered "holy" by the faithful, these beliefs have a sacred quality. Because they are frequently translated into constitutions, political ideology, and educational doctrine, these beliefs are important not only to the religions themselves but also in the nonreligious affairs of a society.

AN ORGANIZATION OF BELIEVERS

An organization of believers is needed to ensure the continuity and effectiveness of the religious experience. Conducting rituals, building places of worship, and choosing specialists such as priests, monks, and ministers to cultivate and safeguard the sacred all call for some kind of organization. For example, the Second Methodist Church of Great Falls, Montana, builds the church building, selects and pays the minister, buys the hymnals and the organ, and recruits the choir. The culmination of these activities is that the believers can go to church on Sunday morning and share their experience of the sacred.

Types of Religious Organizations

Sociologists have commonly divided religious organizations into four types: ecclesia, church, sect, and cult. Max Weber (1922/1963) introduced the distinction between a church and a sect; his student Ernest Troeltsch (1931) was the first to make this typology important in the sociological study of religion. Although we can distinguish among the organizational types as concepts, in practice it is not always easy to tell them apart.

An **ecclesia** is a religious organization that claims as its membership the entire population of a society. Generally, the ecclesia is recognized as the country's official religion, and in some cases the ecclesia has a powerful influence on governmental policies and practices. Membership in the ecclesia is not voluntary; one is born into it as the result of one's citizenship. While there are probably no true ecclesia in the modern world, Roman Catholicism in the Republic of Ireland and Islam in Iran are close approximations.

A **church** is a relatively stable, institutionalized organization of religious believers. It is characterized by a well-defined administrative and clerical hierarchy; elaborate doctrines, or **dogma,** which usually cover most ordinary human situations; and an extensive body of detailed ritual. Many sociologists prefer to use the less confusing term **denomination** when referring to what Weber called churches. Unlike ecclesia, denominations co-exist relatively comfortably within society with various other organized religions, a condition commonly referred to as *religious pluralism.*

Denominations display several other distinctive characteristics. They draw most of their recruits from the children of present members, a practice that helps ensure continuity of membership but risks allowing the pews to be occupied by lukewarm parishioners who have not made a "heart" decision to join the group. Denominational leadership tends to be formally trained and credentialed. Finally, most denominations draw more support from the middle and working classes than from the poor, a fact that may help explain the observation that, whereas denominations may regard the larger society as to some extent sinful, they usually counsel their members to become actively involved in making the world a better place rather than withdraw from it, as do most sects.

A **sect** is less formally organized than a denomination. Its leaders normally lack formal training and in many cases rely heavily on personal charisma as the basis for their authority. Typically, many of the functions carried out by religious specialists in denominations are performed by the ordinary members of sects: They may recruit and instruct new members, conduct services and other rituals, and even interpret sacred beliefs and practices. Because sect members are actively involved in the organization, they are often more committed to it than are members of a denomination.

While the denomination secures its new recruits primarily from the children of present members, sects actively solicit converts. Those who join a sect are typically of lower occupational and educational status than those who join a denomination. They are also more likely to be discontented with their position in life, a factor that may be involved in their typically strong commitment to the religion (Johnstone, 1988).

Many sects emphasize depth and purity of religious feeling. Faith and fervor are important sectarian values. Because sects refuse substantially to compromise their religious principles, they often conflict with other social institutions over questions of belief. According to one observer: "A church is a religious group that accepts the social environment in which it exists. A sect is a religious group that rejects the social environment in which it exists" (Johnson, 1963).

Sects are usually formed by people who reject some aspects of an established religion. The new group generally splits from the older, established body and attacks it for straying from basic doctrines. The sect often calls for a return to the "purity" of earlier forms or ways.

Such religious groups as the Presbyterians, Baptists, and Seventh-day Adventists all began as sects. Most sects that survive tend to move away from their pure state and become new denominations. In the course of their evolution, sects may even come to resemble the organizations from which they originally separated. As sects grow larger, they tend to become increasingly bureaucratic; the result is that the sect's initial spontaneity and flexibility begin to disappear. And as the sect becomes more like a denomination, members dissatisfied with doctrine or dogma may break away yet again to found a new sect (Niebuhr, 1929; Stark & Bainbridge, 1985).

The last type of religious organization is the **cult,** a term that has been used extensively in recent years by the media and the general public. Within the discipline of sociology, cults have traditionally been defined as groups that, like sects, reject some aspects of established religion. They also share several other important characteristics with sects, but they differ from the sectarian model in that they have not broken away from established religious

Marshall Herff Applewhite was the leader of "Heaven's Gate," a religious group that was based in Rancho Santa Fe, California. Most of the group's members died in a mass suicide on the promise by Applewhite that their deaths would free them and that they would ascend to a higher place.

bodies but, rather, constitute more or less entirely new religions. Rather than calling for a return to the old ways, cults frequently devise new sacred symbols, rituals, and belief systems. Typically the cult places a special emphasis on the individual, concentrating on allowing its adherents to attain a desired spiritual experience.

In popular usage, however, the term *cult* has a very different meaning. It is typically used to describe small, unconventional religions that have aroused extensive social disapproval, often because they are believed to employ brainwashing techniques to secure new members. The primary message being conveyed is that the members of the group are strange people who are probably being manipulated by a religious charlatan. Some of the religions that are popularly regarded as cults, including the Branch Davidians and the Hare Krishnas, are, in fact, breakaway groups from more established religions and should be properly classified as sects. On the other hand, some relatively mainstream groups that sociologists would characterize as cults, such as Christian Science, are virtually always popularly identified as sects or even as denominations. For these reasons, many sociologists feel that the term *cult* has become so confused and value-laden that we would be better off classifying all small, informal, and relatively unconventional religions as sects and simply abandoning the concept of cults.

In any event, the groups that sociologists have traditionally labeled as cults are usually founded on a new revelation, the insight of a new prophet, or the discovery of a fragment of "lost" scripture. They have historically

been headed by strong, flamboyant leaders, such as Father Divine, Mary Baker Eddy, Aimee Semple McPherson, Jim Jones, the Reverend Moon, David Koresh, and Herff Applewhite. Because of their unorthodox lifestyles, cults typically exist outside the mainstream of society. Most of them tend to be short-lived, but several have evolved into major established denominations.

Why and how are sects and cults formed? According to one theory, people are driven to form new religious groups in an attempt to alleviate their feelings of *deprivation* (Barker, 1982; Glock, 1964; Stark & Bainbridge, 1985). Several types of deprivation can promote the growth of new religions. Deprivation can be economic if an individual's income is inadequate and access to material goods is limited, or social, if people lack status, power, prestige, and the ability to join certain organizations or participate in certain activities. Deprivation can also be psychological, if one feels dissatisfaction with or rejection by society, even though one shares in its material rewards.

According to this theory, religious movements develop into sects when stimulated by economic deprivation and into cults when inspired by psychological deprivation. The subsequent development of the movement is influenced by the way the group copes with deprivation, and by whether or not deprivation continues in the larger society, thus providing potential new members. For example, movements that arise in response to economic deprivation, as during a depression, tend either to disappear quickly or to change their organizational form in order to survive. They do so either because the deprivation itself has been eliminated or because the group has been successful in helping members overcome it.

RELIGION IN AMERICAN LIFE

In this section, we consider selected characteristics of religion and religious life in American society. Religious attitudes and institutions in the United States strongly reflect the Judeo-Christian tradition. But American religious institutions have also been shaped by social and cultural factors unique to the United States. The democratic structure of government, widely accepted values such as toleration and optimism, and the mixed ethnic and racial composition of the population have all exerted some influence on American religion.

Religion and American Culture

The outstanding single feature of American religious life is its diversity. At present, there are roughly 78 organized religious denominations in the United States with at least 50,000 members each, and there are hundreds more with smaller memberships (*Yearbook of American* and Canadian Churches, 1999). This diversity reflects America's cultural pluralism, the origins of which reach far back into the nation's history. This is in sharp contrast with the situation in many other nations of the world, where one religion is dominant, where there is an official religion or ecclesia, or where there is no separation between church and state.

Because many early American settlers had been religious dissenters in Europe, religious tolerance was part of American culture even before it was guaranteed by the Bill of Rights. In the colonial settlements, however, this tolerance was relatively limited. Most groups of dissenters wanted to make their own religion an official or dominant faith. Yet, as the colonies grew, religious diversity became so great that all groups eventually had to learn to tolerate the others. No single group was able to dominate. By the late eighteenth century, this tolerance had become such an essential part of the society that it was written into the Constitution.

The United States was founded on the principle of separation of church and state. As part of the Constitution, this principle has been followed closely. Unlike England, Italy, and many other countries, the United States has no official religion. Moreover, the government neither supports nor suppresses any particular religion. Although some people feel that Supreme Court interpretations of the separation principle, such as those banning prayer in public schools, have been extreme, over the long run this principle has served to protect the nation's many religions.

Another important feature of religious life in America is its optimism. Religions that place a high premium on self-denial and self-sacrifice are rarely able to secure many members in the United States. American religious beliefs typically focus more on the positive rewards of the religious life—security, peace of mind, and a heavenly afterlife—than on the penalties for religious failings, such as damnation and eternal misery. Peter Berger (1967) has suggested that this positive emphasis in American religion stems partly from our nation's religious pluralism. All churches compete with others for members; doctrines, therefore, must be broadly appealing. Berger expressed this appeal in the language of the marketplace:

> Again, putting it in a somewhat oversimplified way, the "product" of the religious institution must be "saleable." It is one thing to threaten a captive audience of medieval peasants with hellfire and damnation. It is quite another thing to market a doctrine of this sort in a population of suburban commuters and housewives. In other words, the "needs" of the consumer clientele must now be taken into consideration. (p. 375)

Another positive feature of American religion is its relative freedom from *anticlericalism*—the dislike and distrust of priests and ministers. Anticlericalism is especially marked in those countries in which the church once owned much of the land and other property under the feudal system. In such societies, some members of the clergy belonged to a wealthy and oppressive upper class that was feared and disliked by the common people. But this has never been the case in the United States, which was settled after the feudal system had ended.

Robert Bellah (1967, 1970) noted that despite religious diversity and the separation of church and state in the United States, there exists in America an elaborate *civil religion* that is integrated into many aspects of public life and is accepted by most Americans. According to Bellah, this civil religion is based on the Christian orientation of the "Founding Fathers." Although George Washington, John Adams, and Thomas Jefferson avoided public references to Christ, they did frequently refer to God. The deity of this civil religion is vaguely Judeo-Christian, but in no sense specifically Catholic or Baptist, Jewish or Methodist, because he is the God of *all* Americans, not just some. It is this God to whom presidents and other politicians routinely make reference in important political speeches and it is this God in whom, according to our coins and currency, we trust.

Within this American civil religion, democracy and other characteristic forms of American society are seen as having nearly sacred status. Just as the cross and the church building are sacred in Christian religions, the flag and sites such as the White House and Arlington National Cemetery take on sacred meaning for all Americans. Furthermore, the God of civil religion is assumed to take particular interest in America, and our nation is believed to have a special, higher destiny. In a sense, the United States is seen as the new Israel and Americans as the new chosen people. Such beliefs have been used—some would say misused—to justify such doctrines as manifest destiny, which underlay the mid-nineteenth-century expansion of the nation across the North American continent, and more recent military involvements in places like Kuwait and Kosovo undertaken in pursuit of such sacred American values as freedom and democracy. Indeed, the American civil religion has promoted a form of nationalism whereby the nation itself achieves at least quasi-sacred status and becomes the object of religious devotion. This has been called everything from patriotism to idolatry (Chidester, 1988).

RELIGIOUS BELIEFS AND PRACTICES

A number of scholars have argued that the influence of religion is waning in America. But in many ways Americans are as religious as ever. In 1997, 96 percent of

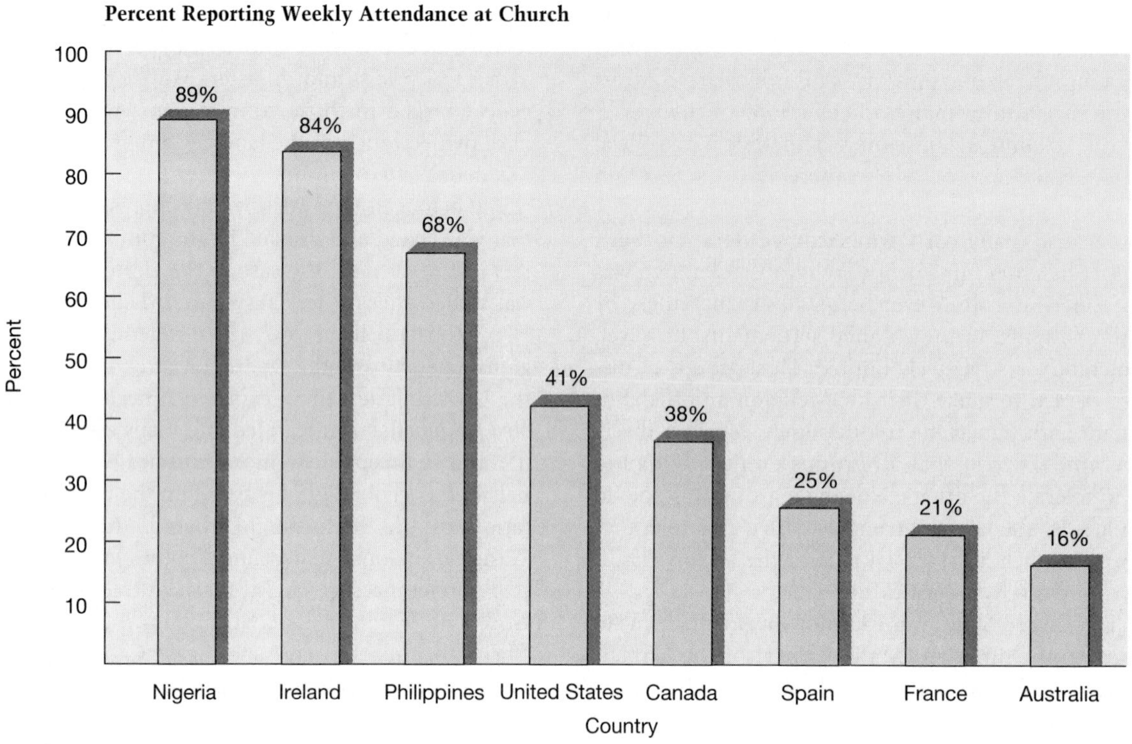

Percent Reporting Weekly Attendance at Church

FIGURE 16.1   The United States ranks among the more actively religious nations in the world, as measured by the percentage of people reporting weekly church attendance.

Source: Russell Shorto, "Belief by the Numbers," *New York Times Magazine*, December 7, 1997, pp. 60–61. Copyright © 1997 by The New York Times. Reprinted by permission.

them said that they believed in God, compared to 95 percent in 1947. Similarly, little has changed in the religious behavior of Americans. In 1947, 90 percent said that they prayed; 43 percent did so before meals. Fifty years later, the overall percentage of Americans who prayed had not changed, but the percentage of those who gave thanks before eating rose to 63 percent (Shorto, 1997).

Cross-cultural comparisons of church attendance also indicate that the United States is one of the most religious nations, especially among industrialized ones. Countries with higher weekly attendance rates included Nigeria (89 percent), Ireland (84 percent), and the Philippines (68 percent). Canada (38 percent), Spain (25 percent), France (21 percent), and Australia (16 percent) all had lower rates. (See Figure 16.1 for a cross-national comparison of weekly church attendance.)

Some measures do seem to indicate a decline in religious commitment in the United States. For example, in 1997 only 68 percent of the population belonged to a church or synagogue, down from 76 percent in 1947. And, yet, today's percentage looks high compared to the figures earlier in American history. In 1776, only 17

percent of the American population belonged to a church or synagogue.

However, some evidence clearly suggests that religion is declining in importance in the United States. In 1957, 82 percent of Americans stated that "religion can answer all or most of today's problems." By 1997, that number had dropped to 61 percent. In 1965, 70 percent of Americans said that religion was very important in their lives. By 1997, that number had dropped to 61 percent. And in 1997, 57 percent of Americans believed that religion as a whole was decreasing, compared to only 14 percent in 1957 (Newport & Saad, 1997).

Religious Membership and Preference

In 1997, over 157 million Americans reported belonging to some religious organization (*Yearbook of American and Canadian Churches, 1999*). This amounts to over 60 percent of the country's population. If the religious organizations are divided into three broad faiths—Protestant, Roman Catholic, and Jewish—then Protestants are the most numerous. But if the figures are considered by denomination, as they are in Table 16.2, the picture is quite different. The number of Roman Catholics in the United States is almost twice that of the next largest group, the Baptists. Since the Baptists are divided among at least 15 different denominational organizations—the American Baptist Association, the Conservative Baptist Association of America, the Free Will Baptists, the General Baptists, and so on—it is clear that Roman Catholics are by far the largest single unified religious group in this country. Methodists, with over 14 million members (about one-fourth the membership of the Roman Catholic Church), constitute the next largest unified religious group.

Data on the membership of American religious organizations are not always reliable. Each group tends to inflate its membership, and not all denominations keep careful records. Also, criteria for membership vary. Some organizations count only active members of congregations; others count all those who have been baptized or confirmed in that faith.

The distribution of religious *preference* in the United States is somewhat different. In 1997, 93 percent of those surveyed expressed a preference for some particular religion. These responses tell us little about levels of religious involvement or commitment, however. To some people, religious preference means total involvement in a religious organization; to others, it means a personal commitment to the beliefs of a religion, without any necessary organizational involvement. And some respondents may identify their religious preference as nothing more than the religion that was practiced by their parents or relatives or by the ethnic group to which they belong. Some people who identify themselves as Jewish, for example, mean to convey only an ethnic identity and not an active religious life.

Older people are far more likely to be affiliated with a religion (DeStefano, 1990; Greeley, 1989). Regional religious differences are fairly well marked. Jews, Catholics, Episcopalians, and Unitarians are more heavily concentrated in the Northeast, whereas Methodists and Baptists are more commonly found in the South and the Midwest. Jews and Catholics are more likely to live in cities; most rural people are Protestants.

Finally, the social status of religious denominations varies: Episcopalians are generally ranked highest in prestige, while Jews tend to have the highest levels of income and education. Throughout much of American history, Catholics held lower occupational status, but the relative social status rankings of Catholics and Protestants in the United States have changed markedly over the last few decades, with Catholics gaining on (and sometimes overtaking) Protestants (Kosmin & Lachman, 1993; Roof, 1979; Roof & McKinney, 1987). (See Table 16.3.)

TABLE 16.2   ESTIMATED U.S. RELIGIOUS MEMBERSHIP, 1998

Religion	Membership
Roman Catholics	61,207,914
Baptists	33,209,484
Methodists	14,183,130
Pentecostals	11,122,982*
Lutherans	8,302,584
Islam	3,332,000
Latter-day Saints (Mormons)	4,977,779
Jews	3,500,000
Presbyterians	4,160,154
Episcopalians	2,536,550
Eastern Orthodox	5,013,821
Churches of Christ	2,250,000
United Church of Christ	1,452,565
Christian Church (Disciples of Christ)	910,297
Jehovah's Witnesses	975,829
Seventh-day Adventists	809,159
Reformed	522,079
Church of the Nazarene	608,008
Salvation Army	453,150
Churches of God	281,673
Mennonites	350,547

All figures rounded to nearest thousand.

*Includes Assemblies of God (2,467,588) and Church of God in Christ (5,499,875).

Note: Although Protestants constitute the largest religious community in the United States, the Roman Catholic Church is the largest unified religious organization.

Source: Reprinted with permission from *The World Almanac and Book of Facts,* 1999. Copyright © 1998 *Primedia* Reference Inc. All rights reserved.

TRENDS IN RELIGIOUS MEMBERSHIP

There are no reliable data on long-term historical changes in religious belief and commitment in the United States, but statistics concerning organizational membership do show a striking trend. In 1997, over 68 percent of Americans belonged to religious bodies, compared to only 37 percent in 1861, 50 percent in 1900, and 76 percent in 1947 (Shorto, 1997). Obviously, there has been a notable increase in religious membership during the past century.

Experts disagree on the meaning of these numbers. There is no evidence of an increase in belief in the supernatural during the last century or of a growing relevance of religious values in the daily lives of Americans. The

TABLE 16.3   INCOME BY RELIGION

Group	Annual Median Household Income
Jewish	$36,700
Unitarian	$34,800
Agnostic	$33,300
Episcopalian	$33,000
Eastern Orthodox	$31,500
Congregationalist	$30,400
Presbyterian	$29,000
Disciples of Christ	$28,800
Buddhist	$28,500
Hindu	$27,800
Catholic	$27,700
No religion	$27,300
Churches of Christ	$26,600
Lutheran	$25,900
Christian Science	$25,800
Mormon	$25,700
Methodist	$25,100
Muslim	$24,700
Seventh-day Adventist	$22,700
Assemblies of God	$22,200
Evangelical	$21,900
Nazarene	$21,600
Jehovah's Witnesses	$20,900
Baptist	$20,600
Pentecostal	$19,400
Brethren	$18,500
Holiness	$13,700

Source: From *One Nation Under God* by Barry A. Kosmin and Seymour P. Lachman. Copyright © 1993 by Seymour P. Lachman and Barry A. Kosmin. Reprinted by permission of Harmony Books, a division of Crown Publishers, Inc.

peaked in the late 1960s, and membership has generally declined since then. One researcher has noted that the church's ability to influence a person's identity and status in a secular society may have been reduced in recent years. Therefore, fewer people may be seeking church membership to enhance their social status (Hammond, 1988). Most of the older established denominations are now growing very slowly, if at all, and the recruitment of new members is a constant concern (Roof & McKinney, 1987; Shorto, 1997; Wuthnow, 1988).

Indeed, the recent decline in membership has been highest among the traditional "high-status" denominations. In contrast, the Catholic community has grown throughout the twentieth century, and the conservative Protestant groups that have traditionally appealed more to working- and lower-middle-class people—such as the Southern Baptists, the Assemblies of God, the Jehovah's Witnesses, and the Pentecostals—have also grown in membership and influence in the past two decades (Shorto, 1997). The reasons for these changes are not entirely clear. Some sociologists feel that, in the face of an increasingly confusing secular culture, people who become members of conservative churches are attracted by the clear and consistent doctrine and practice they advocate. In contrast, the accommodations made by the other churches to the modern secular world seem to have lessened their appeal.

A surprising number of Americans *convert*—that is, change religious membership—during their lifetimes. About 43 percent of all Americans have left the religious group in which they were raised (Roof & McKinney, 1987). The main reasons for this pattern include the desire to worship with people of similar socioeconomic status, the decision to adopt the same religious membership as one's spouse, and the abandonment of established religion by young people. Twenty-seven percent of those who left the religion in which they were raised now claim no religious membership at all (Gallup Organization, 1988d).

Religious Participation

It is important to distinguish religious participation from religious membership and preference. Only about four out of ten Americans report that they attend religious observances in any given week. Twenty years ago, a higher number—almost five out of ten—reported attending services. (See Figure 16.2.) There has been an especially sharp decline in the number of Roman Catholics who go to church weekly: 52 percent in 1989, as compared with 74 percent in 1958 (Gallup Organization, 1989). There are many possible reasons for this decline. When surveyed, many Americans state that it is not necessary to

ratio of clergy to total population and per capita financial support of churches have both declined. Moreover, much "religious" activity of recent years would seem quite secular to the religious men and women of previous generations. Some observers believe that the increase in religious membership is merely one reflection of a desire for status. Having achieved greater economic status, people turn their attention to achieving enhanced social status. They accomplish this by joining socially prestigious religious groups (Demerath & Hammond, 1969).

Membership trends in recent decades paint a different picture, however. Religious organizations increased their membership following World War II, but this trend

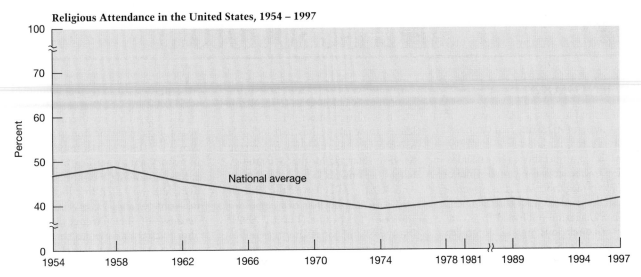

Religious Attendance in the United States, 1954 – 1997

FIGURE 16.2 From the mid-1950s to 1997, levels of attendance at religious services declined in the United States.

Source: The Gallup Poll, *Public Opinion,* annual reports.

attend religious services in order to be a good Christian or a good Jew. And many sociologists believe that the particularly sharp decline in Catholic church attendance represents Catholics' rejection of the Vatican's rigid views on birth control.

As measured by actual church attendance in the United States, both the lower classes and the upper classes tend to be relatively uninvolved with religion. At least among Protestants, church attendance is greatest in the upper-working and the lower-middle classes, especially for those with children. Among Jews, there historically has been a greater degree of religious involvement within the lower classes (Mueller & Johnson, 1975). Some studies, however, suggest more participation by the upper classes (Greeley, 1989). The relationship between social class and religious attendance among Catholics is not clear.

Many reasons have been put forth to account for social class variations in church attendance among Protestants. It has been suggested, for example, that upper-class people lack involvement in religion because they feel less need of the personal and social benefits of religion. The nonparticipation of the lowest classes has been traced in part to an attitude of suspicion toward all institutions and agencies outside the home and immediate family. It is also, of course, limited by such economic factors as inability to afford appropriate clothing for church attendance or to support one's church financially.

A growing body of researchers has come to believe, however, that social class characteristics do not adequately account for group variations in religious participation

(Alston & McIntosh, 1979; Roof & McKinney, 1987). Individuals are far more complex than class position can possibly indicate. A better approach, they suggest, is to examine the nature of people's individual religiosity.

RELIGIOSITY

The problems of defining and measuring the nature of personal religious experience, or **religiosity,** have received extensive attention from sociologists. Religiosity is very difficult to examine because the meaning of the religious experience varies so much from person to person. Membership in a religious body is not an accurate measure of a person's religiosity. Members of the same religion, even of the same congregation, commonly exhibit different levels of commitment to their faith. One person may know a great deal about the doctrines of his or her religion, yet may doubt some of them. Another person may believe strongly in a particular religion, yet be lax about attending services.

Social scientists recognize that people can be religious in various ways. Pioneering work by Joseph Fichter (1951, 1954) suggested that there are four types of religious Roman Catholics: nuclear, modal, marginal, and dormant. *Nuclear* Catholics, the ideal church members, go beyond the minimal requirements of their faith. They are active in parish life, go to communion and mass more than once a week, and send their children to parochial school. At the other end of the spectrum are the *dormant* Catholics: people raised in the religion who do not attend

APPLYING SOCIOLOGY

SCIENTOLOGY

Images of Hollywood stars appear on the covers of magazines sold at newsstands across the country everyday. So what is so unusual about a superstar like John Travolta appearing on the front of *Celebrity* magazine? Well, this magazine is not designed solely for entertainment. It is a magazine published by a controversial religious organization called the Church of Scientology.

It might seem odd for a church to publish a magazine entitled *Celebrity*, but this church draws its flock from Hollywood. And its list of the rich and famous is impressive. In addition to John Travolta, it includes Tom Cruise, Kirstie Alley, Isaac Hayes, Chick Corea, Jenna Elfman, Anne Archer, and Lisa Marie Presley (Frantz, 1998). Ron L. Hubbard, who founded Scientology in 1954, believed that celebrities like these could draw attention to his new religion and hasten its acceptance as a legitimate church. So, beginning in the late 1960s, he built Celebrity Centres that were designed to meet the needs of artists and actors.

And, it appears that Scientology has succeeded in helping a number of them. John Travolta, who joined the Church of Scientology in 1975, attributes his ability to meet personal challenges to what he has learned as a Scientologist. Jenna Elfman, a rising television star, claims that Scientology taught her how to focus on her goals. And Kirstie Alley gives the church credit for helping her overcome her addiction to cocaine (Frantz, 1998). But these kinds of testimonies fail to convince critics of Scientology that it is a legitimate church. They argue that Scientology is nothing more than "a moneymaking enterprise because of the high fees it charges members" (Frantz, 1998, p. A18) And, indeed, most church members would probably agree. Consider, for example, how much money a 36-year-old Scientologist by the name of Lisa McPherson gave to the church. In 1994 she spent $55,767 for Scientology courses. She paid another $41,924 in 1995 (Frantz, 1997). Ironically, she earned this money as an employee of the church. She was paid extraordinarily well—$136,812 in 1994. And, yet, she never seemed to get ahead. So, in order to pay for Scientology courses, she would constantly borrow the money from her employer. In 1995, that amounted to $33,000.

McPherson's involvement with Scientology made the front page of the *New York Times* on December 1, 1997 in a story about her death two years earlier. Following a minor auto accident, she was taken to a local hospital—not because of any injury, but because of her strange behavior. Shortly after paramedics checked her out, she stripped off her clothes and began to wander along the street, insisting that she needed help. Paramedics then took her to the hospital. After refusing psychiatric care, which was a teaching of Scientology, she was released to fellow parishioners, who took her to a church facility. Less than three weeks later she was dead. In the months that followed, her family filed a lawsuit, claiming that McPherson was held against her will and died because she had not received the proper medical treatment.

This was not the first time that the Church of Scientology faced legal problems. In 1981, the convictions of nine Scientologists were upheld by a federal appeals court. Their crime involved a conspiracy to

church or practice the faith in any other way. Modal and marginal Catholics occupy the middle ground. *Modal* Catholics go to church regularly but do not take a serious interest in religion or in parish activities. *Marginal* Catholics consider themselves members of that religion but rarely attend services.

On a more abstract level, religiosity has been analyzed in terms of four main dimensions, each of which is only weakly correlated with the others (Glock, 1959). The *experiential* dimension is the degree of emotional attachment the believer feels toward the supernatural. The *ritualistic* dimension refers to the level of the believer's participation in prayer and attendance at church services. The *ideological* dimension reflects the person's commitment to a group's religious beliefs.

Finally, the *consequential* dimension consists of the ways in which an individual's behavior is affected by religious commitment and involvement.

Thomas Luckmann (1967) has suggested that many individuals who are critical of organized religion (and therefore do not attend religious services) may actually be deeply religious people. Luckmann coined the term *invisible* (private) *religion* to refer to the widespread practice of considering religion to be a personal or subjective experience rather than a group or community experience. This sort of religion is "private" because it takes place in the mind of the individual rather than in a public place of worship or devotion. The existence of private religion can help to explain why only 41 percent of Americans regularly attend religious services, even steal government documents about the church (Singer, 1996). In 1992, the church faced more criminal charges in Canada. That court found it guilty of breach of trust and imposed a $250,000 fine.

Legal problems like these fuel the debate surrounding the question of whether Scientology is a religion, a cult, or a profit-making organization. In fact, for 25 years the Internal Revenue Service refused to grant the Church of Scientology the tax exemption allowed for churches, arguing that it was a commercial enterprise (Frantz, 1997). The church considered it a major victory when it won this exemption in 1993.

Is Scientology a religion? Is it a cult? Or is it, as many critics claim, a profitable business? In many ways it sounds like a religion. Much like other religions, it explains where we came from. According to its version of creation, we were sent to Earth 75 million years ago by an intergalactic ruler. Since then, human beings, who are considered immortal spirits, have continued to evolve, learning from the experiences in each life. Scientology also has its own sacred text, *Dianetics,*

which was written by the church's founder, Ron L. Hubbard. Contained within the pages of this book are the prescriptions for leading a happy and productive life.

But some experts argue that Scientology is not a religion but a cult that can harm members and isolate them from friends and family (Singer, 1995). These critics argue that, unlike mainstream religions, Scientology aims to control it members. Stephen Kent, who has studied this organization extensively, described the church this way:

> For members who are deeply involved, Scientology becomes a totalistic institution. It provides them with everything from occupation, pseudomedical treatments, entertainment and a justice system to an overarching purpose for their lives" (Frantz, 1997p. A14)

Sociologists and theologians would agree that the term *religion* can be used to describe many kinds of behaviors. The descriptions that celebrities give of Scientology fit what scholars would call a world-affirming religion—one that provides a philosophy

Much controversy has ensued over the Church of Scientology. Is it a religion, a cult, or a profit-making organization?

designed to help people succeed in this life, not the afterlife (Frantz, 1998). This emphasis may well explain why many segments of the public have not yet accepted Scientology as a legitimate church.

though 96 percent of them express a belief in God (Shorto, 1997).

The New Religious Consciousness

In the face of what seem to be overall declines in religious membership, participation, and belief among broad segments of American society over the past few decades, religion has shown surprising vitality. Indeed, several polls have found evidence of a "new religious consciousness" in America (Gallup & Newport, 1991).

Such religious experiences are especially associated with the growth of *evangelical* Christianity. In general, evangelicals believe in the literal word of the Bible, have had experiences of spiritual rebirth (are "born again"),

and are committed to spreading the message of salvation to others. Some estimate that there are as many as 40 million evangelical Christians in America today (Balmer, 1989) and claim that they are the fastest-growing, most visible, ambitious, and politically active religious group in the country (Roof & McKinney, 1987).

Increasingly, evangelical ministers have turned to television to spread their message. In 1997, there were 257 religious television programs, and 16 percent of all television programming was religious (Shorto, 1997). Program content varies from the traditional preaching of evangelist Billy Graham to the entertainment and talk-show orientation of Rex Humbard. These programs, and the sophisticated marketing techniques that support them, allow television evangelists to reach out for followers in every home across the country and to raise millions of dollars annually.

The evangelical movement had a pronounced effect on the nation's political life in the 1980s that has continued, although in a more subdued manner today (Mathisen & Mathisen, 1988; Silk, 1988). Evangelical Christian groups have become a strong force in the right-wing political movement that has been characterized as "the revival of backlash moralistic politics" (Balmer, 1989; Lipset & Raab, 1981; Vidich, 1987).

While these fundamentalist groups have not persuaded Congress to accept constitutional amendments prohibiting abortion and permitting school prayer, they did help to sponsor a successful bill in 1984 permitting students to hold religious meetings in school buildings, though not during school hours, if meetings on other noncurricular matters were also permitted. And some of their views are popular with the general public: In a 1988 national poll, 68 percent of the respondents favored an amendment allowing school prayer, compared to 26 percent who opposed the amendment (Gallup Organization, 1988a). According to some analysts, fundamentalists have succeeded in partially shifting the focus of American public opinion from concerns about social justice to concerns about public morality (Baker, Moreland, & Steed, 1989). These efforts, some maintain, have also led to increased polarization between religious conservatives and religious liberals (Hunter, 1991; Wuthnow, 1988).

Attempts to account for this new political–religious alliance point to the many similarities between religious fundamentalism and right-wing political viewpoints. For example, both tend to accept a conspiratorial view of the world and to be strongly critical of secularism. Both are based on a philosophy of absolutes: absolute good and absolute evil, with few gray areas. And both stress individual effort—whether the goal be spiritual or economic. This is one basis for the conservative condemnation of social welfare programs and government intervention in private enterprise (Balmer, 1989). Despite the increased influence of fundamentalists, however, some sociologists have seen signs of a decline in religious orthodoxy on the right as a new generation of evangelical leaders confronts the issues of family, work, morality, and the self in a political context (Hunter, 1987).

The prevalence and growth of religious sects and cults is an additional aspect of the new religious consciousness. Twenty-one American sects now have more than 500,000 members each, but hundreds more are relatively small, often with fewer than 2,000 members. Cults generally have a much smaller membership than sects. They can be grouped into three distinct categories: countercultural, personal growth, and neo-Christian. *Countercultural* cults are typically offshoots of non-Western or non-Christian

traditions. Examples include Zen Buddhism, Hare Krishna, and Sufism (the mystical tradition of Islam). Asian religions seem to be the source of most countercultural cults. Often, they involve charismatic leadership and emphasize direct religious experience. They offer adherents a complete way of life guided by the precepts of the cult and in opposition to mainstream American culture (Galanter, 1982; Glock & Bellah, 1976).

Neo-Christian cults include groups such as the Children of God and Jews for Jesus (Stark & Bainbridge, 1985; Wuthnow, 1976). American history is filled with similar groups that blossomed and died away. Examples are the Oneida Perfectionists, the Shakers, and the Pillar of Fire. Other such groups, though, have thrived—the Jehovah's Witnesses, for example.

Personal-growth cults are Western in origin and quasi-religious in nature. Neutral toward the Christian tradition, they attempt to put their followers in touch with some form of ultimate meaning. Cults in this group include Scientology and Transcendental Meditation. Charismatic leadership is central to some personal-growth cults, but because members do not live in cult-sponsored communities away from the rest of society, the leaders of these movements generally have less authority over the lives of their followers than do leaders of countercultural and neo-Christian cults. Many adherents to personal-growth cults do not give over their lives to these groups but become involved only in an attempt to solve specific personal problems or to gain "control" over their lives (Glock & Bellah, 1976; Mosatche, 1983).

A diffuse personal-growth cult that has thrived in recent years is the New Age movement (Jorstad, 1990). This is not a cult in the traditional sense but, rather, a religious movement with some cultlike characteristics. Unlike most of the groups mentioned here, which tend to be located on the fringe of society, this movement seems to be especially popular among members of the middle class. It has many adherents, for example, among executives in business and industry. Subscribing to such spiritual practices as Eastern mysticism and the occult, New Age believers expect that dramatic social change will occur when enough people undergo a process of "inner transformation." Pyramids, crystals, and gemstones are often integral parts of New Age rituals and are thought to have special healing powers.

RELIGION IN SOCIETY: THE LONG VIEW

In order to obtain a full understanding of the sociology of religion, it is important to examine this institution in very broad historical context. In this final section, we consider the origins and development of religion and the contemporary trend toward secularization.

Origins and Development

In the early stages of human society, religion was practiced primarily within the extended family group (Johnstone, 1988; Wallace, 1966). Sacred objects were those with special meaning to the family—the well that furnished water, burial sites, ancestral relics. Ritual was developed and performed by family members. The deity, who was thought to reside either in the home or on family-owned land, protected and supported the members of the family.

This family orientation of religion was still important in the West in the early days of the Roman civilization. At that time, each extended family had its own special gods, some of whom later came to be worshiped by the whole society. A similar orientation is still evident in the East in the form of the Shinto shrines in many Japanese homes, where the family's ancestors are worshiped.

The main unit of religious organization eventually broadened to include the whole tribe or village, but religion was still for the most part an integral part of other social institutions rather than an institution in itself. The head of the family, and later the head of the tribe, usually was assigned the task of learning, and then teaching his successor, the correct way to perform critical religious rituals. But the leader was not considered any more religious than other members of the group. He carried on the same nonreligious activities as other people and was not a true religious specialist.

In these early societies (and in some societies today), there was no religious pluralism. Each community had only one religion, and all children were included in its rituals and taught its beliefs from a very early age. Religion was inseparable from home, family, and community, and it played a part in nearly every aspect of life. Planting, harvesting, hunting, entering adulthood, marrying, falling ill, building new houses, preparing and eating food—almost every activity was linked to some religious ritual or belief. Religion provided a link between the material world and the "other" world, an integration of that "otherness" with ordinary life. To renounce one's religion in such a setting would be to abandon one's entire social identity.

Throughout the course of history, however, social institutions have tended to break away from the family. Religion has not been exempt from this trend. Over time, religion has become a separate institution, with its own specialized organizations and roles, and a separation has arisen between religious and secular activity. Participation in religious activity, and even the selection of a religious faith, have increasingly become matters of personal choice in modern societies (Demerath & Hammond, 1969; Roof & McKinney, 1987).

The development of the role of priest may have been the first step in the institutional differentiation of religion. As beliefs became more sophisticated and rituals more complicated, certain people—priests—began to specialize in interpreting and explaining them. The priest no longer divided his attention among many responsibilities but gave full time to religious activities. Eventually, religions developed hierarchies of officials to look after their affairs. For example, the Episcopal church in the United States today has several hundred bishops and thousands of ministers.

The creation of full-time priests led to a second change: the expanded separation of sacred and secular realms. The priests, now specialists, were no longer allowed to provide leadership and guidance in other fields. Formerly, the village chief decided when to plant in the spring and then conducted a religious ritual as a part of the planting. Over time, the two aspects—secular planting and religious ritual—became separated. The chief gave planting instructions; the priest held religious ceremonies. This division both symbolized and promoted a reduction in the influence of religion in everyday affairs.

Once the sacred and the secular had been split into two separate worlds, a third change was inevitable. People began to choose whether or not they would participate in religion. When religion and secular activities were fully intermixed, people could not avoid religious involvement. Following their separation, however, people could reject religious activity and, eventually, religion itself (Bellah, 1964).

The Secularization Debate

Like all social institutions, religion has had to adapt to the changing conditions of the modern world. Many scholars have argued that this process of adaptation has resulted in a long, continuous decline in religion's influence (Hammond, 1985; Martin, 1978). In support of this view, Peter Berger (1970) has suggested that the only important sphere of influence that religion retains in advanced societies is the family. Religion today is largely irrelevant to government, education, and the marketplace. It is no longer the primary cohesive force in societies, having been displaced by nationalism and other secular and political ideologies. The process by which religion becomes increasingly marginal to society and culture is called **secularization.**

As religion has declined as an institution, it has been argued, religious norms and values have lost much of their force. Important days on religious calendars are no longer holy days but simply holidays. Heaven and hell, sin and salvation, have lost much of their importance. Moral rules concerning interfaith marriage, divorce, and sexual activities—once enforced by strict religious sanctions—have been relaxed. Religious belief in general has become more a matter of personal than social conviction.

The most important aspects of secularization may be what many see as the weakening of belief in a transcendental being and the removal of supernatural sanctions from secular beliefs and institutions. As one observer has noted, "If commentators on the contemporary situation of religion agree about anything, it is that the supernatural has departed from the modern world" (Berger, 1969). In 1997, 57 percent of Americans surveyed agreed that religion is losing influence in American life (Newport & Saad, 1997).

Like most social trends, secularization must compete with trends that oppose it. We have already noted the significant increase in religious affiliation in this century and the marked vitality of some religious sects, such as the Pentecostal groups, among the working and lower middle classes. A second countertrend to secularization is the widespread interest in Eastern religions and in the many quasi-religious activities associated with personal-growth and New Age movements. A third is the new role of conservative religion in America's political life.

Whether trends like these will slow secularization, or even reverse it, remains to be seen. Berger (1977) believes that people are unhappy with a secularized view of the world because it provides no acceptable explanations for human suffering, injustice, or death, and he anticipates that, as a reaction against secularization, a religious revival might take place in the not too distant future. Some scholars agree with Berger, predicting that there will soon be a profound religious awakening and a return to the sacred—a time when science and technology will lose credibility as solutions to personal and world problems (Cox, 1988; Falk, 1988). Other theorists hold an even grander view and believe that religious boundaries are becoming increasingly blurred and that the world may be moving toward the evolution of a "new global consciousness" in which the barriers between the East and West will be broken down (Kung, 1986). Still others argue that the secularization of American society is a myth, and that overall participation in organized religion has changed little over the past 50 years (Hout & Greeley, 1987).

Other scholars, however, think the secularization of American life will proceed much further, and point to the deterioration in religious life that has taken place in many European countries as an example of what could happen to America. They envision a fragmented and alienated America where extreme individualism and self-preoccupation will lead to a continued breakdown of common values and community.

A middle ground, in the words of one sociologist, is that "neither mass religiosity nor complete secularism appear to be permanent historical possibilities" (Williams, 1970). There is good reason to believe that religion will never again be at the center of modern societies, as it was in traditional societies. But religion will probably continue to lend people emotional support and give meaning to their lives.

CHAPTER REVIEW

1. How would you define religion? Does your definition suggest that religion and science are incompatible?

2. What functions does religion serve?

3. Religion can be an instrument of either stability or change. Provide examples of how it does both.

4. Why is religion so closely linked to the institution of the family?

5. Identify and discuss the four basic elements of religion. Do any other social groups have similar elements? If so, what are they and what functions do they serve?

6. Describe the four main types of religious organizations. Is this a useful typology for modern societies? Why or why not?

7. How has the separation of church and state shaped American society?

8. How would you characterize the religious makeup of the United States today? What factors have contributed to this ever-changing religious composition?

9. How would you explain the relationship between religious affiliation and social class?

10. Could you argue that religion is just another form of politics? Why or why not?

11. How will religion change in the twenty-first century?

INTERNET EXERCISE

The Web destinations for Chapter 16 cover various aspects of religion. To start your explorations, go to the Prentice Hall Companion Web site **http://www.prenhall. com/popenoe.** Next, choose **Chapter 16** (Religion) from the menu on the left side of the screen. There are several sites to investigate. We suggest you begin with the **Scientology and Dianetics Field Auditors** and **Scientology Lies** sites. The former site has been created by the Vigil Field Group and is a licensed distributor of products and information relevant to Scientology, including books written by L. Ron Hubbard. The latter site has been assembled by Kristi Wachter and is, essentially, a formal protest against Scientology. By comparing the two sites, you should be able to evaluate Scientology in an objective fashion. After you have done this, answer the following questions:

- Is Scientology a *religion?* In your judgment, why or why not?
- Do you believe that Scientology poses any threat in our society? Why or why not?

KEY TERMS

religion	simple supernaturalism	dogma
theism	rites of passage	denomination
monotheism	sacred	sect
polytheism	profane	cult
transcendental idealism	ritual	religiosity
totemism	ecclesia	secularization
totem	church	

CHAPTER 17

Power, Politics, and Government

If you were a student attending a college for the deaf, would you want the president of your school to be hearing or deaf?

The majority of the students at Gallaudet University, in Washington, D.C., believed that a deaf president would be much more responsive and sympathetic to the needs of the school's hearing-impaired student body. When, in 1988, a woman with no hearing impairment and lacking sign language skills was appointed president, many students and faculty were outraged. With support from the National Association for the Deaf, Gallaudet's students campaigned to replace the new president with an equally qualified hearing-impaired person. Their campaign was successful. One week after the protest began, Dr. I. King Jordan, a deaf man, was appointed president.

The student and faculty movement that was instrumental in Dr. Jordan's appointment could not have been successful if it had not had significant political backing. This is not to say that the government was called in to decide the issue, or that citizens went to the polls to vote on the matter. Rather, Gallaudet's students and faculty used the political resources at their disposal to make their feelings known, and took steps to ensure that their wishes were respected and acted upon by the university's administration. In response to this political pressure, the changes demanded by the faculty and student body were made.

In small groups, political processes are informal. But in large groups—such as nations—political processes are part of a highly structured institution called *government*. To an extent that few of us realize, the governmental policies brought about through politics establish people's rights, list their responsibilities, affect their opportunities, and control their use of and access to resources. Because the main political system in modern societies is the state or government, it is on this topic that we focus in this chapter. First, we discuss power, authority, and the state in general terms; then we examine particular types or forms of government. We continue with a detailed discussion of politics and government in the United States, and end with a humanistic perspective on society and the state.

POWER, AUTHORITY, AND THE STATE

If the varied interests of human beings and social groups never came into conflict, and if resources were unlimited, political systems would not be needed. But this is not the case. Every society must reconcile the conflict between human desires and interests, on the one hand, and the scarcity of resources and desired items, on the other. There must always be ways of deciding who gets what, when, and how. This is the function of the political system, or **politics**—the process by which some people and groups acquire power and exercise it over others.

Politics is typically a matter of common concern. Decisions that affect the way we organize our social life are frequently political decisions. Politics, then, may also be thought of as the activity by which collective decisions are reached and implemented. Those with power make, enforce, and implement these decisions (Bogdanor, 1987; Miller, 1987).

Power

The essence of politics is power. **Power** is the capacity of people or groups to control or influence the actions of others, whether those others wish to cooperate or not. Although a person acting alone can exert power, most commonly power is exercised by a person acting on behalf of a group. Typically, the power holder acts as an officer of the group; power is vested in the position or office and not in the person who happens to hold it at any one time. Thus, when that person ceases to hold the job, he or she loses the power that comes with it.

There are three main mechanisms for controlling the actions of others. First, a valued object may be offered as a *reward* for obedience. A father may offer his children a snack of homemade cookies and chocolate milk in return for good behavior on a shopping trip. The workers in a tire factory may be given a large Christmas bonus for good attendance and a high rate of production. The supporters of a successful presidential candidate may be offered jobs in the new administration.

A second mechanism of control threatens a *punishment* for noncompliance. A football player who breaks training rules knows he will be fined or benched. A student caught cheating on an exam expects to be expelled from school. And outspoken critics of a dictator know that they risk their lives.

Power can also be exercised less directly by controlling and manipulating information, attitudes, and feelings. Whether controlled by the state or by private organizations, the flow of information to the public is a potent force for molding opinions and behavior. Many national leaders, for example, attempt to maintain the power of their governments by making speeches that are designed to shape the political attitudes of their listeners. Similarly, the managing editors of TV news programs exert power by choosing which items will be reported on their programs, and, even more crucially, how they will be presented. This less direct type of power is sometimes called *influence.*

Because power cannot be directly observed or measured, it is hard to study. One sociologist has drawn an analogy between power in the social sphere and energy in the physical world:

SOCIOLOGY OF THE MEDIA

MEDIA POWER

In his book, *Who's Running America? The Clinton Years,* Thomas Dye (1995) argues that the mass media hold an enormous amount of power in America. He writes:

> Television is the major source of information for the vast majority of Americans, and the people who control this flow of information are among the most powerful in the nation. Indeed, today the leadership of the mass media has successfully established itself as equal in power to the nation's corporate and governmental leadership. (1995, p. 108)

Dye's argument is particularly compelling when you consider who own the media. Ultimately, these owners control the content of the media: They have the power to hire and fire the people who report the news, they decide which projects will receive funding, and they can provide a media platform for speakers of their choice (Croteau & Hoynes, 1997). Another way of thinking about it is in terms of how the media set the agenda (White, 1973). That is, they have the power to determine what Americans think about and talk about. According to Theodore White, that kind of authority is reserved for "tyrants, priests, parties, and mandarins."

The increasing concentration of media ownership in fewer and fewer hands gives us even more cause for concern. Consider, for example, the trend described by Ben Bagdikian (1992). In 1992, 20 national and multinational corporations dominated the media industry. There are over 3,000 book publishers in the United States, but only five of these control more than 50 percent of the book market. Two corporations account for most of the revenue made by magazines, and 11 companies control most daily American newspapers.

This increasing concentration of the media has been accompanied by another troubling trend—the acquisition of media operation by corporations with diverse business interests (see Table 17.1). Today each of the major television networks in America is owned by a major corporate conglomerate (Ryan & Wentworth, 1999). Westinghouse acquired CBS a day after Disney bought ABC. And General Electric, which has a major interest in the defense industry, owns NBC.

Do these parent companies exert influence on the stories that air on the evening news? Because of defense, GE's ownership of NBC makes this question particularly troubling. Determining whether these powerful companies do have this kind of influence is hard to determine. And well-paid network journalists, who believe they control the content of their stories, are not likely to admit it. But some evidence suggests that corporate owners expect to have a say and that this has created some conflict (Auletta, 1991). For example, when General Electric purchased NBC, the new owners did not understand why the News Division maintained its distance from the rest of the company. From a business perspective, it made more sense for all divisions to cooperate. Jack Welsh, the chairman of General Electric, wanted Willard Scott, the weatherman for NBC's *Today* program, to refer to GE light bulbs during the show. But for the journalists, this kind of cooperation raised serious concerns about objectivity, conflict of interests, and the proper role of television news. In this case, the evidence ultimately suggested that the owner's will triumphed over that of the journalists. Even if the influence of media owners cannot be established directly—for example, by orders to pull a story that would be damaging to the corporation's business interests—we must still assume that journalists concerned about their jobs will practice some form of self-censorship.

Wherever we look we observe [energy's] effects, and all activities are in one sense an expression of it. We talk freely about the uses of energy and power, but when we attempt to specify more precisely what either of these phenomena is, we encounter difficulties. The main reason is that neither energy nor power can be directly observed or measured. Their existence, nature, and strength can only be inferred from their effects. (Olsen, 1968, p. 72)

Power and Authority

Max Weber (1919/1946) made a distinction between power that involves force and the kind that people regard as legitimate. An example can clarify this distinction. Gangsters who demand and receive protection money from a shopkeeper by threatening violence are using force. Government agencies that demand and receive a

TABLE 17.1   MARKET SHARE AND HOLDINGS OF THE MAJOR TELEVISION NETWORKS

Company	Percent of Market	Media Holdings
Westinghouse/CBS	31	CBS Radio Network, CBS Television Network, 82 radio stations, Eyemark, Maxam Entertainment, Group W Productions, Group W Satellite Communications, Westinghouse Broadcasting International
GE/NBC	25	NBC Television Network, CNBC, MSNBC, A&E, History Channel (joint venture with Hearst and Disney/ABC), American Movie Classics (joint venture with TCI and Cablevision), NewSport and Prime Sports channel networks (joint ventures with Liberty Media and Rainbow Holdings), NBC SuperChannel Europe, NBC Asia, CNBC Europe
Disney/ABC	24	ABC Radio Networks, ABC Television Network, Walt Disney Pictures, Touchstone Pictures, Hollywood Pictures, Caravan Pictures, Miramax Films, Walt Disney Television, Buena Vista Television, Touchstone Television, Disney Channel, 21 radio stations, 14% Young Broadcasting (14th largest holder of TV stations), 80% of ESPN/ESPN2 (which owns Creative Sports marketing, 80% of ESPN/ESPN2 (which owns creative sports marketing, 80% of SportsTicker, 33% of Eurosport, and 20% of Japan Sports Network), 37.5% of A&E and History Channel (joint venture with Hearst and NBC), Hearst-ABC Video services (joint venture with TCI and Cablevision), 7 daily newspapers (including *Kansas City Star* and *Fort Worth Star-Telegram*), Diversified Publishing Group (more than 100 periodicals), weekly newspapers in Illinois, Michigan, Oregon, and Pennsylvania, Fairchild Publications (14 periodicals), Institutional Investor (4 publications), International Medical News group (6 publications), Chilton Enterprises, interests in German Tele-Munchen (50%) and RTL-2 (23%), French Hamster Productions and TV Sports of France, Tesauro of Spain, Scandinavian Broadcasting System (23%)

Source: John Ryan and William M. Wentworth, *Media and Society: The Production of Culture in Mass Media* (Boston: Allyn & Bacon, 1999).

sales tax from the same shopkeeper are exercising **legitimate power,** or what Weber called **authority.**

Weber was particularly interested in understanding why people willingly allowed others to exercise power over them. This led him to classify the main sources of authority into three major types:

1. **Traditional authority** is authority that is conferred by custom and accepted practice. In a hereditary monarchy, the power of the head of the government is legitimated by birth. The person who becomes the monarch does so solely because a parent or some other ancestor reigned before. The ancient Chinese believed that the ruling elite (called the *mandarins*) of their society received their authority from a heavenly order that permitted them to govern in accordance with the ethical rules of the prevailing religion, Confucianism.

Pope John Paul's authority is legitimated by all three of Weber's classifications of authority: traditional, legal-rational, and charismatic.

2. **Charismatic authority** is authority that is a consequence of the ability of a leader to establish a special relationship with his or her followers. Such a leader is believed to have exceptional and extraordinary, even God-given, abilities. The leaders of many important social and political movements—George Washington, Martin Luther King, Jr., the Ayatollah Ruhollah Khomeini, and Nelson Mandela—are examples of people whose authority was or is based partly on their *charisma*. Literally, charisma is defined as a "gift of grace" from heaven, bestowed upon unique individuals.

3. **Legal-rational authority** is authority that is based on rationally established rules—rules that reflect a systematic attempt to make institutions do what they are supposed to do. The elected and appointed government officials and officers of a formal organization hold this type of authority. In the United States, political legitimacy is based on the ultimate consent of the people through such "rational" mechanisms as the Constitution and popular elections.

Although one type usually predominates—as legal-rational authority does in the United States—all three types of authority are present in most societies. Pope John Paul II is an example of a person whose authority is legitimated by all three sources. As an older male, he has a degree of traditional authority. As the head of a large and complex religious organization, the Roman Catholic Church, he has legal-rational authority. And as a person of wisdom and personal magnetism, he has charismatic authority. Even in societies where power is legitimated mainly in legal-rational ways, political leadership is usually most successful when that source of legitimation is combined with some charismatic authority. This has been demonstrated in modern times by the highly successful political careers of Winston Churchill, Charles de Gaulle, John F. Kennedy, and Ronald Reagan.

The State

Some authority is found in every group or organization. But in modern societies, the **state** is the institution that holds supreme power in society and that claims a monopoly over the legitimate use of force (Weber, 1919/1946; Williams, 1970). It dictates when, where, and how much physical force may be rightfully used.

In early human societies, which were organized principally around family and clan, the state had not yet emerged as a distinct institution. What were to become the distinguishing functions of the state were closely joined with those of other aspects of society: religion, economics, and education. All institutions and most activities were normally regulated by the same person, who was not only the head of the family or clan but also a religious and cultural leader, as well as the chief educator.

From about 3000 B.C. until the end of the Middle Ages (about A.D. 1500), the *city-state* (a political unit made up of an independent city and the territory directly controlled by it) was the basic form of political organization in the Western world. The governmental powers of the city-state typically extended into the surrounding farmlands, which supplied the city with food, labor, and tax revenues. Even empires, such as those of the Romans and the Persians, were little more than collections of loosely assembled city-states held together by military might and numerous political concessions to local authorities. When these empires fell, their city-states continued to exist independently, freed from the need to pay tribute to a foreign overlord, but also lacking the protection, trade, institutions, and technology that had been provided by the empire.

Especially during the last centuries of the Middle Ages, the city-states of Europe gradually evolved into *nation-states* (Bendix, 1964, 1978; Tilly, 1975). The formation of nation-states depends on a number of specific social and political circumstances. There must be a geographic definition of a country, coupled with the ability to defend it. There must be some way to carry on trade and communication throughout the nation. (In this respect, technological advances help to speed up a nation's political integration.) People in different parts of a nation-state must have some sense of mutual loyalty and, usually, a common language. And older forms of political organization, such as the family or the independent city-state, must come under the control of the national organization. Each of these factors not only promotes the emergence of a strong central government but is also, in turn, promoted by it.

The emergence of the nation-state is one of the most important developments of the modern world (Carnoy, 1984; Skocpol, 1979). National states, as well as the associated ideology of nationalism, have become powerful motivating and organizing forces in the urban-industrial period (Skocpol & Amenta, 1986). They have been central both to the rise of complex, technologically oriented societies and to the gravest instances of international conflict.

Recent developments have led some scholars to ask whether the nation-state will remain the fundamental political unit in the modern world. The European Community, an economic alliance among most of the major nation-states of Western Europe, is gradually bringing those countries under a common set of laws and agreements. In contrast, the dissolution of communism in the East European nations has sparked disunification as ethnically diverse segments of those populations have declared their independence.

Two of these nations, Czechoslovakia and Yugoslavia, have fragmented into several smaller ethnic states. Czechoslovakia's dissolution was peaceful, but the breakup of Yugoslavia led to the reemergence of deep-rooted ethnic hostilities and the outbreak of prolonged and bloody conflict within its former borders. These events may be interpreted as the breakup of two nation-states, but it is important to stress that both Czechoslovakia and, in particular, Yugoslavia were artificial rather than organic states, held together more by the power of the former Soviet Union than by any true sense of national identity. Perhaps what we are now seeing is simply the reemergence of nation-states that had been unwillingly welded into an uneasy federation.

Similar comments apply to the fragmentation of the former Soviet Union. As the once-monolithic Soviet state crumbled, the non-Russian republics demanded and attained political autonomy. The three Baltic nations of Latvia, Lithuania, and Estonia broke away completely; most of the remaining 12 states remained tied to Russia economically and in the loose political confederation of the Commonwealth of Independent States. Furthermore, a number of long-suppressed ethnic territories within Russia and in some of the other former Soviet states have also begun to demand at least partial independence. The outcome of these conflicts remains highly uncertain.

Perspectives on the Distribution of Political Power

Nation-states exert an enormous amount of control over the lives of their citizens. They have the power to tax, to write laws, to punish violators, and to wage war against other states. Scholars have examined the power of the state and the distribution of political power in societies from three perspectives: *pluralist, elitist,* and *class conflict.*

THE PLURALIST PERSPECTIVE

The pluralist perspective views society as composed of many different interest groups—including social classes, political parties, unions, economic organizations, and consumers. These different groups continually make demands on, and attempt to influence, the state's leaders and officials. Pluralists assume that no one interest group gets its own way most or all of the time. The role of the state is to mediate among the interest groups, achieve a public consensus, and pass laws that reflect that consensus, thereby maintaining social order. The state performs these tasks through the political system, which is seen as a continuous process of bargaining, or give-and-take, among interest groups (Dahl, 1961; Rose, 1967).

In some cases, very little bargaining is necessary. For instance, there is a strong consensus within most societies that murder should not be tolerated. Thus, the state easily acts to outlaw murder and to protect its citizens against murderers. But a consensus is not so easily formed in other instances. Consider the issue of slavery in the United States. From the time of the nation's founding, numerous interest groups attempted to compel the state to abolish this practice as other equally powerful interest groups fought to maintain it. Political leaders were unable to mediate among the demands successfully, and no public consensus emerged. Eventually, a bloody and costly civil war settled the issue.

The pluralist view sees the state as made up of agencies and bureaus created as a result of particular instances of bargaining between the state and interest groups. These organizations preside over a jumble of overlapping jurisdictions and are in constant competition for resources such as personnel and money. Each organization must be responsive to the interest groups it serves, to the organization that controls it, and to the state's democratic political process. If any state agency or bureau seriously violates the social consensus, it will eventually be forced to change.

THE ELITIST PERSPECTIVE

Pluralists believe that the complexity of modern democratic societies creates a need for compromise and cooperation. The elitists, however, contend that this complexity is an illusion, at least in one basic sense. To them, one fact stands out amid the profusion of interest groups: All are dominated by a small, even tiny, minority.

The so-called classic elitists—notably Robert Michels, Gaetano Mosca, and Vilfredo Pareto—tended to see the masses as "apathetic, incompetent, and unwilling or unable to govern themselves" (Marger, 1981). These conditions, they believed, naturally led to **oligarchy,** or rule by a select few. What has become known as the "iron law of oligarchy" asserts that elite rule will eventually prevail in every large-scale, bureaucratic grouping, no matter how democratic the grouping may appear to be.

The originator of the "iron law" was Robert Michels, a contemporary and friend of Max Weber. In his classic study *Political Parties* (1911), Michels showed how the iron law operated in an analysis of the German Social Democratic party, then the largest and most powerful socialist force in the world. Disillusioned by the gap between the party's democratic goals and its nondemocratic day-to-day workings, Michels viewed the party as dominated by a small number of trade union leaders and intellectuals who failed to represent the wishes of the rank and file.

Drawing on this example, he argued that leaders in any bureaucratic organization tend to become attached to their high positions of responsibility and that, by controlling the organizational machinery, they use their skills behind the scenes to benefit themselves—in particular, to retain their positions of power and influence. In the final analysis, Michels suggested, the power of the few over the many rests on the apathy and lack of involvement of most organization members who are unwilling to take the time and effort to challenge the control of the oligarchy.

Most contemporary versions of elitist theory assume that the masses, though capable of governing themselves, are "manipulated and exploited by elites who rule in their own interests, not those of the larger society" (Marger, 1981). Building on Max Weber's theory of bureaucracy, modern elitists point out that every facet of modern life is dominated by large, complex organizations, such as universities, corporations, government agencies, trade unions, and political parties. An elite armed with special knowledge controls these organizations and their vast resources and thereby dominates society.

Modern elitists deny that the elites of different organizations compete with one another, as the pluralists believe (Domhoff, 1990, 1998; Dye, 1995). Rather, these people often share a common education and upbringing, and routinely move from bureaucracy to bureaucracy; not uncommonly, for example, the head of a large company will become a cabinet officer, or a cabinet officer will take a high position in private industry. The pluralists see many elites, but the elitists tend to see only one, and they believe that this group holds onto power by shaping society to fit its own needs, thus making people regard it as indispensable. These ideas are all associated with C. Wright Mills, whose book *The Power Elite* (1956) was one of the first, and most influential, academic assaults on pluralism.

THE CLASS CONFLICT PERSPECTIVE

The class conflict view of the state derives from the work of Karl Marx. In *The Communist Manifesto,* Marx and his colleague Friedrich Engels (1848/1969) outlined their conviction that all history can be described as the struggle between the rulers and the ruled:

> The history of all hitherto existing society is the history of class struggles. Freeman and slave, patrician and pleibian, lord and serf, guildmaster and journeyman, in a word, oppressor and oppressed, stood in constant opposition to one another, carried on an uninterrupted, now hidden, now open fight, a fight which each time ended, either in a revolutionary reconstitution of society at large, or in common ruin of the contending classes. (p. 9)

When Marx speaks of opposition between lord and serf, or guildmaster and journeyman, he is dividing people into economic classes. Throughout history, Marx believed, fundamental class differences have been based on economic position. In the Middle Ages, for instance, the economy revolved around the feudal manor, so the main classes were the lords, or landowners, and the serfs, or agricultural workers.

In Marx's own time, the 1800s, Western economies had become largely based on industrial production and the exchange of goods. According to Marx, the industrial age brought about a simplification of age-old class struggles by consolidating power in the hands of those who own the means of production (the "bourgeoisie"):

> Our epoch . . . has simplified the class antagonisms. Society as a whole is more and more splitting up into two great hostile camps, two great classes directly facing each other—bourgeoisie and proletariat. (Marx & Engels, 1848/1969, p. 9)

According to Marx, the proletariat, or the industrial working class, will continue to grow as members of the bourgeoisie lose their holdings during economic depressions. As the number of owners decreases and falling rates of profit force employers to treat their employees more harshly, the proletariat will grow in number and in political awareness. The result predicted by Marx is a workers' revolution and the establishment of a new economic order, communism, in which the workers own the means of production. More than a century after Marx, we can see that his predictions were not accurate. Nevertheless, his thinking provides many insights into the nature of class conflict and political struggle.

In Marx's view, political conflicts are basically economic struggles: "Political power . . . is merely the organized power of one class for oppressing another." Control of the system of property ownership, he believed, meant control of the state. Engels put it more graphically when he said that the state is the executive committee of the bourgeoisie. Governments lay down the rules of ownership, giving legitimate power to those who control property.

While broadly accepting the Marxist view of politics as based on economic conflict, modern neo-Marxian theorists have sought to incorporate into class conflict theory the economic and political developments that have taken place since Marx's time (Miliband, 1969; Offe, 1984; Poulantzas, 1973). One relatively recent development is the growth of giant corporations and monopolies and their dominance of industrial, financial, and commercial life—developments neo-Marxians see as further concentrating economic power in the hands of the few. Another important trend concerns the changing character of the modern state. Neo-Marxians believe that the state now is responsible for a range of activities that extends well beyond economic concerns, and at the same time has gained some autonomy from the economic ruling class. However, neo-Marxian theorists still regard the state in Western societies as operating, either directly or indirectly, mainly in the interests of the economic ruling class and in support of capitalism in general (see Parenti, 1978, 1988).

FORMS OF GOVERNMENT

The state exercises control over a society through the agency of *government*. Some societies maintain a distinction between a state and its government. In England, for example, a constitutional monarch, Queen Elizabeth II, is the head of state, but a politically elected leader, the prime minister, is the head of government. But in many societies, such as the United States, one person, the president, heads both state and government.

History provides us with examples of many governmental forms. The three most significant today are democratic, totalitarian, and authoritarian regimes.

The elections of state representatives demonstrate a democratic government in which citizens vote for political officials to represent them.

Democracy

Democracy means literally "rule of the people." The adjective *democratic* has become a popular label, with widely differing governments called "democratic" by their leaders. But two features distinguish true democracies from other kinds of governments: In a true democracy, the powers of government derive from the formal consent of the governed, and citizens have a right to participate in a meaningful way in decision-making processes.

In a *representative democracy,* the most common type, citizens vote for officials to represent them. Once in office, representatives make political decisions using democratic voting procedures. The success of a democratic system rests on universal acceptance of the principle of majority rule.

A democratic government does not demand exclusive obedience from its citizens. Rather, people are permitted to retain strong attachments to their family, religion, and any number of other groups. Thus, a democratic society has many centers of power.

Ideally, free and open debate among all citizens in a representative democracy leads to the adoption of those policies that are most beneficial to the public interest. In practice, however, the representatives are granted the right to make political choices once a certain amount of discussion has taken place. This ensures that important decisions will actually be made, not merely endlessly discussed.

Only in very small democratic systems can each citizen affect government by direct involvement; this type of democracy is called *participatory,* or *direct, democracy.* The New England town meeting is an example of a setting in which direct participation in the democratic process is possible. A similar type of democracy existed in ancient Greek city-states, although these governments did not reflect the views of all adults, since women and slaves were barred from political participation.

The democracy that has developed in most Western societies, including the United States, is called *liberal democracy*. Liberal democracy supports both the principle of liberty, which holds that individuals have certain rights that a just society should not violate, and the principle of democracy, which holds that a just society must ensure that all people have an equal say in the decisions that affect their lives (Bowles & Gintis, 1986). These principles are frequently at odds, because what is best for the individual may not always be what is best for society as a whole.

In liberal democracies, the principles of liberty and democracy are applied to the state (that is, to the public sphere of politics, which is concerned with the common interests of all citizens), but only the principle of liberty is applied to the economy (the private sector, in which people are free to pursue their individual, sometimes selfish, interests). A liberal democracy, then, is a political—but not an economic—democracy. As a result, many important decisions—the relocation of a factory employing thousands of workers, for instance, or a corporation's investment strategy—are not made democratically, even though their consequences will affect the lives of many people. The right to make such decisions is vested in private ownership. The owners of the factory or the corporation are free to decide many such questions without taking into account the popular will. On the other hand, modern liberal democracies have found it necessary to restrict the rights of property owners in a number of ways in order to promote the public interest. Examples include

Fidel Castro's Cuba has a totalitarian form of government. The totalitarian state creates an official ideology, a total worldview, and a set of rules of behavior.

laws restricting the freedom of employers to discriminate in hiring practices and the wide range of environmental regulations that have been legislated in recent decades.

Totalitarianism

Totalitarianism is a form of government, run by a single party, in which there is governmental surveillance and control over all aspects of life. Totalitarianism is not a new concept; a number of Roman emperors tried to set up a totalitarian state. Because the technological means for widespread control were not available, however, a very high level of totalitarianism did not become possible until the twentieth century. With the advent of modern communications and advances in propaganda and spying techniques, nearly complete control of an entire society can now be achieved. Indeed, several twentieth-century societies—notably Hitler's Germany and Stalin's Russia—came close to achieving full totalitarianism. Today, Saddam Hussein's regime in Iraq illustrates the extent to which a dictator can control an entire society.

The totalitarian state creates an official ideology, a total worldview, and a set of rules of behavior. Rival worldviews are suppressed, religious groups are persecuted, and the works of many artists and intellectuals are censored. Because patriotism serves to blind people to totalitarianism's defects, *nationalism* (the belief that national interests and security are more important than international considerations) is usually an important aspect of this governmental form.

Conventional government organization is inadequate to ensure totalitarian control. An effective totalitarian state must establish special control mechanisms. One such mechanism is an official political party that becomes the arena for most of the political process. The political party trains, chooses, and legitimates the ruling political elite. No other party is allowed to organize, and attempts to form one are condemned as treason. In Hitler's Germany, the National Socialist (Nazi) party was the one and only channel of legal political expression. In the former Soviet Union, from the October Revolution of 1917 to March 1990, only the Communist party was able to function legally.

Under the Soviet system, regular elections were held, but the voters were not allowed to choose between candidates representing several parties advocating different policies. Instead, they were merely offered the opportunity to rubber-stamp the decisions made by the leaders of the Communist party. Thus, this totalitarian system did not base its legitimacy on popular approval expressed through open democratic elections but, rather, claimed legitimacy principally on the grounds that "it was the legatee of a communist revolution, . . . the repository of history, . . . the most rational and efficient force in the state, [and] represented the best and most progressive elements of the national tradition" (Schöpflin, 1990, p. 6). As events within the communist world from the mid-1980s on undermined these claims, the party was left with only a weak defense of its monopoly over political power.

The immediate cause of the collapse of the Soviet Communist party was a severe economic crisis. Controlled by a central planning system accountable only to the party, the Soviet economy lacked the efficiency and innovative ability essential to compete successfully in rapidly changing, technologically sophisticated world markets. An economy moving quickly toward collapse combined with a steady erosion of political support to threaten the very foundations of totalitarian rule.

When Mikhail S. Gorbachev came to power as leader of the Communist party in 1985, he pledged to devote his highest priority to dealing with the ills of the economy. As a part of this effort he called for *perestroika,* or the "restructuring" of society. A prominent part of this restructuring was the gradual introduction of private enterprise and market mechanisms and incentives into the Soviet economy. In addition, in 1986, Gorbachev initiated a new policy of *glasnost,* or "openness." This policy encouraged open discussion and criticism of government officials, organizations, and policies (Nove, 1989).

With Gorbachev's support, free elections were held in Soviet-influenced totalitarian countries like Poland, Czechoslovakia, and the former East Germany, which led to the ouster of communist regimes in those nations. By early 1990, the same antiparty spirit surged across the Soviet Union. As tensions mounted, party leaders had Gorbachev arrested and took control of the government in August 1991. Their effort to reestablish totalitarian rule lasted only three days, undermined by an explosion of popular resistance led by Russian President Boris Yeltsin.

In the aftermath of the failed coup, the Communist party—once the centerpiece of Soviet totalitarianism—was dismantled. Gorbachev resigned as secretary-general of the party (though he remained leader of the Soviet Union); the party's Central Committee was abolished and its extensive holdings—presses, newspapers, and private hospitals—were appropriated (*The Economist,* August 31, 1991). In December 1991, despite Gorbachev's opposition, Yeltsin joined with the leaders of two other republics to announce that "the Union of Soviet Socialist Republics, as a subject of international law and geopolitical reality, is ceasing its existence" (*Time,* December 23, 1991, p. 19). People around the world believed that the collapse of the Soviet Union would bring peace and prosperity, but today many of the former Soviet republics have a standard of living far below that of developed capitalist countries, and conflict among ethnic groups in different regions around the globe suggests that global peace is not near at hand.

It is too soon to say what will become of the 15 former Soviet republics, whose 300 million people inhabit one-sixth of the world's landmass. Nevertheless, what happened to the Soviet Union is of great historic significance. While totalitarian regimes continue to exist (most notably in North Korea and in Fidel Castro's Cuba), totalitarian rule is no longer the major force in the modern world that it was only a decade ago.

Authoritarianism

Authoritarianism is a form of government in which ultimate authority is vested in a single person. The ruler may be either a *monarch* (a hereditary ruler) or a *dictator* (someone who typically holds power by means of force). Ideology and political parties do not play a major role in an authoritarian regime. Instead, politics becomes an expression of devotion to the dominant authority figure (Andrain, 1970).

Authoritarian regimes lack the constitutional and procedural bases of democracy. Regular elections, a system of representative government, and basic civil rights (such as the right to vote) are typically absent in authoritarian systems. Opposition is usually greeted with the quick exercise of force—one reason for the relatively fragile character of most authoritarian governments. There are important differences between authoritarian and totalitarian regimes:

> An authoritarian regime is one that does not tolerate political opposition but is prepared to allow institutions and sectors of society to function free of the state provided they do not engage in political activity. A totalitarian regime is one that seeks to impose state control over every institution of society, regardless of whether it engages in political activity or not and with the intention of . . . integrating society as a whole within an all-embracing political design. (Berger, 1986, pp. 83–84)

Authoritarian systems are thus not as inclusive as their totalitarian counterparts. Indeed, many authoritarian governments have existed alongside capitalist economies. Today this combination of authoritarian political rule and capitalist economic freedom continues, albeit in a relatively mild form, in such countries as Singapore.

POLITICS AND GOVERNMENT IN THE UNITED STATES

On March 18, 1990, as citizens in what was then East Germany voted in their country's first democratic election since 1933, the *New York Times* began a series of articles on politics in the United States. "As America's democratic visions and values seem to triumph around the world," the reports began, "an unhappy consensus has emerged at home that domestic politics has become so shallow, mean and even meaningless that it is failing to produce the ideas and leadership needed to guide the United States in a rapidly changing world. . . . [T]he American political system is unable to define and debate critical questions, let alone resolve them."

Are such criticisms valid? The United States is the oldest, most stable, and one of the most open democracies ever known. Its political system has long served as a model for other countries starting on the road to democratic government. But robust democracies require the active political participation of their citizens, strong political parties committed to the education and mobilization of their members, sustained political discussion and debate, and a general sense of shared purpose or common good that overrides, or at least moderates, selfish special interests. Many American social scientists and politicians believe that these requirements are not being fulfilled in the United States today as adequately as they were in the past.

Historical and Cultural Background

Americans are among the most individualistic of modern peoples. Freedom and personal liberty rank very high in the American scheme of values, partly because of the country's background as a nation that took in many refugees fleeing persecution in other societies. Americans know they have the right to engage in free enterprise, read uncensored newspapers, assemble peacefully for any cause, and live without fear of needless search or seizure. At the same time, they have a real fear that the government, the local community, and even their neighbors will tell them what to do and thus dominate their lives.

This strong individualism has made the United States one of the most politically conservative of the advanced nations. Many Americans remain staunch believers in capitalism and the "free market," and seek to avoid "government solutions" and government control as much as possible. Such phrases as "government is the problem, not the solution" and "the government that governs best, governs least" are widely heard (and widely believed).

While these powerful individualistic currents have helped make the United States one of the world's most economically successful nations, some believe that they have also contributed to a diminished sense of civic pride and duty. When government is viewed as a "necessary evil," as it often is in the United States, commitment to the common good may be weak and the obligations of citizenship may

not be taken very seriously. Strong individualism, then, may produce what one scholar has called a "thin democracy" (Barber, 1984) in which **civic privatism**—a focus on the private pursuits of family, career, and leisure—replaces civic concern and appreciation for the value of the common life shared by all citizens (Habermas, 1973).

Civic privatism may lead to a widespread refusal to take part in many aspects of the political process. The authors of *Habits of the Heart,* an examination of American social and political life (see Chapter 3), found that middle-class Americans typically regard the political sphere as intimidating, uninviting, and meaningless. As a result, political participation is generally shunned. Rather, most people become politically involved solely in response to threats and challenges to their private life, and then only reluctantly (Bellah et al., 1986). Under conditions of strong individualism, then, democracy may become simply a means by which individuals and groups seek to express and satisfy their particular interests.

Political Participation

Classic democratic theory enthusiastically supports regular and widespread citizen participation in the process of political decision making. Active political participation, classic theorists argue, enables citizens to protect themselves and their interests against an otherwise unaccountable state. More importantly, though, regular involvement in the political process is believed to make people more virtuous, more informed and tolerant, and more skilled in the art of self-government.

But is this theory realistic? Another version of democratic theory offers, according to its proponents, a far more accurate assessment of political participation. This *realistic* or *empirical* theory of democracy cautions against strong encouragement of active citizen involvement in politics on a number of grounds. First, the average citizen is not well informed, and his or her active participation may bring irrational elements into the political process. Second, modern governments confront enormously complex and highly technical problems, matters best dealt with by trained professionals insulated from the pressures of an uninformed electorate. Third, given the likelihood that increased citizen participation would place greater demands for special services, benefits, and programs on an already overburdened government, there is much to be said for a certain level of citizen apathy. The downward turn in political participation rates in the United States during the past 40 years would surely upset the classic democratic theorist but please the realistic democratic theorist.

Political participation can be divided into three general categories. *Gladiatorial activities,* ranging from contributing time to a campaign to holding public office, entail the greatest level of citizen involvement. *Transitional activities,* ranging from contacting a public official to attending a political meeting or rally, require less participation. *Spectator activities,* such as voting, engaging in a political discussion, and displaying a bumper sticker, require the least involvement (Milbrath, 1965). One well-known study conducted in the 1960s found that about one-third of the American voting-age population was apathetic, unaware of, or indifferent to the world of politics. Only 1 to 3 percent engaged in gladiatorial activities, and only 7 to 9 percent were involved in transitional activities. Nearly 60 percent fell into the low-involvement spectator category (Milbrath, 1965). Later studies have produced nearly identical findings (Davis & Smith, 1986; Verba & Nie, 1972).

By some measures, political participation has been dropping in recent years. Results of a 1993 Roper study showed that the percentage of Americans who have "attended a public meeting or town or school officers" dropped from 23 percent in 1973 to 16 percent in 1993 (Lipset, 1997; Putnam, 1995). And data gathered by the National Opinion Research Center show that the "proportion who attended a political rally or speech, who served on a committee, or who were officers of a club or organization also fell over this twenty year period" (Lipset, 1997, p. 280).

Citizen participation is influenced by a number of social factors. The most important of these is socioeconomic status (SES). The rate of political participation increases as one moves up the stratification hierarchy. This observation holds true for each of the individual factors employed to operationalize SES—occupation, level of education, and family income—as well as for the three combined (Orum, 1988). The most common explanation of the link between class and citizen participation is that high SES is usually accompanied by factors that enhance political interest and involvement—for instance, a better understanding of the workings and the impact of politics and government, a greater stake in society and the policies that would preserve or alter established arrangements, and greater economic and educational resources (Bennett, 1986).

Citizen involvement also varies by gender, age, and race. Women have generally reported lower rates of political involvement than men. Some believe that this is a result of traditional hostility to women's participation in public affairs and the constraints of the homemaking and parenting responsibilities that continue to fall largely on women. It may also be that women are socialized to participate less in politics (see Chapter 13).

Age also contributes to differences in political interest and involvement. Studies have found a rise in political

When education is taken into account, the difference in political participation between women and men and between blacks and whites virtually disappears.

interest and participation during high school and a significant drop in interest during young adulthood, followed by a rapid and substantial increase that is maintained through the mature years, and finally, a decline of interest after retirement (Bennett, 1986). Today the highest rate of political apathy is found among young adults.

Finally, political involvement in the United States varies by race. Overall, whites display higher levels of political participation than blacks. However, this phenomenon appears to be related to socioeconomic status; when blacks are compared with whites who are similarly situated in the stratification hierarchy, blacks show higher involvement rates.

Of the three dimensions of SES (occupation, income, and education), education appears to have the greatest impact on interest and involvement in political affairs. Indeed, when level of education is taken into account, the differences in participation levels between women and men and between blacks and whites virtually disappear (Bennett, 1986; Sapiro, 1983). More specifically, education is the single most powerful predictor of voting: The more education a person has completed, the more likely he or she is to vote (Lewis, McCracken, & Hunt, 1994; Putnam, 1995). As the population has become better educated, then, one would expect a corresponding increase in voter turnout. Since 1960, however, this has not generally been the case.

VOTING

Voting is one of the least demanding forms of political participation. Yet statistics show a decline in voter turnout throughout the last four decades (see Figure 17.1 on page 400). Many scholars have seen this decline in electoral participation as a sign that more and more people are unwilling to assume one of the most minimal and least

APPLYING SOCIOLOGY

EXIT POLLS

Are voters less likely to vote if the polls indicate their candidate has a substantial lead? What if their candidate is hopelessly behind? Do poll results cause voters to change their minds about candidates? Are they more likely to go with the expected winner? Or will they shift their support to the underdog?

These kinds of questions have led researchers to investigate how political polls influence voters (Owen, 1991). They raise concern because polls conducted prior to elections rely to some extent on guesswork. And, despite the scientific advances in polling methods, it is hard to forget the polls whose predictions turned out to be way off the mark. Take, for example, the 1936 Literary Digest poll, which predicted that Alf Landon, the Republican candidate, would win by a wide margin. In fact, however, Franklin D. Roosevelt, the Democratic candidate, won by a landslide—62 to 32 percent.

But one kind of poll that is conducted during elections is highly reliable (Sabato, 1997). It is an exit poll. Instead of predicting how Americans will vote, it explains why they voted in certain ways. The respondents in this kind of poll consist of a sample of voters who are randomly selected as they

leave the polling place. These polls are conducted by media organizations, particularly television networks, that use the results for stories that attempt to explain why the public voted for certain candidates.

To illustrate how exit polls are used, consider the results from the 1996 presidential election exit poll (see Table 17.2). A cross-tabulation of variables shows that Bill Clinton won his second term with the support of female voters (Sabato, 1997). In contrast to male voters, who favored Dole by a narrow margin (44 to 43 percent), female voters voted for Clinton by a wide margin (54 to 38 percent). African-Americans also gave Clinton their overwhelming support. The breakdown of their votes turned out to be 84 percent for Clinton, 12 percent for Dole, and 4 percent for Perot.

In addition to showing how particular demographic groups voted, exit polls also shed light on how the issues influenced the electorate. In 1996, the most important issue turned out to be the economy. Not only did more voters identify it as the top issue in their vote, but their responses to a number of other questions indicate that the state of the economy influenced the direction of their vote. Thus, for example, an analysis of the exit poll data showed that Clinton won 64 percent of the

votes among the 55 percent of voters who rated the national economy as "excellent" or "good" (Sabato, 1997). Of the voters who said the economy was "not good" or "poor," Dole captured only 52 percent of the vote. Slightly more than half of the electorate indicated that the country was "generally going in the right direction." And Clinton captured 69 percent of their votes. About 4 in 10 voters thought the nation was "seriously off on the wrong track." Among these voters, 61 percent voted for Dole; 23 percent voted for Clinton.

time-consuming—but still one of the most important—obligations of democratic citizenship.

Voting in presidential elections, typically higher by half than participation in off-year elections, has declined sharply since 1960, when nearly 63 percent of the voting-age population cast ballots. Just 49.1 percent of all potential voters turned out in 1996.

Several theories have been offered to account for the decline in voter turnout. Seymour Martin Lipset (1994, 1997) suggests that it could partly be attributed to what he calls "populism." Thus, he writes:

The prolonged, multi-year campaigns, the frequency with which Americans are called to the polls . . . and the mud-slinging, character-assassination tactics inherent in contests which necessarily focus on individuals rather than the weak parties, all appear to discourage participation. (1995, p. 45)

Another explanation points to the relatively burdensome and complex registration procedures that distinguish America's electoral system from that of other Western democracies. According to this view, simplifying registration procedures by making them more

TABLE 17.2   SAMPLE OF PRESIDENTIAL ELECTION EXIT POLL RESULTS

Question	Horizontal %				Question	Horizontal %			
	All Voters	Clinton	Dole	Perot		All Voters	Clinton	Dole	Perot
Vote by Gender					Clinton Honest and Trustworthy?				
Men	48	43	44	10	Yes	41	88	6	4
Women	52	54	38	7	No	54	18	67	12
Vote by Race					Clinton and Whitewater				
Whites	83	43	46	9	Told the truth	33	89	6	4
African-Americans	10	84	12	4	Did not tell the truth	60	24	62	13
Hispanics	5	72	21	6	Which Is More Important?				
Asians	1	43	48	8	Issues	58	69	20	8
Other	1	64	21	9	Character	38	18	71	10
Party Identification					Concerned about Clinton Scandals				
Democrat	39	84	10	5					
Republican	35	13	80	6	Yes	49	24	64	10
Independent	26	43	35	17	No	49	73	20	6
Condition of National Economy					Top Issue in Vote				
Excellent	4	78	17	4	Taxes	11	19	73	7
Good	51	62	31	6	Medicare	15	67	26	6
Not good	36	34	52	12	Foreign policy	4	35	56	8
Poor	7	23	51	21	Federal deficit	12	27	52	19
Direction of Country					Economy/jobs	21	61	27	10
Right direction	53	69	24	5	Education	12	78	16	4
Wrong track	43	23	61	13	Crime/drugs	7	40	50	8

Source: "Presidential Election Exit Poll Results," CNN/Time AllPolitics, 1996, <http://allpolitics.com/elections/natl.exit.poll/index1.html> (November 8, 1996). The Voter News Service interviewed 16,359 voters at 300 precincts across the United States to produce this exit poll, which has a margin of error of plus or minus about 1.3 percent.

accessible—for example, permitting mail-in registration, allowing people to register to vote at the same time as they register their automobiles, or allowing social service agencies to encourage and assist their clients to register—would substantially increase voter turnout (Piven & Cloward, 1989).

But this explanation has recently been challenged (Lipset, 1997; Putnam, 1994). Lipset points out that reducing restrictions on registration procedures, which many states have done since the 1960s, has not improved voter participation. And Martin P. Wattenberg (1998)

cites data showing that the percentage of registered voters has increased since 1964, while the percentage of Americans who vote has decreased (see Figure 17.2). With respect to recent efforts to increase voter registration, Wattenberg adds:

Although the Motor Voter Act led to the largest four-year increase in registration ever recorded, the turnout rate of registered voters fell sharply—indicating that many of the new registrants did not make it to the polls in 1996. (1998, p. 236)

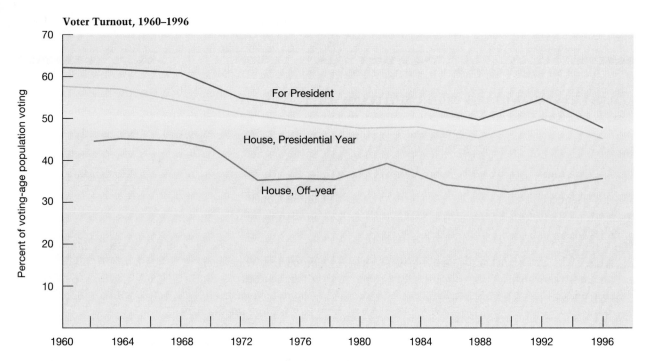

Voter Turnout, 1960–1996

FIGURE 17.1   Except for slight increases in 1982, 1984, and 1992, the percentage of the voting-age population voting in elections for president and the House has declined every election year since 1960.

Sources: U.S. Bureau of the Census, *Statistical Abstract of the United States, 1993* Washington, D.C.: U.S. Government Printing Office, 1993); Normal J. Ornstein, Thomas Mann, and Michael J. Malbin, *Vital Statistics on Congress* (Washington, D.C.: U.S. Government Printing Office, 1989), p. 46; U.S. Bureau of the Census, *Statistical Abstract of the United States, 1998* (Washington, D.C.: U.S. Government Printing Office, 1998).

A third explanation, citing demographic changes, notes that since 1960 the American population has become more single and more mobile—two factors that work to reduce voter turnout. Over the same time, though, the population has also become more educated—a factor strongly related to increased political involvement. To account for this seeming anomaly, a fourth explanation concentrates on attitudinal changes that have occurred since 1960. Studies have shown that Americans today are more skeptical and uncertain and that they display weaker partisan identities and a weaker sense of political competence than they did in 1960 (Valelly, 1990).

In 1964, 29 percent of Americans surveyed in the University of Michigan's election study said that "the government is pretty much run by a few big interests looking out for themselves" (Lipset, 1997, p. 282). By 1992, 8 in 10 Americans expressed this kind of cynicism. According to Lipset, these kinds of attitudes contributed not only to lower voter participation but also to the erosion of the two-party system.

Political parties, themselves, offer yet another explanation for lower participation rates. Since the turn of the century, political parties in the United States have been devoting fewer resources and less time to mobilizing and organizing potential and existing voters (Wattenberg, 1998). Until the 1970s, the partisan loyalties forged during the Civil War and the Great Depression continued to exist, as did real differences in the ideologies of the Democratic and Republican parties. Since the 1970s, however, these differences have receded as the Democrats have moved steadily toward the more conservative politics of the Republican party. In so doing, they may have lost much of the support of the poor and the working class to the fastest-growing political group in the United States—the "party of nonvoters" (Valelly, 1990).

Political Parties

Political participation in the United States has traditionally centered around political parties. A **political party** is an organization, usually composed of people with similar attitudes and interests, whose purpose is to gain and hold legitimate control of the government. In pursuit of these objectives, political parties engage in the nomination of candidates for political office (Dowse & Hughes, 1972).

Surprisingly enough, the framers of the American Constitution were strongly opposed to political parties. Despite this hostility, however, parties developed rapidly in the early 1800s. By the middle of the nineteenth century, parties were commonly viewed as the "heart and soul" of America's democratic process. During the last quarter of the nineteenth century, party affiliation was a central facet of the political identity of most Americans, and, as a result of strong, effective party organizations, voter turnout for presidential elections hit record highs of between 78 and 82 percent of the eligible population.

Toward the end of the nineteenth century, however, key segments of the upper class (as well as proponents of more efficient government) began to feel threatened by the high levels of citizen involvement that had been achieved by the political parties. Citizen participation had always threatened concentrations of wealth, but that danger became more serious as disaffected groups, such as the Knights of Labor and the farmers' alliances, turned to electoral politics to solve their economic problems (Valelly, 1990).

In order to weaken the parties and thereby to make the electoral process more predictable, a series of legislative changes was enacted over the next several decades. Voter registration was made more difficult; parties were subjected to greater regulation by the state in the name of more efficient government; and party control over the nomination process was reduced by the introduction of direct primaries. These changes set in motion the forces that have led to the decline in party strength, effectiveness, loyalty, and identification that has taken place in the United States in later years (Burnham, 1984).

As the influence of political parties has declined, so too has party membership (Wattenberg, 1998). Partisan attachment among those who continue to identify with one of the two major parties has weakened considerably. In addition, independents now make up 35 percent of the American electorate (U.S. Census Bureau, *Statistical Abstract of the United States, 1998*). The growing sense of dissatisfaction with politics and politicians that has accompanied these developments received clear expression during the 1996 presidential campaign.

THE NEW POLITICAL TECHNOLOGY

As the organizational strength of parties has weakened, the resources they once relied on in pursuit of political power—party workers and the capacity to mobilize electoral support—have been increasingly replaced by

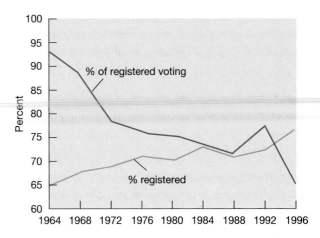

FIGURE 17.2 Voter registration and turnout of registered voters

Sources: Federal Election Commission; Martin P. Wattenberg, *The Decline of American Political Parties 1952–1996* (Cambridge, Mass.: Harvard University Press).

electronic communication techniques. The key forms of the new political technology include the following (Allen, 1996; Ginsberg, 1984; Paletz, 1999):

1. *Polling.* Surveys of voter opinion are now the fundamental basis on which campaign strategies are fashioned and issues selected and presented.

2. *Broadcast Media.* Television advertising designed to promote name identification, a positive image of the candidate, and a negative image of the opponent is a key media technique.

3. *Phone Banks.* Using computerized dialing systems and prepared scripts, callers trained to add a "personal touch" to the campaign contact members of targeted groups with a poll-inspired version of the candidate's stand on the issues.

4. *Direct Mail.* Computerized mailing lists are used to select voters likely to be sympathetic to the candidate. These voters receive regular, seemingly personalized appeals for financial contributions and electoral support.

5. *Professional Public Relations.* Professional managers and consultants are the mainstays of virtually all campaigns for state and national offices, using their expertise to conduct and analyze polls, to orchestrate media coverage and produce commercials, and to target the recipients of personalized phone and direct-mail appeals.

6. *The Internet.* Web sites provide instant information on political candidates—their biographies, their positions on key issues, texts of their speeches, news releases, and even campaign advertisements.

The new political technology makes the candidate much less dependent on the political party than ever before. Popular support requires, candidates have learned, not the organizational strength of traditional parties but, rather, the large reserves of cash necessary to take advantage of the new political technology. "Campaign tasks that were once performed by masses of party workers and a modicum of cash," one scholar notes, "now require fewer personnel but a great deal more money, to operate the polls, computers, and other electronic paraphernalia upon which the new political style depends" (Ginsberg, 1984, p. 170). The result, according to some scholars, has been not simply a substantially reduced role for parties in the American political process but also a marked right-wing or conservative shift in American politics (Edsall, 1984). Because the country's wealth is concentrated among those with conservative political leanings, the high cost of the new political technology has forced the traditionally numerically strong but dollar-poor Democratic party to become more conservative in order to raise enough money for its campaigns.

THE SHIFT RIGHTWARD

The difference in America between "conservative" and "liberal" political views relates in part to the habit of dividing the world into a private sphere of business and economics, on the one hand, and a public sphere of government and politics, on the other. Questions of prosperity, inflation, employment, investment, productivity, economic growth, and personal savings are generally associated with the private sphere. Issues of justice, social security, welfare, civil rights, and equal opportunity are regarded as aspects of the public sphere. Traditionally, the Republican party has been the conservative defender of the private sphere, offering policies designed to minimize strong government intervention into the economy. The Democratic party, in contrast, has been the liberal defender of the public sphere, espousing a larger and more active government that can help to minimize the harsher consequences of economic change on individuals and families. Generally, those who would benefit the most from the reduced tax rates that accompany lowered government spending—that is, the financially secure—have tended to support Republicans. Those less secure—the poor, the victims of discrimination, the working class—have tended to support the Democrats (Reich, 1983).

Starting in the 1970s, however, the Democratic party became less liberal and the Republican party became more conservative. During these years, more people described themselves as "conservative" and fewer people called themselves "liberal." Indeed, by the 1988 presidential election, liberalism had taken on strong negative connotations for many people. A central element of George Bush's successful campaign was to paint his Democratic opponent, Michael Dukakis, as a liberal. Whether or not, as some critics charge, the Democratic and Republican parties have converged so closely that on many issues they offer not choices but merely echoes of each other, the clear rightward shift in American politics has made the political spectrum (not especially broadly drawn to begin with) narrower than ever before.

Some believe that the growing popularity of politically conservative values in the United States over the past two decades has led to a polarization of the U.S. electorate that pits taxpayers against benefit recipients, supporters of the free market against advocates of the welfare state, and whites against blacks. Racial polarization, one study documents

> helped create a political climate receptive to an economic agenda based on the conservative principle that sharply increasing incentives and rewards for those people and interests at the top of the economic pyramid and decreasing government support for those at the bottom would combine to spur economic expansion and growth. To the degree that divisions between blacks and whites overlapped divisions between the poor and the affluent, between the dependent and the successful, and between city and suburb, race became an ally of conservatism. (Edsall & Edsall, 1991, p. 158)

In other words, racial polarization set the context within which wealthy, middle-class, and working-class whites overcame class differences to unify into a solid conservative majority.

Other scholars look to changes in the economy to explain the rightward shift in political attitudes. One economist has argued that when issues of efficiency and cost become prominent—as they did in the 1970s and 1980s—the voters' inclination is to support market solutions and the conservative politics consistent with those solutions. Later, when these market solutions intensify problems of injustice and inequality, liberal politics gain support and remain popular until problems of efficiency, cost, and economic growth arise again (Hirschman, 1982). In any event, given the economic boom of the 1990s, there are few signs yet that the rightward shift has ended.

Interest Groups and Lobbying

Interest groups are organizations and social movements that attempt to influence government policy and legislation on behalf of their members. Interest groups commonly seek to exert their influence through **lobbying,** a process (usually controlled by professional lobbyists) that involves directly communicating with legislators and

.NET INTERNET/TECHNOLOGY

ONLINE POLITICS

What will politics look like in the twenty-first century? Well, like just about everything else, the biggest changes are expected to involve the Internet—that is, its ability to create virtual politics. In fact, the Internet has already changed the way that politicians and political parties communicate. During the 1996 national nominating conventions, Web sites provided instant information, including vote counts in real time, the texts of speeches, news releases, delegate biographies, and state rosters (Allen, 1996; Paletz, 1999). Web sites for the presidential candidates, Bill Clinton and Bob Dole, presented their positions on issues, as well as some of their commercials. They were also used to solicit contributions and recruit volunteers.

Web sites offer a particular advantage to candidates for state and local positions who do not have the resources for expensive media coverage. Through their own home pages, candidates can now reach voters directly with information on their experience, records, platforms, and texts of their speeches. In turn, e-mail allows voters to communicate directly with them. On election night, voters no longer have to wait for the networks to release election results. The Internet provides an alternative source of information— one that was designed to cover all races, not just the big ones.

Voting online will be the next big step for virtual politics. And it is bound to happen sooner than you think. Kevin Phillips (1995), a respected political analyst, predicts that this will happen by 2020. He bases this prediction on the assumption that a nationwide identification system, which could identify eligible voters, will be in place within the next few years. Advanced technologies such as voice identification, face scans, and finger images would prevent voting fraud. This system could increase voter turnout from the current 50 to 55 percent for presidential elections to 65 to 75 percent. Philips also predicts that Internet technology will make it possible for Americans to vote on selected major national issues.

However, the extent to which the Internet will allow Americans to participate in policymaking could be more difficult than Philips thinks. While the White House's Web site allows Americans to express their opinions on the president's policy decisions, some issues might be too complicated to address over the Internet (Paletz, 1999). For example, in 1995 the federal Nuclear Regulatory Commission created a site on the Web to gather ideas from electric utilities, safety groups, reactor manufacturers, and interested Americans. Unfortunately, the legal and technical jargon used made it difficult for the average person to participate. Conducting town meetings on the Internet, which,

presumably, would involve less jargon, could offer a forum for debating and voting on issues. But the value of this will ultimately depend on the way questions and answers are handled. What is more, some critics doubt that electronic forums will forge the kinds of bonds that strengthen democracies. Political scientist Robert Putnam has expressed his doubts, writing: "My hunch is that meeting in an electronic forum is not the equivalent of meeting in a bowling alley—or even in a saloon" (1995, pp. 65–75).

New technologies undoubtedly can produce a number of unexpected problems. But Philips is optimistic about the use of the Internet as a tool in the political process, and he expects online politics to produce a number of positive consequences. Perhaps most importantly, he believes that Americans will experience the kind of enthusiasm for politics that past generations have felt. Active political participation via the Internet could transform apathetic attitudes and feelings of powerlessness. With information about important issues at citizens' fingertips, including the positions taken by their representatives, the Internet has the power to revitalize democracy—to make citizens feel that their voice is heard in Washington. And that, according to Philips, could even make Washington popular again with Americans.

---

their staffs, mobilizing grass-roots support, and donating campaign funds through political action committees (discussed below).

All organized groups—religious organizations, universities, corporations, the military—have political interests and act to pressure the government to act in ways that will support these interests. In this sense, there are a vast number of lobbies in the United States. The

most influential are those organized by large corporations, business associations, labor unions, public interest groups, and single-issue groups.

In addition to supporting business and trade associations that lobby on behalf of industry-wide interests, most large corporations employ a full-time staff of lobbyists in Washington to represent their particular concerns. The National Association of Manufacturers represents

The National Rifle Association is one of the most active single-issue groups in the United States, noted for its highly successful resistance to gun-control legislation.

about 13,000 large corporations. Each of the major labor unions—such as those represented by the American Federation of Labor–Congress of Industrial Organizations (AFL–CIO), the United Auto Workers, and the Teamsters—finances large-scale lobbying activities.

Public interest groups (such as the Sierra Club, Common Cause, and the various consumer and environmental associations created by Ralph Nader) claim to represent not the special interests of particular segments of society but, rather, the general public good. These groups work for such goals as an unspoiled wilderness, an uncorrupted political process, and safe consumer products.

Single-issue groups, the number of which has grown dramatically over the past 30 years, concentrate on one relatively narrowly defined interest. Two of the most active single-issue groups in the United States are the National Rifle Association (NRA), noted for its highly successful resistance to gun-control legislation, and the American Association of Retired Persons (AARP). All

interest groups try to shape the formulation of government policy and legislation through the use of money, votes, and information campaigns (Stone & Barke, 1985).

Many observers regard interest groups as essential to democratic government. According to this view, such groups perform a number of useful functions. They enable people to express their views between elections, thus forcing elected officials to remain responsive to the public will. In addition, interest groups are said to encourage the development of the skills, attitudes, knowledge, and awareness that characterize an informed and active citizenry (see Etzioni, 1984).

A different view is offered by sociologist Amitai Etzioni, who believes that the dramatic growth of interest groups since the 1960s reflects the decaying foundations of the American political system:

> Unrestrained, interest groups will tend to hinder the development of a nationwide consensus and of shared politics. And they will promote policies that neglect needs that are not in the interest of any group, as well as the common good. They will escalate intergroup conflict until the system is unable to function effectively and becomes frustrating and alienating, if not violent. This seems to be the direction in which the United States has been moving. (1984, pp. 187–188)

Many, including some who hold a generally favorable view of interest group politics, attribute the corrupting influence of interest groups to the rise of political action committees. **Political action committees (PACs)** were first created by labor unions, but over the past 25 years PACs set up by and for the business community have played an especially important role in American politics (see Table 17.3). Interest group members make voluntary (usually small) donations to a PAC, which pools the money and then donates up to $5,000 to various senatorial and congressional candidates.

Two factors have increased the significance of the PACs' ability to accumulate and distribute large sums of money. The first is a limitation on the amount individuals can contribute to a political campaign: $1,000 for each candidate and $25,000 per year to all candidates for all federal offices combined. The second is the soaring cost of campaigns driven by the new political technologies.

According to the Center for Responsive Politics, the 1996 presidential race cost about $800 million—three times the amount spent in 1992. An additional $800 million was spent on congressional races (Bagby, 1997). Of all money raised for political campaigns, businesses raised $242.4 million, which was mostly donated to Republicans (see Table 17.4). Another $35 million was raised by organized labor and donated mostly to Democrats.

TABLE 17.3   NUMBER OF POLITICAL ACTION COMMITTEES, BY TYPE, 1974–1996

Year	Total	Corporate	Labor	Other*
1974	608	89	201	318
1976	1,146	433	224	489
1978	1,653	785	217	651
1980	2,551	1,206	297	1,048
1982	3,371	1,469	380	1,522
1984	4,009	1,682	394	1,933
1986	4,157	1,744	384	2,029
1988	4,268	1,816	354	2,098
1990	4,172	1,795	346	2,031
1992	4,195	1,735	347	2,113
1994	3,954	1,660	333	1,961
1996	4,079	1,642	332	2,105

*Includes trade/membership/health, nonconnected, cooperative, and corporations without stock PACs.

Source: U.S. Bureau of the Census, *Statistical Abstract of the United States* (Washington, D.C.: U.S. Government Printing Office, 1993, 1998).

Over the last 20 years, the amount of money contributed by PACs has increased dramatically. In 1978, $34.1 million was donated by 1,653 PACs; more than 4,000 PACs donated a total of $217.9 million in 1996 (U.S. Bureau of the Census, *Statistical Abstract of the United States, 1998*). Over $159 million was donated to candidates running for the House of Representatives in 1996. Neither Democrats nor Republicans were favored by these PAC contributions; both parties received virtually equal amounts. But PAC contributions are not given without some favoritism. Incumbent candidates running for the House of Representatives received over $117 million, while their challengers received only $21.4 million. Incumbent senators gained the same kind of financial advantage. PACs donated over $55 million to candidates running for the Senate, but incumbents were given $28.6 million of this while challengers received only $7.5 million (U.S. Bureau of the Census, *Statistical Abstract of the United States, 1998*).

One scholar has argued that PACs subvert the democratic character of American politics in several ways. First and foremost, money becomes a more important determinant of a group's influence than either the size of the group's membership or the objective merit of its positions. Second, PACs make congressional and senatorial representatives less dependent on and less responsive to both their political parties and their constituents. Finally, and perhaps most importantly, PAC-influenced policies place substantial costs on the population as a whole. In 1985, for instance, a bill supporting dairy subsidies that would cost American consumers about $3 billion a year was passed by the House by a margin of 78 votes. All the House members who had received more

TABLE 17.4   TOP 10 OVERALL CAMPAIGN CONTRIBUTORS, 1996

Rank	Contributor	Total*	Democrat	Republican
1	Philip Morris	$2,741,659	$608,704	$2,131,955
2	AT&T	2,130,045	858,462	1,270,583
3	Association of Trial Lawyers of America	2,106,325	1,747,725	353,600
4	Teamsters Union	2,097,410	2,005,250	87,160
5	Laborers Union	1,938,250	1,778,750	153,500
6	International Brotherhood of Electrical Workers	1,821,710	1,785,260	31,950
7	RJR Nabisco	1,765,306	341,406	1,423,900
8	National Education Association	1,661,960	1,618,110	38,850
9	American Medical Association	1,633,530	321,114	1,309,166
10	American Federation of State/County/Municipal Employees	1,616,125	1,578,700	32,425

*Includes soft money to the national parties, PAC money to candidates, PAC and individual contributions to the Clinton and Dole campaigns and individual campaign contributions to all federal candidates.

Source: Center for Responsive Politics. With permission.

than $30,000 over the years from the dairy lobby, 97 percent of those who had received between $20,000 and $30,000, and 81 percent of those who had received between $10,000 and $20,000 supported the bill. Of representatives who had received no money from dairy PACs, only 23 percent voted in favor of the subsidies (Stern, 1988). To the extent that PACs make the political process excessively responsive to special interest money, they undermine the basis of representative government.

Who Rules in America?

To whom are elected and appointed officials most responsive? Who actually rules America? To answer these questions, we can apply the theoretical perspectives on the distribution of power that were introduced earlier in this chapter, as well as a fourth perspective that has recently emerged.

THE PLURALIST PERSPECTIVE

The pluralist perspective holds that political power in America is divided among a number of groups, each representing a different set of interests or values. Since each group tries to appeal to a wide audience for support, extremism is usually discouraged. However, a pluralist system can be destroyed if the balance of competition is upset by an extremely powerful interest group, or if a stalemate between groups renders government ineffective.

The U.S. Constitution lays out the basic design for a pluralist system. Constitutional checks and balances keep each branch of the government—the legislative, the judiciary, and the executive—from assuming too much power. In theory at least, this separation of powers encourages decentralized political control. Many different political factions thus have a chance to influence government decisions.

American society consists of numerous subgroups formed along occupational, racial, religious, ethnic, and geographic lines. According to pluralist theory, such groups develop their own formal associations to represent them in the political process. Occupational subgroups, for example, organize into trade unions or professional associations. Local communities form neighborhood associations and community clubs. All these associations pursue their members' interests and defend them against others.

Pluralism thus views politics as the state-supervised interplay of competing interest groups. When the occasion demands, the state enters into this political competition as a neutral mediator, arbitrator, or conciliator, seeking to create policies responsive to the demands of organized citizen groups (Dahl, 1961).

THE ELITIST PERSPECTIVE

The most forceful critique of pluralist theory is contained in C. Wright Mills' classic book *The Power Elite* (1956). Mills suggests that most of the power in the United States is held by an elite group consisting of the leaders of the biggest corporations, top officials of the executive branch of government, and key military officers. Most members of the power elite are drawn from the same social backgrounds, attend the same universities, are members of the same clubs, and hence share essentially the same worldview. Furthermore, they frequently move around during their careers between important positions in the corporate, governmental, and military sectors, so that what appears to be three somewhat distinct groups is in fact a single, homogeneous, and cohesive elite. According to Mills, this small group of no more than a few thousand people determines the "size and shape of the national economy, the level of employment, the purchasing power of the consumer, the prices that are advertised, [and] the investments that are channeled" (1956). In essence, they dominate the state and make all important decisions. Mills did not feel that the power elite was necessarily evil, but it does act in order to promote its own ends, which may or may not benefit the general public.

More recent analyses broaden the notion of the power elite to include those at the top of the large institutions—corporations, banks, utilities, government bureaucracies, broadcasting networks, law firms, universities, foundations, and cultural and civic organizations—in which America's power and resources are concentrated (Domhoff, 1998; Dye, 1995). Where Mills described the power elite as only a "handful of men," Thomas Dye identifies 7,314 elite positions. As Mills argued, the holders of these positions (overwhelmingly white, well-to-do men) have—in addition to similar values and beliefs—easy access to, regular interaction with, and often personal knowledge of one another. According to this view, the state responds readily to the interests of this power elite, many of whose members once occupied, now occupy, or soon will occupy top positions in state and federal government.

THE CLASS CONFLICT PERSPECTIVE

Influenced by Marxist theory, the class conflict perspective regards the United States as a class state that acts invariably, almost automatically, to perpetuate the capitalist system. Class conflict theorists believe that power is rooted in ownership of the means of production—not in top institutional positions—and that this power is exercised by a ruling capitalist *class,* not a power elite. Acting to promote conditions that advance capital accumulation, minimize subordinate class opposition, and defuse tensions within the capitalist class, the state formulates policies and employs resources in a way that ultimately benefits the economically dominant class.

But because the state has two primary tasks—preserving order and strengthening the circumstances favorable to the accumulation of capital—it is not simply a passive instrument in the hands of the capitalist class (Miliband, 1977). To accomplish both tasks, it sometimes becomes necessary for the state to act contrary to the immediate desires of the dominant class. Because the state has a degree of independence from this class, it is able to overcome the shortsighted interests of capitalists in order to take the actions required for the long-term stability of the capitalist system. Thus, the New Deal policies introduced during the Great Depression against the wishes of the capitalist class—policies that promoted higher levels of unionization, business regulation, and social welfare—served the long-range interests of the ruling class by strengthening the economy and pacifying the increasingly militant subordinate classes (Skocpol, 1980).

THE STATIST PERSPECTIVE

The classic pluralist, elitist, and class conflict perspectives view the state as doing what it does in *reaction* to the interests of organized groups, a power elite, or a dominant class. In contrast, the *statist perspective* sees the American state as a powerful, authoritative, resource-laden organization with distinctive interests and the capacity to act on them, even when such actions run counter to the interests of outside groups, elites, or classes. Those favoring this perspective see the state as an independent, self-interested, powerful actor in its own right. Public officials use the authority and resources of the state to create policies that support the interests of the state itself (Nordlinger, 1981). These officials do not use their offices for personal gain. Rather, they act on behalf of the state with the knowledge that the strength of their positions depends on the strength of the state.

SOCIOLOGY AND THE STATE: A HUMANISTIC PERSPECTIVE

Both conservatives and liberals agree that society, as the sphere where people learn and practice their social obligations and responsibilities to one another, has been weakened by modern liberal democracy. Conservatives attribute this weakening to the expansion of the state. Liberals trace the erosion of societal bonds to the increasing importance of the market. Both are probably right. Society has been invaded both by the modern state and by the modern market (as we will see in the next chapter). Increasingly, people in liberal democracies rely less and less on themselves, their friends, families, and communities, and more and more on the impersonal structures of the market and the state (Putnam, 1995). If we wish to strengthen society, we may have to restrain both the market and the state.

In all modern liberal democracies, including the United States, the state has grown dramatically in size, scope, power, and authority. As it has grown, the state has come to assume many of the tasks—caring for the elderly, the young, the sick, and the abandoned—once thought to be the responsibility of family and friends. This is both necessary and humanitarian.

As the state expands and society contracts, political obligation based on the coercive authority of the state gradually replaces social obligation based on cooperation. As the bases of social obligation weaken, we find it more difficult to count on, trust, and cooperate with one another. When the power of social obligation fades, the power of the state begins to shine more brightly. Impersonal, coercive political control moves into the vacuum created by the failure of society to take care of and control itself. In this way, the state assumes a greater responsibility for regulating the lives of its citizens.

CHAPTER REVIEW

1. Using examples from current events, identify and discuss the three types of authority that were described by Max Weber.

2. Compare and contrast the three perspectives used to analyze the power of the state and the distribution of political power in societies.

3. Identify a country whose form of government is either totalitarian or authoritarian. What would its citizens have to overcome if they wanted a democratic form of government?

4. Describe the nature of political participation in the United States today. Why are some people more likely than others to take a more active role in politics?

5. Evaluate the theories offered to explain the low rate of voter turn out in the United States. What advice would you give a political candidate who wanted to capture the votes of Americans between the ages of 18 and 22?

6. Describe the factors that have contributed to the decline in political parties over the last half century in the United States. Have media organizations assumed any of the functions previously performed by politial parties? If so, which ones?

7. How do Republicans differ from Democrats today? Use current controversial issues to illustrate the differences you identify.

8. Are interest groups essential to the democratic process, or do they threaten national unity and stability?

9. Who rules America? Use one of the perspectives presented in this chapter to support your argument.

INTERNET EXERCISE

The Web destinations for Chapter 17 cover various aspects of power, politics, and government. To begin your explorations, go to the Prentice Hall Companion Web site **http://www.prenhall.com/popenoe.** Next, choose **Chapter 17** (Power, Politics, and Government). Then, select **web destinations** from the menu on the left side of the screen. There are several sites to choose from. We suggest you begin with **Right Magazine.** This site is related to an ultra-conservative publication with the same name and you will find a variety of articles on a wide range of topics relevant to current political issues. Be sure to click on "Bob Lang's Editorial Cartoons" and "Letters to the Editor." You will also find links to other politically conservative sites. After you have explored the Right Magazine site, answer the following questions:

- In this chapter, there is a selection entitled *The Shift Rightward,* which deals with liberal and conservative politics. Do you agree with the assessment that America is becoming more politically conservative? Why or why not?

- Where do you place yourself on the liberal-conservative political continuum?

KEY TERMS

politics	legal-rational authority	civic privatism
power	state	political party
legitimate power	oligarchy	interest groups
authority	democracy	lobbying
traditional authority	totalitarianism	political action
charismatic authority	authoritarianism	committee

CHAPTER 18

The Economy
and Work

Having succeeded with great difficulty and heroism in killing a fierce wild pig, a hunter from the Semai tribe of Malaysia lugs the carcass to his village, where it is divided equally among all the people. He gets no more and no less than anyone else. No one even thanks him for his efforts; to do so would violate an important Semai norm.

Long before Columbus landed in North America, wealthy men in a number of Native American cultures in the Pacific Northwest regularly engaged in competitive feasts called potlatches in which their social status was validated by how much food and other valued goods they could afford to give away. Some virtually bankrupted themselves in the effort.

At the same time but far to the south, long-established trade relations between North American groups like the Hopi and Zuni and other people living in what is now Mexico brought brightly colored macaws and tropical fruit north in exchange for turquoise and cornmeal.

Jessica hangs up her apron after a long day behind the counter at McDonald's and picks up her minimum wage paycheck before catching a bus home.

Fred finishes repairing his neighbor Jerry's automobile transmission; tomorrow Jerry will use his carpentry skills to rebuild Fred's back porch in exchange. No cash will be involved in the transaction.

Sarah stares at her VDT for a moment and then phones a sell order to her associate on the floor of the New York Stock Exchange. Within the next two hours, she will earn several hundred thousand dollars for her clients and a tidy fee for herself.

All of these are examples of ways in which different people participate or have participated in the **economy,** defined as those organizations and processes through which goods and services are produced and distributed. Economic systems vary greatly. Some are based on simple exchange or barter; others involve complex systems of redistribution. Some are conducted without money as we know it; others could not proceed without sophisticated financial calculations. Yet every known society has some sort of economic institution; the economy is one of the most important human cultural universals.

Not only is the economy universal, it is also crucially important. If a random sample of people were asked which of the five basic social institutions—religion, government, the economy, the family, and education—is most important, the majority would probably say the family. Certainly this answer makes sense, as our daily lives are normally played out very much within the family sphere. But if we think of "most important" in another way, asking which of the major institutions has the most influence on the overall character of society, a different answer might emerge. Many sociologists, especially those working in the conflict tradition, would argue that, looked at this way, the economy is the most crucial of all social institutions.

Like all other institutions, economic systems must solve a number of problems. Resources, both natural and human, are limited. Who will decide which goods and services will be produced? Who will produce which products?

Every society in the world has adopted an economic system that provides answers to these questions. Some systems dictate each individual's particular work role; others allow limited options; still others provide boundless opportunity. Individuals' work lives, in turn, help define their personal identities and social values. Economic systems influence relationships between people, too; economic inequities frequently emerge, and these inequities lead to social inequalities—between social classes, racial and ethnic groups, and the sexes.

Many of these topics have been discussed in previous chapters. Here we concentrate on the components of economic systems: how they developed, what they consist of, and how they function. We then turn to an extended discussion of the dominant features of the American economy. To conclude, we address the sociology of work and end with a humanistic perspective on society and the market.

THE ECONOMY

Historical Evolution of the Economy

Historically, the economic system of the simplest societies rarely extended beyond the family. Labor was divided among family members, who hunted, gathered, or grew and harvested food and who produced the basic goods needed for survival. The result was that families had little, if any, *surplus* of commodities left over after their needs were filled. In this *subsistence economy,* trade, marketing, and taxation were nonexistent. Social roles were based mainly on age and sex rather than rooted in the economy.

With the domestication of plants and animals, the potential for producing surplus goods increased. Larger areas of land were devoted to specific purposes, such as farming and animal husbandry. Families found that they could produce more by concentrating on certain crops, and surpluses led to exchange. In simple agricultural societies, however, most material goods were still produced at home. The priest, the healer, and the metalworker were among the few specialists who offered their services to the community at large.

As the productive advantages of specialization became increasingly apparent, a family might try to produce a surplus of, say, wine or wool or pottery. The first stage of a market economy was probably a regular, perhaps weekly, gathering for the exchange of surplus goods. These exchange centers developed into a new focus for social life as well. People began increasingly to devote themselves to particular tasks, to earn a living by meeting the demands of the marketplace. In this way, the *division of labor* was extended beyond the family and across a village or even an entire district. More and more, a person's social role came to be determined by the nature of his or her participation in the economy.

The system just described eventually evolved into a highly sophisticated economic order. Landowners rented space to craftworkers. Rulers levied taxes on trade to support a professional army, which defended the increasingly complex society from competing rulers and armies. Luxury trade—for instance, in spices or imported cloth—became a regular feature of the economy. Wars of conquest were fought to satisfy the demands of an ever more active market. Finally, a merchant class rose to significant status. These merchants produced no goods themselves but bought goods where they were plentiful and sold them for profit where they were rare and costly.

Components of the Modern Economy

Concerned with the production and distribution of goods and services, modern economies must confront several basic issues: what and how much is to be produced, the resources and technologies to be used in production, and the choice of methods of distribution (Samuelson, 1970). An economic system's response to these issues depends on five general factors: the available resources and technology; the degree to which economic power is centralized; whether the economy operates under a market system or a planned system; the prevailing rules of property ownership; and the incentives that the economy relies on to motivate production and distribution.

RESOURCES AND TECHNOLOGY. Economists distinguish three sectors of the economy: a **primary,** largely agricultural, sector; a **secondary,** manufacturing sector; and a **tertiary,** or service, sector. In a *preindustrial economy,* the primary sector dominates. Raw materials constitute the preindustrial economy's major economic resources. The technology used to extract these resources from nature—in order to farm, fish, and mine—is *labor-intensive* (that is, it relies heavily on human labor). In an *industrial economy,* the secondary sector is the most important source of wealth. The manufacturing and construction industries that drive an industrial economy depend on *capital-intensive* technology (that is, on machine production) more than on human labor. As a consequence, the key resource of the industrial economy is energy. In a *postindustrial economy* (see Chapter 22), the tertiary sector is the principal source of both jobs and

The economy is often divided into three general components: the primary sector, which is largely agricultural; the secondary sector, which produces manufactured goods; and the tertiary sector, which provides services.

.NET   INTERNET/TECHNOLOGY

LET YOUR FINGERS DO THE SHOPPING

From the earliest days of capitalism, businesses have recognized that success depends on the size of their market.

During the nineteenth century, Sears and Roebuck and Montgomery Ward came up with a similar idea to accomplish this. To expand their businesses, they both designed catalogs filled with illustrations and descriptions of their merchandise, and they distributed them to prospective customers in rural areas. Initially, both companies had to work hard to persuade customers to buy their goods (Ryan & Wentworth, 1999). An industrial society depended on the consumption of goods, but convincing Americans, who were shaped by the hardships of an agricultural society, would be a challenge. Making it easier for rural customers to buy merchandise was one of the strategies that the two companies used. And it worked.

Businesses would capitalize on this idea over and over again. By the middle of the twentieth century, the telephone had become the instrument for saving time and effort. And Americans were bombarded with a jingle that reminded them of the most convenient way to shop: "Let your fingers do the walking through the Yellow Pages."

Today, the Internet is rapidly replacing the telephone as the most convenient way to shop. Although online sales constitute only a small fraction of the American economy, they are expected to grow as Internet users become more familiar with business Web sites. In 1997, American Express estimated that consumers would spend between $4 billion and $6 billion in Internet credit card

FIGURE 18.1 Research shows that Americans are buying a variety of goods and services over the Internet—from shoes to computers.

Sources: Forrester Research, Inc.

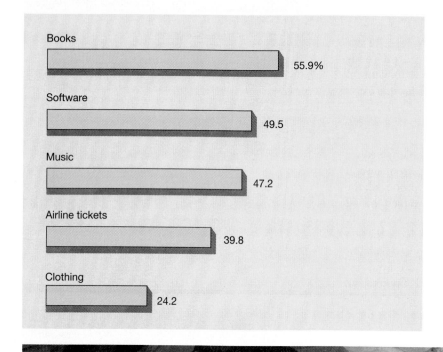

- Books — 55.9%
- Software — 49.5
- Music — 47.2
- Airline tickets — 39.8
- Clothing — 24.2

wealth. The tertiary sector includes workers and industries that provide *services* rather than manufactured goods. Bankers, doctors, writers, scientists, broadcasters, and educators work in the service sector, as do security guards, hospital orderlies, building custodians, hairdressers, and waiters. Information is the major resource in a postindustrial society, and information processing or *knowledge-intensive* technology (computers, robotics, telecommunications) is central (Bell, 1973).

CENTRALIZATION AND DECENTRALIZATION. An economy's fundamental character is also influenced by the distribution of economic power. When the decision-making power in an economy is held by a large number of individuals, households, or firms, the economy is **decentralized.** When such power is concentrated in the hands of a small number of individuals or firms, the economy is **centralized.** A perfectly centralized economy is responsive to one center of command, usually governmental in character. A perfectly decentralized economy, in contrast, would be responsive to the individually expressed preferences of its active participants (Elliott, 1985).

MARKET ECONOMIES VERSUS PLANNED ECONOMIES. In a **market economy,** consumers are the key decision makers: The economy responds to consumer preferences expressed in the market. In a **planned economy,** the ultimate decision makers are the planners: The purchases, and that Internet sales would increase at a rate exceeding 400 percent annually (Hansell, 1997). And Americans are buying a wide variety of goods and services over the Internet (See Figure 18.1). Over half of the people surveyed by Forrest Research indicated that they had bought books over the Internet. Almost half of them said they bought software or music. Four in ten had purchased airline tickets, and one in four had bought clothing this way.

Some direct-sales businesses are discouraging their sales force from marketing products online, including Amway, Mary Kay, and Electrolux (Napoli, 1998). Companies like these argue that while the Internet can serve as a good source of information, it does not provide the personal touch or the kind of service that they value. But you can decide for yourself. Here is a list of popular shopping Web sites (Freeze & Freeze, 1998):

Internet shopping is rapidly becoming the "catalog" shopping of the twenty-first century. Reprinted by permission.

Internet Malls

www.internet-mall.com
www.realmalls.com

Videos, Computer Games, and Audio CDs and Cassettes

www.columbiahouse.com

Greeting Cards

www.cyberpanda.com/postcard

Travel

Airfare
www.travelocity.com
www.flifo.com
www.amtrak.com

Hotels

www.travelweb.com
www.traveler.net/htio
www.kidsuites.com

Books

www.amazon.com
www.barnesandnoble.com

planned economy responds to and is coordinated by a planning agency.

Market economies are less centralized than planned economies. Substantial centralization is possible in the absence of economic planning, however. In many advanced market economies, including that of the United States, a great deal of decision-making power is concentrated in a small number of large corporations. In Japan, a similar concentration of corporate power is wielded in the context of a national industrial policy fashioned by a state that plays an active and powerful role in the economy. The results, in both the United States and Japan, are highly centralized market economies (Gregory & Stuart, 1989).

PROPERTY OWNERSHIP. An economy's performance is also affected by its system of property, resource, and technology ownership. Property ownership carries with it several important rights: the right to transfer title of ownership to others; the right to use the property as the owner sees fit; and the right to full use of the products, services, or surpluses the property generates. In a system of *private ownership,* these rights belong to individuals or groups of individuals. In a system of *public ownership,* these rights belong to a government. In a system of *cooperative ownership,* these rights are held by a *cooperative enterprise*—a voluntary economic association created for the mutual benefit of its members—that owns the property in question. Cooperative ownership is collective (like public ownership) but nongovernmental (like private ownership) (Elliott, 1985; Gregory & Stuart, 1989).

INCENTIVES. The final factor influencing the production of goods and services in an economy is the economic system's *reward structure* or *incentive system.* In the absence of force, people must be motivated to act—to buy and sell, to produce and consume, to use their resources and technology in particular ways and for particular purposes. Generally, an economic system motivates desired performances by employing either *material incentives* (wages, profits, bonuses, and other monetary rewards) or *moral incentives,* which appeal to people's sense of responsibility to the community, society, or religion.

Market economies rely almost exclusively on material incentives. Planned socialist economies, seeking to reduce both the hold that material incentives have on people and the inequality that results from differences in income, have tried to subordinate material incentives to moral incentives. In Mao's China, for instance, the chief moral incentive was the call to "Serve the people!"; in Castro's Cuba, it was the promise of an enhanced sense of solidarity and brotherhood (Elliott, 1985; Gregory & Stuart, 1989; Lindblom, 1977).

ECONOMIC SYSTEMS

The five factors of the modern economy just described are essential to an understanding of the major types of economic systems in the modern world: capitalism, socialism, and mixed economies (Elliott, 1985; Gregory & Stuart, 1989).

Capitalism

THE RISE OF CAPITALISM

Capitalism is an economic system based on the private ownership of wealth. The capitalist system grew out of a simple, agrarian market economy, and began taking modern form in the West in the late Middle Ages (Wallerstein, 1979). Although all the elements of capitalism were present at that time, commodities were largely agricultural. The major source of marketable goods was trade between societies rather than manufacture within any one society. With most of the population still involved in small-scale agrarian production, the "capitalists" were generally merchants and financiers. Their economic power had to coexist with power based on the older, feudal order of the economy.

Capitalism in its industrial form came into being with the discovery of nonhuman sources of energy. The harnessing of steam was a significant turning point because it made possible, for the first time, the large-scale

centralization of manufacturing. Thereafter, the production of goods moved out of the home and into the factory. At the same time, the tremendous population growth of the European nations provided a labor force that had to turn to manufacture for survival, whether it welcomed the new order or not. Thousands of people migrated to manufacturing centers, away from the soil that could no longer directly support their numbers.

Today capitalism is widely regarded as having brought unsurpassed wealth to the world. It may be, as Peter Berger (1986) has asserted, the most successful economic mechanism ever devised for improving the material standards of large numbers of people. Even the socialist nations of the world, such as China, are now seeking to emulate many of capitalism's successes. And the former socialist countries of Eastern Europe, including those that once constituted the Soviet Union, are trying to establish the bases of a capitalist economy. At the same time, however, capitalism has generated numerous unresolved problems, some of which are discussed below.

THE ELEMENTS OF CAPITALISM

Private property is a cornerstone of the capitalist system. In capitalism, almost all goods are owned by individuals or groups, as opposed to the society as a whole or political rulers. By owning such property as real estate, the materials needed to make a marketable product, or the product itself, individuals (or groups) obtain the freedom to use these goods to their best advantage. Under pure capitalism, nothing restricts the owners of capital from pitting their ingenuity against that of competitors in order to derive the greatest possible personal profit from their holdings.

Profit is the goal of those who own and manage the means of production. In capitalist theory, owners are free to decide how they will use their profits. Depending on whether they want to ensure their present or their future comfort, they may raise their own standards of living right away, expand their enterprises, or invest in other areas of the economy. In principle, the amount of profit that can be made is not restricted by the government.

Through *competition,* different producers of a particular commodity seek to appeal to the greatest possible number of buyers. Competitors are continually changing their prices and the character of their goods to capture a greater portion of the market. Ideally, competition inspires technological progress as manufacturers try to outdo one another. Meanwhile, they are generally careful not to outdo *themselves,* since the continual, gradual improvement of an item may ensure its future popularity more than a radical change. Both great profits and great losses have been incurred by companies that surprised competitors and consumers alike with "revolutionary" items. Witness what happened when Coca-Cola changed its time-proven formula. A public outcry forced the corporation to stop tampering with the success of its most important product.

The French term *laissez-faire*, which roughly means "let (them) do (as they wish)," summarizes the common belief that capitalism functions best in those societies in which the government interferes the least in the marketplace. In this view, the forces of competition and consumer demand, which are inherent in the capitalist system, are believed to be "natural controls" that will sufficiently regulate the economy's operation.

The basic unit of modern capitalism is the *corporation,* an enterprise that has been chartered by a government to perform certain functions or services. A corporation is owned by a group of shareholders who protect their personal capital by legally limiting their liability for the corporation's debts. While the shareholders are entitled to a voice in the decision-making process, in practice most large corporations are characterized by a separation of ownership and control, the latter responsibility being given to management.

Nothing is more characteristic of capitalism in this century than very large corporations. Continual competition has led producers to seek greater control over both the sources of raw materials and the outlets for their products. Weaker producers are commonly bought out by stronger competitors, who then benefit from increased control over the market. These larger producers use their profits to finance their own further development and growth. Much concern has been voiced over the fairness of allowing a relatively small number of corporate leaders to control staggering amounts of assets.

CAPITALISM: ISSUES AND PROBLEMS

THE MARXIST CRITIQUE OF CAPITALISM. Karl Marx offered the most influential nineteenth-century criticism of capitalism. Although his economic views were flawed in major ways, they nevertheless provide useful insights into the problems of capitalism. According to Marx, the capitalist system is riddled with contradictions that will eventually lead to its collapse. The chief contradiction of capitalism, he claimed, is that profit levels tend to decline as production expands. Thus, the industrialist can maintain high profits only by exploiting labor ever more harshly.

For example, in order to produce more goods, industrialists purchase labor-saving machinery. The machinery increases production. But with many laborers left unemployed by automation, there are fewer buyers for the extra goods. Because they are competing with one another for this smaller market, industrialists must lower the wages they pay their workers so that they can cut the prices of their goods.

In this situation, managers could also accept falling profits—sometimes they must do this. But the crisis of falling profits may be so great as to cause a wave of bankruptcies among capitalists, leading in turn to greater unemployment or even full-scale depression. Either way, the workers lose out in the end.

Marx believed that after a series of increasingly severe depressions, impoverished workers would rise up and take control of the state. With political power in their hands, they would take property away from the owners and run it collectively. That is, they would *socialize* private property. The laboring class would then control the means of production, and the exploitation of workers would come to an end.

As noted, there are serious defects in the Marxian analysis of capitalism. Marx predicted that the majority of the working class would be pauperized—reduced to a miserable existence—a prediction that has not been realized. Furthermore, Marx did not foresee that labor unions would continue to be reform-minded instead of becoming revolutionary. Unions in Western Europe and the United States have helped workers win higher wages and better working conditions while accepting the basic legitimacy of capitalism. Also, Marx's view that profits cannot be made through machinery now seems mistaken. The introduction of automated labor-saving machines has led to much higher production without a reduction in profits. In fact, production to meet consumer needs has grown enormously in the past 200 years. In these regards, capitalism has developed in ways that Marx did not foresee.

Marxists have developed a number of explanations for the continued economic success of capitalism in the twentieth century. One of the most important (suggested by Lenin in 1917) is that capitalism has survived because Western industrial nations have been able to dump excess goods in developing nations. Selling their extra production in the underdeveloped world has helped industrialists maintain high prices and profits. But Marxists generally believe that such dumping can only provide a temporary solution for Western capitalists. Eventually, the whole world will be industrialized, and then the contradictions of the capitalist system will inevitably take effect. The workers' revolution, according to this view, has been postponed—but will eventually occur.

CONTEMPORARY PROBLEMS OF CAPITALISM. Marx's criticism of nineteenth-century capitalism had a great impact on the formation of labor movements. Later, Marxist thinking was adopted, with modifications, as the basis for the economic and political systems of the Soviet Union, China, and the nations of Eastern Europe. But to

Some scholars believe that a huge deficit is an inherent defect of capitalism, while others view it as a failure of the U.S. political system. What do you think?

understand many of the problems facing capitalism today, it is necessary to look well beyond the scope of Marxist thought.

The ideas of the British economist John Maynard Keynes brought important changes to the economic and political organization of capitalist systems in this century. Keynes advocated government spending as a means to combat economic downturns. Policies based on Keynes's thinking were adopted by President Franklin D. Roosevelt to lessen the effects of the Great Depression in the United States, and many other nations enacted similar policies at that time. Since then, Keynesian theory has played a major, though now diminishing, role in U.S. economic policy.

The "Keynesian revolution" has led to one problem that has grown in importance in recent years: *deficit spending,* or the tendency for government expenditures to outpace revenues. By 1998, the U.S. national debt had surpassed $5.4 trillion, a historically unprecedented level. Some scholars see this huge deficit as an inherent defect of capitalism (O'Connor, 1973). Others view it as a failure of the American political system: It is politically much easier to pass spending bills than it is to increase taxation. Budget deficits have become a major political issue in many capitalist nations.

If tax revenues are inadequate to cover expenditures, governments must borrow money. This is believed to contribute to the problem of *inflation* (an increase in the general price levels of goods and services). Inflation has been a constant problem of Western industrialized nations since the 1960s and has many origins. These include higher wage demands and extraordinary increases in the cost of such raw materials as oil and gas.

It is difficult to separate the causes of inflation from its effects. Do workers cause inflation by asking for higher wages, or do they demand higher pay to keep up with the inflated cost of living? By now, it has become traditional for American business leaders to accuse labor of fueling inflation by making excessive wage demands, and for labor to charge, in turn, that business raises prices beyond reasonable levels.

Unemployment has been another perennial problem of capitalist nations. Despite general prosperity in the decades after World War II, some nations, including the United States, have at times been plagued by both high unemployment and high inflation. This combination, called *stagflation,* beset the U.S. economy throughout the early 1980s. Both rates dropped to a comparatively low level in the second half of the decade, but the U.S. unemployment rate moved upward again in the early 1990s as the country experienced a *recession* (a downturn in the economy).

Following the Persian Gulf War, a period of economic expansion began in the United States, contributing to one of the longest periods of sustained growth during peacetime in the twentieth century (Bagby, 1998). The stability of the U.S. economy at the end of the century looked encouraging, but experts predict that as we enter the twenty-first century highly technological societies like ours may experience a new kind of unemployment (Rifkin, 1996). Many workers may be "left behind" as their skills fail to keep up with advances in the production process. Those who are victims of such *structural unemployment,* as it is called, may feel bitter and hostile. Retraining programs financed by industry or government could provide a partial solution to structural unemployment. But there is a growing realization that there may never again be full employment. Because of the high skill requirements of available jobs and the typically low level of skills among the unemployed, a jobless rate of at least 3 or 4 percent is accepted by many as the lowest level attainable in capitalist economies.

Production in capitalist economies is based on the demands of the market. But the markets in these economies do not necessarily meet a very broad range of social needs. It may be, for example, that the United States as a whole would benefit from an improved intercity railroad network and highly developed systems of urban rapid transit. Yet because of market demands, a great deal of capital is invested in the production of cars, and less money is made available for public transportation. In a capitalist economy, high-profit businesses generally attract the most investment. Unfortunately, this principle means that important products or social services are often neglected. Money is available to finance the growth of huge fashion or fast-food enterprises, for example, while companies seeking to develop solar energy systems must frequently rely on government aid.

Perhaps the most widely discussed problems of modern capitalist societies, especially the United States, are the persistence of poverty and inequalities in the distribution of wealth. (These issues are fully discussed in Chapters 9 and 10.) It should be realized that the United States is exceptional among advanced capitalist nations in the amount of poverty and the degree of income inequality that exist. In nations that have combined capitalism with stronger welfare-state measures, as have many of the nations of northern Europe, income distributions are more egalitarian and serious poverty is negligible (Eisenstadt & Ahimeir, 1985; Spiro & Yuchtman-Yaar, 1983).

Socialism

The economic system most often considered as an alternative to capitalism is **socialism.** Under socialism, the means of production and distribution in society are owned collectively rather than privately. The state is typically the collective owner, but in some forms of socialism the owner might be a small community or everyone who works for a particular enterprise. In place of the market mechanism for setting prices, socialist theory calls for prices to be set collectively. This typically means that, at least for major goods and services, prices are set by government agencies.

Socialists reject the capitalist belief that the greatest public benefits flow from the unregulated actions of individuals acting through the market in pursuit of individual self-interest. Rather, they believe that in economic (as in social and political) affairs, the important decisions should be made by representatives of all the people and should be coordinated to promote the broader social goals of the state.

Originally founded on the writings of Marx and several nineteenth-century French thinkers, socialism in most modern nations has moved away from strict adherence to Marxist theory and ideology. Socialist parties today are often more practical than theoretical in their approach. Particularly since the end of World War II, the theory and practice of socialism have changed dramatically.

Two major developments in socialism should be stressed. The first is the rise of socialism in very poor agricultural countries, usually following the end of colonial rule (Paige, 1975). Marx was doubtful that a socialist revolution could occur in such societies. He considered the peasants a reactionary (i.e., extremely conservative) force because, he believed, they were interested primarily in protecting their property rights. In Marx's view, it was the industrial workers of the more developed nations who would rise up to defeat capitalism. But in the 1920s, Mao Zedong began to organize the peasants of rural China.

This movement was successful, and the peasants have made up the most important political force in the Chinese socialist state. Since the 1920s, socialist movements in developing countries elsewhere have frequently based their political programs on appeals to the peasantry. Cuba, Algeria, and Vietnam provide good examples of nations in which peasant-oriented socialist movements have won political power (Wolf, 1970).

A second major development in the twentieth century is the collapse of socialism in Eastern Europe and the former Soviet Union, once home to the largest planned economy in the world. In the late 1980s, beset by severe economic stagnation, all the nations of Eastern Europe shifted away from an economy controlled by the central government to a market-oriented system. In large part, this shift was triggered by changes introduced into the Soviet Union by Mikhail Gorbachev's policy of social and economic restructuring (*perestroika*). Although designed to save Soviet socialism by reforming it, the policy ultimately failed.

At the start of 1992, the 15 Soviet republics announced the demise of the Soviet Union. Most also committed themselves to the introduction of a market economy that included private ownership of property, the profit motive, and the setting of prices through the market. These far-reaching transformations plunged these countries into inflation, unemployment, and shortages of food, fuel, and shelter.

Why did the Soviet Union's economic system collapse? At the end of the 1980s, the Soviet economy was the third largest in the world. It employed the largest number of scientists and engineers; it was the world's largest producer of oil, natural gas, and crude steel; and it supported the second-largest military force in the world. At the same time, however, the Soviet economy's rate of productivity had not grown in nearly 20 years. In addition, the Soviet Union's standard of living (ranked 60th in the world) was declining and more and more Soviet people went hungry (Bell, 1991). The dismal performance of the Soviet economy is largely attributable to the inability of the central government to coordinate effectively the millions of interdependent elements that make up a complex modern economy.

The socialist economy of the former Soviet Union depended on extensive government planning of production. In practice, decisions to increase production in one area often caused complications and unforeseen consequences in other areas. Inefficiencies often resulted. As two economists noted:

If the target is 10,000 shirts, the firm might use rough cloth and sew a crooked seam. Stories are told of transportation enterprises that move carloads of water back and forth in order to fulfill their output target of logging so many physical ton-miles. (Samuelson & Nordhaus, 1988, p. 775)

Guided almost exclusively by the goals of the government plan, Soviet managers paid little attention to the costs and quality of their goods or to the efficiency of their production. Innovative ways of responding to the demands of a changing economy were smothered by a cumbersome planning apparatus. Hit throughout the 1970s and 1980s by a series of bad harvests, steeply rising military expenditures, and a new international marketplace that valued flexible innovation (discussed below), the Soviet economy grew increasingly incapable of meeting the basic needs of the Soviet people.

Mixed Economies

Capitalism and socialism are both ideal type models of economic systems; in the real world, neither pure capitalism nor pure socialism has been practiced at the societal level. Instead, virtually all existing societies are characterized by **mixed economies,** incorporating a blend of capitalist and socialist principles. Two special types of mixed economies are market socialism, which is relatively close to the socialist model, and democratic socialism, which incorporates large elements of capitalism.

MARKET SOCIALISM

In market socialist economies, profit-seeking enterprises use publicly owned resources in response to market demand. **Market socialism** thus represents an effort to join some features of socialism—for example, public ownership and a relatively equal distribution of income—with the emphasis on market forces and the decentralized decision-making characteristic of capitalist economies (Gregory & Stuart, 1989). In contrast to planned socialist economies, where production is controlled by government directives, enterprises in a market socialist system are expected to produce goods and services that they can sell at a profit. As in capitalist economies, production in market socialist economies is directed by market demand. But in market socialism, the profits belong to the state, which owns the resources and technology. Part of these profits is used to advance the socialist goal of greater equality.

Market socialists recognize that the market is an efficient device for regulating the production of goods and services. Yet in a fully capitalist system, they argue, the market generates severe inequalities, failing to provide jobs for many people who want to work and creating large income differentials between owners and employees. Market socialism is designed to prevent such inequalities "by the

public regulation of investment to ensure full employment, . . . by encouraging the growth of forms of enterprise (especially workers' cooperatives) in which primary income is distributed more equally, and . . . by using the tax system to implement such further measures of redistribution as command general assent" (D. Miller, 1989, pp. 31–32).

The most systematic attempt to base an entire economy on these principles was initiated in the former Yugoslavia in the early 1950s and proved to be workable for a quarter of a century (Lindblom, 1977). After the collapse of communism in Eastern Europe and the disintegration of the Soviet Union, however, Yugoslavia (weakened by the secession of several of its republics) joined the region's other countries in embracing capitalist principles.

Many people believe that these events spell the end of socialism in Europe. Others, however, are careful to distinguish market socialism from bureaucratic, totalitarian Soviet socialism. Some Western scholars continue to see market socialism as an effective alternative to both capitalism and socialism (Heilbroner, 1991; LeGrand & Estrin, 1989; Nove, 1990).

DEMOCRATIC SOCIALISM

For most of the time since World War II, a number of European nations, including Sweden, Norway, Denmark, and the Netherlands, have been ruled by democratic governments that have grafted some principles of socialism onto basically capitalist economic systems. These **democratic socialist** regimes take as their primary responsibility the elimination of some of the harsher consequences of unrestrained capitalism. As a result, welfare expenditures are much higher, social service programs more comprehensive, and governmental protections for citizens more substantial in social democratic societies than in more capitalistic societies. Still, although public ownership in these nations is more widespread than it is in the United States, close to 90 percent of all economic assets are privately owned. On this score, the difference between democratic socialism and market socialism is significant (Esping-Andersen, 1985; Stephens, 1979).

A guiding objective of social democratic governments is the *decommodification* (reduction of the influence of market forces) of such areas as medical care, housing, and employment. Decommodification, which exists to "the extent to which individuals and families can uphold a normal and socially acceptable standard of living regardless of their performance in the labor market" (Esping-Andersen & Korpi, 1984, p. 183), requires the establishment of strong comprehensive citizenship rights and broad social services to meet those rights. In this context, the distribution of essential goods and services (for instance, health care) rests less on market principles (people get what they can afford to purchase) than on the principle of citizenship rights (people have the right to get what they need—say, adequate medical treatment—whether or not they can afford it) (Rae, 1991; Rosenblum, 1991).

Politically, Western European social democratic systems are completely democratic. They hold free elections in which a number of political parties participate. No social democratic party in the West has ever come to power through violence and the expropriation of private property, the methods endorsed by Marx.

THE ECONOMIC SYSTEM IN THE UNITED STATES

Historical and Cultural Background

The strong individualism that is a distinctive mark of American culture (see Chapter 17) gained popular expression in the advice offered by Benjamin Franklin to his eighteenth-century contemporaries. Take advantage, Franklin urged, of the most special gift America has to offer: the opportunity for the individual to prosper through hard work, persistence, and initiative.

Clearly, many Americans took Franklin's advice to heart. By the start of the twentieth century, an emphasis on individual initiative had come to assume a central place in the American imagination. Read by millions, the stories of Horatio Alger gave a fictionalized account of the journey from rags to riches believed to be made possible by hard work and determination. As one scholar has noted:

> Americans at the turn of the century saw Horatio Alger stories personified all around them. Edward Harriman had begun as a $5.00-per-week office boy and came to head a mighty railroad empire; John D. Rockefeller had risen from a clerk in a commission merchant's house to become one of the world's richest men; Andrew Carnegie had started as a $1.20-a-week bobbin boy in a Pittsburgh cotton mill only to become the nation's foremost steel magnate. Two decades later, when boys were still reading the Alger tales, Henry Ford would make his fortune mass-producing the Model T, and become a national folk hero. (Reich, 1987, p. 106)

These real-life models were all self-reliant and self-made men. Their success, like Horatio Alger's, did not depend on government assistance but rather was achieved within an open, competitive marketplace. The life histories of Rockefeller, Carnegie, and Ford seemed to legitimate an economy free of governmental interference.

Ironically, the Horatio Alger stories peaked in popularity at a time when the highly competitive capitalism that had prevailed through much of the nineteenth century was giving way to a much less competitive, more managed capitalism increasingly dependent on government intervention. Since the end of the nineteenth century, the size and power of the government and its influence on the market have increased greatly. Unrestricted capitalist development during the nineteenth century had resulted in the exploitation of many workers and eventually led to government regulations designed to end the worst abuses. The introduction of the progressive income tax in 1913 was another indicator of the increasing power of government. Even more important, however, were the economic and social programs of the 1930s, designed partly to fight the Depression. When the Depression ended, most of these programs endured. Other times of great government expansion were World War II and the 1960s, the latter notable for the growth of new social programs.

Corporate Capitalism

The relatively unchecked free enterprise system of nineteenth-century America gradually gave way to a modern industrial state in which government came to regulate some aspects of the economy. Advances in technology made the production process increasingly complex, and partly in order to manage this complexity, large-scale organizations emerged. In nineteenth-century capitalism, the key figure was the individual entrepreneur who made his fortune either by astutely investing his capital—in railroads, for example—or by promoting a clever invention, like the automobile. But in the industrial society of the late twentieth century, the key actor is the corporation.

Corporations became very powerful in the mass-production industries between 1900 and 1920. *Mass production* is based on enormous investments in specialized equipment and workers geared to the production of large quantities of particular products. However, when the demand for these products drops, the corporation is placed in serious jeopardy because it is unable to deploy its resources in other ways. Classic mass production is therefore profitable only with markets that are "large enough to absorb an enormous output of a single, standardized commodity, and stable enough to keep the resources involved in the production of that commodity continuously employed" (Piore & Sabel, 1984). In response to these concerns, the modern corporation has made continuous efforts to (1) reduce market risks and fluctuations resulting from fierce competition and (2) develop the large and stable markets it requires.

SOCIOLOGY OF THE MEDIA

"GOTTA HAVE IT"

By the end of the twentieth century, the advertising industry had accomplished something that was not only unthinkable but actually morally suspect at the beginning of the nineteenth century. It had convinced the American public that consumption was good for them—You "gotta have it," and just to make sure, "VISA is everywhere you go."

The only things resembling slogans at the turn of the nineteenth century were perhaps adages, which encouraged hard work, self-denial, thrift, and the simple life. Benjamin Franklin penned many of these common expressions, capturing what Max Weber called the Protestant work ethic (1930). Even though they seem anachronistic in today's consumer society, many are still recited verbatim or translated into simpler terms. They include:

A penny earned is a penny saved.
The second Vice is Lying, the first
    is running into Debt.
Industry, Perseverance,
    and Frugality make
        Fortune Yield.

The behavior that this kind of wisdom shaped—saving money rather than spending it—ironically contributed to the rise of industrial capitalism and to our present day consumer society.

Convincing people who were born and raised in an agricultural society to buy goods when they did not need them was difficult (Ryan & Wentworth, 1999). They had experienced hardship and scarcity firsthand. "Waste not, want not" was crucial to their very survival. But capitalist industry could not grow unless the market expanded, and that meant that people had to buy more than they actually needed to survive. Persuading the public to consume became the sole focus of a new industry—advertising.

Over the years, advertisers have tried many strategies for persuading consumers to buy certain products. Many of the methods suggest that the basic strategy has not changed very much. Consider, for example, the way that advertisers appealed to Victorian women with fantasies of getting married. "Ads for tightly laced corsets, fashionable clothing, and perfumes offered one means to do so. . . . Promotions for beauty soaps, cosmetics, and creams also promised love and romance as a prelude to marriage (Sivulka, 1998, p. 53). In 1925, Listerine appealed to young women and their eagerness to marry with a warning about bad breath. The catchphrase read: "Often a bridesmaid but never a bride" (Sivulka, 1998, p. 161). Young brides make great copy even today—from Estee Lauder ads for the fragrance Pleasures, which depict Elizabeth Hurley as a sexy bride, to Diet Pepsi commercials that show a bride who was stranded at the altar tearfully asking: "Is this really diet?"

Today's ads clearly suggest that "we've come a long way" since the early days of capitalism. But how far, and has it been in the right direction? Critics argue that advertising has taken us in the wrong direction, that ads do more

Do you believe that advertising has taken us in the wrong direction? Are companies selling an image or a product? How would you get public interest for a product?

harm than good. Linking beauty, youth, and sexuality to American hopes and dreams convinces consumers that they "gotta have it"—that is, if they want to belong, if they want to be happy. But do they? Drinking the right beer will not produce a beach full of beautiful women. A soda will offer you little comfort, if you are stranded at the altar. And while smoking cigarettes might help you keep off the pounds, it is more likely to take some years off your life. As critics suggest, the role that advertising has played in producing a consumer society might have cost Americans more than they ever imagined.

The first decade of the twentieth century saw a merger frenzy in which corporations consolidated with their competitors in order to stabilize and enlarge their markets. The first giant American corporations—Alcoa Aluminum, U.S. Steel, General Electric, American Telephone and Telegraph, Standard Oil, and General Motors—arose in this fashion (Reich, 1983). Once consolidated, the large corporation sought to incorporate tasks (such as supplying and distributing) that were once external to it. As a result, the industries in which the large corporations were operating often became *oligopolistic* (see Chapter 17). Dominated by a few giant corporations, oligopolistic industries erect strong barriers against entry by other firms, and thus typically encounter little competition over the long run.

Possessing considerable investment capital and easy access to credit, many oligopolistic corporations used a two-part strategy of diversification to stabilize and enlarge their markets after World War II. The first part involved *industrial diversification*—moving into new industries by creating or acquiring different product lines. A steel company, for instance, might diversify by acquiring a chemical company, an oil company, or an appliance manufacturer. The result is the formation of a *conglomerate,* a large corporation encompassing a number of smaller companies usually engaged in producing a variety of different types of goods and services. In this way, the parent corporation protects itself against disaster should the market for one of its products decline. The second part of the diversification strategy entailed the penetration of foreign markets: American firms were transformed into *multinational corporations* with divisions located throughout the world (Hearn, 1988).

Multinationals have many advantages. These corporations are able to produce goods in areas where labor is cheap, such as Taiwan, Korea, and Hong Kong. For this reason, many domestic companies manufacture products in the Far East and import them back to the United States. Many multinational arrangements have been beneficial in some ways to both the foreign investor and the host nation. Developing countries, especially, have received extensive technological training and income in this way.

Nevertheless, many critics view the great power of these corporations with concern. They feel that multinationals often avoid responsibility for the effects of their investments on the host countries. In the developing countries of South America, Africa, and Asia, the multinationals may extract resources and exploit cheap labor without contributing to the development of independent national economies. The economies of such nations can become dependent on a single product or industry and thus are rendered vulnerable to the policies of foreign investors (Harrison, 1984).

Economic Concentration and the Dual Economy

In the nineteenth century, *monopolies* (single enterprises controlling an industry or market) could often set prices at an artificially high level because they had no competition. This situation led to government "trust-busting"—moves to break up the monopolies. The first antitrust law was the Sherman Act of 1890, which prohibited "combinations in restraint of trade" and made it illegal to "monopolize or attempt to monopolize any interstate or foreign commerce." In the early twentieth century, price discrimination, exclusive contracts, acquisition of stock in competitors' corporations, and other unfair practices that limit competition were outlawed. After World War II, laws were passed to prevent monopoly-forming mergers between firms.

Despite these efforts, the American economy today is more centralized than it has been at any time since the turn of the century. Corporate power and wealth have become highly concentrated. **Economic concentration,** the degree to which a disproportionately large share of a nation's economic resources is controlled by a relatively small number of corporations, has increased steadily since the end of the Great Depression. According to one estimate, only about 4,300 individuals (0.002 of 1 percent of the American population) exercise formal authority over more than half of the nation's industrial assets, two-thirds of all banking assets, more than half of all assets in communications and utilities, and more than two-thirds of all insurance assets (Dye, 1995).

Although the American economy is dominated by a relatively small number of large corporations, it also includes millions of small and medium-sized businesses that operate in competitive markets. In a very real sense, then, the American economy is a *dual economy* made up of two distinct sectors: a highly concentrated and managed sector composed of the big corporations, and a highly competitive sector composed of much smaller firms. These two sectors have been labeled, respectively, the *center* and the *periphery* (Averitt, 1968). Firms in the periphery rarely compete against firms in the center. Indeed, smaller firms usually do not even compete with the large corporations for the same workers, for labor market segmentation has accompanied the growth of the dual economy.

The labor market brings together workers looking for jobs and employers seeking to hire workers. A *segmented labor market* is one that has been divided into separate sectors, each with its own workers and employers. Those who supply and employ labor in one segment do not compete with their counterparts in other segments. The modern American labor market is divided into three relatively distinct sectors: a secondary market, most closely associated with the peripheral economy; a subordinate primary market; and an independent primary market. Both of the latter are tied largely to the center economy.

The *secondary labor market* provides jobs that offer the least steady employment, the poorest working conditions, and the fewest opportunities for job advancement. These include the low-paid, low-skill jobs found in small, nonunion enterprises and clerical jobs in large firms in the center economy. The suppliers of labor in this market are disproportionately women and minorities, people who prefer to or are forced to work part time, and newcomers to the job market awaiting vacancies in one of the two primary markets.

The *subordinate primary labor market* consists of jobs that offer greater security, higher wages, more stable employment, and some opportunity for job advancement. Most of these advantages are derived from the relatively high degree of unionization characteristic of this sector. Production jobs in unionized industries (such as auto manufacturing and steelmaking) and unionized clerical and administrative jobs in the center economy fall into this category.

The jobs provided by the *independent primary labor market* offer relatively high pay, job security, and well-defined routes of career advancement. They usually require skills or knowledge acquired through specialized study. Craftsworkers (machinists and electricians, for example), professionals (accountants, lawyers, and engineers), and those who staff the sales and technical positions of large firms find their jobs in this segment (Rossides, 1998; Rothman, 1998).

Studies have found that racial and sex discrimination has occurred most frequently in hiring for primary jobs and in admission to schools, apprenticeship programs, and other institutions that qualify workers for jobs in this sector (Bowles & Edwards, 1985). Women and minority workers are overrepresented in the secondary labor market and thus do not have the same access that white men have to the more stable employment, the greater opportunities for job advancement, and the higher wages and salaries provided by the larger corporations in the center economy.

Although some white females with family responsibilities do choose to enter low-paying, nondemanding occupations (Polacheck, 1984), the most important factor responsible for the limited access of women and minorities is the center economy's preference for workers willing and able to make long-term commitments. Recruitment criteria based on this preference serve to discriminate against women—who may leave their jobs to have children—and to exclude many minority workers—who, like others employed in the low-level jobs found in the secondary labor market, commonly have erratic employment records (Katz, 1989).

The Roles of Government and Organized Labor

The early efforts by U.S. corporations to construct larger and more stable markets received indispensable assistance from both the government and organized labor. Indeed, for nearly 40 years between the end of the Great Depression and the start of the 1980s, corporate interests were closely allied with those of both the government and the nation's largest and most powerful unions.

GOVERNMENT. One of the major lessons of the Great Depression was that a capitalist economy is not fully capable of regulating, correcting, and stabilizing itself. If left to its own devices, it will regularly ride the roller coaster of inflation ups and depression downs. Beginning with Franklin Delano Roosevelt's New Deal policies in the 1930s, the American government started to take increased responsibility for stabilizing the economy as advocated by economist John Maynard Keynes. By manipulating the money supply and interest rates, by increasing or decreasing tax rates and federal spending, and by altering levels of unemployment compensation and welfare payments, the government was able to keep the economy on a more or less even keel.

As the government grew, it became a much more active consumer than it had been in the past. Government programs supporting housing and highway construction substantially increased the demand for building supplies, consumer goods, automobiles, and gas and oil—all markets dominated by large corporations (Piore & Sabel, 1984). In addition, the government facilitated the multinationalization of U.S. corporations by providing military protection for their investments around the world.

ORGANIZED LABOR. The 1935 Wagner Act is often referred to as "Labor's Bill of Rights." One of the Depression-era New Deal reforms, the Wagner Act created the legal framework for *collective bargaining* (negotiations between organized workers and their employers regarding working conditions, pay, and benefits). By protecting union supporters against employer reprisals, by legalizing certain types of strike activity, and by requiring companies to bargain in good faith with unions representing their employees, the Wagner Act encouraged the growth of the trade union movement.

Unions grew most rapidly in the industries controlled by large corporations. With their large concentrations of workers in one place, such firms were relatively easily organized. Moreover, because they encountered little competition, these corporations could easily pass on union-won wage increases to their customers in the form of higher prices. Unions achieved higher wages, better benefits, improved work conditions, and more job stability for their members. The unions also worked in the interests of the large corporations by supplying them with a less disruptive, more stable work force (Hearn, 1988).

LARGE CORPORATIONS VERSUS GOVERNMENT AND ORGANIZED LABOR. In the late 1970s, the large corporations began to act, often in concert, to weaken the government's influence on the economy and to reduce the power of organized labor. Once valued by the corporate sector for their contributions to large and stable markets, the government and the unions came to be viewed as profit-draining burdens. Corporations successfully fought for reductions in taxes, domestic government spending, and government regulations. Corporate lobbies and funding were also instrumental in the election of Ronald Reagan, whose administration's labor policies were widely regarded as antiunion in intention and effect (Bluestone & Harrison, 1982; Edsall, 1984).

Union membership grew steadily and significantly after passage of the Wagner Act, reaching a high of 34 percent of the nonagricultural labor force in 1956. Although this figure declined to 31.5 percent in 1960 and to 25.2 percent in 1980, the total number of organized workers in the economy grew from slightly over 18 million in 1960 to nearly 23 million in 1980. Throughout this period, the union movement remained a major force in politics and in the economy. All this changed in the 1980s. By 1998, only 13.9 percent of all workers were union members (U.S. Bureau of Labor Statistics, 1998). Should this trend continue, unions' share of the nonfarm work force could drop to below 13 percent by the year 2000—a share lower than that which existed prior to passage of the Wagner Act in the mid-1930s (Ford, 1988; Hearn, 1988).

This decline in union strength has led to a weakened bargaining position for organized labor. Throughout the 1980s and 1990s, unionized workers were forced to accept wage and benefit reductions and to accept concessions ("give-backs") on a number of previously won gains, such as protective work rules (rules that protect workers against arbitrary treatment by management) and cost of living agreements (in which automatic wage increases are tied to the inflation rate).

One of the major causes of this decline was the effective "union-avoidance" strategy adopted by many large corporations during the 1980s. Combining a number of elements—including an anti-union public relations campaign, illegal termination of employees seeking to organize labor unions, and the persistent threat (often acted on) of firing workers and moving jobs and production facilities to nonunion areas of the world—this strategy enabled the large corporations to appreciably decrease unions' size and influence (see Table 18.1) (Bluestone & Harrison, 1982; Freeman & Medoff, 1984).

Why have the large corporations, which once relied on government and organized labor, come to oppose both? The reasons are straightforward enough. In the 1970s, America's large corporations began to face ever-increasing international competition. Ford, General Motors, and Chrysler now had to compete against Japanese automakers. The large steel producers were compelled to compete against German, Japanese, and Korean steel producers. The government and unions could do little to stabilize this competition and its accompanying risks. Once allies of the large corporation, they came to be viewed by most corporate managers as obstacles to profit in an increasingly competitive global marketplace.

The Globalization of the Economy

For 30 years after World War II, America's large corporations not only controlled domestic markets but also had easy access to cheap foreign resources and foreign markets. During the 1970s, however, the dominant position held by American corporations was challenged from several directions. Ravaged during the war, the Japanese and European economies had rebounded sufficiently to compete successfully in both the world and U.S. markets. At the same time, many Third World countries adopted more aggressive development strategies. Those in the Pacific Rim—South Korea and Taiwan, for instance—used an export-oriented strategy that brought them into direct competition with U.S. corporations at home and abroad. Many Latin American countries, wishing to develop their own industries, insisted that U.S. multinationals use more Latin American products in their production process. Finally, raw material–exporting nations, primarily those in the Third World, created *cartels* (groups of producers that work together to favorably influence the market for their products) that substantially raised the cost of essential resources (Bowles, Gordon, & Weisskopf, 1983; Piore & Sabel, 1984). The best known of these cartels, OPEC (Organization of Petroleum Exporting Countries), was formed by oil-exporting nations.

As a result of these developments, U.S. corporations have found themselves part of a newly emerging global marketplace in which goods are produced wherever they can be made most cheaply. The least costly and most efficient sites for the manufacture of a wide range of mass-produced goods are Third World countries. These nations provide not only cheap labor, strict trade union restrictions, and low tax rates but also the fastest-growing markets for such goods as appliances and basic carbon steel. To remain competitive in mass-production industries, the very area of the economy in which the large U.S. corporations first rose to prominence, American companies increasingly have shifted their manufacturing facilities to the developing nations (Reich, 1983).

Central to the global marketplace is the *international division of labor*, in which developing countries are becoming the centers of production while the more advanced nations are transformed into international centers of corporate strategy, design, and finance. In the United States, the result has been "the evolution of a new kind of company: manufacturers that do little or no manufacturing. . . . They may perform a host of profit-making

TABLE 18.1   MEMBERSHIP IN SELECTED UNITED STATES UNIONS, 1975–1991

Labor Organization	1975	1985	1991	Labor Organization	1975	1985	1991
Total (in thousands)	**14,070**	**13,109**	**13,923**	Laborers	475	383	406
Actors and Artists	—	100	99	Letter Carriers (NALC)	151	186	210
Automobile, Aerospace and Agriculture (UAW)	—	974	840	Machinists and Aerospace (IAM)	780	537	534
Bakery, Confectionery and Tobacco	149	115	101	Office and Professional Employees	—	90	89
Boiler Makers, Iron Ship-Builders	123	110	66	Oil, Chemical, Atomic Workers (OCAW)	145	108	90
Bricklayers	143	95	84	Painters	160	133	124
Carpenters	712	616	494	Paperworkers Int'l.	275	232	202
Clothing and Textile Workers (ACTWU)	377	228	154	Plumbing and Pipefitting	228	220	220
Communication Workers (CWA)	476	524	492	Postal Workers	249	232	228
Electrical Workers (IBEW)	856	791	730	Retail, Wholesale Department Store	120	106	128
Electronic, Electrical and Salaried	255	198	160	Rubber, Cork, Linoleum, Plastic	173	106	89
Engineers, Operating	300	330	330	Seafarers	—	80	80
Firefighters	123	142	151	Service Employees (SEIU)	490	688	881
Food and Commercial Workers (UFCW)	1,150	989	997	Sheet Metal Workers	—	108	108
Garment Workers (ILGWU)	363	210	143	State, County, Municipal (AFSCME)	647	997	1,191
Glass, Molders, Pottery, and Plastics	—	104	80	Steelworkers	1,062	572	459
Government, American Federation (AFGE)	255	199	151	Teachers (AFT)	396	470	573
Graphic Communications	198	141	113	Teamsters	—	(X)	1,379
Hotel Employees and Restaurant Employees	421	327	269	Transit Union	—	94	98
Ironworkers	160	140	101	Transport Workers	95	85	85
				Transportation/ Communications International	—	102	73

[X] = not applicable.

Source: U.S. Bureau of the Census, *Statistical Abstract of the United States, 1993* (Washington, D.C.: U.S. Government Printing Office, 1993).

functions—from design to distribution—but lack their own production base. In contrast to traditional manufacturers, they are hollow corporations" (*Business Week*, March 3, 1986, p. 57).

Those corporations that continue to produce do so on a global scale, with production facilities spread across the world. As a consequence, the focus of these companies is more on their position in the world market than in the American market, and they are more responsive to changes in the world economy than to those in the U.S.

domestic economy (Cohen, 1988). Also, because it is such an important part of the global marketplace, the contemporary American economy is very sensitive to political, social, and economic developments throughout the world.

THE SOCIOLOGY OF WORK

Work has been regarded differently throughout the ages. The ancient Greeks saw labor as a necessary evil, to be left as much as possible to women and slaves while men engaged in lofty political and philosophical discussion. The early Christians regarded work as punishment inflicted on people as a result of original sin. In contrast, the work ethic espoused by the seventeenth-century Protestant Reformers envisioned work not as punishment but as a duty to God, the primary means of building God's kingdom on earth. In the secularized version of this notion, popular among the supporters of early capitalism, work became a duty to oneself and one's family.

All of these views continue to find expression in modern society. Some people experience work as a curse or a punishment, others as a duty to self, family, community, or cause, and still others as a mode of self-expression and a source of inner satisfaction.

The premise of an influential 1973 report, *Work in America,* issued by the then-Department of Health, Education, and Welfare, is that work, in addition to its obvious economic and social consequences, is a primary source of meaning in most people's lives. The report begins by identifying two important contributions that work makes to self-esteem:

> The first is that, through the inescapable awareness of one's efficacy and competence in dealing with objects of work, a person acquires a sense of mastery over both himself and his environment. The second derives from the view . . . that an individual is working when he is engaging in activities that produce something valued by other people. That is, the job tells the worker day in and day out that he has something to offer. (pp. 4–5)

To what degree does work in modern societies serve these functions? Is work ultimately satisfying or dissatisfying? These are the questions we try to answer in the sections that follow.

Worker Alienation and Satisfaction

Most sociological analyses of work have been influenced by Marx's writings on this topic. He was at his most passionate when criticizing capitalism for intensifying what he called the **alienation of labor.** Marx described dissatisfying, alienated labor as labor that is

> *external* to the worker, i.e., [work that] does not belong to his essential being. . . . [I]n his work, therefore, [the worker] does not affirm himself but denies himself, does not feel content but unhappy, does not develop freely his physical and mental energy but mortifies his body and ruins his mind. . . . His labor is therefore not voluntary, but coerced; it is *forced* labor. . . . Lastly, the external character of labor for the worker appears in the fact that it is not his own, but someone else's, that it does not belong to him, that in

it he belongs, not to himself, but to another. (Marx, 1964, pp. 110–111)

In other words, according to Marx, workers in industrial society have no control over their work. The machinery they use is owned by someone else, the products they make belong to someone else, and the processes they use to make the products are dictated by someone else. In this sense, workers are *alienated* from both their labor and the goods or services that they produce. For Marx, satisfying, nonalienated labor—that is, labor undertaken freely and cooperatively and as an end in itself—would be widely available only under communism. While few today agree with Marx in regarding capitalism as the fundamental cause of worker alienation, his ideas continue to influence the effort to understand what makes work more or less satisfying.

WORKER ALIENATION. One of the most common definitions of worker alienation includes four elements. The first is *powerlessness,* or the inability to control the work process or to influence the character of one's job. *Meaninglessness,* the second dimension, refers to the absence of a sense of purpose: The worker is unable to relate his or her job either to personal goals or to the larger purposes of the organization. The third dimension, *isolation,* occurs when the worker lacks a sense of belonging to the organization itself or of being connected to his or her fellow workers. The fourth dimension is *self-estrangement,* or alienation from self, which occurs when the job prevents the worker from expressing unique personal characteristics such as creativity and independent judgment (Blauner, 1964; Israel, 1971; Seeman, 1961).

Sociological studies of the relation between patterns of work organization and worker alienation have generally found that powerlessness, meaninglessness, isolation, and self-estrangement are experienced more strongly by those who labor in large bureaucratic corporations (see Chapter 7). Commonly, although not always, the larger the workplace, the higher the degree of worker alienation. Alienation becomes stronger as jobs become more simplified, as worker participation in influencing the work process decreases, and as work relations and job tasks become more formal (that is, more limited by explicitly stated and rigidly prescribed rules that minimize individual discretion) (Blauner, 1964; Ritzer & Walczak, 1986; Seeman, 1961).

The costs of job dissatisfaction are high. Worker alienation often leads to low self-esteem, low morale, sabotage at the workplace, and high absenteeism and turnover rates. All these factors detract from productivity. Consequently, many large corporations, stimulated in part by the growing competition created by the global economy, have sought to develop less alienating, more satisfying, and more productive work arrangements.

WORKER SATISFACTION. The *Work in America* report listed eight important factors associated with worker satisfaction (pp. 94–96):

1. High-status jobs that offer prestige, control, and personal satisfaction

2. Challenging jobs that provide variety and autonomy

3. Supervisory behavior that is considerate, thoughtful, and consultative

4. Jobs that allow peer interaction

5. High wages

6. Jobs with clearly defined opportunities for advancement

7. Good work conditions

8. Security of employment

Partly in response to the report and partly in an effort to raise productivity, a number of U.S. corporations have redesigned their work arrangements to incorporate some of the conditions that promote greater job satisfaction. These efforts have included three major reforms: job enlargement, job enrichment, and the establishment of relatively autonomous work groups (Derber & Schwartz, 1988; Kanter, 1983; Miller & Form, 1980).

Many modern jobs, especially those in factories and manufacturing plants, have been highly *routinized*—that is, they have been reduced to sets of simple, repetitive actions that require little experience, training, knowledge, or skill (Blau, 1974). Job enlargement is designed to overcome the fragmentation and job simplification caused by routinization. **Job enlargement** increases the number of tasks workers are expected to perform, makes the work experience more varied, and involves the workers in a wider range of work activity.

Job enrichment adds greater authority and responsibility, as well as additional tasks, to a job. Enriched jobs afford workers more room for initiative, discretion, creativity, and self-supervision. Like job enlargement, job enrichment creates more complex, challenging, and skilled jobs, and gives the individual worker greater control over his or her work.

In a system making use of **autonomous work groups,** relatively independent groups of 7 to 12 members each are assigned a complete set of tasks necessary to accomplish a broadly defined segment of the work process. Rotation from job to job, including the supervisor's job, occurs regularly within the group. In addition, each group is given substantial authority to decide on matters relating to recruitment, training, job evaluation, discipline, work design, and quality control.

Sociological research has shown that these reforms have resulted in increased job satisfaction, improved worker performance, and higher productivity. One review of many studies found strong support for "the proposition that increased worker job control increases job satisfaction and reduces worker alienation. [That] this is associated with increased worker performance and productivity [is supported by] . . . significant correlations between increased autonomy and participation, reduced absenteeism and turnover, and improved labor productivity and product quality" (Derber & Schwartz, 1988, p. 221).

Work Trends in the United States

WOMEN'S LABOR FORCE PARTICIPATION

Women's participation in the labor force has risen significantly since the end of World War II (see Chapter 13). In 1970, only 43.3 percent of all women 16 years and over were in the labor force. This figure jumped to 51.5 percent in 1980 and 59.8 percent in 1997. In contrast, the rate of men's labor force participation has been gradually decreasing, from 79.7 percent in 1970 to 75 percent 27 years later. Even more dramatic has been the sharp increase in the labor force involvement of married women and mothers of small children. The proportion of married women in the labor force rose from 40.5 percent in 1970 to 49.8 percent in 1980 and 62.1 percent in 1997. In 1975, the participation rate of married women with children under 6 years of age was only 36.7 percent. By 1997, that figure reached 63.6 percent (U.S. Bureau of the Census, *Statistical Abstract of the United States, 1998*).

The increase in the rate of women's labor force participation is a reflection of the growing gender equality in American society. Over the past two decades especially, women's career opportunities have sharply increased. But their greater level of participation in the labor force is also a sign of broader demographic and occupational changes. The rise of women's participation has paralleled the growth of single-parent and female-headed families, suggesting that more women have found it necessary to join the labor force. A similar type of pressure has been generated by the loss of relatively high-paying manufacturing jobs and their replacement by lower-paying service jobs. The loss in income to male workers brought about by these changes has forced many wives and mothers to enter the labor force.

DEINDUSTRIALIZATION

Deindustrialization, the systematic withdrawal of private investment from manufacturing, exploded on the American economy in the early 1970s and continued at an accelerated pace throughout the 1980s (Bluestone & Harrison, 1982; Mishel, 1989). Deindustrialization has seriously eroded the manufacturing basis of the economy. Over 1 million jobs in manufacturing, mining, and construction have been lost since 1989 (Mishel, Bernstein, & Schmitt, 1997).

The deterioration of the American industrial base was sparked by the same developments associated with the globalization of the economy. In the international division of labor that characterizes the global marketplace (discussed earlier), labor and materials are sought wherever they can be obtained most cheaply. Thus, U.S. manufacturers, seeking to cut costs, either shifted productive facilities and jobs to low-wage developing countries or phased out production of noncompetitive lines completely. In addition, there is some evidence that deindustrialization was promoted by corporate managers in a deliberate effort to weaken unions (Bluestone & Harrison, 1982). The bulk of the jobs lost as a consequence of deindustrialization were middle-wage, unionized, subordinate primary market jobs.

EXPANSION OF THE SERVICE SECTOR

Despite the loss of manufacturing jobs, the American economy experienced a period of job growth in the 1980s and 1990s. Most of the new jobs that emerged during this time were created in the service sector. Today, the number of service jobs outnumbers the number of manufacturing

HOT JOBS	ANNUAL SALARY
Chief information officer	$100,000–$200,000
Wireless engineer	80,000–120,000
Software-development manager	60,000–100,000
Computer-systems architect	60,000–100,000
Database manager	60,000–80,000
Director of e-commerce	50,000–80,000
Webmaster	50,000–70,000
Tool-and-die worker	40,000–70,000
Teacher trainer	35,000–60,000
Telemarketer/customer rep.	20,000–35,000

FASTEST–GROWING JOBS, 1996–2006, PERCENT INCREASE

Database manager	118%
Computer engineer	109
Systems analyst	103
Personal/home aide	85
Physical–therapy assist.	79
Home health aide	76
Medical assistant	74
Desktop publisher	74
Physical therapist	71
Occupational therapist	69

FIGURE 18.2 Job growth at the beginning of the twenty-first century will occur in the service sector. The salaries for specific jobs will span a wide range.

Source: From *Newsweek,* February 1, 1999, p. 44. © 1999 Newsweek, Inc. All rights reserved. Reprinted by permission.

Do you believe that the increase in the participation of women in the labor force is a reflection of growing gender equality or more related to the conditions of the economy?

jobs. And the U.S. Bureau of Labor Statistics projects that 17.6 million of the 18.6 million new jobs that will be added to the U.S. economy between 1996 and 2006 will be generated by the service sector (see Figure 18.2).

The service sector includes a wide range of jobs, and some are relatively well paid. For example, in 1997, the mean annual wage for a systems analyst was $51,360; data base administrators made $47,960. But service workers at the other end, such as sales clerks and fast-food workers, earned minimum wage salaries (U.S. Bureau of Labor Statistics, 1999).

The shift from a goods-producing economy to a service economy has thus brought an increase in high-earnings jobs but an even greater increase in low-paid jobs clearly inferior to the manufacturing jobs lost

GLOBAL SOCIETY

COMPETING IN THE TWENTY-FIRST CENTURY

As the twentieth century came to a close, nations worldwide understood the realities of a global economy. When South Korea's economy nearly collapsed in 1997, members of the international community put together a loan package worth $55 billion in an effort to avoid a disaster (Bagby, 1998). Three world lending institutions—the International Monetary Fund, the World Bank, and the Asian Development Bank—contributed $35 billion. The remaining $20 billion came from the United States and a number of other countries. Japan's economy, which began a downward slide in 1992, sparked additional concern in 1997 when banking difficulties contributed to its own economic plight.

Americans watched the stock market anxiously for months on end, fearing that the United States would feel the impact of the Asian economic crisis. But the U.S. economy remained strong, bolstering the expansion that had begun in March 1991 in the aftermath of the Persian Gulf War. Many analysts described the U.S. economy as booming, reinforcing Clinton's boast to leaders at the G-7 summit in June 1997 that "America's economy is the healthiest in a generation and the strongest in the world" (Bagby, 1998, p. 49).

But Americans had not forgotten the problems that accompanied a troubled economy just a decade earlier. In 1982, the unemployment rate in America had reached as high as 9 percent. American companies, which were struggling to keep up with foreign competition, downsized their work forces. Autoworkers were hit especially hard by Japan's successful invasion of the automobile market. And autoworkers would not soon forget the massive layoffs and plant closings that characterized the late 1980s.

Americans are not the only ones who feel the effects of global competition. The unemployment rates of other industrialized countries have reached levels twice as high as those in the United States (see Figure 18.3). But finding the solution for high unemployment is not easy. While all countries face the same global competitors, variations in the economic systems of individual countries suggest that the solution for one country may not work for another. Consider, for example, how the average number of hours worked per week varies from one country to another. For production workers, the average is 29 hours in Germany but 37.9 in the United States. The average hourly compensation for these workers also varies widely— Germans receive $31.87 while Americans earn only $17.74.

One solution for high unemployment is to increase the number of jobs by reducing the workweek (Tagliabue 1997). This idea is popular in both Italy and France, where the governments plan to reduce the number of hours in the legal workweek. Thinking along this line led Volkswagen to negotiate a deal with a workers' union to cut the average workweek from 36 hours to less than 29. Wages, in return, were cut by up to 15 percent. The agreement also stipulated that VW could increase the workweek up to 35 hours without having to pay overtime. This deal saved 20,000 out of 30,000 jobs.

Another solution, popular with a few European companies, is to

---

through deindustrialization. This shift has increased the proportion of low-wage jobs in the economy.

Yet most experts have argued that the erosion of the American economy's manufacturing base has been more than offset by the dramatic growth of service employment. They believe that America's hope for a prosperous economic future hinges on the continued expansion of the service sector. Some, however, regard this as a false hope, one that is dangerous to the extent that it discourages efforts to revitalize the nation's industrial sector. According to this view, services are a complement to, not a substitute for, manufacturing.

Nearly 70 percent of service employment in the United States is linked directly to manufacturing. Furthermore, most services are best performed in close proximity to the manufacturing facilities that utilize them. Accordingly, continued shrinkage of the economy's manufacturing base will probably mean the eventual loss of service jobs. This has already happened in the steel and electronics industries. Once the leading exporter of high-level services in these areas, the United States now imports these services from Japan and Europe (Cohen & Zysman, 1987).

FLEXIBLE WORK-SYSTEM ORGANIZATION

A revitalized American industrial base may need to rely on principles of work organization different from those used by many large U.S. corporations throughout most of the twentieth century. In the future, work may have to be

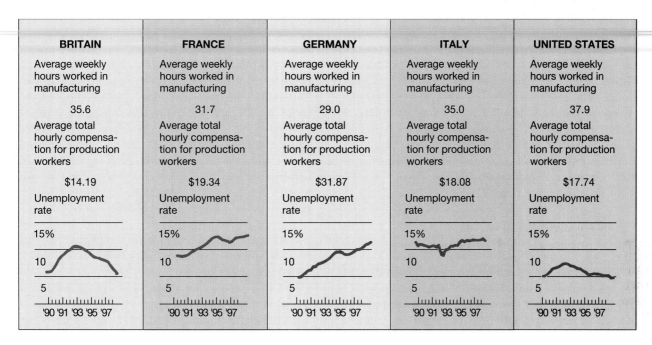

BRITAIN	FRANCE	GERMANY	ITALY	UNITED STATES
Average weekly hours worked in manufacturing	Average weekly hours worked in manufacturing	Average weekly hours worked in manufacturing	Average weekly hours worked in manufacturing	Average weekly hours worked in manufacturing
35.6	31.7	29.0	35.0	37.9
Average total hourly compensation for production workers	Average total hourly compensation for production workers	Average total hourly compensation for production workers	Average total hourly compensation for production workers	Average total hourly compensation for production workers
$14.19	$19.34	$31.87	$18.08	$17.74
Unemployment rate	Unemployment rate	Unemployment rate	Unemployment rate	Unemployment rate

FIGURE 18.3 It is hard to predict how the global economy will impact the varying work conditions of countries around the world.

Source: Bureau of Labor Statistics; DRI/McGraw-Hill; *New York Times,* November 12, 1997, p. C1.

implement more flexible work schedules in an attempt to reduce costs and improve productivity. While it may be difficult to implement this solution in countries that have rigid social structures and strong labor unions, it does reflect the reality of competition in a global economy—the need to respond to a rapidly changing marketplace (Tagliabue, 1997).

organized in such a way as to promote the production of more specialized, higher-quality goods.

The advantage of the United States in the international division of labor lies in its ability to manufacture products that require high-level skills and thus are protected against low-wage competition. Examples of such products include precision dies and tools that demand exacting engineering, testing, and maintenance skills; customized products, such as machine tools and multipurpose robots, designed to satisfy specialized needs; and technology-driven products like computers, fiber optics, and lasers. These types of products all require that traditionally separate business functions (research, design, engineering, purchasing, manufacturing, distribution, marketing, and sales) be merged into a highly integrated system that can respond quickly to new opportunities (Reich, 1983).

Many researchers have argued that the manufacturing of these specialized, sophisticated, high-quality goods requires **flexible-system production.** Flexible-system production achieves its capacity to shift quickly from one project to another by relying on (1) new computer technologies suited to the production of a wide variety of goods and (2) a dedicated work force in possession of skills that are applicable to a wide variety of production tasks. In direct contrast to the large bureaucratic corporation, the flexible-system work organization is characterized by a relatively minimal division of labor. Rather, it encourages teamwork and the diffusion of knowledge and skill; has a flatter hierarchical structure that, in many places, blurs the distinction between managerial and worker responsibilities; and has far fewer formal rules and regulations, thus giving workers more room to use their own creativity and judgment (Hearn, 1988).

Companies in many different industries—steel, papermaking, textiles, banking, chemicals, and computers—already have moved to flexible-system production (Bailey, 1990; Hirschhorn, 1984; Zuboff, 1988). In addition, a number of America's large corporations, including American Telephone and Telegraph, Johnson & Johnson, and Hewlett-Packard, have undertaken massive programs of reorganization in this direction. The extent to which flexible-system production will become a dominant model, however, remains unknown.

Cross-Cultural Perspective: The Economy and Work in Japan

While the United States emerged from World War II as the world's dominant economic and political power, Japan lay in ruins. By the 1980s, however, the Japanese had built the world's second-largest economy. The rapid development and the extraordinary achievements of the Japanese economy have been attributed to a number of factors, most especially to Japanese principles of work organization.

Until the mid-nineteenth century, Japan was a politically and economically isolated nation. The Japanese national character, with its emphasis on cooperation and the common good, can be traced in part to this isolationist tradition. But the nation's modern economy developed as a direct result of Western influences that began to penetrate in the late nineteenth century, after Commodore Perry and his U.S. gunboats forced Japan to open its doors to American trade. Western economic methods and technology were quickly imported and implemented by Japan's leaders. By the 1930s, Japan had become an important second-rank industrial power. World War II destroyed some of Japan's production capacity and deprived the nation of the economic benefits derived from its Asian empire. But with the aid of the Western nations, especially the United States, and the use of the most up-to-date technologies, postwar Japan initiated an intense industrialization drive.

Today the Japanese economy is structured around a number of large industrial groupings—loosely formed organizations typically consisting of 20 to 30 large firms often clustered around a major bank that provides them all with necessary financing. The firms in each grouping generally represent a single major industrial activity—shipping, electronics, steel production, or insurance, for example. Around each of the major firms cluster many smaller companies that supply a particular product or service to the larger firms (Morgan, 1997; Ouchi, 1981).

Although Japanese corporations are strongly oriented to making a profit, the typical firm is less concerned with short-term profits than is its American counterpart. Japanese executives plan for the long-term success of their companies and for the continued employment of their workers. Quick profits are likely to be sacrificed so that resources can be used to build a solid foundation for later, sustained success. The Japanese company will readily invest in training its employees to develop skills that may be needed in the future. Expensive technology is bought or developed if there is a good chance that it will benefit the company at a later date. Money may be spent to modernize plants to meet future needs, even though current production needs are being satisfied (Vogel, 1979). Furthermore, Japanese executives are trained to work for stability and for the overall, long-term growth of their companies. They are rewarded for meeting these goals, not for their ability to earn quick profits.

The Japanese government is intimately involved in business and the economy. Japanese businesses are owned and operated by the private sector, but the government tries to provide a framework that will enable business to prosper. Committed to overall economic success, the public bureaucracy performs many special planning functions and works closely with business to ensure economic growth. Important government officials stand ready to help business in emergencies, and will routinely aid them in locating land, assembling resources, or gaining new, vital technology. The government can also be relied upon not to take legal actions—including antitrust proceedings—that could damage a company's overall ability to operate effectively and profitably.

As these comments suggest, Japanese work organizations evolved differently than their U.S. counterparts. Work in Japan was organized as a series of collective undertakings. A consensus style of management, in which decision making was opened to relatively wide participation, developed. Teamwork at all levels of the organization led to a less fragmented division of labor than is typical in the United States, as did programs of continuous training designed to increase the skills of workers and the knowledge of managers. All this combined with lifetime employment practices to create high levels of employee trust and commitment. In this setting, the resistance to technological change characteristic of many American workers and managers never arose.

But the positive aspects of the Japanese system should not be overemphasized. The most highly publicized features of Japanese work organization are available to only 30 percent of the labor force (those employed in the 1,000 or so largest corporations). Much of the remaining 70 percent finds employment in low-wage, low-skill jobs in small firms that do not provide lifetime job security, consensus management, or continuous training programs. In addition, women, who make up 40 percent of Japan's work force, are overrepresented in these less desirable jobs. Furthermore, those women employed by large companies are usually given menial jobs, have limited opportunities for promotion, and are not covered by the security provisions and training programs made available to their male counterparts (Hearn, 1988).

Moreover, Japan's economy is not as strong as it used to be. Between 1987 and 1991, the Japanese economy was the fastest growing in the world (*The Economist,* March 24, 1992). In 1992, however, it fell victim to global recession and throughout the 1990s has been in a serious economic slump. How the Japanese economy might be redesigned to respond to this slump remains to be seen.

SOCIETY AND THE MARKET: A HUMANISTIC PERSPECTIVE

In the market, as we have seen, people are guided not by the spirit of altruism (unselfish concern for others) but rather by rational, self-interested calculation and the desire for profit. As a result, the market does not nurture—indeed, it discourages—strong moral bonds and deep emotional attachments, for these detract from the ability to calculate rationally the conditions that will best promote one's self-interest (Walzer, 1986; Wolfe, 1989).

Generally accepted standards of honesty, trust, cooperation, and social obligation, which depend on strong ties of altruism and solidarity, once "provided the necessary social binding for an individualistic, nonaltruistic market economy" (Hirsch, 1976, p. 142). In the absence of these social bonds, the market becomes increasingly callous, market relations less dependable, and market participants less concerned with the consequences of their actions. Indeed, sociological research has shown that, as more people guide more of their lives by the rational, self-interested logic of the marketplace, it becomes more and more difficult to sustain a market economy (Etzioni, 1989).

In "civil society"—families, friendships, kinship networks, informal work and religious groups, and voluntary associations—we experience trust, empathy, altruism, and solidarity. We learn how to care for ourselves and for one another. Both the modern state (as we saw in Chapter 17) and the modern market have invaded and weakened civil society. Social obligations are gradually losing their strength.

> Neither the state nor market speaks well of obligations to other people simply as people, treating them instead as citizens or as opportunities. Neither puts its emphasis on the bonds that tie the people together because they want to be tied together without regard for their immediate self-interest or for some external authority having the power to enforce those ties. Finally . . . , neither wishes to recognize . . . that people are capable of participating in the making of their own moral rules. (Wolfe, 1989, p. 12)

The revitalization of social obligation, and indeed the continuation of a rich and meaningful civil society, may require new efforts to curtail the incursions of the market as well as those of the state.

CHAPTER REVIEW

1. Describe the three primary sectors of the economy.

2. Give examples that illustrate each of the following concepts: market economy, planned economy, mixed economy, private ownership, public ownership, cooperative ownership.

3. Identify and discuss the fundamental differences between capitalism and socialism.

4. How has the strong tradition of individualism in the United States shaped Americans' beliefs about economic matters?

5. Describe the economic concentration in the United States today.

6. How has the globalization of the economy changed the way that corporations operate?

7. How can employers decrease worker alienation?

8. Describe the latest work trends in the United States. How will these shape society in the twenty-first century?

INTERNET EXERCISE

The Web destinations for Chapter 18 cover various aspects of the economy and work. To begin your explorations, go to the Prentice Hall Companion Web site **http://www.prenhall.com/popenoe.** Next, select Chapter 18 (The Economy and Work). Then choose **web destinations** from the menu on the left side of the screen. There, you will find a variety of sites to investigate. We suggest you begin with the home page for the **American Federation of Labor–Congress of Industrial Organizations (AFL-CIO).** The AFL-CIO is one of the largest workers' unions in the country. The text points out that the decline in union strength over the past two decades has led to a weakened bargaining position for organized labor. Inside the AFL-CIO Web site, you will be able to explore a wide variety of current issues that affect organized labor today. In particular, you may wish to focus your attention on "union membership and pay." After you have explored the AFL-CIO site, answer the following questions:

- The text points out that one of the major causes of the decline in union strength was the effective "union-avoidance" strategy adopted by many large corporations during the 1980s. What strategies have organized labor unions like the AFL-CIO utilized to combat this trend?
- What do you think the *future* of organized labor will be in the United States?

KEY TERMS

economy	planned economy	alienation of labor
primary sector	capitalism	job enlargement
secondary sector	socialism	job enrichment
tertiary sector	mixed economy	autonomous work groups
decentralized economy	market socialism	deindustrialization
centralized economy	democratic socialism	flexible-system
market economy	economic concentration	production

CHAPTER 19

Population and Ecology

he world is overflowing with people. The total human population increases by three individuals every second, 250,000 per day, and between 90 million and 100 million per year (United Nations Population Fund, 1990). The growth of the world's population has been truly staggering in the twentieth century. It took all of history up to 1815 for the total human population to reach 1 billion. The jump to 2 billion took another 100 years. It then took 35 years for the population to reach 3 billion, 14 years to reach 4 billion, and 12 years to reach 5 billion. Today there are more than 5.9 billion people on Earth, and the number continues to climb relentlessly.

Americans are accustomed to reading about the global population explosion, but the threat may seem a little abstract to many of us because the United States is much less overpopulated than are most other nations. More than 94 percent of the world's population growth is taking place in the developing countries of the Third World. Americans may have to search a little longer for a parking place at the mall because of our rising population; in contrast, a study of Hong Kong showed that almost three decades ago the average person lived in just 43 square feet, 39 percent of Hong Kong residents shared dwelling units with nonrelatives, 28 percent slept three to a bed, and 13 percent slept four or more to a bed (Mitchell, 1971).

Research has led to contradictory findings concerning the effects of such crowding. Some animal studies have found that prolonged exposure to very crowded conditions leads to increases in infant mortality and a wide variety of other forms of pathological behavior (Calhoun, 1962). Studies of humans are less conclusive, but there is no doubt that swelling populations are making it increasingly difficult for some countries, particularly in Africa, to feed and house their people. Population growth also spurs international migration patterns as people seek economic opportunity, and it clearly promotes the massive depletion of natural resources such as clean air and water and fossil fuels.

For these and many other reasons, an understanding of the dynamics of population growth and decline, and of the relationship of human populations to their environments—in modern and premodern countries alike—has never been so important as it is today. In this chapter, we introduce the basic concepts of population change and describe its effects on society. We conclude by considering these dynamics in their *ecological context*—the relationship between human populations and their living and nonliving environments.

THE STUDY OF POPULATION

Only about a century ago, population was studied not by sociologists but by mathematicians, economists, and politicians. With the rise of sociology, however, came an increased awareness of the social factors that influence population size, composition, distribution, and change. In addition, sociologists began to realize that population has important effects on personality, social structure, and culture. Although the study of population—called **demography**—still spans several disciplines, it has become one of the most highly developed and important areas of specialization within sociology.

Demographic research is heavily quantitative; indeed, in this respect, demography is probably the most fully developed area of sociology. But the scientific study of population emerged only recently. Early population specialists had to work with very unreliable data, which were often more the result of guesswork or intuition than of scientific procedure. Today most countries regularly and systematically collect population data, although these data are still far from perfect, especially in developing countries. Scientific demography has also advanced through the development of the computer, which has made the collection and the analysis of population data easier, faster, and more accurate than ever before.

Sources of Population Data

The most important source of population data is a **census,** or periodic head count that also usually gathers such personal data as age, sex, and occupation. Census taking began long ago. The Romans tried to count the number of residents in their empire. England's famous Domesday Book is a report of a national census of property and population taken in 1086, for tax purposes, by order of William the Conqueror. In modern times, censuses have been conducted regularly. The U.S. Constitution established as a duty of the federal government the taking of a census of "all free Persons, including those bound to Service for a Term of Years, and excluding Indians not taxed." Since 1790, a national census has been conducted every 10 years.

A census is an enormous and costly undertaking. In developed nations, censuses are taken periodically as a matter of course. But in less developed countries, lack of funds and skilled personnel make data collection difficult. Although the United Nations, together with countries such as the United States, England, France, and Sweden, have helped developing countries improve their censuses, accurate and up-to-date population data about these countries are often difficult to obtain.

The U.S. census, administered by the Bureau of the Census, collects data about the age, sex, residence, marital status, race, and ethnicity of all people in the United States, both citizens and noncitizens. Additional details on such personal characteristics as occupation, housing, income, and education are collected from a representative sample of the population. On the basis of this sample, estimates are made for the population as a whole. The 1990 census—conducted, processed, and published at a cost of more than $2.6 billion, or about $1,040 per person counted—is the most extensive social survey in American history. A census questionnaire was mailed to nearly 100 million housing units. A staff of more than 315,000 followed up on those who did not respond to the mailing.

The main challenge to the U.S. census is to achieve and maintain a high level of accuracy. Reliable results are vitally important, because the census count is the basis for determining representation in Congress and in state legislatures, as well as being used to allocate federal and state funds for education, health, and other services. Hand tabulation was once a source of substantial census error, but in the last several decades, computerized systems have reduced such problems considerably.

Probably the greatest obstacle to census accuracy is that some parts of the population may be undercounted. Although the 1990 census located 98 percent of the population and is considered one of the most accurate ever conducted, undercounting did occur (U.S. Bureau of the Census, 1992a). The Census Bureau has identified some of the major factors responsible for this problem: fear and suspicion among those who are present in the country illegally or who might be subject to eviction from their dwellings if they were reported; movement from one locality or region to another, with the confusion that such moving entails; and apathy resulting from general ignorance regarding the importance of the census.

Undercounting is especially likely to occur in cities. The Census Bureau estimates that the 1990 census undercounted African-Americans by 4.8 percent, Hispanic-Americans by 5.2 percent, Asian/Pacific Island-Americans by 3.1 percent, and Native Americans by 5.0 percent (U.S. Bureau of the Census, 1990c). Ironically, these groups are among those most in need of services for which private funding is required. When minority areas lose some of their voting strength because of undercounting, the census data can seriously affect the health and welfare of the community.

In addition to census data, demographers also use state and federal government records of **vital statistics**—the number of births, deaths, marriages, and divorces—to document and study population changes. As with census data, the quality of these records varies greatly from state to state and from country to country. In some countries, such as Sweden, accurate vital statistics have been collected for well over a century. In many Third World countries, however, the records are quite unreliable. In the United States, it was not until 1933 that every state required such record keeping. Today the quality of

American vital statistics (compiled separately by each individual state) is very high.

Population Composition: Sex and Age

Population composition refers to significant biological or social characteristics of a population, such as sex, age, race, place of residence, marital status, size of household, occupation, and income. Demographers are particularly concerned with two biological traits, sex and age, because these population characteristics are critically important for the study of such phenomena as fertility and death rates, the employability of the population, and the number of dependent people (children, young people, the elderly) in the society. Age and sex data help demographers analyze a society's needs, target any potential problems, determine growth rates, and make population projections.

SEX RATIO

Census data on the number of males and females in a population are usually expressed in terms of a **sex ratio,** or the number of males for every 100 females. If the sex ratio is exactly 100, there is an equal number of males and females. If it is a number higher than 100, there are more males than females. If it is a number lower than 100, there are more females than males. For example, if the sex ratio is 105, there are 105 males for every 100 females; if the ratio is 87, there are 87 males for every 100 females.

In the United States, as in most of the world, the sex ratio is high at birth. In 1990, there were 2.0 million male births and 1.9 million female births; thus, the sex ratio at birth was 1.05 (U.S. Department of Health and Human Services, 1991). Although boys initially outnumber girls, they gradually lose their lead. Males at every age have higher death rates than females do, and as a result, women in the United States greatly outnumber men. The 1990 census counted almost 21 million more women than men over the age of 65 (U.S. Bureau of the Census, 1990).

Because females tend to live longer, many observers have concluded that they are biologically healthier and stronger than males. But nonbiological factors also contribute to the imbalance. Military combat and other physically dangerous activities have traditionally been the primary or exclusive province of men, so the victims have mostly been male. As a result, unbalanced sex ratios are very common after periods of war. To take another example, throughout the nineteenth century and for a part of the twentieth, the United States had more men than

APPLYING SOCIOLOGY

MEASURING RACE

Every 10 years, the Census Bureau asks all of us to describe ourselves. For the most part, we do not need to give much thought to the questions the bureau asks. The answers are simple and straightforward—sex: male or female; age and year of birth; marital status: now married, widowed, divorced, separated, never married. But for many Americans, one question is not so easy to answer: race.

The 1990 census allowed Americans to fill in only one race (see Figure 19.1). And that created a problem for many people whose parents were of different races. In fact, in 1990, 2.6 million children lived in married-couple households composed of parents of different races, or ones where a Hispanic was married to a non-Hispanic (O'Hare, 1998).

If you are wondering why the Census Bureau needs to ask about race at all, there are many reasons. For one thing, figures on race are required for the Justice Department's review of congressional redistricting. They are also needed for mortgage lending and desegregation (Roberts, 1995).

But racial categories present many problems. The 1990 census included as one racial category "Black or Negro." Because the word Negro had fallen out of favor, some blacks skipped this classification entirely and wrote in "African-American" under the category "other."

The push to revise racial and ethnic categories has come largely from parents of mixed-race school-age children. Their concern was that school systems that allow for only one racial classification put children in the difficult and confusing position of choosing the race of one parent over another (O'Hare, 1998). The push from parents to change racial categories on federal surveys and the census has succeeded. In 1997, the Federal Interagency Committee for the Review of the Racial and Ethnic Standards recommended that respondents to surveys and the census have the option of identifying themselves with more than one race. And, in fact, the 2000 census form is designed to allow Americans to select more than one racial category (see Figure 19.1). Other revisions in the designation of race include the modification of the

"black" category to "black or African American," the Hispanic designation as "Hispanic or Latino," and the division of the single category of Asian or Pacific Islander into two: Native Hawaiian and other Pacific Islander, and Asian.

These changes will create some problems when it comes to comparing populations over time. For example, a racial tabulation of 1990 census data contained five cells: white, black, American Indian, Eskimo or Aleut, Asian or Pacific Islander, and other. Tabulating racial data from the 2000 census could require 64 race cells. These differences will make it difficult to calculate the growth of the black population from 1990 to 2000. And that undoubtedly will contribute to controversies surrounding political redistricting. At the same time, these new racial and ethnic guidelines are expected to provide a wealth of information about the increasingly diverse American population.

women, largely because more men emigrated here. In fact, women did not outnumber men in the United States until the end of World War II. In 1920, the sex ratio was 104.1; by 1940, it had dropped to 100.7; in 1950, after World War II, the sex ratio was 98.6; by 1980, it was only 94.5; by 1990, it was 95.1, and it is expected to be 95.5 by the 2000 census (U.S. Bureau of the Census, *Statistical Abstract of the United States, 1998*).

2000 census

Person 2

What is this person's name? *Print name below.*
Last Name

First Name   MI

Census information helps your community get financial assistance for roads, hospitals, schools, and more.

How is this person related to person 1?
Mark(X) ONE box.
- Husband/Wife
- Natural-born son/daughter
- Adopted son/daughter
- Stepson/stepdaughter
- Brother/sister
- Father/mother
- Grandchild
- Parent-in-law
- Son-in-law/daughter-in-law
- Other relative — *Print exact relationship.*

IF NOT RELATED to Person 1:
- Roomer/boarder
- Housemate, roommate
- Unmarried partner
- Foster Child
- Other nonrelative

What is this person's sex? *Mark (X) ONE box.*
- Male
- Female

What is this person's age and what is this person's date of birth?
Print numbers in boxes.
Age on April 4, 1998   Month   Day   Year of birth

NOTE: Please answer both questions 5 and 6.

Is this person Spanish/Hispanic/Latino? *Mark(X) in the "NO" box if not Spanish/Hispanic/Latino*
- **No,** not Spanish/Hispanic/Latino
- Yes, Mexican, Mexican Am., Chicano
- Yes, other Spanish/Hispanic/Latino—*Print group.*
- Yes, Puerto Rican
- Yes, Cuban

What is this person's race? *Mark(X) one or more races to indicate what this person considers himself/herself to be.*
- White
- Black, African Am., or Negro
- American Indian or Alaska Native—*Print name of enrolled or principal tribe.*
- Asian Indian
- Chinese
- Filipino
- Japanese
- Korean
- Vietnamese
- Native Hawaiian
- Guamanian or Chamorro
- Samoan
- Other Asian—*Print race.*   Other Pacific Islander—*Print race.*
- Some other race — *Print race.*

If more people live here, continue with Person 3.

1990 census

Please fill one column for each person listed in Question 1a on page 1.

Last Name
First Name   Middle Initial

2. How is this person related to PERSON 1?
Fill ONE circle for each person.
If Other relative of person in column 1, fill circle and print exact relationship, such as mother-in-law, grandparent, son-in-law, niece, cousin, and so on.

If a RELATIVE OF PERSON 1:
- Husband/wife
- Natural-born or adopted son/daughter
- Stepson/ stepdaughter
- Brother/sister
- Father/mother
- Grandchild
- Other relative

IF NOT RELATED to person 1:
- Roomer, boarder, or foster child
- Housemate, roommate
- Unmarried partner
- Other nonrelative

3. Sex
Fill ONE circle for each person.
- Male
- Female

4. Race
Fill ONE circle for the race that the person considers himself/herself to be.

If **Indian (Amer.)** print the name of the enrolled or principal tribe.

If **Other Asian or Pacific Islander (API)** print one group, for example: Hmong, Fijian, Laotian, Thai, Tongan, Pakistani, Cambodian and so on.

If **Other race**, print race.

- White
- Black or Negro
- Indian(Amer.) (Print the name of the enrolled or principal tribe.)
- Eskimo
- Aleut

Asian or Pacific Islander (API)
- Chinese
- Filipino
- Hawaiian
- Korean
- Vietnamese
- Japanese
- Asian Indian
- Samoan
- Guamanian
- Other API

- Other race (Print race)

5. Age and year of birth
a. Print the person's age at last birthday. Fill in the matching circle below each box.
b. Print each person's year of birth and fill the matching circle below each box.

a. Age	b. Year of Birth
0 0 0 0 0	0 0 0 0 0 0
1 0 1 0 1 0	1 0 1 0 1 0
2 0 2 0	2 0 2 0
3 0 3 0	3 0 3 0
4 0 4 0	4 0 4 0
5 0 5 0	5 0 5 0
6 0 6 0	6 0 6 0
7 0 7 0	7 0 7 0
8 0 8 0	8 0 8 0
9 0 9 0	9 0 9 0

6. Marital status
Fill ONE circle for each person.
- Now married
- Widowed
- Divorced
- Separated
- Never married

7. Is this person of Spanish/Hispanic origin?
Fill ONE circle for each person.
If Yes, other Spanish/Hispanic, print one group.
- No (not Spanish/Hispanic)
- Yes, Mexican, Mexican-Am., Chicano
- Yes, Puerto Rican
- Yes, Cuban
- Yes, other Spanish/Hispanic (Print one group, for example: Argentinean, Colombian, Dominican, Nicaraguan, Salvadoran, Spaniard, and so on.)

FOR CENSUS USE →

FIGURE 19.1 The 2000 census form will offer Americans far more options for racial classification than the 1990 form.

Source: American Demographics, April 1998, p. 43.

Sex ratios may be unbalanced regionally. In Alaska, which is still a frontier in some respects, there are 301,000 males and only 270,000 females. In Florida, there are 6.4 million males and 6.85 million females (U.S. Bureau of the Census, 1992a). As a general rule, in economically advanced nations, the sex ratio is lower in cities than in rural areas because of urban employment opportunities that attract more women than men. In cities with a great

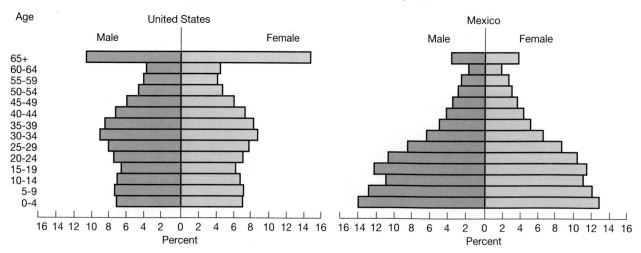

FIGURE 19.2 The age structure of the Mexican population is much different from that of the United States. This difference can be seen by comparing the two countries' population pyramids.

Source: U.S. Bureau of the Census, *International Data Base, 1992.*

deal of heavy industry, however, males often predominate. And in many cities in developing countries, such as India, the sex ratio tends to be high.

An important implication of sex ratios is the availability of marriage partners. The number of marriages in an age group depends partly on the number of available men and women. This is especially evident today in our elderly population, in which there are many more widows than widowers because of the greater longevity of women.

AGE

Historically, the American population has been heavily composed of young people. In the nineteenth century, both the birth rate and the death rate were high, so most of the population was concentrated in the younger age ranges. Since 1900, this state of affairs has gradually changed, for both the birth rate and the death rate have fallen considerably. Today the median age of the population is 34.9 years, and it is going up every year. In 1980, it was 30 years (U.S. Bureau of the Census, 1998).

The **age structure** (the relative proportions of different age categories) of a country's population can be represented by a *population pyramid.* Figure 19.2 shows population pyramids for Mexico and the United States. Each bar on the pyramids represents an **age cohort**—a grouping of people of a given age. In this case, the cohorts are five-year age groupings, and the percentage within each cohort is a portion of the total population (both male and female). Males are represented on the left side, females on the right.

The shape of the population pyramid for the United States is expected to change substantially. The U.S. population structure is fast becoming rectangular in shape, a phenomenon known as "squaring the pyramid." Fewer people are dying in the early years of life, and Americans are, on the average, living longer. If these trends continue, the result will be an almost perfectly rectangular population pyramid by the year 2030 (U.S. Department of Health and Human Services, 1991). However, the shape of the population pyramid will undoubtedly be influenced by migration, a factor that renders future trends less predictable.

The members of a given age cohort share certain experiences throughout their lives (Easterlin, 1980). For example, the bulge in the American population pyramid for the age groupings 25 through 39 represents cohorts born during the post–World War II baby boom. Because of its large size, this segment of the population has experienced special problems, including strong competition for jobs and housing.

A population's age structure has a major impact on a society's level of economic productivity, or its ability to produce goods and services. In industrial societies, the very young and the very old are usually not economically productive. Although children and the elderly can help with some of the chores on a farm, their services are generally not needed in factories and offices. In fact, many advanced societies have enacted laws specifically preventing children from working at many kinds of jobs. People in certain age categories thus become increasingly dependent on the productivity of others. If the number of dependents becomes too large relative to the number of productive people, serious economic problems can arise.

An analysis of the 1990 census data shows that almost 21 percent of the population in the United States is under 15 and about 12 percent over 65. To this group of relatively nonproductive citizens must be added another 13.5 percent or more of the population aged 15 to 24 who are in high school, college, vocational training, or business apprenticeships and are therefore still economically dependent. Thus, 46.5 percent of the total population of the United States is dependent (U.S. Bureau of the Census, 1992a).

This figure may seem large, but it is significantly smaller than those found in some developing nations. Recall the radically different age structures of the United States and Mexico, as shown in the population pyramids in Figure 19.2. In Mexico, 38 percent of the population was under the age of 15 in 1992, compared with 21 percent in the United States. In Mexico, the 15–19 age group is the largest single cohort. In the United States, the largest age group is 30–34 (U.S. Bureau of the Census, 1992a).

The huge population of young people presents Mexico with many current and future problems. Perhaps the greatest is the prospect of another century of population growth. The "population momentum" established by a youthful age structure is an extremely powerful social force. Even if all Mexican women currently of childbearing age had only enough children to replace themselves and their husbands, the country's population would not stop growing until 2075 (Merrick, 1986).

ELEMENTS OF POPULATION CHANGE

Like a still photograph capturing one moment of a continuous action, the *decennial* census, taken every 10 years, provides a snapshot of the population at one point in time. To understand the way a population is changing in size and composition, the demographer tries to construct an explanation of the events that happened before the census and of events that can be expected to take place after it.

Demographers commonly make **population projections,** or extrapolations, that estimate future population trends. Projections can be wrong; the history of demographic analysis is replete with mistaken estimates of population trends. For example, census data collected in 1950 and 1960 showed that the population of the United States had increased by 18.6 percent between those years. A projection made in the 1960s and based on that rate of increase, predicted that the U.S. population would hit 220 million in 1970. Because of a substantial drop in the birth rate during the last few years of the 1960s, however, this projection was too high; the actual population in 1970 was only about 203 million.

In contrast to a projection, a **population forecast** is an estimate of the future population based on assumptions about how social, economic, and technological developments will affect demographic trends (Peterson, 1975, 1985). For example, a forecast assuming that medical innovations will continue to extend longevity in the United States would predict a larger future population than a forecast assuming that the average longevity will stay unchanged.

Three basic factors cause a population to grow or decline: fertility (births), mortality (deaths), and migration. They are the keys to explaining past patterns and to predicting trends in the future. Let us examine each in turn.

Fertility

The rate of **fertility,** or the frequency with which births occur in a population, depends on both biological and social factors. The most important biological factor is the number of women of childbearing age in the population. To determine the fertility rate, demographers choose age ranges, such as 14 to 44 or 15 to 49, that roughly match the biological limits of the childbearing years. They then count the number of women within those age ranges to find the number of potential bearers of children.

Another biological factor influencing fertility is the general health of women of childbearing age. If, for example, an epidemic of rubella (German measles) strikes a community, the birth rate will drop because more pregnancies will end in miscarriages. Similarly, the women of a community hit hard by severe famine will be biologically restricted in their ability to bear children.

The greatest influence on a society's fertility rate, however, results from social attitudes toward reproduction. There has never been a society whose actual fertility rate came close to its level of **fecundity,** or the maximum biological capacity of the women in the population to produce children. Demographers have identified three general categories of means by which fertility may be controlled (Davis & Blake, 1956; see also Easterlin & Crimmins, 1988). The first category consists of factors that constrain sexual intercourse, such as the socially acceptable age at first marriage, norms of premarital sexual behavior, and the value placed on chastity. In the second category are factors that limit conception: artificial birth-control methods and ideals regarding family size. The last category consists of factors affecting the actual birth and survival of infants, such as abortion and infanticide.

For most of human history, societies have struggled to overcome both high death rates and underpopulation. Most traditional societies encouraged the highest practical rates of reproduction; the biblical command of "be

Planned Parenthood clinics have aided millions of American women to control their own reproductive lives.

meaning that at present rates the average U.S. woman will bear 2.0 children over the course of her life (Population Reference Bureau, 1999). The nation's total fertility rate has held fairly steady for the last decade.

Fertility varies from one segment of a population to the next. In the United States, for example, because of differing class attitudes about reproduction and family size, as well as differing levels of knowledge about, and access to, safe and effective methods of birth control, lower-class families tend to be larger than middle- and upper-class families. Also, rural birth rates are almost always higher than urban birth rates. Catholics have had higher fertility rates than Protestants and Jews, although these differences have narrowed greatly in recent decades. Blacks have higher fertility rates than whites, although this reflects class more than racial differences. And women who are not in the labor force tend to have higher fertility rates than do working women. Understanding these kinds of factors helps demographers predict future trends.

fruitful and multiply" was widely reflected in social norms. Only recently has this state of affairs changed. Thanks to medical advances that prolong life and technological discoveries that have made it easier to cope with the natural environment, the populations of most of the world's societies are large and growing. Although a high national fertility rate is no longer desirable, attitudes and norms in many societies have not completely shifted to encourage fewer births. How to change these social attitudes is one of the most difficult problems facing developing nations today.

In the United States and other developed nations, this change in attitudes has, for the most part, already taken place. The number of people who practice birth control has greatly increased. Most Americans consider a two-child family ideal. And the average age at first marriage has been steadily rising, reducing the number of married women of childbearing age. (This effect has been temporarily offset, however, by the large number of women of childbearing age in the baby boom cohorts.)

Birth rates are commonly expressed in terms of the number of births per year for every 1,000 members of the total population. This figure is called the **crude birth rate.** The **age-specific birth rate** is determined by counting the number of births for every 1,000 women in a specific age group, such as 20 to 24.

One of the demographic measures used most commonly today is the **total fertility rate (TFR)**—the average number of children a woman will have, assuming the current age-specific birth rate remains constant throughout her childbearing years (roughly ages 15 through 49). The total fertility rate in the United States was 2.0 in 1999,

Mortality

A society's level of mortality is based on its technological and medical knowledge and its willingness to use that knowledge to make good health and long life available to its people. The United States invests heavily in programs designed to control the causes of death—more heavily, in fact, than in programs devoted to controlling fertility. The result has been a steady decrease in death rates.

Like fertility rates, mortality rates vary among different segments of the population. The highest rates are found among the lower classes, mainly because of poor environmental conditions and limited access to health care (see Chapter 10).

During the twentieth century, there has been a dramatic change in the major causes of death in the United States, a shift from death by communicable diseases to death by degenerative and human-caused illnesses. In 1900, the leading causes of death were pneumonia, influenza, tuberculosis, and diarrhea. In 1997, the leading causes were heart disease, cancer, and stroke (National Center for Health Statistics, 1998). All of these are related to environment and lifestyle. Smoking, drinking, stress, lack of exercise, diet, and pollution have been linked to the diseases that now claim the lives of most Americans (see Table 19.1).

There are a number of ways to measure mortality. We discuss three of them here.

CRUDE DEATH RATE. The **crude death rate** is the number of deaths per year for every 1,000 members of a population. For example, if a country had a total population of 10,000,000 and 110,000 of its people died in any

TABLE 19.1   TEN LEADING CAUSES OF DEATH, 1900 AND 1990

1900 Rank	Percent of Total Deaths	1990 Rank	Percent of Total Deaths
1. Pneumonia and influenza	11.8	1. Heart disease	33.5
2. Tuberculosis	11.3	2. Cancer	23.4
3. Diarrhea and enteritis	8.3	3. Stroke	6.7
4. Heart disease	8.0	4. Accidents	4.3
5. Stroke	6.2	5. Chronic obstructive pulmonary disease	4.1
6. Nephritis	5.2	6. Pneumonia and influenza	3.6
7. All accidents	4.5	7. Diabetes	2.3
8. Diseases of early infancy	4.2	8. Suicide	1.4
9. Cancer	3.7	9. Homicide	1.2
10. Senility	2.9	10. Chronic liver disease and cirrhosis	1.2

Sources: U.S. Bureau of the Census, *Historical Statistics of the United States, Colonial Times to 1970* (Washington, D.C.: U.S. Government Printing Office, 1976); U.S. Department of Health and Human Services, National Center for Health Statistics, 1991.

one year, its crude death rate would be 11: (110,000 divided by 10,000,000) × 1,000. The crude death rate is not very precise because it does not take into account the age structure of the population. An older population naturally has a higher crude death rate than a youthful one.

AGE-SPECIFIC DEATH RATE. The **age-specific death rate** is determined by counting the number of deaths for every 1,000 persons in a given age group. Age-specific death rates reveal some important patterns commonly found in advanced societies. The first year of life is a high-risk period, but it is followed by a sharp decline in death rates. The lowest rate is for those in the age group 5 to 14 years. The rate then slowly climbs with each year, until by age 60 it again reaches the level of the first year of life. After age 60, the rate climbs rapidly.

The age-specific death rate for infants is widely regarded as one of the best indicators of a society's general level of health and the quality of its medical care. A frequently used measure is the **neonatal mortality rate.** This is the age-specific death rate for children less than one month old, an age group that has a very high risk of death. The most commonly used measure is the crude **infant mortality rate,** or the number of deaths among infants less than one year old per 1,000 live births in a given year.

Although the infant mortality rate in the United States is low by international standards, it is by no means the lowest in the world. In 1997, the rate in the United States was 7.0, but Japan's was only 3.7 and Sweden's was 3.6. Canada, Australia, Ireland, and the United Kingdom also have rates lower than that of the United States (Population Reference Bureau, 1999). The higher U.S. rate is thought to result mainly from the lack of a comprehensive public health care system and inequalities in the availability of medical care (see Chapter 12) (Weber, 1988).

The developing nations are plagued by extremely high rates of infant mortality. India's rate is 72 and Egypt's is 52. In several of the smaller African and Asian nations, the figures are well over 100. Afghanistan's infant mortality rate is 150, Gambia's is 130, and Somalia's is 126 (Population Reference Bureau, 1999).

LIFE EXPECTANCY. **Life expectancy** refers to the average number of years of life remaining for persons of any given age. The great international variations in life expectancy among younger age groups reflect the progress each nation has made in combating infant and childhood diseases. In older age groups, there is less variation in life expectancy. For example, life expectancy for 70-year-old men is nearly the same in every country.

Life expectancy should not be confused with **life span,** which is the maximum length of life possible for any given species. The human life span has remained relatively constant over the centuries; very few people live past the age of 100. Life expectancy at birth, however, has risen dramatically, especially during the twentieth century, as communicable diseases have been conquered. Data for the United States are shown in Table 19.2, where it can be seen that women live longer than men and whites live longer than blacks. Women outlive men in virtually all countries of the world.

TABLE 19.2   LIFE EXPECTANCY IN THE UNITED STATES BY RACE AND SEX, 1900–1990

| | Life Expectancy | | | |
| | White | | Black and Other | |
Year	Male	Female	Male	Female
1990	72.6	79.3	68.4	76.3
1980	70.7	78.1	65.3	73.6
1970	68.0	75.6	61.3	69.4
1960	67.4	74.1	61.1	66.3
1950	66.5	72.2	59.1	62.9
1940	62.1	66.6	51.5	54.9
1930	59.7	63.5	47.3	49.2
1920	54.4	55.6	45.5	45.2
1910	48.6	52.0	33.8	37.5
1900	46.6	48.7	32.5	33.5

Note: Since 1990, life expectancy at birth has risen dramatically for all groups in the United States.

Sources: U.S. Bureau of the Census, *Historical Statistics of the United States, Colonial Times to 1970* (Washington, D.C.: U.S. Government Printing Office, 1976); U.S. Department of Health and Human Services, National Center for Health Statistics, 1991.

Migration

Migration is the movement of people from one geographic area to another. Migration is usually classified into two basic categories: international (movement from one country to another) and internal (movement within a country). When people *leave* a country to take up permanent residence elsewhere, their movement is called **emigration.** When they *enter* a country in order to take up permanent residence there, it is called **immigration.** The annual **migration rate** (sometimes called the *net migration rate*) is the yearly difference between the number of immigrants and the number of emigrants per 1,000 members of the total population.

INTERNATIONAL MIGRATION

One of the first great international migrations occurred during and after the fall of the Roman Empire, when nomadic tribes from eastern Europe and central Asia moved westward, often impelling further migrations by people who had been living in the lands they invaded. Some experts believe that drought and the rise of the Chinese Empire touched off this mass movement of population.

The more recent migrations of European and African peoples to North and South America in the seventeenth, eighteenth, and nineteenth centuries is one of the most important international migrations in history. It is estimated that during this 300-year period, more than 60 million Europeans left for overseas destinations, especially in North and South America (Heer, 1975; Kammeyer & Ginn, 1986). This migratory stream peaked between 1901 and 1910, when almost 9 million Europeans arrived in the United States, and still continues at a more modest rate. The largest recent short-term migration began in 1947, when Pakistan, a predominantly Muslim country, was officially separated from India, a predominantly Hindu nation. Over the next three years, 10 million Hindus and Sikhs migrated from Pakistan to India, and 7.5 million Muslims moved from India to Pakistan (Sutton, 1987).

Almost 57 million people have immigrated to the United States since 1820. Although more immigrants come to the United States today than to any other country, some nations receive more immigrants relative to the size of their populations. The foreign-born made up only 6 percent of the American population in the late 1980s, but they constituted 16 percent of Canada's and New Zealand's, 21 percent of Australia's, and over 40 percent of Israel's (Population Reference Bureau, 1989).

Migration is not always permanent. Men often migrate alone with the intention of sending money home and returning after they have "made good." Sometimes when migrants find that they cannot adjust to their new country they give up and return home. Changed social or political conditions at home can also bring about the return of migrants who were forced to leave. According to one study of world population movement, 30 percent of the immigrants who entered the United States between 1821 and 1924 returned to their countries of origin (Carr-Saunders, 1936).

Migration can benefit both the immigrant and the native populations, but it can also pose problems. Because economic improvement is a major incentive for immigration, immigrants often provide a willing labor force in their newly adopted countries. When unemployment is high, however, immigrants may compete with natives for jobs. Immigrants may also find themselves on welfare simply because they lack the skills necessary to obtain a decent-paying job. Almost all countries, therefore, limit the number of immigrants admitted annually.

IMMIGRATION TO THE UNITED STATES. In the United States, restrictions on immigration have been in place for centuries. An act passed in 1789 enabled the president to expel "dangerous" immigrants, and the Naturalization Act of 1790 provided that only free white people "of good moral character" who had resided in

INTERNET/TECHNOLOGY

WHO ARE WE? THE WORLDWIDE WEB PROVIDES SOME ANSWERS

If you were asked to describe the American population, where would you begin? What characteristics would you consider? And where could you find a ready source of reliable information on a population that currently exceeds a quarter of a billion people? The Census Bureau, of course, which is required by law to conduct a national census every 10 years.

As you can imagine, compiling data on the American population is a complicated, expensive task. In 1990, it took over half a million people to gather data on the nation's vital statistics at a cost of $2.6 billion.

If you are wondering whether America gets its money's worth, consider the kinds of questions that data gathered from a census allow us to answer:

- What is the median family income in the United States?

- How long should you expect to live?

- How many Americans are over the age of 100?

- What are you most likely to die from?

- Who is most likely to commit suicide?

- What is the median age at first marriage?

- What is the average family size?

- How many Americans have completed four or more years of college?

- How many Americans live below the poverty level?

- How many Americans lack health insurance?

- How much money is spent on health care in the United States each year?

- How many Americans have access to the Internet?

You could write a book based entirely on census data. In fact, a number of people have. In his book *Who We Are,* an analysis of the bicentennial census, Sam Roberts (1995) reveals some surprising facts about Americans. For example, did you know that the proportion of children raised in single-parent families more than doubled between 1970 and 1990? You might not realize that even though the number of single-parent families was greater among black women, the steepest rise in single-parent families was among white women. And did you know that half of poor people work, but that more than 25 percent of them receive no government benefits? You might also be surprised to learn that 1 in 250 Americans live in jails and prisons. That almost equals the number of Americans who live in college dormitories and nursing homes.

If you need the most up-to-date information about the American population, you do not have to wait for the next census. The Census Bureau also conducts surveys of the American population every month. And you can retrieve this information as soon as it is released by logging on to the Census Bureau's Web site (http://www.census.gov/).

Navigating this site is easy. Subjects are arranged in alphabetical order and can be located by clicking on the "A to Z" subject icon. Say, for example, that you are interested in the median age at which men and women marry. You simply click on marital status and then choose the specific information you want—perhaps historical trends on this variable. In some cases, tables must be downloaded and read through Adobe Acrobat Reader. While that might sound like a lot of work, it is not. It requires a simple procedure that costs you nothing.

One of the most valuable sources of information on the Census Bureau's Web site is the annual *Statistical Abstract of the United States.* You can locate this under "S" in the "A to Z" subject list, or go to it directly (http://www.census.gov/stat_abstract/).

If you find the Census Bureau's Web site interesting, you might want to check out a number of other Web sites that provide data on the American population. One of the best is Fedstats (http://www.fedstats.gov/), where you can find data that have been collected by just about every federal agency—from the FBI to the Centers for Disease Control.

Finally, two online publications provide information on a number of subjects not necessarily gathered by the government. These include the sites for *American Demographics* magazine (http://www.demographics.com/publications/ad/index.htm/) and *Demographics Journal* (http://www.amcity.com/journals/demographics/).

Sources: Anne Cronin, "Census Bureau Tells Something about Everything," *New York Times,* December 1, 1997, p. C10; and Sam Roberts, *Who We Are* (New York: Times Books, 1995).

the United States for two years could acquire citizenship (Bouvier & Gardner, 1986; Zolberg, 1987). In 1882, an infamous act barring the immigration of unskilled laborers (but not of persons with skills) from China was passed. (This act was not rescinded until 1943, when the United States and China were wartime allies.) During the 1920s, in response to growing anti-immigrant attitudes, quotas were established. Nationalities were admitted to the United States on the basis of their share of the American population in 1910. This meant that 82 percent of the immigrants in the late 1920s came from northwest Europe, 16 percent from southeast Europe, and only 2 percent from other nations. Asians were effectively excluded.

After very low rates of immigration during the 1930s and the World War II years, immigration picked up again after World War II. A 1952 act reaffirmed the quota system and added a new provision: Half of the visas assigned to each country could be claimed by highly skilled immigrants (plus their families) "whose services are urgently needed in the United States." Later, special provisions were enacted to permit the immigration of political refugees, and spouses and children of immigrants, beyond the quotas. While maintaining immigration ceilings, a new act in 1965 abolished the national origins provisions and ended discrimination against Asians. Since that time, Asia and Latin America have become the major sources of U.S. immigration. During the period between 1981 and 1990, only 10.4 percent of all immigrants arrived from Europe, compared to 37.3 percent from Asia. Almost 50 percent of U.S. immigrants came from Central and South America (*World Almanac, 1991*). The Immigration Act of 1990 increased the number of persons allowed to enter the United States annually to 714,000.

Vast numbers of immigrants continue to enter the United States illegally. The Bureau of the Census estimated that there were about 5 million illegal immigrants living in the United States in 1996 (U.S. Bureau of the Census, *Statistical Abstract of the United States, 1998*). Like legal immigrants, most illegal immigrants have left their native countries hoping to find job opportunities, political freedom, education, and a generally more desirable lifestyle. Illegal immigrants enter the country in a variety of ways, from contracting sham marriages with Americans to jumping from passing ships and swimming ashore. Many are admitted on short-term student or tourist visas and then stay on after the visas expire. Large numbers simply cross the border from Mexico or Canada.

Most of the illegal aliens in the United States today are Mexicans, driven from their own country by lack of jobs and low pay. By crossing the Rio Grande, Mexican agricultural workers can expect to earn considerably more than they could at home (Brooks, 1989). Most illegal aliens tend to stay close to the border or to migrate to such large Sun Belt cities as Houston, Miami, San Antonio, or Los Angeles. Many are also attracted to New York City and Chicago. Although they are often classified as manual laborers, quite a few hold semiskilled jobs.

Illegal immigration is a complicated issue because it poses so many economic, social, and ethical problems. Some agricultural and business interests, eager to exploit this supply of cheap labor, have opposed strict enforcement of immigration laws. Others have pointed out that ending illegal immigration could have negative effects: It might lead even more industries to relocate to foreign countries where labor is cheap, cause the rate of inflation to rise, and damage diplomatic relations (Sutton, 1987). Labor unions, on the other hand, fearing a possible loss of jobs for Americans, have favored a crackdown on illegal immigration. And population-minded groups have insisted that the influx of immigrants is canceling out the benefits that have accrued from recent declines in the U.S. birth rate.

In coming years, the number of people who hope to immigrate to the United States (and other advanced nations) is likely to increase, especially in Third World nations. Population growth in these societies is far outstripping economic growth, causing their people to look elsewhere for a better life.

POLITICAL REFUGEES. Refugees make up a special category of migrants. The United Nations High Commissioner for Refugees defines a *refugee* as a person who "is outside his or her country of origin and has a 'well-founded' fear of persecution if he or she returns." The refugee population around the world is estimated at 13.5 million (*World Almanac, 1998*). The Middle East has the largest concentration of refugees in the world, followed by Africa.

INTERNAL MIGRATION

Migration can also take place within a country. Historically, the westward movement has been an especially significant stream of internal migration in the United States. Americans have traditionally tended to look to the West for better opportunities and living conditions. In many western states today, the population consists largely of people who have relocated from other areas.

Another major internal migration in the United States was the northward and westward flow of southern African-Americans. This migration began during World War I, when northern industry began recruiting African-Americans for jobs because the supply of immigrant labor was cut off by the war. After World War II, the pace of this migration greatly accelerated. By 1970, about 24 percent of the total population of southern-born African-Americans lived in another region of the country. For those between the ages of 30 and 34, the figure was 51 percent (U.S. Bureau of the Census, 1978). The 1990 census indicated, however, that this flow has begun to reverse itself: Increasing numbers of African-Americans are now leaving northern cities and returning to the South.

The Sun Belt—the band of states that stretches across the southern rim of the country from Virginia to California—continues to draw population from the North and East. Since 1930, the southern and western Sun Belt states have grown faster than the states of the North. The West grew by 22.3 percent and the South by 13.4 percent during the 1980s (U.S. Bureau of the Census, 1991). Florida's population increased by 32.7 percent, while New York's grew by only 2.5 percent. According to the 1990 census, the five states with the fastest-growing populations were Nevada (50.1 percent), Alaska (36.9 percent), Arizona (34.8 percent), Florida (32.7 percent), and California (25.7 percent). Three states—California, Florida, and Texas—accounted for more than half of the nation's population growth.

Migrants to the Sun Belt include native southerners returning from northern cities, white-collar workers employed by large corporations, and many retired persons. As a result of this population shift, the geographic distribution of political and economic power in the United States is undergoing dramatic changes. For example, in the U.S. House of Representatives, the Northeast is losing seats and the West and Sun Belt are gaining representatives.

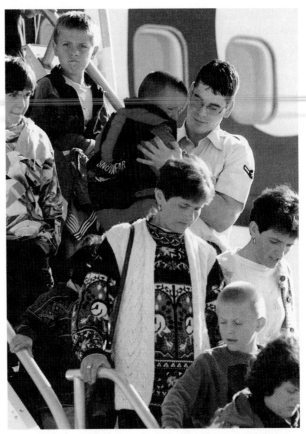

The unrest in Kosovo, Yugoslavia, has displaced many families. This group of refugees was temporarily relocated to Fort Dix, New Jersey.

CAUSES OF MIGRATION

Many factors, both positive and negative, influence people's decisions to migrate. One common motive is the desire to obtain better job opportunities. Another is the preference for a more favorable climate, a factor that has drawn many Americans to the Sun Belt. Superior housing and school systems have attracted many city dwellers to the suburbs. Freedom from religious or political repression has frequently been a motive for international migration, and sometimes for internal migration as well.

Migration can be understood as caused by "push and pull" factors. "Push" factors are negative conditions present in the country or area of origin, including overpopulation, harsh climate, inadequate housing, limited opportunity, or religious persecution. The "pull" factors are those conditions that attract migrants to a different area: plentiful jobs, good weather, an attractive lifestyle, cheap land, and political freedom (Bouvier, 1977; Kammeyer & Ginn, 1986).

Many intervening concerns can mediate these push and pull factors (Stouffer, 1940; World Bank, 1985). Distance, the expense of relocating a family, the age and health status of the would-be migrants, and the strength of family ties all influence decisions to migrate. Legal and physical restrictions can also play a role. In late 1989, the gates of the Berlin Wall, which had separated the populations of East and West Germany and had virtually halted migration for 28 years, were opened. Free passage was permitted, and thousands of East Germans left their country. In early 1990, the wall was torn down, and chunks of it were sold as souvenirs in airports and gift shops.

POPULATION GROWTH AND SOCIETY

The character of a society is profoundly affected by the size, composition, and rate of change of its population. These population factors are, in turn, affected by the character of the society. This interrelationship has long been of great interest to sociologists and demographers.

In this section, we look at one of its most significant aspects: population growth.

World Population Growth

Thomas Malthus

The first person to develop a widely debated theory about the possible consequences of population growth was the English clergyman and economist Thomas Robert Malthus (1766–1834). In a classic essay first published in 1798, Malthus theorized that human populations grow at a geometric rate (2, 4, 8, 16), but that food supplies only increase at an arithmetic rate (2, 3, 4, 5). When population growth exceeds the food supply, disasters such as famine, plague, and war elevate the death rate and reduce the population to a level that can be supported by the available food supply. Malthus referred to those factors that reduce the size of the population by raising the death rate as *positive checks*. Although he was generally pessimistic about the future, Malthus hoped that population might someday be limited primarily by *preventive checks*, such as late marriage and sexual abstinence, which control population growth by reducing fertility, rather than by escalating mortality.

While Malthus's influence on the study of population has been substantial, his theories are not without detractors. Malthus did not foresee the development of effective methods of birth control. Nor did he predict the revolutionary changes in agricultural technology that have increased food production. One contemporary scholar argues in response to Malthus that population growth and increasing personal incomes force the prices of natural resources to rise, which, in turn, stimulates the search for substitutes for those resources as they become scarce. Eventually, new resources are found and the world is better off (Simon, 1990).

Demographic Transition Theory

Population growth patterns in the United States and Western Europe during the period of modernization have been extensively analyzed. The basic pattern characteristic of this era, called the **demographic transition,** has been summarized as follows:

> Premodern populations maintain stability of numbers by balancing high, though fluctuating, death rates with high birth rates. As they begin to experience the effects of modernization, improvements in nutritional and health standards reduce mortality while fertility remains high and rapid growth ensues. Later, urbanization and other social changes associated with the more "mature" states of industrialization create pressure favoring smaller families, and the birth rate falls, once again approaching balance with the death rate, but at low (though fluctuating) rather than high levels. (Wrong, 1964, pp. 18–19)

Thus, nations beginning the demographic transition are initially characterized by high birth and death rates; as a result, there is little if any natural increase in their populations. Then the death rate—but not the birth rate—declines, causing a population explosion. Next, population growth begins to slow down as the birth rate declines. Finally, both birth and death rates stabilize at low levels, again resulting in populations with very low, or even negative, growth rates. The final stage, with low birth and death rates, is typical of modern industrial societies. Figure 19.3 offers a graphic depiction of demographic transition theory.

The theory of the demographic transition is based on the history of the industrialized nations of the West during the two centuries that preceded World War II. At the end of that period, the Western nations appeared to be in the final stage. But during the period of rapid economic growth after World War II, birth rates in these societies rose sharply and remained high for two decades. As a result, demographers questioned whether the relationship between birth and death rates and industrialization was really as simple as visualized in the model.

A revised interpretation of the demographic transition emphasizes the distinction between the short-run and long-run effects of industrial development and economic growth (Heer, 1975; Robinson, 1981). This view assumes that there may be a short-run increase in the birth rate during periods of economic growth. But in the long run, such growth is associated with a number of factors that clearly cause the birth rate to fall. For example,

FIGURE 19.3 The Demographic Transition.
While demographic transition theory has gained wide acceptance in the West, the model does not seem to be equally applicable to the population growth patterns of many non-Western societies.

Source: Copyright © Harry Robinson from *Population and Resources* by Harry Robinson. Reprinted with permission of St. Martin's Press, Incorporated.

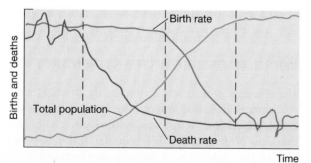

parents have smaller families because more children survive to adulthood, and because they want to give their children expensive advantages that are important in industrialized societies, such as a college education. Moreover, governments in economically developed societies generally provide social security systems, so parents no longer must depend on their children for support in old age. And the high urban population densities common in industrial societies make family living quarters more crowded and children, therefore, less desirable.

The demographic transition was once thought to be universally associated with the process of modernization, but demographers are now less certain that this is the case. The societies that are currently becoming industrialized display widely varying birth and death rates, and many do not seem to be following the Western model closely.

POPULATION AND ECONOMIC DEVELOPMENT

Just as important as the impact of economic development on population growth is the impact of population growth on a nation's capacity for economic development. Many developing countries today are expanding in population much too rapidly for their economic well-being. Economic growth is barely able—and in some cases is unable—to keep up with population growth. For example, Switzerland, Belgium, and other countries with stable or even declining populations can raise their average per capita incomes by 2 percent if they can increase their economic growth at the same rate. But for countries in sub-Saharan Africa, whose population is expected to more than double over the next 20 to 30 years, the situation is quite different. In Nigeria, for example, the population is growing at a rate of 3.0 percent annually (Population Reference Bureau, 1999). There, a 2 percent economic growth rate would lead to a steady decline in income and living standards.

One important negative economic consequence of overpopulation is that it drains away funds needed for capital investment. Every country requires capital to construct and maintain highways, communication systems, factories, power generators, and other such facilities. A country's investment capital usually is drawn from the savings of its citizens. When wages must support large families, very little money can be saved. And when the work force is much larger than the number of jobs available, the unemployed live hand to mouth and can save nothing. As a result, many developing nations must rely on foreign investment or loans for capital investment funds. But foreign investment drains profits from a country, and loans can accumulate at interest rates that intensify a nation's burden of debt.

Economic development is thus seriously hampered by rapid population growth in many industrializing nations. One such country is Pakistan. In 1997, Pakistan's population was estimated at 135.1 million, making it one of the most populous nations in the world (*World Almanac, 1998*). A high birth rate of 43 per 1,000 and a low death rate of 11 per 1,000 keeps Pakistan in a condition of severe overpopulation.

The Pakistani economy is strained not only because of the nation's large population but also because of the high proportion of dependent people in that population. Half of all Pakistanis are under the age of 15. With so many young people, and with the death rate declining as a result of modernization, the population is growing rapidly. If the current rate of increase continues, the population of Pakistan will almost double by the year 2050 (*World Almanac, 1998*). To feed twice the current population, agricultural productivity must be increased substantially. Huge sums will have to be invested to upgrade farming techniques and bring unused lands into cultivation. This means that the country will have little left to spend on the kind of industrialization needed to create jobs, increase personal incomes, and improve the general quality of life.

Highly industrialized nations, on the other hand, can benefit economically from population growth. Larger families mean an increase in the demand for consumer goods, and this increased consumption can be an important stimulus to business expansion. Business executives and economists cite the prosperity generated by the post–World War II baby boom in the United States as an example of the way population growth can promote the growth of the economy.

TRENDS IN WORLD POPULATION

Although the average rate of population growth in the developed countries is much lower than 1 percent per year, in the developing countries the rate is typically well over 2 percent. In fact, in recent years a population explosion has taken place in the nonindustrialized Asian, African, and Latin American nations. A decline in death rates is the most important factor explaining the high rate of population growth in these countries, where the average mortality rate has dropped from 23 per 1,000 in 1950 to 11 or 12 per 1,000 today. Currently, population growth in developing countries accounts for more than 94 percent of the world's total population growth.

The dramatic decline in death rates in the developing world can be attributed to modern drugs, expanded health services, and improved sanitation, food, and water (United Nations, 1988). The decline has been most pronounced among children and young adults, the age

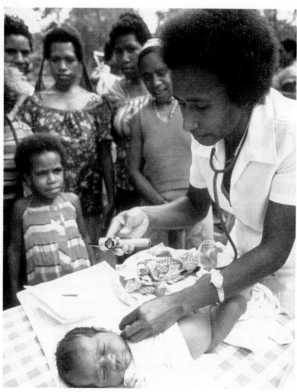

Advances in medical technology have caused the death rates in developing countries to fall dramatically in recent decades. As a result, the rate of world population growth has more than doubled since 1940.

groups that typically are characterized by the highest death rates from infectious diseases such as malaria, yellow fever, smallpox, and cholera. Today public health procedures have controlled—and, in the case of smallpox, virtually eliminated—these diseases.

As a result of the reduction in death rates, the world's annual *growth rate*—the difference (usually expressed as a percentage) between the number of births and the number of deaths in the population—rose from 0.9 percent between 1940 and 1950 to 1.8 percent between 1950 and 1960. Correspondingly, the *doubling time* (the amount of time it takes for a population to double in size) dropped from 77 years between 1940 and 1950 to 39 years between 1950 and 1960.

In the mid-1970s, however, the annual growth rate stabilized at 1.8 percent; since then, it has declined to about 1.4 percent. This is an event some demographers regard as a major turning point in world history, because prior to this downturn, world population had been growing at a steadily increasing rate. Currently, the world's population is estimated to be over 5.9 billion, with a doubling time of 49 years (U.S. Bureau of the Census, 1991f; *World Almanac, 1998;* Population Reference Bureau, 1999). The reasons for

this historic change are not yet entirely clear, but one important factor seems to be the success of fertility-control programs in some developing nations.

Despite these positive trends, the results of the Third World population explosion will be felt for years to come. High fertility rates of the past mean that women entering childbearing age today constitute an exceptionally large proportion of the total population of the developing countries. Thus, even though the fertility rate in these societies is declining—meaning that women are having fewer children—the numbers of women having babies are so great that the total number of births is still actually rising. For example, Brazil's birth rate fell from 5.8 in 1965 to 4.0 in 1980, a decline of about 30 percent. Yet the total number of births increased from 2.9 million a year in the late 1950s to 3.7 million a year in the early 1980s (Easterlin & Crimmins, 1988).

Fertility Control

METHODS OF BIRTH CONTROL

Most demographers believe that the expanded use of birth control is a crucial key to reducing the size of the world's population. Some of the methods of birth control in use today are several thousand years old. Others have been developed and introduced in the twentieth century. Still other methods are now being tested. Unfortunately, the perfect birth-control method has yet to be invented.

Abortion and infanticide (the killing of babies) may be the world's oldest methods of controlling populations; certainly they have been practiced since ancient times. Some societies have placed taboos on sexual intercourse during the two or more years when a child is being nursed. And in European countries since the Industrial Revolution, relatively late marriage has become increasingly customary.

Only recently has the use of contraceptive devices become widespread. Today, a wide variety of birth-control devices are available, most of them designed for women. The birth-control pill has proved to be the most effective single method of contraception. When taken faithfully, it is close to 100 percent effective. Despite the convenience and effectiveness of the pill, there has been considerable concern about its negative side effects and the possible long-term consequences of its use. Other common birth-control devices used by women include intrauterine devices (IUDs), diaphragms, sponges, and spermicidal foams, jellies, and creams. Pills and IUDs now constitute more than half the contraceptive devices used in developing countries.

For men, the condom is a widely used technique of birth control, especially among Europeans. The condom can also provide some protection against sexually transmitted diseases. Its use has grown rapidly since the onset of the AIDS epidemic. New methods of male contraception, such as a birth-control pill and removable clamps that cut off the flow of sperm, are in the testing stage. But the most common method of contraception among married American men is vasectomy, or sterilization.

Sterilization of both men and women was once considered a drastic and largely unacceptable form of birth control. Now, however, it is the most common method of contraception employed by married couples in the United States. And its use is growing faster than that of any of the other birth-control methods. About 9.6 million women have chosen sterilization as their method of birth control (Hatcher et al., 1994).

Sterilization has also rapidly become increasingly popular in the other industrialized nations of the West and in the developing countries. In fact, today it is the most common method of birth control in the world. In 1990, an estimated 138 million women throughout the world had been sterilized. South Korea has the highest reported rate of female sterilization: 37 percent of married women of reproductive age. In China, 30 percent of married women have chosen sterilization, and in India, 21 percent have made this decision. The practice is much less popular in the Near East and Africa (Johns Hopkins University Population Information Program, 1990). These data strongly suggest that people throughout the world have become increasingly motivated to limit births. It is important to note, however, that sterilization is used mainly by women in their later years of childbearing; most have already had as many children as they desire (U.S. Bureau of the Census, 1989).

Abortion is another widespread method of birth control. Worldwide, an estimated one out of every four pregnancies is terminated by this procedure (Francome, 1984). Practiced for centuries, abortion has often been a common, if not the most common, method of birth control. Some techniques that have been used, such as the ingestion of herb or plant solutions, are generally ineffective. Other techniques, such as the insertion into the body of sharp objects or the use of harsh chemicals, pose serious risks—including death—to the woman's health.

In the early 1970s, abortion was legalized in many areas of the United States. Initially, it was permitted only under special conditions, which had to be verified by the woman's doctor—specifically, if continuing the pregnancy would seriously endanger the mother's physical or mental health. In 1973, however, the U.S. Supreme Court ruled in Roe v. Wade that the decision to have an abortion should be left primarily to the mother. Then, in 1989, a subsequent Supreme Court ruling allowed states to place certain restraints on a woman's right to have an abortion.

Both Court decisions have provoked heated controversy. Many people condemn the "antilife" aspects of legal abortion on religious or moral grounds; others insist that the social benefits of abortion outweigh its possible moral costs.

Over 1.4 million abortions were performed in the United States in 1996 (U.S. Bureau of the Census, *Statistical Abstract of the United States, 1998*). That turns out to be 22.9 abortions per 1,000 women between the ages of 15 to 44. Not surprisingly, one-fourth of all abortions in 1994 were performed on women under age 20. Another 32.8 percent were performed on women between 20 and 24 (*World Almanac, 1998*).

FERTILITY CONTROL IN DEVELOPING NATIONS

Recognizing the serious consequences of overpopulation, many developing countries today are actively working to control their populations through *antinatalist programs* (public policies designed to discourage births). These programs are often expensive and difficult to carry out. The populations of developing nations are largely uneducated, poor, and superstitious—factors that frequently undermine official efforts to promote birth control. As a result, effective fertility-control programs must be designed to fit with the established traditions and lifestyles of the local population. In India, for example, most people regard hospitals only as places to die. Sterilization clinics attract more business if they are set up in railway stations—traditional places for large groups to congregate (Easterlin & Crimmins, 1988; Ehrlich & Ehrlich, 1972). In addition, family-planning festivals are held, during which sterilizations are performed and other methods of contraception are publicized. Candidates for sterilization are often paid or given gifts such as transistor radios, a highly successful incentive in a poor nation.

Indonesia and Thailand are among the many other developing countries that have implemented successful fertility-control programs. Thailand has been a leader in family planning since the 1960s. Between 1969 and 1984, contraceptive use by married Thai women aged 15 to 44 expanded from 15 to 65 percent; in the same period, fertility dropped from 6.0 to 2.4. In Indonesia, the fifth most populous country in the world, the fertility rate has dropped by over one-third in 15 years, from 5.6 in the early 1970s to 3.4 in 1987. Forty-two percent of all married Indonesian women aged 15 to 44 now use modern contraceptive measures (Easterlin & Crimmins, 1988).

Attitudes toward fertility control are strongly influenced by political, religious, and social ideologies. In the past, for example, Christian churches generally adhered to the belief that procreation is one of the primary goals of marriage, and therefore were opposed to birth control.

As part of its population control efforts, the Chinese government has sponsored billboards emphasizing the importance of keeping families small.

Within the past 50 years, though, most Protestant churches have become much more liberal on this issue. Other religions that traditionally have lacked sharply defined doctrines concerning fertility control have moved in recent years toward support of family planning. In Thailand, for instance, Buddhists encourage and respect the autonomy of women, and therefore believe that they are entitled to make their own decisions regarding fertility control.

But liberal religious attitudes toward fertility control are not universal. Islam, with its strong patriarchal history, considers birth control a sin, encourages large families, and regards the combined role of wife and mother as properly a woman's master status. However, traditional Muslim values may be changing somewhat. Egypt and Pakistan, two Muslim countries with serious population problems, have embarked on successful national family planning programs (Knodel, Aphichat, & Debevalya, 1987).

The Roman Catholic church remains adamantly opposed to artificial birth control. Survey research suggests that most American Catholics ignore the teachings of the church in this matter; in fact, researchers have found virtually no significant difference between the contraceptive practices of Catholics and Protestants in the United States. However, in heavily Catholic Latin America some advocates of family planning regard the church's posture as a key factor intensifying that region's severe overpopulation problems.

Political ideology and policy can also greatly influence population control. In a dramatic example of antinatalist policy, the Chinese government has developed a national program aimed at achieving a stable population by the year 2000. Couples who have only one child, who pledge that they will not have more, and who prove that they are using birth-control measures receive a fixed amount of money each month until their child is 14 years old. Also, the couple is given preferential treatment in housing, and their child receives priority in school admissions and job applications. At retirement, the couple receives a larger pension than they would ordinarily be allocated.

In some Chinese provinces, fines are imposed on couples who do not limit the size of their families to two children. The minimum fine is 6 percent of the couple's income, and the percentage increases with each additional child. Exceptions may be permitted for multiple births or, in some cases, if the first child is a girl. Unauthorized pregnancies have been known to result in forced abortions and even in the sterilization of the mother (Coleman & Schofield, 1986). Some reports indicate that, in outlying areas, conflict between the state-mandated policy of one-child families and the traditional Chinese preference for males has led many parents to practice female infanticide if their first child is not a boy. This custom could seriously distort the ratio of males to females in the coming generation, with possibly serious repercussions on many dimensions of social life. In any event, the Chinese population will continue to grow for many years to come despite the government's stringent antinatalist measures, mainly because of the extremely high birth rates that accompanied the Cultural Revolution of the 1960s.

Population Growth and Change in the United States

The results of the first U.S. census, which was taken in 1790, reveal a way of life very different from that which we experience today. At that time, the United States was a nation of large families; there were 5.79 people in the average household and only one-tenth of the population lived alone. In 1997, the average U.S. household contained 2.64 persons and one-fourth of all households included only one person (U.S. Bureau of the Census, *Statistical Abstract of the United States, 1998*).

Other contrasts are equally striking. In 1790, only one out of every five Americans lived in a city. New York was the largest city, and the center of population was near Baltimore. There were only three other important urban centers: Philadelphia, Boston, and Charleston. In 1996, 70 percent of the U.S. population lived in metropolitan areas containing over 1 million people, and more than three-quarters lived in metropolitan areas of all sizes. Today's six largest cities are New York, Los Angeles, Chicago, Houston, Philadelphia, and San Diego (*World Almanac, 1998*). In 1790, the center of population was 23 miles east of Baltimore. Today it is more than 818.6 miles away, some 9.7 miles northwest of Steelville, Missouri (U.S. Bureau of the Census, 1992).

GLOBAL SOCIETY

AGING IN THE TWENTY-FIRST CENTURY

In 1968, an ecologist by the name of Paul Ehrlich wrote a book entitled *The Population Bomb,* in which he predicted that the rapidly rising population rates would cause a worldwide calamity. He wrote:

> In order just to keep living standards at the present inadequate level, the food available for the people must be doubled. . . . The amount of power must be doubled. The capacity of the transport system must be doubled. The number of trained doctors, nurses, teachers, and administrators must be doubled. This would be a fantastically difficult job in the United States—a rich country with a fine agricultural system, immense industries, and rich natural resources. Think of what it means in a country with none of these. (pp. 22–23)

In fact, the world's population, which began to rise rapidly after World War II, was cause for concern. Although the growth rate slowed in industrialized, developed countries, it continued to expand rapidly in less developed countries. Growing at rates from 2 to 3.5 percent a year, the populations in these countries were expected to double every 20 to 35 years. This "population explosion" concerned demographers, ecologists, and economists, who warned of global disasters. In 1972, another influential book entitled *The Limits to Growth* (Meadows et al.) predicted that the world's raw materials would be used up in just a few years and that the world would experience mass famine and energy shortages.

But these predictions never materialized. In fact, changes in human behavior led to declining fertility rates worldwide, putting them at or below replacement levels in 61 countries (*U.S. News & World Report,* March 1, 1999). Today the composition of the population worldwide is changing in another way—we are getting older. In 1972, the average life expectancy worldwide was 49.5 years. Today it exceeds 63 years. Based on projections made by the United Nations, this means that the world's population will grow at an average rate of 1.3 percent a year for the next 50 years. And if fertility rates continue to fall, the worldwide population could start to decline by the middle of the twenty-first century.

In the year 2000, the number of people over the age of 60, for the first time in history, will exceed the number aged 14 or under. As new technologies continue to extend the human life span, industrialized countries are beginning to wonder how they will pay for the costs of health care that accompany old age. In developed countries today, total public spending for one older person is two to three times more than that for one child.

Some countries are raising the age of eligibility for benefits; some have also raised the contribution rates. But this may not be enough. China may face a particularly serious situation in the next 20 years. Its policy of one child per family, which began in the late 1970s, means that one child will have to support two parents and four grandparents. As it makes the transition into a market economy, many worry that even that one child will not have time to take care of his or her parents.

The only countries not facing an aging crisis are Muslim ones in North Africa and the Middle East. But many people are hesitant to take the issue seriously. Why, they ask, should we trust demographers' predictions when their predictions failed to materialize in the past? In his book *Gray Dawn,* Peter Peterson (1999) argues that we should pay attention to demographers now because human fertility doesn't influence the current fiscal projections that indicate an impending crisis. While he claims that social and cultural changes could alter predictions of an aging crisis, he believes it would be wise to play it safe and listen to the experts.

At the time of the first census, the United States had a very youthful population; the median age was just 16. With many women in their childbearing years, the crude birth rate was high, 55 per 1,000, which is considerably greater than the birth rate in India today. Life expectancy at that time was 35 years. The United States has a much older population today. In 1997 the median age was 34.9 years and the birth rate was 14.6 per 1,000 (U.S. Bureau of the Census, *Statistical Abstract of the United States, 1998*).

These population shifts both cause and reflect changes in American life and values. Some women today are giving up motherhood for careers; many others are postponing marriage. The increasing number of older people has created new problems concerning retirement policies, Social Security, and health care. A heavily urbanized population has resulted in special difficulties for cities. These are all issues that were relatively unfamiliar to earlier generations of Americans. Let us look closely at some contemporary population trends.

THE CHANGING BIRTH RATE

According to the demographic transition theory discussed earlier, economic growth is normally accompanied by a decline in fertility. This pattern only holds over the long run, however. In the short run, sharp fluctuations in fertility can and frequently do occur. We can see this clearly in the history of American fertility during the twentieth century, generally a period of rapid economic growth. The birth rate gradually dropped during the first decades of the century, reaching a low point of 75.8 births per 1,000 women of childbearing age during the Depression of the 1930s. After World War II, fertility substantially and unexpectedly increased, climbing to a high of 122.7 births (using the same measure) during the 1950s baby boom. Then, in the mid-1960s, fertility began to drop sharply again, and the decline has continued with some minor fluctuations to the present day. The number of births per 1,000 women of childbearing age in 1995 was 61.4.

Why do such fluctuations occur? Some economists believe that changes in the fertility rate result mainly from the size of the age cohort that is of childbearing age (Choucri, 1984; Easterlin, 1980; Simon, 1986). When members of the small cohort born during the Depression came of age after the end of World War II, in 1945, jobs were plentiful. Economically secure during the 1950s and early 1960s, they felt ready to marry and start large families at an early age. But their children reached adulthood in the tight job market of the 1970s and early 1980s. Because of the overpopulation resulting from the baby boom, applicants outnumbered available positions. Uncertain about their earning power, many of these youths have delayed parenthood or strictly limited the size of their families.

Other social scientists emphasize that decisions about childbearing reflect the personal experiences of women as they pass through adolescence (Kasun, 1988; Masnick & McFalls, 1978). These experiences are shaped by prevailing norms and economic conditions. During the Depression, economic insecurity led many couples to choose to limit the size of their families, so most of them practiced birth control faithfully. These attitudes continued into World War II. During the period of prosperity that began with the war and extended into the 1950s and 1960s, however, increased economic security made many couples more lax about contraception.

We cannot be certain whether the baby boom was the result of a rebound from the Depression years and World War II, or whether it would have occurred anyway because the early postwar years were distinguished by unexpected and remarkable economic prosperity. Both of these explanations probably have some validity, and other factors may have been involved as well. In any event, it is clear that the long-term trend in the United States and other industrialized nations has been toward declining birth rates. Fertility in these nations, in fact, has been dropping not only during this century but fairly steadily for the last 200 years (Brown & Jacobson, 1987; Westoff, 1978).

A major reason for the fertility decline of the last few decades has been the rapid increase in the number of married women who have joined the labor force. In the United States, the proportion of married women working outside the home increased from 30 percent in 1960 to 57.5 percent in 1990, and this figure is expected to continue to rise (U.S. Bureau of the Census, 1991). Contributing to this trend has been the wider availability of birth-control pills and other inexpensive and effective means of contraception.

ZERO POPULATION GROWTH

In the early 1970s, the total fertility rate in the United States dropped below the replacement level of 2.1 children per woman. The replacement level is the number of children that each woman must have if the current population is to be maintained. The level must be higher than 2.0 because not all children survive to childbearing age; in nations with high infant mortality rates, it must be considerably above 2.0. If the replacement level were to be maintained indefinitely, it would lead to **zero population growth (ZPG)**, the point at which there is no natural increase in the population.

By the early 1980s, the fertility rate had dropped still further, to 1.8. Since then, it has increased only slightly, to 2.0 in 1999. Yet ZPG will almost certainly not be attained in the United States any time soon. The children born during the baby boom are now of childbearing age. Even with the low fertility rate, the fact that they make up so large a portion of the population will lead the number of births to exceed the number of deaths for some years to come.

Migration also affects population growth and can cause a population to grow even though the natural rate of increase is at zero. In 1997, an estimated 26 million people in the United States were foreign born—the highest level since 1930. If the rate of immigration remains constant, and if the fertility rate drops to 1.6 children per woman, experts predict that ZPG could be achieved in the United States in about 50 years.

THE END OF THE U.S. POPULATION EXPLOSION

Many observers predict that in the future the changes brought about by the declining American birth rate will be dramatic (Peterson, 1999). Almost every aspect of life—the economy, fashion, land use, recreation, education, medical care, retirement policy, music—will be affected. And with more than 20 percent of all votes being cast by people over 65, politics in particular will strongly reflect the "graying of America."

Some of these changes are already evident. Colleges are placing increased emphasis on adult education. Toy manufacturers and baby-food companies have diversified their product lines to include new goods and services, including insurance, cosmetics, and games for adults. And the Social Security system is considering major changes to accommodate the increasing numbers of retirees, whose benefits will have to be financed by fewer and fewer workers. Some of these trends will be temporarily set aside in the next few years, as the children of the baby boomers move through the life cycle. This phenomenon has popularly been labeled the "baby boom echo." But this "echo" will eventually fade away, and the long-term trend toward an older society seems certain to continue.

Will an older America be stagnant, uncreative and conservative? Will rapid economic growth continue in a nation dominated by the elderly? Will younger people have adequate opportunity to advance in a labor market top-heavy with old and experienced workers? These are some of the questions that concern demographers and social planners.

ECOLOGY AND ENVIRONMENTAL SOCIOLOGY

Ecology is the study of the relationships between organisms and their environment. The study of ecology began in the nineteenth century as a branch of biology. It was greatly stimulated by Charles Darwin's discovery that organisms evolve in response to their environmental conditions.

In 1893, Émile Durkheim developed a "social morphology" to study the ways in which population and environment are related to social structure. But it was not until after World War I that American sociologists realized that social behavior can be viewed as an adaptation to the environment, and began seriously to apply ecological perspectives to the discipline of sociology. As human beings adapt, they cooperate and compete among themselves and with other life forms for the use of scarce resources. Their adaptations are similar in some ways to the animal behaviors studied by biological ecologists.

The ecological perspective was introduced into American sociology by Robert Park of the University of Chicago. Chicago dominated the discipline in the United States during the years between the two world wars—that is, in the 1920s and 1930s. Much of the sociological

research done there was ecologically oriented. The foremost examples of this approach are studies of the ecological patterns and processes that occur in large cities. This research is discussed in Chapter 20.

After World War II, sociological interest in ecology declined. One exception was *Human Ecology* (1950), Amos Hawley's pioneering work focusing on community structure, which was based on the assumption "that there is a continuity in the life patterns of all organic forms." Recently, however, there has been renewed interest in ecology and in what has come to be called *environmental sociology*. This revival has been caused partly by the growing national and international concern about environmental problems (Dunlap & Catton, 1979; Robinson, 1981).

Social ecologists and environmental sociologists have somewhat different research interests. Social ecologists have traditionally focused on the spatial distribution of social and cultural phenomena. For example, ecological research has examined how such "social facts" as suicide and mental illness are distributed geographically (Harf, 1986; Short, 1971). Social ecology is closely related to demography. Both specialties emphasize quantitative approaches to the analysis of social issues and use many of the same methods and data sources.

Environmental sociology is a more recent development. Like social ecologists, environmental sociologists pay less attention to cultural values and norms than do most other sociologists. The main concern of environmental sociologists is the effect of the environment on social organization and social behavior. For example, one researcher studied how people in villages responded to a specific natural disaster, in this case a severe flood in Bangladesh that forced extensive resettlement (Zaman, 1986). Other environmental studies have examined responses to the disaster at the Soviet Chernobyl nuclear facility and the fears associated with nuclear power and radiation (Gale, 1987; Rosa, Machilis, & Keating, 1988). Another environmental sociologist has examined the responses of people in Haiti to the ecological consequences of increasing crowding on the island. The annual loss of 10 percent of Haiti's forests as a result of crowding is particularly significant because most Haitians depend on wood for cooking and heating fuel (Woodward, 1983).

Population Density and Human Behavior

Another important focus of ecological and environmental research in sociology is the relationship between population density and human behavior. Evidence from experiments conducted with animals indicates that severe overcrowding can produce pathological behavior. One well-known study examined the effects of overcrowding on the behavior of rats. The rats were given sufficient food and water, but the density of the population was much higher than it was in their natural habitat. Under these conditions, the following effects were observed: an increased death rate, especially among the very young; lowered fertility rates; neglect of the young by their mothers; overly aggressive behavior, including cannibalism; and sexual aberration (Calhoun, 1962).

Although there are those who believe that the findings of animal research should not be applied to humans (Simon, 1981), the striking results of such studies, together with increased concern about the declining environmental quality in many large cities, have inspired many investigations into the effects on human behavior of high urban densities.

Sociologists commonly distinguish between *density* (the objective number of people in a given space) and *crowding* (subjective perceptions regarding whether or not too many people are present). Some research has concluded that high levels of density, although often uncomfortable, are not necessarily a cause of social pathology (Fischer et al., 1975; Freedman, 1975). This conclusion has been strenuously debated by other sociologists, however. Some studies have found that high levels of density in the home have deleterious effects, including physical and psychological withdrawal, and that they produce a general feeling of being "washed out" (Gove, Hughes, & Galle, 1979) as well as increased levels of hostility (Zeedyk-Ryan & Smith, 1983). One pioneering study, conducted in the Chicago area, found that high population density was associated with high death rates, high fertility rates, increased tension in the home, less effective child care, and juvenile delinquency (Galle et al., 1972). Another study has suggested that density promotes stress resulting from increased competition for scarce resources (Jain, 1987).

The Ecosystem

One of the most important concepts in social ecology is that of the ecosystem, the complex web of relationships between living things and their environment. Otis Dudley Duncan (1959), a leading social ecologist, has suggested that the **ecosystem**—which he calls the "ecological complex"—consists of four main elements: population, organization, environment, and technology (commonly referred to by the acronym POET). An analysis of the interplay among these elements is often prominent in the work of ecologists.

An example of the complex interaction characteristic of the ecosystem was provided by Duncan (1961) in his analysis of the smog problem in the Los Angeles basin of southern California. During and after World War II,

when there was a large influx of population and industry into the Los Angeles area, residents began to notice a blue-gray haze that reduced visibility and irritated their eyes and noses. As the smog became worse, it led to more serious health problems, as well as causing extensive damage to local plant life. Scientists eventually discovered that smog is produced when sunlight converts certain by-products of combustion, particularly those found in automobile exhaust fumes, into toxic chemicals. In Los Angeles, the problem is magnified by atmospheric conditions that often prevent the polluted air from rising into the atmosphere and by a ring of mountains that traps the local air. Duncan (1961) noted how the smog problem is closely related to the Los Angeles area's population size and patterns of settlement:

> The problem, severe enough at onset, was hardly alleviated by the rapid growth of population in the Los Angeles area, spreading out as it did over a wide territory, and thereby heightening its dependence on the already ubiquitous automobile as the primary means of local movement. Where could one find a more poignant instance of the principle of circular causation, so central to ecological theory, than that of the Los Angelenos speeding down their freeways in a rush to escape the smog produced by emissions from the very vehicles conveying them? (p. 91)

The Planet as an Ecosystem

The concept of an ecosystem can be extended to include the entire planet. Like all other animals, humans need an adequate supply of fresh water and clean air, as well as a food supply provided directly or indirectly by green plants that can make their own carbohydrates using the sun's energy. People also need a certain amount of space.

Human beings have traditionally acted as though the earth held an infinite supply of these basic resources. The limits of the environment have become increasingly apparent, however, as many of our natural resources are now diminishing rapidly. As the air, water, and soil have become polluted by chemicals, radioactive materials, and garbage, it has become evident that Earth may eventually be pushed beyond its natural capacity for the regeneration of natural resources.

Kenneth Boulding expressed the resultant dilemma metaphorically by suggesting that we must move from a "cowboy" economy toward a "spaceman" economy. A cowboy economy assumes limitless frontiers and encourages recklessness and exploitation. The spaceman economy views Earth as a gigantic yet finite spaceship, an ecological whole of which the human species is an organic part. At the core of the spaceman economy is an emphasis on conserving the planet's capital stock of basic resources. This contrasts with the cowboy economy, which emphasizes continually increasing economic production (Boulding, 1966).

Ironically, many attempts to improve on nature have ultimately helped to destroy the natural environment. Fertilizing crops to increase yield often upsets the balance of life in nearby water sources, for example. Similarly, the conversion of green land into cities may have reduced the oxygen content of the atmosphere.

A United Nations study reported that many formerly productive lands in Africa, India, and South America have been overcultivated for centuries and are now turning into desert. Another United Nations study concluded that "about 35 percent of the earth's land surface, containing 850 million people, was threatened by desertification and that some 407 million people, or about 10 percent of the world's population, were already affected by at least moderate desertification" in which the land has lost up to 25 percent of its productive capability (United Nations, 1988). When periodic droughts are added to the human misuse of land, as was the case in Ethiopia in the 1980s, famines become a reality, killing hundreds of thousands of people and endangering millions more (Correa, El Torky, & Were, 1989; Watson, 1984).

A widely publicized report by a team of researchers from the Massachusetts Institute of Technology estimated that if current trends in population growth, pollution, and food production continue, we will reach the limits of growth on this planet by the end of the twenty-first century. The consequences could include a sudden, drastic decline in population and industrial output. The report does not predict that these events will happen, but it does present projections and analyses of present trends, both as a warning and as a basis for making political, economic, and social policy decisions to ensure that the crisis will not

As air, water, and soil have become polluted, it is possible that the Earth may eventually be pushed beyond its natural capacity for the regeneration of natural resources.

occur (Tyler, 1975; see also Raunikar & Huang, 1987). According to this report, the only way to avoid a bleak future is to begin to limit our expansion while there is still time (Meadows et al., 1972).

Even if this "limits to growth" perspective is excessively pessimistic, the natural environment is clearly being stretched to its limits. Sociologists of the future may have to consider environmental factors more seriously, perhaps giving them much the same importance that they now give to culture.

CHAPTER REVIEW

1. What kinds of businesses and organizations rely on the information collected by demographers?

2. For what purposes are census data used?

3. What can a population's sex ratio tell you?

4. Why should our political leaders be concerned about America's age structure?

5. What is the difference between a population projection and a population forecast?

6. What measures determine the growth or decline of a population?

7. What do infant mortality rates and life expectancies indicate about a society?

8. Consider the problems that societies with aging populations will face over the next 50 years. How will their immigration rates affect those problems?

9. Is zero population growth ideal for all societies?

10. How do you expect the field of ecology to change as we enter the twenty-first century?

INTERNET EXERCISE

The Web destinations for Chapter 19 deal with various aspects of population and ecology. To start your explorations, go to the Prentice Hall Companion Web site **http://www.prenhall.com/popenoe.** Next, choose **Chapter 19** (Population and Ecology). Then, select **web destinations** from the menu on the left side of the screen. There are several sites to choose from. We suggest you begin with **International Migration.** This site is sponsored by the Organization for Economic Cooperation and Development, which monitors trends in international migration movements and policies worldwide. Among the recent issues covered are temporary labor migration, the labor market integration of immigrants, illegal migration, and demographic and economic aspects of migration. The site also offers access to a number of "working papers," on-line newsletters, and other relevant Web sites. After you have explored this site, answer the following questions:

- Based upon the text's discussion, what major problems are associated with international migration?
- What are the societal implications of illegal migration?

KEY TERMS

demography	fecundity	life span
census	crude birth rate	migration
vital statistics	age-specific birth rate	emigration
sex ratio	total fertility rate (TFR)	immigration
age structure	crude death rate	migration rate
age cohort	age-specific death rate	demographic transition
population projections	neonatal mortality rate	zero population growth
population forecast	infant mortality rate	ecology
fertility	life expectancy	ecosystem

CHAPTER 20

Cities, Urbanization, and Community Change

mericans have long maintained a love-hate relationship with the city. Although one hears an occasional voice raised in praise of the advantages of urban life, historically most observers have described cities in overwhelmingly negative terms. Writing more than a hundred years ago, social critic and reformist minister Josiah Strong sounded themes that seem entirely modern except for the slightly quaint language in which they are expressed:

> Here is heaped the social dynamite; here roughs, gamblers, thieves, robbers, lawless and desperate men of all sorts congregate; men who are ready on any pretext to raise riots for the purpose of destruction and plunder; here gather foreigners and wage-workers; here skepticism and irreligion abound; here inequality is the greatest and most obvious, and the contrast between opulence and penury the most striking. (1885, pp. 128–138)

Numerous nineteenth- and twentieth-century writers voiced similar sentiments, condemning the city as the incubator of every dark and sinful impulse in the American soul. Dirt, disarray, riots, danger, disease, crime, and corruption—these appear to be the essence of urban life as viewed by generation after generation of social commentators.

Yet, despite this relentless drumbeat of criticism, Americans have been voting for the cities with their feet just as long as they have been speaking out against them. In the colonial era, America was a predominantly rural and agricultural society. However, with industrialization, there began a massive migration into urban regions, primarily motivated by the quest for employment opportunities, which has resulted in a nation whose population is today well over 70 percent urban.

Most of the migrants initially settled close to the center of the large cities, where rents were cheapest. As these inner-city areas became increasingly crowded and less desirable, those who could afford to do so began to move outward to the suburbs, which provided easy access to the economic and cultural advantages of the city while re-creating some of the atmosphere of small-town or rural life.

Although some population analysts expected the suburban trend to decline, Americans have continued to move to the suburbs in increasing numbers. One of the reasons is that owning a home is now possible for unprecedented numbers of people. And most prospective home buyers prefer a single-family house with a yard (Rybczynski, 1995). Another reason is that many businesses have also moved to the suburbs. And suburbs are now designed to provide the kinds of goods and services

that were at one time only available in the central city (Macionis & Parrillo, 1998).

Other Americans, especially in the South and the West, have moved still farther out, often settling in small towns. While a few former suburbanites have been lured back to restored sectors of the central city, a sizable majority of modern Americans seems to continue to regard cities much as Reverend Strong did over a century ago.

Why do so many people have negative attitudes toward city life? Why did American cities grow so dramatically over the past 200 years despite widespread antiurban sentiments? Have the residents of suburbs and others who have moved entirely away from urban areas found what they were looking for? Can the central city be revived? We explore these issues in this chapter, as well as examine the social structure of urban life, major urban problems, and the distinctive lifestyles of the people who live in metropolitan areas.

THE ORIGIN AND GROWTH OF CITIES

Life in the modern world revolves around cities. They are the centers of government, finance, and industry. To understand modern urban life fully, however, we need to know something about the historical processes that have shaped it.

The First Human Communities

The earliest humans were organized into roving bands of foragers and hunters and lacked stable, settled communities. This pattern of group life can be seen today among the few remaining nomadic tribes, which continually shift from place to place. Such mobile foraging is a relatively effective way of adapting to an environment whose soil will not reward planting or grazing for more than a short time.

About 10,000 years ago, in what is called the *neolithic revolution,* permanent settlements based on agriculture first appeared. The development of simple farming techniques, such as the planting and harvesting of grain, greatly increased the available food supply. Once they began to stay in one place for a long time, people also learned how to tame animals. Besides serving as pets, guardians, and draft animals, domesticated animals increased the food supply. The new stability of life in settled villages meant more food, more safety, and more leisure. Urban historian and critic Lewis Mumford (1961) suggested that this change allowed vastly more time for the domestic arts to develop.

Partly because they could produce only a limited amount of food, few of these early settlements contained more than 200 people. The residents were usually closely related, so the community was organized principally on a kinship basis. Archeological evidence of the existence of such villages has been found throughout the world. Even today, in nearly every country, including the United States, one can find settlements broadly similar to these early communities: small villages in which almost everyone farms the land and in which there is little economic specialization (see also Bairoch, 1988).

The Birth of Urban Places

As agriculture became somewhat more productive some time after 5000 B.C., a few neolithic settlements grew into small towns and cities. This change, one of the most important in history, is sometimes called the *urban revolution* (Benevolo, 1980; Childe, 1951). The most significant factor in defining an urban place is not its size but the way its residents earn a living. In an urban community, a large number of the residents do not grow their own food. Such communities can arise only where there is a surplus of food beyond that needed to feed the people who farm (Bender, 1975; Schaedel, Hardy, & Kinzer, 1978; Ucko et al., 1972).

Because early urban dwellers needed to find ways to obtain a regular supply of food from frequently reluctant peasants, new specialists, including soldiers and tax collectors, appeared. And because some people no longer had to produce their own food, still other types of specialists emerged, such as artisans, traders, and religious officials. City life could no longer be regulated solely by the kinship norms and informal methods of social control that were adequate in the neolithic villages. The new urban conditions required the development of new governing institutions and legal systems.

With the birth of the first towns and cities, the social process known as urbanization began. **Urbanization** is the movement of people from rural to urban areas. But it was not until modern times that a substantial portion of any society's population lived in urban places. Throughout most of human history, the vast majority of the people remained in the countryside.

The first urban communities were built along the banks of the Tigris and Euphrates rivers, in what is now Iraq. They were not large by modern standards, although they were enormous in comparison to any human settlements that had previously existed. Ur, one of the oldest known cities, is thought to have contained, at its peak, 10,000 to 20,000 people (Bairoch, 1988; Whitehouse, 1977). City growth was greatly restricted by poor transportation (the wheel was not invented until about 3000 B.C.), by the difficulty of earning a living in the city, and by unsanitary conditions, which promoted the spread of infectious diseases. Most of the early cities also were very unstable. They were easily captured and sacked,

quick to revolt against their leaders, and occasionally subject to unexplained calamities. Little is known about why many of the great cities of the ancient world were finally abandoned.

The development of early cities was not limited to the Middle East. In what is now India and Pakistan, cities with advanced amenities such as plumbing arose between 2400 and 1500 B.C. In China, cities began to appear after 1800 B.C. (Wheeler, 1968). The early cities of the New World—that is, North and South America—although they developed later (about 1000 B.C.), were fully as impressive as their Old World counterparts.

About 1000 B.C., iron came into widespread use, leading to improved transportation, expanded economic production, and thus ultimately larger urban populations. The exchange of ideas among people in cities stimulated new inventions and discoveries—writing, the calendar, mathematics, money, bronze, copper, and brass—which in turn encouraged still additional growth. Yet, even after centuries of urban development, no city, except for ancient Rome, was occupied by more than a few hundred thousand people (Adams, 1966; Davis, 1955).

Preindustrial Urban Development in Europe

The roots of European urban development lie in the great classical cities of the Mediterranean area: Athens and Rome. A few centuries before the birth of Christ, Athens grew into an independent city-state with a tradition of political democracy and artistic achievement. Indeed, historians trace the beginnings of Western democracy to Athens, despite the fact that only free males (and not women or slaves) were allowed to vote. Public issues were debated and decided at weekly meetings open to everyone who could vote. In time, Athens became a colonial power, ruling the surrounding city-states and islands and demanding tribute in return for military protection (Benevolo, 1980; Mumford, 1961).

Athens was a small city compared to Rome, however. By the second century A.D., as many as 1 million people may have lived in Rome, the center of an empire that included much of Europe, the Near East, and North Africa. A series of Roman emperors spent huge sums on vast construction projects. Extensive water and sewage systems, for example, served the apartment buildings in which most of Rome's residents lived. Yet security was a constant problem, and guards patrolled the streets to maintain law and order (Rabb & Rotberg, 1981; Toynbee, 1967; Vance, 1977).

After the fall of Rome, urban centers across Europe lost people and influence; they remained weak and unstable throughout the early Middle Ages. In the eleventh and twelfth centuries, however, cities again began to play an increasingly active commercial and cultural role, but they continued to be very small. The size of the area that any city could control was limited by the distance its inhabitants could comfortably travel in order to protect their land. In 1377, London had a population of only 30,000 (Girouard, 1985; Pirenne, 1925). In the fourteenth century, urban growth was slowed abruptly by the "Black Death," a series of bubonic plague epidemics that sometimes killed as much as half of a city's population. After the plague subsided, urban growth continued at a slow but steady pace through the Renaissance.

The modern era of rapid urbanization did not begin until the eighteenth century, when changes in farming and industry revitalized Europe's economy. Called the Industrial Revolution, this transformation began in England. By 1800, the population of London had shot up to 1 million. Urban growth in this period was based on "improvement in agriculture and transport, the opening of new lands and trade routes, and above all, the rise in productive activity, first in highly organized handicraft and eventually in a revolutionary new form of production—the factory run by machinery and fossil fuel" (Davis, 1955, p. 433; see also Konvitz, 1985).

THE SOCIAL STRUCTURE OF PREINDUSTRIAL CITIES

Cities before the Industrial Revolution were unlike modern industrial cities in several important ways (Sjoberg, 1960). Although both preindustrial and modern cities are characterized by relatively dense populations and social diversity, the social structure of the preindustrial city was more like that of a rural village. Family and kinship networks were still an important form of social organization. The social stratification system allowed little social mobility. Industry was organized around craftworkers and artisans working in their homes. A small elite controlled the government. And social order was based more on a strict traditional hierarchy of social positions and custom than on written laws or police forces. Each of these characteristics reflects the influence of traditional rural social systems, to which most of the early cities were still tied (Laslett, 1984).

Partly owing to underdeveloped means of transportation, the preindustrial city was usually divided into districts, or quarters. Government officials and upper-class people typically lived in one quarter (usually the one closest to the city's center), foreigners in another, and the lower classes in still another. Metalsmiths, weavers, tailors, and other artisans each had their own districts. Traces of this sort of patterning can be seen today on London's Fleet Street, where printers and journalists still work and, in some cases, live.

Although districts were often specialized in the preindustrial city, buildings were not. People normally lived and worked under the same roof. A local store might also serve as a school and perhaps a government office as well. Nor was there a high degree of occupational specialization in the modern sense. The same merchant bought raw materials, transformed them into manufactured articles, and then sold them to customers.

URBANIZATION AFTER THE INDUSTRIAL REVOLUTION

The towns and cities of Western Europe began to grow very rapidly during the late eighteenth century as a result of the Industrial Revolution. New industries were located in urban places so as to benefit from the well-established systems of commerce that developed as medieval towns grew into craft and trade centers. Advanced technology made farming more efficient and reduced the need for rural labor, thus encouraging migration to urban centers. And the workers, attracted by the opportunity to work in the new urban industries, provided a growing market for goods and services.

In 1700, less than 2 percent of England's population lived in cities. By 1900, a majority were urban dwellers. Other European countries began city growth later but achieved the same level of urbanization in a shorter period. This growth was strongly encouraged by the development of modern medicines and public health measures that finally eradicated most of the endemic diseases that had always made the city an unhealthy environment in which to live. Geographic and environmental factors strongly influenced where new cities were located and how existing cities grew. Typically, the largest cities were located where the costs of transportation were lowest: along seacoasts, beside large rivers, or near deposits of natural resources.

Along with the growth of industrial cities came a number of far-reaching social and cultural changes. Public education became more accessible and also more necessary, leading to improved levels of literacy and a more highly skilled work force. Immigrants, people from the countryside, and ethnic and regional minorities were all at least partially absorbed into a single urban culture. And urban and industrial conditions strongly affected systems of social stratification. For example, a growing industrial middle class of urban managers, merchants, and professionals replaced the small preindustrial middle class of artisans, traders, and rural, small-property owners (Rabb & Rotberg, 1981; Roebuck, 1974). This growth of the middle class is closely associated with the rise of capitalism.

Urbanization in the United States

Although the United States remained a largely rural nation long after rapid urbanization had begun in England, it became highly urbanized in a much shorter time—chiefly between 1860 and 1920. In 1860, less than 20 percent of Americans lived in urban areas. By 1920, a majority lived in cities. Only 25 percent of the total work force was employed in farming in 1920, down from 72 percent a century earlier (Chudacoff & Smith, 1988).

Because of its early industrial development, the Northeast, including New York, Massachusetts, and Pennsylvania, was the first region of the country to become highly urbanized. In 1900, six of the eight states that were more than 50 percent urban were located in the Northeast. Western cities, which depended mainly on trade, lagged behind those of the Northeast until World War II, at which time the rapid expansion of defense industries caused them to grow rapidly.

This trend continued after World War II. In the last decade, the highest rates of urban growth have been found in Sun Belt cities, while the populations in midwestern and northeastern cities have generally declined. Austin, Phoenix, San Diego, San Jose, and San Antonio—all in the South and West—have grown significantly. But Detroit, Cleveland, Washington, D.C., and Baltimore—midwestern and northeastern cities—have lost a substantial number of people. Three cities did not fit this overall pattern: New York City, whose population increased, and New Orleans and Memphis, which both lost people.

Today, the United States is one of the most highly urbanized nations in the world. About three-quarters of the American population lives in urban communities, and nearly 90 percent lives within an hour's driving distance of an urban center. Even those who do not live in urban places are closely tied to an urban way of life as a result of the rapid expansion of modern media of communication and transportation. Worldwide, cities are home to almost half of the population. By 2025, this figure is expected to reach two-thirds (Brockerhoff, 1996).

Urbanization in Developing Nations

Western urbanization and industrialization took place over several generations. The developing nations of Africa, Asia, and Latin America are trying to achieve the same result in a much shorter period of time and under very different conditions from those that prevailed in the West. Whereas the Western nations were the wealthiest in the world even before industrialization, today's developing nations are extremely poor. As they industrialize, they must attempt to compete with the highly sophisticated economies of the developed societies.

Vast slums populated by millions of people living in dangerous and unhealthy shanties like these characterize many of the large cities in the Third World.

The internal situation in the newly developing nations also differs markedly from that which characterized the West during the era of rapid city growth. For one thing, contemporary Third World urbanization involves a more rapid movement of people into cities than did Western urbanization. Indeed, the growth of cities in the developing nations is truly explosive. It is estimated that nine-tenths of all city growth in the next 20 years will take place in this part of the world (Brown & Jacobson, 1987). This rapid growth is largely a result of the enormous population increases that are occurring in the developing nations today.

The reverse process seems to be taking place in the United States and other industrial nations, where technologically advanced transportation and communication systems have encouraged the population to disperse now that goods can be transported and information sent rapidly from one end of a country to the other (Harvey, 1989). This decentralization process has also been promoted by the ability of sophisticated social organizations such as corporations to coordinate the activities of employees dispersed around the world. In contrast, transportation and communication in Third World nations are much less sophisticated.

Economic development in Third World nations typically lags far behind urban population growth. High in population and low in employment opportunities, rural areas are characterized by huge labor surpluses. Surplus labor crowds into the cities in numbers far exceeding the cities' capacity to provide jobs and homes. This phenomenon is sometimes called **overurbanization:** a disparity between the number of people moving into cities and the opportunities and services available there.

WINDOW ON SOCIOLOGY

CITY OF HOPE
OR CAPITAL DECAY?

In this city, non-taxpayers are more privileged than the ones who are paying the taxes.
—Joe Corey (restaurateur)

You can't let children out by themselves, and the playground is littered with intravenous needles.
—Sheila Stamps (widowed mother)

Where can I go? Even if I find somebody who wants to buy my house, I won't have enough money even for a downpayment anywhere else.
—Benjamin Thomas (homeowner)

Few Americans see the city that these residents describe (Murphy, 1997). It is a place that remains invisible, hidden in the shadows of grand monuments. Far from what our founding fathers had envisioned, critics call Washington, D.C., a national disgrace and draw attention to the social problems that plague it. In 1995, Philip Murphy identified the most serious ones, writing:

Among all U.S. states, the District has the highest per capita murder and violent-crime rates, the highest percentage of residents on public assistance, the highest-paid school board, the lowest SAT scores, and the most single-parent families. (1997, p. 141)

How could problems like these escape the attention of the most powerful people in the United States? The president and Congress are literally surrounded by the results of these problems, but, yet, they appear untouched. They seem to live and work in a different city, one that was designed over 200 years earlier to serve as the epicenter of this new nation's governing body. Its designer, a French soldier by the name of Charles L'Enfant, saw a city whose avenues would be crowded with people and lined with noble buildings, like the Champs Elysées in Paris. He believed that his plan would "give Washington a superiority of [amenities] over most of the cities of the world" (Antoniou, 1994, p. 96).

Forty years after the construction of Washington, D.C., had begun, Alexis de Toqueville visited the new capital—the most prominent city being built in the United States and the first one to be planned by a trained professional (Rybczynski, 1995). He was not impressed. The avenues were not filled with people; nor were they lined by magnificent buildings. In disbelief, Tocqueville wrote: "They have already rooted up trees for ten miles around, lest they should get in the way of the future citizens of this imagined capital" (Rybczynski, 1995, p. 97). This city was growing slowly and at that time had a population of less than 20,000.

But by the end of World War II, Washington was a beautiful place. It was also a city that promised bright futures for all Americans. One longtime resident described the way it was in 1944:

The city was a thriving community of educated descendants of freed slaves, flourishing family businesses, and urban sophistication. It was also a magnet of opportunity for blacks seeking to escape rural poverty. (Murphy, 1997, p. 141)

At its peak, Washington was home to 800,000 people, but by 1996, the population had dwindled to 543,000. A local businessman in Washington once described the city as an incubator of America's black middle class—the promised land. By the mid-1990s, the flight from this city had already begun. Black homeowners, entrepreneurs, and role models were departing in huge numbers to live in surrounding suburbs.

The departure of the middle class from cities into surrounding areas is not new. Demographers had observed this trend around the turn of the nineteenth century. It accelerated in the 1940s and was called "white flight" because it seemed to occur as southern blacks moved north. In this case, observers were calling the exodus from Washington "black flight," and they wanted to reverse the trend.

But doing that will not be easy. Murphy suggests the following. First, in order to keep middle-class families, Washington must provide services that middle-class taxpayers expect. This includes quality public education and public safety. Second, the city must also understand and respond to the needs of small businesses. According to Murphy, this will require a "competitive regulatory climate for entrepreneurs and a low-capital point of entry to the economy" (1997, p. 145). And, third, Washington must eliminate projects and services that do not meet the needs of people who simply want to raise families there. Murphy is optimistic about the future of our nation's capital, noting not only that other cities have succeeded in revering the exodus of the middle class but adding that Washington is the kind of place where people would like to live.

The growth of Western cities was largely unregulated by government; in contrast, urbanization in developing nations is often managed by centralized governments.

These governments find themselves caught between a desire to increase economic efficiency and strong pressures to maintain traditional social structures. In the face of this conflict, the management of urban growth is often inadequate, a problem made worse by lack of money and other resources.

Housing is a special problem. Typically, new urban dwellers live in makeshift "squatter settlements" surrounding large cities. These settlements are undesirable, often miserable places to live—severely crowded and lacking in such basic services as running water, waste disposal, and electricity (Gilbert & Gugler, 1983). Despite such conditions, squatter settlements do serve an important function by easing migrants' transition from rural to urban life (Berry & Kasarda, 1977; Bromley, 1988). In Nairobi, where one-fifth of the population lives as squatters, many people have become part of an informal "street work force," peddling food, providing services, and engaging in illegal activities such as prostitution (Gugler, 1988). The highest percentage of squatters is found in the cities of sub-Saharan Africa, where 66 percent of the urban population lives in squatter settlements. Squatters also account for 52 percent of the population in some Middle Eastern cities, 37 percent of many Latin American cities, and 27 percent of some South Asian cities (Castells, 1988).

METROPOLITAN STRUCTURE AND DEVELOPMENT IN THE UNITED STATES

Urban sociologists apply the term *community* to small villages, urban neighborhoods, and large cities alike. To them, a **community** is a cluster of people located in a particular geographic area whose lives are organized around daily patterns of interaction. These patterns involve such activities as work, shopping, and recreation and such institutions as education, religion, and government. (The term *community* is also used, in a different but related sense, to refer to places or groups in which people feel strong bonds of common identity and solidarity.)

In the nineteenth century, the typical urban community was a dense, compact city. But in the modern era, major urban communities take the form of **metropolitan areas**—one or more large cities, together with their surrounding suburbs. In the United States, the Bureau of the Census uses the concept of a *metropolitan statistical area (MSA)* to analyze urban life. An MSA is defined as a city and its suburbs that together contain a total population of at least 50,000 people. Currently, more than 75 percent of the American population lives in MSAs.

The Metropolitan Community

Metropolitan areas develop when cities expand outward into less populated regions. Their growth in the twentieth century was greatly aided by the widespread use of the automobile, which has given people the ability to live outside the city in relatively uncrowded areas and still enjoy easy access to urban jobs and services. The first people to leave the central cities and move to the suburbs were the well-to-do, followed by large numbers of middle-class families. Metropolitan growth has led to increased geographic segregation of people by social class, race, and other social variables (Saunders, 1981; Scargill, 1979). Many of the urban poor—including African-Americans, Hispanic-Americans, and elderly people—remain in the central cities, whereas the white middle class is concentrated in the suburbs.

For many decades, suburban communities have been the fastest-growing parts of American metropolitan areas. The central cities themselves have grown very little and in many cases have actually declined in total population. There has been a high turnover of population in the central cities, however, as middle-class whites have left and rural African-Americans, immigrants, and other newcomers have replaced them. Some native-born minorities and older immigrants are also moving to the suburbs (Riche, 1991). In addition, a great many people have moved directly from farms and small towns to suburban communities without ever passing through the cities. Today only about 30 percent of all Americans live in central cities, whereas 45 percent live in suburbs. Americans are not so much urbanized, therefore, as they are *sub*urbanized.

THE CENTRAL CITIES

The core of most metropolitan areas is heavily devoted to commerce. Because the central city is normally the hub of the local transportation network, it is the ideal location for such industries and services as advertising, publishing, finance, entertainment, and some specialized types of retail businesses. These activities require face-to-face interaction, a large work force, and a place where clients, customers, or audiences can meet easily. The central cities meet all these requirements.

The people who live in the American central city are disproportionately likely to be members of poor minority groups. This is due in part to the flight of the white middle class to the suburbs and in part to the migration of the poor into the cities in search of low-skill jobs and such services as welfare and health care. But this migration of minorities—especially African-Americans—to urban areas has slowed in recent years. Of the nearly 5 million blacks, Hispanics, and Asians who immigrated to the United States between 1976 and 1986, almost half settled in suburban or nonmetropolitan areas rather than in central cities (Macionis & Parrillo, 1998).

Inner-city housing developments have become traps for many disadvantaged minorities. Lack of employment and educational opportunities often prevent the residents from leaving.

The urban poor are often concentrated in areas of substandard, usually overcrowded, housing. These neighborhoods house newcomers to the city, who commonly plan to stay only until their economic situation improves enough to permit them to move out. Unfortunately, however, these areas become traps for many disadvantaged minorities. Lack of employment opportunities and education often prevents these people from saving enough money to leave. And even when they acquire the means to do so, they frequently experience discrimination when they attempt to rent or purchase suburban housing (W. J. Wilson, 1978, 1987).

The central cities house more than just the poor, however. Indeed, they are the home of a wide variety of people and lifestyles. In an influential analysis, Herbert Gans (1962a) identified five distinct groups of people who may be found in many American central cities:

1. *The cosmopolites.* Members of this group tend to be well educated and to work in the professions or in businesses related to literature and art, such as advertising, publishing, and design. Their incomes are typically high. They choose to live in the city in order to be near its cultural offerings, but they do not have strong ties to local neighborhoods.

2. *The unmarried or childless.* These people live in the city by choice, primarily because it is a good place to meet people and to enjoy an active social life. They move often, and many leave the city altogether when they have children.

3. *The ethnic villagers.* This group is made up of immigrants from other countries who remain largely unintegrated into the American way of life and continue to follow many of the ways of their native villages. They tend to stay within their own neighborhoods and have little interest in the rest of the city. As Gans says,

"Although they reside in the city, they isolate themselves from significant contact with most city facilities, aside from workplaces" (p. 309).

4. *The deprived.* The poor, the nonwhite, and unmarried mothers make up the majority of this group. They live in the city because they can find cheap housing there. Furthermore, welfare payments are usually higher in cities than in rural areas. Finally, many deprived people hope that they will be able to find jobs and improve their economic situations in the city.

5. *The trapped.* This group consists mainly of elderly people who live on pensions and cannot afford to move. Many of these people have lived in the city all their lives. Like the ethnic villagers, they identify strongly with their neighborhoods and seldom leave them.

Although first developed in the early 1960s, these categories are still relevant to today's urban centers. Even so, certain social trends in the last two decades are noteworthy. Many European ethnic villagers have moved to the suburbs, and their places in the center city have been taken by more recent immigrants of Hispanic and Asian origin. Especially in the older cities of the East and Midwest, the deprived now account for a dramatically increased share of the total population. They make up what some call the "underclass," characterized by high rates of drug use, unemployment, crime, and teenage pregnancy (Jencks, 1972; Kasarda, 1989; Wilson, 1987). In small areas of many cities, a process known as "gentrification" has increased the number of cosmopolites and middle-class unmarried and childless persons. And a new group—the homeless—has become a familiar sight in the central cities.

THE SUBURBS

A **suburb** is a relatively small community that is near to, and dependent on, a central city. Although cities have had suburbs throughout history, the suburb has flourished in the twentieth century. The modern growth of suburbs was made possible by advances in transportation, especially the development of the automobile and mass transit. The suburbs have been described as one of the most distinctive aspects of American society (Jackson, 1985).

From one point of view, the suburbs are a solution to problems associated with the dense concentration of people in cities. With high density, public facilities become overcrowded and housing becomes expensive and scarce. To meet the growing need for goods and services, commercial and government activities expand and take over living space, causing even more crowding in residential areas. The most common solution to this vicious circle has been to establish new residential areas on the outer edges of the city. This allows the economic advantages of urbanization to be maintained, while some of the problems of density and crowding are reduced.

In the United States, the very rapid growth of the suburbs has been fueled by rising personal incomes and the strong desire to own a single-family home, together with government policies that promote suburbanization (Jackson, 1985). Eager to facilitate the American dream of homeownership, the government created the Home Owners Loan Corporation in the 1930s to protect homeowners from foreclosure, and after World War II made low-cost mortgages available to veterans, provided Federal Housing Administration (FHA) loans for housing renovation and development, and offered income tax deductions for mortgage interest. Furthermore, to ease the suburbanites' commute, the Department of Transportation provided funds to build roads and to support the expansion of commuter railroads. Suburbanization has also been spurred in America by the relatively poor living conditions in the central cities. Many people regard a move to the suburbs as an escape from the negative aspects of city life.

Increasingly, central city jobs and stores have moved to the suburbs along with people. Industries are attracted to the suburbs by the open space and lower taxes they offer. And most downtown department stores have established suburban branches; some have even moved out of the city entirely, many to suburban malls, which function not only as centralized shopping areas but also as informal recreational and social centers. Thus, the suburbs today are less dependent on the central cities than they once were. If anything, the central cities are becoming increasingly dependent on the suburbs. This pattern of dependency is clearest in the younger cities, such as Los Angeles, Houston, and Phoenix. Consisting mainly of a series of residential suburbs mixed with outlying office and shopping malls, these cities are no longer centered around downtown areas.

Suburbs tend to be highly differentiated by social class. Some, such as Darien (Connecticut), Grosse Point (Michigan), and Franklin Lakes (New Jersey), are mostly upper class. Others, like Evanston (Illinois), Arlington (Virginia), and Stanford (California), are upper middle class. But most suburbs are middle class or upper working class.

Middle-class minorities began to move to the suburbs following the federal fair housing legislation of 1968 (Macionis & Parrillo, 1998). By 1980 it seemed that laws alone could not integrate neighborhoods. Census data for that year showed that whites and blacks lived in racially segregated suburbs. Since then, however, suburbs have become increasingly racially diverse, and more and more African-Americans are moving to suburbs. In 1990,

For several generations city dwellers have been flocking to the suburbs in search of better schools, safer neighborhoods, and more living space.

census data showed that 27 percent of African-Americans lived in the suburbs.

Metropolitan Expansion and Decline

MEGALOPOLIS

The growth and decentralization of metropolitan regions have created a new type of urban area, the **megalopolis**— an urban concentration of two or more metropolitan areas that have grown until they overlap. The result is a continuous strip of urban and suburban development that may stretch for hundreds of miles (Gottman, 1964; Scott, 1988). Analysts have identified more than a dozen megalopolitan areas in the United States. The best known is the "Boswash Corridor," the complex of cities lying between Boston and Washington, D.C. Another is the expanse along the West Coast between San Francisco and San Diego.

In a megalopolis, the distinctions between rural, suburban, and urban areas are blurred. The whole region is a patchwork of industrial, suburban, and urban sectors. High-speed highways take workers from home to job and back in trips that may cover more than 100 miles. People tend to live, work, and play in different places. Because regional problems must be confronted by many local and state governments, each with its own interests, it is not easy to coordinate public policies and programs. The megalopolis, therefore, poses major difficulties for city and regional planners. Yet it is likely to be the characteristic urban community of the future as Americans try to

TABLE 20.1   THE MOST TROUBLED CITIES IN AMERICA

Cities of 25,000–50,000 Population	Cities over 50,000 Population
1. Prichard, AL	1. Brownsville, TX
2. Pharr, TX	2. Camden, NJ
3. East St. Louis, IL	3. Laredo, TX
4. Edinburg, TX	4. Saginaw, MI
5. Mission, TX	5. Lawrence, MA
6. Bell Gardens, CA	6. Detroit, MI
7. Greenville, MS	7. Gary, IN
8. New Iberia, LA	8. Cleveland, OH
9. Bell City, CA	9. Pontiac, MI
10. East Chicago, IN	10. Youngstown, OH

Source: Chris Kelley. "In Search of New Life: Once-Proud Industrial Cities Pursue Answers to a Changing Economy," *The Dallas Morning News,* December 3, 1995, pp. A1, A32. Reprinted with permission of *The Dallas Morning News.*

combine the advantages of city life with those of low-density suburbs.

METROPOLITAN DECLINE

Just as it appeared that America was on the way to becoming a completely metropolitan nation, the populations of many of its metropolitan areas have begun to decrease. In the 1970s, major cities experienced a loss of approximately 13 million residents (Fishman, 1987). This decline has continued over the past 30 years, leaving many urban areas strapped for the resources needed to revive their economies (see Table 20.1) (Kelley, 1995). The most troubled cities in the United States face common problems. According to a study conducted by the *Dallas Morning News*, these problems include the following (Kelley, 1995, p. A1):

- More than one in five U.S. cities of more than 25,000 population has a poverty rate of 20 percent or greater.

- In 1968, three in ten poor Americans lived in cities. This concentration has increased: the figure is now more than four in ten.

- Job creation is moving away from traditional urban cores. About seven in ten new jobs are being created outside of cities.

- Smaller cities, with populations of 25,000 to 100,000, may be feeling the worst economic pinch, but they have fewer resources than larger cities.

As we enter the twenty-first century, the economy of the Information Age is expected to contribute to the decline of urban areas. Technological changes now allow people to live and work where they want. And so far they are choosing new suburbs.

THE GENTRIFICATION OF CENTRAL CITIES

At the same time that large numbers of people were moving away from metropolitan areas in the 1970s, analysts noted that a growing number of middle-class men and women—especially single people, childless couples, and "cosmopolites"—were choosing to remain in the central cities (Baldassare, 1986; James, 1977). As a result, many previously marginal neighborhoods in cities that are considered especially exciting and desirable, including New York, Philadelphia, Boston, Washington, San Francisco, and Chicago, are being **gentrified.** In other words, poor residents of these neighborhoods are being displaced by professional people (Gerard, 1984; Laska & Spain, 1980).

The reasons for this trend include the high cost of suburban housing and a large increase in the number of very small households, as more and more young people postpone marriage and childbearing. Gentrification does not involve a return of suburban families to the city. Rather, the "gentry" (a British term that originally referred to well-to-do landowners) appear to be primarily people who were raised in the suburbs, who moved to the city as young adults, and who now have chosen not to leave. In some cities, the trend has produced a central city "revival." Many speculate that gentrification may help to lessen the long-term economic decline of the cities.

Gentrification usually proceeds in three stages. First, a few "pioneering" families move into a deteriorating area

The burned-out buildings of the South Bronx in New York City have become a national symbol of urban decay.

and purchase and renovate existing structures. A year or two later, these families are followed by others who are attracted by housing possibilities and investment potential. Rents go up, and the poor, unable to afford the new rates, are gradually forced to move (Zukin, 1987). Finally, developers and speculators arrive and renovate on a large-scale basis. Developers are often lured by such federal subsidies as the Urban Development Action Grants, enticed by tax credits, and encouraged by local governments that provide assistance in the form of advertising and the building of support facilities—shops, parking lots, office buildings, and parks—near the development (Feagin & Parker, 1990).

In recent years, the transformation of renovated buildings into condominiums, where occupants own rather than rent their units, has become popular and profitable for developers, but costly for residents. In Philadelphia, an apartment that rented for $560 a month required an average monthly mortgage and maintenance cost of $1,200 when it was converted to a condominium. Many people simply cannot afford condominium maintenance fees and are forced to move when their buildings are converted.

A national housing consultant estimates that gentrification displaces approximately 100,000 people per year (Feagin & Parker, 1990). But gentrification is only one factor making it difficult for the urban poor to secure affordable housing. Scholars identify two other trends that contribute to this problem (Grier & Grier, 1980). One is *disinvestment*—the abandonment of housing by landlords because it no longer is profitable. When housing is abandoned, it falls into disrepair. The burned-out buildings of the South Bronx in New York City have become a national symbol of urban decay. The second factor is increased competition for the remaining sound housing. As disinvestment reduces the supply of inexpensive housing, the cost of the sound housing that remains increases, often beyond the ability of the poor to pay.

EDGE CITIES

A most significant change in metropolitan growth patterns over the last half century has been the development of what Joel Garreau (1992) calls *edge cities*. According to him, American cities that are growing resemble the pattern observed in Los Angeles. He describes these new cities as follows:

> These new hearths of our civilization—in which the majority of metropolitan Americans now work and around which we live—look not at all like our old downtowns. Buildings rarely rise shoulder to shoulder, as in Chicago's Loop. Instead, their broad, low outlines dot the landscape like mushrooms, separated by greensward and parking lots. Their office towers, frequently guarded by trees, gaze at one another from respectful distances through bands of glass that mirror the sun in blue or silver or green or gold, like antique drawings of "the city of the future." (1991, pp. 3–4)

Garreau calls these new urban centers "edge cities" because they serve the functions that cities always have—albeit along the spread-out borders of an already existing urban area.

Urban Ecology

Urban ecologists are sociologists who take a special interest in the social and spatial organization of urban communities. Classic urban ecologists have identified several processes that contribute to urban change and explain the distribution of kinds of people and activities in specific areas and neighborhoods of the city (McKenzie, 1926).

URBAN ECOLOGICAL PROCESSES

ECOLOGICAL SEGREGATION. The process by which different areas of a city become increasingly specialized with regard to land use, services, or population is called **ecological segregation.** The most obvious example is the formation of "ghettos" (areas of a city in which members of a particular ethnic group are concentrated), but there are many other kinds of segregation. Childless couples or single people commonly locate in places that feature rental apartments. Public housing projects segregate people by income. Chicago's Old Town, San Francisco's Castro Street, and New York's Greenwich Village are segregated on the basis of lifestyles: They attract people who choose nontraditional or bohemian ways of life. New York's SoHo district, home to many artists, is substantially segregated by profession.

Commercial, governmental, and other facilities and services also tend to cluster in specific parts of cities. For example, New York has the garment district, Los Angeles has television studio districts, and suburbs have "industrial parks." Urban ecologists have also noted that related services frequently locate near each other. Courts are usually close to jails, and smaller retail shops commonly are near major department stores; theaters and restaurants are clustered in entertainment districts. Segregated neighborhoods such as these, which emerge without deliberate planning, are sometimes called *natural areas.*

INVASION AND SUCCESSION. Invasion refers to the entrance of one social group or type of land use into territory currently occupied by another. In ecological **succession,** one social group or type of land use replaces a rival as the dominant one in an area. These concepts are borrowed directly from biological ecology (Schwirian, 1983).

The concepts of invasion and succession can be illustrated by the history of Cleveland's downtown Hough neighborhood. Once an Indian hunting territory, this area became farmland during the colonial period. As the city grew, farms gave way to houses—first, small houses set far apart, then, as the population grew, larger houses located closer together. Later, the area's proximity to the central business district attracted wealthy people who built expensive town houses or brownstones. After many years as one of Cleveland's high-status neighborhoods, the area began to decay. When the rich left, their places were taken by the poor, attracted by the inexpensive rents charged for Hough's large old buildings. These buildings were gradually subdivided into multiple-family dwellings and sometimes into rooming houses. Eventually, the area decayed so seriously that many buildings were condemned and became homes for drug addicts, drifters, and the poorest of the poor.

As "natural" changes like these took their toll, Hough was also undermined by pressures arising from urban redevelopment, which in Cleveland, as elsewhere, disproportionately displaced African-Americans. Government money was used to redevelop largely black central districts adjoining Hough; many African-Americans were evicted and forced into Hough, which thus became more black and more crowded.

As housing became cheaper, it was snapped up by real estate developers, some of whom deliberately created a panic atmosphere. The remaining white residents sold out, usually at extremely low prices, to these developers, who in turn resold the houses at a profit to the incoming blacks. Black homeowners found that banks were unwilling to lend them money for repairs and rebuilding—a common although illegal policy known as *redlining*—which made it almost impossible to reverse the neighborhood's decline (Snow & Leahy, 1980).

URBAN SPATIAL STRUCTURE

Ecological processes such as segregation and invasion-succession commonly lead to the emergence of distinct and identifiable physical patterns in cities. Between the 1920s and the 1940s, a number of urban ecologists attempted to construct models of these patterns.

The best known of these models was developed in the 1920s by Ernest Burgess, who based his work on the growth of Chicago (Park, Burgess, & McKenzie, 1925). Burgess's *concentric zone model* visualizes the city as a series of rings surrounding a central business district. Moving outward from the core, these zones consist of a light manufacturing district, a "zone in transition" consisting

principally of lower-class residences, working-class neighborhoods, and finally middle-class suburbs. The more central residential zones contain many newcomers and single people and are characterized by high rates of crime and other social problems. The outer zones contain more families. Movement away from the central city is seen as an indicator of upward social mobility.

Critics charged that the concentric zone model was too closely based on Chicago and too determinate. In response to such criticisms, successive generations of urban ecologists proposed a series of increasingly generalized and indeterminate models (Harris & Ullman, 1945; Hoyt, 1939), but even these revisions proved too tied to patterns characteristic of particular cities at particular stages of urban development.

Modern urban ecologists no longer construct fixed models of urban spatial structure but seek, instead, to understand the general principles that determine how the spatial structure of cities takes shape over time. A useful quantitative approach to this inquiry called *social area analysis* was proposed in the 1950s by Eshref Shevky and Wendell Bell (Shevky & Bell, 1955). This technique uses three measures to describe how social groups are spatially distributed within cities: class, stage in the life course, and ethnicity. Data are taken from the census. Applied in different cities, this approach provides a very effective explanation of the ways people cluster together.

CONTEMPORARY URBAN ECOLOGY

More recent work by urban ecologists, as well as by geographers and economists, involves the use of computers to develop and test more elaborate models. The newer models include a wide range of social and cultural factors to reflect more accurately the complexity of the real world (Janson, 1980).

Most of today's urban ecologists have switched their focus from the central city to the metropolitan area as a whole (Berry & Kasarda, 1977; Bookchin, 1987; Glass, 1989; Hawley, 1981). They now view the metropolis as a complex and expanding social system. Of particular interest are the kinds of changes in transportation, communication, and community power that occur as a metropolis grows or contracts.

URBAN LIFE AND CULTURE

Urban sociologists are interested in many things besides the movement of populations into and out of cities and urban ecology. They are also concerned with the changes in culture and social structure that are promoted by urbanization and with how lifestyles differ in various types of communities.

Percent of U.S. Population Living in Urban Areas: 1790–1990

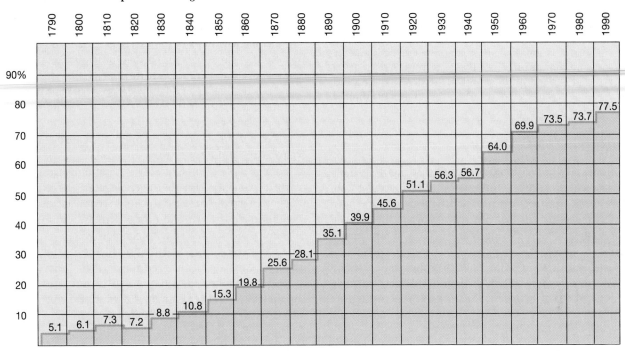

FIGURE 20.1 The Urbanization of America.
With each passing decade, American society has become increasingly urbanized.
Yet the data in the graph can be misleading. The figures include persons who live
in suburbs as well as central cities, and no distinction is made between towns as
small as 5,000 people and large cities of several million residents.
Sources: Historical Statistics of the United States and *U.S. Bureau of the Census, 1984, 1989, 1991.*

Changes in Community Life

In the past 200 years, patterns of community life in the
United States have undergone major changes. The small
town, which is so much a part of America's social heritage, is pretty much a thing of the past (Lyon, 1987;
Warren, 1972). (See Figure 20.1). This transformation is
important, and many of its aspects have been discussed
elsewhere in this book. However, this is a suitable place to
summarize them:

1. Interpersonal activities and relationships have
   become more and more fragmented. People may
   work in one area, spend their leisure time in a second,
   and eat and sleep in a third. Each activity typically
   involves a separate and unrelated set of organizations,
   roles, and people.

2. Community organizations and institutions have
   become larger and more bureaucratic. At the same
   time, many of them have developed a national focus
   that effectively puts them outside the control of the
   local community. What was once the corner grocery

store is now a supermarket owned by a national or
international corporation.

3. Functions once performed in the home, or by volunteers outside the home, have increasingly been taken
   over by business or government. Many of a family's
   recreational activities now take place in commercial
   establishments; schools perform most educational
   functions; and people in need of financial help turn to
   the public welfare office. More and more food is eaten
   in restaurants.

4. Communities of all sizes have become more interrelated. Much as families can no longer be fully self-
   sufficient, neither can towns or cities. State and federal
   governments have taken over many functions from
   local authorities. As a result, local communities are
   subject to increasingly strong federal and state controls. A community may be ordered to build a more
   modern sewage system or to modify the courses
   taught in its schools.

5. Communities have also become culturally interrelated. In America today, the attitudes characteristically
   found in cities, especially in New York and Hollywood,

tend to dominate the culture of small towns and rural areas. The mass media are carriers of urban culture. Millions of Americans regularly read national news-magazines, watch network television programs, and spend Saturday nights at the movies. These media are produced in cities like New York, Los Angeles, Chicago, and Washington, and they tend to reflect and to impart to society as a whole the values and attitudes typical of the urban way of life.

Perspectives on Urbanism

What exactly *is* the urban way of life? Sociologists have long been interested in **urbanism**—the patterns of culture and social structure characteristic of cities—and how it differs from small-town and rural ways of life. One of the first sociologists to study urbanism was Ferdinand Tönnies, whose writings became the basis for a great deal of later research on this topic. Much of the classic work in this area was done in the 1920s and 1930s by Chicago School sociologists such as Robert Park, Ernest Burgess, and Louis Wirth. Their writings on urban life and culture have had a lasting impact on the field.

GEMEINSCHAFT AND GESELLSCHAFT

Ferdinand Tönnies (1855–1936) believed that societies could be classified into two distinct types. In the *Gemeinschaft,* social relationships are based on personal ties of friendship and kinship. By contrast, the *Gesellschaft* is a type of society in which social relationships are formal, contractual, impersonal, and specialized.

In the *Gemeinschaft,* personal interactions are normally frequent and intense. People tend to be family- and community-oriented. In the *Gesellschaft,* however, personal interactions are limited in number and often quite impersonal. People tend to be oriented toward individual rather than group goals. Generally speaking, rural or farm life, in which most members of the community know one another and interact frequently, typifies *Gemeinschaft.* Modern urban living, with its emphasis on privacy and individuality, typifies *Gesellschaft.*

THE DETERMINIST PERSPECTIVE

The Chicago School's perspective on urban life, influenced by the writings of Tönnies, is probably best expressed in a classic article by Louis Wirth entitled "Urbanism as a Way of Life" (1938). Wirth believed that the large size, high density, and cultural heterogeneity characteristic of cities combine to produce a distinctive "culture of urbanism." This view has been called the *determinist perspective* (Fischer, 1975; Gottdiener, 1985) because it implies that the demographic features of cities substantially *determine* the behavior and attitudes of their people.

According to Wirth, city dwellers interact with one another primarily as role players, not in relationships that involve the whole person. Formal mechanisms of social control are more important in the city than informal ones. Finally, kinship and family groups play a less important part in cities than they do in small towns. Under these conditions, urbanites may experience substantial levels of *anomie*—a social condition in which norms and values are conflicting, weak, or absent. In a state of anomie, people cannot agree on a common standard of correct behavior. Wirth's overall image of city life depicted a mass of nameless people, separated from their neighbors and relating to others primarily in order to maximize their own personal economic gain.

Spurred by the escalating problems of large cities, scholars working in the tradition of Wirth have continued to explore the unique features of urban life. Psychologist Stanley Milgram (1970), for example, combined Wirth's perspective with similar observations made by classic German theorist Georg Simmel to conclude that many urban dwellers are faced with *psychic overload,* or the inability to handle all the sensory and cognitive information that constantly bombards them.

Milgram identifies several ways in which city dwellers commonly adapt to psychic overload. Because they normally encounter hundreds of people in a single day, urbanites conserve their psychic energy by maintaining only superficial and short-term relationships with most other people. Relationships that seem irrelevant are avoided entirely; that is why, for example, people walk around drunks lying on city pavements rather than stopping to offer help.

According to the determinist perspective, such methods of adaptation reduce the city dweller's moral and social involvement with others. A classic example is the 1964 murder of Kitty Genovese in front of her New York City apartment building. Thirty-eight of her neighbors heard her screams but failed to respond; no one even telephoned the police. Milgram believes this inaction may have been due in part to the fact that the victim appealed to the public at large rather than to any one person. Urban residents, he feels, do not get involved with others unless they are connected to them in a specific, personal way.

A survey conducted in Germany seems to support Milgram's theory. When asked if they would investigate screams they heard from another apartment, only 36 percent of the respondents said that they would do so (Hastings & Hastings, 1989). However, others have argued that behavior in public settings among people who do not know one another requires a special etiquette—careful, impersonal, and nonintrusive—that is often incorrectly *interpreted* as indifference (Fischer, 1982).

THE COMPOSITIONAL PERSPECTIVE

Sociologists who disagree with Wirth's view of urbanism have developed an alternative interpretation that has come to be called the *compositional perspective* (Fischer, 1984). This view explains the special qualities of urban life as the result of the distinctive social and cultural traits of the kinds of people who live in the city. Those who accept the compositional perspective see the city as a "mosaic of social worlds" (Fischer, 1984) made up of different groups, each of which shares such factors as kinship, ethnic origins, or social class. In contrast to Wirth and his followers, these sociologists deny that urbanism necessarily weakens social solidarity. For example, when immigrants from other countries settle in large cities, they normally develop and maintain strong social ties with one another. These bonds help to insulate them from some of the pressures of urban life.

Indeed, many researchers have found much more social unity and community structure in cities than would be predicted by Wirth's analysis. A study of two Los Angeles neighborhoods, for example, reported that half of the residents included in the sample visited relatives at least once a week (Greer, 1956). Herbert Gans's *The Urban Villagers* (1962a)—a study of how rural Italians adapted to life in Boston—indicates that many of them maintained much of their former social structure in the new environment. This practice provided the immigrants with a sense of identity and preserved their bonds with other Italian-Americans. Other classic sociological studies have identified strong feelings of community in several lower- and working-class neighborhoods in Chicago (Hunter, 1974; Suttles, 1968).

THE SUBCULTURAL PERSPECTIVE

Claude Fischer (1984) has proposed a third perspective on urbanism, the *subcultural perspective,* which combines selected features of the determinist and the compositional perspectives. Fischer agrees with Wirth that the physical and social realities of urban life—size, density, and the mixing of people from diverse backgrounds—do affect the structure and strength of social groups. But, in contrast to Wirth, and more in accord with the compositional perspective, he argues that urban life does not destroy the unity of subgroups but rather strengthens them and increases their importance. In fact, urban life actually creates subcultures that might not exist otherwise, because it brings together people with common backgrounds and interests. In a large city, for example, it

Sociologists favoring the compositional perspective note that there are typically strong feelings of community solidarity and extensive patterns of mutual aid in immigrant neighborhoods such as Chinatown.

might be possible to form a group of left-handed tuba players—certainly more possible than it would be in a small town. Unfortunately, the same holds true for left-handed drug dealers and car thieves.

Empirical Studies of Urbanism

COMPARING URBAN AND NONURBAN LIFE

Just how different is urban life from that style of life which is characteristic of nonurban areas? Is there empirical justification for thinking of the city in problematic terms, as Wirth did? An immense amount of research comparing urban and nonurban life has been conducted over the years, but the results have generally been inconclusive.

Two well-supported empirical generalizations are that urban living is associated with high crime rates, especially property crimes, and also with a weakening of the institution of the family (Farley, 1987; Fischer, 1984). The reasons for these patterns, however, remain unclear. There is also empirical evidence that urban social relationships are more "privatized," relations among neighbors are less frequent and less positive, and people are substantially less helpful and considerate to strangers. Yet urbanites apparently have at least as many friends and acquaintances as do nonurban dwellers (Fischer, 1982; Hill, 1987; Keller, 1968; Korte, 1980). Thus, it may be said that the real difference between urban and nonurban

INTERNET/TECHNOLOGY

.NET

HIGH-TECH CITIES

As we enter the Information Age, technology is allowing many people to live and work where they want (Kelley, 1995). As a result, many are abandoning cities to work in the suburbs. Some are even creating their own virtual workplaces at home. This trend is bad news for many urban areas, which face the possibility of becoming modern-day ghost towns. But all urban areas are not expected to share the same fate. In fact, cities with a concentration of knowledge-intense industries are expected to flourish. For them, urban areas provide ideal places to exchange information and ideas (Kotlin, 1996).

Designing cities to meet the needs of the twenty-first century is not easy. But a handful of high-tech cities have already started to emerge (*Newsweek*, November 9, 1998). They include

> Austin, Texas
> Boise, Idaho
> Boston, Massachusetts
> Champaign–Urbana Illinois
> Salt Lake City, Utah
> Seattle, Washington
> Washington, D.C.
> Bangalore, India
> Cambridge, England
> Tel Aviv, Israel

What do high-tech cities like these require? Steven Levy (1998) has identified six components:

1. A major research institution
2. At least one megasuccess story
3. High-tech talent
4. The proper 'tude
5. Venture capital
6. Infrastructure

These basic elements made Silicon Valley the model for all high-tech cities. Alone, none of them is likely to give birth to a high-tech city, but when they are combined, success is all but inevitable. Consider, for example, Silicon Valley. It is the birthplace of Hewlett-Packard, a recognized leader in the microelectronics business (Morgan, 1997). In the 1940s, Bill

TABLE 20.2   HIGH-TECH CITIES

City	Number of High-Tech Firms	Anchor Companies	Star
Austin, TX	1,750	Dell Computer AMD (Advanced Micro Device)	Michael Dell, founder of Dell
Bangalore, India	250	Texas Instruments Infosys	N. R. Narayana Murthy, chairman and CEO of Infosys
Boise, ID	300	HP, Micron Technology	Ray Smelek, brought HP to Boise
Boston, MA	3,600	Lotus (IBM), Lycos	Mitch Kapor, founder of Lotus
Cambridge, England	1,159	Acorn, Cambridge Display Tech.	Peter Dawe, founder of PIPEX
Champaign–Urbana, IL	70	Wolfram Research	Larry Smarr, director of National Center for Supercomputing Applications
Salt Lake City, UT	2,120	Novell, Iomega, Evans & Sutherland	Ray Noorda, founder of Novell
Seattle, WA	2,500	Microsoft	Bill Gates
Tel Aviv, Israel	1,000	ECI, Formula Group, Point Software Technologies	Dan Goldstein, CEO of Formula Group
Washington, DC	3,000	AOL, Comsat, UUNET (MCI WorldCom)	Mario Marino, formerly of Legent Software

Hewlett and Dave Packard started their company in Bill's garage. Stanford University contributed to their success in a number of ways. To begin with, both were graduates of this research institution. What is more, a university professor by the name of Frederick Terman had encouraged them to start their business (*Newsweek,* November 9, 1998). Today, similar Stanford-seeded companies account for half of Silicon Valley's revenues.

Megasuccess stories like Hewlett and Packard draw talented people to high-tech cities, where they may eventually start up their own companies. And that is, in fact, what happened in Silicon Valley. But success depends on a number of other related factors.

Hewlett and Packard also created an organizational culture that nurtured talent, team commitment, and a philosophy of innovation. A number of other attitudes contribute to high-tech success. They include a willingness to take risks, an openness to innovation, enthusiasm, and idealism.

While risk taking might come naturally to the kind of people attracted to designing innovative products, finding lenders to invest in a high-tech business is a challenge. Megasuccess stories like Bill Gates and Michael Dell show that nothing succeeds like success and that the rewards can well outweigh the risks of a business venture.

The last component on the list illustrates why urban areas may provide

fertile soil for the growth of high-tech industries. They are ideal for providing the necessary infrastructure—for example, lawyers and bankers with special expertise.

Many of the most rewarding occupations in the twenty-first century will be located in new high-tech cities. While they will resemble one another in terms of the key components that Levy identifies, each city is, nonetheless, destined to create its own unique identity (see Table 20.2).

City	Social Scene	Status Symbol	Median Home Price
Austin, TX	Ginger Man (happy hour); Las Minitas (breakfast)	$30,000 Skinatique water-skiing boat	$123,000
Bangalore, India	Black Cadillac Pub; exclusive country clubs	Home theater system	50,000
Boise, ID	Boise River; Bar Guernica	None	160,000
Boston, MA	Au Bon Pain in Kendall Square; Muddy Charles (MIT bar)	Any wireless Internet access device	400,000 in Brookline; $206,000 in Waltham
Cambridge, England	CBI cybercafe; the Six Bells (online Internet pub)	Psion Series 5 Palmtop	320,000
Champaign–Urbana, IL	Cafe Kopi; Radio Maria	Cannondale bicycle	150,000
Salt Lake City, UT	The mountains	Mountain bike	129,800
Seattle, WA	Airport gate at Sea-Tac for flights departing for the San Francisco Bay area	Land Rover	203,500
Tel Aviv, Israel	Budapest restaurant in Herzliya industrial zone	Recordable compact discs	300,000
Washington, DC	Car Pool (bar)	Ricochet wireless Internet connection	275,000

places is found in the public lives, not the private lives, of their residents (Fischer, 1981).

Urban-nonurban comparisons of psychological stress and mental health have also arrived at few firm conclusions (Fischer, 1984). In the United States, people who live in more populous places tend to be less content with their environments, but most indicators of mental health and psychological stress are not very different in urban and nonurban settings.

It may be that in advanced societies urbanism is now so pervasive that rural-urban comparisons no longer have much meaning. As we have previously noted, the ease of travel and communication today makes all of us urbanites to a substantial extent. This may help explain why the differences found between urban and nonurban life are not more striking.

SOCIAL NETWORK ANALYSIS

Social network analysis, introduced in Chapter 5, is an approach to the study of social life that has gained a following among urban sociologists. A *social network* consists of all the relationships, formal and informal, that one person has with others. We can use network analysis to reanalyze some long-standing issues, such as Wirth's perspective on urbanism.

One aspect of Wirth's perspective that has been subject to considerable scrutiny by network analysis is what has been called "the community question," or the issue of how urbanization and urbanism affect the solidarity of local communities (Silverman, 1986; Wellman, 1979). It has been suggested that many studies of this issue have confused "community" with "neighborhood" (Wellman & Leighton, 1979). In other words, sociologists often assume that in order to form a cohesive community, people must live close to one another.

But if we consider communities in terms of social networks, we do not have to think of them as based in neighborhoods. That is, groups of people can participate in strong, cohesive social networks even if their members are scattered around a city. What matters is the strength and number of the interpersonal ties among the members. Using this perspective, network analysts have argued that local urban communities are well adapted to the geographical mobility which is typical of modern life (Wellman, 1988).

Suburban Life

If the nineteenth century can be called the "age of the great cities," one scholar has noted, the second half of the twentieth century may be labeled the "age of the great suburbs" (Fischer, 1982). In 1970, for the first time in history, there were more suburbanites than city dwellers. Between 1950 and 1980, 18 of the 25 largest cities in the United States suffered a net population loss and the suburbs gained more than 60 million residents. By 1990, 46 percent of the U.S. population lived in the suburbs compared to 40 percent in central cities and 14 percent in nonurban areas.

Much has been written about the culture of American suburbs, often contrasting it with life in large cities. In the 1950s and 1960s, suburbia was frequently portrayed as an overly conformist community made up of status seekers. Suburban residents were characterized as neurotic, sexually permissive, and prone to heavy drinking. These traits were thought to be caused by the unique features of suburbs, particularly their low density, their cultural sameness, and their distance from urban services and jobs (Donaldson, 1969; Fishman, 1987).

But one study of working-class families that moved to the suburbs concluded that this view of suburban culture was mostly a myth (B. Berger, 1968; see also Feagin & Parker, 1990). And Gans (1962a, 1962b) has argued forcefully that suburban culture is mainly a product of the social class and life course status of the sorts of people who are most likely to live in the suburbs (the compositional perspective), rather than being directly caused by living in a suburb as opposed to some other type of community. The typical suburban dweller is married and has children living at home, so suburban culture naturally centers on the family. Suburbanites may put a premium on getting ahead financially, but this is a trait of middle-class people regardless of where they live. Gans notes that moving to the suburbs is often part of the process of advancing socially. It is, therefore, not surprising that suburbanites show more upward mobility than do people who live in the central city.

Yet others have argued that suburban living itself probably does have some negative effects—not, however, the same negative effects noted by early observers. A study comparing American suburbs with their planned, medium-density Swedish counterparts, for example, found that suburban life in the United States had negative consequences for teenagers and working women. Teenagers suffered from the lack of public transportation and community facilities, and working women from the lack of transportation and employment opportunities (Popenoe, 1977).

The suburbanization of jobs in recent decades—prompted by the fact that an increasing number of businesses have moved to the suburbs—has modified these negatives to some extent (Jackson, 1985). More and more retailers, high-technology organizations, and corporate headquarters have made the suburbs their home, enabling some suburban neighborhoods to grow into self-sufficient economic entities. Commuter patterns have changed as people have begun to travel from one suburb to another, as well as from the suburbs to the city, for work. Today, for example, the suburban Alexandria–Arlington–Fairfax area outside of Washington, D.C., has a population of 1 million people and provides services and a lifestyle for the residents of northern Virginia that make regular travel into Washington unnecessary (Fishman, 1987).

As the suburbs have become increasingly urbanized, suburban dwellers have encountered many of the problems experienced by residents of larger cities. These include congestion, pollution, heavy traffic, a faster pace of life, and ethnic, racial, and class tensions (Baldassare, 1986).

AMERICAN METROPOLITAN PROBLEMS AND THE URBAN CRISIS

Urban problems can be divided into two broad categories: those of the central city and those of the metropolis as a whole. The phrase *urban crisis* is usually applied only to the first type. But because the two sets of problems are closely linked, solutions to the central city's crisis may involve changes in the entire metropolitan area.

Problems of Older Central Cities

In recent years, extensive public attention has been focused on the growing problems of older American cities—Boston, Cleveland, Detroit, and New York. Many of these problems are economic and physical in nature. These cities are caught in a spiral of forces they find very hard to escape. For example, while the need for such public facilities as hospitals and schools is increasing as a result of the influx into the cities of low-income groups, the cost of operating these facilities is increasing even more rapidly. Yet the funds available to meet these needs are actually decreasing because the local tax base is declining.

A good starting point for explaining the urban crisis is an understanding of the impact on the city of the movement of middle-class families to the suburbs. People who live in the suburbs and commute to work in the city pay no city property taxes and often no city income tax. Sometimes they pay no city taxes at all, yet they use many of the city's facilities, including public transportation, streets and sidewalks, police and fire services, and libraries, thus adding to the city's costs. Yet if the city government were to raise its tax rates, even more middle-income families might leave. Business and industry might also move out, and the city's fiscal problems would become even worse. Instead of raising taxes, therefore,

cities have been forced to cut costs by reducing services. Outmoded transportation systems cannot be modernized, adequate police protection cannot be provided in some places, and schools cannot afford to hire the most qualified teachers.

The lower quality of public services has the same impact as higher taxes: Residents must either adapt or leave, and middle-class families have been choosing to leave the cities in ever-larger numbers. The major exodus of the middle class from the cities began in the 1950s and has continued to the present. As a result, the income gap between city residents and suburbanites has steadily increased.

Those who stay in the cities include primarily the rich and the very poor. The rich remain because they enjoy the cultural advantages of the city and have enough money to send their children to private schools, take taxicabs instead of buses or subways, and hire security guards to protect their property. The poor remain because they cannot afford to leave. Moving to the suburbs requires having enough money to make a down payment on a house and a good credit rating to obtain a mortgage. Suburban living usually requires a car, too. Even the cost of the move itself is often beyond the means of poor families.

Middle-class families who leave the city are replaced by low-income people from rural areas or immigrants from foreign countries. The new residents need city services more than middle-class people do, but they cannot afford to pay for them. The cities thus face a seemingly endless spiral of rising needs and costs, dwindling resources, and decay.

THE HOMELESS

Many of the social problems that are concentrated in the older central cities, such as crime, poverty, and racial tension, have been discussed in earlier chapters. Another serious problem facing American cities today is homelessness. More people are seeking refuge in temporary shelters now than at any time since the Great Depression. And homelessness is not solely an American phenomenon; it is, in fact, a problem throughout the world, in the cities and communities of both the developed and the developing nations.

Nobody really knows how many homeless people there are in the United States today. An accurate head count of this highly transient population is impossible, so we must make do with approximations (Jencks, 1995). In 1984, during the Reagan presidency, the federal Department of Housing and Urban Development maintained that there were somewhere between 250,000 and 300,000 homeless Americans. On the other hand, advocates for the homeless routinely argue that there may be between 2 million and 3 million homeless Americans (Redburn & Buss, 1986). The truth almost certainly lies somewhere between these two figures.

Today the cities of Los Angeles and New York are widely assumed to have the largest populations of the homeless, conservatively estimated at 34,000 and 30,000 individuals, respectively, on any given day. However, the homeless are by no means confined to run-down sections of America's largest cities; there are homeless people living on the streets of suburban communities from Easthampton, New York, to Santa Barbara, California.

Who are the homeless? In the simplest terms, anyone who lacks a fixed address falls into this category. However, this definition does not fully reflect the level of economic and social deprivation that usually accompanies homelessness. Taking these factors into account, the National Institute of Mental Health proposed an alternative definition that characterizes a homeless person as "anyone who lacks adequate shelter, resources, and community ties" (Bingham, Green, & White, 1987). Homeless people are isolated individuals with poor records of employment who have difficulty with relationships, suffer from emotional problems, and report a variety of past or present family problems (Basnik, Rubin, & Lauriat, 1986).

The homeless include people of all races, ages, and educational levels (Baxter & Hopper, 1984). The average age of the homeless is estimated to be between 33 and 36; homeless men outnumber homeless women by a margin of about four to one. One study reported that 45 percent of the homeless population had a high school diploma and that, of this 45 percent, nearly one-half had at least started college (Redburn & Buss, 1986). There are currently more African-Americans and Hispanics than there are whites among the homeless, although the percentages vary from city to city.

A closer look suggests that the homeless include many different kinds of people. Among these are mentally ill persons who have been released from hospitals but are unable to care for themselves; runaways; substance abusers; and families, principally unmarried or divorced women and their children. Many homeless people are the "new poor," individuals who have been left without homes as a result of personal or economic crises (Jencks, 1995; Momeni, 1989).

Several researchers have isolated the main factors that cause or are associated with homelessness. In one study, 48 percent of the respondents reported severe economic problems (unemployment, reduced welfare benefits, eviction), 26 percent listed personal crises, and 7.3 percent indicated substance abuse as the primary cause of their homelessness (Redburn & Buss, 1986). Another study added several other important factors: poor interpersonal relationships, emotional problems, domestic

violence, and recent release from jail (Basnik, Rubin, & Lauriat, 1986). A third study found lack of low-income housing and mental health care to be the strongest predictors of homelessness (Elliott & Krivo, 1991). Many critics consider the homeless to be the victims of changing government policy; they especially blame federal cutbacks in subsidized low-income housing, unemployment, and Social Security benefits (Belcher & Singer, 1987).

The provisions made for the homeless by local, state, and federal governments have proved inadequate. To solve the problem of homelessness, a full range of social services may be necessary: counseling, transitional housing, substance abuse programs, referrals, case management, job training, and placement (Jencks, 1995; Redburn & Buss, 1986).

Metropolitan Fragmentation and Sprawl

Government in metropolitan areas is normally broken up into a large number of competing and overlapping agencies. The Chicago metropolitan area, for example, contains more than 1,000 governmental units; New York has more than 1,400. Such fragmentation makes it difficult to plan for and coordinate the metropolitan area as a whole.

Similarly, economic and political conflict between the central city and its suburbs makes it extremely difficult to allocate resources fairly. As noted earlier, the daily use of urban facilities by workers and shoppers who return to the suburbs at night increases costs to the city. Yet commuters in most metropolitan areas bear few of these expenses. The central cities, therefore, are forced to pay for basic services such as police and sanitation at the expense of other functions such as education. Thus, central cities spend much less on education per pupil than do typical suburban areas, although their educational needs are undoubtedly far greater. In short, the cities have the needs and the suburbs have the resources.

The distribution of jobs within metropolitan areas is another example of the poor match between needs and resources. Many of the jobs that are best suited to the central city's labor force (that is, jobs that are relatively high-paying but require little formal education—in particular, those in manufacturing) have moved to the suburbs. But the frequent lack of adequate public transportation makes it difficult for urban workers to get to the suburbs. At the same time, many of the jobs for which suburban dwellers tend to be best qualified remain in the central city.

The unplanned growth of American metropolitan areas has resulted in what is often called *urban sprawl*. Sprawl, which, as noted previously, is not found to the same degree in other postindustrial societies, has been encouraged by such federal programs as highway subsidies and home mortgage insurance. Although it is apparently favored by most Americans, early research showed that uncontrolled urban growth had important social disadvantages. In 1974, a National Research Council report suggested that metropolitan sprawl appeared to have reduced the ability of governments to function effectively, and that a more equitable sharing of costs was needed—not only between the suburbs and the cities but also among suburbs. The report also noted that there was good reason to consider ending or modifying the subsidies that have in practice favored single-family suburban dwelling.

In recent years, however, new perspectives on suburban sprawl have arisen:

> Some urban researchers and policy analysts have taken issue with the idea that suburban sprawl is problematical. For example, a [recent report] argues that the physical landscape of older cities is technologically obsolete, that the new polycentered (sprawl) landscape better fits in with the modern technologies associated with an auto-centered transport system and modern communications. [The] report also asserts that the low-density suburban residential sprawl increases energy consumption by only 3 percent compared with higher-density construction. According to the report, suburbia even reduces the exposure of people to pollution, because people are spread out more and thus per capita exposure to pollution is less than it otherwise would be. And suburbanization, by means of a trickle-down process, has allegedly brought better housing to the central-city poor. (Feagin & Parker, 1990, p. 228)

However, many sociologists still believe that urban sprawl must be carefully monitored. One way to contain (or at least control) sprawl is through city planning.

City Planning and Urban Rebuilding

The United States was among the last of the world's developed nations to put city planning into practice. **City planning** is the process of deliberately and explicitly formulating goals regarding an urban community's future physical structure. Government bodies establish objectives for community development, and plans are prepared that are designed to promote the attainment of those goals. Only plans that are consistent with the goals, sometimes outlined in the form of a *master plan,* are approved and put into practice (Bairoch, 1988).

The British have been especially innovative city planners, influencing the development of this field throughout the world. In 1945, London's city planners decided to limit the growth of the city by creating a permanent greenbelt and a ring of planned towns around the city. These new towns grew and developed much as the planners had hoped. Soon thereafter, the Swedes and Japanese adopted some aspects of the British model (Sutcliffe, 1981).

Dislike of government intervention has prevented city planning from gaining a strong foothold in the United States. City planners in America tend to serve mainly as advisers at the state and local levels, assisting transportation, housing, health and human services, economic development, and environmental departments. Typically, the city planner's job entails analyzing data concerning the needs, land use, and living patterns of urban residents and determining the costs and benefits of various proposed programs or improvements. Most city planners view their objective as the maximization of the use of city space for the benefit of all (Burns & Friedmann, 1985).

Many American communities have drawn up master plans, but these plans typically have not been implemented to any significant extent (Burchell & Sternlieb, 1978). Nevertheless, most American communities do use one important city planning tool: *zoning.* Zoning laws, which give local governments the power to control the way land is used, have been successful in keeping certain land uses—for example, mobile home parks, low-cost housing, and noxious industries—out of many communities.

Government officials, business leaders, and real estate developers share a concern about maintaining the attractiveness, vitality, and economic viability of urban centers because these districts usually house the commercial nucleus of the city. These entities often sponsor *urban redevelopment* programs, which typically involve razing rundown buildings and constructing an entirely new neighborhood where they stood. Although urban redevelopment programs have given new life to some inner-city areas, such as Philadelphia's Society Hill, these programs have not been very effective overall. Many critics have argued that urban redevelopment all too often forces low-income people from their homes without giving them access to decent homes elsewhere. Some have even declared that the cure is worse than the disease, claiming that urban redevelopment saps the vitality and diversity that are the lifeblood of any city (Burns & Friedmann, 1985; J. Jacobs, 1961). Over the years, many urban redevelopment programs have been replaced by *urban rehabilitation* efforts. These programs are designed to preserve existing areas rather than tear them down and build from scratch.

Some experts have proposed that many urban problems could be solved by creating new towns on land that is not currently developed and by encouraging people to move to these new towns from the cities. But although new towns provide exciting opportunities for creative urban design and hold out the promise of substantially reducing urban sprawl, it would take more money than is presently available to reduce the population of cities by a significant amount. Woodlands, a multi-million-dollar development community constructed outside of Houston, Texas, was designed to demonstrate how urban problems can be solved through the construction of new towns, but many of its planned middle- and low-income houses have not been built because they proved to be unprofitable (Gottdiener, 1985). Although most of the new towns that have been built have run into financial difficulty, there has recently been some renewed interest in private-sector development of such towns.

The urban crisis is so severe and so complex that its solution does not seem to lie in any single program or set of programs. It appears that the only long-run solution may involve the redistribution of more income to the cities and to the poor and the restructuring of urban growth. These measures have been proposed by sociologists who favor conflict perspectives.

Conflict Theory and the Urban Crisis

Conflict theorists argue that the only way to improve our cities is to eradicate many of the basic inequalities in American society. Sometimes called the "new urban sociology," this school of thought focuses attention on the relationship between urban problems and the political and economic structure of the society as a whole. Conflict theorists argue that attempts to solve the urban crisis at the local level are bound to fail, because our capitalist system severely limits the gains that any local political activity can achieve (Castells, 1977, 1983; Molotch, 1979).

Some conflict-oriented urban sociologists identify the root cause of the urban crisis as the fact that economic resources are now concentrated more than ever in the hands of a few multinational companies (Hill, 1978; Saunders, 1981). These companies build factories where they will get the best return on their investment. This often means that they abandon facilities located in older cities and build new ones where costs are lower. The older cities are thus left with a shrinking economy and a growing population of the poor and unemployed (Feagin & Parker, 1990; Smith & Feagin, 1987).

A number of conflict theorists have also analyzed the role of local real estate developers and bankers in urban change, concluding that the growth and decline of cities are largely a result of uneven real estate investment patterns (Feagin & Parker, 1990). These theorists argue that state and local governments are effectively controlled by groups of powerful business and real estate leaders who remain out of the public eye. These individuals are principally interested in profit and in maintaining the commercial viability of the city—interests, the critics assert, that frequently conflict with housing and other basic human needs of the inner-city poor (Patel, 1988; Redburn & Buss, 1986).

Neo-Marxist conflict theorists assume that each of us confronts the economic system less as an individual than as a member of a social class (Jaret, 1983). Factory owners derive their profit not so much from personal initiative as from their ownership of capital and membership in the propertied class. Workers subsist on low wages not because they lack personal merit but because society is organized along class lines.

In this view, urban problems derive not from the failure of social institutions to work properly but, rather, from the way the system actually is intended to work under capitalism. The propertied class can maintain its power only if the majority of the people, who lack property, are politically divided (and thus unable to exercise political power). In India, for example, the economically and socially disadvantaged are divided into segregated groups: 100 million are "untouchables" and another 50 million are members of various tribes. Some believe that this separation is deliberately encouraged to prevent the disadvantaged groups from gaining power (Glass, 1989).

Also, the propertied class depends on cheap labor to maintain high profits. Such urban (though not exclusively urban) problems as poverty and racism serve the interests of the propertied class by not only providing it with a large number of low-paid workers but by also turning these workers against one another politically.

The Future of American Cities: An Assessment of Trends

What hope is there for the older central cities of the United States? Can they be restored to their former vitality? The last few decades have witnessed a strong resurgence of business interest in the central cities, with new office buildings and hotels springing up in downtown areas across the nation. This has helped to bring new life to many central business districts. But this vitality is largely a daytime phenomenon; at night, with such notable exceptions as New York, San Francisco, and a few other cosmopolitan places, the cities go dark. If cities are to become more than places housing the lower classes and the dispossessed, it is necessary for large numbers of the middle and upper classes to return to live in them.

There is at least one positive trend in this regard. A substantial number of young, middle-class people now entering the housing market have been buying houses in decaying inner-city neighborhoods and renovating them. Because they are often childless, they are not deeply concerned about safety or the quality of inner-city schools-concerns that have driven many families to the suburbs (Culver, 1979; Lowry, 1980). Whether these people will stay in the city after they have school-age children, however, remains to be seen.

In the aftermath of the destruction in South Central Los Angeles in the spring of 1992 following the Rodney King verdict, public attention has refocused on the need to address the underlying economic and social causes of disaffection and hopelessness among the inner-city poor and, in the process, to revitalize the older central cities. There is also an increased awareness that such revitalization requires the protection of inner-city residents, workers, and store owners from the violence that often characterizes city life.

Nevertheless, the most probable urban scenario in the near future is the continued decentralization of America, to the suburbs and beyond. As the baby boom generation reaches middle age, there is no reason to suppose that it will act differently from its predecessors. Most people still cling to the American dream of a freestanding, single-family house in the suburbs with two cars in the garage (Rybczynski, 1995; Sternlieb & Hughes, 1986). As long as this dream holds its popularity, the prospects for the nation's older cities are not bright.

CHAPTER REVIEW

1. Trace the emergence and development of urbanization over time. Identify the functions that cities serve and how changes in the economy have influenced the way urban areas develop.

2. Describe your community. In what way has it shaped your life?

3. Is gentrification the best solution for decaying central cities? Why or why not?

4. Consider the cities of the twenty-first century. Predict what urban ecologists are likely to discover.

5. In your opinion, where is the best place to raise children—in a city or a suburb? Why?

6. If you were asked to plan a city, what would be your major considerations?

7. Is homelessness a problem in the United States today? If so, what should be done?

INTERNET EXERCISE

The Web destinations for Chapter 20 cover various aspects of cities, urbanization, and community change. To start your explorations, go to the Prentice Hall Companion Web site **http://www.prenhall.com/popenoe**. Next, choose **Chapter 20** (Cities, Urbanization, and Community Change). Then, select **web destinations** from the menu on the left side of the screen. There are several sites to choose from. We suggest you begin with **Citizens Against Urban Sprawl Everywhere (C.A.U.S.E.).** C.A.U.S.E. is based in Durham, North Carolina. Most recently, the organization has filed suit against Urban Retail Properties in opposition to the plan to build a "mega-mall" in the city of Durham. This fight has gained national attention through the *CBS News Sunday Morning* television program. The C.A.U.S.E. site provides a fascinating history of concerned citizens' efforts to oppose urban sprawl, which is discussed in this chapter in a section entitled *Metropolitan Fragmentation and Sprawl*. After you have explored the Citizens Against Urban Sprawl Everywhere site, answer the following questions:

- What are your personal reactions to the problem of *urban sprawl?*
- Many people would say, "I would like to have a mega-mall to shop at." On the other hand, might you feel differently if that mall were located in your "backyard"?

KEY TERMS

urbanization
overurbanization
community
metropolitan area
suburbs

megalopolis
gentrification
urban ecology
ecological segregation
invasion

succession
urbanism
city planning

Collective Behavior and Social Movements

hree young people enter a well-known alternative music club in New York City late one Saturday night to dance to bands with names like Smashing Pumpkins, White Zombies, and Prong. The two men wear Caesar haircuts—cut very short and combed down over their foreheads—sideburns, T-shirts, baggy shorts hanging down below their knees, and heavy Doc Marten shoes. Their female companion has long, straight hair and is wearing a granny dress over tights, lots of rings and bracelets, and heavy boots. All three sport numerous tattoos and jewelry worn through holes pierced in their eyebrows, noses, lips, and other parts of their bodies. They work their way through the packed club to the front, where the mosh pit is located. Fifty or sixty alternative rockers are dancing wildly and aggressively in the pit, frequently climbing on top of each other and allowing themselves to be passed around atop the crowd. Once in awhile someone jumps up on the stage and plunges head first into the mosh pit. Similar scenes have been common in alternative clubs throughout the United States since the early 1990s.

In Poland, in the late summer of 1980, workers at factories, mines, and shipyards organized a mass strike. In defiance of the Communist Party, Polish workers united to form the Solidarity movement, dedicated to the freedom and democratic treatment of workers. Even though the leaders of the Communist Party eventually imposed martial law, Solidarity remained the symbol of the people's movement for democracy in Poland. Today it is an important constituent of the new Polish regime.

These two events, the alternative rock scene and the Solidarity social movement in Poland, are different in most respects. Yet there is an element common to both that interests sociologists: Each occurred outside the institutional framework of everyday life. In this chapter, we consider the main forms of noninstitutionalized social behavior, ranging from relatively spontaneous behavior like fads, hysterias, and crazes (which sociologists call "collective behavior") to the more purposeful behavior known as "social movements." We also discuss the role of communication and public opinion in helping to shape the development of collective behavior and social movements.

THE NATURE AND CONDITIONS OF COLLECTIVE BEHAVIOR

The phrase *collective behavior,* taken literally, could refer to the main subject of sociology: the behavior of people in groups and societies. But sociologists use the term in a narrower sense: **Collective behavior** is behavior that occurs in response to a common influence or stimulus in relatively spontaneous, unpredictable, unstructured, and unstable situations.

Collective behavior should not be confused with organizational or institutional behavior. *Organizational behavior* (for example, that characteristic of clubs and corporations) is behavior within groups that is governed by established rules and procedures. *Institutional behavior* (for example, that concerned with education or religion) is behavior that is guided by institutionalized norms. Collective behavior, in contrast, lacks predefined organizational procedures and institutional norms. Furthermore, collective behavior is dynamic; it is continually changing (Turner & Killian, 1987).

The Nature of Collective Behavior

It helps to think of collective behavior as one end—the less structured one—of a wide spectrum of social behavior that ranges from the most structured to the least structured. Collective behavior occurs in many forms, including crowds, riots, fads and fashions, and panics. But although these phenomena are different in some ways, they are similar in others: The goals and expectations of the people involved are relatively unclear, the social situation is poorly defined, and the mechanisms of social control are weak (Genevie, 1975).

We can better understand the nature of collective behavior by comparing it with behavior in highly structured situations, such as a high school fire drill. The goals of the fire drill have been spelled out in advance. The people in each classroom are expected to walk outside the building through a specified exit. Not only is the goal clear in each person's mind, but so is the precise way in which the goal is to be accomplished. The definition of the situation is clear as well; students have gone through the procedure before and may even have received advance notice of the drill from the principal's office. Everyone knows there is no real fire and that in 15 minutes they will be back in their seats. Furthermore, methods of social control are in force. Students who step out of line are likely to receive negative sanctions from the teachers.

Compare this event to a real fire, say, in a nightclub. At the first smell of smoke or sight of flames, the social situation changes dramatically. Here the goals and means are vague, and the situation is poorly defined. The patrons do not know what to expect, since they have probably never been in a fire before. Moreover, they lack knowledge about the size of the fire, how fast it will spread, and the efforts being made to control it. Group goals are replaced by conflicting individual goals—some people may try to save their own lives, some may try to help others, and the management may try to pretend everything is under control. There are few rules that people are expected to follow and few methods of social control to enforce conformity to any rules that do exist.

And so a hysterical crowd of people may trample one another as they fight to escape the fire.

Although relatively spontaneous, collective behavior is not completely without structure or pattern. Indeed, the social structure that emerges in collective behavior is precisely the focus of the sociologist's attention. At the scene of a traffic accident, for example, certain social roles soon emerge. Some onlookers simply stand on the sidelines watching events unfold. Others assist in rerouting traffic away from the accident. Still other people render emergency assistance to the injured.

In themselves, collective behavior and social movements are of great inherent interest. But social scientists are also aware that collective behavior can be an important source of social change. Many institutions begin as social movements; today's fads may be tomorrow's customs. From the crowds of the present may emerge the highly structured and long-lasting social groups of the future. The study of collective behavior is thus also the study of some of the processes by which people seek, and often achieve, major social change.

Conditions of Collective Behavior

Because collective behavior takes so many forms, it is not easy to generalize about the social conditions that cause or promote it. Although the following conditions have been identified as important generators of collective behavior, they do not all need to be present at once, nor is any one factor essential to all forms of collective behavior.

ENVIRONMENTAL FACTORS

Certain environmental factors increase the chances that people will respond in a spontaneous way to a common stimulus. Any arrangement of people that enables them to communicate quickly and easily, for example, increases the likelihood of spontaneous behavior (Turner & Killian, 1987). One such arrangement is a mass gathering in a public space such as a square, stadium, or hall.

Timing is also a crucial factor. According to the Kerner Commission, which examined the urban riots of the 1960s, most of the disturbances began on weekends or in the evenings. These are the periods when most people are free from other demands on their time (McPhail, 1971; see also Bray, 1988). The spring 1992 disturbances in Los Angeles, which began at night, also fit this pattern.

NORMLESSNESS

Some situations are so new or occur so rarely that few norms have developed to cover them. There are almost no norms to guide the behavior of people involved, for

This crowd demonstrates collective behavior: spontaneous, unpredictable, unrestricted, and unstable.

example, in a shipwreck, except perhaps the idea of "women and children first." Other situations of relative "normlessness" include those in which an individual's usual ties to the social structure are loosened—for example, at vacation resorts, rock festivals, and conventions. Temporary absence from family and occupational roles can be very conducive to collective behavior.

Even during the most chaotic events, however, a pattern of normative behavior gradually emerges. The first bombing raids on London during World War II produced a great deal of collective behavior, as people poured out of their homes and into bomb shelters for protection through the night. But as the raids continued, norms evolved. Some informality of dress—bathrobes, slippers, even bare feet—became acceptable attire for the bomb shelter. Hair could be uncombed, or left in curlers, although neither would be acceptable on the street the following morning. It was considered bad manners not to share in the camaraderie of the shelter, but people were given some privacy if they wanted it. Over time a set of regulations developed to govern behavior in the shelters. In short, when groups of people had to adapt to a recurring situation, they found it desirable to bring order and routine into their lives. They accomplished this by developing more social structure.

CONFLICTING VALUES AND NORMS

Conflicting values and norms can also give rise to collective behavior. Such conflicts commonly are the consequence of rapid social change or of the introduction of contradictory elements into a culture.

The rapid modernization of traditional societies often breeds collective behavior. The overthrow of the

Shah of Iran in 1979, for example, was achieved by a broad coalition of interest groups. Some objected to specific policies of the Shah; others to his overall program of modernization. Yet his overthrow was just the beginning of an ongoing struggle over values. The new government tried to bring back traditional patterns of Islamic culture, particularly with regard to women and the family. Traditional rules were revived that required women to wear the chador (a head-to-toe veil). Men were allowed to get a divorce simply by telling a notary public that they wanted one and to take a second wife without the consent of the first one. Some Iranian women, who had long since gained the freedoms enjoyed by Western women, and who had also fought in the revolution, found their values threatened. As a result, these women engaged in various forms of collective behavior to protest the attack on their lifestyles and values. They refused to adopt the chador, continued to wear Western dress, and appeared in public places considered off limits to women.

RELATIVE DEPRIVATION

Relative deprivation is another common factor underlying civil strife and other forms of collective behavior (Davies, 1969; Foss & Larkin, 1986; Gurr, 1969, 1970; Haines, 1988). *Relative deprivation* is a condition in which people do not have what they think they deserve. Whether those involved seek economic security, political rights, self-expression, or a sense of belonging, society has taught them that these goals can be achieved if they act in certain ways. But under conditions of relative deprivation, people feel that they are not making adequate progress toward their goals. The system, as they see it, is not giving them what they deserve.

There are several different types of relative deprivation. In *aspirational relative deprivation,* people's expectations rise, but they do not see their life circumstances becoming significantly better. The birth of the American civil rights movement, for example, has been explained in part by rising expectations among African-Americans after the 1954 U.S. Supreme Court ruling in the *Brown* case, which outlawed school segregation. White opposition stalled the implementation of the Court's decision and fueled escalating levels of aspirational deprivation and movement activity.

Another important type is termed *J-curve relative deprivation* (Davies, 1969). This occurs when, after a period during which people's rising expectations have been accompanied by what they see as real progress, the authorities suddenly reverse direction and start taking away some of the recent gains. Under these circumstances, expectations continue to rise while the situation is seen as actually deteriorating (rather than just remaining the same, as in the aspirational model). J-curve relative deprivation is a particularly intense stimulus for collective action and has been shown to have been an important factor underlying many violent social movements, including the Iranian revolution, the French revolution, and both of the Russian revolutions.

Usually, it is not the most severely deprived people who are the most likely to engage in collective action. The most deprived are often the least active. Those who are somewhat less deprived, who are the most aware that their situations can be improved, are usually the most active.

BREAKDOWNS IN MECHANISMS OF SOCIAL CONTROL

Social control is a continuing function of every social system. When the mechanisms of control weaken, people may lose confidence in the existing system and try to reform or restructure it through collective behavior. One example is vigilantism, in which people take the law into their own hands when they feel some injustice has not been officially corrected. Collective behavior such as rioting can also result when harsh measures of social control are suddenly relaxed (Turner & Killian, 1987).

Social control can break down because the *formal* agents of social control—such as the police and the courts—fail to perform their roles adequately. Fearful of crime and lacking confidence in the police force's ability to keep their neighborhoods safe, many citizens have formed patrols to monitor residential areas. Social control can also break down because the *informal* mechanisms of social control are weakened. The breakdown of informal controls is apparent in some urban neighborhoods, where there are few watchful neighbors safeguarding the streets and where many parents cannot control their children.

SMELSER'S VALUE-ADDED PERSPECTIVE

Neil Smelser (1962) has outlined six social conditions that must be present in order for any type of collective behavior or social movement to arise. Smelser calls his theory a **value-added approach** because it is similar to a concept of the same name in economics. Smelser's theory assumes that an episode of collective behavior will occur only when each of six specific conditions combine or interact in a given situation. These determinants may actually arise in any order, but they only become relevant in the following sequence:

The first determinant is *structural conduciveness:* The social structure must be so organized as to permit or allow a movement or an episode of collective behavior to take place. For example, a prison riot cannot occur if all of the prisoners are confined to their cells 24 hours a day. It should be emphasized that structural conduciveness refers to general background factors that make collective behavior possible in a particular situation; it is entirely separate from any sense that there is anything wrong.

The second determinant is *structural strain,* the perception that something is wrong in one's social environment. Most commonly, this strain takes the form of relative deprivation. Prison riots are often sparked by discontent over bad food, cramped conditions, and ethnic hostilities.

The growth of a *generalized belief,* Smelser's third determinant, helps the participants to interpret the structural strain that they are perceiving. It includes an analysis of what has gone wrong, a vision of how things ought to be, a set of strategies and tactics designed to correct the problem, and sometimes a negative vision of what could happen if improvement does not take place. The generalized belief makes the situation personally meaningful to the participants and prepares them for collective action. The generalized belief that underlies prison riots may suggest that rioting could draw public attention and eventually remediation to many of the conditions that are felt to be oppressing the prisoners.

Precipitating factors, the fourth determinant, actually spark the collective action. Often a dramatic event provides a concrete stimulus for collective behavior. Such an event may confirm the fears expressed in the generalized belief, or it may exaggerate the severity of a condition of structural strain. Prison riots are sometimes precipitated by incidents in which individual prisoners are reported to have been severely and unjustly punished by the authorities. Similarly, the not-guilty verdict in the case of four white police officers accused of brutality in the beating of black motorist Rodney King precipitated four days and nights of mob violence in Los Angeles. On the other hand, some episodes of collective behavior seem to lack clear precipitating factors.

The fifth of Smelser's determinants is the *mobilization of the participants for action.* This factor simply means that once the first four determinants are in place, the action gets underway. Given conditions of conduciveness, strain, a generalized belief, and (usually) an appropriate precipitating incident, a riot breaks out. During the process of mobilization, some relatively vague conduct norms and patterns of leadership typically emerge.

Mechanisms of *social control,* the sixth and final determinant, shape the other five factors and help determine the outcome of the collective behavior. The actions of prison authorities may make the situation more or less structurally conducive to a riot, may contribute directly to a sense of structural strain, may have a great deal to do with the generalized belief that develops, and frequently

Fear of crime and the lack of confidence in the police force have led many citizens to form neighborhood crime patrols to monitor residential areas.

constitute the precipitating factor that sparks a riot. Social control mechanisms may be either preventive (affecting the chances that an episode of collective behavior will occur) or emergent (arising after the event has begun and affecting the extent and character of the episode). Emergent social control in the form of more or less effective official response to an ongoing prison riot is a crucial determinant of how long the riot will continue and how much damage will be done by the rioters.

Smelser's theory is essentially a means of classifying into meaningful categories the factors that lead to an outbreak of collective behavior. Occasionally, social scientists have been unable to identify all six determinants in a given situation. However, the value-added perspective is widely acknowledged to constitute an important first step in identifying and organizing the conditions that underlie social movements and collective behavior.

CROWDS AND MASS BEHAVIOR

Of all the forms of collective behavior, the crowd is the most common and perhaps the one of which people are the most aware. A **crowd** is a temporary grouping of people, physically close together and sharing a common focus of attention. The characteristics that distinguish a crowd from a more conventional social grouping include feelings of uncertainty and a sense of urgency. Not everyone in a crowd shares the same expectations. The situation is relatively ambiguous and unstructured. The goals are uncertain. Yet crowd participants share a feeling that something is about to happen.

In their behavior, the participants in a crowd may sometimes ignore normal social constraints. In this sense,

The expressive crowd in Times Square may appear unrestrained; the roles and norms are still present, however, and most times crowd behavior remains acceptable in the context of the festivities.

the crowd can be *permissive*. In adopting new behavior and attitudes, crowd participants typically become open to suggestions that are conveyed by the mood of the crowd.

Types of Crowds

The most loosely structured type of crowd is what Herbert Blumer (1939), in an early and influential work on the subject, called the *casual crowd*—a relatively passive crowd involving a minimum level of emotional engagement and interaction by the participants. In this type of crowd, people drift in and pass on. They pay temporary attention to something, such as a traffic accident or a department store's holiday display. They may or may not talk to one another.

The *conventional crowd* is more structured and its behavior is quite predictable. Conventional crowds include audiences at concerts and passengers on an airplane, situations that are planned in advance. In these situations, people mostly follow conventional norms and the interaction among members of the crowd is often minimal.

Sociologists take greater interest in those types of crowds in which more extensive collective behavior develops: expressive crowds, solidaristic crowds, and acting crowds.

EXPRESSIVE CROWDS

Crowds that are designed to provide opportunities for emotional expression and release are called **expressive crowds.** Most preliterate cultures hold periodic festivals

to celebrate the harvest, some great military victory, or a day of religious significance. So that as large a crowd as possible can assemble, tribal members from miles around may be invited. These crowds engage in activities such as dancing, drinking, feasting, singing, shouting, and competing in games and tests of skill. Because such behavior would be considered disruptive under ordinary circumstances, the occasion gives the participants an emotional release, one that they normally cannot achieve in their everyday lives.

Some anthropologists think that such festivities are especially important in societies whose cultures are characterized by a great deal of emotional repression. They cite as an example the Native American tribes of the Southwest, who from time to time punctuated the emotional control normally required of them with bouts of unrestrained emotionalism in religious ceremonies such as rain dances or curing rituals (Benedict, 1959).

Expressive crowds are quite common in modern American society. Examples are the raucous gatherings in New York City's Times Square on New Year's Eve, the festive crowds celebrating the Mardi Gras in New Orleans, and the stadiums full of cheering fans at Super Bowl games. Such expressive crowds may appear unrestrained, even wild. But roles and norms are still present in these situations; people know which kinds of behavior are acceptable in the context of the festivity and which are not.

SOLIDARISTIC CROWDS

Many expressive crowds have social functions that go beyond the expression of emotions. The term **solidaristic** has been used to describe crowds that provide their members with a strong sense of social solidarity or unity (Turner & Killian, 1987). Those who attended the rock festival near Woodstock, New York, in the summer of 1969, for example, came away speaking of a "Woodstock nation." The one-half million people who gathered at Woodstock seemed representative of the 1960s counterculturists, the "flower children" who opposed the Vietnam War and hoped to work together for peace, love, and understanding.

Most evangelical religious rallies are probably best analyzed as conventional crowds in which the seemingly spontaneous emotionality of the "born-again" participants is in fact highly predictable and virtually choreographed by the organizers, but on occasion these rallies or revivals may "catch fire" and generate high levels of collective energy and excitement. Such events include strong expressive and solidaristic elements and may be viewed by their participants as enormously meaningful and soul-stirring experiences.

Governments sometimes sponsor rallies or mass meetings that will attract large crowds in a deliberate effort to build a sense of social unity. Adolf Hitler was particularly adept at this technique and used political rallies successfully to consolidate his power during the 1930s. Other examples include the crowds that gather in Cuba to hear the public speeches of Fidel Castro and the crowds that assembled in Iraq in support of the Iraqi government during the Persian Gulf War. Official use of this tactic requires some certainty regarding the political climate, for such crowds always have the potential of turning into mobs hostile to the government.

ACTING CROWDS

The **acting crowd** is typically angry and hostile. The two most dramatic types of acting crowds are mobs and riots.

A **mob** is an acting crowd whose emotionally aroused members focus their anger on a single target, frequently disbanding after they have achieved their aim. Most mobs have leaders, and mob action is often somewhat structured. But because they are temporary and unstable, mobs are considered a kind of collective behavior. Lynchings, fire bombings, and the terrorist activities of groups such as the Ku Klux Klan are examples of mob action.

Like a mob, a **riot** is a violent acting crowd; unlike members of a mob, rioters are expressing a more generalized anger and typically move from target to target, often over many hours or even several days. Rioting usually involves an attack on groups that are disliked, the looting and destruction of property, and a general flouting of authority. Some rioters may have specific goals, such as the destruction of homes or businesses owned by unpopular people. For example, in the 1992 Los Angeles disturbances, many Korean stores in the central city were destroyed.

Some norms do emerge to govern riot behavior, though they are often not easily identified. Riots frequently involve looting, which may seem to constitute a total breakdown of norms and values. But looting in civil disorders is frequently guided by an emergent set of norms. When publicly engaged in by members of a local community, looting can amount to a collective protest directed toward the larger society (Quarantelli & Dynes, 1970). Community values concerning property are temporarily set aside, and plundering becomes the socially accepted thing to do.

Those who take part in riots and mob actions are typically under great social strain. In order to spark an acting crowd, the strain must be pervasive and widespread. Economic stress, it is commonly thought, was a key factor underlying the 1992 Los Angeles riots.

Rioters are often members of an ethnic or racial group that has been the target of discrimination. They tend to believe that no quick or certain remedy to their problems is in sight and that the power structure either cannot or will not listen to their complaints. In other words, rioters are frequently people experiencing social problems for which there seem to be no effective institutional solutions (Paige, 1971).

Theories of Crowd Behavior

One of the most commonly cited characteristics of crowd behavior is the apparent abandonment of individual beliefs and attitudes and the substitution of new, collectively generated patterns. Although crowd members may be drawn from very different backgrounds, their behavior in the crowd often conforms to a common new set of norms. A unified crowd spirit may develop. Dominated by a common impulse, the crowd behaves as if it has a mind of its own. How does this phenomenon come about? Why do crowd conditions inhibit individuality and encourage acceptance of the attitudes and actions of the mass? Three main theories have been proposed to answer these questions.

CONTAGION THEORY

In 1896, Gustave Le Bon published *The Crowd,* a pioneering analysis of crowd behavior (Le Bon, 1896/1946). Le Bon viewed the crowd as a single organism with one collective mind. He suggested that the crowd's ability to "hypnotize" individuals was based on three factors: (1) a feeling of *invincibility,* the great power that comes from sheer numbers; (2) *contagion,* the rapid spread of new ways of thinking, analogous to the spread of disease through a population; and (3) *suggestibility.* Le Bon believed that, in a crowd, people's minds are easily reduced to a low level of activity and that people are inclined to accept passively and to mimic, without question, the behaviors and attitudes of others in the crowd.

Later research has found that people in crowds are not as uniform in their behavior as Le Bon assumed; the idea of a "collective mind" has long been discounted by sociologists. Ideas like Le Bon's are still prevalent in popular thought, however. They show up in the media, in political rhetoric, and even in police tactics. One can still hear crowd members spoken of as "irrational animals."

The concept of a "collective mind" is fallacious for two reasons. First, it denies the individual differences of the members of a crowd. When people report that "the mob attacked the intruders" or that "the crowd went crazy," they are ignoring significant individual differences in behavior, attitudes, and actions. Second, this view falsely attributes to the group such qualities as a mind, a conscience, or a lack of self-control. It is incorrect to say "The crowd changed its mind." Psychological attributes of an individual cannot be applied to a group.

Frequently accompanying the fallacious concept of a collective mind is the depiction of crowd behavior as "irrational." Sociologists point to two errors in viewing collective behavior in this way. First, irrationality is a characteristic of an individual's state of mind; it is not an attribute that can be applied to groups. Second, the use of the term *irrational* is value-laden (Turner & Killian, 1987). The same behavior may be deemed irrational or rational by different parties. Many Iranians, for example, believe that death in the service of their religion is the highest good. To many Americans, however, this type of martyrdom seems fanatical or irrational.

The description of collective action as irrational often reflects a failure to think carefully about the social situations in which crowd members find themselves. For example, it was widely reported in the media that an irrational, out-of-control crowd caused the stampede at a 1979 Who concert that resulted in the death of 11 young people and the injury of many others. One sociologist has refuted this theory by carefully examining the reasons for the stampede and the actions of the crowd. The problem, apparently, was twofold: The large number of tickets sold for unreserved seating and the late opening of the stadium doors caused people to rush to compete for seats. This sociologist also pointed out that many members of the crowd acted rationally; for example, when some young people were knocked down, others formed a ring around the fallen to protect them (Johnson, 1987b).

Other theories using some elements of contagion theory in slightly modified form, have been developed. *Circular reaction theory,* originated by Herbert Blumer (1939), suggests that people in a crowd lose their ability to interpret interaction accurately. One person becomes excited, and others "pick up" on this excitement. Seeing the agitation exhibited by others then causes the first individual to become even more emotional. In this theory, crowd behavior is still regarded as irrational and emotional, as Le Bon argued, but the irrationality is seen as stemming from social interaction, not from a "group mind." Circular reaction theory has limited acceptance today, and is subject to the same criticisms that apply to contagion theory.

CONVERGENCE THEORY

A second major perspective explains the apparent similarity of the members of a crowd much more simply. According to convergence theory, the people who join a crowd already share tendencies to see things the same way and to act in a similar fashion; in fact, it was these common tendencies that brought them together as a crowd in the first place (Form & Bae, 1988; Wright, 1978). Thus, if the demonstrators in a crowd outside the Israeli Embassy share common negative attitudes toward Israel, convergence theory explains this similarity by the fact that people who are opposed to Israel will be motivated to come and join such a demonstration, not by the emergence of a shared mentality as a result of collective contagion.

EMERGENT NORM THEORY

According to the emergent norm approach, unanimity seems to prevail in a crowd because one set of behavioral norms gradually becomes accepted by the entire group (Turner & Killian, 1987). Social pressure is used against those who do not conform to the emergent norms. For example, a crowd of people protesting high prices at a supermarket might decide to enter the market and throw high-priced items off the shelves. People who do not agree with this action but remain silent or passive unintentionally lend their support to the norm. Those who voice their disapproval of the idea may be shouted down or heckled by the supporters. Norms that limit certain types of behavior may also emerge. People in the supermarket crowd may agree not to engage in any acts of physical violence, for example.

EVALUATION OF CROWD BEHAVIOR THEORIES

In the past few decades, a great deal of empirical information has been gathered about the behavior of crowds (Graumann & Muscovici, 1986; McPhail & Wohlstein, 1983). We now know that

1. Most crowds are not very homogeneous; crowd members typically vary in their attitudes and degree of participation.
2. Crowd behavior is not inherently irrational; crowd members are not hypnotized, nor are they out of touch with reality.
3. Crowd behavior, like all social behavior, is guided by norms (Turner & Killian, 1987; Wright, 1978).

In view of these findings, the emergent norm approach seems to offer the best explanation of crowd behavior. The members of crowds do not, as contagion theories predict, whip themselves into an emotional frenzy. Nor is their unanimity necessarily reflective only of their views prior to the formation of the crowd, as suggested by convergence theory. Rather, their behavior is controlled by emerging norms. Crowds are made up of social beings, who act according to the definitions they develop of what is happening and what needs to be done.

Mass Behavior

Not all collective behavior takes place exclusively in face-to-face groupings. Uncertainty, suggestibility, and urgency can also characterize the behavior of widely dispersed people in what might be described as "diffuse crowds." Collective behavior in diffuse social groupings is called **mass behavior;** it involves people who do not personally know, and have little contact with, one another.

PANICS

One of the better known types of mass behavior is the **panic,** a flight to secure safety in the face of imminent danger. Panics typically occur only when escape routes are available, but limited in number or closing off so that it appears that some, but not all, of the people who are in danger will be able to escape. The classic examples take place in theaters, restaurants, and nightclubs when a fire breaks out and people are trampled in a desperate effort to reach the exits. The worst of these incidents have claimed many hundreds of lives.

But panics need not involve people who are confined in the same physical space. The stock market crash of 1929 was an economic panic. As stockholders saw the value of their assets eroding, they panicked and sold their stocks, driving prices down even further. In the Depression that followed, banks closed and unemployment rose to alarming heights. A more recent financial panic, on a much smaller scale, occurred in 1985 when the Ohio Home State Savings Bank lost a large sum of money in a failed investment. Depositors, fearing that the bank might collapse, rushed to withdraw their savings. Their panic, in turn, led depositors at other banks to withdraw their money also (Johnson, 1987a).

MASS HYSTERIA

Mass hysteria is a form of collective behavior that occasionally occurs when people find themselves in ambiguous, threatening, and anxiety-creating situations. Rumors circulate, are accepted, and lead to an irrational belief in an imminent danger. Mass hysteria can be limited to small communities or can spread through an entire society. The momentum of mass hysteria eventually subsides when it becomes apparent that the perceived threat is nonexistent.

During a period of less than a week in the summer of 1962, 62 employees of a textile manufacturing firm in the South experienced brief but severe symptoms of illness, including dizziness, chills, and nausea (Kerckhoff & Back, 1968). The afflicted workers strongly believed that they had become ill as a result of being bitten by some sort of poisonous insect. The plant was thoroughly fumigated, but no evidence of any abnormal infestation was found. Puzzled investigators eventually concluded that what had occurred was in fact a case of mass hysteria brought on by overwork and rumors of layoffs. Unable to develop an effective way of responding to the tensions that they were experiencing, the mill workers, instead, relieved their anxiety, if only temporarily, through collective behavior.

In 1938, mass hysteria combined with panic developed in the New York area when thousands of radio listeners misinterpreted the broadcast of a work of fiction as news of an actual event. H. G. Wells's powerful story "The War of the Worlds," which describes an attack from outer space, was broadcast in such a realistic manner that people took it for actual news reporting. Many people reportedly jumped into their cars and drove as far as they could from the site of the supposed invasion; others locked themselves in their homes, armed with shotguns, and prepared to defend themselves against the aliens.

DISASTER BEHAVIOR

Another form of mass behavior is **disaster behavior**—behavior that follows natural or other types of disasters. Disasters include such natural events as epidemics, famines, droughts, hurricanes, earthquakes, and floods, as well as such man-made events as bombings, explosions, and fires. Disasters typically create drastically disrupted,

Behavior in disasters is an important aspect of the field of collective behavior. Here volunteers come to the aid of the Oklahoma tornado victims.

usually chaotic, environments in which people are unable to carry on their normal activities (Turner & Killian, 1987).

A heterogeneous group of people usually arrives at the scene of the disaster: those who live in the area but were not present at the time of the disaster; those who are concerned about friends and family residing in the area; volunteers; and the merely curious.

By virtue of their numbers, the newcomers may create significant problems in the disaster area. Usually, however, disaster behavior is very positive. Leaders and plans emerge and relief supplies arrive, though often in an uneven or unorganized manner. The extent to which disaster relief is provided to the victims varies; in some cases, governments and other types of organizations abandon the victims after the emergency phase of relief operations (Othman-Chande, 1987). If the disaster is prolonged, as in a famine or a plague, the spontaneous social structure that emerges in the wake of the disaster can come into conflict with the preestablished social order.

FASHION, FADS, AND CRAZES

The forms of mass behavior discussed so far all tend to involve unpleasant circumstances. This is not always the case, however.

Fashion is a temporarily popular style of dress or behavior. It is a "customary" departure from custom— that is, it is an attempt to be new and different but at the same time to stay within the bounds of accepted behavior (Sapir, 1937). Most examples of fashion involve items— particularly articles of clothing—that become popular at particular times. Faded jeans, designer T-shirts, and sweat suits, as well as chains, beads, and certain types of shoes, are examples.

Fashions are temporary and have mass appeal. Although fashions are often considered to be of trivial importance, as symbols of social status they can be a significant element in a society's system of stratification. As the nineteenth-century American social critic Thorstein Veblen (1899/1967) noted, fashion can serve as an index of a society's values and attitudes. For example, the popularity of miniskirts in the 1960s dramatically symbolized that era's relative openness concerning sexual matters; furthermore, at the individual level, wearing currently trendy fashions is an effective way of proving to others that one has the taste and financial ability to keep up with ever-changing styles of popular culture.

A **fad** is an activity that large numbers of people enthusiastically pursue for short periods of time. One sociologist has identified four types of fads: *object fads,* such as posters, bumper stickers, and novel types of clothing; *idea fads,* such as astrology; *activity fads,* such as snowmobiling; and *fad heroes,* such as singers like Jewel,

Alanis Morissette, and Ricky Martin (Lofland, 1985). In the United States, fads have included hula-hoops and numerous dances.

A **craze** is an intense fad with serious and lasting consequences. A classic example is the wave of fanatical enthusiasm for tulips that swept Holland in the 1630s (MacKay, 1841/1932). This so-called "tulipmania" was so intense that speculators willingly paid fortunes equivalent to thousands of dollars for prized bulbs. So much land was devoted to the growing of tulips that food had to be imported in order to meet the needs of the people.

Another example is the wild popularity of video arcades in the 1980s. It seemed like every third store in any mall was a new arcade packed with teenagers lined up to pump quarters into the latest game. Like tulipmania, the video arcade craze had a significant effect on the national economy. Furthermore, in both cases the craze became established as a permanent element in the culture after it subsided: Tulips remain popular among the Dutch to this day, and video games still captivate adolescents.

COMMUNICATION AND COLLECTIVE BEHAVIOR

Rumor, gossip, propaganda, and public opinion are all ways by which people share information and ideas. They can be viewed as types of collective behavior in their own right or as elementary processes that contribute to more complex types of collective behavior such as panics and riots.

Rumor and Gossip

The least structured types of information sharing, rumor and gossip, typically arise in situations in which people lack access to greatly needed or desired information. Instead of simply accepting this lack of information, people commonly seek out any source of guidance, even if unsubstantiated.

A **rumor** is an unverified report that is informally communicated from person to person, usually by word of mouth (Murphy, 1985). It is sometimes, although not always, inaccurate and usually much easier to start than to stop (Rosnow & Fine, 1976). For example, when the world's first atomic bomb was dropped on Hiroshima, there was a rumor that the city had been sprayed with gasoline. This rumor, although false, helped the victims to understand the explosion and fire as well as the sickness and poisoned water that ensued (Shibutani, 1966). Although the horror of the bombing remained, the rumor marginally eased people's fear of the unknown.

On a much less significant level, rumors have circulated ever since the death of Elvis Presley in 1977 at the age of 42. To this day, over 30 years later, fans are still debating the truthfulness of reports that their idol is still alive; the tabloids are filled with stories of people who claim to have seen or talked to the singer.

Gossip, which has been called "intellectual chewing gum" (Lumley, in Rosnow & Fine, 1976), is idle talk about the personal or private affairs of others. It amounts to a preoccupation with the nonessential. Yet what makes something "nonessential" depends on its social context. A social worker who tells a supervisor that a client is pregnant and not married is conveying important information. That same information passed between neighbors is gossip.

Gossip about media personalities has long been a staple of American life (Levin & Arluke, 1987). Television, which regularly brings celebrities into the living room, creates for some people some sense of "relationship" with the stars. Followers of specific celebrities sometimes make a hobby of collecting and sharing information about their favorites. Early in 1990, when a California couple announced the publication of a new magazine, called *The Doll,* which would profile everything about singer and film star Dolly Parton, 6,000 people subscribed immediately.

Gossip can play an important role in social life. One anthropologist examined gossip in the rural Figi Indian village of Bhatagon and concluded that the ambiguous nature of gossip (it may be true, or it may not) allows people to feel a sense of commonality without necessarily being in agreement with one another (Brenneis, 1984).

Public Opinion

Who or what is the "public," whose opinions are so often and so carefully solicited? Defined sociologically, a **public** is a dispersed grouping of people who share a common interest, concern, or focus of opinion.

In modern society, publics form around many different issues: abortion, pollution, consumer protection, political preference, and energy policy are examples. Although members of a public are sometimes organized—for example, voters may be registered Democrats, and moviegoers may be members of the Brad Pitt Fan Club—more often they are not. It is thus difficult to determine the exact size of a public.

In spite of its vague composition, a public is neither unimportant nor powerless. We may not know exactly who supports the Democratic ticket, but we know that the next president will be a Republican if the Democratic public is too small. Similarly, Brad Pitt's fans may be faceless and uncounted, but it is their "votes" at the box office that make him a star and keep him in demand with the movie studios.

The attitudes that are held by a public are called **public opinion.** Public opinion is usually more firmly based on reliable information than are rumors. But this information may be interpreted in a biased or misleading way. Also, public opinion is less fleeting than rumor. Whether in politics, entertainment, or business, public opinion can have great and lasting impact.

FORMING PUBLIC OPINION

There has long been speculation concerning the exact process by which public opinion is formed. It would seem reasonable to assume that public opinion is a direct expression of underlying values and social attitudes, but this is not always so. Although people's basic values remain relatively constant, public opinion changes rapidly; very different public opinions can be based on the same values.

Public opinion is heavily influenced by social background and group membership (Blumer, 1948; Cantril, 1980). In many cases nearly all of the members of a particular group (such as Seventh-day Adventists or executives of IBM) tend to have similar opinions on many issues. So do members of the same social class and persons with similar ethnic or educational backgrounds. For example, polls have shown that opinions concerning nuclear power are strongly influenced by an individual's level of education and income. People with graduate school training are more likely to favor nuclear power than are people with less education; and as people's income levels increase, the likelihood that they support nuclear power also goes up (Ginsberg, 1986).

Everyone belongs to more than one social group; and some groups are much more important than others in shaping public opinion. How effective a group is depends on such factors as its purpose, its organization, and the strength of its members' allegiance. The significance of most group memberships is limited to certain topics, however. Membership in the Catholic Church might greatly affect a person's opinions on abortion but may have little effect on his or her opinions about economic policies.

The influence exerted by particular people is another important factor in opinion formation. Every community includes a number of **opinion leaders**—people who have a particularly strong influence over public opinion. Each issue may have a different set of opinion leaders. One pioneering study found that, at least on some issues, personal influence is the single most important factor in the formation of opinion (Katz & Lazarsfeld, 1955). Research has also found that charismatic news commentators and anchorpersons exert considerable influence on public opinion (Rein, Kotler, & Stoller, 1987).

GLOBAL SOCIETY

TRUTH OR PROPAGANDA?

How can you tell the difference between news and propaganda. Sometimes it seems obvious. Consider, for example, editorial cartoons, which are designed to demonize the enemy. This form of propaganda dehumanizes the enemy by linking them to negative images and symbols (see cartoon). Editorial cartoonists rely heavily on stereotypes to convey a message instantly. And when it comes to portraying the "faces of the enemy," it often turns out that commonly recognized symbols of evil—monsters, serpents, barbarians, and various renditions of death—are used. (Keen, 1986).

In many cases, however, it is hard to distinguish news from propaganda. In fact, propaganda is designed to intentionally mislead the public. Just consider some of the many different names used to identify it:

Source: © Jerry Buckley. Courtesy Express Newspapers

- black propaganda
- disinformation
- doublethink
- indoctrination
- brainwashing
- dogma
- hidden agenda
- ideology
- dirty tricks campaign
- doublespeak
- psychological warfare

Of these, let us examine more closely what experts call black propaganda. Richard Nelson (1996) defines it this way: "The use of fabrications, deceptions, BIG LIES, and false source attributions (p. 128). How likely are you to spot black propaganda? Maybe you think you are pretty good, but many

people do not recognize it. It just seems to fit their expectations about an evil enemy.

In fact, several examples show that we frequently accept black propaganda as the truth. One is a common form of black propaganda about an atrocity committed by the enemy. "During World War I, for example, the Allies said (falsely) that the Germans were chopping off the hands of Belgian babies and turning corpses into soap" (Nelson, 1996, p. 128). And the American public believed it.

But could that happen today? After all, communications technology has come a long way since World War I. Perhaps you think that the American public could detect a BIG LIE like that today. If so, consider the horror stories that circulated during the Persian Gulf War. One widely reported story maintained that Iraqi soldiers took Kuwaiti babies from their hospital incubators and left them to die

(Nelson, 1996). This story now seems to have been fabricated and used to provoke war. Originally the source of the story was a refugee by the name of "Nayirah." Later, it turned out that the source was the teenage daughter of the Kuwaiti ambassador to the United States.

Sorting out the truth—recognizing the difference between news and propaganda—is always difficult. Today, the Internet can provide alternative sources of information. But it still takes a lot of time and effort to absorb information. And it takes some experience to determine what is propaganda and what is truth.

Regional differences in public opinion have become less pronounced over the last 40 years, principally because television and other forms of mass communication have helped to homogenize the American public. Before World War II, southern opinion on many important issues was known to differ sharply from the overall national opinion. This is no longer the case. While some regional differences of opinion remain, national similarities of opinion are now increasingly common (Ginsberg, 1986).

INFLUENCING PUBLIC OPINION

Many people and groups would like to shape public opinion. Manufacturers and retailers want to sell products, politicians want to be elected, and governments seek the support of the people. How can they influence public opinion in their favor?

One of the strongest forces shaping public opinion in modern societies is the *mass media:* television, radio, newspapers, and magazines (Biagi, 1989; Jeffres, 1997; McQuail, 1985). Television has an especially strong influence on public opinion. For this reason, access to the media is crucial to any person or organization that wants to influence the public.

In some cases, the media can legitimate social movements and alter public opinion about them. The coverage of the Vietnam War is a good example. Initially, media coverage supported the government's position on the war and disparaged the growing opposition to it. But when reporters began to corroborate the claims of the war's critics, the antiwar movement gained credence, and pressure to end the war grew (Gitlin, 1980; Hallin, 1984). Media coverage of the Persian Gulf War followed a somewhat similar sequence.

Gaining access to the media is one way to *reach* the public. But reaching the public and *persuading* it are two different things. One of the most effective means of persuasion is propaganda.

Propaganda refers to the deliberate manipulation of ideas in a way that appeals to people's emotions and prejudices (Ellul, 1966; Jowett, 1987; Nelson, 1996). Propaganda is used to create a public that sees the world in a way that benefits those who sponsor the propaganda. Between 1974 and 1977, for example, South Africa spent $75 million to finance propaganda abroad. It hired public relations agencies, made contributions to American election campaigns, provided legislators with free trips to South Africa, and attempted to purchase American news media (Windrich, 1989). The goal of this propaganda was, of course, to garner support for the racist policies of the South African government.

Playing on the fears and anxieties of the public, propaganda typically makes a strong emotional appeal and

During World War II, the United States government used propaganda to encourage people to support the war effort by buying U.S. Savings Bonds.

then offers the assurance that accepting a certain point of view will prevent the feared outcome. Hitler's Nazi regime, for example, played on Germans' fear of economic collapse in the 1930s and offered the Nazi political philosophy as the only way to avoid a catastrophe.

One appeal of propaganda is that it gives people an intellectual framework that helps them to understand life. People are constantly surrounded with "news," or accounts of events. The events that most often make news are problems, disasters, and catastrophes. People need a way to handle all this negative information, and propaganda can serve such a purpose. According to one scholar, "News loses its frightening character when it offers information for which the listener already has a ready explanation in his mind, or for which he can easily find one" (Ellul, 1966).

When propaganda is successful, it is not thought of as propaganda at all. Most Americans think of propaganda exclusively as something used by other countries, not by the United States. This is not the case, however; the

American government promotes its ideas in at least three different ways. One is through the educational system, which reinforces the dominant political values of American society. A second area is public relations, on which the government spends hundreds of millions of dollars each year. The third area is the mass media, including televised presidential addresses and press conferences (Weissberg, 1976).

During World War II, the U.S. government used propaganda to induce a major shift in traditional views about women. At the outbreak of the war, the government realized that it would need to attract large numbers of women into the work force in order to maintain the necessary levels of war production. The problem was to encourage the public to alter its traditional image of men as breadwinners and women as homemakers. To accomplish its goals, the government sought the cooperation of family and women's magazines. During the war, these magazines were filled with messages designed to influence women's attitudes on a wide range of issues—from encouraging the rationing of goods to reflecting a positive vision of women as patriots working for and serving their country. The effort was so successful that it required energetic strategies at the end of the war to reemphasize the importance of women's homemaking role, because the jobs taken by women would be needed for the returning war veterans (Honey, 1984; Jowett, 1987).

SOCIAL MOVEMENTS

One of the most distinctive characteristics of modern society is the extent to which people today are willing to act collectively and purposefully in order to promote social and cultural change. Among the most important ways this is accomplished is the **social movement**—a collective effort to produce social change that relies heavily on relatively noninstitutionalized methods.

Sociologists traditionally have stressed the similarities between social movements and collective behavior. In recent years, however, most scholars have paid more attention to the differences between the two (Foss & Larkin, 1986). Although both collective behavior and social movements tend to be relatively unstructured, movements are of much longer duration, feature more firmly established patterns of leadership and internal organization, and are characterized by much more deliberate mobilization of resources. Furthermore, because they are committed to the righting of what their supporters perceive as injustices, unlike most forms of elementary collective behavior, nearly all social movements have significant political implications.

Social movements that have flourished in the United States in recent decades include the civil rights, antiwar, feminist, antinuclear, environmental, pro-life, pro-choice, and gay rights movements, among many others. Most of these movements include various types of elementary collective behavior within their compass. For example, rumors about the plans of their opponents have played an important role in the mobilization of supporters of many mass movements. One of the principal goals of virtually all contemporary movements is to utilize propaganda techniques effectively to influence public opinion on critical issues. And the mass demonstrations and marches favored by modern movements not infrequently turn into riots or other types of acting crowds.

In a sense, social movements function as social experiments. If the movement is ultimately unsuccessful, as was the temperance movement in its struggle to outlaw permanently the sale and use of alcohol, it loses most of its support and gradually withers away. But if it succeeds in attaining its major goals, as did the movement for women's suffrage, then it becomes a lasting part of the social structure. Because of their crucial role in promoting social change, social movements may be thought of as institutions in embryonic form or as seedbeds for the generation of new groups and organizations.

Social movements include several crucial elements: ideologies, strategies and tactics, and leadership. Each may be illustrated by the civil rights movement that fought for equal treatment of African-Americans in the 1950s, 1960s, and 1970s.

The civil rights movement's ideology originally stressed the importance of gaining basic *political* rights, such as the rights to vote, to attend the same schools as whites, and to be able to eat at the same public lunch counters as anyone else. As most of these basic rights were gained (despite fierce and often violent resistance by segregationists), the movement gradually shifted toward a commitment to broader *economic* goals, such as the right to equal opportunity in employment and housing. Belief in the movement's ideology and in its vision of a better future helped to sustain its followers during the difficult periods when the movement was meeting great opposition from representatives of the established social order.

Just as the movement's ideology shifted over time, so did its strategy and tactics. In the early days, the favored approach was legalistic. The National Association for the Advancement of Colored People (NAACP), the leading civil rights organization throughout the 1950s, won a number of court battles to compel local, state, and federal government agencies to guarantee African-Americans the rights promised to all citizens in the Constitution. Beginning in the early 1960s, new organizations, such as the Student Nonviolent Coordinating Committee (SNCC), emerged that favored a more activist strategy, including dramatic tactics such as marches, sit-ins, freedom rides, and mass demonstrations. These attracted extensive media attention and expanded the movement's support base. By the late 1960s, radical groups like the Black Panthers had adopted even more controversial and aggressive tactics such as marching fully armed into the California State Legislature in order to publicize their demands for fair treatment and an end to police harassment of the black community.

Finally, different segments within the civil rights movement were characterized by different types of leaders. By far the best known of the movement's leaders was the highly charismatic Martin Luther King, Jr., who attracted millions of followers by virtue of his impassioned oratory and willingness to accept martyrdom for the civil rights cause. In contrast, many of the young leaders of SNCC and the Congress of Racial Equality (CORE) preferred to remain relatively anonymous, emphasizing the importance of their cause by shunning the limelight and concentrating on building effective organizations. Similarly, the principal Black Panther leaders, including Bobby Seale and Eldridge Cleaver, strongly emphasized the importance of ideas as the primary basis of their claim to leadership.

Types of Social Movements

Social movements take a number of different forms. A list of the main types includes reform, revolutionary, resistance, and expressive movements.

REFORM MOVEMENTS

Some social movements seek to improve society by changing selected aspects of the social structure but do not seek to alter basic economic or political arrangements or to change substantially the stratification hierarchy. These are known as **reform movements.** Because of its relatively democratic structure, American society has been a breeding ground for many such movements. Reform movements generally center on one issue, but the changes they seek can be far-reaching.

The disabled rights movement, which works on behalf of the 13 million to 14 million Americans who suffer from severe handicaps, is a small but growing reform movement. This movement fought for the implementation of the first national legislation passed to assist disabled people, the 1973 Vocational Rehabilitation Act. One section of that act prohibits employment discrimination against the handicapped by any organization receiving federal funds. The movement won another significant victory with the passage of the Americans with Disabilities Act of 1990, which imposes substantial obligations on employers and providers of public transportation, telecommunications, and other public services to accommodate people with disabilities.

Other reform movements in the United States today include most components of the environmental movement, the anti–drunk driving campaign being waged by Mothers Against Drunk Driving (MADD), the victims' rights movement, and the antipornography movement.

REVOLUTIONARY MOVEMENTS

Other movements seek more fundamental change in society. The goal of these **revolutionary movements** is to overthrow the existing social structure and replace it with a new one. Typically, revolutionary movements arise where reform is not seen as a viable alternative. Many governments in the world today began as revolutionary movements.

The socialist revolution that took place in Iran in 1979 was the work of a revolutionary movement that brought drastic changes to an entire society. Iran today is very different from what it was like before 1979. Most Iranians, with the exception of a small group of Westernized elites, felt excluded under the repressive and autocratic rule of the Shah. Long-established ties between two powerful segments of society—bazaar shopkeepers and the Shi'ite clergy—led them to combine against the Shah after he began to attack both groups in order to consolidate further his power during the early 1970s. Anger over the Shah's militarism, modernization programs, lack of respect for Islamic traditions, and ties to the West—especially the United States—had been smoldering for years. His targeting of the bazaars and the Shi'ite religious establishment triggered the mass protests that led to his overthrow and the establishment of a militant Islamic republic (Buraway & Skocpol, 1982).

RESISTANCE MOVEMENTS

Not all social movements try to promote change. **Resistance movements** aim to prevent change or to reverse a change that has already been achieved. These movements typically develop during periods of rapid social transformation such as that which occurred in American society during the 1950s and 1960s. The successes of the civil rights movement, for example, led to backlash movements that opposed the integration of schools and other public facilities.

Pro-life groups have mobilized to overturn *Roe* v. *Wade*, the Supreme Court decision that granted women the right to abort a fetus in the first two trimesters of pregnancy. Groups such as Operation Rescue have organized mass demonstrations outside abortion clinics in hopes of attracting public support for their position and to close down these clinics.

EXPRESSIVE MOVEMENTS

Because they seek to alter the existing power structure in some way, reform, revolutionary, and resistance movements are usually more or less explicitly political in nature. Some movements, however, are oriented less toward changing the structure of a society and more toward changing the people who compose it. These **expressive movements** attempt to provide their members with some type of personal transformation, which may include emotional satisfaction, a new identity, or a different ideology. Expressive movements can be either religious or secular in nature.

A study of one religiously oriented expressive movement, the following gathered around Meher Baba, found that the movement resolved for its members many of the conflicts between the youth culture and the requirements associated with adult society (Robbins & Anthony, 1972). With society as a whole growing more impersonal and bureaucratic, many young people experience difficulty entering adulthood and seek out the support of members of a close primary group. The atmosphere provided by the Meher Baba movement appears informal, friendly, and humane. New members are received warmly, and relationships are supportive. Instead of further alienating its members from adult society, this expressive movement was found to subtly support and encourage them to assume adult responsibilities.

The "human potential" movement of the 1960s and 1970s is a good example of a secular expressive movement focused on inner liberation. Members of the movement attended encounter groups, group therapy, and sensory awareness sessions. People flocked to the Esalen Institute (the California personal growth center at the heart of the movement) and to other therapeutic centers across the country to "get in touch with themselves," to become aware of their feelings, and to learn to connect better with others. The movement grew in a time of increased alienation, when people felt isolated from society, from one another, and from themselves (Lieberman, Yalom, & Miles, 1973). The more recent New Age movement similarly seeks to provide its members with some type of personal transformation linked to physical and spiritual health.

The Life Course of Social Movements

Although social movements differ in their aims and in many other characteristics, those that are successful often have much in common. Many successful movements pass through a series of four stages, culminating in acceptance by society (Bakuniak & Nowak, 1987; Blumer, 1939; Dawson & Gettys, 1948; Hopper, 1950). In sociological terms, the movements become *institutionalized*.

The *preliminary stage* of a social movement is marked by a restlessness in the society, conflict between various groups, and inefficient and insufficient efforts at responding to social problems. The people who are most affected, the restless and the discontented, have no clear focus for their energy. Leaders who emerge at this time are likely to be agitators rather than organizers.

Second comes the *popular stage*. The discontented become aware that others share their views and realize that united action, through a social movement, is possible. The leaders most likely to emerge at this stage are prophets and reformers. Prophets speak with a sense of authority and confidence and can sway the masses with their vision of the future. Reformers focus the masses on specific problems and solutions.

In the third phase, the *formal organization stage,* ideologies are developed that help to give the movement direction and unity. Values and goals become increasingly clear. At the same time, the movement develops an organizational structure with a hierarchy of leaders, a set of policies, and programs for action. Leadership by prophets and reformers gives way to leadership by strategists, people who can take the movement to the final stage.

In the *institutional stage,* the movement becomes an accepted part of society. The idealism and fervor of the members are dulled or lost, and decision making becomes divided among several bodies within the movement. The administrator-executive proves to be the characteristic leader at this point.

A Modern Theory of Social Movement Development: Resource Mobilization

For many years, sociologists emphasized collective frustrations and grievances as the most crucial factors in explaining the origin of social movements. Perhaps the best example of this perspective is the central place given to the concept of structural strain in Neil Smelser's value-added theory, discussed earlier in this chapter. This concept can just as effectively account for social movement activity as it can explain the growth of elementary forms of collective behavior.

In the past several decades, however, a number of scholars have argued that the traditional orientation is incomplete. While not denying that relative deprivation plays a role in the development of social movements, they note that most people constantly experience some degree of strain, yet movements only arise at certain times and places. What seems to make the crucial difference

SOCIOLOGY OF THE MEDIA

ORGANIZING FOR THE MEDIA

What do you think is the most important problem facing this country today? Public opinion polls ask Americans to answer this question regularly. Over the years their answers have included many social problems—prejudice and discrimination, drugs, crime, unemployment. For years, no one wondered why some social problems attracted national attention while others did not. Presumably, Americans identify problems that directly affect their lives. But, in fact, many other factors operate in leading the public to identify certain problems as the nation's most important. John Ryan and William Wentworth argue that

> For an issue to become defined as an important social problem a number of things must occur. Principal among them is that an individual or group must adopt the issue as their own and actively work to promote the issue to the public and to policy makers. Groups that are likely to be most successful are those that mobilize such resources as volunteers, money, communication networks, and, most importantly . . . media attention. (1999, p. 79)

In fact, research strongly suggests that the problems the public regards as the nation's most important are the ones that receive prominent media attention (Iyengar & Kinder, 1987). That suggests that grassroots

organizers must know how the media operate (Ryan, 1991). Understanding what constitutes news and how to get it covered is the key to building a successful social movement. The first thing that social activists must understand is that drawing attention to their cause can do as much harm as good—it all depends on how reporters frame the story. Consider, for example, how the media cover demonstrations. More often than not, they are framed to discredit the participants (Ryan & Wentworth, 1999). The Million Man March on Washington was in general framed positively. But the Promise Keepers March in 1997 was not.

There are many ways to slant a story (Ryan & Wentworth, 1999). To begin with, reporters choose which elements to include and which to exclude. Reporters intent on choosing an interesting soundbite can fundamentally alter a speaker's words. The selection and presentation of visual images can distort meaning as well. In short, reporters control the way a story is framed.

Once social activists understand how the media operate, they can design a media strategy to mobilize support for their cause. In her book, *Prime Time Activism*, (1991), Charlotte Ryan outlines some key strategies for grassroots organizers. To help activists get their message across with minimum media bias, she advises the following:

- *Clarify your political goals.* Begin by assessing the extent to which the public recognizes the issue.

Then determine your audience and the targets you should pressure.

- *Prepare your message.* Decide how you want to frame the issue. Choose the images and cultural themes that you will use. And gather documentation that you will need.

- *Weigh your resources.* Assess your relationships with the mainstream media. Are your staff/members trained to deal with reporters and producers? Do they understand newsroom norms?

- *Determine the general direction of the media coverage desired.* Identify the media that can best reach your potential supporters, activists, and decision makers.

- *Set your priorities and consider alternative media outlets.* In addition to regular news coverage, consider other avenues of communication. These would include letters to the editor, op-ed pages, talk shows, and opinion columns.

- *Focus on developing a relationship with key reporters.* Keep key reporters updated on your issue. Suggest possible stories. Invite reporters to meet members and arrange workshops that cover important aspects of your issue.

---

is the availability of adequate resources—money, followers, access to the media, and so forth—to allow discontent to be translated into movement formation. These sociologists have developed what is termed the **resource mobilization approach,** which focuses on the political and economic resources that are available to movement activists and asks such questions as: How do

the organizations that coalesce out of movement activism obtain and mobilize the resources they need and utilize them to promote the attainment of their goals (Foss & Larkin, 1986; Oberschall, 1973)?

Several key differences between the resource mobilization perspective and traditional approaches to social movement analysis may be identified (Zald & McCarthy,

1979). The first concerns the character of a movement's support base. According to the traditional perspective, the most crucial source of movement support is a large aggrieved population. It is assumed that the movement develops principally because there are substantial numbers of people who are seeking social change. In contrast, resource mobilization theorists note that some movements may achieve substantial success despite having, at least initially, little popular support, if they are able to secure the backing of a relatively small number of committed individuals. The key resources for such groups are typically the allegiance of a cadre of upper-middle-class supporters together with the assistance of private foundations, government agencies, universities, and the mass media (Haines, 1988; McCarthy & Zald, 1973; Zald & McCarthy, 1979). Far from being built on the discontent of the masses, these movements must actively work to mobilize popular discontent (which then becomes one of the key resources that they use to move toward their goals).

A second difference concerns movement strategies. According to the traditional view, movements must devote most of their time and energy to bargaining with, and sometimes threatening, the authorities in order to compel them to institute the changes desired by the movement activists. Without denying that such activities are important, the resource mobilization school adds that movement leaders must also spend a great deal of time recruiting supporters, obtaining funds, and developing relationships with other organizations that are seeking similar goals.

One of the great strengths of the resource mobilization perspective is its recognition of the increasing reliance of modern movements on the mass media, public mailings, lobbying, and the like for their success. Such techniques require the evolution of a new type of movement leader: less fiery orator and more media specialist. Such leaders have been termed *social movement entrepreneurs* (McCarthy & Zald, 1973). Not infrequently, these individuals shift from movement to movement during their careers, seemingly more committed to activism itself than to any particular cause.

Resource mobilization theory was developed principally from the analysis of the major movements of the 1960s and reflects the intimate knowledge of movement dynamics that many contemporary sociologists derived from their own experiences as activists during their college years. However, there are varied themes within the general resource mobilization perspective (Jenkins, 1983; Picharro, 1988). For instance, some scholars take a long-term position, emphasizing gradual changes over the years in the availability of resources for movement development, whereas others focus more on day-to-day access to committed workers and adequate funding. Some analysts devote most of their attention to broad currents of movement activism (such as the civil rights movement in general), and others focus primarily on specific movement organizations (like the NAACP or CORE).

CHAPTER REVIEW

1. Identify and discuss incidents of collective behavior that have been reported in the news.

2. What kinds of social conditions give rise to collective behavior?

3. College students often find themselves in a crowd. Describe experience you have had in different kinds of crowds.

4. Discuss the three major theories that explain crowd behavior.

5. How do the following forms of mass behavior differ from one another—panic, mass hysteria, disaster behavior?

6. Describe the fashions, fads, and crazes that are popular among college students.

7. Why do sociologists consider gossip and rumor a form of collective behavior? Do they serve a function?

8. What role does public opinion play in the emergence of a social movement?

9. Consider the kinds of social problems that we are likely to see in the twenty-first century. Will any of these give rise to a social movement? If so, what will it be?

INTERNET EXERCISE

The Web destinations for Chapter 21 cover various aspects of collective behavior and social movements. To begin your investigation, go to the Prentice Hall Companion Web site **http://www.prenhall.com/popenoe.** Next, select **Chapter 21** (Collective Behavior and Social Movements). Then, choose **web destinations** from the menu on the left side of the screen. There are several sites to choose from. We suggest you begin with the **Propaganda Analysis Home Page.** This site provides an opportunity to substantially expand your knowledge on this subject. For example, you will find an excellent discussion of the major forms of propaganda (e.g., *glittering generalities, transfer, testimonial,* etc.); you can learn more about the Institute for Propaganda Analysis, the Internationalist Socialist Organization, and the John Birch Society; and you can actually view videoclips in a "Propaganda Gallery." After you have explored the Propaganda Analysis Home Page, answer the following questions:

- What are the central dangers of propaganda?
- Do you think you are a victim of propaganda? If so, how?

KEY TERMS

collective behavior	panic	opinion leaders
value-added approach	mass hysteria	propaganda
crowd	disaster behavior	social movements
expresssive crowd	fashion	reform movements
solidaristic crowd	fad	revolutionary movements
acting crowd	craze	resistance movements
mob	rumor	expressive movements
riot	gossip	resource mobilization
emergent norm theory	public	approach
mass behavior	public opinion	

CHAPTER 22

Social
and Cultural Change

hange, sometimes subtle and sometimes dramatic, has always been an integral part of the American way of life. In order to appreciate fully how much social and cultural change this country has experienced, let's look at the lifestyles of two college students, related by blood but separated by 120 years.

John Wilson was a college sophomore in 1875. In this era, higher education was a privilege available to only a minute fraction of Americans; John's parents were able to afford to send him to college only because they were very well-to-do. John journeyed to school by train, passing mostly through wooded areas and farmlands on the way. He communicated with his parents and his five brothers and sisters while at college through the mail. He studied by gaslight and handwrote all of his assignments and term papers. There were no women on campus because higher education was considered inappropriate for them. When John went home on vacation, he visited his betrothed at the home of her parents.

John Wilson IV is a student in 1995. Since his parents' divorce, he has lived with his mother and brother, who see him off for college at the airport. During the flight, the plane passes over a megalopolis that stretches for hundreds of miles. Higher education is the norm among John's friends, most of whom are members of America's greatly expanded middle class. To communicate with his family while he is at school, John simply picks up a phone and pushes some buttons; a computer processes his call in a fraction of a second. Electricity lights his room and powers his personal computer. Women make up about half of the student body, and John's dorm is coed. He dates several women, one of whom asked him out.

Both John Wilson and his descendant have experienced rapid social and cultural change. The first John Wilson saw America transformed from an agrarian society to an urban society, and he witnessed the advent of numerous inventions that made transportation and communication far more rapid and available. John Wilson IV takes technological change for granted. He is aware that shortages in fossil fuels may someday alter the world he knows, but postindustrial America's computer technology and service economy are familiar to him, even if they are a little unsettling at times. He has learned that change is normal and inevitable, but occasionally he wonders what lies ahead.

The study of social change is one of the most important areas of interest to sociologists. Developing an understanding of this universal process and how it affects us are the goals of this final chapter.

SOURCES OF SOCIAL CHANGE

Let us begin by introducing the main sources of social change. Possibilities range from the impersonal to the very personal. At one extreme is a natural cataclysm, such as a volcanic eruption that buries fertile farmland under tons of lava and forces local inhabitants to develop new ways of providing food for themselves. At the other extreme is the dedicated effort of a single individual, such as Mahatma Gandhi, who worked to end colonial rule in India.

Sociologists and anthropologists have focused their attention on seven main causes of social change: the physical environment, population, technology, nonmaterial culture, cultural processes, economic development, and deliberate efforts to promote change.

The Physical Environment

One of the most striking, although not the most common, causes of social change is a natural disaster, such as a flood or an earthquake. The social effects of one such event, the Buffalo Creek flood in West Virginia, were discussed in Chapter 1. This flood forced the abrupt relocation of the people who had lived in the valley below a ruined dam. The results: A once tightly knit community broke up into isolated individuals and family units, and people found it very difficult to establish new social ties.

Not all changes in the environment are this sudden and dramatic. Industrial pollution, for example, may build up gradually yet be just as important in changing the life of a community. Consider what can happen to a fishing village when the waters become polluted and the fish become contaminated or die off.

Population

Changes in the size and composition of a society's population can have an enormous impact, as discussed in Chapter 19.

The most compelling evidence of the ability of population growth to promote social change is found in the world's developing societies, which are presently undergoing dramatic population increases as they pass through the middle phases of the demographic transition. These increases have led directly to the growth of huge cities throughout the Third World and have contributed materially to important changes in virtually all institutions in these societies. Population growth also has directly contributed to the depletion of natural resources, which has led, in turn, to a wide range of changes in economic and political systems worldwide.

Industrial pollution is one of the many factors of social change. Although the change is gradual, the lasting effects can dramatically alter the lives of people in a community.

Changes in population composition also can have an enormous impact on social life. For example, the aging of the U.S. population is reshaping nearly all aspects of American society, as discussed in detail in Chapter 12. Imbalanced sex ratios among the first wave of some immigrant groups entering the United States and in response to government-mandated population control programs in present-day China are other examples that have had important effects on a variety of spheres of social and cultural life.

Technology

Social change that results from **technology**—knowledge and tools used to manipulate the environment for practical ends—often has an unplanned, seemingly inevitable, quality. As soon as a new technique or invention is developed, it is normally put to use, regardless of its larger moral and social implications. Take, for example, the introduction of the snowmobile into the society of the Skolt Lapps (a group in northeastern Finland) in the 1960s. The Lapps quickly became dependent on an external source of energy, gasoline, as the snowmobile

displaced native reindeer for transportation. As a result, the cost of living went up. A new category of "have-nots"—those who could not afford fuel for snowmobiles—was created in this formerly egalitarian society. At the same time, though, the snowmobile extended the group's range of social contacts and speeded the delivery of such services as emergency medical aid (Pelto, 1973; Pelto & Müller-Wille, 1972).

During the past few decades, many technological developments have been adopted with surprisingly little planning or thought about their long-range effects; the development of nuclear power, gene-splicing technology, and space exploration vehicles are some examples.

William Ogburn, a pioneering American theorist of social change, introduced (1950) an important concept that is still very useful in thinking about the social effects of technology. He suggested that the adoption of new elements of material culture and technology is usually quite rapid because it is relatively easy to demonstrate their advantages in comparison to those of more traditional methods. However, the adoption of modified elements of nonmaterial culture, made necessary by the acceptance of the new technologies, is frequently much slower, creating what Ogburn called a **cultural lag**—a period of maladjustment between the adoption of material or technological advances and the compensatory changes in nonmaterial culture that they necessitate.

The concept of cultural lag offers especially useful insights into some recent and historical dilemmas of American social change. For example, acceptance of the automobile (material culture) was very rapid, but we are still resisting some of the changes in nonmaterial culture that the automobile has made necessary. For example, we may need to modify further our norms regarding premarital sex, which is now much more prevalent than it once was, in part because of the privacy afforded by the automobile. Similarly, some observers argue that we need to develop new forms of metropolitan government (nonmaterial culture) in response to the fact that nineteenth-century urban political boundaries have been rendered all but meaningless by the expansion and decentralization of urban regions, which was made possible in turn by the widespread acceptance of the automobile. Some scholars, following Ogburn's logic, have suggested that modern nuclear and biochemical technologies, which have transformed warfare from a relatively rational policy in pursuit of national interests to a likely mechanism of species extinction, have rendered war itself unthinkable; yet we have barely begun to transform our political and military institutions and related values (such as patriotism and nationalism) in response to this new technological reality. As a final example, American educational systems are only beginning to respond to the instructional opportunities inherent in the widespread availability of personal computers.

Nonmaterial Culture

Many sociologists have emphasized, in contrast to Ogburn, that changes in nonmaterial culture often *precede* changes in material culture. The classic analysis of cultural values and ideology as sources of social change is Max Weber's interpretation of the social impact of values and beliefs associated with Protestantism (1905/1930; see Chapter 16). Weber suggested that the then-new Protestant beliefs regarding work, savings, and prosperity encouraged the development of capitalism in European society. To take another example, the spread of the ideologies of communism and socialism has had a massive impact on many of the world's societies.

Cultural Processes

As noted in Chapter 3, social change can be set in motion either by developments within a culture or by the influence of foreign cultures. Two common sources of social change within a culture are discovery and invention, which are sometimes grouped together under the term *innovation. Discovery* refers to becoming aware of something that was always present but had not previously been recognized, such as Watson and Crick's discovery of the DNA molecule. *Invention,* in contrast, results from the combination of existing elements of a culture in a new way—for example, the development of the personal computer or the VCR.

The process by which cultural traits spread from one group or society to another, as in the case of Christianity, is called **cultural diffusion.** Popular among anthropologists in the early twentieth century, the theory of cultural diffusion remains of enormous importance today.

Economic Development

Another important set of social change factors accompanies economic development. These factors are often included within the concept of **modernization,** which refers to the broad internal social changes that typically occur when a traditional preindustrial society becomes industrialized and urbanized.

Three key factors are commonly subsumed within the concept of modernization: industrialization, urbanization, and bureaucratization. **Industrialization** refers to a shift from human to nonhuman sources of energy and the rise of the factory system of economic production (Blumer, 1990). An example would be the process by which shoes, previously made by hand in small shops,

Modernization has brought an enormous change to industry. The once labor intensive assembly line factories have been replaced with the ease of high-tech manufacturing.

came to be manufactured in factories by electrically powered machines. **Urbanization** (see Chapter 20) means the movement of people from rural areas into towns and cities (where factories tend to be located). **Bureaucratization** (see Chapter 7) refers to the rise of large-scale formal organizations. These three components of modernization, in turn, lead to changes in such social institutions as religion, politics, and the family. We discuss sociological theories of economic development and modernization later in this chapter.

Deliberate Efforts to Promote Change

A final source of change, largely unknown before the Industrial Revolution but of great importance today, consists of deliberate efforts to transform society and culture. Through most of history, people thought of change, if they thought of it at all, as something that happened to them, not as something that they could bring about. But

.NET   INTERNET/TECHNOLOGY

REVOLUTIONS: LESSONS FOR THE FUTURE

Revolutions are the most spectacular manifestations of social change. They mark fundamental ruptures in the historical process, reshape human society from within and remould the people. They leave nothing as it was before; they close epochs and open new ones. (Sztompka, 1993)

In this brief description, Piotr Sztompka distilled the defining characteristics of revolutions. The revolutions that fit this description have occurred at different times, but most are linked to the modern period. The greatest ones include the English (1640), the American (1776), the French (1789), the Russian (1917), the Chinese (1949), and the anticommunist revolution in eastern and central Europe (1989) (Sztompka, 1993).

Most experts on revolutions believe that they involve violence and coercion. But, in fact, these elements do not necessarily characterize all revolutionary change (Vago, 1999). Scientific discoveries also have the power to "leave nothing as it was before"—"to close epochs and open new ones." Consider, for example, Copernicus's discovery that the earth revolves around the sun, which fundamentally altered the way people thought. Or Gutenberg's invention of movable type, which revolutionized the dissemination of information.

As we enter a new millennium, scientific discoveries as profound as these promise to fundamentally alter society. At a White House conference in 1998, Stephen Hawking spoke about one of the most controversial scientific possibilities—the ability to change human DNA (Isaacson, 1998). While this revolutionary achievement is now well within our reach, our ability to deal with its moral consequences is far more remote. Some experts have expressed concern, but others seem more focused on its scientific and technological aspects. For them, the study of revolutions can provide some valuable lessons.

Overall, experts who study revolutions realize that our understanding of them is limited. Even though scholars' analyses seem to provide some insight into the conditions that gave rise to them, the next revolution always seems to surprise us. The most important lesson of all, however, is probably this: "Revolutions never end in what was dreamed of by the revolutionaries. By some irony of history, they often end in its opposite, resulting in more injustice, inequality, exploitation, oppression and repression" (Sztompka, 1993, p. 303). While we generally do not expect technology to alter human relationships in this way, our ability to alter DNA clearly offers that opportunity. It was, in fact, what Aldous Huxley warned us about in *Brave New World*. And that is something that deserves serious thought.

---

in the modern world, with our vastly expanded understanding of social life, people are increasingly attempting to mold society in desired directions.

An outstanding example of this is the development in recent decades of research and development (R&D) divisions of major corporations. It is an explicit function of these divisions to prepare corporations to do business in a future that, it is assumed, will be fundamentally different in important ways from the present. The fact that we take such planning for granted today should not obscure the novelty of such activities in historical context.

The increased importance of a wide variety of social movements, as discussed in Chapter 21, is another example of how social and cultural change have become more deliberate in modern times. Outstanding movement leaders, from Gandhi to Martin Luther King, Jr., have succeeded in enlisting their followers in the promotion of large-scale changes in the public sector. Other movements, such as feminism, have produced equally extensive changes in the private sphere.

THEORIES OF SOCIAL CHANGE

Theories of social change range from explanations of specific factors that cause small-scale changes to abstract and wide-ranging attempts to discern broad underlying trends in the evolution of human societies. The development of such theories was a major goal of the founders of the discipline. Today many sociologists are still actively engaged in proposing empirically based explanations of how and why societies change and of the directions in which they are moving. This is not to say that sociologists have been completely successful in their attempts to answer such "big questions." But our understanding does grow with each passing year.

Four broad types of social change theory have been proposed: sociocultural evolutionary theory, cyclical theory, the functionalist perspective, and the conflict perspective.

Sociocultural Evolutionary Theory

The most widely accepted of all perspectives on social change is probably the theory of **sociocultural evolution,** which holds that societies and cultures develop gradually over time, changing from simpler to more complex forms (Lenski & Lenski, 1987; Parsons, 1966).

The concept of evolution dominated the work of most classical sociologists (see Chapter 1), who assumed that all social change took place in a *unilinear* fashion—that is, along a single path of development. This assumption led its supporters to argue that Western civilization must be the culmination of a process of change that all non-Western societies would eventually emulate, and thus to the conclusion that the United States and the nations of Western Europe were inherently more advanced than any other societies. This early evolutionism developed into an ideology justifying the economic and political domination of many of the world's peoples under the colonial system.

In part because of its ideological underpinnings and in part because of a lack of empirical support for the theory, unilinear evolution fell into disrepute through much of the twentieth century. In recent years, however, evolutionary thinking has undergone a rebirth of popularity. Modern evolutionists assume, however, that social change is *multilinear,* meaning that while the general trend is still from the simple to the complex, change can and does occur in different ways in different societies. Modern evolutionary thought is very useful in helping to suggest guidelines that may assist Third World nations as they undergo rapid economic development.

Contemporary sociocultural-evolutionists point to the special significance of three "master" evolutionary trends:

1. The increasing ability of societies to control the environment as a result of *technological developments.*

2. The increasing specialization of groups, organizations, and institutions—a process called *social differentiation.*

3. *Functional interdependence* of the component elements of society, with each unit relying more on the others to help it perform its task.

The vast changes in society that resulted from the Industrial Revolution in England reflect these master trends. Major technological developments included the introduction of the steam engine and the mechanization of textile production. Increased social differentiation was exemplified by the emergence of new social classes-owners (capitalists) and wage workers (proletarians). Increasing functional interdependence may be illustrated by the loss of independence by family units. Families no longer made their own clothing, for example. Instead, they became dependent on the developing textile industry to produce what they needed. In turn, the textile industry depended on families to buy its products and to provide it with a steady supply of workers.

Modern scholars who study such master evolutionary trends are careful to avoid some of the mistakes of their predecessors. They do not suggest that these trends always increase human happiness. Nor do they believe that these patterns of change are inevitable: They are subject to a certain degree of human control (Sanderson, 1990).

In addition, modern evolutionists believe that these trends might reverse direction in the future. Some parts of societies today are apparently becoming more alike rather than more diverse—the opposite of social differentiation. There is, for example, a growing standardization of culture promoted by the mass media, and some geographic, class, ethnic, and religious differences seem to be lessening. Some observers even believe that a "world culture" is emerging, with American values, products, and technologies influencing lifestyles all over the globe (McCord & McCord, 1986).

Cyclical Theory

Unlike the evolutionists, who believe that major social trends normally proceed in a particular direction, other theorists have held that cultures and societies continually experience directionless patterns of growth and decay, challenge and response. *Cyclical theories* were especially popular during the first half of the twentieth century. The three theories discussed here are so broad in scope that they are often thought of as philosophies of history rather than as scientific theories of social change. Yet they have significantly influenced scientific thinking about the growth and change of civilizations.

The German historian Oswald Spengler (1880–1936), whose most famous work was *The Decline of the West* (1918/1965), viewed societies as living organisms. According to Spengler, each society has a birth; a period of childhood during which it develops rapidly; a maturity, or "golden age"; a long and slow decline; and a final period of relatively rapid disintegration leading, as in any organism, to death. As the title of his work suggests, Spengler believed that Western civilization was in the period of decline and pessimistically declared that nothing could reverse this trend. Although few sociologists today agree with Spengler, more than 80 years after its publication his philosophy still attracts much popular interest.

The major work of Arnold Toynbee (1889–1975), an English historian, was the massive *A Study of History* (1964). Like Spengler, Toynbee thought that societies develop cyclically. But Toynbee felt that the cycles could be repeated many times over and was rather optimistic about the future.

Toynbee believed that each cycle begins with some sort of "challenge"—initially to establish a regular pattern of economic subsistence, later to adjust to various social conditions. Each challenge is met by a "response," which is mounted by the "creative elite" within a given culture. If the response is successful, the society survives and continues on to face the next challenge. If the response is unsuccessful, the society will collapse. Toynbee viewed this cycle of challenge and response as leading to progress toward a better civilization. He maintained that modern Western—and especially English—society had reached the highest level of civilization possible, thus providing a guide for others to follow. Because of this view, reminiscent of the position of the nineteenth-century unilinear evolutionists, some critics have charged Toynbee with ethnocentrism. Those who support his theory, however, point to the fact that the use of Western technology—particularly in agriculture, industry, and medicine—has raised the standard of living throughout the world today to the highest level ever attained.

Pitirim Sorokin (1889–1968) was a Russian-American sociologist whose theory of history, contained in the multivolume work *Social and Cultural Dynamics* (1941), was based on a detailed, partly quantitative comparison of a large number of historical societies. Sorokin suggested that there are two basic types of culture. In a "sensate" culture, human institutions and symbolic expression are designed primarily to gratify the senses. Art is pictorial and philosophy is based on what can be learned or perceived empirically; science is a key institution. The "ideational" culture, in contrast, appeals mostly to faith. Ideational art is abstract, and ideational philosophy is based on the nonempirical or transcendent; religion is a key institution. Sorokin believed that all societies alternate in their development between sensate and ideational cultures. The modern West, according to Sorokin, is a perfect example of a "late sensate" culture. Although Sorokin viewed this era quite negatively, he was optimistic that it would eventually be replaced by a more ideational type of culture.

Sorokin's theory has caused much debate among sociologists. It is often criticized for failing to explain specifically why and how cultures change. Despite such objections, Sorokin's work remains a landmark of sociological scholarship.

The Functionalist Perspective

It will be recalled that in order to understand why a given part of a social system exists—a group, an institution, a class—functionalists ask what function it performs in maintaining the social order as a whole. Their main focus is thus on what preserves a social system, not on the kinds of change that may occur within one. However, if all elements of a society are assumed to be relatively stable and integrated and to serve important functions, where does change come from?

Talcott Parsons (1951), a leading functionalist, conceived of society as a system of interdependent parts, each of which makes some contribution to the maintenance of the system. The natural condition of a social system, he stated, is *equilibrium,* a balance between or among all elements of the system. But change can arise, according to Parsons, from two sources. It can originate outside a particular social system—that is, in other systems—or it can be generated by tensions and strains within the system.

Since a system is made up of interdependent parts, a change in one part will necessarily cause changes in the other parts. It may even change the system as a whole, thus creating a temporary disequilibrium. Consider, for example, the high school viewed as a social system. The various parts of the school—the students, the faculty, the administration, the staff—are interdependent. A change in one of these parts would be felt in all the others. Let us say that the administration suddenly becomes more concerned with the quality of teaching as a result of a new commitment to academic rigor introduced from outside the school system. This change would first be felt among teachers, who might strengthen academic requirements. Students, in turn, would respond with changes in their own behavior. But after all the parts of the system had adjusted to the change, Parsons felt, an equilibrium would be restored.

Parsons emphasized that culture—the shared beliefs, norms, and values of a society—is the "glue" that holds society together because it is particularly resistant to change. A change in social structure is likely to be very slow if it conflicts with culture. Politicians, for example, are not likely to propose an amendment to the Constitution forbidding the consumption of alcohol. The norms in this country tolerating moderate alcohol use are so strong that significant social change in this area probably cannot be achieved through the political institution.

The Parsonian approach to social change has been carefully scrutinized by functionalists themselves, among others. The most common criticism has been that functionalism places too much emphasis on the external environment as a source of social change. Although Parsons clearly stated that social change could be generated by tensions and strains within the system, it seems only logical that the most likely source of change must lie outside the system when one begins with the assumption that a social system is normally in a state of equilibrium. Critics point out that while a functioning society may be meeting the needs of its members and is therefore in a temporary state of equilibrium, those needs may only be met minimally. If this is the case, the society is subject to serious internal strains and inconsistencies. Critics have suggested, therefore, that functionalists should pay more attention to analyzing sources of change originating within the social system (Moore, 1960).

The Conflict Perspective

Many sociologists have found functionalism too limiting. It has been argued that real societies display less stability than functionalist theory implies and that this perspective is unable to account for many kinds of change. Foremost among the sociologists who find the functionalist approach too limiting are those who view social change from the conflict perspective.

Ralf Dahrendorf (1959) proposed the following assumptions as the basis for a conflict theory of social change:

1. Every society, at every point, is subject to processes of change; social change is ubiquitous.

2. Every society, at every point, displays dissension and conflict; social conflict is ubiquitous.

3. Every element in a society renders a contribution to its disintegration and change.

4. Every society is based on the coercion of some of its members by others. (p. 162)

The main body of conflict theory rests on the theories of Karl Marx, whose work has been discussed in earlier chapters. Whereas Marx focused principally on conflict between economically determined social classes within societies, Dahrendorf and other contemporary conflict theorists have greatly expanded the number of areas in which they see conflict at work. Ethnic and racial groups, political parties, and religious groups enter into conflict as well. In all these areas, the basic source of conflict is assumed to be the unequal distribution of power and authority (Vago, 1999). Social change is typically viewed by conflict theorists, therefore, as involving a struggle to implement a redistribution of power. Such power changes can occur rapidly, as they did in the complete and sudden restructuring of the Soviet social system that followed the Bolshevik Revolution of 1917 and that occurred again in 1989–1991; or they can take place

slowly, as they have in response to the growing popularity of environmentalism in the contemporary United States.

ECONOMIC DEVELOPMENT IN THE THIRD WORLD

One of the most important examples of social change over the last few centuries has been the rapid economic development of many of the world's societies. An area of major interest to sociologists in recent years has been the search for theories capable of explaining this economic development and the social changes associated with it. Much of this interest has focused on the most rapidly developing nations today—those of the Third World, which includes most of Asia, Africa, and Latin America.

Conditions of Economic Development in the Third World

The societies of the Third World, sometimes called the "developing nations," are currently undergoing a process of economic growth similar to that which occurred in the West over the past two centuries. The patterns of development in the Third World today, however, are strikingly different from those that characterized Western nations. In the West, economic development was a slow, evolutionary process. In the Third World, the pace is much more rapid: Nations expect to move from the ox cart to the airplane in only a few generations. For this reason, development in the Third World has often entailed major cultural lags. Material development has been swift, but social and cultural adjustment, which takes much longer, has lagged behind. This has resulted in considerable social disruption and even strong resistance to industrialization in some nations.

Among the most difficult elements to change are deeply rooted traditional values and beliefs such as those concerning religion, the family, and the proper role of the sexes. Scholars have pointed out that the values of many Third World cultures today are significantly different from those that were found in the West at the time of the Industrial Revolution. Third World religious orientations and attitudes toward work and even toward prosperity make these nations less responsive to industrialization (Gill, 1987; Myrdal, 1968; Repetto, 1985). For example, when the Italian-based Fiat Motor Company opened a plant in Egypt in the 1960s, the Italians learned that thinking of time in terms of seconds and minutes, an attitude deeply ingrained in most Westerners, and one that is critical for industrial development, was almost completely absent in the Egyptian culture (McCord & McCord, 1986).

There is a dramatic contrast in many Third World nations between traditional agricultural production and a rapidly expanding industrial sector.

Another factor that makes Third World economic development distinctive is the serious problem of overpopulation. Many developing nations were already overpopulated when they first began to industrialize, and every step of economic growth has been matched by a jump in population. In many cases, sharp increases in population have kept per capita incomes unchanged even though national productivity has risen.

In addition, Third World economic development is almost always planned and managed by centralized governments. This was not the case in the West, where governments have tended to avoid large-scale involvement in the marketplace. Unfortunately, Third World regimes often lack the political stability and popular support that they need in order to carry out their ambitious plans (Griffin, 1989; Moore, 1963, 1979). Furthermore, these societies commonly lack adequate numbers of highly skilled and motivated professionals and technicians—engineers, managers, agricultural specialists, doctors—without whom economic development is unlikely to succeed.

Finally, many of the Third World's nation-states are still very young. Most of Africa's nations did not become independent until the 1960s, and many are still in the process of establishing their legitimacy. Most lack cultural cohesion as well as economic stability, and few have been able to establish educational systems adequate to permit rapid economic development. Systems of communication are also inadequate; in fact, intra-African telephone, telegraph, and postal service is so inefficient that mail is frequently routed through Europe rather than directly from one African capital to another. For Africa to realize its economic potential, some believe, its 53 nations will have to be replaced by a much smaller number of regional economic entities or perhaps by a single continental unit (Martin & Kandal, 1989).

The Economic Plight of the Third World: Conflict Perspectives

Why does much of the Third World remain poor? Many analysts, especially those who are labeled "modernization theorists," seek the explanation in some combination of the factors discussed above. Conflict theorists, however, have argued that additional conditions must be taken into account. Third World nations, they point out, face a very different international environment than the Western nations did when they were developing (Walton, 1987).

Many of today's developing nations are former colonies whose economies and political structures were once directly controlled by foreign powers. Although most overt colonialism has ended, the nations of the Third World now find themselves locked into yet another foreign-dominated system—the complex web of global economic and political interdependence. In this new world order, called a *world system* by some sociologists, the developing nations seem to have little if any more opportunity for self-determination than they had when they were actually colonies (Bergesen, 1980; see also Wang & Dissanayatce, 1984). More to the point, according to conflict theorists, the advanced nations—particularly the United States—are in effect preventing economic development from occurring in the Third World. In this new form of *imperialism* (the process by which a nation seeks to control other societies in order to exploit their natural resources), the economically developed nations have maintained indirect control over the economic and political life of their former colonial possessions (Alcalde, 1989; Baran, 1957; Frank, 1969).

Imperialist policies toward the Third World began during the colonial era. The Western capitalist countries that seized control of the Third World were not interested in industrializing these societies. Rather, their main goal was to obtain the raw materials they needed to promote their own economic growth. The colonial economies they established were run by Westerners mainly for the benefit of the colonial powers (Anderson, 1974; Gill & Law, 1988). Little if anything was done to help the Third World countries become self-sufficient.

As a result, these societies came to depend on the export of a small number of raw materials and needed to import almost all manufactured goods. Moreover, colonization divided up Third World territories based on the arbitrary whims of the imperial powers. Traditional cultural boundaries were generally ignored, and as a result the newly created colonial nations commonly contained several antagonistic groups of people.

When colonial rule ended, very little changed for most Third World people (Anderson, 1974; McCord & McCord, 1986). The colonial-era economic order was maintained, either directly by Western economic interests or indirectly by Westernized native leaders. This perpetuation of Western economic rule is called *neocolonialism*.

In recent decades, conflict theorists argue, the advanced capitalist nations have thus shifted their objective from the establishment of new colonies to the attempt to continue to exploit as many of the resources of their former colonies as possible. They do this—according to a viewpoint known as **dependency theory**—by keeping their former colonies economically and financially dependent upon them. Many dependency theorists see the United States as the organizer and leader of this modern neocolonial imperialism. Through its foreign aid and military policies, they argue, the United States strives to prevent developing countries from reaching economic maturity (Frank, 1969).

Many of the preceding arguments have been pulled together in global and historical context under the label **world systems theory**. Based principally on the work of Immanuel Wallerstein, world systems theory asserts that contemporary nations play either dominant or subordinate roles within a global economy that had its beginnings in northwestern Europe about 400 years ago (Wallerstein, 1974, 1979, 1980, 1990; see also Hopkins et al., 1982; Rostow, 1987).

The *core* nations are characterized by advanced technologies and economies, powerful state bureaucracies and military establishments, and high standards of living. The *peripheral* nations supply the core nations with cheap raw materials and manual labor, and at the same time serve as markets for many of their products. Today the dominant, or core, nations include Western Europe together with the United States, Canada, and Japan. The subordinate, or peripheral, nations are located in Latin America, Asia, and Africa. World systems theory also identifies a third category of nations—*semiperipheral*—which includes such partially developed nations as Brazil, Taiwan, and South Korea.

At the heart of world systems theory is the observation that the core nations are able to dominate the course of global social change, often to the detriment of the peripheral nations. The theory also emphasizes that one of the main instruments of this domination is the multinational corporation, and adds that the core nations are able to shift much of the cost of downturns in the world economy to the peripheral nations. World systems theorists use these ideas to explain why the majority of the world's developing countries have experienced declines in trade, economic conditions, and gross national product since 1973 (Martin & Kandal, 1989).

There is some empirical support for world systems theory. For example, a significant relationship has been found between the extent of economic control over peripheral nations by multinational corporations and the level of income inequality that is found in those nations. The greater the economic control, the higher the level of inequality (Bornschier & Ballmer-Cao, 1979; Evans & Timberlake, 1980; Gill & Law, 1988). Another study (Kentor, 1981) found that their peripheral position contributes to the overurbanization of many Third World nations (see Chapter 20).

Critics of world systems theory argue, however, that this perspective does not adequately account for the actual patterns of development in the Third World (Chirot, 1986; Chirot & Hall, 1982; Harper, 1989). According to the conflict perspective, those countries most closely bound to the capitalist world economy should be the poorest. But, in fact, they are often among the more prosperous of the Third World societies. Cases in point include the Latin American nations of Brazil, Argentina, Venezuela, and Mexico. Despite such criticisms, few would deny that the conflict perspective has opened up many challenging areas of sociological theory and research (So, 1990).

Comparative Studies in Economic Development

The economic development of China and India—the two most populous countries in the world—has been the subject of extensive sociological analysis. And for good reason: Because of their size, changes in these countries' economies, populations, and political and social systems have serious repercussions around the world. Dramatic economic growth in either or both nations could shift the balance of world power, while a serious economic decline in either could lead to a significant reallocation of world resources.

INDIA

The effort to industrialize India began after World War II, when British colonial rule ended and Jawaharlal Nehru became prime minister. With the aid of foreign capital and technological assistance, India developed industries to produce cloth, fertilizer, cement, and other needed products. As these industries grew, others were set up. The products of India's factories today are often quite sophisticated and include jet planes, antibiotics, and heavy machinery (McCord & McCord, 1986).

However, Indian society is still a long way from being fully industrialized. In 1996, 65 percent of the country's labor force was engaged in agricultural work (*World Almanac,* 1999). About three-quarters of the population still live in small agricultural villages, where most of the work is still done the traditional way—by hand. The nation remains very poor, with a 1996 per capita gross domestic product of just $1,600 compared to $28,600 for the United States (*World Almanac,* 1999; *World Factbook,* 1997).

In India, as in much of the Third World, overurbanization is a major problem. The cities are growing much more rapidly than the society's ability to economically support an urban population. Bombay is home to more than 15 million people, and the population of

India has made significant progress toward modernization. However, the nation still remains very poor. Some sociologists believe that the long-standing closed system of social stratification (caste system) has prevented more rapid economic development.

Calcutta is nearly 12 million, making them two of the ten most populous cities in the world (*World Almanac,* 1999).

In contrast to what happened in the West during the Industrial Revolution, the rural population of India is also growing very rapidly. Overpopulation, along with food shortages, contributes to a constant threat of mass starvation. Because of this rapid increase in the population, India's economy has shown little economic growth on a per capita basis since World War II. Furthermore, food-grain production per capita is actually lower today than it was at the turn of the twentieth century (Repetto, 1987). Since 1977, nationwide programs of birth control have contributed to a slight decline in the birth rate. But it will be many years before the Indian population will stop growing.

What are the main factors, aside from overurbanization and overpopulation, that keep India from advancing economically? Sociologists have long noted that India has been hampered by its caste system, a closed system of social stratification that has been officially outlawed but many remnants of which still exist. In the West during industrialization, people could move relatively easily from one class to another. Traditional Indian culture, however, did not allow individual advancement. Furthermore, the Indian value system gives low priority to some of the personal and social qualities that are important to industrialization, such as the acquisition of wealth and power, and technological initiative (Anderson, 1974; McCord & McCord, 1986).

Conflict theorists argue that India's plight stems as much from its colonial legacy and from international economic dependency as it does from internal problems. India has relied heavily on U.S. foreign aid during much of the time it has been trying to modernize, and this aid may not always have been applied in India's best interests.

The future of Indian economic development is not entirely bleak, however. Beginning in the mid-1980s, previously strict trade restrictions were lifted as India began to woo the multinationals. India also has begun to enter into joint ventures with Japan, another traditionally closed culture. It is expected that the rise of a new Indian middle class will further promote India's current emphasis on business and economic development (McCord & McCord, 1986).

CHINA

Before World War II, India and China were at approximately the same stage of economic development. Both were extremely poor nations with predominantly rural, technologically simple economies overwhelmed by high rates of population growth and low rates of literacy. Since

World War II, however, India and China have followed very different roads to modernization. In India, economic planning has been guided by democratic principles and a mixture of private and public enterprise. In China, on the other hand, an authoritarian regime has held control, and economic planning has been highly centralized.

The restructuring of China's economy began with the founding of the People's Republic of China in 1949. The new country's economic plan was based on a strict communist model borrowed from the Soviet Union. All major industrial and financial enterprises were brought under direct state control and agriculture was collectivized. However, both administration and production remained inadequate. A new ideology was imposed on an old bureaucratic structure, but many of the old system's inefficiencies remained. Rigidities in the system, along with a lack of technical expertise on the part of managers, reduced efficiency. And because the Chinese population lacked technical skills, industrialization got a late start—not really getting into full gear until around 1958. In 1996, 54 percent of China's labor force was still engaged in agriculture, compared to only 26 percent working in industry and commerce (*World Almanac*, 1999).

Partly as a result of this late industrialization, China's rate of urbanization has been somewhat slower than that of most of the other developing countries. The population of China's largest cities, Shanghai and Beijing, actually experienced a slight decline in the early 1980s.

The Chinese have made several adjustments in their approach to development over the last 50 years. The collective farms originally set up in the 1950s were replaced by communes in the 1960s. Unlike the collectives (which were organized into huge "production brigades" that practically abolished the family), the communes were based on smaller "production teams" of about 33 household units, allowing more emphasis on self-sufficiency and the family. As a result, agricultural production increased, slowly but steadily.

Then, during the 1980s, China's policies took yet another turn. Reforms that linked payment to output resulted in further improvements in the rural economy. In 1983, rural communes were disbanded, and by the late 1980s, 60 percent of all Chinese agriculture was free of state controls (*World Factbook*, 1989). Substantial progress was also made in industrialization. Between 1992 and 1996, the Chinese GDP increased—averaging more than 10 percent annually (*World Factbook*, 1997). And, like India, China has begun to seek more extensive trade relationships with other countries. Negotiations to allow multinational corporations to operate on Chinese soil have even taken place, although so far with only modest results.

A COMPARISON

How do India and China compare today? After more than 50 years of development, the two nations have similar per capita GDPs: $2,800 for China and $1,600 for India (*World Almanac*, 1999). But, in recent years, China's economic growth rate has been almost twice that of India. Analysts are quick to note, however, that China's higher economic growth rate is explained mainly by that country's considerable success in slowing population growth.

To continue expanding, India needs more qualified workers and a stronger educational system. In 1995, India's literacy rate was only 52 percent; China's, on the other hand, was 82 percent (*World Almanac*, 1999). China's prospects for future expansion seem to rest heavily on the introduction of more market incentives into its economic system.

Although both India and China have come close to achieving self-sufficiency in food production—quite an accomplishment—both still rank among the poorest countries in the world. Like many other developing nations, India and China continue to struggle with cumbersome bureaucracies and traditions that hamper economic development and social change.

ECONOMIC SUCCESS ON THE PACIFIC RIM

The most successful Third World economies are found in the newly industrialized countries of the Pacific Rim, especially Hong Kong, Korea, Singapore, and Taiwan. The cultures of these countries emphasize hard work, competitive pricing of labor, and pragmatic government. In fact, the rapid economic growth and dynamic and aggressive performances of these four small states have earned them an important position in the world economy. Hong Kong has become an entrepreneurial paradise and a world financial, manufacturing, and trade center; Korea makes more microwave ovens than Japan; Singapore has gone from slums to skyscrapers and has created an environment so supportive of the growth of high-tech industries that it has earned the nickname "Silicon Island"; and Taiwan has developed a wide variety of export industries (Rowan & Hammes, 1989). Currently, Malaysia, Thailand, and Vietnam are aggressively developing market economies and hope to strengthen further the economic power of the Pacific Rim (Veit, 1987).

THE COMPONENTS OF MODERNIZATION

Economic development is the primary force behind the process known as modernization. As we noted earlier, *modernization* refers to the internal social changes that

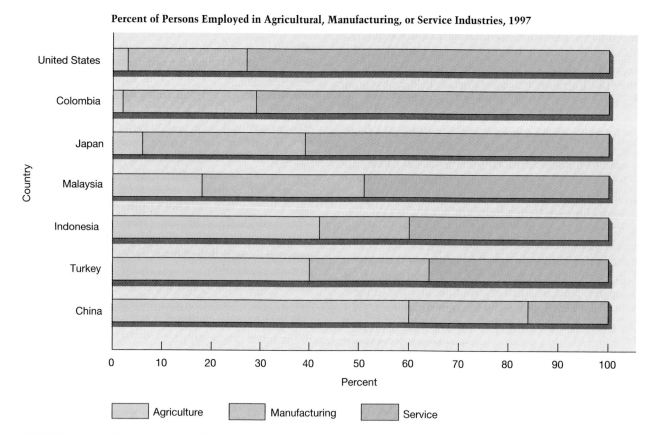

FIGURE 22.1 Modernization typically entails a decrease in the proportion of workers employed in agriculture and corresponding increases in the proportion working in industry and service.

Source: Yearbook of Labour Statistics, 1998 (Geneva: International Labour Office). Copyright © International Labour Organization 1998.

typically occur when a traditional preindustrial society develops economically. In trying to construct models of this process, sociologists have analyzed both the historical experience of the West and the experiences of the developing nations today (Harper, 1989; Hoselitz & Moore, 1963; Kerr et al., 1960; Moore, 1979; Smelser, 1959). They have also relied heavily on the evolutionary theories of social change outlined previously in this chapter. The main components of modernization include the following:

- Economic relationships become separated from other aspects of social life. In preindustrial societies, economic relationships are frequently based on family or kinship ties, on caste or class connections, or on religious identities. In industrial societies, economic behavior is largely independent of other elements of the social web.

- The factory system changes the relationship between employees and their work. Karl Marx, one of the first

to observe this change, wrote that industrial technology and the resulting specialization of tasks often made workers powerless and alienated. In preindustrial times, the quality of the end product depended mainly on the workers' skills, judgment, and experience. But in a factory, the quality of production is determined by machines to which workers must fit their actions.

- The main economic activity of the labor force shifts from the primary sector—agriculture and the extraction of natural resources—to secondary sector manufacturing and later to tertiary services, such as clerical work, sales, and teaching. Figure 22.1 shows the proportion of economic activities in each of these three sectors in a number of nations.

- Modernization leads to the development of many new occupational roles. People leave traditional positions to take newly created jobs as skilled and semiskilled factory workers, clerks, salespeople, and business managers.

- The specialization of occupational roles makes a new type of economic activity necessary: administrative organization. The workers in this sector are managers and supervisors who coordinate and integrate the many occupational specialties, making sure that they mesh efficiently and productively. Over time, these administrative activities become increasingly specialized, leading to a never-ending cycle of differentiation, integration or coordination, further differentiation, and additional integration (Smelser, 1968; see also Hearn, 1988).

- The evolution of new occupational roles causes an increase in both geographic and social mobility. Industrial employment typically requires rural families to leave their traditional surroundings and move to the cities. This, in turn, commonly leads to upward social mobility.

- The system of social stratification changes. Wealth and occupation become more important than birth and kinship. That is, ascribed statuses tend to be replaced by achieved statuses, and closed systems of social stratification become more open (see Chapter 9). There is often some redistribution of power within the society as well.

- Because the nuclear family is better adapted to industrial society, the extended family is undermined, though it never disappears entirely. Because they cannot work in highly skilled jobs, the very old and the very young, who had been able to contribute productive labor in an agricultural or a handicraft economy, are rendered unproductive. They are, therefore, no longer economic assets but, rather, liabilities. Women, conversely, are able to find employment outside the home in large numbers. Their greater independence changes the nature of the marital relationship, a change that, in turn, alters the character of family life. Family structure becomes less authoritarian and more democratic. The family becomes less a center of activity throughout the day and more a home base to which one returns at night.

- The informal social control mechanisms of family and kin become weakened by the pressures of social and residential mobility. Informal control is replaced by the formal mechanisms of the state.

- In the process of secularization, some religious beliefs are replaced by rationality and science. As religion becomes less important, it is increasingly separated from other aspects of life, especially economics and politics.

- There is an expansion of mass communications, mass education, and ultimately mass culture. Some art forms (music, for example) tend to become standardized and commercialized. These developments do not necessarily mean that cultural forms degenerate. Rather, culture is communicated in new ways and to a wider audience.

- In most modernizing societies, centralized bureaucratic political power expands markedly. In the Western nations, most governments adopted a laissez-faire economic policy. In the contemporary Third World, government control of the economy is more common. Political participation increases.

- Finally, modernization is accompanied by characteristic changes in psychology and values. Some theorists argue that these changes do not just accompany modernization but are actually a precondition for it—in other words, modernization can occur only among people whose values and psychological makeup are conducive to it (Hagen, 1962; Harman, 1988; McClelland, 1967). The changes include increased openness to new experiences and innovation, a democratic orientation, belief in personal and human dignity, and faith in science and technology (Inkeles, 1966; Inkeles & Smith, 1974).

Convergence Theory

Like early supporters of evolutionary theory, early proponents of modernization saw it as a process that would ultimately affect all the world's peoples; every society, it was assumed, would eventually experience the social changes outlined above. This view is summed up in Karl Marx's statement, "The country that is more developed industrially only shows to the less developed the image of its own future." The idea that all societies are becoming more alike as a result of the process of modernization lies at the heart of *convergence theory*.

The fact that the societies of the world are so diverse and occupy so many different stages of the development process means that there are bound to be many exceptions to the broad generalizations listed above. These exceptions have provided plenty of ammunition to the critics of convergence theory. It has been pointed out, for example, that convergence theory does not sufficiently take into account the vast environmental differences around the world, such as in the availability of arable land and energy sources. Also, many developing nations are choosing to preserve their traditional values and behaviors. Saudi Arabia, for example, has a per capita income level equivalent to that of the economically advanced societies of the West but maintains an almost feudal structure in which the rights of women are weak, the extended family is still very powerful, and there is no Western-style democracy.

In addition, say the critics, other developing nations have serious problems with overurbanization and no hope of creating a strong enough economic base to provide a decent standard of living for the millions of people who have moved to urban areas. For this and other reasons, these nations are giving greater priority to

WINDOW ON SOCIOLOGY

THE IMPACT OF CHANGE

> As centuries go, this has been one of the most amazing. (Isaacson, 1998)

Few would dispute that claim. Some might even say it understates the remarkable achievements of the twentieth century. A short list of them, compiled by Walter Isaacson, makes the point.

> To name just a few random things we did in a hundred years: We split the atom, invented jazz and rock, launched airplanes and landed on the moon, concocted a general theory of relativity, devised the transistor and figured out how to etch millions of them on tiny microchips, discovered penicillin and the structure of DNA, fought down fascism and communism, bombed Guernica and painted the bombing of Guernica, developed cinema and television, built highways and wired the world. Not to mention the peripherals these produced, such as sitcoms and cable channels, "800" numbers and Websites, shopping malls and leisure time, existentialism and modernism, Oprah and Imus. Initials spread like graffiti: NATO, IBM, ABM, UN, WPA, NBA, NFL, CIA, CNN, PLO, IPO, IRA, IMF, TGIF. And against all odds, we avoided blowing ourselves up. (1998, p. 70)

What other century could compare to this one? And yet, it has not been without its problems. Indeed, while we assume that social change advances society, it also brings many unintended consequences. Its impact is enormous. It complicates life—changes the rules, shifts standards, calls traditional values into question, and affects behavior patterns (Vago, 1999).

Consider, for example, how mass media have changed American life. The effects attributed to it range from the outcomes of political elections to consumer choices to random acts of violence. Vice president Dan Quayle launched a crusade for family values after Murphy Brown, a character in a television sitcom, chose to become a single mother (Jeffres, 1997). And after repeated incidents of school violence involving the massacre of innocent students, the role of media again came under question.

The impact of technology should not be underestimated. In an assessment of its increasing impact, Donald Schon wrote:

> Individuals must somehow confront and negotiate, in their own persons, the transformations which used to be handled by generational change. . . . While technological change has been continuing exponentially for the last two hundred years, it has now reached a level of pervasiveness and frequency uniquely threatening to the stable state. (1971, pp. 27–28)

What will a future generation write about the twenty-first century? Unlike Isaacson's summary of the twentieth, which focused on what we discovered, invented, and built, they may very well take a more philosophical approach and write about how society dealt with the moral and political problems that accompanied new technologies. That, hopefully, will allow them to similarly write that "against all odds, we avoided blowing ourselves up."

---

rural than to urban development, and they could end up with populations that are considerably more rural than those of the West.

Finally, there are important differences between capitalist and socialist societies. These differences extend beyond economics and into basic cultural values and beliefs. For example, in socialist Cuba, where equality and the subordination of the private sector to the state are emphasized, people's earnings and consumption habits have been restricted. In capitalist Singapore, on the other hand, where individual entrepreneurism is rewarded, the standard of living is the second highest in Asia (exceeded only by Japan's), and consumerism is a way of life. Today Singapore ranks twelfth in the world in the number of computers per capita (*1998 Information Please Almanac,* 1999).

In short, the idea that all societies are converging toward a common form has been seriously challenged. Even modernization theorists have come to agree that their original formulations were too pat. One of the founders of convergence theory later put two questions to himself: Are all societies becoming alike? Is there a trend toward a common destination? His answer to the first question: More than they used to be. His answer to the second: No (Moore, 1979). But even if all societies are not headed toward a common destiny, it is surprising just how regularly the characteristics of modernization outlined above recur around the world today. Indeed, as socialist regimes find it increasingly difficult to maintain themselves in the face of recent global transformations—Cuban socialism, for example, is threatened by the loss of critical economic support from the former Soviet Union—these traits may appear with even greater frequency.

THE FUTURE OF ADVANCED SOCIETIES

There are very few nations of the Third World that do not want to develop economically as fast as possible, however different their approaches to economic growth may be. Some of these nations can expect to reach the present economic level of the fully industrialized nations in the next few generations—perhaps 50 or 75 years. By the year 2000, most of the world will have passed through at least the early and most difficult phases of industrial development. But while this development is taking place in the Third World, what will be happening to the Western societies? They, too, continue to experience massive social change.

A Postindustrial Society?

Some sociologists argue that the developed nations are now entering a "postindustrial" period—an era that, they maintain, will be as different from the industrial period as the industrial was from the preindustrial. They use the concept of *postindustrial society* to summarize some of the main trends that are occurring in the West. Daniel Bell (1976) is a leading advocate of this perspective. The following are some of the major ways in which Bell and others think the postindustrial era will differ from the industrial age:

1. The economic activities most characteristic of industrial societies are manufacturing, agriculture, and extractive enterprises such as mining. In the postindustrial period, the *service sector* of the economy will become dominant. The service sector includes such diverse activities as business, government, transportation, communication, health, and education. In several advanced societies, including the United States, the majority of all workers are already employed in the service sector of the economy.

2. If the industrial period is the age of the machine, the postindustrial era is the age of the computer. Many forms of labor, including learning and communicating, are radically affected by automation and computerization.

3. In the industrial age, most workers held blue-collar status. The postindustrial labor force, however, will be made up largely of white-collar, middle-class workers.

This trend is closely related to the growth of service jobs and to automation and computerization, both of which remove people from the direct work of production. There will be a sharp increase in the need for administrators, computer programmers, systems analysts, and other white-collar employees.

4. The problems of postindustrial societies typically require highly technical solutions. A premium, therefore, will be placed on intellectual and technical knowledge, and long educational preparation will become necessary for almost all important social positions. Instead of the entrepreneurs of the industrial age, who often lacked formal education, the key postindustrial workers will be scientists and other highly educated specialists.

5. As business dominated the industrial era, government will dominate the postindustrial period. Centralized political direction will tend to replace decentralized decision making through the market. The public (government-owned or -controlled) sector of the economy will increase, and the line between it and the private sector will become increasingly blurred. More people will work for government at all levels, especially in agencies dealing with social services, the regulation of industry, and the protection of the natural environment.

The concept of a postindustrial society was developed during the 1960s and early 1970s. Recent events, however, have cast some doubt on its validity. The current political climate in many advanced societies, for example, is hostile to the idea of increased centralization and government control (Eisenstadt, 1992).

Furthermore, critics note that many features of the postindustrial society are not fundamentally different from those of industrial societies. Such phenomena as class conflict, worker alienation, racial segregation, and substandard living conditions are still in evidence today, and probably will continue to be present in the foreseeable future.

Predicting the Future

Social scientists differ in their expectations for the future of society. Some are optimistic; others are pessimistic. But how much confidence should we place in their predictions? Is it really possible to predict social change? Can we predict a population explosion, a rising crime rate, or the future of religion? Are we able to anticipate the next social movement? Can we forecast changes in the economy?

The track record for past predictions shows that many of them have been wrong. Indeed, some events occurred that caught everyone off guard. For example, almost no social scientist predicted the sudden collapse of the Soviet Union. Analyses of current trends give social scientists the ability to predict the course of certain kinds of social change, and it is possible to predict how certain technologies will develop. But we often fail to anticipate the unintended consequences of technology—and these can have an enormous impact on the future development of society as we have certainly found out over the course of the twentieth century.

CHAPTER REVIEW

1. Advances in technology have far-reaching and often unintended consequences. Identify and discuss the social problems that today's technologies have created.

2. What role does the Internet play in cultural diffusion?

3. Which theory of social change do you favor? Discuss its strengths and weaknesses and compare it to other theories of social change.

4. How does economic development in the Third World differ from the pattern taken in the West?

5. Why is it difficult to predict the future course of society? What tools can social scientists use to help them anticipate the future?

INTERNET EXERCISE

The Web destinations for Chapter 22 cover various aspects of social and cultural change. To start your explorations, go to the Prentice Hall Companion Web site **http://www.prenhall.com/popenoe.** Next, choose **Chapter 22** (Social and Cultural Change). Then, select **web destinations** from the menu on the left side of the screen. There are several sites to choose from. We suggest you begin with **New Democracy and Democratic Revolution.** This site is the home page for an organization called "New Democracy," reflecting a publication with the same name. This organization is surely controversial because it believes that a revolution is necessary in American society in order to achieve a truly equal and democratic society. You can click on "Our Statement of Principles" to glimpse the essence of this organization. There are a variety of articles and "democracy flyers" that can be accessed by clicking on the titles. After you have explored the *New Democracy* site, answer the following questions:

- Do you agree with the editors of the publication *New Democracy?* Why or why not?

- Some critics believe that there will never be another revolution in American society. Do you agree? Why or why not?

KEY TERMS

technology	industrialization	dependency theory
cultural lag	urbanization	world systems theory
cultural diffusion	bureaucratization	
modernization	sociocultural evolution	

achieved status A social position that can be obtained over the course of one's life as a result of individual effort or lack of effort.

acting crowd A crowd that is typically angry and hostile.

affirmative action Policies that grant preference to minority group members in order to make up for the effects of prior discrimination.

age cohort A grouping of people of a given age.

age deviance Behavior that violates the age norms of a group or society.

ageism The ideology that holds that the elderly are biologically or socially inferior and the discrimination that results from the acceptance of this belief.

age norms Social norms or standards that define what people at a given age should think and do.

age roles Expectations about the behavior of people occupying particular age statuses.

age-specific birth rate The number of births per 1,000 women in a specific age group.

age-specific death rate The number of deaths per 1,000 members of a specific age group.

age status A status based on a person's age.

age status inconsistency Inconsistency among the social expectations or definitions of the various age statuses a person holds.

age structure The relative proportions of different age categories in a country's population.

agents of socialization Those persons, groups, or institutions that contribute significantly to the socialization of the individual.

aggregate A number of people who find themselves face-to-face in a particular setting but do not interact and lack more than a minimal social structure.

alienation of labor Marx's term for a condition in which workers feel they have lost control over their work.

amalgamation The biological merging of an ethnic or a racial group with the dominant population.

animism A type of religion that recognizes active ("animistic") spirits operating in the world.

annihilation The process by which a dominant group causes the deaths of a large number of minority group members.

anomie A social condition in which norms and values are conflicting, weak, or absent.

anticipatory socialization Socialization that is directed toward learning future roles.

applied research Research designed to provide answers for the solution of immediate practical problems.

ascribed status A social position to which an individual is assigned and which normally cannot be changed.

assimilation The absorption of newcomers into the dominant society.

authoritarianism A form of government in which ultimate authority is vested in a single person.

authority Legitimate power that is institutional in nature.

autonomous work group A relatively independent small work group that works together on a set of tasks and that has the authority to make decisions on work-related matters.

basic research Research that is concerned with knowledge for its own sake, without regard to the uses and applications of that knowledge.

bilateral descent Kinship and lineage are traced through both the mother and the father's families; both male and female children are entitled to inherit.

bureaucracy A hierarchical authority structure that operates on the basis of explicit rules and procedures.

bureaucratization The rise of large-scale formal organizations.

capitalism An economic system based on the private ownership of wealth.

case study A detailed record of a single event, person, or social grouping.

caste system A system of stratified inequality in which status is determined at birth and in which people generally cannot change their social position.

census A periodic population head count that usually includes personal data such as age, sex, and occupation.

centralized economy One in which decision-making power is concentrated in the hands of a small number of individuals or firms.

charismatic authority Authority that is a consequence of the ability of a leader to establish a special relationship with his or her followers.

chromosomes The threadlike structures in the nucleus of every cell that hold genes that carry the programming for all inherited traits.

church A relatively stable, institutionalized organization of religious believers.

city planning The process of deliberately and explicitly formulating goals regarding an urban community's future physical structure.

civic privatism A focus on the private pursuits of family, career, and leisure.

class conflict Struggle between competing classes.

class consciousness The shared awareness that members of a social class have about their common situation and interests.

class divisions   The perceived and real differences between a society's classes.

class system   A relatively open form of stratification based mainly on economic status.

coercion   A type of social interaction in which one person or group forces its will on another.

collective behavior   Behavior that occurs in response to a common influence or stimulus in relatively spontaneous, unpredictable, unstructured, and unstable situations.

community   A cluster of people located in a particular geographic area whose lives are organized around daily patterns of interaction.

community control   The ability of residents to influence the actions of public institutions serving their community.

community study   A case study focusing on an entire community.

comparative analysis   Research involving the comparison of several social systems or of the same social system at more than one time.

competition   A kind of cooperative conflict governed by rules that make the goal being sought more important than the defeat of one's opponents.

concept   A generalization, a way of labeling similar things or processes.

conflict   The struggle for a prized object or value.

conflict perspective   A theoretical perspective that emphasizes struggle over limited resources, power, and prestige as a permanent aspect of societies and a major source of social change.

conformity   Action in accordance with customs, rules, or prevailing opinion.

conspicuous consumption   People's demonstration of their socioeconomic status by displaying their status symbols blatantly.

content analysis   A research strategy that involves examining any form of communication and applying it to a systematic coding scheme to identify issues of interest to the researcher.

control group   In an experiment, the group that is not exposed to the independent variable and is compared with the experimental group.

controlled experiment   An experiment that is designed to isolate the specific effect of the independent variable by controlling the effects of other variables that may influence the dependent variable.

conversation analysis   The study of naturally occurring talk in interaction.

cooperation   Interaction in which people or groups act together in order to achieve common interests or goals that might be difficult or impossible to attain alone.

correlation   A regular, recurrent relationship between variables in which a change in one variable is associated with a change in another variable.

counterculture   A subculture that directly challenges the values, beliefs, ideals, institutions, or other aspects of a dominant culture.

craze   An intense fad with serious and lasting consequences.

credentialism   An emphasis on the specific requirements of a job for employment.

crime   Behavior that is prohibited by governmental authority and that can be punished through the application of formal sanctions.

crowd   A temporary grouping of people, physically close together and sharing a common focus of attention.

crude birth rate   The number of births per year for every 1,000 members of the total population.

crude death rate   The number of deaths per year for every 1,000 members of the total population.

cult   A loosely organized religious movement, without well-developed doctrines, that typically stresses attainment of a desired spiritual experience.

cultural diffusion   The process by which cultural traits spread from one group or society to another.

cultural integration   The logical consistency of cultural traits.

cultural lag   A period of maladjustment between the adoption of material or technological advances and the compensatory changes in nonmaterial culture that they necessitate.

cultural pluralism   A pattern in which minorities achieve full participation in the dominant society yet retain many of their social and cultural differences.

cultural relativity   The principle that a culture should be judged on its own terms and not by the standards of another culture.

cultural universals   Similar basic practices and beliefs shared by all of the world's cultures.

culture   The shared products of a human group or society, including values, language, knowledge, and material objects.

culture of poverty   A set of norms and values common to poor people.

decentralized economy   One in which decision-making power is held by a large number of individuals, households, cooperatives, or firms.

de facto segregation   Segregation that results from residential patterns.

deindustrialization   The systematic withdrawal of private investment from manufacturing.

de jure segregation   Segregation based on local law.

democracy   A form of government in which authority derives from the formal consent of the governed and in which citizens have the right to participate in decision-making processes.

democratic socialism   A type of mixed economy that takes as its primary responsibility the elimination of some of the harsher consequences of unrestrained capitalism.

demographic transition   The pattern of population growth and change, resulting from industrialization, which over the long run tends to produce low birth and death rates.

demography   The study of population size, composition, distribution, and change.

denomination   See *church*.

dependency theory   An explanation of the Third World's economic plight that emphasizes the consequences of its subordination to the world's wealthier nations.

dependent variable   A variable that is thought to be the effect of one or more independent variables.

descriptive studies   Research designed to find out what is happening to whom, where, and when.

deviant career   The adoption of a deviant identity and lifestyle within a supporting deviant subculture.

disaster behavior   Behavior that follows natural of other types of disasters.

discrimination   The unfair or unequal treatment of people because of the groups or categories of which they are members.

dogma   A fixed body of doctrine that usually covers most ordinary human situations.

dramaturgical perspective   Erving Goffman's approach to the study of social interaction, which views people as though they were actors in a theater.

dual-earner families   Families in which both partners work outside the home.

dyad   A group of two members.

dysfunctional   Preventing society, or one of its parts, from meeting its needs.

ecclesia   A religious organization that claims as its membership the entire population of a society.

ecological segregation   The process by which different areas of a city become increasingly specialized with regard to land use, services, or population.

ecology   The study of the relationships between organisms and their environment.

economic concentration   The control of a disproportionately large share of a nation's economic resources by a relatively small number of corporations.

economy   Those organizations and processes through which goods and services are produced and distributed.

ecosystem   The complex web of relationships between living things and their environment.

education   The formal institution that directs many learning experiences within a particular society.

egalitarian family   A family in which the husband and wife are roughly equal in authority and privilege.

emigration   The departure of individuals or groups from one country to take up permanent residence in another country.

empirical generalization   A statement, supported by empirical evidence, about the relationship between two or more variables.

empirical method   The approach to knowledge that involves using the human senses to make observations.

endogamy   Marriage within one's own group.

estate system   A system of stratification associated with feudal society in which dominant power is held by land-owning nobles, and peasants are bound to the noble's land in a vassal relationship.

ethnic group   Any group that is socially distinguished from other groups, has developed a distinct subculture, and has a shared feeling of peoplehood.

ethnocentrism   The tendency to evaluate other cultures in terms of one's own and to automatically evaluate one's own culture as superior.

ethnomethodology   A sociological approach that seeks to analyze the full range of rules that people follow in everyday social interaction.

exchange relationship   A relationship in which a person or group acts in a certain way toward another in order to receive a reward or return.

exogamy   Marriage outside one's own group.

experimental group   In an experiment, the group into which the independent variable is introduced.

explanatory studies   Research that answers the questions "why" and "how."

expressive crowd   A crowd that provides opportunities for emotional expression and release.

expressive movement   A movement that attempts to provide members with some type of personal transformation.

expulsion   The forcing of people—for example, a minority group—out of an area or a society.

extended family   A family group that consists of three or more generations.

fad   An activity that large numbers of people enthusiastically pursue for short periods of time.

false consciousness   Any situation in which a person's subjective understanding of reality is inconsistent with the objective facts of the situation.

family   A relatively small domestic group of kin (or people in a kinlike relationship) who function as a cooperative unit.

family of orientation   The family into which people are born and in which the major part of their socialization takes place.

family of procreation   The family that people create when they marry and have children.

fashion   A temporarily popular style of dress or behavior.

fecundity   The maximum biological capacity of the women in a population to produce children.

fertility   The frequency with which births occur in a population.

flexible-system production   Using the greater efficiencies created by new computer technologies and a highly skilled workforce to shift quickly from one project to another.

folkways   Weakly held norms or social customs that are not considered to be morally significant and are not strictly enforced.

formal organization   An organization in which the formal structure is dominant.

formal structure   The stated set of rules, regulations, and procedures that guides the activities of an organization's members.

functionalist perspective   A theoretical perspective that emphasizes the way in which each part of a society contributes to the whole so as to maintain stability.

Gemeinschaft   A society in which individual relationships are based on common feeling, kinship, or membership in the community.

gender   The social and psychological traits associated with masculinity and femininity.

gender identity   Our conception of ourselves as either male or female.

gender role   A social role associated with being male or female.

generalized other   An individual's conception of the demands and expectations of people in general.

genocide   The deliberate and systematic destruction of an entire ethnic or racial group.

gentrification   The displacement of poor residents by professional people in marginal neighborhoods of desirable cities.

gerontology   The multidisciplinary study of aging and the special problems of the elderly.

Gesellschaft   A society in which social relationships are formal, contractual, impersonal, and specialized.

goal displacement   A process that occurs when the members of an organization become more concerned with perpetuating the organization itself and their positions in it than with meeting the actual goals of the organization.

gossip   Idle talk about the personal or private affairs of others.

group   Two or more people who have a common identity and some feeling of unity, and who share certain goals and expectations about each other's behavior.

Hawthorne effect   Changes in the behavior of research subjects resulting from their knowledge that they are being studied.

health care system   All the people and formal organizations that deliver, finance, and regulate health care.

homogamy   Marriage between individuals having similar social characteristics.

hormones   Chemical substances that promote or restrain biological processes vital to growth and body functioning.

hypothesis   A tentative statement about the way in which two or more variables are related.

ideal type   A description of the most essential or characteristic qualities of a phenomenon.

ideology   A set of cultural beliefs that legitimates or justifies the interests of a class, group, or other sector of society in its struggle with other groups for prestige or dominance.

illegitimate power   Power used without social approval.

immigration   The entry of persons or groups into a country in order to take up permanent residence there.

impression management   The attempt to display ourselves to others so they will see ourselves as we wish to be seen.

incest taboo   A powerful moral prohibition against sexual relations between certain categories of relatives.

income   The gain derived from the use of human or material resources.

independent variable   A variable that is thought to be the cause or explanation of one or more dependent variables.

industrialization   A shift from human to nonhuman sources of energy and the rise of the factory system of economic production.

infant mortality rate   The number of deaths among infants less than one year old per 1,000 live births within a given year.

informal structure   The personal relationships in an organization that form as members interact.

ingroups   Groups to which individuals belong.

instincts   Complex, fixed, biologically inherited behavior patterns.

institutional racism   Policies that appear to be race-neutral or color-blind, and that are usually not the result of intentional efforts to discriminate, but nevertheless have the effect of limiting the opportunities of members of minority groups.

interactionist perspective   A theoretical perspective that focuses on how people interact in their everyday lives and on how they make sense of this interaction.

interest group   A voluntary organization that attempts to influence government policy and legislation on behalf of its members.

internalization   The acceptance of the norms of a group or society as part of one's identity.

invasion   The entrance of one social group or type of land use into territory currently occupied by another.

job enlargement   Adding to a job the tasks associated with one or more other jobs to make the work experience more varied and involve the worker in a larger portion of the work process.

job enrichment   Bringing greater authority and responsibility, as well as additional tasks, to a job.

kinship   A social network of people who are related by common ancestry or origin, or by marriage and adoption; although they do not all necessarily reside in a single household, they recognize certain obligations and responsibilities toward one another.

language   Human speech in both its spoken and written forms.

latent function   An unrecognized and unintended consequence of a unit of a social structure.

laws   Norms, usually mores, that have been enacted by the state to regulate human conduct.

learning   The lifelong process of social and personal experiences that alters an individual's knowledge, attitudes, and behavior.

legal-rational authority   Authority that rests on rationally established rules.

legitimate power   Power that is used in a way that is generally recognized as socially acceptable.

life chances   The likelihood of obtaining important goals in life.

life expectancy   The average number of years of life remaining for persons of a given age.

life span   The maximum length of life possible for any given species.

lobbying   A process (usually controlled by professional lobbyists) that involves direct communication with legislators and their staffs, mobilizing grass-roots support, and donating campaign funds through political action committees.

looking-glass self   Cooley's term for the sense of self that reflects what people think others think of them.

male dominance   The social situation in which more power and prestige are given to men than to women.

manifest function   A recognized and intended consequence of a unit of a social system.

market economy   One that responds to consumer preferences expressed in the market.

market socialism   An economic system that attempts to join features of socialism, such as public ownership of resources and a relatively equal distribution of income, with the emphasis on market forces and decentralized decision making characteristic of capitalism.

marriage   A socially approved mating arrangement, usually involving sexual activity and economic cooperation between a man and a woman.

marriage gradient   The tendency of men to marry women who are younger than they are, have less education, and work at less prestigious occupations.

mass behavior   Collective behavior involving people who do not know, and have little contact with, one another.

mass hysteria   A form of collective behavior that occasionally occurs when people find themselves in ambiguous, threatening, and anxiety-creating situations.

master status   An important status that determines a person's general social position.

material culture   The physical objects produced by a society that reflect nonmaterial cultural meanings.

matriarchal family   A family structure in which most of the authority is in the hands of the oldest female.

matrifocal family   A family in which a woman is the central and most important member.

matrilineal descent   Kinship and lineage are traced through the mother's side of the family; property is passed from mother to daughter.

matrilocal residence   The custom for a married couple to live in the household or community of the wife's parents.

mechanical solidarity   A term used to describe societies that are held together because their members perform very similar economic roles and therefore share the same values.

megalopolis   An urban concentration of two or more metropolitan areas that have grown until they overlap.

methodology   The system of procedures that helps sociologists develop knowledge.

metropolitan area   One or more large cities, together with their surrounding suburbs.

migration   The movement of people from one geographic area to another.

migration rate   The yearly difference between the number of immigrants and the number of emigrants per 1,000 members of the total population.

military-industrial complex   The combination of top civilian and military officials in the Department of Defense, the large private corporations profiting from military contracts, and sympathetic members of Congress.

minority group   Any group in society that consists of people who are identified by some biological, social, or cultural trait and who are singled out as objects of prejudice and discrimination.

mixed economy   Any economic system that blends capitalist and socialist principles.

mob   An acting crowd whose members focus their anger on a single target.

modernization   The internal social changes that typically occur when a traditional preindustrial society becomes industrialized and urbanized.

monogamy   Marriage between one man and one woman.

monotheism   The belief in only one god.

mores   Strongly held norms that provide the moral standards of a social system and are strictly enforced.

multivariate analysis   Research in which more than two variables are involved. The search for cause and effect focuses on finding the relative importance of a number of variables that together have an overall effect.

natural science   The systematized study of the physical world.

neolocal residence   The custom for a married couple to live apart from either spouse's parents or other relatives.

neonatal mortality rate   The age-specific death rate for infants less than one month old.

nonmaterial culture   Shared cultural creations that are abstract or intangible.

nonparticipant observation   A research method in which the observer does not take part in the activities or social situation under study.

nonverbal communication   Communication that is carried on in symbols other than language.

norms   Expectations of how people are supposed to act, think, or feel in specific situations.

nuclear family   A two-generation family group that consists of a couple and their children, usually living apart from other relatives.

oligarchy   Rule by a select few.

operationalizing the variable   Translating general concepts into specific, measurable variables.

opinion leaders   People who have a strong influence over public opinion.

organic solidarity   A term used to describe societies that are held together because their members perform very specialized economic roles and are therefore highly dependent upon one another.

organization A social group that has been deliberately constructed to achieve specific goals.

outgroup A group to which a person does not belong, as distinct from an ingroup.

overurbanization A disparity between the number of people moving into cities and the actual opportunities and services available in those cities.

panic A flight to secure safety in the face of imminent danger.

paramedicals Medical support personnel, such as nurses, pharmacists, and laboratory technicians, who generally work under the supervision of a physician.

participant observation A research method in which the observer is personally involved in the social situation under observation.

partition The political reorganization of a nation in order to make political boundaries correspond more closely to ethnic or racial ones.

patriarchal family A family structure in which most of the authority is held by the oldest male.

patrilineal descent Kinship and lineage are traced through the father's side of the family; males inherit property through the male side of the family and females are generally not permitted to inherit.

patrilocal residence The custom for a married couple to live in the household or community of the husband's parents.

peer group A group of people who have roughly equal social status and who are usually of similar ages.

personality The particular pattern of thoughts, feelings, and self-concepts that make up the distinctive qualities of a particular individual.

planned economy One that responds to and is coordinated by a planning agency.

political action committee (PAC) An interest group whose members make voluntary (usually small) donations, which the PAC pools and uses

to donate to senatorial, congressional, and presidential candidates.

political party An organization, usually composed of people with similar attitudes and interests, whose purpose is to gain and hold legitimate control of the government.

politics The process by which some people and groups acquire power and exercise it over others.

polyandry A polygamous marriage in which one woman has more than one husband at the same time.

polygamy Marriage involving more than one man or woman at the same time.

polygyny A polygamous marriage in which one man has more than one wife at the same time.

polytheism The belief in more than one god.

population In research the total group of people to be studied.

population forecast An estimate of the future population based on assumptions about how social, economic, and technological developments will affect demographic trends.

population projections Extrapolations from prior demographic patterns to estimate future population trends.

poverty A condition of scarcity or deprivation of material resources characterized by a lack of the necessities of life.

poverty level A specific income that is used in order to identify who will officially be regarded as poor.

power The capacity of people or groups to control or influence the actions of others, whether those others wish to cooperate or not.

prejudice The judgment of people, objects, or situations in a stereotyped way.

presentation of self See *impression management*.

prestige The favorable evaluation and social recognition that a person receives from others.

primary group A relatively small, multi-purpose group in which the

interaction is intimate and there is a strong sense of group identity.

primary relationship A personal, emotional, and not easily transferable relationship that includes a variety of roles and interests of each individual. It involves free and extensive communication and the interaction of whole personalities.

primary sector of the economy Agricultural activity.

primary socialization The basic preparation for the various roles of adult life that takes place during the early years.

profane All the elements of everyday life that are considered part of the ordinary physical (natural) world.

propaganda The calculated manipulation of ideas in a way that appeals to people's emotions and prejudices.

public A dispersed grouping of people who share a common interest, concern, or focus of opinion.

public opinion The attitudes about an issue that are held by a public.

qualitative methods Research methods designed to describe reality in accurate verbal terms rather than in numbers.

quantitative methods Research methods designed to study variables that can be measured in numbers.

race A group of people who are believed to share certain physical traits and to be genetically distinct.

racism An ideology that holds that one race is inherently inferior or superior to another.

random sampling A sample chosen so that every member of the population has an equal chance of being picked for inclusion.

rationalization The gradual process by which older, traditional methods of social organization are replaced by explicit, abstract, and numerous formal rules and procedures.

reference group A group that is especially important in shaping a person's beliefs, attitudes, and values.

reform movement A type of social movement that tries to improve society by changing selected aspects of the social structure but does not seek to alter basic economic or political arrangements or to change substantially the stratification hierarchy.

reliability   The degree to which a study or research instrument provides consistently accurate results.

religion   A system of beliefs and practices by which a group of people interprets and responds to what they feel is sacred and, usually, supernatural as well.

religiosity   Personal religious experience.

replication   Repetition of the same experiment with different population samples to test the validity of the results of the original study.

resistance movement   A social movement that aims to prevent change or reverse a change that has already been achieved.

resocialization   A process in which old values and behavior patterns are unlearned and new ones are adopted.

resource mobilization   An approach to the analysis of social movements that emphasizes the political and economic resources that are available to activists.

revolutionary movement   A movement that seeks to overthrow the existing social structure and replace it with a new one.

riot   An acting crowd whose members typically shift from target to target.

rites of passage   Ceremonies marking major transitional events in an individual's life, such as birth, marriage, or death.

ritual   An established pattern of behavior closely associated with the experience of the sacred.

role   The behavior expected of someone occupying a given status in a group or society.

role conflict   A situation in which opposing demands are made on an individual by two or more roles linked with two or more entirely separate social statuses.

role expectation   Society's definition of the way a role ought to be played.

role performance   The way a person actually plays a role.

role set   The whole set of roles associated with a single status.

role strain   Personal stress caused by the opposing demands of a single role.

role taking   Pretending to take or actually taking the role of another person so that one can see oneself and the world from the point of view of another.

rumor   An unverified report that is informally communicated from person to person, usually by word of mouth.

sacred   Anything set apart from everyday life that is capable of evoking deep respect and awe.

sample   In a research study, a limited number of cases selected to represent the entire population being studied.

sanction   A reward (positive sanction) or punishment (negative sanction) intended to encourage or enforce conformity to norms.

secondary analysis   The reanalysis of previously collected data.

secondary group   A specialized group designed to achieve specific goals.

secondary relationship   A relationship that is specialized, lacks emotional intensity, and involves only a limited aspect of one's personality.

secondary sector of the economy   Manufacturing activity.

sect   A type of religious organization that is less formal than a church, emphasizes faith and fervor, and is usually formed by people who reject some aspects of an established religion.

secularization   A process by which many areas of social life become increasingly separated from religious connections and influences.

segregation   The separation of residential areas, services, or other facilities on the basis of the ethnic or racial characteristics of the people using them.

self   A person's awareness of, and feelings about, his or her personal and social identities.

self-control theory   A theoretical perspective that emphasizes the role of restraining impulses and desires.

self-fulfilling prophecy   A belief or prediction that comes true as a result of the behavior it produces.

self-segregation   The process by which a minority group voluntarily tries to keep itself separated from the dominant society.

separatism   The most extreme form of self-segregation, in which a minority group aspires to set up a totally independent society of its own.

sex   The biological traits that distinguish the male and female members of a species.

sexism   The ideology that supports gender inequality and justifies male dominance.

sex ratio   The number of males for every 100 females in a population.

significant others   People who have the greatest influence, particularly in childhood, on the development of the self.

simple supernaturalism   A type of religion that does not recognize specific gods or spirits but that does believe in supernatural forces that influence humanity.

slavery   An extreme system of stratified inequality in which freedom is denied to one group in society that is owned by another and may be regarded as subhuman.

small group   A group that is small enough to allow its members to relate to one another on an individual basis.

social category   A collection of people who share a particular social trait.

social control   Efforts intended to discourage deviance and encourage conformity.

social deviance   Behavior that violates the significant norms of a group or society.

social disorganization   A breakdown of social institutions.

social epidemiology   The study of the social distribution of disease and the relationship of this distribution to social and environmental characteristics.

social institution A relatively stable cluster of social structures that is intended to meet the basic needs of a society.

social interaction The process in which people act toward or respond to others in a mutual and reciprocal way.

socialism An economic and political system based on collective ownership of the means of production and collective planning and control of the economy.

socialization The process of social interaction through which people acquire personality and learn the ways of a society or group.

social control theory A theoretical perspective that emphasizes people's bonds to social institutions.

social mobility A change on the part of an individual or a group of people from one status or social class to another.

social movement A collective effort to produce or resist social change that relies heavily on relatively noninstitutionalized means.

social network An intricate web of ties among individuals.

social science The application of scientific methods to the study of society and human behavior.

social stratification An enduring pattern based on the ranking of groups or categories of people into social positions according to their access to desirables.

social structure The ways in which the components of a group or society relate to one another.

social system A social group conceived of strictly as a set of interrelated statuses and roles, distinct from the individuals who make up the group.

social welfare A system of programs, benefits, and services that seeks to enable people in need to attain a minimum level of social and personal functioning.

society A comprehensive, territorially based social grouping that includes all the social institutions required to meet basic human needs.

sociocultural evolution Theory that holds that societies and cultures develop gradually over time, from simpler to more complex forms.

socioeconomic status (SES) A measure of social status that takes into account a person's educational attainment, income level, and occupational prestige.

sociological imagination A way of understanding ourselves through locating our positions in society and the social forces that affect us.

sociology The systematic and objective study of human society and social interaction.

solidaristic crowd A crowd that provides its members with a strong sense of social solidarity or unity.

spurious correlations Correlations that are not based on causal connections.

state The institution that holds the supreme power in a society and that claims a monopoly over the legitimate use of force.

status A socially defined position in a group or society.

status consistency The tendency for people who rank high in one area to also rank high in other status hierarchies.

status inconsistency A condition that occurs when a person ranks high in one dimension of status and low in another.

status symbol Anything that communicates to others that an individual displaying it occupies a particular level of status.

stereotype A simplified or unsubstantiated generalization applied to an entire category of people.

stigma A label that identifies a deviant as socially unacceptable.

structural explanations of poverty Explanations that attribute poverty to persistent inequalities in society.

structural mobility The upward mobility that results from changes in the social or economic system rather than from personal achievement.

structural strain A theory that explains deviance as the product of social strains that put pressure on people to deviate from their society's norms.

subculture The culture of a group that has a style of living that includes features of the main culture and also certain distinctive cultural elements not found in other groups.

suburbs Relatively small communities that are near to, and dependent on, a central city.

succession The replacement of one social group or type of land use by a rival as the dominant one in an area; completion of the process of invasion.

survey The systematic questioning of large numbers of people about their opinions, attitudes, or behavior.

symbol Anything that a group of people have agreed upon as a way of meaningfully representing something other than itself.

symbolic interactionism A theoretical perspective that emphasizes the importance of symbols and meaning at the microsociological level.

technology The knowledge and tools used to manipulate the environment for practical ends.

tertiary sector of the economy Services.

theism The belief in a god or gods.

theory A comprehensive explanation of observed relationships among variables.

total fertility rate (TFR) The average number of children a woman will have, assuming the current age-specific birth rate remains constant throughout her childbearing years.

total institution A place where people are confined 24 hours a day under the complete control of an administrative staff for the purpose of radical resocialization.

totalitarianism A form of government, run by a single political party, in which there is governmental surveillance and control over all aspects of life.

totem A sacred object (usually an animal, but in rare cases a plant).

totemism The veneration of an animal (or, in rare cases, a plant) as both a god and an ancestor.

tracking   Dividing students into different groups or classes on the basis of academic ability.

traditional authority   Authority that is conferred by custom and accepted practice.

transcendental idealism   A type of religion that does not worship a god and that centers around a set of ethical, moral, or philosophical principles.

triad   A group of three members.

urban ecologist   A social scientist who has a special interest in the social and spatial organization of urban communities.

urbanism   The patterns of culture and social structure characteristic of cities.

urbanization   The movement of people from rural to urban areas.

validity   The degree to which a study or research instrument actually measures what it is attempting to measure.

value   An idea shared by the people in a society about what is good and bad, right and wrong, desirable and undesirable.

value-added approach   A theory of collective behavior that assumes such behavior occurs only when six levels of determinants combine or interact in a particular situation.

variables   Concepts that refer to change across time or space, or from one person or group to another.

vital statistics   Publicly recorded data about the number of births, deaths, marriages, and divorces.

victimless crime   Crimes that result from using the criminal law to attempt to prohibit the exchange between consenting adults of strongly desired goods and services.

voluntary association   An organization that is constructed by its members to pursue some common interest and that has few formal control mechanisms.

wealth   All the economic assets of a person—not only money but also material objects such as land, natural resources, and productive labor services.

world system   The system of economic, political, and cultural relationships that links all the societies in the world.

world systems theory   A theory that asserts that the world's nations are either dominant or subordinate within a historically determined global economy that had its beginnings in northwest Europe about 400 years ago.

zero population growth (ZPG)   The point at which there is no natural increase in the population.

References

Abbott, M. M., N. Kitovitch-Winer, and Judith Worrell. 1986. "Three voices in opposition." *Society* 23 (September/October): 15–21.

Abelman, Robert, and Kimberly Neuendorf. 1985, "How religious is programming?" *Journal of Communications* 35 (Winter): 98–110.

Abrahamson, Mark. 1979. "A functional theory of organizational stratification." *Social Forces* 58:128–145.

Ackelsberg, Martha A., Bennett M. Berger, Karol H. Borowski, Raymond Lee Muncy, Charles F. Petranek, Shulamit Reinharz, Laurence Veysey, and Carol Weisbrod. 1988. "Communal lives and utopian hopes." *Society* 25(2):29–65.

Adams, R. M. 1966. *The Evolution of Urban Society: Early Mesopotamia and Pre-Hispanic Mexico.* Chicago: Aldine.

Adelson, J. 1980. *Handbook of Adolescent Psychology.* New York: Wiley.

Adler, Patricia A., Peter Adler, and Andrea Fontana. 1987. "Everyday life sociology." *Annual Review of Sociology* 13:217–235.

Adler, Peter, and Patricia Adler. 1980. "Symbolic interactionism." In Jack D. Douglas et al., *Introduction to the Sociologies of Everyday Life.* Boston: Allyn & Bacon.

Administration on Aging. 1998. U.S. Department of Health and Human Services. Washington, D.C.

Adorno, T. W., et al. 1950. *The Authoritarian Personality.* New York: Harper & Row.

Akers, Ronald. L. 1994. *Criminological Theories: Introduction and Evaluation.* Los Angeles: Roxbury.

Alba, Richard D. 1985. *Italian Americans: In the Twilight of Ethnicity.* Englewood Cliffs, N.J.: Prentice Hall.

Albonetti, Celesta. 1991. "An integration of theories to explain judicial discretion." *Social Problems* 38:247–266.

Albrecht, Stan L., Howard M. Bahr, and Kristen L. Goodman. 1983. *Divorce and Remarriage.* Westport, Conn.: Greenwood Press.

Alcalde, Javier Gonzalo. 1989. *The Idea of Third World Development: Emerging Perspectives in the United States and Britain, 1900–1950.* Lantham, Md.: University Press of America.

Alcorn, M. D., J. S. Kinder, and J. R. Schunert. 1970. *Better Teaching in Secondary Schools.* Chicago: Holt, Rinehart & Winston.

Alderman, Ellen, and Caroline Kennedy. 1991. *In Our Defense: The Bill of Rights in Action.* New York: Avon Books.

Alexander, J., B. Giesen, R. Munch, and R. Smelser. 1987. *The Macro-Micro Link.* Berkeley: University of California Press.

Allen, Mike. 1996. "On-line access to G.O.P. convention." *New York Times,* August 12, C4.

Allison, M. T. 1979. "On the ethnicity of ethnic minorities in sport." *Quest* 31:50–56.

Allott, Susan. 1985. "Soviet rural women: Employment and family life." In Barbara Holland (ed.), *Soviet Sisterhood.* Bloomington: Indiana University Press.

Allport, Gordon. 1958. *The Nature of Prejudice.* New York: Doubleday.

Almond, Gabriel A. 1950. *The American People and Foreign Policy.* New York: Harcourt Brace & World.

Alston, Jon P., and William A. McIntosh. 1979. "An assessment of the determinants of religious participation." *Sociological Quarterly* 20:49–62.

Alston, Letitia. 1986. *Crime and Older Americans.* Springfield, Ill.: Charles C. Thomas.

Alwin, Duane. 1988. "From obedience to autonomy: Changes in traits desired in children, 1924–1978." *Public Opinion Quarterly* 52:33–52.

Am-Ad, Zvi. 1988. "Investment patterns of the kibbutz elders in their life domains." *Institute for Study and Research and Kibbutz and Cooperative Idea* 12:157–173.

American Association of University Women. 1992. *The AAUP Report: How Schools Shortchange Girls.* Prepared by the Wellesley College Center for Research on Women. Washington, D.C.: AAUW Educational Foundation.

American College Testing Program. 1986. *Demographics, Standards and Equity: Challenges in College Admissions.* Iowa City, Iowa: American College Testing Program.

Amir, Menachem, and Yitzchak Berman. 1970. "Chromosomal deviation and crime." *Federal Probation* 34:55–62.

Anderson, Charles. 1974. *Toward a New Sociology: A Critical View.* Homewood, Ill.: Dorsey Press.

Anderson, Kurt. 1983. "Private violence." *Time,* September 5, pp. 18–22.

Anderson, Margaret L. 1997. *Thinking about Women: Sociological Perspectives on Sex and Gender,* 4th ed. Boston: Allyn & Bacon.

Andersson, Bengt Erik. 1989. "Effects of public day-care: A longitudinal study." *Child Development* 60:857–866.

Andrain, Charles F. 1970. *Political Life and Social Change.* Belmont, Calif.: Wadsworth.

Andrews, Richard L. 1987. "The school-community interface: Strategies of community involvement." In John I. Goodlad (ed.), *The Ecology of School Renewal.* 86th Yearbook of the National Society for the Study of Education. Chicago: University of Chicago Press.

Ann-Ping, Chin. 1988. *Children of China: Voices from Recent Years.* New York: Knopf.

Antoniou, Jim. 1994. *Cities: Then and Now.* New York: Macmillan.

Apple, Michael. 1993. *Official Knowledge.* New York: Routledge.

Arasaratnam, Sinnappah. 1987. "Sinhala-Tamil relations in modern Sri Lanka." In Jeff Boucher, Dan Landis, and Karen Arnold Clark (eds.), *Ethnic Conflict: International Perspectives.* Newbury Park, Calif.: Sage.

Ariès, Philippe. 1981. *The Hour of Our Death.* New York: Knopf.

Armor, David J. 1989. "After busing: Education and choice." *The Public Interest* 95 (Spring): 24–37.

Asch, Solomon. 1955. "Opinions and social pressure." *Scientific American* 193(5):31–55.

Asmussen, L., and C. L. Shehan. 1992. "Gendered expectations and behavior in dating relationships." Paper, 54th Annual Conference of the National Council on Family Relations, Orlando, Fla.

Astin, Alexander W., et al. 1984. *The American Freshman: National Norms for Fall, 1984.* Los Angeles: Higher Education Research Institute, University of California.

Astrachan, Anthony. 1986. *How Men Feel: Their Response to Women's Demands for Equality and Power.* Garden City, N.Y.: Anchor/Doubleday.

Atchley, Robert C. 1988. *Social Forces and Aging.* Belmont, Calif.: Wadsworth.

Atkins, Richard N. 1986. "Single mothers and joint custody: Common ground." In Michael W. Yogman and T. Berry Brazelton (eds.), *In Support of Families.* Cambridge, Mass.: Harvard University Press.

Auletta, Ken. 1991. *Three Blind Mice: How the TV Networks Lost Their Way.* New York: Random House.

Averitt, Robert. 1968. *The Dual Economy.* New York: Norton.

Avison, William R., and Pamela L. Loring. 1986. "Population diversity and cross-national homicide: The effects of inequality and heterogeneity." *Criminology* 24:733–749.

Axelrod, Morris. 1956. "Urban structure and social participation." *American Sociological Review* 21:13–18.

Azicri, Max. 1988. *Cuba: Politics, Economics, and Society.* London: Pinter.

Azumi, Koya. 1977. "Japan's changing world of work." *Wilson Quarterly* (Summer):72–80.

Babbie, Earl. 1995. *The Practice of Social Research.* New York: Wadsworth.

Bachman, Jerald G., Lee Sigelman, and Greg Diamond. 1987. "Self-selection, socialization, and distinctive military values: Attitudes of high school seniors." *Armed Forces and Society* 13:169–187.

Bachofen, Johann Jacob. 1967. *Myth, Religion, and Mother Right.* Translated by Ralph Mannheim. Princeton, N.J.: Princeton University Press. (Originally published in 1861.)

Bagby, Meredith. 1997. *Annual Report of the United States of America.* New York: McGraw-Hill.

Bagby, Meredith. 1998. *Annual Report of the United States of America.* New York: McGraw-Hill.

Bagdikian, Ben. 1992. *The Media Monopoly,* 4th ed. Boston: Beacon Press.

Bagley, Christopher. 1989. "Aggression and anxiety in day-care graduates." *Psychological Reports* 64:250.

Bahr, Howard M., Bruce A. Chadwick, Reuben Hill, and Margaret Holmes Williamson. 1982. *Middletown Families: Fifty Years of Change and Continuity.* Minneapolis: University of Minnesota Press.

Bailey, Thomas. 1990. "Jobs of the future and the skills they will require." *American Educator* (Spring):10–15, 40–44.

Bainbridge, W. S., and R. Stark. 1979. "Cult formation: Three compatible models." *Sociological Analysis* 40:283–295.

Bairoch, Paul. 1988. *Cities and Economic Development from the Dawn to the Present.* Chicago: University of Chicago Press.

Baker, Keith A., and Adriana de Kanter. 1983. "An answer from research on bilingual education." *American Education* 19(6):40–48.

Baker, T. A., L. W. Moreland, and R. S. Steed. 1989. "Party activists and the new religious right," pp. 161–175. In C. W. Dunn (ed.), *Religion in American Politics.* Washington, D.C.: CQ Press.

Bakuniak, Grezegorzi, and Krzysztof Nowak. 1987. "The creation of a collective identity in a social movement." *Theory and Society* 16:401–429.

Baldassare, Mark. 1986. *Trouble in Paradise: The Suburban Transformation in America.* New York: Columbia University Press.

Bales, Robert F. 1951. *Interaction Process Analysis: A Method for the Study of Small Groups.* Cambridge, Mass.: Addison Wesley.

Bales, Robert F. 1953. "The equilibrium problem in small groups." In Talcott Parsons et al. (eds.), *Working Papers in the Theory of Action.* Glencoe, Ill.: Free Press.

Bales, Robert F., and Fred L. Strodtbeck. 1951. "Phases in group problem solving." *Journal of Abnormal and Social Psychology* 46:485–495.

Bales, William D., and Linda G. Dees. 1992. "Mandatory minimum sentencing in Florida: Past trends and future implications." *Crime and Delinquency* 38(3) (July): 309–329.

Ballantine, Jeanne H. 1997. *The Sociology of Education,* 4th ed. Upper Saddle River, N.J.: Prentice Hall.

Balmer, Randall. 1989. *Mine Eyes Have Seen the Glory.* New York: Oxford University Press.

Bamberger, Joan. 1974. "The myth of matriarchy: Why men rule in primitive society." In M. Z. Rosaldo and L. Lamphere (eds.), *Women, Culture, and Society.* Stanford, Calif.: Stanford University Press.

Bandura, Albert. 1973. "Social learning theory of aggression." In J. F. Knudson (ed.), *The Control of Aggression.* Chicago: Aldine.

Banner, Lois W. 1984. *Women in Modern America: A Brief History.* San Diego, Calif.: Harcourt Brace Jovanovich.

Banton, Michael. 1988. *Racial Consciousness.* London: Longman.

Baran, P. 1957. *The Political Economy of Growth.* New York: Monthly Review Press.

Barash, David P. 1977. *Sociobiology and Behavior.* New York: Elsevier.

Barber, Benjamin. 1984. *Strong Democracy.* Berkeley: University of California Press.

Barkan, Steven E. 1997. *Criminology: A Sociological Understanding.* Upper Saddle River, NJ: Prentice Hall.

Barker, Eileen. 1982. *New Religious Movements: A Perspective for Understanding Society.* New York: Edwin Mellen Press.

Barney, Gerald O. 1980. *The Global 2000 Report to the President of the United States: Entering the 21st Century. The Summary Report.* Vol. 1. New York: Pergamon.

Baron, James N., and William T. Bielby. 1986. "The proliferation of job titles in organizations." *Administrative Science Quarterly* 31:561–586.

Barr, Robert D. 1982. "Magnet schools: An attractive alternative." *Principal* 61(3):37–40.

Barrow, Georgia M., and Patricia A. Smith. 1979. *Age, Ageism, and Society.* St. Paul, Minn.: West.

Barry, Herbert, Margaret K. Bacon, and Irvin L. Child. 1957. "A cross-cultural survey of some sex differences in socialization." *Journal of Abnormal and Social Psychology* 55:327–332.

Bart, Pauline B. 1981. "A study of women who both were raped and avoided rape." *Journal of Social Issues* 37(4):123–137.

Barwise, Patrick, and Andrew Ehrenberg. 1988. Television and Its Audience. Beverly Hills, Calif.: Sage.

Basnik, Ellen L., Lenoire Rubin, and Alison S. Lauriat. 1986. "Characteristics of sheltered homeless." *American Journal of Public Health* 76(9):1097–1107.

Basow, Susan A. 1984. "Ethnic group differences in educational achievement in Fiji." *Journal of Cross-Cultural Psychology* 15:435–451.

Basow, Susan A., and Nancy T. Silberg. 1987. "Student evaluations of college professors: Are female and male professors rated differently?" *Journal of Educational Psychology* 79:308–314.

Baum, Alice S., and Donald W. Burnes. 1993. *A Nation in Denial: The Truth about Homelessness.* Boulder, Colo.: Westview.

Baumrind, Diana. 1980. "New directions in socialization research." *American Psychologist* 35:639–652.

Baxter, Ellen, and Kim Hopper. 1984. In John A. Talbott (ed.), *The Chronic Mental Patient: Five Years Later.* New York: Grune & Stratton.

Beach, Stephen W. 1977. "Religion and political change in Northern Ireland." *Sociological Analysis* 38(1):37–48.

Beck, Melinda. 1993. "Thy kingdom come." *Newsweek*, March 15, pp. 52–55.

Becker, Howard S. 1952. "Social class variations in the teacher-pupil relationship." *Journal of Educational Psychology* 25:457.

Becker, Howard S. 1963. *Outsiders: Studies in the Sociology of Deviance.* New York: Free Press.

Becker, Howard S. 1967. "Whose side are we on?" *Journal of Social Problems* 14:239–247.

Belcher, John R., and Jeff Singer. 1987. "Homelessness: A cost of capitalism." Social Policy 18:44–48.

Bell, Daniel. 1973. *The Coming of Post-Industrial Society.* New York: Basic Books.

Bell, Daniel. 1976. *The Post-Industrial Society: A Venture in Social Forecasting.* New York: Basic Books.

Bell, Daniel. 1978. *The Cultural Contradictions of Capitalism.* New York: Basic Books.

Bell, Daniel. 1991. "Behind the Soviet economic crises." *Dissent* (Winter): 46–54.

Bell, Wendell, and Robert V. Robinson. 1980. "Cognitive maps of class and racial inequalities in England and the United States." *American Journal of Sociology* 86:321–342.

Bellah, Robert N. 1964. "Religious evolution." *American Sociological Review* 29:358–374.

Bellah, Robert N. 1967. "Civil religion in America." *Daedalus* (Winter).

Bellah, Robert N. (1970). *Beyond Belief.* New York: Harper & Row.

Bellah, Robert N., Richard Madsen, William M. Sullivan, Ann Swidler, and Steven M. Tipton. 1986. *Habits of the Heart: Individualism and Commitment in American Life.* New York: Harper & Row.

Bellah, Robert, Richard Madsen, William Sullivan, Ann Swidler, and Steven Tipton. 1991. *The Good Society.* New York: Knopf.

Bellas, Marcia L. 1993. "Faculty salaries: Still a cost of being female." *Social Science Quarterly* 74(1):62–75.

Belsky, Jay. 1987. "Risks remain." *Zero to Three* 7:22–24.

Belsky, Jay. 1988a. "The 'effects' of infant day care reconsidered." *Early Childhood Research Quarterly* 3:235–272.

Belsky, Jay. 1988b. "Infant day care and socioemotional development: The United States." *Journal of Child Psychology and Psychiatry and Allied Disciplines* 29:397–406.

Belsky, Jay. 1988c. "Nonmaternal care in the first year of life and the security of infant-parent attachment." *Child Development* 59:157–167.

Benard, Cheryl, and Zalmay Khalilzad. 1979. "Secularization, industrialization, and Khomeini's Islamic republic." *Political Science Quarterly* 94:229–241.

Bender, B. 1975. *Farming in Pre-History: From Hunter-Gatherer to Food Producer.* New York: St. Martin's Press.

Bendix, Reinhard. 1964. *Nation-Building and Citizenship: Studies of Our Changing Social Order.* Berkeley: University of California Press.

Bendix, Reinhard. 1978. *Kings or People: Power and the Mandate to Rule.* Berkeley: University of California Press.

Benedict, Ruth. 1959. *Patterns of Culture,* 2nd ed. Boston: Houghton Mifflin.

Benet, Sula. 1976. "Why they live to be 100 or even older in Abkhasia." In Cary S. Kart and Barbara B. Manard (eds.), *Aging in America.* Port Washington, N.Y.: Alfred.

Benevolo, Leonardo. 1980. *The History of the City.* Cambridge, Mass.: MIT Press.

Bennett, Neil G., Ann Klimas Blanc, and David E. Bloom. 1988. "Commitment and the modern union: Assessing the link between premarital cohabitation and subsequent marital stability." *American Sociological Review* 53(1):127–139.

Bennett, Richard R., and James P. Lynch. 1990. "Does a difference make a difference: Comparing cross-national crime indicators." *Criminology* 28:153–181.

Bennett, Stephen. 1986. *Apathy in America.* Dobbs Ferry, N.Y.: Transnational.

Benokraitis, Nijole V. 1999. *Marriages and Families: Changes, Choices, and Constraints,* 3rd ed. Upper Saddle River, N.J.: Prentice Hall.

Bensman, Joseph, and Israel Gerver. 1963. "Crime and punishment in the factory: The function of deviancy in maintaining the social system." *American Sociological Review* 28:588–598.

Bensman, Joseph, and Arthur Vidich. 1971. *New American Society: The Revolution of the Middle Class.* New York: Times Books.

Berger, Bennett M. 1968. *Working Class Suburb: A Study of Auto Workers in Suburbia.* Berkeley: University of California Press.

Berger, Brigitte, and Peter J. Berger. 1983. *The War over the Family: Capturing the Middle Ground.* New York: Anchor.

Berger, Peter L. 1963. *Invitation to Sociology: A Humanistic Perspective.* Garden City, N.Y.: Doubleday/Anchor.

Berger, Peter L. 1967. "Religious institutions." In Neil J. Smelser (ed.), *Sociology: An Introduction.* New York: Wiley.

Berger, Peter L. 1969. *A Rumor of Angels.* Garden City, N.Y.: Doubleday.

Berger, Peter L. 1977. "'A great revival' coming for American churches."

Interview in *U.S. News & World Report,* April 11, pp. 70–72.

Berger, Peter L. 1986. *The Capitalist Revolution.* New York: Basic Books.

Berkowitz, L. 1962. *Aggression: A Social-Psychological Analysis.* New York: McGraw-Hill.

Bernard, Jessie. 1956. *Remarriage: A Study of Marriage.* New York: Dryden Press.

Bernard, Jessie. 1981. *The Female World.* New York: Free Press.

Bernard, Jessie. 1982. *The Future of Marriage.* New Haven, Conn.: Yale University Press. (Originally published in 1973.)

Bernstein, Nina. 1997. "On line, high-tech sleuths find private facts." *New York Times,* September 15, A1, A12.

Berreman, Gerald D. 1960. "Caste in India and the United States." *American Journal of Sociology* 66:120–127.

Berrick, Jill. 1995. *Faces of Poverty: Portraits of Women and Children on Welfare.* New York: Oxford University Press.

Berrueta-Clement, John R., Lawrence J. Schweinhart, W. Steven Barnett, Ann S. Epstein, and David P. Weikart. 1984. *Changed Lives: The Effects of the Perry Preschool Program on Youths through Age 19.* Ypsilanti, Mich.: High/Scope Press.

Berry, Brian J. L., and J. D. Kasarda. 1977. *Contemporary Urban Ecology.* New York: Macmillan.

Best, Raphaela. 1983. *We've All Got Scars: What Boys and Girls Learn in Elementary School.* Bloomington: Indiana University Press.

Bettelheim, Bruno. 1969. *The Children of the Dream.* New York: Macmillan.

Biagi, Shirley. 1989. *Media Reader: Perspectives on Mass Media Industry Effects and Issues.* Belmont, Calif.: Wadsworth.

Biblarz, T. J., and A. E. Rafferty. 1993. "The effects of family disruption on social mobility." *American Sociological Review* 58 (February): 97–109.

Bidwell, Charles E. 1965. "The school as a formal organization." In James G. March (ed.), *Handbook of Organizations.* New York: Rand McNally.

Bielby, William T., and James N. Baron. 1986. "Men and women at work: Sex segregation and statistical discrimination." *American Journal of Sociology* 91:759–799.

Bielby, William T., and Denise D. Bielby. 1989. "Family ties: Balancing commitments to work and family in dual earner households." *American Sociological Review* 54:776–789.

Birdwhistell, Ray L. 1970. *Kinesics and Context: Essays on Body Motion Communication.* Philadelphia: University of Pennsylvania Press.

Bissinger, H. G. 1990. *Friday Night Lights.* New York: Harper.

Black, Donald J. 1971. "The social organization of arrest." *Stanford Law Review* 23:1087–1111.

Blackburn, M., and D. Bloom. 1985. "What is happening to the middle class?" *Demographics* (January): 18–25.

Blackwell, James E. 1991. *The Black Community,* 3rd ed. New York: HarperCollins.

Blain, Jenny, and Jerome Barkow. 1988. "Father involvement, reproductive strategies, and the sensitive period." In Kevin B. MacDonald (ed.), *Sociological Perspectives on Human Development.* New York: Springer-Verlag.

Blake, Judith, and Kingsley Davis. 1964. "Norms, values and sanctions." In R.E.L. Faris (ed.), *Handbook of Modern Sociology.* Chicago: Rand McNally.

Blank, R. K., and D. A. Archibald. 1992. "Magnet schools and issues of educational quality." *The Clearinghouse* 82:81–86.

Blau, Francine O., and Carol L. Jusenius. 1976. "Economists' approaches to sex segregation in the labor market: An appraisal." *Signs: Journal of Women in Culture and Society* 1:181–200.

Blau, Peter M. 1964. Exchange and Power in Social Life. New York: Wiley.

Blau, Peter. 1974. "Parameters of social structure." *American Sociological Review* 39(5):615–635.

Blau, Peter M. 1987. "Contrasting theoretical perspectives." In J. Alexander, J. B. Giesen, et al. (eds.), *The Macro-Micro Link.* Berkeley: University of California Press.

Blau, Peter M., and O. D. Duncan. 1967. *The American Occupational Structure.* New York: Wiley.

Blau, Peter M., and W. Richard Scott. 1962. *Formal Organizations: A Comparative Approach.* San Francisco: Chandler.

Blau, Zena S. 1981. *Aging in Changing Society,* 2nd ed. New York: Franklin Watts.

Blauner, Robert. 1964. *Alienation and Freedom.* Chicago: University of Chicago Press.

Blauner, Robert. 1969. "Internal colonialism and ghetto revolt." *Social Problems* 16(4):612–617.

Blendon, Robert J. 1985. "Policy choices for the 1990s." In E. Ginzburg (ed.), *The U.S. Health Care System: A Look to the 1990s.* Totowa, N.J.: Rowman & Allenheld.

Bloch, Ruth H. 1978. "Untangling the roots of modern sex roles: A survey of four centuries of change." *Signs: Journal of Women in Culture and Society* 4(2):237–252.

Block, Jeanne H. 1976. "Issues, problems, and pitfalls in assessing sex differences." *Merrill-Palmer Quarterly* 22:283–308.

Bloom, David E., and Geoffrey Carliner. 1988. "The economic impact of AIDS in the United States." *Science* 239, 4840 (February 5): 604–610.

Bluestone, Barry, and Bennett Harrison. 1982. *The Deindustrialization of America: Plant Closings, Community Abandonment, and the Dismantling of Basic Industry.* New York: Basic Books.

Blum, Marian. 1983. *The Day-Care Dilemma.* Lexington, Mass.: D. C. Heath.

Blumberg, A. S. 1970. *Criminal Justice.* Chicago: Quadrangle.

Blumberg, Rae Lesser. 1978. *Stratification: Socioeconomic and Sexual Inequality.* Dubuque, Iowa: William C. Brown.

Blumer, Herbert, 1939. "Collective behavior." In Alfred Lee (ed.), *Principles of Sociology.* New York: Barnes and Noble.

Blumer, Herbert. 1948. "Public opinion and public opinion polling." *American Sociological Review* 13:542–549.

Blumer, Herbert. 1962. "Society as symbolic interaction." In Arnold Rose (ed.), *Human Behavior and Social Processes: An Interactionist Approach.* Boston: Houghton Mifflin.

Blumstein, Philip, and Pepper Schwartz. 1983. *American Couples.* New York: Morrow.

Bodovitz, Kathy. 1991. "Black America." *American Demographics Desk Reference Series No. 1* (July): 8–10.

Bogdanor, Vernon (ed.). 1987. *The Blackwell Encyclopedia of Political Institutions.* Oxford: Basil Blackwell.

Bohannan, Paul. 1985. *All the Happy Families: Exploring the Varieties of Family Life.* New York: McGraw-Hill.

Bonvillain, Nancy. 1998. *Women and Men: Cultural Constructs of Gender.* Upper Saddle River, N.J.: Prentice Hall.

Boocock, Sarane. 1980. *Sociology of Education: An Introduction,* 2nd ed. Boston: Houghton Mifflin.

Bookchin, Murray. 1987. *The Rise of Urbanization and the Decline of Citizenship.* San Francisco: Sierra Club.

Booth, Alan, David R. Johnson, and Harvey M. Choldin. 1977. "Correlates of city crime rates: Victimization surveys versus official statistics." *Social Problems* 25:187–197.

Bornschier, Volker, and Thanh-Huyven Ballmer-Cao. 1979. "Income inequality: A cross-national study of the relationships between MNC-penetration, dimensions of the power structure and income distribution." *American Sociological Review* 44:487–506.

Boroughs, Don L., and Betsy Carpenter. 1991. "Cleaning up the environment." *U.S. News & World Report,* March 25, p. 45ff.

Botwinick, J. 1967. *Cognitive Processes in Maturity and Old Age.* New York: Springer-Verlag.

Boucher, Jeff, Dan Landis, and Karen Arnold Clark (eds.). 1987. *Ethnic Conflict: International Perspectives.* Newbury Park, Calif.: Sage.

Boulding, Kenneth E. 1966. "The economics of the coming spaceship earth." In Henry Jarrett (ed.), *Environmental Quality in a Growing Economy.* Baltimore: Johns Hopkins University Press.

Bouvier, Leon F., and Robert W. Gardner. 1986. "Immigration to the U.S.: The unfinished story." *Population Bulletin* 44:4.

Bouvier, Leon F., with Henry S. Shryock and Harry W. Henderson. 1977. "International migration: Yesterday, today, and tomorrow." *Population Bulletin* 32:26.

Bowen, Gary Lee, and Dennis K. Orthner. 1983. "Sex-role congruency and marital quality." *Journal of Marriage and the Family* 45:223–229.

Bowerman, C. E., and J. W. Kinch. 1959. "Changes in family and peer orientation of children between the fourth and tenth grades." *Social Forces* 37:201–211.

Bowes, A. M. 1989. *Kibbutz Goshen: An Israeli Commune.* Prospect Heights, Ill.: Waveland Press.

Bowles, Samuel, and Richard Edwards. 1985. *Understanding Capitalism.* New York: Harper & Row.

Bowles, Samuel, and Herbert Gintis. 1976. *Schooling in Capitalist America: Educational Reform and the Contradictions of Economic Life.* New York: Basic Books.

Bowles, Samuel, and Herbert Gintis. 1986. *Democracy and Capitalism.* New York: Basic Books.

Bowles, Samuel, David Gordon, and Thomas Weisskopf. 1983. *Beyond the Wasteland.* New York: Doubleday.

Boyer, Richard, and David Savegeau. 1989. *Places Rated Almanac.* New York: Prentice Hall.

Braithwaite, John, and Valerie Braithwaite. 1980. "The effect of income inequality and social democracy on homicide." *British Journal of Criminology* 20:45–53.

Brandreth, Gyles. 1985. *Super Silly Riddles.* New York: Wings Books.

Braverman, H. 1975. *Labor and Monopoly Capital.* New York: Monthly Review Press.

Bray, Thomas J. 1988. "Reading America the riot act." *Policy Review* 43:32–36.

Bredin, Alice. 1996. *Virtual Office Survival Handbook.* New York: Wiley.

Brenneis, Donald. 1984. "Grog and gossip in Bhatagon: Style and substance in Fiji Indian conversation." *American Ethnologist* 11:487–505.

Bretl, Daniel J., and Joanne Cantor. 1988. "The portrayal of men and women in U.S. television commercials: A recent content analysis and trends over 15 years." *Sex Roles* 18:595–609.

Brim, Orville G., Jr. 1968. "Adult socialization." In David Sills (ed.), *International Encyclopedia of the Social Sciences.* New York: Macmillan.

Brim, Orville G., Jr., and Jerome Kagan. 1980. *Constancy and Change in Human Development.* Cambridge, Mass.: Harvard University Press.

Brittan, Arthur. 1989. *Masculinity and Power.* London: Blackwell.

Broadstreet, Simon, and Susanna Segnit. 1975. "Is anybody out there?" *View* (November).

Brockerhoff, Martin. 1996. "'City summit' to address global urbanization." *Population Today* 24 (March): 4–5.

Brody, Jacob A. 1989. "Toward quantifying the health of the elderly." *American Journal of Public Health* 79:685–686.

Brofman, Rob. 1989. "Red hot. Soviet watches are fad in Italy." *Life,* December, p. 8.

Bromley, Ray. 1988. "Work in the streets: Survival strategy, necessity, or unavoidable evil?" In José Gugler (ed.), *Urbanization of the Third World.* New York: Oxford University Press.

Bronfenbrenner, Urie. 1958. "Socialization and social class through time and space." In Eleanor E. Maccoby et al. (eds.), *Readings in Social Psychology,* 3rd ed. New York: Holt, Rinehart & Winston.

Bronner, Ethan. 1998. "U.S. 12th graders rank poorly in math and science, study says." *New York Times,* February 25, A1, C20.

Brooks, John (ed.). 1989. *South American Handbook.* Bath, England: Trade and Travel Publications.

Broom, Leonard, and Robert Cushing. 1977. "A modest test of an immodest theory: The functional theory of stratification." *American Sociological Review* 42:157–169.

Broudy, H. S. 1987. *Becoming Educated in Contemporary America.* National Society for the Study of Education. Chicago: University of Chicago Press.

Brower, Brock. 1988. "The pernicious power of the polls." *Money* (March): 144–163.

Brown, Arnold S. 1990. *Social Processes of Aging and Old Age.* Englewood Cliffs, N.J.: Prentice Hall.

Brown, L. R., and J. L. Jacobson. 1987. "The future of urbanization: Facing the ecological and economic constraints." *Worldwatch Paper 77* (May). New York: Worldwatch Institute.

Brown, Lester R. 1988. *State of the World.* New York: Norton.

Brown, Phil. 1987. "Popular epidemiology: Community response to toxic waste-induced disease." *Science, Technology, and Human Value* 12 (Summer/Fall): 78–85.

Brown, Richard Maxwell. 1990. "Historical patterns of American violence." In Neil Alan Weiner, Margaret A. Zahn, and Rita J. Sagi (eds.), *Violence, Patterns, Causes, Public Policy,* pp. 4–15. San Diego: Harcourt Brace Jovanovich.

Browne, M. Neil, and Stuart M. Keeley. 1990. *Asking the Right Questions:*

A Guide to Critical Thinking. Upper Saddle River, N.J.: Prentice Hall.

Brunner, Borgna. 1998. *Information Please Almanac 1998.* Boston: LLC.

Buell, Emmett H. 1980. "Busing and the defended neighborhood: South Boston 1974–1977." *Urban Affairs Quarterly* 16:161–188.

Bulmer, Martin. 1984. *The Chicago School of Sociology: Institutionalization, Diversity, and the Rise of Sociological Research.* Chicago: University of Chicago Press.

Burawoy, Michael. 1984. "Organizing consent on the shop floor: The game of making out." In Frank Fisher and Carmen Sirianni (eds.), *Critical Studies in Organization and Bureaucracy.* Philadelphia: Temple University Press.

Burawoy, Michael, and Theda Skocpol (eds.). 1982. *Marxist Inquiries: Studies of Labor, Class, and States.* Chicago: University of Chicago Press.

Burchell, Robert, and George Sternlieb. 1978. *Planning Theory in the 1980s: A Search for Future Directions.* New Brunswick, N.J.: Rutgers University Press.

Burnham, Walter. 1981. "The 1980 earthquake." In T. Ferguson and J. Rogers (eds.), *The Hidden Election.* New York: Pantheon.

Burnham, Walter. 1984. "The appearance and disappearance of the American voter." In T. Ferguson and J. Rogers (eds.), *The Political Economy.* Armonk, N.Y.: M. E. Sharpe.

Burns, Leland S., and John Friedmann. 1985. *The Art of Planning.* New York: Plenum Press.

Burridge, Kenelm O. L. 1957. "Disputing in Tangu." *American Anthropologist* 59:763–780.

Buss, David M. 1984. "Toward a psychology of person-environment (PE) correlation: The role of spouse selection." *Journal of Personality and Social Psychology* 47:361–377.

Butsch, Richard. 1992. "Class and gender in four decades of television situation comedy: Plus ça change. . . . *Critical Studies in Mass Communication* 9:387–399.

Cabezas, Amado, Larry Hajime Shinagawa, and Gary Kawaguchi. 1986–87. "New inquiries into the socioeconomic status of Philippino Americans in California." *Amerasia Journal* 13:3–7.

Calhoun, J. 1962. "Population density and social pathology." *Scientific American* (February): 139–148.

Callender, C., and L. Kochems. 1987. "The North American berdache." *Current Anthropology* 24:443–456.

Camara, Kathleen A. 1986. "Family adaptation to divorce." In Michael W. Yogman and T. Berry Brazelton (eds.), *In Support of Families.* Cambridge, Mass.: Harvard University Press.

Camden, Thomas M., and Susan Schwartz. 1995. *How to Get a Job in Chicago.* Chicago: Surrey Books.

Cameron, Kim S., and R. E. Quinn. 1996. *Diagnosing and Changing Organizational Culture.* San Francisco: Jossey-Bass.

Campbell, Angus. 1981. *The Sense of Well-Being in America.* New York: McGraw-Hill.

Campbell, Anne. 1991. *The Girls in the Gang,* 2nd ed. Cambridge, Mass.: Basil Blackwell.

Campbell, Bernard. 1985. *Human Evolution,* 3rd ed. New York: Aldine.

Campbell, Ernest. 1971. "On desegregation and matters sociological." *Phylon* (Summer): 140–142.

Campbell, Joseph. 1988. *The Power of Myth.* New York: Doubleday.

Cancian, Francesca M. 1987. *Love in America.* New York: Cambridge University Press.

Cantril, Albert H. (ed.). 1980. *Polling on the Issues.* Cabin John, Md.: Seven Locks Press.

Caplan, Nathan, Marcella H. Choy, and John Whitmore. 1992. "Indochinese refugee families and academic achievement." *Scientific American* 266:36–42.

Caplow, Theodore. 1969. *Two against One: Coalitions in Triads.* Englewood Cliffs, N.J.: Prentice Hall.

Caplow, Theodore, H. M. Bahr, B. A. Chadwick, R. Hill, and M. H. Williamson. 1982. *Middletown Families: Fifty Years of Change and Continuity.* Minneapolis: University of Minnesota Press.

Cardozo, Arlene Rossen. 1986. *Sequencing: Having It All but Not All at Once.* New York: Atheneum.

Carey, James T. 1978. *Introduction to Criminology.* Englewood Cliffs, N.J.: Prentice Hall.

Carey, Marx, and James Franklin. 1991. "Industry output and job growth continue slow into the next century." *Monthly Labor Review* (November): 45–63.

Carlen, Pat, and Anne Worrall (eds.). 1987. *Gender, Crime, and Justice.* Philadelphia: Open University Press.

Carmichael, Stokely, and Charles V. Hamilton. 1967. *Black Power.* New York: Vintage.

Carnoy, Martin. 1984. *The State and Political Theory.* Princeton, N.J.: Princeton University Press.

Carr-Saunders, A.M. 1936. *World Population.* New York: Oxford University Press.

Castells, Manuel. 1977. *The Urban Question.* Cambridge, Mass.: MIT Press.

Castells, Manuel. 1983. *The City and the Grassroots: A Cross-Cultural Theory of Urban Social Movements.* Berkeley: University of California Press.

Castells, Manuel. 1988. "Squatters and the state in Latin America." In José Gugler (ed.), *Urbanization of the Third World.* New York: Oxford University Press.

Castive, George Pierre, and Gilbert Kushner (eds.). 1981. *Persistent Peoples: Cultural Enclaves in Perspective.* Tucson: University of Arizona Press.

Caton, Carol L. M. 1990. *Homeless in America.* New York: Oxford University Press.

Cazenave, Noel A., and Murray A. Straus. 1979. "Race, class, network embeddedness and family violence: A search for potent support systems." *Journal of Comparative Family Studies* 10:281–300.

CBS/New York Times Poll. 1993. "How we classify ourselves." *American Enterprise* 4 (May–June): 82.

Centers for Disease Control. 1998. http:\\www.cdc.gov

Centerwall, Brandon S. 1993. "Our cultural perplexities: Television and violent crime." *The Public Interest* 111:56.

Chafetz, Janet Saltzman. 1988. *Feminist Sociology: An Overview of Contemporary Theories.* Itsaca, Ill.: Peacock.

Chambliss, William J. 1973. "The Saints and the Roughnecks." *Society* 2(1).

Chapman, Anthony J. 1973. "Funniness of jokes, canned laughter, and recall performance." *Sociometry* 36:569–578.

Chase, Ivan D. 1975. "A comparison of men's and women's intergenerational mobility in the United States." *American Sociological Review* 40:483–505.

Cherlin, Andrew. 1983. *Marriage, Divorce, Remarriage.* Cambridge, Mass.: Harvard University Press.

Chidester, David. 1988. *Patterns of Power, Religion, and Politics in American Culture.* Englewood Cliffs, N.J.: Prentice Hall.

Childe, V. Gordon. 1951. *Man Makes Himself.* New York: New American Library.

Chinoy, Ely. 1968. *Sociological Perspective: Basic Concepts and Their Application,* rev. ed. New York: Random House.

Chirot, Daniel. 1986. *Social Change in the Modern Era.* San Diego: Harcourt Brace Jovanovich.

Chirot, Daniel, and Thomas D. Hall. 1982. "World system theory." *Annual Review of Sociology* 8:81–106.

Chodorow, Nancy. 1978. *The Reproduction of Mothering.* Berkeley: University of California Press.

Chodorow, Nancy. 1989. *Feminism and Psychoanalytic Theory.* New Haven, Conn.: Yale University Press.

Choldin, H. M. 1984. *Cities and Suburbs.* New York: McGraw-Hill.

Chomsky, Noam. 1965. *Aspects of the Theory of Syntax.* Cambridge, Mass.: MIT Press.

Chomsky, Noam. 1975. *Reflections on Language.* New York: Pantheon.

Choucri, Nazl (ed.). 1984. *Multidisciplinary Perspectives on Population and Conflict.* Syracuse, N.Y.: Syracuse University Press.

Christopher, David. 1983. *The Japanese Mind: The Goliath Explained.* New York: Linden Press/Simon & Schuster.

Chudacoff, Howard, and J. Smith, 1988. *The Evolution of American Urban Society,* 3rd ed. Englewood Cliffs, N.J.: Prentice Hall.

Clark, Burton R. 1962. *Educating the Expert Society.* San Francisco: Chandler.

Clark, Charles S. 1993. "TV violence." *CQ Researcher* 3(12):267–284.

Clarke-Stewart, K. Alison. 1988. "The 'effects' of daycare reconsidered." *Early Childhood Research Quarterly* 3:293–318.

Clarke-Stewart, Alison, and Susan Friedman. 1987. *Child Development: Infancy through Adolescence.* New York: Wiley.

Clayton, R. C. 1975. *The Family, Marriage, and Social Change.* Lexington, Mass.: D. C. Heath.

Clegg, Stewart, and David Dunkerley. 1980. *Organization, Class and Control.* London: Routledge & Kegan Paul.

Clinard, Marshall B. 1979. *Illegal Corporate Behavior.* Washington, D.C.: U.S. Government Printing Office.

Cloward, Richard A. 1960. "Social control in the prison." In *Theoretical Studies in the Social Organization of the Prison.* New York: Social Science Research Council.

Cloward, Richard A., and Lloyd E. Ohlin. 1964. *Delinquency and Opportunity.* New York: Free Press.

Coakley, Jay J. 1986. *Sport in Society: Issues and Controversies.* St. Louis, Mo.: Mosby.

Coche, Judith M., and Erich Coche. 1986. "Leaving the institutional setting to enter private practice: A mid-life crisis resolution." *Psychotherapy in Private Practice* 4:43–50.

Cockerham, William C. 1991. *This Aging Society.* Englewood Cliffs, N.J.: Prentice Hall.

Cockerham, William C. 1998. *Medical Sociology,* 7th ed. Upper Saddle River, N.J.: Prentice Hall.

Cogan, John, Judith Torney-Purta, and Douglas Anderson. 1988. "Knowledge and attitudes toward global issues: Students in Japan and the United States." *Comparative Education Review* 32:282–297.

Cohen, Albert. 1966. *Deviance and Control.* Englewood Cliffs, N.J.: Prentice Hall.

Cohen, Carl I., and Jay Sokolovsky. 1989. *Old Men of the Bowery: Strategies of Survival among the Homeless.* New York: Guilford Press.

Cohen, Jere Z. 1979. "High school subcultures and the adult world." *Adolescence* 16:491–502.

Cohen, R. B. 1988. "The new international division of labor and multinational corporations." In Frank Hearn (ed.), *The Transformation of Industrial Organization.* Belmont, Calif.: Wadsworth.

Cohen, Stephen S., and John Zysman. 1987. *Manufacturing Matters.* New York: Basic Books.

Colasanto, Diane, and Linda DeStefano. 1989. "Religion: Public image of TV evangelists deteriorates." *The Gallup Poll Monthly* (September): 16–19.

Cole, William S. 1995. "Readers for sale! What newspapers tell advertisers about their audience. *Extra!* 8(3): 6–7.

Coleman, James. 1987. "Families and schools." *Educational Researcher* 32 (August/September): 32–38.

Coleman, James S. 1961. *The Adolescent Society.* New York: Free Press.

Coleman, James S., et al. 1966. *Equality of Educational Opportunity.* Washington, D.C.: U.S. Department of Health, Education, and Welfare.

Coleman, James S., and Thomas Hoffer. 1986. *Public and Private High Schools: The Impact of Communities.* New York: Basic Books.

Coleman, James S., Thomas Hoffer, and Sally Kilgore. 1982. *High School Achievement: Public, Catholic, and Private Schools Compared.* New York: Basic Books.

Coleman, James S., Sara D. Kelly, and John A. Moore. 1975. "Recent trends in school integration." Paper presented at American Sociological Association Meeting, April 2.

Coleman, James William, and Donald R. Cressey. 1999. *Social Problems,* 7th ed. New York: Addison-Wesley Longman.

Coleman, John C., and Leo Hendry. 1990. *The Nature of Adolescence,* 2nd ed. New York: Routledge, Chapman, and Hall.

Coleman, Richard, and Lee Rainwater. 1978. *Social Standing in America.* New York: Basic Books.

Collins, Randall. 1981. "On the micro-foundations of macrosociology." *American Journal of Sociology* 86:984–1014.

Collins, Randall. 1990. "Market dynamics as the engine of historical change." *Sociological Theory* 8(Fall): 111–135.

Collins, Randall. 1992. *Sociological Insight: An Introduction to Non-Obvious Sociology,* 2nd ed. New York: Oxford University Press.

Coltrane, Scott. 1988. "Father-child relationships and the status of women: A cross-cultural study." *American Journal of Sociology* 93:1060–1095.

Comstock, George, and Victor C. Strasburger. 1990. "Deceptive appearances: Television violence and aggressive behavior." *Journal of Adolescent Health Care* 11(1):31–44.

Comte, Auguste. 1877. *System of Positive Polity.* London: Longmans, Green.

Congressional Quarterly. 1986. *The Soviet Union,* 2nd ed. Washington, D.C.: Congressional Quarterly.

Congressional Quarterly Almanac. 1988. Vol. 44.

Connors, John H. 1987. "Ranks of the poor swell with women and children." *State Government News* 29:4–7.

Conrad, Peter, and Rochelle Kern. 1990. "The social and cultural meanings of illness." In Peter Conrad and Rochelle Kern (eds.), *Sociology of Health and Illness: Critical Perspectives.* New York: St. Martin's Press.

Conrad, Peter, and Joseph W. Schneider. 1980. *Deviance and Medicalization: From Badness to Sickness.* St. Louis, Mo.: Mosby.

Constantine, B. L., and J. M. Constantine. 1973. *Group Marriage: A Study of Contemporary Multilateral Marriage.* New York: Macmillan.

Converse, Jean M., and Stanley Presser. 1986. *Survey Questions: Handcrafting the Standardized Questionnaire.* Beverly Hills, Calif.: Sage.

Cookson, Peter W., Jr., and Caroline Hodges Persell. 1985. *Preparing for Power: America's Elite Boarding Schools.* New York: Basic Books.

Cooley, Charles Horton. 1902. *Human Nature and the Social Order.* New York: Scribner's.

Cooley, Charles Horton. 1909. *Social Organization.* New York: Scribner's.

Coon, Carleton S. 1982. *Racial Adaptation.* Chicago: Nelson-Hall.

Cooney, J. G. 1966. *The Potential Uses of Television in Preschool Education.* New York: Carnegie Corporation of New York.

Cooney, J. G., with L. Gottlieb. 1968. *Television for Preschool Children: A Proposal.* New York: Carnegie Corporation of New York.

Cornish, Edward. 1987. "The social consequences of AIDS." *The Futurist* 21(6):45–46.

Corr, Charles A. 1993. "Coping with dying: Lessons that we should and should not learn from the work of Elisabeth Kubler-Ross." *Death Studies* 17(1) (January/February): 69–83.

Correa, Hector, Mohammed Al El Torky, and Miriam K. Were. 1989. "Ecological upheavals with special reference to desertification and predicting health impact." *Social Science and Medicine* 18(3):357–367.

Corsaro, William. 1985. *Friendship and Peer Culture in the Early Years.* Norwood, NJ: Ablex.

Corsaro, William. 1992. "Interpretive reproduction in children's peer cultures." *Social Psychology Quarterly* 55:160–177.

Corsaro, William. 1997. *The Sociology of Childhood.* Thousand Oaks, Calif.: Pine Forge Press.

Corsaro, William, and Donna Eder. 1990. "Children's peer cultures. *Annual Review of Sociology* 16:197–220.

Corsaro, William, and T.A. Rizzo. 1988. "Discussion and friendship: Socialization processes in the peer culture of Italian nursery school children." *American Sociological Review* 53:879–894.

Coser, Lewis. 1956. *The Functions of Social Conflict.* New York: Free Press.

Costa, Joseph J. 1984. *Abuse of the Elderly: A Guide to Resources and Services.* Lexington, Mass.: D. C. Heath.

Cottrell, Fred. 1974. *Aging and the Aged.* Dubuque, Iowa: William C. Brown.

Cowgill, Donald O. 1986. *Aging around the World.* Belmont, Calif.: Wadsworth.

Cox, Christopher. 1983. "Second marriages: Better while they last." *Psychology Today* (February): 72.

Cox, Harold G. 1996. *Later Life: The Realities of Aging.* Upper Saddle River, N.J.: Prentice Hall.

Cressey, Donald R. 1953. *Other People's Money: A Study in the Social Psychology of Embezzlement.* Montclair, N.J.: Patterson Smith.

Crewdson, John. 1988. *By Silence Betrayed: Sexual Abuse of Children in America.* Boston: Little, Brown.

Crohn, Joel. 1995. *Mixed Matches.* New York: Fawcett Columbine.

Crosbie, Paul V. (ed.). 1975. *Interaction in Small Groups.* New York: Macmillan.

Croteau, David, and William Hoynes. 1997. *Media/Society: Industries, Images, and Audiences.* Thousand Oaks, Calif.: Pine Forge Press.

Crouse, James, and Dale Trusheim. 1988. "The case against the SAT." *The Public Interest* 93 (Fall): 97–110.

Crouter, Ann C., and Maureen Perry-Jenkins. 1986. "The impact of working mothers on children's attitudes and gender development." In Michael W. Yogman and T. Berry Brazelton (eds.), *In Support of Families.* Cambridge, Mass.: Harvard University Press.

Cruse, Harold. 1987. *Plural but Equal: A Critical Study of Blacks and Minorities in America's Plural Society.* New York: Morrow.

Crystal, David. 1988. *The Cambridge Encyclopedia of Language.* New York: Cambridge University Press.

Culver, Lowell W. 1979. "America's troubled cities: Better times ahead?" *The Futurist* (August): 275–286.

Cumming, Elaine, and William E. Henry. 1961. *Growing Old: The Process of Disengagement.* New York: Basic Books.

Curran, Jeanne, and Carol Telesky. 1980. *Up the Job Market: Controlling the Ascent.* Washington, D.C.: American Sociological Association.

Currie, Elliot, and Jerome Skolnick. 1984. *America's Problems.* Boston: Little, Brown.

Curtis, Richard, and Elton Jackson. 1977. *Inequality in American Communities.* New York: Academic Press.

Cyert, Richard, and David Mowery. 1989. "Technology, employment, and U.S. competitiveness." *Scientific American* 260(5):54–62.

Dahl, Robert. 1961. *Who Governs? Democracy and Power in an American City.* New Haven, Conn.: Yale University Press.

Dahl, Robert. 1990. "Social reality and 'free' markets." *Dissent* (Spring): 224–228.

Dahrendorf, Ralf. 1958. "Out of utopia: Toward a reorganization of sociological analysis." *American Journal of Sociology* 64:115–127.

Dahrendorf, Ralf. 1959. *Class and Class Conflict in Industrial Society.* Stanford, Calif.: Stanford University Press.

Dalgard, Odd Steffen, and Einar Kringlen. 1976. "A Norwegian twin study of criminality." *British Journal of Criminality* 16(3):213–232.

Dambrot, Faye H., Diana C. Reep, and Daniel Bell. 1988. "Television sex roles in the 1980s: Do viewers' sex and sex role orientation change the picture?" *Sex Roles* 19:387–401.

Daniels, Roger. 1988. *Asian America: Chinese and Japanese in the U.S. since 1850.* Seattle: University of Washington Press.

Daniels, Roger, and Harry H. L. Kitano. 1970. *American Racism: Exploration of the Nature of Prejudice.* Englewood Cliffs, N.J.: Prentice Hall.

Daniloff, Nicholas. 1983. "The posh world of Russia's ruling class." *U.S. News & World Report,* September 5, pp. 43–44.

Darby, John, Nicholas Dodge, and A. C. Hepburn (eds.). 1990. *Political Violence: Ireland in Comparative Perspective.* Ottawa: University of Ottawa Press.

Darden, Joe T. 1989. "Afro-American inequality within the urban structure of the United States, 1967–1987." *Journal of Developing Societies* 5(1):1–14.

Darwin, Charles. 1859. *On the Origin of Species.*

Da Silva, Tomaz Tadeu. 1988. "Distribution of school knowledge and social reproduction in a Brazilian urban setting." *British Journal of Sociology of Education* 9:55–79.

Dautrich, Ken, and Jennifer Necci Dineen. 1996. "When is a poll newsworthy?" *The Media and Campaign 96 Briefing by the Media Studies Center No. 3* (September). New York: Media Studies Center.

Davies, James C. 1969. "The J-curve of rising and declining satisfactions as a cause of some great revolutions and a contained rebellion." In H.D. Graham and T.R. Gurr (eds.), *Violence in America.* New York: Bantam.

Davis, James A., and Tom W. Smith. 1983. *General Social Survey Cumulative File, 1972–1982.* Ann Arbor, Mich.: Inter-University Consortium for Political and Social Research.

Davis, James, and Tom W. Smith. 1986. *General Social Surveys: 1972–1986.* Storrs, Conn.: National Opinion Research Center.

Davis, Karen. 1986. "Aging and the health-care system: Economic and structural issues." *Daedalus* 115 (Winter): 227–246.

Davis, Kingsley. 1940. "Extreme social isolation of a child." *American Journal of Sociology* 45:554–565.

Davis, Kingsley. 1947. "A final note on a case of extreme isolation." *American Journal of Sociology* 52:432–437.

Davis, Kingsley. 1955. "The origin and growth of urbanization in the world." *American Journal of Sociology* 60:431.

Davis, Kingsley (ed.). 1985. *Contemporary Marriage.* New York: Russell Sage Foundation.

Davis, Kingsley, and Judith Blake. 1956. "Social structure and fertility: An analytic framework." *Economic Development and Cultural Change* 4 (April): 211–235.

Davis, Kingsley, and Wilbert Moore. 1945. "Some principles of stratification." *American Sociological Review* 10:242–249.

Davis, Robert C. 1987. "Studying the effects of services for victims in crisis." *Crime and Delinquency* 33:520–531.

Dawkins, Richard. 1976. *The Selfish Gene.* New York: Oxford University Press.

Dawson, Carl A., and Werner E. Gettys. 1948. *An Introduction to Sociology.* New York: Ronald Press.

Deal, Terrence E., and Allan A. Kennedy. 1982. *Corporate Cultures: The Rites and Rituals of Corporate Life.* Reading, Mass.: Addison-Wesley.

Dedman, Bill. 1998. "It isn't just big brother who is watching." *New York Times,* January 12, p. C3.

Demerath, N.J. III, and Phillip E. Hammond. 1969. *Religion in Social Context: Tradition and Transition.* New York: Random House.

Demo, David H., and Alan C. Acock. 1988. "The impact of divorce on children." *Journal of Marriage and the Family* 50:619–648.

Dennis, Everette E. 1989. *Reshaping the Media: Mass Communication in an Information Age.* Newbury Park, Calif.: Sage.

DeNora, Tina. 1986. "How is extra-musical meaning possible? Music as a place and space for 'work.'" *Sociological Theory* 4:84–94.

Denzin, Norman K. 1978. *The Research Act.* New York: McGraw-Hill.

Denzin, Norman K. 1984. "Retrieving the small social group." In N. K. Denzin (ed.), *Studies in Interaction* (Vol. 15). Greenwich, Conn.: JAI Press.

Denzin, Normal K. 1986a. "Behaviorism and beyond." *Contemporary Sociology* 15:553–556.

Denzin, Norman K. 1986b. *The Recovering Alcoholic.* Beverly Hills, Calif.: Sage.

Denzin, Norman K., and Charles M. Keller. 1981. "Frame analysis reconsidered." *Contemporary Sociology* 10(1):52–60.

Derber, Charles, and William Schwartz. 1988. "Toward a theory of worker participation." In Frank Hearn (ed.), *The Transformation of Industrial Organization.* Belmont, Calif.: Wadsworth.

DeStefano, Linda. 1990. "Church synagogue membership and attendance levels remain stable." *The Gallup Poll Monthly* (January): 32–33.

de Toqueville, Alexis. 1945. Democracy in America. 2 vols. New York: Knopf.

Deviney, Stanley, and Angela M. O'Rand. 1988. "Gender-cohort succession and retirement among older men and women, 1951 to 1984." *Sociological Quarterly* 29:525–540.

Diamond, Milton. 1982. "Sexual identity: Monozygotic twins reared in discordant sex roles and a BBC follow-up." *Archives of Sexual Behavior* 11:181–186.

DiCanio, Margaret. 1989. *The Encyclopedia of Marriage, Divorce, and the Family.* New York: Facts on File.

Digest of Education Statistics. 1997. "The annual Gallup poll of the public's attitudes toward the public schools."

Dilip, Hiro. 1985. *Iran under the Ayatollahs.* New York: Praeger.

Dinnerstein, Dorothy. 1977. *The Mermaid and the Minotaur: Sexual Arrangements and Human Malaise.* New York: Harper & Row.

Dion, K., et al. 1972. "What is beautiful is good." *Journal of Personality and Social Psychology* 24:285–290.

DiPrete, Thomas A., and Whitman T. Soule. 1988. "Gender and promotion in segmented job ladder systems." *American Sociological Review* 53:26–40.

Dobbins, Gregory H., Robert L. Cardy, and Donald M. Truxillo. 1986. "Effect of ratee sex and purpose of appraisal on the accuracy of performance evaluations." *Basic and Applied Psychology* 7:225–241.

Domhoff, G. William. 1978. *Who Really Rules?* New Brunswick, N.J.: Transaction.

Domhoff, G. William. 1983. *Who Rules America Now?* Englewood Cliffs, N.J.: Prentice Hall.

Domhoff, G. William. 1990. *The Power Elite and the State: How Policy Is Made in America.* New York: Aldine.

Domhoff, G. William. 1998. *Who Rules America? Power and Politics in the Year 2000,* 3rd ed. Mountain View, Calif.: Mayfield.

Donaldson, Scott. 1969. *The Suburban Myth.* New York: Columbia University Press.

Douglas, Jack D., et al. 1980. *Introduction to the Sociology of Everyday Life.* Boston: Allyn & Bacon.

Dowse, Robert, and John Hughes. 1972. *Political Sociology.* New York: Wiley.

Dreeban, Robert. 1968. *On What Is Learned in Schools.* Reading, Mass.: Addison-Wesley.

D'Souza, Neila, and Ramini Natarjan. 1986. "Women in India: The reality." In Lynn B. Iglitzin and Ruth Ross (eds.), *Women in the World, 1975–1985: The Women's Decade.* Santa Barbara, Calif.: ABC-Clio.

Dubin, Robert, and Daniel Goldman. 1972. "Central life interests of American middle managers and specialists." *American Journal of Vocational Behavior* 2:133–141.

Duley, Margot I. 1986. "Women in India." In Margot I. Duley and Mary I. Edwards (eds.), *The Cross-Cultural Study of Women: A Comprehensive Guide.* New York: Feminist Press.

Duncan, Greg. 1984. *Years of Poverty, Years of Plenty.* Ann Arbor, Mich.: Institute for Social Research.

Duncan, G., M. Hill, and S. Hoffman. 1990. "Welfare dependents within and across generations." *Science* 239:467–471.

Duncan, Otis Dudley. 1959. "Human ecology and population." In Philip M. Hauser and Otis Dudley Duncan, *The Study of Population.* Chicago: University of Chicago Press.

Duncan, Otis Dudley. 1961. "From social system to ecosystem." *Sociological Inquiry* 31 (Spring): 140–149.

Dunlap, Riley E., and William R. Catton, Jr. 1979. "Environmental sociology." *Annual Review of Sociology* 5.

Durkheim, Émile. 1915. *The Elementary Forms of the Religious Life.* Translated by Joseph Ward Swain. New York: Macmillan.

Durkheim, Émile. 1950. *The Rules of Sociological Method.* Glencoe, Ill.: Free Press. (Originally published in 1894.)

Durkheim, Émile. 1950. *Suicide.* Glencoe, Ill.: Free Press. (Originally published in 1897.)

Durkheim, Émile. 1893. *The Division of Labor in Society.* New York: Free Press.

Dutton, Diane. 1989. "Social class, health, and illness." In Phil Brown (ed.), *Perspectives in Medical Sociology.* Belmont, Calif.: Wadsworth.

Dye, Thomas. 1986. *Who's Running America?* Englewood Cliffs, N.J.: Prentice Hall.

Dye, Thomas. 1995. *Who's Running America? The Clinton Years.* Upper Saddle River, N.J.: Prentice Hall.

Dye, Thomas R. 1990. *Who's Running America: The Bush Era,* 5th ed. Englewood Cliffs, N.J.: Prentice Hall.

Easterlin, Richard A. 1980. *Birth and Fortune: The Impact of Numbers on Personal Welfare.* New York: Basic Books.

Easterlin, Richard A., and Ellen M. Crimmins. 1988. *Fertility Revolution.* Chicago: University of Chicago Press.

Eder, Donna. 1991. The Role of Teasing in Adolescent Peer Culture. Pp. 181–97, in *Sociological Studies of Child Development*, vol. 4, ed. S. Cahill. Greenwich, Conn.: JAI Press.

Eder, Donna, with Catherine Colleen Evans and Stephen Parker. 1995. *School Talk: Gender and Adolescent Culture.* New Brunswick, N.J.: Rutgers University Press.

Edidin, Peter. 1989. "Perros caliente." *Psychology Today* 23:36.

Edmonds, T. R. 1976. "On the mortality of infants in London." *Lancet* 1 (1835):692.

Edsall, Thomas. 1984. *The New Politics of Inequality.* New York: Norton.

Edsall, Thomas, and Mary Edsall. 1991. *Chain Reaction.* New York: Norton.

Edwards, Richard. 1979. *Contested Terrain.* New York: Basic Books.

Ehrenhaus, Peter. 1989. "Commemorating the unknown war: On not remembering Vietnam." *Journal of Communication* 39:96–107.

Ehrlich, Paul. 1968. *The Population Bomb.* New York: Ballantine Books, pp. 22–23.

Ehrlich, Paul R., and Anne H. Ehrlich. 1972. *Population, Resources, Environment: Issues in Human Ecology,* 2nd ed. San Francisco: Freeman.

Eisenstadt, S. N. 1956. From Generation to Generation. Glencoe, Ill.: Free Press.

Eisenstadt, S. N. 1971. Social Differentiation and Stratification. Glenview, Ill.: Scott, Foresman.

Eisenstadt, S. N. 1992. "The breakdown of communist regimes." *Daedalus* 121(2):21–41.

Eisenstadt, S. N., and Ora Ahimeir (eds.). 1985. *The Welfare State and Its Aftermath.* London: Croom Helm.

Ekman, P., and W. V. Friesen. 1971. "Constants across cultures in the face and emotion." *Journal of Personality and Social Psychology* 17:124–129.

Elam, Stanley M., and Alec M. Gallup. 1989. "The 21st annual Gallup Poll of the public's attitudes toward the public schools." *Gallup Monthly Report* (September):31ff.

Elder, Glen H. 1974. *Children of the Great Depression—Social Change in Life Experience.* Chicago: University of Chicago Press.

Elder, Glen H., Jr. 1975. "Age differentiation and the life course." *Annual Review of Sociology* 1.

Elkin, Frederick, and Gerald Handel. 1978. *The Child and Society,* 3rd ed. New York: Random House.

Elkind, David. 1968. "Giant in the nursery: Jean Piaget." *New York Times Magazine,* May 26.

Elkind, David. 1970 "Erik Erikson's eight ages of man." *New York Times Magazine,* April 5.

Elliott, John. 1985. *Comparative Economic Systems.* Belmont, Calif.: Wadsworth.

Elliott, Marta, and Lauren J. Krivo. 1991. "Structural determinants of homelessness in the United States." *Social Problems* 38:113–131.

Ellul, Jacques. 1966. *Propaganda: The Foundations of Men's Attitudes.* New York: Knopf.

Else, John F., and Martha J. Sanford. 1987. "Nonsexist language in social work journals: Not a trivial pursuit." *Social Work* 32:52–59.

Engels, Friedrich. 1977. *The Origin of the Family, Private Property and the State.* New York: International Publishers. (Originally published in 1884.)

England, Paula, and Lori McCreary. 1987. "Gender inequality in paid employment." In Beth B. Hess and Myrna Marx Ferree (eds.), *Analyzing Gender: A Handbook of Social Science Research.* Beverly Hills, Calif.: Sage.

Entertainment Weekly. 1996. April 12.

Entman, Robert. 1992. "Blacks in the news: Television, modern racism, and cultural change." *Journalism Quarterly* 69(2):341–361.

Entwisle, Doris R., Karl L. Alexander, Aaron M. Pallas, and Doris Cadigan. 1987. "The emergent academic self-image of first graders: Its response to social structure." *Child Development* 58:1190–1206.

Epstein, Cynthia Fuchs. 1986. "Symbolic segregation: Differences in the language and non-verbal communication of women and men." *Sociological Forum* 1:27–49.

Epstein, Cynthia Fuchs. 1988. *Deceptive Distinctions: Sex, Gender, and the*

Social Order. New Haven, Conn.: Yale University Press.

Ergas, Yasmine. 1987. "The social consequences of the AIDS epidemic." *Social Science Research Council* 41(3/4):33–39.

Erikson, Erik. 1963. *Childhood and Society,* 2nd ed. New York: Norton.

Erikson, Erik, 1982. *The Life Cycle Completed: A Review.* New York: Norton.

Erickson, Kai T. 1966. *Wayward Puritans.* New York: Wiley.

Erikson, Kai T. 1977. *Everything in Its Path.* New York: Simon & Schuster.

Erlanger, Howard S. 1974. "Social class and corporal punishment in child rearing: A reassessment." *American Sociological Review* 39:68–85.

Esping-Andersen, Gosta. 1985. *Politics against Markets: The Social Democratic Road to Power.* Princeton, N.J.: Princeton University Press.

Esping-Andersen, Gosta, and Walter Korpi. 1984. "Social policy as class politics in post-war capitalism: Scandinavia, Austria, and Germany," pp. 179–208. In John Goldthorpe (ed.), *Order and Conflict in Contemporary Capitalism.* New York: Clarendon Press.

Etzioni, Amitai. 1975. *A Comparative Analysis of Complex Organization: On Power, Involvement, and Their Correlates,* rev. ed. New York: Free Press.

Etzioni, Amitai. 1984. *Capital Corruption.* New York: Harcourt Brace Jovanovich.

Etzioni, Amitai. 1989. *The Moral Dimension.* New York: Free Press.

Etzioni, Amitai, and Edward W. Lehman. 1980. *Complex Organizations,* 3rd ed. New York: Holt, Rinehart & Winston.

Evans, Peter B., and Michael Timberlake. 1980. "Dependence, inequality, and the growth of the tertiary: A comparative analysis of less developed countries." *American Sociological Review* 45:531–552.

Eysenck, Hans. 1977. *Crime and Personality.* London: Routledge & Kegan Paul.

Falk, Richard. 1988. "Religion and politics: Verging on the postmodern." *Alternatives* 13:379–394.

Fallows, James. 1983. "Immigration: How it's affecting us." *Atlantic Monthly,* November, pp. 45–106.

Fallows, James. 1988. "A talent for disorder." *U.S. News & World Report,* 21 February 8, pp. 83–84.

Family Economics Review. 1989. "Population growth of the middle aged and elderly." 2:21.

Farley, John E. 1987. "Suburbanization and the central city crime rates: New evidence and a reinterpretation." *American Journal of Sociology* 93(3):688–700.

Farley, John E. 1995. *Majority-Minority Relations.* Upper Saddle River, N.J.: Prentice Hall.

Fausto-Sterling, Anne. 1986. *Myths of Gender: Biological Theories about Men and Women.* New York: Basic Books.

Fava, Sylvia F., and Rosalie G. Genovese. 1983. "Family, work, and individual development in dual-career marriages: Issues for research." *Research in the Interweave of Social Roles: Jobs and Families* 3:163–185.

Fawcett, James T., and Benjamin V. Carino. 1987. *Pacific Bridges: The New Immigration from Asia and the Pacific Islands.* New York: Center for Migration Studies.

Feagin, Joe R. 1989. *Racial and Ethnic Relations,* 3rd ed. Englewood Cliffs, N.J.: Prentice Hall.

Feagin, Joe R., and Clairece Booher Feagin. 1999. *Racial and Ethnic Relations,* 6th ed. Upper Saddle River, N.J.: Prentice Hall.

Feagin, Joe R., and Robert Parker. 1990. *Rebuilding American Cities: The Urban Real Estate Game,* 2nd ed. Englewood Cliffs, N.J.: Prentice Hall.

Feagin, Joe R., and Melvin Sikes. 1994. *Living with Racism.* Boston: Beacon.

Featherman, David L., and Robert M. Hauser. 1978. *Opportunity and Change.* New York: Academic Press.

Federal Bureau of Investigation. 1989. *Uniform Crime Reports, 1989.* Washington, D.C.: Government Printing Office.

Federal Bureau of Investigation, 1991. *Uniform Crime Reports, 1991.* Washington, D.C.: Government Printing Office.

Feinberg, Andrew. 1987. "Sleeping dragons." *Venture* 9(7):50–52.

Felson, Richard B. 1991. "Blame analysis: Accounting for the behavior of protected groups." *American Sociologist* 22(2):5–23.

Fennema, Elizabeth. 1976. "Women and girls in the public schools: Defeat or liberation?" In Joan J. Roberts, *Beyond Intellectual Sexism: a New Woman, a New Reality.* New York: McKay.

Fersko-Weiss, Henry. 1988. "A man, a ship, and a dream to sail by." *Sierra* 73:66–72.

Festinger, Leon. 1954. "A theory of social comparison processes." *Human Relations* 7:117–140.

Fichter, Joseph. 1951. *Southern Parish.* Chicago: University of Chicago Press.

Fichter, Joseph. 1954. *Social Relations in the Urban Parish.* Chicago: University of Chicago Press.

Filene, Peter. 1987. *Men in the Middle.* Englewood Cliffs, N.J.: Prentice Hall.

Filson, Glen G. 1988. "Ontario teachers' deprofessionalization and proletarianization." *Comparative Education Review* 32:298–317.

Fine, Mark, John Moreland, and Andrew I. Schwebel. 1984. "Long term effects of divorce on parent-child relationships." *Developmental Psychology* 19(5):703–713.

Finkelhor, David, and Linda Meyer Williams, with Nanci Burns. 1988. *Nursery Crimes: Sexual Abuse in Day Care.* Newbury Park, Calif.: Sage.

Finn, Chester, Jr. 1981. "Why public and private schools matter. Report analysis." *Harvard Educational Review* 51:483–525.

Firestone, Shulamith. 1971. *The Dialectic of Sex.* New York: Bantam.

Fischer, Claude S. 1975. "Toward a subcultural theory of urbanism." *American Journal of Sociology* 80(6):1319–1341.

Fischer, Claude S. 1981. "The public and private worlds of city life." *American Sociological Review* 46(2):306–316.

Fischer, Claude S. 1982. *To Dwell among Friends: Personal Networks in Town and City.* Chicago: University of Chicago Press.

Fischer, Claude S. 1984. *The Urban Experience,* 2nd ed. New York: Harcourt Brace Jovanovich.

Fischer, Claude S., et al. 1975. "Crowding studies and urban life: A critical review." *Journal of the American Institute of Planners* 41 (November): 406–418.

Fischer, Claude S., et al. 1977. *Networks and Places.* New York: Free Press.

Fischer, David H. 1978. *Growing Old in America,* exp. ed. New York: Oxford University Press.

Fischer, Frank. 1984. "Ideology and organization theory." In Frank Fischer and C. Siriani (eds.), *Organization* and Bureaucracy. Philadelphia: Temple University Press.

Fischman, Joshua. 1986. "A journey of hearts and minds." *Psychology Today* (July): 42–47.

Fishman, Robert. 1987. *Bourgeois Utopias.* New York: Basic Books.

Fitch, Ed. 1987. "Is red carpet treatment plush enough?" *Direct Marketing* 50:20–21.

Foner, Anne, and Karen Schwab. 1981. *Aging and Retirement.* Monterey, Calif.: Brooks/Cole.

Fontana, Lynn. 1988. "Television and the social studies." *Social Education* 52:348–350.

Foote, Nelson. 1953. "Love." *Psychiatry* 16:247.

Forbes. 1998. October 12.

Ford, F. Scott. 1986. "Favorable intergroup contact may not reduce prejudice: Inconclusive journal evidence, 1960–1984." *Sociology and Social Research* 70:256–258.

Ford Foundation. 1989. *Social Welfare and the American Future.* New York: Ford Foundation.

Ford, Ramona. 1988. *Work, Organization and Power.* Boston: Allyn & Bacon.

Fore, William F. 1987. *Television and Religion: The Shaping of Faith, Values, and Culture.* Minneapolis: Augsburg.

Form, William, and Kyu Han Bae. 1988. "Convergence theory and the Korean connection." *Social Forces* 66:618–640.

Foss, Daniel A., and Ralph Larkin. 1986. *Beyond Revolution. A New Theory of Movements.* South Hadley, Mass.: Bergin & Garvey.

Fox, Daniel. 1987. "The cost of AIDS from conjecture to research." *AIDS and Public Policy Journal* 2:25–27.

Fox, Kenneth. 1986. *Metropolitan America: Urban Life and Urban Policy in the United States 1940–1980.* Jackson: University of Mississippi Press.

Fox, Mary F. 1995. "Women and higher education: Gender differences in the status of students and scholars." In Jo Freeman, ed., *Women: A Feminist Perspective.* Mountain View, Calif.: Mayfield.

Fox, Renee C. 1989. *The Sociology of Medicine.* Englewood Cliffs, N.J.: Prentice Hall.

Fox, Thomas G., and S.M. Miller. 1965. "Economic, political and social determinants of mobility: An international cross-sectional analysis." *Acta Sociologica* 9:76–93.

Fox, Stephen. 1983. *The Mirror Makers: A History of American Advertising and Its Creators.* New York: Vintage.

Francome, Colin. 1984. *Abortion Practice in Britain and the United States.* London: Allen & Unwin.

Frank, A. G. 1969. *Latin America: Underdevelopment and Revolution.* New York: Monthly Review.

Franke, Richard H., and James D. Kaul. 1978. "The Hawthorne experiments: First statistical interpretation." *American Sociological Review* 43:623–643.

Frankl, Razelle. 1987. *Televangelism: The Marketing of Popular Religion.* Carbondale: Southern Illinois University Press.

Frantz, Douglas. 1998. "Scientology's star roster enhances image." *New York Times,* February 13, A1, A18.

Freedman, Jonathan J. 1975. *Crowding and behavior.* San Francisco: Freeman.

Freeman, James M. 1989. *Hearts of Sorrow: Vietnamese-American Lives.* Stanford, Calif.: Stanford University Press.

Freeman, Richard, and James Medoff. 1984. *What Do Unions Do?* New York: Basic Books.

Freeze, Jill T., and Wayne T. Freeze. 1998. *Introducing Webtv.* Redmond, Wash.: Microsoft Press.

Freidson, Eliot. 1970. *Profession of Medicine.* New York: Dodd, Mead.

Freidson, Eliot. 1979. "The organization of medical practice." In Howard E. Freeman, Sol Levine, and Leo G. Reeder (eds.), *Handbook of Medical Sociology,* 3rd ed. Englewood Cliffs, N.J.: Prentice Hall.

Freud, Sigmund. 1962. *Civilization and Its Discontents.* Translated by James Strachey. New York: Norton. (Originally published in 1930.)

Frey, William, and Alden Speare, Jr. 1988. *Regional and Metropolitan Growth and Decline in the United States.* New York: Russell Sage Foundation.

Friedan, Betty. 1963. *The Feminine Mystique.* New York: Norton.

Friedan, Betty. 1981. *The Second Stage.* New York: Summit.

Frieden, Bernard J. 1980. "Housing allowances: An experiment that worked." *The Public Interest* 69:15–35.

Friedlander, Walter A., and Robert Z. Apte. 1980. *Introduction to Social Welfare,* 5th ed. Englewood Cliffs, N.J.: Prentice Hall.

Frost, Peter. 1986. "Skin color preference, sexual dimorphism, and sexual selection: A case of gene culture co-evolution?" *Ethnic and Racial Studies* 9:87–113.

Frost, Richard, and John Stauffer. 1987. "The effects of social class, gender, and personality on physiological responses to filmed violence." *Journal of Communication* 37:29–45.

Fuchs, Victor R. 1988. *Women's Quest for Economic Equality.* Cambridge, Mass.: Harvard University Press.

Gabrielli, William, Barry Hutchings, and Sarnoff Mednick. 1984. "Genetic influences in criminal convictions: Evidence from an adoption cohort." *Science* 224:891–894.

Gaensbauer, Theodore, and Susan Hiatt. 1984. *The Psychobiology of Affective Development.* Hillsdale, N.J.: Laurence Erlbaum.

Gale, Robert Peter. 1987. "Calculating risk: Radiation and Chernobyl." *Journal of Communication* 37:68–75.

Galinsky, Ellen. 1986. "Family life and corporate politics." In Michael W. Yogman and T. Berry Brazelton (eds.), *In Support of Families.* Cambridge, Mass.: Harvard University Press.

Galinsky, Ellen. 1989. "A case for intergenerational child care." *Journal of Children in Contemporary Society* 20:239–243.

Galle, Omar R., et al. 1972. "Population density and pathology: What are the relations for man?" *Science* (April): 23–30.

Gallup, Alec M., and David L. Clark. 1987. "The 19th annual Gallup poll of the public's attitudes toward the public schools." *Phi Delta Kappan* (September): 17–30.

Gallup, George H. 1983. *The Gallup Poll: Public Opinion, 1983.* Wilmington, Del.: Scholarly Resources.

Gallup, George, Jr., and Alec Gallup. 1988. *The Gallup Youth Survey.* Princeton, N.J.: Associated Press.

Gallup Organization. 1988a. As reported by *Emerging Trends* 10:1. Princeton, N.J.: Princeton Religious Research Center.

Gallup Organization. 1988b. As reported by *Emerging Trends* 10:4. Princeton, N.J.: Princeton Religious Research Center.

Gallup Organization. 1988d. "The undivided American—10 years later." As reported in *Emerging Trends* 10:12. Princeton, N.J.: Princeton Religious Research Center.

Gallup Organization. 1989. *Religion in America.* Princeton, N.J.: Princeton Religious Research Center.

Gallup Poll Monthly. 1990. *Twenty-Fifth Anniversary Edition.* Princeton, N.J.: The Gallup Poll.

Gallup Poll. 1991. August.

Gallup Poll. 1997. Many women cite spousal abuse; job performance affected.

Gallup Poll. 1998. Most Americans would soften U.S. military's rules against adultery. June 13. August.

Gann, L. H., and Peter J. Duignan. 1986. *The Hispanic in the United States: A History.* Boulder, Colo.: Westview.

Gans, Herbert J. 1962a. *The Urban Villagers.* New York: Free Press.

Gans, Herbert J. 1962b. "Urbanism and suburbanism as ways of life." In Arnold M. Rose (ed.), *Human Behavior and Social Processes: An Interactionist Approach.* Boston: Houghton Mifflin.

Gans, Herbert J. 1971. "The uses of poverty: The poor pay all. *Social Policy* 2: 21–23.

Gans, Herbert J. 1980. *Deciding What's News.* New York: Vintage Books.

Garbarino, J. 1989. "The incidence and prevalence of child maltreatment. In *Family Violence,* eds. L. Ohlin and M. Tonry, pp. 219–261. Chicago: University of Chicago Press.

Gardner, R. A., and B. T. Gardner. 1975. "Early signs of language in child and chimpanzee." *Science* 187:752–753.

Garfinkel, Harold. 1967. *Studies in Ethnomethodology.* Englewood Cliffs, N.J.: Prentice Hall.

Garfinkel, Irwin, and Sara S. McLanahan. 1986. *Single Mothers and Their Children: A New American Dilemma.* Washington, D.C.: Urban Institute Press.

Garreau, Joel. 1992. *Edge City: Life on the New Frontier.* New York: Anchor Books.

Garten, Helen A. 1987. "Insider trading in the corporate interest." *Wisconsin Law Review* 4:573–640.

Geiger, Jack. 1971. "Poor hungry babies." *New South* 26:4.

Gelles, Richard J. 1978. "Violence in the American family." In J.P. Martin (ed.),

Violence and the Family. New York: Wiley.

Gelles, Richard J., and Murray A. Straus. 1988. *Intimate Violence: The Definitive Study of the Causes and Consequences of Abuse in the American Family.* New York: Simon & Schuster.

General Social Surveys 1972–1988: Cumulative Codebook. 1988. Storrs, Conn.: Roper Center for Public Opinion Research, University of Connecticut.

Genevie, Louis E. (ed.). 1975. *Collective Behavior and Social Movements.* Itasca, Ill.: Peacock.

Gerard, Karen. 1984. *American Survivors.* New York: Harcourt Brace Jovanovich.

Gerson, Mary Joan. 1984. "Feminism and the wish for a child." *Sex Roles* 11:389–397.

Gibbons, Don C. 1977. *Society, Crime, and Criminal Careers,* 3rd ed. Englewood Cliffs, N.J.: Prentice Hall.

Gibbons, Don C., and Joseph F. Jones. 1975. *The Study of Deviance.* Englewood Cliffs, N.J.: Prentice Hall.

Gibbs, Jack. 1966. "Sanctions." *Social Problems* 14:147–159.

Gibbs, Jack P. 1975. *Crime, Punishment and Deterrence.* New York: Elsevier.

Gibbs, Jack P. 1981. *Norms, Deviance, and Social Control.* New York: Elsevier.

Gibson, Margaret A., and Parminder K. Bhachu. 1988. "Ethnicity and school performance: A comparative study of South Asian pupils in Britain and America." *Ethnic and Racial Studies* 11:239–262.

Gilbert, Alan, and Joseph Gugler. 1983. *Cities, Poverty, and Development.* New York: Oxford University Press.

Gilbert, Dennis, and Joseph A. Kahl. 1992. *The American Class Structure: A New Synthesis,* 4th ed. Belmont, Calif.: Wadsworth.

Gill, Lesley. 1987. *Peasants, Entrepreneurs, and Social Change: Frontier Development in Lowland Bolivia.* Boulder, Colo.: Westview.

Gill, Stephen, and David Law. 1988. *Global Political Economy: Perspectives, Problems, and Policies.* Baltimore: Johns Hopkins University Press.

Gillette, Howard, Jr., and Zanel Miller (eds.). 1987. *American Urbanism.* Westport, Conn.: Greenwood Press.

Gilligan, Carol. 1993. *In a Different Voice.* Cambridge, Mass.: Harvard University Press.

Gilligan, Carol, Janie Victoria Ward, and Jill McLean Taylor (eds.). 1989. *Mapping the Moral Domain.* Camabridge, Mass.: Harvard University Press.

Ginsberg, Benjamin. 1984. "Money and power: The new political economy of American elections." In T. Ferguson and J. Rogers (eds.), *The Political Economy.* Armonk, N.Y.: M. E. Sharpe.

Ginsberg, Benjamin. 1986. *The Captive Public: How Mass Opinion Promotes State Power.* New York: Basic Books.

Girouard, Mark. 1985. *Cities and People: A Social and Architectural History.* New Haven, Conn.: Yale University Press.

Giroux, H. A. 1994. "Educational reform and the politics of teacher empowerment." In Joseph Kretovics and Edward J. Nussel (eds.), *Transforming Urban Education.* Boston: Allyn & Bacon.

Gitlin, Todd. 1980. *The Whole World Is Watching.* Berkeley: University of California Press.

Gitlin, Todd. 1987. *The Sixties: Years of Hope, Days of Rage.* New York: Bantam.

Glass, Ruth. 1989. *Cliches of Doom and Other Essays.* New York: Basil Blackwell.

Glenn, N. D. 1982. "Interreligious marriage in the United States: Patterns and recent trends. *Journal of Marriage and the Family* 44 (August): 555–566.

Glenn, Norval D. 1987. "The trend in 'no religion' respondents to U.S. national surveys: Late 1950s to early 1960s." *Public Opinion Quarterly* 51:293–314.

Glenn, Norval D., and Charles N. Weaver. 1981. "The contribution of marital happiness to global happiness." *Journal of Marriage and the Family* 43:161–168.

Glick, Paul C. 1990. "American families: As they are and were." *Social Science Research* 74(3):139–145.

Glock, Charles Y. 1959. "The religious revival in America." In Jane Zahn (ed.), *Religion and the Face of America.* Berkeley: University of California Press.

Glock, Charles Y. 1964. "The role of deprivation in the origin and evolution of religious groups." In Robert Lee and Martin Marty (eds.), *Religion and Social Conflict.* New York: Oxford University Press.

Glock, Charles Y., and Robert N. Bellah (eds.). 1976. *The New Religious Consciousness.* Berkeley: University of California Press.

Gluckman, Tim Jacob. 1988. "The census and data privacy." *Network* 42:7–8.

Goffman, Erving. 1959. *The Presentation of Self in Everyday Life.* New York: Anchor.

Goffman, Erving. 1961. *Asylums: Essays on the Social Situation of Mental Patients and Other Inmates.* Chicago: Aldine.

Goffman, Erving. 1971. *Relations in Public.* New York: Basic Books.

Goffman, Erving. 1976. *Gender Advertisements.* New York: Harper & Row.

Goffman, Erving. 1980. Reprint of 1963 ed. *Behavior in Public Places.* Westport, Conn.: Greenwood Press.

Goffman, Erving. 1986. *Encounters: Two Studies in the Sociology of Interaction.* New York: Macmillan.

Goldsmith, Seth. 1984. *Theory Z Hospital Management: Lessons from Japan.* Rockville, Md.: Aspen Systems Corp.

Goldthorpe, John H. 1987. *Social Mobility and Class Structure in Modern Britain,* 2nd ed. Oxford: Clarendon Press.

Golembiewski, Robert T. 1962. *The Small Group: An Analysis of Research Concepts and Operations.* Chicago: University of Chicago Press.

Goode, Erich. 1990. *Deviant Behavior,* 3rd ed. Englewood Cliffs, N.J.: Prentice Hall.

Goode, William J. 1959. "The theoretical importance of love." *American Sociological Review* 24(6):38–46.

Goode, William J. 1960. "Encroachment, charlatanism, and the emerging profession: Psychology, sociology, and medicine." *American Sociological Review* 25:902–914.

Goode, William J. 1963. *Revolution and Family Patterns.* New York: Free Press.

Goode, William J. 1982. *The Family,* 2nd ed. Englewood Cliffs, N.J.: Prentice Hall.

Goode, William J. 1984. "Individual investments in family relationships over the coming decades." *The Tocqueville Review* 6:51–83.

Goodstein, Laurie. 1997. "Has television found religion? Not exactly." *New York Times,* November 30, Arts and Leisure Sec., p. 37.

Goody, Jack. 1983. *The Development of the Family and Marriage in Europe.* Cambridge: Cambridge University Press.

Gordon, Milton M. 1964. *Assimilation in American Life.* New York: Oxford University Press.

Gorer, Geoffrey. 1965. *Death, Grief, and Mourning.* New York: Doubleday.

Gornick, Vivian. 1990. "Who says we haven't made a revolution?" *New York Times Magazine,* April 15, 1990.

Goslin, David A. 1965. *The School in Contemporary Society.* Glenview, Ill.: Scott, Foresman.

Gottdiener, Mark. 1985. *The Social Production of Urban Space.* Austin: University of Texas Press.

Gottfredson, Michael, and Travis Hirschi. 1990. *A General Theory of Crime.* Stanford, CA: Stanford University Press.

Gottman, Jean. 1964. *Megalopolis: The Urbanized Northeastern Seaboard of the United States.* Cambridge, Mass.: MIT Press.

Gough, Kathleen. 1975. "The origin of the family." In R.R. Reiter (ed.), *Toward an Anthropology of Women.* New York: Monthly Review Press.

Gould, M. S., and D. Shaffer. 1986. "The impact of suicide in television movies: Evidence of imitation." *New England Journal of Medicine* 315:690–694.

Gould, Stephen J. 1971. *Ever since Darwin: Reflections in Natural History.* New York: Norton.

Gould, Stephen J. 1981. *The Mismeasure of Man.* New York: Norton.

Gouldner, Alvin W. 1962. "Anti-minotaur: The myth of a value-free sociology." *Social Problems* 9:199–213.

Gouldner, Alvin. 1970. *The Coming Crisis of Western Sociology.* New York: Basic Books.

Gove, Walter R. 1985. "The effect of age and gender on deviant behavior: A biopsychosocial perspective." In Alice S. Rossi (ed.), *Gender and the Life Course.* New York: Aldine.

Gove, Walter, Michael Hughes, and Omar Galle. 1979. "Overcrowding in the home: An empirical investigation of the possible pathological consequences." *American Sociological Review* 44 (February): 59–80.

Graber, Steven (ed.). 1998. *Electronic Job Search: Almanac 1998.* Holbrook, MA: Adams Media Corporation.

Gracey, Harry L. 1970. "Kindergarten as academic boot camp." In Dennis Wrong and Harry L. Gracey (eds.), *Readings in Introductory Sociology,* 2nd ed. New York: Macmillan.

Graham, Sazon, and Leo G. Reeder. 1979. "Social epidemiology of chronic diseases." In Howard E. Freeman, Sol Levine, and Leo G. Reeder (eds.), *Handbook of Medical Sociology,* 3rd ed. Englewood Cliffs, N.J.: Prentice Hall.

Graham, Thomas W. 1988. "The pattern and importance of public knowledge in the nuclear age." *Journal of Conflict Resolution* 32(2):319–334.

Graña, César. 1987. "The bullfight and Spanish national decadence." *Society* 24:33–37.

Granovetter, Mark. 1973. "The strength of weak ties." *American Journal of Sociology* 78:1360–1380.

Grant, Carl, and Christine E. Sleeter. 1988. "Race, class, and gender and abandoned dreams." *Teachers College Record* 90:19–40.

Graumann, Carl F., and Serge Muscovici. 1986. *Changing Conceptions of Crowd Mind and Behavior.* New York: Springer-Verlag.

Gray, Francine du Plessix. 1990. *Soviet Women: Walking the Tightrope.* New York: Doubleday.

Grayson, Betty, and Morris I. Stein. 1981. "Attracting assault: Victim's nonverbal cues." *Journal of Communication* 31:68–75.

Greeley, Andrew M. 1989. *Religious Change in America.* Cambridge, Mass.: Harvard University Press.

Greenberg, David F. 1986. "Marxist criminology." In Bertell Ollman and Edward Vernoff (eds.), *The Left Academy: Marxist Scholarship on American Campuses,* Vol. 3. New York: Praeger.

Greene, Maxine, and Mary Anne Raywid. 1987. "Changing perspectives on schools and schooling." In Kenneth D. Benne and Steven Tozer (eds.), *Society as Educator in an Age of Transition.* 86th Yearbook of the National Society for the Study of Education. Chicago: University of Chicago Press.

Greer, Scott. 1956. "Urbanism reconsidered: A comparative study of local areas in a metropolis." *American Sociological Review* 21:19–25.

Gregory, Paul, and Robert Stuart. 1989. *Comparative Economic Systems.* Boston: Houghton Mifflin.

Gribben, John, and Mary Gribben. 1988. *The One Percent Advantage.* New York: Basil Blackwell.

Grier, George, and Eunice Grier. 1980. "Urban displacement: A reconnaissance." In S.B. Laska and D. Spain (eds.), *Back to the City.* New York: Pergamon.

Griffin, Keith. 1989. *Alternate Strategies for Economic Development.* New York: St. Martin's Press.

Gromkin, Victoria, Stephen Krashen, Susan Curtiss, David Rigler, and Marilyn Rigler. 1974. "The development of language in Genie: A case of language acquisition beyond the critical period." *Brain and Language* I:81–107.

Grossman, Andrew. 1989. "A radical departure." *Marketing and Media Decisions* 24:30.

Gugler, José (ed.). 1988. *Urbanization of the Third World.* New York: Oxford University Press.

Gummer, Burton. 1985–1986. "'Committing the truth': Whistle-blowing, organizational dissent, and the honorable bureaucrat." *Administration in Social Work* 9 (Winter): 89–102.

Guppy, Neil, and John C. Goyder. 1984. "Consensus on occupational prestige: A reassessment of evidence." *Social Forces* 62:709–723.

Gurr, Ted Robert. 1969. "A comparative study of civil strife." In H.D. Graham and T.R. Gurr (eds.), *Violence in America.* New York: Bantam.

Gurr, T. R. 1970. *Why Men Rebel.* Princeton, N.J.: Princeton University Press.

Gusfield, Joseph R., and Jerzy Michalowicz. 1984. "Secular symbolism: Studies of ritual, ceremony, and the symbolic order in modern life." *Annual Review of Sociology* 10:417–435.

Habermas, Jurgen. 1973. *Legitimation Crisis.* Boston: Beacon Press.

Hacker, Andrew. 1998. *Money: Who Has How Much and Why.* New York: Touchstone.

Hagen, Everett E. 1962. *On the Theory of Social Change.* Homewood, Ill.: Dorsey Press.

Hagestad, Gunhild. 1986. In A. Pifer and L. Bronte, *Our Aging Society: Paradox and Premise.* New York: Norton.

Haines, Herbert H. 1988. *Black Radicals and the Civil Rights Mainstream, 1954–1970.* Knoxville: University of Tennessee Press.

Halberstam, David. 1986. *The Reckoning.* New York: Morrow.

Hall, Edward T. 1966. *The Hidden Dimension.* New York: Doubleday.

Hall, Edward T. 1988. "The hidden dimension of time and space in today's world." In F. Poyatos (ed.), *Cross-Cultural Perspectives in Nonverbal Communication.* New York: Hogrefe.

Hall, G. Stanley. 1904. *Adolescence.* New York: Appleton.

Hall, Richard H. 1999. *Organizations: Structures, Processes, and Outcomes,* 7th ed. Upper Saddle River, N.J.: Prentice Hall.

Hallin, Daniel C. 1984. "The media, the war in Vietnam, and political support: A critique of the thesis of oppositional media." *Journal of Politics* 46:2–29.

Hammond, Margo. 1997. "Race and the nation." *St. Petersburg Times,* November 23, p. 6D.

Hammond, Phillip E. (ed.). 1985. *The Sacred in a Secular Age.* Berkeley: University of California Press.

Hammond, Phillip E. 1988. "Religion and the persistence of identity." *Journal for the Scientific Study of Religion* 27:1–11.

Handy, Charles. 1995. *Gods of Management: The Changing Work of Organizations.* New York: Oxford University Press.

Hannan, Michael T., and John H. Freeman. 1989. *Organizational Ecology.* Cambridge, Mass.: Harvard University Press.

Hansell, Saul. 1997. "Money starts to show in Internet shopping." *New York Times,* December 1, C1, C4.

Hare, A. Paul. 1962. *Handbook of Small Group Research.* New York: Free Press.

Hare, A. Paul. 1976. *Handbook of Small Group Research,* 2nd ed. New York: Free Press.

Harf, James L. 1986. *The Politics of Global Resources: Population, Food, Energy, and Environment.* Durham, N.C.: Duke University Press.

Harkins, Stephen G., and Kate Szymanski. 1989. "Social loafing and group evaluation." *Journal of Personality and Social Psychology* 56:934–941.

Harlow, Harry F. 1959. "Love in infant monkeys." *Scientific American* 200:68–74.

Harlow, Harry F. 1962. "The heterosexual affectional system in monkeys." *American Psychologist* 17:1–19.

Harlow, Harry F. 1965. "Sexual behavior in the rhesus monkey." In Frank A. Beach (ed.), *Sex and Behavior.* New York: Wiley.

Harman, Willis. 1988. *Global Mind Change.* Sausalito, Calif.: Knowledge Systems.

Harmon, Amy. 1997. "On the office PC, bosses opt for all work, and no play." *New York Times,* September 22, A1, C11.

Harper, Charles L. 1989. *Exploring Social Change.* Englewood Cliffs, N.J.: Prentice Hall.

Harris, C. C. 1983. *The Family and Industrial Society.* London: Allen & Unwin.

Harris, Chauncey, and Edward L. Ullman. 1945. "The nature of cities." *Annals of the American Academy of Political and Social Science* 242 (November): 7–17.

Harris, Louis. 1987. *Inside America.* New York: Vintage.

Harris, Louis, and associates. 1991. "The first year: New teachers' expectations and ideals. From *Teacher Survey.* Boston: Massachusetts Teachers' Association.

Harris, Marvin. 1977. *Cannibals and Kings: The Origins of Cultures.* New York: Random House.

Harris, Marvin. 1988. *Culture, People, and Nature,* 5th ed. New York: Harper & Row.

Harris, Marvin. 1989. *Our Kind.* New York: Harper & Row.

Harris, T., M. G. Kovar, R. Suzman, J. C. Klein, and J. J. Feldman. 1989. "Longitudinal study of physical ability in the oldest old." *American Journal of Public Health* 79:698–702.

Harrison, Bennett, and Barry Bluestone. 1988. *The Great U-Turn: Corporate Restructuring and the Polarization of America.* New York: Basic Books.

Harrison, J. Richard. and Glenn R. Carroll. 1991. "Keeping the faith: A model of cultural transmission in formal organizations." *Administrative Science Quarterly* 36:552–582.

Harrison, Paul. 1984. *Inside the Third World: The Anatomy of Poverty.* New York: Penguin Books.

Hartmann, Heidi. 1976. "Comment on Marnie W. Mueller's 'The economic determinants of volunteer work by women.'" *Signs: Journal of Women in Culture and Society* 1:773–776.

Harvey, David. 1989. *The Condition of Postmodernity.* New York: Basil Blackwell.

Hastings, Philip K., and Elizabeth Hann Hastings. 1989. *Index to International*

Public Opinion, 1987–1988. New York: Greenwood Press.

Hastings, Philip K., and Elizabeth Hann Hastings. 1991. *Index to International Public Opinion, 1987–1988.* New York: Greenwood Press.

Hastings, Philip K., and Dean R. Hoge. 1986. "Religious and moral attitude trends among college students, 1948–1984." *Social Forces* 65:370–377.

Hatcher, R. A., F. Stewart, J. Trussell, D. Kowal, F. Guest, G. K. Stewart, and W. Cates. 1994. *Contraceptive Technology,* 16th ed. New York: Irvington Publishers.

Haub, Carl. 1989. "Understanding population projections." *Population Bulletin* 42:4.

Havighurst, Robert J., and Bernice L. Neugarten. 1978. *Society and Education,* 5th ed. Boston: Allyn & Bacon.

Havighurst, Robert J., Bernice L. Neugarten, and Sheldon S. Tobin. 1968. "Disengagement and patterns of aging." In Bernice L. Neugarten (ed.), *Middle Age and Aging.* Chicago: University of Chicago Press.

Hawkins, John N. 1988. "The transformation of education for rural development in China." *Comparative Education Review* 32:266–281.

Hawley, Amos. 1950. *Human Ecology.* New York: Ronald Press.

Hawley, A. 1981. Urban Society, 2nd ed. New York: Wiley.

Hayes, Robert, and William Abernathy. 1988. "Managing our way to economic decline," pp. 129–139. In Frank Hearn (ed.), *The Transformation of Industrial Organization.* Belmont, Calif.: Wadsworth.

Hazelrigg, L. E., and M. A. Garnier. 1976. "Occupational mobility in industrialized societies: A comparable analysis of differential access to occupational ranks in seventeen countries." *American Sociological Review* 41:498–511.

Health, United States, 1998. 1999. U.S. Department of Health and Human Services.

Hearn, Frank. 1985. *Reason and Freedom in Sociological Thought.* Boston: Unwin Hyman.

Hearn, Frank (ed.). 1988. *The Transformation of Industrial Organization.* Belmont, Calif.: Wadsworth.

Heaton, T. B., and E. L. Pratt. 1990. "The effects of religious homogamy on marital satisfaction and stability." *Journtal of Family Issues* 11:191–207.

Heer, David M. 1975. *Society and Population,* 2nd ed. Englewood Cliffs, N.J.: Prentice Hall.

Heidensohn, Frances. 1987. "Women and crime: Questions for criminology." In Pat Carlen and Ann Worrall, *Gender, Crime, and Justice.* Philadelphia: Open University Press.

Heilbroner, Robert. 1991. "Symposium: From Sweden to socialism." *Dissent* (Winter): 96–110.

Heilbrun, Alfred B., Jr., and Mark R. Heilbrun. 1986. "The treatment of women within the criminal justice system: An inquiry into the social impact of the women's rights movement." *Psychology of Women Quarterly* 10:240–251.

Hemming, Heather. 1985. "Women in a man's world: Sexual harassment." *Human Relations* 38:67–79.

Hendershot, Heather. 1998. *Saturday Morning Censors: Television Regulation before the V-Chip.* Durham, NC: Duke University Press.

Hendrick, Clyde. 1977. "Social psychology as an experimental science." In Clyde Hendrick (ed.), *Perspectives on Sociology.* Hillsdale, N.J.: Lawrence Erlbaum.

Hendricks, Jon, and C. Davis Hendricks. 1986. *Aging in Mass Society: Myths and Realities,* 3rd ed. Boston: Little, Brown.

Hendry, Joy. 1987. *Understanding Japanese Society.* New York: Croom Helm.

Henry, Jules. 1955. "Docility, or giving teacher what she wants." *Journal of Social Issues* 11:33–41.

Henry, Susan. 1984. "Juggling the frying pan and the fire: The portrayal of employment and family life in seven women's magazines, 1975–1982." *Social Sciences Journal* 23:87–107.

Henry, W. E. 1965. "Engagement and disengagement: Toward a theory of adult development." In R. Kastenbaum (ed.), *Contributions to the Psychology of Aging.* New York: Springer-Verlag.

Hensley, Thomas R., and Glen W. Griffin. 1986. "Victims of groupthink: The Kent State University Board of Trustees and the 1977 gymnasium controversy." *Journal of Conflict Resolution* 30:497–531.

Herbers, John. 1986. *The New Heartland: America's Flight Beyond the Suburbs and How It Is Changing Our Future.* New York: Times Books.

Hertz, Rosanna. 1986. *More Equal Than Others: Women and Men in Dual-Career Marriages.* Berkeley: University of California Press.

Hewlett, S. A. 1990. "The feminization of the work force." *New Perspectives Quarterly* 7 (Winter): 13–15.

Hill, Gretchen. 1987. "Close personal relationships at work and with kin: Testing an urban subculture theory." *Mid-American Review of Sociology* 12(2):51–70.

Hill, Richard Child. 1978. "Fiscal collapse and political struggle in decaying central cities in the United States." In William K. Tabb and Larry Sawers (eds.), *Marxism and the Metropolis.* New York: Oxford University Press.

Hill, Susan, and Tim Hill. 1990. *The Collaborative Classroom: A Guide to Co-Operative Learning.* Portsmouth, N.H.: Heinemann.

Hinds, Michael de Courcy. 1990. "Pulling families out of welfare is proving to be an elusive goal." *New York Times,* April 2, A1.

Hinkle, Roscoe, Jr., and Gisela J. Hinkle. 1954. *The Development of Modern Sociology.* New York: Random House.

Hirschhorn, Larry. 1984. *Beyond Mechanization.* Cambridge, Mass.: MIT Press.

Hirschhorn, Larry. 1988. *The Workplace Within.* Cambridge, Mass.: MIT Press.

Hirschi, Travis. 1969. *Causes of Delinquency.* Berkeley, Calif.: University of California Press.

Hirschman, Albert. 1982. *Shifting Involvements.* Princeton, N.J.: Princeton University Press.

Hite, Shere. 1987. *Women and Love: A Cultural Revolution in Progress.* New York: Knopf.

Hochschild, Arlie, with Anne Machung. 1989. *Second Shift: Inside the Two-Job Marriage.* New York: Penguin.

Hockett, C. F., and R. Ascher. 1964. "The human revolution." *Current Anthropology* 5:135–147.

Hodge, Robert W., Paul M. Siegel, and Peter H. Rossi. 1964. "Occupational prestige in the United States, 1925–1963." *American Journal of Sociology* 70:286–302.

Hogan, Dennis P., and Nan Marie Astone. 1986. "The transition to adulthood." *Annual Review of Sociology* 12:109–130.

Holland, Dorothy C., and Margaret A. Eisenhart. 1990. *Educated in Romance:*

Women, Achievement, and College Culture. Chicago: University of Chicago Press.

Höllinger, Franz, and Max Haller. 1990. "Kinship and social networks in modern societies: A cross-cultural comparison among seven nations." *European Sociological Review* 6(2):102–124.

Hollinger, Richard C., and John P. Clark. 1982. "Formal and informal social controls of employee deviance." *Sociological Quarterly* 23:333–343.

Holloway, Mark. 1966. *Heavens on Earth: Utopian Communities in America 1680–1880.* New York: Dover.

Hollowell, Christopher. 1999. *Playing the Odds,* Time, January 11.

Holmes, William, and Lenore, Olsen. 1984. "Abused teens." *Psychology Today* (July): 8.

Homans, George C. 1958. "Social behavior as exchange." *American Journal of Sociology* 62:597–606.

Homans, George C. 1974. *Social Behavior: Its Elementary Forms,* rev. ed. New York: Harcourt, Brace, Jovanovich.

Honey, Maureen. 1984. *Creating Rosie the Riveter: Class Gender and Propaganda during World War II.* Amherst: University of Massachusetts Press.

Hooten, Ernest. 1939. *Crime and the Man.* Cambridge, Mass.: Harvard University Press.

Hoover, Sally L., and Jacob S. Siegel. 1986. "International demographic trends and perspectives on aging." *Journal of Cross-Cultural Gerontology* 1:5–30.

Hopkins, Terence K., Immanuel Wallerstein, et al. 1982. *World Systems Analysis: Theory and Methodology.* Beverly Hills, Calif.: Sage.

Hopper, Rex D. 1950. "Revolutionary movements." *Social Forces* 28:270–279.

Horn, Patricia. 1991. "A market: But what kind?" *Dollars and Sense* (December): 6–9.

Horowitz, Rose A. 1989. "California beach culture rides wave of popularity in Japan." *Journal of Commerce and Commercial* 381:1–2.

Hoselitz, Bert F., and Wilbert E. Moore (eds.). 1963. *Industrialization and Society.* Paris and the Hague: UNESCO, Mouton.

Hotchkiss, Lawrence, and Linda Eberst Dorsten. 1987. "Curriculum effects on early post-high school outcomes." *Research in the Sociology of Education and Socialization* 7:191–219.

Houghland, James G., Kyong-Dong Kim, and James A. Christenson. 1979. "The effects of ecological and socio-economic status variables on membership and participation in voluntary organizations." *Rural Sociology* 44:602–612.

Hout, Michael, and Andrew Greeley. 1987. "The center doesn't hold: Church attendance in the United States." *American Sociological Review* 52:325–345.

Howard, Michael C. 1986. *Contemporary Cultural Anthropology,* 2nd ed. Boston: Little, Brown.

Howe, Louise Kapp. 1978. *Pink Collar Workers: Inside the World of Women's Work.* New York: Avon.

Hoyt, Homer. 1939. *The Structure and Growth of Residential Neighborhoods in American Cities.* Washington, D.C.: Federal Housing Administration.

Huber, Bettina J. 1984. *Career Possibilities for Sociology Graduates.* Washington, D.C.: American Sociology Association.

Hudson, Ray, and Allen M. Williams. 1989. *Divided Britain.* New York: Belhaven Press.

Hughes, Everett. 1945. "Dilemmas and contradictions of status." *American Journal of Sociology* 50:353–359.

Hughes, Everett C., Howard S. Becker, and Blanche Geer. 1962. "Student culture and academic effort." In Nevitt Sanford (ed.), *The American College: A Psychological and Social Interpretation of Higher Learning.* New York: Wiley.

Hughes, Michael, and Bradley Hertel. 1990. "The significance of color remains: A study of life chances, mate selection, and ethnic consciousness among black Americans." *Social Forces* 68(4):1105–1120.

Hughes, Patrick H. 1977. *Behind the Wall of Respect: Community Experiments in Heroin Control.* Chicago: University of Chicago Press.

Humphreys, Laud. 1970. *Tearoom Trade: Impersonal Sex in Public Places.* Chicago: Aldine.

Hunt, Janet G., and Larry L. Hunt. 1982. "The dualities of careers and families: New integrations or new polarizations?" *Social Problems* 29:499–509.

Hunt, Jennifer. 1985. "Police accounts of normal force." *Urban Life* 13(4):315–341.

Hunt, Morton. 1985. *Profiles of Social Research: The Scientific Study of Human Interactions.* New York: Russell Sage Foundation.

Hunter, Albert. 1974. *Symbolic Communities: The Persistence and Change of Chicago's Local Communities.* Chicago: University of Chicago Press.

Hunter, James Davison. 1987. *Evangelicalism: The Coming Generation.* Chicago: University of Chicago Press.

Hunter, James Davison. 1991. *Culture Wars: The Struggle to Define America.* New York: Basic Books.

Huxley, Aldous. 1969. *Brave New World.* Harper & Row.

Hyman, H. H. 1953. "The value systems of different classes: A social psychological contribution to the analysis of stratification." In R. Bendix and S.M. Lipset (eds.), *Class, Status, and Power.* New York: Free Press.

Iga, Mamoru. 1986. *The Thorn in the Chrysanthemum: Suicide and Economic Success in Modern Japan.* Berkeley: University of California Press.

Illich, Ivan. 1976. *Medical Nemesis.* New York: Pantheon.

Imbrogno, Salvatore, and Nadia Ilyin Imbrogno. 1986. "Marriage and family in the USSR: Changes are emerging." *Social Casework* 67:245–259.

Information Please Almanac. 1998. Boston: LLC.

Inkeles, Alex. 1966. "The modernization of man." In M. Weiner (ed.), *Modernization: The Dynamics of Growth.* New York: Basic Books.

Inkeles, Alex. 1978. "National differences in individual modernity." In Richard F. Tomasson (ed.), *Comparative Studies in Sociology.* Greenwich, Conn.: JAI Press.

Inkeles, Alex, and Peter H. Rossi. 1956. "National comparisons of occupational prestige." *American Journal of Sociology* 61:329–339.

Inkeles, Alex, and D.H. Smith. 1974. *Becoming Modern.* Cambridge, Mass.: Harvard University Press.

Insko, Chester A., Richard H. Smith, Mark D. Alicke, et al. 1985. "Conformity and group size: The concern with being right and the concern with being liked." *Personality and Social Psychology Bulletin* 11:41–50.

Intelligence Report. 1998. Special Issue: *1997 The Year in Hate* (Winter). Montgomery, Ala. Southern Poverty Law Center.

Irish, Richard K. 1978. *Go Hire Yourself an Employer.* Garden City, N.Y.: Anchor.

Irvine, S. H., and J. W. Berry. 1988. *Human Abilities in Cultural Context.* New York: Cambridge University Press.

Isaacson, Walter. 1998. "Our century and the next one." *Time,* April 13.

Israel, Joachim. 1971. *Alienation.* Boston: Allyn & Bacon.

Iyengar, Shanto, and Donald R. Kinder. 1987. *News That Matters.* Chicago: The University of Chicago Press.

Jacklin, Carol Nagy, Janet Ann DiPietro, and Eleanor E. Maccoby. 1984. "Sex-typing behavior and sex-typing pressure in child/parent inter-action." *Archives of Sexual Behavior* 13:413–425.

Jackson, Kenneth T. 1985. *Crabgrass Fron-tier: The Suburbanization of the United States.* New York: Oxford University Press.

Jacobs, Jane. 1961. *The Death and Life of Great American Cities.* New York: Random House.

Jacobs, Jerry A. 1989. *Revolving Doors: Sex Segregation and Women's Careers.* Stanford, Calif.: Stanford University Press.

Jain, Uday. 1987. "Effect of population density and resources in the feeling of crowding and personal space." *Jour-nal of Social Psychology* 127:331–338.

James, Franklin J. 1977. *Back to the City: An Appraisal of Housing Reinvestment and Population Change in America.* Washington, D.C.: U.S. Department of Housing and Urban Development, Office of Policy Development and Research.

James, Franklin J., Betty I. McCummings, and Eileen A. Tynan. 1984. *Minori-ties in the Sunbelt.* New Brunswick, N.J.: Rutgers University.

Janis, Irving. 1972. *Victims of Groupthink.* Boston: Houghton Mifflin.

Janis, Irving. 1983. *Groupthink: Psycho-logical Studies of Policy Decisions and Fiascoes,* 2nd ed., rev. Boston: Houghton Mifflin.

Janson, Carl-Gunnar. 1980. "Factorial social ecology: An attempt at summary and evaluation." *Annual Review of Soci-ology* 6:433–456.

Jeffres, Leo W. 1997. *Mass Media Effects.* 2nd ed., rev. Prospect Heights, Ill.: Waveland Press.

Jencks, Christopher. 1985. "Affirmative action for blacks: Past, present, and future." *American Behavioral Scien-tist* 28(6):751–760.

Jencks, Christopher. 1995. *The Homeless.* Cambridge, Mass.: Harvard Univer-sity Press.

Jencks, Christopher, and David Riesman. 1977. *The Academic Revolution.* Chicago: University of Chicago Press.

Jencks, Christopher, et al. 1972. *Inequal-ity: A Reassessment of the Effect of Family and Schooling in America.* New York: Basic Books.

Jencks, Christopher, et al. 1979. *Who Gets Ahead? The Determinants of Economic Success in America.* New York: Basic Books.

Jenkins, J. Craig. 1983. "Resource mobi-lization theory and the study of social movements." *Annual Review of Soci-ology* 9.

Jensen, Arthur. 1969. "How much can we boost IQ and scholastic achievement?" *Harvard Educational Review* 39:1–23.

Jensen, Arthur. 1973a. *Educability and Group Differences.* New York: Harper & Row.

Jensen, Arthur. 1973b. "The differences are real." *Psychology Today* (Decem-ber): 80–86.

Jensen, Gary, and Eve Raymond. 1976. "Sex differences in delinquency." *Criminology* 13:427–448.

Johnson, Benton. 1968. "On church and sect." *American Sociological Review* 28:539–549.

Johnson, Colleen Leahy, and Frank A. Johnson. 1980. "Parenthood, mar-riage, and careers: Situational con-straints and role strain." In Fran Pepitone-Rockwell (ed.), *Dual-Career Couples.* Beverly Hills, Calif.: Sage.

Johnson, David W., and Roger T. John-son. 1987. *Learning Together and Alone: Cooperative, Competitive, and Individualistic Learning.* Upper Sad-dle River, NJ: Prentice Hall.

Johnson, David W., Roger T. Johnson, and E. J. Holubec. 1993. *Circles of Learn-ing: Cooperation in the Classroom,* 4th ed. Edina, Minn.: Interaction Books.

Johnson, Doyle Paul. 1979. "Dilemmas of charismatic leadership: The case of the People's Temple." *Sociological Analysis* 40:315–323.

Johnson, Elizabeth S., and John B. Williamson. 1987. "Retirement in the United States." In K. S. Makjides and C. L. Cooper (eds.), *Retirement in Industrialized Societies.* New York: Wiley.

Johnson, Norris R. 1987a. "Panic and the breakdown of social order: An empir-ical assessment." *Sociological Focus* 20(3):171–183.

Johnson, Norris R. 1987b. "Panic at 'The Who concert stampede': An empir-ical assessment." *Social Problems* 34(4):362–373.

Johnstone, Diana. 1999. "U.S. media pro-motes biased coverage of Bosnia." In Peter Phillips (ed.), *Censored 1999.* New York: Seven Stories Press.

Johnstone, Ronald L. 1988. *Religion and Society in Interaction,* 3rd ed. Engle-wood Cliffs, N.J.: Prentice Hall.

Jolly, Clifford J., and Fred Plog. 1979. *Phys-ical Anthropology and Archaeology.* New York: Knopf.

Jorstad, Erling. 1990. *Holding Fast/Press-ing On: Religion in America in the 1980s.* New York: Praeger.

Jowett, Garth S. 1987. "Propaganda and communications: The re-emergence of a research tradition." *Journal of Communication* 37:97–114.

Joy, L. A., M. M. Kimball, and M. L. Zabrack. 1986. "Television and chil-dren's aggressive behavior." In T. M. Williams (ed.), *The Impact of Tele-vision: A Natural Experiment in Three Communities.* Orlando, Fla.: Acade-mic Press.

Kahn, Alfred J., and Sheila B. Kamerman. 1987. *Child Care: Facing the Hard Choices.* Dover, Mass.: Auburn House.

Kahn, Herman. 1984. *The Coming Boom.* New York: Simon & Schuster.

Kaiser, Robert G. 1976. *Russia: The People and the Power.* New York: Pocket Books.

Kamerman, Sheila B. 1991. "Child care policies and programs: An interna-tional overview." *Journal of Social Issues* 47(2):179–196.

Kamerman, Sheila B., and Alfred J. Kahn. 1981. *Child Care, Family Benefits and Working Parents: A Study in Com-parative Policy.* New York: Columbia University Press.

Kamin, Leon J. 1974. *The Science and Pol-itics of IQ.* New York: Wiley.

Kammeyer, Kenneth C., and Helen Ginn. 1986. *An Introduction to Population.* Chicago: Dorsey Press.

Kanter, Rosabeth Moss. 1977. *Men and Women of the Corporation.* New York: Basic Books.

Kanter, Rosabeth. 1983. The Change Makers. New York: Simon & Schuster.

Kantrowitz, Barbara. 1993a. "The messiah of Waco." Newsweek, March 15, pp. 56–58.

Kantrowitz, Barbara. 1993b. "Day of judgment." Newsweek, May 3, pp. 22–27.

Kantrowitz, Barbara, with Pat Wingert, Patrick Rogers, Nadine Joseph, and Shawn D. Lewis. 1991. "A is for Ashanti, B is for black . . . and C is for curriculum which is starting to change." Newsweek, September 13, pp. 45–46.

Kasarda, John D. 1989. "Urban industrial transition and the underclass." Annals of the American Academy of Political and Social Science 501:26–47.

Kassebaum, Gene, David A. Ward, and Daniel M. Wilner. 1971. Prison Treatment and Parole Survival. New York: Wiley.

Kasun, Jacqueline R. 1978. The War against Population: The Economics and Ideology of World Population Control. San Francisco: Ignatius Press.

Katz, Elihu, and Paul Lazarsfeld. 1955. Personal Influence. New York: Free Press.

Katz, Michael. 1986. In the Shadow of the Poorhouse: A Social History of Welfare in America. New York: Basic Books.

Katz, Michael. 1989. The Undeserving Poor. New York: Pantheon.

Katz, Richard. 1997. "More commercials than ever in prime daytime." Mediaweek, March 24, p. 10.

Kaufman, Debra R. 1995. "Professional women: How real are the recent gains?" In Jo Freeman (ed.), Women: A Feminist Perspective. Mountain View, Calif.: Mayfield.

Keen, Sam. 1986. Faces of the Enemy: Reflections of the Hostile Imagination. New York: Harper & Row.

Keller, Suzanne. 1968. The Urban Neighborhood. New York: Random House.

Kelley, B. T., T. P. Thornberry, and C. A. Smith. 1997. In the Wake of Childhood Maltreatment. U.S. Department of Justice, Office of Justice Programs, Office of Juvenile Justice and Delinquency Prevention, August.

Kelley, Chris. 1995. "In search of new life: Once-proud industrial cities pursue answers to a changing economy." Dallas Morning News, December 3, A1.

Kempf, Kimberly L. 1993. "The empirical status of Hirschi's control theory." In Freda Adler and William S. Laufer (eds.), New Directions in Criminological Theory, vol. 4, pp. 143–185. New Brunswick, N.J.: Transaction.

Keniston, K. 1970. "Youth as a stage of life." American Scholar 39:631–654.

Kennedy, Paul. 1987. The Rise and Fall of the Great Powers: Economic Change and Military Conflict from 1500 to 2000. New York: Random House.

Kentor, Jeffrey. 1981. "Structural determinants of peripheral urbanization: The effects of international dependence." American Sociological Review 46:201–211.

Kephart, William M., and William W. Zellner. 1994. Extraordinary Groups, 5th ed. New York: St. Martin's Press.

Kerckhoff, Alan C. 1986. "Family position, peer influences, and schooling." In John G. Richardson (ed.), Handbook of Theory and Research for the Sociology of Education. New York: Greenwood Press.

Kerckhoff, Alan C., and Kurt W. Back. 1968. The June Bug. New York: Appleton Century Crofts.

Kerr, C., et al. 1964. Industrialization and Industrial Man. New York: Oxford University Press.

Kerr, Clark, et al. 1960. The Problem of Labor and Management in Economic Growth. Cambridge: Harvard University Press.

Kessler, Ronald C., and Paul D. Cleary. 1980. "Social class and psychological distress." American Sociological Review 45:463–478.

Khalilzad, Zalmay, and Cheryl Benard. 1984. The Government of God: Iran's Islamic Republic. New York: Columbia University Press.

Khullar, Gurdeep S. 1988. "Retirement, social participation, and social integration." International Review of Modern Sociology 18:107–137.

Kidder, Louise, Joanne L. Boell, and Marilyn M. Moyer. 1983. "Rights consciousness and victimization prevention: Personal defense and assertiveness training." Journal of Social Issues 39(2):155–170.

King, Bruce M. 1996. Human Sexuality Today, Upper Saddle River, N.J.: Prentice Hall.

King, Haitung, and Frances B. Locke. 1980. "Chinese in the United States: A century of occupational transition." International Migration Review 14:15–42.

Kirby, David J., et al. 1973. Political Strategies of Northern School Desegregation. Lexington, Mass.: Lexington Books.

Kitano, Harry H.L. 1985. Race Relations, 3rd ed. Englewood Cliffs, N.J.: Prentice Hall.

Kitcher, Philip. 1987. "Confessions of a curmudgeon." Behavioral and Brain Sciences 10:89–99.

Kitson, Gay C., Karen B. Babri, and Mary J. Roach. 1985. "Who divorces and why?" Journal of Family Issues 6(3):255–293.

Kjøller, Susanne, Bente Hansen, and Erling Segest. 1989. "Free condoms in the schools of Copenhagen, Denmark." Journal of School Health 59:66–68.

Klass, Perri. 1988. A Not Entirely Benign Procedure. New York: NAL/Penguin.

Klassen, Albert D., Colin J. Williams, and Eugene E. Levitt. 1989. Sex and Morality in the United States: An Empirical Enquiry under the Auspices of the Kinsey Institute. Middletown, Conn.: Wesleyan University Press.

Kleke, Philip R., William D. Marder, and Anne B. Silberger. 1990. "The growing proportion of female physicians: Implications for U.S. physician supply." American Journal of Public Health 80:300–304.

Kluckhohn, Clyde. 1961. "The study of values." In D.N. Barrett (ed.), Values in America. South Bend, Ind.: University of Notre Dame Press.

Kluegel, James R. 1987. "Macroeconomic problems, beliefs about the poor, and attitudes toward welfare spending." Social Problems 34:82–91.

Knight, Robin. 1989. "Just you move over, 'Enry 'Iggins." U.S. News & World Report, April 24, p. 40.

Knodel, John, Chamratrithirong, Aphichat, and Nibhon Debevalya. 1987. Thailand's Reproductive Revolution: Rapid Fertility Decline in a Third World Setting. Madison: University of Wisconsin Press.

Kochen, Manfred (ed.). 1989. The Small World. Norwood, N.J.: Ablex.

Kohlberg, Lawrence. 1963. "The development of children's orientations toward a moral order." I. Sequence in the development of moral thought." Vita Humana 6:11–33.

Kohn, Alfie. 1988. "You know what they say . . ." Psychology Today 22:36–41.

Kohn, M. L. 1963. "Social class and parent-child relationships: An interpretation." *American Journal of Sociology* 68:471–480.

Komarovsky, Mirra. 1964. *Blue-Collar Marriage.* New York: Random House.

Konvitz, Josef. 1985. *The Urban Millennium.* Carbondale: Southern Illinois University Press.

Koppel, Herbert. 1987. "Likelihood of victimization." *Bureau of Justice Statistics Technical Report NCJ-104274.* Washington, D.C.: U.S. Department of Justice.

Korte, Charles. 1980. "Urban-nonurban differences in social behavior and social psychological models of urban impact." *Journal of Social Issues* 36(3):29–51.

Kosmin, Barry A., and Seymour P. Lachman. 1993. *One Nation under God.* New York: Crown.

Kotlin, Joel. 1996. "Still the best places to do business." *Inc.* (July): 42–44, 46, 48, 50.

Kovar, Mary Grace. 1986. "Expenditures for the medical care of elderly people living in the community in 1980." *Milbank Quarterly* 64:100–132.

Kovar, Mary Grace, Gerry Hendershot, and Evelyn Mathis. 1989. "Older people in the U.S. who receive help with basic activities of daily living." *American Journal of Public Health* 79:778–779.

Krahn, Harvey, Timothy F. Hartnagel, and John W. Gartrell. 1986. "Income inequality and homicide rates: Cross-national data and criminological theories." *Criminology* 24:269–295.

Krauskopf, Joan A., and Mary Elise Burnett. 1983. *Trial.*

Krymkowski, Daniel H., and Russell Middleton. 1987. "Social stratification in East Africa: Bases of respect among Kipsigis and Kikuyu men in rural Kenya." *Rural Sociology* 32:379–388.

Kubey, Robert, and Mihaly Csikszentmihalyi. 1990. *Television and the Quality of Life: How Viewing Shapes Everyday Experience.* Hillsdale, N.J.: Laurence Erlbaum.

Kubler-Ross, Elisabeth. 1969. *On Death and Dying.* New York: Macmillan.

Kung, Hans. 1986. *Christianity and the World Religions.* New York: Doubleday.

Kunkel, Dale. 1998. "Policy battles over defining children's educational television." *Annals of the American Academy of Political and Social Sciences* 557:39–54.

Kurz, D. 1993. "Physical assaults by husbands: A major social problem." In R. J. Gelles and D. R. Loseke (eds.), *Current Controversies on Family Violence,* pp. 88–103. Thousand Oaks, Calif.: Sage.

Kurz, D. 1997. "Doing parenting: Mothers, care work, and policy." In T. Arendell (ed.), *Contemporary Parenting: Challenges and Issues,* pp. 92–118. Thousand Oaks, Calif.: Sage.

Kutscher, Ronald. 1991. "Outlook 1990–2005: Findings and implications." *Monthly Labor Review* (November): 3–12.

Landis, Suzanne E. 1987. "Sick child care options: What do working mothers prefer?" *Women and Health* 1:61–77.

Lane, Christel. 1987. "The impact of the economic and political system on social stratification and social mobility: Soviet lower white-collar workers in a comparative perspective." *Sociology* 21:171–198.

Lane, David. 1984. "Social stratification and class." In Erik P. Hoffmann and Robbin F. Laird (eds.), *The Soviet Polity in the Modern Era.* New York: Aldine.

Langley, Lester D. 1988. *Mex America: Two Countries, One Future.* New York: Crown.

Lapidus, Gail Warshofsky (ed.). 1982. *Women, Work, and Family in the Soviet Union.* Armonk, N.Y.: M. E. Sharpe.

Lasch, C. 1977. *Haven in a Heartless World.* New York: Basic Books.

Lasch, Christopher. 1979. *The Culture of Narcissism.* New York: Warner.

Laska, Shirley B., and Daphny Spain (eds.). 1980. *Back to the City.* New York: Pergamon.

Laslett, P. 1977. *Family Life and Illicit Love in Earlier Generations.* Cambridge: Cambridge University Press.

Laslett, Peter. 1984. *The World We Have Lost: England before the Industrial Age,* 3rd ed. New York: Scribner's.

Laslett, P. (ed.), with R. Wall. 1972. *Household and Family in Past Time.* Cambridge: Cambridge University Press.

Lassey, Marie L., William R. Lassey, and Martin J. Jinks. 1997. *Health Care Systems around the World: Characteristics, Issues, Reforms.* Upper Saddle River, N.J.: Prentice Hall.

Latane, Bibb, Kipling Williams, and Stephen Harkins. 1979. "Many hands make light the work: The causes and consequences of social loafing." *Journal of Personality and Social Psychology* 37:822–832.

La Torre, R. P., and K. Kear. 1977. "Attitudes toward sex in the aged." *Archives of Sexual Behavior* 6:203–213.

Laumann, E. O., J. Gagnon, R. T. Michael, and S. Michaels. 1994. *The Social Organization of Sexuality: Sexual Practices in the United States.* Chicago: University of Chicago Press.

Lawton, M. Powell. 1977. "Environments for older persons." *The Humanist* (September/October): 20–24.

Lazarsfeld, Paul. 1945. "The discussion goes on." *Public Opinion Quarterly* 9 (Winter 1945–1946): 404.

Leba, John Kong, John H. Leba, and Anthony T. Leba. 1985. *The Vietnamese Entrepreneurs in the U.S.A.: The First Decade.* Houston, Tex.: Zieleks.

Le Bon, Gustave. 1946. *The Crowd: A Study of the Popular Mind.* New York: Macmillan. (Originally published in 1896.)

Lee, Martin A., and Norman Solomon. 1991. *Unreliable Sources: A Guide to Detecting Bias in News Media.* New York: Carol.

Lee, Motoko. 1976. "The married woman's status and role in Japanese: An exploratory sociolinguistic study." *Signs* 1:991–999.

Lee, Valerie E., and Anthony S. Bryk. 1988. "Curriculum tracking as mediating the social distribution of high school achievement." *Sociology of Education* 61:78–94.

LeGrand, Julian, and Saul Estrin (eds.). 1989. *Market Socialism.* New York: Oxford University Press.

Leishmann, Katie. 1983. "Child abuse: The extent of the harm." *The Atlantic* 252:23–32.

Lemann, Nicholas. 1991. *The Promised Land.* New York: Knopf.

Lemert, Edwin. 1951. *Social Pathology.* New York: McGraw-Hill.

Lemert, Edwin. 1967. *Human Deviance, Social Problems, and Social Control.* Englewood Cliffs, N.J.: Prentice Hall.

Lenaghan, Donna D., and Michael J. Lenaghan. 1987. "AIDS and education: The front line of prevention." *The Futurist* 21(6):17.

Lengermann, Patricia M., Katherine M. Marconi, and Ruth Wallace. 1978. "Sociological theory in teaching sex roles: Marxism, functionalism and phenomenology." *Woman's Studies International Quarterly* 1:375–385.

Lengermann, Patricia Madoo, and Ruth A. Wallace. 1985. *Gender in America: Social Control and Social Changes.* Englewood Cliffs, N.J.: Prentice Hall.

Lenin, V. I. 1917. *Imperialism: The Highest Stage of Capitalism.* New York: Path Press.

Lenski, Gerhard. 1966. *Power and Privilege: A Theory of Social Stratification.* New York: McGraw-Hill.

Lenski, Gerhard. 1984. *Power and Privilege: A Theory of Social Stratification,* 2nd ed. Chapel Hill: University of North Carolina Press.

Lenski, Gerhard, and Jean Lenski. 1987. *Human Societies: An Introduction to Macrosociology.* New York: McGraw-Hill.

Lenski, Gerhard, Jean Lenski, and Patrick Nolan. 1991. *Human Societies: An Introduction to Macrosociology,* 6th ed. New York: McGraw-Hill.

Leonard, Eileen B. 1982. *Women, Crime, and Society: A Critique of Theoretical Criminology.* New York: Longman.

Lersch, Rainer. 1988. "Praktisches Lernen und Bildungsreform: Zur Dialektik von Nähe und Distanz der Schule zum Leben." *Zeitschrift für Pädagogik* 34:781–797.

Levenson, Richard L., Jr. 1984. "Incestuous fathers." *Psychology Today* (April): 14.

Levin, Jack, and Arnold Arluke. 1987. *Gossip: The Inside Scoop.* New York: Plenum Press.

Levine, Daniel U., and Rayna F. Levine. 1996. *Society and Education,* 9th ed. Boston: Allyn & Bacon.

Levinger, George. 1979. "A social exchange view on the dissolution of pair relationships." In Robert L. Burgess and Ted L. Huston, *Social Exchange in Developing Relationships.* New York: Academic Press.

Levinson, Daniel J., et al. 1978. *The Seasons of a Man's Life.* New York: Knopf.

Levinson, Mark. 1992. "Our economy keeps limping." *Dissent* (Winter): 5–6.

Lévi-Strauss, Claude. 1969. *The Elementary Structures of Kinship.* Boston: Beacon Press.

Levy, Frank S., and Richard C. Michel. 1991. *The Economic Future of American Families: Income and Wealth Trends.* Washington, D.C.: Urban Institute.

Levy, Steven. 1998. "The hot new tech cities." *Newsweek,* November 9, pp. 45–48, 50.

Lewin, Tamar. 1998. "Men assuming bigger share at home, new survey shows." *New York Times,* April 15.

Lewis, Oscar. 1959. *Five Families: Mexican Case Studies in the Culture of Poverty.* New York: Basic Books.

Lewis, Oscar. 1961. *The Children of Sanchez.* New York: Random House.

Lewis, Oscar. 1964. *Pedro Martinez.* New York: Random House.

Lewis, Oscar. 1966. *La Vida: A Puerto Rican Family in the Culture of Poverty—San Juan and New York.* New York: Random House.

Lewis, Peirce, Casey McCracken, and Roger Hunt. 1994. "Politics: Who cares?" *American Demographics* 16 (October): 20–26.

Lewontin, R. C., S. Rose, and L. J. Kamin. 1984. *Not in Our Genes: Biology, Ideology, and Human Nature.* New York: Pantheon.

Lickona, Thomas. 1989. "Educating the moral child." *Education Digest* 55:45–47.

Lieberman, Morton A., Irvin D. Yalom, and Matthew B. Miles. 1973. *Encounter Groups: First Facts.* New York: Basic Books.

Liebow, Elliot. 1967. *Tally's Corner.* Boston: Little, Brown.

Light, Donald W. 1989. "Social control and the American health care system." In Howard E. Freeman and Sol Levine (eds.), *Handbook of Medical Sociology,* 4th ed. Englewood Cliffs, N.J.: Prentice Hall.

Lincoln, James R., and Arne L. Kalleberg. 1990. *Culture, Control, and Commitment: A Study of Work Organization and Work Attitudes in the United States and Japan.* New York: Cambridge University Press.

Lindblom, Charles. 1977. *Politics and Markets.* New York: Basic Books.

Lindsey, Linda L. 1997. *Gender Roles: A Sociological Perspective,* 3rd ed. Upper Saddle River, N.J.: Prentice Hall.

Link, Bruce G., and Francis T. Cullen. 1990. "The labeling theory of mental disorder: A review of the evidence." *Research in Community and Mental Health* 6:75–105.

Linton, Ralph. 1936. *The Study of Man.* New York: Appleton Century Crofts.

Linton, Ralph. 1937. "The one hundred percent American." *American Mercury* 40:427–429.

Linz, Daniel G., and Edward Donnerstein. 1989. "The effects of violent messages in the mass media." In James Bradac (ed.), *Message Effects in Communication Science.* Sage Annual Reviews of Communication Research, vol. 17. Beverly Hills, Calif.: Sage.

Lipman-Blumen, Jean. 1984. *Gender Roles and Power.* Englewood Cliffs, N.J.: Prentice Hall.

Lippit, Ronald, and Ralph K. White. 1952. "An experimental study of the effect of democratic and authoritarian group atmospheres." *University of Iowa Studies in Child Welfare* 16:43–195.

Lipset, Martin N. 1987. "Blacks and Jews: How much bias?" *Public Opinion* 10:4–5.

Lipset, Seymour M. 1963. *The First New Nation: The United States in Historical and Comparative Perspective.* New York: Basic Books.

Lipset, Seymour M. 1994. "Why Americans refuse to vote." *Insight,* February 7, pp. 24–26.

Lipset, Seymour M. 1997. *American Exceptionalism.* New York: Norton.

Lipset, Seymour M., and Reinhard Bendix. 1959. *Social Mobility in Industrial Society.* Berkeley: University of California Press.

Lipset, Seymour M., and Earl Raab. 1981. "The election and the evangelicals." *Commentary* 71:25–31.

Lipset, Seymour, Martin Trow, and James Coleman. 1956. *Union Democracy.* Glencoe, Ill.: Free Press.

Litwak, Eugene, and Henry Meyer. 1966. "A balance theory of coordination between bureaucratic organizations and community primary groups." *Administrative Science Quarterly* 11 (March): 31–58.

Livingston, Jay. 1996. *Crime and Criminology,* 2nd ed. Upper Saddle River, N.J.: Prentice Hall.

Loehlin, John, Gardner Lindzey, and J.N. Spuhler. 1975. *Race Differences in Intelligence.* San Francisco: Freeman.

Lofland, John. 1971. *Analyzing Social Settings.* Belmont, Calif.: Wadsworth.

Lofland, John. 1977. "'Becoming a world-saver' revisited." *American Behavioral Scientist* 20(6):805–18.

Lofland, John. 1985. *Protest: Studies of Collective Behavior and Social Movements.* New Brunswick, N.J.: Transaction.

Logan, John R., and Mark Schneider. 1984. "Racial segregation and social change in American suburbs, 1970–1980." *American Journal of Sociology* 89:874–888.

Lombroso-Ferrero, Gina. 1911. Criminal Man According to the Classification of Cesare Lombroso. New York: Putnam's.

Lopata, Helena. 1986. "Becoming and being a widow: Reconstruction of the self and support systems." *Journal of Geriatric Psychiatry* 19:203–214.

Lopata, Helena Z. (ed.). 1987. *Widows.* Vol. I. Durham, N.C.: Duke University Press.

Lorber, Judith. 1994. *Paradoxes of Gender.* New Haven, Conn.: Yale University Press.

Los Angeles Times. 1999. "Study puts to rest notion of 'midlife crisis.'" February 17, A4.

Loveman, Gary, and Chris Tilly. 1988. "Good jobs or bad jobs: What does the evidence say?" *New England Economic Review* (January–February): 46–65.

Lowry, Ira S. 1980. "Dismal future." In A.P. Solomon (ed.), *The Prospective City.* Cambridge, Mass.: MIT Press.

Luckenbill, David F. 1986. "Deviant career mobility: The case of male prostitutes." *Social Problems* 33:283–296.

Luckmann, Thomas. 1967. *The Invisible Religion.* New York: Macmillan.

Ludeman, Kate. 1981. "The sexuality of the older person: Review of the literature." *The Gerontologist* 21:203–208.

Luker, Kristen. 1984. *Abortion and the Politics of Motherhood.* Berkeley: University of California Press.

Luker, Richard, and Jerome Johnston. 1988. "TV and teens: Television in adolescent social development." *Social Education* 52:350–353.

Lund, Dale A. (ed.). 1989. *Older Bereaved Spouses: Research with Practical Applications.* New York: Hemisphere.

Lund, Dale A., Michael S. Caserta, and Margaret F. Dimond. 1986. "Gender differences through two years of bereavement among the elderly." *The Gerontologist* 26:314–320.

Lundin, T. 1984. "Morbidity following sudden and unexpected bereavement." *British Journal of Psychiatry* 144:84–88.

Lynch, Michael J., Graeme R. Newman, and W. Byron Groves. 1993. "Control theory and punishment: An analysis of control theory as a penal philosophy." In Freda Adler and William S. Laufer (eds.), *New Directions in Criminological Theory,* vol. 4, pp. 337–361. New Brunswick, N.J.: Transaction.

Lynd, Robert S., and Helen M. Lynd. 1929. *Middletown.* New York: Harcourt Brace & World.

Lynd, Robert S., and Helen M. Lynd. 1937. *Middletown in Transition.* New York: Harcourt Brace & World.

Lynn, Naomi B. 1984. "Women and politics: The real majority." In Jo Freeman (ed.), *Women: A Feminist Perspective.* Palo Alto, Calif.: Mayfield.

Lyon, Larry. 1987. *The Community in Urban Society.* Chicago: Dorsey Press.

Lystard, Mary. 1986. *Violence in the Home: Interdisciplinary Perspectives.* New York: Brunner/Mazel.

Maccoby, Eleanor Emmons (ed.). 1966. *The Development of Sex Differences.* Stanford, Calif.: Stanford University Press.

Maccoby, Eleanor Emmons, and Carol Nagy Jacklin. 1974. *The Psychology of Sex Differences.* Stanford, Calif.: Stanford University Press.

Maccoby, Eleanor Emmons, and Carol Nagy Jacklin. 1980. "Sex differences in aggression: A rejoinder and reprise." *Child Development* 51:964–980.

Macionis, John J., and Vincent N. Parrillo. 1998. *Cities and Urban Life.* Upper Saddle River, N.J.: Prentice Hall.

MacKay, Charles. 1932. *Extraordinary Popular Delusions and the Madness of Crowds.* New York: Farrar, Straus, & Giroux. (Originally published in 1841.)

Mackinnon, Carol E., and Donna King. 1988. "Day care: A review of literature, implications for policy, and critique of resources." *Family Relations* 37(2):229–236.

Magaziner, Ira, and Mark Patinigin. 1989. *The Silent War: Inside the Global Business Battles Shaping America's Future.* New York: Random House.

Malloy, Ruth. 1989. *Fielding's People's Republic of China.* New York: Morrow.

Malmaud, Roslyn K. 1984. *Work and Marriage: The Two-Profession Family.* Ann Arbor: University of Michigan Press.

Mangan, J. A., and Roberta J. Park. 1987. *From Fair Sex to Feminism: Sport and the Socialization of Women.* London: Frank Cass.

Manning, Peter K. 1974. "The police: Mandate strategies and appearances." In Richard Quinney (ed.), *Criminal Justice in America.* Boston: Little, Brown.

Marger, Martin N. 1981. *Elites and Masses: An Introduction to Political Sociology.* New York: Van Nostrand.

Margolis, Maxine L. 1990. "From mistress to servant: Downward mobility among Brazilian immigrants in New York City." *Urban Anthropology* 19(3):215–231.

Maris, Ronald W. 1981. *Pathways to Suicide: A Survey of Self-Destructive Behaviors.* Baltimore: Johns Hopkins University Press.

Markowski, E. M., J. W. Croake, and J. F. Keller. 1978. "Sexual history and present sexual behavior of cohabitating and married couples." *Journal of Sex Research* 14:27–39.

Marlin, John T. 1988. *Cities of Opportunity: Finding the Best Place to Work, Live, and Prosper in the 1990s.* New York: National Civic League.

Marlin, John T., Immanuel Ness, and Stephen T. Collins. 1986. *The Book of World City Rankings: The Quality of Life and Work in over 100 Urban Centers.* New York: Free Press.

Marrett, Cora Bagley, and Cheryl Leggon (eds.). 1985. *Research in Race Relations.* Vol. 4. Greenwich, Conn.: JAI Press.

Marsh, Dave. 1981. *Born to Run.* New York: Dell.

Martin, David. 1978. *A General Theory of Secularization.* New York: Harper Colophon.

Martin, L. John. 1984. "The genealogy of public opinion polling." *Annals of the American Academy of Political and Social Science* 472:12–23.

Martin, Michael T., and Terry R. Kandal, 1989. *Studies of Development and Change in the Modern World.* New York: Oxford University Press.

Marx, Karl. 1964. *The Economic and Philosophic Manuscripts of 1844.* New York: International Publishers.

Marx, Karl, and Friedrich Engels. 1969. *The Communist Manifesto.* Baltimore:

Penguin. (Originally published in 1848.)

Masnick, George S., and Joseph A. McFalls, Jr. 1978. "Those perplexing U.S. fertility swings." *PRB Report,* November.

Massagli, Michael P., and Claire McCullough. 1979. "Policy research and politics: Some inferences from the 'Coleman Report' for the policy role of the social scientist." *Sociological Focus* 12:87–101.

Massey, Douglas, and Nancy A. Denton. 1995. *American Apartheid.* Cambridge, Mass.: Harvard University Press.

Masters, Brooke. 1994. "Staying the science course." *Washington Post Education Review,* April 3, 8, 10.

Masters, William H., and Virginia E. Johnson. 1966. *Human Sexual Response.* Boston: Little, Brown.

Masters, William H., and Virginia E. Johnson. 1970. *Human Sexual Inadequacy.* Boston: Little, Brown.

Mathisen, Gerald S., and James A. Mathisen. 1988. "The new fundamentalism: A socio-historical approach to understanding theological change." *Review of Religious Research* 30:18–32.

Matras, Judah. 1984. *Social Inequality, Stratification and Mobility,* 2nd ed. Englewood Cliffs, N.J.: Prentice Hall.

McCarthy, J. D., and M. N. Zald. 1973. *The Trends of Social Movements in America: Professionalization and Resource Mobilization.* Morristown, N.J.: General Learning Press.

McClelland, David G. 1967. *The Achieving Society.* New York: Free Press.

McConahay, John B., and Joseph C. Hough, Jr. 1976. "Symbolic racism." *Journal of Social Issues* 32:23–45.

McCord, William, and Arline McCord. 1986. *Paths to Progress: Bread and Freedom in Developing Societies.* New York: Norton.

McCormick, J. 1994. "Why parents kill." *Newsweek,* November 14, pp. 31–34.

McCormick, Teresa. 1984. "Multiculturalism: Some principles and issues." *Theory into Practice* 23(2) (Spring).

McKeachie, W. J. 1954. "Student centered versus instructor centered instruction." *Journal of Educational Psychology* 45:143–150.

McKenzie, Roderich D. 1926. "The scope of human ecology." In E.W. Burgess (ed.), *The Urban Community.* Chicago: University of Chicago Press.

McKeon, Thomas. 1976. *The Modern Rise of Population.* New York: Academic Press.

McKinley, John, and John Stoeckle. 1988. "Corporation and the social transformation of doctoring." *International Journal of Health Services* 18:191–205.

McLuhan, Marshall. 1964. *Understanding Media.* New York: McGraw-Hill.

McLuhan, Marshall. 1967. *The Medium Is the Massage.* New York: Bantam.

McNeil, Kenneth. 1978. "Understanding organizational power: Building on the Weberian legacy." *Administrative Science Quarterly* 23(1):65–90.

McPhail, Clark. 1971. "Civil disorder participation: A critical examination of recent research." *American Sociological Review* 36:1058–073.

McPhail, Clark, and Ronald T. Wohlstein. 1983. "Individual and collective behaviors within gatherings, demonstrations, and riots." *Annual Review of Sociology* 9.

McQuail, Denis. 1985. "Sociology of mass communication." *Annual Review of Sociology* 11:93–111.

Mead, George Herbert. 1934. *Mind, Self, and Society.* Charles W. Morris (ed.). Chicago: University of Chicago Press.

Mead, George Herbert. 1964. "The psychology of primitive justice." In Lewis A. Coser and Bernard Rosenberg (eds.), *Sociological Theory: A Book of Readings.* New York: Macmillan.

Mead, Lawrence M., and Laurence E. Lynn, Jr. 1990. "Should workfare be mandatory? What research says." *Journal of Policy Analysis and Management* 9(3):400–404.

Mead, Margaret. 1935/1963. *Sex and Temperament in Three Primitive Societies.* New York: Morrow.

Mead, Margaret. 1975. *Male and Female: A Study of the Sexes in a Changing World.* New York: Morrow. (Originally published in 1949.)

Mead, Margaret. 1977. *Letters from the Field: 1925–1975.* New York: Harper & Row.

Meadows, Dennis L., Donella Meadows, et al. 1972. *The Limits to Growth.* New York: New American Library.

Meadows, Donella, Dennis L. Meadows, Jorgen Randers, and William W. Behrens. 1972. *The Limits to Growth: A Report for the Club of Rome's Projection on the Predicament of Mankind.* New York: Universe Books.

Mechanic, David. 1986. *From Advocacy to Allocation.* New York: Free Press.

Melville, Keith. 1988. *Marriage and the Family Today.* New York: Random House.

Merrick, T. 1986. *Population Pressure in Latin America* 41(3). Washington, D.C.: Population Reference Bureau.

Merrick, Thomas W., and Stephen J. Tordella. 1988. "Demographics: People and markets." *Population Bulletin* 43:1.

Merton, Robert K. 1956. "Bureaucratic structure and anomie. *American Sociological Review* 3:672–682.

Merton, Robert K. 1956. "Bureaucratic structure and personality." In *Social Theory and Social Structure,* rev. ed. Glencoe, Ill.: Free Press.

Merton, Robert K. 1968. *Social Theory and Social Structure,* enl. ed. New York: Free Press.

Merton, Robert K. 1976. "Social problems and sociological theory." In Robert K. Merton and Robert A. Nisbet (eds.), *Contemporary Social Problems,* 4th ed. New York: Harcourt Brace Jovanovich.

Merton, Robert K. 1984. "Scientific fraud and the fight to be first." *The Times Literary Supplement,* November 2, pp. 1–2.

Messner, Steven F. 1982. "Societal development, social inequality, and homicide: A cross-national test of a Durkheim model. *Social Forces* 61:225–240.

Metheny, E. 1977. *Vital Issues.* Washington, D.C.: American Association for Health, Physical Education, and Recreation.

Meyrowitz, Joshua. 1985. *No Sense of Place: The Importance of Electronic Media on Social Behavior.* New York: Oxford University Press.

Michaels, Robert. 1911. *Political Parties.*

Milbrath, Lester. 1965. *Political Participation.* Chicago: Rand McNally.

Milgram, Stanley. 1963. "Behavioral study of obedience." *Journal of Abnormal and Social Psychology* 67:371–378.

Milgram, Stanley. 1970. "The experience of living in cities." *Science* 167:1462.

Miliband, Ralph. 1969. *The State in Capitalist Society.* New York: Basic Books.

Miliband, Ralph. 1977. *Marxism and Politics.* Oxford: Oxford University Press.

Miller, Carol. 1975. "American Rom and the ideology of defilement." In Farnham Rehfisch, ed., *Gypsies, Tinkers, and Other Travelers*. New York: Academic Press.

Miller, David (ed.). 1987. *The Blackwell Encyclopedia of Political Thought*. Oxford: Basil Blackwell.

Miller, David. 1989. "Why markets?" In Julian LeGrand and Saul Estrin (eds.), *Market Socialism*, pp. 25–49. New York: Oxford University Press.

Miller, Delbert, and William Form. 1980. *Industrial Sociology*. New York: Harper & Row.

Miller, Jeannie. 1979. *Six Years with God: Life Inside Reverend Jim Jones' People's Temple*. New York: A & W.

Miller, Mark Crispin. 1986. "Deride and Conquer." In Todd Gitlin (ed.), Watching Television, New York: Pantheon.

Miller-Jones, Dalton. 1989. "Culture and testing." *American Psychologist* 44:360–366.

Mills, C. Wright. 1951. *White Collar: The American Middle Classes*. New York: Oxford University Press.

Mills, C. Wright. 1956. *The Power Elite*. New York: Oxford University Press.

Mills, C. Wright. 1977. *The Sociological Imagination*. New York: Oxford University Press.

Minor, W. William., and Joseph Harry. 1982. "Deterrent and experimental effects in perceptual research: Replication and extension." *Journal of Research in Crime and Delinquency* 19:190–203.

Mintz, Steven, and Susan Kellogg. 1988. *Domestic Revolutions: A Social History of American Life*. New York: Free Press.

Mishel, Lawrence. 1989. "The late great debate on deindustrialization." *Challenge* (January–February): 35–43.

Mishel, Lawrence, Jared Bernstein, and John Schmitt. 1997. *The State of Working America, 1996–97*. Armonk, NY: M. E. Sharpe.

Mitchell, Robert E. 1971. "Some social implications of high-density housing." *American Sociological Review* 36:18–29.

Mitroff, Ian I. 1987. *Business Not As Usual*. San Francisco: Jossey Bass.

Molotch, Harvey. 1979. "Capital and neighborhood in the United States: Some conceptual links." *Urban Affairs Quarterly* 14:289–312.

Momeni, Jamshid A. (ed.). 1989. *Homelessness in the United States*. Vol. 1. *State Surveys*. New York: Greenwood Press.

Monette, Duane P., Thomas J. Sullivan, and Cornell R. De Jong. 1986. *Applied Sociological Research*. New York: Holt, Rinehart & Winston.

Money, John. 1977. "Destereotyping sex roles." *Society* 14(5):25–28.

Money, John. 1986. "Gender: History, theory, and usage of the term in sexology and its relationship to nature/ nurture." *Journal of Sex and Marital Therapy* 11:71–79.

Money, John. 1988. *Gay, Straight, and In-Between: The Sexology of Erotic Orientation*. New York: Oxford University Press.

Money, John A., and Anke A. Ehrhardt. 1972. *Man & Woman, Boy & Girl*. Baltimore: Johns Hopkins University Press.

Mooney, Linda A., and Sarah Brabant. 1988. "Birthday cards, love, and communication." *Sociology and Social Research* 72:106–109.

Moore, David W. 1994. "One in seven Americans victim of child abuse." *Gallup Poll Monthly*, May 8–12.

Moore, David W. 1997. "AIDS Issue Fades Among Americans." Gallup Poll Archives, October 3–5, http: www.gallup.com.

Moore, David W. 1999. "AIDS issue fades among Americans." *Gallup Poll Archives*.

Moore, David, and Lydia Saad. 1998. The Gallup Poll, June 5–7.

Moore, Timothy E., and Leslie Cadeau. 1985. "The representation of women, the elderly and minorities in Canadian television commercials." *Canadian Journal of Behavioral Sciences* 17:215–225.

Moore, Wilbert E. 1960. "A reconsideration of theories of social change." *American Sociological Review* 25:810–818.

Moore, Wilbert E. 1963. *Social Change*. Englewood Cliffs, N.J.: Prentice Hall.

Moore, Wilbert E. 1979. *World Modernization: The Limits of Convergence*. New York: Elsevier.

Morgan, Gareth. 1997. *Images of Organization*, 2nd ed. Thousand Oaks, Calif: Sage.

Morgan, Gwen G. 1986. "Supplemental care for young children." In Michael W. Yogman and T. Berry Brazelton (eds.), *In Support of Families*. Cambridge, Mass.: Harvard University Press.

Morgan, Hal. 1987. *Symbols of America*. New York: Penguin.

Morgan, Lewis Henry. 1964. *Ancient Society*, L. A. White (ed.). Cambridge, Mass.: Harvard University Press. (Originally published in 1877.)

Morison, Robert S. 1979. "Life extending technologies." In Robert M. Veatch (ed.), *Life Span*. New York: Harper & Row.

Morris, Desmond. 1977. *Manwatching: A Field Guide to Human Behavior*. New York: Abrams.

Morris, Peter A., and J. P. Wheeler. 1976. *Rural Renaissance in America*. Washington, D.C.: Population Reference Bureau.

Morrison, Terri, Wayne A. Conaway, and George A. Borden. 1994. *Kiss, Bow, or Shake Hands: How to Do Business in Sixty Countries*. Holbrook, Mass.: Adams Media Corp.

Mosatche, Harriet. 1983. *Searching: Practices and Beliefs of the Religious Cults and Human Potential Movements*. New York: Stravon Educational Press.

Moynihan, Daniel P. 1965. *The Negro Family: The Case for National Action*. Washington, D.C.: U.S. Department of Labor.

Mueller, Charles W., and Weldon Johnson. 1975. "Socioeconomic status and religious participation." *American Sociological Review* 40:785–800.

Mueller, Gerhard. 1983. "The United Nations and criminology." In Elmer H. Johnson (ed.), *International Handbook of Contemporary Developments in Criminology*. Westport, Conn.: Greenwood Press.

Mumford, Lewis. 1961. *The City in History: Its Origins, Its Transformations, and Its Prospects*. New York: Harcourt Brace Jovanovich.

Munnell, Alicia. 1983. "Financing options for social security." In Herbert S. Parnes (ed.), *Policy Issues in Work and Retirement*. Kalamazoo, Mich.: W. E. Upjohn Institute for Employment Research.

Murdock, G. P. 1949. *Social Structure*. New York: Macmillan.

Murdock, George. 1956. "How culture changes." In Harry L. Shapiro (ed.), *Man, Culture & Society*. New York: Oxford University Press.

Murphy, Michael D. 1985. "Brief communications." *Human Organization* 44(3):132–135.

Murphy, Philip. 1997. "Black flight." *Policy Review* (Spring 1995): 28, 30–33.

Murray, Charles. 1984. *Losing Ground: American Social Policy 1950–1980.* New York: Basic Books.

Mussen, Paul H., John J. Conger, and Jerome Kagan. 1974. *Child Development and Personality.* New York: Harper & Row.

Musto, David F. 1987. *The American Disease,* expanded ed. New York: Oxford University Press.

Myrdal, Gunnar. 1962. *An American Dilemma.* New York: Harper & Row.

Myrdal, Gunnar. 1968. *Asian Drama: An Inquiry into the Poverty of Nations.* 3 vols. New York: Random House.

Nadelman, Ethan. 1992. "America's drug problem." *Dissent* (Spring):205–212.

Naipaul, Shiva. 1980. *Journey to Nowhere.* New York: Simon & Schuster.

Naisbitt, John. 1982. *Megatrends: Ten New Directions Transforming Our Lives.* New York: Warner.

Naisbitt, John, and Patricia Aburdene. 1990. *Megatrends 2000: Ten New Directions for the 1990s.* New York: William Morrow.

Nanda, Serena. 1990. *Neither Man nor Woman: The Hijras of India.* Belmont, Calif.: Wadworth.

Napoli, Lisa. 1998. "Staying with the pitch: Stalwarts of face-to-face sales reluctant to peddle on line." *New York Times,* February 23, C1.

Nash, June. 1986. "A decade of research on women in Latin America." In June Nash and Helen I. Safa (eds.), *Women and Change in Latin America.* South Hadley, Mass.: Bergin & Garvey.

National Center for Education Statistics. 1987. *Digest of Educational Statistics.* Washington, D.C.: U.S. Department of Health, Education and Welfare, Education Division.

National Center for Education Statistics. 1995. *Digest of Educational Statistics.* Washington, D.C.: U.S. Department of Health, Education and Welfare, Education Division.

National Center for Education Statistics, 1997. *Digest of Educational Statistics.* Washington, D.C.: U.S. Department of Health, Education and Welfare, Education Division.

National Center for Health Statistics. 1988. *Health United States, 1987.* Washington, D.C.: U.S. Government Printing Office.

National Center for Health Statistics. 1989. *National Vital Statistics Report. Series 21, No. 46.* Washington, D.C.: U.S. Department of Health, Education, and Welfare.

National Center for Health Statistics. 1997. *Health United States, 1997.* Washington, D.C.: U.S. Government Printing Office.

National Center for Health Statistics. 1998. Advance Data No. 289. Hyatsville, Maryland: Public Health Service. p. 3.

National Institute of Mental Health. 1982. "Television and behavior: Ten years of scientific progress and implications for the eighties." Washington, D.C.: U.S. Government Printing Office.

National Research Council. 1974. *Toward an Understanding of Metropolitan America.* New York: Harper & Row.

Natriello, Gary, Aaron M. Pallas, and Karl Alexander. 1989. "On the right track? Curriculum and academic achievement." *Sociology of Education* 62:109–118.

Near, Janet P., and Marcia P. Miceli. 1989. "The incidence of wrongdoing, whistle-blowing, and retaliation: Results of a naturally occurring field experiment." *Employee Responsibilities and Rights Journal* 2:91–108.

Nelson, Richard Alan. 1996. *A Chronology and Glossary of Propaganda in the United States.* Westport, Conn.: Greenwood Press.

Neugarten, Bernice L., and Gunheld, O. Hagestad. 1976. "Age and the life course." In Robert H. Binstock and Ethel Shanas (eds.), *Handbook of Aging and the Social Sciences.* New York: Van Nostrand Reinhold.

Neugarten, Bernice L., and Joan W. Moore. 1968. "The changing age-status system." In Bernice L. Neugarten (ed.), *Middle Age and Aging.* Chicago: University of Chicago Press.

Newcomb, T. M. 1943. *Personality and Social Change.* New York: Holt, Rinehart & Winston.

Newell, Colin. 1988. *Methods and Models in Demography.* New York: Guilford Press.

Newman, Katherine S. 1988. *Falling from Grace.* New York: Macmillan.

Newport, Frank. 1996. "Americans generally happy with their marriages." *Gallup Poll Monthly,* September.

Newport, Frank, and Lydia Saad. 1997. "Religious faith Is widespread but many skip church." *Gallup Poll Monthly,* March.

Newsweek. 1996. "The end of AIDS?" December 2.

Newsweek. "Off to a Good Start," Barbara Kantrowitz, Special Issue, pp. 7–9.

Newsweek. 1997. "The web: Infotopia or marketplace?" Peter McGrath, January 27.

New York Times. 1997a. "Equal pay for equal work is no. 1 goal of women." September 5, p. A20.

New York Times. 1997a. "How much has Texaco changed?" November 2, Sec. 3, p. 1.

New York Times. 1998. Cell rejuvenation may yield rush of medical advances." January 20, B11, B13.

Niebuhr, H. Richard. 1929. *The Social Sources of Denominationalism.* New York: Henry Holt.

Niemi, Richard C., John Mueller, and Tom W. Smith (eds.). 1989. *Trends in Public Opinion: A Compendium of Survey Data.* New York: Greenwood Press.

1998 Information Please Almanac. 1998. Borgna Brunner, (ed.). Boston: Houghton Mifflin.

Nisbet, Robert A. 1966. *The Sociological Tradition.* New York: Basic Books.

Nisbet, Robert A. 1970. *The Social Bond.* New York: Knopf.

Nixon, Howard L. 1979. *The Small Group.* Englewood Cliffs, N.J.: Prentice Hall.

Noble, Trevor. 1981. *Structure and Change in Modern Britain.* London: Batsford.

Nock, Steven L., and Paul W. Kingston. 1989. *The Sociology of Public Issues.* Belmont, Calif.: Wadsworth.

Noell, Jay. 1982. "Public and Catholic schools: A reanalysis of 'Public and Private Schools.'" *Sociology of Education* 55 (April/July):123–132.

Nordhøy, F. 1962. "Group interaction in decision making under risk." Cited in Stephen Wilson. 1978. *Informal Groups: An Introduction.* Englewood Cliffs, N.J.: Prentice Hall.

Nordlinger, Eric. 1981. *On the Autonomy of the Democratic State.* Cambridge, Mass.: Harvard University Press.

Norris, William P. 1984. "Coping with poverty in urban Brazil: The contribution of patron-client relationships." *Sociological Focus* 17:259–273.

Notestein, Frank W. 1945. "Population: The long view." In Theodore W. Schultz (ed.), *Food for the World.* Chicago: University of Chicago Press.

Nove, Alec. 1982. *Political Economy and Soviet Socialism,* 2nd ed. London: Allen & Unwin.

Nove, Alec. 1989. *Glasnost in Action.* Boston: Unwin Hyman.

Nove, Alec. 1990. "Market socialism and free economy." *Dissent* (Fall): 443–446.

Oberschall, Anthony. 1973. *Social Conflict and Social Movements.* Englewood Cliffs, N.J.: Prentice Hall.

Ochs, E. 1988. *Culture and Language Development: Language Acquisition and Language Socialization in a Samoan Village.* New York: Cambridge University Press.

O'Connor, James. 1973. *The Fiscal Crisis of the State.* New York: St. Martin's Press.

Offe, Claus. 1984. *Contradictions of the Welfare State.* Cambridge, Mass.: MIT Press.

Ogburn, William. 1950. *Social Changes with Respect to Culture and Original Nature,* rev. ed. New York: Viking.

O'Hare, William P. 1987. "America's welfare population: Who gets what?" *Population Trends and Public Policy* 13, Population Reference Bureau.

O'Hare, William. 1998. "Managing multiple-race data." *American Demographics,* April.

Oldham, G. R., and D. J. Brass. 1979. "Employee reactions to an open-plan office: A naturally occurring quasi-experiment." *Administrative Science Quarterly* 24:267–284.

Olsen, Marvin E. 1968. *The Process of Social Organization.* New York: Holt, Rinehart & Winston.

Olsen, Marvin E., and Michael Micklin (eds.). 1981. *Handbook of Applied Sociology: Frontiers of Contemporary Research.* New York: Praeger.

Olson, Elizabeth B. 1997. "As hate spills onto the web, a struggle over whether, and how, to control it." *New York Times,* November 24, C11.

Organization for Economic Cooperation and Development. 1998. Aging Working Paper 1.4.

Ornstein, Allan. 1985. *Foundations of Education,* 3rd ed. Boston: Houghton Mifflin.

Ornstein, Allan C. 1988. "The changing status of the teaching profession." *Urban Education* 23:261–279.

Ornstein, Norman, Andrew Kohut, and Larry McCarthy. 1988. *The People, the Press, and Politics.* Reading, Mass.: Addison-Wesley.

Ornstein, Norman J., Thomas Mann, and Michael J. Malbin. 1989. *Vital Statistics on Congress.* Washington, D.C.: Government Printing Office.

Orum, Anthony. 1988. *An Introduction to Political Sociology,* 3rd ed. Englewood Cliffs, N.J.: Prentice Hall.

Ostrander, Susan A. 1984. *Women of the Upper Class.* Philadelphia: Temple University Press.

Othman-Chande, M. 1987. "The Cameroon volcanic gas disaster: An analysis of a makeshift response." *Disaster* 11(1):96–101.

O'Toole, Richard, and Stephen Webster. 1988. "Differentiation of family mistreatment." *Deviant Behavior* 9:346–368.

Otten, Mac W., Steven M. Teutsch, David E. Williamson, and James S. Marks. 1990. "The effect of known risk factors on the excess mortality of black adults in the United States." *Journal of the American Medical Association* 268:845–850.

Ouchi, William G. 1981. *Theory Z: How American Business Can Meet the Japanese Challenge.* Reading, Mass.: Addison-Wesley.

Owen, Diana. 1991. *Media Messages in American Presidential Elections.* Westport, Conn.: Greenwood Press.

Oxford Analytica. 1986. *America in Perspective.* Boston: Houghton Mifflin.

Page, Charles H. 1969. *Class and American Sociology.* New York: Schocken.

Page, Ellis. 1981. "Coleman Report 'just plain wrong.'" *Phi Delta Kappan* 63 (September): 74.

Paige, Jeffrey M. 1971. "Political orientation and riot participation." *American Sociological Review* 36:810–820.

Paige, Jeffrey M. 1975. *Agrarian Revolution.* New York: Free Press.

Paik, Haejung, and George Comstock. 1994. "The effects of television violence on antisocial behavior: A meta-analysis." *Communications Research* 21(40):516–546.

Paletz, David L. 1999. *The Media in American Politics: Contents and Consequences.* New York: Addison Wesley Longman.

Palgi, Michael, J. R . Blasi, M. Rosen, and M. Safir (eds.). 1983. *Sexual Equality: The Israeli Kibbutz Tests the Theories.* Norwood, Pa.: Norwood Editing.

Palmer, C. Eddie, and Sheryl M. Gonsoulin, 1990. "Paramedics, protocols, and procedures: 'Playing doc' as deviant role performance." *Deviant Behavior* 11(3):207–219.

Pampel, Fred J., Kenneth C. Land, and Marcus Felson. 1977. "A social indicator model of changes in the occupational structure of the United States, 1947–1974." *American Sociological Review* 42(6):951–964.

Parelius, Ann Parker, and Robert J. Parelius. 1987. *The Sociology of Education,* 2nd ed. Englewood Cliffs, N.J.: Prentice Hall.

Parenti, Michael. 1978. *Power and the Powerless.* New York: St. Martin's Press.

Parenti, Michael. 1988. *Democracy for the Few,* 5th ed. New York: St. Martin's Press.

Park, Robert E., and Ernest W. Burgess. 1921. *Introduction to the Science of Sociology.* Chicago: University of Chicago Press.

Park, Robert E., Ernest W. Burgess, and R. D. McKenzie. 1925. *The City.* Chicago: University of Chicago Press.

Parker, Gordon. 1985. "The search for intimacy in mid-life: An exploration of several myths." *Australian and New Zealand Journal of Psychiatry* 19:326–371.

Parkin, Frank. 1971. *Class Inequality and Political Order.* New York: Praeger.

Parkinson, C. Northcote. 1964. *Parkinson's Law.* New York: Ballantine.

Parnes, Herbert S. 1981. *A Longitudinal Study of Men, Work, and Society.* Cambridge, Mass.: MIT Press.

Parnes, Herbert S. (ed.). 1983. *Policy Issues in Work and Retirement.* Kalamazoo, Mich.: W. E. Upjohn Institute for Employment Research.

Parrot, Andrea. 1988. *Date Rape and Acquaintance Rape.* New York: Rosen.

Parsons, Talcott. 1951. *The Social System.* Glencoe, Ill.: Free Press.

Parsons, Talcott. 1955. "The American family: Its relations to personality and social structure." In Talcott Parsons and R. F. Bales (eds.), *Family,*

Socialization and Interaction Process. New York: Free Press.

Parsons, Talcott. 1959. "The school system." *Harvard Educational Review* 29.

Parsons, Talcott. 1964. *Social Structure and Personality.* New York: Free Press.

Parsons, Talcott. 1966. Societies: *Evolutionary and Comparative Perspectives.* Englewood Cliffs, N.J.: Prentice Hall.

Parsons, Talcott. 1967. *Sociological Theory and Modern Society.* New York: Free Press.

Parsons, Talcott, and Robert F. Bales. 1955. *Family Socialization and Interaction Process.* Glencoe, Ill.: Free Press.

Parsons, Talcott, and Gerald M. Platt. 1973. *The American University.* Cambridge, Mass.: Harvard University Press.

Parsons, Talcott, and Edward A. Shils (eds.). 1951. *Toward a General Theory of Action.* Cambridge, Mass.: Harvard University Press.

Parsons, Talcott, and Neil J. Smelser. 1956. *Economy and Society.* New York: Free Press.

Passel, Jeffrey S., and Karen A. Woodrow. 1984. "Geographic distribution of undocumented immigrants." *Internal Migration Review* 18:642–671.

Patel, Diana. 1988. "Some issues of urbanization and development in Zimbabwe." *Journal of Social Development* in Africa 3(2):17–31.

Patterson, J., and P. Kim. 1991. *The Day America Told the Truth: What People Really Believe about Everything That Really Matters.* Upper Saddle River, N.J.: Prentice Hall.

Paulos, John Allen. 1995. *A Mathematician Reads the Newspaper.* New York: Anchor.

Pearson, Landon. 1990. *Children of Glasnost: Growing Up Soviet.* Seattle: University of Washington Press.

Peers, Jo. 1985. "Workers by hand and womb: Soviet women and the demographic crisis." In Barbara Holland (ed.), *Soviet Sisterhood.* Bloomington: Indiana University Press.

Pelto, Pertti J. 1973. *Technology and Social Change in the Arctic.* Menlo Park, Calif.: Cummings.

Pelto, Pertti J., and Ludger Müller-Wille. 1972. "Snowmobiles: Technological revolution in the Arctic." In H. Russell Bernard and Pertti J. Pelto (eds.), *Technology and Social Change.* New York: Macmillan.

Pelton, Joseph N. 1988. "Tele-education: The future." *Social Education* 52:366–369.

People. 1999. "Heaven help us!" February 22.

Perevendentev, Victor Ivanovich. 1983. "The Soviet family today." *Sociology and Social Research* 67:245–259.

Perkins, H. Wesley, and James L. Spates. 1986. "Mirror images? Three analyses of values in England and the United States." *International Journal of Comparative Sociology* 27:31–50.

Perrow, Charles. 1979. *Complex Organizations: A Critical Essay,* 2nd ed. Glenview, Ill.: Scott Foresman.

Perrow, Charles. 1984. *Normal Accidents: Living with High-Risk Technologies.* New York: Basic Books.

Pescosolido, Bernice A., and Sharon Georgianna. 1989. "Durkheim, suicide and religion: Toward a network theory of suicide." *American Sociological Review* 54(1):33–48.

Peter, Laurence J. 1985. *Why Things Go Wrong, or, The Peter Principle Revisited.* New York: Morrow.

Peter, Laurence J., and Raymond Hull. 1969. *The Peter Principle: Why Things Always Go Wrong.* New York: Morrow.

Peterman, D., C. Ridley, and S. Anderson. 1974. "A comparison of cohabiting and noncohabiting college students." *Journal of Marriage and the Family* 36:344–354.

Peters, Thomas J., and Robert H. Waterman, Jr. 1982. *In Search of Excellence.* New York: Harper & Row.

Peterson, Peter G. 1999. *Gray Dawn: How the Coming Age Wave Will Transform America—And the World.* New York: Times Books.

Peterson, William. 1975. *Population,* 3rd ed. New York: Macmillan.

Peterson, William. 1985. *Dictionary of Demographics.* Westport, Conn.: Greenwood Press.

Petranek, Charles F. 1988. "Recruitment and commitment." *Society* 25(2):48–51.

Pettigrew, Thomas. 1971. *Racially Separate or Together.* New York: McGraw-Hill.

Pettigrew, Thomas F., et al. 1982. *Prejudice.* Cambridge, Mass.: Harvard University Press.

Pettigrew, Thomas F., and Joanne Martin. 1987. "Shaping the organizational context for American inclusion." *Journal of Social Issues* 43(1):41–78.

Pfeffer, Jeffrey, and Gerald R. Salancik. 1978. *The External Control of Organizations: A Resource Dependence Perspective.* New York: Harper & Row.

Pfuhl, Erdwin H., Jr. 1987. "Computer abuse: Problems of instrumental control." *Deviant Behavior* 8:113–130.

Phillips, David P., and Lundie L. Carstensen. 1988. "The effect of suicide stories on various demographic groups, 1968–1985." *Suicide and Life Threatening Behavior* 18 (1) (Spring): 100–114.

Phillips, David P., and Daniel Paight. 1987. "The impact of televised movies about suicides: A replicative study." *New England Journal of Medicine* 317 (13) (September 24): 809–811.

Phillips, David P., and John S. Wills. 1987. "A drop in suicides around major national holidays." *Suicide and Life Threatening Behavior* 17:1–12.

Phillips, Kevin. 1995. "Virtual Washington." *Time,* Spring, pp. 65–68.

Picharro, Nelson A. 1988. "Resource mobilization: An analysis of conflicting theoretical visions." *Sociological Quarterly* 29(1):97–118.

Pieraccini, Tina. 1987. "Sexism and the media." In Alan Wells (ed.), *Mass Media and Society.* Lexington, Mass.: D. C. Heath.

Pines, Maya. 1981. "The civilization of Genie." *Psychology Today* 15 (September): 28–34.

Pinkney, Alphonso. 1984. *The Myth of Black Progress.* New York: Cambridge University Press.

Piore, Michael, and Charles Sabel. 1984. *The Second Industrial Divide.* New York: Basic Books.

Pirenne, Henri. 1925. *Medieval Cities.* Princeton, N.J.: Princeton University Press.

Piven, Frances Fox. 1996. "Welfare and the transformation of electoral politics." *Dissent* (Fall): 61–67.

Piven, Frances Fox, and Richard A. Cloward. 1982. *The New Class War.* New York: Pantheon.

Piven, Frances, and Richard Cloward. 1989. *Why Americans Don't Vote.* New York: Pantheon.

Platt, John. 1987. "The future of AIDS." *The Futurist* 21(6):10–17.

Pleck, Joseph H. 1985. "Husbands' paid work and family roles: Current research issues." In H. Lopata (ed.), *Research in the Interweave of Social Roles, Jobs, and Families.* Beverly Hills, Calif.: Sage.

Pleck, Joseph H., Michael E. Lamb, and James A. Levine. 1986. "Epilog: Facilitating future change in men's family roles." *Marriage and Family Review* 9:11–16.

Pol, Louis G. 1987. *Business Demography: A Guide for Business Planners and Marketers.* New York: Quorum Press.

Polacheck, Soloman. 1984. "Women in the economy: Perspectives on gender equality." *Comparable Worth* (June): 53–68.

Pollock, Jocelyn M., and Barbara Ramirez. 1995. "Women in the legal profession." In Alida V. Merlo and Jocelyn M. Pollack (eds.), *Women, Law, and Social Control.* Boston: Allyn & Bacon.

Pool, John Charles, and Stephen C. Stamos, Jr. 1989. *International Economic Policy: Beyond the Trade and Debt Crisis.* Lexington, Mass.: Lexington Books.

Pope, Whitney. 1976. *Durkheim's Suicide: A Classic Reanalyzed.* Chicago: University of Chicago Press.

Popenoe, David. 1977. *The Suburban Environment: Sweden and the United States.* Chicago: University of Chicago Press.

Popenoe, David. 1988. *Disturbing the Nest: Family Change and Decline in Modern Societies.* New York: Aldine.

Popham, James W., and Elaine Lindheim. 1981. "Implications of a landmark ruling on Florida's minimum competency test." *Phi Delta Kappan* 63:18–20.

Popkin, Susan J. 1990. "Welfare: View from the bottom." *Social Problems* 37:64–73.

Population Reference Bureau. 1991. *1991 World Population Data Sheet.* Washington, D.C.: Population Reference Bureau.

Population Reference Bureau. 1992. *1992 World Population Data Sheet.* Washington, D.C.: Population Reference Bureau.

Population Reports. Johns Hopkins University. 1990. "Voluntary female sterilization: Number one and growing." Series C, no. 10. Baltimore: Population Information Program.

Porter, Bruce D. 1980. "Parkinson's law revisited: War and the growth of American government." *Public Interest* 60:50–68.

Portes, Alejandro, and Ruben G. Rumbaut. 1990. *Immigrant America: A Portrait.* Berkeley: University of California Press.

Portes, Alejandro, and Cynthia Truelove. 1987. "Making sense of diversity: Recent research on Hispanic minorities in the United States." *Annual Review of Sociology* 13:359–385.

Postman, Neil. 1981. "TV's 'disastrous' impact on children." *U.S. News & World Report* 90:43–45.

Postman, Neil. 1982. *The Disappearance of Childhood.* New York: Delacorte.

Postman, Neil. 1985. *Amusing Ourselves to Death.* New York: Penguin.

Postman, Neil. 1993. *Technopoly: The Surrender of Culture to Technology.* New York: Vintage Books.

Postman, Neil. 1995. *The End of Education.* New York: Vintage Books.

Poulantzas, Nicos. 1973. *Political Power and Social Classes.* London: New Left Books.

Premack, David. 1985. *The Future History of the Animal Language Controversy.* Cambridge, Mass.: MIT Press.

Press, Aric, et al. 1985. "The war against pornography." *Newsday,* March 18, pp. 58–66.

Price-Bonham, S., and J. O. Balswick. 1980. "The noninstitutions: divorce, desertion, and remarriage." *Journal of Marriage and the Family* 42: 959–972.

Public Opinion. 1985. "Opinion roundup." 7(6):23–42.

Pullin, Diana. 1981. "Minimum competency testing and the demand for accountability." *Phi Delta Kappan* 63:20–22.

Putnam, Jo Anne. 1997. *Cooperative Learning in Diverse Classrooms.* Upper Saddle River, N.J.: Prentice Hall.

Putnam, Robert. 1995. "Bowling alone: America's declining of social capital." *Journal of Democracy* (January).

Quarantelli, F. I., and Russel R. Dynes. 1970. "Property norms and looting: Their patterns in community crises." *Phylon* 31:168–182.

Quittner, Joshua. 1998. "Free speech for the net: A panel of federal judges overturns the communications decency act." In Michael Petracca and Madeleine Ssorapure (eds), *Common Culture.* Upper Saddle River, N.J.: Prentice Hall.

Rabb, Theodore K., and Robert Rotberg (eds.). 1981. *Industrialization and Urbanization.* Princeton, N.J.: Princeton University Press.

Radcliffe-Brown. A.R. 1952. *Structure and Function in Primitive Society.* New York: Free Press.

Rae, Bob. 1991. "A socialist credo." *Dissent* (Winter): 43–45.

Raine, Philip. 1974. *Brazil: Awakening Giant.* Washington, D.C.: Public Affairs Press.

Rapoport, Robert, and Rhona Rapoport. 1978. *Working Couples.* New York: Harper & Row.

Raskin, Marcus G. 1972. "The channeling colony." In Martin Carnoy (ed.), *Schooling in a Corporate Society.* New York: McKay.

Raunikar, Robert, and Chung-Liang Huang. 1987. *Food Demand, Analysis Problems, Issues, and Empirical Evidence.* Ames: Iowa State University Press.

Reckless, Walter. 1967. *The Crime Problem.* New York: Appleton Century Crofts.

Redburn, F. Stevens, and Terry F. Buss. 1986. *Responding to America's Homeless: Public Policy Alternatives.* New York: Praeger.

Reeves, Phil. 1996. "Russian children learn capitalism is a teddy bear's picnic." *The Independent,* November 29, 15.

Reich, Charles A. 1970. *The Greening of America.* New York: Random House.

Reich, Robert. 1983. *The Next American Frontier.* New York: Penguin.

Reich, Robert. 1987. *Tales of a New America.* New York: Vintage.

Reich, Robert. 1991. *The Work of Nations.* New York: Knopf.

Rein, Irving J., Philip Kotler, and Martin Stoller. 1987. *High Visibility.* New York: Dodd, Mead.

Reiss, Albert J., Jr. 1968. "Sociology." *International Encyclopedia of the Social Sciences.* Vol. 15. New York: Crowell Collier and Macmillan.

Repetto, Robert (ed.). 1985. *The Global Possible: Resources, Development, and the New Century.* New Haven, Conn.: Yale University Press.

Repetto, Robert. 1987. "Population, resources, and environment: An uncertain future." *Population Bulletin* 42:2.

Reskin, Barbara F. 1988. "Bringing the man back in: Sex differentiation and the devaluation of woman's work." *Gender and Society* 2:58–81.

Resnick, Daniel P., and Lauren B. Resnick. 1983. "Improving educational standards in American schools." *Phi Delta Kappan* 65(3):178–80.

Reynolds, Michael. 1994. *Groupwork in Education and Training: Ideas in Practice.* London: Kegan Page.

Reynolds, Vernon. 1976. *The Biology of Human Action.* San Francisco: Freeman.

Riche, Martha F. 1981. "Demographic supermarkets of the eighties." *American Demographics* 3:15–21.

Riche, Martha F. 1991. "We're all minorities now." *American Demographics* 13 (October): 36–34.

Riesman, David. 1961. *The Lonely Crowd.* New Haven, Conn.: Yale University Press.

Rifkin, Jeremy. 1996. *The End of Work: The Decline of the Global Labor Force and the Dawn of the Post-Market Era.* New York: Putnam's.

Riley, Matilda White. 1987. "Aging, health, and social change." In Matilda Riley, Joseph D. Matarazzo, and Andrew Baum (eds.), *The Aging Dimension.* Hillsdale, N.J.: Laurence Erlbaum.

Riley, Matilda White, Anne Foner, and Joan Waring. 1988. "Sociology of age." In Neil J. Smelser (ed.), *Handbook of Sociology.* Newbury Park, Calif.: Sage.

Riley, Matilda White, Marilyn Johnson, and Anne Foner. 1972. *Aging and Society.* New York: Russell Sage Foundation.

Rist, Marilee C. 1989. "Should parents choose their child's school?" *The Education Digest* 55:3–6.

Ritzer, George. 1993. *The McDonaldization of Society.* Thousand Oaks, Calif.: Pine Forge Press.

Ritzer, George, and David Walczak. 1986. *Working: Conflict and Change,* 3rd ed. Englewood Cliffs, N.J.: Prentice Hall.

Riulin, Alice M., and P. Michael Timpane. 1975. *Ethical and Legal Issues of Social Experimentation.* Washington, D.C.: Brookings Institution.

Rix, Sara E. (ed.). 1989. *The American Woman 1988–89. A Status Report.* Women's Research and Education Institute. New York: Norton.

Roberts, Sam. 1995. *Who We Are: A Portrait of America Based on the Latest U.S. Census.* New York: Times Books.

Robbins, Thomas, and Dick Anthony. 1972. "Getting straight with Meher Baba: A study of mysticism, drug rehabilitation and postadolescent conflict." *Journal for the Scientific Study of Religion* 7:122–128.

Robinson, Harry. 1981. *Population and Resources.* New York: St. Martin's Press.

Robinson, John P., and Mark Levy. 1987. "Interpersonal communication and news comprehension." In Michael Gurevitch and Mark Levy (eds.), *Mass Communication Review Yearbook.* Vol 6. Beverly Hills, Calif.: Sage.

Rodgers, Harrell R., Jr. 1982. *The Cost of Human Neglect: America's Welfare Failure.* Armonk, N.Y.: M. E. Sharpe.

Roebuck, Janet. 1974. *The Shaping of Urban Society.* New York: Scribner's.

Roethlisberger, F. J. 1949. *Management and Morale.* Cambridge, Mass.: Harvard University Press.

Rogers, David. 1969. *110 Livingston Street: Politics and Bureaucracy in the New York City School System.* New York: Random House.

Rokeach, Milton. 1968. "The role of values in public opinion research." *Public Opinion Quarterly* 32(4) (Winter 1968–1969): 549.

Rokeach, Milton. 1973. *The Nature of Human Values.* New York: Free Press.

Rokeach, Milton (ed.). 1979. *Understanding Human Values.* New York: Free Press.

Roniger, Luis. 1987. "Coronelismo, Caciquismo and Oyabunkobun bonds: Divergent implications of hierarchical trust in Brazil, Mexico, and Japan." *British Journal of Sociology* 38:310–330.

Roof, Wade C. 1979. "Socioeconomic differentials among white socio-religious groups in the United States." *Social Forces* 58:280–289.

Roof, Wade C., and William McKinney. 1987. *American Mainline Religion: Its Changing Shape and Future.* New Brunswick, N.J.: Rutgers University Press.

Roopnarine, Jaipaul L., and Lynn M. Hempel. 1988. "Day care and family dynamics." *Early Childhood Research Quarterly* 3:427–438.

Roos, Patricia A. 1985. *Gender and Work: A Comparative Analysis of Industrial Societies.* Albany: State University of New York.

Rosa, Eugene A., Gary E. Machilis, and Kenneth M. Keating. 1988. "Energy and society." *Annual Review of Sociology* 14:149–172.

Roscoe, Will. 1992. *The Zuni Man-Woman.* Albuquerque: University of New Mexico.

Rose, A. M. 1965. "The subculture of the aging: A framework in social gerontology." In A.M. Rose and W.A. Peterson (eds.), *Older People and Their Social World.* Philadelphia: Davis.

Rose, A. M. 1967. *The Power Structure.* New York: Oxford University Press.

Rosenberg, Charles E. 1987. *The Care of Strangers: The Rise of American Hospitalization.* New York: Basic Books.

Rosenberg, Dorothy. 1991. "Shock therapy: GDR women in transition from a socialist welfare state to a social market economy." *Signs* 17:129–152.

Rosenberg, Morris. 1956. "Misanthropy and political ideology." *American Sociological Review* 21:690–695.

Rosenberg, Morris. 1990. "The self-concept: Social product and social force." In Morris Rosenberg and Ralph H. Turner (eds.), *Social Psychology: Sociological Perspectives.* New York: Basic Books.

Rosenberg, Morris, and Roberta Simmons. 1971. *Black and White Self-Esteem: The Urban School Child. American Sociological Association Monograph Series.*

Rosenblum, Simon. 1991. "Social Democrats win in Ontario." *Dissent* (Winter): 19–21.

Rosener, Judy B. 1990. "Ways women lead." *Harvard Business Review* 68:119–25.

Rosenfeld, Anne, and Elizabeth Stark. 1987. "The prime of our lives." *Psychology Today* (May): 162–172.

Rosenfeld, Rachel A. 1978. "Women's intergenerational occupational mobility." *American Sociological Review* 43:36–46.

Rosenthal, Robert, and Lenore Jacobson. 1968. *Pygmalion in the Classroom: Teacher Expectation and the Pupil's Intellectual Development.* New York: Holt, Rinehart & Winston.

Rosnow, Ralph L., and Gary Alan Fine. 1976. *Rumor and Gossip.* New York: Elsevier.

Ross, Heather L., and Isabel V. Sawhill. 1975. *Time of Transition: The Growth of Families Headed by Women.* Washington, D.C.: Urban Institute.

Rossell, Christine H., and Charles L. Glenn. 1988. "The Cambridge controlled choice plan." *The Urban Review* 20:75–94.

Rossi, Alice S. 1984. "Gender and parenthood." *American Sociological Review* 49:1–16.

Rossi, Peter H., James D. Wright, and Sonia R. Wright. 1978. "The theory and practice of applied social research." *Evaluation Quarterly* 2:171–191.

Rossides, Daniel M. 1990. *Social Stratification: The American Class System in Comparative Perspective.* Upper Saddle River, N.J.: Prentice Hall.

Rossides, Daniel. 1997. *Social Stratification: The Interplay of Class, Race, and Gender,* 2nd ed., Upper Saddle River, N.J.: Prentice Hall.

Rostow, W. W. 1987. *Rich Countries, Poor Countries: Reflections on the Past, Lessons for the Future.* Boulder, Colo.: Westview.

Rothman, Barbara Katz. 1989. *Recreating Motherhood: Ideology and Technology in a Patriarchal Society.* New York: Norton.

Rothman, Robert. 1978. *Inequality and Stratification in the United States.* Englewood Cliffs, N.J.: Prentice Hall.

Rothstein, Stanley William. 1987. "Schooling in mass society." *Urban Education* 22:267–285.

Rowan, Roy, and Sara Hammes. 1989. "A Guide to the Pacific rim." *Fortune* 120: 72–82.

Rubin, Jeffrey Z., Frank J. Provenzano, and Zella Luria. 1974. "The eye of the beholder: Parents' views on sex of newborns." *American Journal of Orthopsychiatry* 44:512–519.

Rubin, Lillian. 1976. *Worlds of Pain: Life in the Working-Class Family.* New York: Basic Books.

Ryan, Charlotte. 1991. *Prime Time Activism: Media Strategies for Grassroots Organizing.* Boston: South End Press.

Ryan, John and William M. Wentworth. 1999. *Media and Society: The Production of Culture in the Mass Media.* Boston: Allyn & Bacon.

Ryan, William. 1976. *Blaming the Victim,* rev. ed. New York: Vintage.

Rybczynski, Witold. 1995. "Culture's urban fortunes." *Civilization* (November/December): 33–35.

Rybczynski, Witold. 1995. *City Life.* New York: Touchstone.

Ryder, Judith, and Harold Silver. 1985. *Modern English Society,* 3rd ed. New York: Methuen.

Sabato, Larry J. 1997. *Toward the Millenium: The Elections of 1996.* Boston: Allyn & Bacon.

Sadker, David, and Myra Sadker. 1988. *Teachers Make the Difference,* 2nd ed. New York: Random House.

Sadker, Myra, and David Sadker. 1994. *Failing at Fairness: How Schools Cheat Girls.* New York: Touchstone.

Sadker, Myra, David Sadker, and Susan S. Klein. 1986. "Abolishing misconceptions about sex equity in education." *Theory into Practice* 25:219–226.

Sagarin, Edward. 1975. *Deviants and Deviance.* New York: Praeger.

Sahlins, Marshall. 1978. *The Use and Abuse of Biology.* Ann Arbor: University of Michigan Press.

Saltzman, Linda, Raymond Paternoster, Gordon P. Waldo, and Theodore G. Chiricas. 1982. "Deterrent and experiential effects: The problem of causal order in perceptual deterrence research." *Journal of Research in Crime and Delinquency* 19:172–189.

Samuel, Maurice. 1943. *The World of Sholom Aleichem.* New York: Knopf.

Samuelson, Paul. 1970. *Economics.* New York: McGraw-Hill.

Samuelson, Paul, and William Nordhaus. 1988. *Economics.* New York: McGraw-Hill.

Sanders, Jimmy M. 1990. "Public transfers: Safety net or inducement into poverty?" *Social Forces* 68:813–834.

Sanders, Richard J. 1985. "Teaching apes to ape language: Explaining the imitative and nonimitative signing of a chimpanzee." *Journal of Comparative Psychology* 99:197–210.

Sanderson, Stephen K. 1990. *Social Evolutionism: A Critical History.* Cambridge, Mass.: Basil Blackwell.

Saney, Parviz. 1986. *Crime and Culture in America.* Westport, Conn.: Greenwood Press.

Sanjian, Andrea Stevenson. 1991. "Social problems, political issues: Marriage and divorce in the USSR." *Soviet Studies* 43(4):629–649.

Sapir, Edward. 1937. "Fashion." *In Encyclopedia of the Social Sciences.* New York: Macmillan.

Sapiro, Virginia. 1983. *The Political Integration of Women.* Urbana: University of Illinois Press.

Sapiro, Virginia. 1988. *Women, Political Action, and Political Participation.* Washington, D.C.: American Political Science Association.

Sarbin, Theodore, and Jeffrey E. Miller. 1970. "Demonism revisited: The chromosomal abnormality." *Issues in Criminology* (Summer): 195–207.

Saunders, John. 1971. *Modern Brazil: New Patterns and Development.* Gainesville: University of Florida Press.

Saunders, Peter. 1981. *Social Theory and the Urban Question.* New York: Holmes and Meyer.

Saxe, Leonard. 1986. "Policymakers' use of social science research." *Knowledge: Creation, Diffusion, Utilization* 8(1):59–78.

Saxe, L. D. Dougherty, and K. Esty. 1985. "Alcoholism: A public policy perspective." In J. Mendelson and N. Mello (eds.), *The Diagnosis and Treatment of Alcoholism.* New York: Wiley.

Scanlan, Christopher. 1993. "Reality awaits leave bill: Most US workers won't be covered." *Wichita Eagle,* February 5.

Scargill, D. I. 1979. *The Form of Cities.* London: Bell and Hyman.

Schaedel, Richard P., Jorge E. Hardy, and Nora Scott Kinzer. 1978. *Urbanization in the Americas from Its Beginning to the Present.* The Hague: Mouton.

Schaffer, Jeffrey, and Suzy Blackaby. 1984. "How to gain status and intimidate people." *Wall Street Journal,* November 26.

Schatzman, Leonard, and Anselm L. Strauss. 1973. *Field Research.* Englewood Cliffs, N.J.: Prentice Hall.

Schein, Edgar. 1961. *Coercive Persuasion.* New York: Norton.

Schieffelin, B. 1990. *The Give and Take of Everyday Life: Language Socialization of Kaluli Children.* New York: Cambridge University Press.

Schiff, Michael, and Richard Lewontin. 1986. *Education and Class: The Irrelevance of IQ Genetic Studies.* Oxford: Clarendon Press.

Schiller, Herbert. 1973. *The Mind Managers.* Boston: Beacon Press.

Schlapentokh, Vladimir. 1988. "The XXVII Congress: A case study in the shaping of a new party ideology." *Soviet Studies* 40:1–20.

Schlemmer, Lawrence. 1991. "A challenge of political transition in South Africa: Majority vs. minority rights." *South African Journal of Sociology* 22(1):16–23.

Schmalleger, Frank. 1997. *Criminal Justice Today: An Introduction for the Twenty-First Century.* Upper Saddle River, N.J.: Prentice Hall.

Schneider, Benjamin (ed.) 1990. *Organizational Climate and Culture.* San Francisco: Jossey-Bass.

Schneller, Raphael. 1985. "Heritage and changes in the nonverbal language of Ethiopian newcomers." *Israel Social Science Research* 3:33–54.

Schon, Donald. 1971. *Beyond the Stable State.* New York: W. W. Norton.

Schöpflin, George. 1990. "The end of communism in Eastern Europe." *International Affairs* 66(1):3–16.

Schram, Wilbur, Jack Lyle, and Edwin B. Parker. 1961. *Television in the Lives of Our Children.* Stanford, Calif.: Stanford Universtiy Press.

Schultz, Sandra. 1981. "Adjusting marriage tradition: Greeks to Greek-Americans." *Journal of Comparative Family Studies* 7:205–218.

Schuman, Howard, and Stanley Presser. 1981. *Questions and Answers in Attitude Surveys: Experiments on Question Form, Wording, and Context.* New York: Academic Press.

Schur, Edwin M. 1971. *Labelling Deviant Behavior.* New York: Harper & Row.

Schutz, Alfred. 1962. *Collected Papers I: The Problem of Social Reality.* The Hague: Martinus Nijhoff.

Schwartz, Barry. 1967. "The social psychology of privacy." *American Journal of Sociology* 73:741–752.

Schwartz, Barry. 1975. *Queuing and Waiting: Studies in the Social Organization of Access and Delay.* Chicago: University of Chicago.

Schwartz, Felice N. 1989. "Management women and the new facts of life." *Harvard Business Review* 89:65–76.

Schwartz, Mary Ann, and Barbara Marliene Scott. 1997. *Marriages and Families: Diversity and Change.* Upper Saddle River, N.J.: Prentice Hall.

Schwirian, Kent P. 1983. "Models of neighborhood change." *Annual Review of Sociology* 9:83–108.

Scitovsky, Anne A., and M. Cline. 1986. "Medical care costs of patients with AIDS in San Francisco." *Journal of the American Medical Association* 256(3):3107–3109.

Scott, Allen J. 1988. *Metropolis: From the Division of Labor to Urban Form.* Berkeley: University of California Press.

Scott, W. Richard. 1998. *Organizations: Rational, Natural, and Open Systems.* Upper Saddle River, N.J.: Prentice Hall.

Sears, David O., Carl P. Hensler, and Leslie K. Speer, 1979. "White opposition to 'busing': Self-interest or symbolic politics?" *American Political Science Review* 73:161–188.

Seeman, Melvin. 1961. "On the meaning of alienation." *American Sociological Review* 26:753–758.

Select Committee on Children, Youth, and Families, U.S. House of Representatives. 1989. *U.S. Children and Their Families: Current Conditions and Recent Trends.* Washington, D.C.: U.S. Government Printing Office.

Selvin, Hanan C., and Warren O. Hagstrom. 1960. "Determinants of support of civil liberties." *British Journal of Sociology* 11 (March):51–73.

Sewell, William H. 1971. "Inequality of opportunity for higher education." *American Sociological Review* 36:793–808.

Sewell, William H., Robert M. Hauser, and Wendy C. Wolf. 1980. "Sex, schooling and occupational status." *American Journal of Sociology* 86:551–583.

Shanas, Ethel, and George R. Maddox. 1976. "Aging, health, and the organization of health resources." In Robert H. Binstock and Ethel Shanas (eds.), *Handbook of Aging and the Social Sciences.* New York: Van Nostrand Reinhold.

Shapiro, Judith. 1992. *The Industrial Labour Force.* In Mary Buckley (ed.), *Perestroika and Soviet Women.* Cambridge: Cambridge University Press.

Shaw, Clifford R., and Henry O. McKay. 1929. *Delinquency Areas.* Chicago: University of Chicago Press.

Shaw, John W., Peter G. Nordie, and Richard M. Shapiro (eds.). 1987. *Strategies for Improving Race Relations: The Anglo-American Experience.* Manchester, England: Manchester University Press.

Shaw, Marvin E. 1976. *Group Dynamics: The Psychology of Small Group Behavior,* 2nd ed. New York: McGraw-Hill.

Sheehy, Gail. 1976. *Passages: Predictable Crises of Adult Life.* New York: Dutton.

Sheldon, William H., et al. 1949. *Varieties of Delinquent Youth.* New York: Harper & Brothers.

Sherif, Muzafer. 1936. *The Psychology of Social Norms.* New York: Harper & Row.

Sherif, Muzafer, and Carolyn Sherif. 1953. *Groups in Harmony and Tension: An Introduction to Studies in Intergroup Relations.* New York: Harper & Row.

Sherwood, Mrs. John. 1887. *Manners and Social Usages.* New York: Harper & Brothers.

Shevky, Eshrev, and Wendell Bell. 1955. *Social Area Analysis.* Stanford, Calif.: Stanford University Press.

Shibutani, Tomatsu. 1966. *Improvised News: A Sociological Study of Rumor.* Indianapolis, Ind.: Bobbs-Merrill.

Shipler, David K. 1989. *Russia: Broken Idols, Solemn Dreams.* New York: Penguin.

Short, James F. 1971. *The Social Fabric of the Metropolis.* Chicago: University of Chicago Press.

Shorto, Russell. 1997. "Belief by the numbers." *New York Times,* December 7, 60–61.

Sibley, Elbridge. 1971. "Scientific sociology at bay?" *American Sociologist* 6:13–17.

Sidel, Victor W., and Ruth Sidel. 1982. *A Health State: An International Perspective on the Crisis in United States Health Care,* 2nd ed. New York: Pantheon.

Siegal, Michael. 1987. "Are sons and daughters treated more differently by fathers than by mothers?" *Developmental Review,* no. 3:83–209.

Signorielli, Nancy. 1983. "Health, prevention, and television: Images of the elderly and perceptions of social reality." *Prevention in Human Services* 3:97–117.

Signorielli, Nancy. 1985. *Role Portrayal and Stereotyping on Television.* Westport, Conn.: Greenwood Press.

Signorielli, Nancy. 1989. "Television conceptions about sex roles: Maintaining conventionality and the status quo." *Sex Roles* 21:341–360.

Silberman, Charles E. 1978. *Criminal Violence and Criminal Justice.* New York: Random House.

Silk, Mark. 1988. *Spiritual Politics.* New York: Simon & Schuster.

Sills, David. 1968. "Voluntary associations." In *International Encyclopedia of the Social Sciences.* Vol. 16. New York: Crowell Collier.

Sills, David. 1970. "Preserving organizational goals." In Oscar Grusky and George Miller (eds.), *The Sociology of Organizations.* New York: Free Press.

Silverman, Carol J. 1986. "Neighborhoods and urbanism: Commonality vs. friendship." *Urban Affairs Quarterly* 22(2):312–328.

Simenauer, David, and Jacqueline Carroll. 1982. *Singles: The New Americans.* New York: Simon & Schuster.

Simmel, Georg. 1955. *Conflict and the Web of Group Affiliations.* Translated by Kurt H. Wolff & Reinhard Bendix. New York: Free Press.

Simon, Barbara Levy. 1987. *Never Married Women.* Philadelphia: Temple University Press.

Simon, Julian L. 1981. *The Ultimate Resource.* Princeton, N.J.: Princeton University Press.

Simon, Julian L. 1986. *Theory of Population and Economic Growth.* Oxford: Basil Blackwell.

Simon, Julian L. 1990. *Theory of Population Control,* 2nd ed. New York: Basil Blackwell.

Simon, Rita, and Jean Landis. 1991. *The Crimes Women Commit, the Punishments They Receive.* Lexington, Mass.: Lexington Books.

Simpson, George E., and J. Milton Yinger. 1972. *Racial and Cultural Minorities,* 4th ed. New York: Harper & Row.

Singer, Margaret Thaler. 1996. *Cults in Our Midst: The Hidden Menace in Our Everyday Lives.* San Francisco: Jossey-Bass.

Sivulka, Juliann. 1998. *Soap, Sex, and Cigarettes: A Cultural History of American Advertising.* Belmont, Calif.: Wadsworth.

Sjoberg, Gideon. 1960. *The Preindustrial City.* New York: Free Press.

Skidmore, Rex A., M. Hon, G. Thackeray, and O. William Farley. 1988. *Introduction to Social Work,* 4th ed. Englewood Cliffs, N.J.: Prentice Hall.

Skocpol, Theda. 1979. *States and Social Revolutions.* New York: Cambridge University Press.

Skocpol, Theda. 1980. "Political response to capitalist crises." *Politics and Society* 10:155–201.

Skocpol, Theda, and Edwin Amenta. 1986. "States and social policies." *Annual Review of Sociology* 12:131–157.

Skogan, Wesley G. 1979. "Crime and crime rates." In Wesley G. Skogan (ed.), *Sample Surveys of the Victims of Crimes.* Cambridge, Mass.: Ballinger.

Skolnik, Jerome. 1966. *Justice without Trial.* New York: Wiley.

Sloan, Allen. 1997. "The new rich." *Newsweek,* August 4, pp. 48–55.

Smelser, Neil J. 1959. *Social Change in the Industrial Revolution.* Chicago: University of Chicago Press.

Smelser, Neil J. 1962. *Theory of Collective Behavior.* New York: Free Press.

Smelser, Neil J. 1968. *Essays in Sociological Explanation.* Englewood Cliffs, N.J.: Prentice Hall.

Smircich, Linda. 1985. "Is the concept of culture a paradigm for understanding organizations and ourselves?" In Peter J. Frost, Larry F. Moore, Meryl Reis Louis, Craig C. Lundberg, and Joanne Martin (eds.), *Organizational Culture* pp. 55–72. Beverly Hills, Calif.: Sage.

Smith, A. Emerson. 1981. "Work roles of applied sociologists." Paper presented at the American Sociological Association Workshop on Directions in Applied Sociology.

Smith, Hedrick. 1976. *The Russians.* New York: Ballantine.

Smith, Hedrick. 1995. *Rethinking America: Innovative Strategies and Partnerships in Business and Education.* New York: Avon.

Smith, Michael P., and Joe R. Feagin (eds.). 1987. *The Capitalist City: Global Restructuring and Community Politics.* New York: Basil Blackwell.

Smith, R.E. 1979. *The Subtle Revolution: Women at Work.* Washington, D.C.: Urban Institute.

Snow, David A. 1988. "On the precariousness of measuring sanity in insane contexts." *Social Problems* 35:192–196.

Snow, D., and P. Leahy. 1980. "The making of a black slum-ghetto: A case study of neighborhood transition." *Journal of Applied Behavioral Sciences* 16(4).

Snyder, Benson R. 1971. *The Hidden Curriculum.* Cambridge, Mass.: MIT Press.

Snyder, Thomas D. 1987. *Digest of Educational Statistics, 1987.* Washington, D.C.: National Center for Education Statistics.

So, Alvin Y. 1986. "The math/reading gap among Asian American students: A function of nativity, mother tongue, and SES." *Sociology and Social Research: An International Journal* 70(1):76–77.

So, Alvin Y. 1990. *Social Change and Development: Modernization, Dependency, and World-System Theories.* Newbury Park, Calif.: Sage.

Solomon, Lewis C., and Paul Wachtel. 1975. "The effects on income of type of college attended." *Sociology of Education* 48:75–90.

Sorokin, Pitirim A. 1941. *Social and Cultural Dynamics.* New York: American Books.

Sowell, Thomas. 1981. *Ethnic America: A History.* New York: Basic Books.

Spade, Joan Z., and Carole A. Reese. 1991. "We've come a long way, maybe: College students' plans for work and family." *Sex Roles* 24:309–321.

Spates, James L. 1983. "The sociology of values." *Annual Review of Sociology* 9:27–49.

Spender, Dale. 1980. *Man Made Language.* London: Routledge & Kegan Paul.

Spengler, Oswald. 1965. *The Decline of the West.* New York: Modern Library. (Originally published in 1918.)

Spiering, Frank. 1984. *Lizzie.* New York: Random House.

Spiro, M. E. 1958. *Children of the Kibbutz.* Cambridge, Mass.: Harvard University Press.

Spiro, S. E., and Ephraim Yuchtman-Yaar (eds.). 1983. *Evaluating the Welfare State.* New York: Academic Press.

Spitz, René A. 1945. "Hospitalism: An inquiry into the genesis of psychiatric conditions in early childhood." *The Psychoanalytic Study of the Child* 1:53–74.

Sreenivasan, Sreenath. 1998. "Corporate intelligence: A cloakhold on the web." *New York Times,* March 2, C4.

Stack, C. B. 1974. *All Our Kin.* New York: Harper & Row.

Stack, John F., Jr. 1986. *The Primordial Challenge: Ethnicity in the Contemporary World.* Westport, Conn.: Greenwood Press.

Stack, S. 1987. "Celebrities and suicides: A taxonomy and analysis." *American Sociological Review* 52:401–412.

Stack, Steven. 1990. "New micro-level data on the impact of divorce on suicide, 1959–1980: A test of two theories." *Journal of Marriage and the Family* 52(1):119–127.

Stagner, Ross. 1987. "Group conflicts." In Jeff Boucher, Dan Landis, and Karen Arnold Clark (eds.), *Ethnic Conflict: International Perspectives.* Newbury Park, Calif.: Sage.

Staples, Robert (ed.). 1991. *The Black Family,* 4th ed. Belmont, Calif.: Wadsworth.

Starer, Daniel. 1995. *Hot Topics.* New York: Simon & Schuster.

Stark, Rodney, and William Sims Bainbridge. 1979. "Of churches, sects, and cults: Preliminary concepts for a theory of religious movements." *Journal for the Scientific Study of Religion* 18:117–133.

Stark, Rodney, and William Sims Bainbridge. 1985. *The Future of Religion: Secularization, Revival, and Cult Formation.* Berkeley: University of California Press.

Starkey, Marion L., 1946. *The Cherokee Nation.* New York: Knopf.

Starr, Paul. 1982. *The Social Transformation of American Medicine.* New York: Basic Books.

Stavrianos, L.S. 1983. *A Global History: The Human Heritage,* 3rd ed. Englewood Cliffs, N.J.: Prentice Hall.

Steffensmeier, Darrell, and Cathy Streifel. 1991. "Age, gender, and crime across three historical periods: 1935, 1960, and 1985." *Social Forces* 69(3):869–894.

Steffensmeier, Darrell J., and Robert M. Terry. 1973. "Deviance and respectability: An observational study of reactions to shoplifting." *Social Forces* 51:417–426.

Stein, Barry. 1979. "Occupational adjustment of refugees: The Vietnamese in the United States." *International Migration Review* 13:25–45.

Steinem, Gloria. 1983. *Outrageous Acts and Everyday Rebellions.* New York: Holt, Rinehart & Winston.

Steiner, Gilbert Y. 1981. *The Futility of Family Policy.* Washington, D.C.: Brookings Institution.

Stephens, John. 1979. *The Transition from Capitalism to Socialism.* London: Macmillan.

Stern, Phillip. 1988. *The Best Congress Money Can Buy.* New York: Pantheon.

Sternlieb, George, and James W. Hughes. 1986. "Demographics and housing in America." *Population Bulletin* 41:1.

Stevens, William K. 1992. "Humanity confronts its handiwork: An altered planet." *New York Times,* May 5.

Steward, Julian. 1955. *Theory of Cultural Change.* Urbana: University of Illinois Press.

Stipp, Horst, and J. Ronald Milavsky. 1988. "U.S. television programming's effects on aggressive behavior of children and adolescents." *Current Psychology Research and Reviews* 7:76–92.

Stockard, Jean, and Miriam M. Johnson. 1980. *Sex Roles.* Englewood Cliffs, N.J.: Prentice Hall.

Stone, Alan, and Richard Barke. 1985. *Governing the American Public.* New York: St. Martin's Press.

Stone, John. 1985. *Racial Conflict in Contemporary Society.* Cambridge, Mass.: Harvard University Press.

Stone, Joseph L., and Joseph Church. 1975. *Childhood and Adolescence,* 3rd ed. New York: Random House.

Stone, Lawrence. 1985. "Sex in the West." *The New Republic,* July 8, pp. 25–37.

Stoner, J. A. F. 1961. "A comparison of individual and group decisions including risk." Cited in Stephen Wilson. 1978. *Informal Groups: An Introduction.* Englewood Cliffs, N.J.: Prentice Hall.

Stouffer, S. A. 1940. "Intervening opportunities: A theory relating mobility and distance." *American Sociological Review* 5:845–867.

Stouffer, Samuel A., et al. 1949. *The American Soldier.* Princeton, N.J.: Princeton University Press.

Stowe, Harriet B. 1962. *Uncle Tom's Cabin.* New York: Macmillan. (Originally published in 1852.)

Straub, Carrie. 1998. *jobsearch.net.* Menlo Park, Calif.: Crisp Publications.

Straus, Murray A., and Richard J. Gelles. 1988. "Societal change and change in family violence from 1975 to 1985 as revealed by two national surveys." *Journal of Marriage and the Family* 48:465–479.

Straus, Murray A., Richard J. Gelles, and Suzanne K. Steinmetz. 1980. *Behind Closed Doors: Violence in the American Family.* Garden City, N.Y.: Doubleday/Anchor Books.

Strauss, Anselm. 1956. George Herbert Mead: *On Social Psychology.* Chicago: University of Chicago Press.

Strong, Josiah. 1885. *Our Country: Its Possible Future and Its Present Crisis.* New York.

Sugden, John. 1987. "The exploitation of disadvantage: The occupational subculture of the boxer." *Sociological Review Monograph* 33:187–209.

Sullivan, Gary L., and P. J. O'Connor. 1988. "Women's role portrayals in magazine advertising: 1958–1983." *Sex Roles* 18:181–188.

Sumner, William G. 1960. *Folkways.* New York: New American Library. (Originally published in 1906.)

Survey Research Consultants International. 1981. *Index to International Public Opinion,* 1980–1981.

Sutcliffe, Anthony. 1981. *Towards the Planned City: Germany, Britain, the*

United States, and France, 1790–1914. New York: St. Martin's Press.

Sutherland, Edwin M. 1940. "White-collar criminality." *American Sociological Review* (February): 1–12.

Sutherland, Edwin. 1947. *Principles of Criminology,* 4th ed. Chicago: Lippincott.

Suttles, Gerald D. 1965. *The Social Order of the Slum.* Chicago: University of Chicago Press.

Sutton, Frances X. 1987. "Refugees and mass exodus: The search for a humane, effective policy." In William Alonso (ed.), *Population in an Interacting World.* Cambridge, Mass.: Harvard University Press.

Swanson, Guy. 1967. *Religion and Regime: A Sociological Account of the Reformation.* Ann Arbor: University of Michigan Press.

Sykes, Gresham. 1978. *Criminology.* San Diego: Harcourt Brace Jovanovich.

Sykes, Gresham, and David Matza. 1957. "Techniques of neutralization: A theory of delinquency." *American Sociological Review* 22:664–670.

Syme, S. Leonard, and Lisa F. Berkman. 1986. "Social class, susceptibility, and sickness." In Peter Conrad and Rochelle Kern (eds.), *The Sociology of Health and Illness: Critical Perspectives,* 2nd ed. New York: St. Martin's Press.

Szalai, Julia. 1991. "Some aspects of the changing situation of women in Hungary." *Signs* 17(1):153–170.

Sztompka, Piotr. 1993. *The Sociology of Change.* Cambride, Mass.: Blackwell.

Tagliabue, John. 1997. "Buona notte, guten tag: Europe's new workdays." *New York Times,* November 12, C1, C6.

Tajfel, H., and J. Turner. 1979. "An interpretive theory of intergroup conflict." In W.G. Austin and S. Worchel (eds.), *The Social Psychology of Intergroup Relations.* Monterey, Calif.: Brooks/Cole.

Tannahill, Reay. 1980. *Sex in History.* New York: Stein & Day.

Tannen, Deborah. 1990. *You Just Don't Understand: Men and Women in Conversation.* New York: Morrow.

Tapscott, Don. 1998. *Growing Up Digital: The Rise of the Net Generation.* New York: McGraw-Hill.

Tavris, Carol, and Carole Wade. 1984. *The Longest War.* New York: Harcourt Brace Jovanovich.

Taylor, Ann Siegris, and John W. Louns-bury. 1988. "Unconventional commuter marriages: Living in different cities." *Human Relations* 41:407–423.

Taylor, Ella. 1989. *Prime-Time Families: Television Culture in Postwar America.* Berkeley, Calif.: University of California Press.

Taylor, Howard. 1975. "Quantitative racism: A partial documentation." *Journal of Afro-American Issues* 3:19–42.

Taylor, Howard. 1980. *The IQ Game.* New Brunswick, N.J.: Rutgers University Press.

Teixeira, Ruy. 1990. "Things fall apart." In Maureen Hallinan, David Klein, and Jennifer Glass (eds.), *Changes in Social Institutions,* pp. 239–255. New York: Plenum Press.

Television Audience Assessment. 1983. *Methodology Report.*

Terman, Lewis M., and Leona E. Tyler. 1954. "Psychology of sex differences." In L. Carmichael (ed.), *Manual of Child Psychology,* 2nd ed. New York: Wiley.

Terrance, Herbert S. 1979. *Nim: A Chimpanzee Who Learned Sign Language.* New York: Knopf.

Theen, Rolf H. W. 1984. "Party and bureaucracy." In Erik P. Hoffmann and Robbin F. Laird (eds.), *The Soviet Polity in the Modern Era.* New York: Aldine.

Thernstrom, Stephan. 1973. *The Other Bostonians: Poverty and Progress in the American Metropolis, 1880–1970.* Cambridge, Mass.: Harvard University Press.

Thomas, W. I., with Dorothy Swaine Thomas. 1928. *The Child in America.* New York: Knopf.

Thompson, William E. 1983. "Hanging tongues: A sociological encounter with the assembly line." *Qualitative Sociology* 6:215–237.

Thorne, Barrie. 1986. "Girls and boys together . . . but mostly apart: Gender arrangements in elementary school." W. Hartup and A. Rubin. (eds.), In *Relationships and Development,* pp. 167–184. Hillsdale, N.J.: Laurence Erlbaum.

Thorne, Barrie. 1995. *Gender Play: Girls and Boys in School.* New Brunswick, N.J.: Rutgers University Press.

Thornton, Arland, and Deborah Freedman. 1983. *The Changing American Family.* Washington, D.C.: Population Reference Bureau.

Thornton, W., and J. James. 1979. "Masculinity and delinquency revisited." *British Journal of Criminology* 19:225–241.

Thorton, Russell. 1987. *American Indian Holocaust and Survival.* Norman: University of Oklahoma Press.

Tiger, L., and J. Shepher. 1975. *Women in the Kibbutz.* New York: Harcourt Brace Jovanovich.

Tilly, Charles (ed.). 1975. *The Formation of Nation-States in Western Europe.* Princeton, N.J.: Princeton University Press.

Timar, Thomas. 1989. "The politics of school restructuring." *Phi Delta Kappan* 71:265–275.

Time. 1995. "Welcome to cyberspace," by Philip Elmer-DeWitt. Spring.

Time. 1998. "Time 100 special issue: Builders and titans of the 20th century." December 7.

Time. 1999. "The end of the nightmare." February 22, pp. 32–37.

Time. 1999. "A shot for aging body parts?" by Clare Thompson. January 11, p. 90. Special Issue: The Future of Medicine.

Tittle, Charles R. 1980. *Sanctions and Social Deviance: The Question of Deterrence.* New York: Praeger.

"TNC commission focuses on environment and development." 1991. *UN Chronicle.* 36ff.

Tönnies, Ferdinand. 1963. *Community and Society.* New York: Harper & Row.

Toffler, Alvin. 1983. *Previews and Premises.* New York: Morrow.

Tomeh, Aida K. 1974. "Formal voluntary organizations: Participation, correlates, and interrelationships." In M.P. Effrat (ed.), *The Community: Approaches and Applications.* New York: Free Press.

Toynbee, Arnold. 1964. *A Study of History.* New York: Oxford University Press.

Toynbee, Arnold (ed.). 1967. *Cities of Destiny.* London: Thames & Hudson.

Travers, Jeffrey, and Stanley Milgram. 1969. "An experimental study of the 'small-world' problem." *Sociometry* 32:425–443.

Treas, Judith. 1979. "Socialist organization and economic development in China: Latent consequences for the aged." *Gerontologist* 19:34–42.

Treiman, D. J. 1970. "Industrialization and social stratification." In E.O. Laumann (ed.), *Social Stratification.* Indianapolis, Ind.: Bobbs-Merrill.

Treiman, Donald J., and Kermit Terrell. 1975. "Sex and the process of status attainment: A comparison of working women and men." *American Sociological Review* 40:174–200.

Trimble, Joseph E. 1987. "American Indians: Interethnic conflict." In Jeff Boucher, Dan Landis, and Karen Arnold Clark (eds.), *Ethnic Conflict: International Perspectives.* Newbury Park, Calif.: Sage.

Troeltsch, Ernst. 1931. *The Social Teaching of the Christian Churches.* New York: Macmillan.

Tsui, Kai Yuen. 1991. "China's regional inequality." *Journal of Comparative Economics* 15(1):1–21.

Tuchman, Gaye. 1979. "Women's depiction by the mass media." *Signs: Journal of Women in Culture and Society* 4(3):528–542.

Tumin, Melvin. 1953. "Some principles of stratification: A critical review." *American Sociological Review* 18:387–394.

Tumin, Melvin M. 1985. *Social Stratification: The Forms and Functions of Inequality,* 2nd ed. Englewood Cliffs, N.J.: Prentice Hall.

Turk, Austin T. 1969. *Criminality and the Legal Order.* Chicago: Rand McNally.

Turnbull, Colin. 1972. *The Mountain People.* New York: Simon & Schuster/Touchstone.

Turner, Barbara F., and Catherine G. Adams. 1988. "Reported change in preferred sexual activity over the adult years." *Journal of Sex Research* 25:289–303.

Turner, Ralph H. 1960. "Sponsored and contest mobility and the school system." *American Sociological Review* 25:855–857.

Turner, Ralph. 1978. "The role of the person." *American Journal of Sociology* 84:1–23.

Turner, Ralph H. 1990. "Role change." *Annual Review of Sociology* 16:87–110.

Turner, Ralph H., and Lewis M. Killian. 1987. *Collective Behavior,* 3rd ed. Englewood Cliffs, N.J.: Prentice Hall.

Tyler, Leona. 1965. *The Psychology of Human Differences,* 3rd ed. New York: Appleton Century Crofts.

Tyler, Miller G., Jr. 1975. *Living in the Environment: Concepts, Problems, and Alternatives*. Belmont, Calif.: Wadsworth.

Tyler, William B. 1985. "The organizational structure of the school." *Annual Review of Sociology* 11:49–73.

Tyree, Andrea, Moshe Semyonov, and Robert Hodge. 1979. "Gaps and glissandos: Inequality, economic development, and social mobility in 24 countries." *American Sociological Review* 44:410–424.

Ucko, Leonora Greenbaum. 1986. "Perceptions of aging, East and West: Soviet refugees see two worlds." *Journal of Cross-Cultural Gerontology* 1:411–428.

Ucko, P. J., et al. (eds.). 1972. *Man, Settlement, and Urbanism*. London: Duckworth.

United Nations. 1988. *World Population Trends and Policies, 1987 Monitoring Report*. New York: United Nations.

United Nations Human Development Programme. *Human Development Report, 1997*. New York: Oxford University Press.

United Nations Population Fund. 1990. *The State of the World Population, 1990*. New York: United Nations.

U.S. Advisory Board on Child Abuse and Neglect. 1995. *A Nation's Shame: Fatal Child Abuse and Neglect in the United States*. Washington, D.C.: Department of Health and Human Services, Administration for Children and Families.

U.S. Bureau of the Census. 1978. "The source and economic status of the black population in the United States: A historical view 1790–1978." *Current Population Reports, Series P-23:80*. Washington, D.C.: U.S. Government Printing Office.

U.S. Bureau of the Census. 1983. "Money income and poverty status of families and persons in the U.S.: 1983." *Current Population Reports, Series P-60*. No. 145.

U.S. Bureau of the Census. 1987. "Estimates of the population of the United States: 1970 to 1983." *Current Population Reports, Series P-25*. No. 957.

U.S. Bureau of the Census. 1989a. *Statistical Abstract of the United States, 1989*, 109 ed. Washington, D.C.: U.S. Government Printing Office.

U.S. Bureau of the Census. 1989b. *Current Population Report: The Hispanic Population in the United States. March 1988, Series P-20*. No. 438. Washington, D.C.: U.S. Government Printing Office.

U.S. Bureau of the Census. 1990a. "Marital status and living arrangements: 1989 and 1990." *Current Population Reports, Series P-20*. No. 445.

U.S. Bureau of the Census. 1990b. "Child support and alimony: 1987." *Current Population Reports, Series P-23*. No. 167.

U.S. Bureau of the Census. 1991. "Geographical mobility, March 1987 to March 1990." *Current Population Reports, Series P-20*. No. 456.

U.S. Bureau of the Census. 1991d. "Ethnic origin of the population, state by state." Washington, D.C.: U.S. Government Printing Office.

U.S. Bureau of the Census. 1991e. *World Population Profile, 1991*. Washington, D.C.: U.S. Government Printing Office.

U.S. Bureau of the Census. 1992. "Studies in the distribution of income." *Current Population Reports, Consumer Income, Series P-60*. No. 183.

U.S. Bureau of the Census. 1992. "Summary of social, economic, and housing characteristics: United States." *1990 Census of Population and Housing*. Washington, D.C.: U.S. Government Printing Office.

U.S. Bureau of the Census. 1992. *Statistical Abstract of the United States, 1992*. Washington, D.C.: Government Printing Office.

U.S. Bureau of the Census. 1992. "General housing characteristics of the United States: 1990." *1990 Census of Housing*. Washington, D.C.: Government Printing Office.

U.S. Bureau of the Census. 1992. *International Data Base, 1992*. Accessed through CompuServe.

U.S. Bureau of the Census. 1993. *Statistical Abstract of the United States, 1993*. Washington, D.C.: Government Printing Office.

U.S. Bureau of the Census. 1993. "Poverty in the United States: 1992." *Current Population Reports, Consumer Income, Series P-60*. No. 185.

U.S. Bureau of the Census. 1993. "Asians and Pacific Islanders in the United States." *1990 Census of Population. 1990 CP-3-5*. Washington, D.C.: U.S. Government Printing Office.

U.S. Bureau of the Census. 1998. *Statistical Abstract of the United States, 1998*. Washington, D.C.: U.S. Government Printing Office.

U.S. Bureau of the Census. 1995. *Statistical Abstract of the United States, 1994*. Washington, D.C.: U.S. Government Printing Office.

U.S. Bureau of Labor Statistics. 1998. http://stats.bls.gov

U.S. Bureau of Labor Statistics. 1984. *Demographic and Socioeconomic Aspects of Aging in the U.S.* Washington, D.C.: U.S. Government Printing Office.

U.S. Commission on Civil Rights. 1988. *The Economic Status of Americans of Asian Descent*. Washington, D.C.: Clearinghouse Publications.

U.S. Conference of Mayors. 1988. *A Status Report on Children in America's Cities*. Washington, D.C.: U.S. Conference of Mayors.

U.S. Department of Education. 1984. *Survey of Magnet Schools: Analyzing a Model for Quality Integrated Education*. Washington, D.C.: U.S. Government Printing Office.

U.S. Department of Education. 1997. National Center for Education Statistics. *Digest of Education Statistics, 1997, NCES 98-015*, by Thomas D. Snyder. Production Manager, Charlene M. Hoffman. Program Analysts, Claire M. Geddes. Washington, D.C.

U.S. Department of Education. 1999. National Center for Education Statistics. Schools and Staffing Survey: 1987–88 (Administrator Questionnaire), 1990–91 (Administrator Questionnaire), 1993–1994 (Principal Questionnaire). http://nces.ed.gov/pubs/ppsp/97455-2.html.

U.S. Department of Health, Education, and Welfare. 1973. *Work in America*. Cambridge, Mass.: MIT Press.

U.S. Department of Health and Human Services. 1991. National Center for Health Statistics. Accessed through CompuServe, 1992.

U.S. Department of Health and Human Services. 1996. National Center on Child Abuse and Neglect. *Third National Incidence Study of Child Abuse and Neglect: Final Report (NIS-3)*. Washington, D.C.: Government Printing Office.

U.S. Department of Health and Human Services. 1997. National Center on Child Abuse and Neglect. *Child Maltreatment 1995: Reports from the States to the National Child Abuse and Neglect Data ystem*. Washington, D.C.: U.S. Government Printing Office.

U.S. Department of Justice. 1987. *Crime in the United States: 1986 Uniform Crime Reports.* Washington, D.C.: U.S. Government Printing Office.

U.S. Department of Justice. 1994. *Violence against Women, A National Crime Victimization Survey Report,* January. Washington, D.C.: U.S. Government Printing Office.

U.S. Department of Justice. Bureau of Justice Statistics. Prisoners in State and Federal Institutions on December 31.

U.S. Department of Justice. 1998. *Uniform Crime Reports for the United States, 1997.* Washington, D.C.: U.S. Government Printing Office.

U.S. Health Care Financing Administration. 1997. *Health Care Financing Review, Fall.* http://www.hcfa.gov/stats/stats.htm.

U.S. Immigration and Naturalization Service. 1997.

U.S. National Institute of Justice. *Drug Use Forecasting. Quarterly.*

U.S. News & World Report. 1999. "How global aging will challenge the world's economic well-being." March 1, pp. 30–39.

Vago, Steven. 1999. *Social Change,* 4th ed. Upper Saddle River, N.J.: Prentice Hall.

Valelly, Richard. 1990. "Vanishing voters." *The American Prospect* (Spring): 140–150.

Valentine, Charles A. 1968. *Culture and Poverty: Critique and Counterproposals.* Chicago: University of Chicago Press.

Valentine, Charles A. 1971. "The 'culture of poverty': Its scientific significance and its implications for action." In Eleanor B. Leacock (ed.), *The Culture of Poverty: A Critique.* New York: Simon & Schuster.

Vance, James E., Jr. 1977. *The Scene of Man: The Role and Structure of the City in the Geography of Western Civilization.* New York: Harper's College Press.

Van den Berghe, Pierre L. 1990. "South Africa after thirty years." *Social Dynamics* 16(2):16–37.

Van Dijk, Jan J. M., Pat Mayhew, and Martin Killias. 1991. *Experiences of Crime across the World: Key Findings from the 1989 International Crime Survey.* Duventer: Kluwer Law and Taxation Publishers.

Vandivort, Rita, Gaile M. Kurren, and Kathryn Braun. 1984. "Foster family care for frail elderly: A cost-effective quality care alternative." *Journal of Gerontological Social Work* 7:110–114.

Van Hasselt, Vincent B., Randall L. Morrison, Alan S. Bellack, and Michel Hersen. 1988. *Handbook of Family Violence.* New York: Plenum Press.

Van Oudenhoven, Jan Pieter, and Tineke M. Willemsen (eds.). 1989. *Ethnic Minorities: A Social Psychological Perspective.* Berwyn, Pa.: Swets North America.

Veblen, Thorstein. 1967. *The Theory of the Leisure Class.* New York: Viking. (Originally published in 1899.)

Veit, Lawrence A. 1987. "Time of the new Asian tigers." *Challenge: The Magazine of Economic Affairs* 30:49–55.

Verba, Sidney, and Norman Nie. 1972. *Participation in America.* New York: Harper & Row.

Vidich, Arthur. 1987. "Religion, economics, and class in American politics." *International Journal of Comparative Sociology* 1:4–22.

Violence Against Women. 1994. *A National Crime Victimization Survey Report.* Washington, D.C.: U.S. Department of Justice, January [online].

Vogel, Ezra. 1979. *Japan as Number One: Lessons for America.* New York: Harper & Row.

Wade, Nicholas. 1998. "Cell rejuvenation may yield rush of medical advances." *New York Times,* January 20, B11, B13.

Wagley, Charles. 1971. *An Introduction to Brazil.* New York: Columbia University Press.

Waldrop, Judith, and Thomas Exter. 1990. "What the 1990 census will show." *American Demographics* 12 (January): 20–34.

Walker, Elaine M. 1987. "Understanding minority students' mathematics learning gains in computer-assisted instruction." *Journal of Negro Education* 56:557–569.

Walker, J. C. 1988. "The way men act: Dominant and subordinate male cultures in an inner-city school." *British Journal of Sociology of Education* 9:3–18.

Walker, Samuel. 1994. *Sense and Nonsense about Crime and Drugs: A Policy Guide,* 3rd ed. Belmont, Calif.: Wadsworth.

Wallace, A. F. C. 1966. *Religion: An Anthropological View.* New York: Random House.

Wallace, A. F. C. 1970. *Culture and Personality,* 2nd ed. New York: Random House.

Wallace, Ruth A. (ed.). 1989. *Feminism and Sociological Theory.* Newbury Park, Calif.: Sage.

Wallace, Ruth A., and A. Wolf. 1986. *Contemporary Sociological Theory,* 2nd ed. Englewood Cliffs, N.J.: Prentice Hall.

Wallach, M. A., N. Kogan, and D. J. Bem. 1962. "Diffusion of responsibility and level of risk taking in groups." *Journal of Abnormal and Social Psychology* 68:263–274.

Waller, Willard. 1961. *The Sociology of Teaching.* New York: Russell & Russell. (Originally published in 1932.)

Wallerstein, Immanuel. 1974. *The Modern World System.* New York: Academic Press.

Wallerstein, Immanuel. 1979. *The Capitalist World-Economy.* Cambridge: Cambridge University Press.

Wallerstein, Immanuel. 1980. *The Modern World System II.* New York: Academic Press.

Wallerstein, Immanuel. 1990. "Societal development, or development of world-system?" In Martin Albrow and Elizabeth King (eds.), *Globalization, Knowledge, and Society: Readings from "International Sociology."* Newbury Park, Calif.: Sage.

Wallerstein, Judith S., and J. B. Kelly. 1981. *Surviving the Breakup.* New York: Basic Books.

Wallerstein, Judith S., and Sandra Blakeslee. 1989. *Second Chances: Men, Women, and Children a Decade after Divorce.* New York: Ticknor & Fields.

Walster, Elaine, and William G. Walster. 1978. *A New Look at Love.* Reading, Mass.: Addison-Wesley.

Walters, Pamela Barnhouse. 1993. *Education in Social Problems,* ed. Craig Calhoun and G. Ritzer. New York: McGraw-Hill.

Walther, A. N. 1991. *Divorce Hangover.* New York: Pocket Books.

Walton, John. 1987. "Theory and research on industrialization." *Annual Review of Sociology* 13:89–103.

Walum, Laurel Richardson. 1974. "The changing door ceremony: Notes .on the operation of sex roles in everyday life." *Urban Life and Culture* 2:506–516.

Walzer, Michael. 1982. "Socialism and the gift relationship." *Dissent* (Fall): 431–441.

Walzer, Michael. 1986. "Toward a theory of social assignments." In W. Knowlton and R. Zeckhauser (eds.), *American Society*. Cambridge: Ballinger.

Wang, Georgette, and Wimal Dissanayatce. 1984. *Continuity and Change in Communication Systems: An Asian Perspective*. Norwood, N.J.: Ablex.

Warner, W. Lloyd, et al. 1949. *Social Class in America*. New York: Harper & Row.

Warren, Roland L. 1972. *The Community in America*, 2nd ed. Chicago: Rand McNally.

Warwick, Donald P., and S. Osherson. 1973. *Comparative Research Methods*. Englewood Cliffs, N.J.: Prentice Hall.

Watkins, Steve. 1997. *The Black O: Racism and Redemption in an American Corporate Empire*. Athens: University of Georgia Press.

Watson, Russell. 1984. "An African nightmare." *Newsweek*, November 26, pp. 50–55.

Wattenberg, Martin P. 1998. *The Decline of American Political Parties, 1952–1996*. Cambridge, Mass.: Harvard University Press.

Weatherford, M. Stephen. 1980. "The politics of school busing: Contextual effects and community polarization." *Journal of Politics* 42:747–765.

Webb, E. J., et al. 1966. *Unobtrusive Measures*. Chicago: Rand McNally.

Weber, Max. 1922/1968. *Economy and Society*. Translated by Ephraim Fischoff et al. New York: Bedminster Press.

Weber, Max. 1930. *The Protestant Ethic and the Spirit of Capitalism*. Translated by Talcott Parsons. New York: Scribner's.

Weber, Max. 1946. "Politics as a vocation." In Hans H. Gerth & C. Wright Mills (eds.), *From Max Weber: Essays in Sociology*. London: Oxford University Press. (Originally published in 1919.)

Weber, Max. 1963. *The Sociology of Religion*. Boston: Allyn & Bacon. (Originally published in 1922.)

Weber, Susan (ed.). 1988. *USA by Numbers*. Washington, D.C.: Zero Population Growth.

Webster, Paula. 1975. "Matriarchy: A vision of power." In R.R. Reiter (ed.), *Toward an Anthropology of Women*. New York: Monthly Review Press.

Weeks, John R. 1988. "The demography of Islamic nations." *Population Bulletin* 43:4–53.

Weick, K. 1976. "Educational organizations as loosely-coupled systems." *Administrative Science Quarterly* 21:1–19.

Weinstein, Grace W. 1980. "How secure is social security?" *American Demographics* 2:14–17.

Weis, Robert S. 1988. "Loss and recovery." *Journal of Social Issues* 44:37–52.

Weiss, Carol H. 1987. "Evaluating social programs: What have we learned?" *Society* 25:40–45.

Weiss, Carol H., and Eleanor Singer, with the assistance of Phyllis Endreny. 1987. *Reporting of Social Science in the National Media*. New York: Russell Sage Foundation.

Weiss, R. 1989. "Teen suicide clusters: More than mimicry." *Science News* 136:342.

Weissberg, Robert. 1976. *Public Opinion and Popular Government*. Englewood Cliffs, N.J.: Prentice Hall.

Wellman, Barry. 1979. "The community question: The intimate networks of East Yorkers." *American Journal of Sociology* 84:1201–1231.

Wellman, Barry. 1988. "The community question re-evaluated." In Michael P. Smith (ed.), *Power, Community and the City*. New Brunswick, N.J.: Transaction.

Wellman, Barry, and Barry Leighton, 1979. "Networks, neighborhoods, and communities: Approaches to the study of the community question." *Urban Affairs Quarterly* 4:363–390.

Wellman, Barry, and Scot Wortley. 1990. "Different strokes from different folks: Community ties and social support." *American Journal of Sociology* 96:558–588.

Wentworth, M. 1980. *Context and Understanding: An Inquiry into Socialization Theory*. New York: Elsevier.

Wershow, H. J. 1969. "Aging in the Israeli kibbutz." *Gerontologist* 14:300–304.

Wertheimer, Barbara M. 1984. "Union is power: Sketches from women's labor history." In Jo Freeman (ed.), *Women: A Feminist Perspective*. Palo Alto, Calif.: Mayfield.

Westergaard, John, and Henrietta Resler. 1976. *Class in a Capitalist Society: A Study of Contemporary Britain*. New York: Basic Books.

Westermarck, Edward A. 1894–1901. *History of Human Marriage*. London: Macmillan.

Westley, William A. 1970. *Violence and the Police: A Sociological Study of Law, Custom, and Morality*. Cambridge, Mass.: MIT Press.

Westoff, Charles F. 1978. "Marriage and fertility in the developed countries." *Scientific American* 239 (December): 51–57.

West's Federal Practice Digest. 1987. 3rd ed., Vol. 112. St. Paul, Minn.: West.

Whalen, Marilyn R., and Don H. Zimmerman. 1987. "Sequential and institutional contexts in calls for help." *Social Psychology Quarterly* 50(2):172–185.

Wheeler, Michael. 1976. *Lies, Damn Lies, and Statistics: The Manipulation of Public Opinion in America*. New York: Liverwright.

Wheeler, Mortimer. 1968. *The Indus Civilization*, 3rd ed. Cambridge: Cambridge University Press.

White, Theodore. 1973. *The Making of the President, 1972*. New York: Bantam.

Whitehouse, Ruth. 1977. *The First Cities*. New York: Dutton.

Whiting, Beatrice B., and Carolyn Edwards. 1973. "A cross-cultural study of sex differences in the behavior of children aged three through eleven." *Journal of Social Psychology* 91:171–188.

Whiting, Beatrice B., and John W.M. Whiting. 1975. *Children of Six Cultures: A Psychocultural Analysis*. Cambridge, Mass.: Harvard University Press.

Whorf, Benjamin Lee. 1941. "The relation of habitual thought and behavior to language." In Leslie Spier (ed.), *Language, Culture, and Personality*. Menasha, Wis.: Sapir Memorial Education Fund.

Whyte, William Foote. 1981. *Street Corner Society: The Social Structure of an Italian Slum*, 3rd ed. Chicago: University of Chicago Press. (Originally published in 1943.)

Wicklund, R.A., and J.W. Brehm. 1976. *Perspectives on Cognitive Dissonance*. Hillsdale, N.J.: Lawrence Erlbaum.

Wierzbicka, Ann. 1986. "Does language reflect culture? Evidence from Australian English." *Language in Society* 15:349–374.

Wiese, D. and D. Daro. 1995. *Current Trends in Child Abuse Reporting and Fatalities: The Results of the 1994 Annual*

Fifty State Survey. Chicago: National Committee to Prevent Child Abuse.

Wiggins, Lee M. 1955. "A panel study of automobile buying." Report of a conference at the Center for Advanced Study of the Behavioral Sciences.

Wilensky, Harold L. 1975. *The Welfare State and Equality: Structural and Ideological Roots of Public Expenditures.* Berkeley: University of California Press.

Wilensky, Harold L., and Charles N. Lebeaux. 1965. *Industrial Society and Social Welfare.* New York: Free Press.

Wilkie, Jane Riblett. 1981. "The trend toward delayed parenthood." *Journal of Marriage and the Family* 43:583–590.

"Will earth survive man?" 1988. *UN Chronicle.* June, 40ff.

Williams, Dennis A. 1984. "Why teachers fail." *Newsweek,* September 24.

Williams, John E., and John R. Stabler. 1973. "If white means good, then black . . ." *Psychology Today* 7(2):50–54.

Williams, J. R., and Martin Gold. 1972. "From delinquent behavior to official delinquency." *Social Problems* 20:209–229.

Williams, Juanita H. 1987. *Psychology of Women: Behavior in a Biosocial Context.* New York: Norton.

Williams, Kipling D., Steve A. Nida, Lawrence D. Baca, and Bibb Latané. 1989. "Social loafing and swimming: Effects of identifiability on individual and relay performance of intercollegiate swimmers." *Basic and Applied Social Psychology* 10:73–81.

Williams, Robin M., Jr. 1964. *Strangers Next Door.* Englewood Cliffs, N.J.: Prentice Hall.

Williams, Robin M., Jr. 1970. *American Society: A Sociological Interpretation,* 3rd ed. New York: Knopf.

Williams, Sarah. 1985. "Long-term care alternatives: Continuing care retirement communities." *Journal of Housing for the Elderly* 3:15–34.

Willie, Charles Vert. 1984. *School Desegregation Plans That Work.* Westport, Conn.: Greenwood Press.

Willis, Paul. 1981. *Learning to Labor: How Working Class Kids Get Working Class Jobs.* New York: Columbia University Press.

Wilson, Carter A. 1986. "Affirmative action defended: Exploding the myths of a slandered policy." *The Black Scholar* 17(3):19–24.

Wilson, Clint C., and Felix Gutierrez. 1995. *Race, Multiculturalism, and the Media: From Mass to Class Communication,* 2nd ed. Thousand Oaks, CA: Sage.

Wilson, David S. 1988. "Computer's role in class expands." *Report of National Assessment of Educational Progress.*

Wilson, Edward O. 1975. *Sociology: The New Synthesis.* Cambridge, Mass.: Harvard University Press.

Wilson, Edward O. 1978. *On Human Nature.* Cambridge, Mass.: Harvard University Press.

Wilson, James Q. 1968. *Varieties of Police Behavior.* Cambridge, Mass.: Harvard University Press.

Wilson, James Q., and Richard J. Herrnstein. 1985. *Crime and Human Nature.* New York: Simon & Schuster.

Wilson, Stephen. 1978. *Informal Groups: An Introduction.* Englewood Cliffs, N.J.: Prentice Hall.

Wilson, W. Cody. 1975. "The distribution of selected sexual attitudes and behaviors among the adult population of the United States." *Journal of Sex Research* 11(1):44–64.

Wilson, William Julius. 1978. *The Declining Significance of Race: Blacks and Changing American Institutions.* Chicago: University of Chicago Press.

Wilson, William Julius. 1987. *The Truly Disadvantaged: The Inner City, the Urban Underclass, and Public Policy.* Chicago: University of Chicago Press.

Wilson, William Julius, 1996. *When Work Disappears: The World of the New Urban Poor.* New York: Vintage Books.

Windrich, Elaine. 1989. "South Africa's propaganda war." *Africa Today* 36(1):51–60.

Wingert, Pat, and Barbara Kantrowitz. 1990. "The day care generation." *Newsweek.* Special Issue: The Twenty-first Century Family (Winter/Spring): 86–92.

Wise, Gordon L., and J. Paul Merenski. 1974. "Reactions to sexy ads vary with age." *Journal of Advertising Research* 14:11–16.

Wiseman, Jacqueline P. 1979. *Stations of the Lost: The Treatment of Skid Row Alcoholics.* Chicago: University of Chicago Press.

Wolf, Eric. 1970. *Peasant Wars of the Twentieth Century.* New York: Harper & Row.

Wolfe, Alan. 1989. *Whose Keeper?* Berkeley: University of California Press.

Wolfe, Alan. 1991. *The Terms of Power, Contemporary Sociology* 20 (March): 244–245.

Wolfe, Alan. 1998. *One Nation After All.* New York: Penguin/Putnam.

Wolff, Kurt H. 1950. *The Sociology of Georg Simmel.* New York: Free Press.

Wolfinger, Raymond, and Steven Rosenstone. 1980. *Who Votes?* New Haven, Conn.: Yale University Press.

Wood, Floris W. (ed.). 1990. *An American Profile—Opinions and Behavior, 1972–1989: Opinion Results Derived from the General Social Survey Conducted by the National Opinion Research Center.* New York: Gale Research.

Wood, W., D. Polek, and C. Aiken. 1985. "Sex differences in group task performance." *Journal of Personality and Social Psychology* 48:63–71.

Woodward, Herbert N. 1983. *Human Survival in a Crowded World.* London: McFarland.

World Almanac and Book of Facts, 1990. 1989. New York: Scripps Howard.

World Almanac and Book of Facts, 1991. 1990. New York: Scripps Howard.

World Almanac and Book of Facts, 1992. 1991. New York: World Almanac.

World Almanac and Book of Facts, 1994. 1993. New York: World Almanac.

World Almanac and Book of Facts, 1998. 1999. New York: World Almanac.

World Bank. 1985. *Population Change and Economic Development.* New York: Oxford University Press.

World Bank. 1991. *World Development Report.* New York: Oxford University Press.

World Bank. 1998. *World Development Report.* http://www.worldbank.org

World Factbook. 1989. Washington, D.C.: Central Intelligence Agency.

World Factbook. 1990. Washington, D.C.: Central Intelligence Agency.

World Factbook. 1991. Washington, D.C.: Central Intelligence Agency.

World Factbook. 1997. Washington, D.C.: Central Intelligence Agency.

World Factbook. 1998. Washington, D.C.: Central Intelligence Agency.

Wright, Erik Olin, and Bill Martin. 1987. "The transformation of the American class structure, 1960–1980." *American Journal of Sociology* 93:1–29.

Wright, James D. 1989. *Address Unknown: The Homeless in America.* New York: Aldine.

Wright, Robert. 1999. "Who gets the good genes." *Time*, January 11, p. 67.

Wright, Sam. 1978. *Crowds and Riots.* Beverly Hills, Calif.: Sage.

Wrong, Dennis H. 1959. "The functional theory of stratification: Some neglected considerations." *American Sociological Review* 24:772–782.

Wrong, Dennis H. 1961. "The oversocialized conception of man in modern sociology." *American Sociological Review* 26:183–193.

Wrong, Dennis H. 1964. *Population and Society.* New York: Random House.

Wuthnow, Robert. 1976. "The new religions in social context." In Charles Y. Glock and Robert N. Bellah (eds.), *The New Religious Consciousness.* Berkeley: University of California Press.

Wuthnow, Robert. 1988. *The Restructuring of American Religion.* Princeton, N.J.: Princeton University Press.

Yampolsky, Helene Boas. 1958. "Excerpts from the letter diary of Franz Boas on his first trip to the Northwest coast." *International Journal of American Linguistics* 24.

Yankelovich, Daniel. 1981. *New Rules: Searching for Self-Fulfillment in a World Turned Upside Down.* New York: Random House.

Yankelovich, Daniel. 1991. *The Affluence Effect.*

Yankelovich, Daniel. 1994. "How changes in the economy are reshaping American values." In Henry J. Aaron, Thomas E. Mann, and Timothy Taylor (eds.), *Values and Public Policy,* pp. 16–53. Washington, D.C.: Brookings Institution.

Yanowitch, Murray, and Wesley A. Fisher. 1973. *Social Stratification and Mobility in the USSR.* White Plains, N.Y.: International Arts & Sciences Press.

Yearbook of American and Canadian Churches, 1999. 1999. New York: National Council of the Churches in the United States of America.

Yearbook of Labor Statistics, 1991. 1991. Geneva: International Labor Office.

Yin, Peter, and Kwok Hung Lai. 1983. "A reconceptualization of age stratification in China." *Journal of Gerontology* 38:608–613.

Young, Michael, and Peter Willmott. 1974. *The Symmetrical Family.* New York: Pantheon.

Yu, Vivienne W. S., and Paul A. Atkinson. 1988. "An investigation of the language difficulties experienced by Hong Kong secondary school students in English-medium schools: I. The problems." *Journal of Multilingual and Multicultural Development* 9:267–284.

Zaccaro, Stephen J. 1984. "Social loafing: The role of task attractiveness." *Personality and Social Psychology Bulletin* 10:99–106.

Zald, Mayer, and John McCarthy (eds.). 1979. *The Dynamics of Social Movements.* Cambridge, Mass.: Winthrop.

Zaman, M. Q. 1986. "The role of social relations in response to riverbed erosion hazards and population resettlement in Bangladesh." *Studies in Third World Societies* 36:177–199.

Zarbatany, Lynne, and Michael E. Lamb. 1985. "Social referencing as a function of information source: Mothers vs. strangers." *Infant Behavior and Development* 8:28–33.

Zaretsky, Eli. 1976. *Capitalism, the Family, and Personal Life.* New York: Harper & Row.

Zaretsky, Eli. 1978. "Capitalism, the family, and personal life." In A.M. Jagger and P.R. Struhl (eds.), *Feminist Frameworks: Alternative Theoretical Accounts of the Relations between Women and Men.* New York: McGraw-Hill.

Zastrow, Charles. 1986. *Introduction to Social Welfare Institutions: Social Problems, Services, and Current Issues.* Chicago: Dorsey Press.

Zawitz, M. 1994. *Violence between Intimates. NCJ-149259.* U.S. Department of Justice, Office of Justice Programs, Bureau of Justice Statistics, November.

Zeedyk-Ryan, Janice, and Gene F. Smith. 1983. "The effects of crowding on hostility, anxiety, and desire for social interaction." *Journal of Social Psychology* 120:245–252.

Zelnick, Melvin, John F. Kantner, and Kathleen Ford. 1981. *Sex and Pregnancy in Adolescence.* Beverly Hills, Calif.: Sage.

Zimbardo, Philip. 1971. "The psychological power and pathology of imprisonment." A statement prepared for the U.S. House of Representatives, Committee on the Judiciary, Subcommittee 3: Hearings on Prison Reform, San Francisco, October 25.

Zimbardo, Philip. 1972. "Pathology of imprisonment." *Society* 9 (April): 4–8.

Zimmerman, Carle G., and Lucius F. Cervantes. 1960. *Successful American Families.* New York: Pageant Press.

Zimring, Franklin E., and Gordon Hawkins. 1973. *Deterrence: The Legal Threat in Crime Control.* Chicago: University of Chicago Press.

Zola, I.K. 1972. "Medicine as an institution of social control." *Sociology Review* 20:487–504.

Zolberg, Aristide. 1987. "Wanted but not welcome: Alien labor in western development." In William Alonso (ed.), *Population in an Interacting World.* Cambridge, Mass.: Harvard University Press.

Zuboff, Shoshanna. 1988. *In the Age of the Smart Machine.* New York: Basic Books.

Zuckerman, Harriet. 1988. "The sociology of science." In Neil J. Smelser (ed.), *Handbook of Sociology.* Beverly Hills, Calif.: Sage.

Zukin, Sharon. 1987. "Gentrification: Culture and capitalism in the urban core." *Annual Review of Sociology* 13:129–147.

Photo Credits

Chapter 1: **2** Remi Benali/Stephen Ferry/ Liaison Agency, Inc.; **3** Comstock; **7** Franck Spooner/Liaison Agency, Inc.; **11** Lewis Hines/ Corbis; **16** Frank Siteman/Stock Boston; **22** Scott Cunningham/Merrill Education.

Chapter 2: **29** (top) Mark Richards/Photo-Edit; **29** (bottom) Robert Brenner/PhotoEdit; **30** Ken Karp/Pearson Education/PH College; **34** Will Faller; **41** (top) Will Hart; **41** (bottom) Jeff Maloney/PhotoDisk, Inc.; **45** Mark Mangold/U.S. Bureau of the Census; **48** Michael Newman/PhotoEdit.

Chapter 3: **54** Susan Kuklin/Science Source/ Photo Researchers, Inc.; **55** Shostak/Anthro-Photo; **57** (top) Michael S. Yamashita/ Corbis; **57** (bottom) Richard Rowan/Photo Researchers, Inc.; **61** Tomi/PhotoDisk, Inc.; **62** Dr. Ralph Solecki; **67** Dave Bartruff/ Corbis; **68** AP/Wide World Photos.

Chapter 4: **80** Mark Richards/PhotoEdit; **83** Steve Kagan Photography; **84** Steve Mason/PhotoDisk, Inc.; **88** Renee Lynn/ Photo Researchers, Inc.; **92** AP/Wide World Photos.

Chapter 5: **97** Benali/Liaison Agency, Inc.; **101** Lawrence Migdale/Stock Boston; **104** (top left) Christopher Briscoe/Photo Researchers, Inc.; **104** (top right) Richard Hutchings/ PhotoEdit; **104** (bottom left) Will Hart; **104** (bottom right) Tony Freeman/PhotoEdit; **108** Mark C. Burnett/Photo Researchers, Inc.

Chapter 6: **116** Will Faller; **117** Harlow Primate Laboratory, University of Wisconsin; **123** M. Siluk/The Image Works; **125** Frank Siteman/PhotoEdit; **128** Joseph Schuyler/ Stock Boston; **131** (left) Photofest; **131** (right) Twentieth Century Fox/Neal Peters Collection; **133** Laimute Druskis/Pearson Education/PH College; **135** David Burnett/ Stock Boston; **137** Voyager Foundation.

Chapter 7: **141** Sidney/Monkmeyer Press; **142** Chuck Keeler/Tony Stone Images; **146** (top) Jeff Greenberg/PhotoEdit; **146** (bottom) J. Gerard Smith/Monkmeyer Press; **147** P. G. Zimbardo, Inc.; **149** Alexandra Milgram; **151** Robert Brenner/PhotoEdit; **155** Time Life Syndication. © 1997 Time Inc. Reprinted by permission; **161** Jonathan Nourok/PhotoEdit.

Chapter 8: **168** Charles Gatewood/Pearson Education/PH College; **170** APTV/AP/Wide World Photos; **174** John Garrett/Woodfin Camp & Associates; **176** Stephen Frisch/ Stock Boston; **179** Robert Yager/Tony Stone Images; **181** John Maher/Stock Boston; **189** A. Ramey/Woodfin Camp & Associates.

Chapter 9: **193** Lefteris Pitarakis/AP/Wide World Photos; **195** Morry Gash/AP/ Wide World Photos; **199** Tannen Maury/ AP/Wide World Photos; **201** Richard Abarno/The Stock Market; **208** Rick Bowmer/AP/Wide World Photos; **210** Sue Klemens/Stock Boston; **211** David R. Frazier Photolibrary, Inc.

Chapter 10: **217** (top) T. Savino/The Image Works; **217** (bottom) Lennox McLendon/ AP/Wide World Photos; **222** Alex Quesada/ Matrix International, Inc.; **223** Mark Richards/PhotoEdit; **229** National Archives; **230** Hays/Monkmeyer Press.

Chapter 11: **236** Jim Hubbars/Corbis; **237** Lawrence Migdale/Pix; **240** Karen R. Preuss/ The Image Works; **243** Rafael Macia/Photo Researchers, Inc.; **244** AP/Wide World Photos; **245** Lionel Delevingne/Stock Boston; **247** Tony Savino/Sygma Photo News; **253** Russell Lee/FSA/Library of Congress.

Chapter 12: **265** Michael Hayman/Stock Boston; **271** John A. Rizzo/PhotoDisk, Inc.; **273** Joe Carini/The Image Works; **275** Bill Horsman/Stock Boston; **276** Robert Brenner/PhotoEdit; **277** Bob Daemmrich/The Image Works; **288** A. Lichtenstein/The Image Works.

Chapter 13: **293** J. Griffin/The Image Works; **294** (top) Myrleen Ferguson/PhotoEdit; **294** (bottom) Lenore Weber/Omni-Photo Communications, Inc.; **299** (top) Jeff Parsons/ Stock Boston; **299** (bottom) M. Antman/The Image Works; **303** Laura Dwight/PhotoEdit.

Chapter 14: **317** Penny Gentieu/Tony Stone Images; **318** (top) Leo de Wys, Inc.; **318** (bottom) John Isaac/United Nations. UN Photo 152770/John Isaac; **320** United Nations; **323** David Young-Wolff/PhotoEdit; **326** Shoneman, Stanley R/Omni-Photo Communications, Inc.; **328** Tom McCarthy/PhotoEdit.

Chapter 15: **337** (left) R. Termine/CTW/ Everett Collection, Inc.; **337** (right) CBS Television Network/Photofest; **340** (top) Will Faller; **340** (bottom) David R. Frazier/Photo Researchers, Inc.; **347** Amy E. Conn/AP/Wide World Photos; **349** Najlah Feanny/SABA Press Photos, Inc.; **356** K. Knudson/PhotoDisk, Inc.

Chapter 16: **365** Corbis; **369** Mathias Oppersdorff/Photo Researchers, Inc.; **372** (top) David R. Austen/Stock Boston; **372** (bottom) Sepp Seitz/Woodfin Camp & Associates; **374** AP/Wide World Photos; **381** Lee Snyder/Corbis.

Chapter 17: **390** Luc Novovitch/Reuters/ Corbis; **393** J. Scott Applewhite/AP/Wide World Photos; **394** AP/Wide World Photos; **397** Brooks Kraft/Sygma Photo News; **404** Eric Gay/AP/Wide World Photos.

Chapter 18: **411** (top) Joe Traver/Liaison Agency, Inc.; **411** (middle) Ted Horowitz/ The Stock Market; **411** (bottom) Blair Seitz/ Science Source/Photo Researchers, Inc.; **413** L.L. Bean; **416** Richard Ellis/Sygma Photo News; **420** L. Stone/Sygma Photo News; **427** Keith Brofsky/PhotoDisk, Inc.

Chapter 19: **440** Sidney/Monkmeyer Press; **445** Jeff Zelevansky/AP/Wide World Photos; **448** David Austen/Stock Boston; **450** M. E. Warren/Uniphoto Picture Agency; **455** Edmond Van Hoorick/PhotoDisk, Inc.

Chapter 20: **461** Maggie Steber/Stock Boston; **464** Don Hogan Charles/New York Times Pictures; **465** Tony Freeman/Photo-Edit; **466** C. Vergara/Photo Researchers, Inc.; **471** David Carmack/Stock Boston.

Chapter 21: **483** Corbis; **485** Tony Freeman/PhotoEdit; **486** Michael Schmelling/AP/ Wide World Photos; **489** Paul B. Southerland/Daily Oklahoman/SABA Press Photos, Inc.; **493** Library of Congress.

Chapter 22: **502** Tony Freeman/PhotoEdit; **503** (top) Hulton Getty; **503** (bottom) Saturn Corporation, used with permission; **508** Alex Quesada/Matrix International; **510** Ben Edwards/Tony Stone Images.

Author Index